THE LIBRARIES, MUSEUMS AND ART GALLERIES YEAR BOOK 1976

EDITORS

Adrian Brink &
Derry Watkins

JAMES CLARKE & CO. LTD.,
Cambridge

Published by James Clarke & Co. Ltd.
7 All Saints' Passage, Cambridge, CB2 3LS, England

Distributed in the United States by R. R. Bowker Company
(A Xerox Education Company)
1180 Avenue of the Americas, New York, N.Y., 10036, U.S.A.

Printed in Great Britain by Unwin Brothers Limited
The Gresham Press, Old Woking, Surrey GU22 9LH

CONTENTS

INTRODUCTION

During the eight decades since the 'Libraries, Museums and Art Galleries Year Book' was first published, there have been many changes in librarianship and in museum and art gallery management, but at no time have there been developments as important as those since 1971, when the last edition of the 'Year Book' was published.

BRITISH LIBRARY A major development in British librarianship was the creation of a national library, the British Library, in July 1973. This absorbed the departments of the British Museum Library, the National Library for Science and Invention, the National Central Library, the Library Association Library and various smaller bodies. With the choice of a site at Somers Town, in between St. Pancras and Euston Stations, the idea of a single, centralised national reference library with adequate space and facilities became for the first time a real possibility.

PUBLIC LIBRARIES The early 1970s saw a rearrangement of local government, which affected England and Wales in 1974, and Scotland in 1975. A few county and borough authorities were left virtually unaltered, but the only substantial area to be unaffected was Greater London. Partly as a result of local difficulties, Northern Ireland was not subject to government reorganisation, except for the library and education system, responsibility for which was divided among five new Area Boards. It is perhaps too early to say whether these changes have led to improvements in the service that libraries give, but from an administrative point of view they have unquestionably produced benefits. Another major change still in prospect at the time of going to press is the introduction of the principle of a public lending right.

Organisational change was matched by growth in the budgets of both central and local government, and the early 1970s saw a massive expansion in the budgets of public libraries, not only in monetary terms, but in real terms also. In common with other branches of local government, an increasing proportion of the enlarged budget of the libraries was spent on salaries and wages, giving library staff an unprecedented —but perhaps overdue—increase in remuneration. The organisational changes make comparative figures hard to compute, but a representative sample suggests that the remuneration of the average librarian rose by over 260 per cent between 1970 and 1975, in comparison with an increase in national average earnings of just over 200 per cent.

There was at the same time a relative fall in the value of book budgets to under 25 per cent of total expenditure, a development which suggests that there may be increasing questioning of the role of the free public library system in a relatively wealthy and educated modern society. This questioning, serious in itself, can only be increased by the cuts in public expenditure that were made in some counties during the course of 1975-76, cuts which are likely to be followed in many areas during 1976-77 and almost everywhere in 1977-78. These cuts, coming after decades of almost continuous growth in expenditure, present a potential threat to the library system as it has developed in Britain and an almost inevitable challenge to received orthodoxies not only among librarians, but among library users also.

SPECIAL LIBRARIES Changes in the public library system have not been matched among special libraries. The era of rapid growth in educational institutions in Britain appears to have come to an end, and indeed, at the time of going to press, mergers between training colleges were being announced by the Department of Education and Science. Elsewhere, the threat to library budgets as a result of cuts in government expenditure is likely to make itself felt over a period of years.

MUSEUMS AND ART GALLERIES With the exception of the ill-fated attempt by the Conservative government to impose charges for admission to national collections, museums too have in general escaped the brunt of the expenditure cuts which are affecting public libraries. Financial pressures are, however, making themselves felt, due partly to escalating administrative costs and partly to the difficulty of purchasing major works of art for the country as the value of sterling declines.

The gap of five years since the publication of the 1971 edition of the 'Libraries, Museums and Art Galleries Year Book' is due in large measure to the substantial changes that have taken place in the library world during that time. These changes have necessitated an alteration in the arrangement of the 'Year Book', with the creation of a new section to cover the British Library. A number of other modifications have been made. Most noticeable is the change in format; it was felt that a larger page size would make the book easier to use, as well as helping to control production costs during a period of rapid inflation. In recent editions of the 'Year Book' there have been separate indexes for the different sections. This has meant considerable extra work for anyone who wanted to trace a particular subject through British libraries and museums. We have, therefore, taken the opportunity of producing a single index for all the sections, as we feel that this will facilitate the use of the book. The information on which the index is based is taken from the questionnaires, and since standards differ, some important collections have almost certainly been omitted from the index, while other relatively unimportant ones have been included. It must be stressed that we are dependent for all the information in the 'Year Book' on what we have been told be Librarians, Curators and Keepers.

There has been a considerable increase in the number of museum entries included in the edition, although the problems of the definition of a museum, and the criteria for including stately homes, have continued to present difficulties.

Another serious problem has been caused by the failure of a few libraries and museums to return the questionnaires reasonably quickly, and this has resulted in some delay in production. We are, however, grateful for the promptitude with which most of the questionnaires were returned. While every effort has been made to ensure that the entries are free of errors, it is inevitable that in a book of this size some mistakes will have crept in. In a few cases this is due to handwriting that has defeated all efforts to decipher it.

It is hoped that the next edition of the 'Year Book' will be published in 1978.

In conclusion we would like to thank the following for their assistance: Mr E. V. Corbett MA, FLA for the compilation of the questionnaires; Mrs Alison Dobb MA and Mrs Sarah Silcock BA for editorial assistance; Miss Heather Morris BA for compilation of the index; and above all Miss Faith Fowles for typing enormous quantities of often illegible handwriting, almost without error. We would also like to thank Unwin Brothers for handling the highly complicated typesetting.

ADRIAN BRINK
DERRY WATKINS

ABBREVIATIONS

ad ldg - adult lending
ALS - Automated Library Systems
ANSLICS - Aberdeen & North of Scotland Library & Information Co-operative Service
ARLIS - Art Libraries Society
Aslib - Association of Special Libraries
asst - assistant
BARDIS - Barnsley & District Information Service
BC - Borough Council
BIALL - British & Irish Association of Law Libraries
BLCMP - Birmingham Libraries Co-operative Mechanization Project
BLG - Berkshire Libraries Group
BLib - Branch Library
B-LINK - Birmingham Libraries & Information Network
BLL - British Library Lending Division
BMS - Background Materials Scheme
BNBC - British National Book Centre
BRASTACS - Bradford Scientific, Technical & Commercial Service
BUCOP - British Union Catalogue of Periodicals
c. - circa
CADIG - Coventry & District Information Group
CC - County Council
CCL - Canterbury Circle of Librarians
CEIL - Council of Engineering Institutions Libraries
cent - century
CICRIS - Co-operative Industrial & Commercial Reference & Information Service
coll - college
colln - collection
COPAEP - see SCE, COPAEP
CTIS - Cornwall Technical Information Service
DC - District Council
dep - deputy/depute
dept - department
dir - director
div - division
DLIS - Dublin Library Information Service
EDC - European Documentation Centre
EMRLB - East Midland Regional Library Bureau
ETCLS - Essex Technical & Commercial Library Service
exc - except/excluding
GLASS - Greater London Arts Specialisation Scheme
GLC - Greater London Council
GLGCL - Greater London Group of College Libraries
GTIS - Gloucestershire Technical Information Service
HADIS - Huddersfield & District Information Service
HALDIS - Halifax & District Information Service
HASL - Hertfordshire Association of Special Libraries

HATRICS - Hampshire Technical, Research, Industrial & Commercial Service
HERTIS - Hertfordshire County Technical Information Service
HMSO SSS - HM Stationery Office, Selective Subscription Service
hols - holidays
hon - honorary
HULTIS - Hull Technical Interloan Service
IADIS - Irish Association of Documentation & Information Services
ICLS - Irish Central Library for Students
ILEA - Inner London Education Authority
inc - including
inf - information
JLG - Japan Library Group
KULOP - Kent Union List of Periodicals
LADSIRLAC - Liverpool & District Scientific, Industrial & Research Library Advisory Council
LAMedSectExch - Library Association Medical Section Exchange scheme
LASER - London & South East Regional system
LEA - Local Education Authority
LETIS - Leicestershire Technical Information Service
lib - library
libn - librarian
LINK - Lambeth Information Network
LINOSCO - Libraries in North Staffordshire in Co-operation
LISE - Libraries of Institutes & Schools of Education
LIST - Library & Information Services, Teesside
MAFF - Ministry of Agriculture, Fisheries & Food
MBC - Metropolitan Borough Council
MDC - Metropolitan District Council
MEDLARS - Medical Literature Analysis & Retrieval System
MISLIC - Mid-Staffordshire Libraries in Co-operation
MJFR - Metropolitan Joint Fiction Reserve
MLA of USA - Medical Library Association of U.S.A.
MoD - Ministry of Defence
MSC - Metropolitan Special Collections
mss - manuscripts
NANTIS - Nottingham & Nottinghamshire Technical Information Service
NEMROC - Newcastle Media Resources Organising Committee
NICS - Northern Ireland Counties Scheme
NINES - Norfolk Information Exchange Scheme
NLS - National Library of Scotland
NRLB - Northern Regional Library Bureau
NWRLB - North West Regional Library Bureau
OAPs - old age pensioners

ohp - overhead projector
pa - per annum
pd - per day
poly - polytechnic
PSA - Property Services Agency
pw - per week
ref - reference
SCE - Scottish Colleges of Education
SCE, COPAEP - SCE, Co-operative Purchase of American Educational Periodicals
SCOLCAP - Scottish Libraries Co-operative Automation Project
SCOLMA - Standing Conference on Library Materials for Africa
SCONUL - Standing Conference on National & University Libraries
SCOPELC - Standing Conference on Physical Education Library Co-operation
SEAL - South East Area Libraries
sec - secretary
SELRL - South East London Reference Libraries
SINTO - Sheffield Interchange Organisation
SKeLLeM - Sheffield, Keele, Liverpool, Leeds & Manchester University Libraries
SOSCOL - South Staffordshire College Libraries
STC - Short Title Catalogue
S3RB - Southampton, Surrey, Sussex, Reading & Brunel University Libraries
SWALCAP - South West Academic Libraries Co-operative Automation Project
SWRLB - South West Regional Library Bureau
TALIC - Tyneside Association of Libraries for Industry & Commerce
univ - university
WANDPETLS - Wandsworth Public Educational & Technical Library Service
WATL - Worcestershire Association of Technical Libraries
WESLINK - West Midlands Library & Information Network
WMRLB - West Midlands Regional Library Bureau
WRLS - Wales Regional Library Service
UCABE - Union Catalogue of Art Books in Edinburgh
UCISE - Union Catalogue of Institutes & Schools of Education
UCoPIL - Union Catalogue of Periodicals in Irish Libraries
YHJLS - Yorkshire & Humberside Joint Library Service
YRLB - Yorkshire Regional Library Bureau

THE BRITISH LIBRARY

BRITISH LIBRARY, established 1 July 1973 by the British Library Act (1972). Managed by *The British Library Board*, Store St, London WC1E 7DG (01-636 0755), Chairman: Viscount Eccles DC, KCVO; Dep Chairman & Chief Exec: Dr H. T. Hookway.
Divided into three main operating divisions (Reference, Lending & Bibliographic Services), augmented by the Central Administration Branch & the Research & Development Dept.

REFERENCE DIVISION, Gt Russell St, London WC1B 3DG (01-636 1544), Dir General: Mr D. T. Richnell CBE, FLA.
Scope: comprises the former library departments of the British Museum (inc the Science Reference Library); contains the largest single colln of material printed in English (a copy of every book, periodical, newspaper, map & piece of music published in UK must by law be deposited here); foreign material obtained by exchange or purchase. **Stock:** c. 10,000,000 vols. **Purchases:** £877,345. Construction of new building in Euston Rd at Somers Town to house all parts of the Reference Division, to start in 1979. **Services:** electrostatic copies (of post-1800 material other than mss), microfilm, photographs & photocopies available on request; information services; 4 exhibition galleries. **Admission** to all departments (exc Science Ref Lib) is by ticket only. Tickets available to those over 21 on application. All departments closed Dec 24-26, Jan 1 & Good Friday.

DEPARTMENT OF PRINTED BOOKS, Gt Russell St, Keeper: Mr J. L. Wood BA.
Scope: printed books & periodicals in all languages except those of Asia. **Special Collections:** Thomason colln of civil war tracts; Croker colln of French Revolution tracts; Cracherode colln of fine editions; Ashley Library of English literature; Burney colln of pre-1800 English newspapers; important colln of postage stamps. **Stock:** c. 9,000,000 books; c. 64,400 serials; over 10,000 incunabula. **Includes:** *Official Publications Library* (formerly the State Paper Room): largest colln in Europe of official papers from all periods & countries, & from inter-governmental organisations (UN, OEEC etc). *Map Library:* historical colln of maps, charts, plans & topographical views, (40,000 vols; 700,000 sheets); modern maps of all countries; King George III topographical colln; largest extant colln of Ordnance Survey material. *Music Library:* printed music of all countries & periods (over 1,000,000 items); Royal Music Library colln (inc Handel autographs); Paul Hirsch Music Library. **Hours:** Mon-Sat 9.00-17.00 (21.00 Tues-Thurs). **Total Staff:** 652.
Branches: *Newspaper Library,* Colindale Ave, London NW9 5HE (01-205 6039). **Scope:** newspapers & weekly periodicals of all countries from 1800 onwards; British provincial papers from before 1800. **Hours:** Mon-Sat 10.00-17.00. *Library Association Library,* 7 Ridgemount St, London WC1E 7AE (01-636 7543; telex 21897). **Scope:** librarianship; information science; book trade; annual library reports. **Stock:** c. 50,000 books; c. 850 current periodicals; 30 films; 30 fimstrips; 5,000 microtexts. **Hours:** Mon-Fri 9.00-18.00 (20.00 Tues & Thurs, mid Sept-mid July only).

DEPARTMENT OF MANUSCRIPTS, Gt Russell St, Keeper: Dr D. P. Waley PhD, FRHistS.
Scope: hand-written books & documents of every kind (inc maps & music) & of all periods, in European languages. **Special collections:** illuminated mss; 10th-cent Benedictional of St Ethelwold; 14th-cent Queen Mary Psalter; Luttrell Psalter; Lindisfarne Gospels; Magna Carta; 4th-cent Codex Sinaiticus; early mss of Beowulf & Chaucer; heraldic mss; literary & historic autographs (inc English royalty & Shakespeare); Nelson's memorandum on Trafalgar & logbooks of HMS Victory. **Stock:** c. 100,000 mss; c. 100,000 charters & rolls; 18,000 seals & casts; 3,000 Greek & Latin papyri; Egyptian papyri. **Hours:** Mon-Sat 10.00-16.45. **Total staff:** 56.

DEPARTMENT OF ORIENTAL MANUSCRIPTS AND PRINTED BOOKS, Gt Russell St, Keeper: Dr G. E. Marrison BA, PhD.
Scope: literature of the Oriental world & northern Africa (especially Hebrew, Arabic, Persian & Indo-Persian mss, many illustrated). **Special collections:** Stein colln (over 6,000 Chinese mss & printed rolls, inc Diamond Sutra of 868 AD, the oldest dated printed document in the world); Japanese block-printed books. **Stock:** c. 250,000 books; 30,000 mss. **Hours:** Mon-Fri 10.00-16.45, Sat 10.00-12.45. **Total staff:** 47.

SCIENCE REFERENCE LIBRARY (formerly the National Reference Library of Science & Invention), Dir: Mr M. W. Hill MA, BSc, ARIC.
Scope: natural sciences; all branches of engineering; all industrial technologies & associated skills; no clinical medicine, no history or philosophy of science, no student level books; nearly all material (exc bibliographies & patents) is post-1910. **Stock:** 850,000 books; c. 40,000 current serials; official patent trademarks & design publications of c. 100 countries; trade literature of 2,500 companies; 17,000,000 patent specifications. **Staff:** non-manual 348; graduates & chartered libns 65.
Housed in 2 branches: *Holborn Branch* (formerly the Patent Office Library), 25 Southampton Buildings, Chancery Lane, London WC2A 1AW (01-405 8721; telex 266959). **Scope:** mainly industry-oriented books & journals; most comprehensive colln of patent specifications in UK; foreign patent annexe. **Hours:** Mon-Fri 9.30-21.00, Sat 10.00-13.00; closed on public holidays. *Bayswater Branch,* 10 Porchester Gardens, Queensway, London, W2 4DE (01-727 3022; telex 22717). **Scope:** life sciences; scientific literature in Slavonic & Oriental languages. **Hours:** Mon-Fri 9.30-17.30; closed on public holidays.

LENDING DIVISION (formerly the National Lending Library for Science & Technology & the National Central Library), Boston Spa, Wetherby, West Yorkshire, LS23 7BQ. (0937-843434; telex 557381), Dir General: Mr M. B. Line MA, FLA.
Scope: largest lending library in the world; UK centre for national & international inter-library loans & photocopy service; contains most significant books in English; books & periodicals in all languages; loans not made to individuals, but material can be consulted in the Reading Room; medical search & retrieval service (MEDLARS); translation service from Russian & Oriental languages. **Stock:** over 2,300,000 vols; over 1,500,000 microforms; 45,169 current serials. **Purchases:** £914,828. **Requests handled:** 2,164,000. **Total staff:** 556.

BIBLIOGRAPHIC SERVICES DIVISION (formerly the British National Bibliography Ltd), Store St, London WC1E 7DG (01-636 0755; telex 22787), Dir General: Mr Richard E. Coward FLA.
Function: processes & catalogues acquisitions of the British Library; produces current listings of all British publications; computer-based system for storing & handling bibliographic information; British Library Copyright Receipt Office; UK National Serials Data Centre. Publishes 'General Catalogue of Printed Books & Subject Index', 'British Catalogue of Music', 'British Education Index', 'Books in English', 'British Union Catalogue of Periodicals'. **Total staff:** 160.

RESEARCH AND DEVELOPMENT DEPARTMENT (formerly the Office of Scientific & Technical Information), Sheraton House, Gt Chapel St, London W1V 4BH (01-734 6767), Dir: Mr John C. Gray.
Function: promotes research on & development of library & information operations in all subjects.

CENTRAL ADMINISTRATION, Sheraton House, Gt Chapel St, London W1V 4BH (01-437 0196), Head: to be appointed.
Function: finance, administration, staffing, accommodation & legal services. *Press and Public Relations Section,* Store St, London WC1E 7DG (01-636 0755).

PUBLIC LIBRARIES

All entries are arranged alphabetically under the name of the local authority (except for the Northern Ireland entries which are grouped together under 'Northern Ireland'). The whole of the Greater London area is included under 'London'. The Channel Islands and the Isle of Man entries follow the United Kingdom entries. Irish entries are arranged under 'Republic of Ireland', after the Museums and Art Galleries Section.

Public libraries are not open on bank holidays.

As a result of government reorganisation in Scotland, much information on Scottish public libraries was not available at the time of going to press. Nearly all the financial figures given for Scotland are for a 10½ month period (16 May 1975-31 March 1976), rather than a full year.

PUBLIC LIBRARIES: QUESTIONNAIRE

1. Name of Local Authority   2. Population served   3. Full postal address of Central Library or Administrative Headquarters   4. Telephone number of above; Telex number   5. Name of Chief Librarian, with designation and qualifications (if responsible for a wider service than libraries alone, please state)   6. Name of deputy to (5) with designation and qualifications   7. Committee responsible for libraries   8. If the officer named in (5) is subordinate to some other officer, state designation of the latter together with name and qualifications 9. Opening hours of main libraries: Monday to Friday: adult lending, reference, children's; Saturday: adult lending, reference, children's

10. Basis of organisation   11. Names, addresses and telephone numbers of Regional or District Libraries within the system, together with name and qualifications of Librarian in charge   12. Names and addresses of full-time Branch Libraries (excluding question 11) open at least 30 hours per week   13. Number of part-time libraries; number of mobiles

14. List any Special Collections of significance other than those which are regional or national commitments (exclude collections covered in questions 15 to 17)   15. Gramophone records: Number of Record Libraries; Issues 1974/75: (a) Records, (b) Cassettes etc; Stock: (c) Records, (d) Cassettes etc; (e) Loan charges or subscription, if any; (f) Scale of fines 16. Picture loan collection: Stock; Charges, if any   17. Does the Library provide any of the following services: Schools, Housebound, Prisons, Hospitals, Old People's Homes, other extramural services   18. Is the Library, or the department of which it is part, responsible for: Cultural activities? Entertainments? (Give total estimated expenditure on cultural activities and entertainments for 1975/76, including salaries, wages and administration; designation of officer directly in charge of these activities; number of staff employed in this field (a) officer; (b) manual)   19. Name issue methods employed for adult lending other than Browne   20. Lending Library loan period if other than 2 weeks   21. Lending Library fine scale: (a) Adult; (b) Children; (c) Old Age Pensioners   22. Name any purely local co-operative scheme in which Library participates   23. Stock: (a) Adult Lending; (b) Adult Reference; (c) Children's (excluding schools); (d) Schools; (e) Number of individual periodical titles taken   24. Issues 1974/75 (issues from mobiles and to housebound to be included in as appropriate): (a) Adult Lending (excluding institutions); (b) Junior Lending (excluding schools); (c) Schools; (d) Institutions

25. Staff (figures given should relate to established posts including vacancies, if any; where part-time staff are employed their total weekly working hours should be divided by the hours normally worked by full-time members of staff, usually 35 or 36, and thus converted to the equivalent of full-time staff): (a) Total officers; (b) Total manual; (c) Number of chartered librarians actually employed (including graduate chartered librarians); (d) Number of graduates actually employed   26. Finance (based on annual estimates for 1975/76): (a) Total expenditure (including cultural activities if part of Library budget); (b) Total income other than from rate; (c) Expenditure per head of population (total expenditure divided by population served); (d) Expenditure on books, binding and periodicals; (e) Total expenditure on gramophone records and allied material; (f) Total expenditure on salaries and wages (including superannuation and national insurance but excluding Town Hall establishment charges)   27. Capital Projects approved for start in 1975 or 1976 and costing more than £250,000.

PUBLIC LIBRARIES

UNITED KINGDOM

ABERDEEN CITY DISTRICT COUNCIL (pop 213,000) Central Library, Rosemount Viaduct, Aberdeen, Aberdeenshire, AB9 1GU (0224-28991). City Libn: Mr Peter Grant ALA; Dep City Libn: B.J.R. Gregory DPA, ALA. **7** Libraries. **9** Mon-Fri: 9.30-20.00 (ref 21.00); Sat: 9.30-17.00. **10** Central; Area HQ. **11 Area HQs:** Airyhall Lib, Springfield Rd, AB1 7RF, Libn: Mr Norman Low ALA; Linksfield Lib, King St, Libn: Mr Fraser Adam ALA; Bucksburn Lib, Kepplehills Rd, AB2 9DG, Libn: Mr Jeffrey Dyce ALA; Torry Lib, Victoria Rd, AB1 3NJ, Libn: Mr Alan Rennie ALA. **12** Sir John Anderson Lib, Clifton Rd, Woodside; Ruthrieston & Ferryhill Lib, Fonthill Rd; G. M. Fraser Lib, Byron Sq, Northfield; Mastrick Lib, Greenfern Rd; Kincorth Lib, Provost Watt Dr; 189 North Deeside Rd, Culter, Aberdeenshire; North Deeside Rd, Cults. **13** P-t 5; mobiles 2. **15** 8; (a) 65,738; (c) 5,000; 65p for carrying case; (f) 10p pw or part. **16** 750; none. **17** Housebound, prisons, hospitals, old people's homes. **19** Check book. **20** 4 weeks. **21** (a,b & c) 2½p pw. **22** ANSLICS. **23** (a) 260,000; (b) 132,000; (c) 90,000. **24** (a) 1,178,547; (b) 271,482; (d) 34,671 **25** (a) 103; (b) 11; (c) 24 (establishment 28); (d) 12. **26** (a) £535,665; (b) £9,085; (c) £2.51; (d) £143,000; (e) £11,000; (f) £287,710.

ANGUS DISTRICT COUNCIL (pop 82,000) Administrative Headquarters, County Buildings, Forfar, Angus, DD8 3LF (0307-3661). Dir of Libs & Museums: Mr Gavin N. Drummond ALA; Dep Dir: Mr Gerald Moore BA, ALA. **7** Leisure & Recreation. **9** Mon-Fri: 10.00-18.00; Sat: 10.00-17.00. **10** HQ; Sub District; Branch. **11 Sub Districts:** North: Montrose Lib, High St, Montrose, DD10 8PJ (0674-3256), Libn: Miss Moira A. Stephen MA, ALA; South: Arbroath Lib, Hill Terrace, Arbroath, DD11 1EJ (02414-2248), Libn: Mr Gerald Moore BA, ALA; West: Forfar Lib, Meffan Institute, 20 West High St, Forfar, DD8 1BB (0307-3468). **12** St Ninians Sq, Brechin; High St, Carnoustie; Town Hall, Kirriemuir. **13** P-t 5; mobiles 1. **17** Schools, housebound, prisons, hospitals, old people's homes, lighthouses. **21** (a,b & c) 1p pw or part. **23** (a,b,c & d) 296,600. **25** (a) 39; (b) 8; (c) 7; (d) 4. **26** (a) £225,500; (c) £2.75; (d) £66,950; (f) £76,190.

ARGYLL AND BUTE DISTRICT COUNCIL (pop c. 65,000) Argyll & Bute District Library, Argyll House, Alexandra Parade, Dunoon, Argyll, PA23 8AJ (0369-4000). District Libn: Mr Donald C. Reid. **7** Tourism, Leisure & Recreation. **8** Dir of Tourism, Leisure & Recreation: Mr James E. Moran. **9** Varies; Mon-Fri: 10.00-19.00, or 9.45-12.30, 14.00-20.00; Sat: ad ldg & ref 10.00-17.00, children 10.00-12.00, or all depts 9.45-12.30, 14.00-17.00. **10** HQ; Branch; Mobile; Centre. **12** The Moat, Stuart St, Rothesay, Isle of Bute; Campbeltown; Tulloch Lib, Castle House, Dunoon; Corran Halls, Oban. **13** P-t 2; mobiles 4; Volunteer centres 20. **14** Local colln; Gaelic books; Clyde steamers. **17** Schools, housebound, hospitals, old people's homes, lighthouses, playgroups. **18** Cultural activities, entertainments (Dir of Tourism, Leisure & Recreation). **20** 3 weeks. **21** (a) 1p pw for 1st week, 1p pd thereafter; (b & c) at discretion. **23** (a,b,c & d) 251,500; (e) 30. **24** (a) 800,000; (b) 40,000; (c) 200,000. **25** (a) 26; (b) 3; (c) 2.

AVON COUNTY COUNCIL (pop 915,300) Central Library, College Green, Bristol, Avon, BS1 5TL (0272-26121; telex Bristol 44200). Dir of Libs: Mr R. E. Grimshaw FLA; Principal Libns: Mr. P. D. Pocklington FLA (Admin & Support); Mr A. D. Mortimore MA, FLA (Services). **7** Community Leisure. **9** Mon-Fri: 9.30 (or 10.00)-19.00 (or 20.00); Sat: 9.30 (or 10.00)-17.00. **10** HQ; Area; Branch. **11 Areas:** Bristol: Central Lib, College Green, BS1 5TL (0272-26121), Area Libn: Mr Peter Heaton; Bath/Wansdyke: Lewis House, Manvers St, Bath BA1 1JQ (0225-28144), Area Libn: Mr John Kite FLA; Kingswood/Northavon: Yate Lib, West Walk, Yate, BS17 4AX (0454-312475), Area Libn: Miss Frances Blandford BA, ALA; Woodspring: Central Lib, The Boulevard, Weston-super-Mare, BS23 1PL (0934-24133), Area Libn: Mr John Loosley ALA. **12** Bedminster Lib, East St, Bristol, BS3 4HY; Bishopsworth Rd, Bristol, BS13 7LN; Clifton Lib, Princess Victoria St. Bristol, BS8 4BX; Eastville Lib, Muller Rd, Bristol, BS5 6XP; Filwood Broadway, Bristol, BS4 1JN; Fishponds Rd, Bristol, BS16 3UH; Peterson Sq, Hartcliffe, Bristol, BS13 0EE; Crow Lane, Henbury, Bristol, BS10 7DW; Henleaze Lib, Northumbria Dr, Bristol, BS9 4HP; Hillfields Lib, Summerleaze, Fishponds, Bristol, BS16 4HL; Horfield Lib, Filton Ave, Bristol, BS7 0BD; Knowle Lib, Redcatch Rd, Bristol BS4 2EP; Stile Acres, Lawrence Weston, Bristol, BS11 0QA; Marksbury Road Lib, Bedminster, Bristol, BS3 5LG; North District Lib, Cheltenham Rd, Bristol, BS6 5QX; Redland Lib, Whiteladies Rd, Bristol, BS8 2PY; St George Lib, Church Rd, Bristol, BS5 8AL; St Philips Lib, Trinity Rd, Bristol, BS2 0NW; Sea Mills Lib, Sylvan Way, Bristol, BS9 2NA; Shirehampton Lib, Station Rd, Bristol, BS11 9TU; Southmead Lib, Greystoke Ave, Bristol, BS10 6AS; Westbury Lib, Falcondale Rd, Bristol, BS9 3JZ; Wick Road Lib, Brislington, Bristol, BS4 4HE; Southmead Hospital, Westbury-on-Trym, BS10 5NB; Linden Rd, Clevedon, BS21 7SN; Somerset Sq, Nailsea, BS19 2EX; 12 High St, Portishead, Bristol, BS20 9EW; The Maltings, Worle, Weston-super-Mare, BS22 0JB; Buckingham Gardens, Downend, BS16 5TW; Filton Lib, Gloucester Rd North, Bristol, BS12 7PT; Kingswood Lib, High St, Bristol, BS15 4AR; Oldland Parkwall Lib, School Rd, Cadbury Heath, Bristol, BS15 5EN; Patchway Lib, Rodway Rd, Bristol, BS12 5HY; Staple Hill Lib, Broad St, Bristol, BS16 5LR; Thornbury Lib, St Mary St, BS12 2AA; Bath Ref Lib, Queen Sq, Bath, BA1 2HN; Bath Central Lending Lib, Bridge St, Bath, BA2 4AT; Keynsham, Bristol, BS18 1ED; Midsomer Norton Lib, High St, Bath, BA3 2DP; Moorland Road Lib, Bath, BA2 3PL; The Street, Radstock, BA3 3PR. **13** P-t 14; mobiles 10. **14** Bristol Ref Lib. Thomas Chatterton; S. T. Coleridge; Stuckey Lean colln (folk lore & proverbs); Somerset (Emmanuel Green colln); Sabin colln & other private press books; fine arts (inc local artists' directory); local history; music; commercial library (inc BSI & British patents filed for 20 years); HMSO SSS. Bath Ref Lib:- local history; Napoleonic colln; Oppenheim & Miles colln (19th cent travels); Jenyns & Broome colln (botanical & scientific books). Weston-s-Mare Lib:- Wood colln (history & natural history); local history. **15** 2; (a) 112,432; (c) 14,450; (e) 8p pw; (f) 1p pd. **16** 4,470; none. **17** Schools, housebound, prisons, hospitals, old people's homes. **19** Weymouth system (adapted Browne) (Weston-super-Mare); family issue mobiles (adapted Browne); Photocharging (Bath). **20** 3 weeks. **21** (a&c) 1½p pd; (b) 1 p pw or part. **23** (a) 906,000; (b) 398,300; (c) 262,500; (d) 88,680; (e) 650. **24** (a) 8,494,989; (b) 1,865,514; (c) 1,386,159; (d) 177,900. **25** (a) 429; (b) 90; (c) 93; (d) 35. **26** (a) £1,770,610; (b) £183,070; (c) £1.93; (d) £365,670; (e) £8,015; (f) £1,184,820.

BARNSLEY METROPOLITAN BOROUGH COUNCIL (pop 226,701) Central Library, Shambles St, Barnsley, South Yorkshire, S70 2JF (0226-83241/4; telex 547369). Chief Libn: Mr T. R. Hayes ALA; Dep Libn: Mr C. T. Nicholls ALA. **7** Education. **8** Dir of Education: Mr T. Brooks BSc. **9** Mon-Fri: ad ldg & ref 9.30-20.00, children 9.30-18.00; Sat: 9.30-17.00 **10** HQ; Area; Branch. **11 Area HQs:** Goldthorpe Lib, Goldthorpe, Rotherham (070-989 3278), Area Libn: Mrs M. Turton ALA; Penistone B Lib, High St, Penistone, Sheffield, S30 6BR (022 676-2313), Area Libn: Miss G. M. Peace ALA; Worsbrough B Lib, Elm Tree Estate, Worsbrough, Barnsley (0226-2372), Area Libn: Miss E. Naylor ALA; Wombwell B Lib, Station Rd, Wombwell, S73 0BA (0226-75 3421), Area Libn: Mr H. Welburn. **12** Lindhurst Rd, Athersley, Barnsley; Carr Head Lane, Bolton-on-Dearne, Goldthorpe; Barnsley Rd, Cudworth, Barnsley; Church St, Darfield, Barnsley; High St, Dodworth, Barnsley; High St, Grimethorpe, Barnsley; Miners Welfare Hall, Hoyland Nether, Barnsley; Birch Rd, Kendray, Barnsley; 22 Blacker Rd, Mapplewell, Darton, Barnsley; Lamb Lane, Monk Bretton, Barnsley; Midland Rd, Royston, Barnsley; Shepherd Lane, Thurnscoe, Barnsley. **13** P-t 8; mobiles 3. **14** Barnsley colln; Yorkshire colln. **15** 6; (a&b) 10,249; (c&d) 1,500; (e) 3p pw. **16** 125; 30p for 3 months. **17** Schools, housebound, old people's homes, WEA. **18** Cultural activities (£2,000; Admin & Arts Officer). **19** Plessey computer photocharging 'Islington'. **21** No fines. **22** BARDIS. **23** (a) 250,000; (b) 125,000; (c) 30,000; (d) 50,000; (e) 190. **24** (a) c.1,102,000; (b) c.932,000; (c) c.15,000; (d) 5,500. **25** (a) 106; (b) 18; (c) 25; (d) 13. **26** (a) £673,160; (b) £102,260; (c) £3.012; (d) £132,730; (e) £1,060; (f) £318,420.

BEARSDEN AND MILNGAVIE DISTRICT (pop 37,000) Administratrive Headquarters, Drymen Rd, Bearsden, Glasgow, G61 3RJ (041-942 6811). Chief Libn: Mrs Sheena V. Peters FLA; Chief Asst: Mr John Dysart ALA. **7** Leisure & Recreation. **8** Dir of Technical Services: Mr W. W. Dudgeon. **9** Mon-Fri: 10.00-20.00; Sat: 10.00-17.00. **10** HQ; District; Branch. **11 District Libraries:** Brookwood, Drymen Rd, Bearsden, Libn: Miss Janet Chisholm MA; Hillfoot, Milngavie Rd, Bearsden, Libn: Miss M. Murray City & Guild; Westerton, Maxwell Ave, Bearsden, Libn: Miss S. Smart; Milngavie, Muddock Rd, Milngavie, Libn: Miss F. Sage. **13** P-t 1. **14** Local history. **17** Schools, housebound, hospitals, old people's homes. **20** 3 weeks. **21** No fines. **23** (a) c.59,000; (b) c.11,000; (c) c.20,000; (e) 10. **25** (a) 25; (b) 17; (c) 4; (d) 2. **26** (a) £119,345; (c) £3.22; (d) £43,400; (f) £58,000.

BEDFORDSHIRE COUNTY COUNCIL (pop 484,300) Bedfordshire County Library, County Hall, Cauldwell St, Bedford, Bedfordshire, MK42 9AP (0234-56181; telex 82244). County Libn: Mr Colin Muris MA, FLA; Dep County Libn: Mr W. J. H. Watson FLA, AMBIM; Asst County Libns: Mr E. May ALA (principal); Mr W. K. A. Child ALA (book supply); Mr A. Threadgill ALA (ref & inf); Mrs C. J. Wright (youth). **7** Leisure. **9** Mon-Fri: 9.30-20.00; Sat: 9.30-17.00. **10** HQ (functional); District; Community. **11 Districts:** Bedford: Central Lib, Harpur St, Bedford, MK40 1PG (0234-50931), Libn: A. E. Baker ALA; Luton: Central Lib, Bridge St, Luton, LU1 2NG (0582-30161), Libn: R. P. Hawkes ALA; Mid-Bedfordshire: Biggleswade Lib, Chestnut Ave, Biggleswade, SG18 0LL (0767-31234), Libn: P. Catcheside BA, ALA; South Bedfordshire: Dunstable Lib, Vernon Pl, Dunstable, LU5 4HA (0582-65861), Libn: B. S. George ALA. **12** County Hall Lib, Bedford; Library Walk, Putnoe St, Bedford; Marsh Rd, Leagrave, Luton; Tomlinson Ave, Lewsey, Luton; Marsh Farm Lib, Purley Centre, Luton; Stopsley Lib, Hitchin Rd, Luton; Sundon Park, Hill Rise, Luton; Luton & Dunstable Hospital, Dunstable Rd, Luton; Saunders Piece, Ampthill; Market Sq, Sandy; Bedford Sq, Houghton Regis; Lake St, Leighton Buzzard. **13** P-t 6; mobiles 11. **14** Dr Fowler Library (History); Thomas Bagshawe Library; Mott Harrison (John Bunyan) Library; Offor (John Bunyan) Library; Shaw colln. **15** 10; (c) 16,000; (e) £3.00 pa (exc

VAT), OAPs no charge; (f) None. **16** 475; £2.00 pa (inc VAT). **17** Schools, housebound, prison, hospitals, old people's homes, playgroups, fire stations, police station, approved school, remand centre, youth clubs. **19** Photocharging; Plessey light pen computerised; token. **20** 3 weeks. **21** (a, b&c) 3p pw; Urban mobile users—1p pw; Rural mobile users—none. **23** (a, b, c&d) 1,165,000; (e) 750. **25** (a) 339; (b)24.5; (c) 109; (d) 30. **26** (a) £1,709,390; (b) £278,920; (c) £3.5; (d&e) £364,800; (f) £774,570. **27** Leighton Buzzard Library.

BERKSHIRE ROYAL COUNTY COUNCIL (pop 658,000) Abbey Mill House, Abbey Sq, Reading, Berkshire, RG1 3BH (0734-55981; telex 847392). County Libn: Mr Vernon Jennings FLA; Asst County Libns: Mr A. G. Walters ALA (bibliographic services); Mr M. E. Asser FLA (admin); Mrs P. Heeks FLA (children & education). **7** Education (Libraries Sub-Committee). **9** Mon-Fri: 9.30-17.00 (ref or 19.00); Sat: 9.30-17.00. **10** HQ; District; Branch. **11 Districts:** Public Lib, Carnegie Rd, Newbury, RG14 5DW (0635-40972; telex 849315), District Libn: Miss C. M. Steer ALA; Central Lib, Belgrave St, Reading, RG1 1QL (0734-55981; telex 842 9421), District Libn: Mr I. J. Lewis BA, ALA; County B Lib, Montague House, Broad St, Wokingham, RG11 1AU (0734-781368; telex 849 423), Libn: Miss D. M. Woods FLA; Public Lib, St Ives Rd, Maidenhead, SL6 1QU (0628-25657; telex 849319), District Libn: Mr J. C. Powell FLA; Central Lib, 84 High St, Slough, SL1 1EA (0753-35166; telex 848149), District Libn: Miss J. V. Cook FLA; County B Lib, Town Sq, Bracknell, RG12 1AT (0344-23149; telex 849317), Libn: Mr S. R. Thomas ALA. **12** Palmer Park Lib, St Bartholomew's Rd, Reading, RG1 3QB; Whitley Lib, Northumberland Ave, Reading, RG2 7PX; Battle Lib, Oxford Rd, Reading, RG3 1EE; Southcote Lane, Reading, RG3 3BA; School Rd, Tilehurst, Reading, RG3 5AS; Church St, Caversham, Reading, RG4 8AU; Elmshott Lane, Cippenham, Slough, SL1 5RB; Trelawney Ave, Langley, Slough, SL3 7UF; Lower Broadmoor Rd, Crowthorne; St Leonards Rd, Windsor, SL4 3BY; Library House, The Green, Datchet, Slough; 42 Church Rd, Woodley, Reading. **13** P-t 25; mobiles 11. **14** Music; drama. **15** 3; (a) c.36,000; (c) 6,500; (e) £3.00 pa; (f) 5p pw or part. **17** Schools, housebound, prisons, hospitals, old people's homes, WEA. **19** ALS computer charging (Reading Central); tokens for adult fiction. **20** 3 weeks. **21** (a) 1st week 2p, 2nd week 5p, 3rd week 7p, 4th week 10p, max 35p; (b) 1p pw or part; (c) none. **22** LASER. **23** (a) 583,123; (b) 75,000; (c) 66,782; (d) 277,720; (e) 625. **24** (a) 4,750,486; (b) 1,123,741; (c) 152,133; (d) c.10,000. **25** (a) 233½; (b) 33; (c) 87; (d) 10. **26** (a) £1,382,665; (b) £43,530; (c) £2.37; (d) £374,050; (e) £3,240; (f) £722,280.

BIRMINGHAM METROPOLITAN DISTRICT COUNCIL (pop 1,087,660) Central Libraries, Paradise, Birmingham, B3 3HQ (021-235 4511; telex 33455). City Libn: Mr W. A. Taylor OBE, MC, FLA; Dep City Libn: Mr E. Hargreaves FLA. **7** Leisure Services. **9** Mon-Fri: ad ldg & ref 9.00-20.00, children 9.00-19.00; Sat: 9.00-17.00. **10** HQ; Branch. **12** Acocks Green, Shirley Rd, B27 7XH; Aston, Albert Rd, B6 5NQ; Aston Cross, Lichfield Rd, B6 5RW; Balsall Heath, Moseley Rd, B12 9BX; Birchfield, Birchfield Rd, B20 3BX; Bloomsbury, Nechells Parkway, B7 4PT; Boldmere, Boldmere Rd, B73 5TU; Erdington, Orphanage Rd, B24 9HP; Glebe Farm, Glebe Farm Rd, B33 9NA; Hall Green, 1221 Stratford Rd, B28 9AD; Handsworth, Soho Rd, B21 9DP; Harborne, High St, B17 9QG; Kings Heath, High St, B14 7SW; Kings Norton, Pershore Rd South, B30 3EU; Kingstanding, Kingstanding Rd, B44 9ST; Mere Green, Mere Green Rd, B75 5BP; Northfield, Church Rd, B31 2LB; Perry Common, College Rd, B44 0HH; Quinton, Community Centre, Ridgacre Rd, N32 2TW; Selly Oak, 669 Bristol Rd, B29 6AE; Shard End, Shustoke Rd, B34 7BA; Sheldon, Brays Rd, B26 2RJ; Small Heath, Green Lane, B9 5DB; South Yardley, Yardley Rd, B25 8LT; Sparkhill, Stratford Rd, B11 4EA; Spring Hill, Spring Hill, B18 7BH; Stirchley, Bournville Lane, B30 2JT; Sutton Coldfield, Lower Parade, B72 1YA; Tower Hill, Tower Hill, B42 1LG; Ward End, Washwood Heath Rd, B8 2HF; Yardley

CODE: 1 Local authority. 2 Population. 3 Postal address of HQ. 4 Telephone & telex. 5 Chief Libn. 6 Deputy. 7 Committee responsible. 8 Officer to whom Libn is responsible (if any). 9 Hours. 10 Organisation. 11 Area libraries. 12 Branches. 13 Part-time libraries; mobiles. 14 Special collections. 15 Gramophone records: number of libraries, (a) record issues (b) cassette issues (c) record stock (d) cassette stock (e) loan charges (f) fines. 16 Pictures: stock; charges. 17 Other services. 18 Cultural activities (expenditure, officer in charge, staff: (a) officers (b) manual). 19 Issue method (if not Browne). 20 Loan period (if not 2 weeks). 21 Fines: (a) adult (b) children (c) OAPs. 22 Co-operative schemes. 23 Stock: (a) adult lending (b) adult reference (c) children (d) schools (e) current periodical titles. 24 Issues: (a) adult (b) children (c) schools (d) institutions. 25 Staff: (a) officers (b) manual (c) chartered libns (d) graduates. 26 Finance: (a) total expenditure (b) non-rate income (c) per capita expenditure (d) expenditure for books (e) expenditure for records etc (f) salaries & wages. 27 Capital projects.

BIRMINGHAM METROPOLITAN DISTRICT COUNCIL
—continued
Wood, Highfield Rd, B14 4DU. **13** P-t 13.
14 Shakespeare lib (over 40,000 vols in 86 languages); Stone colln (photographs); Milton; Johnson; Cervantes; children's literature; war poetry; early printed books; fine bindings & private press books; Boulton & Watt colln.
15 2; (a&b) c. 88,000 (c) 20,500; (d) 1,500; (e) £2 pa (£5 pa corporate membership); (f) as books. **16** 375,000 sheets of mounted illustrations; 450 paintings; £2 pa for paintings.
17 Schools, housebound, prisons, hospitals, old people's homes, community centres, voluntary local house visiting services. **19** Computer charging (central libs).
20 4 weeks. **21** (a) 5p pw or part; (b & c) none.
22 WESLINK; B-LINK. **23** (a) 1,217,978; (b) 963,050; (c) 340,812; (f) 3,101. **24** (a&d) 6,909,600 books; 182,539 sheets of mounted illustrations; (b) 1,977,785.
25 (a) 578; (b) 113; (c) 207; (d) 70. **26** (a) £3,179,850; (b) £79,120; (c) £2.92; (d) £497,760; (e) £14,380; (f) £1,396,400.

BOLTON METROPOLITAN BOROUGH COUNCIL (pop 261,800) Central Library, Le Mans Crescent, Bolton, Lancashire, BL1 1SD (0204-22311/23543; telex 635001). Dir of Arts, Libraries, Museums, Entertainments: Miss Dorothy Noel Pearce FLA, FRSA; Principal Libn: Mr Francis Norman Parker FLA. **7** Arts. **9** Mon-Fri: ad ldg & children 9.30-19.30; ref 9.30-20.00; Sat: 9.30-17.00 (District Libs 9.30-12.30).
10 HQ; District; Branch. **11** **District Libraries:** Farnworth: Market St, Farnworth, Bolton (0204-72790), Libn: Miss H.M. Makin FLA; Harwood: Gate Fold, Harwood, Bolton, BL2 3HN (0204-54565), Libn: Mrs J.R. Pritchard ALA; Westhoughton: Library St, Westhoughton, Bolton, BL5 3AU (052 36-811222), Libn: Mrs A.J. Smith FLA. **12** Astley Bridge Lib, Moss Bank Way, Bolton, BL1 8NP; Church St, Blackrod, Bolton, BL6 5EQ; Brazley Lib, Cedar Ave, Horwich, Bolton, BL6 6EU; Breightmet Dr, Bolton, BL2 6EE; The Crescent, Toppings Estate, Bromley Cross, Bolton, BL7 9JU; Horsfield St, Deane, Bolton, BL3 4LU; Great Lever Lib, Bradford Rd, Bolton, BL3 2HF; Halliwell Lib, Hatfield Rd, Bolton, BL1 3BU; Heaton Lib, New Hall Lane, Bolton BL1 5LF; High St, Bolton, BL3 6SZ; Jones St, Horwich, Bolton, BL6 7AJ; Oakes St, Kearsley, Bolton, BL4 8DJ; Coronation Sq, Little Lever, Bolton, BL3 1LP; Marsh Lane, Farnworth, Bolton, BL4 0AP; Tonge Moor Rd, Bolton, BL2 2LE. **13** P-t 1; mobiles 1.
14 Walt Whitman Colln in Central Ref Library; Bowyer Bible (19th-cent grangerised Bible in 46 vols inc over 5,000 unique illustrations); Rev P.H. Ditchfield Colln (memoirs & miscellaneous writings). **15** 1; (a) 21,110; (c) 3,655; (e) £2.16; (f) as books. **16** 220; £1.00 pa & 25p per picture (usually 6 months). **17** Schools, housebound, hospitals, old people's homes. **18** Cultural activities, entertainments (£31,385; Entertainments Officer; (a) 3). **19** Automated Library Systems Label Based System (Central). **20** 3 weeks.
21 (a) 1p pd; (b) 1p pw; (c) none. **23** (a) 410,108; (b) 68,872; (c) 83,475; (d) 55,000; (e) 466. **24** (a) 2,407,497; (b) 508,797; (d) 6,880 (old people's homes).
25 (a) 130; (b) 29; (c) 29; (d) 14. **26** (a) £572,835; (b) £36,205; (c) £2.19; (d) £127,595; (e) £1,650; (f) £349,670.

BORDERS REGIONAL COUNCIL (pop 100,000) Regional Library Headquarters, Public Library, Lawyers Brae, Galashiels, Selkirkshire, TD1 3JQ (0896-2512). Regional Libn: Mr Alan Carter FLA, FSA (Scot); Dep Regional Libn: Mrs L.M. McLachlan BA, ALA. **7** Education. **8** Dir of Education: Mr J. McLean BSc. **9** Mon-Fri: 9.00-20.00;

Sat: 9.00-13.00.
10 HQ; Area; Branch. **11** **Area Libraries:** Galashiels: Lawyers Brae, Galashiels, TD1 3JQ (0896-2512); Duns Area: 49 Newtown St, Duns, TD11 3AY (036 12-2338), Libn: Mr J. Luby ALA; Peebles: Chambers Institution, Peebles, EH45 8AG (0721-20123), Libn: Mr P. Taylor BSc, ALA; St Boswells: Old School, St Boswells, TD6 0AG (08352-3260), Libn: Mr J.G. Allan; Hawick: North Bridge St, Hawick, TD9 9QT (0450-2637), Libn: Miss R.M. McIvor MA, FLA. **13** P-t 13; mobiles 2.
15 2; (c) 2,000. **17** Schools, housebound, hospitals, old people's homes, playgroups. **20** 4 weeks. **21** No fines.
25 (a) 43; (b) 15; (c) 14; (d) 8. **26** (a) £243,190; (b) £1,350; (c) £2.43; (d) £67,720; (e) £3,600; (f) £113,160.

BRADFORD METROPOLITAN DISTRICT COUNCIL (pop c. 461,000) Central Library, Prince's Way, Bradford, West Yorkshire, BD1 1NN (0274-33081; telex 51480). Chief Libn: Mr W. Davies FLA; Principal Libns: B.B. Smith ALA (support); G.J. Wood FLA (circulation); N.V. Tilley ALA (inf); R.E. Wilkes FLA (young people's). **7** Educational Services (Cultural Activities Panel). **8** Dir of Educational Services: W.R. Knight. **9** Mon-Fri: ad ldg & ref 9.00-21.00, children 9.00-19.00; Sat: 9.00-18.00.
10 HQ; Area; Branch. **11** **Area Libraries:** Baildon/Bingley/ Shipley: Shipley Lib, Victoria Rd, Saltaire, Shipley (0274-54084), Libn: K. Harries ALA; Keighley: Keighley Lib, North St, Keighley (053 52-2309/61453), Libn: G. Kitching ALA; Wharfedale: Ilkley Lib, Station Rd, Ilkley (09433-2721/4), Libn: D.E. Gadsby ALA. **12** Bolton Rd, Eccleshill, Bradford, BD2 4SR; Myrtle Walk, Off Chapel Lane, Bingley, BD16 1EW; Kelcliffe, Baildon, Shipley, BD16 6ND; North Rd, Wibsey, Bradford, BD6 1TR; Cross Lane, Great Horton, Bradford, BD7 3JT; Carlisle Rd, Manningham, Bradford, BD8 8BB; Huddersfield Rd, Wyke, Bradford, BD12 8HS; Main St, Menston, LS29 6LG; Grange Rd, Burley-in-Wharfedale, LS29 7HD; Memorial Gardens, Silsden, Keighley, BD20 0PH.
13 P-t 30; mobiles 2.
14 Philip Snowden Colln (c. 1,000 vols); Bronte Colln (c. 200 vols); Federer Colln (c. 9,000 vols); Dickons Colln (c. 400 vols vols); Lees Botanical Colln (c. 500 vols). **15** 4; (a) 89,024; (c) 12,716; (e) £1.00 pa, £0.50 per 6 months, OAPs £0.25 pa; (f) as books. **17** Schools, housebound, hospitals, old people's homes, immigrant centres, social services day centres, council service. **18** Cultural activities.
19 Plessey Computerised (Central, soon 5 other libs); photocharging; token. **20** 3 weeks. **21** (a) 1p pd (exc Sun) 1st week; 5p pw thereafter; (b&c) none (cost of overdues only).
22 BRASTACS. **23** (a) Total adult: 908,923; (c) 132,293; (d) 151,520; (e) 962. **24** (a) 4,456,418; (b) 798,589; (c) 91,734; (d) 78,274.
25 (a) 250; (b) 43; (c) 57; (d) 13. **26** (a) £1,479,540; (b) £53,540; (c) £3.2; (d) £250,520; (e) £5,120; (f) £681,910.

BUCKINGHAMSHIRE COUNTY COUNCIL (pop 507,000) County Library Headquarters, Walton St, Aylesbury, Buckinghamshire, HP20 1UU (0296-4671; telex 83101). Libn: Mr C. Rippon FLA; Dep: Mr H. Westacott FLA. **7** Education. **8** Chief Education Officer: Mr R.P. Harding BSc, FIMA, DPA. **9** Mon-Fri: 9.00-20.00 (Mon 17.00); Sat: 9.00-17.00.
10 HQ; Division; Branch. **11** **Divisional Libraries:** Walton St, Aylesbury, HP20 1UU (0296-5000); Westfield Rd, Bletchley, MK2 2RA (0908-72797; telex 82115); Queen Victoria Rd, High Wycombe, HP11 1BD (0494-23981; telex 837333).
12 Chiltern Ave, Amersham, HP6 5AH; Reynolds Rd, Beaconsfield, HP9 2NJ; Wakeman Rd, Bourne End, SL8 5SX; Verney

BUCKINGHAMSHIRE COUNTY COUNCIL *—continued*
Close, Buckingham, MK18 1JP; Windsor Lane, Burnham Park,
Burnham, SL1 7HR; High St, Chalfont St Peter, SL9 9QA;
Elgiva Lane, Chesham, HP5 2JB; 38 Station Rd, Gerrards
Cross, SL9 8EL; High St, Great Missenden, HP16 0AL; New
Pond Rd, Holmer Green, HP15 6SU; Institute Rd, Marlow SL7
1BL; St John St, Newport Pagnell, MK16 8HQ; Church St,
Princes Risborough, HP17 9AA; Bells Hill Green, Stoke Poges,
SL2 4BY; Church St, Stony Stratford, MK11 1JR; High St,
Wendover, HP22 6DU; 122 Church St, Wolverton, MK12 5JR.
13 P-t 20; mobiles 8 & 1 spare.
14 Local history; drama; music; foreign texts.   **15** 1;
(a) 8, 606; (c) 1, 683; (e) £1.75 pa; (f) 5p pw.   **17** Schools,
housebound, prisons, hospitals, old people's homes, WEA
classes.   **19** Token (for fiction).   **20** 4 weeks (simplified
weekly issue).   **21** (a & c) 5p pw, max 70p & postage;
(b) 1p pw, max 6p.   **23** (a) 358, 880; (b) 72, 359; (c) 78, 010;
(d) 335, 992; (e) 751.   **24** (a) 4, 060, 036; (b) 1, 150, 576.
25 (a) 223; (b) 24; (c) 81.5; (d) 6.   **26** (a) £1, 023, 850
(+ £209, 780 Agency Service); (b) £978, 700 (+ £45, 150);
(c) £2; (d) £85, 255 (+ £87, 560); (e) £1, 450; (f) £600, 650
(+ £59, 630).

BURY METROPOLITAN BOROUGH COUNCIL (pop 181, 000)
Central Library, Manchester Rd, Bury, Lancashire BL9 0DG
(061-764 4110/761 4021). Dir of Libs & Arts: Mr P.
Chadwick FLA; Principal Libn: Mr F. Sunderland ALA.
7 Recreation & Amenities.   **9** Mon-Fri: 9.30-19.30; Sat:
ad ldg & children 9.30-16.00, ref 9.30-16.30.
10 HQ; District; Branch.   **11 Districts:** Prestwich Lib,
Longfield Centre, Prestwich, M25 5AY (061-773 8920), Div
Libn: Mr H. B. Wilkinson BA, ALA; Radcliffe Lib, Stand Lane,
Radcliffe M26 9WR (061-723 2344), Div Libn: Mr P. J. Morgan
ALA; Ramsbottom Lib, Carr St, Ramsbottom BL0 9AE (070
682-2484), Div Libn: Mrs J. Garstang ALA.   **12** Brooklands
Lib, Bury Old Rd, Prestwich; Polefield Rd, Prestwich;
Unsworth Lib, Sunnybank Rd, Bury; Pinfold Lane, Whitefield;
Market St, Tottington.   **13** P-t 4.
15 2; (a) 13, 459; (c) 2, 571; (e) resident, rated or employed
in Borough £2.00 + VAT, others £2.50 + VAT; (f) 1p pd.
16 410; £1.50 + VAT.   **17** Schools, hospitals, old people's
homes.   **19** Tokens (adult fiction at Central & Unsworth).
20 3 weeks.   **21** (a) 1p pd; (b & c) no fines.   **23** (a) 255,
423; (b) 25, 005; (c) 47, 162; (d) 150, 503; (e) 94.   **24** (a)
1, 554, 700; (b) 266, 739.
25 (a) 91; (b) 10; (c) 24; (d) 8.   **26** (a) £409, 500; (b) £29, 450;
(c) £2.26; (d) £62, 320; (e) £1, 150; (f) £229, 000.

CALDERDALE METROPOLITAN BOROUGH COUNCIL (pop
190, 736) Libraries Department, Wellesley Park, Gibbet St,
Halifax, West Yorkshire, HX2 0BA (0422-63561). Chief Libn:
Mr D. Williamson FLA; Dep Chief Libn: Miss D. E. Wood ALA.
7 Recreation & Amenities.   **9** Mon-Fri: 10.00-20.00 (Weds
12.00); Sat: 10.00-17.00.
10 HQ; Area; Branch.   **11 Areas:** Central & Mid: Central
Lib, Belle Vue, Lister Lane, Halifax, HX1 5LA (0422-60425),
Central Libn: Mr D. Taylor ALA, Mid Libn: Mr C. W.
Staples ALA; East: Brighouse B Lib, Halifax Rd, Brighouse,
HD6 2AF (048 47-4740), Libn: Mr J. R. Jebson ALA; West;
Hebden Bridge B Lib, Cheetham St, Hebden Bridge HX7 8EP
(042 284-2151), Libn: Miss M. G. Morgan BA, ALA.
12 Coronation St, Elland, HX5 0DF; Council Offices, Leeds
Rd, Hipperholme, Halifax, HX3 8ND; Crowtrees Lane, Ras-
trick, Brighouse, HD6 3NE; Akroyd B Lib, Bankfield, Boothtown
Rd, Halifax, HX3 6HG; Harrison House, 10 Harrison Rd,
Halifax, HX1 2AF; 237-9 King Cross Rd, Halifax HX1 3JL;
Mixenden Rd, Mixenden, Halifax, HX2 8PU; Lydgate, Northo-
wram, Halifax HX3 7EJ; Beechwood Rd, Holmfield, Halifax,
HX2 9BU; Skircoat Green Rd, Halifax, HX3 0LQ; Hollings Mill
Lane, Sowerby Bridge, HX6 2QG; Strand, Rochdale Rd,
Todmorden, Lancashire, OL14 7LB.   **13** P-t 24; 1 mobile;
1 travelling library.
15 3; (a&b) 6, 950; (c) 868; (d) 292; (e) £2.00 pa, or 10p per
issue (3 weeks); (f) 3p pw, max 30p.   **16** 204; 25p per
picture (3 months).   **17** Schools, housebound, hospitals,
old people's homes.   **20** 3 weeks   **21** (a) 3p pw, max 30p;
(b) 1p pw, max 10p.   **23** (a) 462, 958; (b) 32, 934; (c) 59, 646;
(d) 35, 000; (e) 217.   **24** (a) 2, 120, 767; (b) 299, 337.
25 (a) 110; (b) 15; (c) 24; (d) 5.   **26** (a) £481, 500; (b)

£17, 460; (c) £2.524; (d) £100, 380; (e) £1, 750; (f) £297, 060.

CAMBRIDGESHIRE COUNTY COUNCIL (pop 542, 525)
Cambridgeshire Library Headquarters, Princes St, Hunting-
don, Cambridgeshire, PE18 6NS (0480-52181; telex 32180).
County Libn: R. Brown FLA, AMBIM; Dep County Libn: B. A.
Dwyer BA, ALA.   **7** Leisure & Amenities.   **9** Mon-Fri:
10.00-19.00; Sat: 10.00-17.00.
10 HQ; Divisions; Groups; Service Points.   **11 Divisional
HQs:** Eastern: Gordon Ave, March, PE15 8AL (03542-3349/
4749), Asst County Libn: A. T. Bates ALA; Peterborough:
Broadway, Peterborough, PE1 1RX (0733-69105/6), Asst
County Libn: B. Hall FLA; Cambridge: Lion Yard, Cambridge,
CB2 3QD (0223-65252), Asst County Libn: A. J. Armour FLA;
Huntingdon: Princes St, Huntingdon, PE18 6PH (0480-52181),
Asst County Libn: J. T. Rowland ALA.   **12** Arbury Court,
Cambridge, CB4 2JQ; High St, Cherry Hinton, Cambridge,
CB1 4HZ; Mill Rd, Cambridge, CB1 2AZ; Milton Rd BLib,
Ascham Rd, Cambridge, CB4 2BD; Rock Rd, Cambridge,
CB1 4UG; School Lane, Ramsey, Huntingdon, PE17 1AF;
Bible Orchard, North Rd, St Ives, Huntingdon, PE17 4PS;
Huntingdon Rd, St Neots, Huntingdon, PE19 1BG; New Rd,
Chatteris, PE16 6BJ; Ely City Lib, Palace Green, Ely, CB7
4EW; 15 Market St, Whittlesey, Peterborough, PE7 1BA;
Stanground B Lib, Southfields Ave, Peterborough, PE2 8RZ;
Walton B Lib, Mountsteven Ave, Peterborough, PE4 6HX;
Westwood B Lib, Hampton Court, Peterborough, PE3 7JB;
Alexandra Rd, Wisbech, PE13 1HQ; Dogsthorpe Newark B
Lib, Central Ave, Peterborough, PE1 4LH; 10-12 Woollards
Lane, Great Shelford, Cambridge, CB2 5LZ; Townsend Rd,
Wittering, Peterborough, PE8 6BD.   **13** P-t 31; mobiles 8.
14 Cambridgeshire colln; Peterborough colln; John Clare
colln.   **15** 5; (a) 57, 300; (c) 7, 132; (e) £3 pa; (f) 5p pw.
16 400; none.   **17** Schools, housebound, prisons, hospitals,
old people's homes.   **18** Cultural activities.   **19** Photocharging; tokens.   **20** 4 weeks.   **21** (a&c) 5p; (b) none.
23 (a, b, c&d) 1, 120, 177 (e) 589.   **24** (a, b&d) 5, 368, 779
(exc schools).
25 (a) 220; (b) 12; (c) 48; (d) 13.   **26** (a) £1, 165, 350;
(b) £126, 240; (c) £2.15; (d) £330, 740; (f) £550, 140.

CHESHIRE COUNTY COUNCIL (pop 904, 600) Cheshire
Libraries & Museums, County Library HQ, 91 Hoole Rd,
Chester, Cheshire, CH2 3NG (0244-20055; telex 61355). Dir
of Libs & Musuems: A. Wilson FLA; 1st Dep Dir: Mr P. D.
Gee FLA; 2nd Dep Dir: G. A. Carter FLA.   **7** Library &
Arts.   **9** Mon-Fri: District Libs: 9.30-19.00, BLibs:
9.30-13.00, 14.00-19.00 (2 days 17.00); Sat: District Libs:
9.30-17.00, BLibs: 9.30-13.00, 14.00-17.00.
10 HQ; Division; Branch.   **11** Divisions: Chester/
Ellesmere Port: Ellesmere Port Lib, Civic Way, Ellesmere
Port (051-355 8101: telex 627348); Crewe/Congleton: Crewe
Lib, Prince Albert St, Crewe, CW1 2DH (0270-2156/3354;
telex 36648), Div Libn: Mr J. Sankey FLA; Halton/Vale
Royale: Runcorn Lib, Egerton St, Runcorn, WA7 1JN
(09285-74495; telex 627072), Div Libn: Miss S. Challinor
ALA; Macclesfield: Wilmslow Lib, South Dr, Wilmslow, SK9
1NW (099-64 28977/28034; telex 667102), Div Libn: Mr L.
Murray ALA; Warrington: Museum St, Warrington, WA1 1JB
(0925-5439; telex 628 278), Div Libn: Mr W. B. Leeming FLA.
12 St John St, Chester; Parkgate Rd, Neston, Wirral; Moody
St, Congleton; Beam St, Nantwich; Witton St, Northwich;
Victoria Rd, Widness; High St, Winsford; Park Green,
Macclesfield; Western Ave, Blacon; Great Boughton, Green
Lane, Vicars Cross; 31 Hoole Rd, Chester; Ivor Johnson, Hope
Farm Rd, Ellesmere Port; Lache Park Ave, Chester; Chester
Rd, Little Sutton; Wealstone Lane, Upton, Chester; Sandbach
Rd North, Alsager; London Rd, Holmes Chapel, Crewe; The
Common, Sandbach; Townfield Lane, Barnton; Queens Ave,
Ditton, Widnes; Rock Chapel, Main St, Frodsham; Sandiway,
Mere Lane, Cuddington, Northwich; Russett Rd, Weaverham,
Northwich; Palmerston St, Bollington; Handforth Green, Hand-
forth; Brook St, Knutsford; Park Lane, Poynton, Stockport;
Warrington Rd, Culcheth; Davies Way, Off Brookfield Rd,
Lymm; Poplars Ave, Orford, Warrington; Honiton Way,
Penketh; Alexandra Park, Stockton Heath; Holes Lane,
Woolston; Educational Resources Lib, High St, Winsford;
Research Lib, Commerce House, Chester.   **13** P-t 10;
mobiles 7 & 2 trailers & 4 school mobiles.

CODE: 1 Local authority. 2 Population. 3 Postal address of HQ. 4 Telephone & telex. 5 Chief Libn. 6 Deputy. 7 Committee responsible. 8 Officer to whom Libn is responsible (if any). 9 Hours. 10 Organisation. 11 Area libraries. 12 Branches. 13 Part-time libraries; mobiles. 14 Special collections. 15 Gramophone records: number of libraries, (a) record issues (b) cassette issues (c) record stock (d) cassette stock (e) loan charges (f) fines. 16 Pictures: stock; charges. 17 Other services. 18 Cultural activities (expenditure, officer in charge, staff: (a) officers (b) manual). 19 Issue method (if not Browne). 20 Loan period (if not 2 weeks). 21 Fines: (a) adult (b) children (c) OAPs. 22 Co-operative schemes. 23 Stock: (a) adult lending (b) adult reference (c) children (d) schools (e) current periodical titles. 24 Issues: (a) adult (b) children (c) schools (d) institutions. 25 Staff: (a) officers (b) manual (c) chartered libns (d) graduates. 26 Finance: (a) total expenditure (b) non-rate income (c) per capita expenditure (d) expenditure for books (e) expenditure for records etc (f) salaries & wages. 27 Capital projects.

CHESHIRE COUNTY COUNCIL—*continued*
14 Cheshire Salt Colln; local studies; early printed books (to 1640); early shorthand systems; complete BSI; Warrington Academy colln; Broadbent colln (early children's books); books printed in Warrington, inc Eyres Press to 1800; Penketh Society of Friends (Quakers) Colln. **15** 11; (a&b) 120,000; (c) 25,000; (d) 1,500; (e) none; (f) as books. **16** 383; £2.20 pa. **17** Schools, housebound, prisons, hospitals, old people's homes, local government inf service, Cheshire inf service, WEA classes, post-entry training school for County Council. **18** Cultural activities; entertainments (£54,000 Arts & Community Officer (a) 1). **19** Photocharging with Plessey Light Pen Attachment. **20** 3 weeks. **21** (a) 1p pd; (b&c) none. **22** LADSIRLAC; LINOSCO. **23** (a) 1,331,879; (b) 165,413; (c) 152,239; (d) 310,000; (e) 625. **24** (a) 7,620,916 (inc records & pictures); (b) 1,570,320. **25** (a) 355; (b) 66; (c) 97; (d) 43. **26** (a) £2,038,000; (b) £69,000; (c) £2.25; (d) £445,000; (e) £20,000; (f) £1,007,630. **27** Kuntsford Library—replacement District Library (estimated cost £333,000).

CLACKMANNAN DISTRICT COUNCIL (pop c.46,000) Clackmannan District Library, 17 Mar St, Alloa, Clackmannanshire, FK10 1HT (02592-2160 ext 288). District Chief Libn: Mr W. McK. Murray ALA; Asst District Chief Libn: Mr M. Mitchell ALA. **7** District Council. **8** Chief Executive Officer: Mr Allan Stewart MA, LLB. **9** Mon-Fri: 10.00-19.00 (Tues 16.30); Sat: 9.00-12.30. **10** District HQ; Branch. **12** Alloa B Lib, 17 Mar St, Alloa, FK10 1HT (in same building as District Lib). **13** P-t 16. **14** Music; local history. **17** Schools, housebound, prisons (detention centre), hospitals, old people's homes. **23** (a) 101,921; (b) 2,683; (c) 19,134. **25** (a) 15; (b) 2; (c) 3. **26 Finance** (10½ months only): (a) £66,280; (b) £660; (c) £1.44; (d) £22,540; (f) £33,400.

CLEVELAND COUNTY COUNCIL (pop 579,000) Central Library, Victoria Sq, Middlesbrough, Cleveland, TS1 2AY (0642-45294; telex 58439). County Libn: Mr F. Regan FLA, FRSA; Asst County Libns: Mr L. Still ALA; Mr G. R. Fletcher ALA. **7** Leisure & Amenities. **8** Dir of Leisure & Amenities: Mr J. W. Pinches DipMus. **9** Mon-Fri: ad ldg & children 9.30-19.00, ref 9.30-20.00; Sat: 9.30-17.00. **10** HQ; District; Branch. **11 District Libraries:** Hartlepool: Clarence Rd, Hartlepool, TS24 7EW (0429-2905/ 63778); Stockton: Church Rd, Stockton-on-Tees, TS18 1TU (0642-62680), District Libn: Mr L. R. Meynell ALA; Middlesbrough District HQ, Victoria Sq, Middlesbrough, TS1 2AY (0642-45294), District Libn: Mr F. Jenkins ALA; Langbaurgh: Coatham Rd, Redcar, TS10 1RP (06493-72162), District Libn: Mr J. V. Fairbrother ALA. **12** Foggy Furze B Lib, Stockton Rd, Hartlepool; Northgate, Hartlepool; Owton Manor B Lib, Wynyard Rd, Hartlepool; Station Lane, Seaton Carew; Glamorgan Grove, Throston Grange Hartlepool; West View B Lib, Miers Ave, Hartlepool; Bedale Ave, Billingham; Butterfield Dr, Orchard Est, Egglescliffe; Fairfield Rd, Stockton; Blue Hall Recreation Ground, Leven Rd, Norton; Roseberry B Lib, The Causeway, Billingham; Roseworth B Lib, Redhill Rd, Stockton; George St, Thornaby, Stockton; Wrightson House B Lib, New Town Centre Thornaby; High St, Yarm; Acklam Rd, Acklam, Middlesbrough; Berwick Hills B Lib, Ormesby Rd, Middlesbrough; Easterside B Lib, Broughton Ave, Middlesbrough; Grove Hill B Lib, The Gables, Marton Rd, Marton, Middlesbrough; The Willows, Marton, Middlesbrough; Melbourne House, Newport Rd, Middlesbrough; Kings

Rd, North Ormesby, Middlesbrough; Beresford Crescent, Thorntree, Middlesbrough; Whinney Banks B Lib, Harehills Rd, Middlesbrough; High St, Brotton, Saltburn by the Sea; 3 Farndale Sq, Dormanstown, Redcar; 248 Normanby Rd, Eston, Middlesbrough; Birchington Ave, Grangetown, Middlesbrough; Westgate, Guisborough; Laburnum Rd, Redcar; Hall Grounds, Loftus, Saltburn by the Sea; Marske B Lib, Windy Hill Lane, Marske by the Sea, Redcar; The Crescent, Nunthorpe, Middlesbrough; Orchard Way, Ormesby, Middlesbrough; Roseberry Sq, Redcar; Saltburn B Lib, Windsor Rd, Saltburn by the Sea; Skelton B Lib, Coniston Rd, Skelton in Cleveland, Saltburn. **13** P-t 8; mobiles 5. **14** Kelly Colln (Bibles & related work); local collns & archives. **15** 5; (a) 58,840; (b) 531; (c) 9,600; (d) 300; (e) £2 pa; (f) as books. **17** Schools, housebound, hospitals, old people's homes, WEA & university extramural classes collns. **18** Cultural activities, entertainments (£297,466; Dir of Leisure & Amenities; (a) 22). **19** Photocharging (1 lib). **20** 4 weeks. **21** (a & c) 1p 1st week, 5p pw thereafter, max 50p; (b) none. **22** LIST. **23** (a) 815,000; (b) 95,000; (c) 200,000; (e) 1,300. **24** (a) 5,199,439; (b) 1,236,675. **25** (a) 278; (b) 40; (c) 58; (d) 16. **26** (a) £1,428,329; (b) £32,484; (c) £2.46; (d) £328,330; (e) £10,000; (f) £725,798.

CLWYD COUNTY COUNCIL (pop 360,000) Headquarters Library, County Civic Centre, Mold, Clwyd, CH7 6NW (0352-2121; telex 61454). County Libn: Mr Glyn Davies FLA, FRSA; Dep County Libns: Miss D. Roberts ALA; Mr W. G. Williams ALA, MInstAM. **7** Cultural, Recreation & Amenities. **9** Mon-Fri: 9.30-19.00; Sat: 9.00-17.00. **10** HQ; Area; Branch, Mobile. **11 Area Libraries:** Alyn & Deeside: Wepre Dr, Connah's Quay, Deeside, CH5 4HA (024 451-3485; telex 61535), Area Libn: Mrs A. Jenkins; Colwyn: Woodlands Rd West, Colwyn Bay, LL29 7DH (0492-2358, telex 61533), Area Libn: Mr W. R. Flint FLA; Delyn: Church St, Flint, CH6 5AP (035 26-3168, telex 61537), Area Libn: Mrs M. J. Cottington ALA; Glyndwr: 46 Clwyd St, Ruthin, LL15 1HP (082 42-3040/3648, telex 61531), Area Libn: Miss E. O. Edwards ALA; Rhuddlan: Wellington Rd, Rhyl (0745-53814, telex 61539), Area Libn: Mr P. A. Kerrigan ALA; Wrexham: Llwyn Isaf, Wrexham, LL11 1AU (0978-2351, telex 61551), Area Libn: Mrs M. Roberts ALA. **12** Market St, Abergele; Aston B Lib, Larch Ave, Shotton, Deeside; Broughton CP School, Broughton Hall Rd, Broughton; Mold Rd, Buckley; Derby Rd, Caergwrle; Plas Kynaston, Cefn Mawr, Wrexham; Chapel Lane, Chirk, Wrexham; Parish Hall, Coedpoeth; Lenton Pool, Denbigh; Sealand Ave, Garden City, Deeside; Vicarage Lane, Gresford; The Old Rectory, Rectory Lane, Hawarden; North Rd, Holywell; Castell Alun High School, Hope; Parade St, Llangollen; Mancot Lane, Mancot, Deeside; Daniel Owen Centre, Earl Road, Mold; Nant Hall Rd, Prestatyn; Rhosllanerch B Lib, Princess St, Rhosllanerchrugog, Wrexham; Vicarage Lane, Rhuddlan; High St, Ruabon, Wrexham; The Roe, St Asaph; Salisbury Ave, Saltney, Chester. **13** P-t 25; mobiles 15. **14** Arthurian literature colln (1,800 items); local history colln (4,740 items). **15** 11; (a) 23,299; (c) 10,000; (d) 30; (e) £1 pa per ticket; (f) 2p pw or part. **16** 500; £1 pa. **17** Schools, housebound, hospitals, old people's homes, WEA. **19** Token (2 Area Libs). **20** 2 weeks. **21** (a&c) 2p pw or part; (b) none. **22** WRLS. **23** (a) 491,291; (b) 118,704; (c) 144,209; (d) 286,553; (e) 520. **24** (a) 3,595,346; (b) 610,474; (c) 2,964,600; (d) 365,400. **25** (a) 191; (b) 28; (c) 45; (d) 12. **26** (a) £1,176,040;

CLWYD COUNTY COUNCIL—*continued*
(b) £137, 280; (c) £3. 12; (d) £240, 870; (e) £4, 750;
(f) £583, 260.

CLYDEBANK DISTRICT COUNCIL (pop 59, 173) Central
Library, Dumbarton Rd, Clydebank, Dumbartonshire, G81 1XH
(041-952 1416). District Chief Libn: Mr John Brogan ALA;
Asst Chief Libn: Mr John McLaughlin ALA.   **7** Environmental Services.   **8** Dir of Environmental Services: Mr
John McPherson MRSanA, MCIT, AMInstTA.   **9** Mon-Fri
ad ldg & ref 10. 00-20. 00, children's 14. 30-18. 00; Sat: ad
ldg, & ref 10. 00-17. 00, children's 10. 00-13. 00.
10 HQ; Branch.   **12 Branches:** Milldam Rd, Faifley, Clydebank; Hawthorn St, Parkhall, Clydebank; Swindon St, Dalmuir,
Clydebank; Glenhead Leisure Centre, Duntiglennan Rd,
Duntocher.   **13** P-t 1.
14 Local history.   **15** 3; (a) 31, 160; (b) 7, 942; (c) 5, 500;
(d) 700; (e) non-ratepayers £1. 50 pa.   **17** Schools, housebound, old people's homes, playgroups, storytelling.
21 (a) 5p pw; (b) 2p pw; (c) at discretion.   **23** (a) 80, 132;
(b) 6, 000; (c) 20, 000; (d) 5, 000; (e) 95.   **24** (a) 394, 085;
(b) 71, 370; (c) 8, 456; (d) 26, 400.
25 (a) $32\frac{1}{2}$; (b) $6\frac{1}{2}$; (c) 8; (d) 2.   **26** (a) £162, 000;
(b) £1, 800; (c) £2. 74; (d) £34, 400; (e) £4, 475; (f) £92, 788.

CORNWALL COUNTY COUNCIL (pop 400, 310) Cornwall
County Library, County Hall, Station Rd, Truro, Cornwall,
TR1 3HG (0872-4282; telex 45305). County Libn: Mr R. D.
Hale BA, FLA; Dep Libn: J. E. Farmer ALA.   **7** Library
Sub-Committee.   **8** Sec for Education: K. Cruise MA.
9 Mon-Fri 9. 30-17. 00 (or 19. 00); Sat: 9. 30-16. 00.
10 HQ; Area; Branch; Mobile.   **11 Areas:** West: Penzance
Lib, 62 Morab Rd, Penzance, TR18 4EY (0736-5012), Libn:
P. F. Byrne ALA; Central: St Austell Lib, Carlyon Rd, St
Austell (0726-3348), Libn: R. M. Nott ALA; East: Bodmin Lib,
Lower Bore St, Bodmin (0208-2286), Libn: M. G. Thomas
ALA.   **12** The Castle, Bude; The Cross, Camborne:Muni-
cipal Offices, The Moore, Falmouth; Commercial Rd, Hayle;
Trengrouse Way, Helston; Bounsall's Lane, Launceston;
Barras St, Liskeard; Sea Front, East Looe; Marcus Hill,
Newquay; The Institute, Padstow; Clinton Rd, Redruth;
Gabriel St, St Ives; Callington Rd, Saltash; Fore St, Torpoint;
Pydar St, Truro.   **13** P-t 8; mobiles 10; 2 Container Libs.
14 Local colln (at Redruth).   **15** 4; (a) 23, 277; (c) 7, 575;
(e) 10p per record or set of records; (f) 5p pw, max 25p.
16 121; 50p & 15p for each loan.   **17** Schools, housebound,
hospitals, old people's homes, evening classes.   **19** Photocharging (5 libs).   **20** 3 weeks.   **21** (a&c) 5p pw, max 25p;
(b) no fines.   **22** CTIS.   **23** (a, d&e) 669, 468.   **24** (a&b)
5, 377, 037.
25 (a) $143\frac{1}{4}$; (b) $24\frac{1}{2}$; (c) 44; (d) 9.   **26** (a) £818, 765;
(b) £108, 965; (c) £1. 8172; (d) £211, 590; (e) £2, 990;
(f) £420, 425.

COVENTRY METROPOLITAN DISTRICT COUNCIL (pop
336, 000) Administration, Reference Library, Bayley Lane,
Coventry, West Midlands, CV1 5RG (0203-25555 ext 2317;
telex 31469). Dir Libs, Arts & Museums Dept: Mr Anthony
Davis ALA; Dep Dirs: J. L. Atkins ALA (Libs, Inf & Archives);
Dr T. Werner (Arts & Museums).   **7** Libraries, Arts &
Leisure.   **9** Mon-Fri: ad ldg & children's 9. 00-20. 00
(closed Wed), ref 9. 00-21. 00; Sat: 9. 00-16. 30.
10 HQ; Central Departments; Community Area; Branch.
11 Community Areas: North: Foleshill Lib, Broad St, Coventry
CV6 5BG (0203-87562), Libn: Mr P. Jackson **ALA**; East:
Stoke Lib, Kingsway, Coventry (0203-452059), Libn: Mr R.
Major ALA; West: Tile Hill Lib, Jardine Crescent, Coventry
(0203-464994), Libn: Mr R. Heath ALA.   **12** Roseberry Ave,
Bell Green; Prior Deram Walk, Canley, Coventry; Central
Lending Lib, Trinity Church Yard, Coventry; Central Ref Lib,
Bayley Lane, Coventry; Earlsdon Ave, Earlsdon, Coventry;
Droylesdon Park Rd, Finham, Coventry; Briscoe Rd,
Holbrook, Coventry; Jubilee Crescent, Radford, Coventry;
Moseley Ave, Radford, Coventry; Stoke Lib, Walsgrave Rd,
Coventry; 192 Remembrance Rd, Willenhall; Coventry Informa-
tion Centre, 6 Broadgate, Coventry.   **13** P-t 10; mobiles 1.
14 Coventry & Warwickshire local history colln, (inc
George Eliot colln); Bartleet colln (bicycles & bicycling).
15 1, (but records in 10 branches); (a) 217, 872; (b) 70, 046;

(c) 15, 520; (d) 4, 353; (e&f) fee/fine 6p per item pw.
16 374; 50p pa per picture.   **17** Schools, housebound,
hospitals, old people's homes.   **18** Cultural activities
(Art Gallery, Museums & Arts Centre; £282, 050; Dep Dir
(Arts & Museums); a 21; b 25).   **19** Photo-charging;
Plessey computer charging.   **21** (a) 5p pw; (b)1p pw; (c)
no fines.   **22** CADIG.   **23** (a) 261, 167; (b) 19, 243;
(c) 72, 662; (d) 83, 204; (e) 474.   **24** (a&b) 3, 254, 153;
(c) 10, 235; (d) hospitals 35, 981.
25 (a) 154; (b) 21; (c) 23; (d) 7.   **26** (a) £794, 560;
(b) £80, 530; (c) £2. 36; (d) £126, 850; (e) £11, 000; (f)
(f) £437, 470

CUMBERNAULD AND KILSYTH DISTRICT LIBRARY (pop
54, 500) 8 Allander Walk, Cumbernauld, Glasgow, G677 1EE
(023 67-25664). District Libn: Miss Jean Dawson ALA;
Dep: Mr John Macalpine ALA.   **7** Leisure & Recreation.
9 Mon-Fri; ad ldg & ref 10. 00 (Wed 9. 00)-21. 00 (Wed. 17. 00),
children's 10. 00 (Wed 9. 00)-19. 00 (Wed 17. 00); Sat closed.
10 District; Branch.   **12** Burngreen B Lib, Kilsyth;
Abronhill B Lib, Pine Rd, Cumbernauld.   **13** P-t 1; mobiles
1.
15 1; (a&b) 13, 663; (e) £2. 00 non-returnable deposit (50p
for senior citizens).   **17** Housebound, old people's homes.
20 3 weeks.   **21** No fines.   **23** (a) 85, 950; (b) 1, 645;
(c) 27, 966; (e) 53.   **24** (a) 368, 969; (b) 80, 007.
25 (a) $26\frac{1}{2}$; (b) 4; (c) $7\frac{1}{2}$; (d) 2.   **26 Finance** (for $10\frac{1}{2}$
months only): (a) £123, 210; (b) £526; (c) £2. 26; (d) £26, 064;
(e) £2, 000; (f) £61, 000.

CUMBRIA COUNTY COUNCIL (pop 476, 500) Cumbria County
Library Headquarters, 1-3 Portland Sq, Carlisle, Cumbria,
CA1 1PS (0228-32161; telex 64316). County Libn: Mr John S.
Smith FLA; Dep County Libn: Mr Stuart A. Brewer MA, ALA.
7 Arts & Amenities.   **9** Mon-Fri 9. 00-19. 00; Sat: 9. 00-
17. 30.
10 HQ; Division; Branch.   **11 Divisions:** North East: Tullie
House, Castle St, Carlisle, CA3 8TR (0228-24166; telex
64317), Div Libn: Mr H. W. Hodgson FRSA, FLA; South:
Barrow-in-Furness Lib, Ramsden Sq, Barrow-in-Furness,
LA14 1LL (0229-20650; telex 65240), Div Libn: Mr D. F.
James FLA; West: Workington Lib, Vulcans Lane, Working-
ton (0900-3744/5311; telex 64318), Div Libn: Mr H. J.
Chandler BEM, FLA.   **12** Kelsick Rd, Ambleside; Low
Wiend, Appleby, CA16 6QP; Charles Edmonds Lib, Egremont,
CA22 2DH; Market Sq, Cleator Moor, CA25 5AP; Main St,
Cockermouth, CA13 9LU; Nelson St, Dalton-in-Furness;
Grange Fell Rd, Grange-over-Sands; Stricklandgate, Kendal;
Heads Lane, Keswick; Lawson St, Maryport, CA15 6ND; St
George's Rd, Millom; Portland Pl, Penrith, CA11 7QN;
Roose Rd, Barrow-in-Furness; Gosforth Rd, Seascale, CA20
1PN; Main St, Seaton, Workington; Kings Rd, Ulverston;
Central Dr, Walney, Barrow-in-Furness; High St, Wigton;
Ellerthwaite, Windermere; Lowther St, Whitehaven, CA28 7QZ.
13 P-t 27 (inc 10 centres); mobiles 17 (inc 2 for School
Library Service).
14 Local collns: for Furness (at Barrow, inc archives), for
Cumberland & Westmorland (at Carlisle, inc Jackson Library),
for Westmorland (at Kendal), Whitehaven, Workington;
drama & playsets (at HQ); geology of North West England
(at Kendal); Technical Library (at Barrow); Wordsworth colln
(at Carlisle).   **15** 2; (a) 8, 028; (b) 3, 731; (c) 2, 512; (d)
264; (e) 5p per record pw; (f) 3p pw or part, max 30p.
16 30.   **17** Schools, housebound, prisons, hospitals, old
people's homes, pre-school play groups, community homes,
further education classes.   **19** Tokens (for fiction in some
libs).   **20** 4 weeks.   **21** (a) 3p pw or part, max 30p
(b&c) no fines.   **23** (a) 907, 900; (b) 58, 844; (c) 164, 948;
(d) 141, 414; (e) 460.   **24** (a) 4, 707, 485; (b) 754, 538;
(c) 1, 853, 160.
25 (a) 270; (b) 39; (c) 52; (d) 15.   **26** (a) £998, 500;
(b) £14, 500; (c) £2. 10; (d) £270, 000; (e) £1, 000; (f) £576, 700.

CUMNOCK AND DOON VALLEY DISTRICT (pop 49, 000)
Bank Glen, Camnock, Ayrshire, KA18 1PH (0292-22024).
District Libn: Miss I. C. Crawford ALA; Asst District Libn:
Miss I. C. Kerr.   **8** Chief Executive: Mr Douglas Hemmings
DPA.
10 HQ; Branch.

CODE: 1 Local authority. 2 Population. 3 Postal address of HQ. 4 Telephone & telex. 5 Chief Libn. 6 Deputy. 7 Committee responsible. 8 Officer to whom Libn is responsible (if any). 9 Hours. 10 Organisation. 11 Area libraries. 12 Branches. 13 Part-time libraries; mobiles. 14 Special collections. 15 Gramophone records: number of libraries, (a) record issues (b) cassette issues (c) record stock (d) cassette stock (e) loan charges (f) fines. 16 Pictures: stock; charges. 17 Other services. 18 Cultural activities (expenditure, officer in charge, staff: (a) officers (b) manual). 19 Issue method (if not Browne). 20 Loan period (if not 2 weeks). 21 Fines: (a) adult (b) children (c) OAPs. 22 Co-operative schemes. 23 Stock: (a) adult lending (b) adult reference (c) children (d) schools (e) current periodical titles. 24 Issues: (a) adult (b) children (c) schools (d) institutions. 25 Staff: (a) officers (b) manual (c) chartered libns (d) graduates. 26 Finance: (a) total expenditure (b) non-rate income (c) per capita expenditure (d) expenditure for books (e) expenditure for records etc (f) salaries & wages. 27 Capital projects.

CUNNINGHAME DISTRICT AUTHORITY (pop 125,000) District Library Headquarters, St, Mary's, Springvale St, Saltcoats, Ayrshire (0294-68111/2). Libn: Miss Jane G. McMillan ALA; Dep: Miss Janice F. Martin MA, ALA. **7** Leisure & Recreation. **8** Dir of Leisure & Recreation: Mr David P. Webster DPE, LCSP. **9** Hours under review. **10** HQ; Branch. **12** Montgomery St, Ardrossan; The Strand, Beith; James St, Dalry; Town Hall, Irvine; Avils Pl, Kilbirnie; Howgate, Kilwinning; Bath St, Largs; Springvale St, Saltcoats; Main St, Stevenston; The Institute, West Kilbride. **13** P-t 6; mobiles 1. **15** 3; (a) 2,700; (c) 1,500 (e) none; (f) as books (damage: 10p per scratch up to value of record). **17** Housebound, hospitals, old people's homes. **18** Entertainments (Dir of Leisure & Recreation). **21** (a, b&c) 2p pw. **23** (a) 147,773; (b) 2,647; (c) 24,332; (e) 25. **24** (a) 919,206; (b) 132,929. **25** (a) 36; (b) 16; (c) 6; (d) 2. **26** (a) £171,630; (c) £133; (d) £46,500; (e) £2,000; (f) £90,500.

CYNON VALLEY BOROUGH COUNCIL (pop 68,690) Central Library, High St, Aberdare, Mid-Glamorgan, CF44 7AG (068588-2441). Libn: G. Davies; Dep: R. Arnold ALA. **7** Libraries. **9** Mon-Fri: ad ldg & ref 10.00-18.00 (Mon & Fri 20.00); Sat: ad ldg & ref 9.00-13.00, children's 10.00-13.00. **10** HQ; Branch. **12** Duffryn Rd, Mountain Ash; High St, Hirwaun, Aberdare; Walter St, Abercynon, Mountain Ash; Workmen's Institute, Ynysybwl; Workmen's Hall, Penrhiwceiber, Mountain Ash. **13** P-t 2; mobiles 1. **15** 1; (a) 3,076; (c) 1,200; (e) £1.00 pa & 10p per record; (f) 3p pw. **20** 4 weeks. **21** (a&c) 3p pw; (b) 2p pw. **23** (a) 171,001; (b) 10,825; (c) 21,186; (e) 146. **24** (a, b, c&d) 522,964. **25** (a) 31; (b) 8; (c) 3; (d) 1. **26** (a) £161,370; (b) £4,210; (c) £2.03; (d) £26,815; (e) £3,320; (f) £87,250.

DERBYSHIRE COUNTY COUNCIL (pop 892,300) Derbyshire County Library, Central Office, County Offices, Matlock, Derby, DE4 3AG (0629-3411; telex 377596). County Libn: P.D. Gratton BA, DPA, FLA; Dep County Libn: R.E. Marston FLA; Asst County Libn: C.R. Field FLA, FAMS. **7** Leisure. **9** Mon-Fri: ad ldg 9.00-10.00, ref 9.00-20.00, children's 9.00-18.00; Sat 9.00-17.00. **10** HQ; Area; Branch. **11** Areas: Amber Valley & Erewash: Central Lib, Market Pl, Ilkeston, DE7 5RN (060 72-3361), Libn: A. Germany ALA; Bolsover, Chesterfield & N.E. Derbyshire: Central Lib, Corporation St, Chesterfield, S41 7TY (0246-2047), Libn: R.J.Webb ALA; Derby & South Derbyshire: Central Lib, The Wardwick, Derby, DE1 1HF (0322-31111), Libn: L.Greaves FLA; High Peak & West Derbyshire: Public Lib, The Crescent, Buxton, SK17 6BQ (0298-5331), Libn: P.H. Turner ALA. **12** Blagreaves Lane, Littleover, Derby; Civic Centre, Swadlincote, Burton-on-Trent; Park Farm Centre, Birchover Way, Allestree; Sitwell St, Spondon, Derby; Chaddesden Park, Derby; Wollaton Road Lib, Greenwood Ave, Chaddesden, Derby; Burton Rd, Littleover, Derby; Peartree Rd, Derby; Memorial Hut, Station Rd, Mickleover, Derby; Nunsfield House Lib, Boulton Lane, Alvaston, Derby; High St, Alfreton; Bridge St, Belper, Derby; Heanor BLib, Ilkeston Rd, Langley Mill, Nottingham; Tamworth Rd, Long Eaton, Nottingham; Grosvenor Rd, Ripley, Derby; Wirksworth Rd, Duffield, Derby; Cotton St, Bolsover, Chesterfield; Kenning Park, Holmgate Rd, Clay Cross, Chesterfield; Rectory Rd, Clowne, Chesterfield; Manor House, Dronfield, Chesterfield; Main St, Shirebrook, Nottingham; Hall Lane,

Staveley, Chesterfield; 9 Littlemoor Centre, Newbold, Chesterfield; New St, Bakewell, DE4 1DY; Victoria Hall, Glossop; Steep Turnpike, Matlock. **13** P-t 52; mobiles 12. **14** Derbyshire colln (inc Devonshire & Bemrose collns, at Derby); drama library (Matlock); D.H. Lawrence colln (Ilkeston); Sitwell colln (Derby); George Stephenson colln (Chesterfield). **15** 6; (a) 16,000; (c) 5,362; (e) 10p per loan. **16** 189; none. **17** Schools, housebound, prisons, hospitals, old people's homes, WEA, Police Authority. **19** Photocharging; Derby system. **20** 4 weeks. **21** (a) 4p 1st week, 2p pw thereafter, max 20p; (b&c) none. **22** NANTIS; EMRLB. **23** (a) 1,085,915; (b) 118,660; (c) 244,287; (d) 665,941; (e) 700. **24** (a&b) 9,410,079. **25** (a) 439; (b) 76; (c) 79; (d) 19. **26** (a) £1,867,203; (b) £36,070; (c) £2.08; (d) £458,835; (e) £880; (f) £940,415.

DEVON COUNTY COUNCIL (pop 931,000) Administrative Centre, Barley House, Isleworth Rd, Exeter, Devon EX4 1RQ (0392-74142; telex 42933). County Libn: R.G. Charlesworth ALA. **7** Amenities & Countryside. **9** No overall pattern as yet. **10** Administrative Centre; Area; Division; Branch. **11** Areas: North: Area Lib, Vicarage St, Barnstaple, EX32 7EJ (0271-71886), Area Libn: K.Hunt FLA; East: Central Lib, Castle St, Exeter, EX4 3PQ (0392-73047), Area Libn: I.G.Hardy FLA; South: Central Lib, Lymington Rd, Torquay, TQ1 3DT (0803-211251), Area Libn: J.R. Pike FLA; West: Central Lib, Drake Circus, Plymouth, PL4 8AL (0752-68000), Area Libn: J.R. Elliott FLA. **12** South St, Axminster; The Square, Barnstaple; New Rd, Bideford; Abbey Rd, Bovey Tracey; Chaloners Rd, Braunton; Market St, Brixham; Station Rd, Budleigh Salterton; Broadsands Rd, Paignton; 37 High St, Crediton; Plumer Rd, Crownhill; Newcomen Rd, Dartmouth; 2 Old Town St, Dawlish; Duke St, Devonport; Efford Lane, Plymouth; Exeter Rd, Exmouth; 48/50 New St, Honiton; Brookfield Pl, Ilfracombe; Ilbert Rd, Kingsbridge; Bank St, Newton Abbot; Fore St, Northam; 3 Station Rd, Okehampton; Old Town Hall, Ottery St. Mary; Courtland Rd, Paignton; Harewood, Ridgeway, Plympton; Horn Cross Rd, Plymstock; Pounds House, Outlands Rd, Peverell, Plymouth; The Square, Victoria Rd, St Budeaux, Plymouth; St Thomas, Station Yard, Cowick St, Exeter; The Esplanade, Seaton; Blackmore Dr, Sidmouth; 351 Southway Dr, Plymouth; Outram House, Albert Rd, Stoke, Plymouth; Bedford Sq, Tavistock; Fore St, Teignmouth; Angel Hill, Tiverton; The Square, Torrington; 4 The Plains, Totnes; Woodland Fort, Crownhill Rd, Honicknowle, Plymouth. **13** P-t 32; mobiles 18. **14** Local history collns (East & West Devon Area Libraries); naval history colln (Plymouth). **15** 2; (a) 60,653; (c) c.14,500; (e) 10p per record, 20p per set. (f) 5p pw. **16** c.22,000 (also local history photographs & prints at Plymouth). **17** Schools, housebound, prisons, hospitals, old people's homes, WEA, lighthouses. **19** Photocharging; Bookamatic; token. **20** 3 weeks. **21** (a&c) 5p pw; (b) 2p pw. **23** (a) 1,600,000; (b) 250,000; (c) 400,000; (e) c.650. **24** (a&d) 13,250,000. **25** (a) 367; (b) 100; (c) 64; (d) 6. **26** (a) £2,024,525; (b) £302,775; (c) £2.175; (d) £614,750; (e) £6,450; (f) £992,575.

DONCASTER METROPOLITAN BOROUGH COUNCIL (pop 285,000) Central Library, Waterdale, Doncaster, South Yorkshire, DN1 3JE (0302-69123/4/5; telex 54425). Chief Libn: Mr E.J.Chapman BA, ALA; Dep Chief Libn: Mr J.H. Coster ALA. **7** Education (Libraries, Museums & Arts Sub-Committee). **8** Dir of Education: Mr M.J. Pass MA. **9** Mon-Fri: Central 9.00-18.00 (ref 20.00); main branches

DONCASTER METROPOLITAN BOROUGH COUNCIL
—continued
9.30-19.00; Sat: Central 9.00-17.00; main branches 9.30-
17.00.
10 Central Library (HQ); Circulation HQ; Branch.
11 Carcroft Circulation HQ, Skellow Rd, Carcroft, Doncaster,
DN6 8HF (030 272-2327/8898), Libn-in-charge: Miss A.
Gardner ALA.   **12** Church St, Armthorpe, Doncaster;
Youth Centre, Selby Rd, Askern, Doncaster; High Rd, Balby,
Doncaster; Doncaster Rd, Bawtry, Doncaster; Cooke St,
Bentley, Doncaster; Ellers Ave, Bessacarr, Doncaster;
Church Hall, Community Centre, Sturton Close, West
Bessacarr; Goodison Boulevard, Cantley, Doncaster; 11 West
St, Conisbrough, Doncaster; Church Rd, Denaby Main, Doncas-
ter; 120 Thorne Rd, Edenthorpe, Doncaster; 7 The Crescent,
Edlington, Doncaster; High St, Hatfield, Doncaster, DN7 6RY;
Hayfield Community Library, Hayfield Comprehensive School,
Hurst Lane, Auckley, Doncaster; Community Centre, Shadyside,
Hexthorpe, Doncaster; Montrose Ave, Intake, Doncaster;
Church Hall, Kirk Sandall, Doncaster; Bank St, Mexborough,
Doncaster; The Circle, Moorends, Doncaster; County Primary
School, Norton, Doncaster; McConnel Crescent, Rossington,
Doncaster; Amersall Rd, Scawthrope, Doncaster, DN5 9PQ;
Sprotbrough Rd, Doncaster; Church Rd, Stainforth, Doncaster,
DN7 5PW; Fieldside, Thorne, Doncaster DN8 4BQ; Castle
Gate, Tickhill, Doncaster; Edlington Lane, Warmsworth,
Doncaster; Parkway South, Wheatley, Doncaster; Miners
Welfare Hall, Welfare Rd, Woodlands, Doncaster; Doncaster
Royal Infirmary, Thorne Rd, Doncaster.   **13** P-t 12; mobiles
2.
14 Local history; railways; coal-mining; horse-racing.
15 3; (a) 29, 216; (b) 3, 125; (c) 3, 155; (d) 500; (e) 6p per
record or cassette, per fortnight.   **16** 321; 30p per print,
for 13 weeks.   **17** Schools, housebound, hospitals, old
people's homes.   **19** Islington System.   **20** 3 weeks.
21 (a, b&c) none.   **22** YHJLS.   **23** (a, b, c, d&e) 571, 904.
24 (a, b, c&d) 2, 935, 175.
25 (a) 135; (b) 20½; (c) 31; (d) 8.   **26** (a) £806, 150;
(b) £18, 150; (c) £2.84; (d) £217, 830; (e) £5, 700; (f) £360, 650.

DORSET COUNTY COUNCIL (pop 566, 360) Dorset County
Library, Colliton Park, Dorchester, Dorset DT1 1XJ (0305-
3131; telex 417201). County Libn: Mr H.E. Radford FLA;
Dep County Libn: Mr K. Carter ALA, AMBIM.   **7** Amenities.
9 Mon-Fri: ad ldg & children 9.30-19.00, ref 9.30-20.00;
Sat: 9.30-17.00.
10 HQ; Area HQ; Group; Branch.   **11 Area HQs:** West:
Dorset County Lib, Colliton Park, Dorchester, DT1 1XJ
(0305-3131), Asst County Libn: Miss J.M. Rhodes ALA;
Central: Poole Central Lib, Arndale Centre, Poole, BH15 1QE
(02013-3919), Asst County Libn: Miss S.J. Senior BA, FLA,
DMA; East: Bournemouth Central Lib, Lansdowne, Bourne-
mouth, BH1 1RU (0202-26603), Asst County Libn: Mr H.N.
Heissig FLA.   **12** Anderson House, Bovington Camp,
Wareham; 51 East St, Bridport; Bell St, Shaftesbury; Digby
Hall, Hound St, Sherborne; Bath Road, Sturminster Newton;
High St, Swanage; Unitarian Church Schoolroom, South St,
Wareham (Mon closed); Portlands Underhill Library, East
St, Fortuneswell, Portland; Westwey Rd, Weymouth (Thurs
closed); The Tabernacle, Blandford (Wed closed); Steel House,
5th Army Education Corps Centre, Blandford Camp (Sat
closed); Britannia Rd, Parkstone, Poole (Thurs closed);
Hanham Rd, Wimborne, Dorset; Heathcote Rd, Boscombe,
Bournemouth; Strouden Ave, Bournemouth; Druitt Buildings,
High St, Charminster; Gordon Rd, Highcliffe; Wimborne Rd,
Winton, Bournemouth; Wimborne Rd, Kinson, Bournemouth;
East Howe Lib, Cunningham Crescent, Bournemouth; Seabourne
Rd, Southbourne, Bournemouth; Westbourne Lib, Alum Chine,
Bournemouth; Library Rd, Ferndown, Wimborne; Station Rd,
West Moors (Wed closed); Canford Heath Lib, Mitchell Rd,
Poole (Thurs closed).   **13** P-t 11; mobiles 7.
14 Local history (at Dorchester, Bournemouth, Weymouth
& Poole); Thomas Hardy colln; Powys family colln; files of
local newspapers.   **17** Schools, housebound, prisons,
hospitals, old people's homes; adult education classes,
borstals.   **19** Computer via Olivetti RP50.   **20** 3 weeks.
21 (a&c) 3p pw; (b) none.   **22** HATRICS.   **23** (a) 856, 816;
(b) 104, 337; (c) 175, 056.   **24** (a) 7, 948, 719; (c) 142, 372;
(d) 73, 683.

25 (a) 281; (b) 79; (c) 73; (d) 14.   **26** (a) £1, 372, 995;
(b) £35, 335; (c) £2. 326; (d) £234, 600; (f) £703, 525.

DUDLEY METROPOLITAN BOROUGH COUNCIL (pop
297, 760) Central Library, St James's Rd, Dudley, West Midlands, DY1 1HR (0384-56321 telex 339831). Dir of Leisure &
Recreation: Mr John Hoyle FLA; Asst Dir (Libs): Mr P.J.
Bullock ALA.   **7** Recreation & Amenities.   **9** Mon-Fri:
9.00-19.00; Sat: 9.00-17.00.
10 HQ/Central; District; Branch.   **11 Districts:** Moor St,
Brierley Hill DY5 3ET (0384-77457), Libn: Mr S.R. Masters
ALA; The Precinct, Halesowen, B63 4AJ (021-550 6188; telex
338385), Libn: Mr B.N. Kirby FLA; Market St, Kingswinford
(038 44-3906), Libn: Mrs J. Noons: Ladies Walk, Sedgley,
DY3 3UA (09073-3462), Libn: Mr G. Baker ALA; Hagley Rd,
Stourbridge (03843-4004; telex 337145), Libn: Mr D.C.
Hickman ALA.   **12** Old Meeting Rd, Coseley; Colley Lane,
Cradley; Long Lane, Halesowen; Chapel St, Lye; Information
Centre, Churchill Precinct, Dudley.   **13** P-t 6; mobiles 2.
14 Brierley Hill Glass colln, (books on 'Stourbridge' glass
industry); Francis Brett Young colln, (Halesowen Lib).
15 4; (a&b) 122, 041; (c) 12, 431; (d) 1, 134; (e) 15p per 2 weeks,
& £1.08 pa for non-residents; (f) 2p pd.   **17** Schools,
housebound, hospitals, old people's homes.   **18** Cultural
activities, entertainments (Asst Dir Research, Admin &
Dev).   **19** Photocharging, computerised (Plessey).
20 3-4 weeks.   **21** (a) 4p pw or part; (b&c) none.
22 MISLIC; WESLINK.   **23** (a) 413, 306; (b) 34, 562;
(c) 139, 415; (d) 110, 500; (e) c. 300.   **24** (a&b) 3, 204, 611.
25 (a) 111; (b) 12; (c) 35; (d) 4.

DUMBARTON DISTRICT LIBRARIES (pop 79, 000) Dumbarton
District Libraries, Levenford House, Helenslee Rd,
Dumbarton, Glasgow, G82 4AJ (0389-63136). District Libn:
Mr William M. Martin ALA; Dep District Libn: Mr Brian D.
Osborne ALA.   **7** Civic Amenities.   **8** Dir of Civic
Amenities: Mr Ian Owen.   **9** Mon-Fri: ad ldg & children's
10.00-19.30, ref 9.00-19.30; Sat: 10.00-17.00.
10 HQ; Branch.   **12** Gilmour St, Alexandria; Carrochan Rd,
Balloch; Strathleven Pl, Dumbarton; John St, Helensburgh;
Ladyton Estate, Bonhil.   **13** P-t 5; mobiles 2.
14 Local history.   **17** Hospitals, old people's homes.
18 Cultural activities, entertainments.   **20** 4 weeks.
21 (a, b&c) none.
25 (a) 46; (b) 7½; (c) 6; (d) 5.   **26** (d) £51, 370; (f) £125, 170.

DUMFRIES AND GALLOWAY REGIONAL LIBRARY SERVICE
(pop 143, 000) Ewart Library, Catherine St, Dumfries, Dumfries-
shire DG1 1JB (0387-3820). Regional Libn: Mr Desmond
Donaldson FLA, FRSA, FSA (Scot); Asst Regional Libn: Mr
Hugh Macpherson ALA.   **7** Education.   **8** Dir of Education:
J.K. Purves MA, DipEd.   **9** Mon-Fri: 10.00-19.30; Sat:
10.00-17.00.
10 HQ; Large Branch; Small Branch; Mobile.   **11 Large
Branches:** Ewart Lib, Catherine St, Dumfries DG1 1JB
(0387-3820), Libn: Mr A. Fulton ALA; Annan B Lib, Charles
St, Annan, DG12 5AG (04612-2809), Libn: Miss J. Sinclair
ALA; Castle Douglas B Lib, Market Hill, Castle Douglas, DG7
3AY, Libn: Mr M. McColl; Stranraer B Lib, London Rd,
Stranraer, DG9 8ES (0776-2153), Libn: Mr A. Wilson ALA.
13 P-t 21; mobiles 5.
14 Dumfries & Galloway collns; Frank Mills colln (ballads);
Dumfries Burns Club collns; R.C. Reid Genealogical colln.
17 Schools, housebound, prisons, hospitals, old people's
homes.   **21** (a&c) 2½p pw; (b) 1p pw.
25 (a) 51; (b) 4; (c) 12; (d) 6.   **26** (a) £293, 200; (c) £2.50;
(d) £68, 500; (f) £150, 000.

DUNDEE CITY DISTRICT LIBRARIES (pop 203, 000) Central
Library, Albert Institute, Albert Sq, Dundee, Angus, DD1 1DB
(0382-24938/9). Chief Libn: Mr Duncan M. Torbet FLA;
Dep Chief Libn: Mr David Crichton.   **7** Civic Amenities
(Libraries Sub-Committee).   **8** Dir of Civic Amenities:
Mr H.E. Rubidge ALA.   **9** Mon-Fri: Central 9.30-19.00
(ref 21.00), Branches 9.00-19.00 (Thurs 13.00); Sat: Central
9.30-17.00, Branches 9.00-13.00.
10 HQ; Branch.   **12** Central Junior Lib & Art, Music &
Architectural Lib, Ward Rd, Dundee; High St, Lochee, Dundee;
Arthurstone Terrace, Dundee; Blackness B Lib, 225 Perth
Rd, Dundee; Coldside B Lib, 150 Strathmartine Rd, Dundee;

CODE: 1 Local authority. 2 Population. 3 Postal address of HQ. 4 Telephone & telex. 5 Chief Libn. 6 Deputy. 7 Committee responsible. 8 Officer to whom Libn is responsible (if any). 9 Hours. 10 Organisation. 11 Area libraries. 12 Branches. 13 Part-time libraries; mobiles. 14 Special collections. 15 Gramophone records: number of libraries, (a) record issues (b) cassette issues (c) record stock (d) cassette stock (e) loan charges (f) fines. 16 Pictures: stock; · charges. 17 Other services. 18 Cultural activities (expenditure, officer in charge, staff: (a) officers (b) manual). 19 Issue method (if not Browne). 20 Loan period (if not 2 weeks). 21 Fines: (a) adult (b) children (c) OAPs. 22 Co-operative schemes. 23 Stock: (a) adult lending (b) adult reference (c) children (d) schools (e) current periodical titles. 24 Issues: (a) adult (b) children (c) schools (d) institutions. 25 Staff: (a) officers (b) manual (c) chartered libns (d) graduates. 26 Finance: (a) total expenditure (b) non-rate income (c) per capita expenditure (d) expenditure for books (e) expenditure for records etc (f) salaries & wages. 27 Capital projects.

DUNDEE CITY DISTRICT LIBRARIES —*continued*
St Roques B Lib, 1 Blackscroft, Dundee; Queen St, Broughty Ferry, Dundee; Camperdown B Lib, 58 Craigmount Rd, Lochee, Dundee; Findcastle St, Fintry, Dundee; 24 Balmoral Ave, Douglas, Dundee; Orleans Pl, Menzieshill, Dundee; Derwent Ave, Kirkton, Dundee; Whitfield B Lib, Montpelier House, Drumgeith Rd, Dundee; 20 Union St, Monifieth; Ardler B Lib, Turnberry Ave, Dundee.   **13** P-t 1; mobiles 1.
14 Wighton colln (early printed music); Wilson colln (19th-20th cent photographs of Dundee & district inc negatives).   **15** 2; (c) 714; (d) 303; (e) £1.00 returnable deposit; (f) as books.   **17** Schools, housebound, hospitals, old people's homes, playgroups.   **18** Cultural activities, entertainments.
21 (a&b) 1st week ½p, 2nd week 1p, 3rd week 2p, 4th week 2½p, max 25p (children 5p); (c) none.   **23** (a) 320, 776; (b) 113, 609; (c) 59, 153; (d) 13, 000; (e) 790.   **24** (a) 1, 490, 175; (b) 238, 713; (d) 41, 326.
25 (a) 100; (b) 28; (c) 12; (d) 7.   **26** (a) £497, 595; (b) £16, 350; (c) £2.45; (d) £98, 130; (e) £2, 700; (f) £321, 750.
27 New Central Library £1, 970, 400.

DUNFERMLINE DISTRICT COUNCIL (pop 124, 000) Central Library Headquarters, Abbot St, Dunfermline, Fife, KY12 7NW (0383-23661/2). Dir of Libs, Museums & Art Galleries: Mr James K. Sharp FLA; Asst Dir: Mr John J. Jamieson ALA.
7 Leisure & Recreation.   **9** Mon-Fri: ad ldg 10.00-19.00 ref 10.00-13.00, 14.00-20.00, children's 10.00-12.00, 14.00-19.00; Sat: 10.00-13.00, 14.00-17.00.
10 Central HQ; Group; Branch.   **11** **Group Libraries:** Cowdenbeath, Libn: Miss P.A. Sutherland MA, ALA; Lochgelly, Libn: Mrs I. Taylor ALA; Inverkeithing, KY11 1LG, Libn: Mrs C. Stuart ALA; West Fife, Kincardine.
12 Rosyth; Lochore; Kelty; Abbey View.   **13** P-t 7; mobiles under consideration
14 Murison Burns colln; George Reid colln (Mediaeval mss); local history (West Fife).   **15** 1; (a) 21, 453; (b) 6, 193; (c) 2, 010; (d) 621; (e) £2 returnable deposit; (f) as books.   **17** Housebound, hospitals, old people's homes.   **20** 3 weeks.   **21** (a&c) 2p pw or part & cost of notices; (b) none, except cost of notices.   **23** (a) c. 220, 000; (b) c. 5, 000; (c) c. 30, 000; (e) 50.
25 (a) 52; (b) 2 & cleaners; (c) 9; (d) 1.   **26** Finance (10½ months only): (a) £223, 000; (b) £5, 420; (c) £1.80; (d) £63, 000; (e) £1, 750; (f) £110, 000.

DURHAM COUNTY COUNCIL (pop 610, 000) County Library, PO Box, County Hall, Durham, DH1 5TY (0385-64411; telex 53-281). County Libn: Mr A.H. Good FLA; Dep County Libn: Mr S.C. Dean FLA.   **7** Education (Libraries, Museums & Arts Sub-Committee).   **9** Mon-Fri: 10.00-19.00; Sat: 10.00-17.00.
10 HQ; District; Branch.   **11** **Districts:** Market Pl, Crook, DL15 8QH (038 882-2269), Libn: Mr R.A. Bell ALA; Crown St, Darlington, DL1 1ND (0325-2034), Libn: Miss S.I. Cairns ALA; South St, Durham City, DH1 4QS (0385-64003), Libn: Mr J. Main ALA; Burnhope Way, Peterlee, SR8 1NT (078 323-2279), Libn: Mr C. Ferguson ALA; 24 Cheapside, Spennymoor, DL16 6DJ (038 881-2394), Libn: Mr L. Maughan ALA; High St, Stanley, DH9 0DQ; (02073-2128), Libn: Mr. G.H. Watson ALA.   **12** North Rd, Annfield Plain, Stanley, DH9 8EZ; Witham Hall, Barnard Castle, DL12 8LY; Cheveley Park Shopping Centre, Belmont, DH1 2AA; Lightfoot Institute, Bishop Auckland, DL14 7JN; Back Middle St, Blackhall Colliery, Hartlepool, Cleveland, TS27 4HD; Durham Rd, Bowburn, DH6 5AB; Lowland Rd, Brandon, DH7 8NN; Station Rd, Chester-le-Street, DH3 3PB; Durham Rd, Chilton, Ferryhill, DL17 0EX; Cockerton Green, Darlington, DL3 9AA; Victoria Rd, Consett, DH8 5AT; Seaside Lane, Easington Colliery, Peterlee, SR8 3PN; North St, Ferryhill, DL17 8HX; Sunderland Rd, Horden, Peterlee, SR8 4PF; Barnes Rd, Murton, Durham, SR7 9QR; Dalton Way, Newton Aycliffe, DL5 4PD; Newbiggen Lane, Lanchester, DH7 0NT; Alnwick Rd, Newton Hall, DH1 5NL; Ouston Lane, Pelton, Chester-le-Street, DH2 1EZ; Plawsworth Rd, Sacriston, Durham, DH7 6HJ; St John's Sq, Seaham, SR7 7JE; Front St, Sedgefield, Stockton-on-Tees, Cleveland, TS21 3AT; 'Hallgarth', Shildon, DL4 1AH; Co-operative Terrace, Shotton, Durham, DH6 2LW; Severn Crescent, South Moor, Stanley; High St, Thornley, Durham, DH6 3EL; Church Rd, Trimdon, Trimdon Station, TS29 6PY; 73 High St, Willington, Crook, DL15 0PF; Front St, Wingate, TS28 5AG; Woodhouse Close B Lib, Woodhouse Lane, Bishop Auckland, DL14 6JX.
13 P-t 36; mobiles 12.
14 Railway colln; local colln (Durham & Darlington).
15 7; (a) 16, 393; (c) 11, 144; (e) £2.00 pa; (f) 4p pw or part.
17 Schools, housebound, prisons, hospitals, old people's homes.   **18** Cultural activities; entertainments (County Libn).   **19** Photocharging (1 lib).   **20** 3 weeks.
21 (a) 4p pw or part; (b&c) 1p pw or part.   **22** LIST.
23 (a&b) 1, 173, 369; (c) 172, 983; (d) 257, 446; (e) 330.
24 (a) 5, 866, 456; (b) 886, 699; (c) 1, 716, 000; (d) 291, 604.
25 (a) 238; (b) 48; (c) 32; (d) 3.   **26** (a) £1, 224, 620 (net); (b) £120, 200; (c) c. £2.00; (d) £300, 000; (e) £4, 000; (f) £679, 360.

DYFED COUNTY COUNCIL (pop 243, 200) Public Library, St Peter's St, Carmarthen, Dyfed, SA31 1LN (0267-7488/89). County Libn: Mr Alun R. Edwards MA, FLA.   **7** Education (Library Sub-Committee).   **9** Mon-Fri: Aberystwyth 9.30-18.00; Carmarthen 10.00-19.00; Haverfordwest 9.30-17.00; Sat: Aberystwyth 9.30-17.00; Carmarthen 10.00-17.00; Haverfordwest 9.30-13.00.
10 HQ; Regional; Branch.   **11** **Regional Libraries:** Haverfordwest: Dew St, Haverfordwest, SA61 1SU (0437-2070/4920), Libn: Iorweth Davies; Ceredigion: Corporation St, Aberystwyth, SY23 2BU (0970-7464/7557), Libn: Mr John T. Richards ALA; Carmarthen: St Peter's St, Carmarthen, SA31 1LN (0267-7488/89), Libn: Mr W.D. Griffiths ALA.
12 Hamilton Terrace, Milford Haven; High St, Fishguard; Greenhill Crescent, Tenby; Iscennen Rd, Ammanford; Meyrick St, Pembroke Dock; Guildhall, Cardigan.   **13** P-t 37; mobiles 12.
14 Francis Green mss (solicitor's papers of genealogical nature, notes, wills etc); Henry Owen (solicitor's library held in trust, historical & local); part of Carmarthenshire Antiquarian Society's library.   **15** 2; cassette libraries: 6; (a) 15, 987; (b) 26, 613; (c) 4, 614; (d) 9.665, (e) £1.00 & VAT; (f) 5p pw max 40p.   **17** Schools, housebound, hospitals, old people's homes, adult education classes.   **18** Cultural activities (£17, 500; Cultural Services Libn; a 5).   **19** Token charging (Aberystwyth only).   **20** 3 weeks.   **21** (a) 5p pw max 40p; (b&c) none.   **23** (a) 710, 327; (b) 32, 250; (c) 75, 500; (d) 505, 250; (e) 110.   **24** (a) 2, 923, 848; (b) 472, 599; (d) 39, 777.
25 (a) 120; (b) 7; (c) 24; (d) 14.   **26** (a) £681, 120 (exc schools); (b) £8, 580; (c) £2.80; (d) £118, 695; (e) £7, 830; (f) £381, 780.

EAST KILBRIDE DISTRICT COUNCIL (pop 80, 000) Central Library, Alexandra Arcade, East Kilbride, Lanarkshire, G74 1LX (0355 22-20046). Chief Libn: Mr Donald E. Harrison FLA; Asst Chief Libn: Mr J. Loudon Craig ALA.   **7** Halls,

EAST KILBRIDE DISTRICT COUNCIL—*continued*
Entertainments & Libraries.   **8** Acting Dir of Leisure &
Recreation: Mr Kenneth Love IPFA.   **9** Mon-Fri: 9.45-19.45
(Wed 13.00); Sat: 9.45-17.00.
10 Central; Branch.   **12** St Leonard's Lib, Neighbourhood
Centre, East Kilbride G74 2AT; 14/16 Calderwood Sq, East
Kilbride G74 3BQ; Glasgow Rd, Strathaven, ML10 6LZ; 133
Westwood Sq, East Kilbride, G75 8JQ.   **13** Mobiles 1.
15 2; (a&b) 31,486; (c) 4,094; (d) 350.   **17** Housebound,
hospitals, old people's homes.   **20** 4 weeks.
21 (a, b&c) none.   **23** (a) 109,951; (b) 4,000; (c) 29,925;
(e) 33.   **24** (a) 854,516; (b) 191,516; (d) 8,000.
25 (a) 46; (b) 9; (c) 8; (d) 4.   **26 Finance** (10½ months only):
(a) £198,400; (b) £620; (c) £2.48; (d&e) £54,790; (f)
£99,000.

EAST LOTHIAN DISTRICT COUNCIL (pop 78,000) Library
Headquarters, Haddington, East Lothian, EH41 4DU (062
082-2370). Asst Dir of Leisure & Recreation, & District Libn:
Mr Brian M. Gall BA, ALA; Asst District Libn: Mr John G
Hunter ALA.   **7** Leisure & Recreation.   **8** Dir of Leisure
& Recreation.   **9** Mon-Fri: 10.00-19.00; Sat: 10.00-16.00.
10 HQ; Branch; Mobile.   **12** Castellau, Dunbar, EH42 1DA;
Newton Port, Haddington, EH41 3NA; Bridge St, Musselburgh;
Hope Rooms, Forth St, North Berwick, EH39 4JD; West Loan,
Prestonpans, EH32 9NX; 3 Civic Sq, Tranent, EH33 1LH.
13 P-t 5; mobiles 2.
14 Local history; Robert Louis Stevenson.   **15** 1 (3 planned);
(e) none; (f) 1p pd.   **17** Schools, housebound, hospitals,
old people's homes, playgroups, lighthouses.   **18** Cultural
activities, entertainments (Dir of Leisure; a 1).
21 (a) 2p pw; (b&c) variable.   **23** (a) c.75,000; (b) c.3,000;
(c) c.42,000; (e) c.30.   **24** (a&b) c.775,000; (c) 15,000;
(d) c.2,900.
25 (a) 36; (b) 13; (c) 6; (d) 3.   **26** (a) £160,150; (b) £7,000;
(c) £2.05; (d) £49,000; (e) £4,400; (f) £81,200.

EAST SUSSEX COUNTY COUNCIL (pop 660,000) East Sussex
County Library, Southdown House, 44 St Anne's Crescent,
Lewes, East Sussex, BN7 1SQ (079 16-5400; telex 877515).
Chief Libn: Mr J.N. Allen BA, FLA; Dep Chief Libn: Mr J.F.
Saunders FLA.   **7** Libraries Sub-Committee.   **9** Mon-
Fri: 10.00-19.00; Sat: 10.00-17.00.
10 HQ; Area; District.   **11 Major Areas:** Bexhill: Western
Rd, Bexhill-on-Sea, TN40 1DY (0424-212546), Libn: Mrs P.G.
Haines ALA; Brighton: Church St, Brighton, BN1 14E (0273-
62801), Libn: Mr C. Batt ALA; Eastbourne: Grove Rd,
Eastbourne, BN21 4TL (0323-22834), Libn: Miss M.L.
Butler BA, FLA; Hastings: Brassey Institute, 13 Claremont,
Hastings, TN34 1HE (0424-420501), Libn: Mr B.G. Purdey
ALA; Hove: 182-6 Church Rd, Hove, BN3 2EG (0273-70472),
Libn: Mr E.P. Scott ALA.   **12 District Libraries:** Beatty
Ave, Coldean, Brighton; The Broadway, Crowborough, TN6
1DA; Western Rd, Hailsham, BN27 3DN; West Way, Hangleton,
Hove, BN3 8LD; Carden Hill, Hollingbury, Brighton, BN1 8DA;
Albion St, Lewes, BN7 2ND; The Highway, Moulscomb,
Brighton, BN2 4PA; Church Hill, Newhaven, BN9 9LR;
Victoria Dr, Old Town, Eastbourne, BN20 8QJ; Ladies Mile
Rd, Patcham, Brighton, BN1 8TA; Windsor Way, Polegate,
BN26 6QF; Old Shoreham Rd, Portslade, BN4 1XR; The
Grange, Rottingdean, Brighton; Lion St, Rye, TN31 7LB; The
Lido, Saltdean, Brighton, BN2 8SP; 17 Park Rd, Seaford,
BN25 1QX; Firle Rd, 168 Seaside, Eastbourne, BN22 7QW;
Luxford's Field, High St, Uckfield, TN22 1AR; Bankside,
Westdene, Brighton, BN1 5GN; Whitehawk Community Centre,
Whitehawk Rd, Brighton, BN2 5GZ; Coppice Ave, Lower
Willingdon, BN20 9PN; Warren Rd, Woodingdean, Brighton,
BN2 6BA.   **13** P-t 13 (+ 142 centres); mobiles 2.
14 Local history (HQ, Bexhill, Brighton, Eastbourne,
Hastings, Hove, Lewes); at Brighton: Elliott colln (theology),
Bloomfield colln (mss, incunabula, printed works from 1500),
Lewis colln (arts, in European languages), Long colln (19th
cent editions of classics), Mathews (Hebrew & oriental
classics); at Hastings: Thomas Brett (mss history of
Hastings), Oscar Browning (music & correspondence), Lord
Brassey's Library, Betham Edwards (her novels); at Hove:
Viscount Wolseley's letters.   **15** 4; (a) 161,545; (b) 17,762;
(c) 18,000; (d) 1,770; (e) £1.29 pa (2 tickets) inc VAT;
(f) as books.   **17** Schools, housebound, prisons, hospitals,

old people's homes, WEA.   **19** Plessey; ALS; token.   **20** 3
weeks.   **21** (a&c) 1p 1st day; 2p pd thereafter; (b) none.
22 LASER; SASLIC.   **23** (a) 1,135,000; (b) 195,000;
(c) 146,000; (d) 124,000; (e) 850.   **24** (a) 7,220,000;
(b) 993,000; (c) 179,844; (d) 10,400.
25 (a) 319; (b) 17; (c) 81; (d) 15.   **26** (a) £1,524,700;
(b) £83,600; (c) £2.31; (d) £365,000; (e) £9,800; (f) £846,800.

EASTWOOD DISTRICT LIBRARIES (pop 50,000) Capelrigg
House, Capelrigg Rd, Newton Mearns, Glasgow, G77 6NH
(041-639 4555/6677). Chief Libn: Miss Helen B. Young ALA;
Senior Libn: Miss Mary M.W. Ballantyne MA, ALA.
7 Libraries Sub-Committee.   **8** Chief Executive Officer:
M.D. Henry MA, LLB.   **9** Mon, Wed & Fri: 14.00-20.00,
Tues 10.00-17.00, Thurs 10.00-13.00; Sat: 10.00-17.00.
10 HQ; Branch.   **12** Clarkston Rd, Clarkston, Glasgow, G76
8NA; Rhuallan House, Montgomerie Dr, Giffnock, Glasgow,
G46 6PY; Mearns Cross, Ayr Rd, Newton Mearns, Glasgow.
13 P-t 4.
14 Local colln.   **15** 3; (a) 32,057; (c) 3,663; (e) £1.50 pa
(OAPs & students - no charge); (f) as books.   **17** Housebound, old people's homes, playgroups, children's home,
old people's club, sheltered housing unit.   **20** 3 weeks.
21 (a, b&c) 1p pw or part + 10p for overdue notice.
23 (a) 86,345; (b) 1,497; (c) 15,078.   **24** (a) 575,122;
(b) 106,035; (d) 1,857.
25 (a) 32; (b) 5; (c) 9; (d) 6.   **26 Finance** (10½ months
only): (a) £159,935; (b) £3,500; (c) £3.2; (d) £37,000;
(e) £3,000; (f) £69,880.

EDINBURGH CITY DISTRICT COUNCIL (pop 489,000) Central Library, George IV Bridge, Edinburgh EH1 1EG (031-225
5584). City Libn: A.P. Shearman FLA, BA; Asst City Libn:
A.G.D. White ALA.   **7** Recreation.   **8** Dep Dir of
Recreation (Head of Cultural Services): J.A. Howe FLA.
9 Mon-Fri: ad ldg 9.00-20.30, ref 9.00-21.00, children's
9.30-18.00; Sat: 9.00-13.00
10 Central; Branch.   **12** Newsroom, Trinity College Church
Apse, 81 High St, Edinburgh, EH1 1SR; Balgreen Rd, Balgreen,
Edinburgh, EH12 3AT; Hillhouse Rd, Blackhall, Edinburgh,
EH4 5EG; Thorburn Rd, Colinton, Edinburgh EH13 0BQ; Kirk
Loan, Corstorphine, Edinburgh, EH12 7HD; Niddrie Mains
Terrace, Craigmillar, Edinburgh, EH16 4NT; Dundee St,
Fountainbridge, Edinburgh, EH11 1BG; Wardieburn Terrace,
Granton, Edinburgh, EH5 2DA; Ferry Rd, Leith, Edinburgh,
EH6 4AE; Leith Walk, McDonald Rd, Edinburgh, EH7 4LU;
Morningside Rd, Morningside, Edinburgh, EH10 4PU; Pennywell
Court, Muirhouse, Edinburgh, EH4 4TZ; Rosefield Av,
Portobello, Edinburgh, EH15 1AU; Sighthill Wynd, Sighthill,
Edinburgh EH11 4BL; Hamilton Pl, Stockbridge, Edinburgh,
EH3 5BA.   **13** P-t 5; mobiles 4.
14 Edinburgh; Scottish; music; fine arts; illustrations; slides;
Sanderson Bequest (etchings etc); Moir Library (bee-
keeping); Scottish family histories; Sir Walter Scott; R.L.
Stevenson; Sir Arthur Conan Doyle.   **15** 1; (c) 5,500;
(d) 1,000; (e) £3.00 deposit; (f) as books.   **17** Schools,
housebound, prisons, hospitals, old people's homes.   **18** Cultural activities, entertainments, (£18,325, Asst City Libn, a
1, b 3).   **19** Plessey Data Pen System.   **20** 3 weeks.
21 (a, b&c) 1p 1st week, 3p pw or part thereafter.   **22** NLS;
SCOLCAP.   **23** (a) 612,283; (b) 278,186; (c) 91,060;
(d) 211,402; (e) c.1,000.   **24** (a) 3,695,620; (b) 1,697,727;
(c) 1,814,825; (d) hospitals 54,628.
25 (a) 260; (b) 50; (c) 36; (d) 33.   **26** (a) £1,170,720;
(b) £95,560; (c) £2.39; (d) £228,940; (e) £20,000; (f) £694,530.

ESSEX COUNTY COUNCIL (pop 1,415,000) County Library
Headquarters, Goldlay Gardens, Chelmsford, CM2 0EW
(0245-51141/4; telex 99223). County Libn: K.J. Lace FLA;
Dep County Libn: Mr Barry Langton ALA.   **7** Library,
Museums & Records.   **8** County Education Officer: J.A.
Springett MA.   **9** Mon-Fri: 9.00-19.00 (or 20.00); Sat:
9.00-17.00.
10 HQ; Group; Branch.   **11 Group Libraries:** Basildon
Central Lib, Fodderwick, Basildon, SS14 1DP, Libn: N.D.
Humphries FLA; 180 London Rd, Hadleigh, Benfleet, SS7 2PD,
Libn: M.C.B. Nugent ALA; 13/15 Coggeshall Rd, Braintree,
CM7 6JB, Libn: B.M. Cheater ALA; Coptfold Rd, Brentwood,
CM14 4BN, Libn: J.D. Lewis FLA; High St, Canvey Island,

CODE: 1 Local authority. 2 Population. 3 Postal address of HQ. 4 Telephone & telex. 5 Chief Libn. 6 Deputy. 7 Committee responsible. 8 Officer to whom Libn is responsible (if any). 9 Hours. 10 Organisation. 11 Area libraries. 12 Branches. 13 Part-time libraries; mobiles. 14 Special collections. 15 Gramophone records: number of libraries, (a) record issues (b) cassette issues (c) record stock (d) cassette stock (e) loan charges (f) fines. 16 Pictures: stock; charges. 17 Other services. 18 Cultural activities (expenditure, officer in charge, staff: (a) officers (b) manual). 19 Issue method (if not Browne). 20 Loan period (if not 2 weeks). 21 Fines: (a) adult (b) children (c) OAPs. 22 Co-operative schemes. 23 Stock: (a) adult lending (b) adult reference (c) children (d) schools (e) current periodical titles. 24 Issues: (a) adult (b) children (c) schools (d) institutions. 25 Staff: (a) officers (b) manual (c) chartered libns (d) graduates. 26 Finance: (a) total expenditure (b) non-rate income (c) per capita expenditure (d) expenditure for books (e) expenditure for records etc (f) salaries & wages. 27 Capital projects.

ESSEX COUNTY COUNCIL—*continued*
SS8 7RB, Libn: A. E Gravatt ALA; Central Lib, The Drive, Loughton, IG10 1HD, Libn: B. W. Tuck ALA; Central Lib, Station Rd, Clacton-on-Sea, CO15 1SF; Libn: T. A. Baker ALA; Central Lib, Shewell Rd, Colchester, CO1 1JB, Libn: P. R. Gifford ALA; Hemnal St, Epping, CM16 4LS, Libn: B. Pratt ALA; 121/3 Connaught Ave, Frinton, CO13 9PS, Libn: S. A. Sullivan ALA; Bridge St, Halstead, CO9 1HU, Libn: D. E. Couch ALA; Central Lib, The High, Harlow, CM20 1HA: Libn: L. A. Ward ALA; Waddesdon Rd, Harwich, CO12 3BA: Libn: S. S. Cornish ALA; St Peter's Room, High St, Maldon, CM9 7PZ Libn: K. J. McGowan Docherty ALA; 132/4, High St, Rayleigh, SS6 7BX, Libn: E. Marshall ALA; Civic Centre, Duke St, Chelmsford, CM1 1JF, Libn: S. M. Jarvis FLA; Southend Rd, Hockley, SS5 4PZ, Libn: F. Makepeace-Lott ALA; 2 King St, Saffron Walden, CB10 1ES, Libn: H. J. Ridler ALA; Central Lib, Victoria Ave, Southend-on-Sea, SS2 6EX, Libn: L. Helliwell, FLA; MBE; Central Lib, Orsett Rd, Grays, RM17 5DX; 32/4 Highbridge St, Waltham Abbey, EN9 1BS, Libn: J. C. Cridland ALA. **12** Market Rd, Wickford, SS14 1DP; High St, Billericay, CM12 9AB; Fryerns B Lib, Whitmore Way, Basildon, SS14 2NN; Vange B Lib, Southview Rd, Basildon; 48 Laindon Centre, Basildon, SS15 5TQ; Great Tarpots B Lib, 127 London Rd, Benfleet, SS7 5HD; Hutton Rd, Shenfield, Brentwood, CM15 8NJ; 165 Queens Rd, Buckhurst Hill; Debden B Lib, Rectory Lane, Loughton; Hainault Rd, Chigwell; 118 High St, Ongar, CM5 9AR; 138 High Rd, North Weald, Epping; Mark Hall B Lib, The Stow, Harlow, CM20 3AP; Tye Green B Lib, Bush Fair, Harlow, CM18 6LU; Great Parndon B Lib, Staple Tye, Harlow, CM18 7LZ; 30 High St, Old Harlow, CM17 0DW; Leigh B Lib, Broadway West, Leigh-on-Sea, SS9 2DA; Kent Elms B Lib, 1 Rayleigh Rd, Leigh-on-Sea, SS9 5UU; Friars B Lib, Constable Way, Shoeburyness; Thorpedene B Lib, Delaware Rd, Thorpe Bay, SS3 9NW; Southchurch B Lib, 221 Lifstan Way, Southend-on-Sea, SS1 2XG; Temple Sutton B Lib, 11 Cluny Sq, Southend-on-Sea, SS2 4AF; Westcliff B Lib, 649 London Rd, Westcliff-on-Sea, SS0 9PD; Purfleet Rd, Aveley; Belhus B Lib, Derry Ave, South Ockendon; Blackshots Lane, Grays; Brentwood Rd, Chadwell St Mary, Grays; St Johns Way, Corringham; High St, Standford-le-Hope; Civic Square, Tilbury. **13** P-t 189 inc village centres; mobiles 18. **14** Taylor & Cunnington colln; music & drama; Harsnett Library (1631); Castle Library (1745). **15** 11; (a) 338, 752; (b) 350; (c) 47, 650; (d) 1, 525; (e) £2 + VAT pa; (f) 3p pw max 36p. **16** £4 pa. **17** Schools, housebound, prisons, hospitals, old people's homes, pre-school playgroups. **19** Photocharging (Chelmsford, Colchester); Plessey Light Pen (Southend). **20** 3 weeks. **21** (a&c) 3p pw or part, max 36p; (b) none. **22** ETCLS. **23** (a, b, c&d) 3, 527, 665; (e) 2, 000. **24** (a) 12, 324, 625; (b) 2, 683, 699; (c) 3, 163, 793; (d) 158, 697. **25** (a) 615; (b) 103; (c) 129; (d) 30. **26** (a) £3, 501, 735; (b) £150, 930; (c) £2.47; (d&e) £778, 335; (f) £1, 603, 250.

FALKIRK DISTRICT COUNCIL (pop 142, 000) Falkirk Library, Hope St, Falkirk, Stirling, FK1 5AU (0324-24911). District Chief Libn: Mr Alex Howson ALA; Dep Chief Libn: Mr N. W. Turner. **7** Leisure & Recreation. **9** Mon-Fri: 9.30-20.00 (Wed & Fri 17.00); Sat: 9.30-17.00. **11** Boness Libn, Town Hall, Boness, (050682-2264); Grangemouth Lib, Boness Rd, Grangemouth, (0324-3291), Libn: Mr A. C. Barker ALA; Larbert Lib, Main St, Stenhousemuir, EK5 4ET (03245-2865), Libn: Miss M. Cameron BA, ALA. **12** Bridge St, Bonnybridge; Nisbet St, Denny; The Cross, Slamannan. **13** P-t 1; mobiles 3. **15** 2; (a) 19, 000; (c) 4, 000; (e) £2 pa; (f) as books. **17** Housebound, hospitals, old people's homes. **19** Photo-

charging. **20** 3 weeks. **21** (a, b&c) 3p pw. **23** (a) 250, 000; (b) 14, 000; (c) 40, 000; (e) 70. **24** (a) 1, 250, 000; (b) 200, 000; (d) 75, 000. **25** (a) 66; (b) 6; (c) 19; (d) 5. **26** (a) £394, 000; (b) £13, 550; (c) £2.77; (d) £99, 000; (e) £3, 000; (f) £195, 250.

GATESHEAD METROPOLITAN BOROUGH COUNCIL (pop 223, 000) Central Library, Prince Consort Rd, Gateshead, Tyne and Wear, NE8 4LN (0632-773478; telex 537379). Borough Libn & Arts Officer: Mr T. S. Cardy FLA, AMBIM; Dep Borough Libn: Mr W. A. Cairns ALA. **7** Libraries & Arts. **9** Mon-Fri: 10.00 (ref 9.30)-20.00 (Wed: 17.00 Central, 13.00 Branches); Sat: 10.00 (ref 9.30)-12.30, 13.30-17.00. **10** HQ; Branches. **12** 16 Durham Rd, Birtley, Chester Le Street; Shibdon Rd, Blaydon, NE21 5AE; Derwent St, Chopwell, NE17 7NZ; Brompton House, Dunston, Gateshead, NE11; Tarlton Crescent, Felling, Gateshead, NE10 9HU; Leam Lane B Lib, Colegate, Gateshead, NE10 8PP; Lobley Hill Rd, Gateshead, NE11 0AL; Low Fell B Lib, 710 Durham Rd, Gateshead, NE9 6HT; Redheugh Rd, Gateshead NE8 2HT; Norman Rd, Rowlands Gill, NE39 1JT; Grange Rd, Ryton, NE40 3LT; Sunderland Rd B Lib, Lindisfarne Dr, Gateshead, NE8 3LB; Chase Park, Whickham, NE16 4EE; Church St, Winlaton, Blaydon on Tyne, NE21 6AR; Ebchester Ave, Wrekenton, Gateshead NE9 7LP. **13** P-t 8; mobiles 1. **14** Railways. **15** 13; (a) 25, 133; (b) 1, 087; (c) 6, 488; (d) 228; (e&f) under revision. **16** 376; charges under revision. **17** Schools, housebound, hospitals, old people's homes, sheltered housing. **18** Cultural activities, entertainments (£4, 233; Arts & Entertainments Officer; a 2). **19** Token charging (for adult fiction). **20** 3 weeks. **21** (a, b&c) under revision. **22** NRLB. **23** (a) 290, 305; (b) 41, 171; (c) 55, 620; (d) 9, 948; (e) 603. **24** (a) 1, 808, 757; (b) 316, 873; (c) 59, 737; (d) 22, 185. **25** (a) 130; (b) 11; (c) 35; (d) 15. **26** (a) £640, 440; (b) £14, 280; (d) 114, 300; (e) 5, 000; (f) £369, 350.

GLASGOW CITY DISTRICT COUNCIL (pop 825, 668) The Mitchell Library, North St, Glasgow G3 7DN (041-248 7121/8; telex 778732). Dir of Libs: Mr W. A. G. Alison FLA; Dep Dir of Libs: Mr A. Miller FLA. **7** Library. **9** Mon-Fri: ad ldg & children 10.00-20.00, ref 9.30-21.00; Sat: ad ldg & children's 10.00-13.00, 14.00-17.00, ref 9.30-17.00. **10** HQ; Division; Branch. **11** **Divisional Libraries:** Stirlings Lib, Queen St, G1 3AZ (041-221 1876), Libn: Miss O. Scott FLA; Hillhead Lib, 348 Byres Rd, G12 8AP (041-339 7223/4) Libn: Miss A. Martin ALA; Dennistoun Lib, Craigpark, G31 2NA (041-554 0055) Libn: Miss I. McEwan ALA; Shettleston Lib, 154 Wellshot Rd, G32 7AX (041-778 1221), Libn: Miss E. Allan ALA; Rutherglen Lib, 163 Main St, G73 2HB (041-647 6453), Libn: Miss I. Hardie ALA; Langside Lib, 2 Sinclair Dr, G42 9QE (041-632 0810), Libn: Mrs A. Kelly ALA; Cardonald Lib, 1113 Mosspark Dr, G53 3BU (041-882 1381), Libn: Mr E. Voy ALA. **12** Baillieston Lib, 141 Main St, G69 6AA; 80 Barlanark Rd, G33 4PT; Barmulloch Lib, 99 Rockfield Rd, G21 3DY; Bridgeton Lib, 23 Landressy St, G40 1BP; Cambuslang Lib, 6 Glasgow Rd, G72 7BW; Castlemilk Lib, 5 Dougrie Dr, G45 9AD; Cathkin Lib, 21 Lovat Pl, G73 5HS; Couper Institute Lib, 84 Clarkston Rd, G44 3DA; Drumchapel Lib, 65 Hecla Ave, G15 8LX; Easterhouse Lib, 5 Shandwick St, G34 9DP; Elder Park Lib, 228a Langlands Rd, G51 3TZ; Gorbals Lib, 100 Norfolk St, G5 9EJ; Govanhill Lib, 170 Langside Rd, G42 7JU; Hutchesontown Lib, 27-29 Cumberland Arcade, G5 0SD; King's Park Lib, 275 Castlemilk Rd, G44 4LE; Kingston Lib, 336 Paisley Rd, G5 8RD; Knightswood Lib, 27 Dunterlie Ave, G13 3BB; 1508 Maryhill

GLASGOW CITY DISTRICT COUNCIL—*continued*
Rd, G20 9AD; Milton Lib, 163 Ronaldsay St, G22 7AP
Mosspark Lib, 35 Arran Dr, G52 1JR; Parkhead Lib, 64
Tollcross Rd, G31 4XA; Partick Lib, 305 Dumbarton Rd,
G11 6AB; Pollok Lib, 100/106 Peat Rd, G53 6DH; Pollokshaws
Lib, 50/60 Shawbridge St, G43 1RW; Pollokshields Lib, 30
Leslie St, G41 2LF; Possilpark Lib, 127 Allander St, G22 5JJ;
Riddrie Lib, 1020 Cumbernauld Rd, G33 2QS; Springburn Lib,
179 Ayr St, G21 4BW; Townhead Lib, 192 Castle St, G4 0SR;
Whiteinch Lib, 14 Victoria Park Dr, South, G14 9RL; Woodside Lib, 343 St George's Rd, G3 6JQ.   **13** P-t 4; mobiles 1.
14 Commercial; Glasgow; music; science & technology;
Scottish poetry; early Glasgow printing; Robert Burns; Moir;
foreign languages; Jeffrey; Braille.   **15** 2 (in preparation);
(c) 9,000; (d) 6,000.   **17** Residential schools, prisons,
hospitals, old people's homes, university, art galleries,
museums.   **19** Plessey Library Pen, 'Live'.   **20** 4 weeks.
21 (a, b&c) none.   **22** SCOLCAP.   **23** (a) 844,578;
(b) 1,030,111; (c) 176,245; (e) 650 (Branches) + 1,300
(Mitchell).   **24** (a) 5,950,003; (b) 1,219,691; (d) 262,072.
25 (a) 421; (b) 179; (c) 108; (d) 16.   **26** (a) £1,986,003;
(b) £39,375; (c) £2.40; (d) £483,355; (e) £42,500;
(f) £1,530,629.   **27** Darnley Library, £290,000; Ibrox
Library, £320,000.

GLOUCESTERSHIRE COUNTY COUNCIL (pop 487,000)
County Library Headquarters, Quayside Wing, Shire Hall,
Gloucester GL1 2HY (0452-21444; telex 43155). County Libn:
B. Stradling FLA; Dep County Libn: D. F Parker FLA.
7 Recreation & Leisure.   **9** No general pattern.
10 HQ; Division; Local.   **11 Divisions:** Cheltenham Lib,
Clarence St, Cheltenham, GL50 3JT (0242-22476/55636/52131)
Libn: Mr J.R. Wood FLA; Gloucester Lib, Brunswick Rd,
Gloucester, GL1 1HT (0452-20020/20684), Libn: Mr V.A.
Woodman ALA; Stroud Lib, Lansdown, Stroud, GL5 1BL
(04536-4053), Libn: Mr A.M. Morley FLA; Moreton-in-Marsh
Lib, Mann Institute, Oxford St, GL56 0LA (0608-50780), Libn:
Miss L. Knight FLA; Cinderford Lib, Belle Vue Rd, Cinderford
GL14 2BZ (0594-22581), Libn: Miss B. Griffith BA, ALA;
Cirencester Lib, The Waterloo, Cirencester, GL57 2PP
(0285-3582), Libn: Mr A. Welsford BA, ALA.   **12** Tobysfield
Rd, Bishops Cleeve; Moorfield Rd, Brockworth, Gloucester;
May Lane, Dursley; Hesters Way Lib, Goldsmith Rd, Chelten-
ham; Hucclecote Rd, Gloucester; Hill St, Lydney; Matson
Library, Winsley Rd, Gloucester; Church St, Tewkesbury;
Tuffley Lib, Windsor Dr, Gloucester.   **13** P-t 23; mobiles 7
(inc 2 school).
14 Gloucestershire colln; Hartland colln (herbals); Day colln
(natural history); Hitching's colln (bibles); Hanham-Clark
colln (Palestine); Birchall colln (American Civil War).
15 2; (a) 43,374; (b) 3,926; (c) 8,163; (d) 549; (e) £1.50 +
VAT pa; (f) as books.   **16** 50; under review.   **17** Schools,
housebound, prisons, hospitals, old people's homes.
18 Cultural activities, (£2,700 exc salaries, wages & administration).   **19** Token; photo-charging (to be replaced by
computer-based (Plessey) system).   **20** 3 weeks.
21 (a&c) 3p pw or part; (b) none.   **22** WESLINK.
23 (a&b) 897,375; (c) 250,049; (d) 143,043; (e) 242.
24 (a) 4,778,505; (b) 1,010,541; (c) 1,971,270; (d) 28,100.
25 (a) 208; (b) 32; (c) 74; (d) 20.   **26** (a) £1,030,570;
(b) £36,160; (c) £2.14; (d) £228,180; (e) £6,720; (f) £566,190.

GWENT COUNTY COUNCIL (pop 442,303) Cambria House,
Caerleon, Newport, Gwent, NP6 1XG (0633-421018). County
Libn: Mr M.F.A. Elliott FLA, LRAM.   **7** Library Sub-Com-
mittee.   **8** Dir of Education: Mr T.M. Morgan MA.
9 Mon-Fri: 9.30-17.30; Sat: 9.30-16.00.
10 HQ; Regional; Branch.   **11 Regions:** Newport: John
Frost Sq, Newport, NPT 1PA (0633-65539), Libn: Mrs R.
Hayward FLA; Torfaen: Gwent House, Gwent Sq, Cwmbran,
NP4 3HS (063 33-3240), Libn: Mr G. Hiatt ALA; Monmouth:
Shire Hall, Monmouth, NP5 3DY (0600-3248), Libn: Mrs F.
Key ALA; Blaenau Gwent: Bethcar St, Ebbw Vale, NP3 6HS
(0495 21-3069), Libn: Miss J. Colwell ALA; Islwyn: Park
P1, Risca, NP1 6AT (0633-612462), Libn: Mrs K. Niblett BA.
12 Baker St, Abergavenny; Oak St, Abertillery; Bettws
Shopping Centre, Newport; Gordon Rd, Blackwood; Reading
Institute, High St, Blaina; Newport Rd, Caldicott; Carnegie B
Lib, Corporation Rd, Newport; Upper Nelson St, Chepstow;
Maindee B Lib, Chepstow Rd, Newport; Hanbury Rd, Pontypool;
Ringland B Lib, Ringland Centre, Newport; Stow Hill,
Newport; Workmen's Institute, Morgan St, Tredegar.   **13** P-t
12; mobiles 11.
14 Local history (over 13,000 Gwent, Monmouthshire, items);
Quaker material; Arthur Machen Special colln.   **15** 1;
(e) 50p pa + 5p per record; (f) 2p pw.   **17** Schools, hospitals,
old people's homes.   **19** Photocharging (Cwmbran).
21 (a&b) 2p pw; (c) none.   **23** (a, b, c&d) 763, 927; (e) 147.
24 (a, b, c&d) 3, 685, 465.
25 (a) 176; (b) 36; (c) 31; (d) 12.   **26** (a) £1, 003, 500;
(b) £24, 200; (c) £2.02; (d) £182, 100; (f) £437, 300.

GWYNEDD COUNTY COUNCIL (pop 224, 240) Gwynedd
Library Headquarters, Maesincla, Caernarfon, Gwynedd,
LL55 1LH (0286-4441). County Libn: Mr Geoffrey Thomas
BA, FLA; Asst County Libn: J.M. Griffiths ALA (Admin &
Dev.).   **7** Recreation, Amenities & Culture.   **9** No general
pattern.
10 HQ; Area HQ; Branch.   **11 Area Library HQs:** Aber-
conwy: Public Lib, 44 Mostyn St, Llandudno, LL30 2RS (0492-
77304), Asst County Libn: W.J. Jones ALA; Arfon/Dwyfor:
Maesincla, Caernarfon, LL55 1LH (0286-4441 ext 95), Asst
County Libn: T.E. Griffiths, BA, ALA; Meirionnydd: Fron
Serth, Dolgellau, LL40 1LE (0341-422771), Asst County Libn:
G.W. Griffiths ALA; Môn: Lôn y Felin, (Mill St), Llangefni
(024881-723262 ext 63), Asst County Libn: J.C. Jones ALA.
12 Town Hall, Conway; Plough St, Llanrwst; Ffordd Gwynedd,
Bangor; Pavilion Hill, Caernarfon; Church St, Blaenau
Ffestiniog; Neptune Rd, Tywyn; Newry Fields, Holyhead.
13 P-t 31; mobiles 7.
14 Local collns in all areas; D. Lloyd George (Arfon/Dwyfor
Area).   **15** 6; (a&b) 11, 389; (c) 4, 256; (d) 80; (e) £1 pa;
(f) as books.   **17** Schools, housebound, hospitals, old people's
homes.   **18** Cultural activities (£400 exc salaries & wages;
Asst County Libns-Areas).   **21** (a&b) 2p pw; (c) none.
23 (a&c) 741, 165; (b) 31, 352.   **24** (a&b) 2, 243, 417 (exc
schools).
25 (a) 94; (b) 13; (c) 21; (d) 10.   **26** (a) £627, 570;
(b) £15, 400; (c) £2.70; (d) £117, 270; (e) £3, 000; (f) £297, 070.

HAMILTON DISTRICT COUNCIL (pop 104, 629) Hamilton
District Libraries, Central Library, Cadzow St, Hamilton,
Lanarkshire, ML3 6HQ (06982-21188). Chief Libn: Mr C.
Smith ALA; Principal Asst Chief Libn: Mr G.C. Stewart DPA,
FSA, ALA.   **7** Leisure & Recreation.   **9** Mon-Fri:
10.00 (ref 9.00) - 19.30 (Wed 17.00); Sat: 10.00 (ref 9.00)-
17.00.
10 Central (District HQ); Branch.   **12** Calder St, Blantyre;
Main St, Bothwell; 76 Burnbank Centre, Hamilton; Fairhill
Lib, Neilsland Rd, Hamilton; Hillhouse Rd, Hamilton; Muir St,
Larkhall; Green St, Stonehouse; 131 Main St, Uddingston;
Whitehill Lib, Margaret Rd, Hamilton.   **13** mobiles 1.
14 Hamilton (local history); civic film library (local events).
15 3; (c) 6, 516; (d) 1, 141.   **16** 123; none.   **17** Housebound,
old people's homes.   **21** (a, b&c) none.   **23** (a) 201, 000;
(b) 13, 500; (c) 53, 000.
25 (a) 65; (b) 26; (c) 11; (d) 2.   **26 Finance** (10½ months
only): (a) £320, 835; (b) £2, 145; (c) £3.00; (d) £55, 610;
(e) £8, 160; (f) £201, 864.

HAMPSHIRE COUNTY COUNCIL (pop 1, 445, 300) 81 North
Walls, Winchester, Hampshire, SO23 8BY (0962-3301; telex
47121). County Libn: Mr R.R. Lawson FLA; Dep County Libn:
Mr J.C. Beard FLA.   **7** Recreation.   **9** Mon-Fri: HQ
8.30-18.30, Portsmouth 9.30-19.00 (ref 20.00), Sat: HQ
8.30-17.00, Portsmouth 9.30-17.00.
10 HQ, District:Branch.   **11 District Libraries:** Basingstoke: County Lib, 19/20 Westminster House, Potters Walk,
Basingstoke (0256-3901; telex 858391), Libn: Mr Paul Dix
ALA; East Hants: County Lib, Winton House, High St, Petersfield (0730-3451), Libn: Mr F.E. Dovey ALA; Eastleigh:
County Lib, 40 Chamberlayne Rd, Eastleigh, SO5 5JH (042
126-3727; telex 477220), Libn: Mr L.A. Duffner ALA; Fareham:
County Lib, Osborn Rd, Fareham (03292-4018/6718; telex
86430), Libn: Mr A. Bullen ALA; Gosport: County Lib, High
St, Gosport (070 17-80432/87952; telex 86359), Libn: Miss
J.C. Lockhart AMBIM; Hart: County Lib, 236 Fleet Rd, Fleet
GU13 8BX (02514-4213), Libn: Mr M. Owen BA, ALA; Havant:

CODE: 1 Local authority. 2 Population. 3 Postal address of HQ. 4 Telephone & telex. 5 Chief Libn. 6 Deputy.
7 Committee responsible. 8 Officer to whom Libn is responsible (if any). 9 Hours. 10 Organisation. 11 Area libraries.
12 Branches. 13 Part-time libraries; mobiles. 14 Special collections. 15 Gramophone records: number of libraries,
(a) record issues (b) cassette issues (c) record stock (d) cassette stock (e) loan charges (f) fines. 16 Pictures: stock;
charges. 17 Other services. 18 Cultural activities (expenditure, officer in charge, staff: (a) officers (b) manual). 19 Issue
method (if not Browne). 20 Loan period (if not 2 weeks). 21 Fines: (a) adult (b) children (c) OAPs. 22 Co-operative
schemes. 23 Stock: (a) adult lending (b) adult reference (c) children (d) schools (e) current periodical titles. 24 Issues:
(a) adult (b) children (c) schools (d) institutions. 25 Staff: (a) officers (b) manual (c) chartered libns (d) graduates.
26 Finance: (a) total expenditure (b) non-rate income (c) per capita expenditure (d) expenditure for books (e) expenditure
for records etc (f) salaries & wages. 27 Capital projects.

HAMPSHIRE COUNTY COUNCIL —*continued*
County Lib, 20 Stockheath Lane, Leigh Park, Havant PO9 3BE
(07012-4716; telex 86523), Libn: Miss P. I. Cooper ALA;
New Forest: County Lib, Cannon St, Lymington SO4 9BR
(05907-3050; telex 477634), Libn: Mr N. M. Gannaway ALA;
Portsmouth: County Lib, Guildhall Sq, Portsmouth, PO1 2DX
(0705-21441/27089; telex 86382), Libn: Mrs M. J. Guy ALA;
Rushmoor: County Lib, Pinehurst Ave, Farnborough (0252-
513838; telex 858695) Libn: Mr H. H. Bamber ALA; South-
hampton: County Lib, Civic Centre, Southampton SO9 4XP
(0703-23855; telex 47331), Libn: Mr H. A. Richards BA, ALA,
AMBIM; Test Valley: County Lib, Chantry Way, Andover
(0264-2807/66540), Libn: Mr G. C. Attenborough; Winchester:
County Lib, Jewry St, Winchester, SO23 8RX (0962-3909/
62748), Libn: Mr D. G. Dine ALA. 12 Paddock Rd, South
Ham, RG22 6QB; New Church Rd, Tadley, Basingstoke, RG26
6HN; School Lane, Yateley; 103-113 High St, Aldershot;
Station Rd, Romsey, SO5 8DN; Vicarage Hill, Alton, GU34 1HT;
Gore Rd, New Milton, BH26 6RW; Library Rd, Totton, SO4 3AP;
New Rd, Hythe, SO4 6BP; Christchurch Rd, Ringwood, BH24
1DW; Shirley Lib, Redcar St, Southampton; Portswood Rd,
Southampton; Burgess Rd, Southampton; Woolston Lib,
Portsmouth Rd, Southampton; Eastern Lib, Bitterne Rd,
Southampton; Bitterne Lib, Cobbett Rd, Southampton; Leigh
Rd, Eastleigh, SO5 4DE; Hursley Rd, Chandlers Ford, East-
leigh, SO5 2FT; Community Centre, St John's Rd, Hedge End,
SO3 4AF; Chalky Walk, Portchester, PO16 9BB; Stubbington
Lane, Fareham, PO14 2PP; High St, Lee-on-Solent; Nobes
Ave, Bridgemary, Gosport; Elm Grove, Southsea, PO5 1LJ;
North End Lib, Gladys Ave, Portsmouth, PO2 9AX; Carnegie
Lib, Fratton Rd, Portsmouth, PO1 5EZ; Cosham Lib, Spur Rd,
Portsmouth, PO6 3EB; Milton Rd, Southsea, PO4 8PR; Alla-
way Ave, Paulsgrove, Portsmouth, PO6 4HH; Alderman Lacey
Lib, Tangier Rd, Portsmouth, PO3 6HU; 31 North St, Havant,
PO9 1PW; Elm Grove, Hayling Island, PO11 9EE; North St,
Emsworth, PO10 7BY; 16 Greywell Rd, Leigh Park, PO9 5AL;
The Precinct, Waterlooville, PO7 7DT. 13 P-t 30; mobiles
20 (inc 6 urban vehicles).
14 Pitt colln bequest (Southampton); Naval colln (Portsmouth);
Dickens colln (Portsmouth); Brune colln (organ music,
Winchester); transport (mainly railway, Winchester).
15 13; (c) 10, 000; (e) £3 pa + £1.50 for 2nd record at same
time; (f) 10p pw or part. 16 302; 50p deposit + 16p per
loan. 17 Schools, housebound, prisons, hospitals, old
people's homes. 19 Plesseypen; Delayed Browne; Selective Token. 20 4 weeks. 21 (a) 10p pw; (b&c) none.
22 HATRICS. 23 (a) 1, 347, 721; (b) 68, 495; (c) Junior
331, 992; (d) 359, 200; (e) 1, 296. 24 (a) 12, 903, 995;
(b) 2, 934, 625; (c) 2, 367, 018; (d) 23, 095 (old people's homes,
prisons, hospitals).
25 (a) 551; (b) 93; (c) 184; (d) 30. 26 (a) £3, 294, 910;
(b) £118, 690; (c) £2.28; (d) £653, 450; (e) £12, 450;
(f) £1, 589, 500.

HEREFORD AND WORCESTER COUNTY COUNCIL (pop
594, 800) Hereford and Worcester County Library, Love's
Grove, Castle St, Worcester, WR1 3BY (0905-23400; telex
Colib. H. Q. Worc. 336713). County Libn: Miss A. P. Barnes
MA, FLA; Dep County Libn: Mr C. L. Phipps FLA.
7 Libraries, Museums & Arts Sub-Committee. 9 No
pattern.
10 HQ; Division; Area; Branch. 11 Divisional HQs: North-
East Worcestershire: Reddich Central Lib, Church Green
West, Redditch, B97 4DT (0527-63291), Libn: Mr B. Hart ALA;
North-West Worcestershire: Kidderminster Lib, Market St,
Kidderminster DY10 1AD (0562-62832/3), Libn: Mr R.

Parish ALA; South Worcestershire & East Herefordshire:
Worcester City Lib, Foregate St, Worcester WR1 1DT (0905-
22154/24853), Libn: Mr N. H. Parker, FLA; Herefordshire:
Widemarsh St, Hereford, HR4 9EX (0432-3206), Libn: Mr F. A.
Milligan MA, FLA. 12 Load St, Bewdley, Worcestershire
DY12 2EQ; Stratford Rd, Bromsgrove, B60 1AP; Ombersley St,
Droitwich, WR9 8QS; Market Pl, Evesham, WR11 4RW;
Worcester Rd, Hagley, Stourbridge, BY9 0NW; Broad St,
Hereford, HR4 9AU; Market St, Kidderminster, DY10 1AB;
South St, Leominster, Herefordshire, HR6 8JB; Graham Rd,
Malvern, WR14 2HW; Old Infants' School, New Rd, Pershore,
WR10 1BY; Church Green West, Redditch, B97 4DT; Woodrow
Centre, Studley Rd, Redditch, B98 7RY; Market House, Ross-
on-Wye, Herefordshire, HR9 5NX; 7 Library Way, Rubery,
Rednal, Birmingham, B45 9JS; County Buildings, Stourport-on-
Severn, BY13 9AA; Foregate St, Worcester, WR1 1DT; St
Johns, Bromyard Rd, Worcester, WR2 5BS; Cranham Dr, Warn-
don, Worcester WR4 9PA; Wythall, Maylane, Hollywood,
Birmingham B47 5PD. 13 P-t 18; mobiles 14.
14 Grainger-Stuart colln & Willis-Bund colln (mainly
archaeology & history) (both at Worcester City Lib); carpets
& textiles (at Kidderminster Lib); early agricultural books
(at Hereford City Lib). 15 5; (a&b) 58, 794; (c&d) 12, 507;
(e) £1.50 pa; (f) as books. 17 Schools, housebound, prisons,
old people's homes, pre-school playgroups, Sheltered Housing
Units; not systematically served: nursing homes, nursing
unit, handicapped persons, Darby & Joan groups. 19 Photocharging (7 libs); cheque book charging (1 lib). 20 4/5
weeks. 21 (a) 2p pw, max 50p; (b&c) none. 23 (a, b&c)
1, 104, 000; (d) c. 200, 000. 24 (a, b&d) 6, 020, 812.
25 (a) 225; (b) 36; (c) 60; (d) 25. 26 (a) £1, 169, 900; (b)
£31, 500; (c) £1. 97; (d&e) £284, 200; (f) £587, 500.

HERTFORDSHIRE COUNTY COUNCIL (pop 946, 000) County
Library, County Hall, Hertford, SG13 8EJ (099 25-54242; telex
81272). County Libn: Miss L. V. Paulin, OBE, MA, FLA; Dep
County Libn: Mr J. H. Jones FLA. 7 Cultural & Recreational Facilities. 9 Mon-Fri: 9. 30-20. 00; Sat: 9. 30-17. 00.
10 HQ; Division; Branch. 11 Divisions: East Herts: Central Lib, Southgate, Stevenage, SG1 1HD (0438-2941/2; telex
826723), Senior Asst County Libn: Mr G. L. Evans ALA;
Libn (Stevenage): Mr J. P. O'Reilly ALA; Mid Herts: Central
Lib, Campus West, Welwyn Garden City, AL8 6AJ (070
73-32331; telex 263212), Senior Asst County Libn: Mr M. R.
Hughes, FLA; Libn (Welwyn Garden City): Mr R. P. Head ALA;
West Herts: Central Lib, Combe St, Hemel Hempstead, HP1
1HJ (0442-3331/2; telex 82224), Senior Asst County Libn:
Mr L. C. Burton ALA; Libn (Hemel Hempstead): Miss A. M.
Phillips ALA. 12 Bell Row, Baldock, SG7 6AP; Kings Rd,
Berkhamsted, HP4 3BD; The Causeway, Bishop's Stortford,
CM23 2EJ; Elstree Way, Boreham Wood, WD6 1JX; Sparrows
Herne, Bushey, WD2 3HA; Central Lib, Turners Hill, Cheshunt,
EN8 8LB; Lower Rd, Chorleywood, WD3 5LB; Barton Way,
Croxley Green, WD3 3HB; 207 Cell Barnes Lane, Cunningham,
St Albans; 237 Hatfield Rd, Fleetville, St Albans; The
Community Centre, Middlefields Grange, Letchworth; Vaughan
Rd, Harpenden, AL5 4EN; Queensway, Hatfield, AL10 0LT;
Old Cross, Hertford; Hitchin; 'Lowewood' High St, Hoddesdon;
The Nap, Kings Langley, WD4 8ET; St Martin's Rd, Knebworth,
SG3 6ER; Central Lib, The Broadway, Letchworth, SG6 3PF;
The Ridgeway, Marshalswick, St Albans, AL4 9TU; St Albans
Rd, North Watford, W22 5RE; Bridlington Rd, Oxhey, WD1 6AG;
Mutton Lane, Potters Bar, EN6 3AA; High St, Potter's Bar,
EN6 5BZ; Aldenham Ave, Radlett, WD7 8HL; High St, Rick-
mansworth, WD3 1EH; Market Hill, Royston, SG8 9JN; Central
Lib, Victoria St, St Albans, AL1 3JQ; 38 High St, Stevenage,

HERTFORDSHIRE COUNTY COUNCIL—*continued*
SG1 3HD; 87 High St, Ware, SG12 9AD; Central Lib, Hempstead
Rd, Watford WD1 3EU; Cole Green Lane, Woodhall, AL7 3JA.
13 P-t 13; mobiles 15.
14 Drama (playsets & single copies); music (sets & single
copies); local history; technical books. **15** 6; (c) 20,000;
(f) 5p pw, max 40p. **17** Schools, housebound, hospitals,
old people's homes, old people's clubs, youth clubs, playgroups, nurses homes. **19** Photocharging. **20** 3 weeks.
21 (a) 5p pw, max 40p; (b) 2p pw, max 10p; (c) discretion not
to charge. **22** HERTIS. **23** (a, b&c) 2,040,000;
(d) 2,410,000; (e) 1,100. **24** (a&d) 9,882,667;
(b) 1,892,370.
25 (a) 491; (b) 46; (c) 132; (d) 28. **26** (a) £2,656,275;
(b) £79,850; (c) £2.81; (d) £702,200; (e) £3,135;
(f) £1,416,920. **27** Hoddesdon Library.

HIGHLAND REGIONAL COUNCIL (pop 178,000) Regional
Buildings, Inverness, Inverness-shire, IV3 5NX (0463-34121).
Regional Libn: Mr Thomas M. Gray DPA, FLA. **7** Leisure
& Recreation. **8** Dir of Leisure & Recreation: H. Wilkin-
son MA. **9** Mon-Fri: 9.30-20.00; Sat: 9.30-17.00.
10 HQ; Division; Branch. **11 Divisions:** Caithness/Suther-
land: Carnegie Public Library, Wick, Caithness (0955-2864),
Div Libn: Mr David Morrison ALA; Ross & Cromarty: Old
Academy, Tulloch St, Dingwall, Ross-shire (0349-3163), Div
Libn: Mr Michael G. O'Brien; Inverness: Regional Buildings
Inverness, IV3 5NX (0463-34121), Div Libn: Mr Donald
Anderson. **12** Brova; Portree; Alvess; Tain; Fort William;
Nairn; Portree; Invergorden. **13** P-t 7; mobiles 7.
14 Fraser-Mackintosh (Highland history). **15** 3; (a) 4,201;
(c) 2,010; (e) £1.00 deposit. **17** Schools, housebound, old
people's homes. **20** 4 weeks. **23** (a) 335,939; (b) 13,603;
(e) 149. **24** (a) 1,330,797; (b) 253,231.
25 (a) 71; (c) 17; (d) 5. **26 Finance** (10½ months only);
(a) £352,675; (c) £1.99; (d&e) £98,875; (f) £197,734.

HUMBERSIDE COUNTY COUNCIL (pop 838 685) Central
Library, Albion St, Hull, HU1 3TF (0482-223344; telex 52211).
Dir of Leisure Services: R. G. Roberts DMS, FLA, FIMEnt;
Asst Dirs: A. S. McCubbin BA (Admin & Dev); P. J. Ainscough
DMS, ALA (Supplies & Resources). **7** Leisure Services.
9 Mon-Fri: 9.00-20.00; Sat: 9.00-17.30.
10 HQ; Division; Area; Branch. **11 Divisions:** Hull: Cen-
tral Lib, Albion St, Hull, HU1 3TE (0482-223344); North: 10
Lord Roberts Rd, Beverley, Hull, HU17 9BE (0482-885167),
Div Officer: R. Richards ALA; South: Central Lib, Carlton
St, Scunthorpe, DN15 6TA (0724-60161); Div Officer: J.I.
Davies ALA. **12** Ings Lib, Savoy Rd, Hull; Shopping Centre,
Garden Village, Hull; Greatfield Lib, Elmbridge Parade,
Annandale Rd, Hull; James Reckitt Lib, Holderness Rd, Hull;
Shannon Rd, Longhill, Hull; Preston Rd, Hull; Ada Holmes
Circle, Greenwood Ave, Hull; The Greenway, Anlaby High Rd,
Hull; Carnegie Lib, West Park, Anlaby Rd, Hull; Derringham
Bank Lib, Wold Rd, Hull; Gipsyville Lib, North Rd, Hull;
Northern Lib, Beverley Rd, Hull; Western Lib, The Boulevard,
Hull; Champney Rd, Beverley; The Green, Cottingham; St
Augustine Gate, Hedon; Town Hall, Hessle; The Institute,
Main Rd, Willerby; Market Sq, Goole; King St, Bridlington;
Cross Hill, Driffield; Newbegin, Hornsea; Barton-on-Humber
Lib, Providence House, Holydyke, Barton; Princes St,
Brigg; Ashby High St, Scunthorpe; Park Lib, Ave Vivian,
Scunthorpe; Willoughby Rd, Scunthorpe; Isaacs Hill, Clee-
thorpes; Town Hall Sq, Grimsby; Church Lane, Humberston,
Grimsby; Civic Centre, Pelham Rd, Immingham; Grant
Thorold Lib, Durban Rd, Grimsby; Nunsthorpe Lib, Sutcliffe
Ave, Grimsby; Scartho Lib, St Giles Ave, Grimsby; Wingate
Rd, Willows Estate, Grimsby; Yarborough Lib, Cromwell Rd,
Grimsby. **13** P-t 40; mobiles 12.
14 Local history; Wesley (600 items) (Scunthorpe); Shakes-
peare (250 items) (Scunthorpe); foreign literature (especially
Urdu & Bengali) (Scunthorpe); fisheries (600 vols) (Grimsby);
Civil War (Hull); Napoleon (Hull); regimental histories (Hull);
non-conformist religions in the reign of Charles I (Hull);
slavery (Hull); whaling (Hull); Winifred Holtby (Hull); Andrew
Marvell (Hull). **15** Available through any branch;
(a) 132,638; (f) as for books. **16** No charges for lending,
fines as for books. **17** Schools, housebound, prisons,
hospitals, old people's homes; Area Health Authority Staff

Medical Library. **18** Cultural activities; entertainments
(£184,250; Entertainments Officer, Sport & Recreation
Officer; (a) 9 (b) 2). **19** ALS; Plessey; photocharging.
20 4 weeks. **21** (a) 3p pw; (b&c) none. **22** HULTIS.
23 (a, b, c&d) 2,044,021; (e) 367. **24** (a) 7,270,522;
(b) 1,478,459.
25 (a) 403; (b) 67; (c) 125. **26** (a) £2,234,590;
(b) £74,910; (c) £2.664; (d&e) £521,640; (f) £1,017,930.

INVERCLYDE DISTRICT COUNCIL Central Library, Clyde
Sq, Greenock, Renfrewshire, PA15 1NA (0475-26211/2).
Chief Libn & Cultural Services Officer: Mr J. T. Hamilton MA,
FLA; Dep Chief Libn & Cultural Services Officer: Miss I. J.
Monteith ALA. **7** Leisure & Recreation. **9** Mon-Fri: ad
ldg & ref 10.00-20.00 (Wed 13.00), children's 16.00-20.00;
Sat: 10.00-13.00.
10 HQ; Branch. **12 Branches:** East B Lib, Bawhirley Rd,
Greenock; South-West B Lib, Inverkip Rd, Greenock; John
Reid Lib, Burns Sq, Greenock; Watt Monument Lib, Union St,
Greenock; Boglestone Lib, Dubbs Rd, Port Glasgow; King St,
Port Glasgow; Gamble Institute, Gourock; Kilmacolm
Institute, Kilmacolm; Inverskip Primary School, Inverskip.
14 Local history & archives (Watt Library, 40,000 titles on
Greenock & district & Scottish material). **15** 5; (a) 35,000
(b) 15,000; (c) 5,000; (d) 1,500; (e) £2.00 deposit; (f) as books.
17 Housebound, prisons, hospitals, old people's homes.
18 Cultural activities (£20,000; Chief Libn & Cultural Services Officer; (a) 4 (b) 1). **21** (a) 3p pw or part; (b&c) 1p pw
or part. **23** (a) 120,000; (b) 10,500 (exc Watt Lib);
(c) 28,000; (e) 120. **24** (a) 558,000; (b) 123,000; (d) 60,000.
25 (a) 55; (b) 15; (c) 8; (d) 3. **26 Finance** (10½ months
only); (a) £298,200; (b) £1,200; (c) £3.01; (d) £68,688;
(e) £6,125; (f) £139,125.

ISLE OF WIGHT COUNTY COUNCIL (pop c.112,000) County
Library Headquarters, Parkhurst Rd, Newport, PO30 5TX
(098381-2324). Dir of Cultural Services: Mr L. J. Mitchell
BA, FLA; Libs Officer: Mr M. R. Howley, ALA. **7** Amenities & Leisure Services. **9** Mon-Fri: 9.30-18.00; Sat:
9.30-17.00.
10 HQ; Branch. **12** Upper St James St, Newport; George
St, Ryde; Beckford Rd, Cowes; High St, Ventnor; School Green
Rd, Freshwater; 8 Clarence Rd, East Cowes; High St, Bembridge; High St, Sandown; Victoria Rd, Shanklin. **13** P-t
2; mobiles 2.
14 Printing & illustrations (from 16th cent, c.100 items).
17 Schools, housebound, prisons, hospitals, old people's
homes. **18** Cultural activities (Dir of Cultural Services).
20 4 weeks. **21** (a) 5p 1st week, 10p 2nd week, 5p pw
thereafter; (b) none; (c) as adult, but concessionary loan
period. **22** SWRLB; HATRICS. **23** (a) 187,454;
(b) 6,500; (c) 23,654; (d) 20,142; (e) 213. **24** (a) 1,085,692;
(b) 197,398; (c) 24,976; (d) 4,200.
25 (a) 52; (b) 6; (c) 16; (d) 7. **26** (a) £348,060 (libs only);
(b) £22,860 (libs only); (c) £3.10; (d) £94,480; (f) £177,490
(lib staff only).

KENT COUNTY COUNCIL (pop 1,449,000) Kent County
Library, Springfield, Maidstone, ME14 2LH (0622-54371 ext
385; telex 965212). County Libn: Mr Dean Harrison MA,
FLA; Dep: Mr M. S. Crouch BA, FLA. **7** Libraries,
Museums & Archives Sub-Committee. **8** Chief Education
Officer: Mr W. H. Petty MA, BSc. **9** Mon-Fri: ad ldg &
ref 9.30-19.00 (Wed 13.00), children's varies; Sat: 9.30-
17.00
10 HQ; Division; Branch. **11 Divisional HQs:** Ashford:
Church Rd, Ashford, TN23 1QX (0233-20649), Libn: Mrs J.
Tindale FLA; Canterbury: High St, Canterbury, CT1 2JF
(0227-63608), Libn: Mr V. Ralph ALA; Dartford: Central
Park, DA1 1EU (08043-21133), Libn: Mr C. Crook ALA;
Dover: Maison Dieu House, Dover, CT16 1DW (0304-204201),
Libn: Mr T. Ricketts ALA; Gillingham: High St, Gillingham
ME7 1BG (0634-51066), Libn: Mr N. Tomlinson FLA;
Gravesham: Windmill St, Gravesend DA12 1AQ (0474-52578),
Libn: Mr W. T. W. Woods FLA; Maidstone: St Faiths St,
Maidstone, ME14 1LH (0622-52344), Libn: Mr C. H. Sneddon
DMA, ALA; Medway: Riverside, Chatham ME4 4HL (0634-
43580), Libn: Mr G. Fordham ALA; Sevenoaks: The Drive,
Sevenoaks, TN13 3AB (0732-53118), Libn: Mr G. Lawrence

CODE: 1 Local authority. 2 Population. 3 Postal address of HQ. 4 Telephone & telex. 5 Chief Libn. 6 Deputy. 7 Committee responsible. 8 Officer to whom Libn is responsible (if any). 9 Hours. 10 Organisation. 11 Area libraries. 12 Branches. 13 Part-time libraries; mobiles. 14 Special collections. 15 Gramophone records: number of libraries, (a) record issues (b) cassette issues (c) record stock (d) cassette stock (e) loan charges (f) fines; charges. 17 Other services. 18 Cultural activities (expenditure, officer in charge, staff: (a) officers (b) manual). 19 Issue method (if not Browne). 20 Loan period (if not 2 weeks). 21 Fines: (a) adult (b) children (c) OAPs. 22 Co-operative schemes. 23 Stock: (a) adult lending (b) adult reference (c) children (d) schools (e) current periodical titles. 24 Issues: (a) adult (b) children (c) schools (d) institutions. 25 Staff: (a) officers (b) manual (c) chartered libns (d) graduates. 26 Finance: (a) total expenditure (b) non-rate income (c) per capita expenditure (d) expenditure for books (e) expenditure for records etc (f) salaries & wages. 27 Capital projects.

KENT COUNTY COUNCIL—*continued*
FLA; Shepway: Grace Hill, Folkestone, CT20 1HD (0303-57583), Libn: Mr R. Dawe ALA; Swale: Central Ave, Sittingbourne, ME10 4AH (0795-76545), Libn: Mr K. F. W. Chatfield FLA; Thanet: Cecil Sq, Margate, CT9 1RE (0843-23626), Libn: Mr J. Walters BA, ALA; Tonbridge: 4 High St, Tonbridge, TN9 1EL (07322-2754), Libn: Miss S. J. Hardy FLA; Tunbridge Wells: Mount Pleasant, Tunbridge Wells, TN1 1NS (0892-22352/3), Libn: Miss J. K. Page ALA. **12** The Square, Stanhope, Ashford; The Pebbles, High St, Tenterden; High St, Herne Bay; Herne Bay Rd, Swalecliffe; 31-33 Oxford St, Whitstable; 158 Colney Rd, Dartford; Fleetdown, Swaledale Rd, Dartford; Summerhouse Dr, Bexley; Temple Hill Sq, Dartford; Victoria Lodge, 11 Wellington Rd, Deal; 13 Market St, Sandwich; Birling Ave, Rainham; Twydall Green, Gillingham; Fairview Ave, Wigmore; Kings Farm, Kitchener Ave, Gravesend; Marling Cross, Mackenzie Way, Gravesend; River View Park, The Alma; Gravesend; Coldharbour Rd, Northfleet; 1 London Rd, Northfleet; Shepway, Northumberland Court, Northumberland Rd, Maidstone; The Parade, High St, Staplehurst; Lordswood Lane, Chatham; Walderslade Rd, Chatham; St Werburgh Crescent, Hoo; Central Lib, Northgate, Rochester; Leake House, The Fairway, Rochester; 32 Bryant Rd, Strood; Church St, Edenbridge; Ash Rd, Hartley, Longfield; Dippers Close, Kemsing; High St, Seal; Whiteoak, London Rd, Swanley; London Rd, Westerham; Cheriton High St, Cheriton, Folkestone; Sandgate High St, Sandgate, Folkestone; Wood Ave, Folkestone; Stade St, Hythe; High St, New Romney; High St, Milton; Newton Rd, Faversham; 395 Minster Rd, Minster-in-Sheppey; 44 Trinity Rd, Sheerness; Alpha Rd, Birchington; Queen Elizabeth Ave, Cliftonville; Minster Rd, Westgate; Pierremont Gardens, Broadstairs; Guildford Lawn, Ramsgate; Newington Rd, Ramsgate; 5 York Parade, Tonbridge; Martin Sq, Larkfield; Holborough Rd, Snodland; 24 High St, West Malling; Lower Green Rd, Rusthall, Tunbridge Wells; Showfields Estate, Tunbridge Wells; Carriers Rd, Cranbrook; 2 Commercial Rd, Paddock Wood; Yew Tree Rd, Southborough. **13** P-t 34; mobiles 13.
14 Local history; music; drama. **15** 14; (a) 112, 314; (b) 2, 733; (c) 16, 000; (d) 150; (e) £2 pa; (f) as for books. **16** Charges variable, max £2 pa. **17** Schools, housebound, prisons, hospitals, old people's homes, WEA & other classes. **18** Cultural activities. **19** Token in 1 division. **20** 4 weeks. **21** (a) 2p pw, max 50p; (b) none. **23** (a, b, c&d) 3, 500, 000; (e) 800. **24** (a&b) 15, 272, 349. **25** (a) c. 600; (c) c. 200; (d) 20. **26** (a) £3, 143, 000; (b) £203, 000; (c) £2. 16; (d) £767, 900; (e) £25, 000; (f) £1, 610, 700.

KILMARNOCK AND LOUDOUN DISTRICT COUNCIL (pop 89, 000) Dick Institute, Elmbank Ave, Kilmarnock, Ayrshire, KA1 3BU (0563-26401). Manager, Cultural Services Dept: J. F. T. Thomson MBE, MA, FLA; Chief Libn: Mr John Preston BA, ALA. **7** Leisure. **9** Mon-Fri: ad ldg & ref 9.00-20.00 (Wed 17.00), children's 12.30-17.30 (Wed 17.00); Sat: ad ldg & ref 9.00-17.00, children's 10.00-17.00. **10** HQ; District; Branch. **11** Districts: Stewarton: Cunningham Institute, Stewarton, Libn: Mrs Ulla-Brita Dunn ALA; Galston: Henrietta St, Galston, Libn: Miss Silvja Ledaunieks BA. **12** Bellfield B Lib, 87 Whatriggs Rd, Kilmarnock; Dean B Lib, Deanhill Rd, Kilmarnock; 1 Tourhill Rd, Kilmarnock. **13** P-t 5.
14 Hutton colln (early printed Bibles); Braidwood colln (incunabula & early printed books); Ayrshire colln; Burns colln (books & mss); John Galt colln. **15** 1; (a) 11, 819; (c) 2, 192; (d) 716; (e) none; (f) 2p pw or part. **17** Schools,

housebound, old people's homes, old people's clubs. **18** Cultural activities (£34, 690; Manager of Cultural Services; a 4, b 1). **19** Photo-charging. **21** (a&c) 2p pw or part; (b) 1p pw or part. **23** (a) 81, 420; (b) 5, 905; (c) 17, 260; (e) 44. **24** (a&d) 371, 484; (b) 58, 869. **25** (a) 37; (b) 6; (c) 9; (d) 8. **26** (a) £175, 000; (b) £4, 000; (c) £1. 967; (d) £40, 400; (e) £1, 000; (f) £85, 800.

KIRKCALDY DISTRICT COUNCIL (also serving **North East Fife District Council** on an agency basis) (pop 236, 099) District Library Headquarters, East Fergus Place, Kirkcaldy, Fife, KY1 1XT (0592-68386). Asst Dir of Leisure & Recreation: Mr Ronald McLaren ALA; Senior Libn: Miss Anne Gardner ALA. **7** Leisure & Recreation (Kirkcaldy DC); Recreation & General Purposes (North East Fife DC). **8** Dir of Leisure & Recreation: A. Sneddon LLB. **9** Mon-Thurs: 10.00-19.00, Fri: 10.00-17.00; Sat: 10.00-19.00. **10** HQ; Group: **11** Group Libraries: Glenwood Lib, Glenwood Shopping Centre, Glenrothes (0592-755866), Libn: Miss M. McKenna ALA; Central Lib, War Memorial Gardens, Kirkcaldy (0592-60707), Libn: Miss I. McKinlay ALA; Methil Lib, Wellesley Rd, Methil (0333-23117), Libn: Mr D. Spalding ALA; St Andrews Lib, Church St, St Andrews (033481-3381), Libn: Mr A. Rodden ALA. **12** Cupar; Templehall; Leven; Sinclairtown; Burntisland; Auchmuty. **13** P-t 25; mobiles 2.
14 Local history. **15** 3; (e) £2 deposit. **17** Housebound, hospitals, old people's homes. **20** 3 weeks. **21** (a, b&c) 2p pw or part, max 24p inc postage. **23** (a, b&c) 400, 000; (e) 35.
25 (a) 100; (b) 28 (some part-time); (c) 15; (d) 6.
26 Finance (10½ months only): (a) £387, 000; (b) £86, 850; (c) £1. 64; (d) £97, 000; (e) £400; (f) £175, 470.

KIRKLEES METROPOLITAN BOROUGH COUNCIL (pop 375, 200) Headquarters Kirklees Libraries & Museums Service, Princess Alexandra Walk, Huddersfield, West Yorkshire, HD1 2SU (0484-21356; telex 517463). Chief Libn & Curator: Mr Stanley T. Dibnab AMBIM, MILGA, FLA; Principal Assts: Mr H. White ALA (Major Libs); Mr V. C. Smith FGS, FMA (Major Museums); Mr P. J. Arnold ALA (Circulation); Mr F. W. Smith FLA (Bibliographical). **7** Education (Libraries & Museums). **8** Dir of Educational Services: Mr Ernest T. Butcher MA. **9** Mon-Fri: ad ldg 9.00-19.30, ref 9.00-20.30, children's 12.00-14.00, 15.30-19.30; Sat: 9.00-16.00.
10 HQ; Major Libraries; Area Teams; Branches. **11** Major Libraries: Princess Alexandra Walk, Huddersfield, HD1 2SU (0484-21356), Libn: Mrs J. Madden ALA; Market Pl, Batley, WF17 5DF (092 44-3141), Libn: Mrs J. M. Hodge ALA; Whitcliffe Rd, Cleckheaton BD19 3DX (097 62-3856), Libn: Mr Edward Hobson ALA; Wellington Rd, Dewsbury, WF13 1HW (092 42-5151), Libn: Mr Peter Gill-Martin MA, ALA. **Area Teams:** Eastthorpe Lodge, Mirfield (0924-2030), Acting Libn: Mr Peter Jennings ALA; Walkley Lane, Heckmondwyke (0924-3764), Libn: Mr I. Stringer ALA; 8 Britannia Rd, Slaithwaite, HD7 5HG (048 484-2564), Libn: Mr J. Blinston ALA; 47 Huddersfield Rd, Holmfirth, HD7 1JH (048 489-2231), Libn: Mr G. Peach ALA. **12** Market Pl, Birstall, Batley; Carlisle Institute, Meltham. **13** P-t 21; mobiles 10.
14 Asian language books (Urdu, Punjabi, Hindi, Gujurati, Bengali, Marthati); local history & archives. **15** 3; (a) 31, 731; (b) 3, 558; (c) 8, 971; (d) 715; (e) £1 per ticket pa (max 2 tickets); (f) none (except postage for reminders). **16** 563; none. **17** Schools, housebound, hospitals, old people's homes, play groups. **19** Plessey library pen.

KIRKLEES METROPOLITAN BOROUGH COUNCIL—*continued*
20 4 weeks. **21** (a, b&c) none. **22** YHJLS. **23**
(a) 588, 850; (b) 58, 849; (c) 176, 975; (d) 109, 668; (e) 722.
24 (a) 3, 178, 256; (b) 617, 932; (c) 1, 000, 000; (d) 51, 173.
25 (a) 155; (b) 21; (c) 44; (d) 12. **26** (a) £799, 500;
(b) £9, 100; (c) £2.13; (d) £217, 600; (e) £4, 500; (f) £431, 000.
27 Rebuilding Mirfield Library.

KNOWSLEY METROPOLITAN BOROUGH COUNCIL (pop
193, 000) Knowsley Library Service, 'Blacklow', Roby Rd,
Huyton, Liverpool, Merseyside, L36 4HA (051-480-8585).
Borough Libn: Mr Nicholas Holbrook ALA; Principal Libn:
Mr Alan S. Ronalds ALA, FRSA, AMBIM. **7** Library
9 No general pattern.
10 HQ; Branch. **12** 1 The Withens, Cantril Farm, Liverpool, L28 1SU; 4 Childwall Parade, Pilch Lane, Huyton, L14
6TT; Leathers Lane, Halewood, Liverpool, L26 0TS; Westmorland Rd, Huyton, L36 9UN; Newtown Gardens, Kirkby, Liverpool, L32 8RR; 54 Hillside Rd, Longview, Huyton, L36 8BJ;
Princess Dr, Page Moss, Huyton, L14 9ND; High St, Prescot,
L34 3LD; St Johns B Lib, 19 Manor Farm Rd, Huyton, L36
0UB; Dragon Dr, Whiston, Prescot, L35 3QW. **13** Mobiles
1.
16 100 framed prints; £1 pa. **17** Schools, housebound,
hospitals, old people's homes. **18** Cultural activities
(£5, 000; Borough Libn). **19** Photocharging (Kirkby)
20 4 weeks. **21** (a) 4p pw or part, max £1; (b&c) none.
22 NWRLB. **23** (a) 239, 750; (b) 8, 065; (c) 73, 056;
(d) primary 95, 000; (e) 80. **24** (a) 995, 510; (b) 298, 439.
(b) 298, 439.
25 (a) 96; (b) 14; (c) 35; (d) 7. **26** (a) £456, 929;
(b) £53, 885; (c) £2.36; (d) £105, 200; (f) £232, 273.

KYLE AND CARRICK DISTRICT COUNCIL (pop 113, 611) 12
Main St, Ayr, Ayrshire, KA8 8ED (0292-69148). Dir of Lib
Services: Mr Allan Leach BA, DPA, FLA; Dep Dir: Mr David
Hynd ALA. **7** Leisure & Recreation. **9** Mon-Fri:
10. 00-19. 30; Sat: 10. 00-17. 30.
10 HQ; Area; Branch; Mobile. **11 Area Libraries:** Central Lib, 12 Main St, Ayr, KA8 8ED (0292-69141 ext 34);
B Lib, Girvan, Ayrshire. **13** P-t 8.
14 Ayrshire (books, maps & plans, newspapers, illustrations);
Robert Burns. **15** 2; (c) 600; (f) as books. **17** Housebound, hospitals, old people's homes, lighthouses.
18 Exhibitions (Organiser of Museums & Galleries; staff 3½).
19 Computer (Automated Library Systems). **20** 3 weeks
21 (a&c) 1st 2 weeks 3p per book; further 2 weeks 5p per
book; further 2 weeks 13p per book; further 2 weeks 25p per
book; (b) 1st 2 weeks overdue, free, thereafter as above.
23 (a&c) 196, 803; (b) 22, 420. **24** (a, b&d) 1, 102, 969.
25 (a) 53; (c) 6; (d) 7. **26** (a) £282, 790; (b) £9, 310;
(c) £2.49; (d) £70, 780; (f) £137, 240.

LANARK DISTRICT COUNCIL (pop 53, 109) Lanark District
Libraries, Lindsay Institute, Hope St, Lanark, Lanarkshire
(0555-2828). Chief Libn: Mr R. S. Davidson ALA; Principal
Asst: Mr J. J. Douglas ALA. **7** Halls, Entertainments &
Libraries. **8** Dir of Environmental Health & Recreation:
G. B. S. Craig MInstSWM. **9** Mon-Fri: 10. 00-19. 45; Sat:
10. 00-17. 00.
10 HQ; District; Mobile; Centre. **11 District Libraries:**
Carluke Lib, Carnwath Rd, Carluke (0555-72134), Libn-in-
charge: Mr J. Dempster MA; Forth Lib, Forth Primary School,
Main St, Forth, M11 8AE (055 581-594), Libn-in-charge: Miss
C. McManus. **13** Mobiles 4.
14 Robert Owen colln; William Smellie colln. **15** 3;
(c) 1, 659. **17** Housebound, prisons, hospitals, old people's
homes. **18** Cultural activities; Entertainments (Parks &
Cemeteries Manager). **20** 4 weeks. **21** (a, b&c) none.
23 (a) 50, 330; (b) 7, 300; (c) 18, 044.
25 (a) 28; (b) 3; (c) 2; (d) 2. **26** (a) £172, 000; (c) £3.25;
(d) £29, 610; (e) £2, 190; (f) £90, 140.

LANCASHIRE COUNTY COUNCIL (pop 1, 370, 100) 143 Corporation St, Preston, Lancashire PR1 8RH (0772-54868;
telex 67349). County Libn: Mr Alan Longworth FLA; Dep
County Libn: Mr James Brown FLA. **7** Library & Leisure.
9 Mon-Fri: 9. 30-19. 30; Sat: 9. 30-17. 00.
10 HQ; District; Branch. **11** Districts: Blackburn: Library

St, Blackburn BB1 7AJ (0254-59511), Libn: Mr J. B. Darby-
shire FLA; Blackpool: Queen St, Blackpool, FY1 1PX
(053 834-23977), Libn: Mr P. Dunderdale FLA; Burnley:
Grimshaw St, Burnley, BB11 2BD (0282-33540), Libn: Mr R.
Pickles FLA; Chorley: Avondale Rd, Chorley, PR7 2EH
(025 72-77222/3), Libn: Mr A. Clarkson ALA; Fylde: 254
Clifton Dr South, St Annes-on-Sea, FY8 1NR (039 15-724711),
Libn: Mr D. B. Timms ALA; Hyndburn: St James St,
Accrington, BB5 1NQ (0254-32411), Libn: Mr B. Ashton
ALA; Lancaster: Market Sq, Lancaster, LA1 1HY (0524-2800),
Libn: Mr E. H. Lowe FLA; Pendle: Market Sq, Nelson, BB9
7PU (0282-692511/2), Libn: Mr W. B. Richardson ALA;
Preston: Harris Lib, Market Sq, Preston PR1 2PP (0772-
53191), Libn: Mr R. F. Watson FLA; Ribble Valley: Abbey
Rd, Whalley, BB6 9RS (025 482-2446), Libn: Miss B. R. Snell
FLA; Rossendale: Rawtenstall, BB4 6QU (07062-2911/2 or
7777), Libn: Mr J. Elliott ALA; South Ribble: Watkins Lane,
Lostock Hall, Preston PR5 5TU (0772-39775/6), Libn: Mrs
M. Latham ALA; West Lancashire: Burscough St, Ormskirk,
L39 2EN (0695-76843), Libn: Miss M. Williams ALA; Wyre:
Victoria Rd, Thornton, FY5 3SZ (039 14-77931/2), Libn:
Mr G. D. Williams ALA. **12** Knott St, Darwen, BB3 2RN;
Cherry Tree Lane, Livesey, BB2 5NX; Mill Hill Centre,
New Chapel St, Blackburn BB2 4DT; Shadsworth Community
Centre, Shadsworth, Blackburn, BB1 2HT; Luton Rd, Anchors-
holme, Blackpool, FY5 3RS; Devonshire Rd, Bispham,
Blackpool, FY2 0HH; Claremont Rd, Claremont, Blackpool,
FY1 2QJ; Dinmore Ave, Grange Park, Blackpool, FY3 7RW;
Hawes Side Lane, Blackpool, FY4 5AJ; Highfield Rd, Black-
pool, FY4 2JF; Talbot Rd, Layton, Blackpool, FY3 7BD;
Waterloo Rd, Marton, Blackpool, FY4 4BL; Bowness Ave,
Mereside, Blackpool, FY4 4TE; Central Dr, Revoe, Black-
pool, FY1 5HS; Lytham Rd, South Shore, Blackpool, FY1 6ET;
Jubilee St, Briercliffe, Burnley, BB10 2JD; Colne Rd, Burn-
ley, BB10 1LL; Town Hall, Padiham, BB12 8BS; Lowerhouse
Lane, Rosegrove, Burnley, BB12 6HU; Coal Clough, Burnley;
Railway Rd, Adlington, PR6 9RG; Spendmore Lane, Coppull,
PR7 5DF; St Mary's Gate, off Runshaw Lane, Euxton, PR7
6AH; Station Rd, Kirkham, PR4 2HD; Clifton St, Lytham, FY8
5EP; Library St, Church, BB5 4JY; Pickup St, Clayton-le-
Moors, BB5 5NT; Queen St, Great Harwood, BB6 7AL; Union
Rd, Oswaldtwistle, BB5 3HS; School St, Rishton, BB1 4DN;
Central Dr, Morecambe, LA4 5DL; Council Offices, Heysham
Rd, Heysham, LA3 2BJ; Memorial Hall, Slyne-with-Hest,
LA2 6BJ; Lancaster Moor Hospital; Albert Rd, Colne, BB8
0AP; Fern Lea Ave, Barnoldswick, BB8 5DW; Ann St, Barrow-
ford, BB9 8QH; Colne Rd, Brierfield, BB9 5HW; Garstang Rd,
Fulwood, PR2 4RQ; Sharoe Green Lane, Fulwood, PR2 4ED;
Ribbleton Hall Dr, Ribbleton, Preston, PR2 6EE; West Park
Ave, Savick; Preston, PR2 1UH; Church St, Clitheroe, BB7
2DG; Berry Lane, Longridge, PR3 3JA; St James Sq, Bacup,
OL13 9OH; Deardengate, Haslington, BB4 5QJ; Lloyd St,
Whitworth, OL12 8AA, Station Rd, Bamber Bridge, PR5 6LA;
Lancastergate, Leyland, PR5 1EX; Kingsfold, Hawksbury Dr,
Penwortham, PR1 9EH; Liverpool Rd, Penwortham, Preston,
PR1 9XE; High St, Skelmersdale, WN8 8AP; Hall Green, Up
Holland, WN8 0PB; Chatsworth Ave, Fleetwood, FY7 8EA;
Rossall Rd, Cleveleys, FY5 1EE; Dock St, Fleetwood, FY7
6AQ; Market Pl, Garstang, PR3 1ZA; Lancaster Rd,
Knott End, FY6 0AU; Blackpool Old Rd, Poulton, FY6 7DH;
Welbeck, Poulton Rd, Fleetwood, FY7 7BS. **13** P-t 51;
mobiles 16.
14 Stocks-Massey (music); Fuller-Maitland (music); Dr
Shepherd (10, 000 vols bequeathed to Preston 1759); Spencer
(18th & 19th cent children's books & chapbooks); Dunn (18th
& 19th cent art books); Burnley Grammar School (16th, 17th,
& 18th cent books); Colonel Whalley (military history; fine
bindings). **15** 7; (a) 70, 198; (b) 3, 127; (c) 15, 289; (d) 829;
(e) £2.00 pa; (f) as books. **16** £1.25 pa. **17** Schools,
housebound, prisons, hospitals, old people's homes, training
centres. **18** Cultural activites partly (£3, 170 exc salaries
etc; District Libn). **19** Reverse Browne; token (fiction
only); Photocharging; computer (ALS label-based). **20** 3
weeks. **21** (a) 2p first week, 1p pd thereafter, max 50p;
(b&c) none. **22** NWRLB. **23** (a, b, c&d) 3, 089, 000.
24 (a) 13, 894, 357; (b) 2, 185, 627; (d) 256, 495.
25 (a) 640; (b) 77½; (c) 166; (d) 51. **26** (a) £3, 515, 570;
(b) £196, 170; (c) £2. 57; (d) £703, 850; (e) £8, 490;
(f) £1, 733, 000. **27** Skelmersdale.

CODE: 1 Local authority. 2 Population. 3 Postal address of HQ. 4 Telephone & telex. 5 Chief Libn. 6 Deputy. 7 Committee responsible. 8 Officer to whom Libn is responsible (if any). 9 Hours. 10 Organisation. 11 Area libraries. 12 Branches. 13 Part-time libraries; mobiles. 14 Special collections. 15 Gramophone records: number of libraries, (a) record issues (b) cassette issues (c) record stock (d) cassette stock (e) loan charges (f) fines. 16 Pictures: stock; charges. 17 Other services. 18 Cultural activities (expenditure, officer in charge, staff: (a) officers (b) manual). 19 Issue method (if not Browne). 20 Loan period (if not 2 weeks). 21 Fines: (a) adult (b) children (c) OAPs. 22 Co-operative schemes. 23 Stock: (a) adult lending (b) adult reference (c) children (d) schools (e) current periodical titles. 24 Issues: (a) adult (b) children (c) schools (d) institutions. 25 Staff: (a) officers (b) manual (c) chartered libns (d) graduates. 26 Finance: (a) total expenditure (b) non-rate income (c) per capita expenditure (d) expenditure for books (e) expenditure for records etc (f) salaries & wages. 27 Capital projects.

LEEDS CITY COUNCIL (pop 738, 931) Central Library, Municipal Buildings, Leeds, LS1 3AB (0532-31301). Dir of Lib Service: A. B. Craven FLA; Libn: R. G. Benjamin, ALA (Central Book & Inf Services). **7** Leisure Services. **8** Dir of Leisure Services: M. C. Palmer-Jones MA. **9** Mon-Fri: 9.00-20.00; Sat: 9.00-16.00. **10** HQ; Area; Branch. **11 Area Library HQs: North:** 2 Newstead Rd, Otley, LS21 3JB (094 34-3349), Area Libn: J. B. Shackleton MA, ALA; East: York Road Lib, York Rd, Leeds, LS9 9AA (0532-454391), Area Libn: Mr G. Edmundson ALA, FLA; South: Hunslet B Lib, Waterloo Rd, LS10 2NS (0532-716282), Libn: D. B. Glover ALA. **12** Headingley, North Lane, Leeds, LS6 3HG; Holt Park, Ralph Thoresby High School, Farrar Lane, Leeds 16; Horsforth, Town St, Horsforth, LS18 5BL; 4 Boroughgate, Otley, LS21 1AL; Woodhouse Carr, Craven Rd, Leeds LS6 2SN; Burley, Cardigan Rd, Leeds, LS6 1QL; Otley Rd, Guiseley, LS20 8AH; Ireland Wood, 19 Iveson Approach, off Otley Old Rd, Leeds LS16 6LJ; Micklefield House, Rawdon, LS19 6DF; Town Hall Sq, Yeadon; Chapel Allerton, 106 Harrogate Rd, Leeds LS7 4LZ; Compton Rd, Harehills Lane, Leeds, LS9 7BG; Crossgates, Farm Rd, Leeds LS15 7LB; Lidgett Lane, Garforth, Leeds LS25 1EH; 1 Oakwood Lane, Leeds, LS8 2PZ; Seacroft Crescent, Leeds, LS14 6PA; 17 Westgate, Wetherby, LS22 4LL; Halton, 257-259 Selby Rd, Leeds, LS15 7JR; Westfield Lane, Kippax, LS25 7JP; Armley, 2 Stocks Hill, Leeds LS12 1UQ; Beeston, Hugh Gaitskell School, St Anthony's Dr, Leeds LS11 8AB; Bramley, Hough Lane, LS13 3ND; 112 Dewsbury Rd, Leeds LS11 6XD; Commercial St, Morley, LS27 8HZ; Central Lib, Church Lane, Pudsey, LS28 7TY; Marsh St, Rothwell, LS26 0AE; 36 Heights Dr, Armley Heights, LS12 3SU; Aberfield Gate, Belle Isle Rd, Belle Isle, LS10 3QH; Thornhill St, Calverley, Pudsey; Cow Close, 4 Whincover Dr, Leeds LS12 5JR; Old Rd, Farsley, LS28 5DH; Middleton Park Ave, Acre Close, Leeds LS10 4HT. **13** P-t 28; mobiles 4; 1 travelling lib. **14** Music; art; law; local history (Leeds & Yorkshire); Gott Bequest (early gardening & illustrated flower books); modern fine printing; Yorkshire Ramblers' Club (mountaineering & potholing); Leeds Philatelic Society Library; Porton Room (Judaica); Civil War tracts; British & foreign patents; illustrations (for school use); archives (at Sheepscar). **15** 6; (a) c. 183, 421; (b) 8, 084; (c) c. 23, 187; (d) 704; (e) £1.00 pa (2 tickets); (f) 3p pw or part. **16** 470 (run in conjunction with Art Gallery); £2.00 residents, £3.50 non-residents. **17** Schools, housebound, prisons, hospitals, old people's homes. **18** Cultural activities, entertainments (£572, 420, Dir of Leisure Services, a 35, b 79). **19** Photo-charging in some branch libs. **21** (a, b&c) 1p pw or part. **23** (a) 868, 295; (b) 481, 508; (c) 231, 133; (d) 106, 251; (e) 1, 870. **24** (a) 7, 532, 433; (b) 1, 477, 012; (d) 172, 702. **25** (a) 302; (b) 65; (c) 65; (d) 35. **26** (a) £1, 630, 490; (b) £50, 550; (c) £2.17; (d) £464, 030; (e) £8, 520; (f) £810, 400.

LEICESTERSHIRE COUNTY COUNCIL (pop 838, 000) Leicestershire Libraries & Information Service, Lee Circle, Leicester, LE1 3RW (0533-22012; telex 34307). County Libn: Mr G. E. Smith FLA; Dep: Mr W. R. M. McClelland FLA. **7** Libraries & Museums. **9** Mon-Fri: 9.00-19.30; Sat: 9.00-16.00. **10** HQ; Area; Branch. **11 Areas:** Information Centre, Bishop St, Leicester, LE1 6AA (0533-20644), Libn: Mr D. Palmer MA, FLA; Granby St, Loughborough, LE11 3DZ (05093-2985), Libn: Mr P. Oldroyd BA, ALA; Oakham Lib, Catmos St, Oakham, LE15 6HW (0572-2918), Libn: Miss M. Harper FLA; Oadby Lib, Sandhurst St, Oadby, LE2 5AR (0533-715066), Libn: Mr D. Adams ALA; Hinckley Lib, Lancaster Rd, Hinckley, LE10 1AS (04553-35106), Libn: Mr K. H. Ceeney ALA; Wigston Magna Lib, Oadby Rd, Wigston, LE8 1PT (0533-887381), Libn: Mr R. Eaton ALA; Coalville Lib, New Broadway, Coalville, LE6 2ET (05303-37010), Libn: Mrs V. Biddiscombe ALA; Syston Lib, Upper Church St, Syston, LE7 8HR (053723-3647), Libn: Mr G. W. Belton ALA. **12** Stadon Rd, Anstey, LE7 7AY; Kilwardby St, Ashby de la Zouch, LE6 5FX; Belgrave Lib, Cossington St, Leicester, LE4 6JD; Wanlip Lane, Birstall, Leicester, LE4 4JU; Lutterworth Rd, Blaby, Leicester LE8 3DW; Braunstone Av, Leicester, LE3 1LE; Welcombe Ave, Ravenhurst Rd, Braunstone, Leicester, LE3 2TA; Delven Lane, Castle Donington, Derby DE7 2LJ; Wood St, Earl Shilton, LE9 7NE; 200 Evington Lane, Leicester, LE5 6DH; Gavendon St, Leicester LE2 0AH; Stamford St, Glenfield, Leicester, LE3 8DL; Leicester Rd, Groby, Leicester, LE6 0DQ; Knighton Lib, Clarendon Park Rd, Leicester, LE2 3AJ; Central Lending Lib, Belvoir St, Leicester, LE1 6QG; Central Children's Lib, Wellington St, Leicester, LE1 6QG; Goldsmith Music & Gramophone Record Lib, Belvoir St, Leicester, LE1 6QG; Leicester Forest East Lib, Holmfield Ave West, Leicester, LE3 3FF; Coventry Rd, Lutterworth, LE17 4SH; 53 The Square, Market Harborough, LE16 7PA; Wilton Rd, Melton Mowbray, LE13 0UJ; New Parks Lib, Dillon Rd, Leicester, LE3 9PF; Rushey Mead Lib, Lockerbie Walk, Leicester, LE4 7ZX; St Barnabas Rd, Leicester LE5 4AH; Hall Croft, Shepshead, Loughborough, LE12 9AN; Cossington Rd, Sileby, Loughborough, LE12 7RS; Southfields Lib, Saffron Lane, Leicester, LE2 6QS; Church Hill Rd, Thurmaston, Leicester, LE4 8DE; Westcotes Lib, Narborough Rd, Leicester, LE3 0BQ; Woodgate Lib, Leicester, LE3 5GE. **13** P-t 39; mobiles 9. **15** 22; (a) 293, 826; (c) 22, 175; (e) 5p pw. **17** Schools, housebound, prisons, hospitals, old people's homes. **18** Cultural activities. **20** 4 weeks. **21** (a, b&c) $\frac{1}{2}$p pd for 2 weeks, 1p pd thereafter, max 24p (short loans double). **22** EMRLB. **23** (a) 1, 255, 270; (b) 69, 153; (c) 342, 339; (d) 558, 994; (e) 630. **24** (a) 6, 560, 000; (b) 1, 554, 000. **25** (a) 318; (b) $30\frac{3}{4}$; (c) 97. **26** (a) £1, 532, 005; (b) £65, 205; (c) £1.83; (d) £387, 425; (e) £13, 450; (f) £855, 580.

LINCOLNSHIRE COUNTY COUNCIL (pop 524, 000) Lincolnshire County Library, Brayford House, Lucy Tower St, Lincoln, LN1 1XN (0522-26287; telex 56306 LIB LINCS). County Libn: Mr E. H. W. Roberts FLA; Principal Asst County Libn: Mr R. M. Lyle ALA. **7** Education (Library Sub-Committee). **8** County Education Officer: Mr G. V. Cooke MA. **9** Mon-Fri: 9.30-19.00; Sat: 9.30-17.00 **10** HQ; Division; Group; Branch. **11 Divisional Libraries:** Boston: 10 Haverfield Rd, Spalding, LN1 1EY (0775-3729), Libn: Mr B. Field FLA; Lincoln: Freeschool Lane, Lincoln, LN2 1EY (0522-33541), Libn: Mr D. E. Hayward FLA; Louth: Victoria Hall, Victoria Rd, Louth, LN11 0BX (0507-2218), Libn: Mr A. R. Foster ALA; Sleaford: Westholme, Sleaford (052 93-2691), Libn: Miss N. Goom FLA. **12** County Hall, Boston; South St, Bourne; The Parade, Cherry Willingham; The Park, High St, Deepings; Cobden St, Gainsborough; St Peter's Hill, Grantham; Church St, Holbeach; Wharf Rd, Horncastle; County Hospital, Sewell Rd, Lincoln; Newark Rd, Bracebridge, Lincoln; Lincoln Central Lib, Free School Lane, Lincoln; Ermine Lib, Ravendale Dr, Lincoln; 12 Upgate, Louth; 32 Victoria Rd, Mablethorpe; Mill Rd, Market Rasen; 1 East St, Nettleham; Middle St, North Hykeham; 23 Roman Bank, Skegness; Watergate, Sleaford; Victoria St, Spalding; High St, Stamford; Students Lib, Westholme, Sleaford. **13** P-t 25; mobiles 13. **14** Sir Joseph Banks mss; Tennyson colln; agricultural colln;

LINCOLNSHIRE COUNTY COUNCIL—*continued*
Sir Isaac Newton colln; Newcome colln; music (inc. vocal
scores); drama.   **15** 5; (a&b) 15, 171 (exc schools); (c&d)
4, 590 (+5, 115 in schools); (e) 50p pa + 10p per record; free
to O.A.P. s, blind, handicapped; (f) 5p pw or part.
17 Schools, housebound, prisons, hospitals, old people's
homes, adult education classes, H.M. Forces, youth clubs,
playgroups, police, handicapped, offshore rigs, nature reserve.   **19** Cheque book (in ex-Lincoln City area only).
20 4 weeks.   **21** (a&c) 5p pw or part; (b) none.
23 (a&b) 938, 865; (c) 190, 469; (d) 215, 086; (e) 524.
24 (a) 5, 063, 265; (b) 955, 774; (d) 244, 590.
25 (a) 297; (b) 22; (c) 62; (d) 9.   **26** (a) £1, 060, 655;
(b) £73, 165; (c) £2. 024; (d) £309, 610; (e) £1, 742 (exc
schools); (f) £602, 360.

LIVERPOOL CITY COUNCIL (pop 561, 000) Liverpool City
Libraries, William Brown St, Liverpool, Merseyside L3 8EW
(051-207 2147; telex 62500). City Libn: Mr Ralph Malbon
FLA; Asst City Libn: Mr J.R Cowan FLA.   **7** Libraries
& Leisure Activities.   **9** Mon-Fri: ad ldg & ref 9.00-
21.00, children's 9.00-18.00 (Thurs 17.00 most branches);
Sat: ad ldg & ref 9.00-17.00, children's 9.00-13.00.
10 HQ; Branch.   **12** Allerton Rd, Allerton, L18 6HG; Child-
wall Fiveways, Childwall, L15 6YG; Lodge Lane, Edge Hill,
L8 0QH; St Domingo Rd, Everton, L5 0RB; Longmoor Lane,
Fazakerley, L10 7LN; Bowden Rd, Garston, L19 1QN; Moss
Way, Gillmoss, L11 0BL; Great Homer St, Liverpool, L5 3LF;
Kensington, L7 2RJ; Stanley Rd, Kirkdale, L5 7QQ; Dovecot
Pl, Knotty Ash, L14 9PH; Queens Dr (Hewitson Rd), Larkhill,
L13 0DB; Childwall Valley Rd, Netherley, L27 3YA; Towns-
end Ave, Norris Green, L11 5AF; Old Swan, Prescot Rd, L13
5XG; Rawdon, Breck Rd, Anfield, L4 2QS; Aigburth Rd, Sefton
Park, L17 4JS; Central Ave, Speke, L24 0TW; County Rd,
Spellow, L4 3QF; Windsor St, Toxteth, L8 1XF; Evered Ave,
Walton, L9 2AF; Picton Rd, Wavertree, L15 4LP; Green Lane,
West Derby, L13 7EB; West Derby Village Hall Lib, Town Row,
L12 5HG; Allerton Rd, Woolton, L25 7RQ.   **13** Mobiles 3.
14 Autograph letters (from 16th cent); bookplate colln (one
of largest in world); fine bindings; children's books; press
books; Walter Crane colln; Edward Lear colln; fine prints
& engravings; early 17th cent English printed books.   **15** 1;
(a) 32, 529; (b) 2, 929; (c) 5, 000; (d) 340; (e) residents £2. 30
+ VAT pa, non-residents £4. 60 + VAT pa, OAP's £1. 15 +
VAT pa; (f) as books.   **17** Schools, housebound, prisons,
hospitals, old people's homes, youth clubs, remand homes,
musical societies & groups, amateur dramatic societies,
technical, industrial & commercial undertakings (through
LADSIRLAC).   **18** Library extension activities.   **20** 4
weeks.   **21** (a) 10p pw or part; (b&c) none.
22 LADSIRLAC.   **23** (a) 961, 923; (b) 1, 285, 459;
(c) 250, 884; (e) 2, 765.   **24** (a) 5, 494, 794; (b) 2, 209, 522.
25 (a) 353; (b) 150; (c) 80; (d) 61.   **26** (a) £1, 834, 300;
(b) £29, 239; (c) £3. 27; (d&e) £326, 150; (f) £1, 028, 040.
27 Central Libraries Extension, commenced 1 Jan 1974
(to complete in 1976) £1, 058, 700.

LLANELLI BOROUGH COUNCIL (pop 76, 900) Public Library,
Vaughan St, Llanelli, Dyfed, SA15 3TY (05542-3538). Borough
Libn & Curator: Mr H.A. Prescott FLA; Senior Libn: Mr
W.A. Doughty ALA.   **7** Devlopment & Leisure.   **9** Mon-
Fri: ad ldg 9.30-15.00, ref 9. 30-16.00, children's 9.30-
18.00; Sat: 9. 30-18. 00.
10 HQ; Branch.   **13** P-t 11; mobiles 2.
14 Local colln (slides, prints & films (16 mm) of local
events, industry, etc); paintings (by local artists of local
scenes); Llanelli pottery; paintings (Parc Howard).   **15** 1;
(a&b) 13, 454; (c) 7, 000; (d) 850; (e) £2. 00 deposit (returnable); (f) 3½p pw.   **17** Housebound, hospitals, old people's
homes, university extra-mural & WEA classes.   **18** Cultural activities (£4, 500, Borough Libn & Curator, a 1, b 1).
20 4 weeks (students 12).   **21** (a&c) 3½p pw for 3 weeks,
7p pw thereafter; (b) ½p pw for 3 weeks, 1p pw thereafter.
23 (a) 138, 331; (b) 30, 000; (c) 25, 000; (e) 269.
24 (a) 873, 893; (b) 49, 598; (d) 76, 983.
25 (a) 33; (b) 4; (c) 14; (d) 1.   **26** (a) £213, 405; (b) £2, 350;
(c) £2. 78; (d) £45, 670; (e) £2, 550; (f) £92, 845.

LONDON (GLC AREA)

BARKING, LONDON BOROUGH OF (pop 157, 600) Central
Library, Barking, Essex, IG11 7NB (01-594 9135/9; telex
897605). Borough Libn: Mr E. W. McManus FLA; Dep: Mr
Leslie Cannon FLA, DipSoc.   **7** Libraries.   **9** Mon-Fri:
ad ldg & ref 9.30-20.00 (Wed 17.00), children's 9.30-19.00
(closed Wed); Sat: 9. 30-17. 00.
10 Central; Branch.   **12** Valence Lib, Becontree Ave,
Dagenham, RM8 3HT; Rectory Rd, Dagenham, RM10 9SA;
Whalebone Lib, High Rd, Chadwell Heath, Romford, RM6 6AS;
Fanshawe Lib, Barnmead Rd, Dagenham, RM9 5DX; Woodward
Rd, Dagenham, RM9 4SP; Wantz Lib, Rainham Rd North,
Dagenham, RM10 7DX; Markyate Rd, Dagenham, RM8 2LD;
Goresbrook Rd, Dagenham, RM9 6UR; Dagenham Rd, Rush
Green, Romford, RM7 0TL; Thames View Lib, 2a Farr Ave,
Barking, IG11 0NZ; John Preston Annexe, Rose Lane, Chadwell Heath, Romford, RM6 5NJ.   **13** P-t 4.
14 Local colln (Barking & Essex).   **15** 2; (a&b) 43, 088;
(c) 13, 902; (d) 854; (e&f) none.   **16** 849; none.   **17** Schools,
housebound, hospitals, old people's homes.   **21** (a, b&c)
none.   **23** (a) 281, 646; (b) 33, 058; (c) 76, 027; (d) 162, 298;
(e) 334.   **24** (a&d) 1, 478, 817; (b) 374, 472.
25 (a) 93; (b) 22; (c) 27; (d) 5.   **26** (a) £644, 970;
(b) £17, 835; (c) £4. 09; (d) £104, 665; (e) £4, 000; (f) £348, 745.
27 Rebuilding Wantz Library & Community Centre (joint
project).

BARNET, LONDON BOROUGH OF (pop 297, 200) Ravens-
field House, The Burroughs, Hendon, London NW4 4BE
(01-202 5625; telex 25665). Borough Libn: Mr David A.
Ruddom ALA.   **7** Libraries & Arts.   **8** Dir of Educational
Services: Mr J. Dawkins BA, MEd.   **9** Mon-Fri: 9.00-
20.00; Sat: 9.00-18.00.
10 HQ; Branch/Special Sections.   **12** Burnt Oak Lib,
Watling Ave, Edgware, Middlesex, HA8 0UB; The Burroughs,
Hendon, London NW4 4BQ; Church End Lib, 24 Hendon Lane,
Finchley, London N3 1TR; Hale Lane, Edgware, Middlesex,
HA8 8NN; Friern Barnet Rd, London N11 3DS; 156 Golders
Green Rd, London NW11 8HE; Childs Hill Lib, 320 Crickle-
wood Lane, London NW2 2QE; Chipping Barnet Lib, Church
Passage, Barnet, Hertfordshire; East Finchley Lib, 226
High Rd, London N2 9BB; Hampstead Garden Suburb Lib, 15
Market Pl, London NW11 6LB; Mill Hill Lib, Hartley Ave,
London NW7 2HX; North Finchley Lib, Ravensdale Ave,
London N12 9HP; Osidge Lib, Brunswick Park Rd, London
N11 1EY; 85 Brookhill Rd, East Barnet, Hertfordshire;
South Friern Lib, Colney Hatch Lane, London N10 1HD;
'Dollisfield', Totteridge Lane, London N20 8DZ.
13 Mobiles 3.
15 3; (a) 132, 126; (c) 31, 375; (f) 1p pd.   **16** 240 K + 362 N;
originals £1 for 4 months; reproductions 50p for 3 months.
17 Schools, housebound, hospitals, old people's homes.
18 Cultural activities.   **19** Plessey Light Pen; photocharging.   **20** 3 weeks.   **21** (a&c) 1p pd; (b) none.
22 CICRIS; GLASS.   **23** (a) 565, 964; (b) 37, 287; (c) 133, 456;
(e) 444.   **24** (a) 3, 725, 773; (b) 712, 859; (d) playgroup 8, 400.
25 (a) 214; (b) 31; (c) 61; (d) 29.   **26** (a) £1, 100, 000;
(b) £67, 150; (c) £3. 70; (d) £230, 410; (e) £7, 610; (f) £666, 750.

BEXLEY, LONDON BOROUGH OF (pop 216, 900) Central
Administrative Offices, Bexley Library Service, Hall Pl,
Bourne Rd, Bexley, Kent, DA5 1PQ (0322-526574; telex
896119). Borough Libn: Mr P. E. Morris, FLA; Dep: Miss
J. E. Cloke FLA.   **7** Civic Amenities (& Allotments).
9 Mon-Fri: 9.30-20.00; Sat: 9. 30-17. 00.
10 HQ; Branch.   **12** Mayplace Rd East, Barnehurst, DA7
6EJ; Bourne Rd, Bexley, DA5 1LU; Broadway, Bexleyheath,
DA6 8DB; Blackfen Lib, Cedar Ave, Sidcup, DA15 8NJ;
Bostall Lib, 115 King Harold's Way, Bexleyheath, DA7 5RE;
Crayford Rd, Crayford, DA1 4ER; Walnut Tree Rd, Erith,
DA8 1RS; Newacres Lib, Binsey Walk, Thamesmead, SE3 9TS;
North Heath Lib, 200 Bexley Rd, Erith, DA8 3HF; Nelson Pl,
Sidcup, DA14 6D2; Upper Belvedere Lib, Woolwich Rd,
Belvedere, DA17 5EQ; Churchfield Rd, Welling, DA16 3PA;
Ref Lib, Townley Rd, Bexleyheath, DA6 7HJ.   **13** P-t 2;
mobiles 2.
14 Local history (Bexley & Kent); small museum above

CODE: 1 Local authority. 2 Population. 3 Postal address of HQ. 4 Telephone & telex. 5 Chief Libn. 6 Deputy. 7 Committee responsible. 8 Officer to whom Libn is responsible (if any). 9 Hours. 10 Organisation. 11 Area libraries. 12 Branches. 13 Part-time libraries; mobiles. 14 Special collections. 15 Gramophone records: number of libraries, (a) record issues (b) cassette issues (c) record stock (d) cassette stock (e) loan charges (f) fines. 16 Pictures: stock; charges. 17 Other services. 18 Cultural activities (expenditure, officer in charge, staff: (a) officers (b) manual). 19 Issue method (if not Browne). 20 Loan period (if not 2 weeks). 21 Fines: (a) adult (b) children (c) OAPs. 22 Co-operative schemes. 23 Stock: (a) adult lending (b) adult reference (c) children (d) schools (e) current periodical titles. 24 Issues: (a) adult (b) children (c) schools (d) institutions. 25 Staff: (a) officers (b) manual (c) chartered libns (d) graduates. 26 Finance: (a) total expenditure (b) non-rate income (c) per capita expenditure (d) expenditure for books (e) expenditure for records etc (f) salaries & wages. 27 Capital projects.

LONDON—*continued*

Erith B Lib (mainly local geology & history). **15** 4 service points; (a) 25,010; (c) 6,001; (d) 816; (e) 12p per record or set; (f) 5p pw or part. **16** Available from twice yearly exhibitions; £1 (6 months). **17** Schools, housebound, hospitals, old people's homes, veterans' club, WEA. **18** Cultural activities (Borough Libn). **20** 29 days. **21** (a&c) 4p pw or part; (b) none. **22** SEAL. **23** (a) 316,313; (b) 92,666; (c) 82,717; (e) 515. **24** (a) 2,002,340; (b) 441,861; (c) 15,974; (d) 8,876. **25** (a) 139; (b) 29; (c) 39; (d) 6. **26** (a) £703,633; (b) £28,801; (c) £3.24; (d) £107,430; (e) £4,250; (f) £450,925.

BRENT, LONDON BOROUGH OF (pop 275,000) Central Library, High Rd, Willesden Green, London NW10 2ST (01-459 5242; telex 923595). Borough Libn & Curator: Mr B. H. Baumfield FLA, FRSA, MBIM; Principal Libn: Miss C. M. Wares BA, ALA, MILGA. **7** Amenities & Works (Libraries Sub-Committee). **8** Dir of Amenities & Works: E. E. Shirley CEng, FIEE, FIERE, MBIM. **9** Mon-Fri: 9.00-20.00 (Wed 13.00 except ref); Sat: 9.00-18.00. **10** Central; Branch. **12** Brent Town Hall, Forty Lane, Wembley, HA9 9HU; Barham Park, Harrow Rd, Wembley, HA0 2HB; Olive Rd, Cricklewood, NW2 6UY; Ealing Rd, Wembley, HA0 4BR; Craven Park Rd, Harlesden, NW10 8SE; Bathurst Gardens, Kensal Rise, NW10 5JA; Salusbury Rd, Kilburn, NW6 6NN; Stag Lane, Kingsbury, NW9 9AE; North Circular Rd, Neasden, NW2 7OG; Preston, Carlton Ave East, Wembley, HA9 8PL; Queensbury, 35-36 South Parade, Mollison Way, Edgware, HA8 5QL; Tokyngton, Monks Park, Wembley; Patients' Lib, Central Middlesex Hospital, Park Royal, NW10. **13** Mobiles 1 (shared with Harrow). **14** Railway history; local history. **15** 2; (a&b) 109,754; (c&d) 19,897; (e) none; (f) as books. **16** 259; no loan charges; fines 10p 1st week or part, 15p pw thereafter. **17** Schools, housebound, hospitals, old people's homes. **18** Cultural activities entertainments £140,800, Arts & Entertainments Manager, a 12). **19** Photocharging, to be replaced by Plessey Computer Charging. **20** 3 weeks. **21** (a) 3p pw or part; (b&c) none. **22** CICRIS. **23** (a) 600,000; (b) 60,000; (c) 117,000; (d) 194,507; (e) 303. **24** (a) 2,367,398; (b) 721,532; (c) 584,450; (d) 29,320. **25** (a) 148; (b) 17; (c) 54; (d) 31. **26** (a) £782,990; (b) £63,370; (c) £2.84; (d) £174,180; (e) £7,210; (f) £418,950.

BROMLEY, LONDON BOROUGH OF (pop 301,500) Bromley Central Library, Bromley, Kent, BR1 1EX (01-460 9955; telex 896712). Borough Libn: Mr D. M. Laverick FLA; Dep Borough Libn: Mr R. G. Surridge MA, FLA. **7** General Purposes. **9** Mon-Fri: ad ldg & ref 9.00-18.00 (Mon & Thurs 20.00), children: term 11.30 (Thurs 9.15)-13.00, 15.30-18.00, vac 9.15-13.00, 14.30-17.00; Sat: 9.00-17.00. **10** Central; District; Branch. **11 District Libraries:** Beckenham Rd, Beckenham, Kent, BR3 4PE (01-650 7292/3), District Libn: Miss P. Beardsall BA, ALA; The Priory, Church Hill, Orpington, Kent, BR6 0HH (0689-31551), District Libn: Mr R. W. Martyn FLA. **12** 206D Anerley Rd, London SE20 8TH; Frankwood Ave, Petts Wood, Orpington, BR5 1BP; Glebe Way, West Wickham, BR4 0SH; Red Hill, Chislehurst, BR7 6DA; Mickleham Rd, St. Paul's Cray, Orpington, BR5 2RW; Southborough Lane, Bromley, BR2 8AP; Hayes St, Hayes, Bromley, BR2 7LH; Burnt Ash Lane, Bromley, BR1 5AF; 186 Maple Rd, London SE20 8HT; 31 Mottingham Rd, Mottingham, London SE9 4QZ; 110 Shortlands Rd, Shortlands, Bromley, BR2 0JP. **13** P-t 2; mobiles 3 & 1 standby. **14** Walter De la Mare; H. G. Wells; Harlow Bequest (Orping-

ton & Kent); 400 first issues of periodicals (c. 1900-1950); Crystal Palace colln. **15** 6; (a) 157,700; (c) 19,613; (e) 5p per record, 10p per set (2 weeks), + £1.00 pa for non-residents; (f) 1½p pd. **17** Housebound, hospitals, old people's homes, museum. **19** ALS computer based (Central); token (for fiction in all others). **20** 3 weeks. **21** (a&c) 1p pd (mobile lib 2p pw); (b) none (exc postage for overdue notices). **22** SELRL. **23** (a) 584,408; (b) 82,374; (c) 141,335; (e) 376. **24** (a) 3,042,123; (b) 727,506; (d) 105,092. **25** (a) 189; (b) 22; (c) 63; (d) 14. **26** (a) £1,089,770; (b) £35,360; (c) £3.61; (d) £146,280; (e) £12,000; (f) £587,630.

CAMDEN, LONDON BOROUGH OF (pop c. 190,400) St Pancras Library, 100 Euston Rd, London NW1 2AJ (01-278 4444; telex 24323). Dir of Libs & Arts: Mr F. D. Cole FLA. **7** Leisure Services (Libs & Arts Sub-Committee). **9** Mon-Fri: ad ldg 9.30-20.00, ref 9.30-21.00, children's 9.30-19.00 (16.00-19.00 in smaller libraries); Sat: 9.30-17.00. **10** HQ; Branch. **12** Swiss Cottage Lib, 88 Avenue Rd, NW3 3HA; Holborn Lib, 32-38 Theobalds Rd, WC1X 8PA; Belsize Lib, Antrim Rd, NW3 4XN; Heath B Lib, Keats Grove, NW3 2RR; Kilburn B Lib, Cotleigh Rd, NW6 2NP; West Hampstead B Lib, Dennington Park Rd, NW6 1AU; 198 High Holborn, WC1V 7BD; Camden Town B Lib, 12 Camden High St, NW1 0JH; Chalk Farm B Lib, Sharpleshall St, NW1 8YN; Highgate B Lib, Chester Rd, N19 8YN; 262-6 Kentish Town Rd, NW5 2AA; Athlone St, NW5 4LT; Regents Park B Lib, Compton Close, Robert St, NW1 3QT. **13** P-t 14; mobiles 1. **14** Keats & the Romantic poets; Kate Greenaway; Eleanor Farjeon. **15** 8; (a&b) 403,312; (c) 71,021; (d) 1,911; (e) none; (f) none. **16** 700; none. **17** Housebound, hospitals, old people's homes. **18** Cultural activities, entertainments (£276,155; Asst Dir (Arts); a 9). **19** Photocharging; bookamatic; Plessey Light Pen; ALS. **20** 1 month. **21** (a, b&c) none. **23** (a) 703,000; (b) 119,000; (c) 109,500; (e) 1,777. **24** (a) 2,469,708; (b, c&d) 404,789. **25** (a) 300; (b) 22; (c) 123; (d) 81. **26** (a) £2,378,270; (b) £104,310; (c) £12.39; (d) £193,300; (e) £19,000; (f) £1,119,200. **27** Queen's Crescent Library £250,000; Highgate Library £254,000.

CITY OF LONDON (pop 5,300) Guildhall Library, London EC2P 2EJ (01-606 3030; telex 887955). City Libn: Mr W. G. Thompson FLA; Dep: Mr E. W. Padwick FLA. **7** Library. **9** Mon-Fri: ad ldg & children's 9.30-17.30, ref 9.30-17.00; Sat: 9.30-17.00. **11 Reference Libraries:** City Business Lib, Gillett House, 55 Basinghall St, EC2V 5DU (01-638 8215), Libn: Mr M. J. Campbell ALA; St Bride Printing Lib, Bride Lane, Fleet St, EC4Y 8EQ (01-353 4660), Libn: Mr J. Mosley MA. **14** Comprehensive colln on the City & on London; official archive repository for deposited records of City; London Municipal Society colln (election literature & tracts); Hackney College colln (18th cent sermons & theology); Chapman & Hamilton bequests (19th cent plays, London & provincial playbills); Gresham music library; Institute of Masters of Wine; Clockmakers', Gardeners', Fletchers' & Glaziers' Companies Libraries; Cock colln (Sir Thomas More); Company of Makers of Playing Cards colln; Willshire colln (ancient prints & engravings). **17** Housebound. **19** Photocharging. **20** 3 weeks. **21** (a&c) 1p pd; (b) none. **23** (a) 236,304; (b) 317,658; (c) 3,454; (e) 2,125. **24** (a) 1,176,830; (b) 11,939. **25** (a) 117; (b) 10; (c) 34; (d) 20. **26** (a) £1,132,270; (b) £21,045; (c) £213.63; (d) £152,960; (f) £386,740.

LONDON—*continued*
CROYDON, LONDON BOROUGH OF (pop 329,300) Central Library, Katharine St, Croydon, Surrey, CR9 1ET (01-688 3627). Chief Libn: A.O.Meakin FLA; Dep Chief Libn: B.D.C. Totterdell FLA. **7** Libraries. **9** Mon-Fri: ad ldg & ref 9.30-19.00, children's 9.30-18.00; Sat: Central 9.00-17.00, Branches 9.30-17.00.
10 HQ; Branch. **12** Ashburton, Ashburton Park, Lower Addiscombe Rd, Croydon, CR0 6RX; Bradmore Green, Bradmore Way, Old Coulsdon, CR3 1PE; Brighton Rd, Coulsdon, CR3 2NH; Mitcham Rd, Canterbury Rd, Croydon, CR0 3JN; Central Parade, New Addington, CR0 0JB; London Rd, Beatrice Ave, Norbury, London SW16; Banstead Rd, Purley, CR2 3YH; Sanderstead Hill, Sanderstead, CR2 0HL; Addington Rd, Selsdon, CR2 8LA; Wickham Rd, Hartland Way, Shirley, CR0 8BH; Lawrence Rd, South Norwood, London SE25; Brigstock Rd, Thornton Heath, CR4 7JB. **13** Mobiles 1.
15 1; (a) 46,122; (c) 7,050; (e) 4p per record; (f) as books.
17 Housebound, hospitals, old people's homes, handicapped people's work centres; homes for young disabled people.
19 Photocharging (Central & larger branches). **20** 4 weeks. **21** (a&c) 1p pd 1st week; 4p pw thereafter (mobile lib 1p per visit); (b) none **23** (a) 409,329; (b) 97,911; (c) 110,778. **24** (a) 2,439,653; (b) 572,439.
25 (a) 130½; (b) 27½; (c) 49½; (d) 8. **26** (a) £749,000; (b) £45,000; (c) £2.27; (d) £148,000; (e) £3,380; (f) £485,100.

EALING, LONDON BOROUGH OF (pop 294,000) Central Library, Walpole Park, Ealing, London W5 5EQ (01-579 2424; telex 262289). Borough Libn: Mr Norman E.Binns FLA; Dep Borough Libn: Mr E.L.J.Smith FLA. **7** Amenities.
8 Chief Education Officer: Mr R.J.Hartles BSc, CEng.
9 No general pattern.
10 HQ; District; Branch. **11** **District Libraries:** High St, Acton, W3 6NA (01-992 3295), Libn: Mr P.E.Jones ALA; Osterley Park Rd, Southall, Middlesex, UB2 4BL (01-574 3412), Libn: Mr C Mandelstam ALA; Oldfield Lane, Greenford, Middlesex, UB6 9LG (01-578 1466), Libn: Miss M.Hulbert ALA **12** Hanger Hill Lib, Fernlea House, Ealing, W5 1EF; Hanwell Lib, Cherington Rd, W7 3HL; Jubilee Gardens Lib, Southall, Middlesex, UB1 2TJ; Northfields Lib, Northfield Ave, W5 4UA; Church Rd, Northolt, Middlesex, UB5 5AS; Horsenden Lane South, Perivale, Middlesex, UB6 7NT; 145 Pitshanger Lane, W5 1RH; West Ealing Lib, Melbourne Ave, W13 9BT; Wood End Lib, Whitton Ave West, Greenford, Middlesex, UB6 0EE. **13** Mobiles 5.
14 Selborne Society Library (ref only); Middlesex colln; Martinware colln. **15** 5; (a) 97,824; (c) 19,354; (f) as books. **17** Schools, housebound, hospitals, old people's homes. **19** Photocopying with mechanical sorting; token.
20 4 weeks. **21** (a&c) 5p pw or part; (b) none.
22 CICRIS. **23** (a) 542,304; (b) 77,758; (c) 116,284; (d) 204,027; (e) 1,467 (inc non-current items).
24 (a) 2,191,584; (b)646,484, (d) 33,773
25 (a) 160; (b) 17; (c) 56; (d) 10. **26** (a) £960,040; (b) £70,050; (c) £3.2; (d) £171,000; (e) £4,000; (f) £549,800.

ENFIELD, LONDON BOROUGH OF (pop 263,700) Central Library, Cecil Rd, Enfield, Middlesex, EN2 6TW (01-366 2244). Dir of Libs, Arts & Entertainment: A.E.Brown FLA; Dep Borough Libn: P.N.Turner FLA. **7** Leisure & Amenities. **9** Mon-Fri: ad ldg 9.00-20.00 (closed 1 day), ref 9.00-20.00 (17.00, 1 day), children's 9.00-18.00 (closed 1 day); Sat: 9.00-17.00.
10 HQ; Main; Branch. **11** **Main Libraries:** Edmonton Lib, Fore St, London N9 0NU (01-807 3618); Palmers Green Lib, Broomfield Lane, London N13 4EY (01-886 3728).
12 Bowes Rd, London N11; Bush Hill Park, Fourth Ave, Enfield; De Bohun, Green Rd, London N14; Enfield Highway, Hertford Rd, Enfield; Merryhills, Enfield Rd, Enfield; Bush Hill, Ridge Ave, London N21; Southgate Circus, High St, London N14; Winchmore Hill, Green Lanes, London N21; Houndsfield, Houndsfield Rd, London N9; College Court, High Rd, Ponders End; Weirhall, Silver St, London N18; Bullsmoor, Kempe Rd, Enfield. **13** P-t 1; mobiles 1.
14 Charles Lamb colln (Edmonton Lib); local history (Main Libs). **15** 10; (a) 113,000; (b) 20,000; (f) as books.
17 Schools, housebound, old people's homes. **18** Cultural activities, entertainments (£62,950 (income £6,100),

Chief Asst Arts & Entertainments, a 6, b 1½). **20** 3 weeks. **21** (a) none (but 11p per overdue notice); (b) 6p per notice; (c) none. **23** (a) c.510,000; (b) c.55,000; (c) c.120,000; (d) c.220,000; (e) 359. **24** (a&b) 2,344,000; (b) 578,000.
25 (a) 165; (b) 33½; (c) 38; (d) 8. **26** (a) £987,300; (b) £31,600; (c) £3.71; (d) £179,400; (e) £10,000; (f) £589,000.

GREENWICH, LONDON BOROUGH OF (pop 215,300) Greenwich Library, Woolwich Rd, London SE10 0RL (01-858 6656). Borough Libn & Curator: Mr H.Davis FLA.
7 Recreational Services. **8** Dir of Recreational Services: Mr C.H.Field. **9** Mon-Fri: ad ldg & ref 9.00-20.00, children's 9.00-19.00; Sat: 9.00-17.00.
10 HQ; Branch. **11** **District Libraries:** Eltham High St, Eltham, SE9 1TS (01-850 2268) Libn: Mr J.S.Hicks ALA; Plumstead High St, Plumstead, SE18 1JL (01-854 1728), Libn: Mr H.G.Walsh FLA; Calderwood St, Woolwich, SE18 6OZ (01-854 8888/1939), Libn: Mr F.K.Harrison BA, ALA. **12** Eynsham Dr, Abbey Wood, SE2 9PT; St John's Park, Blackheath, SE3 7JP; Charlton House, Charlton, SE7 8RE; William Barefoot Dr, Coldharbour, SE9 3AY; Brook Lane, Kidbrooke, SE3 0EA; Southwood Rd, New Eltham, SE9 3QT; Bushmoor Crescent, Shrewsbury House, SE18 3EG; Erindale, Slade, SE18 2QQ; Greenwich High Rd, West Greenwich, SE10 8NN. **13** P-t 4; mobiles 2.
14 Local collns (Greenwich & Kent). **15** 5; (a&b) 167,000; (c) 34,500; (d) 3,400; (f) 4p pw. **16** 370; none. **17** Housebound, hospitals, old people's homes. **18** Art Exhibitions (£11,500, J.Bunston AMA, a 2, b 2). **19** Photocharging (part). **20** 3 weeks. **21** (a&c) 4p pw; (b) none.
22 SEAL Business & Technical Information Service.
23 (a) 385,000; (b) 33,500; (c) 110,500; (e) 367. **24** (a) 2,005,000; (b) 413,000; (d) 97,000 (hospitals, old people's homes).
25 (a) 174; (b) 26; (c) 36; (d) 7. **26** (a) £937,460; (b) £30,950; (c) £4.35; (d) £191,500; (c) £18,500; (f) £499,630.

HACKNEY, LONDON BOROUGH OF (pop 208,000) Hackney Central Library, Mare St, London E8 1HG (01-985 8262/6). Borough Libn: C.J.Long FLA; Dep Borough Libn: F.E.Ayley ALA. **7** Libraries & Amenities. **9** Mon-Fri: ad ldg 9.00-20.00 (Wed closed), ref 9.00-21.00, children's 12.00-14.00, 15.30-19.00; Sat: 9.00-17.00.
10 HQ; District; Branch. **11** **Districts:** Central Lib, Mare St, London E8 1HG, Libn: A.R.Pickering FLA; Stoke Newington Church St, Stoke Newington, N16 0JS, Libn: F.Hume ALA; Pitfield St, Shoreditch, N1 6EX, Libn: G.Harding ALA.
12 Northwold Rd, Clapton, E5 8RA; Dalston Lane, Dalston, E8 3AZ; Homerton High St, Homerton, E9 6AS; Victoria Park Rd, Parkside, E9 7JL; Howards Rd, Howard, N16 8PR; Brownswood Rd, Brownswood, N4 2ST; Woodberry Grove, Woodberry Down, N4 2SB; Portland Ave, Stamford Hill, N16 6SB; Farleigh Rd, Somerford Grove, N16 7TH; Goldsmith's Row, E2 9BE; Murray Grove, Wenlock, N1 7QP; Rose Lipman B Lib, De Beauvoir Rd, N1 5SQ; Kate Greenaway B Lib, Weymouth Terrace, E2 8LR. **13** P-t 2.
14 Daniel Defoe; Edgar A.Poe; Dr Isaac Watts; John Dawson colln. **15** 4; (a) 76,799; (c) 24,450; (f) 5p pw. **16** 922; none. **17** Housebound, hospitals, old people's homes, playgroups. **18** Cultural activities, entertainments (£22,350, Cultural Activities Organizer, a 2, b 1).
19 Token (1 branch). **20** 4 weeks. **21** (a) 3p pw or part 1st 2 weeks, 5p pw thereafter; (b&c) none.
23 (a) 452,199; (b) 93,262; (c) 68,614. **24** (a) 1,641,058; (b) 637,472; (c) 1,723; (d) 23,232.
25 (a) 172; (b) 46; (c) 43; (d) 16. **26** (a) £1,237,740; (b) £16,130; (c) £5.94; (d) £156,600; (e) £5,400; (f) £762,800.
27 Eastway Library.

HAMMERSMITH, LONDON BOROUGH OF (pop 170,000) Central Library, Shepherds Bush Rd, Hammersmith, London W6 7AT (01-748 6032). Dep Borough Libn: T.J.Rix FRSA, FLA. **7** Leisure & Recreation Services. **8** Dir of Leisure & Recreation. **9** Mon-Fri: 9.15-20.00; Sat: 9.15-17.00.
10 Central; Branch. **12** 598 Fulham Rd, Fulham, SW6 5NX;

CODE: 1 Local authority. 2 Population. 3 Postal address of HQ. 4 Telephone & telex. 5 Chief Libn. 6 Deputy.
7 Committee responsible. 8 Officer to whom Libn is responsible (if any). 9 Hours. 10 Organisation. 11 Area libraries.
12 Branches. 13 Part-time libraries; mobiles. 14 Special collections. 15 Gramophone records: number of libraries,
(a) record issues (b) cassette issues (c) record stock (d) cassette stock (e) loan charges (f) fines. 16 Pictures: stock;
charges. 17 Other services. 18 Cultural activities (expenditure, officer in charge, staff: (a) officers (b) manual). 19 Issue
method (if not Browne). 20 Loan period (if not 2 weeks). 21 Fines: (a) adult (b) children (c) OAPs. 22 Co-operative
schemes. 23 Stock: (a) adult lending (b) adult reference (c) children (d) schools (e) current periodical titles. 24 Issues:
(a) adult (b) children (c) schools (d) institutions. 25 Staff: (a) officers (b) manual (c) chartered libns (d) graduates.
26 Finance: (a) total expenditure (b) non-rate income (c) per capita expenditure (d) expenditure for books (e) expenditure
for records etc (f) salaries & wages. 27 Capital projects.

LONDON—*continued*
North End Crescent, Baron's Court, W14 8TG; Clem Attlee
Court, Lillie Rd, SW6 7PU; Cobb's Hall, Fulham Palace Rd,
SW6 6LL; Sands End B Lib, 132 Wandsworth Bridge Rd,
SW6 2UL; Uxbridge Rd, Shepherds Bush, W12 8LG; Warm-
holt B Lib, Westway, W12 0PP; Askew Rd B Lib.
13 Mobiles 2.

HARINGEY, LONDON BOROUGH OF (pop 230,000) Central
Offices, Bruce Castle, Lordship Lane, London N17 8NU
(01-808 8772; telex 263257). Controller of Libs, Museum &
Arts: Mr W.S.H.Ashmore FLA; Principal Libn: Mr P.E.
Dunklin FLA. **7** Civic Amenities (Libs Museum & Arts
Panel). **8** Coordinator of Civic Amenities. **9** Mon-
Fri: ad ldg & ref 9.30-20.00, children's: term 15.30-18.00,
vac 9.30-17.00; Sat: 9.30-17.00.
15 2; (a&b) 108,876; (c&d) 24,000; (f) 1p pd. **16** 1,100;
none. **17** Housebound, prisons, hospitals, old people's
homes, day centres, sheltered housing. **18** Cultural
activities, entertainments, (Civic Entertainments Officer).
20 3 weeks. **21** (a&c) 1p pd; (b) none. **22** CICRIS.
23 (a) 252,220; (b) 105,563; (c) 69,550; (e) 725.
24 (a) 1,302,450; (b) 356,734.
25 (a) 136; (b) 18; (c) 52; (d) 12. **26** (a) £892,110;
(b) £20,995; (c) £5.25; (d) £120,750; (e) £6,500; (f) £461,020.
10 Main; District; Branch. **11** District: Haringey Park,
Hornsey, N8 9JA, Exec Libn (Circulation): Mr. M.K.Bentley
ALA; 391 High Road, Tottenham, N17 6QR, Exec Libn
(Bibliographical): Miss W.R.Evans ALA; Brabant Rd, Wood
Green, N22 6XD; Queens Ave, Muswell Hill, N10 3PE.
12 Alexandra Park Rd, N22 4UJ; Coombes Croft Lib, High
Rd, N17 8AG; Devonshire Hill Lib, Compton Crescent,
N17 7LD; Highgate Lib, Shepherds Hill, N6 5QT; Stroud
Green Lib, Quernmore Rd, N4 4QR; St Ann's Lib, Cissbury
Rd, N15 5PU; West Green Lib, Vincent Rd, N15 3QA.
13 Mobiles 1.
14 Official repository for archives; postal history. **15** 4;
(a) 78,315; (c) 23,823; (f) as books. **16** 160; none.
17 Schools, housebound, hospitals, old people's homes.
18 Cultural activities, (£26,980, Arts & Extension Officer
(Libs), Arts Organiser (Arts Council), a 4, b 3 pt).
19 Cheque book (1 lib). **20** 3 weeks. **21** (a) 5p pw:
(b) none; (c) ½ rate, rounded down to 2p pw.
23 (a) 384,000; (b) 59,000; (c) 67,000; (e) 470.
24 (a) 1,596,720; (b) 378,100; (d) 12,705.
25 (a) 191; (b) 28; (c) 34; (d) 13. **26** (a) £1,126,710 (exc
Museum); (b) £46,350 (exc Museum); (c) £4.89; (d) £190,060;
(c) £4,060; (f) £575,390 (exc Museum). **27** New Central
Library (scheduled start Autumn 1975).

HARROW, LONDON BOROUGH OF (pop 199,000) The Civic
Centre, PO Box 4, Station Rd, Harrow, HA1 2UU (01-863 5611;
telex 923826). Borough Libn: Mr A.W.Ball FLA; Dep Borough Libn: Mr L.E.S.Darby FLA. **7** Leisure. **8** Dir of
Education: Mr M.Johnson MA. **9** Mon-Fri: 9.00-20.00;
Sat: 9.00-17.00.
10 HQ; Branch. **12** Gayton Rd, Harrow; Uxbridge Rd, Hatch
End; Kenton Lane, Kenton; Marsh Rd, Pinner; Imperial Dr,
Rayners Lane; Northolt Rd, South Harrow; Honeypot Lane,
Stanmore; Grant Rd, Wealdstone; Pinner Rd, West Harrow.
13 P-t 1; mobiles 1.
14 Local colln. **15** 1; (a) 56,502; (c) 12,676; (e) £2.00 pa;
(f) 10p pw. **17** Schools, housebound, old people's homes.
19 Token (adult & junior fiction). **20** 3 weeks. **21** (a) 5p
pw; (b&c) none. **22** CICRIS. **23** (a) 286,865; (b) 26,584;
(c) 72,100; (d) c.191,000; (e) 485. **24** (a) 2,091,020;

(b) 467,785; (d) 45,718.
25 (a) 125; (b) 9; (c) 42; (d) 23. **26** (a) £811,550;
(b) £29,035; (c) £4.07; (d) £169,280; (e) £6,000; (f) £364,565.

HAVERING, LONDON BOROUGH OF (pop 245,610) Central
Library, Romford, Essex, RM1 3AR (0708-44297). Borough
Libn & Arts Officer: G.H.Humby ALA; Dep Borough Libn &
Arts Officer: D.A.Partridge FLA. **7** Community &
Recreation. **9** Mon-Sat: 9.30-20.00.
10 HQ; Branch. **12** 45 Collier Row Rd, Romford, RM5
3NR; Balgores Lane, Gidea Park, Romford, RM2 6BS;
Hilldene Ave, Harold Hill, Romford, RM3 8DJ; 44 North St,
Hornchurch, Essex, RM11 1TB; 26 Corbets Tey Rd, Upminster,
Essex, RM14 2BB; Arundel Rd, Harold Wood, Romford, RM3
0RX; 7-11 The Broadway, Rainham, Essex, RM13 9YW; South
Hornchurch, Rainham Rd, Rainham, Essex, RM13 7RD; St
Nicholas Avenue, Elm Park, Hornchurch, Essex, RM12 4PT.
14 Local history (old County of Essex with emphasis on
London Borough of Havering); microfilms of archives;
Council's archives (from 1840). **15** 4; (a&b) 108,000;
(c&d) 22,000; (f) 5p pw. **16** 850. **17** Schools, housebound, old people's homes. **18** Cultural activities
(Asst Arts Officer; a 3½). **19** On-line Circulation
Control System (computer based). **20** 3 weeks.
21 (a) 5p pw or part; (b&c) none. **23** (a) 400,000;
(b) 38,000; (c) 110,000; (d) 280,000; (e) 400. **24** (a&b)
2,500,000; (d) housebound 60,000.
25 (a) 122; (c) 51; (d) 4. **26** (a) £646,625; (b) £25,525;
(c) £2.63; (d) £117,385; (e) £5,000; (f) £418,090.

HILLINGDON, LONDON BOROUGH OF (pop 235,500)
Libraries Arts and Information Services, 22 High St,
Uxbridge, Middlesex, UB8 1JN (0895-37446; telex 934224).
Borough Libn: Mr Philip Colehan FLA; Principal Asst
Borough Libn: Mr W.R.Hill ALA, ALAA. **7** Leisure.
9 Mon-Fri: 9.30-20.00 (Wed 13.00); Sat: 9.30-17.00.
10 HQ; Branches. **12** 88 Field End Rd, Eastcote,
HA5 1RL; Park Lane, Harefield, UB9 6BJ; Bedwell Gardens,
Harlington, UB3 4EF; Golden Crescent, Hayes, UB3 1AQ;
Hayes End, 1346 Uxbridge Rd, Hayes, UB4 8JQ; Long Lane,
Ickenham, UB10 8RE; Kingshill, Bury Ave, Hayes, UB4 8LF;
Northwood Hills, Potter St, Northwood, HA6 1QQ; Oak Farm,
Sutton Court Rd, Hillingdon, UB10 9PB; Oaklands Gate, Green
Lane, Northwood, HA6 3AB; Bury St, Ruislip, HA4 7SU;
Ruislip Manor, Victoria Rd, Ruislip, HA4 9BW, Victoria Rd,
South Ruislip, HA4 0JE; Station Rd, West Drayton, UB7 7JF;
Yeading Lane, Hayes, UB4 0EW; High St, Yiewsley, UB7 7BE.
13 Mobiles 1.
15 2; (a) 28,037; (c) 5,603; (e) £1.30 pa (non-resident £2.60
inc VAT); (f) 3p pw, max 50p. **16** 30; none. **17** Schools,
housebound, hospitals, old people's homes, playgroups.
18 Cultural activities (arts £24,861, entertainments £45,334
(net); Arts Development Officer; a 2). **19** Browne
delayed discharge using "addressograph" tickets; tokens.
20 3 weeks. **21** (a) 3p pw; (b&c) none. **22** CICRIS.
23 (a) 349,709; (b) 20,733; (c) 85,786; (e) 610 (inc annuals).
24 (a) 2,357,389; (b) 512,411; (d) 62,708.
25 (a) 158; (b) 11; (c) 43; (d) 6. **26** (a) £767,377 (net, exc
Arts); (b) £30,030; (c) £3.26; (d) £146,517; (e) £2,645;
(f) £470,954.

HOUNSLOW, LONDON BOROUGH OF (pop 205,000) Hounslow
Civic Centre, Lampton Rd, Hounslow, Middlesex, TW3 4DN
(01-570 7728). Chief Libn: Miss F.M.Green FLA; Dep Chief
Libn: Mr B.R.Walkinshaw BA, ALA. **7** Education (Libraries Sub-Committee). **9** Mon-Fri: ad ldg 9.00-20.00

LONDON—*continued*
(13.00 1 day Districts, closed 1 day Branches), ref 9.00-
20.00 (17.00 1 day), children's: term 14.00-19.00, vac 9.00-
17.00 (term & vac: closed 1 day); Sat: 9.00-17.00.
10 HQ; District: Branch. **11 District Libraries:** Chiswick: Duke's Ave, Chiswick W4 2AB (01-994 1008/9), Libn:
Mr R.P.C. Jones ALA; Feltham: 210 The Centre, Feltham,
Middlesex, TW13 4BX (01-890 3506/5273), Libn: Mr E.A. Body
ALA; Hounslow: Treaty Rd, Hounslow, Middlesex, TW3 1DR
(01-570 0622/7510), Libn: Mrs S. Knight ALA. **12** 103
Salisbury Rd, Hounslow, TW4 7NW; Staines Rd, Bedfont,
Feltham, TW14 8DB; Boston Manor Rd, Brentford, TW8 8DW;
Bath Rd, Cranford, Hounslow, TW5 9TL; 2-12 Hampton Rd
West, Hanworth, Feltham, TW13 6AW; New Heston Rd, Heston,
Hounslow, TW5 0LW; Twickenham Rd, Isleworth, TW7 7EU;
St Mary's Crescent, Osterley, Isleworth, TW7 4NB.
15 3; (a) 90,997; (b) 5,699; (c) 18,747; (d) 1,329; (e) non-
residents only £1.50 + VAT pa; (f) as books. **17** Schools,
housebound, prisons, old people's homes. **18** Cultural
activities (£4,525 for publicity & grants to local cultural
organisations). **19** Photocharging (7 libs); Token/Browne
20 3 weeks. **21** (a) 1p 1st week, 5p pw thereafter, max
50p; (b) none; (c) at discretion. **22** CICRIS.
23 (a) 320,416; (b) 38,796; (c) 102,640; (d) 184,898; (e) 344.
24 (a) 1,934,716; (b) 469,446.
25 (a) 129½; (b) 14½; (c) 47; (d) 11½. **26** (a) £741,055;
(b) £17,530; (c) £3.615; (d) £123,055; (e) £6,000;
(f) £433,570.

ISLINGTON, LONDON BOROUGH OF (pop 171,035) 68 Holloway Rd, London N7 8JN (01-607 4038; telex 263674). Chief
Libn: Mr C.A. Elliott FLA; Dep Mr A.W.C. Wright FLA.
7 Arts & Recreation. **8** Co-Ordinator of Recreation:
Mr Spencer Hudson MA. **9** Mon-Fri: ad ldg 9.00-20.00
(13.00 Weds in Branches), ref 9.00-20.00, children's
16.00-19.00; Sat: 9.00-17.00.
10 HQ; Branch. **12** North Lib, Manor Gardens
London N7 6JX; South-East Lib, Essex Rd, London N1 2SL;
West Lib, Lofting Rd, London N1 1BD; Archway Lib, Archway
Close, London N19 3UB; Mildmay Lib, 19-23 Mildmay Park,
London N1 4NA; Arthur Simpson Lib, Hanley Rd, London
N4 3DL; Finsbury Lib, 245 St John St, London EC1; St Lukes
Lib, Lever St, London EC1V 3TB; John Barnes Lib, 275
Camden Rd, London N7 0JN; Dick Whittington Lib, Giesbach
Rd, London N19 3DA; Lewis Carroll Junior Lib, Copenhagen
St, N1 0ST. **13** Mobiles 1.
14 Physics & chemistry, Dewey Class 530-549, 770-779;
MJFR author's surname COM-CRH, GRI-HOY; Islington &
Finsbury local history; Sadlers Wells colln; W.R. Sickert
colln. **15** 3; (a) 49,692; (c) 15,758; (e) none; (f) 2p pd.
17 Schools, housebound, prisons, hospitals, old people's
homes. **18** Cultural activities, entertainments (£39,350;
Entertainments Manager, a 2). **19** Islington Charging
System. **20** 3 weeks. **21** (a) 3p pw or part; (b&c) none.
23 (a) 287,644; (b) 52,354; (c) 126,912; (e) 846.
24 (a) 1,122,678; (b) 475,994; (c) 2,592; (d) 204,518.
25 (a) 172½; (b) 32; (c) 52; (d) 13. **26** (a) £1,109,128;
(b) £25,050; (c) £6.48; (d) £132,260; (e) £5,000; (f) £664;754.

KENSINGTON AND CHELSEA, ROYAL BOROUGH OF
(pop 162,500) Central Library, Phillimore Walk, London
W8 7RX (01-937 2542). Borough Libn & Arts Officer:
Mr Melvyn Barnes, DMA, ALA, AMBIM, MILGA. **7** Libraries & Amenities. **9** Mon-Fri (exc Wed): ad ldg & ref
10.00-20.00, children's 10.00-13.00, 14.00-18.30; Wed &
Sat: ad ldg & ref 10.00-17.00, children's 10.00-13.00, 14.00-
17.00.
10 HQ; Branch. **12** 108 Ladbroke Grove, North Kensington,
W11 1PZ; 1 Pembridge Sq, Notting Hill, W2 4EW; 210 Old
Brompton Rd, Brompton, SW5 0BS; Manresa Rd, Chelsea,
SW3 6LU. **13** P-t 1; mobiles 1.
14 Local history (Central & Chelsea); early children's books,
book plates, illustrations (Chelsea); illustrations, portraits,
heraldry (Central); paintings & drawings by Lord Leighton
& contemporary Victorians, Victorian furniture, De Morgan
pottery (Leighton house). **15** 2; (a) 106,662; (c) 28,000;
(f) 1p pd. **17** Housebound with WRVS, old people's homes.
18 Cultural activities (grants in aid £6,075, Borough Libn).
20 4 weeks. **21** (a&c) 1p pd; (b) none. **23** (a) 332,797;

(b) 154,459; (c) 71,401; (e) 894. **24** (a) 1,234,808;
(b) 224,047.
25 (a) 144; (b) 16; (c) 49; (d) 12. **26** (a) £976,550;
(b) £32,660; (c) £6.00; (d) £182,400; (e) £7,900; (f) £522,555.

KINGSTON-UPON-THAMES, LONDON BOROUGH OF (pop
136,500) Central Library, Fairfield Rd, Kingston-upon-
Thames, Surrey, KT1 2PS (01-549 0226; telex 928544).
Borough Libn & Curator: W.G.B. Brown FLA; Dep: M.W.
Lunt FLA. **7** Arts & Recreation. **9** No general pattern.
10 HQ; District; Branch. **11 Districts:** Kingston Rd, New
Malden, KT3 3LY (01-942 0814); Ewell Rd, Surbiton; KT6
6AG (01-399-2331). **12** Moor Lane, Chessington; Hook Rd,
Hook, Chessington; Tudor Dr, Kingston-upon-Thames; Old
Malden B Lib, Church Rd, Worcester Park; 65 Warren Dr
North, Tolworth, Surbiton. **13** P-t 1; mobiles 1.
15 3. **17** Schools, housebound, hospitals, old people's
homes. **18** Cultural activities (Arts Liaison Officer, a 1).
20 3 weeks. **22** LASER.

LAMBETH, LONDON BOROUGH OF (pop 299,380) 14 Knights
Hill, West Norwood, SE27 0HY (01-761 0901/5 or 1931/5).
Senior Asst Dir (Libs): Mr B. Usherwood ALA; Principal
Libn: Ms Janet Hill ALA (Zone Co-ordinator).
7 Amenities. **8** Dir of Amenity Services: Mr R. McColvin.
9 No general pattern.
10 Zone; Neighbourhood. **11 Zones:** Central: Tate Central
Lib, Brixton Oval, SW2 1JG (01-274 7451), Libn: Mr Nigel
Bouttell ALA; North Lambeth: Durning Lib, 167 Kensington
Lane, SE11 4HF (01-735 2349), Libn: Mr Peter Norman ALA;
Streatham: Tate Lib, Streatham High Rd, SW16 (01-769 1021),
Libn: Ms Doris Mann FLA; West Norwood: West Norwood
Lib & Nettlefold Hall, Norwood High St, SE27 9JX (01-670
8104), Libn: Ms Jill Goring LA. **12** Clapham Lib, Clapham
Common North Side, SW4; Jeffreys Lib, Jeffreys Rd, SW4;
Tate Lib, South Lambeth Rd, SW8; Minet Lib, Knatchbull Rd,
SE5; North Lambeth Lib, Lower Marsh, SE1; Clapham Park
Lib, Poynders Rd, SW4; Streatham Vale Lib, Eardley Rd,
SW16; Carnegie Lib, Herne Hill Rd, SE24; St Martins Lib,
220 Upper Tulse Hill, SW2. **13** Mobiles 1.
14 Surrey colln of archives. **15** 6; (c) 12,000; (d) 4,000;
(f) as books. **17** Housebound, prisons, hospitals, old
people's homes, sports centres, pre-school playgroups, day
nurseries, clinics, community organizations. **18** Cultural
activities, entertainments (£94,240). **19** Token.
20 4 weeks. **21** (a) 2½p pw or part; (b&c) none.
22 MSC; MJFR (Speciality); GLASS **23** (a, b&c) 972,090;
(d) none; (e) c.500. **24** (a, b, c&d) 2,234,102.
25 (a) 118; (b) 39; (c) 76. **26** (a) £1,478,570; (b) £16,110;
(c) £5.02; (d) £259,940; (e) £15,440; (f) £710,190.

LEWISHAM, LONDON BOROUGH OF (pop 258,000) Bromley
Road Library, 170 Bromley Rd, Catford, SE6 2UZ (01-698
7347). Dep Borough Amenities Officer & Chief Libn: R.A.
Greenhill, FLA. **7** Amenities. **8** Borough Amenities
Officer: W.A.C. Copp FCIS, MIRM, MMBIM. **9** Mon-Fri:
ad ldg & ref 9.30-20.00 (Wed 13.00 ad ldg), children's 12.00-
14.00, 15.30-19.00; Sat: 9.30-17.00.
10 HQ; Branch. **12** Blackheath Village Lib, Tranquil
Passage, SE3 0BJ; Brockley Rd, SE4 2AF; Deptford Lib,
Lewisham Way, SE14 6PF; Moorside Rd, Downham, Kent
BR1 5EP; Forest Hill Lib, Dartmouth Rd, SE23 3HZ; Grove
Park Lib, Somertrees Ave, SE12 0BX; Hither Green Lib,
Torridon Rd, SE6 1RQ; Lewisham High St, SE13 6LG; Manor
House Lib, Old Rd, SE13 5SY; New Cross Lib, New Cross Rd,
SE14 5BA; Old Town Lib, Clyde St, SE8 5LW; Pepys Lib,
Foreshore, SE8 3AQ; St Catherine's Lib, Kitto Rd, SE14 5TY;
300 Stanstead Rd, SE23 1DE; Sydenham Rd, SE26 5SE.
13 P-t 1; mobiles 1.
14 Education Library; archives & local history. **15** 6;
(a) 187,693; (c) 35,370; (f) as books. **16** 1,275. **17** Housebound, hospitals, old people's homes, clubs, community
centres. **18** Cultural activities, (£12,000, Libn in charge of
Extension Activities, a 2). **19** Photocharging. **20** 4
weeks + 6 weeks without fine. **21** (a) 50p if not returned
within two weeks of overdue notice (sent at end of eight
weeks); (b) none; (c) discretionary. **22** LASER; SEAL.
23 (a) 525,952; (b) 47,000; (c) 139,455; (e) 1,670.
24 (a) 1,806,762; (b) 522,080; (d) 104,490.
25 (a) 207 (inc trainees); (b) 17; (c) 58; (d) 18.

CODE: 1 Local authority. 2 Population. 3 Postal address of HQ. 4 Telephone & telex. 5 Chief Libn. 6 Deputy.
7 Committee responsible. 8 Officer to whom Libn is responsible (if any). 9 Hours. 10 Organisation. 11 Area libraries.
12 Branches. 13 Part-time libraries; mobiles. 14 Special collections. 15 Gramophone records: number of libraries,
(a) record issues (b) cassette issues (c) record stock (d) cassette stock (e) loan charges (f) fines. 16 Pictures: stock;
charges. 17 Other services. 18 Cultural activities (expenditure, officer in charge, staff: (a) officers (b) manual). 19 Issue
method (if not Browne). 20 Loan period (if not 2 weeks). 21 Fines: (a) adult (b) children (c) OAPs. 22 Co-operative
schemes. 23 Stock: (a) adult lending (b) adult reference (c) children (d) schools (e) current periodical titles. 24 Issues:
(a) adult (b) children (c) schools (d) institutions. 25 Staff: (a) officers (b) manual (c) chartered libns (d) graduates.
26 Finance: (a) total expenditure (b) non-rate income (c) per capita expenditure (d) expenditure for books (e) expenditure
for records etc (f) salaries & wages. 27 Capital projects.

LONDON—*continued*
26 (a) £1, 243, 385; (b) £6, 555; (c) £4. 8; (d) £193, 275;
(c) £8, 800; (f) £691, 020.

MERTON, LONDON BOROUGH OF (pop 175, 000) Merton
Cottage, Church Path, Merton Park, SW19 3HH (01-542 6211).
Borough Libn: Mr D. S. Hope FLA; Dep: M. J. Saich FLA.
7 Libraries & Further Education Sub-Committee. **9** Mon-
Fri: ad ldg & ref 9.00-19. 45 (Wed 17. 00), children's 9.00-
12. 45, 13. 45-18. 30 (Wed 17. 00); Sat: ad ldg & ref 9.00-17.00,
children's 9.00-12. 45, 13. 45-17.00.
10 HQ; Branch. **12** London Rd, Mitcham, CR4 2YR; Morden
Rd, Morden, SW19 3DA; Wimbledon Hill Rd, Wimbledon,
SW19 7NB; High St, Colliers Wood, SW19 2HR; Morden Park
Lib, Lower Morden Lane, Morden, Surrey; Pollards Hill Lib,
South Lodge Ave, Mitcham, Surrey, CR4 1LT; Approach Rd,
Raynes Park, SW20 8BA; West Barnes Lane, New Malden,
Surrey; Arthur Rd, Wimbledon Park, SW19 8AD. **13** Mobiles
1.
14 Tennis; cricket; Nelsoniana. **15** 1; (a) 59, 971;
(c) 11, 000; (e) £2 (refundable deposit); (f) 1p pd. **17** Schools,
housebound, old people's homes, library club, lectures,
exhibitions. **18** Cultural activities, partially (£7, 700).
19 Computer (Wimbledon); photocharging (Morden).
20 3 weeks. **21** (a) ½p pd 1st 3 days, 2p pw 1st 2 weeks,
3p pw thereafter; (b&c) none. **23** (a) 299, 314; (b) 81, 004;
(c) 73, 328;, (d) 42, 000; (e) 640. **24** (a) 1, 661, 055;
(b) 343, 421; (d) 1, 747.
25 (a) 94; (b) 13; (c) 27; (d) 6. **26** (a) £547, 725;
(b) £34, 195; (c) £3. 13; (d) £91, 800; (e) £3, 740; (f) £329, 485.

NEWHAM, LONDON BOROUGH OF (pop 230, 000) East Ham
Library, High St South, London E6 4EL (01-472 1430 ext 42).
Borough Libn: Mr James Green ALA; Dep Borough Libn:
F. Sainsbury BEM, ALA, ARHistS. **7** Education (Libraries
& Cultural Activities Sub-Committee). **9** Mon-Fri: 9.00-
20. 00 (Wed 17. 00, exc ref); Sat: 9.00-17. 00.
10 HQ; Branch. **12** Boleyn Lib, Claughton Rd, E13;
Canning Town Lib, Barking Rd, E16; Custom House Lib,
Prince Regent Lane, E16; Forest Gate Lib, Woodgrange Rd,
E7; Manor Park Lib, Romford Rd, E12; North St, Plaistow,
E13; Plashet Lib, Plashet Grove, E6; Silvertown Lib, 14 Constance St, E16; Stratford Lib, Water Lane, E15; North Woolwich Lib, Pier Rd, E16. **13** Mobiles 3.
14 Essex & London; road transport history. **15** (a) 24, 585;
(c) 8, 394. **17** Schools, housebound, hospitals, old people's
homes. **18** Cultural activities (£10, 370, Arts Development
Officer, a 1). **20** 4 weeks. **21** (a&c) 1p 1st week or part,
3p pw thereafter; (b) none. **23** (a) 253, 294; (c) 95, 244;
(e) 818. **24** (a) 1, 386, 878; (b) 433, 581; (c) 47, 000;
(d) 13, 322.
25 (a) 123; (b) 33; (c) 28; (d) 19. **26** (a) £881, 780;
(b) £21, 630; (c) £3. 83; (d) £153, 300; (e) £2, 250; (f) £415, 800.

REDBRIDGE, LONDON BOROUGH OF (pop 235, 200) Central
Library, Oakfield Rd, Ilford, Essex, IG1 1EA (01-478 0017/8
or 8993; telex 897778). Borough Libn: F. C. Kennerley FLA,
FRSA; Dep Borough Libn: N. Maxwell FLA. **7** Libraries.
9 Mon-Fri: ad ldg & ref 9.00 (or 9. 30)-20.00, children's:
term 13.00-18. 30, vac 9. 30-12.00, 13.00-17.00; Sat: 9. 30-
17.00.
10 Central; Branch. **12** Central Ref Lib, 112b High Rd,
Ilford, Essex, IG1 1BY; Fullwell Cross Lib, 140 High St,
Barkingside, Ilford, Essex, IG6 2EA; 490 Cranbrook Rd,
Gantshill, Ilford, Essex, IG2 6LA; Hainault Lib, 100 Manford
Way, Chigwell, Essex, IG7 4DD; 633-639 Longbridge Rd,
Dagenham, Essex, RM8 2DH; 785 High Rd, Seven Kings,

Ilford, Essex, IG3 8RR; South Woodford Lib, 116 High Rd,
E18 2QS; Wanstead Lib, Spratt Hall Rd, London E11 2RQ;
Snakes Lane, Woodford Green, Essex, IG8 0DX.
13 P-t 2; mobiles 2.
14 Brand colln (local history); photography; music scores
& plays. **15** 3; (a) 61, 694; (c) 14, 436; (f) 2p pd.
16 1, 007 (schools & libs only, no loans to individuals).
17 Schools, housebound with WRVS, old people's homes,
clinic, playgroups, nursery schools, teacher's centre.
18 Cultural activities (£12, 250, Asst Sec Redbridge Arts
Council, responsible to Borough Libn, a 2). **20** 3 weeks.
21 (a&c) 1p pd 1st month, 2p pd thereafter (OAP's
allowed 1 weeks grace), (fines remitted in cases of illness);
(b) 2p pw. **23** (a) 405, 000; (b) 26, 000; (c) 135, 000;
(d) 40, 000; (e) 362. **24** (a) 2, 464, 954; (b) 645, 524; (c) books
exchanged 17, 270.
25 (a) 139; (b) 30; (c) 39; (d) 6. **26** (a) £940, 644;
(b) £35, 025; (c) £3. 999; (d) £150, 000; (e) £1, 925; (f) £475, 950.

RICHMOND UPON THAMES, LONDON BOROUGH OF (pop
167, 400) The Retreat, Retreat Rd, Richmond, Surrey, TW9
1PH (01-940 0031; telex 917174). Borough Libn: Mr Derek
Jones MA, FLA; Dep Borough Libn: Mr Robert A. Hardman
BA, ALA. **7** Amenities. **9** Mon-Fri: ad ldg & ref 9.00-
19.00, children's 9.00-13.00, 14.00-18.00; Sat: 9.00-17.00.
10 HQ; Branch. **12** Little Green, Richmond; Garfield Rd,
Twickenham; Sheen Lane, East Sheen; Waldegrave Rd,
Teddington; 75 Castelnau; Ham St, Ham; Rosehill, Hampton;
Windmill Rd, Hampton Hill; Percy Rd, Heathfield; North Rd,
Kew; Nelson Rd, Whitton. **13** P-t 1.
14 Sir Richard Burton colln; Alexander Pope colln; Douglas
Sladen colln; Capt George Vancouver colln. **15** 3;
(a) 118, 933; (b) 7, 199; (c) 11, 320; (d) 692; (e) £2. 00 pa;
(f) as books. **17** Schools, housebound, prisons, hospitals, old
peopel's homes. **19** Local adaptation of Browne.
20 3 weeks min, 3 weeks & 6 days max. **21** (a) 1p pd
1st 4 weeks, 2p pd thereafter, max 85p; (b&c) none.
22 CICRIS. **23** (a) 247, 238; (b) 43, 469; (c) 69, 827;
(d) 121, 146; (e) 354. **24** (a) 1, 676, 434; (b) 370, 404;
(d) 26, 398.
25 (a) 104; (b) 9; (c) 39; (d) 6. **26** (a) £582, 900; (c) £3. 48;
(d) £85, 450; (e) £4, 250; (f) £315, 900. **27** New Richmond
Central Library.

SOUTHWARK, LONDON BOROUGH OF (pop 241, 700) Library
Services Administration Dept, 20/22 Lordship Lane, London
SE22 8HN (01-693 9221). Borough Libn & Curator: Mr K. A.
Doughty FLA; Asst Borough Libns: Mr W. J. Lowles FLA;
Mr P. W. Taylor MA, FLA (& Dep Curator). **7** Libraries
& Amenities. **9** Mon-Fri: ad ldg & ref 9. 30-20. 00 (Wed
9. 30-13. 00), children's: term 15. 30-19. 00 (Wed closed),
vac 9. 30-12. 00, 14. 00-19. 00 (Wed 9. 30-13. 00); Sat: 9. 30-
17. 00.
10 HQ; District; Branch. **11** District Libraries: 368
Lordship Lane, Dulwich, London SE22 (01-693 5171/2),
District Libn: Mr C. A. Part FLA; 155/157 Walworth Rd,
Newington, London SE17 (01-703 3324/5529/6514), District
Libn: Miss J. Hermann ALA. **12** Bessemer Grange Lib,
8 Crossthwaite Ave, SE5 8ET; 17 Camberwell Church St,
SE5 8TR; 25/27 Grove Vale, SE22 8EQ; Kingswood Lib,
Seeley Dr, SE21 8QR; Music Lib, 34 Peckham Rd, SE5 8PX;
North Peckham Lib, Civic Centre, 600 Old Kent Rd, SE15
1JB; Nunhead Lib, 138 Gordon Rd, SE15 3RW; 167 Peckham
Hill St, SE15 5JZ; Bermondsey Lib, Spa Rd, SE16 3QW;
Blue Anchor Lib, Market Pl, Southwark Park Rd, SE16; 7/12
Borough Rd, SE1 0AF; Brandon Lib, Maddock Way, SE17

LONDON—*continued*

3NH; 168/170 Old Kent Rd, SE1 5TY; 191 Harper Rd, SE1
6AF; North Camberwell Lib, Wells Way, SE5 0PX; Rotherhithe
Lib, Community Centre, Albion St, SE16; Southwark Bridge
Rd, SE1 0AS.   **13** Mobiles 2 + 1 schools.
14 Southwark (archives & local history).   **15** 5;
(a) 256, 236; (b) 680; (c) 46, 515; (d) 1, 409; (f) as books.
17 Housebound, hospitals, old people's homes, children's
activities, film shows, exhibitions, twinning links.
20 3 weeks.   **21** (a) ½p pd; (b&c) none.   **22** GLASS;
LASER; SEAL; SELRL.   **23** (a) 373, 061; (b) 55, 063;
(c) 166, 484; (e) 459.   **24** (a) 1, 946, 321; (b) 640, 931.
25 (a) 184; (b) 29; (c) 60; (d) 14.   **26** (a) £1, 156, 180;
(b) £18, 330; (c) £4.78; (d) £204, 000; (e) £16, 000;
(f) £748, 930.   **27** Branch Library, Borough High Street.

SUTTON, LONDON BOROUGH OF (pop 168, 210) Central
Library, St Nicholas Way, Sutton, Surrey, SM1 1EA (01-643
4461). Borough Libn: Mr R. P. Smith FLA.   **7** Leisure &
Recreation.   **8** Dir of Education: Mr Charles Melville
MA, MEd.   **9** Mon-Fri: ad ldg & ref 9.30-20.00 (Wed &
Thurs 19.00, Mon closed), children's 14.00-19.00; Sat:
9.30-17.00.
10 HQ; Branch.   **12** Church Rd, Cheam, Surrey; Windsor
Rd, Worcester Park, Surrey; Ridge Rd, Sutton, Surrey;
Middleton Circle, Carshalton, Surrey; Mollison Way, Round-
shaw, Wallington, Surrey; Shotfield, Wallington, Surrey;
The Square, Carshalton, Surrey.   **13** P-t 1; mobiles 1.
15 2; (a) 142, 002; (c) 17, 513; (e) 5p per record or set; (f) 1p
pd.   **16** 606; 5p per picture.   **17** School, housebound, old
people's homes.   **18** Cultural activities, entertainments
(£22, 460, Borough Libn, a 2).   **19** Datapen; photocharging.
20 4 weeks.   **21** (a&c) 1p pd; (b) none.   **23** (a) 305, 569;
(b) 49, 800; (c) 74, 816; (d) 42, 122; (e) 183.   **24** (a) 1, 878, 151;
(b) 460, 723.
25 (a) 123; (b) 11; (c) 45; (d) 20.   **26** (a) £1, 082, 860;
(b) £46, 500; (c) £6.304; (d) £137, 000; (e) £15, 503;
(f) £513, 000.

TOWER HAMLETS, LONDON BOROUGH OF (pop 150, 000)
Central Library, Bancroft Rd, London, E1 4DQ (01-980 4366).
Borough Libn: Mr Herbert Ward FLA.   **7** Amenities.
8 Dir of Community Services: Mr Edward P. Webber.
9 Mon-Fri: ad ldg & ref 9.00-20.00, children's 16.30-
18.00; Sat: 9.00-17.00.
10 Central; Area; Branch.   **11 Area Libraries:** Central:
Bancroft Rd, E1 4DQ (01-980-4366), Libn: H. A. Vincent;
Bethnal Green: Cambridge Heath Rd, E2 0HL (01-980-3902),
Libn: G. Bliss ALA; Limehouse: 638 Commercial Rd,
E14 7HS (01-987-3183), Libn: F. Smith ALA; Poplar:
Brunswick Rd, E14 6RJ (01-987-3234), Libn: E. Bodley;
Whitechapel: 77 High St, E1 (01-247-5272).   **12** Bow Lib,
Stafford Rd, E3; Cubitt Town Lib, Strattondale St, E14; Dorset
Estate, Hassard St, E2; Fairfoot Rd, E3; Lansbury Lib,
23/25 Market Way, E14; 369 Roman Rd, E3; St George's Lib,
Library Pl, Cable St, E1; Sidney Street Lib, Lindley St, E1;
Music & Gramophone Record Lib, Mayfield House, Cambridge
Heath Road, E2.   **13** Pt-1; mobiles 1.
14 Local history (Central) (6, 684 vols); art library (Whitechapel) (6, 000 vols); Indian languages colln (Whitechapel)
(2, 370 vols in Urdu, Bengali, Punjabi, Hindi, & Gujarti).
15 7; (a) 62, 463; (b) 7, 581; (c) 19, 954; (d) 480; (f) as books.
17 Schools, housebound, hospitals, old people's homes.
18 Cultural activities, entertainments.   **20** 3 weeks.
21 (a) 1p pw or part; (b&c) none.   **23** (a) 321, 601;
(b) 22, 114; (c) 72, 825; (e) 220.   **24** (a) 1, 084, 223; (b&c)
304, 543; (d) 27, 264.
25 (a) 132; (b) 38; (c) 29; (d) 18.   **26** (a) £796, 780;
(b) £12, 365; (c) £5.23; (d) £132, 700; (e) £6, 050; (f) £524, 915.

UPPER NORWOOD JOINT LIBRARY (pop 40, 000) Upper
Norwood Public Library, Westow Hill, London SE19 1TJ
(01-670 2551/5468). Chief Libn: Mr L. H. Cudby FLA;
Dep Libn: Mr H. H. Hanton ALA.   **7** Joint Library.
9 Mon-Fri: ad ldg & ref 9.00-19.00, children's 10.00-18.00
(Wed 13.00); Sat: ad ldg & ref 9.00-17.00, children's 9.30-
17.00.
14 Crystal Palace.   **15** 1 (languages only); (a) 592; (c) 300;
(e) £1 deposit; (f) 2p pd.   **17** Hospitals, old people's homes.
19 Full token charging.   **20** 3 weeks.   **21** (a) 2p 1st

week (or part), 5p 2 weeks, 8p 3 weeks, 10p 4 weeks, 12p 5
weeks, 15p 6 weeks; (b&c) none.   **23** (a) 69, 651; (b) 6, 097;
(c) 14, 551; (e) 77.   **24** (a) 212, 267; (b) 29, 253; (c) 175;
(d) 7, 934.
25 (a) 13; (b) 2; (c) 5; (d) 2.   **26** (a) £84, 516; (b) £1, 200;
(c) £2.11; (d) £13, 840; (e) £50; (f) £41, 000.

WALTHAM FOREST, LONDON BOROUGH OF (pop 230, 700)
Central Library, High St, Walthamstow, London E17 7JN
(01-520 3031/4733). Borough Libn & Curator: Mr H. L.
Chambers FLA; Dep Borough Libn & Curator: Mr J. W.
Howes FLA.   **7** Further Education & Libraries.
9 Mon-Fri: 9.00-20.00 (Wed closed); Sat: 9.00-17.30.
10 Central; Branch.   **12** North Chingford Lib, The Green,
Chingford, E4 7EN; Friday Hill, Chingford, E4 6EL; Hale End
Lib, Castle Ave, Highams Park, E4 9QD; South Chingford Lib,
Hall Lane, Chingford, E4 8EU; Higham Hill Lib, Countess Rd,
Walthamstow, E17 5HF; Wood Street Lib, Forest Rd,
Walthamstow, E17 4AA; St James Street Lib, Coppermill
Lane, Walthamstow, E17 7HA; Central Junior Lib, Linden Rd,
Walthamstow, E17 7LA; Schools & Teachers' Library,
Teachers' Centre, Queens Road, Walthamstow, E17 8QS
(not open to the public); Lea Bridge Rd, Leyton, E10 7HU; High
Rd, Leyton, E10 5QH; Church Lane, Leytonstone, E11 1HG;
Harrow Green Lib, Cathall Rd, Leytonstone, E11 4LF.
14 Local collns (Essex, Chingford, Leyton, Walthamstow,
Waltham Forest); play sets.   **15** 3; (a) 79, 485; (b) 6, 324;
(c) 18, 148; (d) 1, 563; (f) 2½p 1st week, 5p pw thereafter.
16 1, 053; deposit 50p, charge 20p for 3 months, fines 2p
pw.   **17** Schools, housebound, hospitals, old people's homes,
playgroups.   **18** Cultural activities, (£21, 158 (excluding
costs of Vestry House Museum and William Morris Art
Gallery); Libn i/c Special Activities; a 2).   **20** 4 weeks.
21 (a) 1½p 1st week, 5p pw thereafter; (b&c) none.
23 (a) 442, 726; (b) 73, 428; (c) 127, 698; (d) 209, 808; (e)
c.425.   **24** (a) 2, 279, 837; (b) 558, 097; (d) 57, 778.
25 (a) 150; (b) 31; (c) 36; (d) 11.   **26** (a) £903, 810;
(b) £24, 740; (c) £3.91; (d) £176, 800; (e) £8, 640; (f) £499, 090.

WANDSWORTH, LONDON BOROUGH OF (pop 291, 000)
West Hill Library, West Hill, Wandsworth, London SW18 1RZ
(01-874 1143; telex 25632). Borough Libn: Mr E. V. Corbett
MA, FLA, FRSA; Asst Borough Libn: Mr E. C. Transom ALA.
7 Recreation.   **8** Dir of Recreation: Mr L. T. Garrett.
9 Mon-Fri: ad ldg & children's 10.00-20.00 (Wed or Thurs
13.00), ref 9.00-20.00; Sat: 9.00-17.00.
10 HQ; District; Branch.   **11 District Libraries:** West
Hill: West Hill, Wandsworth, SW18 1RZ (01-874 1143), Libn:
Mr K. R. Kirby ALA; Battersea: Lavender Hill, SW11 1JB
(01-228 3474), Libn: Mr T. W. Ottway ALA; Balham: Ramson
Rd, SW12 8QY (01-673 4119), Libn: Mr A. E. Goring FLA.
12 Putney Lib, Disraeli Rd, SW15 2DR, Roehampton Lib,
Danebury Ave, SW15 4HD; Southfields Lib, Wimbledon Park
Rd, SW19 6NL; Alvering Lib, Allfarthing Lane, SW18 2PQ;
Earlsfield Lib, Magdalen Rd, SW18 3NY; Tooting Lib,
Mitcham Rd, SW17 9PD; Battersea Park Rd, SW11 4NF;
Northcote Rd, SW11 6HW; Southlands Lib, Battersea High St,
SW11 3HR, Winstanley Junior Lib, Fenner Sq, Winstanley
Estate, SW11 2HQ; York Lib, Wye St, SW11 2SP.   **13** Mobiles
2.
14 Early children's books; MJFR; MSC.   **15** 5; (a&b)
269, 783; (c&d) 34, 256; (f) 1p pd 1st week, 2p pd thereafter.
17 Schools, housebound, prisons, hospitals, old people's
homes.   **18** Cultural activities, entertainments (£116, 560,
Cultural Activities Officer, a 21, b 8).   **19** Photocharging;
Plessey Pen System.   **20** 15-21 days.   **21** (a) 1½p 1st
week, 2½p 2nd week, 4p 3rd week, c.5p pw thereafter, max
50p; (b&c) none.   **22** WANDPETLS.   **23** (a) 581, 090;
(b) 121, 531; (c) 185, 739; (e) 695.   **24** (a) 2, 644, 446;
(b) 786, 688; (c) 6, 423; (d) 336, 362.
25 (a) 189; (b) 43; (c) 59; (d) 17.   **26** (a) £1, 446, 210;
(b) £35, 110; (c) £4.97; (d) £263, 269; (e) £12, 366;
(f) £816, 590.

WESTMINSTER CITY COUNCIL (pop 218, 500, c. 800, 000
daytime population) Marylebone Library, Marylebone Rd,
London NW1 5PS (01-828 8070 ext 4025; telex 263305).
City Libn: K. C. Harrison MBE, FLA; Dep City Libn: F. N.

CODE: 1 Local authority. 2 Population. 3 Postal address of HQ. 4 Telephone & telex. 5 Chief Libn. 6 Deputy. 7 Committee responsible. 8 Officer to whom Libn is responsible (if any). 9 Hours. 10 Organisation. 11 Area libraries. 12 Branches. 13 Part-time libraries; mobiles. 14 Special collections. 15 Gramophone records: number of libraries, (a) record issues (b) cassette issues (c) record stock (d) cassette stock (e) loan charges (f) fines. 16 Pictures: stock; charges. 17 Other services. 18 Cultural activities (expenditure, officer in charge, staff: (a) officers (b) manual). 19 Issue method (if not Browne). 20 Loan period (if not 2 weeks). 21 Fines: (a) adult (b) children (c) OAPs. 22 Co-operative schemes. 23 Stock: (a) adult lending (b) adult reference (c) children (d) schools (e) current periodical titles. 24 Issues: (a) adult (b) children (c) schools (d) institutions. 25 Staff: (a) officers (b) manual (c) chartered libns (d) graduates. 26 Finance: (a) total expenditure (b) non-rate income (c) per capita expenditure (d) expenditure for books (e) expenditure for records etc (f) salaries & wages. 27 Capital projects.

LONDON—*continued*
McDonald FLA.　7 General Purposes.　9 Mon-Fri: ad ldg 9.30-19.00, ref 10.00-19.00, children's 10.00-18.30; Sat: ad ldg 9.30-17.00, ref & children's 10.00-17.00. 10 HQ; District (Branch).　12 Victoria Lib, 160 Buckingham Palace Rd, SW1 9UD; Mayfair Lib, 25 South Audley St, W1Y 5DJ; Great Smith Street Lib, SW1P 3DG; Charing Cross Lib, 4 Charing Cross Rd, WC2H 0HG; Portland Lib, 6 Little Portland St, W1N 5AG; Pimlico Lib, Rampayne St, SW1V 2PU; Maida Vale Lib, Sutherland Ave, W9 2QT; Paddington Lib, Porchester Rd, W2 5DU; Queen's Park Lib, 666 Harrow Rd, W10 4NE; St John's Wood Lib, 20 Circus Rd, NW8 6PD; Church Street Lib, NW8 8EU; Central Ref Lib, St Martin's St, WC2H 7HP; Churchill Gardens (Children's Lib), Lupus St, SW1V 3EN.　13 P-t 1.
14 Music; fine arts; archives & local history; medical library; Preston Blake colln (William Blake).　15 3 (+1 cassette library); (a) 215,072; (b) 31,753; (c&d) 43,900; (f) as books.　17 Schools (private), housebound, old people's homes.　18 Cultural activities (£32,000, Arts & Recreations Officer, a 3).　19 Tokens.　20 3 weeks. 21 (a&c) 1p pd; (b) none.　23 (a) 848,830; (b) 308,700; (c) 113,180; (d) private schools 300; (e) 1,872. 24 (a) 2,683,064; (b) 384,915. 25 (a) 248; (b) 61; (c) 91; (d) 81.　26 (a) £1,775,310; (b) £32,270; (c) £8.31; (d) £335,250; (e) £18,500; (f) £866,680.　27 Paddington District Library (1976).

MANCHESTER CITY COUNCIL (pop 528,500) Central Library, St Peter's Sq, Manchester, M2 5PD (061-236 9422; telex 667149/669475). Dir of Libs: Mr K.D. King BA, ALA. 7 Cultural.　8 Dir of Cultural Services: Mr L.G. Lovell FLA.　9 Mon-Fri: 9.00-21.00; Sat: 9.00-17.00. 10 HQ; District; Branch.　11 District Libraries: Crumpsall District Lib, Abraham Moss Centre, M8 6UH (061-740 1491), Libn: Mr I. Wallman FLA; Chorlton District Lib, Manchester Rd, M21 1PN (061-881 3179), Libn: Mrs M. Sumner ALA; East Area: Levenshulme Lib, Cromwell Grove, M19 3QE (061-224 2775), Libn: Mrs P. Coleman BA, ALA; Hulme District Lib, Stretford Rd, M15 5FQ (061-226 1006), Libn: Mr S. Macwilliam BA, ALA; North Area: Harpurhey Lib, Park View, M9 1TS (061-205 2637), Libn: Miss S. Ross ALA; Precinct Centre Lib, Booth St East, Manchester, M13 9BH (061-273 6346), Libn: Miss C. Lister ALA; South East Area: Withington District Lib, 410 Wilmslow Road, M20 9BM (061-445 1991), Libn: Mr B. Stevenson ALA; Wythenshawe Central Lib, The Forum, M22 5RT (061-437 8211), Libn: Mr M. Moss ALA; Didsbury District Lib, 692 Wilmslow Rd, M20 0DN (061-445 3220).　12 4 Maple Rd, Brooklands, M23 9HJ; Burnage Lane, Burnage, M19 1EW; Cambert Lane, Gorton, M18 8HJ; Victoria Ave, Higher Blackley, M9 3RH; Trevor St, Higher Openshaw, M11 1EQ; Hollyhedge Rd, Wythenshawe, M22 4QN; Haley St, Longsight, M12 4EX; Moston Lane, Moston, M10 9NB; 333 Hollinwood Ave, New Moston, M10 0JA; Church Rd, Northendon, M22 4WL;

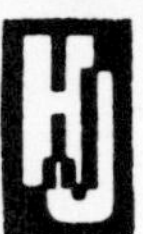

MANCHESTER CITY COUNCIL—*continued*
103 Sale Rd, Rackhouse, M23 0BQ; Waverton Rd, Wilbraham,
M14 7FB.   **13** Mobiles 4.
14 Commercial; arts; Watson Music library; technical;
local history; social sciences; language & literature;
archives dept.   **15** 2; (a&b) 47, 382; (c&d) 9, 164; (e) £1.00
pa (residents), £3.00 pa (non-residents); (f) 1p pd.
16 957; none.   **17** Housebound, prisons, hospitals, old
people's homes.   **18** Cultural activities (£212, 590, Dir of
Productions, a 79).   **20** 4 weeks.   **21** (a) 1p pd; (b) 1p pd,
max 5p; (c) none.   **22** Manchester Technical Information
Service.   **23** (a) 1, 016, 134; (b) 767, 493; (c) 143, 153;
(e) 4, 500.   **24** (a) 3, 942, 562; (b) 700, 023; (d) 89, 235.
25 (a) 405; (b) 111; (c) 82; (d) 31.   **26** (a) £2, 274, 100;
(b) £2, 490; (c) £4.30; (d&e) £402, 030; (f) £1, 273, 650.

MERTHYR TYDFIL BOROUGH COUNCIL (pop 61, 500)
Central Library, High St, Merthyr Tydfil, Mid Glamorgan,
CF47 8AF (0685-3057). Borough Libn & Curator: T. R.
Whitney.   **7** Leisure Services.   **8** Chief Leisure
Services Officer: F. P. Ryder FInstPRA(Dip).   **9** Mon-
Fri: ad ldg & children's 10. 00-18. 30, ref. 9. 00-18. 30; Sat:
9. 00-12. 00.
10 Central; Branch.   **12** Brewery Lane, Cefn Coed;
Church St, Dowlais; Perrott St, Treharris; Tyntaldwyn Rd,
Troedyrhiw.   **13** Mobiles 2.
17 Old people's homes.   **20** 3 weeks.   **21** (a&c) 3p pw
or part; (b) cost of notices only.   **23** (a) 90, 766; (b) 5, 707;
(c) 15, 136; (e) 125.   **24** (a) 332, 868; (b) 56, 220; (d) 5, 900.
25 (a) 21; (b) 4½; (c) 2.   **26** (a) £109, 950; (b) £3, 810;
(c) £1.79; (d) £21, 630; (f) £67, 070.

MID GLAMORGAN COUNTY COUNCIL (pop 304, 000)
Coed Parc, Park St, Bridgend, Mid Glamorgan, CF31 4BA
(0656-4210/55889). County Libn: Mr D. G. Williams FLA;
Dep County Libn: Mr R. W. Davies FLA.   **7** Education
(Libraries & Arts Sub-Committee).   **8** Dir of Education:
Mr J. L. Brace MA.   **9** Mon-Fri: 10. 00-18. 00 (Fri 19. 30);
Sat: 10. 00-17. 00.
10 HQ; District; Branch.   **11** District Libraries: Ogwr:
Coed Park, Park St, Bridgend, CF31 4BA (0656-4210/55889
ext 1), District Libn: I. Rowley ALA; Rhymney Valley: Morgan
Jones Park, Caerphilly, CF8 1AP (0222-882358), District
Libn: Mr P. F. Tobin BA, ALA; Taff Ely: Public Lib, Library
Rd, Pontypridd, CF37 2DY (0443-402821/402823), District
Libn: R. B. Watkins FLA.   **12** The Square, Bargoed;
Wyndham St, Bridgend, CF31 1EF; North's Lane, Maesteg,
CF34 9AA; Penybont Rd, Pencoed, CF35 5RA; Heol-y-Felin,
Pontyclun; Church Pl, Porthcawl, CF36 3AG; Ffald Rd, Kenfig
Hill, Pyle, CF33 6BF; Rhydyfelin, Pontypridd; Victoria Rd,
Rhymney, Gwent; High St, Tonyrefail; Ystrad Mynach.
13 P-t 12; mobiles 3 & 1 exhibition van & 1 schools' van.
15 1; (a) 3, 809; (c) 2, 486; (e) 50p + VAT pa; (f) 2p pw or
part.   **17** Schools, housebound, hospitals, old people's
homes, playgroups.   **19** Photo-charging (Bridgend).
20 3 weeks.   **21** (a, b&c) 2p pw or part (& postage).
23 (a) 532, 036; (b) 26, 328; (c) 122, 851; (d) 9, 637; (e) 166.
24 (a) 1, 481, 155; (b) 360, 084 (exc schools)
25 (a) 140; (b) 30; (c) 30; (d) 7.   **26** (a) £757, 510;
(b) £12, 015; (c) £2.49; (d) £199, 240; (e) £1, 525; (f) £377, 070.

MIDLOTHIAN DISTRICT COUNCIL (pop c. 73, 000) District
Library Headquarters, Fisherrow School, South St, Musselburgh, Midlothian EH21 6AU (031-665 2931). District Libn:
Mr Andrew Fraser ALA; Dep: Miss J. C. McLeod MA, ALA.
7 Leisure & Recreation.   **8** Dir of Recreation: Mr John
A. L. Gilfillan MA, DipEd.   **9** Mon-Fri: 10. 00-12. 30, 14. 00-
19. 30; Sat: closed.
10 HQ; Branch.   **12** Polton St, Bonnyrigg; Whitehard St,
Dalkeith; Newton Church Rd, Danderhall; Hunterfield, Gore-
bridge; George Ave, Loanhead; Combined Schools, Mayfield;
St David's, Newtongrange; Bellman's Rd, Penicuik.
13 Mobiles 2.
14 Local history; primary education.   **15** 8; (c) 1, 500;
(d) 350; (e) £1.00 pa; (f) 5p per scratch, 1p pd overdue.
17 Schools, housebound, hospitals, old people's homes, playgroups.   **20** 3 weeks.   **21** (a) 1p pd; (b&c) discretionary.
22 NLS.   **23** (a) 253, 804; (b) 4, 890; (c) 51, 842; (d) 51, 079;
(e) 55.   **24** (a) 1, 002, 240; (b) 188, 584; (c) 41, 293; (d) 7, 431.

MIDLOTHIAN DISTRICT COUNCIL —*continued*
25 (a) 56; (b) 10; (c) 7; (d) 4.   **26** (a) £174, 230; (b) £13, 600;
(c) £2.38; (d&e) £47, 620; (f) £102, 100.

MONKLANDS DISTRICT COUNCIL (pop 110, 000) Monklands
District Library Services, Public Library, Wellwynd, Airdrie,
Lanarkshire, ML6 0AG (02366-63221). Chief Libn: Mr
John Fox DMS, ALA, AMBIM.   **7** Leisure & Recreation.
9 Mon-Fri: 9. 30-20. 00 (closed Wed); Sat: 9. 30-17. 00.
10 HQ; District.   **11** Airdrie Lib, Wellwynd, Airdrie,
ML6 0AG (02366-63221), Libn: Mrs M. A. Black ALA;
Coatbridge Lib, Academy St, Coatbridge (0236-24150), Libn:
Mr G. L. Carter ALA.   **13** P-t 3; mobiles 2.
15 2; (a) 26, 357; (b) 15, 108; (c) 7, 002; (d) 2, 097; (e&f) none.
16 248; none.   **17** Housebound, hospitals, old people's
homes, remand home.   **19** Plessey pen & photocharging.
20 4 weeks.   **21** (a, b&c) none.   **23** (a) 190, 860;
(b) 10, 972; (c) 45, 331; (e) 120.   **24** (a) 735, 322; (b) 103, 658;
(d) 5, 444.
25 (a) 50; (b) 7; (c) 7; (d) 2.   **26** (a) £255, 845; (b) £1, 000;
(c) £2.33; (d) £72, 240; (e) £6, 650; (f) £101, 355.

MORAY DISTRICT COUNCIL (pop 77, 000) Dept of Libraries,
Grant Lodge, Cooper Park, Elgin, Morayshire IV30 1HS.
(0343-2746). Director of Libs: Miss Moira Innes ALA;
Dep Libn: Mr Fred J. Guthrie ALA; Chief Asst: Mrs
Elizabeth Rae, MA, ALA.   **7** Recreation & Libraries.
9 Mon-Fri: 10. 00-20. 00; Sat: 9. 00-12. 30.
10 HQ; Branch.   **12** Grant Lodge, Cooper Park, Elgin;
Forres House, High St, Forres.   **13** P-t 10; mobiles 4.
17 Housebound, hospitals, old people's homes.   **19** Simplified Newark; photo-charging.   **20** 4 weeks.   **21** (a, b&c)
none.   **22** ANSLICS.   **23** (a) 139, 931; (b) 6, 497;
(c) 31, 549; (e) 65.   **24** (a) 724, 586; (b) 123, 188.
25 (a) 38; (b) 4; (c) 12; (d) 4.   **26 Finance** (10½ months
only): (a) £269. 360; (c) £4.00; (d) £67, 550; (e) £11, 550;
(f) £118, 000.

MOTHERWELL DISTRICT COUNCIL. Motherwell Public
Library, Hamilton Rd, Motherwell, Lanarkshire ML1 3BZ
(0698-51311/12). Chief Libn: H. I. Hunt FLA; Dep: G.
McDonald ALA.   **7** Leisure & Recreation.   **9** Mon-Fri:
9. 00-17. 00; Sat: 9. 00-17. 00.
10 HQ; Branch.   **12** Hamilton Rd, Motherwell; YMCA
Building, Main St, Wishaw; Craigneuk Public Lib, Shieldmuir
St, Wishaw; 250 Main St, Bellshill; Manse Rd, Newmains;
4 Kirkhill Rd, Newarthill; 228 Clydesdale St, New Stevenston;
14 Thorniewood Rd, Tannochside; 25 Main St, Cleland; 35
Station Rd, Shotts.   **13** Mobiles 2.
15 3; (a) 11, 488; (b) 7, 295; (c) 3, 946; (d) 795; (e&f) none.
16 772, none.   **17** Housebound, hospitals, old people's
homes.   **19** Plessey Library Pen.   **20** 4 weeks.
21 (a, b&c) none.   **23** (a) 52, 319; (b) 4, 852; (c) 10, 475.
24 (a) 350, 347; (b) 36, 079.
25 (a) 60; (b) 17; (c) 8; (d) 1.   **26** (a) £341, 000; (b) £120;
(c) £2.10; (d) £80, 015; (e) £5, 000; (f) £162, 000.
27 Wishaw.

NEWCASTLE UPON TYNE CITY COUNCIL (pop 299, 800)
Central Library, PO Box 1MC, Newcastle upon Tyne, NE99
1MC (0632-610691; telex 53373, Library N/Tyne). City
Libn: Mr A. Wallace DMA, FLA, MILGA; Dep: Mr T. Mann
FLA.   **7** Arts & Recreation.   **9** Mon-Fri: 9. 00-21. 00;
Sat: 9. 00-17. 00.
10 Central; Area; Branch.   **11** Area Libraries: Gosforth:
Regent Farm Rd, NE3 1JN (0632-841224), Libn: P. Bradley
ALA; Denton Park: West Denton Way, NE5 2LF (0632-677922),
Libn: A. D. Walton ALA.   **12** Atkinson Rd, Benwell; Bins-
wood Ave, Blakelaw; Brinkburn St, Byker; Park Rd, Cruddas
Park; West Rd, Denton; Elswick Rd, Elswick; Fawdon Park
Rd, Fawdon; Fenham Hall Dr, Fenham; Heaton Park View,
Heaton; Newton Pl, High Heaton; St Georges Terrace,
Jesmond; Halewood Ave, Kenton; Shopping Precinct, New-
biggin Hall; High St, Newburn; Armstrong Rd, Scotswood;
Welbeck Rd, Walker; Appletree Gardens, Walkerville.
13 P-t 1; mobiles 2.
14 Thomas Bewick colln; Joseph Cowen papers; Greenwell
deeds.   **15** 1; (a) 19, 890; (b) 546; (c) 7, 300; (d) 360;

CODE: 1 Local authority. 2 Population. 3 Postal address of HQ. 4 Telephone & telex. 5 Chief Libn. 6 Deputy. 7 Committee responsible. 8 Officer to whom Libn is responsible (if any). 9 Hours. 10 Organisation. 11 Area libraries. 12 Branches. 13 Part-time libraries; mobiles. 14 Special collections. 15 Gramophone records: number of libraries, (a) record issues (b) cassette issues (c) record stock (d) cassette stock (e) loan charges (f) fines. 16 Pictures: stock; · charges. 17 Other services. 18 Cultural activities (expenditure, officer in charge, staff: (a) officers (b) manual). 19 Issue method (if not Browne). 20 Loan period (if not 2 weeks). 21 Fines: (a) adult (b) children (c) OAPs. 22 Co-operative schemes. 23 Stock: (a) adult lending (b) adult reference (c) children (d) schools (e) current periodical titles. 24 Issues: (a) adult (b) children (c) schools (d) institutions. 25 Staff: (a) officers (b) manual (c) chartered libns (d) graduates. 26 Finance: (a) total expenditure (b) non-rate income (c) per capita expenditure (d) expenditure for books (e) expenditure for records etc (f) salaries & wages. 27 Capital projects.

NEWCASTLE UPON TYNE CITY COUNCIL—*continued*
(e) £2.50 + VAT pa, OAP's £1.00 + VAT pa; (f) 1½p pd.
16 980; 65p + VAT pa & 16p per issue of 2 pictures.
17 Housebound, hospitals, old people's homes, play group picture book lending. 19 Computer charging (Plessey light pen). 20 4 weeks. 21 (a&c) 1p pd, max £1; (b) none. 22 TALIC. 23 (a) 624, 595; (b) 191, 025; (c) 144, 256; (e) 1, 081. 24 (a&b) 3, 600, 000; (d) old people's homes 29, 360; hospitals 12, 819.
25 (a) 206; (b) 33; (c) 52; (d) 16. 26 (a) £1, 086, 290; (b) £30, 130; (c) £3.62; (d) £184, 000; (e) £2, 700; (f) £569, 950.

NORFOLK COUNTY COUNCIL (pop 654, 000) County Library, County Hall, Martineau Lane, Norwich, NR1 2DH (0603-22288 ext 309; telex 975083). County Libn: D. P. Mortlock FLA; Dep: A. H. Coles FLA. 7 Leisure Services (Library & Arts Sub-Committee).
10 HQ; Division; Branch. 11 Divisions: Central Norfolk: County Hall, Martineau Lane, Norwich, NR1 2DH (0603-22288 ext 5363), Libn: I. Mollard ALA; Norwich: Central Lib, Bethel St, NR2 1NJ (0603-22233), Libn: P. Hepworth MA, FLA; East Norfolk: Central Lib, Tolhouse St, Great Yarmouth, NR20 2SH (0493-4551/2279), Libn: A. Bridges FLA; West Norfolk: Central Lib, London Rd, King's Lynn, PE30 5EZ (0553-2568), Libn: R. Wilson FLA. 12 Dyes Loke, Aylsham, Norwich, NR11 6EH; Beach Rd, Caister, Gt Yarmouth, NR30 5EX; Breckland Rd, New Costessey, Norwich, NR5 0RW; Prince of Wales Rd, Cromer, Norfolk; Church St, Diss, Norfolk; Bridge St, Downham Market, PE38 9DW; Church St, East Dereham, Norwich, NR19 1DN; Oak St, Fakenham, Norfolk, NR21 9DY; 1 Lowestoft Rd, Gorleston, Norfolk, NR31 6SG; Middleton's Lane, Hellesdon, Norwich, NR6 5SR; Westgate, Hunstanton, Norfolk, PE36 5AL; New Rd, North Walsham, Norfolk, NR28 9DE; New Rd, Sheringham, Norfolk, NR26 8EB; Recreation Ground Rd, Sprowston, Norwich, NR7 8EW; The Pightle, Swaffham, Norfolk, PE37 7DF; Raymond St, Thetford, Norfolk, IP24 2EA; St Williams Way, Thorpe St Andrew, Norwich, NR7 0AR; Norwich Rd, Wroxham, Norwich, NR12 8RX; Becket's Chapel, 2 Church St, Wymondham, Norfolk, NR18 0PH; 52, Thorpe Rd, Norwich, NR1 1RY; Earlham B Lib, Colman Rd, Norwich, NR4 7GH; Lazar House B Lib, Sprowston Rd, Norwich, NR3 4HZ; Mile Cross B Lib, Aylsham Rd, Norwich, NR3 2RJ; Thorpe B Lib, Plumstead Rd, Norwich, NR1 1RY. 13 P-t 18; mobiles 14.
14 Colman & Rye local history collns; Peter Henry Emerson colln (photography); East Anglian library of Soc of Chartered Accountants; Norfolk & Norwich Incorp Law Soc Library; Shipdham Church library; City Library (mss etc, founded 1608); American Memorial Room colln; (all at Norwich Central Lib); Stanley library; St Margaret's colln (both at King's Lynn); William de Castre mss colln (Gt Yarmouth); Thomas Paine colln; local material (Thetford). 15 2; (a) 24, 976; (b) 4, 422; (c) 3, 140; (d) 633; (e) £1.50 pa; (f) 1p pd.
17 Schools, housebound, prisons, hospitals, old people's homes. 19 Photocharging (Norwich Central); Worthing Token (Gt Yarmouth, Gorleston, Earlham); Westminster Token (King's Lynn). 20 3 weeks. 21 (a, b&c) 1p pd, max 50p.
23 (a) 1, 097, 266; (b) 111, 958; (c) 197, 161; (d) 237, 738; (e) 666. 24 (a) 6, 411, 140; (b) 1, 029, 540.
25 (a) 237; (b) 24; (c) 87; (d) 27. 26 (a) £1, 338, 840; (b) £31, 560; (c) £2.05; (d) £311, 210; (e) £3, 720; (f) £615, 670.

NORTHAMPTONSHIRE COUNTY COUNCIL (pop 505, 000) Northamptonshire Libraries, 27 Guildhall Rd, Northampton, Northamptonshire, NN1 1EF (0604-34833; telex 311278 Northampton Central Library). County Libn: Mr R. Wright

FLA; Dep County Libn: Mr J. A. J. Munro ALA. 7 Leisure & Libraries. 9 Mon-Fri: ad ldg & ref 10.00-20.00 (closed Thurs afternoons), children's variable; Sat: 10.00-17.00.
10 HQ; District; Branch. 11 Districts: Corby: George St, Corby, NN17 1PZ (053 66-3304), Libn: Mr M. Sharman ALA; Daventry: Ashworth St, Daventry, NN11 4AR (032 72-3130), Libn: Mr D. Bond ALA; Eastern: Midland Rd, Higham Ferrers, Wellingborough, NN8 4HR (093 33-4842), Libn: Mr M. Davison ALA; Kettering: Sheep St, Kettering, NN16 0AY (0536-2315), Libn: Mr J. Burden FLA; Northampton: Central Lib, Abington St, Northampton, NN1 2BA (0604-34833), Libn: Mr J. Kennedy FLA; South: Regional Lib HQ, Roads & Bridges Depot, Brackley Rd, Towcester, NN12 7DH (032 75-50398), Libn: Miss B. Hudson MA, ALA; Wellingborough: Pebble Lane, Wellingborough, NN8 4HR (093 33-5365), Libn: Miss H. D. Parker ALA. 12 Abington Lib, Lindsay Ave, Northampton; High St, Burton Latimer, Kettering; High St, Desborough, Kettering; Far Cotton Lib, Towcester Rd, Northampton; High St, Irthlingborough, Wellingborough; Kingsthorpe Lib, Harborough Rd, Northampton; Market Sq, Rothwell, Kettering; Newton Rd, Rushden; The Square, St James, Northampton. 13 P-t 14; mobiles 8.
14 John Clare Colln; Charles Bradlaugh Colln; H. E. Bates Colln; leather & footwear colln. 15 6; (a) 103, 670; (c) 21, 100; (d) 588; (e) £2.70 pa; (f) 1p 1st week, 5p pw thereafter. 17 Schools, housebound, prisons, hospitals, old people's homes, university & WEA classes. 19 Photocharging (2 libs); manual transaction slips (1 lib).
20 3 weeks. 21 (a) 1p 1st week, 5p pw thereafter, max 75p; (b) 1p pw, max 5p; (c) none. 23 (a) 832, 912; (b) 78, 265; (c) 173, 352; (d) 251, 598; (e) 972. 24 (a, b&d) 5, 704, 289; (c) 102, 421.
25 (a) 234; (b) 17; (c) 58; (d) 28. 26 (a) £1. 070, 630; (b) 36, 820; (c) £2.12; (d) £237, 000; (e) £12, 100 (inc audiovisual); (f) £573, 500.

NORTH EAST FIFE DISTRICT COUNCIL (see Kirkcaldy District Council)

NORTH EAST SCOTLAND LIBRARY SERVICE (pop 160, 000) 14 Crown Terrace, Aberdeen, Aberdeenshire, AB9 2BH (0224-572658/9). Chief Libn: Mr Neil R. McCorkindale DFM, ALA. 7 Joint Committee from Banff/Buchan, Gordon, & Kincardine/Deeside.
10 HQ; District; Branch. 11 14 Crown Terrace, Aberdeen, AB9 2BH (0224-572658/9), Area Libn (South): Mr G. Johnson ALA; Fraserburgh Lib, King Edward St, Fraserburgh, AB4 5PY (03462-2197), Area Libn (North): Mr B. Kelly ALA.
12 King Edward St, Fraserburgh; St Peter St, Peterhead; Town Hall, Inverurie. 13 P-t 23; mobiles 7.
14 George Macdonald mss (Brander Lib, Huntly).
15 11; (c) c. 8, 000; (d) c. 150; (f) fines under review.
16 c. 1, 000; none. 17 Family Book Service (housebound), prisons, hospitals, old people's homes, lighthouses, RAF Station. 20 4 weeks. 21 (a) Fines under review.
22 ANSLICS. 23 (a) c. 420, 000.
25 (a) 63.5; (b) 9.25; (c) 13; (d) 3. 26 (a) £292, 050; (b) £1, 500; (c) £1.83; (d) £77, 600; (e) £5, 000; (f) £152, 750.

NORTHERN IRELAND

BELFAST EDUCATION AND LIBRARY BOARD (pop
416,000) Central Library, Royal Ave, Belfast, BT1 1EA (0232-
43233; telex 747359). Chief Libn: I. A. Crawley FLA; Asst
Chief Libns: T. Watson ALA; T. W. Parker ALA; J. N. Montgomery ALA.   **7** Library.   **8** Chief Officer, Education
& Lib Board: W. C. H. Eakin MSc.   **9** Ad ldg & children's:
Mon & Thurs 13.30-20.00, Tues, Wed & Fri 9.30-17.30,
ref: Mon-Fri 9.30-17.30 (Mon & Thurs 20.00); Sat: 9.30-
13.00.
10 Central; Branch.   **12** Slievegallion Dr, Andersons-
town, Belfast BT5 4FP; 19-35 Templemore Ave, Ballyma-
carrett, Belfast BT5 4FP; 4 Chichester Rd, Belfast BT15 5EJ;
121 Donegall Rd, Belfast BT12 5JL; 49 Falls Rd, Belfast
BT12 4PD; 13 Finaghy Rd South, Belfast BT10 0BW; 85-89
Holywood Rd, Belfast BT4 3BD; Knock Branch, 514 Upper
Newtonards Rd, Belfast BT4 3HB; 53-55 Ligoniel Rd, Belfast
BT14 8BW; Derwent House, 440 Lisburn Rd, Belfast BT9
6GR; 46 Oldpark Rd, Belfast BT14 6FS; Ormeau Rd Embankment Belfast BT7 3GG; 298-300 Shankill Rd, Belfast BT13
1FT; Whiterock Rd, Belfast B12.   **13** P-t 4; mobiles 2.
14 Music (5,600 vols, 22,250 scores); Irish & local history
(32,000 vols); fine books colln (1,245 vols).   **15** 1;
(a) 48,270; (b) 4,119; (c) 14,000; (d) 1,000; (e) £3.00 pa;
(f) as books.   **16** 4,000 (not loaned at present).
17 Schools, housebound, prisons, hospitals, old people's
homes, playgroups.   **19** Plessey SPC Library System.
20 3 weeks.   **21** (a) 2p pw or part; (b&c) 1p pw or part.
22 IJFR.   **23** (a&c) 331,667; (b) 460,228; (d) 150,000;
(e) 1,860.   **24** (a&b) 2,010,185; (d) 27,564.
25 (a) 216; (b) 51; (c) 21; (d) 39.   **26** (a) £1,110,100;
(b) £35,100; (c) £2.34; (d) £360,700; (e) £5,000; (f) £550,000.

NORTH EASTERN EDUCATION AND LIBRARY BOARD
(pop 320,000) County Library, Demesne Ave, Ballymena,
Co. Antrim, BT43 7BG (0266-41531/3; telex 747371).
Chief Libn: Mr J. P. E. Francis FLA. Asst Chief Libns:
Mr P. R. Craddock FLA (Central); Miss M. McIlroy ALA
(Adult); Mr T. V. O'Hara ALA (Youth).   **7** Library.
8 Chief Officer: Dr R. J. Dickson MA, PhD.   **9** Mon-Sat:
10.00-17.30 (or 18.00).
10 HQ; Division; Branch.   **11 Divisions:** Central: County
Lib, Demesne Ave, Ballymena BT43 7BG (0266-41531/3)
Libn: Mr M. McQuitty ALA; North: County Lib, County Hall,
Castlerock Rd, Coleraine, BT52 3HS (0265-4111), Libn:
Mr P. Reid ALA; South: Divisional Lib, Carnmoney Rd,
Glengormley, Newtownabbey (023 13-3797), Libn: Mr M.
Chandler ALA.   **12** Courthouse, Antrim; 43 Castle St,
Ballycastle; Rodden Foot, Ballymoney; 2 Joymount,
Carrickfergus; Queen St, Coleraine, BT52 1BE; Glassilan
Grove, Greenisland; Greystone Rd, Antrim; Victoria Rd,
Larne; Main St, Maghera; Queens' Ave, Magherafelt; Dunluce
St, Portrush; Town Hall, Port Stewart; 22a The Diamond,
Rathcoole, Newtownabbey; Edward Rd, Whitehead.
13 P-t 10; mobiles 9.
15 1; (a) 857; (c) 4,070 (inc schools); (d) 571; (e) £3 pa;
(f) as books.   **17** Schools, housebound, hospitals, old people's
homes.   **21** (a) 2p pw (unless returned within 2 months);
(b) 1p pw (unless returned within 2 months); (c) none.
22 Northern Ireland Cooperative Scheme.   **23** (a) 382,322;
(b) 43,510; (c) 83,742; (d) 421,461; (e) 360.
24 (a) 1,711,483; (b) 730,521; (c) c.1,000,000; (d) hospitals
12,490.
25 (a) 159; (b) 12; (c) 18½; (d) 7.   **26** (a) £1,117,600;
(c) £3.49; (d) £448,700; (e) £28,000; (f) £346,800.

SOUTH EASTERN EDUCATION AND LIBRARY BOARD (pop
299,000) Library Headquarters, Windmill Lane, Bally-
nahinch, Co. Down, BT24 8DH (0238 56-2639; telex 747325).
Chief Libn: D. H. Welch FLA; Chief Asst Libn (Central):
C. D. Wort ALA.   **7** Library.   **8** Chief Officer to the
Board: F. H. Ebbitt BA, HDipEd.   **9** Mon-Fri: 10.00-20.00
(Wed or Thurs 13.00); Sat: 10.00-17.00.
10 HQ; District; Branch.   **11 Districts:** 80 Hamilton Rd,
Bangor, BT20 4LH (0247-5591), Libn: Miss J. Barfoot ALA;
Railway St, Lisburn (02382-6749), Libn: Miss C. O'Neill ALA;
Mount Oriel Lib, Saintfield Rd, Belfast, BT8 4HL (0232-

643440), Libn: Miss P. McMillen ALA; Tullycarnett Lib,
Kinross Ave, Belfast, 5 (023 121-5079), Libn: Miss K. B. F.
Smyth ALA.   **12** Main St, Ballynahinch, BT24 8DN;
Belvoir Park Lib, Drumart Sq, Belfast, BT8 4EY; Braniel
Lib, Glen Rd, Belfast, BT5 7JH; Newtownards Rd, Comber,
BT23 5AU; Cregagh Lib, 7 Elesington Court, Bell's Bridge,
Belfast, BT6 9JY; The Mall, English St, Downpartrick,
BT30 6AE; Church Rd, Dundonald, BT16 0RJ; Upper Dunmurry
Lane, Dunmurry, BT17 0AA; Queen's Hall, Sullivan Pl,
Holywood, BT18 9JH; Annesley Mansions, Central Promenade,
Newcastle, BT33 0AA; Queen's Hall, Regent St, Newtownards,
BT23 4AB.   **13** P-t 5; mobiles 5.
14 Irish & local history colln.   **15** 4; (a&b) 4,500;
(c) 4,560; (d) 60; (e) none; (f) 2p pw or part.   **17** Schools,
housebound, prisons, hospitals, old people's homes, lighthouses, Open University study centres.   **20** 3 weeks.
21 (a&b) 1p pw or part; (b) none.   **22** IJFR.   **23** (a&b)
267,678; (c) 118,521; (d) 164,804; (e) 331.   **24** (a) 1,245,416;
(b) 501,993; (c) primary schools c.156,454; (d) 34,980.
25 (a) 150; (b) 7; (c) 20; (d) 18.   **26** (a) £655,000;
(b) £5,000; (c) £2.19; (d) £203,000; (e) 4,000; (f) £353,000.

SOUTHERN EDUCATION AND LIBRARY BOARD (pop
284,000) Library Service, Library Headquarters, Brownlow Rd, Legahory, Craigavon, Co. Armagh, BT65 8DP
(0762-42312/4). Chief Libn: W. R. H. Carson FLA; Asst
Chief Libns: R. Dougan ALA (Central); A. Marrow ALA
(Adult).   **7** Library.   **8** Chief Officer: W. J. Dickson.
9 Mon-Fri: 10.00-18.00 (2 days 20.00); Sat: 10.00-17.00.
10 HQ; Branch.   **12** Market St, Armagh; Downshire Rd,
Banbridge; Church Rd, Bessbrook; Brownlow B Lib, Tully-
gally, Craigavon; The Square, Coalisland; Burn Rd, Cooks-
town; Scotch St, Dungannon; 28 Greencastle St, Kilkeel, Downshire High School, Belfast Rd, Newry; Edward St, Portadown;
Market St, Tandragee; Summerhill; Warrenpoint.
13 P-t 4; mobiles 5 & 3 schools.
17 Schools, housebound, prisons, hospitals, old people's
homes, playgroups.   **18** Cultural activities (Extension
Activities Libn).   **20** 4 weeks.   **21** (a, b&c) none.
22 IJFR.   **23** (a) 264,947; (b) 5,780; (e) 439.   **24** (a)
941,123; (b) 576,444; (c) 284,698; (d) 12,392.
25 (a) 126; (b) 16; (c) 9; (d) 11.   **26** (a) £641,000;
(b) £641,000; (c) £2.26; (d) £289,500; (e) £10,000;
(f) £279,200.

WESTERN EDUCATION AND LIBRARY BOARD (pop
230,000) Library Headquarters, Dublin Rd, Omagh, Co.
Tyrone, BT78 1HG (0662-2107/3858; telex 747097). Chief
Libn: Mr R. T. A. Farrow ALA; Asst Chief Libns: Mr
W. K. McCoubrey ALA (Adult); Ms Rosemary A. Adams
BA, ALA (Central); Mr W. D. Strahan ALA (Youth).
7 Library.   **8** Chief Officer: Mr M. H. F. Murphy BA,
HDipEd.   **9** Mon-Fri: 10.00-18.00; Sat: 9.30-13.00
(under review).
10 HQ; Division; Branch.   **11 Divisions:** 39 Great James
St, Londonderry, BT48 7DF (0504-2445/3651; telex 747518),
Div Libn: Miss J. Sterling BA, ALA; c/o Library HQ, Dublin
Rd, Omagh, Co. Tyrone, BT78 1HG (0662-2107/3858; telex
747097), Div Libn: Mr R. W. Adams BA, ALA; Darling St,
Enniskillen, Co. Fermanagh, BT74 7DD (0365-2886/4383;
telex 747517), Div Libn: Mr F. J. Nawn MBE.   **12** The
Pavilion, Showgrounds, Sedan Ave, Omagh; County Buildings,
Newtown St, Strabane; Main St, Irvinestown; Fairview,
Enniskillen; Drumhaw, Lisnaskea; Brooke Park, Londonderry; Bishop St, Londonderry; Racecourse Rd, Shantallow,
Londonderry; Strathfoyle, Londonderry; Waterside, Londonderry; 33-35 Main St, Limavady; Main St, Dungiven.
13 Mobiles 6.
14 Local history.   **15** (a) 6,969; (e&f) none.
17 Schools, housebound, prisons, hospitals, old people's
homes.   **20** 4 weeks.   **21** (a, b&c) none.   **22** IJFR;
ICLS.   **23** (a) 509,900; (b) c.20,000; (c) 75,421;
(d) 256,274; (e) 411.   **24** (a&b) 1,362,994; (c) 367,815;
(d) 52,351.
25 (a) 275; (b) 20; (c) 12; (d) 9.   **26** (a) £547,376; (c) £2.37;
(d) £103,000; (e) £12,000; (f) £312,000.

CODE: 1 Local authority. 2 Population. 3 Postal address of HQ. 4 Telephone & telex. 5 Chief Libn. 6 Deputy. 7 Committee responsible. 8 Officer to whom Libn is responsible (if any). 9 Hours. 10 Organisation. 11 Area libraries. 12 Branches. 13 Part-time libraries; mobiles. 14 Special collections. 15 Gramophone records: number of libraries, (a) record issues (b) cassette issues (c) record stock (d) cassette stock (e) loan charges (f) fines. 16 Pictures: stock; · charges. 17 Other services. 18 Cultural activities (expenditure, officer in charge, staff: (a) officers (b) manual). 19 Issue method (if not Browne). 20 Loan period (if not 2 weeks). 21 Fines: (a) adult (b) children (c) OAPs. 22 Co-operative schemes. 23 Stock: (a) adult lending (b) adult reference (c) children (d) schools (e) current periodical titles. 24 Issues: (a) adult (b) children (c) schools (d) institutions. 25 Staff: (a) officers (b) manual (c) chartered libns (d) graduates. 26 Finance: (a) total expenditure (b) non-rate income (c) per capita expenditure (d) expenditure for books (e) expenditure for records etc (f) salaries & wages. 27 Capital projects.

NORTH TYNESIDE METROPOLITAN BOROUGH COUNCIL (pop 207, 000) Central Library, Northumberland Sq, North Shields, Tyne & Wear, NE30 1QU (089 45-82811; telex 53134). Chief Libn: Mr Richard Blundell FLA; Asst Chief Libn: Mr John Brian West ALA (Library Services). **7** Information, Libraries & Arts. **9** Mon-Fri: 9.00-19.00 (or 19.30); Sat: 9.00-17.00. **10** HQ; Area; Branch. **11 Area Libraries:** North Shields: Central Lib, Northumberland Sq, North Shields, Tyne & Wear, NE30 1QU (089 45-82811), Libn: Dr J.P. Devine ALA; Killingworth: Communicare House, Citadel East, Killingworth Town Centre, Newcastle upon Tyne, NE12 0UP (0632-681883) Libn: Miss E. Mallabar ALA; Wallsend: Ferndale Ave, Wallsend, NE28 7NB (0632-623438), Libn: Mrs E. Penton ALA; Whitley Bay: Park Rd, Whitley Bay, NE26 1EJ (089 44-25209/32926), Libn: Miss J. Scott ALA. **12** 26 Front St, Tynemouth, North Shields, NE30 4DZ; St George's Rd, Cullercoats, North Shields, NE30 3JY; 27 Coast Rd, North Shields, NE29 7PG; 27 Buttermere Rd, Marden Estate, North Shields, NE30 3AS; 41 Avon Ave, Meadow Well Estate, North Shields, NE29 7QT; The Shopping Centre, West Farm Ave, Longbenton, Newcastle-upon-Tyne, NE12 8SE; Whitfield Rd, Forest Hall, Newcastle-upon-Tyne, NE12 0LJ; Park Lane, Shiremoor, Northumberland, NE27 0LB; Canterbury Way, Wideopen, Newcastle-upon-Tyne, NE13 6JJ; Howdon B Lib, Churchill St, Wallsend, NE28 7TG; Berwick Dr, Battle Hill Estate, Wallsend, NE28 9EF; Woodleigh Rd , Monkseaton, Whitley Bay. **13** P-t 2. **14** Edington colln (engravings by British artists); Roddam collns (19th cent playbills & 19th cent Northumberland election materials). **15** 3; (a&b) 70, 000; (c&d) 17, 400; (e) residents £1.08 pa (inc VAT), non-residents £2.70 pa (inc VAT), + 5p per record; (f) as books. **16** 268; 17p per month. **17** Schools, housebound, old people's homes. **18** Cultural activities, entertainments (£50, 750; Chief Libn; a 4; b 1). **19** Token; photo-charging. **20** 4 weeks. **21** (a) 2p pd, max 60p (+postage); (b) 1p pw or part, max 7p (+postage); (c) none. **22** TALIC. **23** (a&b) 370, 404; (c) 94, 500; (e) 351. **24** (a) 2, 288, 128; (b) 424, 573. **25** (a) 118½; (b) 21¼; (c) 26; (d) 14. **26** (a) £695, 191; (b) £21, 612; (c) £3.6; (d) £137, 202; (e) £23, 487; (f) £637, 143.

NORTHUMBERLAND COUNTY COUNCIL (pop 285, 700) County Central Library, The Willows, Morpeth, Nothumberland, NE61 1TA (0670-2385/6/7; telex 53439). County Libn: Mr G.E. Laughton FLA; Dep County Libn: G.S. Payne ALA. **7** Amenities. **8** Dir of Education: Mr M.H. Trollope MA. **9** Mon-Fri: ad ldg & ref 10.00-20.00, children's 10.00-18.30; Sat: 10.00-17.00. **10** HQ; Area; Branch. **11 Areas:** Alnwick: Green Batt, Alnwick, NE66 1TU (0665-2689) Area Libn: Mr R. Hall ALA; Berwick: Marygate, Berwick-upon-Tweed, TD15 1MG (0289-7320) Area Libn: Miss M. Simpson ALA; Blyth Valley: Bridge St, Blyth, NE24 2DJ (06706-61352; telex 53446), Area Libn: Miss M. Taylor ALA; Castle Morpeth: Gas House Lane, Morpeth, NE61 1TA (0670-2385; telex 53439), Area Libn: Miss M. Burdon ALA, BA; Tynedale: Beaumont St, Hexham, NE46 3LU (0434-3156), Area Libn: Mrs J. Brown ALA; Wansbeck: Kenilworth Rd, Ashington, NE63 8AA (067081-813245; telex 53450), Area Libn: Mr G. Andrew ALA. **12** Queen St, Amble, Morpeth, NE65 0DQ; Forum Way, Civic Precinct, Cramlington, NE23 6QD; Elsdon Ave, Seaton Delaval, Whitley Bay, Tyne & Wear, NE25 0BW; Thornhill Rd, Ponteland, Newcastle upon Tyne, NE20 9PZ; Station Bank, Prudhoe on Tyne, NE42 5PR; Glebe Rd, Bedlington; Jubilee Terrace, Newbiggin-by-the-Sea, NE64 6AA. **13** P-t 13; mobiles 10.

14 Northern Arts Poetry Library (all English poetry from 1968); Open University colln of background reading. **15** 4; (a) 3, 250; (c) 3, 200; (d) 450; (e) £2 pa; (f) 5p pw or part. **17** Schools, housebound, prisons, hospitals, old people's homes, adult classes, Open University, music & drama societies, LEA & WEA classes. **19** Tokens for adult fiction. **20** 4 weeks. **21** (a&c) 5p pw or part, max 15p; (b) 1p pw or part, max 10p. **22** TALIC. **23** (a) 475, 060; (b) 17, 644; (c) 73, 777; (d) 197, 675; (e) 385. **24** (a) 3, 316, 400; (b) 540, 528; (c) 946, 981; (d) 183, 600. **25** (a) 134; (b) 15; (c) 30; (d) 7. **26** (a) £654, 850; (b) £11, 680; (c) £2.29; (d) £150, 280; (e) £5, 320; (f) £316, 590.

NORTH YORKSHIRE COUNTY COUNCIL (pop 648, 600) County Library Headquarters, 21 Grammar School Lane, Northallerton, North Yorkshire, DL6 1DF (0609-5381; telex 58257). County Libn: Miss D.M. Hudson FLA; Dep County Libn: Mr J.A. Saunders ALA. **7** Library Archives & Museums. **9** Mon-Fri: 10.00-19.00; Sat: ad ldg & children's 10.00-17.00, ref 10.00-19.00. **10** HQ; Division; Branch. **11 Divisions:** 21 Grammar School Lane, Northallerton, DL6 1DF (0609-5381), Asst County Libn A Div: Miss A.E.E. McDougle FLA; Central Lib, Vernon Rd, Scarborough, YO11 2NL (0723-64285), Asst County Libn B Div: Mr A. Dearden FLA; Central Lib, Victoria Ave, Harrogate, HG1 1EG (0423-2744), Asst County Libn C Div: Mr H. Whittleston FLA; Central Lib, Museum St, York, YO1 2DS (0904-55631), Asst County Libn D Div: Mr O.S. Tomlinson FLA. **12** Front St, Acomb, York; 3 Pickering Rd, West Ayton, Scarborough; Old Vicarage, Bilton Lane, Harrogate; Gough Rd, Catterick Garrison; Rawcliffe Lane, Clifton, York; The Broadway, Colburn, Catterick Garrison; Tadcaster Rd, Dringhouses, York; 105b High St, Great Ayton, Middlesbrough; Station Rd, Haxby, York; Garth Rd, Huntington, York; Market Pl, Knaresborough; St Michael St, Malton; 72 High St, Northallerton; Commercial St, Norton, Malton; 36 Market Pl, Pickering; Queens Rd, Richmond, North Yorkshire; Skellgarths, Ripon; 450 Scalby Rd, Newby, Scarborough; James St, Selby; Finkle Hill, Sherburn in Elmet, Leeds; High St, Skipton; College Sq, Stokesley, Middlesbrough; Fifth Ave, Tang Hall, York; Castlegate, Thirsk; The Village, Upper Poppleton, York; Windsor Terrace, Whitby. **13** P-t 36; mobiles 27. **14** Petyt colln (Skipton); local history. **15** 2; (a) 35, 518; (b) 3, 647; (c) 6, 752; (d) 300; (e) £2.00 pa, £10 for Society; (f) as books. **16** 351; £2 pa. **17** Schools, housebound, prisons, hospitals, old people's homes. **19** Photocharging. **20** 3 weeks. **21** (a) 1p pd 1st week, 5p pw thereafter. **22** LIST. **23** (a) 754, 410; (b) 98, 330; (c) 179, 930; (d) 284, 666; (e) 709. **24** (a, b&c) 8, 689, 208; (d) 8, 445. **25** (a) 336; (b) 32; (c) 79; (d) 21. **26** (a) £1, 573, 000; (b) £41, 400; (c) £2.425; (d) £413, 300; (e) £4, 680; (f) £827, 800. **27** County Library Headquarters and Branch, Northallerton.

NOTTINGHAMSHIRE COUNTY COUNCIL (pop 984, 190) County Hall, West Bridgford, Nottingham NG2 7QP (06902-863366). Asst Dir (Libs): Mr John N. Taylor FLA. Asst County Libns: Mr G. Hare ALA (Development); Mr J.T. Boyd ALA (Bibliographic); Miss L.E. Green ALA (Education & Youth); Mr L.F. Craik FLA (Central Resources). **7** Leisure Services. **8** Dir of Leisure Services: Mr Wyndham Heycock BA. **9** No general pattern. **10** HQ; District; Branch. **11 Districts:** Ashfield: Devonshire Mall, Sutton-in-Ashfield, Nottingham, NG17 1BP

NOTTINGHAMSHIRE COUNTY COUNCIL—*continued*
(06235-3241), Libn: Mr S. J. Riley ALA; Bassetlaw: Memorial
Ave, Worksop, S80 2BP (0909-2408), Libn: Miss B. M. Atten-
borough FLA; Broxtowe: Foster Ave, Beeston, Nottingham,
NG9 1AE (0602-255168/255084), Libn: Mr F. G. Barnes ALA;
Gedling: Nottingham Rd, Arnold, Nottingham, NG5 6JN (0602-
264114/264115), Libn: Mr K. M. Negus ALA; Mansfield:
Leaming St, Mansfield, NG18 1NH (0623-23861/34208), Libn:
Mrs A. J. Wright ALA; Newark: Castlegate, Newark-on-Trent
(0636-3966/6367), Libn: Mr A. J. Cook ALA; Nottingham:
Central Lending Lib, South Sherwood St, Nottingham, NG1 4DA
(0602-43591), Libn: Mr R. Earlam FLA; Rushcliffe: Bridgford
Rd, West Bridgford, Nottingham NG2 6AT (0602-816506/
816780), Libn: Mr H. E. Rowlinson.   **12** Market Pl, Hucknall,
Nottingham NG15 7BS; Sutton Rd, Huthwaite, Sutton-in-Ash-
field, Nottingham; Ashfield Precinct, Kirkby-in-Ashfield,
Nottingham, NG17 7BQ; Skegby & Stanton Hill Lib, Mansfield
Rd, Skegby, Sutton-in-Ashfield, Nottingham; Churchgate, Ret-
ford, DW22 6PE; 47 Nottingham Rd, Eastwood, Nottingham
NG16 3AN; Main St, Kimberley, Nottingham NG16 2LY;
Warren Ave, Stapleford, Nottingham, NG9 5EY; Meadow Lane,
Burton Joyce, Nottingham; St Wilfred Square, Calverton,
Nottingham, NG14 6FP; Manor Rd, Carlton, Nottingham NG4
3AZ; 341 Carlton Hill, Nottingham, NG4 1JE; Gedling Lib,
Wollaton Ave, Carlton, Nottingham, NG4 4HX; Mapperley Lib,
Westdale Lane, Nottingham, NG4 3JF; Milton Court, Ravens-
head, Nottingham NG15 9BD; Ladybrook Lane, Mansfield;
Woodhouse Lib, Church St, Mansfield; High St, Warsop, Mans-
field; Main St, Old Balderton, Newark; New Lane, Blidworth,
Mansfield; High St, Edwinstowe, Mansfield; Forest Rd, New
Ollerton, Newark; King St, Southwell; Clifton Lib, Southchurch
Dr, Nottingham NG11 8AB; Radford/Lenton Lib, Lenton
Boulevard, Nottingham, NG7 2BY; Wollaton Lib, Bramcote
Lane, Nottingham NG8 2NA; Aspley Lib, Nuthall Rd, Notting-
ham, NG8 5DD; Bilborough Lib, Bracebridge Dr, Nottingham,
NG8 4PN; Sherwood Lib, Spondon St, Mansfield Rd, Notting-
ham, NG5 4AB; Northern Lib, Highbury Vale, Bulwell, Notting-
ham, NG6 9AE; St Ann's Lib, Robin Hood Chase, Nottingham;
Eaton Pl, Bingham, Nottingham; Church Dr, Keyworth
Nottingham, NG12 5FF.   **13** P-t 35; mobiles 9.
14 D. H. Lawrence (inc Hopkin colln); Byron; Cecil Roberts.
15 39; (a) 99, 027; (c) 24, 144; (e) none; (f) as books.
17 Schools, housebound, prisons, hospitals, old people's
homes.   **18** Cultural activities, entertainments (£278, 000;
Asst Dirs Arts, Sports; a 2).   **19** Photocharging.   **20** 3
weeks.   **21** (a) 1p 1st week, 4p pw thereafter; (b&c) none.
22 NANTIS.   **23** (a&b) 1, 706, 595; (c) 361, 239;
(d) 876, 761; (e) c. 1, 000.   **24** (a) 8, 749, 520; (b) 2, 332, 044.
25 (a) 393; (b) 122; (c) 130.   **26** (a) £2, 136, 667;
(b) £61, 795; (c) £2. 17; (d) £477, 172; (e) £16, 071;
(f) £1, 166, 728.

OLDHAM METROPOLITAN BOROUGH COUNCIL (pop
230, 000) Central Library & Art Gallery, Union St, Oldham,
Lancashire, OL1 1DM (061-624 3633; telex 667779). Dir of
Libraries, Art Galleries & Museums: Mr James Carter FLA;
Dep Dir: Ms Deirdre Heywood BA, ALA.   **7** Arts & Recreation.   **9** Mon-Fri; 10. 00-19. 00 (Wed 13. 00); Sat: 10. 00-13. 00.
10 HQ; Branch.   **12** Middleton Rd, Chatterton, Oldham;
Beal Lane, Crompton, Oldham; Main St, Failsworth, Manchester; Rochdale Rd, Royton, Oldham; High St, Uppermill,
Oldham;   **13** P-t 5; mobiles 1.
15 3; (a) 18, 558; (c) 3, 937; (e) £3 pa; (f) 10p pw or part,
max 50p.   **16** 956; none.   **17** Schools, housebound, old
people's homes.   **18** Cultural activities, Art galleries and
Museums.   **19** Computer-ALS.   **20** 4 weeks.   **21** (a) 2p
pd, max 50p; (b&c) none.   **23** (a) 303, 174; (b) 9, 453;
(c) 77, 321; (d) 55, 677; (e) 308.   **24** (a) 1, 721, 177; (b) 389,
660; (c) 51, 731.
25 (a) 105; (b) 26; (c) 14; (d) 7.   **26** (a) £622, 000 (inc art
gallery & museum); (b) £46, 500; (c) £2. 70; (d) £134, 200
(inc schools); (e) £4, 700; (f) 303, 160 (inc art gallery &
museum).

ORKNEY ISLANDS COUNCIL (pop 17, 109) The Orkney
Library, Laing St, Kirkwall, Orkney, KW15 1NW (0856-3141
ext 7). Chief Libn: Mr David M. N. Tinch ALA; Dep Libn:
Mr Robert K. Leslie ALA.   **7** Education.   **8** Dir of

Education: A. Bain BSc.   **9** Mon-Fri: 9. 00-20. 00; Sat:
9. 00-17. 00.
10 HQ; Branch.   **13** P-t 1; mobiles 1.
15 1; (a) 2, 000; (c) 850; (e&f) none.   **17** Schools, housebound,
hospitals, old people's homes.   **19** Tokens.   **21** (a, b&c)
none.   **23** (a) 83, 000; (b) 14, 600; (c) 12, 000; (d) 7, 000;
(e) 25.   **24** (a) 245, 000; (b) 18, 000; (c) 51, 000; (d) 3, 300.
25 (a) 9½; (c) 3 & 1 archivist; (d) 1.   **26** (a) £52, 200;
(c) £3. 05; (d) £16, 280; (e) £500; (f) £25, 000.

OXFORDSHIRE COUNTY COUNCIL (pop 535, 300) Central
Library, Westgate, Oxford, Oxfordshire, OX1 1DJ (0865-
722422; telex 837439). County Libn: Mr J. P. Wells MA, FLA;
Dep County Libn: Mr L. White FLA; Asst County Libn: Mr
G. M. Elliott ALA.   **7** Libraries, Museums & Archives.
9 Mon-Fri: ad ldg & children's 9. 15-19. 00; ref 9. 15-20. 00;
Sat: 9. 15-17. 00.
10 HQ; Region; Branch.   **11** **Regions:** Central: Central
Lib, Westgate, Oxford, OX1 1DJ (0865-722422), Libn: Mr S. B.
Clennett MA, ALA; East: Holton Park, Oxford, OX9 1QQ
(08677-2234), Libn: Mrs E. G. Atkinson ALA; North West:
Marlborough Rd, Banbury OX16 8DF (0295-2282), Libn: Mr
M. Elsom BA, ALA; South West: Welch Way, Witney, OX8 7HH
(0993-3659), Libn: Mr D. J. Darvill ALA.   **12** High St,
Abingdon; Old Palace Yard, Bicester, OX6 7AU; Elms Court,
Botley, Oxford; Bury Knowle Lib, North Pl, Headington,
Oxford, OX3 9HY; Station Rd, Chinnor; Goddards Lane, Chipp-
ing Norton, OX7 5NH; Mereland Rd, Didcot; Town Hall, Henley-
on-Thames, RG6 2AQ; 25 Oxford Rd, Kidlington, OX5 2BP;
Community Centre, Hilton Rd, Neithrop, Banbury; Northcourt
Rd, Abingdon; Redefield Lib, Blackbird Leys Rd, Oxford,
OX4 5HT; Grove Rd, Sonning Common, RG4 9RH; Summertown
Lib, South Parade, Oxford OX2 7JN; Temple Rd, Cowley, OX4
2EZ; Rookes Lane, Southern Rd, Thame, OX9 2DY; High
St, Wallingford; The Cloisters, Wantage.   **13** P-t 38;
mobiles 8.
14 Local history.   **15** 1; (a) 30, 397; (c) 5, 000; (e) £2 pa &
10p per record pw; (f) 5p pw.   **17** Schools, housebound,
prisons, hospitals, old people's homes, WEA classes.
19 Computer; token.   **20** 3 weeks (4 weeks on rural mobile
libs).   **21** (a) 2p 1st week, 5p 2nd week, 10p 3rd week, 5p
pw thereafter, max 50p (Rural mobile libraries 2p per visit,
max 50p); (b) 1p pw, max 10p; (c) none.   **23** (a) 676, 000;
(b) 34, 500; (c) 153, 000; (d) 196, 000; (e) 231.
24 (a) 4, 589, 405; (b) 1, 073, 958.
25 (a) 219; (b) 16; (c) 51; (d) 29.   **26** (a) £1, 215, 390;
(b) £31, 950; (c) £2. 27; (d) £289, 010; (e) £2, 780; (f) £600, 080.

PERTH AND KINROSS DISTRICT COUNCIL (pop 117, 911)
District Libraries, 7 Rose Terrace, Perth, Perthshire, PH1
5HE (0738-22318). District Libn: Mr A. A. Jeffress FLA;
Chief Asst: Mr M. C. G. Moir BA, ALA; Sandeman Libn: Mr
A. F. Bryce FLA.   **7** Leisure & Recreation.   **9** Mon-Fri:
9. 30-18. 00 (Fri 19. 00) (children's closed 12. 00-14. 00);
Sat: 9. 30-13. 00.
10 HQ; Branch:Mobile; Centre,   **12** Leslie St, Blairgowrie;
6 Comrie St, Crieff; Sandeman Lib, 16 Kinnoull St, Perth.
13 P-t 6; mobiles 2.
14 Perthshire colln; Atholl colln (music); Mackintosh colln;
Brough colln (fine arts).   **17** Schools (agency service);
housebound, prisons, hospitals, old people's homes.
19 Photo-charging (1 lib).   **20** 2-3 weeks (photo-charging
only).   **21** (a, b&c) none.   **23** (a) 241, 823; (b) c. 30, 000;
(c) 57, 663; (d) c. 50, 000.   **24** (a) 1, 002, 508; (b&c) 127, 773.
25 (a) 37; (b) 4½; (c) 9; (d) 3.   **26** (a) £216, 384; (b) £1, 850;
(c) £1. 92; (d) £70, 070; (f) £107, 639.

POWYS COUNTY COUNCIL (pop 100, 200) County Library
Headquarters, Cefnllys Rd, Llandrindod Wells, Powys, LD1
5LD (0597-2212). County Libn: Mr George Llewellyn FLA;
Dep County Libn: Miss Elizabeth Ducker ALA.   **7** Libraries
& Museums.   **9** Mon-Fri: 10. 00-17. 00 (2 eves 19. 00); Sat:
10. 00-12. 30
10 HQ; Area; Branch.   **11** **Area Libraries:** Brecon: Ship
St, Brecon, LD3 9AE, (0874-3346), Area Libn: Mr K. Jones
ALA; Montgomery: Park Lane, Newtown, SY16 1EJ (0686-
6934), Area Libn: Mr R. J. Hampson ALA; Radnor: County
Lib HQ, Cefnllys Rd, Llandrindod Wells, LD1 5LD, (0597-2212),
Area Libn: Mr R. M. Foulkes.   **12** The Cross, Newtown; Red

CODE: 1 Local authority. 2 Population. 3 Postal address of HQ. 4 Telephone & telex. 5 Chief Libn. 6 Deputy. 7 Committee responsible. 8 Officer to whom Libn is responsible (if any). 9 Hours. 10 Organisation. 11 Area libraries. 12 Branches. 13 Part-time libraries; mobiles. 14 Special collections. 15 Gramophone records: number of libraries, (a) record issues (b) cassette issues (c) record stock (d) cassette stock (e) loan charges (f) fines. 16 Pictures: stock; charges. 17 Other services. 18 Cultural activities (expenditure, officer in charge, staff: (a) officers (b) manual). 19 Issue method (if not Browne). 20 Loan period (if not 2 weeks). 21 Fines: (a) adult (b) children (c) OAPs. 22 Co-operative schemes. 23 Stock: (a) adult lending (b) adult reference (c) children (d) schools (e) current periodical titles. 24 Issues: (a) adult (b) children (c) schools (d) institutions. 25 Staff: (a) officers (b) manual (c) chartered libns (d) graduates. 26 Finance: (a) total expenditure (b) non-rate income (c) per capita expenditure (d) expenditure for books (e) expenditure for records etc (f) salaries & wages. 27 Capital projects.

POWYS COUNTY COUNCIL—*continued*
Bank, Salop Rd, Welshpool.   **13** P-t 20; mobiles 6.
14 Local history.   **15** 3; (a) 7,500; (c) 3,193; (d) 43; (e) none; (f) as books.   **17** Schools, housebound, hospitals, old people's homes.   **18** Art exhibitions.   **20** 3 weeks.
21 (a&c) 3p pw or part; (b) none.   **23** (a, b&c) 526,000; (d) 85,000; (e) 155.   **24** (a) 976,000; (b) 138,300.
25 (a) 51; (b) 8; (c) 10; (d) 9.   **26** (a) £264,094; (b) £43,494; (c) £2.635; (d) £57,145; (e) £1,150; (f) £145,150.

RENFREW DISTRICT COUNCIL (pop 207,800) Renfrew District Library Headquarters, Marchfield Ave, Paisley, Renfrewshire, PA3 2RJ (041-887 2468/9). Chief Libn: Mr Joseph D. Hendry FLA, FSA(Scot); Senior Dep: Mr James B. Hood ALA; Junior Dep: Mrs Barbara Ann Abernethy ALA.
7 Arts.   **9** No general pattern.
10 HQ; Branch.   **12** Glen St, Barrhead; Central Lib, High St, Paisley; Foxbar B Lib, Ivanhoe Rd, Paisley; Glenburn B Lib, Fairway Ave, Paisley; Houston Court, Johnstone; Ardlamont Sq, Town Centre, Linwood; Paisley Rd, Moorpark, Renfrew; Todholm B Lib, Lochfield Rd, Paisley.   **13** P-t 17.
15 9; (a) 57,088; (b) 3,558; (c) 8,235; (d) 620; (e) £1.00 (non-returnable deposit); (f) none.   **17** Schools, housebound, hospitals, old people's homes; convent.   **19** Plessey computer charging.   **20** 4 weeks.   **21** (a, b&c) none.
23 (a) 250,789; (b) 31,031; (c) 61,179; (e) 176.
24 (a) 1,498,242; (b) 298,982; (d) 12,314.
25 (a) 101; (b) 26; (c) 19; (d) 15.   **26** (a) £466,500; (b) £5,000; (c) £2.24; (d) £118,700; (e) £10,400; (f) £269,000.

RHONDDA BOROUGH COUNCIL (pop 87,100) Treorchy Library, Station Rd, Treorchy, Rhondda, Mid Glamorgan, CF42 6UA (044372-2204). Borough Libn: Miss E. Davies ALA; Senior Asst Libn: Miss S. Scott ALA.   **7** Recreation & Amenities.   **8** Chief Executive: Mr G. Evans IPFA.
9 Mon-Thurs: 9.30-17.15; Fri: 13.00-20.00; Sat: 9.00-12.00.
10 HQ; Branch.   **12** Treherbert B Lib; Ton Pentre B Lib; Tonypandy B Lib; Porth B Lib; Tylorstown B Lib; Ferndale B Lib.   **13** P-t 1.
14 Local history; music.   **15** 2; (a) 20,987; (c) 6,130; (e) £1 (refundable); (f) as books.   **17** Schools.   **20** 3 weeks.
21 (a&c) 3p pw or part; (b) 2p pw or part.   **23** (a, b&c) 167,385; (d) 49,694; (e) 120.   **24** (a) 475,256; (b) 76,810; (c) 16,855.
25 (a) 39; (b) 4; (c) 7; (d) 3.   **26** (a) £212,870; (b) £9,000; (c) £2.44; (d) £42,500; (e) £1,600; (f) £124,460.

ROCHDALE METROPOLITAN BOROUGH COUNCIL (pop 210,600) Libraries & Arts Headquarters, Council Offices, Wardle Rd, Rochdale, Lancashire, OL12 9ER (0706-46966; telex 635144). Dir of Libs & Arts Services: G. E. Thornber ALA; Dep Dir Libs & Arts Services: J. Milne FLA.
7 Recreation & Amenities.   **9** Mon-Fri: 9.30-20.00 (Tues & Fri 18.00) (Wed 17.00); Sat: 9.30-13.00, 14.00-16.00.
10 HQ; Area; Branch.   **11** Area Central Libraries: Heywood: Church St Heywood, OL10 1LL (0706-60947), Libn: P. G. Fish, BA, ALA; Middleton: Long St, Middleton, Manchester, M24 3DU (061-643 5228), Libn: D. L. Martin ALA, MIPM; Rochdale: Esplanade, Rochdale, OL16 1AQ (0706-47474), Libn: W. Moss BA, ALA.   **12** Alkrington B Lib, Kirkway, Middleton, Manchester; Balderstone B Lib, Balderstone Park, Rochdale; Castleton B Lib, Manchester Rd, Rochdale; Darnhill B Lib, Argyle Parade, Heywood; Langley B Lib, Windermere Rd, Middleton, Manchester; Harehill Park, Littleborough; Newhey Rd, Milnrow; Smallbridge B Lib, Stevenson Sq, Rochdale; Spotland B Lib, Ings Lane, Rochdale.

13 P-t 10.
14 Tim Bobbin (John Collier); local history for Heywood, Middleton, Rochdale.   **15** 2; (a) 16,804; (c) 4,246; (e) residents £1.50, non-residents £3.00; (f) as books.   **17** Schools, housebound, old people's homes, playgroups.   **18** Cultural activities, entertainments. (£189,700; Asst Dir, Arts & Entertainments; a 12; b 8).   **20** 29 days.   **21** (a&c) 2p pd; (b) 1p pw.   **23** (a) 305,871; (b) 29,822; (c) 83,753; (e) 405.
24 (a) 1,500,421; (b) 338,087; (d) 86,481.
25 (a) 107; (b) 26; (c) 26; (d) 5.   **26** (a) £649,900; (b) £53,100; (c) £3.09; (d) £89,750; (e) £1,250; (f) £334,400.

ROTHERHAM METROPOLITAN BOROUGH COUNCIL (pop 248,100) Howard St, Rotherham, South Yorkshire, S65 1JH (0709-65674; telex 54483). Dir of Libs, Museum & Arts: Mr Christopher Williams DMA, ALA; Dep Dir of Libs, Museum & Arts: Mr Antony Wilson.   **7** Libraries, Museum & Arts.   **9** Mon-Fri: ad ldg & ref 9.00-20.00 (Wed 13.00), children's 16.00-18.00 (Wed 9.00-13.00); Sat: 9.00-17.00.   **12** Broom Valley Rd, Rotherham; Laughton Rd, Dinnington, Sheffield; Coach Rd, Greasborough, Rotherham; F. J. Boardman B Lib, Browning Rd, Herringthorpe, Rotherham; High St, Kimberworth, Rotherham; Frances Green B Lib, Wheatey Rd, Kimberworth Park, Rotherham; Wales Rd, Kiveton Park, Sheffield; Percy Wright B Lib, Herringthorpe Valley Rd, Mowbray Gardens, Rotherham; Rawmarsh Hill, Parkgate, Rotherham; Station St, Swinton, Rotherham, Montgomery Rd, Wath, Rotherham.   **13** P-t 11; mobiles 3.
15 5; (a) 50,203; (b) 26,853; (c) 10,985; (d) 2,753; (e) 4p pw; (f) 8p pw.   **16** 1,682; 20p for 2 months, 25p for 3 months.
17 Schools, housebound, hospitals, old people's homes.
18 Cultural activities (£57,445; Arts Officer; a 3).
19 Photocharging (1 branch only).   **20** 3 weeks.
21 (a) 5p pw; (b&c) none.   **23** (a&b) 386,435; (c) 85,466; (d) 128,865; (e) 430.   **24** (a&b) 2,312,512; (c) 50,676; (d) 6,731.
25 (a) 113; (b) 15; (c) 26; (d) 18.   **26** (a) £848,005; (b) £27,435; (c) £3.42; (d) £184,165; (e) £10,195; (f) £355,985.

ST HELENS METROPOLITAN DISTRICT COUNCIL (pop 190,332) Central Library, Victoria Sq, St Helens, Merseyside, WA10 1DY (0744-24061; telex 627813). Dir of Libs, Museum & Arts: Mr G. K. Senior FLA; Dep Dir of Libs, Museum & Arts: Ms Hilda Nock FLA.   **7** Leisure & Recreation.
9 Mon-Fri: 10.00-19.00; Sat: 10.00-17.00 (13.00 at District Libs).
10 HQ; District.   **12** (District Libraries): Ashtons Green Dr, Ashtons Green, St Helens, WA9 2AP; Main St, Bilinge, Wigan; Broadway, Eccleston, St Helens; Four Acre Lib, Chester Lane, St Helens; Clipsley Lane, Haydock, St Helens; Haydock East Lib, Church Rd, Haydock, St Helens; Eskdale Ave, Moss Bank, St Helens; Carnegie Crescent, Sutton; Crow Lane East, Newton-Le-Willows; Thatto Heath Rd, St Helens; Newtown Lib, Horace St, St Helens; Parr Library, Chancery Lane, St Helens; Church Rd, Rainford; View Rd, Rainhill, Liverpool.   **13** P-t 1.
15 1; (a) 21,873; (c) 4,041; (e) £1 deposit; (f) as books.
17 Schools, housebound, hospitals, old people's homes, exchange colln at Vulcan Foundry.   **18** Cultural Activities (£8,214; Dir of Libs, Museum & Arts; a 3, b 2).   **20** 3 weeks.
21 (a) 2p pw or part; (b&c) none.   **23** (a) 173,401; (b) 26,422; (c) 35,723; (e) 183.   **24** (a) 395,643; (b) 95,436; (c) 7,000; (d) 1,173.
25 (a) 96; (b) 4 (& cleaners); (c) 27; (d) 4.
26 (a) £516,445; (b) £8,128; (c) £2.72; (d) £104,550; (e) £2,650; (f) £275,381.

SALFORD CITY COUNCIL (pop 288,000) Cultural Services Dept, Civic Offices, Astley Rd, Irlam, Manchester, M30 5LL (061-775 3981; telex 669800). Cultural Services Manager: M.W. Devereux FLA.   **7** Cultural Services.   **9** Mon-Fri: 9.00-19.00 (or 20.00) (Wed or Thurs 13.00); Sat: 9.00-13.00 (or 17.00).
10 HQ; Area; District; Branch.   **11 Areas:** Eccles & Irlam: Central Lib, Church St, Eccles, Manchester M30 0EP (061-789 1430) Area Libn: Mr A. Jones ALA; Swinton & Worsley: Central Lib, Chorley Rd, Swinton, Manchester, M27 2AF (061-794 7449) Area Libn: Mrs M. Roberts; Salford: Central Lib, Peel Park, Salford, Manchester (061-736 4246) Area Libn: Mr B. Kelly ALA.   **12** Height B Lib, King St, Salford, M6 7GY; Charlestown B Lib, Cromwell Rd, Salford, M6 6SR; Langworthy B Lib, Chadesworthy House, Eccles New Rd, Salford 5; Broughton District Lib, 400-404 Bury New Rd, Salford, M7 0EA; Ordsall District Lib, Tatton St, Salford, 5; Winton B Lib, Parrin Lane, Eccles, M28 4PB; Peel Green District Lib, Liverpool Rd, Peel Green, Eccles; Hope B Lib, Eccles Old Rd, Salford, M6 8FH; Worsley Village B Lib, Worsley Court House, Worsley Rd, Worsley, M28 4PB; Irlam District Lib, Hurst Fold, Liverpool Rd, Irlam, M30 6FF; Cadishead B Lib, 126 Liverpool Rd, Cadishead, M30 5BY; Walkden District Lib, Memorial Rd, Walkden, Worsley, M28 5AQ; Little Hulton B Lib, Longshaw Dr, Little Hulton, Worsley, M28 6BA.   **13** P-t 6; mobiles 1.
14 Ghosh; Trinity; Cowan; Davies; Nasmyth; Brighouse; Chess; Lowry; Lancastrian pottery.   **15** 3; (a) 27,768; (c) 4,582; (e) £1.00 deposit; (f) 1p pd.   **16** 310; charges as for records.   **17** Schools, housebound, old people's homes.   **18** Cultural activities, entertainments (£5,000; Asst Manager (Admin & Cultural Activities); a 1).   **19** Islington (1 lib).   **20** 4 weeks.   **21** (a) 1p pd, max £1.00; (b&c) none.   **23** (a) 411,185; (b) 71,948; (c) 86,558; (d) 212,863; (e) 211.   **24** (a) 1,786,619; (b) 353,358; (d) 23,096.   **25** (a) 148; (b) 25½; (c) 30; (d) 7.   **26** (a) £747,710; (b) £52,670; (c) £2.60; (d) £149,300; (e) £3,950; (f) £437,400.

SANDWELL METROPOLITAN BOROUGH COUNCIL (pop 316,300) Central Library, High St, West Bromwich, West Midlands, B70 8DZ (021-569 2325; telex 338392). Borough Libn: Mr R.B. Ludgate ALA; Chief Asst Libns: Miss A.M. Price ALA; Miss M.J. Higgs ALA, JP.   **7** Libraries & Museums Sub-Committee.   **8** Dir of Education: Mr G.A. Brinsdon MA.   **9** Mon-Fri: 9.00-19.00 (Branches close 13.00-14.00); Sat: 9.00-17.00 (Branches close 13.00-14.00).
10 Central; District; Branch.   **11 District Libraries:** Central Lib, High St, West Bromwich, B70 8DZ (021-569 2325), Libn: Mrs R.J. Bailey ALA; Langley: Barrs St, Oldbury, Warley, B68 8QT (021-552 1680) Libn: Mr A. Blakeway ALA; Smethwick: High St, Smethwick, Warley, B66 1AB (021-558 0497), Libn: Miss R.J. Armstrong ALA; Tipton: Victoria Rd, Tipton, DY4 8SR (021-557 1796), Libn: Mrs O.T. Herbert FLA; Wednesbury: Walsall St, Wednesbury, WS10 9EH (021-556 0351), Libn: Mr A.R. Billington ALA.   **12** Blackheath B Lib, Carnegie Rd, Rowley Regis, Warley, B65 8BY; Bleakhouse Rd, Oldbury, Warley, B68 9DS; Brandhall B Lib, Tame Rd, Oldbury, Warley, B68 0JT; Charlemont Farm B Lib, Beacon View Rd, West Bromwich; Upper High St, Cradley Heath, Warley, B64 5JU; Glebefields B Lib, St Mark's Rd, Tipton, DY4 0SZ; Birmingham Rd, Great Barr, Birmingham, B43 6NW; Sheepwash Lane, Great Bridge, Tipton; Hamstead B Lib, Broome Ave, Great Barr, Birmingham, B43 5AL; Oakham B Lib, Poplar Rise, Tividale, Warley, B69 1RD; Municipal Buildings, Oldbury, Warley, B69 2AB; Rounds Green B Lib, Martley Rd, Oldbury, Warley, B69 1DZ; Beverley Rd, Stone Cross, West Bromwich, B71 2LH; Thimblemill Rd, Smethwick, Warley, B67 5RJ; Toll End Rd, Tipton, DY4 0HE; West Smethwick Shopping Precinct, Oldbury Rd, Smethwick, Warley, B66 1JQ; Windmill Precinct, Smethwick, Warley, B66 3QX; Yew Tree B Lib, Redwood Rd, Walsall, WS5 4LB.   **13** P-t 1; mobiles 2.
14 Local studies; Sandwell pictorial record; archives; maps; slides; books in Hindi, Urdu & Punjabi.   **15** 1; (a) 20,135; (c) 4,400; (e) 3p per record, non-residents 55p pa; (f) as books.   **16** 150.   **17** Schools, housebound, prisons, old people's homes.   **18** Cultural activities, entertainments (£20,000, Borough Libn, a 5, b 1).   **20** 4 weeks.   **21** (a) 10p pw or part; (b&c) none.   **22** MISLIC; WESLINK; Association of West Midlands Metropolitan District Chief

Librarians.   **23** (a&c) 834,196; (b) 46,608; (d) 5,326; (e) 379.   **24** (a) 2,468,816; (b) 804,970; (c) 9,763.   **25** (a) 152; (b) 17¼; (c) 24; (d) 5.   **26** (a) £683,170; (b) £23,460; (c) £2.10; (d) £175,507; (e) £1,400; (f) £377,690.

SEFTON METROPOLITAN BOROUGH COUNCIL (pop 306,300) Bootle Library, Oriel Rd, Bootle, Merseyside, L20 7AG (051-922-4040 ext 245).   Libn & Arts Services Officer: A.R. Hardman FLA, FRSA.   **7** Libraries & Arts.   **9** Mon-Fri: 10.00-19.30; Sat: 10.00-17.00.
10 HQ; Area.   **11 Areas:** South: Crosby Lib, Crosby Rd North, L22 0LQ (051-928 6487), Libn: Mr J.A. Miller FLA; North: Atkinson Lib, Lord St, Southport, PR8 1DJ (0704-33133 ext 223), Area Libn: Mr J.R. Livesey FLA.   **12** Liverpool Ave, Ainsdale, Southport, PR8 3NE; 240-244 Liverpool Rd, Birkdale, Southport, PR8 4PD; Mill Lane, Churchtown, Southport, PR9 7PL; Duke St, Formby, L37 4AN; Altway, Aintree, Liverpool, L10; College Rd, Crosby, Liverpool, L23 3DP; Pendle Dr, Ford, Liverpool, L21 0HY; Litherland Lib, Linacre Rd, Liverpool, L21 6NR; Liverpool Rd North, Maghull, L31 2HJ; The Marian Way, Netherton, L30 3TQ; Orrell Lib, Linacre Rd, Bootle, L20 6ES; 128-130 Peel Rd, Bootle, L20 4LB; Crescent Rd, Seaforth, Liverpool, L21 4LJ.   **13** P-t 3; mobiles 3.
14 Local history; battle of Waterloo; cinema; motor manuals.   **15** 2; (a) 66,344; (b) 8,826; (c) 8,367; (d) 990; (e) residents no charge (£1 for special carrying case), non-residents £2 pa; (f) as books.   **17** Schools, housebound, hospitals, old people's homes.   **18** Cultural activities (Librarian & Arts Services Officer; a 4, b 6).   **19** Photo-charging (Crosby); token (fiction only, North Area).   **20** 4 weeks.   **21** (a&c) 4p pw or part; (b) 1p per 2 days.   **23** (a) 459,000; (b) 76,000; (c) 107,000; (d) 85,000; (e) 167.   **24** (a) 3,580,354; (b) 559,453; (c) 1,071,000.   **25** (a) 145; (b) 42½; (c) 54; (d) 16.   **26** (a) £774,630 (net); (b) £82,320; (c) £2.53; (d) £140,140; (e) £4,520; (f) £441,160.

SHEFFIELD METROPOLITAN DISTRICT COUNCIL (pop 565,500) Sheffield City Libraries, Central Library, Surrey St, Sheffield, S1 1XZ (0742-734711/3; telex 54243).   Dir of Libs: Mr R.F. Atkins FLA; Dep Dir of Libs: Mr D.W. Bromley FLA.   **7** Libraries & Arts.   **9** Mon-Fri: ad ldg 10.00-20.00, ref 9.00-21.00, children's 10.00-20.00 (Tues, Wed, Thurs 18.00); Sat: ad ldg & children's 9.30-16.30, ref 9.00-20.30.
10 HQ; Area; Branch.   **11 Areas:** Hillsborough: Middlewood Rd, Hillsborough, S6 4HD (0742-343757), Area Libn: Mr A.E. Speight ALA; Greenhill: Highfield House, 20 St Barnabas Rd, Greenhill, S2 4TF (0742-56582), Area Libn: Miss B. Padley ALA; Manor: Ridgeway Rd, Manor, S12 2SS (0742-399044), Area Libn: Mr G. Robson FLA; Firth Park: Firth Park Rd, Firth Park, S5 6WS (0742-386490), Area Libn: Mr A.E. Woodroffe ALA; Mobile & Special Services: 443 Handsworth Rd, Sheffield, S13 9DD (0742-695633), Div Officer: Mr I. Vincent ALA.   **12** Leeds Rd, Attercliffe, S9 3TS; Taptonville Rd, Broomhill, S10 5BR; Gower St, Burngreave, S4 7HA; Lound Side, Chapeltown, S30 4UN; Ecclesall Rd South, Ecclesall, S11 9PL; Smalldale Rd, Frecheville, S12 4YD; White Lane, Gleadless, S12 3GH; 12 Four Wells Dr, Hackenthorpe, S12 4JB; Hall Rd, Handsworth, S13 9AG; Blackstock Rd, Hemsworth, S14 1FX; London Rd, Highfield, S2 4NF; 15 Jordanthorpe Centre, Jordanthorpe, S8 8DX; Barnsley Rd, Lane Top, S5 0QF; Gleadless Rd, Newfield Green, S2 2BT; Duke St, Park, S2 5QP; Parson Cross, Margetson Crescent, S5 9NP; Moonshine Lane, Southey, S5 8RB; Manchester Rd, Stocksbridge, S30 5DH; Bawtry Rd, Tinsley, S9 1UE; 205 Baslow Rd, Totley, S17 4DT; Upperthorpe, S6 3GA; South Rd, Walkley, S6 3TD; Tannery St, Woodhouse, S13 7JU; Chesterfield Rd, Woodseats, S8 0SH.   **13** P-t 8; mobiles 5 & 1 travelling lib.
14 Wentworth Woodhouse, Arundel, Spencer Stanhope (mss); Carpenter (Edward) Library; Fairbank colln (draft plans, surveying books etc.); Jackson Antiquaries; private press books; foreign specifications & standards (iron & steel).   **15** 1; (a) 99,295; (c) 17,692; (d) 948; (e) £1.50; (f) 5p pw.   **17** Schools, housebound, hospitals, old people's homes, WEA.   **18** Cultural activities.   **19** Plessey Light Pen (1 lib).   **20** 3 weeks.   **21** (a&c) 5p pw; (b) none.   **22** SINTO; Sheffield Media Resources Organising Committee.

CODE: 1 Local authority. 2 Population. 3 Postal address of HQ. 4 Telephone & telex. 5 Chief Libn. 6 Deputy. 7 Committee responsible. 8 Officer to whom Libn is responsible (if any). 9 Hours. 10 Organisation. 11 Area libraries. 12 Branches. 13 Part-time libraries; mobiles. 14 Special collections. 15 Gramophone records: number of libraries, (a) record issues (b) cassette issues (c) record stock (d) cassette stock (e) loan charges (f) fines. 16 Pictures: stock; charges. 17 Other services. 18 Cultural activities (expenditure, officer in charge, staff: (a) officers (b) manual). 19 Issue method (if not Browne). 20 Loan period (if not 2 weeks). 21 Fines: (a) adult (b) children (c) OAPs. 22 Co-operative schemes. 23 Stock: (a) adult lending (b) adult reference (c) children (d) schools (e) current periodical titles. 24 Issues: (a) adult (b) children (c) schools (d) institutions. 25 Staff: (a) officers (b) manual (c) chartered libns (d) graduates. 26 Finance: (a) total expenditure (b) non-rate income (c) per capita expenditure (d) expenditure for books (e) expenditure for records etc (f) salaries & wages. 27 Capital projects.

SHEFFIELD METROPOLITAN DISTRICT COUNCIL—*continued*
23 (a) 734, 697; (b) 265, 714; (c) 208, 040; (d) 394, 909; (e) 1, 658.
24 (a) 4, 403, 276; (b) 1, 116, 842; (c) 1, 031, 983; (d) 173, 641.
25 (a) 318½; (b) 78; (c) 81; (d) 26.　　**26** (a) £1, 807, 400;
(b) £181, 000; (c) £3. 22; (d) £433, 000; (e) £4, 500; (f) £989, 900.

SHETLAND ISLANDS COUNCIL (pop c. 18, 623) County Library Headquarters, Lower Hillhead, Lerwick, Shetland, ZE1 0EL (0595-3868; telex 75218). County Libn: Mr George W. Longmuir FLA; Dep: Miss A. M. Sutherland ALA.　　7 Education.
8 Dir of Education: Mr R. A. B. Barnes MA, DipEd.
9 Mon-Fri: 10.00-13.00, 14.30-17.00 (Mon, Weds, Fri 18.00-20.00), (closed Thurs afternoon); Sat: 10.00-13.00, 14.30-17.00.
10 HQ.　　**13** P-t 1; mobiles 2.
14 Shetland local colln; Icelandic saga literature; Faroese colln.　　**15** 1; (a) 1, 747; (c) 1, 050; (e) £1.00 deposit.
16 300; £1.00 deposit per print.　　**17** Hospitals, old people's homes, playschool groups, service units.　　**23** (a) c. 50, 000; (b) c. 5, 000; (c&d) c. 17, 000; (e) 40.　　**24** (a) 222, 000; (b) 30, 000; (c) 20, 000; (d) 3, 000.
25 (a) 9; (b) 2; (c) 2.

SHROPSHIRE COUNTY COUNCIL (pop 357, 000) Shropshire County Library, Column House, 7 London Rd, Shrewsbury, Shropshire SY2 6NW (0743-52561; telex 35187). County Libn: Miss O. S. Newman FLA; Dep County Libn: Mr A. J. Crowe FLA.　　7 Leisure Activities.　　9 Mon-Fri: 9.30-19.30; Sat: 9.30-17.00.
10 HQ; Area; Branch; Trailer.　　**11 Areas:** Caldecott Lib, High St, Whitchurch, SY13 1EE (0948-2238; telex 35188), Area Libn: Miss E. Daniel BA, ALA; Shrewsbury Public Lib, Castle Gates, Shrewsbury, SY1 2AS (0743-59503/54876), Area Libn: Mr A. L. Marsh ALA; Listley St, Bridgnorth, WV16 4AW (07462-3358; telex 338886), Area Libn: Mr A. P. MacNaughtan ALA; 10 Old St, Ludlow, SY8 1NP (0584-2619; telex 35189), Area Libn: Mr Webb ALA; Arthur St, Oswestry, SY11 1JN (0691-3211; telex 35234), Area Libn: Mr W. Walpole ALA; 23 Walker St, Wellington, Telford, TF1 1BD (082347-44013), Area Libn: Mr M. F. Donnelly ALA.　　**12** Station Rd, Albrighton, Wolverhampton, Staffordshire, WV7 3QH; Mary Webb Lib, Lythwood Rd, Bayston Hill, Shrewsbury, SY3 0NA; Church St, Church Stretton, SY6 6DQ; King St, Dawley, Telford; Turreff Ave, Donnington, Telford; 10 Gladstone House, High St, Hadley, Telford; Meadow Farm Dr, Harlescott, Shrewsbury; 21 Russell Sq, Madeley, Telford; Clive Lib, Cheshire St, Market Drayton, TF9 1PH; 137 High St, Newport; 3-4 Limes Walk, Oakengates, Telford; Broadway, Shifnal, TF11 8AZ; Community Centre, Sutton Hill, Telford.　　**13** P-t 15; mobiles 6.
14 Parochial libraries (10, 000); local history; music library; creative writing (West Midlands colln); UK statistics.
15 13; (a) 14, 055; (c) 7, 000; (e) £3.15 (inc VAT) pa.
16 60; 50p for 3 months.　　**17** Schools, housebound, prisons, old people's homes.　　**18** Cultural activities (£1, 100; Area Libns & Display Artist).　　**19** Camera Issue method; Olivetti Computer issue.　　**20** 3 weeks.　　**21** (a&c) 1p pd 1st week, 2p pd thereafter; after 4 weeks, 1p per service day, after 5 weeks, 2p per service day; (b) none.　　**22** WESLINK.
23 (a&b) 533, 755; (c) 130, 289; (d) 125, 857; (e) 270.
24 (a&b) 3, 198, 416; (d) c. 12, 500.
25 (a) 127; (b) 21; (c) 37; (d) 15.　　**26** (a) £651, 680;
(b) £19, 190; (c) £1.83; (d) £169, 790; (e) £2, 000; (f) £337, 400.

SOLIHULL METROPOLITAN BOROUGH COUNCIL (pop 200, 000) Central Library, Church Hill Rd, Solihull, West Midlands, B91 3RG (021-705 1838/6447). Chief Libn: J. W.

Lendon FLA; Dep Chief Libn: B. J. Chase FLA.　　7 Education.
8 Dir of Education: D. B. Love LLB.　　9 Mon-Fri: Chelmsley Wood 9.30-19.00 (ref 20.00), Solihull 10.00-18.30 (Fri 20.00); Sat: Chelmsley Wood 9.30-17.00, Solihull 9.00-17.00.
10 HQ; Area; Branch.　　**11 Areas:** Central Lib, Church Hill Rd, Solihull, West Midlands, B91 3RG (021-705 1838/6447), Libn: G. Mustoe FRSA, FLA; Chelmsley Wood Lib, Stephenson Dr, Chelmsley Wood, Birmingham, B37 5TA (021-770 5551), Libn: N. P. Guy ALA.　　**12** Hobs Moat Lib, Ulleries Rd, Solihull, B92 8EB; Church Rd, Shirley, Solihull, B90 2AX; 48 St John's Way, Knowle, Solihull, B93 0LE; Olton Lib, 183-185 Warwick Rd, Solihull, B92 7AW; Hurst Lane North, Castle Bromwich, Birmingham, B36 0EY; Marston Dr, Kingshurst, Birmingham, B37 6BD.　　**13** P-t 4; mobiles 2.
15 1; (a) 806; (c) 400; (e) 50p pa + 10p per record; (f) 2p pd.
17 Schools, housebound, hospitals, old people's homes.
19 Photocharging; Plessey Library Pen System.　　**20** 4 weeks.　　**21** (a) 2p pd; (b&c) none.　　**22** WMRLB; WESLINK.
23 (a) 205, 363; (b) 10, 634; (c) 79, 018; (d) 61, 613; (e) 307.
24 (a) 1, 683, 797; (b) 440, 932; (c) 8, 002; (d) old people's homes 7, 200.
25 (a) 105; (b) 1; (c) 27; (d) 10.　　**26** (a) £580, 800;
(b) £28, 100; (c) £2.89; (d) £103, 300; (e) £600; (f) £263, 110.
27 New Central Library & Theatre, started 1974, completion Sept 1976, £1, 800, 000.

SOMERSET COUNTY COUNCIL (pop 403, 000) County Library Headquarters, Mount St, Bridgwater, Somerset, TA6 3ES (0278-51201/4). County Libn: Mr C. R. Eastwood FLA; Dep County Libn: Mr Roy J. Collis ALA, DMA.　　7 Education & Cultural Services.　　9 No general pattern.
10 Ad hoc area organisation.　　**11 Areas:** Binford Pl, Bridgwater, TA6 3LF (0278-2597), Libn: Mr G. Mort FLA; Boden St, Chard, TA20 2AX (04606-3321), Libn: Mr M. G. Ball ALA; Scott Rd, Frome, BA11 1AL (0373-2215), Libn: Mrs S. A. Bane ALA; 1 Leigh Rd, Street, BA16 0HA (045 84-2032), Libn: Miss P. J. Haydon ALA; Corporation St, Taunton, TA1 4AN (0823-84077), Libn: Mr J. Morley FLA; Union St, Wells, BA5 2PU (0749-72292), Libn: Miss J. K. F. Swinyard; Area Lib Office, 4 Priest St, Williton, TA4 4NJ (09843-740), Libn: Mrs J. M. Stephens ALA; 7 Carrington Way, Wincanton, BA9 9JS (09633-32173), Libn: Mrs G. J. Norman BA, ALA; King George St, Yeovil, BA20 1PY (0935-3144), Libn: Mr K. L. Plumridge ALA.　　**12** Adam St, Burnham-on-Sea, TA8 1PG; Council Offices, Crewkerne; 19 Northload St, Glastonbury; Local History Lib, Taunton Castle, Taunton, TA1 4AD; Eastwick Rd, Taunton, TA2 7HD; 16 Fore St, Wellington, TA21 8AQ; 22 High St, Shepton Mallet, BA4 5AN; Bancks St, Minehead, TA24 5DJ.
13 P-t 17; mobiles 12.
14 Early children's books (1, 200); Laurence Housman colln (Street).　　**15** 1 (Taunton); (a) 28, 854; (c) 4, 481.　　**16** 370.
17 Schools, housebound, prisons, mental hospitals, old people's homes, WEA, music & drama.　　**18** Cultural activities (Area Libns).　　**20** 4 weeks.　　**21** (a&c) 5p pw, max 25p; (b) none.　　**22** SWRLB.　　**23** (a&b) 603, 294; (c) 99, 406.
24 (a&d) 4, 165, 464.
25 (a) 144; (b) 31; (c) 37; (d) 3.　　**26** (a) £763, 053;
(b) £20, 918; (c) £1.89; (d) £156, 936; (e) £1, 500; (f) £430, 096.

SOUTH GLAMORGAN COUNTY COUNCIL (pop 394, 600) Central Library, The Hayes, Cardiff, CF1 2QU (0222-22116; telex 497416). County Libn: G. A. C. Dart FLA; Dep County Libn: P. D. John ALA.　　7 Libraries.　　9 Mon-Fri: ad ldg, ref 9.30-18.30 (or 19.00), ref 9.30-20.00; Sat 9.00-17.30.
10 HQ; District; Branch.　　**11 Districts:** City of Cardiff: Central Lib, The Hayes, Cardiff, CF1 2QU (0222-22116),

SOUTH GLAMORGAN COUNTY COUNCIL—*continued*
County Libn; Borough of Vale of Glamorgan: Central Lib, King Sq, Barry, Dep County Libn. **12** Cathays Branch, Whitchurch Rd/Fairoak Rd, Cardiff; Roath Branch, Newport Rd/Four Elms Rd, Cardiff; Canton Branch, Cowbridge Rd/Library St, Cardiff; Grangetown Branch, Clive St/Redlaver St, Cardiff; Splott Branch, Singleton Rd/Hinton St, Cardiff; Gabalfa Branch, 213 North Rd, Cardiff; Ely Branch, Grand Ave/Pendine Rd, Cardiff; Roath Park Branch, Penylan Rd/Ninian Rd, Cardiff; Fairwater Branch, Doyle Ave/Fairwater Rd, Cardiff; Llanrumney Branch, Countisbury Ave, Cardiff; Rhydypennau Branch, Llandennis Rd, Cardiff; Trelai Branch, Heol Ebwy/Bishopston Rd, Cardiff; Llandaff North Branch, College Rd/Gabalfa Ave, Cardiff; Whitchurch Branch, Park Rd/Velindre Rd, Cardiff; Rhiwbina Branch, Pen-y-dre, Heol-y-Deri, Cardiff; Rumney Branch, Brachdy Rd/Wentloog Rd, Cardiff; Llanedeyrn Branch, 74 Maelfa, Cardiff; Trowbridge Branch, 26 Abergele Rd, Cardiff; Penarth, Stanwell Rd, Vale of Glamorgan; Llantwit Major, Boverton Rd, Vale of Glamorgan; Cowbridge, Old Hall Complex, Vale of Glamorgan; Dinas Powis, The Murch, Vale of Glamorgan. **13** P-t 12; mobiles 3.
14 Welsh (c. 80,000 vols); research & mss (4,000 mss, 3,500 deeds & documents); incunabula (129); fine press books. **15** 2; (a&b) 42,760; (c) 6,950; (d) 354; (e) £2.25 pa, £3.50 for 2 records; (f) 2p pd. **16** c. 100,000. **17** Schools, housebound, prisons, hospitals, old people's homes, lightships, lighthouses. **21** (a) 1p 1st day, 3p pw (1st-5th weeks), 4p pw (6th-10th weeks), 5p (11th week), max 40p; (b) 1p pw, max 11p; (c) discretionary. **23** (a) 590,000; (b) 340,000; (c) 120,000; (e) 792. **24** (a) 3,608,605; (b) 400,000; (d) 78,975.
25 (a) 189; (b) 40; (c) 34; (d) 2. **26** (a) £920,745; (b) £32,015; (c) £2.3; (d) £221,000; (e) £4,300; (f) £504,840. **27** New Central Library, Cardiff.

SOUTH TYNESIDE METROPOLITAN DISTRICT COUNCIL (pop 180,000) South Tyneside Libraries, Central Library, Ocean Rd, South Shields, Tyne & Wear, NE33 2JA (08943-4321 ext 36). Asst Dir of Culture & Leisure Activities: Mr R. Hill ALA; Chief Asst Libn: Mr A. Bishop ALA. **7** Cultural & Leisure Activities. **9** Mon-Fri: ad ldg & ref 10.00-19.00, children's: term 10.00-11.30, 16.00-19.00, vac 10.00-19.00; Sat: ad ldg & ref 10.00-17.00, children's 10.00-13.00, 14.30-17.00.
10 HQ; Branch. **12** Boldon B Lib, Back Western Terrace, East Boldon; Boldon Lane, South Shields; Cleadon Park B Lib, Sunderland Rd, South Shields; Station Rd, Hebburn; Cambrian St, Jarrow; Glasgow Rd, Primrose, Jarrow; Mill Lane, Whitburn. **13** P-t 3.
14 Local history; photographs of South Shields & district. **17** Schools, housebound, old people's homes, day centre, hostels, children's homes. **18** Cultural activities, entertainments (£1,413,160, Dir of Cultural & Leisure Activities, a 96, b 69). **20** 4 weeks. **21** (a) ½p pd; (b&c) none. **23** (a) 96,547; (b) 25,000; (c) 7,162; (d) 13,640; (e) 102. **24** (a) 418,571; (b) 25,627; (c) 13,437; (d) 1,160. **25** (a) 61; (b) 10; (c) 18. **26** (a) £456,550 (libs only); (b) £44,900; (c) £2.54; (d) £75,000; (f) £166,440.

STAFFORDSHIRE COUNTY COUNCIL (pop 984,620) County Library Headquarters, Friars Terrace, Stafford, ST17 4AY (0785-53653; telex 36255). County Libn: Mr S. Barton FLA; Dep County Libn: Mr L. J. Livesey FLA; Asst County Libn: Mr G. Bradley FLA. **7** Libraries, Records & Museums. **9** Mon-Fri: 9.30-19.00; Sat: 9.30-17.00.
10 HQ; Area; Branch. **11 Area HQs:** Cannock Chase: Cannock Lib, Manor Ave, Cannock, WS11 1AA (05435-2019/71114; telex 338850), Principal Area Libn: Mr R. H. Whiting MA, ALA; East: Burton Lib, Union St, Burton upon Trent, DE14 1AH (0283-3042/44996; telex 341737), Principal Area Libn: Mr K. F. Stanesby FLA; Lichfield: Lichfield Lib, Bird St, Lichfield, WS13 6PN (05432-22177), Principal Area Libn: Mr T. M. Rogers ALA; Newcastle-under-Lyme: Newcastle Lib, Ironmarket, Newcastle, ST5 1AT (0785-618125; telex 36123), Principal Area Libn: Miss A. England ALA; South: Brewood Lib, Newport St, Brewood, Stafford, ST19 9DT (0902-850087), Dep Area Libn: Mr G. L. King FLA; Stafford: Stafford Lib, The Green Stafford, ST17 4BJ (0785-2151), Principal Area

Libn: Mr H. Doyson ALA; Staffordshire Moorlands: Leek Lib, Nicholson Institute, Leek, ST13 6DW (05382-382615), Dep Area Libn: Miss E. Jerram ALA; Stoke-on-Trent: City Centre Lib, Bethesda St, Hanley, Stoke-on-Trent, ST1 3RS (0782-25108/263568/23187/21242/23122; telex 36132), Principal Area Libn: Mr V. Tyrrell ALA; Tamworth: Tamworth Lib, Corporation St, Tamworth, B79 7DW (0827-53244/5), Principal Area Libn: Mr C. H. Williams ALA, AMBIM. **12** Main Rd, Brereton, Rugeley; Hednesford Rd, Heath Hayes, Cannock; Anglesey Crescent, Hednesford; Burntwood Rd, Norton Canes, Cannock; Anson St, Rugeley; Red Gables, High St, Uttoxeter; Sankey's Corner, Chase Terrace, Walsall; Main St, Shenstone, Lichfield; Deer Park Rd, Fazeley, Tamworth, B78 3SY; St Matthews Hospital, Burntwood, Walsall; Hall St, Audley, Stoke-on-Trent, ST7 8BD; Community Centre, London Rd, Chesterton, Newcastle; Dartmouth Ave, Clayton, Newcastle; Meadows Rd, Kidsgrove, ST7 1BS; High St, Silverdale, Newcastle; Chester Rd, Talke Pits, Stoke-on-Trent, ST7 1SW; Bradwell Lodge, Bradwell Lane, Wolstanton, Newcastle, ST5 8PS; High St, Cheslyn Hay, Walsall, WS6 7AE; Histon's Hill, Codsall, Wolverhampton, WV8 1AA; Johns Lane, Great Wyrley, Walsall, WS6 6BY; Bell Brook, Penkridge, Stafford, ST19 5DL; Windmill Bank, Wombourne, Wolverhampton, WV5 9JD; High St, Stone, ST15 8AT; High St, Eccleshall, Stafford, ST21 6BZ; Holmcroft Rd, Stafford, ST16 1JG; Stafford South Lib, Merrey Rd, Stafford, ST17 9LX; Baswich Lib, Lynton Ave, Stafford, ST17 0EA; Tunstall Rd, Biddulph, Stoke-on-Trent, ST8 6HH; Uttoxeter Rd, Blythe Bridge, Stoke-on-Trent, ST11 9JR; Leek Rd, Cheadle, Stoke-on-Trent, ST10 1JF; Ash Bank Rd, Werrington, Stoke-on-Trent, ST9 0JS; Wedgwood Institute, Queen St, Burslem, Stoke-on-Trent, ST6 3EF; Baker St, Fenton, Stoke-on-Trent, ST4 3AF; Sutherland Institute, Lightwood Rd, Longton, Stoke-on-Trent, ST3 4HY; London Rd, Stoke-on-Trent, ST4 7QE; Victoria Institute, The Boulevard, Tunstall, Stoke-on-Trent, ST6 6BD; Caledonian, Glascote, Tamworth, B77 2ED. **13** P-t 25; mobiles 12.
14 Staffordshire history; Esperanto; Samuel Johnson; music scores; pottery. **15** 27; (a) 70,802; (b) 105; (c) 32,500; (d) 252; (e) 10p per record (4 weeks); (f) 3p pw. **16** 787; reproductions 27p, originals 55p for 3 months; fines: 5p pw or part. **17** Schools, housebound, prisons, hospitals, old people's homes, adult classes, adult illiterates. **19** Photocharging; computer (Olivetti). **20** 4 weeks. **21** (a, b&c) 2p pw (children & OAP's not charged if returned before 1st notice). **22** LINOSCO; MISLIC. **23** (a, b&c) c. 2,214,051; (d) 552,130. **24** (a&b) 8,578,251; (d) 262,906. **25** (a) 427; (b) 66; (c) 95; (d) 29. **26** (a) £2,054,045; (b) £59,850; (c) £2.08; (d) £424,475; (e) £8,000; (f) £1,155,500.

STIRLING DISTRICT LIBRARY (pop 75,000) Administrative Headquarters, Stirling District Library, Spittal St, Stirling, Stirlingshire, FK8 1DY (0786-64127/9). District Libn: Miss C. E. Morrice ALA; Chief Asst (Branches & Mobiles): Mr Hugh Ferguson ALA. **7** Leisure & Recreation. **9** No general pattern.
10 Administrative HQ; Central; Branch. **11 Central Library:** Corn Exchange Rd, Stirling, FK8 2HX (0786-3969). **12** Bannockburn; Bridge of Allan; Dunblane. **13** P-t 7; mobiles 2.
14 Local history (Admin HQ & Central); Scottish history (Central). **17** Housebound, prisons, old people's homes, playgroups, family book service. **21** (a, b&c) none (for trial period). **22** Proposed inter-district loans within Central Region. **23** (a) 201,838; (b) 7,119; (c) 29,009; (e) 90.
25 (a) 44; (b) 2; (c) 11; (d) 2. **26** (a) £247,645; (c) £3.30; (d) £55,780; (f) £133,320. **27** Combined Administrative Headquarters & Central Library Building.

STOCKPORT METROPOLITAN BOROUGH COUNCIL (pop 296,554) Dept of Culture, Torkington Lodge, Torkington Rd, Hazel Grove, Stockport, Cheshire, SK7 4QP (061-483 1234; telex 667184 Central Library). Asst Dir of Culture: R. E. G. Smith FLA. **7** Recreation & Culture. **8** Dir of Recreation & Culture Division: H. Hitchcock IPFA, FRVA, MInstRM. **9** Mon-Fri: 9.00-20.00 (Branches 10.00-20.00); Sat: 9.00-17.00 (Branches 10.00-17.00).
10 HQ; Area; Branch. **11 Areas:** North: Central Lib, Wellington Rd South, Stockport, SK1 3RS (061-480 2966/

CODE: 1 Local authority. 2 Population. 3 Postal address of HQ. 4 Telephone & telex. 5 Chief Libn. 6 Deputy. 7 Committee responsible. 8 Officer to whom Libn is responsible (if any). 9 Hours. 10 Organisation. 11 Area libraries. 12 Branches. 13 Part-time libraries; mobiles. 14 Special collections. 15 Gramophone records: number of libraries, (a) record issues (b) cassette issues (c) record stock (d) cassette stock (e) loan charges (f) fines. 16 Pictures: stock; charges. 17 Other services. 18 Cultural activities (expenditure, officer in charge, staff: (a) officers (b) manual). 19 Issue method (if not Browne). 20 Loan period (if not 2 weeks). 21 Fines: (a) adult (b) children (c) OAPs. 22 Co-operative schemes. 23 Stock: (a) adult lending (b) adult reference (c) children (d) schools (e) current periodical titles. 24 Issues: (a) adult (b) children (c) schools (d) institutions. 25 Staff: (a) officers (b) manual (c) chartered libns (d) graduates. 26 Finance: (a) total expenditure (b) non-rate income (c) per capita expenditure (d) expenditure for books (e) expenditure for records etc (f) salaries & wages. 27 Capital projects.

STOCKPORT METROPOLITAN BOROUGH COUNCIL—*continued*
3038/7297), Area Libn: M. R. Farnsworth MA, ALA; West: Ashfield Rd, Cheadle, SK8 1BB (061-428 7169), Area Libn: A. Maddock ALA; East: Memorial Park, Marple, SK6 6BA (061-427 3236), Area Libn: E. Wilcock ALA. **12** Bramhall Lane, South, Stockport; George Lane, Bredbury; The Arcade, Taunton Ave, Brinnington; Mellor Rd, Cheadle Hulme, Cheadle; Alexandra Park, Edgeley, Stockport; Gladstone St, Great Moor, Stockport; Beech Ave, Hazel Grove, Stockport; Finney Lane, Heald Green, Cheadle; Thornfield Rd, Heaton Moor, Stockport; Gorton Rd, Reddish, Stockport. **13** P-t 8; mobiles 1. **14** Stockport; dogs. **17** Schools, housebound, hospitals, old people's homes. **18** Cultural activities (a 8, b 4). **19** Photocharging (Central). **20** 3 weeks. **21** (a) 1p pd; (b&c) none. **23** (a, b&c) 501, 000; (d) 117, 000; (e) 900. **24** (a&b) 3, 564, 000.
25 (a) 144; (b) 26; (c) 51; (d) 15. **26** (a) £758, 060; (b) £57, 530; (c) £2, 492; (d) £136, 200; (f) £402, 820.

STRATHKELVIN DISTRICT COUNCIL (pop 80, 000) Bishopbriggs Library, 170 Kirkintilloch Rd, Bishopbriggs, Glasgow, G64 2LX (041-772 4513). Chief Libn: Mrs Alice A. MacKenzie FLA; Principal Assts: Mr J. Fergusson BA, ALA; Mr C. Roberton ALA; Miss J. Simpson ALA. **7** Recreation & Leisure. **8** Dir of Environmental & Recreational Services: Mr W. Neil. **9** Mon-Fri: 10.00-19.30; Sat: 10.00-17.00. **10** HQ; Branch. **12** William Patrick Memorial Lib, Camphill Ave, Kirkintilloch, Glasgow, G66 1DW. **13** P-t 3; mobiles 2. **15** 1; (c) 1, 105. **17** Schools, housebound, hospitals, old people's homes, pre-school playgroups. **18** Cultural activities. **20** 3 weeks. **21** (a, b&c) none. **23** (a) 65, 126; (b) 1, 477; (c) 18, 182; (e) 40. **24** (a) 457, 761; (b) 111, 303. **25** (a) 32; (b) 4; (c) 11; (d) 6.

SUFFOLK COUNTY COUNCIL (pop c. 567, 300) Suffolk County Library, Central Administrative Unit, County Hall, Ipswich, Suffolk, IP4 2JS (0473-55801; telex 987708 SCC Ipswich). County Libn: E. F. Ferry FLA. **7** Libraries, Museums, Records & Amenities. **9** Mon-Fri: 9.30-18.00 (or 20.00); Sat: 9.00 (or 9.30)-17.00 (or 17.30). **10** Central Administrative Unit; Area; Division; Branch. **11** Areas: Bury St Edmunds: Central Lib, Cornhill, Bury St Edmunds, IP33 1BT (0284-5340/64503), Libn: Mr H. I. Hammond FLA; Ipswich: Central Lib, Northgate St, Ipswich (0473-53561/214370), Libn: Mr P. R. Labdon FLA; Lowestoft: Central Lib, Clapham Rd, Lowestoft (0502-66325), Libn: Mr W. James FLA. **12** Newmarket Division Lib, Fitzroy St, Newmarket; Sudbury Division Lib, Market Hill, Sudbury; Ipswich Division, Chantry Lib, Hawthorn Dr, Ipswich; Bury St Edmunds District General Hospital, Hardwick Lane, Bury St Edmunds; Lower Downs Slade, Haverhill; Local History Lib, Area Record Office, Shire Hall, Bury St Edmunds; Chestnut Close, Mildenhall; Council Offices, Stowmarket; Crescent Rd, Felixstowe; Gainsborough Lib, Clapgate Lane, Ipswich; Beccles Division Lib, Blyburgate, Beccles; George St, Hadleigh; Rosehill Lib, Tomline Rd, Ipswich; Westbourne Lib, Sherrington Rd, Ipswich; New St, Woodbridge; Council Offices, Bridge Rd, Oulton Broad, Lowestoft; Community Centre, Bury Rd, Brandon. **13** P-t 25; mobiles 10 & 3 Schools Service. **15** 14; (a&b) 36, 693; (c) 12, 153; (d) 143; (e) £2.00 annual subscription; (f) as books. **17** Schools, housebound, prisons, hospitals, old people's homes. **19** Token. **20** 4 weeks. **21** (a&c) 3p pw, max 50p; (b) none. **23** (a) 667, 006; (b) 58, 656; (c) 145, 915; (d) 187, 783. **24** (a, b&d) 5, 497, 140.

25 (a) 180; (b) 53; (c) 49; (d) 13. **26** (a) £1, 052, 000; (b) £30, 000; (c) £1.85; (d&e) £260, 000; (f) £491, 000.

SUNDERLAND METROPOLITAN DISTRICT COUNCIL (pop 293, 600) Central Library, Borough Rd, Sunderland, Tyne & Wear, SR1 1PP (0783-41235/8). Asst Dir of Arts: Mr E. W. Kirtley ALA; 1st Principal Asst Libn: Mr D. J. Johnston BA, ALA. **7** Leisure (Libraries & Arts Sub-Committee). **8** Dir of Arts. **9** Mon-Fri: 9.30-19.30; Sat: 9.30-16.00. **10** HQ; Division; Branch. **11** Divisions: East: West B Lib, Kayll Rd, Sunderland, SR4 7TW (0783-73829), Libn: Mrs J. Robertson ALA; North: Fulwell B Lib, Dene Lane, Sunderland, SR6 8EH (0783-70248), Libn: Mrs J. Holman ALA; West: Houghton B Lib, Mautland Sq, Houghton-le-Spring, Sunderland DH4 4BJ (0783-3380), Libn: Miss J. Tobitt ALA. **12** Easington Lane; Atlantis Rd, East Herrington; Grindon B Lib & Museum, Grindon Lane, Sunderland; Hendon B Lib, Toward Rd, Sunderland; Hetton-le-Hole B Lib, Houghton Rd, Hetton; Hylton Castle B Lib, Cranleigh Rd, Sunderland; Monkwearmouth B Lib, Church St, Sunderland; Ryhope St, Ryhope; Chester Rd, Shiney Row; Vane St, Silksworth; Beaumont St, Southwick; Victoria Rd, Washington; The Green, Washington. **13** P-t 1; mobiles 1. **14** Teachers centre colln; shipbuilding; marine engineering; development of printing & book illustration; local (Sunderland & Durham). **15** 1; (a) 30, 452; (b) 54; (c) 3, 908; (d) 98; (e) £1.75 pa; (f) 1p pd. **16** 890; £2.16 pa (now operated by County Museum Service). **17** Schools, housebound, hospitals (2 only), old people's homes, playgroups, aid to youth services. **18** Cultural activities, entertainments (facilities offered—but come under Leisure Committee's Miscellaneous Services and not charged to Libraries Dept). **19** Photocharging. **20** 3 weeks. **21** (a) 1p pd; (b&c) none. **22** NRLB. **23** (a) 354, 174; (b) 31, 945; (c) 82, 147; (d) 43, 823; (e) 451. **24** (a) 2, 773, 445; (b) 500, 337; (c) 17, 450 (& 611 project colln sets); (d) 9, 681. **25** (a) 143.5; (b) 27.25; (c) 40; (d) 5. **26** (a) £762, 925; (b) £97, 334; (c) £2.59; (d) £203, 852; (e) £4, 050; (f) £409, 645.

SURREY COUNTY COUNCIL (pop 1, 005, 900) County Library Headquarters, 140 High St, Esher, KT10 9QR (0372-63585/7; telex 922061). County Libn: Mr Robert F. Ashby FLA. **7** Education (Library Sub-Committee). **8** County Education Officer: Mr J. W. Henry MA. **9** Mon closed (exc 3 largest libs), Tues-Fri 10.00-20.00 (2 days 17.00); Sat: 9.30-17.00. **10** HQ; Group; Branch. **11** Groups: North: Church St, Weybridge, KT13 8DX (0932-43812), Asst County Libn: Mr G. E. Mawson FLA; North West: Town Sq, Woking, GU21 1EP (04862-70591/2), Asst County Libn: Mr W. P. J. Critcher ALA; South West: North St, Guildford, GU1 4AL (0483-68496), Asst County Libn: Miss P. M. St J. Brewer ALA; Central: Bourne Hall, Ewell, Epsom, KT17 1UF (01-394 0088), Asst County Libn: Mr J. F. Viles ALA; South East: 33 London Rd, Reigate, RH2 9PY (073 72-44272), Asst County Libn: Mr T. W. A. Faulkner ALA. **12** Church Rd, Addlestone, KT15 1RW; Ash St, Ash, Aldershot, Hants, GU12 6LF; Church Rd, Ashford, Middlesex, TW15 2XB; Woodfield Lane, Ashtead, KT21 2BQ; Bolters Lane, Banstead, SM7 2AW; Bookham Grove, Lower Shott, Great Bookham, KT23 4NS; High St, Bramley, Guildford, GU5 0HG; High Rd, Byfleet, Weybridge, KT14 7QN; Knoll Rd, Camberley, GU15 3SY; Caterham Hill B Lib, Westway, Caterham, CR3 5TP; Caterham Valley B Lib, Stafford Rd, Caterham, CR3 6JG; Guildford St, Chertsey, KT16 9BE; Hollyhedge Rd, Cobham, KT11 3DQ; Lady Peek Institute, Cranleigh, GU6 8AS; Dittons B Lib, Watts Rd, Thames Ditton,

SURREY COUNTY COUNCIL—*continued*
KT7 0BX; Pippbrook, Dorking, RH4 1SL; High St, Egham, TW20
9EA; 12/14 Waterloo Rd, Epsom, KT19 8BN; Old Church Path,
Esher, KT10 9NS; Ewell Court B Lib, Ewell Court House,
Lakehurst Rd, Ewell, Epsom, KT19 0EB; Vernon House, 28
West St, Farnham, GU9 7DR; 2 Beech Rd, Frimley Green,
Camberley, GU16 6LQ; Bridge St, Godalming, GU7 1HT; 91
Wey Hill, Haslemere, GU27 1HP; Molesey Rd, Hersham, KT12
4RF; Victoria Rd, Horley, RH6 7AG; Station Parade, Ockham
Rd South, East Horsley, Leatherhead, KT24 6QR; High St,
Knaphill, Woking, GU21 2PE; The Mansion, Church St,
Leatherhead, KT22 8DP; The Guest House, Vicarage Lane,
Lingfield, RH7 6HA; Weldon Way, Merstham, RH1 3QB; The
Forum, West Molesey, KT8 0HZ; The Broadway, New Haw,
Weybridge, KT15 3HA; 12 Gresham Rd, Oxted, RH8 0BQ;
Fairfax Ave, Redhill, RH1 1HX; High St, Shepperton, Middle-
sex, TW17 9AU; Clarence St, Staines, Middlesex, TW18 4TF;
Hadrian Way, Stanwell, Middlesex; 1 The Broadway, Stoneleigh,
Epsom, KT17 2JA; The Parade, Staines Rd West, Sunbury-on-
Thames, Middlesex, TW16 7AB; Tattenham Crescent, Epsom
Downs, Epsom, KT18 5NU; Station Parade, Virginia Water,
GU25 4AB; High St, Walton-on-Thames, KT12 1HZ; Shelton
Ave, Warlingham, CR3 9NF; The Corner, West Byfleet,
Weybridge, KT14 6NY; Trehaven Parade, Woodhatch, Reigate,
RH2 7LL.   **13** P-t 21; mobiles 14.
14 Music & play sets; government publications (selected
subscription service).   **15** All branches (a) 55, 962;
(c) 22, 040; (e) £1.60 per ticket pa; (f) as books.   **16** 140
(Woking); originals 75p (3 months), reproductions 50p (3
months).   **17** Schools, housebound, prisons, hospitals, old
people's homes, blind & partially sighted.   **19** Token (adult
fiction & junior only); photocharging (Woking).   **20** 3 weeks.
21 (a&c) 2p pd, max 60p; (b) 1p pd.   **22** SASLIC.
23 (a) 1, 459, 686; (b) 101, 511; (c) 309, 814; (d) 419, 451;
(e) 450.   **24** (a) 10, 026, 095; (b) 1, 950, 831.
25 (a) 451; (b) 54½; (c) 104; (d) 61.   **26** (a) £2, 471, 060;
(b) £93, 620; (c) £2.45; (d) £647, 190; (e) £15, 140;
(f) £1, 244, 240.   **27** Redhill Library.

TAMESIDE METROPOLITAN BOROUGH COUNCIL (pop
223, 000) Libraries & Arts, Stamford House, Jowett's Walk,
Ashton-under-Lyne, Lancashire, OL7 0BB (061-330 5636;
telex 669991). Chief Libn & Arts Officer: T. M. Featherstone
BA, FLA; Asst Chief Libn: R. K. Bluhm FLA (Bibliographical);
N. A. Simpson MA, ALA (Operational).   **7** Libraries &
Arts.   **9** Mon-Fri: 9.00-20.00; Sat: 9.00-16.00.
10 HQ; District; Branch.   **11 Areas:** Old St, Ashton-under-
Lyne, OL6 7SG (061-330 2151), Area Libn: Mr J. Benson;
Peel St, Denton, M34 3JY (061-336 6431 ext 104), Area Libn:
Mrs J. Gromada ALA; Manchester Rd, Droylsden (061-370
1282); Union St, Hyde, SK14 1NF (061-368 2447); Trinity St,
Stalybridge, SK15 2BN (061-338 2708), Area Libn: Mr C.
Heathcote ALA.   **12** Town Lane, Dukinfield; Hattersley Rd
East, Hattersley; Mancunian Rd, Haughton Green, Denton;
Wyre St, Mossley; Ryecroft Hall Lib, Manchester Rd, Auden-
shaw; West End Lib, Windsor Rd, Denton.   **13** P-t 15;
mobiles 1.
15 2; (a&b) 34, 074; (c&d) 4, 683; (e) £1.10 pa; (f) as books.
17 Schools, housebound, hospitals, old people's homes, pre-
school playgroups.   **18** Cultural activities (£21, 600;
a 2, b 1).   **20** 4 weeks.   **21** (a) 3p pw; (b&c) none.
23 (a) 282, 088; (b) 25, 867; (c) 81, 926; (d) 100, 000; (e) 236.
24 (a) 1, 643, 033; (b) 321, 582.
25 (a) 120; (b) 17; (c) 40.   **26** (a) £707, 310; (b) £39, 010;
(c) £3.17; (d) £165, 800; (e) £11, 030; (f) £299, 810.

TRAFFORD BOROUGH COUNCIL (pop 299, 700) Birch House,
Talbot Rd, Old Trafford, Manchester, M16 0GH (061-872
6133/6177). Borough Libn: Mr J. W. H. Watters ALA; Asst
Borough Libn: Mr J. J. Wade ALA (bibliographical).
7 Recreation & Amenities.   **9** Mon-Fri: 10.00-19.30
(or 20.00) (Wed 10.00-13.00 or 16.00); Sat: 10.00-17.00.
10 HQ; Division; Branch.   **11 Divisions:** Altrincham:
Public Lib, 8-10 Kingsway, Altrincham, Cheshire, WA14 1PJ,
Libn: Miss F. Walmsley ALA; Sale: Public Lib, Tatton Rd,
Sale, Cheshire, M33 1YH (061-973 3142), Libn: Mr G. Yeoman
ALA; Stretford: Public Lib, Kingsway, Stretford, Manchester,
M32 8AP (061-865 2218/9), Libn: Mr P. N. C. Ford ALA;
Urmston: Public Lib, Crofts Bank Rd, Urmston, Manchester,

M31 1TZ (061-748 0774), Libn: Miss D. E. B. Simpson ALA.
12 Leigh Rd, Hale; Park Rd, Timperley; Coppice Ave, Sale;
Firswood B Lib, Great Stone Rd, Stretford; Lostock B Lib,
Barton Rd, Stretford; Shrewsbury St, Old Trafford, Manchester
16; Hayeswater Rd, Davyhulme; Brook Rd, Flixton; Woodsend
Rd, Flixton; Central Rd, Partington.   **13** P-t 4; mobiles 1.
16 205; 50p pa; fines 1p pd.   **17** Schools, housebound, old
people's homes.   **18** Cultural activities (£1, 500; Borough
Libn).   **20** 3 weeks.   **21** (a) 1p pd; (b&c) none.
23 (a) 357, 375; (b) 28, 695; (c) 100, 731; (d) 33, 451; (e) 143.
24 (a) 2, 185, 278; (b) 485, 597; (c) 10, 704.
25 (a) 136; (b) 22; (c) 41; (d) 11.   **26** (a) £805, 685;
(b) 60, 532; (c) £3.51; (d) £134, 000; (f) £380, 767.

WAKEFIELD METROPOLITAN DISTRICT COUNCIL (pop
306, 000) Library Headquarters, Balne Lane, Wakefield,
West Yorkshire, WF2 0DQ (0924-71231; telex WAKLIB
557330). Chief Libn: Mr L. J. Feiweles BA, ALA; Dep Libn:
Miss M. G. Pyle FLA.   **7** Education.   **8** Chief Education
Officer: Mr R. Eyles BSc.   **9** Mon-Fri: 9.30-19.30; Sat:
9.30-17.00.
10 HQ; Area; Branch.   **11 Areas:** Carlton St, Castleford,
WG10 1BB (09775-59552), Area Libn: Miss F. M. Milnes ALA;
Hemsworth Area Lib, Balne Lane, Wakefield, WF2 0DQ
(0924-71231), Area Libn: Miss M. Bennett ALA; Salter Row,
Pontefract, WF8 1BD (0977-3948), Area Libn: Mr N. Lloyd
ALA; Wakefield Area Lib, Drury Lane, Wakefield, WF1 2TD
(0924-75157), Area Libn: Mr N. Willox.   **12** The Square,
Airedale, Castleford; Green Lane, Featherstone, Pontefract;
Flanshaw Lane, Dewsbury Rd, Wakefield; Cow Lane, Haver-
croft, Wakefield; Market St, Hemsworth, Pontefract; Westfield Rd, Horbury, Wakefield; Wakefield Rd, Kinsley, Pontefract; Chapel St, Knottingley; Castleford Rd, Normanton;
Station Rd, Ossett; Sandal Lib, Sparable Lane, Wakefield;
Barnsley Rd, South Elmsall, Pontefract; White Apron St, South
Kirkby, Pontefract.   **13** P-t 17; mobiles 3.
14 Local history (inc George Gissing colln); Frank Green
colln (art & architecture); archives (inc Pilkington colln).
15 5; (a) 18, 438; (c) 6, 844; (e) £1.25 pa (2 records) (free
to OAP's, chronically sick & disabled); (f) as books.
16 550.   **17** Schools, housebound, prisons, hospitals, old
people's homes.   **20** 4 weeks.   **21** (a) none (exc 1st class
postage for overdue notices); (b&c) none.   **23** (a) 440, 000;
(b) 45, 000; (c&d) 239, 000; (e) c.585.   **24** (a&b) 2, 832, 020;
(c) 855, 000; (d) 39, 223.
25 (a) 155; (b) 35; (c) 54; (d) 9.   **26** (a) £867, 000;
(b) £137, 590; (c) £2.83; (d) £198, 000; (e) £6, 500;
(f) £426, 660.

WALSALL METROPOLITAN BOROUGH COUNCIL (pop c.
273, 500) Central Library, Lichfield St, Walsall, West Midlands,
WS1 1TR (0922-21244). Dir of Lib & Museum Services: Mr
F. H. Lamb ALA; Dep Dir of Lib & Museum Services: Mr D. J.
Guy ALA.   **7** Recreation.   **9** Mon-Fri: 9.30-19.00; Sat:
9.30-17.30.
10 HQ; District; Branch.   **11 District Libraries:** The
Manor House, High St, Aldridge (0922-52601), Libn: Mr E. R.
Mitchell ALA; Elmore Row, Bloxwich, Walsall WS3 2HR
(0922-76959), Libn: Mrs J. Wood ALA; Brickiln St, Brownhills
WS8 6AU (054 33-3017), Libn: Miss J. Kendrick ALA; Town
Hall, Victoria Rd, Darlaston, WS10 8AA (021-526 2391), Libn:
Mrs V. Wheeler ALA; Walsall St, Willenhall, WV13 2EX (0902-
65613), Libn: Mrs C. Meredith ALA.   **12** South Walsall
B Lib, West Bromwich Rd, Walsall; Pleck B Lib, Darlaston
Rd, Walsall; Pheasey B Lib, Collingwood Dr, Birmingham;
Blackwood Rd, Streetley; Pelsall Lane, Rushall, Walsall;
Shelfield B Lib, Birch Lane, Pelsall; High St, Pelsall; Lichfield Rd, Walsall Wood.   **13** P-t 4.
15 1; (a&b) 21, 750; (c) 4, 623; (d) 454; (e) none; (f) as books.
17 Schools (agency arrangements), housebound, old people's
homes.   **18** Cultural activities, entertainments (£3, 180;
Admin Officer).   **20** 3 weeks.   **21** (a) 5p pw or part;
(b&c) none.   **22** WESLIB; WESLINK.   **23** (a) 283, 234;
(b) 43, 940 (inc pamphlets); (c) 105, 898; (e) 130.
24 (a) 1, 718, 860; (b) 568, 880.
25 (a) 102; (b) 15; (c) 27; (d) 1.   **26** (a) £581, 950;
(b) £68, 380; (c) £2.14; (d) £118, 500; (e) £4, 690; (f) £333, 100.

CODE: 1 Local authority. 2 Population. 3 Postal address of HQ. 4 Telephone & telex. 5 Chief Libn. 6 Deputy. 7 Committee responsible. 8 Officer to whom Libn is responsible (if any). 9 Hours. 10 Organisation. 11 Area libraries. 12 Branches. 13 Part-time libraries; mobiles. 14 Special collections. 15 Gramophone records: number of libraries, (a) record issues (b) cassette issues (c) record stock (d) cassette stock (e) loan charges (f) fines. 16 Pictures: stock; charges. 17 Other services. 18 Cultural activities (expenditure, officer in charge, staff: (a) officers (b) manual). 19 Issue method (if not Browne). 20 Loan period (if not 2 weeks). 21 Fines: (a) adult (b) children (c) OAPs. 22 Co-operative schemes. 23 Stock: (a) adult lending (b) adult reference (c) children (d) schools (e) current periodical titles. 24 Issues: (a) adult (b) children (c) schools (d) institutions. 25 Staff: (a) officers (b) manual (c) chartered libns (d) graduates. 26 Finance: (a) total expenditure (b) non-rate income (c) per capita expenditure (d) expenditure for books (e) expenditure for records etc (f) salaries & wages. 27 Capital projects.

WARWICKSHIRE COUNTY COUNCIL (pop 470, 000) County Central Library, The Butts, Warwick, Warwickshire, CV34 4SS (0926-43431; telex 31621). County Libn: T. W. Howard FLA; Dep County Libn: P. G. Gill FLA. 7 Education. 8 County Education Officer: M. L. Ridger MA. 9 Mon-Fri: 9.00-19.00; Sat: 9.00-17.00. 10 HQ; Divisional; Branch. 11 **Divisional Libraries:** North: Church St, Nuneaton, CV11 4DR (0682-4027/8; telex 311280), Div Libn: T. Birch ALA; East: St Matthew St, Rugby, CV21 3BZ (0788-2687; telex 31488), Div Libn: J. Haiste FLA; South: 12 Henley St, Stratford-upon-Avon, CV37 6PZ (0789-2209; telex 311317), Div Libn: H. S. A. Smith MA, FLA; Central: Avenue Rd, Leamington Spa, CV31 3PP (0926-25873; telex 311319), Div Libn: R. A Howard ALA. 12 Long St, Atherstone, CV9 1AX; 30 High St, Bedworth, CV12 8NG; 141 High St, Coleshill, Birmingham, B46 3AY; 11 Smalley Pl, Kenilworth, CV8 1QG; Valley Rd, Lillington, Leamington Spa, CV32 7SJ; 10 Church St, Warwick, CV34 4AL. 13 P-t 37; mobiles 7. 14 Warwickshire colln; Warwick local history; George Eliot; Robert Burton & Michael Drayton—Nuneaton local history; Fowler colln (theatre). 15 4; (a) 22, 000; (c) 7, 000; (e) £1.45 pa; (f) as books. 16 1, 573; residents 54p pa, non-residents £1.08 pa. 17 Schools, housebound, hospitals, old people's homes. 19 Photocharging. 20 4 weeks. 21 (a) 6p pw or part; (b&c) none. 22 CADIG. 23 (a, b&c) 1, 219, 806; (d) 145, 575; (e) 375. 24 (a, b&d) 5, 447, 922; (c) 167, 720 25 (a) 199; (b) 69; (c) 78. 26 (a) £862, 647; (b) £124, 578; (c) £1.83; (d) £210, 799; (e) £2, 481; (f) £547, 266.

WESTERN ISLES ISLANDS COUNCIL (pop 30, 000) Public Library, Stornoway, Isle of Lewis, PA87 2XF (0851-3488; telex 75164). Chief Libn: A. M. Morrison; Dep: Miss J. M. Morrison MA, ALA. 7 Education. 8 Dir of Education: Mr Angus Macleod MA. 9 Mon-Fri: 9.30-17.30 (Tues & Fri 19.30); Sat: 9.30-12.30. 10 Regional HQ. 13 P-t 3; mobiles 3. 14 Morrison mss; Scottish Gaelic colln; local history; T. B. Macaulay colln (photographs). 15 1; (a) 839; (b) 190; (c) 476; (d) 60; (e) £1.00 deposit. 17 Schools, housebound, hospitals, old people's homes. 21 (a&b) 2p pw; (c) none. 25 (a) 13; (c) 3; (d) 3. 26 (a) £68, 100; (b) £1, 000; (c) £2.16; (d) £23, 000; (e) £1, 000; (f) £36, 000.

WEST GLAMORGAN COUNTY COUNCIL (pop 374, 900) West Glamorgan County Libraries, Alexandra Rd, Swansea, West Glamorgan, SA1 5DX (0792-54065/6; telex 48396). County Libn: Mr J. A. Davies FLA; Dep County Libn: Mr B. Thomas ALA. 7 Education. 8 Dir of Education: Mr J. Beale MA. 9 Mon-Fri: ad ldg & children 9.30-18.00 (Fri 19.00 or 19.30); ref 9.00-19.00 (Thurs 17.00); Sat: ad ldg & children 9.30-17.00 (or 13.00), ref 9.30-17.00 10 HQ; District; Branch; Centre; Mobile. 11 **Districts:** Afan: Taibach Lib, Commercial Rd, Port Talbot (0792 94-4521), Libn: Mr B. J. Croft ALA; Neath: Victoria Gardens, Neath, SA11 3BA (079298-4604), Libn: Mr L. Edwards ALA; Swansea: Central Lib, Alexandra Rd, Swansea, SA1 5DX (0792-54065/6), Libn (1): A. M. Hodgetts ALA, Libn (2): Mrs A. Stone ALA. 12 Bethany Vestry, Station Rd, Aberavon, Port Talbot; Laurel Ave, Baglan, SA12 8PA; Briton Ferry, SA11 2AQ; Llangyfelach Rd, Brynhyfryd, Swansea, SA5 9LH; Depot Rd, Cwmavon, SA12 9OF; Fforestfach, Kings Head Rd, Gendros, Swansea, SA5 8DA; Glynneath; West St, Gorseinon, SA4 2AA; Mansel St, Gowerton, SA4 3BU; Treharne Rd, Morriston, Swansea, SA6 7AA; Dunn's Lane, Oystermouth, Swansea, SA3 4AA; Southgate, Pennard; 9 Herbert St, Pontardawe, SA8 4EB; St Michael's Ave, Pontardulais, SA4 1TE; Morrison Rd, Sandfields Estate, Port Talbot, SA12 6TG; Vivian Rd, Sketty, Swansea, SA2 0UN; Miers St, St Thomas, Swansea SA1 8BZ; New Rd, Skewen, SA10 6UU; Powys Ave, Town Hill, Swansea. 13 P-t 15; mobiles 3. 14 Dylan Thomas. 15 2; (a&b) 33, 976; (c) 8, 000; (d) 160; (e) £1.00 & VAT; (f) 2p pw. 17 Schools, housebound, prisons, hospitals, old people's homes. 19 Photocharging. 20 3 weeks. 21 (a) 2p pw; (b&c) 2p max. 23 (a, b&c) 606, 750; (e) 566. 24 (a, b&d) 2, 900, 605. 25 (a) 173; (b) 15; (c) 22; (d) 7. 26 (a) £813, 374; (b) £17, 580; (c) £2.16; (d) £200, 100; (e) £4, 000; (f) £429, 135.

WEST LOTHIAN DISTRICT COUNCIL (pop 112, 000) West Lothian District Library Headquarters, Wellpark, 66 Marjoribanks St, Bathgate, West Lothian EH48 1AN (0506-52866). Chief Libn: Mr William S. Walker ALA; Dep Chief Libn: Mr George D. Kerr ALA. 7 Leisure & Recreation. 8 Dir of Administration: Mr W. N. Fordyce MA, LLB. 9 Mon-Fri: 9.30-18.00 (Tues & Thurs 20.00); Sat: 9.30-16.00. 10 District HQ; Branch. 12 West Main St, Armadale; Hopetoun St, Bathgate; Ashgrove, Blackburn; West Main St,, Broxburn; Lanrigg Rd, Fauldhouse; The Vennel, Linlithgow; West Main St, Whitburn; Almondbank B Lib, Livingston; West Calder. 13 P-t 3; mobiles 2. 14 J. G. B. Henderson bequests (local material donated by the late county clerk of West Lothian). 15 4; (a) 4, 000; (c) 2, 120; (d) 30; (e) £1.00 returnable deposit; (f) 1p pd. 16 300; £1.00 returnable deposit. 17 Schools, hospitals, old people's homes, playgroups. 21 (a, b&c) none. 23 (a) 207, 500; (b) 1, 500; (c) 52, 000; (e) 46. 24 (a) 596, 550; (b) 111, 000; (c) 153, 460. 25 (a) 49½; (c) 12; (d) 1. 26 (a) £230, 000; (b) £150; (c) £2.00; (d) £38, 000; (e) £600; (f) £102, 000.

WEST SUSSEX COUNTY COUNCIL (pop 612, 000) Library Service, Tower St, Chichester, Sussex, PO19 1QJ (0243-86563/85100; telex 86279). County Libn: Mr R. J. Huse FLA; 1st Dep Libn: Mr R. J. Stoakley FLA; 2nd Dep Libn: Mr J. N. Harris FLA. 7 Library & Archives. 9 Mon-Fri: 9.30-19.30; Sat: 9.30-17.00. 10 HQ; Division; Branch. 11 **Divisions:** South-Eastern: Richmond Rd, Worthing (0903-206961), Libn: Mr R. E. Hodder FLA; North-Eastern: County Buildings, Crawley, RH10 1XG (0293-23234), Libn: Miss E. M. Hosking ALA; Western: Tower St, Chichester, PO19 1QJ (0243-86563/85100), Libn: Mr D. W. Liddle ALA. 12 Maltravers St, Arundel, BN18 9BQ; Mill Lane, Billingshurst, RH14 9JZ; London Rd, Bognor Regis, PO21 1DE; Dominion Rd, Broadwater, BN14 8JL; The Martlets, Burgess Hill, RH15 9NN; Salvington Rd, Durrington, BN13 2JD; Southwick House, London Rd, East Grinstead, RH19 1PQ; Ferring St, Ferring, BN12 5HL; Lime Tree Ave, Findon, BN14 0HD; Mulberry Lane, Goring-by-Sea, BN12 4NR; Stafford House, Keymer Rd, Hassocks, BN6 8QJ; 34 Boltro Rd, Haywards Heath, RH16 1BN; Off High St, Henfield, BN5 9HN; North St, Horsham, RH12 1RJ; Penstone Park, Lancing, BN15 9DL; Maltravers Rd, Littlehampton, BN17 5NA; Knockhundred Row, Midhurst, GU29 9DQ; High St, Petworth, GU28 0NS; Off Lower St, Pulborough, RH20 2BP; Claigmar Rd, Rustington, BN16 2NL; School Lane, Selsey, PO20 9EH; St Mary's Rd, Shoreham, BN4 5ZA; Church St, Steyning, BN4 3YB; Ryecroft Lane, Storrington, RH20 4NZ; Oakfield Ave, Witterings, PO20 8BT; Pryors Lane, Willowhale, Bognor Regis, PO21 4JF. 13 P-t 5; mobiles 7. 14 Guermonprez colln (mainly 19th cent natural history);

WEST SUSSEX COUNTY COUNCIL—*continued*
Sussex colln.   **15** 3; (a&b) 91, 024; (c) 9, 500; (d) 500;
(e) reservation fee 10p; (f) 1p pd.   **17** Schools, housebound,
prisons, hospitals, old people's homes.   **19** Computer—ALS
& Plessey.   **20** 3 weeks (2 weeks if demand).   **21** (a&c) 1p
pd; (b) none.   **22** SASLIC.   **23** (a, b, c&d) 1, 276, 7971;
(e) 600.   **24** (a, b, c&d) 7, 882, 400.
25 (a) 295; (b) 15; (c) 99; (d) 10.   **26** (a) £1, 383, 620;
(b) £107, 660; (c) £2.24; (d) £276, 875; (e) £6, 500;
(f) £739, 960.

WIGAN METROPOLITAN BOROUGH COUNCIL (pop 306, 200)
Dept of Leisure, 9/10 Bridgeman Terrace, Wigan, Lancashire,
WN1 1SZ (0942-36141). Asst Dir of Leisure: Mr Noel E.
Willis FLA; Bibliographic Libn: Mr C. M. Caley ALA; Schools
& Children's Libn: Mr Derrick Scott ALA; Service Points Libn:
Mr T. F. Houghton ALA.   **7** Recreation & Amenities.
8 Dir of Leisure: Mr Gil Swift BA, MSc.   **9** Mon-Fri: ad
ldg 9.30 (or 10.00)-19.00 (or 19.30), ref 9.30-19.30,
children's 12.00-13.00, 14.30-18.00; Sat: ad ldg & ref 9.30-
17.00, children's 9.30-13.00, 14.30-18.00.
10 HQ; Group; Branch.   **11 Groups:** Wigan: Central Lib,
Rodney St, Wigan, WN1 1DQ (0942-41387), Principal Libn:
Mr F. Howard; Leigh: The Lib, Leigh, WN7 1ED (052 35-4131),
Group Libn: Mr J. Blackburn FLA; Standish: Cross St, Stan-
dish, Wigan, WN6 0HQ (0257-421755), Group Libn: Mr T. C.
Miller ALA; Hindley/Golborne: Market St, Hindley, Wigan,
WN2 3AN (0942-55287), Group Libn: Mrs S. M. Folkes.
12 Golborne, Warrington, WA3 3BU; Vicarage Rd, Abram,
Wigan, WN2 5QX; The Meadows, Hesketh Meadow Estate,
Lowton, WA3 2LR; Gathurst Lane, Shevington, Wigan WN6 8HA;
Orrell Post, Wigan, WN5 8LY; Oakfield Crescent, Aspull,
Wigan, WN2 1XJ; Atherton Lib, York St, Manchester, M29 9JH;
Tyldesley, Manchester, M29 8AH; Buckely St West, Beech
Hill, Wigan WN6 7PQ; Harrow Rd, Marsh Green, Wigan;
Ormskirk Rd, Pemberton, Wigan WN5 9DM; Wigan Rd,
Ashton-in-Makerfield, Wigan WN4 9BH; Children's Lib,
Powell Building, Station Rd, Wigan WN1 1YQ.   **13** P-t 2;
mobiles 3.
14 Wigan local history; Dootson local history (Leigh colln);
incunabula & STC colln; record office & genealogical collns.
15 4; (a) 43, 582; (c) 8, 243; (e) 10p pa (non-residents £2 pa) +
3p per record or set (two weeks); (f) as books.   **16** 65;
£1 pa individual, £5 pa corporate.   **17** Schools, housebound,
prisons, old people's homes.   **18** Cultural activities, entertainments (£94, 650; Asst Dir, Leisure Dept (Development);
a 6).   **19** Reverse Browne (Leigh).   **20** 4 weeks.
21 (a) 1p pd 1st week, 6p pw thereafter; (b&c) none.
23 (a) 381, 000; (b) 127, 000; (c) 97, 000; (d) 114, 442; (e) 350.
24 (a&d) 2, 089, 000; (b) 455, 073; (c) 417, 924.
25 (a) 141; (b) 30; (c) 57; (d) 10.   **26** (a) £1, 024, 650;
(b) £14, 050; (c) £3.34; (d) £209, 850; (e) £6, 600; (f) £493, 900.

WILTSHIRE COUNTY COUNCIL (pop 512, 000) Library &
Museum Headquarters, Bythesea Rd, Trowbridge, Wiltshire,
(02214-3641; telex 44297). Dir of Lib & Museum Service:
F. Hallworth FLA, FRGS; Asst Dirs: C. W. Franklin FLA
(Research & Admin); P. W. H. Pickup FLA (Public Services);
K. A. Wood ALA (Central Services).   **7** Library & Museum.
9 Mon-Fri: 10.00-20.00; Sat: 10.00-17.00.
10 HQ; Division; Area; Branch.   **11 Divisional Libraries:**
Eastern: Central Lib, Regents Circus, Swindon, SN1 1QG
(0793-27211), Div Libn: E. A. Stevens FLA, DMS; Southern:
Public Lib, Salisbury, SP1 1BL (0722-4167), Div Libn: B. M.
Little FLA; Western: Public Lib, Timber St, Chippenham,
SN15 3EJ (024972-50536), Div Libn: A. L. Bamber ALA.
12 Smithfield St, Amesbury; St Margaret St, Bradford-on-
Avon; New Rd, Calne; Pickwick Rd, Corsham; Sheep St,
Devizes; Eastrop, Highworth; Cross Hayes, Malmesbury;
91 High St, Marlborough; Lowbourne, Melksham; Church
Walk North, Moredon; Victoria Rd, Old Swindon; Cavendish Sq,
Park; Penhill Dr, Penhill; The Circle, Pinehurst; 10 Army
Education Centre, Tidworth; Hill St, Trowbridge; Beechcroft
Rd, Upper Stratton; Somerville Rd, Walcot; 31 Portway,
Warminster; Edward St, Westbury; South St, Wilton; High St,
Wootton Bassett; High St, Wroughton.   **13** P-t 21; mobiles
11.
14 Richard Jefferies colln (Swindon); railways (Swindon);
Wiltshire colln (Devizes); Salisbury colln (Salisbury);

agricultural & horticultural colln (Lackham); cricket
(Chippenham).   **15** 4; (a) 12, 045; (c) 8, 000; (d) 2, 000;
(e) £1 pa & 10p per record; (f) as books.   **16** 473 (for
schools only).   **17** Schools, housebound, prisons, hospitals,
old people's homes, adult education.   **19** Photocharging
(Southern Divisional Lib).   **20** 3 weeks.   **21** (a, b&c) 2p
pd.   **22** SWRLB; Wiltshire Technical Information Service.
23 (a&b) 864, 360; (c) 249, 294; (d) 498, 417.
24 (a) 5, 159, 852; (b) 1, 150, 464.
25 (a) 277; (b) 38; (c) 89; (d) 23.   **26** (a) £1, 480, 000;
(b) £47, 950; (c) £2.89; (d&e) £338, 310; (f) £694, 225.

WIRRAL METROPOLITAN BOROUGH (pop 355, 000) Birkenhead Central Library, Borough Rd, Cheshire, L41 2XB
(051-652 6106/7/8; telex 628136). Chief Libn & Arts
Officer (Asst Dir of Leisure Services): Mr H. H. G. Arthur
FLA, FRSA, MBIM; Principal Libns: Mr J. K. Burkitt ALA
(Support Services); Mr J. I. Coles ALA (Operational Services).
7 Leisure Services.   **8** Dir of Leisure Services: Mr
Brian J. Barnes MInstBM, ARM(M), MInstRM.   **9** Mon-Fri:
ad ldg, ref 9.30-20.00, children's 9.30-19.00; Sat: 9.30-
13.00, 14.00-17.00.
10 HQ; Central; Branch.   **11 Central Libraries:** Civic
Way, Bebington, L63 7PN (051-645 2080), Libn-in-charge:
Mrs H. Davies ALA; Earlston Rd, Wallasey, L45 5DX (051-
638 2334/5), Libn-in-charge: Mr H J. Hotchkiss ALA.
12 Allport Lane, Bromborough; Mill Park Dr, Eastham; 16
Ford Precinct, Ford; 158a Greasby Rd, Greasby; Telegraph
Rd, Heswall; Higher Bebington Rd, Higher Bebington; Market
St, Hoylake; Thurstaston Rd, Irby; Twickenham Dr, Leasowe;
Pasture Rd, Moreton; Pensby Rd, Pensby; Dickens Ave, Pren-
ton; Grove Rd, Rock Ferry; Liscard Rd, Seacombe; St Anne
St, Birkenhead; St James Lib, Laird St, Claughton; Ford Rd,
Upton; St Georges Rd, Wallasey Village; Sandlea Park, West
Kirby; Home Farm Rd, Woodchurch.   **13** P-t 3; mobiles 1
(schools only).
14 Actuarial science; American poetry; botany; English poetry;
ethics; floriculture; history of painting; food & confectionery;
local history; insurance; psychology; Shakespeare: shipbuilding & armament; transportation.   **15** 3; (a) 78, 717;
(b) 10, 509; (c) 10, 702; (d) 821; (e) £2.16 pa, £1.35 per 6
months (non-resident £3.24 pa, £2.16 per 6 months); (f)
as books.   **16** 750; £1 pa.   **17** Schools, housebound,
hospitals, old people's homes, youth clubs.   **18** Cultural
activities, entertainments (£158, 500; Entertainments Officer;
a 12 b 60).   **20** 4 weeks.   **21** (a&b) ½p pd; (c) none.
22 LADSIRLAC   **23** (a) 600, 000; (b) 65, 000; (c) 100, 000;
(d) 50, 000; (e) 660.   **24** (a) 3, 505, 211; (b) 752, 890; (c)
(c) 180, 000; (d) 20, 000.
25 (a) 171; (b) 31; (c) 49; (d) 15.   **26** (a) £926, 100;
(b) £52, 100; (c) £2.71; (d) £191, 200; (e) £4, 800; (f) £444, 000.

WOLVERHAMPTON BOROUGH COUNCIL (pop 268, 000) Cen-
tral Library, Snow Hill, Wolverhampton, West Midlands,
WV1 3AX (0902-20109/26988/24905). Chief Libn: F. Mason
BSc, DPA, FLA; Dep: A. Rowberry FLA.   **7** Leisure &
Amenities.   **8** Mon-Fri: 10.00-19.00; Sat: 10.00-17.00.
10 Central; Branch.   **12** Ashmore Park, Griffiths Dr,
Wednesfield, WV11 2JW; Mount Pleasant, Bilston, WV14 7LU;
Brierley Lane, Bilston, WV14 8TU; Bushbury, Probert Rd,
Oxley, WV10 6UF; Willenhall Rd, Eastfield, WV1 2HW; White-
oak Dr, Finchfield, WV3 9AF; Tudor Rd, Heath Town, WV10
0LT; Long Knowle, Wood End Rd, Wednesfield, WV11 1YG;
Showell Circus, Low Hill, WV10 9JL; Coalway Ave, Penn, WV3
7LT; Regis Rd, Tettenhall, WV6 8RU; School Rd, Tettenhall
Wood, WV6 8EJ; Warstones Rd, Penn, WV4 4LP; Church St
Wednesfield, WV11 1SR; Bargate Dr, Evans St, Whitmore
Reans; Woodcross, 108 Childs Ave, Bilston, WV14 9XB; Bevan
Ave, Springvale, WV4 6SG.   **13** P-t 3; mobiles 2.
15 1; (a) 67, 000; (b) 7, 000; (c) 9, 000; (d) 600; (e) 7p per
record (45's 5p); (f) as books.   **16** 218; 50p (6 months); fines
1p pd.   **17** Schools, housebound, hospitals, old people's homes.
19 Islington (Central & Penn).   **20** 4 weeks.   **21** (a) 5p pw
or part; (b) ½p pw or part; (c) none.   **23** (a) 297, 000;
(b) 57, 000; (c) 110, 000; (d) 45, 000; (e) 273.   **24** (a) 1, 871, 000;
(b) 552, 000; (d) hospital 3, 900.
25 (a) 97; (b) 15; (c) 24; (d) 3.   **26** (a) £499, 050;
(b) £17, 940; (c) £1.85; (d) £115, 410; (e) £3, 000; pictures
£460; (f) £269, 430.

CODE: 1 Local authority. 2 Population. 3 Postal address of HQ. 4 Telephone & telex. 5 Chief Libn. 6 Deputy. 7 Committee responsible. 8 Officer to whom Libn is responsible (if any). 9 Hours. 10 Organisation. 11 Area libraries. 12 Branches. 13 Part-time libraries; mobiles. 14 Special collections. 15 Gramophone records: number of libraries, (a) record issues (b) cassette issues (c) record stock (d) cassette stock (e) loan charges (f) fines. 16 Pictures: stock; charges. 17 Other services. 18 Cultural activities (expenditure, officer in charge, staff: (a) officers (b) manual). 19 Issue method (if not Browne). 20 Loan period (if not 2 weeks). 21 Fines: (a) adult (b) children (c) OAPs. 22 Co-operative schemes. 23 Stock: (a) adult lending (b) adult reference (c) children (d) schools (e) current periodical titles. 24 Issues: (a) adult (b) children (c) schools (d) institutions. 25 Staff: (a) officers (b) manual (c) chartered libns (d) graduates. 26 Finance: (a) total expenditure (b) non-rate income (c) per capita expenditure (d) expenditure for books (e) expenditure for records etc (f) salaries & wages. 27 Capital projects.

CHANNEL ISLANDS AND THE ISLE OF MAN

ALDERNEY LIBRARY COMMITTEE (pop c. 2,000) The Alderney Library, Royal Connaught Square, Alderney, Channel Islands. **7** Library. **9** Mon-Fri: 10.00-12.30, 14.15-16.30; Sat: 10.00-12.30, 18.00-20.30. **20** 1 week. **21** (a) 2p pw; (b) 1p pw. **23** (a) c.30,000; (c) c.4,500. **24** (a) c.37,300; (b) c.1,350. **25** No salaried staff. **26** (a) £1,414; (b) £1,415; (c) c. £0.70; (d) £910; (f) £0.

DOUGLAS CORPORATION (pop 20,385) Public Library, Ridgeway St, Douglas, Isle of Man (0624-23021). Borough Libn: Mr John R. Bowring BA, ALA; Chief Asst: Mrs T. J. Williamson. **7** Library. **9** Mon-Sat: ad ldg & children's 10.00-17.30, ref 9.00-17.00. **10** HQ only. **14** Manx colln. **17** Prisons. **21** (a, b&c) 1p pd. **23** (a) 80,000; (b) 3,000; (c) 4,000; (e) 40. **24** (a) 184,000; (b) 7,000. **25** (a) 3; (c) 1; (d) 1. **26** (a) £22,690; (b) £730; (c) £1.11; (d) £4,980; (f) £11,200.

GUERNSEY STATE OF (pop 45,000) Priaulx Library, Candie Rd, St Peter Port, Guernsey, Channel Islands (0481-21998). Chief Libn: Mr J.M.Y. Trotter BA; Dep: Miss D.C. Cook ALA. **7** Priaulx Library Council **9** Mon-Sat: 10.30-13.00, 14.00-16.30. **14** Local colln (books, deeds, diaries, letters, maps, photographs, book plates, mss etc). **20** 2 weeks, renewal allowed. **21** (a, b&c) none. **22** BLL. **23** (a, b, c&d) 25,000. **24** (a, b&c) 8,000. **25** (a) 3; (b) 1; (c) 1; (d) 1.

ISLE OF MAN BOARD OF EDUCATION (pop 56,000) Rural Library Headquarters, Burtons' Chambers, 18a Victoria St, Douglas, Isle of Man (0624-3123). Chief Libn: Ms Sheila M. Cowin; Dep: Ms Marjorie L. Dugdale. **7** Special Services. **8** Dir of Education: Mr Alun Davies LLB. **9** Mon-Fri: 9.30-17.30; Sat: 9.30-17.00. **10** HQ; Branch; Mobile. **12** Ramsey Public Lib, Parliament Sq, Ramsey, Isle of Man. **13** P-t 4; mobiles 1. **14** Leslie Berrisford music colln. **17** Schools, housebound, prisons, hospitals, old people's homes, lighthouses & beacons; playgroups. **21** (a&c) 2p 1st week, 1p pd thereafter; (b) none. **23** (a) 68,817; (b) 2,000; (c) 10,000; (d) 8,000; (e) 38. **24** (a&d) 482,846; (b) 40,000; (c) 145,000; **25** (a) 16; (b) 1; (c) 4; (d) 1. **26** (a) £38,850; (b) £2,000; (c) £0,695; (d) £17,100; (f) £14,000 (HQ only).

JERSEY STATES OF (pop c. 75,000) States of Jersey Library Service, Royal Sq, St Helier, Jersey, Channel Islands (0534-33201). Libn: Mr J. Kenneth Antill FLA; Dep Libn: Mr Ian Sutherland ALA; Chief Asst Libn: Miss Margaret Law ALA. **7** Education (Libraries Sub-Committee). **8** Civil Service Structure. **9** Mon-Sat: ad ldg & ref 10.00-17.30 (Fri 20.00), children's 10.00-13.00, 14.00-17.30. **13** P-t 1; mobiles 1. **14** Sea & its surrounds. **17** Schools, prisons, old people's homes & hospitals (help with book stock). **20** 3 weeks. **21** (a, b&c) 1p pd. **23** (a) 75,000; (b) 18,000; (c&d) 43,000; (e) 100. **24** (a) 435,492; (b) 190,962; (c) (book-box loans) 45,341. **25** (a) 25; (b) Govt pool; (c) 8. **26** (a) £135,000; (b) library service funded from taxes; (c) £1.80; (d) £46,000; (f) salaries (inc Jersey Civil Service superannuation & Insular Insurance) £80,000.

SPECIAL LIBRARIES

All entries are arranged alphabetically by town. The whole of the Greater London area is included under 'London'.

Unless specifically stated in the entry (question 11), it should not be assumed that a library is open to the public for reference, borrowing or even viewing. It is always courteous and sometimes essential to ask the Librarian's permission before visiting. Libraries are closed on bank holidays unless otherwise stated.

Some colleges, especially colleges of education, were due to merge in 1975 or 1976. As a result, much of the information about these colleges was not available at the time of going to press. Where the merger was not yet completed, the available information about proposed changes is given in brackets after the name of the college.

SPECIAL LIBRARIES: QUESTIONNAIRE

1. Official title of Library   2. Full postal address   3. Telephone number; Telex number 4. Designation, name and qualifications of officer in charge   5. Designation, name and qualifications of deputy to (4)

6. Name of governing body   7. Branch Libraries, if any, with brief address and telephone number, and name of officer in charge with qualifications   8. Main subjects covered by Library   9. Special Collections of significance 10. Co-operative schemes in which Library participates   11. Is the general public allowed access to the Library (state any special conditions) 12. Hours of opening   13. Stock: (a) Books and bound periodicals, number of volumes; (b) Number of individual periodical titles taken; (c) Other materials in the Library, with number of items if possible   14. Finance: estimated expenditure 1975/76 for books, binding, periodicals and all similar materials such as records, microtexts etc   15. Staff (hours worked by part-time staff per week should be totalled and divided by the number of normal working hours of a full-time member of staff to give the equivalent of full-time working): (a) Total number of full-time staff (excluding manual employees); (b) Number of graduate staff; (c) Number of chartered librarians (including graduates).

SPECIAL LIBRARIES

ABERDEEN, Aberdeenshire

ABERDEEN COLLEGE OF COMMERCE LIBRARY, Holburn
St, Aberdeen, AB9 2YT (Tel 0224-52528).
6 Grampian Regional Council.   **8** Sociology; law; statistics;
business management; accountancy; retailing; computers;
languages; history; geography.   **11** Yes, for ref only.
12 Mon-Thurs 8.30-21.00, Fri 8.30-17.00.   **13** (a) 2,000;
(b) 220.   **14** £6,000.   **15** (a) 3 (b) 1 (c) 2.

ABERDEEN COLLEGE OF EDUCATION LIBRARY, Hilton Pl,
Aberdeen, AB9 1FA (Tel 0224-42345) Principal Libn: Mr
D. McK. Read BA, FLA.
8 General.   **9** Education; children's books; non-book
material.   **10** SCE; inter-library loans.   **11** Only with
permission of Principal Libn.   **12** Term: Mon-Fri 9.00-
21.30, Sat 9.30-12.30; vac: Mon-Fri 9.00-17.15.
13 (a) 60,850; (c) pictures (2,000); filmstrips (1,000);
cassettes; gramophone records; etc.   **15** (a) 10 (b) 2½
(c) 3½.

ABERDEEN UNIVERSITY LIBRARY, King's College,
Aberdeen, AB9 2UB (Tel 0224-40241; Telex 73458) Univ Libn:
Mr J. M. Smethurst BA, ALA; Dep: Mr A. T. Hall MA, ALA.
6 University of Aberdeen.   **7** Science Lib, Meston Walk
(0224-40241, ext 297); Medical Lib, Foresterhill (ext 2740);
Agriculture Lib, School of Agriculture, King Street (ext 390);
Law Lib, Taylor Building (ext 224); Marischal College Lib
(ext 316); Taylor Reading Room, Taylor Building (ext 223).
8 General.   **9** MacBean (Jacobite) Colln; Gregory (science)
Colln; O'Dell (transport) Colln; G. W. Wilson (photographic)
Colln; rare & early printed books; mss; local collns.
11 Yes, on application to Libn.   **12** Term: Mon-Fri 9.00-
23.00, Sat 9.00-17.00, Sun 14.00-17.00; Christmas & Easter
vacs: Mon-Fri 9.00-22.00, Sat 9.00-13.00; summer vac:
Mon-Fri 9.00-17.00, Sat 9.00-13.00.   **13** (a) 650,000;
(b) 7,000; (c) archives; microtexts.   **14** £285,000.
15 (a) 100.

CHRIST'S COLLEGE LIBRARY, 2 Alford Pl, Aberdeen, AB1
1YD (Tel 0224-26426) Coll Libn: Rev J. Mowat MA; Dep:
Mr. A. McLennan.
6 Christ's College Council.   **8** Theological.   **10** NLS.
11 No.   **12** Term: 9.00-17.00; vac: Tues & Thurs 14.00-
17.00.   **13** (a) c.10.000; (b) 21.   **14** £400.   **15** (a) 1.

MACAULAY INSTITUTE FOR SOIL RESEARCH LIBRARY,
Craigiebuckler, Aberdeen, AB9 2QJ (Tel 0224-38611).
8 Soil science; plant sciences; geology; forestry; chemistry;
physics; agriculture.   **10** ANSLICS.   **11** No.   **12** 8.45-
17.15.   **13** (a) 5,000 books; (b) c.350.   **15** (a) 3 (b) 1
(c) 1.

MARINE LABORATORY LIBRARY, PO Box 101, Victoria Rd,
Torry, Aberdeen, AB9 8DB (Tel 0224-29944; Telex 73587
Fishlab Abdn) Libn: Mr John H. Burne ALA; Dep: Mrs Jean
Alcock MA, ALA.
6 Dept of Agriculture & Fisheries for Scotland.   **7** Freshwater Fisheries Laboratory, Faskally, Pitlochry, Perthshire,
PH16 5LB (Tel 0796-2060) Libn: Mrs R. Laurie.   **8** Biology
of fish & marine life; oceanography; ecology & statistics;
fishing methods & instrumentation.   **9** Ogilvie (Diatoma-
ceae) Colln.   **10** Aslib; ANSLICS.   **11** Yes, for ref only.
12 Mon-Thurs 8.30-17.00, Fri 8.30-16.30.   **13** (a)
18,000; (b) 1,600; (c) maps & charts; patents; standards;
slides & reports.   **14** £24,000.   **15** (a) 6 (b) 1 (c) 2.

ROBERT GORDON'S INSTITUTE OF TECHNOLOGY
LIBRARY, St Andrew St, Aberdeen, AB1 1HG (Tel 0224-22338)
Principal Libn: Mr S. R. Latham FLA, FInstPet; Senior Libn:
Mr J. Duncan MA, ALA.
7 Kepplestone Premises, Queens Rd, Aberdeen, Libn: Miss
N. Willox MA, ALA; 252 King St, Aberdeen, Libn: Mr R. C.

Moodie ALA; Gray's School of Art, Garthdee, Aberdeen, Libn:
Mrs E. Dunphy MA; Scott Sutherland School of Architecture,
Garthdee, Aberdeen, Libn: Mr A. Cluer ALA.   **8** Architecture; art; building economics; chemistry; pharmacy; physics;
maths; social studies; speech therapy; librarianship; mechanical engineering; electrical & electronic engineering; business
management; navigation; home economics; nutritional science;
hotel & institutional management; health visiting.   **10** BLL;
NLS; Aslib; ANSLICS.   **11** Yes.   **12** Term: Mon-Fri
9.00-22.00, Sat 9.00-17.00, Sun 14.00-22.00; vac: Mon-Fri
9.00-17.00.   **13** (a) 85,000; (b) 1,110; (c) gramophone
records; microtexts; slides; video-tapes; tape cassettes.
14 £60,000.   **15** a 21; b 3; c 8.

ROWETT RESEARCH INSTITUTE, REID LIBRARY, Bucksburn, Aberdeen, AB2 95B (Tel 0224-71 2751) Libn: Mr J. C. R.
Yeats ALA; Dep: Miss Helen P. Martin.
8 Nutrition (human & animal); physiology; biochemistry;
animal husbandry.   **9** Part of library of Sir Archibald
Grant (18th cent).   **10** BLL; NLS.   **11** Yes, to bona-fide
students & enquirers.   **12** Mon-Fri 9.00-17.25.
13 (a) c.28,000; (b) 750; (c) c.25,000 pamphlets; 100 microtexts; annual reports.   **15** (a) 4 (c) 1.

RUBISLAW ACADEMY LIBRARY, Skene St, Aberdeen, AB9
1HT (Tel 0224-22299) Libn: Ms Patricia A. Fraser.
6 Local Authority.   **8** All academic subjects; hobbies;
general.   **9** Colln of 18th-cent books.   **11** No.
12 8.45-17.00.   **13** (a) 20,000; (b) 40.   **14** £2,600.
15 (a) 1.

ABERYSTWYTH, Dyfed

COLLEGE OF LIBRARIANSHIP WALES LIBRARY,
Llanbadarn Fawr, Aberystwyth, SY23 3AS (Tel 0970-3181;
Telex 35391) Libn: Mr D. Ball FLA; Sub-Libns: Mr H. Davies
BA, FLA; Mr M. Wise FLA.
6 Dyfed CC.   **7** Exhibition & Design Centre.   **8** Library
& information science.   **9** Appleton Colln (19th-cent colour
printing); Oliver Simon Colln (printing).   **10** WRLS.
11 Yes, on application.   **12** Term: Mon-Fri 9.00-22.00,
Sat 10.00-16.30; vac: Mon-Thurs 9.00-17.30, Fri 9.00-17.00.
13 (a) 65,000; (b) 970; (c) 19 art prints; 80 films; 9 film
cassettes; 11 film loops; 224 filmstrips; 37 kits; 67 maps; 79
posters; 135 records; 2,482 slides; 21 slide kits; 49 OHP transparencies; 159 tapes; 321 tape cassettes; 256 texts; 28 wall
charts; 10 video cassettes; 25 slide sound presentations.
14 £47,000.   **15** (a) 23 (b) 6 (c) 11.

NATIONAL LIBRARY OF WALES, (Llyfrgell Genedlaethol
Cymru), Aberystwyth, SY23 3BU (Tel 0970-3816/9; Telex
35165) Libn: Mr David Jenkins MA, JP.
6 Court of Governors of National Library of Wales.
8 Copyright library; world's largest colln of books in Welsh
& relating to Wales; other Celtic countries.   **9** Sir John
Williams Colln (over 25,000 vols); complete set, in fine bindings, of Gregynog Press; Chaucer's 'Canterbury Tales'; mss
of Bede's 'Ecclesiastical History'; Hengwrt-Peniarth mss,
(finest colln of Welsh mss in a single location); Euclid; international folklore; Egyptology & papyrology.   **10** Headquarters of National Bureau for Wales, Regional Libraries
Scheme (WRLS).   **11** Yes, to Gregynog Gallery; to Readers'
Room with Reader's Ticket only.   **12** Gregynog Gallery:
(May-Oct) Mon-Sat 10.00-17.00; Reading Room: Mon-Fri
9.30-18.00, Sat 9.30-17.00.   **13** (a) 2,000,000; (b) 5,500;
(c) 180,000 maps, prints, drawings of photographs; 30,000
mss; 2,000 microfilms; 1,000 slides; 3,500,000 archives.
14 £118,525.   **15** (a) 94 (b) 47 (c) 16.

ABERYSTWYTH, Dyfed—continued

UNIVERSITY COLLEGE OF WALES LIBRARY, Old College, King St, Aberystwyth, SY23 2AX (Tel 0970-2711, ext 26; Telex 35181 LIBRY UCW ABRWTH) Libn: Mr W. W. Dieneman MA, ALA; Senior Sub-Libn: Miss B. T. Clay ALA.
6 Court of Governors of the University College of Wales.
7 Penglais Campus, Aberystwyth (0970-3111); Llandinam (social & earth sciences) Lib; Biology Lib; Institute of Rural Sciences Lib; Physical Sciences Lib; (new Law & Arts/Social Science Libs to be opened in 1975-76). Town libs; Chemistry Lib, Edward Davies Laboratories, Buarth Rd (0970-7645); Education Lib, Alexandra Rd (0970-7872). **8** General; humanities; social sciences; law; sciences (excluding medicine & engineering); agriculture. **9** Law; classical & medieval Latin studies; American (US) studies (c. 6,000 items); J. W. Duff monographs on classical authors (1,080 items); Gregynog Press publications; British govt & UN publications; George Powell colln; John Camden Hotten colln; Richard Ellis mss; David de Lloyd mss. **10** BLL; WRLS; Background Materials Scheme 1857-59. **11** Yes, for ref only. **12** Term: Mon-Fri 9.00-22.00, Sat 9.00-13.00; vac: Mon-Fri 9.00-13.00, 14.00-17.30, Sat 9.00-13.00. **13** (a) c. 300,000; (b) 3,200; (c) microtext sets (190); gramophone records (12); mss (c. 10,000). **14** £124,000. **15** (a) 44 (b) 18 (c) 24.

WELSH PLANT BREEDING STATION LIBRARY, Plas Gogerddan, Aberystwyth, SY23 3EB (Tel 0970-87255) Libn: Miss J. M. Williams.
6 Agricultural Research Council. **8** Developmental genetics; herbage plant breeding; grassland agronomy; seed multiplication & herbage seed research; arable crop breeding; plant pathology; chemistry; cytology; physics; visual aids; statistics; nematology; biochemistry; microbiology.
9 Classical colln of old agricultural & botanical books.
10 Collaborates with libs of University College of Wales & all local research libraries; inter-library loans. **11** No.
12 8.30-17.00. **13** (a) 9,327; (b) 700; (c) theses; map collns; annual reports; reprints; & technical bulletins etc. of the Research Institute itself. **15** (a) 4.

ABINGDON, Oxfordshire

ABINGDON COLLEGE OF FURTHER EDUCATION LIBRARY, Northcourt Rd, Abingdon, OX14 1NN (Tel 0235-21585) Libn: Mrs. P. Webber ALA.
6 Oxfordshire Education Committee. **8** General; engineering. **11** Yes, for ref only. **12** Mon & Wed 9.00-19.30, Tues & Thurs 9.00-21.00, Fri 9.00-17.00. **13** (a) 20,566; (b) 122. **15** (a) 2 (c) 2.

CULHAM LABORATORY LIBRARY, UKAEA Culham Laboratory, Abingdon, OX14 3DB (Tel 0235-21840; Telex 83189) Libn: J. L. Hall BSc, ARCST.
8 Plasma physics & controlled thermonuclear fusion; vacuum technology; electrotechnology; computing; astrophysics; space research. **9** On-line information retrieval.
11 Yes, but only by special arrangement with Libn.
12 8.30-17.00. **13** (a) 14,000; (b) over 400; (c) c. 30,000 scientific reports (many in microfiche). **15** (a) 12 (b) 3 (c) 4.

ABINGER, Surrey

FIRE SERVICE STAFF COLLEGE LIBRARY, Wotton House, Abinger Common, Dorking, RH5 6HT (Tel 0306-730441, exts 34 & 60) Libn: Mr. P. L. Hill ALA.
6 Home Office (Fire Service College Board). **8** Fire fighting & fire prevention; emergency operations & major incidents; fire reports & fire losses; history of the Fire Service, inc fire insurance & fire marks; legislation on fire fighting + fire prevention. **10** BLL; local authority fire brigades; government departmental libraries; inter-library loans. **11** Yes, for ref only, by prior arrangement.
12 Open during normal College sessions. **13** (a) pamphlets 21,000; (b) 150; (c) unpublished reports (16,000).
15 (a) 2 (c) 1.

ALDERSHOT, Hampshire

PRINCE CONSORT'S ARMY LIBRARY, Knollys Rd, Aldershot, GU11 1PS (Tel 0252-24431, ext Montgomery 381/382) Libn: Mrs J. Sears ALA; Clerical Officer: Mr L. Owen.
6 MoD (Army) **8** All military topics; military & general history; biography; general non-fiction. **9** Military history colln of Prince Albert. **10** BLL; Services Central Library.
11 Yes, on written application with references. **12** Mon-Thurs 9.00-13.00, 14.00-17.30, Fri 9.00-13.00, 14.00-17.00. **13** (a) c. 50,000; (b) 24. **15** (a) 3 (c) 1.

ALLOA, Clackmannanshire

CLACKMANNAN COLLEGE OF FURTHER EDUCATION LIBRARY, Branshill Rd, Alloa (Tel 02592-4148) Coll Libn: Mrs J. Horne.
6 Central Region. **8** General. **11** No. **12** Mon-Fri 8.45-16.15. **13** (a) 2,800; (b) 20. **14** £1,000. **15** (a) 1.

ALTRINCHAM, Cheshire

SOUTH TRAFFORD COLLEGE OF FURTHER EDUCATION LIBRARY, Manchester, Altrincham (Tel 061-962 2286).
6 Trafford Borough Council. **7** Sale Adult Centre, Ashfield Rd, Sale. **8** General. **10** BLL; NWRLB. **11** Yes.
12 9.00-17.15. **13** (a) 26,000; (b) 220; (c) filmstrips; slides; illustrations; tapes; cassettes; gramophone records; project files; video-tape. **14** £6,000. **15** (a) 6 (c) 3.

AMBLESIDE, Cumbria

FRESHWATER BIOLOGICAL ASSOCIATION, The Ferry House, Ambleside, LA22 0LP (Tel 09662-2468) Libn: Mr John E. M. Horne BSc, MIInfSc; Dep: Mr Ian Pettman BSc, ALA.
8 Biology, physics & chemistry of fresh waters. **9** Fritsch Colln of illustrations of freshwater algae. **11** No, except by prior arrangement. **12** Mon-Thurs 8.30-16.45, Fri 8.30-15.45. **13** (a) 10,000; (b) 500; (c) offprints of individual papers (over 40,000). **15** (a) 4½ (b) 2 (c) 1.

AMERSHAM, Buckinghamshire

RADIOCHEMICAL CENTRE LTD LIBRARY, Amersham, HP7 9LL (Tel 02404-4444; Telex 83141) Libn: Mr Jolyon Lea; Dep Libn: Mrs Vera Butterworth.
8 Radioactive materials; nuclear & clinical medicine; biochemistry; analytical chemistry. **9** Nuclear medicine.
10 HASL. **11** Yes, by prior arrangement with Libn.
12 Mon-Fri 8.30-17.00. **13** (a) 10,000; (b) 300.
14 £12,000. **15** (a) 4 (c) 1.

ASHFORD, Kent

WYE COLLEGE LIBRARY, Wye, Ashford, TN25 5AH (Tel 0233-812401) Libn: Mr G. P. Lilley MA, DipLib, FLA.
6 University of London. **8** Agriculture, horticulture & related subjects, inc. management & marketing; landscape & environmental subjects. **9** Early books on agriculture & horticulture (1,400); Kentish history (300); mss records of Wye parish and Royal Manor of Wye; Sir E. John Russell Colln of mss. **10** BUCOP; KULOP. **11** Yes, for ref only, by prior arrangement. **12** Term: Mon-Fri 9.00-22.00, Sat 9.30-17.00; Sun 14.00-17.00; vac: Mon-Fri 9.00-19.00, Sat 9.30-12.00, Sun 14.00-17.00. **13** (a) 30,000; (b) 800; (c) pamphlets (c. 20,000). **14** c. £18,400. **15** (a) 7½ (b) 3 (c) 3½.

ASHINGTON, Northumberland

NORTHUMBERLAND COUNTY TECHNICAL COLLEGE LIBRARY, College Rd, Ashington, NE63 9RG (Tel 0903-813248) Tutor-Libn: Mr W. E. Hume ALA; Coll Libn: Miss F. E. Middlemist BA.
6 Northumberland CC. **8** Mining; construction; engineering; business studies; catering; health & fashion; general.
9 BSI. **10** TALIC; NRLB. **11** No, but we do offer a service to industry based on the BSI colln. **12** Term: Mon-Thurs 9.00-20.00, Fri 9.00-17.00; vac: Mon-Fri 9.00-17.00. **13** (a) c. 26,000; (b) 250; (c) 875 gramophone records; filmstrips; cassettes. **14** £9,000. **15** (a) 3 (b) 1 (c) 1.

CODE: 1 Name of Library. 2 Address. 3 Telephone & Telex. 4 Officer in charge. 5 Deputy. 6 Governing body.
7 Branches. 8 Main Subjects. 9 Special Collections. 10 Co-operative Schemes. 11 Open to public? 12 Hours.
13 Stock: (a) books (b) periodicals (c) other. 14 Finance. 15 Staff: (a) non-manual (b) graduate (c) chartered librarians.

AYLESBURY, Buckinghamshire

AYLESBURY COLLEGE OF FURTHER EDUCATION AND
AGRICULTURE LIBRARY, Oxford Rd, Aylesbury, HP22 5TB
(Tel 0296-4571) Tutor-Libn: Miss B. M. Still FLA.
6 Buckinghamshire CC. **8** General. **11** No.
12 Term: Mon-Thurs 9.15-21.00, Fri 9.15-20.00.
13 (a) 21,000; (b) 170. **14** £4,850. **15** (a) 3 (c) 1.

AYR, Ayrshire

CRAIGIE COLLEGE OF EDUCATION LIBRARY, Ayr,
KA9 0SR (Tel 0292-60321) Principal Libn: Mr Geoffrey
Dixon BA, ALA; Sub-Libn: Mr William A. Anderson ALA.
6 Governors of Craigie College of Education. **8** General;
education; child psychology; teaching of various curricular
subjects; children's books. **10** NLS; scheme for co-operative provision of American educational periodicals in the
libraries of Scottish Colls of Education. **11** No, except
for ref to teachers and students. **12** Term: Mon-Fri
9.00-17.00 (19.00 Tues & Thurs); vac: Mon-Fri 9.00-12.30,
13.30-17.00. **13** (a) 45,000; (b) 240; (c) 1,000 filmstrips,
slides, etc; 1,100 gramophone records & tapes; 5,500 wallcharts & illustrations. **15** (a) 6½ (b) 1 (c) 3.

HANNAH RESEARCH INSTITUTE LIBRARY, Ayr, KA6 5HL
(Tel 0292-77292) Libn & Inf Officer: Mr Brian A. Nettlefold
BA, ALA, AIInfSc.
8 Milk production & utilization; biochemistry; animal
physiology; microbiology; chemistry. **11** Yes, with prior
permission. **12** 8.50-17.10 **13** (a) 7,000; (b) 190.
15 (a) 2 (b) 1 (c) 1.

WEST OF SCOTLAND AGRICULTURAL COLLEGE, W. J.
THOMSON LIBRARY, Donald Hendrie Building, Auchincruive,
KA6 5HW (Tel 029-252 331) Libn: Miss M. B. Myers CDH;
Asst Libn: Mrs M. Drummond.
8 Agriculture; horticulture; poultry-keeping; food technology.
11 Yes, for ref only. **12** Mon-Fri 9.00-17.00, & Mon, Tues,
Thurs 18.45-20.45. **13** (a) 12,000; (b) 350; (c) 30,000
pamphlets. **14** £2,300. **15** (a) 2½ (c) 1.

BANBURY, Oxfordshire

ALCAN INTERNATIONAL LTD LIBRARY, Southam Rd, Banbury, OX16 75P (Tel 0295-2821; Telex 83253) Libn: Mr K. K.
Covill; Dep: Mrs M D Cook.
8 Properties, fabrication & uses of aluminium; metallurgy;
chemistry; physics; engineering. **10** BLL; Interlab
(Mintech); Aslib. **11** No. **13** (a) 5,000; (b) 300; (c) 46,000
photographs; 27,000 patents. **15** (a) 9 (b) 1.

BANGOR, Gwynedd

UNIVERSITY COLLEGE OF NORTH WALES LIBRARY,
Bangor, LL57 2DG (Tel 0248-51151; Telex 61100) Libn:
L. G. Heywood MA; Dep Science Libn: Mr R. I. J. Tully FLA;
Dep Arts Libn: Dr R. Gwyn Davies MA, PhD, ALA.
7 Science Lib, Deiniol Rd (0248-51151), Dep Libn: Mr R. I. J.
Tully FLA. **8** Arts: economics; education; English language & literature; French & Romance studies; Italian, German
& Teutonic philology; Russian, Greek, Hebrew & biblical
studies; history; archaeology; Latin; linguistics; music;
philosophy; social theory & institutions; Welsh history, language & literature. Science: agriculture; forest zoology; biochemistry; soil science; chemistry; engineering science;
forestry; marine science; maths; physics; plant biology;
psychology; zoology. **9** Welsh library (books & periodicals); Bangor Cathedral Library (inc 1,100 vols printed
before 1700 & 4 incunabula); Sir Frank Brangwyn Art Colln;
Talfourd-Jones Colln (botanical & zoological); important
archive colln (mainly North Wales inc family & estate
papers). **10** BLL; WRLS. **11** Yes, for ref; borrowing on
application only. **12** Term: Mon-Fri 9.00-22.00 (summer

term 23.00), Sat 9.00-12.30, 14.00-17.00, Sun 14.00-17.00;
vac: Mon-Fri 9.30-17.00 (Easter vac 19.00), Sat 9.00-12.00.
13 (a) c. 400,000; (b) 3,650; (c) c. 300,000 mss; microforms;
records. **15** (a) 46 (b) 18 (c) 13.

BARNSTAPLE, Devon

NORTH DEVON ATHENAEUM LIBRARY, The Square, Barnstaple, EX32 8LN (Tel 0271-2174) Libn: Mr G. A. Morris.
6 Rock Trust. **8** Local history; geography; geology;
topography; travel; classical literature. **10** BLL; SWRLB.
11 Yes, (children under 14 must be accompanied by adult).
12 Mon-Fri 10.00-13.00, 14.15-18.00, Sat 10.00-13.00.
13 (a) c. 30,000; (c) microfilms of local journal. **15** (a) 1
(b) 1.

NORTH DEVON COLLEGE LIBRARY, Sticklepath, Barnstaple,
EX31 2BQ (Tel 0271-5291) Lecturer/Learning Resources:
Miss P. Waterer BA, ALA; Senior Asst Libn: Mrs A. M.
Bidgood ALA.
6 Devon CC. **8** General. **9** Barbour Index; ref set of
Open University course units. **11** Yes for ref only; loans
for local teachers, commerce & industry by arrangement).
12 Mon-Fri 8.45-20.00 (Tues 21.00, Fri 17.00). **13** (a)
25,000; (b) 220; (c) software colln.

BASILDON, Essex

BASILDON COLLEGE OF FURTHER EDUCATION LIBRARY,
Nethermayne, Basildon, SS16 5NN (Tel 0268-25202) Libn:
Mrs J. Hayward ALA.
6 Board of Governors. **8** General engineering; business
studies; nursing; education. **10** LASER. **11** No.
12 Term: Mon-Thurs 9.00-20.00, Fri 9.00-17.30; vac:
9.00-17.00. **13** (a) 6,449; (b) 83. **14** £3,000. **15** (a) 3
(c) 2.

BASINGSTOKE, Hampshire

BASINGSTOKE TECHNICAL COLLEGE LIBRARY, Worting
Rd, Basingstoke, RG21 1TN (Tel 0256-65551) Coll Libn: Miss
M. I. Dawe BA, ALA.
6 Hampshire CC. **8** General; engineering; building; commerce & management; domestic science. **9** BSI.
10 BLL; SWRLB. **11** Yes, by appointment, for ref only.
12 Term: Mon-Thurs 9.00-19.30, Fri 9.00-17.00; vac:
Mon-Fri 9.00-17.00. **13** (a) 17,000; (b) 148; (c) 300 films
strips & film loops. **14** £3,000. **15** (a) 2 (b) 1 (c) 1.

POLICE COLLEGE LIBRARY, Bramshill House, Bramshill,
Basingstoke, RG27 0JW (Tel 025-126 2931 ext 227) Libn:
Mr D. T. Brett FLA; Mr H. M. Barrett MA.
6 Governors of the Police College. **8** General; public
science; crime; punishment; law; criminal law; social problems.
9 Annual reports of H. M. Inspectors of Constabulary from
1857; 'Police & Constabulary Almanac' from 1858; 'Police
Review' from 1893; 'Police Journal' from 1928; 'Punch' from
1841. Exhibits: Dixon, Acworth & Langton collns of trun-
cheons & tipstaves. **11** No, except with Commandant's
permission. **12** Daily: 7.00-midnight. **13** (a) 21,760;
(b) c. 300; (c) microfilm periodicals. **14** £8,000.
15 (a) 7 (b) 1 (c) 1.

BATH, Avon

BATH TECHNICAL COLLEGE LIBRARY, Avon St, Bath,
BA1 1UP (Tel 0225-64191) Tutor-Libn: Mr D. L. Houldridge
MA, FLA.
6 Avon CC. **8** Social science; pure sciences; engineering;
construction industries; catering; English literature.
10 SWRLB. **11** Yes, for ref only. **12** Term: Mon-Fri
8.45-21.00. **13** (a) 20,500; (b) 130. **14** £3,000.
15 (a) 3 (b) 1 (c) 1.

BATH, Avon—*continued*

BATH UNIVERSITY LIBRARY, Claverton Down, Bath,
BA2 7AY (Tel 0225-6941; Telex 44907) Univ Libn: Mr J.H.
Lamble; Mr K.E. Jones BA, ALA.
8 Science; technology; social sciences; management; education; modern languages.   **9** Pitman Colln (history of shorthand, etc).   **10** SWRLB.   **11** Yes, on recommendation.
12 Term: Mon-Fri 9.00-21.00, Sun 10.00-18.00.   **13** (a)
100,000; (b) c. 2,000; (c) video cassettes; slide/tapes; microfilm.   **14** £100,000.   **15** (a) 32 (b) 9 (c) 12.

BATHGATE, West Lothian

WEST LOTHIAN COLLEGE OF FURTHER EDUCATION
LIBRARY, Marjoribanks St, Bathgate, EH48 1QJ (Tel 0506-55801/4) Libn: Miss Evelyn P. Steel MA, DipLib; Asst Libn:
Mrs Dorothy Billinge.
6 Education Dept, Lothian Regional Council.   **8** Engineering; business studies; building; general.   **10** BLL; NLS.
11 Yes, for ref only.   **12** Mon-Thurs 8.30-16.30, 18.00-20.30, Fri 8.30-13.00, 14.00-16.30.   **13** (a) 12,600; (b) 99.
14 £3,000.

BEACONSFIELD, Buckingham

WIGGINS TEAPE RESEARCH AND DEVELOPMENT
LIBRARY, Butler's Court, Beaconsfield, HP9 1RT (Tel 04946-5652; Telex 83612) Technical Inf Officer: Mr S.R. Loynes
FIInfSc, MIRT; Asst Technical Inf Officer: Miss J.R. Smith.
8 Paper technology; science & research.   **9** Company's
technological progress & development reports for over 40
years (part hard copy, part microfilm).   **10** North Atlantic
Paper Libraries Exchange Scheme (Translations).   **11** Yes,
on application to Inf Officer.   **12** Mon-Fri 9.00-17.30.
13 (a) 5,500; (b) 280; (c) internal company reports (90,000).
14 £6,000.   **15** (a) 8½ (b) 3.

BEAULIEU, Hampshire

NATIONAL MOTOR MUSEUM LIBRARY, Beaulieu, SO4 7ZN
(Tel 0590-612 345 ext 38) Libn: Mr Eric A. Bellamy.
8 Motoring, inc motor-cycles & commercial vehicles.
11 No.   **12** Open for enquiries: Mon-Fri 10.00-12.30,
14.00-17.00.   **13** (a) c. 14,000; (b) 35; (c) archives.
14 £50-60 (binding).

BEDFORD, Bedfordshire

AIRCRAFT RESEARCH ASSOCIATION LTD LIBRARY,
Manton Lane, Bedford, MK41 7PF (Tel 0234-50681 ext 233;
Telex 825056) Libn: Mrs F.M. Guinevan BA, ALA; Asst Libn:
Mrs B.M. Couling.
8 Aerodynamics, especially wind tunnel tests & testing;
aeronautics; computing; electronics; maths.   **9** Colln of
reports, mainly British & American.   **10** BLL; Aslib.
11 Yes, on application to Libn.   **12** 8.30-16.50.
13 (a) 2,500; (b) 120; (c) 20,500 reports; microfiche.
15 (a) 2 (b) 1 (c) 1.

BEDFORD COLLEGE OF EDUCATION LIBRARY (will merge
with Mander College & Bedford College of Physical Education
in September 1976 to form the Bedford College of Higher
Education), Polhill Ave, Bedford, MK41 9EA (Tel 0234-51671)
Tutor-Libn: D.S. Redfearn BA, ALA; Asst Libn: Miss N.W.
Griffith BA, ALA.
6 Bedfordshire CC.   **8** Education; art + craft; English
literature & drama; French; geography; history; maths;
music; physical education; science.   **9** Hockliffe colln
(c. 1,200 16th-19th cent children's books).   **11** No.
12 Term: Mon & Thurs 9.00-19.00, Tues & Wed 9.00-18.00,
Fri 9.00-17.00; vac: Mon-Fri 9.00-17.00.   **13** (a) 40,000;
(b) 210.   **14** £9,000.   **15** (a) 3 (b) 2 (c) 2.

MANDER COLLEGE LIBRARY, (will merge with Bedford
College of Education & Bedford College of Further Education,
Sept 1976, to form the Bedford College of Higher Education),
Cauldwell St, Bedford, MK42 9AH (Tel 0234-45151 ext 29)
Tutor-Libn: Mr J.A. Hargreaves FLA.
6 Bedfordshire CC.   **8** Agriculture; commerce; construction & engineering industries; home economics; technical
education.   **10** BLL.   **11** Yes, for ref only.   **12** Term:

8.45-20.00; vac: 9.00-13.00, 14.00-17.00.   **13** (a) 25,000;
(b) 200; (c) 800 film loops; 150 ohp transparencies; 3,000
slides; 200 gramophone records; 350 tapes; 100 maps; 90 study
kits; 100 wall charts.   **14** £11,000.   **15** (a) 6 (b) 1 (c) 3.

NATIONAL COLLEGE OF AGRICULTURAL ENGINEERING
LIBRARY, Silsoe, Bedford, MK45 4DT (Tel 0525-60428 ext 16)
Libn: Mr B.A. Morgan ALA.
8 Agricultural engineering; farm machinery; mechanization;
irrigation; drainage; farm buildings; agricultural environmental control & crop processing; soil conservation; land
resource planning; agricultural systems.   **10** Inter-library
loans.   **11** Yes, for ref to bona-fide enquirers.   **12** Term:
Mon-Fri 9.00-21.00 (Wed 17.30, Fri 18.30); vac: Mon-Fri
9.00-13.00, 14.00-17.30.   **13** (a) 20,000; (b) 280; (c) maps
(546); microtexts (4,200); slides, overhead projector sets and
film loops (950).   **14** £8,000.   **15** (a) 3½ (c) 1.

NATIONAL INSTITUTE OF AGRICULTURAL ENGINEERING
LIBRARY, Wrest Park, Silsoe, Bedford, MK45 4HS (Tel 0525-60000) Libn: Mr W.J. Course CEng, MIMechE, MIInfSc; Asst
Libn: Mrs D.M. Cook.
6 Agricultural Research Council.   **8** Engineering applied
to agriculture.   **11** Yes, by prior arrangement.   **12** Mon-Fri 8.30-17.00 (Fri 16.30).   **13** (a) 10,000; (b) 220.
15 (a) 3.

BELFAST, Northern Ireland

BELFAST LIBRARY AND SOCIETY FOR PROMOTING
KNOWLEDGE (LINEN HALL LIBRARY), 17 Donegall Sq
North, Belfast, BT1 5GD (Tel 0232-21707) Libn: Mr J.W.
Vitty MA; Dep Libn: Dr J.R.R. Adams ALA.
8 History, biography; genealogy; humanities generally
(Irish emphasis).   **9** Irish colln; Belfast & Ulster printing
colln; British printing before 1700; N.I. political ephemera
from 1968; Gibson colln (Burns & Burnsiana); Ewart colln
(textile works); Irish works; Blackwood colln (genealogy &
family history); 'Belfast Newsletter' from 1738.   **10** BLL;
ICLS.   **11** Yes, but identification preferred.   **12** Mon-Fri 9.30-18.00, Sat 9.30-16.00.   **13** (a) 220,000; (b) 226;
(c) c. 135 reels microfilm (mainly 'Belfast Newsletter' files);
c. 3,500 items political ephemera; 100 vols mss (inc typescript).   **14** £10,000.   **15** (a) 9 (b) 1 (c) 2.

MINISTRY OF COMMERCE, DEPARTMENT OF INDUSTRIAL
AND FORENSIC SCIENCE LIBRARY, 180 Newtonbreda Rd,
Belfast, BT8 4QR (Tel 0232-645421) Libn & Inf Officer:
Miss A.B. Smyth BSc.
8 Building science; fuel technology; paint technology; metallurgy; inorganic chemistry; chemical engineering; wood
science; organic chemistry; industrial biology; water pollution
control; environmental science; instrumental methods; forensic science.   **9** Forensic science; BSI; abridgments of British patent specifications from 1956.   **10** Computer-based
ISBN book location system for Northern Ireland; Union list of
current periodicals in Irish libraries.   **11** No, available to
industrialists, others by special arrangement.   **12** Mon-Fri 9.00-12.45, 13.30-17.00.   **13** (a) 7,250; (b) 400; (c)
7,500 pamphlets; reports & reprints.   **14** £5,000.
15 (a) 6 (b) 2.

PARLIAMENT BUILDINGS LIBRARY, Stormont, Belfast,
BT4 3SY (Tel 0232-63210) Libn: Mr Thomas Hamilton; Dep:
Miss A.M. Fowler
6 Northern Ireland Assembly (suspended).   **8** Constitutions
& constitutional law; politics & political science; education;
economics; biographies; parliamentary debates & papers;
law.   **9** Parliamentary debates (Westminster, Northern
Ireland & Republic of Ireland); parliamentary papers (Westminster & N. Ireland).   **11** No.   **12** 9.30-17.00.
13 (a) 29,000; (b) 74.   **14** £12,000.   **15** (a) 10 (b) 1.

QUEEN'S UNIVERSITY LIBRARY, Belfast, BT7 1LS (Tel
0232-45133; Telex 74487) Univ Libn: Mr A. Blamire MA,
ALA.
7 Science Lib, Belfast, BT9 5EQ (0232-45133), Libn: Mr R.T.
Kimber MLS, BSc; Medical Lib, Belfast, BT12 6BJ (0232-22043); Libn: Mr W.D. Linton BLS, BSc, MIBiol; Agriculture
Lib, Belfast, BT9 5BX (0232-61166), Libn: Mrs M. Walsh
NDDT.

CODE: **1** Name of Library. **2** Address. **3** Telephone & Telex. **4** Officer in charge. **5** Deputy. **6** Governing body. **7** Branches. **8** Main Subjects. **9** Special Collections. **10** Co-operative Schemes. **11** Open to public? **12** Hours. **13** Stock: (a) books (b) periodicals (c) other. **14** Finance. **15** Staff: (a) non-manual (b) graduate (c) chartered librarians.

BELFAST, Northern Ireland

8 Humanities; pure & applied science; medicine; law; economics & social sciences; education; agriculture. **9** Thomas Percy Colln; Somerville & Ross (mss) Colln; McDouall (Sanskrit) Colln; Hamilton Harty (Music) Colln; Ross [Rosenweig] (Hebrew) Colln; Hibernica Colln; Gibson-Massie (Scottish) Colln. **10** BLL; ICLS. **11** Yes. **12** Term: Mon-Fri 9.00-23.00, Sat: 9.00-12.30; vac: 9.00-17.30. **13** (a) 688,000; (b) 8,000. **14** £230,000. **15** (a) 108 (b) 39 (c) 30.

STRANMILLIS COLLEGE LIBRARY, Belfast, BT9 5DY (Tel 0232-665271) Libn: Mr F. J. Teskey MA; Dep: Miss M. Ginn ALA.
6 Board of Governors. **8** General. **9** Education. **11** Yes, at libn's discretion. **12** Term: 9.00-22.00; vac: 9.00-17.00. **13** (a) 70,000; (b) 400; (c) Gramophone records; microtexts; slides; film strips; tapes; film loops; pictures. **14** £24,000.

BERKHAMSTED, Hertfordshire

ASHRIDGE MANAGEMENT COLLEGE LIBRARY, Berkhamsted, HP4 1NS (Tel 044284-3491; Telex 28604 ref. 843) Libn: Mrs S. P. Luke ALA; Dep: Miss A. M. Pring BA, ALA.
6 The Governors, Ashridge (Bonar Law Memorial) Trust. **8** Management education; behavioural sciences; general management; economics; finance; personnel management; industrial relations; marketing. **10** HERTIS; Aslib. **11** No. **12** 24 hours a day, but staffed only 8.30-18.00. **13** (a) 15,000 books & pamphlets; (b) 220; (c) management films; Extel Company information service. **14** £5,000. **15** (a) 3½ (b) 1 (c) 2.

BIGGLESWADE, Bedfordshire

SHUTTLEWORTH AGRICULTURAL COLLEGE LIBRARY, Old Warden Park, Biggleswade, SG18 9DX (Tel 076727-441) **6** Richard Ormonde Shuttleworth Remembrance Trust. **8** Agriculture. **9** Agricultural history. **11** No. **13** (a) c. 2,000; (b) 50. **14** £750. **15** (a) ½ (b) ½.

BILLINGHAM, Cleveland

STOCKTON-BILLINGHAM TECHNICAL COLLEGE LIBRARY, The Causeway, Billingham, TS23 2DB (Tel 0642-552101 ext 25) Libn: Miss Jean Shaw BA, ALA.
6 Cleveland CC. **7** Oxbridge Ave Annexe, Oxbridge Ave, Stockton-on-Tees (0642-62317 ext 33). **8** Engineering; construction; business studies; science; domestic sciences; liberal & cultural studies; general. **9** BSI (at Oxbridge Ave). **10** NRLB; LIST. **11** Yes, at Libn's discretion. **12** Mon-Fri 9.00-19.00 (Fri 16.15). Branch varies. **13** (a) 20,000; (b) 183; (c) 175 cassette tapes; 80 slide sets; 30 tape slide sets. **15** (a) 4 (b) 1 (c) 1.

BILSTON, West Midlands

BILSTON COLLEGE OF FURTHER EDUCATION LIBRARY, Westfield Rd, Bilston, WV14 6ER (Tel 0902-42871) Tutor-Libn: Mr P. S. Walkins ALA.
6 Wolverhampton Education Authority. **8** General. **9** Small local colln. **10** WMRLB; Aslib; MISLIC; SOSCOL; WESLINK. **11** Yes, by prior arrangement. **12** Mon-Fri 8.45-19.30. **13** (a) 28,000; (b) 250; (c) 20 microtexts. **14** c. £3,500. **15** (a) 6½ (c) 1.

BIRKENHEAD, Merseyside

BIRKENHEAD COLLEGE OF TECHNOLOGY LIBRARY, Borough Rd, Birkenhead, L42 9QD (Tel 051-652 1521 ext 16) Libn: Mr R. Worsnip ALA.
6 Wirral MBC. **8** Building; chemical, electrical & mechanical engineering; commerce; food technology; science

(particularly chemistry, physics & biology). **9** BSI; examination question papers; syllabuses & prospectuses. **10** BLL; LADSIRLAC. **11** No. **12** Term: Mon-Sat 9.00-20.00; vac: Mon-Fri 9.00-17.00. **13** (a) 17,000; (b) 355. **14** £7,000. **15** (a) 4 (c) 1.

BIRMINGHAM

ALUMINIUM FEDERATION LIBRARY, Broadway House, Calthorpe Rd, Birmingham, B15 1TN (Tel 021-455 0311) Libn: Mr D. J. Keevil ALA; Miss M. Jones ALA.
8 Aluminium. **9** Specifications; statistics; history. **10** Birmingham & District Works Loans Scheme. **11** Yes, by prior arrangement. **12** 9.30-17.00. **13** (a) 5,000; (b) 250; (c) 32,000 pamphlets, reports, specifications; 36,000 frames of microfilm. **15** (a) 3 (c) 2.

AUSTIN MORRIS, BRITISH LEYLAND UK LTD, LIBRARY & INFORMATION DEPARTMENT, Longbridge, Birmingham, B45 9SP (Tel 021-475 2101 ext 151; Telex 33491) Inf Officer: Mr R. H. Trueman; Dep: Miss G. Breakwell.
8 Motor vehicle engineering; metallurgy; management. **9** BSI. **11** No. **12** 8.30-12.30, 13.30-17.00. **13** (a) 5,000; (b) 240; (c) foreign standards, inter Europe.

BIRMINGHAM JEWISH REFERENCE LIBRARY, Education Dept, Singers Hill, Birmingham, B1 1HL (Tel 021-643 6155) Chief-Libn: Rev Dr Reuben S. Brookes; Dep: Mrs E. Marquiss.
6 Birmingham Hebrew Congregation. **8** Judaica; Rabbinica. **11** Yes, for ref only. **12** 10.00-12.30. **13** (a) 4,000; (b) 6; (c) international colln of magazines, booklets & pamphlets of Jewish interest. **14** £300. **15** (a) 1.

BIRMINGHAM LAW LIBRARY, 8 Temple St, Birmingham, B2 5BT (Tel 021-643 9116) Libn: Mr S. P. Lahiri BA, DipLib; Asst Libn: Mrs P. R. Cathcart.
6 Birmingham Law Society. **8** Law. **9** Early law books; statutes; abridgements; procedure & practice; land law & conveyancing; criminal law; year books & law reports; legal encyclopaedias & text books; constitutional law; legal history; biographies; dictionaries; trials. **11** No. **12** Mon-Fri 9.00-17.00. **13** (a) 42,000; (b) 70. **14** £4,000. **15** (a) 1½ (b) 1.

Birmingham University

UNIVERSITY LIBRARY, PO Box 363, Edgbaston, Birmingham, B15 2TT (Tel 021-472 1301; Telex 338160 Univlib Bham). Libn (Designate): Dr M. A. Pegg PhD; Dep Libn: A. Nicholls BA, ALA.
7 Barnes Medical Lib, Birmingham, B15 2TJ (021-472 1301); Harding Law Lib, Birmingham, B15 2TT, Libn-in-Charge: Miss D. M. Blake; Music Lib, Birmingham, B15 2TT, Asst Libn: Mr P. S. Wilson MA, ALA.
8 Humanities; social sciences; science; engineering; medicine; law; music; West African studies; Russian & East European studies. **9** Rare book collns: books printed by John Baskerville (18th cent); books & pamphlets printed at Birmingham School of Printing (1926-53); St Mary's Warwick Library (many 16th & 17th cent books); Wedgwood (philological) colln; Wigan Library (18th cent books). Mss collns: Sir Granville Bantock musical mss; Cadbury papers (1900-60) (printed catalogue); Joseph Chamberlain, Sir Austen Chamberlain & Neville Chamberlain papers; John Galsworthy mss & letters (printed catalogue); Jerningham letters; Harriet Martineau letters & papers; Shishkin papers; Francis Brett Young notebooks, typescripts, mss & letters; John Drinkwater letters & mss; William Withering letters; Joseph Priestley letters; Maria Edgeworth letters; Dolgorukov papers; Sir Oliver Lodge papers. Also responsible for recataloguing books, mss, & muniments of Worcester & Lichfield cathedral libraries. **10** BLL; WMRLB; SCONUL; BMS (1660-69); SCOLMA (Francophone West Africa); BLCMP. **11** Yes,

BIRMINGHAM—*continued*

by prior arrangement.　**12** Term: Mon-Fri 9.00-21.00; Sat 9.00-00.30; Vac: Mon-Fri 9.00-17.00; Sat 9.00-00.30 (exc August).　**13** (a) c. 950,000; (b) c. 7,000; (c) c. 45 archives & mss collns; 6,500 gramophone records; 3,220 microforms; 100 videotapes.　**14** £350,000.　**15** (a) 115 (b) 29 (c) 40.

EXTRAMURAL LIBRARY, Dept of Extramural Studies, PO Box 363, Birmingham, B15 2TT (Tel 021-472 1301 ext 3170) Libn: Mr R. K. Fisher MA, ALA; Asst Libn: Mr R. J. Moore BA, ALA.
8 General; art & architecture; biological sciences; English literature; history & archaeology; industrial studies; music; philosophy; psychology; social studies; theology.　**11** Yes.　**12** Mon-Fri 9.30-12.30, 13.30-17.15.　**13** (a) 75,000; (b) 95; (c) 3,000 aerial photographs (archaeology); 10,000 slides; 1,000 gramophone records.　**14** £6,800.　**15** (a) 5 (c) 2.

NATIONAL DOCUMENTATION CENTRE FOR SPORT, PHYSICAL EDUCATION AND RECREATION, PO Box 363, Edgbaston, Birmingham, B15 2TT (Tel 021-472 7410) Dir: Mr G. A. Bell BSc, DipLib, MInstP, MIInfSc; Asst Dir: Mrs J. E. Parnaby BLib, ALA.
6 Sponsored jointly by University of Birmingham, and Sports Council.　**8** Sport, physical education & recreation.　**11** Yes, for ref only, except in special cases.　**12** Term: Mon-Fri 9.00-17.00.　**13** (a) 1,500; (b) 150; (c) 40 abstract journals; over 150 bibliographies.　**15** (a) 5 (b) 3 (c) 3.

SCHOOL OF EDUCATION LIBRARY, PO Box 363, Edgbaston, Birmingham, B15 2TT (Tel 021-472 1301 ext 2271) Libn: Dr P. Platt MA, PhD, FLA; Dep Libn: Miss E. M. Collins BA, ALA.
8 Education; psychology; sociology.　**9** Historical colln of children's books; textbooks (school); Commonwealth textbooks (school).　**10** BLL; WMRLB; LISE.　**11** Yes, for ref only.　**12** Term: Mon-Fri 9.00-17.00 (20.00 Mon, Tues & Thurs), Sat 9.15-12.30; Vac: Mon-Fri 9.00-17.00.　**13** (a) 60,000; (b) 375.　**14** c. £7,000.　**15** (a) 8½ (b) 2 (c) 3.

BRITISH CAST IRON RESEARCH ASSOCIATION LIBRARY, Alvechurch, Birmingham, B48 7QB (Tel 0527-66414; Telex 337125) Libn: Mrs J. Redgrove.
8 Cast iron; ironfounding industry; control of pollution.　**9** BSI.　**10** BLL; Aslib; CADIG; WMRLB; WESLINK.　**11** Yes, by special arrangement.　**12** Mon-Fri 9.00-17.00.　**13** (a) 5,800; (b) 250; (c) patents; pamphlets etc.　**15** (a) 5.

BROOKLYN TECHNICAL COLLEGE LIBRARY, Aldridge Rd, Great Barr, Birmingham, B44 8NE (Tel 021-360 3543 ext 276) Tutor-Libn: Mrs A. A. B. Gosling ALA.
6 Birmingham MDC.　**8** Building; engineering.　**10** B-Link.　**11** No.　**12** Mon-Fri 9.00-19.00 (Fri 17.50).　**13** (a) 10,500; (b) c. 90.　**15** (a) 2 (c) 1.

CADBURY SCHWEPPES LIBRARY AND INFORMATION SERVICE, Bournville, Birmingham, B30 2LY (Tel 021-458 2000; Telex 33-8011) Inf Manager: Mr F. J. Stanley ALA; Libn: Mr J. R. Sherwell ALA.
6 Cadbury-Typhoo Ltd.　**8** Food science & technology, especially cocoa & chocolate.　**9** William Cadbury colln (history of cocoa & of South America); Cadbury Business Archives (from 1850, Bournville & West Africa).　**10** WESLINK.　**11** Yes, by prior arrangement.　**12** Mon-Fri 8.30-17.00.　**13** (a) 5,000; (c) 250; (c) 6,000 company reports; Cadbury archives.　**14** £5,000.　**15** (a) 8 (b) 1 (c) 2.

CITY OF BIRMINGHAM POLYTECHNIC LIBRARY, Perry Barr, Birmingham, B42 2SU (Tel 021-356 6911 ext 222) Poly Libn: Mr K. J. Rider FLA; Dep Libn: Mr M. M. Hadcroft MA, ALA.
7 Anstey Dept of Physical Education Lib, Chester Rd, Sutton Coldfield, West Midlands (021-373 0095), Libn: Miss M. Tighe ALA; Art & Design Centre Lib, Corporation St, Birmingham, B4 7DX (021-359 6721 ext 236), Libn: Mr L. E. Davies ALA; Art & Design Centre Lib, Margaret St, Birmingham, B3 3BU (021-235 2207), Dep Libn: Miss D. M. Abbott FLA; Commerce Centre Lib, Gosta Green, Birmingham, B4 7HA (021-359 6851 ext 241), Libn: Mr P. S. Pargeter MA, FLA; North Centre (Science & Technology) Lib, Perry Barr, Birmingham, B42 2SU (021-356 6911 ext 223), Libn: Mr M. A. Pearman BA, ALA; Law Annexe Lib, Perry Barr, Birmingham, B42 2SU (021-356 6911 ext 326), Libn: Miss H. C. Boucher ALA; School of Music Lib, Paradise Circus, Birmingham, B3 3HG (021-235 4614), Libn: Miss S. M. Clegg ALA; South Centre Lib, Bristol Rd South, Birmingham, B31 2AJ (021-476 1131 ext 202), Libn: Miss J. D. O'Driscoll ALA; Edgbaston Dept Lib, Centre for Teacher Education & Training, Westbourne Rd, Edgbaston, Birmingham, B15 3TN (021-454 5106) Tutor-Libn: Mr David Cadney BA, FLA; Bordesley Dept of Education Lib, Camp Hill, Birmingham 11 (021-772 5912) Tutor-Libn: Mrs L. Wood BA, ALA.　**8** Law; librarianship; engineering; science; management; social sciences; economics; business; modern languages & literature; fine art; design; fashion & textiles; visual communication; art education; architecture & planning; construction technology; music; maths; education; physical education.　**9** Librarianship; EDC.　**10** BLCMP; WESLINK; WMRLB.　**11** Yes, for ref only.　**12** Term: Mon-Fri 9.00-19.00 (or 21.00); vac: Mon-Fri 9.00-17.00.　**13** (a) c. 275,000; (b) c. 2,412; (c) 321,000 music scores; 1,500 microtexts; 27,500 slides; 4,000 gramophone records.　**14** £128,000.　**15** (a) 49½ (b) 11 (c) 23.

GARRETTS GREEN TECHNICAL COLLEGE LIBRARY, Garretts Green Lane, Birmingham, B33 0TS (Tel 021-743 4471) Tutor-Libn: Mr R. J. Garland BSc, AIM.
6 City of Birmingham Education Department.　**11** Yes, during term.　**12** Term: Mon-Fri 9.00-19.00 (Fri 17.00).　**13** (a) 9,400; (b) 50.　**14** £2,500.　**15** (a) 1.

HALL GREEN TECHNICAL COLLEGE LIBRARY, Colebank Rd, Birmingham, B28 8ES (Tel 021-777 6251 ext 28) Tutor-Libn: Mrs I. A. Clarke ALA.
6 City of Birmingham Education Committee.　**8** Building; engineering; business studies; history; geography; sociology; economics; politics; languages; sciences.　**10** Inter-library loans.　**11** No.　**12** Term: Mon-Fri 9.00-19.00 (Fri 17.00); vac: 9.00-17.00.　**13** (a) 12,000; (b) 60.　**14** £5,000.　**15** (a) 2 (c) 1.

HANDSWORTH AND ERDINGTON TECHNICAL COLLEGE LIBRARY, Whitehead Rd, Aston, Birmingham, B6 6EU (Tel 021-327 1493) Tutor-Libn: Mrs A. E. Daly ALA, CertEd.
6 Birmingham City Council.　**7** Erdington Centre, Edwards Rd, Birmingham, B24 9EW (021-373 4214), Libn: Mrs A. E. Daly; Handsworth Centre, Golds Hill Rd, Birmingham, B21 9DQ (021-554 5614), Libn: Mrs A. E. Daly.　**8** Sciences; mechanical engineering; motor vehicle engineering; electrical engineering; clothing technology; general.　**10** WRLB; Inter-library loans.　**11** No.　**12** Mon-Fri 9.00-16.30 (Fri 15.30). Branches vary.　**13** (a) c. 14,000; (b) 62.　**15** (a) 4 (b) 1.

QUEEN'S COLLEGE AT BIRMINGHAM LIBRARY, Somerset Rd, Edgbaston, Birmingham (Tel 021-454 1527) Libn: Rev J. M. Turner MA; Dep: Mr P. Myers ALA.
6 Council of Queen's College at Birmingham.　**8** Theological studies.　**9** Wesleyan & Methodist history; Anglicana (especially 17th cent).　**11** No.　**12** During college terms.　**13** (a) 25,000; (b) 50.　**14** £1,000.　**15** (c) 1.

SELLY OAK COLLEGES LIBRARY, Birmingham, B29 6LE (Tel 021-472 4231) Libn: Miss F. H. B. Williams MA, ALA, DipLib.
6 Council of Selly Oak Colleges.　**8** Church & mission history; anthropology; development studies; non-Christian religions, especially Islam; oriental studies; social studies & child welfare; overseas social work.　**9** A few incunabula; 16th & 17th cent books; Mingana mss colln (5th to 18th cent,

CODE: 1 Name of Library. 2 Address. 3 Telephone & Telex. 4 Officer in charge. 5 Deputy. 6 Governing body. 7 Branches. 8 Main Subjects. 9 Special Collections. 10 Co-operative Schemes. 11 Open to public? 12 Hours. 13 Stock: (a) books (b) periodicals (c) other. 14 Finance. 15 Staff: (a) non-manual (b) graduate (c) chartered librarians.

BIRMINGHAM—*continued*

Syriac, Christian, Arabic & Islamic mss); Rendel Harris colln of Greek papyri. **10** WMRLB. **11** Yes. **12** Mon-Fri 9.00-13.00, 14.00-17.30. **13** (a) c. 50,000; (b) 100. **14** c. £4,000. **15** (a) 2 (b) 2 (c) 1.

TUBE INVESTMENTS (GROUP SERVICES) LTD, DEPT OF MECHANICAL INFORMATION AND PATENTS LIBRARY, Rocky Lane, Aston, Birmingham, B6 5RH (Tel 021-359 3030 ext 111) Libn: Mrs C. A. Crabtree ALA. **7** STD DED B Lib, The Airport, Aldridge, Walsall, WS9 0QD (0922-28966), Branch Libn: Mrs C. J. Lees AIInfSc. **8** Mechanical engineering; metallurgy; production engineering; electrical engineering. **9** Steel tubes. **10** WESLINK; MISLIC. **11** Yes, by special arrangement. **12** Mon-Fri 8.30-16.45 (Fri 16.15). **13** (a) 8,000; (b) 400; (c) 35,000 patents; 6,000 standards; 10,000 trade literature. **14** £6,000. **15** (a) 8 (c) 2.

UNIVERSITY OF ASTON IN BIRMINGHAM LIBRARY, Birmingham, B4 7ET (Tel 021-359 3611; Telex 336997) Univ Libn: Mr E. H. C. Driver MSc, FLA; Dep Libn: C. R. Burman BA, FLA. **8** Science; technology; social sciences; management. **9** Comrie colln of mathematical tables. **10** Aslib; WMRLB; BLCMP. **11** Yes, with prior application. **12** Term: Mon-Fri 9.00-21.30, Sat 9.00-12.00; Vac: Mon-Fri 9.00-17.00. **13** (a) 144,000; (b) 2,300; (c) 152 films; 577 gramophone records; 267 tapes/slides. **14** £145,000. **15** (a) 42 (b) 7 (c) 15.

WESTHILL COLLEGE OF EDUCATION LIBRARY, Weoley Park Rd, Selly Oak, Birmingham, B29 6QY (Tel 021-472 1563 ext 27) Coll Libn: Mrs M. Bilton ALA; Dep: Mr K. Barker, ALA. **8** Education; religion; art; literature; geography; history; music; maths; science; physical education; sociology; philosophy; psychology; linguistics; biology; environmental science. **11** No. **12** Term: 9.00-19.00; Vac: 9.00-16.30 (closed August). **13** (a) 43,000; (b) 216; (c) slides; gramophone records; pictures; tapes & cassette tapes; kits; filmstrips. **14** £8,000. **15** (a) 4 (c) 3.

BISHOP AUCKLAND, Co Durham

BISHOP AUCKLAND TECHNICAL COLLEGE LIBRARY, Woodhouse Lane, Bishop Auckland, DL14 6JZ (Tel 0388-3052) Libn: Mr B. Marquis ALA; Lib Asst: Mrs S. J. Lowrie. **6** Durham County Education Committee. **8** Engineering; construction; business & general studies; homecraft; hairdressing. **9** BSI; student projects (mainly management); filmstrips. **10** NRLB. **11** Yes, for ref only. **12** Term: Mon-Fri 8.45-19.00 (Fri 16.15); vac: Mon-Fri 8.45-16.45 (Fri 16.15). **13** (a) 9,124 books & pamphlets; (b) 115; (c) 130 filmstrips; 10 microfiche; 63 projects. **15** (c) 1.

BLACKBURN, Lancashire

COLLEGE OF TECHNOLOGY AND DESIGN LIBRARY, Feilden St, Blackburn, BB2 1LH (Tel 0254-64321 ext 6) Head, Lib & Inf Dept: Mr John Oldcorn FLA. **6** Lancashire CC. **8** Art & design; construction & civil engineering; management; business; languages; electronic & electrical engineering; mechanical & production engineering; pure & applied science; sociology; textiles; maths; computing & statistics. **9** Complete BSI. **10** NWRLB. **11** Yes. **12** Term: Mon-Fri 9.00-21.00 (Thurs & Fri 19.30); vac: Mon-Fri 9.00-17.15. **13** (a) 23,000; (b) 250. **14** £7,500. **15** (a) 4½ (b) 1 (c) 3.

BLACKPOOL, Lancashire

BLACKPOOL COLLEGE OF TECHNOLOGY AND ART LIBRARY, Ashfield Rd, Bispham, Blackpool, FY2 0HB (Tel 0253-52352) Senior Tutor-Libn: Mr Charles Oldham FLA, ALCM; Dep Libn: Mrs Sheila Thomas ALA. **6** Lancashire CC. **8** Hotel & catering; mechanical, civil & electrical engineering. **9** Complete set of Shakespeare plays on records. **10** NWRLB. **11** Yes, for ref only. **12** Term: Mon-Fri 9.00-21.00 (Fri 17.00); Vac: Mon-Fri 9.00-12.30, 13.30-17.00. **13** (a) 15,000; (b) 300. **14** £9,000.

BLETCHLEY, Buckinghamshire

BLETCHLEY COLLEGE OF FURTHER EDUCATION LIBRARY, Sherwood Dr, Bletchley, Milton Keynes, MK3 6DR (Tel 0908-79211) Coll Libn: Mrs A. C. Hawkins ALA. **6** Buckinghamshire CC. **8** General education & science; business studies. **11** Yes, for ref only. **12** Term: Mon-Thurs 9.00-19.30, Fri 9.00-16.30. **13** (a) c. 11,500; (b) 75. **14** £2,800. **15** (a) 2 (c) 1.

BOGNOR REGIS, West Sussex

BOGNOR REGIS COLLEGE OF EDUCATION LIBRARY, Bognor Regis, PO21 1HR (Tel 02433-5581) Libn: Mr R. H. Hamlin MA, DipLib, ALA; Dep Libn: Mr R. Heron MA, ALA. **6** West Sussex CC. **8** Education; art & craft; English; environmental sciences; geography; history; maths; movement & dance; music; physical education; religious & social studies. **9** Gerard Young Local History Colln on Bognor & the surrounding region. **11** Yes, to bona-fide students & enquirers by prior arrangement with Libn. **12** Term: Mon-Fri 9.00-21.00, Sat 9.00-12.00; vac: Mon-Fri 9.00-12.30, 13.30-17.00. **13** (a) c. 50,000; (b) 300; (c) microfilm & microfiche. **15** (a) 7 (b) 2 (c) 3.

BOLTON, Lancashire

BOLTON COLLEGE OF EDUCATION (TECHNICAL) LIBRARY, Chadwick St, Bolton, BL2 1JW (Tel 0204-22132) Tutor-Libn: Mr C. H. Bleasdale ALA; Dep: Mrs M. Thompson MA, ALA. **6** Bolton MDC **8** Education. **11** Yes, for ref only. **12** Term: 9.00-21.00; vac: 9.00-17.00. **13** (a) 25,000; (b) 250; (c) 100 microtexts; 4,000 audiovisual materials. **14** £12,500. **15** (a) 7 (b) 3 (c) 3.

BOLTON INSTITUTE OF TECHNOLOGY LIBRARY, Deane Rd, Bolton, BL3 5AB (Tel 0204-28851) Libn: Miss T. Crook FLA; Dep: Mrs A. Woon BSc, ALA. **7** Textile colln at Bolton Technical College, Manchester Rd, Bolton (0204-31411). **8** Civil, electronic & mechanical engineering; pure sciences; social sciences; psychology; business studies; textiles; literature; history; philosophy. **10** BLL; NWRLB. **11** Yes, by prior arrangement. **12** Term: Mon-Thurs 9.30-21.00, Fri 9.30-17.30; Vac: Mon-Fri 9.30-12.30, 1.30-17.00. **13** (a) 60,000; (b) 700; (c) 200 microtexts; 100 audiocassettes & gramophone records. **14** £30,000. **15** (a) 7 (b) 3 (c) 3.

BOLTON SCHOOL LIBRARY, Chorley New Rd, Bolton, BL1 4PA (Tel 0204-40202) Master-in-charge: Mr R. Booth. **6** The Governors, Bolton School. **8** History; English; French; geography; science. **9** Chained library (stall system) 1694, nearly 50 vols retain their chains. **11** No. **12** 9.00-17.00. **13** (a) c. 23,000; (b) 3; (c) programmes, photographs & newspaper cuttings dealing with school functions and buildings; old school registers; cassettes; tapes. **14** £450. **15** (a) 1 (b) 1.

BOREHAMWOOD, Hertfordshire

BUILDING RESEARCH ESTABLISHMENT, FIRE RESEARCH STATION LIBRARY, Boreham Wood, WD6 2BL (Tel 01-953 6177) Libn: Mrs Jill Johnston ALA; Inf Officer: Miss P. Mealing BSc.
6 Dept of Environment.   **8** Ignition & growth of fire; detection, extinction & suppression of fire; special fire hazards in industries & materials; structural aspects of fire in buildings; fire & loss statistics.   **9** Early fire journals, e.g. US National Fire Protection Assoc journals; codes & standards; British Fire Prevention Committee Reports.   **10** HASL.
11 Yes, by prior arrangement.   **12** Mon-Thurs 9.00-17.00, Fri 9.00-16.45.   **13** (a) 11,000; (b) c. 400, (c) microfilm (c. 10 journals).   **15** (a) 8 (b) 1 (c) 1.

JOHN LAING RESEARCH AND DEVELOPMENT LTD, CENTRAL TECHNICAL INFORMATION SERVICE LIBRARY, Manorway, Borehamwood, WD6 1LN (Tel 01-953 6144 ext 230, 231) Libn: Mr C.W. Mathew ALA; Head of Inf Service: Mr R.G. Groeger BSc, ARPS; Dep: Mr P.J. Ellway BA, ALA.
7 Head Office Branch, Block 9, John Laing Construction, London NW7 (01-905 6279), Libn: Mrs A. Bicknell; Manchester Office Library, John Laing Construction Ltd, 2 Warwick Rd, Manchester, M16 0GE (061-872 2373), Libn: Mrs E. Farnsworth.   **8** Building & civil engineering.   **9** BSI; large selection of building industry standards.   **10** HERTIS.
11 Yes, by prior arrangement.   **12** Mon-Fri 8.30-17.00.
13 (a) c. 1,800; (b) c. 450; (c) 100 microfilm; manufacturers literature; c. 6,500 pamphlets.   **15** (a) 6 (b) 1 (c) 3.

BOURNEMOUTH, Hampshire

BOURNEMOUTH AND POOLE COLLEGE OF ART LIBRARY, Royal London House, The Lansdowne, Bournemouth, BH1 3JL (Tel 0202-20772 ext 7) Libn: Mr Nicholas Pollard BA, ALA; Dep: Mr Alan Browning BA, ALA.
6 Dorset CC.   **8** The arts in the widest sense.   **9** Comic strips.   **11** Yes.   **12** 9.00-20.00.   **13** (a) 21,000; (b) 215; (c) 35,000 slides; 1,000 gramophone records.
14 £6,000.   **15** (a) 4 (b) 3 (c) 3.

BOURNEMOUTH COLLEGE OF TECHNOLOGY LIBRARY, (will merge with Weymouth College of Education) The Lansdowne, Bournemouth, BH1 3JJ (Tel 0202-20844 ext 23/30) Libn: Mr A. Sutherland FLA; Dep: Miss P.M. Wilkinson.
7 Norwich Union House, Lansdowne, Bournemouth, BH1 3JJ (0202-20844 ext 43), Libn: Miss M. O'Connor ALA; Knyveton Rd, Bournemouth (0202-20844 ext 29), Libn: Mr P. Kettlewell ALA; Shelley Park, Beechwood Ave, Bournemouth (0202-36614), Libn: Miss L. Gill ALA.   **8** Humanities; social sciences; business; management; tourism; catering; hotels; engineering science; construction; languages.   **10** HATRICS.
11 Yes.   **12** Term: Mon-Fri 9.00-21.00, Sat 9.00-12.00; vac: 9.00-17.00.   **13** (a) 65,000; (b) 800; (c) 600 videotapes; 1,000 audio-tapes; 200 gramophone records; 400 slides & filmstrips.   **14** £38,000.   **15** (a) 16 (b) 2 (c) 9.

BRACKNELL, Berkshire

BRACKNELL COLLEGE OF FURTHER EDUCATION LIBRARY, Church Rd, Bracknell, RG12 1DJ (Tel 0344-20411) Tutor-Libn: Miss D. Smith BA, Cert Ed, ALA, DipLib; Asst Tutor-Libn: Miss A. Stanley BA, Cert Ed, DipLib & Inf Studies.
6 Berkshire Local Education Authority.   **7** Woodley Hill House, Eastcourt Ave, Earley, Reading, Libn: Mrs D. Turner ALA.   **8** Social sciences; languages; pure & applied sciences; mechanical & electrical engineering; art; cookery; commercial subjects; literature; geography; economics.
10 BLG.   **11** No.   **12** Term: Mon-Thurs 9.00-19.30, Fri 9.00-17.00; vac: by arrangement.   **13** (a) 12,600; (b) c. 142; (c) cassette tapes (listening centre).   **14** £3,200.
15 (a) 4 (b) 2 (c) 1.

BUILDING SERVICES RESEARCH AND INFORMATION ASSOCIATION LIBRARY, Old Bracknell Lane, Bracknell, RG12 4AH (Tel 0344-25071) Inf Officer: Mr A.R. Eaves ALA; Libn: Mr S.R. Loyd.
8 Heating; ventilating; air conditioning; other technologies & sciences relating to mechanical & electrical services of buildings.   **10** Representatives of European Heating, Ventilating Associations.   **11** No.   **12** Mon-Fri 9.00-17.30.
13 (a) 2,500; (b) 250; (c) 1,200 pamphlets; manufacturers catalogues.   **14** £2,000.   **15** (a) 3 (c) 2.

BURMAH CASTROL COMPANY PRODUCT DEVELOPMENT LIBRARY, London Rd, Bracknell, RG12 2UW (Tel 0344-20511; Telex 848291) Head of Technical Records: Mr H.C. Claxton; Libn: Mr G. Burger.
8 Lubricating oils; greases; additives; additive manufacture; lubricant development.   **10** BLG.   **11** Yes, by prior arrangement.   **12** 9.00-17.00.   **13** (a) 2,500; (b) 200.
15 (a) 4 (b) 1.

ICI PLANT PROTECTION DIVISION LIBRARY, Jealott's Hill Research Station, Bracknell, RG12 6EY (Tel 0344-24701 ext 261, 260; Telex 668411) Libn: Mr R.J. Smith ALA; Asst Libn: Mrs E. Evison ALA.
7 Associated Lib: Fernhurst, Haslemere, Surrey, GU27 3JE (0428-4061 ext 619), Libn: Miss J.I. Chuter.   **8** Agriculture & agricultural chemicals; crop protection; crop production & soil science; animal husbandry; biology; organic chemistry; ecology & environment.   **9** Nuptown House colln of pre-1850 books on agriculture.   **10** ICI combined list of periodicals; ICI union catalogue (of books); BLG; Bracknell industrial librarians.   **11** Yes, by prior arrangement.   **12** Mon-Fri 8.45-17.00.   **13** (a) c. 14,000; (b) 800; (c) microcards of 'Journal of the Chemical Society' (1893, vol 63 to 1917, vol 112).   **15** (a) 4 (c) 2.

METEOROLOGICAL OFFICE LIBRARY, London Rd, Bracknell, RG12 2SZ (Tel 0344-20242; Telex 848160 & 847010) Head of Library, Publications & Editing: Mr R.P.W. Lewis MA, MSc; Libn: Mr F.A. Seammen.
6 Meteorological Office, MoD.   **7** Meadow House, 231 Corstorphine Rd, Edinburgh (031-334 9721).   **8** Meteorology; climatology; oceanography; hydrology.   **9** Expeditions.
10 BLG.   **11** Yes, by prior arrangement.   **12** Normal office hours.   **13** (a) 120,000; (b) 300; (c) 7,000 slides & photographs.   **15** (a) 19 (b) 5.

BRADFORD, West Yorkshire

BRADFORD COLLEGE LIBRARY, Lecture Block, Trinity Rd, Bradford, BD5 0JE (Tel 0274-33291) Acting Coll Libn: Mr Derek Laverack ALA; Dep: Mrs J. Iredale BA, ALA.
7 Westbrook Site, Great Horton Rd, Bradford 7 (0274-34844), Libn: Miss J. Craven ALA.   **8** Amalgamation of former technical, art & education college libraries.   **9** Complete BSi.
10 BLL; BRASTACS; YRLB.   **11** Yes, for ref only.
12 Term: Mon-Fri 8.45-20.00.   **13** (a) 88,500; (b) 844.
14 £30,000.   **15** (a) 11 (b) 1 (c) 6½.

HEPWORTH AND GRANDAGE LTD, TECHNICAL LIBRARY, St John's Works, Wakefield Rd, Bradford, BD4 8TU (Tel 0274-29595) Technical Libn: Miss S.F. Munro ALA.
8 Engineering, particularly automobile engineering.
9 British, US & German patents on: pistons, piston-rings, crankshafts & other automotive components; SAE preprints; IMechE preprints; MIRA papers, preprints & reports.
10 BRASTACS; Motor Industry Information Group.   **11** No, but queries answered.   **12** Mon-Fri 8.45-12.00, 13.00-17.15 (Fri 16.45).   **13** (a) 2,500; (b) 110; (c) 600 BSI.
15 (c) 1.

UNIVERSITY OF BRADFORD LIBRARY, Richmond Road, Bradford, BD7 1DP (Tel 0274-33466; Telex 51309 University Brad) Univ Libn: Mr F. Earnshaw BA, ALA; Dep Libn: Mr F.H. Ayres BA, FLA.
7 Management Centre Lib, Emm Lane, Bradford, BD9 4JJ (0274-2299 ext 232); Social Sciences & Modern Languages Lib, Wardley House, Little Horton Lane, Bradford, BD5 0AJ (0274-33466 ext 8261).   **8** Pure & applied science; life sciences; engineering; textiles; social sciences; management; languages; humanities.   **10** YHJLS.   **11** Yes, for ref only.
12 Term: Mon-Fri 8.45-22.00, Sat 8.45-17.30, Sun 13.00-17.30; vac: Mon-Fri 8.45-17.30.   **13** (a) 230,000; (b) 2,900; (c) 8,000 microtexts; sound recordings; films & other audiovisual material.   **15** (a) 49 (b) 16 (c) 23.

CODE: 1 Name of Library. **2** Address. **3** Telephone & Telex. **4** Officer in charge. **5** Deputy. **6** Governing body.
7 Branches. **8** Main Subjects. **9** Special Collections. **10** Co-operative Schemes. **11** Open to public? **12** Hours.
13 Stock: (a) books (b) periodicals (c) other. **14** Finance. **15** Staff: (a) non-manual (b) graduate (c) chartered librarians.

BRECON, Powys

WELSH NATIONAL WATER DEVELOPMENT AUTHORITY
LIBRARY (Awdurdod Cenedlaethol Datblygu Dwr Cymru),
Cambrian Way, Brecon, LD3 7HP (Tel 0874-3181; Telex
497428 WNWDA BRECON) Libn & Inf Officer: Mr D. W. Hope
BA, FLA.
8 Water supply; water engineering; control of quality of water;
treatment of sewage; analysis of polluted water; ecology of
waters (inc reservoirs, lakes, rivers, estuaries, coastal
waters); outdoor recreation (especially in area of WNWDA);
law. **12** Mon-Thurs 8. 45-13. 00, 14. 00-17. 15, Fri 8. 45-
13. 00, 14. 00-16. 45. **15** (a) 1½ (b) 1 (c) 1.

BRIDGWATER, Somerset

BRIDGWATER COLLEGE LIBRARY, Broadway, Bridgwater,
TA6 5HW (Tel 0278-55464) Tutor-Libn: Mrs Margaret Wild
ALA, CertEd; Lib Asst: Mrs Valerie Warren BA.
6 Somerset CC. **7** Park Rd, Bridgwater, Libn: Mrs P.
Duffin. **8** General. **10** SWRLB. **11** Yes. **12** 8. 30-
20. 30. **13** (a) 16, 000; (b) 150; (c) some non-book materials.
14 £4, 400.

BRITISH CELLOPHANE LTD LIBRARY, Bath Rd, Bridgwater,
TA6 4PA (Tel 0278-4321; Telex 46266) Inf Officer: Mr W. J.
Coles BSc, MIInfSc.
8 Packaging plastics. **9** Selected British patent abridgments (from 1937); British & foreign patent specifications.
11 No. **12** Mon-Fri 8. 45-17. 15. **13** (a) 4, 000; (b) 180.
14 £2, 000. **15** (a) 4 (b) 1.

SOMERSET COLLEGE OF AGRICULTURE AND HORTI-
CULTURE LIBRARY, Cannington, Bridgwater, TA5 2LS (Tel
0278-652226).
6 Somerset CC. **8** Agriculture; horticulture; dairying;
food technology. **11** No. **12** 24 hours a day. **13** (a)
4, 500; (b) 83. **14** £1, 000. **15** (a) ½.

BRIGHTON, East Sussex

BRIGHTON COLLEGE OF EDUCATION LIBRARY (will
merge with Brighton Polytechnic), Falmer, Brighton, BN1 9PH
(Tel 0273-66622) Acting Chief Libn: Miss C. E. Moon BA,
ALA.
6 East Sussex CC. **8** Education & related topics; children's books; general. **10** Local co-operative schemes.
11 Yes, for ref only. **12** Term: Mon-Fri 9. 00-21. 00
(Thurs 21. 45, Fri 19. 00), Sat 9. 00-17. 00; vac: Mon-Fri 9. 00-
17. 00. **13** (a) c. 100, 000; (b) 250. **14** £15, 000.
15 (a) 8 (b) 3 (c) 4.

BRIGHTON POLYTECHNIC, LEARNING RESOURCES
CENTRE (will merge with Brighton College of Education),
Moulsecoomb, Brighton, BN2 4GJ (Tel 0273-67304) Libn & Dep
Head of Learning Resources: Miss C. R. Lutyens LLB, FLA;
Officer-in-charge (Moulsecoomb): Mr D. E. House BA, ALA.
7 Grand Parade, Brighton, BN2 2JY, Officer-in-charge: Mr
L. G. Willmot MA, FLA; 251 Preston Rd, Brighton, BN1 6SE,
Officer-in-charge: Ms J. B. Carter ALA; 2 Sussex Sq,
Brighton, BN2 1FJ, Officer-in-charge: Ms H. S. Harper.
8 Science; technology; fine arts; graphics; architecture;
management & business; education. **9** Open University,
audio-visual materials, especially video-tape. **10** Local
co-operative schemes in process of formulation. **11** Yes,
for ref only. **12** Term: 9. 00-21. 00; vac: 9. 00-17. 30.
13 (a) 65, 390; (b) 856; (c) video-tapes; tape slides; slides,
microfilms. **14** £104, 700. **15** (a) 27½ (b) 10 (c) 10.

BRIGHTON TECHNICAL COLLEGE LIBRARY, Richmond
Terrace, Brighton, BN2 2SZ (Tel 0273-685971 ext 284) Coll
Libn: Miss N. M. Hobbs ALA; Dep: Miss S. Boyle ALA.
6 East Sussex CC. **7** BLib, Cheapside (0273-685971 ext
280), Libn: Miss S. Boyle ALA. **8** Science; engineering;
construction; business; hotel & catering; domestic studies.

9 Applied biology, journals & books. **10** SASLIC.
11 Yes. **12** Term: Mon-Fri 9. 00-20. 00; vac: Mon-Fri
9. 00-17. 00. **13** (a) 28, 000; (b) 250; (c) c. 200 slides; 20
cassettes. **14** £10, 000. **15** (a) 7 (b) 1 (c) 4.

NATIONAL SOCIETY FOR CLEAN AIR LIBRARY, 136 North
St, Brighton, BN1 1RG (Tel 0273-26313) Inf Officer: Ms
Nicola Walters; Asst: Ms Helene Garner.
8 Air pollution; general environmental subjects (inc
American & French literature). **10** Inter-library loans.
11 Yes, in exceptional cases. **12** Mon-Fri 9. 00-17. 00.
13 (a) 500; (b) 25; (c) numerous local government acts.
14 £400.

ITT CREED LTD, TECHNICAL LIBRARY AND INFORMA-
TION OFFICE, Hollingbury, Brighton, BN1 8AL (Tel 0273-
507111 ext 3273; Telex 87. 169) Technical Inf Officer: Mr
Michael Dudley; Asst Libn: Mrs A. B. Stoakes.
8 Telecommunications; data processing; automation; electronic, electrical & mechanical engineering; optics; computer
technology. **11** No. **12** Mon-Fri 9. 45-17. 00.
13 (a) over 1, 500; (b) 215; (c) standards; specifications;
indexes; microfilms; technical & commercial catalogues.
14 over £4, 000. **15** (a) 3 (b) 1.

University of Sussex

UNIVERSITY LIBRARY, Brighton, BN1 9QL (Tel 0273-
66755; Telex 87394) Libn: Mr P. R. Lewis MA, FLA;
Dep: Mr A. L. Pollard MA.
8 Normal academic disciplines except medicine.
9 Paris Commune (1871) Colln; East Africa Colln;
European Colln (mainly official EEC publications).
10 SCOLMA (Kenya, Uganda, Tanzania); SASLIC.
11 Yes, at Libn's discretion. **12** Term: Mon-Fri 9. 00-
21. 45, Sat 10. 00-18. 00, Sun 13. 30-19. 30; vac: Mon-Fri
9. 00-17. 30. **13** (a) 400, 000; (b) 2, 200; (c) 3, 200 sound
tapes. **15** (a) 70 (b) 25 (c) 26.

INSTITUTE OF DEVELOPMENT STUDIES LIBRARY,
Andrew Cohen Building, Falmer, Brighton, BN1 9RE (Tel
0273-66261; Telex 877151) Libn: Mr M. H. Rogers MA,
ALA.
8 Social & economic development of poorer countries;
relations between rich & poor countries. **9** UN &
UNESCO deposit library. **11** Yes, on application to
Libn. **12** Mon-Fri 9. 00-18. 15. **13** (a) 75, 000;
(b) 10, 000; (c) UN documents (1947-73) (Readex microcard edition); c. 5, 000 other microtexts. **15** (a) 19 (b) 5
(c) 4.

BRISTOL, Avon

AGRICULTURAL RESEARCH COUNCIL, MEAT RESEARCH
INSTITUTE LIBRARY, Langford, Bristol, BS18 7DY (Tel 093
485-661) Libn: Miss S. A. Hutchison BA, ALA; Clerical
Officer: Mrs J. Thompson.
8 Biochemistry; microbiology; physiology; bioengineering
(refrigeration etc); meat quality; anatomy of meat; animals;
slaughtering & dissection techniques; meat. **9** Reprint
collns of Low Temperature Research Station, Cambridge;
Food Research Institute; Meat Research Institute; Torry
Research Station. **11** No. **12** Mon-Fri 8. 30-17. 00.
13 (a) c. 6, 500; (b) 150; (c) 1, 500 pamphlets; microfiche.
14 £7, 500. **15** (a) 2 (c) 1.

BRISTOL POLYTECHNIC LIBRARY (will merge with Red-
land College & the College of St Matthias), Coldharbour Lane,
Stoke Gifford, Bristol, BS16 1QY (Tel 0272-656261) Poly Libn:
Mr J. C. Hartas BCom, ALA; Dep: Mr D. A. Smith BSc, AIEE,
AIInfSc.
6 Avon CC. **7** Clanage Rd, Bower Ashton, Bristol, BS3 2JU
(0272-660222) Libn: Mr J. M. Matthews ALA; Ashley Down Rd,
Bristol, BS7 9BU (0272 41241); Libn: Mrs J. M. Murray BA,
ALA; Unity St, Bristol, BS1 5HP (0272-23016) Libn: Miss M. A.
Black ALA. **8** Science; law; management; economics; social

BRISTOL, Avon—*continued*

sciences; business; accountancy; languages; surveying; construction; town planning; engineering; maths; computing; humanities; art & design.　**10** BLL; SWRLB.　**11** Yes, for ref only.　**12** Mon-Fri 8.30-20.30, Sat 9.00-13.00.　**13** (a) 110,000; (b) 1,650; (c) 100 films; 5,000 microfilms; 500 audiotapes & tape-slide sets; 100 videotapes; 50,000 slides; 10,000 pamphlets.　**14** £120,000.　**15** (a) 33 (b) 7 (c) 14.

BRISTOL UNIVERSITY LIBRARY, Tyndall Ave, Bristol, BS8 1TJ (Tel 0272-24161; Telex 449174) Univ Libn: N. Higham MA, ALA; Dep Libn: J. Lightbown MA.
8 Arts; sciences; medicine; engineering; social sciences; education; law.　**9** British philosophers; early novels; Allen Lane colln (autographed Penguin books); Brunel ms sketch-books, notebooks & letterbooks; Pinney family papers; published business histories; early mathematical, medical, chemical & alchemical books.　**10** SWRLB; SWALCAP.
11 Yes, on written application to Univ Libn.　**12** Mon-Fri 8.45-21.00, Sat 8.45-13.00 branches vary.　**13** (a) 550,000; (b) 4,800; (c) archives; microtexts.　**14** £240,700.
15 (a) 101 (b) 39 (c) 24.

BRUNEL TECHNICAL COLLEGE, HALLETT LIBRARY, Ashley Down, Bristol, BS7 9BU (Tel 0272-41241) Tutor-Libn: Mr Michael Williams.
6 Avon CC Education Dept.　**8** Electrical, electronic & mechanical engineering; marine & aero electronics; navigation & maritime studies; catering & social services; humanities; library studies; education; printing; science & mathematics; building & land administration; fiction.　**9** Brunelia; local history; wide colln of audio-visual learning resources.
11 Yes, on special application.　**12** Term: Mon-Fri 8.30-20.45 (Fri 16.30).　**13** (a) 20,687; (b) 216; (c) 1,028 records and cassettes; 70 video-cassette recordings; 325 sets of 35 mm slides; 48 film loops.　**14** £10,000.　**15** (a) 8 (b) 1 (c) 2.

COLLEGE OF ST MATTHIAS LIBRARY, (will merge with Bristol Polytechnic), Fishponds, Bristol, BS16 2JJ (Tel 0272-655384) Coll Libn: Mr R. James MA, ALA.
8 Education; teaching materials.　**10** BLL; SWRLB.
11 Yes.　**12** Term: Mon-Fri 9.00-21.00, Sat 9.00-12.00, vac: Mon-Fri 9.00-17.00.　**13** (a) 70,000; (b) 350; (c) 200 microtexts; 500 audio cassettes; 20 film loops; 1,000 charts & posters; 1,000 slides; 100 film strips.　**14** £12,000.
15 (a) 6⅔ (b) 3 (c) 3.

FILTON TECHNICAL COLLEGE LIBRARY, Filton Ave, Filton, Bristol, BS12 7AT (Tel 0272-694217) Tutor-Libn: Mrs J. Price ALA; Asst Libn: Mrs L. Brain ALA.
6 Avon CC.　**7** Shield House Lib, Gloucester Rd North, Filton, Bristol (0272 694217) Asst Libn: Mrs L. Brain.
8 General; psychology; sociology; economics & commerce; politics & government; law; social services; education; maths (inc. computer studies); science; technology; mechanical & electrical engineering; human biology & nutrition; building construction; carpentry & joinery; brickwork; gas fitting & utilization; arts (music, photography, painting, sculpture, pottery); English literature; French; German; Spanish; Russian; geography; history; management.　**10** SWRLB.　**11** Yes.
12 Term: Mon-Fri 9.00-21.00 (Fri 17.00); vac: 9.00-16.30. Branch varies.　**13** (a) c. 27,000; (b) 195.

IMPERIAL TOBACCO LTD, RESEARCH DEPARTMENT LIBRARY, Raleigh Rd, Bristol, BS3 1QX (Tel 0272-666961 ext 4084) Libn: Mr E.G.N. Berry.
8 Science & engineering.　**9** Tobacco science & technology.
10 BLL; SWRLB.　**11** No.　**12** Mon-Fri 9.00-16.30.
13 (a) 8,000; (b) 220.　**14** £8,000.　**15** (a) 3 (b) 2 (c) 1.

LONG ASHTON RESEARCH STATION LIBRARY, University of Bristol Research Station, Long Ashton, Bristol, BS18 9AF (Tel 027 580-2181) Libn: Miss I.P. Keeton ALA.
6 University of Bristol Agricultural Research Council.
8 Specialised aspects of pomology & plant breeding; plant nutrition; plant physiology & biochemistry; organic chemistry; physical chemistry; pesticide application; zoology; plant pathology; microclimatology; cider & fruit juices; home food preservation.　**9** Small colln of antiquarian books on cider & horticultural science.　**10** SWRLB.　**11** Yes, in special

circumstances.　**12** Mon-Fri 9.00-17.00.　**13** (a) 8,300; (b) 700.　**15** (a) 3 (c) 1.

REDLAND COLLEGE LIBRARY, (will merge with Bristol Polytechnic), Redland Hill, Bristol, BS6 6UZ (Tel 0272-311251 ext 30) Tutor Libn: Mrs Jennifer Parmenter BA; Libn: Mrs C. Greenwood BA, ALA.
6 Avon CC.　**8** Education; English; geography; history; religion; maths; physical & special education; art & design (inc constructional design); commerce; economics.
9 Children's books (16,735); audio-visual aids (over 20,000).
10 BLL; SWRLB.　**11** No, except for ref, on application.
12 Term: Mon-Fri 9.00-20.00 (Mon & Fri 18.00), Sat 9.00-12.00; vac: Mon-Fri 9.00-17.00.　**13** (a) 36,962; (b) c. 450.
14 c. £21,000.　**15** (a) 7 (b) 3 (c) 2.

SOUNDWELL TECHNICAL COLLEGE LIBRARY, St Stephen's Rd, Soundwell, Bristol, BS16 4RL (Tel 0272-675101) Tutor-Libn: Miss P.A. Symons ALA; Clerical Lib Asst: Miss J.A. Barnett.
6 Avon CC Education Dept.　**8** Technology; engineering; business studies; sociology; economics.　**9** Printing; BSI.
10 GTIS; SWRLB.　**11** Yes.　**12** Mon-Fri 9.00-19.00 (Fri 16.30).　**13** (a) 20,000; (b) 160; (c) 48 slides; 90 ohp transparencies; 50 film loops; 490 charts.　**14** £6,000.
15 (a) 2½ (c) 1.

SOUTH BRISTOL TECHNICAL COLLEGE LIBRARY, Marksbury Rd, Bedminster, Bristol, BS3 5JL (Tel 0272-661105 ext 35) Libn: Miss D.M. Foweraker BLib, ALA; Lib Asst: Mrs M. Seabourn.
6 Avon CC.　**8** General; business studies; engineering & electrical engineering.　**10** BLL; SWRLB.　**11** No.
12 Term: Mon-Fri 8.45-20.00 (Fri 16.00); vac: Mon-Fri 8.45-17.00.　**13** (a) 9,500 (b) 32.　**14** c. £3,000.　**15** (a) 2½ (b) 1 (c) 1.

TRINITY COLLEGE LIBRARY, 14-26 Stoke Hill, Stoke Bishop, Bristol, BS9 1JW (Tel 0272-682803) Libn: Rev C.P. Williams MA, BD.
6 Trinity College Council.　**8** Theology, inc church history & philosophy.　**10** BLL.　**11** No.　**12** Mon-Fri 9.00-17.00.　**13** (a) 25,000; (b) 45.　**14** £1,400.

WESLEY COLLEGE LIBRARY, Henbury Hill, Westbury-on-Trym, Bristol, BS10 7QD (Tel 0272-628495) Coll Libn: Rev Kenneth Wilson MA, MLitt.
8 Theology; Methodism, its history & theology.　**9** Methodist material.　**11** No, except by special arrangement with Libn.　**12** 8.30-16.30.　**13** (a) 20,000; (b) 24.

BROADSTAIRS, Kent

THANET TECHNICAL COLLEGE LIBRARY, Ramsgate Rd, Broadstairs, CT10 1PN (Tel 0843-65111) Tutor-Libn: David Copsey BA, DipLib, ALA.
6 Kent CC.　**7** High St, Ramsgate, CT11 9TT.　**8** Catering; hotel management; building; engineering; hairdressing; welfare; business; general.　**10** KULOP.　**11** Yes, for ref only, to Libn.　**12** 8.45-17.00.　**13** (a) 12,000; (b) 140.
14 c. £4,000.　**15** (a) 2½ (b) 1 (c) 1.

BROMSGROVE, Hereford and Worcester

BROMSGROVE COLLEGE OF FURTHER EDUCATION LIBRARY (will merge with Shenstone New College, Sept 1976), School Dr, Stratford Rd, Bromsgrove, B60 1BB (Tel 0527-76474) Acting Libn: Miss M.M. Taylor ALA.
6 Hereford & Worcester CC.　**8** Engineering; motor vehicle engineering; garage management; transport; business; general & specialized management; social services.　**9** Complete BSI.　**10** WATL; WESLINK.　**11** Yes, for ref only.
12 Term: 9.00-21.00; vac: 9.00-13.00; 14.00-17.00. Closed Aug.　**13** (a) 23,000; (b) 275.　**14** £6,300.　**15** (a) 4½ (b) 1 (c) 3.

BUCKINGHAM, Buckinghamshire

UNIVERSITY COLLEGE AT BUCKINGHAM LIBRARY, Hunter St, Buckingham, MK18 1EG (Tel 02802-4161) Libn: John E. Pemberton BA, FLA, FRSA; Classifier: Mr Richard Newell BA, DipLib.
8 Law; economics; politics.　**9** Alexander MacCallum Scott

CODE: 1 Name of Library. 2 Address. 3 Telephone & Telex. 4 Officer in charge. 5 Deputy. 6 Governing body.
7 Branches. 8 Main Subjects. 9 Special Collections. 10 Co-operative Schemes. 11 Open to public? 12 Hours.
13 Stock: (a) books (b) periodicals (c) other. 14 Finance. 15 Staff: (a) non-manual (b) graduate (c) chartered librarians.

BUCKINGHAM, Buckinghamshire—*continued*

papers relating to Liberalism.   **11** Yes, for ref only.
12 Mon-Fri 9.00-22.00, Sat & Sun 9.00-17.00.   **13** (a)
10,000; (b) 50.   **15** (a) 5 (b) 3 (c) 1.

BURY, Lancashire

BURY AND DISTRICT POSTGRADUATE MEDICAL INSTI-
TUTE LIBRARY, Bury General Hospital, Walmersley Rd,
Bury, BL9 6PG (Tel 061-764 2444 ext 258) Libn: Mrs J. L.
Broughton ALA.
6 Bury Area Health Authority.   **7** Psychiatry, obstetrics &
gynaecology, Fairfield General Hospital, Rochdale Rd, Bury.
8 Medicine.   **11** Yes, for ref only on special application to
Libn.   **12** 24 hours a day.   **13** (a) 2,086; (b) 120; (c)
c. 2,000 transparencies; movies (1 16 mm colour); 10 phono-
tapes.   **14** c.£2,000.   **15** (a) 1 (c) 1.

CAMBERLEY, Surrey

ROYAL MILITARY ACADEMY, SANDHURST, LIBRARY,
Camberley, GU15 4PQ (Tel 0276-63344 ext 367) Chief Libn:
Lt Col G. A. Shepperd MBE; Dep: Mr M. G. H. Wright MA, FLA.
6 MoD.   **7** Narrien (Science) Lib, Faraday Hall, RMA
Sandhurst, Camberley, GU15 4PQ (0276-63344 ext 369), Libn:
J. R. C. Quibell BA, ALA.   **8** War studies; international
affairs; contemporary Britain; Soviet studies; military technology.   **9** Military history & campaigns; Soviet history
(in English & Russian); Le Marchant Colln.   **10** BLL; inter-
library loans.   **11** No.   **12** Mon, Tues & Thurs 8.30-12.30
13.30-19.30, 20.00-22.00, Wed & Fri 8.30-12.30, 13.30-19.00,
Sat 8.30-12.30, Sun 14.00-17.00.   **13** (a) 100,000; (b) 300;
(c) register of cadets RMC Sandhurst 1806-1939; register of
cadets RMA Woolwich.   **15** (a) 11 (b) 2 (c) 2.

STAFF COLLEGE LIBRARY, Camberley, GU15 4NP (Tel
0276-63344) Libn: Mr K. M. White ALA; Dep Libn: Miss M.
Hill ALA.
6 MoD.   **8** Military history; British & Commonwealth
history; biography; international affairs; strategy & study of
war; regimental history.   **9** Staff College Colln.   **11** No,
but assistance given to research workers.   **12** Ref: daily
8.30-22.00; Lending: Mon-Fri 8.30-17.30.   **13** (a)
c. 45,000; (b) 100; (c) archival material; maps; mss.
14 £5,000 (exc binding).   **15** (a) 5 (c) 2.

CAMBRIDGE, Cambridgeshire

CAMBRIDGE INSTITUTE OF EDUCATION LIBRARY, Shaftesbury Rd, Cambridge, CB2 2BX (Tel 0223-69631) Libn: Ms
Marjorie Bucking Bsc, ALA.
8 Education & psychology.   **10** EMRLB; LISE.   **11** Yes.
12 Term: Mon-Fri 10.00-20.00, Sat 9.30-12.30; vac: Mon-
Fri 10.00-18.00.   **13** (a) 18,000; (b) 125; (c) resource
material (mainly school curriculum projects).   **14** £3,685.
15 (a) 3½ (b) 2 (c) 2.

CAMBRIDGESHIRE COLLEGE OF ARTS AND TECHNOLOGY
LIBRARY, Collier Rd, Cambridge, CB1 2AJ (Tel 0223-63271)
Tutor-Libn: Mr F. J. Chambers BA, ALA; Dep Libn: Miss
R. M. Davies ALA.
6 Cambridgeshire CC.   **8** General.   **9** History of fine
art; modern European history & politics.   **10** BLL.
11 Yes, by prior arrangement.   **12** Term: Mon-Fri 9.00-
21.00, Sat 10.00-17.00; variations in lending library & music
library.   **13** (a) 88,000; (b) 800; (c) 50,000 ft microfilm;
5,000 slide transparencies; 300 hrs audio tapes; 900 discs.
14 £42,000.   **15** (a) 25 (b) 8 (c) 8.

CAMBRIDGE UNION SOCIETY LIBRARY, Bridge St, Cambridge, CB2 1UB (Tel 0223-61521/2) Libn: Mr D. J. McKit-
terick MA; Lib Clerk: Miss G. I. Mayhew.
8 Greek; Latin; English literature; law; history; politics;
economics; philosophy; maths; physical & life sciences; biography; fiction; art & architecture; music.   **9** Erskine Allon

Colln (music); Fairfax Rhodes Library; Hugh Anderson
Memorial Colln.   **11** No.   **12** Term: Mon-Fri 12.30-
17.30, Sat 10.00-12.00; vac: 13.30-16.00.   **13** (a) 30,000;
(b) 32; (c) gramophone records.   **14** £1,000.

CAMBRIDGE UNIVERSITY.   The Old Schools, Cambridge,
CB2 1TT (0223-58933). The University's library service
consists of 3 main 'central' libraries & 54 subject libraries in Faculties & Departments. Each library is under
the control of the appropriate Library, Faculty or Departmental authority, subject to the overall jurisdiction of
the General Board of the Faculties. The General Board
has a standing Committee on Libraries (Sec: G. B. Skelsey
MA). The public are not, in general, admitted but scholars
& bona-fide students may be admitted to certain libraries
by special arrangement. The opening hours given may vary
during University vacations. Up-to-date particulars are
given in the 'Cambridge Univesity Libraries Directory'.

UNIVERSITY LIBRARY, West Rd, Cambridge, CB3 9DR
(Tel 0223-61441; Telex 81395) Univ Libn: Mr E. B.
Ceadel MA.
6 Library Syndicate.   **8** As a copyright deposit library
all subjects are covered.   **9** Acton historical library
(50,000 vols); Wade (Chinese) Colln; Bradshaw (Irish)
Colln.   **10** Inter-library loans; SCONUL; Union Catalogue
of Serials in the University.   **11** Yes, for ref only, by
prior arrangement.   **12** Full term: Mon-Fri 9.00-
19.00, Sat 9.00-13.00.   **13** (a) c. 3,000,000; (b) 17,000;
(c) mss, archives, microtexts; maps; music.   **14** £293,000.
15 (a) 114 (b) 47 (c) 18.

AFRICAN STUDIES CENTRE LIBRARY, Sidgwick Ave,
Cambridge, CB3 9DA (Tel 0223-58944) Dir of African
Studies Centre: Dr A. F. Robertson; Libn: Mrs L.
Kratochvil BA.
8 Contemporary African Studies.   **11** No.   **12** Mon-Fri
9.00-18.00.   **13** (a) 18,000; (b) 52.   **14** £1,745.
15 (b) 2.

APPLIED BIOLOGY DEPARTMENT LIBRARY, Downing
St, Cambridge, CB2 3DX (Tel 0223-58381) Libn: Mrs C. A.
Ansorge MA, ALA.
8 Environmental biology; agriculture; nutrition; plant &
animal breeding; entomology.   **10** BLL; inter-library
loans.   **11** No.   **12** Term: 9.00-18.30; vac: 9.00-13.00,
14.00-17.30.   **13** (a) 108,200; (b) 2,294; (c) 58,000 pamphlets.   **14** £3,600.   **15** (a) 3 (b) 1 (c) 1.

ARCHAEOLOGY AND ANTHROPOLOGY FACULTY,
HADDON LIBRARY, Downing St, Cambridge CB2 3BZ (Tel
0223-59714/6) Libn: Dr John Drayton Pickles MA, PhD;
Asst Libn: Mrs F. Wetherell ALA.
8 Archaeology; physical anthropology; social anthropology.
9 Bequests from libraries of A. C. Haddon, Sir James
Frazer & Miles Burkitt.   **10** Inter-library loans.
11 No, except by prior arrangement.   **12** Full term:
Mon-Fri 9.00-17.30, Sat 9.30-12.30; vac: Mon-Fri 9.15-
17.00.   **13** (a) 30,000; (b) 459.   **14** £6,000.   **15** (a)
2 (c) 1.

ARCHITECTURE AND HISTORY OF ART FACULTY
LIBRARY, 1 Scroope Terrace, Cambridge, CB2 1PX (Tel
0223-69501/6 ext 219) Libn: R. D. Middleton PhD; Dep:
Mrs J. Murphy.
6 General Board.   **9** 18th cent architecture, most
source books.   **11** Yes, for ref only.   **12** Full term:
9.15-18.00.   **13** (a) 10,312; (b) 51; (c) 6 rolls microfilm.
14 £3,500.   **15** (a) 2.

ASTRONOMY LIBRARY. The Observatories, Madingley
Rd, Cambridge, CB3 OHA (Tel 0223-62204) Libn: Dr. D. W.
Dewhirst MA, PhD; Lib Asst-in-charge: Miss J. E. Herring.
8 Astronomy & astrophysics; cosmology; related physics;
optics, etc.   **9** John Couch Adams colln; 17th & 18th
cent books on astronomy.   **10** BLL; inter-library loans.
11 No, except qualified individuals, on written application.

CAMBRIDGE UNIVERSITY—*continued*

12 Mon-Fri 9.00-17.30.   **13** (a) 10,000; (b) 550; (c) 10,000 pamphlets & reprints; 10,000 map sheets.   **15** (a) 1 (b) 1 (part time).

BIOCHEMISTRY DEPARTMENT, COLMAN LIBRARY, Tennis Court Rd, Cambridge, CB2 1QW (Tel 0223-51781) Libn: Dr P. K. Tubbs MA, PhD; Asst Libn: Mrs J. Annis.   **8** Biochemistry.   **10** BLL.   **11** No.   **12** Mon-Fri 8.00-19.00, Sat 8.00-13.00.   **13** (a) 10,000; (b) 237. **14** £8,500.

BOTANY SCHOOL LIBRARY, Downing St, Cambridge, CB2 3AE (Tel 0223-61414) Libn: Dr K. R. Sporne MA, PhD; Lib Asst in charge: Mrs M. Heap.   **8** Botany (except agriculture & forestry).   **9** Ethel Sargent Colln; Brooks, Pringsheim, Seward, Hamshaw Thomas, collns of reprints; early herbals.   **10** BLL; inter-library loans.   **11** No. **12** Mon-Fri 8.30-17.30; Sat 8.30-13.00 (full term only). **13** (a) 20,629; (b) 276; (c) 54,525 reprints (other than collns).

CHEMICAL ENGINEERING DEPARTMENT LIBRARY, Pembroke St, Cambridge, CB2 3RA (Tel 0223-58231) Libn: Dr R. M. Nedderman MA, PhD, MIChemE. **8** Chemical engineering.   **11** Yes, on application to Libn. **12** Mon-Fri 9.00-17.30.   **13** (a) 2,400; (b) 37. **14** £2,000.

CHEMICAL LABORATORY LIBRARY, Lensfield Rd, Cambridge, CB2 1EW (Tel 0223-66499 ext 227)   **8** All aspects of chemistry.   **11** Yes, with special permission of Libn. **12** Mon-Fri 8.30-17.30.   **13** (a) 13.000; (b) 170. **14** £15,320.   **15** (a) 1.

CLASSICAL ARCHAEOLOGY (MUSEUM OF) LIBRARY, Little St Mary's Lane, Cambridge, CB2 1RR (Tel 0223-65621 ext 204) Curator: Prof R. M. Cook. **8** Classical archaeology (except numismatics cf Fitzwilliam Museum, & Roman British studies cf Univ Library, Archaeology & Anthropology Faculty Library).   **9** 550 casts of Greek & Roman sculpture; small colln of Greek pots & sherds. **11** Yes, on application to Curator.   **12** Mon-Fri 9.00-13.00, 14.15-17.00 (full term 18.00), Sat 9.00-13.00. **13** (a) 13,145; (b) 75; (c) 8,970 photos; 18,730 slides; 3,920 maps.   **14** £2,300.   **15** (a) 2 (b) 1.

CLASSICAL FACULTY LIBRARY, Mill Lane Lecture Rooms, Mill Lane, Cambridge, CB2 1RX (Tel 0223-65621 ext 205) Libn: Miss J. M. Ethridge ALA; Dep: Miss D. W. Clark. **8** Greek & Latin literature, language, history, philosophy, philology & archaeology; modern Greek language, literature, history & folk-lore.   **9** Mins colln of palaeographical works; Rouse colln on modern Greek.   **10** BLL. **11** No, except with Libn's written permission.   **12** Full term: Mon-Sat 9.00-19.00; vac: Mon-Fri 9.00-13.00, 14.15-17.00, Sat 9.00-13.00.   **13** (a) 18,000; (b) 96. **14** £3,500.   **15** (a) 2 (c) 1.

CLINICAL VETERINARY MEDICINE DEPARTMENT LIBRARY, Madingley Rd, Cambridge, CB3 OES (Tel 0223-55641) Libn: Miss M. L. P. Clarke. **8** Veterinary science; natural sciences; epidemiology; toxicology; immunology; mycology; bacteriology; virology; parasitology; pathology; surgery; agriculture.   **9** 18th & 19th cent works (c. 70 vols); Sir John Hammond colln (nutrition). **10** BLL.   **11** Yes, with Libn's permission.   **12** 8.45-19.00.   **13** (a) 7,600; (b) 292.   **14** £4,615.

CRIMINOLOGY INSTITUTE, RADZINOWICZ LIBRARY, 7 West Rd, Cambridge, CB3 9DT (Tel 0223-68511 ext 34) Libn: Miss R. Perry MA, ALA, DipLibst; Asst Libn: Miss K. Anderson MA. **8** Criminology.   **9** Criminal statistics; annual reports; police annual reports.   **10** BLL; inter-library loans. **11** Yes, by prior arrangement.   **12** Term: Mon-Fri 9.00-13.45, 14.00-22.00 (Fri 17.45), Sat 10.00-12.45; vac: Mon-Fri 9.00-13.00, 14.00-18.00.   **13** (a) 30,727; (b) 192; (c) 70 microtexts; ephemera.

DIVINITY FACULTY LIBRARY, St John's St, Cambridge, CB2 1TW (Tel 0223-58933 ext 333) Libn: Rev J. V. M. Sturdy MA; Asst Libn: Miss Margaret Cawthorne BA. **8** Theology.   **9** Library of Bishop J. B. Lightfoot of Durham. **10** BLL; inter-library loans.   **11** No.   **12** Term: Mon-Fri 9.00-18.45, Sat 9.00-13.00; vac: Mon-Fri 9.00-17.00. **13** (a) c.18,000; (b) 30.   **14** £3,000.   **15** (a) 1.

ECONOMICS FACULTY, MARSHALL LIBRARY, Sidgwick Ave, Cambridge, CB3 9DB (Tel 0223-58944) Sec-Libn: Miss M. Hannigan BA; Dep Libn: Mr A. H. Finkell. **8** Economics; politics.   **9** Pryme colln (political economy before 1864)   **11** No.   **12** Full term: Mon-Fri 9.00-22.00, Sat 9.00-19.00; vac: Mon-Fri 9.00-13.00, 2.15-17.00, Sat 9.00-13.00.   **13** (a) 61,000; (b) 569; (c) Marshall papers. **14** £7,475.   **15** (a) 4.

EDUCATION DEPARTMENT LIBRARY, 17 Brookside, Cambridge, CB2 1JG (Tel 0223-55271). **6** General Board.   **8** Education; sociology; psychology; philosophy; teaching.   **9** Education (16th-19th cent). **11** Yes, for ref with permission of Senior Lib Asst. **12** Term: Mon-Fri 8.30-19.00, Sat 9.00-12.30; vac: Mon-Fri 9.00-13.00, 14.00-17.00.   **13** (a) 20,204; (b) 147. **14** £2,800.   **15** (a) 2 (c) 1.

ENGINEERING FACULTY LIBRARY, Trumpington St, Cambridge, CB2 1PZ (Tel 0223-66466; Telex 812239) Libn: Mr K. A. Knell MA; Dep: Mrs N. Smith. **8** Structures; soil mechanics; materials science; electricity; automatic control; mechanics; fluid mechanics inc aeronautics and hydraulics; thermodynamics & heat engines; management; behavioural sciences.   **9** BSI relevant to engineering; selected NASA publns; NEL reports; ARC R & Ms.   **10** BLL; Aslib.   **11** No.   **12** Mon-Fri 9.00-17.00.   **13** (a) 20,000; (b) 400; (c) 20,000 technical reports, pamphlets & standards.   **14** £12,000.   **15** (a) 4 (b) 1.

EXTRA-MURAL STUDIES (BOARD OF) LIBRARY, Madingley Hall, Cambridge, CB3 8AQ (09542-636) Libn: Mr A. Stripp MA. **8** English literature; economics; local history; art; music; psychology; history; theology; archaeology; astronomy; general. **11** No.   **12** 9.00-17.00.   **13** (a) 25,000.   **14** £1,800. **15** (a) 1.

FITZWILLIAM MUSEUM LIBRARY, Trumpington St, Cambridge, CB2 1RB (Tel 0223-69501) Keeper Libn: Mr P. Woudhuysen. **8** Fine & applied arts; illuminated mss; music (mss & printed); literary mss; autograph letters; finely printed books; private presses.   **9** Music; illuminated mss.   **11** Yes, with special permission.   **12** Tues-Fri 10.00-13.00, 14.15-17.00, Sat (term only) 10.00-13.00.   **13** (a) 60,000; (b) c.150.   **15** (a) 3 (b) 1.

GENETICS DEPARTMENT LIBRARY, Milton Rd, Cambridge, CB4 1XH (Tel 0223-58694) Dept officer responsible: Dr K. J. R. Edwards MA, PhD; Lib asst in charge: Mrs M. Leverton. **8** Genetics & related aspects of biology.   **9** Offprints of most important papers published in genetics (1900-50). **10** Inter-library loans.   **11** No, except by special arrangement.   **12** Mon-Fri 9.00-17.30.   **13** (a) 2,721; (b) 103. **14** £2,600.   **15** (a) 3/4.

GEOLOGY DEPARTMENT, SEDGWICK GEOLOGY LIBRARY, Downing St, Cambridge, CB2 3EQ (Tel 0223-51585) Libn: Mr W. B. Harland MA; Asst Libn: Mrs B. L. Falkner. **8** Geology.   **11** No.   **13** (a) c. 20,000; (c) c. 20,000 pamphlets; c. 10,000 maps.   **15** (a) 1 (b) 1 supervising only.

HISTORY FACULTY, SEELEY HISTORICAL LIBRARY, West Rd, Cambridge, CB3 9EF (Tel 0223-61661) Libn: Prof G. R. Elton LittD; Dep Libn: Miss A. C. Cunninghame ALA. **8** History & allied subjects.   **11** No.   **12** Full term: Mon-Fri 8.45-19.15, Sat 8.45-12.00, 14.00-18.00; vac: Mon-Fri 9.00-17.00.   **13** (a) 43,346; (b) 146; (c) 4,296 microtexts.   **14** £5,400.   **15** (a) 4 (c) 1.

LAND ECONOMY DEPARTMENT LIBRARY, Laundress Lane, Cambridge, CB2 1SD (Tel 0223-55262 ext 10). **8** Housing; agricultural economics; material resources; land law; town & country planning; human settlements; regional economics; land tenure & land reform.   **10** Inter-library loans.   **11** Yes, for ref only.   **12** Mon-Fri 9.00-13.00, 14.00-17.30, Sat (term only) 9.00-12.45.   **13** (a) 9,000; (b) 180.   **14** £2,000.   **15** (a) 1 (b) 1 (c) 1.

LAW FACULTY, SQUIRE LIBRARY, Old Schools, Cambridge, CB2 1TU (Tel 0223-58933) Dep Libn in charge: Mr G. G. E. Hughes. **8** Law.   **9** International law; conflict of laws; comparative

CODE: 1 Name of Library. **2** Address. **3** Telephone & Telex. **4** Officer in charge. **5** Deputy. **6** Governing body.
7 Branches. **8** Main Subjects. **9** Special Collections. **10** Co-operative Schemes. **11** Open to public? **12** Hours.
13 Stock: (a) books (b) periodicals (c) other. **14** Finance. **15** Staff: (a) non-manual (b) graduate (c) chartered librarians.

CAMBRIDGE UNIVERSITY—*continued*

law; legal history. **11** No. **12** Mon-Fri 9.00-22.00,
Sat 9.00-13.00. **13** (a) 85,000; (b) 2,000; (c) microfilms;
microfiche. **14** £18,000. **15** (a) 7.

MEDICINE DEPARTMENT LIBRARY, Level 5, Addenbrooke's
New Site, Hills Rd, Cambridge, CB2 2QQ (Tel 0223-44014)
Libn: Prof Ivor H. Mills; Dep: Mrs V. G. Hotchkiss.
8 Medicine. **11** No. **12** 9.00-17.30. **13** (a) 900;
(b) 14. **14** £100 (books only).

METALLURGY AND MATERIALS SCIENCE DEPARTMENT
LIBRARY, Pembroke St, Cambridge CB2 3QZ (Tel 0223-
65151 ext 328) Academic Libn: Dr J. P. Chilton; Asst Libn:
Mrs J. E. Hillier.
8 Metallurgy & materials science. **10** BLL. **11** No.
12 Mon-Fri 9.00-17.30, Sat 9.00-12.00. **13** (a) c.6,800;
(b) 78.

MINERALOGY AND PETROLOGY DEPARTMENT LIBRARY,
Downing Pl, Cambridge, CB2 3EW (Tel 0223-64131 ext 287)
Libn: Dr R. C. Evans MA, PhD; Dep Libn: Mrs L. P. Hall.
8 Mineralogy; petrology; crystallography (morphological,
x-ray, physical, & structural); geochemistry; geophysics.
9 Early classical works on mineralogy & crystallography
(c. 150 vols); Harker colln (offprints). **10** BLL; inter-
library loans. **11** Yes, by special arrangement.
12 Mon-Fri 8.45-17.30, Sat 8.45-13.00. **13** (a) 3,200;
(b) 52; (c) 25,000 offprints. **14** £1,700. **15** (a) ½ (b) 1.

MODERN AND MEDIEVAL LANGUAGES LIBRARIES,
Sidgwick Ave, Cambridge CB3 9DA (Tel 0223-56411) Libn:
Miss Elizabeth L. Falconer MA.
8 Languages & literatures of most European countries;
linguistics; some history, philosophy, art etc. **9** Beit
Library (German research colln, founded 1913); Slavonic
Library. **10** BLL; inter-library loans. **11** Yes, for ref
only, if recommended & if information not obtainable
elsewhere. **12** Full term: Mon-Fri 9.00-22.00, Sat
9.00-13.00; rest of term & long vacation residence: 9.00-
17.00; vac: closed. **13** (a) over 80,000; (b) under 200;
(c) tape recordings (mostly literary readings). **14** under
£10,000. **15** (a) 3½ (b) 3½ (c) 1

MUSIC FACULTY, PENDLEBURY LIBRARY, University
Music School, Downing Pl, Cambridge, CB2 3EL (Tel 0223-
53322) Libn: Mr R. M. Andrewes MA, DipLib.
8 Music. **9** Papers of R. J. S. Stevens, W. H. Weiss, E. J.
Dent; Picken Gift (early editions of Bach); Bryan Bequest
(musical instruments). **11** Yes, by appointment, for ref
only. **12** Term: 9.30-17.30; vac: 9.30-13.00.
13 (a) 60,000 (inc music); (b) 35; (c) 9,000 gramophone
records; 100 mss; 1,000 early printed books & music.
14 £3,800. **15** (a) 3 (b) 1 (c) 1.

ORIENTAL STUDIES FACULTY LIBRARY, Sidgwick Ave,
Cambridge, CB3 9DA (Tel 0223-62253) Libn: Mrs Jean F.
Lambert ALA.
8 South East Asia; South Asia; Near East, Middle East &
Central Asia; Egyptology; Assyriology; languages; literature;
history; art; archaeology; culture; geography; philosophy;
religion. **9** Abraham's (Hebrew); Queens' College (Hebrew/
Arabic, inc Wright Colln); Arberry; Middle East Centre
Library. **10** BLL; SCONUL. **11** Yes, on application to
Faculty Chairman or Libn. **12** Term: 9.00-18.00; vac:
9.00-17.00. **13** (a) 32,000; (b) 128; (c) maps; gramophone
records. **14** £5,000. **15** (a) 2½ (b) 2 (c) 1.

PATHOLOGY DEPARTMENT, KANTHAK LIBRARY, Tennis
Court Rd, Cambridge, CB2 1QP (Tel 0223-58251) Dept
Officer in charge: Dr D. Franks; Lib Asst in charge: Mrs
P. M. Walker.
8 Pathology; immunology; bacteriology; virology; cancer
research. **11** Yes, by arrangement with Libn. **12** Mon-
Fri 9.00-12.45, 14.00-17.15. **13** (a) 15,453; (b) 126.
15 (a) 1.

PHARMACOLOGY DEPARTMENT LIBRARY, Medical School,
Hills Rd, Cambridge, CB2 2QD (Tel 0223-45171) Libn: Dr M. J.
Waring; Dep Libn: Mr C. Wright.
8 Pharmacology. **11** No. **12** 9.00-17.30. **13** (a) 650;
(b) 35. **14** £2,906. **15** (b) 1.

PHILOSOPHY LIBRARY, Sidgwick Ave, Cambridge, CB3 9DA
(Tel 0223-56411 ext 53) Libn: Dr D. H. Mellor MA, PhD; Asst
Libn: C. A. Mahe BA, ALA.
8 Philosophy; ethics; psychology; logic; philosophy of science.
11 No. **12** Full term: Mon-Fri 9.30-19.00.
13 (a) 4,500; (b) 25. **14** £1,200. **15** (a) 1 (b) 1 (c) 1.

PHYSICS DEPARTMENT, RAYLEIGH LIBRARY, Cavendish
Laboratory, Madingley Rd, Cambridge, CB3 0HE (Tel 0223-
66477 ext 562; Telex 812912) Asst-in-charge: Ms Ruth
Ellam BA, DipLib.
8 Physics & closely related subjects. **9** Napier Shaw
Library (meteorology). **11** No. **12** 8.30-18.00.
13 (a) 10,990; (b) 103. **15** (a) ¾ (b) 1.

PHYSIOLOGICAL LABORATORY LIBRARY, Downing St,
Cambridge, CB2 3EG (Tel 0223-614131) Dept Officer in
charge: Dr J. T. Fitzsimons MA, PhD, MD; Lib Asst in
charge: Mrs A. J. Pine.
8 Physiology; biophysics. **10** BLL. **11** No.
12 Mon-Fri 8.45-17.30, Sat (term only) 9.00-12.15.
13 (a) 10,500; (b) 103. **14** £5,960. **15** (a) 1.

PSYCHOLOGICAL LABORATORY LIBRARY, Downing St,
Cambridge, CB2 3EB (Tel 0223-51386) Hon Libn: Dr P.
Whittle; Asst Libn: Mrs R. E. Sewell.
8 Psychology; psychopathology; physiology; philosophy.
9 Oldfield Colln (general psychology); Maccurdy Library
(psychopathology). **10** BLL. **11** No. **12** Mon-Fri
9.00-13.00, 14.15-17.30 (vac 17.00), Sat 9.00-12.00.
13 (a) Extensive reprint colln. **14** £1,995.

PURE MATHEMATICS LIBRARY, 16 Mill Lane, Cambridge,
CB2 1SB (Tel 0223-65621) Academic Libn: Dr B. Bollobas;
Lib asst: Mrs S. J. Wesson.
8 Pure maths. **11** Yes, by prior arrangement.
12 Mon-Fri 9.00-17.30, Sat (full term only) 9.00-12.30.
13 (a) 6,500; (b) 26. **14** £3,000. **15** (a) 1.

SCIENTIFIC PERIODICALS LIBRARY, Bene't Street,
Cambridge, CB2 3PY (Tel 0223-54724; Telex 81240)
Libn: Miss J. E. I. Larter MA, FLA; Asst Libn: Mr A. B.
Britton MA, ALA.
6 Joint Committee of Cambridge University & Cambridge
Philosophical Society. **8** Science, exc medicine.
10 BLL. **11** No. **12** Mon-Fri 9.30-18.00 (vac
17.00 some eves) Sat 9.30-13.00. **13** (a) 60,000;
(b) 1,960. **15** (a) 9 (b) 3 (c) 3.

SCOTT POLAR RESEARCH INSTITUTE LIBRARY,
Lensfield Rd, Cambridge, CB2 1ER (Tel 0223-66499 ext 413)
Libn: Mr H. G. R. King MA; Dep Libn: Mr C. Holland MA.
8 All aspects of arctic & antarctic regions. **11** Yes, on
application to Libn. **12** Mon-Fri 9.00-17.30; Sat 9.00-
12.45. **13** (b) 850; (c) mss; photographs; art.

SOUTH ASIAN STUDIES CENTRE LIBRARY, Faculty Rooms,
Laundress Lane, Cambridge CB2 1SD (Tel 0223-65621
ext 202) Sec-Libn: A. J. N. Richards MA.
6 Committee of Management/General Board of University.
8 Social sciences in South Asia (India, Pakistan, Sri Lanka,
Burma, Bangladesh, Afghanistan, Nepal) (from c. 1800).
9 Archive of material on British period in India. **10** Inter-
library loans; South Asia Libraries Group (bibliographies).
11 No, unless academically sponsored. **12** Mon-Fri 9.30-
13.00, 14.00-17.30. **13** (a) 10,000; (b) 170; (c) archive
(printed catalogue); 1,500 rolls microfilm of Indian newspapers. **14** £1,870. **15** (a) 1.

CAMBRIDGE UNIVERSITY—*continued*

STATISTICAL (WISHART) LIBRARY, 16 Mill Lane,
Cambridge, CB2 1SB (Tel 0223-65621) Academic Libn:
Dr. A. D. Barbour; Lib asst: Mrs S. J. Wesson.
8 Mathematical statistics. **9** Offprint colln (from 1948).
11 Yes, by prior arrangement. **12** Mon-Fri 9.00-17.30,
Sat (full term only) 9.00-12.30. **13** (a) 3,300; (b) 45;
(c) c.15,000 offprints. **14** £1,800. **15** (a) 1.

WHIPPLE LIBRARY, Free School Lane, Cambridge, CB2
3RH (Tel 0223-58381 ext 383) Libn: Miss Susan M. Scarlett
BA, ALA.
8 History & philosophy of science, inc medicine.
9 R. S. Whipple's colln (works of Robert Boyle & antiquarian science books inc 17th-19th cent books on scientific instruments); A. W. Pollard colln (English instrument
makers printed ephemera, c. 1890-1940); Cambridge
Scientific Instrument Co Ltd Colln (instruction manuals,
catalogues, 1880-1950, some archives & engineering
drawings). **11** Yes, by written appointment only.
12 9.30-13.00, 14.00-17.00. **13** (a) c.10,000; (b)
67; (c) microcards (Landmarks of Science series 1);
Pye of Cambridge engineering drawings. **15** (a) 1 (c) 1.

ZOOLOGY DEPARTMENT, BALFOUR AND NEWTON
LIBRARIES, Downing St, Cambridge, CB2 3EJ (Tel 0223-
58717) Libn: Mr R. Hughes; Asst Libn: Miss J. Sanderson.
8 Zoology; ornithology. **9** Books & periodicals bequeathed by F. M. Balfour & A. Newton; collns of R. A.
MacAndrew, Strickland, J. Gould & others; mss. **10** BLL;
Aslib. **11** No. **12** Mon-Fri 8.30-13.00, 14.15-17.30
(longer during full term), Sat (full term only) 9.00-12.30.
13 (a) c.33,000; (b) c.400. **15** (a) 2.

Cambridge University Colleges

CHRIST'S COLLEGE LIBRARY, Cambridge, CB2 3BU
(Tel 0223-67641) Libn: Dr C. P. Courtney; Sub-Libn: Miss
Gillian Farmer.
8 General. **9** Lesingham Smith (16th & 17th cent
mathematical & scientific books); Robertson Smith Colln
(Oriental Books); Rouse (Indian) Colln; Gazelee (Coptic)
Colln; Rouse Colln (16th & 17th cent English books).
11 No. **12** Mon-Fri 9.00-13.00, 14.15-17.00, Sat
(term only) 9.00-13.00. **13** (a) c.50,000; (c) college &
library archives. **14** c. £3,500. **15** (a) 2 (b) 1.

CHURCHILL COLLEGE, ARCHIVES CENTRE & LIBRARY,
Storey's Way, Cambridge, CB3 0DS (Tel 0223-61200
ext 338) Libn & Keeper of Archives: Dr M. A. Hoskin MA,
PhD, FRAS; Asst Libn: Mr B. S. Purvis BA, ALA;
Archivist: Mrs P. M. Bradford BA.
6 Master, Fellows & Scholars. **8** Bracken Reading
Room (undergraduate texts); Bevin Library (political,
military & scientific history & biography of Churchill
era). **9** Archives Centre: 200 collns of political,
scientific, military & naval papers covering Churchill
era, inc Churchill's own papers. **11** Yes, on application
to, & at discretion of Libn. **12** Mon-Fri 9.00-12.30,
13.30-17.00. **13** (a) 24,000; (b) 112. **14** £5,000.
15 (a) 7 (b) 4 (c) 2.

CLARE COLLEGE, FORBES LIBRARY, Cambridge,
CB2 1TL (Tel 0223-58681 ext 35) Forbes Libn: Dr R. D.
Gooder PhD; Asst Libn: Mrs Dorothy Dingle.
8 General; arts; sciences. **9** Cecil Sharp mss.
11 No. **12** 7.00-02.00. **13** (a) 11,000; (b) 5.
14 £3,500. **15** (a) 1.5.

CORPUS CHRISTI, COLLEGE LIBRARY, Cambridge,
CB2 1RH (Tel 0223-59418) Libn: Dr R. I. Page LittD.
6 Masters & Fellows. **8** General. **9** Over 600 mss,
particularly Anglo-Saxon, later medieval & reformation;
over 600 printed books bequeathed by Matthew Parker in
1575; 142 incunabula; 196 books printed between 1501-20;
Stokes colln of books on Jews especially in England; Lewis
colln of coins; gems, vases etc & books relating to them:
Perowne colln of printed books on military orders of the
Church. **11** Yes, by appointment. **12** Mon-Fri 14.00-
16.00 (or 17.00). **13** (a) 20,000. **15** (a) 1.

DOWNING COLLEGE LIBRARY, Cambridge CB2 1DQ
(Tel 0223-59491 ext 49) Libn: Dr G. P. Chapman MA, PhD;
Sub-Libn: Mrs O. J. Miller BSc.
8 General; English; Law. **9** Naval history.
11 Yes, but only by prior arrangement. **12** 9.00-
17.30. **13** (a) 18,000. **14** £3,500.

EMMANUEL COLLEGE LIBRARY, Cambridge, CB2 3AP
(Tel 0223-65411) Libn: Dr F. H. Stubbings, MA, PhD, FSA.
8 General. **9** Books printed before 1800 (c. 18,000
vols) inc whole library of Archbishop William Sancroft
(d. 1693); W. C. Bishop library (liturgy); mss (printed
catalogue). **11** No, except by prior written agreement.
12 Mon-Fri 9.00-13.00, 14.30-17.30, Sat 9.00-13.00.
13 (a) c. 55,000; (b) c. 70. **15** (a) 1½.

FITZWILLIAM COLLEGE LIBRARY, Huntingdon Rd,
Cambridge, CB3 0DG (Tel 0223-58657) Libn: Dr J. Street
MA, PhD; Asst Libn: Mrs J. Donkin BA, DipLib.
8 General. **11** No. **12** 9.00-23.00. **13** (a) 17,000;
(b) 60. **14** c. £3,000. **15** (a) 1 (b) 1 (c) 1.

GIRTON COLLEGE LIBRARY, Cambridge, CB3 0JG
(Tel 0223-76219) Libn: Mrs Margaret Gaskell; Sub Libn:
Mrs J. A. Taylor.
8 Anglo Saxon; archaeology; anthropology; art; architecture;
biological sciences (inc medicine); classics; economics;
engineering; English; geography; history; law; maths;
modern and medieval languages; music; Oriental studies;
physical sciences; theology. **9** Women's education &
suffrage etc; Scandinavian; Hebrew. **10** Inter-library
loans. **11** No, except by prior arrangement with Libn.
12 9.00-17.00. **13** (a) c. 64,000; (b) 108; (c) archives;
women & education (letters & photographs) (late 19th &
20th cent). **14** £6,000. **15** (a) 1½.

GONVILLE AND CAIUS COLLEGE LIBRARY, Cambridge,
CB2 1TA (Tel 0223-53275) Libn: Mr J. H. Prynne MA.
6 Master & Fellows. **8** General; serials; ref; music;
etc. **9** 800 Western mss (printed catalogue); incunabula
(printed catalogue); other early printed books, inc Bran-
thwaite Library (bequeathed 1619); papers of John Venn,
C. M. Doughty, etc. **11** Yes, by prior arrangement with
Libn, or mss & books can be deposited at Univ Library
for photography & ref. **12** Mon-Fri: 9.00-13.00,
14.00-17.00. **13** (a) 40,000; (b) 84 (serials);
(c) archives form a separate collection. **15** (a) 1¼
(b) 2.

HUGHES HALL LIBRARY, Wollaston Rd, Cambridge,
CB1 2EW (Tel 0223-52866) Libn: Mrs S. E. Lello MA.
6 Council. **8** General. **9** Education. **11** No.
12 Full term. **13** (a) 4,200; (b) 32. **14** £200.
15 (b) ½.

JESUS COLLEGE LIBRARY, Cambridge, CB5 8BL
(Tel 0223-68611) Libn: Dr: M. J. Waring MA, PhD, ScD;
Asst Libn: Mrs I. Tedder.
8 All academic subjects. **11** No. **13** (a) 18,000.
15 (a) 1.

JESUS COLLEGE, THE OLD LIBRARY, Cambridge,
CB5 8BL (Tel 0223-68611) Keeper: Mr D. J. V. Fisher
MA; Asst Libn: Mrs I. Tedder.
9 Some Durham mss; a few letters of S. T. Coleridge;
Civil War tracts; Malthus colln. **11** No, except
visiting scholars by appointment. **13** (a) 10,000.

KING'S COLLEGE LIBRARY, Cambridge, CB2 1ST
(Tel 0223-50411) Coll Libn: P. J. Croft.
6 Provost & Fellows. **8** General. **9** Incunabula
(250); 16-18th cent English literature; Aeschylus; T. S.
Eliot; 20th cent literary papers; history of thought
(Newton, J. S. Mill, etc); Keynes library (6,000 vols);
Rowe music library (especially Handel); papers of C. R.
Ashbee, Rupert Brooke, E. M. Forster. **11** Yes, by prior
arrangement with Libn, for ref only. **12** Term: Mon-
Fri 9.00-17.30, Sat 9.00-13.00; vac: Mon-Fri 9.00-13.00,
14.00-17.30. **13** (a) c. 120,000. **15** (a) 4 (b) 2.

MAGDALENE COLLEGE, PEPYS LIBRARY, Cambridge,
CB3 0AG (Tel 0223-61543 ext 38) Libn: Mr R. C. Latham
CBE, MA; Lib Asst: Mrs E. M. Coleman BA.
8 History; literature; science; music; prints & drawings.

CODE: 1 Name of Library. **2** Address. **3** Telephone & Telex. **4** Officer in charge. **5** Deputy. **6** Governing body.
7 Branches. **8** Main Subjects. **9** Special Collections. **10** Co-operative Schemes. **11** Open to public? **12** Hours.
13 Stock: (a) books (b) periodicals (c) other. **14** Finance. **15** Staff: (a) non-manual (b) graduate (c) chartered librarians.

CAMBRIDGE UNIVERSITY—*continued*

9 Library consists of personal colln of Samuel Pepys (bequeathed 1703): medieval mss; early printed books; naval collns; ballads; calligraphy; shorthand; London topography. **11** Yes, by appointment. **12** 11.30-12.30, 14.30-15.30. **13** (a) 3,000 (inc mss).

NEW HALL LIBRARY, Huntingdon Rd, Cambridge, CB3 0DF (Tel 0223-51721) Coll Libn: Miss S. K. Newman MA, ALA; Asst Libn: Mrs E. A. Davis ALA. **8** General. **11** No. **13** (a) c.30,000; (b) 1. **14** c.£2,750. **15** (a) 1½ (b) 1 (c) 2.

NEWNHAM COLLEGE LIBRARY, Cambridge, CB3 9DF (Tel 0223-62273) Libn: Miss A. Phillips MA; Asst Libn: Miss J. Hilton BA. **6** Principal & Fellows. **8** General. **11** No, except by prior arrangement. **12** Term: 8.00-midnight; vac: 9.00-17.00. **13** (a) c.60,000; (b) 97. **14** c.£4,000. **15** (a) 1 (b) 2.

PEMBROKE COLLEGE LIBRARY, Cambridge, CB2 1RF (Tel 0223-52241) Fellow Libn: Mr Clive Trebilcock MA. **8** General. **9** Thomas Gray, especially commonplace books (inc The Elegy in ms) & diaries. **11** No. **12** Mon-Fri 9.00-17.00. **13** (a) 30,000; (b) c.30. **14** £3,500. **15** (a) 2.

PETERHOUSE, WARD LIBRARY, Cambridge, CB2 1RD (Tel 0223-50256) Libn: R. W. K. Hinton. **6** Master & Fellows. **8** History; natural sciences. **11** No. **12** 12.00-15.00, 17.00-20.00. **13** (a) 25,000; (b) 34. **15** (b) 2 (c) 1.

QUEENS' COLLEGE LIBRARY, Cambridge, CB3 9ET (Tel 0223-65511 ext 249) Libn: Dr J. S. C. Riley-Smith MA, PhD; Asst Libn: Mrs E. Machin MA. **8** General. **9** Early books on theology, science, law & belles lettres. **11** No, except by prior arrangement. **12** Term: 9.00-midnight; vac: shorter hours. **13** (a) c.55,000; (c) medieval mss; college archives. **14** £4,000. **15** (a) 1½ (b) 4.

ST CATHARINE'S COLLEGE LIBRARY, Cambridge, CB2 1RL (Tel 0223-59445, ext 60) Libn: Dr John R, Shakeshaft PhD; Asst Libn: Mrs Avril Pedley MA. **8** General. **9** c.20 mss (13th-17th cent); 30 incunabula; other early printed books; medical works given in 1718 by John Addenbrooke; 1761 Thomas Sherlock bequest, inc large colln of 17th & 18th cent political & religious tracts; c.3,000 vols (mainly medieval Romance literature, especially French & Provencal) from estate of H. J. Chaytor, 1954. **11** No, except by prior arrangement with Libn. **12** Daily in full term. **13** (a) 25,000; (b) c.60; (c) college archives housed separately, under care of Prof E. E. Rich. **14** £5,000. **15** (b) 2.

ST JOHN'S COLLEGE LIBRARY, Cambridge, CB2 1TP (Tel 0223-61621) Libn: Mr A. G. Lee MA; Sub-Libn: Mr N. C. Buck. **6** Master & Fellows. **8** General. **9** Books by, & relating to, Samuel Butler; Otway colln of 17th cent pamphlets; Ferrari colln of early Italian & French books; Souldern Laurence colln of 18th cent law books; Yule colln of editions of 'The Imitation of Christ' by Thomas á Kempis; W. F. Smith colln of Rabelais literature. **11** No, except with Libn's permission. **13** (a) 110,000; (b) 90; (c) c.580 mss; 275 incunabula. **15** (a) 4.

SELWYN COLLEGE, LIBRARY, Grange Rd, Cambridge, CB3 9DQ (Tel 0223-62381) Coll Libn: Dr A. Vlasto; Asst Libn: Rev R. J. C. Gutteridge. **8** General. **9** Liturgics; patristics; 19th cent theology. **11** No. **12** Term: all day. **13** (a) c.25,000; (b) 11. **15** (a) 1 (b) 1.

TRINITY COLLEGE LIBRARY, Cambridge, CB2 1JQ (Tel 0223-58201) Libn: Dr Philip Gaskell; Sub-Libn: Mr T. Kaye. **6** Master & Fellows. **8** General. **9** <u>Printed Books</u>: Isaac Newton colln; Capell colln of Shakespeareiana; Rothschild colln of 18th cent literature; c.750 incunabula. <u>Mss</u>: c.1,500 early mss (printed catalogue); Lord Houghton papers; William Whewell papers; Sir J. G. Frazer papers; Wittgenstein notebooks; Tennyson notebooks. **10** BLL; inter-library loans. **11** Yes, to Wren Library. Admission to reading room by prior arrangement only. **12** Wren Library Mon-Fri: 14.15-16.45 (15.45 in winter), Sat 9.00-12.45 (full term only); Reading Room: Mon-Fri 9.00-17.00, Sat 9.00-12.45 (full term only). **13** (a) c.150,000; (b) c.160; (c) 175,000 other mss. **15** (a) 5 (b) 2 (c) 1.

CRAC/NICEC LIBRARY, Bateman St, Cambridge, CB2 1LZ (Tel 0223-51446) Inf Officer: Mrs Trillia Scoins. **6** Careers Research & Advisory Centre. **8** Careers, guidance & vocational counselling. **9** One of largest collns of such literature in England, especially American works. **11** Yes, by appointment. **12** 9.00-13.00, 14.00-17.00. **15** (a) 1 (b) 1.

HOMERTON COLLEGE LIBRARY, Hills Rd, Cambridge, CB2 2PH (Tel 0223-45931 ext 55) Libn: Miss N. M. Bartlett MA, ALA; Dep Libn: Miss N. E Gatland BA, CertEd, DipLib. **6** Trustees. **8** General; education. **9** Children's books; learning resources material. **10** BLL; Cambridge Institute of Education. **11** Yes, by prior arrangement. **12** Term: Mon-Fri 9.00-22.00, Sat 9.00-12.00, Sun 10.00-19.00; vac: Mon-Fri 9.00-17.30 **13** (a) 50,000; (b) 250; (c) records; film strips; illustrations; charts; packaged materials; slides. **14** £10,000. **15** (a) 5½ (b) 5 (c) 1.

NATIONAL INSTITUTE OF AGRICULTURAL BOTANY LIBRARY, Huntingdon Rd, Cambridge, CB3 0LE (Tel 0223-76381) Libn & Technical Editor: Mr P. R. Colegate BA, ALA; Dep: Mrs M. A. Clarke. **8** Agricultural botany; crop varieties; seeds. **9** Seed catalogues. **10** BLL; Aslib. **11** Yes, for researchers, by arrangement with Libn. **12** Mon-Thurs 8.45-17.15, Fri 8.45-16.45. **13** (a) 5,000; (b) 900; (c) 3,000 pamphlets. **15** (a) 2 (b) 1 (c) 1.

TYNDALE LIBRARY, 36, Selwyn Gardens, Cambridge, CB3 9BA (Tel 0223-52159) Libn: Rev Dr. R. T. France MA, BD, PhD. **6** Universities & Colleges Christian Fellowship. **10** Biblical & theological studies, with emphasis on primary sources & research tools for study of biblical & related cultures. **9** Archaeological & linguistic materials relating to ancient Near East; colln of 16th, 17th & 18th cent theology. **10** BLL; inter-library loans. **11** No, except with reader's ticket issued by Libn. **12** Mon-Sat 9.00-22.30. **13** (a) c.16,000; (b) 112; (c) limited archives & personal papers, of evangelical christian leaders & groups. **14** c £3,000. **15** (a) 3 (b) 2.

WELDING INSTITUTE LIBRARY AND INFORMATION SERVICE, Abington Hall, Abington, Cambridge, CB1 6AL (Tel 0223-891162; Telex 81183) Chief Libn: Mr T. D. Stephens BA, AIInfSc; Asst Libn: Mr J. M. Loader ALA. **8** Technology & practice of welding, brazing, soldering, thermal cutting, weld surfacing, metal spraying; inspection & non-destructive testing; welding design; performance of welded assemblies (fatigue, brittle fracture corrosion); welding metallurgy; fabrication techniques; welded construction; quality control. **10** BLL; inter-library loans. **11** No, but requests from researchers considered. **12** Mon-Fri 8.30-16.30. **13** (a) c.4,000; (b) c.400; (c) 4,000 microfiche technical reports; 30,000 "Weldasearch" Inf Services abstracts cards on microfilm with computerized access to data base. **15** (a) 8 (b) 4 (c) 2.

CANNOCK, Staffordshire

CANNOCK CHASE TECHNICAL COLLEGE LIBRARY,
Stafford Rd, Cannock, WS11 2AE (Tel 05435-5811/2/3) Tutor-
libn: Mr G. C. Paterson FLA.
6 Staffordshire CC.   8 Engineering; mining; commerce &
business studies.   10 MISLIC; SOSCOL.   11 Yes, for ref
only.   12 Term: Mon-Thurs 9.00-19.00, Fri 9.00-17.00;
vac: 9.00-14.00.   13 (a) 12, 146; (b) 136; (c) gramophone
records; film-strips.   14 £1, 450.   15 (a) $2\frac{1}{2}$ (c) 1.

CANTERBURY, Kent

CANTERBURY COLLEGE OF ART LIBRARY, New Dover Rd,
Canterbury, CT1 3AN (Tel 0227-69371 ext 27) Tutor-Libn:
Mr Colin Franck Ball BA, ALA; Asst Libn: Ms Pam Grimsey
BA, ALA.
6 Board of Governers of C.C.A.   8 Architecture; building;
fine arts; philosophy; graphic design; illustrated books;
costume; textiles.   10 ARLIS; CCL.   11 Yes, by arrangement with, & at discretion of, Libn.   12 Term: Mon-Thurs
9.30-18.30, Fri 9.30-17.00; vac: Mon-Fri 9.30-12.00, 14.00-
16.45.   13 (a) c. 20, 000; (b) 164; (c) c. 28, 000 slides;
c. 2, 000 illustrations; 326 maps; 55 reels of microfilms; 45
posters & wallcharts, videocassettes & audiocassettes.
14 £6, 850.   15 (a) $3\frac{1}{2}$ (b) 2 (c) 2.

CANTERBURY COLLEGE OF TECHNOLOGY LIBRARY, New
Dover Rd, Canterbury, CT1 3AJ (Tel 0227-66081) Tutor-Libn:
B. J. Paget FLA, ADB.
6 Kent CC.   8 Business studies; engineering & coal mining; science; building & construction; catering + domestic
science.   10 CCL.   11 Yes, by arrangement.   12 Term:
Mon-Thurs 9.00-18.30, 18.30-20.00 (ref only), Fri 9.00-
17.00.   13 (a) 18, 000; (b) 152; (c) 120 teaching programmes
for Canterbury teaching machine.   14 £5, 150.

CATHEDRAL ARCHIVES AND LIBRARY, The Precincts,
Canterbury, CT1 2EG (Tel 0227-63510) Archivist: Miss Anne
M. Oakley MA.
6 Canterbury Dean and Chapter with the City Council.
8 History; theology; texts & commentaries; some local history; dictionaries; travel books; herbals; Bibles.   9 Coombe
colln of Bibles.   11 Yes, by appointment only.   12 Mon-
Fri 9.30-12.45, 14.00-16.30.   13 (a) 40, 000; (b) 10; (c)
city, diocesan & chapter archives.   15 (a) 4 (b) 1.

CHRIST CHURCH COLLEGE LIBRARY, North Holmes Rd,
Canterbury, CT1 1QU (Tel 0227-65548) Tutor-Libn: Mr A. J.
Edwards BA, ALA.
6 College Governors.   8 General.   9 Historical colln of
text & children's books (825).   10 BLL; KULOP.   11 Yes,
for ref only.   12 Mon-Fri 9.00-17.00.   13 (a) 50, 000;
(b) 200; (c) 650 filmstrips; 1, 200 slides; 2, 500 charts; 260
gramophone records.   14 £10, 000.   15 (a) $5\frac{1}{2}$ (b) 1 (c)
$2\frac{1}{2}$.

ST AUGUSTINE'S COLLEGE LIBRARY, Monastery St, Canterbury, CT1 1NL (Tel 0227-66242/3) Libn: Rev K. S. Mason BSc,
BD, ARCS.
6 King's College, University of London.   8 Theology;
philosophy; patristics; comparative religion.   11 No, except
by special arrangement, on recommendation of an institute
of higher education.   12 Term: 11.30-16.00.   13 (a)
28, 000; (b) 20.   14 £650.   15 (a) 2 (b) 1.

UNIVERSITY OF KENT AT CANTERBURY LIBRARY, Canterbury, CT2 7NU (Tel 0227-66822; Telex 965449) Libn: Mr G. S.
Darlow MA, ALA; Dep Lib: Mr W. J. Simpson BA, DipLibStud,
ALA.
6 Council of the University.   8 Humanities; law; social
sciences; experimental sciences; maths; no engineering or
professional schools, no medicine.   9 Pettingell Colln (mss
& printed plays, mainly 19th cent.); John Crow Colln (pre-
1800 books, booksellers' catalogues); Cartoon Centre (original
political cartoons).   10 BLL; BUCOP; KULOP; SCOLMA
(Malagasy Republic).   11 Yes, by written arrangement.
12 Term: Mon-Fri 9.00-22.00, Sat 9.00-21.00, Sun 14.00-
21.00; vac: Mon-Fri 9.00-21.00, Sat 9.00-17.00.   13 (a)
270, 000 (b) 2, 600; (c) c. 70, 000 microforms; 1, 300 mss;
20, 000 cartoons; 500 unpublished theses.   14 £105, 000.
15 $47\frac{1}{2}$ (b) 14 (c) 16.

CARDIFF, South Glamorgan

COLLEGE OF FOOD TECHNOLOGY AND COMMERCE
LIBRARY, Colchester Ave, Cardiff, CF3 7XR (Tel 0222-
22121) Libn: Ms Brenda G. Hockley ALA; Lib Asst: Ms Freda
Davies.
6 South Glamorgan CC.   8 Business studies; journalism;
social work; catering; bakery; dietetics; languages.
10 WRLS.   11 Yes, for ref only.   12 Term: 9.00-20.00;
vac: 9.00-17.00.   13 (a) 12, 000; (b) 150.   14 £5, 900.
15 (a) 2 (c) 1.

LLANDAFF COLLEGE OF TECHNOLOGY LIBRARY,
Western Ave, Cardiff, CF5 2YB (Tel 0222-561241) Tutor-
Libn: Mr R. Lewis BA, DipEd, ALA; Senior Lib Asst: Mrs
S. M. Marshall.
6 South Glamorgan CC Education Committee.   8 Science;
technology; medical sciences; general.   9 Dental technology.
10 WRLS.   11 Yes, for ref, loans, at Libn's discretion.
12 Term: Mon-Thurs 9.00-19.00, Fri 9.00-17.00; vac: Mon-
Fri 9.00-13.00 (usually).   13 (a) 14, 000; (b) 200.
14 £13, 000.   15 (a) $2\frac{1}{2}$ (b) 1 (c) 1.

NATIONAL MUSEUM OF WALES LIBRARY, Cathays Park,
Cardiff, CF1 3NP (Tel 0222-26241) Libn: Mr William J.
Jones FLA; Dep: Mrs E. C. Bridgeman FLA.
6 Court of Governors of the National Museum of Wales.
7 Dept libs not independant.   8 Archaeology; art; botany;
geology; industry; zoology.   9 Tomlin Colln (Molluscs);
Willoughby Gardner Colln (early natural history); Cardiff
Naturalists' Society Library; Cambrian Archaeological
Association Library.   10 BLL; WRLS.   11 Yes, on presentation of introduction forms or by prior arrangement.
12 Mon-Fri 10.00-13.00, 14.00-17.00.   13 (a) 93, 000;
(b) 510; (c) 6" ordnance survey maps of Wales; microtexts
in dept libraries.   14 c. £10, 000.   15 (a) 4 (b) 1 (c) 2.

UNIVERSITY COLLEGE, CARDIFF, LIBRARY, PO Box 98,
Cardiff, CF1 1XQ (Tel 0222-44211; Telex 49635) Libn: Mr
R. J. Bates MA; Dep Libn: Mr H. A. Cufflin BA, ALA.
7 Science Lib, Cathays Park, Cardiff (0222-44211), Libn:
Mrs O. M. Braund BA; Applied Sciences Lib, Newport Rd,
Cardiff (0222-44211), Libn: Miss J. Chamberlayne BA, ALA;
Education Lib, Senghenydd Rd, Cardiff (0222-44211), Libn:
Mr G. Hughes BA, ALA; Music Lib, Corbett Rd, Cardiff (0222-
44211), Libn: Miss J. Wines BA, FLA.   8 General; arts;
economic & social studies (inc law); education; theology;
science & applied science.   9 Salisbury Library (Welsh
& Celtic Colln); special colln (books printed pre-1800);
Mazzini & Tennyson Collns.   10 SWALCAP.   11 Yes,
for ref enquiries of limited scope.   12 Term: Mon-Fri
9.00-22.00, Sat 9.00-13.00; vac: Mon-Fri 9.00-17.00, Sat
(Easter vac only) 9.00-13.00. Closed about four days at
Christmas & Easter & one week in Aug.   13 (a) 400, 000;
(b) 2, 500.   14 £125, 000.   15 (a) 63 (b) 26 (c) 14.

UNIVERSITY OF WALES INSTITUTE OF SCIENCE AND
TECHNOLOGY LIBRARY, King Edward VII Ave, Cardiff,
CF1 3NU (Tel 0222-42522 ext 210/322) Libn: Mr J. K.
Roberts MSc, ALA; Sub-Libn: T. K. Wall BA, DipLib.
7 Applied Psychology Lib, Llwyn-y-Grant Rd, Cardiff (0222-
40171), Libn: Mr R. Sander; Friary Lib, The Friary, Cardiff
(0222-42522 ext 277), Libn: Miss G. L. Parkinson; Grey
Friars Library, South Wales Institute of Engineers, Park Pl,
Cardiff (0222-42522 ext 267), Libn: Miss L. M. Hinton; Law
Lib, Arts & Social Sciences Lib, University College, Cardiff,
Corbett Rd, Cardiff (0222-44211), Libn: Miss A. G. Palmer.
8 Science; technology; social sciences.   9 Architecture.
11 Yes, for ref only, on application to Libn.   12 Term:
Mon-Fri 8.45-22.00, Sat 9.00-17.00, Sun 14.00-17.00; vac:
Mon-Fri 9.00-17.00.   13 (a) 90, 000; (b) 1, 200; (c) micro-
texts.   14 £70, 000.   15 (a) 24 (b) 9 (c) 10.

WALES GAS LIBRARY, Snelling House, Bute Terrace, Cardiff,
CF1 2UF (Tel 0222-33131; Telex 49416) Libn: Miss P. J.
Beech ALA.
8 Gas industry & technology; management.   9 BSI; British
Gas Research Papers; IGE transactions (1898-1960); Reports
Gas Associations (1905-1939).   10 WRLS.   11 No.
12 Mon-Fri 8.30-13.00, 14.00-17.00.   13 (a) 5, 000; (b)
90.   14 £1, 000.   15 (a) 1 (c) 1.

CODE: 1 Name of Library. **2** Address. **3** Telephone & Telex. **4** Officer in charge. **5** Deputy. **6** Governing body. **7** Branches. **8** Main Subjects. **9** Special Collections. **10** Co-operative Schemes. **11** Open to public? **12** Hours. **13** Stock: (a) books (b) periodicals (c) other. **14** Finance. **15** Staff: (a) non-manual (b) graduate (c) chartered librarians.

CARDIFF, South Glamorgan—*continued*

WELSH FOLK MUSEUM LIBRARY, St Fagans, Cardiff, CF5 6XB (Tel 0222-561357/8). **6** Court of Governors of the National Museum of Wales. **8** All subjects relating to folk life; linguistics. **10** BLL; WRLS. **11** Yes, for ref only. **12** Mon-Fri 9.00-17.00. **13** c. 17,500; (b) 188. **15** (a) 2 (c) 1.

WELSH NATIONAL SCHOOL OF MEDICINE LIBRARY, Heath Park, Cardiff, CF4 4XN (Tel 0222-755944; Telex 49696) Libn: Mr R.J.Dannatt BA, ALA. **6** Council, Welsh National School of Medicine. **7** Dental School Lib, Heath Park, Cardiff, CF4 4XY (0222-755944), Libn: Miss J.Stevens ALA. **8** Medicine & dentistry. **9** Cardiff Medical Society library; historical colln (2,500 books). **10** WRLS. **11** No. **12** Mon-Fri 9.00-21.00, Sat, 9.00-12.30 (July & Aug vary). Branch varies. **13** (a) 36,000; (b) 770. **14** £25,500. **15** (a) 11 (b) 8 (c) 5.

CARLISLE, Cumbria

CARLISLE TECHNICAL COLLEGE LIBRARY, Victoria Pl, Carlisle, CA1 1HS (Tel 0228-24464) Tutor-Libn: Mr K.Hudson FLA. **6** Cumbria CC. **8** Engineering; business studies; science; construction; food. **9** BSI. **10** NRLB. **12** Term: Mon-Thurs 9.00-19.00, Fri 9.00-17.00; vac: Mon-Fri 9.00-16.30. **13** (a) 20,000; (b) 250. **14** £4,500. **15** (a) 3 (c) 1.

CHATHAM, Kent

MEDWAY AND MAIDSTONE COLLEGE OF TECHNOLOGY LIBRARY, Horsted, Maidstone Rd, Chatham, ME5 9UQ (Tel 0634-41001) Coll Libn: Mrs J.M.Crisp ALA. **7** Oakwood Park, Tonbridge Rd, Maidstone, Libn: Mrs B.J.Payne BA, ALA; City Way, Rochester, Libn: Mrs P.Davey BA; Westree Rd, Libn: Mrs E.Prentice. **8** Engineering; building; commerce; management; science; maths; social work; education. **9** Chemistry; chemical abstracts; complete set of BSI. **10** BLL; LASER; inter-library loans **11** Yes, for ref only. **12** Term: Mon-Thurs 9.00-21.00, Fri 9.00-18.30; vac: Mon-Thurs 9.00-12.30, 13.15-17.00, Fri 9.00-12.30, 13.15-16.00. **13** (a) 66,000; (b) c.370; (c) tapes; slides; sets of booklets; wall charts; filmstrips; video tapes. **14** £28,000.

ROYAL ENGINEERS CORPS LIBRARY, Brompton Barracks, Chatham, ME4 4UG. (Tel 0634-44555 ext 309) Head Libn: Lt Col J.E.South; Asst Libn: Mr J.L.Longfield. **6** Institution of Royal Engineers. **8** Military history; corps history; military engineering; fortifications. **10** BLL. **11** Yes, by prior arrangement. **12** Mon-Fri 8.45-12.45, 13.45-16.45. **13** (a) 25,000; (b) 175. **15** (a) 3.

CHELMSFORD, Essex

CHELMSFORD CATHEDRAL LIBRARY, Guy Harlings, New St, Chelmsford, CM1 1NG (Tel 0245-52702) Hon Cathedral Libn: Mr E.O,Reed JP, FLA. **6** Provost & Chapter. **8** Theology; Essex church history. **9** Knightbridge colln of 16th & 17th cent theological works (c.500 vols). **11** Yes. **12** Cathedral Library: Tues 18.30-20.30, other times by arrangement; Chapter House Library (modern works): daily 9.30-17.00. **13** (a) 4,000; (c) c.1,500 pamphlets; c.500 archives; c.750 photographs & plans. **14** £250. **15** (c) 1.

MEDICAL RECORDING SERVICE FOUNDATION LIBRARY, Kitts Croft, Writtle, Chelmsford, CM1 3EH (Tel 0245-421475) Libn: Mrs Barbara Trevor; Dep Libn: Mrs Gwen Alchin. **6** Royal College of General Practitioners. **8** Medical; social services; community health; all material on tape-slide or slide. **11** No. **12** Postal only. **13** (c) 800 medical educational tape-slide programmes; non-book material library. **15** (a) 10

MID-ESSEX TECHNICAL COLLEGE AND SCHOOL OF ART LIBRARY, (will merge with Brentwood College of Education, Sept 1976, to form the Chelmer Institute of Higher Education), Victoria Rd South, Chelmsford, CM1 1LL (Tel 0245-54491) Coll Libn: Miss Margaret Homer LLB, ALA; Dep: Mrs J.A.Symes BA, ALA. **6** Essex CC. **7** Law Lib, Victoria Rd South, Chelmsford, CM1 1LL (0245-54491), Libn: Ms Margaret Homer. **8** Law; business; economics; maths; electrical engineering & electronics; mechanical engineering; construction technology; building; town planning; home economics; art; music. **9** English, American & Commonwealth law (15,000 vols). **10** LASER. **11** Yes, subject to library rules. **12** Mon-Fri 9.00-21.30. **13** (a) 45,000; (b) 500; (c) microfilms; audio tapes; films; filmstrips. **14** £45,000. **15** (a) 8 (b) 3 (c) 4.

CHELTENHAM, Gloucester

CHELTENHAM LADIES' COLLEGE LIBRARY, St George's Rd, Cheltenham, GL50 3EP (Tel 0242-20691) Libn: Mrs M.F.Harries; Asst Libns: Mrs M.Worn; Mrs A.Eldridge **6** Cheltenham Ladies' College Council. **8** General academic; fiction. **9** Books presented by John Ruskin; letters of Dickens, Swinburne, Byron, & others. **11** Yes, on written application to Libn. **12** Term: Mon-Fri 9.15-16.45; vac: 10.00-16.00. **13** (a) c.21,000; (b) 20. **14** c.£1,500. **15** (a) 2

GLOUCESTERSHIRE COLLEGE OF ART AND DESIGN LIBRARY, Pittville, Cheltenham, GL52 3JG (Tel 0242-32501/8) Tutor-Libn: Miss P.Y.Lewis BA, ALA. Asst Libn: Mr E.Shaw ALA. **6** Gloucestershire CC. **7** Brunswick Rd, Gloucester. **8** Fine art; fashion; graphic design; architecture; landscape; town planning. **10** BLL; SWRLB; GTIS; ARLIS. **11** Yes, for ref only. **12** Term: (Cheltenham) Mon-Thurs 9.00-21.00, Fri 9.00-17.00; (Gloucester) Mon-Thurs 9.00-17.30, Fri 9.00-17.00; vac: by appointment. **13** (a) 30,000; (b) 200; (c) 15,000 slides. **15** (a) 7½ (b) 2 (c) 3.

NORTH GLOUCESTERSHIRE COLLEGE OF TECHNOLOGY LIBRARY, The Park, Cheltenham, GL50 2RR (Tel 0242-28021) Tutor-Libn: Mr J.B.Gailey ALA. **6** Gloucestershire CC. **8** Mechanical, production & electrical engineering; building & surveying; business studies & languages; pure & applied science; maths (inc computing); food technology; home economics & nursing; social studies; general. **10** SWRLB; GTIS. **11** Yes, for ref only. **12** Term: Mon-Thurs 9.00-20.00, Fri 9.00-17.00; vac: Mon-Fri 9.00-12.30, 14.00-17.00. **13** (a) 30,000; (b) 250. **15** (a) 4 (c) 1.

CHESHAM, Buckinghamshire

NATIONAL DEFENCE COLLEGE LIBRARY, Latimer, Chesham, HP5 1UD (Tel 02404-2761) Libn: Mr D.Male FLA; Miss C.E.Coulston BA, ALA. **6** MoD. **8** International affairs; strategy; defence economics & management. **11** No. **13** (a) 18,000; (b) 200; (c) 500 microfilms; Rand Papers; reports; research memoranda. **15** (a) 4 (b) 1 (c) 2.

CHESTER, Cheshire

BRITISH NUCLEAR FUELS LIBRARY, Capenhurst Works, Capenhurst, Chester, CH1 6E (Tel 051-339 4101 ext 720; Telex 62002 Nufuel Capenhurst) Libn Inf Officer: Mr G.E.Lowe ALA, AIInfSc; Asst Libn: Mrs C.M.Riley BA, ALA. **8** Chemical, electrical & mechanical engineering; inorganic chemistry, inc mass spectrometry & gas chromatography; maths; computers; physics; especially heat transfer & fluid mechanics; isotope separation & fluorine chemistry; atomic energy. **9** British & foreign technical reports (30,000). **10** BLL; LADSIRLAC; BNBC. **11** Inter-library loans.

CHESTER, Cheshire—*continued*

12 8.30-16.30.   **13** (a) 12,000; (b) 400.   **14** £9,000.
15 (a) 5 (c) 2.
CHESTER CATHEDRAL LIBRARY, Chester, (Tel 051-24756)
Canon Residentiary: Rev K. M. Maltby.
6 Dean & Chapter.   **8** Theology.   **9** Sanders Colln
(mainly works of Chester Bishops pre-1900); Bishop Jacob-
son's Library.   **11** No.   **14** £50.
CHESTER COLLEGE OF FURTHER EDUCATION, JEFFERIES
LONG LIBRARY, Eaton Rd, Chester CH 4 7ER (Tel 051-
26321) Tutor-Libn: Rev L. O. Arridge BA.
8 Business; science; engineering; art; building; general.
11 No.   **12** Mon-Thurs 9.00-19.00, Fri 9.00-17.00.
13 (a) 19,000; (b) 100; (c) 227 filmstrips; 59 audio-tapes;
13 sets slides; 139 records; 3 chp transparencies.
14 £6,500.   **15** (a) 2½ (b) 1.

CHESTERFIELD, Derbyshire

BRITISH CARBONIZATION RESEARCH ASSOCIATION
LIBRARY, Wingerworth, Chesterfield, S42 6JS (Tel 0246-
76821) Inf Officer: Dr D. G. Edwards BSc PhD, AI Inf Sc;
Dep: Mr D. G. Lewis BA, DipLib.
8 Fuel technology; chemistry & applied chemistry.
9 Library of Coke Oven Managers' Association; BSI.
10 SINTO.   **11** Yes, for bona-fide enquirers.   **12** Mon-
Fri 9.00-17.00.   **13** (b) c.100; (c) reports; offprints; patent
specifications.   **14** £1,900.   **15** (a) 2 (b) 2.
CHESTERFIELD COLLEGES OF ART AND TECHNOLOGY
(RESOURCES CENTRE) LIBRARY, Infirmary Rd, Chesterfield, S41 7NG (Tel 0246-70271) Tutor-Libn: Mr R. Slack BA,
ALA; Dep Tutor Libn: Mr M. Wynn BSc, ALA.
8 Art; design; printing; mechanical & electrical engineering;
construction; maths; education; management; humanities;
foundry technology; chemistry; physics; biology.   **9** British
Standard Codes of Practice (complete).   **10** Aslib; NANTIS.
11 Yes, borrowing at discretion of Tutor-Libn: **12** Terms:
8.45-20.30; vac: 8.45-17.15.   **13** (a) 23,220; (b) 400;
(c) records (600); audio-cassettes (200); audio-tapes (35);
video-cassettes (85); slides (6,000); films (20); filmstrips
(25); models (5); ohp transparency sets (50); multi-media kits
(30).   **14** £11,890.   **15** (a) 7 (b) 2 (c) 4.

CHICHESTER, West Sussex

CHICHESTER COLLEGE OF FURTHER EDUCATION
LIBRARY, Westgate Fields, Chichester, PO19 1SB (Tel 0243-
86321 ext 28) Libn: Miss Clare Likeman ALA.
6 West Sussex CC.   **8** General.   **10** SASLIC; Circle of
Sussex College Librarians.   **11** Yes, on application to Libn.
12 Term: Mon-Fri 9.00-19.00 (Fri 17.00); vac: Mon-Fri
9.00-17.00.   **13** (a) 18,000; (b) 180.   **14** £4,000.
15 (a) 2 (c) 1.

CHIGWELL, Essex

CHIGWELL SCHOOL, SWALLOW LIBRARY, High Rd,
Chigwell, IG7 6QF (Tel 01-500 2014).
8 General; English; history; geography; classics; French;
German; religion; science; recreation.   **11** No.   **12**
12 Term: all day.   **13** (a) 4,000; (b) 10.   **14** £500.
15 (b) 1.

CHILTON, Oxfordshire

RUTHERFORD LABORATORY LIBRARY, Chilton, Didcot,
OX11 0QX (Tel 0235-21900; Telex 83159) Libn: Mrs E. Marsh
ALA.
6 Science Research Council.   **8** Elementary particle
physics; cryogenics; superconductivity; computers.
9 World-wide colln of reports on elementary particles
(c.50,000).   **11** Yes.   **12** 24 hours a day.   **13** (a)
25,000; (b) 200; (c) 5,000 microforms.   **14** £20,000.
15 (a) 5 (c) 1.

CHIPPENHAM, Wiltshire

LACKHAM COLLEGE OF AGRICULTURE LIBRARY, Lacock,
Chippenham, SN15 2NY (Tel 0249-50812) Libn: Ms Stella M.
Vain ALA.
6 Wiltshire Library & Museum Service.   **8** Agriculture;

horticulture; home economics.   **10** SWRLB   **11** Yes.
12 Term: Mon 13.00-15.30, 18.15-21.15, Tues 13.00-15.30,
Weds 14.00-17.30, 18.15-21.15, Thurs & Fri 9.30-12.30;
vac: Tues 9.30-12.30, 13.15-17.15.   **13** (a) 8,200; (b) 143.
14 £1,706.   **15** (c) 1.

CHIPPING CAMPDEN, Gloucestershire

CAMPDEN FOOD PRESERVATION RESEARCH ASSOCIATION
LIBRARY AND INFORMATION SERVICE, Chipping Campden,
GL55 6LD (Tel 0386-840319) Libn & Inf Officer: J. J. Gainsley
AIInfSc; Asst to Libn: Mrs E. Keitley.
6 Council of Research Association.   **8** Food preservation,
especially fruit & vegetables.   **9** CFPRA publications.
10 WESLINK.   **11** No.   **12** Mon-Fri 8.30-12.30, 13.15-
17.15.   **13** (a) 2,700; (b) 120; (c) pamphlets on fruit &
vegetable research, worldwide, from research stations &
universities.   **14** £2,000.   **15** (a) 1½.

CHORLEYWOOD, Hertfordshire

FLOUR MILLING AND BAKING RESEARCH ASSOCIATION
LIBRARY, Chorleywood, Rickmansworth, WD3 5SH (Tel
09278-4111) Libn: Mrs C. E. B. French.
8 Science & technology of milling & baking; nutrition; allied
subjects.   **11** Yes, by prior written arrangement.
12 Mon-Fri 9.00-17.00 (Fri 16.30).   **13** (a) c.8,000;
(b) c.300; (c) 2500 slides (2" × 2"); c.4,000 British &
foreign patent specifications.   **14** c. £6,500.

CINDERFORD, Gloucestershire

WEST GLOUCESTERSHIRE COLLEGE OF FURTHER
EDUCATION LIBRARY, College Rd, Cinderford, GL14, 2JY
(Tel 0594-22191) Tutor-Libn: Mrs B. R. Sanigar ALA; Lib
Asst: Mrs E. Wingrave.
8 Engineering (especially motor vehicle engineering);
business & commerce; home economics; computer programming.   **9** BSI (incomplete); British & foreign motor
manuals; 'Autocar' & 'Motor' (from 1965).   **10** GTIS; SWRLB.
11 Yes.   **12** Term: Mon-Thurs 9.00-17.00, 17.30-19.00,
Fri 9.00-17.00; vac: Mon-Fri 9.00-17.00.   **13** (a) 19,500,
(b) 141, (c) art slides; filmstrips; gramophone records.
14 c. £2,700.   **15** (a) 2 (c) 1.

CIRENCESTER, Gloucestershire

ROYAL AGRICULTURAL COLLEGE LIBRARY, Stroud Rd,
Cirencester, GL7 6JS (Tel 0285-2531) Hon Libn; Mr W.
Heatherington BSc; Asst Libn: Mr H. Lewis.
6 Royal Agricultural College Governors.   **8** Agriculture
& estate management.   **11** No, except by prior arrangement.   **12** Term: 10.00-18.30.   **13** (a) 6,000; (b) 200.
14 £2,000.   **15** (a) 2 (b) 1.

CLACTON-ON-SEA, Essex

ST OSYTH'S COLLEGE OF EDUCATION LIBRARY, (will
merge with North East Essex Technical College & School of
Art, Sept 1976), 73 Marine Parade East, Clacton-on-Sea,
CO15 6JQ (Tel 0255-22324) Tutor-Libn: Mr G. Nelson BA,
ALA; Asst Libn: Mrs J. E. Newby ALA.
6 Essex Education Committee.   **8** Education; philosophy;
psychology; religion; sociology; maths; science; home
economics; dress & design; art; music; physical education;
literature; history; geography; children's literature.
10 Essex County Library.   **11** No.   **12** Term: Mon-Fri
9.00-21.00, Sat 9.30-12.00; vac: Mon-Fri 9.00-17.00.
13 (a) 55,000; (b) 220; (c) wallcharts; slides; filmstrips; tape
recordings.   **14** £8,500.   **15** (a) 5¼ (b) 1 (c) 2.

CLECKHEATON, West Yorkshire

BBA GROUP LTD LIBRARY AND INFORMATION SERVICE,
PO Box 20, Whitechapel Rd, Cleckheaton, BD19 6HP (Tel
09762-4444; Telex 51106) Group Libn: Mrs H. Davis ALA.
8 Automotive industry; economics; engineering; plastics;
textiles; materials handling; glass fibres.   **10** BRASTACS;

CODE: **1** Name of Library. **2** Address. **3** Telephone & Telex. **4** Officer in charge. **5** Deputy. **6** Governing body. **7** Branches. **8** Main Subjects. **9** Special Collections. **10** Co-operative Schemes. **11** Open to public? **12** Hours. **13** Stock: (a) books (b) periodicals (c) other. **14** Finance. **15** Staff: (a) non-manual (b) graduate (c) chartered librarians.

CLECKHEATON, West Yorkshire—*continued*

HALDIS; HADIS. **11** No. **12** 8.30-16.30. **13** (a) 7,000; (b) 450. **15** (a) 3 (c) 1.

COLCHESTER, Essex

ESSEX ARCHAEOLOGICAL SOCIETY LIBRARY, Hollytrees Museum, High St, Colchester, Hon Libn: Mr Peter B. Boyden BA.
8 Essex history, archaeology, antiquities & topography; British history & antiquities; British & European archaeology.
10 Inter-library loans. **11** Yes, with Hon Libn or representative in attendance. **12** Summer: Mon-Sat 10.00-13.00, 14.00-17.00; Winter: Mon-Fri 10.00-13.00, 14.00-16.00.
13 (a) c.10,000; (b) c.60; (c) miscellaneous documents; watercolours & prints of Essex buildings & scenes; photographs of Essex churches, etc; rubbings of most Essex brasses (& brasses in other counties), transcripts of many Essex parish registers. **14** £300. **15** (b) 1.

NORTH EAST ESSEX TECHNICAL COLLEGE AND SCHOOL OF ART LIBRARY (will merge with St Osyth's College of Education Sept 1976), Sheepen Rd, Colchester, CO3 3LL (Tel 0206-70271) Tutor-Libn: Mrs B.I. Culpan ALA; Senior Asst Libn: Mrs J.L. Gifford ALA.
6 Essex CC. **7** Endsleigh annexe, Lexden, Colchester, (0206-76382); Music Branch & Art Branch, Sheepen Rd, Colchester. **8** General; science; engineering; arts; humanities. **9** Music Branch (over 11,000 items of performance & recorded music); Art Branch (mainly art history).
10 LASER (via Essex County Library), inter-library loans.
11 Yes, individual enquirers, for ref only. **12** Term: 9.00-20.45; vac: 9.00-13.00, 14.00-17.00. **13** (a) 43,000; (b) c.250; (c) c.1,000 records; c.500 audio-visual sets.
14 c.£11,000. **15** (a) 10 (b) 1 (c) 3.

UNIVERSITY OF ESSEX LIBRARY, PO Box 24, Wivenhoe Park, Colchester, CO4 3UA (Tel 0206-44144; Telex 98440 (UNILIB COLCHSTR)) Libn: Mr P. Long MA.
8 General; art; linguistics; literature; government; history; philosophy; sociology; economics; computing science; maths; biology, chemistry & electrical engineering. **9** S.L. Bensusan colln; John Hassall colln; Rowhedge Ironworks archives; Bassingbourn Parish Library; Gaudier-Brzeska papers. **10** BLL; BMS (1760-64); Essex County Library Union List of Serials. **11** Yes, for ref, on application.
12 Term: Mon-Fri 9.00-22.00, Sat 9.00-18.00, Sun 14.00-19.00; vac: Mon-Fri 9.00-17.30. **13** (a) 230,000; (b) 2,700; (c) microtexts. **14** £132,000. **15** (a) 42 (b) 12 (c) 9.

COLERAINE, Co Londonderry

NEW UNIVERSITY OF ULSTER LIBRARY, Coleraine, BT52 1SA (Tel 0265-4141 ext, 245) Univ Libn: Mr F.J.E. Hurst MA, ALA; DepLibn: Mr B.J.C. Wintour MA, ALA.
6 Council of New University of Ulster. **7** Magee University College, Northland Rd, Londonderry, BT48 7JL (0504-65621) Sub-Libn: G. White MA, FLA. **8** Humanities (inc linguistics, Irish, Russian, French, German, Spanish); social sciences (inc nursing); biological & environmental studies; physical sciences; education. **9** Headlam-Morley (world war I); Paul Ricard (world-war II); Henry Morris (Irish studies); Stelfox (natural history); Galbraith (mediaeval history); Denis Johnston (mss); Henry Davis Gift (incunabula & rare books); Yakut language. **10** BLL; BL bibliographical services. **11** Yes, for ref only; subject to Libn's approval for long-term use. **12** Term: Mon-Fri 9.00-

22.00, Sat 9.00-13.00; vac: Mon-Fri 9.30-17.30. **13** (a) c.150,000; (b) c.2,600; (c) microfilm; microfiche; microcard. **14** £90,000. **15** (a) 30 (b) 16 (c) 9.

COLWYN BAY, Clwyd

LLANDRILLO TECHNICAL COLLEGE LIBRARY, Llandudno Rd, Colwyn Bay, LL28 4HX (Tel 0492-44216) College Libn: Mrs G. Eyton-Jones.
6 Clwyd & Gwynedd CC. **8** General; English; languages; technical subjects; sciences; catering; hairdressing; economics; office arts. **9** Hotel catering; hairdressing.
10 Inter-library loans. **11** Yes if attending evening classes or for genuine inquiries. **12** Mon-Fri 8.45-17.00 (19.30 Tues & Thurs). **13** (a) 12,000; (b) 150.
14 £2,500. **15** (a) 2.

CORBY, Northamptonshire

COUNTY TECHNICAL LIBRARY, George St Corby, NN17 1QF (Tel 05366-3695) Libn: Mr M.G.S. White BA, ALA; DepLibn: Mr N. Butlin.
6 Northamptonshire CC. **8** Science; technology; commerce.
9 Ferrous metallurgy. **10** BLL; CADIG. **11** Yes.
12 Mon-Fri 9.00-20.00. **13** (a) 30,289; (b) 493.
14 £14,400. **15** (a) 6 (b) 1 (c) 2.

COVENTRY, West Midlands

COVENTRY COLLEGE OF EDUCATION LIBRARY, Canley, Coventry, CV4 8EE (Tel 0203-462531) Libn: Ms E.K. Hodson BA, FLA; Dep: Ms P.M. Rowland BA, ALA.
6 Coventry LEA. **8** Arts; sciences. **9** Education; children's books (information, school texts, fiction).
10 BLL, WMRLB, CADIG. **11** Yes, for ref only; teachers & others in education may borrow. **12** Term: Mon-Fri 9.30-21.30 (Fri 17.00), Sat & Sun: 14.00-17.00 (& Sun 18.00-21.30); vac: Mon-Fri 9.00-17.00. **13** (a) 95,000; (b) 780 serials (inc 280 annuals); (c) c.50 microtexts (i.e. actual titles, multiple reels of newspapers). **14** £19,330 (exc audio-visual). **15** (a) 10; (b) 5; (c) 6.

COVENTRY TECHNICAL COLLEGE LIBRARY, The Butts, Coventry, CV1 3GD (Tel 0203-57221) Tutor-Libn: Ms Hilary Temple BA, DipLib, ALA; Dep: Ms Kaye S. Prentice.
6 Coventry Education Authority. **8** Mechanical & electrical engineering; construction; metallurgy; textiles; general.
10 CADIG. **11** Yes, for ref only. **12** Term: 8.30-20.30; vac. 8.30-17.00. **13** (a) 45,000; (b) 400; (c) archives, slides; tape/slides; film loops; teaching machine programmes.
14 £7,000. **15** (a) 7 (b) 1 (c) 2.

LANCHESTER POLYTECHNIC LIBRARY, Priory St, Coventry, CV1 5FB (Tel 0203-24166) Polytechnic Libn: Mr E.G. Baxter MA, FLA; DepLibn: Mr C.B. West BA, ALA.
6 Coventry & Warwickshire Joint Education Committee.
7 Art & Design Lib, Gosford St, Coventry (0203-24166), DepLibn: Mr J.M. Avann BA, FLA; Rugby Site Lib, Eastlands, Rugby (0788-71481), DepLibn: Mrs J.A. Loveridge ALA.
8 Mechanical, production, electrical, electronic & civil engineering; business; law; fine art; industrial design; transportation; building; control systems; computers; physics; biology; chemistry; mathematics; statistics; materials technology; geography; accountancy; social work; regional & urban planning; mechanics; politics; history; social science; modern language; graphic design. **9** F.W. Lanchester Colln; automobiles & aeronautics; EDC; Open University Colln. **10** BLL; CADIG; WMRLB. **11** Yes, for ref;

COVENTRY, West Midlands—*continued*

lending in certain circumstances. **12** Term: Mon-Fri
9.00-21.00, Sat 9.00-12.00; vac: Mon-Fri 9.00-17.15.
13 (a) 145,000; (b) 2,600; (c) 64,000 illustrations; 90 film
loops; 35 discs; 250 film strips; 130 audio tapes; 8 films;
20 tape-slide sets; 300 slides; 3,600 microfiche; 263 microfilms. **14** c. £80,000. **15** (a) 33 (b) 7 (c) 16.

UNIVERSITY OF WARWICK LIBRARY, Coventry, CV4 7AL
(Tel 0203-24011; Telex 31406) Libn: Mr P.E. Tucker BLitt,
MA, ALA; Dep: Mr D. Kelly BA, MA, ALA.
8 Arts; sciences; social studies. **9** Trade & finance
statistics; trade union & other labour history records.
10 WMRLB; CADIG. **11** Yes, on application.
12 Term: Sun-Fri 9.00-21.30, Sat 9.00-18.00. **13** (a)
30,000; (b) 5,500; (c) labour history archives; 4,000 rolls
microfilm; 2,000 sheets microfiche; 50,000 microcards.
14 £130,000. **15** (a) 72 (b) 21 (c) 16.

CRANFIELD, Bedfordshire

BRITISH HYDROMECHANICS RESEARCH ASSOCIATION,
Fluid Engineering Library, Cranfield, Bedford, MK43 0AJ
(Tel 0234-750422; Telex 825059) Libn: Mrs R. Tomlinson
ALA; Dep: Miss A. Feneley.
8 Fluid engineering. **11** No. **13** (a) c. 10,000; (b) 250;
(c) reports; conference papers; British patents; standards;
microfiche. **15** (c) 1.

CRANFIELD INSTITUTE OF TECHNOLOGY LIBRARY,
Cranfield, Bedford, MK43 0AL (Tel 0234-750111; Telex
825072) Institute Libn: Mr Cyril W. Cleverdon FLA; Mr E.J.
MacAdam ALA.
8 Engineering & management. **11** Yes. **12** Mon-Fri
9.00-22.00. **13** (a) 28,000; (b) 750; (c) 50,000 research
reports. **15** (a) 13 (b) 3 (c) 5.

CRANWELL, Lincolnshire

ROYAL AIR FORCE COLLEGE LIBRARY, Cranwell, Sleaford,
NG34 8HB (Tel 04006-201 ext Whittle 329) Coll Libn &
Archivist: Mrs J.M. King ALA; DepLibn & Technical Libn:
Mr D.E. Clarke ALA.
6 MoD (AIR). **8** Aeronautics; military science & history;
air power; RAF history; defence studies; current affairs;
engineering (mechanical, electrical, electronic, materials,
aeronautical); maths; computer science; management.
9 Whittle documents (microfilm); colln of books by & about
T.E. Lawrence; technical reports colln (c. 17,000). **11** No.
12 Mon-Fri 8.15-17.00. **13** (a) 100,000; (b) 400;
(c) c. 25,000 reports; microfilm; coll archives. **15** (a) 11
(c) 4.

CRAWLEY, West Sussex

CRAWLEY COLLEGE OF TECHNOLOGY LIBRARY, College
Rd, Crawley, RH10 1NR (Tel 0293-25686 ext 33) Libn: Mrs
H.N. Elsmere ALA; DepLibn: Mrs M. Peters.
6 West Sussex CC. **8** General. **10** Inter-library loans;
SASLIC; LASER. **11** Yes, for ref only. **12** 9.00-19.30
(closed Aug). **13** (a) 15,000; (b) 320. **14** £4,000.
15 (a) 2½ (c) 1.

DARLASTON, West Midlands

RUBERY OWEN GROUP INFORMATION SERVICE LIBRARY,
PO Box 10, Darlaston, WS10 8JD (Tel 021-526 3131 ext 661;
Telex 338236/7) Group Libn: Miss J. Holt; Enquiry Officer:
Miss L. James.
8 Automobile engineering; management; computers.
9 Trade literature; German 'DIN' specifications; MoD specifications; inter-Europe automotive Regulations; BSI.
10 MISLIC; WESLINK; CADIG. **11** No. **12** Mon-Fri
8.45-17.00 (Mon 16.30). **13** (a) 28,000; (b) 200.
14 £8,000. **15** (a) 4.

DARLINGTON, Co Durham

DARLINGTON COLLEGE OF TECHNOLOGY LIBRARY,
Cleveland Ave, Darlington, DL3 7BB (Tel 0325-67651) Tutor-
Libn: Mr B.S. Bowron BA, FILALA; Senior Lib Asst: Mrs
B.L. Buckley.
6 Durham CC. **8** Maths; physics; chemistry; engineering;
building; catering; hairdressing; accountancy; industrial
management; journalism; law; history; geography; education.
9 Multilingual dictionaries both general and specialised of
major western european languages. **10** LIST. **11** Yes,
borrowing restricted to one book per person. **12** Term:
Mon-Fri 8.45-21.15 (Fri 17.00); vac: Mon-Fri 8.45-12.30,
13.45-17.30 (Fri 17.00). **13** (a) 26,000; (b) 193; (c) 20
microtexts; 30 records; 400 film-slides; 20 filmstrips;
6 16 mm films; 18 8 mm film-loops; 25 kits; 30 tape-record-
ing. **14** £8,620. **15** (a) 4½ (b) 1 (c) 1.

DARTFORD, Kent

DARTFORD COLLEGE OF EDUCATION LIBRARY, (will
merge with Thames Polytechnic), Oakfield Lane, Dartford
DA1 2SZ (Tel 0322-21328 ext 25) Libn: Miss E. Johnston
BA, ALA; DepLibn: Mrs C. Govan ALA.
6 ILEA. **8** Education; physical education; art; music;
history; geography; biology. **11** Yes, for ref only.
12 Term: Mon-Fri 8.45-21.00 (Fri 18.45); vac: Mon-Fri
9.00-16.30. **13** (a) 50,000; (b) 293; (c) 2,000 gramophone
records; filmstrips; slide sets; charts; multi-media kits; tapes.
14 £8,439. **15** (a) 5 (b) 1 (c) 3.

NORTH WEST KENT COLLEGE OF TECHNOLOGY
LIBRARY, Miskin Rd, Dartford, DA1 2LU (Tel 0322-25471
ext 31) Libn: Mr R. Savage.
6 Kent CC. **7** Pelham Rd, Gravesend (0474-65233).
8 Technical & academic studies; industrial crafts; automobile
engineering; business; secretarial & catering studies.
9 BSI. **10** BLL. **11** No, except to local industry for
ref. **12** Mon-Fri 9.00-17.30. **13** (a) 22,600; (b) 58;
(c) gramophone records; film strips; video tapes. **14**
14 £4,030. **15** (a) 4.

DARTMOUTH, Devon

BRITANNIA ROYAL NAVAL COLLEGE LIBRARY, Dartmouth, TQ6 0HJ (Tel 08043-2141 ext 328) Libn: Mr M.M.
Chapman MA, ALA.
6 MoD (Navy). **8** General; defence; naval history; international affairs; engineering. **10** Inter-library loans.
11 Yes, on written application. **13** (a) 28,000; (b) 130.
14 £4,000. **15** (a) 2 (b) 1 (c) 1.

DERBY, Derbyshire

BISHOP LONSDALE COLLEGE LIBRARY (will merge with
Derby College of Art & Technology), Western Rd, Mickleover,
Derby, DE3 5GX (Tel 0332-54911) Libn: Mr P.W. Staton
MA, ALA; Dep Libn: Miss Susan Elwen ALA.
8 American studies; area studies; art & design; French;
maths; science (biology); physical education; music; theology;
education; history; English; geography; literature & society.
9 19th cent children's books; books & pamphlets on Derby &
Derbyshire. **10** BNBC; SCOPELC. **11** No, except for
teachers; students from other colleges for ref only.
12 Term: Mon-Fri 8.45-21.00; vac: Mon-Fri 9.00-12.30,
14.00-17.00. **13** (a) 75,300; (b) 350; (c) college archives;
c. 600 gramophone records; filmstrips; slides; cassettes;
videotapes; charts; illustrations; microfilm (some journals &
educational reports). **14** £10,900. **15** (a) 5½ (b) 1
(c) 3.

BRITISH RAIL RESEARCH AND DEVELOPMENT LIBRARY,
Technical Centre, London Rd, Derby, DE2 8UP (Tel 0332-
49203; Telex 37367) Libn: Miss I.E. Harvey ALA; Dep Libn:
Mrs G. Davis ALA.
8 Railway technology research & development. **10** ASLIB;
EMRLB; VIC (International Union of Railways). **11** Yes,
by appointment. **12** 9.00-13.00, 14.00-17.00. **13** (a)
7,000; (b) 450; (c) 150 microtexts. **14** £12,000. **15** (a) 5
(c) 2.

CODE: 1 Name of Library. 2 Address. 3 Telephone & Telex. 4 Officer in charge. 5 Deputy. 6 Governing body. 7 Branches. 8 Main Subjects. 9 Special Collections. 10 Co-operative Schemes. 11 Open to public? 12 Hours. 13 Stock: (a) books (b) periodicals (c) other. 14 Finance. 15 Staff: (a) non-manual (b) graduate (c) chartered librarians.

DERBY, Derbyshire—*continued*

DERBY COLLEGE OF ART AND TECHNOLOGY LIBRARY (will merge with Bishop Lonsdale College), Kedleston Rd, Derby, DE3 1GB (Tel 0332-47181) Tutor-Libn: Mr R. A. H. O'Neal BA, ALA; Dep Libn: Mr K. A. Harja BSc, ALA. 7 Art Lib, Kedleston Rd, Libn: Mrs T. Sheppard ALA. 8 General. 9 Slides (especially history of art). 10 BLL, EMRLS; NANTIS. 11 Yes, borrowing at Libn's discretion. Term: Mon-Fri 9.00-20.30 (Fri 17.30); Vac: Mon-Fri 09.00-17.30. 13 (a) 40,000; (b) 600; (c) 600 gramophone records. 14 £20,000. 15 (a) 9½ (b) 2 (c) 3. 15 (a) 9½ (b) 2 (c) 3.

ROLLS-ROYCE (1971) LTD, DERBY ENGINE DIVISION LIBRARY, P. O. Box 31, Moor Lane, Derby, DE2 8BJ (Tel 0332-42424 ext 9; Telex 37645) Head of Library & Inf Services: Mr A. C. Firth BA, FLA; Dep Libn: Mr J. B. Martin BA, ALA. 8 Gas turbines; aeronautical engineering; fluid dynamics; advanced materials; computers; management. 10 NANTIS. 11 No. 13 (a) 20,000; (b) 650; (c) 250,000 reports (100,000 in microform). 15 (a) 14 (b) 5 (c) 2.

DOLLAR, Clackmannanshire

DOLLAR ACADEMY LIBRARY, Dollar, FK14 7DU (Tel 02594-2511) Teacher-Libn: Mr S. C. Cannon MA. 6 Governors of Dollar Academy Trust. 8 General. 11 Yes. 12 Mon & Fri 15.30-16.00, Wed 16.00-16.30, Tues & Thurs 18.45-20.15. 13 (a) 14,500; (b) 6. 14 £650. 15 (b) 1.

DONCASTER, South Yorkshire

DONCASTER COLLEGE OF EDUCATION LIBRARY (will merge with Scawsby College of Education & Doncaster Colleges of Technology & of Art, Sept 1976, to form Doncaster Institute of Higher Education), High Melton, Doncaster, DN5 7SD (Tel 070988-2427) Tutor-Libn: Miss J. Moulden BA, FLA; Dep Libn: Mr P. F. Hopwood BA, ALA. 6 Doncaster MBC. 8 General; education. 11 Yes: for ref only. 12 Term: Mon-Fri 9.00-20.30 (Fri 18.00); vac: 9.00-17.00. 13 (a) 80,000; (b) 300 (some microfiche); (c) teaching kits; visual aids; fiche/film reader. 14 £30,000.

DONCASTER COLLEGE OF TECHNOLOGY, HUGH RICHMOND LIBRARY (will merge with Doncaster Colleges of Art & of Education, & Scawsby College of Education, Sept 1976, to form Doncaster Institute of Higher Education), Waterdale, Doncaster, DN1 3EX (Tel 070988-66881) Tutor-Libn: Miss F. M. Armstrong ALA, Cert Ed; Asst Tutor-Libn: Miss M. M. Devine ALA. 6 Doncaster MBC. 7 Annexe, Ellers Rd, Bessacarr, Doncaster, Libn: Mrs A. Hill. 8 Building; business; electrical, mechanical & mining engineering; management; science; maths; social service; hairdressing; catering. 10 Inter-library loans. 11 Yes, for ref only. 12 Term: Mon-Fri 8.45-20.00 (Fri 17.30); vac: Mon-Fri 9.00-12.45, 13.45-17.00 (Fri 16.45). Branch varies. 13 (a) 34,000; (b) 420; (c) c.150 microfilm; c.50 tape slides; c.50 charts. 14 £12,000. 15 (a) 9 (c) 3.

DORCHESTER, Dorset

DORSET COUNTY MUSEUM LIBRARY, Dorchester, DT1 1XA (Tel 0305-2735) Curator & Secretary: R. N. R. Peers MA, FSA, FMA. 6 Dorset Natural History & Archaeological Society. 8 Dorset (all aspects). 9 Thomas Hardy; William Barnes. 11 Yes, by prior arrangement. 12 10.00-17.00. 13 20,000; (b) c.100; (c) tape recordings; water-colours; engravings; maps; mss. 14 £670. 15 (b) ½.

DOUGLAS, Isle of Man

MANX MUSEUM LIBRARY, Douglas, Isle of Man. Libn & Archivist: Miss A. M. Harrison BA, Dip Archive Admin. 6 Trustees of Manx Museum. 11 Yes, for ref only. 12 Mon-Fri 10.00-17.00. 13 c.15,000; (b) c.40; (c) mss (from 1400). 15 (a) 4 (b) 2.

DUDLEY, West Midlands

DUDLEY COLLEGE OF EDUCATION LIBRARY, Castle View, Dudley, DY1 3HR (Tel 0384-59741 ext 49) Coll Libn: Mr H. S. Peake BA, ALA, Cert Ed; Miss A. Mathie ALA. 6 Dudley MBC. 8 Art & design; English language & literature; commerce & economics; geography; maths; music; political & economic history; physical education; religious studies; science; sociology; education. 9 Education & curriculum; local studies on West Midlands; school textbooks & information books. 10 BLL; MISLIC; WESLINK; SOSCOL. 11 Yes, borrowing at discretion of Libn. 12 Term: Mon-Fri 9.00-21.00 (Fri 17.00); vac: Mon-Fri 8.45-17.15 (Mon & Fri 17.00). 13 (a) 65,000; (b) 280; (c) records & tapes; filmstrips & slides; charts; study kits; transparencies. 14 £10,900. 15 (a) 6 (b) 1 (c) 3.

DUDLEY TECHNICAL COLLEGE LIBRARY, The Broadway, Dudley, DY1 4AS (Tel 0384-53585) Tutor-Libn: Miss Margaret Silvers BA, FLA; Asst Libn: Miss Diane O. Sharples ALA. 6 Dudley MBC. 8 Engineering & technical. 10 MISLIC; WESLINK. 11 Yes, for ref only on application to Libn. 12 Term: Mon-Fri 9.00-21.00 (Fri 17.30); vac: 9.00-17.00. 13 (a) 31,000; (b) 250. 14 £7,250. 15 (a) 4½ (b) 1 (c) 2.

DUMFRIES, Dumfriesshire

DUMFRIES TECHNICAL COLLEGE LEARNING RESOURCES CENTRE LIBRARY, Heathhall, Dumfries, DG1 1EB (Tel 0387-61261). Tutor-Libn: Mr Graeme Cockburn. 6 Dumfries CC. 8 Building; commerce & business; engineering; sciences; general. 9 Business administration; marketing; automobile engineering; catering; building construction. 10 BLL. 11 Yes. 12 9.00-17.00. 13 (a) 10,000; (b) 120; (c) c.300 audio-visual materials, cassettes, slides, filmstrips, VCR. 14 £7,000. 15 (a) 2 (c) 1

DUNDEE, Angus

DUNDEE COLLEGE OF EDUCATION, Gardyne Rd, Dundee, DD5 1NY (Tel 0382-453433) Principal Libn: Mr B. H. Gill MA, ALA; Dep Libn: Miss R. P. Lawrence ALA. 6 Board of Governors, Dundee College of Education. 8 Education; psychology, sociology. 11 Yes, for ref only. 12 Term: Mon-Fri 9.00-21.00 (Fri 17.00), Sat 9.00-12.00; vac: Mon-Fri 9.00-17.00, Sat 9.00-12.00. 13 (a) 60,000; (b) 430; (c) 1,800 gramophone records; 400 charts; 1,000 film strips; illustrations; 600 educational packages; slides. 14 £16,000. 15 (a) 14 (b) 5 (c) 7.

DUNDEE COLLEGE OF TECHNOLOGY LIBRARY, Bell St, Dundee, DD1 1HG (Tel 0382-27225 ext 28, 67, 69; Telex 76453) Principal Libn: Mr Neil Craven FLA; Senior Libn: Mr Philip Bradley MA, FLA. 8 Accountancy & finance; building & surveying; business; civil, electrical & electronic engineering; maths & computer studies; mechanical & industrial engineering; molecular & life sciences; physics; textile science. 11 Yes. 12 Term: Mon-Fri 8.45-21.00; vac: Mon-Fri 8.45-17.00. 13 (a) 55,000; (b) 840; (c) microtexts; tape-slides; gramophone records; video-tape recordings. 14 £37,935. 15 (a) 12½ (b) 3 (c) 4.

DUNDEE, Angus—*continued*

SCOTTISH HORTICULTURAL RESEARCH INSTITUTE
LIBRARY, Invergowrie, Dundee, Angus, DD2 5DA (Tel 08267-441).
8 Horticulture. **11** No. **12** Mon-Fri 8.30-17.00 (Fri 16.30). **13** (a) 8,000; (b) 300; (c) microfilm; slides; photographs. **14** £6,000. **15** (a) 2 (b) 1 (c) 1.

UNIVERSITY OF DUNDEE LIBRARY, Dundee, DD1 4HN
(Tel 0382-23181; Telex 76293) University Libn: Mr J.R.
Barker MA, FLA; Dep Libn: Mr M.Shafe BSc, ALA.
7 Law Lib, Bonar House, Bell St, Dundee (0382-24423), Libn:
Mrs H.Charlton LLB; Ninewells Medical Lib, Dundee
(0382-6011), Libn: Mr J.B.Cooper MA, ALA. **8** Arts;
social sciences; medicine; dentistry; law; science; applied
science; engineering; environmental studies. **9** Nicoll
Colln (Fine Art); Leng Colln (Scottish Philosophy); William
Lyon Mackenzie Colln (Canadiana); Brechin Diocesan
Library; Thoms Colln (Mineralogy). **10** BLL. **11** Yes,
on application, for ref only. **12** Term: Mon-Fri 9.00-
22.00, Sat 9.00-12.00; vac: Mon-Fri 9.00-17.00, Sat 9.00-
12.00. **13** (a) 287,000; (b) 4,564; (c) archives; gramophone
records; microtexts; audio-visual material. **14** £120,000.
15 (a) 60 (b) 20 (c) 14.

DURHAM, Co Durham

ARCHDEACON SHARP LIBRARY, The College, Durham, DH1
3EH (Tel 0385-62489) Libn to Lord Crewe Trustees: Rev
Canon Ronald L.Coppin BA; Asst Libn: Mr Roger C.Norris
MA, DipLib.
6 Lord Crewe Trustees. **8** Theology. **11** Yes, borrowing for clergy & christian workers in Newcastle-upon-Tyne
& Durham, & for students of theology. **12** Tues-Fri 9.30-
13.00, 14.15-17.00. **13** (a) c.5,000. **14** c.£250.
15 (a) 1½ (b) 1 (c) 1.

DEAN AND CHAPTER LIBRARY, The College, Durham, DH1
3EH (Tel 0385-62489) Chapter Libn: Rev Canon Ronald L.
Coppin BA; Asst Libn: Mr Roger C Norris MA, DipLib.
6 Dean & Chapter. **8** Theology; bibliography; architecture;
archaeology; history; palaeography; local history; music.
9 Saxon & mediaeval mss from the monastic house; local
history mss collns: Raine, Surtees, Allan, Randall, Longstaffe,
Sharp, Hunter, Henson; mss music from cathedral (organ &
choir part books) (early 17th cent); printed secular music
(17th & 18th cents). **11** Yes, bona-fide researchers &
scholars are encouraged to use the library. **12** Tues-Fri
9.30-13.00, 14.15-17.00. **13** (a) c.45,000; (b) c.100;
(c) mss; photographic material; photostats; microfilms;
transparencies. **15** (a) 2 (b) 1 (c) 1.

Durham University

UNIVERSITY LIBRARY, Palace Green, Durham, DH1 3RN
(Tel 0385-61262; Telex 537351) Univ Libn: Miss A.M.
McAulay BA, FLA; Dep Libn: Mr B.Cheesman MA, ALA.
6 Curators of the Library. **7** Science Section, Science
site, South Rd, Durham (0382-64971), Keeper of Science
Books: Mr W.B.Woodward BSc; Oriental Section, Elvet
Hill, Durham (0865-64371), Keeper of Oriental Books:
Miss L.E.Forbes BA, ALA. **8** All academic subjects
except medicine & architecture. **9** Oriental collns, inc
Sudan Archive, collns of Professor Gunn (Egyptological) &
of Mr H.J.Cant & Professor Yetts (Far Eastern); collns
of older printed books (50,000 vols) & mss, inc those of
Bishop Cosin, Dr Routh & Dr Winterbottom; local material.
10 BLL; English printed BMS; NRLB. **11** Yes, for ref,
on written application.
12 Term: Mon-Fri 8.45-22.00, Sat 9.00-12.30; vac: Mon-
Fri 9.00-17.00, Sat 9.00-12.30. Branches vary. **13** (a)
460,000; (b) 3,350; (c) microforms; mss; official publications. **14** £130,455. **15** (a) 60 (b) 30 (c) 20.

INSTITUTE OF EDUCATION LIBRARY, Old Shire Hall,
Old Elvet, Durham, DH1 3HP (Tel 0385-64466) Libn:
Mr Frank Rutherford MA, FLA.
8 Education; psychology. **10** BLL; NRLB; LISE.
11 Yes, for ref only, by arrangement with Libn.
12 Term: Mon-Fri 9.30-18.30 (Fri 17.00); Sat 9.30-
12.30; Michaelmas term: Tues & Thurs 9.30-21.00.

13 (a) 17,000 (b) 200. **14** £2,500. **15** (a) 2 (b) 1 (c)
1.

ST JOHN'S COLLEGE LIBRARY, Durham, DH1 3EE (Tel
0385-66793) Libn: Rev B.N.Kaye BA, BD.
8 Theology. **11** No. **12** Term: 24 hours a day.
13 (a) 9,500; (b) 27. **14** £900.

USHAW COLLEGE, LIBRARY, Durham. Libn: Rev B.Payne;
Dep: Rev Dr Michael Sharratt PhD.
8 Theology; history. **9** Leadbitter law colln. **11** No.
13 (a) c.45,000.

EASTBOURNE, East Sussex

CHELSEA COLLEGE OF PHYSICAL EDUCATION LIBRARY,
Denton Rd, Eastbourne, BN20 7SR (Tel 0323-22571) Libn:
Miss R.Arkley BA, ALA; Asst Libn: Mrs Sheila Handley
ALA.
6 East Sussex Education Authority. **8** Education; physical
education; dance; drama; arts; physiology; anatomy; kinesiology;
biology; social studies. **11** No. **12** Term: daily 8.30-
22.30; vac: Mon-Fri 9.00-17.00. **13** (a) 30,000; (b) 217;
(c) 160 theses; 80 microfilms (periodicals). **14** £9,600.

EASTBOURNE COLLEGE OF EDUCATION LIBRARY, Darley
Rd, Eastbourne, BN20 7UN (Tel 0323-27633) Libn: Mrs A.D.
Conyers MA, ALA; Dep: Miss R.E.Whiting MA, ALA.
6 East Sussex CC. **8** Education; art; English; French;
geography; history; maths; music; religion; science; children's
books. **11** Yes, for ref only, on application. **12** Term:
Mon-Fri 8.30-21.30, Sat 9.00-17.00; vac: Mon-Fri 9.00-
17.00. **13** (a) 60,000; (b) 250. **15** (a) 4 (b) 2 (c) 3.

EASTHAM, Merseyside

CARLETT PARK COLLEGE OF TECHNOLOGY LIBRARY,
Eastham, Wirral, L62 OAY (Tel 051-327 4331) Tutor-Libn:
Mr J.L.Powell FLA; Asst Tutor-Libn: Mr E.J.Evans ALA.
6 Borough of Wirral Education Committee. **8** Languages;
science; engineering; geography; history; biography; arts;
social sciences; domestic science. **10** LADSIRLAC.
11 No. **12** Term: Mon-Thurs 9.00-19.30, Fri 9.00-17.00.
13 (a) 16,000 (b) 164 (c) other materials currently housed
separately. **14** c.£6000. **15** (a) 3½ (c) 2.

EASTLEIGH, Hampshire

WILLIAM R.WARNER AND CO. LTD LIBRARY, Chestnut
Ave, Eastleigh, SO5 3ZQ (Tel 042126-3131; Telex 47226
(Quikpill Eastlgh)) Libn: Mrs E.Sparks.
8 Pharmaceutical; management; marketing. **9** Medical
journals. **10** HATRICS. **11** No. **12** Mon-Fri 8.30-
17.00 (Fri 15.45). **13** (a) 2,500; (b) 200; (c) microfilm.
15 (a) 2.

EAST MALLING, Kent

EAST MALLING RESEARCH STATION AND COMMON-
WEALTH BUREAU OF HORTICULTURE AND PLANTATION
CROPS, JOINT LIBRARY, East Malling, Maidstone, ME19
6BJ (Tel 0732-843833) Libn: Miss C.A.H.Jolly BSc, DipLib,
ALA.
6 Kent Incorporated Society for Promoting Experiments in
Horticulture, & the Commonwealth Agricultural Bureaux.
8 Horticulture (especially deciduous fruits). **10** BLL.
11 Yes, for ref only, by appointment. **12** Mon-Fri 8.30-
16.30 (Fri 16.00). **13** (a) 16,000; (b) 1,200; (c) 80,000
pamphlets. **15** (a) 3½ (b) 1 (c) 1.

EDINBURGH

ADVOCATES' LIBRARY, Parliament House, Edinburgh,
EH1 1RF (Tel 031-226 5071) Libn: Mr H.Brashaw.
6 Faculty of Advocates. **8** Law. **9** Scots law; 16th-18th
cent Roman, civil & canon law. **11** No, exc for ref at NLS.

ANIMAL BREEDING LIBRARY (Joint Library of Commonwealth Bureau of Animal Breeding & Genetics, & ARC
Animal Breeding Research Organisation), King's Buildings,
West Mains Rd, Edinburgh, EH9 3JX (Tel 031-667 6901 ext
39) Libn: Mrs A.H.Barfield MA
6 Commonwealth Agricultural Bureaux. **8** Animal

CODE: 1 Name of Library. **2** Address. **3** Telephone & Telex. **4** Officer in charge. **5** Deputy. **6** Governing body. **7** Branches. **8** Main Subjects. **9** Special Collections. **10** Co-operative Schemes. **11** Open to public? **12** Hours. **13** Stock: (a) books (b) periodicals (c) other. **14** Finance. **15** Staff: (a) non-manual (b) graduate (c) chartered librarians.

EDINBURGH—*continued*

breeding; genetics.   **11** Yes, to bona-fide scientists.
12 8.45-17.00.   **13** (a) c.5,000; (b) c.480.   **15** (a) 2 (b) 1.
DUNFERMLINE COLLEGE OF PHYSICAL EDUCATION LIBRARY, Cramond Rd North, Edinburgh, EH4 6JD (Tel 031-336 6001).
8 Psychology; education; philosophy; social sciences; medicine & health education; recreation & leisure; physical education inc movement, dance & drama.   **9** Physical education.
11 No.   **12** Experimental basis: Mon-Fri 9.00-20.30 (Fri 16.30), Sat & Sun 14.00-16.00.   **13** (a) 17,000; (b) 200; (c) 5 films; 175 tapes; filmstrips; video tapes; 15 film loops; 1,783 records; 225 slides.   **15** (a) 5 (c) 1.

EDINBURGH COLLEGE OF ART LIBRARY, Lauriston Pl, Edinburgh, 3 (Tel 031-229 9311).
6 Governors of Edinburgh College of Art.   **7** Architecture Library, College of Art, Libn: G.Craig MA, ALA; Town Planning Library, Palmerston Pl, Libn: Ian Watson MA.   **8** Fine & applied art; architecture; town planning; conservation.
10 UCABE; inter-library loans.   **11** Yes, for ref only.
12 Term: Mon-Fri 9.15-20.30 (Fri 17.00), vac: 9.15-16.00.
13 (a) 31,000; (b) 244; (c) 65,000 slides; 900 prints; 12 records; 20 cassettes; 22,000 pamphlets.   **14** £15,000.
15 (a) 12½ (b) 2 (c) 1.

EDINBURGH SCHOOL OF AGRICULTURE LIBRARY, West Mains Rd, Edinburgh, EH9 3JG (Tel 031-667 1041) Libn: Miss Jean Playfair MA.
6 East of Scotland College of Agriculture.   **8** Agriculture & related subjects.   **11** Yes, for ref only.   **12** Mon-Fri 8.45-17.00, some eves 18.00-21.00.   **13** (a) 20,000; (b) 330.   **14** £5,000.   **15** (a) 3 (b) 1 (c) 1.

EDINBURGH UNIVERSITY LIBRARY, George Sq, Edinburgh, EH8 9LJ (Tel 031-667 1011) Univ Libn: Mr E.R.S. Fifoot MA, DipLib, ALA; Dep Libn: Mr V.E.Knight MA.
7 New College Lib, Mound Pl, Edinburgh, 1 (031-225 8400), Libn: Mr J.V.Howard MA, FLA; Central Medical Lib, Teviot Pl, Edinburgh, 8 (031-667 1011), Libn: Miss M.D.Bell MA, ALA; Law Lib, Old College, South Bridge, Edinburgh, 8 (031-667 1011), Libn: Miss M.Sturgeon MA; Reid Music Lib, Alison House, Nicolson Sq, Edinburgh, 8 (031-667 1011), Libn: Mr M.S.Anderson MA, LRAM, ALA; Veterinary Lib, Royal (Dick) School of Veterinary Studies, Summerhall, Edinburgh, EH9 1QH (031-667 1011), Libn: Mrs M.MacIvor.
8 General.   **9** Laing (mss) colln; Halliwell-Phillips (Shakespearian & dramatic) collns.   **10** SCOLMA.
11 Yes, on written application stating special need.
12 Term: Mon-Fri 9.00-22.00 (Fri 19.00), Sat 9.00-12.30, vac: Mon-Fri 9.00-17.00.   **13** (a) 1,150,000; (b) c.7,000; (c) 18,200 vols mss; 35,500 letters; 40,000 maps.
14 £250,000.   **15** (a) 153 (b) 41 (c) 33.

EDUCATIONAL INSTITUTE OF SCOTLAND LIBRARY, 46 Moray Pl, Edinburgh, EH3 6BH (Tel 031-225 6244) General Sec: Mr John D.Pollock BSc, FEIS.
8 Teaching of general subjects; educational psychology; Scottish education; history of Scottish education; nursery schools; teaching children with hearing & speech defects; backwardness.   **11** No.   **12** Mon-Fri 9.15-12.30, 14.00-16.45, some Sats 9.30-12.30.   **13** (a) c.5,500.   **14** Under £50.   **15** (a) 1.

FACULTY OF ACTUARIES LIBRARY, 23 St Andrew Sq, Edinburgh, EH2 1AQ (Tel 031-556 6791) Sec: W.W.Mair MA.
8 Actuarial practice; life contingencies; mortality; investments; maths; statistics.   **9** Transactions of faculty of Actuaries; Journal of Institute of Actuaries.   **11** No.
12 Mon-Fri 9.00-17.00.   **14** £500.

FERRANTI LTD LIBRARY, Ferry Rd, Edinburgh, EH5 2XS (Tel 031-332 2411; Telex 72141) Chief Libn: Miss M.L. Richmond.
8 Electronics & electrical engineering.   **10** NLS.

12 Mon-Fri 8.30-17.00 (Fri 16.30).   **13** (a) 6,700; (b) 250; (c) photocopying machine.   **15** (a) 4.
FERRIER'S MEDICAL LIBRARY, 18 Teviot Pl, Edinburgh, EH1 2RB (Tel 031-225 5689) Libn: Miss C.Scott; Asst Libn: Kim Westgarth.
6 Donald Ferrier Ltd.   **8** Medical textbooks.   **11** No.
12 Mon-Fri 9.00-17.30, Sat 9.00-13.00.   **13** (a) 35,000.
15 (a) 3.

HERIOT-WATT UNIVERSITY, CAMERON SMAIL LIBRARY, Chambers St, Edinburgh, EH1 1HX (Tel 031-225 8432) Univ Libn: Mr Alex Anderson MA, FLA; Dep Libn: Mr N.J.Hunter MA, BSc, ALA.
6 University Senate.   **8** Science; engineering; social sciences; languages; law.   **11** Yes, on application to Libn.
12 Mon-Fri 9.00-21.00.   **13** (a) 70,000; (b) 1,000; (c) microfilm; microfiche.   **14** £77,300.   **15** (a) 25 (b) 13 (c) 7.

INSTITUTE OF CHARTERED ACCOUNTANTS OF SCOTLAND, EDINBURGH LIBRARY, 27 Queen St, Edinburgh, EH2 1LA (Tel 031-225 3687) Edinburgh Libn: Mrs Alison M.Gordon MA, ALA; Asst Libn: Mrs Mary R.Hunter.
8 Accountancy; law; economics.   **9** Accounting history (1494-1930), (700 vols).   **11** No.   **12** Mon-Fri 9.00-17.00.
13 (a) 7,000; (b) 155.   **15** (a) 1 (b) 1 (c) 1.

INSTITUTE OF OCCUPATIONAL MEDICINE LIBRARY, Roxburgh Pl, Edinburgh, EH8 9SU (Tel 031-667 5131) Libn/ Inf Officer: Ms Eliz.B.Duncan, BSc, MSc, MIInfSc.
6 National Coal Board.   **8** Occupational health; lung diseases (pathology & physiology); dust physics; epidemiology; ergonomics.   **10** NLS.   **11** Yes, by prior application to Libn/Inf.Officer.   **12** 9.00-17.00   **13** (a) c.2,500; (b) 60; (c) c.100 slides.   **14** £2,000.   **15** (a) ½ (b) ½ (c) ½.

JOHN BARTHOLOMEW AND SON LTD LIBRARY, Duncan St, Edinburgh, EH9 1TA (Tel 031-667 9341).
8 Cartography; world geography; atlases.   **9** Atlases on various subjects & areas (mainly 1955-75).   **11** No, except bona-fide students on discretionary basis.   **12** Mon-Fri 9.00-17.00.   **13** (a) c.3,500; (b) 80; (c) 600 atlases.
14 £800.   **15** (a) ½ (c) 1.

MORAY HOUSE COLLEGE OF EDUCATION LIBRARY, Holyrood Rd, Edinburgh, EH8 8AQ (Tel 031-556 8455) Principal Libn: Mr A.G.Brown MA, FLA; Dep Libn: Mrs M Kennaway FLA.
8 Education; social studies.   **11** No.   **12** Mon-Fri 8.45-20.00 (Fri 17.00).   **13** (a) 95,000; (b) 550; (c) tapes (cassettes); slides; film strips; kits.   **14** £20,000.   **15** (a) 26 (b) 11 (c) 10.

NAPIER COLLEGE OF COMMERCE AND TECHNOLOGY LIBRARY, Colinton Rd, Edinburgh, EH10 5DT (Tel 031-447 7070) Head of Dept of Lib & Inf Resources: Mr John Bate MA, DipEd, FLA.
6 Napier College Council, Lothian Region Education Committee.   **7** Sighthill Court, Edinburgh (031-443 6061) Libn: Miss A.S.Cowper MA, FLA, FSA.   **8** Biological science; physics; maths; computing science; chemistry; engineering; art & design; modern languages; business; law; banking & insurance; history; librarianship & information science; printing & publishing; catering & tourism.   **9** Edward Clark Colln (printing history); Bernard Newdigate Colln (20th-cent private press books); BSI.   **10** BLL.   **11** Yes, for ref only; BSI & other specialist material lent to industrial firms.   **12** Term: Mon-Fri 8.45-21.00 (Fri 17.00); vac: Mon-Fri 8.45-17.00.   **13** (a) 80,000; (b) 1,200; (c) 1,000 microtexts; gramophone records; cassette tapes; video-tapes & transparencies (held by Dept of Educational Technology).   **14** £50,000.   **15** (a) 22 (b) 9 (c) 7.

NATIONAL LIBRARY OF SCOTLAND, George IV Bridge, Edinburgh, EH1 1EW (Tel 031-226 4531; Telex 72638) Libn: Dr E.F.D.Roberts MA, PhD; Sec of Lib: Dr M.A.Pegg BA, PhD.

EDINBURGH—*continued*

6 Board of Trustees. **7** Map Room, Annexe, 137 Causewayside, Edinburgh, EH9 1PH (031-667 7848) Libn: Miss M. Wilkes MA; Lending Services, Lawnmarket, Edinburgh, EH1 2PJ (031-225 5321; Telex: 72279) Libn: Miss C.E.G. Wright ALA. **8** As a national copyright library all subjects are covered. **9** Rosebery (early & rare Scottish books & pamphlets); Scandinavian (founded on Grimur Thorkelin's library); Nichol Smith (French & English literature & criticism, 16th-18th cent); Graham Brown & Lloyd (alpine & mountaineering); Mason (children's books); Lauriston Castle (chapbooks); Dieterichs & Crawford (German Reformation theses); Wordie (polar exploration); Blaikie (Jacobite material); Glen & Inglis (Scottish music). **10** BLL; BUCOP; Scottish Union Catalogue; Gaelic Union Catalogue; Slavonic Union Catalogue; SCOLCAP; UCABE; Library Co-operation Committee organizes all aspects of library co-operation in Scotland. **11** Yes, 6-month & 3-day tickets for ref for information not available elsewhere; special conditions for undergraduates. Enquiries to Superintendent of Readers Services. **12** Reading Rooms: Mon-Fri 9.30-20.30, Sat 9.30-13.00; Branches vary. **13** (a) c.3,000,000; (b) 8,500; (c) Large colln of mss; records of life in Scotland & of careers of Scotsmen at home & abroad; Western Icelandic mss. **15** (a) 185 (b) 42 (c) 12.

PROPERTY SERVICES AGENCY LIBRARY, Room B110, Argyle House, 3 Lady Lawson St, Edinburgh, EH3 9SD (Tel 031-229 & 9191 ext 5188; Telex 72127; telefacsimile 031-229 9801).
6 Dept of Environment. **7** Angusfield House, 226 Queens Rd, Aberdeen; Montrose House, 187 George St, Glasgow; Hilton Rd, Rosyth. **8** Building; construction; engineering (civil, electrical, mechanical, structural); ancient monuments; architectural design. **9** 250,000 photographic negatives; slides & prints of government buildings & ancient monuments in Scotland. **11** No. **12** Mon-Fri 8.30-17.00 (Fri 16.30). **13** (a) 2,000; (b) 250; (c) microtexts of building & engineering journals; 10,000 pamphlets; 5,000 trade catalogues. **14** £5,000. **15** (a) 2 (c) 2.

ROYAL BOTANIC GARDEN LIBRARY, Edinburgh, EH3 5LR (Tel 031-552 7171) Libn: Mr M.V.Mathew BA, DLSc, ALA.
6 Dept of Agriculture & Fisheries for Scotland. **8** Taxonomic botany & amenity horticulture. **9** Pre-Linnaean botanical literature; garden archives. **10** Inter-library loans. **11** Yes, by appointment, for ref only. **12** Mon-Fri 8.00-13.00, 14.00-17.00 (Fri 16.30). **13** (a) 60,000; (b) c.1,200; (c) large collns of cuttings & illustrations; reprints; separates & pamphlets; portraits & other photographs; journals. **14** £13,500. **15** (a) 5 (b) 2 (c) 2.

ROYAL COLLEGE OF PHYSICIANS LIBRARY, 9 Queen St, Edinburgh, EH2 1JQ (Tel 031-225 5968) Libn: Miss J.P.S. Ferguson MA, ALA; Dep: Mrs S.G. Le Touze BA, DipLib.
8 Medicine & allied sciences. **9** J.Y.Simpson Colln (books & pamphlets on gynaecology & obstetrics), J.W. Ballantyne Colln (foetal pathology pamphlets); mss (18th-cent lecture notes etc). **10** BLL; NLS. **11** Yes, for ref only. **12** Mon-Fri 9.00-17.00. **13** (a) 200,000; (b) 326; (c) college archives; c.1,000 vols mss; portraits; prints. **15** (a) 4 (b) 2 (c) 2.

ROYAL COLLEGE OF SURGEONS OF EDINBURGH LIBRARY, 18 Nicolson St, Edinburgh, EH8 9DW (Tel 031-556 6206) Hon Libn: Dr I.Simson Hall FRCSEd; Libn: Miss D.U. Wardle ALA.
8 Surgery. **11** No. **12** Mon-Fri 9.00-17.00. **13** (a) 28,000; (b) 200. **15** (a) 2 (c) 1.

ROYAL OBSERVATORY LIBRARY, Blackford Hill, Edinburgh, EH9 3HJ (Tel 031-667 3321; Telex 72383).
6 Science Research Council. **8** Astronomy; astrophysics; physics (especially dynamics of gases & fluids, plasma physics, optics, electromagnetism, low-temperature physics, vacuum physics, relativity, gravity); geophysics; meteorology; electrical & electronic engineering; computers; maths. **9** Crawford colln c.11,000 books & mss inc 1st editions of nearly every book important in history of astronomy & related fields. **10** Inter-library loans. **11** Yes, to bona-fide researchers, on application to Dir. **12** Mon-Fri 9.00-17.30 (Fri 17.00). **13** (a) c.3,000 books; (b) c.1,100;

(c) mss of former Astronomers Royal for Scotland; plates of various sky surveys. **14** £7,000-10,000. **15** (a) 2½ (b) 1 (c) 1.

ROYAL SCOTTISH MUSEUM LIBRARY, Chambers St, Edinburgh, EH1 1JF (Tel 031-225 7534) Libn: Miss D.C.F. Smith MA, ALA.
6 Scottish Education Dept. **8** Decorative arts & sculpture (exc 20th cent.); ethnography; archaeology; geology; zoology; history of science & technology. **10** BLL; UCABE; NLS. **11** Yes, to bona-fide scholars, by introduction & appointment. **12** Mon-Fri 10.00-12.30, 14.00-17.00 (Fri 16.30). **13** (a) 65,000; (b) c.900; (c) photographs; maps; microforms; mss; slides; records. **15** (a) 3 (b) 2 (c) 1.

ROYAL SOCIETY OF EDINBURGH LIBRARY, 22-24 George St, Edinburgh, EH2 2PQ (Tel 031-225 6057) Executive Sec & Libn: Mr W.H.Rutherford, FCIS, FRSE, FRZS.
6 Council of RSE. **8** Science. **10** Inter-library loans. **11** Yes, for ref. **12** Mon-Fri 9.30-17.00. **13** (a) c.200,000; (b) c.2,000. **15** (a) 6 (b) 2 (c) 1.

SCOTTISH BEEKEEPERS' ASSOCIATION, MOIR LIBRARY, Central Library, George IV Bridge, Edinburgh, EH1 1EG (Tel 031-225 5584) City Libn: Mr A.P.Shearman FLA, BA; Asst City Libn: Mr A.G.D.White ALA.
6 Council of SBA. **8** Beekeeping; bees & other hymenoptera. **9** Early English books on insects; husbandry. **11** Yes, for ref only. **12** Mon-Fri 9.00-21.00, Sat 9.00-13.00. **13** (a) 5,076; (b) 40. **15** (a) 1.

SCOTTISH CONGREGATIONAL COLLEGE LIBRARY, 29 Hope Terrace, Edinburgh, EH9 2AP (Tel 031-447 1807) Libn: Prof A.Morton Price.
8 Theology & biblical studies. **11** No, except by application to Libn. **12** During college day, or by arrangement. **13** (a) c.10,000; (b) 11.

SCOTTISH HEALTH SERVICE CENTRE LIBRARY, Crewe Rd South, Edinburgh, EH4 2LF (Tel 031-332 2335) Libn: Miss Antonia J. Bunch, FLA; Dep: Miss Eileen Cumming ALA.
6 Common Services Agency for SHS. **8** Health service planning & administration; planning & design of health care buildings; care & welfare of elderly & disabled; international & comparative studies of health care. **10** BLL; NLS. **11** Yes, by prior application. **12** Mon-Fri 9.00-17.00. **13** (a) 8,000; (b) 150. **15** (a) 4 (c) 2.

SCOTTISH OFFICE LIBRARY, Rm 2/64, New St Andrew's House, St James' Centre Edinburgh, EH1 3TG (Tel 031-556 8400 or 5370) Chief Libn: Mr H.A.Colquhoun FLA.
6 Scottish Office. **7** St Andrew's House, Edinburgh, EH1 3DH; Chesser House, Gorgie Rd, Edinburgh, EH11 3AW; Agricultural Scientific Services Station, East Craigs, Edinburgh, EH12 8NJ, Libn: Mrs C.John BA, ALA. **8** Scottish affairs (social, economic, administration); law & criminal justice; agriculture; education; social work; local government; public health; planning; architecture; civil engineering. **10** NLS. **11** No. **12** Mon-Fri 8.30-17.00. **13** (a) 50,000; (b) 1,100; (c) 60,000 pamphlets & reports. **14** £35,000. **15** (a) 21 (b) 6 (c) 7.

SCOTTISH UNITED SERVICES MUSEUM LIBRARY, Crown Sq, The Castle, Edinburgh, EH1 2NG (Tel 031-226 6907) Keeper: Mr William A.Thorborn FSA(Scot); Research Asst: Mr William Boag MA.
6 Scottish Education Dept. **8** Military & armed forces history; costume; organisation; weapons. **9** Rare contemporary publications, documents & pictorial archives related to armed forces of Great Britain; military costume; c.9,000 engravings & lithographs; c.9,000 photographs. **11** Yes, by appointment. **12** Mon-Fri 9.30-12.30, 14,00-17.30 (Fri 17.00). **13** (a) 9,000; (b) c.20; (c) archives of military sounds, music etc; army lists (1760-1975). **15** (a) 5.

SIGNET LIBRARY, Parliament Sq, Edinburgh, EH1 1RF (Tel 031-225 4923) Libn: Mr George H.Ballantyne MA, FLA; S.A.F.Easterbrook WS.
6 Society of Writers to Her Majesty's Signet. **8** Law, especially Scots law; Scottish history; topography; genealogy. **9** Session Papers (2,500 vols, from 1700) (index, 1713-1820); William Roughead colln (400 vols on trials). **11** No.

CODE: 1 Name of Library. **2** Address. **3** Telephone & Telex. **4** Officer in charge. **5** Deputy. **6** Governing body.
7 Branches. **8** Main Subjects. **9** Special Collections. **10** Co-operative Schemes. **11** Open to public? **12** Hours.
13 Stock: (a) books (b) periodicals (c) other. **14** Finance. **15** Staff: (a) non-manual (b) graduate (c) chartered librarians.

EDINBURGH—*continued*

12 Mon-Fri 9.30-16.00, Sat (term only) 9.30-12.00.
13 (a) 120,000; (b) 50. **15** (a) 4 (b) 2 (c) 1.

SOCIETY OF SOLICITORS IN THE SUPREME COURTS
LIBRARY, Parliament House, Edinburgh, EH1 1RF (Tel 031-
225 6268) Keeper of Lib: Mr J. W. Malcolm; Society Officer: Mr
Gill.
8 Scottish legal subjects of all kinds, & UK law. **9** Full
colln of Scottish law reports. **11** Yes, for occasional ref
on special request to Keeper of Library. **12** Mon-Fri
9.30-16.00 **13** (a) 15,000; (b) 25. **14** £500. **15** (a) 2.

STEVENSON COLLEGE OF FURTHER EDUCATION
LIBRARY, Bankhead Ave, Sighthill, Edinburgh, EH11 4DE
(Tel 031-443 7111) Senior Tutor-Libn: Mr G.S. Neil Mochrie
ALA.
6 Lothian Regional Council. **7** Ramsay College Annexe,
Inchview Terrace, Edinburgh (031-669 3580). **8** General;
automobile & electrical engineering; pre-nursing; building;
commerce; science; laboratory technology. **10** BLL.
11 Yes, for ref & information only. **12** Term: Mon-Fri
8.40-21.00 (Fri 16.55); vac: 9.00-16.30. **13** (a) 21,800;
(b) 250; (c) 10 rolls microfilms. **14** £6,650. **15** (a) 8
(b) 1 (c) 2.

TELFORD COLLEGE OF FURTHER EDUCATION LIBRARY,
Crewe Toll, Edinburgh, EH4 2NZ (Tel 031-332 7631) Senior
Tutor-Libn: Mr David Christie ALA; Tutor-Libn: Mr James
Cranstoun ALA.
6 Lothian Regional Council. **8** Engineering; building;
catering; hairdressing; science; commerce. **10** BLL;
inter-library loans. **11** Yes, for ref only. **12** Term:
Mon-Fri 8.30-19.30 (Fri 16.35); vac: Mon-Fri 9.00-16.30.
13 (a) 22,000; (b) 180; (c) 600 gramophone records.
14 £7,750. **15** (a) 6 (b) 1 (c) 4.

EGHAM, Surrey

ROYAL HOLLOWAY COLLEGE LIBRARY, Egham Hill,
Egham, TW20 0EX (Tel 07843-4455; Telex 935504) Libn: Mr
R. J. E. Horrill BA.
6 RHC Council, University of London. **7** Dept Libs in
chemistry, botany, zoology, biochemistry; seminar libs in
other subjects. **8** English; French; German; Italian; history;
music; maths; statistics; computer science; chemistry;
physics; botany; zoology; biochemistry. **11** Yes, by application to Libn. **12** Term: Mon-Fri 9.00-21.00, Sat 9.00-
13.00, Sun 14.00-18.00; vac: Mon-Fri 9.00-17.00. **13** (a)
c. 142,000; (b) c.800. **14** £68,000. **15** (a) 20 (b) 7 (c) 13.

SHOREDITCH COLLEGE LIBRARY, Cooper's Hill, Englefield
Green, Egham, TW20 0JZ (Tel 07843-3981) Libn: Mr E. J.
Haywood ALA; Miss D. Penson BA, ALA.
6 ILEA. **8** Education; liberal arts; handicraft; design
technology. **9** Early material relating to handicrafts
teaching; history of Royal Indian Engineering College.
11 Yes, on application to Libn. **12** Term: Mon-Fri 9.00-
21.00, Sat 9.00-13.00; vac: 9.00-13.00, 14.00-17.00.
13 (a) 65,000; (b) 250; (c) archival material for history of
handicraft teaching; non-book materials; filmstrips; transparencies; cineloops; cassettes; wallcharts; illustrations;
learning packs. **14** £9,100. **15** (a) 6 (b) 2 (c) 4.

ELSTREE, Hertfordshire

ALDENHAM SCHOOL LIBRARY, Elstree, WD6 3AJ (Tel
09276-6131).
6 AS Governors. **8** General. **9** Hertfordshire.
11 No. **12** 8.30-22.00. **13** (a) 18,000; (b) 21.
14 £620. **15** (a) 1.

EWELL, Surrey

EWELL COUNTY TECHNICAL COLLEGE LIBRARY, Reigate
Rd, Ewell (Tel 01-394 1731; Telex 917228) Tutor-Libn: Mrs
E. R. Macdonald ALA; Asst Tutor-Libn: Mrs H. M. Currington.

6 ECTC Board of governors. **8** Biology; construction;
general building; languages; home economics; education &
teacher training; management; business. **9** Trade & technical information covering all aspects of building & construction; trade & technical literature & teaching aids on home
economics & allied subjects; illustration colln. **11** Yes, for
ref only. **12** Term: 9.00-21.00; vac: 9.00-12.30.
13 (a) 30,000; (b) 350; (c) gramophone records; slides & filmstrips; audio tapes; films; filmloops. **14** £17,000.
15 (a) 7½ (c) 3.

EXETER, Devon

DEVON AND EXETER INSTITUTION LIBRARY, 7 The Close,
Exeter (Tel 0392-74727) Libn: Mrs S. Stirling BA, DipLib.
8 South-West studies; topography; genealogy; history.
9 Local newspapers (18th & 19th cent). **11** No. **12** Mon-
Fri 9.00-17.00. **13** (a) 33,000; (b) 38; (c) local maps;
topographical prints. **15** (a) 1 (b) 1 (c) 1.

EXETER CATHEDRAL LIBRARY, Bishop's Palace, Exeter
(Tel 0392-72894) Libn: Mr J. F. Stirling MA; Asst Libn: Miss
J. Packer BA.
6 Dean & Chapter. **8** Theology; liturgy; church history;
biography; history; history of Devon & Exeter; early medicine
& science. **9** Harington Library (Protestant & general
theology); Thomas Glass Colln (early medicine & science).
11 Yes, for ref. **12** Mon-Fri 14.00-17.00. **13** (a)
30,000; (b) 6; (c) large archive colln. **14** £500.

EXETER COLLEGE LIBRARY, Hele Rd, Exeter, EX4 4JS
(Tel 0392-76381) Senior Resource Tutor: Mr Roy Deasy TD,
MA, BD; Dep: Mrs Barabara Harrington ALA; DipEd.
6 Devon CC. **8** General; engineering; building; hairdressing; food; business; child care. **9** Complete BSI; Barber
Index; engineering index; All England Law Reports; laws of
England; Halsbury's Statutes; statutory instruments.
10 SWRLB. **11** Yes, with Libns permission. **12** Term:
Mon-Fri 8.30-18.00. **13** (a) 21,000; (c) print colln (5,500
items inc audio-visual software). **14** £14,650. **15** (a) 5
(b) 1 (c) 1.

Exeter University

UNIVERSITY LIBRARY, Prince of Wales Rd, Exeter, EX4
4PT (Tel 0392-77911; Telex 42894) Libn: Mr J. F. Stirling
MA; Dep Libn: Dr C. F. Scott MA, PhD, ALA.
6 Library Committee, Senate of Exeter University.
8 General. **9** Crediton Parochial Library; Dodderidge
Theological Library; Totnes Parochial Library.
10 BLL; SCOLMA; SWALCAP; SWRLB. **11** Yes, for ref
only. **12** Term: Mon-Fri 9.00-22.00, Sat 9.00-17.30,
Sun 14.00-21.00; vac: hours vary. **13** (a) 355,000; (b)
2,800; (c) microforms; slides & other audio-visual materials. **14** £150,000.

SCHOOL OF EDUCATION LIBRARY, Gandy St, Exeter,
EX4 3LZ (Tel 0392-77911 ext 334; Telex 42894) Libn:
Mr John R. Ruck MA, ALA; Asst Libn: Miss Anne Turner
ALA.
8 Education; psychology; sociology. **10** LISE.
12 Term: Mon-Fri 9.00-18.00, Sat 9.00-12.00; vac: Mon-
Fri 9.00-17.00. **13** (a) 27,000 (excl periodicals); (b)
250; (c) microtexts; tapes; slides. **14** £6,900. **15** (a)
3½ (b) 1 (c) 2.

EXMOUTH, Devon

ROLLE COLLEGE OF EDUCATION LIBRARY, Douglas Ave,
Exmouth, EX8 2AT (Tel 03952-5344) Tutor-Libn: Mr J. Owen
Jones BA, ALA; Asst Libn: Mr K. H. Shafee, ALA.
6 Devon CC. **8** Education; history; geography; literature;
languages (French & English); divinity; sociology; sciences
(maths, physics, chemistry); biology; fine arts; health; physical
education. **11** Yes, for local teachers. **12** Term: Mon-
Fri 9.00-21.00 (Fri 17.00), Sat 9.00-12.00, 13.00-16.00,
Sun 14.00-17.00; vac: Mon-Fri 9.30-16.30. **13** (a) 50,000.
15 (a) 5 (b) 1 (c) 2.

FALKIRK, Stirling

CALLENDAR PARK COLLEGE OF EDUCATION LIBRARY, Falkirk, FK1 1YS (Tel 0324-22982) Principal Libn: Miss D. Atkinson BA, ALA; Asst Libns: Miss I. P. Davidson ALA; Miss M. Ferguson ALA.
6 Governing body of college. **8** Education; educational psychology. **10** SCE, COPAEP. **11** Yes, for ref only, for teachers & others connected with education. **12** Term: Mon-Fri 9.00-20.30 (Fri 17.00); vac: Mon-Fri 9.00-17.00. **13** (a) 7,520; (b) 304; (c) music tapes; cassettes; filmstrips. **14** £3,000-4,000.

FALKIRK COLLEGE OF TECHNOLOGY LIBRARY, Grangemouth Rd, Falkirk, FK2 9AD (Tel 0324-24981) Coll Libn: Ms Margaret J. Sked ALA; Asst Libn: Mr Gordon McCrae BA.
6 Central Region Education Authority. **8** Electrical, construction, foundry, mechanical, mining, automobile engineering; business; chemistry; general. **9** Complete BSI. **10** BLL; NLS; Aslib. **11** Yes. **12** Term: Mon-Fri 9.00-20.15 (Fri 17.30); vac: 9.00-17.00. **13** (a) 26,000; (b) 300; (c) 450 gramophone records; 13 tapes; 16 filmstrips; 50 cassettes; 23 kits; 125 jackdaws; 30 sets of slides; 9 film loops; 150 art prints; 350 maps. **14** £11,000. **15** (a) 7 (b) 2 (c) 1.

FALMOUTH, Cornwall

FALMOUTH SCHOOL OF ART LIBRARY, Woodlane, Falmouth, TR11 4RA (Tel 0326-313269) Libn: Mr Derek Toyne BA, ALA.
6 Cornwall CC. **8** Fine art. **11** Yes, by appointment. **12** Mon-Fri 9.15-12.30, 14.00-17.15. **13** (a) c. 7,000; (b) c. 50; (c) c. 500 gramophone records; 2 microfilm periodical backruns. **14** c. £2,500. **15** (a) 1½ (b) 1 (c) 1.

FAREHAM, Hampshire

FAREHAM TECHNICAL COLLEGE LIBRARY, Bishopsfield Rd, Fareham PO14 1NH (Tel 03292-5631) Libn: Miss D. M. Burndred ALA.
6 Hampshire CC. **8** Sociology; engineering; business. **10** SWRLB. **11** Yes. **12** Term: Mon-Fri 9.00-19.00 (Fri 17.00); vac: Mon-Fri 9.00-17.00. **13** (a) 11,000; (b) 80. **14** £3,800. **15** (a) 1½ (c) 1.

FARNBOROUGH, Hampshire

ROYAL AIRCRAFT ESTABLISHMENT LIBRARY, Q4 Building, Farnborough, GU14 6TD (Tel 0252-24461 ext 2954; Telex 85134) Chief Libn: Mr J. R. Seymour ALA; Libn in Charge, Main Library Services: Mr D. W. Goode ALA.
6 Procurement Executive, MoD. **7** Several branch libraries in RAE Departments at Farnborough & outstations. Contact via Main Library. **8** Aerospace engineering; aeronautics; aerodynamics; electrical & electronic engineering; avionics; materials; structures; weapons; human factors. **9** Aeronautical reports colln; library bibliographies & library translations series produced by RAE library staff; history of aviation technology. **10** HATRICS. **11** No, except on written application to Chief Libn. Requests for reports to Defence Research Information Centre, St Mary Cray, Kent, BR5 3RE. **12** Mon-Fri 8.30-17.00 (Fri 16.30). **13** (a) c. 50,000; (b) c. 1,600; (c) 15,000 specifications & standards, 200,000 reports; several thousand reports on microcard & microfilm.

GALASHIELS, Selkirkshire

SCOTTISH COLLEGE OF TEXTILES LIBRARY, Galashiels, TD1 3HF (Tel 0896-3351; Telex 72416) Senior Libn: Mr Ian C. Monie MSc, FLA; Libn: Miss Jane R. Ogg BSc, DipLib.
6 Board of Governors. **8** Textile technology; textile design; management. **9** Pattern books & fabric samples of selected Scottish tweed firms. **10** BLL; NLS. **11** Yes, on application. **12** Term: Mon-Fri 9.00-20.30 (Fri 16.45); vac: Mon-Fri 9.00-16.45. **13** (a) 10,000; (b) 220; (c) 150 microtexts. **15** (a) 4 (b) 2 (c) 1.

GATESHEAD, Tyne and Wear

CLARKE CHAPMAN LTD GROUP LIBRARY, Saltmeadows Rd Works, PO Box 13, Gateshead, NE8 1YZ (Tel 0632-772271 ext 116; Telex 537107) Group Inf Officer: Mr K. W. Leslie BSc; Dep: Mr A. Worton AMIInfSc.
6 Advanced Technology Division. **7** Advanced Technology Div, Spring Rd, Ettingshall, Wolverhampton, WV4 5JX (0902-41121; Telex 33-212), Libn: Mr A. Worton AMIInfSc; International Combustion Div, Sinfin Lane, Derby, DE2 9GJ (0332-23223), Libn: Mrs R. M. Timmins. **8** Engineering. **9** ASME boiler codes. **10** TALIC; MISLIC; NRLB. **11** No. **12** Mon-Fri 8.30-17.00 (Fri 16.30). **13** (a) 9,000; (b) 250; (c) microfiche—mostly US reports. **14** c. £10,000. **15** (a) 6 (b) 2.

GATESHEAD TECHNICAL COLLEGE LIBRARY, Durham Rd, Gateshead, NE9 5BN (Tel 0632-770524 ext 3) Admin Libn: Mr M. J. M. Hugo ALA.
8 Mechanical & electrical engineering; motor vehicle technology; business & social sciences; humanities. **9** BSI (complete from 1968). **10** NRLB; TALIC. **11** Yes, for ref only. **12** 9.00-18.00. **13** (a) 8,353; (b) 117. **14** £5,000. **15** (a) 3 (c) 1.

GERRARDS CROSS, Buckinghamshire

BEE RESEARCH ASSOCIATION LIBRARY, Hill House, Chalfont St Peter, Gerrards Cross, SL9 0NR (Tel 02813-85011)
6 Bee Research Association Council. **7** Dept of Environmental Biology, University of Guelph, Guelph, Ontario, Canada, Libn: Prof G. F. Townsend; Beekeeping Section, PO Box 62, Tabora, Tanzania; Central Bee Research Institute, Khadi & Village Industries Commission, Shivajinagar, Poona 4, India, Libn: C. V. Thakar. **8** Bees (all species); beekeeping; substances used or produced by bees; pollinating activity; (all on a worldwide scale). **9** 1,450 unpublished English translations of works on bees; theses; trade catalogues. **11** No. **12** Mon-Fri 9.00-17.30. **13** (a) 3,000; (c) c. 3,300 microforms; c. 1,200 slides; c. 9,000 pictures. **15** (a) 1.

GLASGOW

ANNIESLAND COLLEGE LIBRARY, Hatfield Dr, Glasgow, G12 0YE (Tel 041-339 6851) Teacher-Libn: Mr Eric W. M. Simpson ALA; Dep Mrs S. V. Beaton.
6 Strathclyde Regional Council. **8** Engineering (marine); building trades; secretarial practice; English literature; commerce. **11** No, except to persons undertaking leisure-time activities within college. **12** Autumn & winter terms: Mon-Thurs 9.00-13.25, 14.10-17.30, 18.00-19.30, Fri 9.00-13.25, 14.10-16.45; spring term: Mon-Thurs 9.00-13.25, 14.10-17.00; vac: closed. **13** (a) 16,528; (b) 150; (c) 300 gramophone records. **14** £5,000. **15** (a) 2 (c) 1.

BAILLIE REFERENCE LIBRARY, 69 Oakfield Ave, Glasgow, G12 8LP (Tel 041-339 9627) Libn: Mrs M. Manchester.
8 Scottish colln. **9** Foulis Press books (235 titles); autograph letters; MacLean Society Library; Caithness Society Library; Scottish theatre programmes; Glasgow Colln (3,000 vols.). **11** Yes. **12** Mon-Fri 10.00-17.00. **13** (a) 40,000.

BARMULLOCH COLLEGE OF FURTHER EDUCATION LIBRARY, Rye Rd, Glasgow, G21 3JY (Tel 041-558 9071) Senior Teacher-Libn: Miss W. G. Mann DCE; Teacher-Libn: Mr David Millar MI Prod E, AMBIM.
6 Strathclyde Regional Council. **8** Building; commerce; engineering; general. **11** No. **12** College hours. **13** (a) 16,795; (b) 123; (c) gramophone records (600). **14** £4,500. **15** (a) 4.

CARDONALD COLLEGE OF FURTHER EDUCATION LIBRARY, 690 Mosspark Dr, Glasgow, G52 3AY (Tel 041-883 6151) Tutor-Libn: Mr Robert M. McLean BA, ALA.
6 Strathclyde Regional Council. **8** General; commerce; engineering; pre-nursing; education; art & design. **11** Yes, for ref only. **12** Mon-Fri 9.00-16.50 (Sept-May: Mon-Thurs 20.30). **13** (a) 19,300; (b) 155; (c) 280 gramophone records. **14** £6,000. **15** (a) 3½ (b) 2 (c) 3.

CODE: 1 Name of Library. **2** Address. **3** Telephone & Telex. **4** Officer in charge. **5** Deputy. **6** Governing body.
7 Branches. **8** Main Subjects. **9** Special Collections. **10** Co-operative Schemes. **11** Open to public? **12** Hours.
13 Stock: (a) books (b) periodicals (c) other. **14** Finance. **15** Staff: (a) non-manual (b) graduate (c) chartered librarians.

GLASGOW—*continued*

CENTRAL COLLEGE OF COMMERCE LIBRARY, 300
Cathedral St, Glasgow, G1 2TA (Tel 041-552 3941) Senior
Tutor-Libn: Mr S. Sharp BA, DPA, FLA.
6 Strathclyde Regional Council. **8** Economics; accountancy;
management; sociology & politics. **10** BLL. **11** Yes,
by arrangement. **12** Term: Mon-Thurs 9.00-16.45, 17.30-
20.30. **13** (a) 25,000; (b) 60; (c) tape & video-tape.

GLASGOW UNIVERSITY LIBRARY, Hillhead St, Glasgow,
G12 8QE (Tel 041-334 2122; Telex 778421) University Libn &
Keeper of Hunterian Books & Mss: Mr R.O. MacKenna MA,
ALA; Dep Libn: Mr P.A. Hoare MA, ALA.
7 Undergraduate Reading Room, Libn: Miss B.M. Cook BA,
MSc, ALA; Veterinary Hospital, Bearsden Rd, Glasgow,
G61 1QH, Libn: Miss M. Postlethwaite MA; Institute of Soviet
& East European Studies, 10 Southpark Terrace, Glasgow
G12 8LQ, Libn: Dr J.A. Large BSc, PhD, DipLib; Dental
Hospital & School, 211 Renfrew St, Glasgow G2 3JZ, Libn:
Mrs M.H. Drabble.
8 General; arts; social sciences; divinity; law; medicine (inc
dentistry); science; engineering; veterinary medicine.
9 Hunterian (10,000 vols, inc 534 incunabula & 649 mss,
early printing, medical & scientific history); Euing (15,000
vols, inc 2,000 Bibles, 400 Black-letter ballads & many 15th
& 16th cent books); Euing Music (5,300 vols); Stirling-
Maxwell (2,000 vols, emblem literature); Ferguson (7,500
vols, history of chemistry, alchemy & witchcraft); David
Murray (14,500 vols, local history & bibliography); Hamilton
(8,000 vols, philosophy); Wylie (1,000 vols, history &
antiquities of Glasgow); J.A. McNeill Whistler, papers &
mss; Dougan colln (D.O. Hill photographs). **10** NLS;
BMS of Joint Standing Committee on Library Co-operation.
11 Yes, for ref only, to visiting scholars & other accredited
persons. **12** Term: Mon-Fri 9.00-21.30, Sat 9.00-
12.30; vac: Mon-Fri 9.00-17.00, Sat 9.00-12.30.
13 (a) 1,165,000; (b) 7,500; (c) 10,000 mss; 10,000 maps;
55,000 microtexts; 6,650 theses; 2,700 vols of newspapers.
14 £270,000. **15** (a) 150 (b) 64 (c) 33.

INSTITUTE OF CHARTERED ACCOUNTANTS OF
SCOTLAND, CENTRAL LIBRARY, 218 St Vincent St, Glasgow,
G2 5QL (Tel 041-221 2333/4) Libn: Miss D. Henry ALA.
8 Accountancy; management; business; law, especially
commercial law, company law, taxation. **10** NLS.
11 Yes, if introduced by a member or someone known to
the Institute. **12** Mon-Fri 9.30-17.30. **13** (a) 11,717;
(b) 77. **15** (a) 3 (c) 1.

JORDANHILL COLLEGE OF EDUCATION LIBRARY, 76
Southbrae Dr, Glasgow, G13 1PP (Tel 041-959 1232)
Principal Libn: Mr Peter B. Clarke MA, FLA; Dep Libn:
Miss Anne L. Williamson FLA.
6 JCE Board of Governors. **8** General; education &
psychology. **10** BLL; SCE. **11** No. **12** Term: Mon-
Fri 9.00-21.00 (Fri 17.00), Sat 9.00-12.00; vac: Mon-Fri
9.00-17.00. **13** (a) 100,000; (b) 650; (c) audio-visual
materials. **15** (a) 23 (b) 10 (c) 13.

LANGSIDE COLLEGE OF FURTHER EDUCATION
LIBRARY, 50 Prospecthill Rd, Glasgow, G42 9LB (Tel 041-
649 4991) Teacher-Libn: Miss Jeanie D.C. McLeod MA;
Teacher-Libn: Mr John Murray ALA.
6 Strathclyde Regional Council, Education Dept.
8 Pre-school children; sociology; child care; engineering;
building; education; commerce. **11** No. **12** Term:
9.00-17.00, (Sept-May 17.30-19.30). **13** (a) 13,500;
(b) 100; (c) 500 records; 50 cassettes. **14** £4,800.
15 (a) 2 (b) 1 (c) 1.

NATIONAL ENGINEERING LABORATORY LIBRARY, East
Kilbride, Glasgow, G75 0QU (Tel 03552-20222; Telex 77588)
Head of Lib Services: T. Archbold; Dep: Mr J. Revie MIInfSc.
6 Dept of Industry. **8** Engineering. **11** No.

12 Mon-Fri 9.00-17.00. **13** (b) 700. **14** £26,000.
15 (a) 11 (b) 4 (c) 2.

NOTRE DAME COLLEGE OF EDUCATION LIBRARY,
Bearsden, Glasgow, G61 4QA (Tel 041-942 2363) Principal
Libn: Miss E.K. McCreadie ALA; Dep Libn: Wilfrid J.
Downie MAALA.
6 NDCE Board of Governors. **7** Dowanhill College Lib,
74 Victoria Crescent Rd, Glasgow, G12 9JN (041-334 9651),
Sub-Libn: Mrs A.H. Hannah MA, ALA. **8** Religion;
sociology; education; linguistics; literature; modern languages;
maths; biology; physical sciences; history; geography; art;
music; needlework & fabric crafts. **10** BLL; NLS.
11 No. **12** Term: Mon-Thurs 9.00-18.00, Fri 9.00-17.00;
vac: Mon-Fri 9.00-17.00; Branch varies. **13** (a) 56,600;
(b) 360; (c) 2,540 flat pictorial material; 185 audio materials;
988 projectable materials; 23 microtexts; 755 kits etc.
15 (a) 15 (b) 6 (c) 3.

QUEEN'S COLLEGE LIBRARY, 1 Park Dr, Glasgow, G3 6LP
(Tel 041-339 9211) Senior Libn: Miss H.F. Sommerville
ALA; Asst Libn: Miss F. Laverty MA, ALA.
6 Scottish Education Dept. **8** Home economics; catering &
institutional management; dietetics; social welfare.
11 No. **12** Mon-Fri 9.00-20.00 (Fri 17.00).
13 (a) 16,000; (b) 130. **14** £5,000. **15** (a) 4 (b) 1 (c) 2.

ROYAL COLLEGE OF PHYSICIANS AND SURGEONS OF
GLASGOW LIBRARY, 242 St Vincent Street, Glasgow, G2 5RJ
(Tel 041-248 5279) Libn: Mr Alex M. Rodger BA, ALA; Dep:
Miss Nancy Wylie.
8 Medicine; surgery. **9** Mackenzie (ophthalmology); Ross
(tropical medicine); Macewen (surgery). **11** No.
12 Mon-Fri 9.30-17.30 (Fri 21.00). **13** (a) 200,000;
(b) 378; (c) tape/slides on post-graduate medicine.
15 (a) 4 (b) 1 (c) 1.

ROYAL SCOTTISH ACADEMY OF MUSIC AND DRAMA
LIBRARY, St George's Place, Glasgow, G2 1BS (Tel 041-332
4101) Senior Libn: Mr Kenneth F. Wilkins BA, ALA.
6 RSAMD Board of Governors. **8** Music & drama.
9 Choral sets & orchestral parts. **10** BLL; NLS.
11 Yes, at Libn's discretion. **12** Term: Mon-Fri 9.30-
18.00 (Tues & Thurs 19.30, Fri 17.30); vac: Mon-Fri
9.30-17.00. **13** (a) 60,000; (b) 58; (c) 5,000 gramophone
records; 10 tapes. **14** £5,500. **15** (a) 5½ (b) 3 (c) 2.

STOW COLLEGE LIBRARY, Shamrock St, Glasgow, G4 9LD
(Tel 041-332 1786) Teacher Libn: Mr John MacLachlan ALA.
6 Strathclyde Regional Council. **8** Engineering (civil,
mechanical, production, electrical, inc TV & radio); chemistry;
physics; maths; biological sciences; management.
10 BLL; Aslib. **11** No. **12** Mon-Fri 10.00-17.00
(Mon-Wed 19.00, Sept-May). **13** (a) 16,000; (b) 110;
(c) 700 gramophone records; 50 tapes. **15** (a) 2 (c) 2.

UNIVERSITY OF STRATHCLYDE, ANDERSONIAN LIBRARY,
McCance Building, 16 Richmond St, Glasgow, G1 1XQ
(Tel 041-552 4156; Telex 77472 STRATHLIB GLW) Libn:
Mr C.G. Wood MA, FLA; Dep Libn: Miss M.I. Cooper BA,
FLA.
7 Fleck Lib, Thomas Graham Building, 295 Cathedral St,
G1 1XL; Weir Div Lib, James Weir Building, 75 Montrose St,
G1 1XJ; Law Lib, Stenhouse Building, 143 Cathedral St,
G4 0RQ; Short Loan Colln, Collins Building, Richmond St,
G1 1XQ; Scottish Hotel School Lib, 221 Crookston Rd,
G52 3NQ; Chesters Management Centre, Bearsden, G61 4AG.
8 General. **9** Anderson (c. 1,500 vols, private library of
founder, John Anderson, 17th-18th cent scientific & philosophical works); Young (c. 1,300 vols, 16th-18th cent alchemy
chemistry, pharmacy, printed catalogue); Laing (c. 500 vols,
17th-19th cent maths). **10** BLL. **11** Yes, for ref if
need can be shown. **12** Mon-Fri 9.30-17.00 (term 21.00),
Sat 9.30-12.00. **13** (a) 247,000; (b) 4,000; (c) c. 90,000
microtexts; university archives. **15** (a) 65 (b) 21 (c) 26.

GLASGOW—*continued*

WEIR PUMPS LTD LIBRARY, 149 Newlands Rd, Cathcart, Glasgow, G44 4EX (Tel 041-637 7141; Telex 77161/2) Libn: Miss A. Greig ALA.
8 Mechanical engineering, emphasis on fluid mechanics.
11 No.   **12** Mon-Fri 8.30-17.00 (Fri 16.30).
13 (a) 2,500;(b) 100.   **14** £4,500.   **15** (a) 2 (c) 1.

GLOUCESTER, Gloucestershire

GLOUCESTER CITY COLLEGE OF TECHNOLOGY LIBRARY, Brunswick Rd, Gloucester, GL1 1HU (Tel 0452-35881 ext 20) Libn: Miss P.M. Jones BSc, ALA; Asst Libn: Mr P.J. Gray BSc, ALA.
6 Gloucestershire CC.   **8** Building; engineering; hairdressing; public administration; management; science.
10 GTIS; SWRLB.   **11** Yes, for ref only.   **12** Term: Mon-Fri 9.00-20.30 (Fri 17.00); vac: Mon-Fri 9.00-16.45.
13 (a) 16,000;(b) 120.   **14** £6,000.   **15** (a) $4\frac{1}{3}$ (b) 2 (c) $2\frac{1}{3}$.

GLOUCESTERSHIRE COLLEGE OF EDUCATION LIBRARY, Oxstalls Lane, Gloucester, GL2 9HW (Tel 0452-26321) Tutor-Libn: Mrs E. Greenall; College Libn: Mrs P. Kestell.
6 Gloucester CC.   **8** Education; psychology; home economics; art; English literature; history.   **10** GTLS.   **11** No.
12 Term: Mon-Fri 8.45-20.00 (Fri 17.00), Sat 9.00-12.00; vac: Mon-Fri 9.00-16.00.   **13** (a) 47,000; (b) 250; (c) 100 gramophone records; film-strips; slide sets; charts.
14 £7,500.   **15** (a) 4 (b) 1 (c) 1.

GODALMING, Surrey

CHARTERHOUSE LIBRARY, Godalming, GU7 2DN (Tel 04868-6226) Libn: Mrs B. Freake BA.
8 General.   **9** Local colln; history of school & its pupils.
11 No, except for bona-fide researchers, by application to Libn.   **12** Daily during school terms.   **13** (a) c.11,000; (b) c.40; (c) archives.   **15** (b) $\frac{1}{2}$.

INSTITUTE OF OCEANOGRAPHIC SCIENCES LIBRARY, Wormley, Godalming, GU8 5UB (Tel 042 879-2122) Libn: Mr D.W. Privett MSc, AIInfSc; Dep: Mrs P. Simpson ALA.
6 Natural Environment Research Council.   **7** Member Libraries: Bidston (051-652 2396), Libn: Mrs K.D. Jones ALA; Taunton (0832-86211), Libn: Mrs C. Whiteway BA, ALA.
8 Oceanography & related disciplines.   **11** No, except to bona-fide researchers, by prior arrangement.   **12** Mon-Fri 9.00-17.00.   **13** (a) 4,500; (b) 760; (c) 45,000 pamphlets, extracts, offprints; 15,500 reports; 4,000 charts & atlases.
15 (a) $9\frac{1}{2}$ (b) 2 (c) 1.

GRAYS, Essex

THURROCK TECHNICAL COLLEGE LIBRARY, Woodview, Grays, RM16 4YR (Tel 0375-71621) Coll Libn: Ms Louise J.M. Lawrence BA, ALA; Dep Libn: Mr Donald F. Spade.
6 Essex CC.   **7** Aveley Annexe Lib, Back Lane, West Thurrock (040 26-3014), Libn: Mrs Gladys Viney.   **8** Engineering; domestic arts; fine arts; management; social sciences; education; science.   **10** Essex County Library, LASER.
11 No, except to students.   **12** Mon-Fri 9.00-19.45.
13 (a) 26,000; (b) 313; (c) 5,289 slides & transparencies; 29 tapes & cassettes; 34 filmstrips.   **14** £6,000.   **15** (a) 7 (b) 1 (c) 1.

GUILDFORD, Surrey

GUILDFORD COUNTY COLLEGE OF TECHNOLOGY LIBRARY, Stoke Park, Guildford, GU1 13Z (Tel 0483-73201) Tutor Libn: Miss G.M. Drew BA, ALA; Asst Libn: Miss V.H.S. Beresford ALA.
6 Surrey CC.   **7** Building Ref Lib, Dept of Building Surveying, Stoke Park, Guildford, GU1 13Z, Libn: Mrs W.M. Whitney.
8 Engineering (civil, electrical & mechanical); economic & commercial subjects; building; catering; social sciences.
10 SASLIC; Surrey Reference & Information Group; Surrey Librarians Group.   **11** Yes, for ref only.   **12** Term: Mon-Fri 9.00-19.15; vac: Mon-Fri 9.00-16.45.   **13** (a) 23,500; (b) 150; (c) 100 gramophone records; 200 tapes; 1,000 slides;

600 ohp transparencies; 20 filmstrips; 50 videotapes.
14 £7,000.   **15** (a) 4 (b) 1 (c) 2.

GUILDFORD INSTITUTE LIBRARY, Ward St, Guildford, GU1 4LH (Tel 0483-62142)
8 Current fiction & biography.   **11** No.   **12** 11.00-13.30, 15.00-19.00.   **13** (a) 8,000; (b) 10.   **14** £200.

SURREY ARCHAEOLOGICAL SOCIETY LIBRARY, Castle Arch, Guildford GU1 3SX (Tel 0483-32454) Hon Libn: Dr R.A. Christophers MA, PhD, FLA.
8 Archaeology; Surrey   **9** Topographical drawings; Speed's maps of Surrey; miscellaneous collns of transcripts towards county & parish histories.   **11** Yes, on prior application, with suitable recommendations.   **12** Mon-Sat 9.00-17.00.
13 (a) c.9,000; (b) c.100; (c) maps; prints; postcards; transcripts; lantern slides; ephemera.   **14** £300.   **15** (c) 1.

UNIVERSITY OF SURREY LIBRARY, Guildford, GU2 5XH (Tel 0483-71281; Telex 85331) Univ Libn: Mr R.F. Eatwell MA, FLA; Dep Libn: Miss J. Gibson BA, DipLib.
6 U of S Council.   **8** Science; technology; social sciences.
10 S3RB; SASLIC.   **11** Yes, for ref only.   **12** Term: Mon-Fri 9.00-22.00, Sat 9.00-18.00, Sun 14.00-18.00; vac: Mon-Fri 9.00-17.00.   **13** (a) 160,000; (b) 2,600; (c) gramophone records; microtexts; film loops; tape slide programmes.
14 £126,000.   **15** (a) 33 (b) 13 (c) 10.

HAILSHAM, East Sussex

ROYAL GREENWICH OBSERVATORY LIBRARY, Herstmonceux Castle, Hailsham, BN27 1RP (Tel 032-181 3171; Telex 87451) Libn: Miss J.E. Perry; Clerical Officer: Mrs S.A. Hartley.
6 Science Research Council.   **7** Her Majesty's Nautical Almanac Office, Clerical Officer: Mrs V. Bacon.   **8** Astronomy.   **11** No.   **13** (a) 21,000; (b) 137.   **15** (a) $1\frac{1}{2}$ (b) $\frac{1}{2}$.

HALIFAX, West Yorkshire

PERCIVAL WHITLEY COLLEGE OF FURTHER EDUCATION LIBRARY, Francis St, Halifax, HX1 3UZ (Tel 0422-58221 ext 15) Tutor-Libn: Mr K.R. Tomlinson ALA; Dep Miss M. Coates ALA.
6 Calderdale MBC.   **8** Art; building; business; engineering; household studies; science; maths & computing; social services; sociology; education; European languages, literature & history; geography.   **9** Complete BSI.   **10** HALDIS.
11 Yes, by prior arrangement.   **12** Term: Mon-Fri 9.00-20.30 (Fri 19.00); vac: 9.00-17.00.   **13** (a) 34,000; (b) 250; (c) 25,000 slides; 600 records; 200 tapes; 50 reels microfilm; 150 teaching-machine programmes; 300 charts.
14 £4,000.   **15** (a) 5 (c) 3.

HAMILTON, Lanarkshire

BELL COLLEGE OF TECHNOLOGY LIBRARY, Almada St, Hamilton, ML3 OJB (Tel 06982-29221 ext 242) Coll Libn: D.W. Bissett ALA, DBEA; Dep Libn: R.A. Alexander ALA.
6 Strathclyde Regional Council.   **8** Social sciences; maths; physics; chemistry; biology; health administration; mechanical & electrical engineering; metallurgy; building; computer science; literature.   **9** Sir Andrew McCance Colln; government & international agency publications; BSI (7,000).   **11** Yes, by arrangement with Coll Libn.   **12** Term: Mon-Thurs 9.00-19.00 (may be extended to 21.00), Fri 9.00-16.30; vac: Mon-Fri 9.00-17.00 (Fri 16.30).   **13** (a) 26,000; (b) 1,400; (c) 2,500 government publications; 700 gramophone records; 100 cassettes; 200 microforms.   **14** £35,000.   **15** (a) 13 (b) 5 (c) 3.

HAMILTON COLLEGE OF EDUCATION LIBRARY, Bothwell Rd, Hamilton, ML3 OBD (Tel 06982-23241) Principal Libn: Mrs Dorothy H. McLelland MA, FLA.
8 Education; psychology.   **10** SCE, COPAEP.   **11** No.
12 Term: Mon-Fri 9.00-20.00 (Fri 17.00); vac: Mon-Fri 9.00-17.00.   **13** (a) 38,500; (b) 282; (c) illustrations; film-strips; gramophone records; music-cassettes; learning kits; microtexts.   **15** (a) 8 (b) 3 (c) 4.

CODE: 1 Name of Library. **2** Address. **3** Telephone & Telex. **4** Officer in charge. **5** Deputy. **6** Governing body.
7 Branches. **8** Main Subjects. **9** Special Collections. **10** Co-operative Schemes. **11** Open to public? **12** Hours.
13 Stock: (a) books (b) periodicals (c) other. **14** Finance. **15** Staff: (a) non-manual (b) graduate (c) chartered librarians.

HARLOW, Essex

HARLOW TECHNICAL COLLEGE LIBRARY, College Gate,
The High, Harlow, CM20 1LT (Tel 0279-20131 ext 47) Libn:
Ms Moira Jones ALA; Asst Libn: Mr Robert Hill BA, ALA.
6 Essex CC. **8** Engineering (mechanical & electrical);
management; art; journalism; maths; science; catering; education; law; languages; literature; sociology; psychology; commerce. **9** Engineering; maths; science; management; journalism; catering. **10** Essex interloan system. **11** Yes.
12 Term: Mon-Fri 8.45-20.00; vac: Mon-Fri 9.00-17.00.
13 (a) 30,000; (b) 220; (c) 3000 illustrations; newspaper cuttings; some audio-visual materials. **14** £6,000. **15** (a)
4 (b) 2 (c) 3.

SMITH & NEPHEW RESEARCH LTD LIBRARY, Gilston Park,
Harlow, CM20 2RQ (Tel 0279-26751; Telex 81327) Head of
Inf Dept: T. Williams.
8 Pharmacology; biochemistry; ophthalmics; toxicology;
microbiology; organic chemistry; biomedical engineering;
polymers; pressure-sensitive adhesives; wound dressings;
surgical equipment. **11** No. **12** 9.00-17.00. **13** (a)
7,000; (b) 180. **15** (a) 6 (b) 2.

STANDARD TELECOMMUNICATION LABORATORIES, TECH-
NICAL LIBRARY, London Rd, Harlow, CM17 9NA (Tel 0279-
29531; Telex 81151) Libn: Mr G. Allison; Chief Technical Inf
Officer: Mr D. Stanley CEng, MIEE, MIInfSc.
7 STC central library (c. 20 library service points); shares
central library responsibilities for International Telephone
and Telegraph Corporation Europe Companies (c. 25
libraries). **8** Telecommunications; electronic engineering;
related subjects. **10** BLL; Aslib; BNBC; HERTIS; ETCLS.
11 No. **12** Mon-Fri 8.45-17.00. **13** (a) 20,000; (b)
550; (c) 600 reports; 100 translations; 1,000 slides.
14 £20,500. **15** (a) 11 (b) 2.

HARWELL, Oxfordshire

ATOMIC ENERGY RESEARCH ESTABLISHMENT LIBRARY,
Harwell, OX11 ORB (Tel 0235-4141; Telex 83135) Libn: Mr
C. W. J. Wilson FLA.
6 UKAEA. **8** Nuclear physics; reactor science & technology; metallurgy; ceramics & materials; non-destructive
testing; engineering; radiochemistry; inorganic chemistry;
analytical chemistry; isotope technology; chemical engineering; electronics; physics; health physics; computers; particle
accelerators; hazardous materials. **9** Nuclear science &
technology; scientific & technical reports. **10** BLL.
11 No. **12** Mon-Fri 8.30-17.30 (Fri 16.00). **13** (a)
55,000; (b) 2,000; (c) 290,000 reports; 190,000 microcards &
microfiches. **15** (a) 31 (c) 6.

HATFIELD, Hertfordshire

HATFIELD POLYTECHNIC LIBRARY, PO Box 110, Hatfield,
AL10 9AD (Tel 07072-68100; Telex 262413) County Technical
Libn: D. E. Bagley FLA; Dep County Technical Libn: N. F.
McLean BA, DipEd, DipLib.
6 Hertfordshire CC, Education Dept. **8** Science; engineering; management; social sciences; humanities; education.
9 Aeronautical engineering; Far Eastern history (China,
Japan, Indo-China); biology. **10** HERTIS **11** Yes, for
ref only. **12** Term: Mon-Fri 8.45-21.50, Sat 9.30-12.30;
vac: Mon-Fri 9.00-17.00. **13** (a) 100,000; (b) 1,600; (c)
3,000 audio records; several thousand microforms.
14 £90,000. **15** (a) 55 (b) 16 (c) 27.

HAWARDEN, Clwyd

ST DEINIOL'S (RESIDENTIAL) LIBRARY, Hawarden, Deeside,
CH5 3DF (Tel 0244-532350) Warden & Libn: Dr Raymond
Foster PhD, ThD; Sub-Warden: Mr Robert P. Symonds MA.
6 Trustees of St Deiniol's Library. **8** Theology; history;

literature; philosophy; classics. **9** 19th-cent studies.
10 BLL. **11** Yes, by prior arrangement, (testimonial required). **12** Every day: 9.00-22.00. **13** (a) 100,000; (b)
30; (c) Gladstone letters; Archbishop Green archives.
14 £2,000. **15** (a) 2 (b) 2.

HEBBURN, Tyne and Wear

HEBBURN TECHNICAL COLLEGE LIBRARY, Mill Lane,
Hebburn, NE31 2ER (Tel 0632-832741) Libn: Mrs J. Dmytriw
ALA; Lib Asst: Mrs P. Keer.
6 South Tyneside BC. **8** Mechanical & electrical engineering; shipbuilding; mining; fabrication & welding; business &
general. **10** NRLB. **11** Yes, for ref only. **12** Term:
Mon-Fri 9.00-19.00 (Fri 16.30); vac: by arrangement.
13 (a) 15,000; (b) 200; (c) gramophone records; filmstrips.
14 £3,500. **15** (a) 2 (c) 1.

HEREFORD, Hereford and Worcester

HEREFORD CATHEDRAL LIBRARY, Hereford, HR1 2NG
(Tel 0432-3537) Chapter Libn: Rev Canon J. M. Irvine MA;
Hon Libns: Mr F. C. Morgan MA, FSA, FLA; Ms Penelope E.
Morgan FRHistS, FLA.
6 Dean & Chapter. **8** Theological & religious history;
music, inc mss of 17th-20th cents; history. **9** 30,000
archives; 227 mss vols (from c. 800); 1,220 chained printed
books & c. 9,000 other printed books inc 56 incunabula; 800
negatives & 700 lantern slides relating to cathedral.
11 Yes, to chained library. Access to other books by prior
arrangement with Hon Libns. **12** Chained library Easter-
Sept: 10.30-12.30, 14.00-16.00; other times by appointment.
13 (a) c. 11,000; (c) 30,000 archives. **14** £50. **15** (b) 1
(c) 2.

HEREFORD COLLEGE OF EDUCATION LIBRARY, College
Rd, Hereford, HR1 1EB (Tel 0432-65725) Tutor-Libn: Miss
K. J. Eggleston MA, ALA; Asst Libn: Miss S. R. Tomkins BA,
ALA.
8 Education; English; French; history; geography; art; music;
science; maths. **10** BLL; WMRLB. **11** Yes. **12** Term:
Mon-Fri 9.00-21.15, Sat 12.30-16.30, Sun 13.30-16.30,
17.30-21.15; vac: Mon-Fri 9.00-17.00. **13** (c) records;
cassettes; filmstrips; slides; microfilm; microfiche; micro-
print; newspaper cuttings; tapes. **14** £8,000. **15** (a) 4
(b) 2 (c) 2.

HEREFORDSHIRE TECHNICAL COLLEGE LIBRARY, Aylestone Hill, Hereford, HR1 1LS (Tel 0432-67311) Tutor-Libn:
C. R. Randall.
10 WESLINK; WATL. **11** Yes. **12** Term: 9.00-20.00;
vac: 9.00-12.30. **13** (a) 16,000; (b) 200; (c) records;
slides & filmstrips; videotapes etc. **15** (a) 4⅔ (b) 2 (c) 2.

WOOLHOPE NATURALISTS' FIELD CLUB LIBRARY, Hereford Library, Broad St, Hereford, HR4 9AU (Tel 0432-68645)
Hon Libn: Mr B. J. Whitehouse ALA.
8 Archaeology; antiquities; folklore; geology; natural history;
genealogy. **9** Marshall Bequests; books & graphic material on archaeology. **11** Yes, in Hereford Ref Library.
12 As for Hereford Ref Library. **13** (a) 3,500; (b) 35.

HERTFORD, Hertfordshire

MALAYSIAN RUBBER PRODUCERS' RESEARCH ASSOCI-
ATION LIBRARY, Brickendonbury, Hertford, SG13 8NP (Tel
0992-54966) Manager, Inf Systems: Mr Kevin P. Jones FLA,
AlInfSc; Libn: Miss Linda Simpson MA, DipLib.
6 Malaysian Rubber Research & Development Board.
8 Natural rubber: science & technology. **10** HERTIS.
11 Yes, by prior appointment only. **12** Mon-Fri 9.00-
17.00. **13** (a) 10,000; (b) 250; (c) 25,000 indexed reports.
15 (a) 7 (b) 2 (c) 1

HIGH WYCOMBE, Buckinghamshire

G. D. SEARLE AND CO LTD LIBRARY, Lane End Rd, High Wycombe, HP12 4HL (Tel 0494-21124; Telex 83205) Libn: Mrs P. J. Cockram ALA.
8 Medicine; biochemistry; microbiology.   11 No.
12 9.00-17.30.   13 (a) 4,000; (b) 500.   15 (a) 7 (b) 2 (c) 1.

TIMBER RESEARCH AND DEVELOPMENT ASSOCIATION LIBRARY, Hughenden Valley, High Wycombe, HP14 4ND (Tel 024024-3091) Chief Inf Officer: Mr R. T. Allcorn BSc, AIInfSc; Libn: Mrs Anne E. Peters ALA.
8 Timber utilization; timber construction; forestry; trees.
10 BLL; inter-library loans.   11 Yes, for ref only.
12 Mon-Fri 9.15-13.00, 13.45-17.15 (Fri 17.00).   13 (a) 10,000; (b) 196; (c) 3,000 colour transparencies; 30,000 pamphlets, reports etc; 38 16 mm films.   14 £4,000.
15 (a) 4 (b) 1 (c) 1.

HITCHIN, Hertfordshire

HITCHIN COLLEGE LIBRARY, Cambridge Rd, Hitchin, SG4 0JD (Tel 0462-2351) Libn: Mr P. Ryan BSc, ALA, AIInfSc; Dep: Mrs E. Blunden.
6 Hertfordshire CC.   8 Economics; management; retail distribution.   10 HERTIS.   11 Yes, with prior permission.   12 Term: Mon-Fri 8.45-20.00 (Fri 17.00); vac: Mon-Fri 9.00-17.00.   13 (a) 20,000; (b) 160; (c) video tapes; slides; filmstrips.   14 c. £3,000.

HORNCHURCH, Essex

HAVERING TECHNICAL COLLEGE LIBRARY, 42 Ardleigh Green Rd, Hornchurch, RM11 2LL (Tel 04024-55011) Tutor-Libn: Mr Michael J. Rees BA, CertEd, ALA; Asst Libn: Mr David Hare BSc.
6 London Borough of Havering.   8 Mechanical, electrical & automobile engineering; electronics; science; art; design; hairdressing; display; social work; teacher education; social sciences; modern languages; child care; nursery nursing; management; secretarial work; accountancy; banking; law; computers; maths; telecommunications.   11 No.
12 Term: Mon-Thurs 9.00-20.00, Fri 9.00-17.00.
13 (a) 25,000; (b) 175; (c) 4,000 pamphlets; 750 wallcharts; 125 gramophone records; 50 8mm film loops; 475 filmstrips & slides; 13 learning programmes; 2 16 mm films; 50 multi-media kits; 200 ohp transparencies; 150 sound tapes; 125 video tapes; 21 microfilms; c. 75,000 Resource Bank paper multiples.   14 £4,500.   15 (a) 3½ (b) 2 (c) 1.

HUDDERSFIELD, West Yorkshire

HUDDERSFIELD POLYTECHNIC LIBRARY, Queensgate, Huddersfield, HD1 3DH (Tel 0484-30501) Acting Libn: Mr N. Kerrod MA, ALA.
6 Huddersfield Polytechnic Governors.   7 College of Education (Technical) Lib, Holly Bank Rd, Huddersfield (0484-25611) Libn: Miss M. Rooker, BA, ALA; Education Lib, New St, Huddersfield (0484-30501) Libn: Mr R. W. H. B. Pugsley MA.   8 General.   9 G. H. Wood colln (19th cent social & monetary problems)   11 Yes, for ref only.   12 Term: Mon-Thurs 9.00-21.45, Fri 9.00-21.00, Sat 9.00-12.00; vac: Mon-Fri 9.00-17.30.   13 (a) 150,000; (b) 1,500; (c) micro-texts; gramophone records.   14 £136,000.   15 (a) 30 (b) 10 (c) 10.

HULL, see Kingston-upon-Hull

HUNTINGDON, Cambridgeshire

HUNTINGDON TECHNICAL COLLEGE LIBRARY, California Rd, Huntingdon, PE18 7BL (Tel 0480-52346) Libn: Ms Gillian Mead MA, DipLib; Asst Libn: Ms Janice Benson City & Guilds Lib Asst Cert.
6 Cambridgeshire CC.   8 General.   10 EMRLB.
11 Yes.   12 9.00-17.00 (term 19.30, 2 eves per week).
13 (a) 11,000; (b) 99; (c) filmstrips; slides; tape cassettes; records; transparencies.   14 £3,000.

ILKESTON, Derbyshire

SOUTH EAST DERBYSHIRE COLLEGE, WHITFIELD SCORER LIBRARY, Field Rd, Ilkeston, DE7 5RS (Tel 06072-4212) Tutor-Libn: Mr A. J. Aldous FLA.
6 Derbyshire CC.   7 Heanor B Lib, Ilkeston Rd, Heanor (077 37-2482), Tutor-Libn: Mr R. Brown FLA.   8 General; business; mechanical, foundry, automobile, electrical engineering; coal mining; construction.   9 Derbyshire County Library coal mining colln at Heanor branch.   11 Yes.
12 Term: Mon-Thurs 8.50-19.45, Fri 8.45-17.00.
13 (a) 18,000; (b) 200; (c) 100 gramophone records.
14 £2,700.   15 (a) 2½ (c) 1.

INVERNESS, Invernessshire

HIGHLANDS AND ISLANDS DEVELOPMENT BOARD LIBRARY, Bridge House, 27 Bank St, Inverness, IV1 1QR (Tel 0463-34171 ext 290; Telex 75267) Libn: Mr R. J. Ardern BSc, MA, ALA.
8 Rural, regional & industrial development; fisheries; land use; tourism; transport.   9 Area index to bookstock available for identifying material on different parts of the highlands & islands.   11 Yes, researchers admitted, by appointment, for ref only.   12 Mon-Fri 9.00-17.30 (Fri 17.00).   13 (a) 4,500; (b) 240.   15 (a) 1 (b) 1 (c) 1.

IPSWICH, Suffolk

FISONS LTD, FERTILIZER DIVISION LIBRARY, Levington Research Station, Levington, Ipswich, IP10 0LU (Tel 0473-76911; Telex 91840) Head of Lib Services: Mr C. J. Cameron BA.
8 Agriculture; inorganic chemistry; chemical engineering.
10 HERTIS; Aslib.   11 No.   12 Mon-Fri 9.00-17.15.
13 (a) 15,000; (b) 250.   15 (a) 10 (b) 4.

IPSWICH CIVIC COLLEGE LIBRARY, Rope Walk, Ipswich, IP4 1LT (Tel 0473-55885) Tutor-Libn: Mr R. T. M. Wilson BA, DipLib, ALA; Libn: Mr A. H. Teece Dip LB, ALA.
6 Suffolk CC.   8 General.   10 EMRLB.   11 Yes, for ref only.   12 Term: Mon-Fri 9.00-21.00; vac: Mon-Fri 9.00-17.00.   13 (a) 40,000; (b) 380.   15 (a) 8 (b) 3 (c) 3.

KEELE, Staffordshire

University of Keele

UNIVERSITY LIBRARY, Keele, ST5 5BG (Tel 078 271-371; Telex 36113) Libn: S. O. Stewart MA, ALA; Dep: P. G. Tudor MA.
8 Humanities; social sciences; experimental science.
9 Turner colln (history of mathematics & allied subjects); William Blake; Izaak Walton; private presses; Sneyd, Wedgwood & Spode papers; Arnold Bennett mss.
10 BLL; LINOSCO; SKELLEM.   11 Yes, for ref only, on application.   12 Term: 9.00-22.00; vac: 9.30-17.00.
13 (a) 359,000; (b) 2,000; (c) microforms; slides; engravings.   15 (a) 50 (b) 17 (c) 14.

INSTITUTE OF EDUCATION LIBRARY, Keele, ST5 5BG (Tel 078-271 371 ext 206) Tutor-Libn: Mr A. K. D. Campbell MA, FLA; Dep: Mrs M. G. Pritchard MA.
8 Education; sociology; psychology.   9 School counselling (c. 1,000 vols).   10 LISE; LINOSCO.   11 Yes, for ref only.   12 Mon-Fri 9.30-17.00 (21.00, 3 eves per week), Sat 9.30-12.00.   13 (a) 26,000; (b) 2,500.
14 £3,500.   15 (a) 4 (b) 2 (c) 1.

KIDDERMINSTER, Hereford and Worcester

BRITISH CARPET INDUSTRY TECHNICAL ASSOCIATION LIBRARY, Aykroyd House, Hoo Rd, Kidderminster, DY10 1NB (Tel 0562-4053/61684; Telex 338526)
6 Federation of British Carpet Manufacturers & Tufted Carpets Manufacturers Association.   8 Carpets.
9 Carpet technology & patents.   11 No, except by special arrangement.   12 9.00-17.15.   13 (a) 243; (b) 41; (c) patents, mainly British, US & Canadian.   15 (a) ½.

CODE: **1** Name of Library. **2** Address. **3** Telephone & Telex. **4** Officer in charge. **5** Deputy. **6** Governing body.
7 Branches. **8** Main Subjects. **9** Special Collections. **10** Co-operative Schemes. **11** Open to public? **12** Hours.
13 Stock: (a) books (b) periodicals (c) other. **14** Finance. **15** Staff: (a) non-manual (b) graduate (c) chartered librarians.

KIDDERMINSTER, Hereford and Worcester—*continued*

COLLEGE OF FURTHER EDUCATION LIBRARY, Hoo Rd,
Kidderminster,DY10 1LX (Tel 0562-66311) Senior Libn:
Mr W.W. Ovens; Tutor-Libn: Mrs J.A. Edwards ALA.
6 Hereford & Worcester CC. **8** Textiles, especially carpets. **10** WATL. **11** Yes. **12** Mon-Fri 9.00-20.00.
13 (a) 14, 367; (b) 183; (c) 330 records; several thousand
filmstrips & slides. **15** (a) 4 (b) 1 (c) 2.

KINCARDINE, Clackmannanshire

SCOTTISH POLICE COLLEGE LIBRARY, Tulliallan Castle
Kincardine, Alloa, FK10 4BE (Tel 0259-30333) Libn: Miss
M.E.Cook FLA.
6 Scottish Home & Health Dept. **8** Police administration;
criminology; law; central & local government; politics;
sociology; management; history; geography; sport; biography;
computer science; liberal arts. **9** Charles Reith Bequest
Colln (police administration & history). **10** NLS, interlibrary loans. **11** No, except by special permission.
12 Never closes. **13** (a) c. 20, 000 (inc pamphlets); (b)
c. 100; (c) 67 films; a media resources centre; closed circuit
television; TV films on crowd control. **14** £3, 500.
15 (a) 5 (c) 1.

KINGSTON UPON HULL, Humberside

**The following three colleges will merge with the Kingston
upon Hull Colleges of Commerce & of Technology, & the
Nautical College, in Sept 1976, to form the Hull College of
Higher Education & the Hull College of Further Education.**

ENDSLEIGH COLLEGE OF EDUCATION LIBRARY, Inglemire Av, Hull HU6 7LJ (Tel 0482-42157) Tutor-Libn: Miss
P.B.Atkinson.
8 General; Primary, Middle, Secondary teaching.
9 Postgate colln (recusancy). **11** No. **12** Mon-Fri
9.00-21,00, Sat 9.00-12.00. **13** (a) c.60, 000; (b) 360;
(c) gramophone records; microtexts; 3, 845 audio-visual
aids.

KINGSTON UPON HULL COLLEGE OF EDUCATION
LIBRARY, Cottingham Rd, Hull, HU6 7RT (Tel 0482-41451)
Senior Tutor-Libn: Mr David J. Brown BA, ALA; Tutor-Libn: Miss P.Fulcher ALA.
6 College Governors. **8** Education; general. **9** Local
colln on Hull & Humberside; school practice library of
children's books; audio-visual media. **10** BLL; HULTIS.
11 Yes. **12** Term: Mon-Fri 9.00-21.00; vac: Mon-Fri 9.00-12.00, 13.00-17.00. **13** (a) 56, 000; (b) 300.
14 £8, 000. **15** (a) 7 (b) 1 (c) 3.

REGIONAL COLLEGE OF ART LIBRARY, Wilberforce Dr,
Hull HU1 3DQ (Tel 0482-224311) Tutor-Libn: Mr G.R.
Bullock BA, ALA.
6 Humberside CC. **7** School of Architecture Lib,
Brunswick Ave, Hull (0482-25938), Asst Libn: Miss A.
Phillipson ALA. **8** Art & design; architecture.
10 HULTIS. **11** Yes, for ref only. **12** Term: Mon-Thurs: 9.00-20.45, Fri 9.00-19.00; vac: Mon-Fri 9.00-17.00. **13** c.16, 000; (b) c, 200. **15** (a) 3½ (b) 1
(c) 2.

University of Hull

BRYNMOR JONES LIBRARY, Hull, HU6 7RX (Tel 0482-46311; Telex 52530) Libn: Dr P.A. Larkin CBE, MA,
DLitt, FRSL; Dep: Miss B.E. Moon MA, FLA.
7 Social Sciences Faculty Lib, Map Room, Libn: Miss
A.M. Ferrar BSc. **8** General; arts; law; social sciences;
science. **9** Labour history; contemporary papers of
political & social interest; South-East Asia colln.
10 BMS 1860-64. **11** Yes, at discretion of Libn.
12 Term: Mon-Fri 9.00-22.00, Sat 9.00-13.00; vac:
Mon-Fri 9.00-17.30, Sat 9.00-13.00. **13** (a) 474, 535;

(b) 6, 416; (c) archives; mss; maps; gramophone records;
microtexts; audio-visual material; slides. **14** £183, 500.
15 (a) 70 (b) 20 (c) 13.

INSTITUTE OF EDUCATION LIBRARY, Cottingham Rd,
Hull, HU6 7RX (Tel 0482-46311; Telex 52530) Libn: Mr
C.B. Freeman MA, FLA; Asst Libn: Mr J. F. Hooton BA,
FLA.
8 Education; psychology; sociology; general; school books.
9 History of education (source materials), inc children's
books (mostly textbooks). **10** BLL; UCISE; HULTIS.
11 Yes, for ref only. **12** Mon-Fri 9.00-17.30 (Tues-Thurs 19.30), Sat 9.00-12.30. **13** (a) 49, 000; (b) 250;
(c) 65 microfilms; microfiches; tape cassettes.
14 £7, 000. **15** (a) 7 (b) 3 (c) 3.

LAMPETER, Dyfed

SAINT DAVID'S UNIVERSITY COLLEGE LIBRARY, Lampeter, SA48 7ED (Tel 0570-422351) Libn in Charge: Mr
R.C. Rider MA, FLA; Asst Libn: Mr D.S.I. Reynolds BA,
ALA.
7 Old Library (pre-1821 material). **8** General; classics;
English; French; German; geography; history; philosophy;
theology; Welsh. **9** Tracts colln (828 vols containing
11, 395 items, mostly 17th-18th cent); mss colln (inc 15th
cent books of hours); incunabula (over 60, from most important centres of early printing); early Welsh periodicals,
Bibles, prayerbooks, hymnals, catechisms & ballads.
10 WRLS. **11** Yes, for ref only. **12** Term: Mon-Fri
9.00-22.00, Sat 9.00-13.00, 14.00-17.00, vac: Mon-Fri 9.00-17.00, Sat 9.00-12.00 (closed Sat in long vac). **13** (a)
c.90, 000; (b) c.450. **14** c. £22, 700. **15** (a) 9 (b) 4 (c) 4.

LANCASTER, Lancashire

UNIVERSITY OF LANCASTER LIBRARY, Bailrigg, Lancaster,
LA1 4YH (Tel 0524-65201; Telex 65111 (Univlib Lancstr))
Univ Libn: Mr A.Graham Mackenzie MA, ALA; Dep Libns:
Mr Michael Argles MA, ALA; Dr J.S. Andrews MA, PhD,
ALA.
6 Council of the University. **8** General. **9** Arabic &
Islamic Colln; Comenius Library (central & South-east
Europe); Fell & Rock Climbing Club of English Lake District;
Ford Railway colln; Hans Ferdinand Redlich colln (Music);
Quaker colln. **10** BLL; NWRLB. **11** Yes, by application
to Libn. **12** Term: Mon-Fri 8.45-22.00, Sat 9.00-17.00;
vac: Mon-Fri 8.45-17.15. **13** (a) 270, 000; (b) 3, 200; (c)
30, 000 official publications; 5, 500 music scores; 31, 000
(vol equivalents) microtexts; media resources centre.
14 £150, 000. **15** (a) 72 (b) 27 (c) 28.

LEATHERHEAD, Surrey

CENTRAL ELECTRICITY GENERATING BOARD RESEARCH
LABORATORIES LIBRARY, Kelvin Ave, Leatherhead, KT22
7SE (Tel 03723-74488 ext 248; Telex 917338) Inf. Officer/
Libn: Mr David Baynes ALA.
8 Planning, generation, transmission & environmental impact of electrical power. **10** SASLIC. **11** No, except
in exceptional cases. **12** 8.30-17.00. **13** (b) 500; (c)
trade literature; microforms; technical reports; patents.
15 (a) 9 (b) 2 (c) 4.

LEATHERHEAD FOOD RESEARCH ASSOCIATION LIBRARY,
Randalls Rd, Leatherhead (Tel 03723-76761; Telex 929846)
Technical Libn: Mr G.R. Ford ALA; Asst Libn: Miss S.Cavey.
6 Research Association Council comprising member firms.
8 Food science; nutrition; catering; hygiene; pollution; quality
control; microbiology; analytical chemistry; polymer science.
10 SASLIC. **11** No. **12** 8.45-17.00. **13** (a) 5,000;
(b) 500; (c) 12, 000 pamphlets & reprints. **14** c. £12, 000.
15 (a) 5 (c) 2.

LEATHERHEAD, Surrey—*continued*

PIRA INFORMATION GROUP AND LIBRARY, Randalls Rd, Leatherhead, KT22 7RU (Tel 03723-76161; Telex 929810) Inf Group Head: Mrs M. Y. Gates BSc, MIInfSc.
8 Papermaking; printing; packaging. **11** No. **12** Mon-Fri 8. 45-17. 00. **13** (a) 6, 000; (b) 600; (c) 30, 000 reports, standards, translations, pamphlets. **15** (a) 20 (b) 10 (c) 1.

LEEDS, West Yorkshire

CITY OF LEEDS AND CARNEGIE COLLEGE LIBRARY, (will merge with Leeds Polytechnic, Sept 1976), Beckett Park, Leeds, LS6 3QS (Tel 0532-759061) Libn: Mr Robin B. Bateman; Tutor-Libn: Ms Joan Newiss.
6 Local education authority. **8** Education; child psychology; sociology; physical education; movement studies.
9 Carnegie historical colln (books on physical education, sport, recreation & health education published before 1946).
11 Yes, for teachers only. **12** Mon-Fri 8. 45-21. 00, Sat 9. 30-12. 30. **13** (a) 81, 600; (b) 380; (c) 1, 580 gramophone records; 2, 710 filmstrips. **14** £18, 000.

LEEDS LIBRARY, 19 Commercial St, Leeds, LS1 6AL (Tel 0532-453071) Libn: Mr Robert Stuart; Dep: Mrs B. Knight.
6 Trustees & Committee. **8** Biography; history; fiction; humanities. **9** 19th cent fiction; 19th cent periodicals; Wilson colln (Yorkshire & Lancashire pedigrees). **11** No.
12 Mon-Fri 9. 00-17. 30. **13** (a) c. 200, 000; (b) 50.
14 £2, 300.

Leeds Polytechnic (will merge with James Graham College of Education and City of Leeds and Carnegie College, Sept 1976)

POLYTECHNIC LIBRARY, Calverley St, Leeds, LS1 3HE (Tel 0532-41101) Libn: Mr J. H. Flint FLA; Dep Libn: Mr A. M. Clay FLA.
7 Architecture Lib, Claypit Lane, Leeds 2; Town Planning Lib, St Pauls St, Leeds. **8** Management; law; languages; accountancy; social sciences; education; home economics; art & design; electrical & mechanical engineering; computing; building; architecture; town planning; speech therapy; dietetics nursing. **9** 35mm slide colln (mainly art); EDC. **11** Yes, for ref, on application to Libn: **12** Term: 9. 00-21. 00; vac: 9. 00-17. 00.
13 (a) 150, 000; (b) 1, 800; (c) 52, 000 slides; 900 tapes; 350 microtexts. **14** £85, 290. **15** (a) 29 (b) 11 (c) 11.

DEPARTMENT OF LIBRARIANSHIP LIBRARY, 28 Park Pl, Leeds, LS1 2SY (Tel 0532-456696) Libn: Mr R. J. Prytherch MA, ALA.
8 Librarianship; information science; historical bibliography. **11** Yes. **12** Mon-Fri 9. 00-17. 00. **13** (a) 15, 000; (b) 275; (c) 1, 500 slides; 2, 000 microtexts.
14 £7, 250. **15** (a) 5 (b) 2 (c) 4.

LEEDS UNIVERSITY LIBRARY, Leeds, LS2 9JT (Tel 0532-31751) Univ Libn & Keeper of Brotherton Colln: Mr D. Cox BA, ALA; Dep Libn: Mr A. Davies BA, ALA.
7 Medical Lib, Sub-Libn in charge: Miss A. M. Kameen, BSc, ALA; Institute of Education Lib (0532-31751 ext 6102) Sub-Libn in charge: Mr J. R. V. Johnson MA, FLA; Law Lib, Asst Libn in charge: Mr J. M. Porter BA, MA. Clothworkers' Lib (Textiles), Lib Asst in charge: Mrs V. Whitehead ALA.
8 Arts; economics & social studies; law; science; applied science; medicine & dentistry. **9** Brotherton colln (rare books & mss of all periods, especially English 17th & 18th cent); Icelandic; Anglo-French. **10** BLL; YHJLS; LISE.
11 Yes, on application to Libn. **13** (a) 1, 165, 756 (inc pamphlets); (b) 8, 729; (c) maps; 109, 767 microforms; mss; gramophone records; tapes; videotapes. **14** £280, 000.
15 (a) 113 (b) 53 (c) 38.

THORESBY SOCIETY LIBRARY, Claremont, 23 Clarendon Rd, Leeds, LS2 9NZ. Hon Libn: Mrs J. Mary D. Forster.
8 History of Leeds & district. **11** Limited access for ref only. **12** Tues & Thurs 10. 00-14. 00. **13** (c) pictures; maps; plans; slides.

TRINITY AND ALL SAINTS' COLLEGES LIBRARY, Brownberrie Lane, Horsforth, Leeds, LS18 5HD (Tel 070 133-4341) Res Libn: Ms Marlene A. Godfrey.

6 Affiliated with Leeds University. **8** Education; planning & administration; public media; communication; arts & media; drama; economics; English; fine arts; French; geography; history; home economics; maths; music; physical education; psychology; science; sociology; Spanish; theology.
9 Yorkshire colln (inc older items & maps); reading centre; multi-media colln in all subjects. **11** Yes. **12** Term: Mon-Fri 9. 15-21. 00; Sat 10. 00-17. 00; Sun 14. 00-21. 00; vac: Mon-Fri 9. 00-17. 00. **13** (a) 80, 000; (b) 300; (c) 2, 000 filmstrips; gramophone records; tapes; videotapes; microforms; kits; posters; slides. **14** £10, 000. **15** (a) 10 (b) 3 (c) 3.

WOOL TEXTILE INDUSTRIES RESEARCH ASSOCIATION LIBRARY, Headingley Lane, Leeds, LS6 1BW (Tel 0532-759071; Telex 557189) Head of Inf Services: G. A. Feather FIL, LTI; Libn: Mrs M. E. Brain BA.
8 Wool textiles. **11** Yes, for approved research students only. **12** Mon-Fri 8. 30-17. 15. **13** (a) 4, 500; (b) 160. **15** (a) 4 (b) 1.

YORKSHIRE ARCHAEOLOGICAL SOCIETY LIBRARY, Claremont, Clarendon Rd, Leeds, LS2 9NZ (Tel 0532-457910) Libn & Archivist: Mr D. J. H. Michelmore BA.
8 Yorkshire history; British archaeology. **9** Sermons & religious tracts (mostly Yorkshire). **11** Yes, for ref only.
12 Mon (except as below), Thurs & Fri 9. 30-17. 00, Tues & Wed 14. 00-20. 30, 1st & 3rd Sats 9. 30-17. 00 (closed the following Mon); Aug: Tues, Wed & Thurs 10. 00-14. 00.
13 (a) 25, 000; (b) 250; (c) c. 1100 mss; archives. **15** (a) 1 (b) 1.

YORKSHIRE POST NEWSPAPERS LTD LIBRARY, PO Box 168, Wellington St, Leeds, LS1 1RF (Tel 0532-32701; Telex 55425) Libn & Inf Officer: Miss Kathleen Rainford; Dep: Miss Sarah Collis.
8 Newspaper cuttings & photographs. **11** Yes, for limited research at Libn's discretion. **12** 9. 00-17. 00. **13** (a) 1, 500 (ref books), (c) bound files of: 'Yorkshire Post' (from 1866), 'Evening Post' (from 1890) & 'Leeds Intelligencer' (1754-1866). **15** (a) 7.

YORKSHIRE WATER AUTHORITY LIBRARY, West Riding House, 67 Albion St, Leeds, LS1 5AA (Tel 0532-448201 ext 84) Libn: Mrs D. Winstanley BSc.
7 Olympia House, Gelderd Rd, Leeds 12; Rivers Div, 21 Park Sq South, Leeds LS1 2QG. **8** Water resources & supply; pollution; water recreation; fishing; sewerage; law; freshwater biology; civil engineering. **10** BLL; BRASTACS.
11 Yes, by prior arrangement. **12** Mon-Thurs 9. 00-12. 30 (Mon 16. 30), Fri 14. 00-16. 30. Branches vary.
13 (a) 3, 000; (b) 110; (c) 400 local acts. **14** £5, 500.
15 (a) 1 (b) 1.

LEICESTER, Leicestershire

CHARLES KEENE COLLEGE OF FURTHER EDUCATION LIBRARY, Painter St, Leicester, LE1 3WA (Tel 0533-5603) Libn: Mr R. Matthewman FLA; Dep Libn: Miss V. Lovett ALA.
6 Leicestershire CC. **7** Humberstone Gate, Leicester, LE1 3PJ. **8** General. **10** BLL; EMRLB. **11** No.
12 Mon-Fri 8. 45-20. 00. **13** (a) 17, 000; (c) 200.
14 £4, 000. **15** (a) 4 (c) 2.

CITY OF LEICESTER COLLEGE OF EDUCATION LIBRARY, Scraptoft, Leicester, LE7 9SU (Tel 05374-4101) Tutor-Libn: Mr J. A. Bland ALA; Dep: Miss O. M. Reynard ALA.
6 Leicestershire CC. **8** General; education. **10** BLL.
11 Yes, for ref only. **12** Term: Mon-Fri 9. 00-20. 00 (Fri 17. 00), Sun 13. 00-17. 00; vac: Mon-Fri 9. 00-17. 00.
13 (a) 90, 000; (b) 400; (c) 2, 000 gramophone records; cassette tapes; 800 filmstrips, slides, kits, etc. **14** £20, 000.
15 (a) 11 (c) 4.

ENGLISH ELECTRIC CO LTD, ESTATES DIVISION LIBRARY, Cambridge Rd, Whetstone, Leicester, LE8 3LH (Tel 053729-3434; Telex 34611) Chief Libn: Mrs S. M. Spriggs BSc, ALA.
6 GEC Power Engineering Ltd. **8** Electrical, mechanical & nuclear engineering; hydraulics; maths. **9** English Electric Co reports, bibliographies & translations. **10** BLL; EMRLB; LETIS; NANTIS; Aslib. **11** Yes, by appointment.
12 Mon-Fri 8. 30-12. 30, 13. 30-17. 00. **13** (a) 13, 000;

CODE: **1** Name of Library. **2** Address. **3** Telephone & Telex. **4** Officer in charge. **5** Deputy. **6** Governing body.
7 Branches. **8** Main Subjects. **9** Special Collections. **10** Co-operative Schemes. **11** Open to public? **12** Hours.
13 Stock: (a) books (b) periodicals (c) other. **14** Finance. **15** Staff: (a) non-manual (b) graduate (c) chartered librarians.

LEICESTER, Leicestershire—*continued*

(b) 400; (c) 35, 000 confidential reports; 1, 700 microfiche.
15 (a) 5 (b) 2 (c) 2.

LEICESTER POLYTECHNIC LIBRARY, PO Box 143,
Leicester, LE1 9BH (Tel 0533-50181; Telex 34429) Chief
Libn: Mr S. R. Gadsden.
7 Art Lib, Fletcher Building (0533-50181 ext 2312/2405),
Libn: Ms Jill Hall ALA; Technology Lib, Hawthorn Building
(0533-50181 ext 2424, 2321, 2159) Libn: Mr John Glasswell;
Architecture & Building Lib (0533-50181 ext 2346/2160),
Libn: Mr Eric Loveridge BA, ALA. **8** Design & visual
arts; science; social science; technology & construction.
9 Fashion & costume; textile technology. **10** EMRLB.
11 Yes, for ref only. **12** Term: 8. 45-21. 00; summer
term: 8. 45-22. 00; vac: 9. 00-12. 30, 14. 00-17. 30. **13** (a)
94, 344; (b) 1, 687; (c) 987 records; 68, 073 slides; 1, 553 maps;
2, 995 illustrations; 618 microfilms. **14** £91, 000.
15 (a) 35½ (b) 6 (c) 11.

LEICESTERSHIRE ARCHAEOLOGICAL AND HISTORICAL
SOCIETY LIBRARY, Guildhall, Guildhall Lane, Leicester,
LE1 5FQ (Tel 0533-539111) Hon Libn: Mr Dennis H.
Thompson; Dep: Miss W. A. G. Herrington.
8 Local history & archaeology. **11** No. **12** Fri & Sat
11. 00-16. 00. **13** (a) c. 3, 000. **14** £50.

LEICESTER UNIVERSITY LIBRARY, University Rd,
Leicester, LE1 7RH (Tel 0533-50000) Univ Libn: Mr Douglas
G. F. Walker MA, LLB.
7 School of Education Library, 21 University Rd, Leicester,
LE1 7RF (0533-24211), Libn: R. W. Kirk BA, ALA.
8 General; arts; sciences; engineering; social sciences; law;
medicine. **9** English local history (all localities); transport
history (especially railways); official publications (inc EDC).
10 EMRLB. **11** Yes, on written application. **12** Term:
Mon-Fri 9. 00-22. 00, Sat 9. 00-12. 30; vac: Mon-Fri 9. 00-
17. 30, Sat 9. 00-12. 30. **13** (a) c. 430, 000; (b) c. 4, 000;
(c) 2, 100 boxes/reels microtexts (285 titles).
14 c. £240, 000. **15** (a) 80 (b) 29 (c) 25.

MATHEMATICAL ASSOCIATION LIBRARY, University of
Leicester, Leicester, LE1 7RH (Tel 0533-50000) Hon Libn:
Prof R. L. Goodstein.
8 Maths. **11** No. **13** (a) c. 4, 000; (b) 80.

MOUNT SAINT BERNARD ABBEY LIBRARY, Coalville,
Leicester, LE6 3UL (Tel 0530-32298) Rev Dr John Morson
OCR, PhD, DD.
6 Abbot & Community of Mount Saint Bernard Abbey.
8 Theology; studies of monastic, especially Cistercian,
interest. **9** c. 250 rare books (16th & 17th cent), (printed
catalogue). **11** No. **13** (a) c. 17, 000; (b) 43. **14** £800.

NORTH WEST LEICESTERSHIRE TECHNICAL COLLEGE
LIBRARY, Bridge Rd, Coalville, LE6 2QR (Tel 0530-36136)
Tutor-Libn: Miss D. P. Norman BA, MA, ALA.
6 Leicestershire CC. **8** Sociology; law; business;
engineering; building; history; English; mining. **9** BSI
(complete from 1970). **10** EMRLB **11** Yes. **12** Mon-
Fri 9. 00-20. 00 (Fri 17. 00). **13** (a) 20, 000; (b) 140; (c)
150 filmstrips; 12 audiotapes. **14** £1, 200. **15** (a) 2½
(b) 1 (c) 1.

SOUTH FIELDS COLLEGE OF FURTHER EDUCATION
LIBRARY, Aylestone Rd, Leicester, LE2 7LW (Tel 0533-
50191 ext 211) Mrs P. Leahy BA, ALA; Dep Libns: Mrs H.
Hillier BSc, DipLib; Mrs G. Holmes BA.
6 Leicestershire Education Authority. **7** 1 Newarke St,
Leicester, Libn: Mrs G. Holmes BA; Humberstone Dr,
Leicester, Libn: Mrs M. Bryant ALA. **8** Building; catering;
child care; fashion; hairdressing; printing. **10** EMRLB.
11 No. **12** Term: Mon-Fri 9. 00-19. 00 (Fri 17. 00); vac:
9. 00-12. 30, 13. 30-17. 00. **13** (a) 24, 000; (b) 150.
14 £5, 000. **15** (a) 4½ (b) 3 (c) 1½.

LETCHWORTH, Hertfordshire

COLLEGE OF TECHNOLOGY LIBRARY, Broadway, Letchworth, SG6 3PB (Tel 04626-3911; Telex 82139) Tutor-Libn:
Mr A. B. Jackson FLA; Chief Asst Libn: Mrs V. George ALA.
6 Hertfordshire CC. **8** Education; maths & computing;
physics; chemistry; mechanical & electrical engineering;
catering; management. **9** Complete BSI. **10** HERTIS.
11 Yes, for ref only. **12** Term: Mon-Thurs 8. 30-21. 00,
Fri 8. 30-17. 00; vac: Mon-Fri 8. 30-12. 30, 13. 30-17. 00.
13 (a) 23, 000; (b) 260; (c) microfilm; microfiche.
14 £4, 300. **15** (a) 6 (b) 1 (c) 2.

LINCOLN, Lincolnshire

BISHOP GROSSETESTE COLLEGE, SIBTHORP LIBRARY,
Lincoln, LN1 3DY (Tel 0522-27347) Tutor-Libn: Miss E. B.
Dean MA, ALA; Dep: Mr J. C. Child BA, ALA.
8 Education & professional studies; American studies; art
& craft; drama; English; French; geography; history; maths;
music; physical education; religion; science. **10** BLL.
11 Yes, for ref only, on application. **12** Term: Mon-Fri
8. 45-20. 30, Sat 9. 00-12. 00; vac: Mon-Fri 9. 00-13. 00, 14. 00-
17. 00. **13** (a) 55, 000; (b) c. 250; (c) filmstrips; slides;
records; teaching kits; microtexts. **14** £9, 300.
15 (a) 5½ (b) 3 (c) 2.

DEAN AND CHAPTER LIBRARY, The Cathedral, Lincoln
(Tel 0522-21089) Libn: Mrs Naomi Pearman BA.
6 Dean & Chapter. **8** Theology & related subjects; local
history. **9** Wren Library (300 medieval mss); 10, 000 pre-
1800 printed books; 3, 000 17th cent pamphlets; 7, 000 19th cent
tracts. **11** Yes, by appointment. **12** Wren Library:
by appointment; Medieval Library exhibitions, May-Sept:
Tues-Fri 14. 30-16. 30.

LINCOLN THEOLOGICAL COLLEGE, BISHOP'S HOSTEL
LIBRARY, Lincoln, LN1 3BP (Tel 0522-31120) Libn: Rev Dr
D. G. A. Calvert.
6 The Council, Bishop's Hostel. **8** Theology. **11** No.
12 Permanently open to members of College. **13** (a)
15, 000; (b) 35. **14** £1, 000. **15** (b) ½.

LINDSEY COLLEGE OF AGRICULTURE LIBRARY, Rise-
holme, Lincoln, LN2 2LG (Tel 0522-22252) Libn: R. J. Bowler
BSc, NDA.
6 Lincolnshire CC. **8** Agriculture; horticulture; beekeeping; business. **11** No. **12** Open access.
13 (a) 3, 000; (b) 25. **14** £550. **15** (a) ¼.

RUSTON-PAXMAN DIESELS LTD LIBRARY, Research
Centre, Beevor St, PO Box 25, Lincoln, LN5 7BJ (Tel 0522-
21241) Inf Manager: Mr R. E. Hooley; Libn: Mr B. S. C.
Harling ALA.
8 Internal-combustion engines; gas turbines; production
engineering. **9** Classification society rules. **10** NANTIS.
11 Yes, by appointment. **12** Mon-Fri 8. 30-12. 15, 13. 30-
17. 00 (Fri 16. 00). **13** (a) 9, 000; (b) 200; (c) 30, 000 reports;
5, 000 trade catalogues; company archives; standards; patents.
15 (a) 6 (c) 1.

LITTLEHAMPTON, West Sussex

GLASSHOUSE CROPS RESEARCH INSTITUTE LIBRARY,
Worthing Rd, Rustington, Littlehampton, BN16 3PU (Tel
09064-4481 ext 16) Scientific Inf Officer & Acting Libn: Dr
C. R. Worthing BSc, MA, DPhil.
8 Scientific: agricultural, horticultural, biological & chemical
publications. **10** SASLIC. **11** No. **13** (a) 8, 000;
(b) 350; (c) microfilms; microcards; microfiche. **15** (a) 2
(b) 1.

LIVERPOOL, Merseyside

ATHENAEUM, Church Alley, Liverpool, L1 3DD (Tel 051-709
7770) Hon Libn: Mr Ralph Malbon FLA.
6 President, Officers & Committee of Athenaeum.

LIVERPOOL, Merseyside—*continued*

8 General. **9** Local history; Gladstone & Roscoe collns. **10** Inter-library loans. **11** Yes, if suitably recommended, with permission of committee, for specific projects. **13** (a) 50,000. **15** (a) 1 (c) 1.

CHRIST'S COLLEGE OF EDUCATION LIBRARY, Woolton Rd, Liverpool, L16 8ND (Tel 051-722 7331) Tutor-Libn: Miss M. E. Fazakerley BA, ALA; Dep Libn: Mrs J. Greenham. **6** Governors of Christ's College. **8** General; arts; pure science. **9** Education; teaching practice library of children's books & school textbooks. **10** BLL. **11** No. **12** Term: Mon-Fri 9.00-21.00 (Fri 18.30), Sat & Sun 13.30-17.30; vac: Mon-Fri 9.00-17.00. **13** (a) 54,550; (b) 310. **14** £9,900. **15** (a) 6 (b) 1 (c) 2.

EVANS MEDICAL LTD LIBRARY, Speke, Liverpool, L24 9JD (Tel 051-486 1881; Telex 62-673) Libn: Miss O. Dinsdale. **8** Pharmaceutical sciences; medical sciences (inc virology, bacteriology etc); chemistry. **10** NWRLB. **11** No. **12** 8.15-17.00. **13** (a) c. 4,600; (b) 124. **14** £3,000. **15** (a) 1.

LIVERPOOL MEDICAL INSTITUTION LIBRARY, 114 Mount Pleasant, Liverpool, L3 5SR (Tel 051-709 9125) Libn: Mr D. M. Crook ALA. **8** Medicine. **9** Colln of historical medical books (printed catalogue). **11** No. **12** Mon-Fri 9.30-18.00, Sat 9.30-12.00. **13** (a) 40,000; (b) 200. **15** (a) 4 (c) 2.

LIVERPOOL POLYTECHNIC LIBRARY, (will merge with I. M. Marsh College of Physical Education), Walton House, Tithebarn St, Liverpool, L2 2NG (Tel 051-227 1781 ext 39; Telex 628087) Poly Libn: Mr D. H. Revill BSc FLA. **6** Liverpool Education Authority. **7** Humanities Lib, Walton House, Libn: Mrs J. Mander BA; Engineering & Science Lib, Byrom St, Liverpool, Libn: Mr J. Fildes; Construction Lib, Clarence St, Liverpool, Libn: Miss B. Juxon; Art & Design Lib, Hope St, Liverpool, Libn: Miss J. Roberts; Construction Lib, Victoria St, Liverpool, Libn: Mr R. Triplett. **8** Social sciences; law; languages; librarianship; business & management; accountancy; maths; physics; biological sciences; chemistry; medical & pharmaceutical sciences; engineering; maritime studies; sports; science; general; surveying; building; civil engineering; arts; fashions; architecture; town & country planning. **11** Yes, for ref only. **12** Term: 9.00-21.00; vac: 9.00-16.30. Branches vary. **13** (a) 124,042; (b) 2,037; (c) 145 microforms; 3,333 audio-visual aids. **14** £140,000. **15** (a) 40 (b) 11 (c) 17½.

LIVERPOOL SCHOOL OF TROPICAL MEDICINE LIBRARY, Pembroke Pl, Liverpool, L3 5QA (Tel 051-709 7611) Libn: Miss V. M. Nottage BSc. **8** Tropical medicine; tropical community health; parasitology; entomology. **11** Yes. **12** Mon-Fri 9.00-17.00. **13** (a) 14,500; (b) 260; (c) c. 20,000 reprints. **14** £4,000. **15** (a) ½.

NOTRE DAME COLLEGE OF EDUCATION LIBRARY, Mount Pleasant, Liverpool, L3 5SP (Tel 051-709 7454) Tutor-Libn: Mr F. M. Wilson MA, ALA. **8** Education; art; divinity; English; French; geography; history; maths; music; physical education; science; speech & drama. **10** BLL. **11** No. **12** Term: Mon-Fri 9.00-18.30; Sat 9.00-12.00; vac: Mon-Fri 9.00-17.00. **13** (a) 55,000; (b) 180. **15** (a) 3 (b) 1 (c) 1.

MABEL FLETCHER TECHNICAL COLLEGE LIBRARY, Sandown Rd, Liverpool, L15 4JB (Tel 051-733 2214) Mr Barry Jones ALA. **6** Liverpool Education Committee. **8** Health & social services; child care; nursing; fashion; embroidery; music. **10** LADSIRLAC. **11** Yes, by prior arrangement. **12** Mon-Fri 9.00-19.30 (Fri 16.00). **13** (a) 10,000; (b) 300. **14** £3,000. **15** (a) 3 (b) 2 (c) 2.

ST KATHARINE'S COLLEGE LIBRARY, Stand Park Rd, Liverpool, L16 9JD (Tel 051-722 2361/5) Libn: Mr J. F. Williams BA, ALA; Dep: Mrs K. M. Wallace. **6** Church of England. **8** American studies; art & craft; divinity; drama; education; English; French; geography; history; maths; music; physical education; sciences (biology, chemistry, physics). **9** Children's colln. **11** No. **12** Mon-Fri 9.00-20.00. **13** (a) 56,000; (b) 260; (c) filmstrips; slides; teaching kits; illustrations etc. **14** £9,000. **15** (b) 1 (c) 1.

UNIVERSITY OF LIVERPOOL LIBRARY, PO Box 123, Liverpool, L69 3DA (Tel 051-709 6022; Telex 627095) Univ Libn: Mr D. H. Varley MA, FLA; Dep Univ Libn: Mr T. S. Broadhurst MA, FLA. **6** University of Liverpool. **7** Main (Harold Cohen) Lib; Arts Reading Room; School of Education Lib, 22 Aberomby Sq, Liverpool, L69 3BX (051-709 7312 ext 49/50), Libn: Mr J. E. Vaughn MA; 21 subject libs; 2nd main lib (Sydney Jones Lib) to open Oct 1976. **8** General; arts; social & environmental studies; science; medicine; engineering science; veterinary science; law; education; dentistry; business. **9** Parry Latin-American Centre. **10** BLL; NWRLB; SCONUL; Latin-American Centre; SCOLMA (Spanish-speaking Africa); SKELLEM, LISE. **11** Yes, for ref, on written recommendation to Libn. **12** Term: 9.00-21.30; Easter vac: 9.00-18.00 (or 21.30); other vacs: 9.00-13.00. **13** (a) 750,000; (b) 6,000; (c) microfilms; microfiches; music; maps. **14** £250,000. **15** (a) 100 (b) 30 (c) 30.

WALKER ART GALLERY LIBRARY, William Brown St, Liverpool, L3 8EL (Tel 051-207 1371). **6** Merseyside CC. **8** Catalogues of paintings, sculpture, drawings, prints etc. **11** Yes, by appointment. **12** Mon-Fri 10.00-17.00. **13** (c) 10,000 catalogues. **14** £600. **15** (a) ½.

CODE: 1 Name of Library. 2 Address. 3 Telephone & Telex. 4 Officer in charge. 5 Deputy. 6 Governing body. 7 Branches. 8 Main Subjects. 9 Special Collections. 10 Co-operative Schemes. 11 Open to public? 12 Hours. 13 Stock: (a) books (b) periodicals (c) other. 14 Finance. 15 Staff: (a) non-manual (b) graduate (c) chartered librarians.

LONDON (GLC AREA)

ACTON TECHNICAL COLLEGE LIBRARY, High St, Acton, London, W3 6RD (Tel 01-993 2344) Colln Libn: Mrs E. J. Moffatt ALA; Mrs J. Murtagh.
6 Board of Governors. 7 Annexe, Woodlands Ave, High St, Acton, London W3. 8 Science; economics; sociology; computer studies; English language & literature; mechanical, electrical, electronic & automobile engineering; education & teaching methods; technical drawing. 9 BSI (from 1963). 10 BLL; CICRIS. 11 Yes, with introduction. 12 Term: Mon-Thurs 9.00-20.00, Fri 9.00-17.00; vac: Mon-Fri 9.30-16.30. 13 (a) 25,000; (b) 165; (c) tape recordings. 14 £7,500.

ADVERTISING ASSOCIATION LIBRARY, Abford House, 15 Wilton Rd, London, SW1V 1NJ (Tel 01-828-2771) Inf Officer: Miss Beth Rosenbaum MIPR; Dep: Miss Jane Bland BSc.
8 Advertising; marketing; media; related statistics & research material. 9 History of advertising & other historical material (old advertisements); periodicals; news cuttings; information on advertising industry, & applied research. 11 Yes. 12 Mon-Fri 10.00-1300, 14.00-17.00. 13 (a) c.5,500; (b) c.120; (c) 2 films. 15 (a) 2 (b) 1.

AERONAUTICAL RESEARCH COUNCIL LIBRARY, c/o National Physical Laboratory, Teddington, Middlesex, TW11 OLW (Tel 01-977 3222 ext 3324) Libn: Mrs S. D. Bradshaw.
6 MoD Procurement Executive. 8 Aerodynamics; fluid mechanics; aircraft; aircraft operation; materials. 9 Many early reports in aeronautics, aircraft engineering etc. 10 BLL; inter-library loans. 11 Yes, by special arrangement. 12 Mon-Fri 9.00-17.30 (Thurs 17.00, Fri 16.30). 13 (a) c.5,000; (b) c.80; (c) c.100,000 reports.

ANBAR TEAR SHEET LIBRARY, PO Box 23, Wembley, HA9 8DJ (Tel 01-902 4489; Telex 935779 Anbarpub) Tear Sheet Libn: Miss J. Shread.
6 Anbar Publications Ltd. 7 PO Box 8550, Johannesburg 2000, South Africa; Management House, St Leonards Ave, St Kilda, Victoria 3182, Australia. 8 Management; marketing & distribution; personnel & training; accounting & data processing; work study & o & m. 9 The journal articles abstracted in 5 professional abstracting journals (current & 7 preceding vols; earlier articles transferred to Manchester Commercial Library). 11 Yes, occasionally by prior arrangement. 12 Mon-Fri 9.00-17.00. 13 (b) over 200. 15 (a) 3.

ANTIQUARIAN HOROLOGICAL SOCIETY LIBRARY, Guildhall Library, Aldermanbury, EC2P 2EJ (Tel 01-606 3030) Libn of Guildhall Library: Mr Godfrey Thompson FLA.
8 History & technique of clock- and watch-making inc many foreign items; biographical material; related topics, e.g. scientific instruments. 9 Howgrave-Graham slide colln, mainly on turret clocks; H. Alan Lloyd's colln of photographs relating to horological history. 11 Yes. 12 Mon-Sat 9.30-17.00. 13 (a) 1,100; (b) 6; (c) 5,000 illustrations; 1,250 transparencies; 15 mss; 10 boxes of cuttings.

ARCHITECTURAL ASSOCIATION LIBRARY, 34-36 Bedford Sq, London, WC1B 3ES (Tel 01-636 0974) Libn: Miss M. E. Dixon ALA; Dep Libn: Miss E. Underwood.
8 Architecture; building; construction; planning. 9 60,000 slides; technical colln (1,800 books, 14,000 classified periodical articles & trade literature); 41,000 classified periodical articles; some rare books. 10 BLL 11 No. 12 Term: Mon-Fri 10.00-18.00; vac: Mon-Fri 10.00-17.00. 13 (a) 22,000; (b) 300; (c) 600 maps, 150 AA School theses. 14 £7,200. 15 (a) 6(c) 1.

ARMOURIES' LIBRARY, HM Tower of London, London, EC3N 4AV (Tel 01-709 0765) Libn: Ms Sarah Barter BA.
6 Dept of Environment. 8 History of arms & armour, both European & Oriental; history of Tower of London. 9 Sale catalogues of arms & armour (from 18th cent). 11 Yes, to serious students, by appointment. 12 10.00-12.30, 14.00-17.00; Sat mornings by special arrangement. 13 (a) 10,000; (b) 20; (c) mss; prints & drawings; brass rubbings; photographs. 14 £1,250. 15 (a) 1 (b) 1

ARTS COUNCIL OF GREAT BRITAIN POETRY LIBRARY, 105 Piccadilly, London, W1V OAU (Tel 01-629 9495) Libn: Mr Jonathan Barker.
8 English poetry since 1930; poetry in English from Ireland, Scotland, Wales, Australia, USA, West Indies; poetry translated into English. 9 Largest colln of its kind in England; exceptional colln of English & American poetry (free printed catalogue). 10 Inter-library loans. 11 Yes. 12 Mon-Fri 10.00-12.30, 13.30-17.00 (Thurs 19.00). 13 (a) 7,000; (b) 25. 14 c.£1,500. 15 (a) 1.

ASLIB LIBRARY, 3 Belgrave Sq, London, SW1X 8PL (Tel 01-235 5050; Telex 23667) Libn: Miss F. I. Tait ALA; Dep: Mr G. Hynd MA, DipLib.
8 Librarianship; information science; documentation. 11 No. 12 9.00-17.15. 13 (a) 26,000; (b) 375. 15 (a) 5 (b) 2 (c) 3.

ASSOCIATED PORTLAND CEMENT MANUFACTURERS LTD, RESEARCH DEPARTMENT LIBRARY, London Rd, Greenhithe, Kent, DA9 9JQ (Tel 0322-842244; Telex 896335) Head of Lib, Inf & Patent Services: Mr A. E. Beety BA; Dep Head: Mr T. G. Burnham BA, MSc, AIInfSc.
8 Cement; concrete. 9 History of Portland cement. 10 SEAL. 11 No. 12 Mon-Fri 8.30-17.00. 13 (a) 5,500; (b) 250; (c) 12,500 pamphlets, reprints etc. 15 (a) 6½ (b) 2.

ASSOCIATION OF CERTIFIED ACCOUNTANTS LIBRARY, 23 Bedford Sq, London, WC1B 3HS (Tel 01-636 2103) Libn: Miss S. A. Teat ALA; Dep: Miss J. G. Logan ALA.
8 Accountancy; taxation; executorship; bankruptcy; company law; mercantile law; general law; general & industrial management; statistics & other mathematical techniques as applied to management; electronic data processing for business; economics with reference to finance, industry & commerce. 10 Inter-library loans. 11 No. 12 Mon-Fri 10.00-17.00. 13 (a) c.8,000; (b) c.130. 15 (a) 3 (c) 2.

ASSOCIATION OF COMMONWEALTH UNIVERSITIES, REFERENCE LIBRARY, 36 Gordon Sq, London, WC1H OPF (Tel 01-387-8572 ext 52) Libn: Ms Joyce Madden ALA.
8 Education, especially higher education; research in the Commonwealth. 9 Current calendars, prospectuses, reports, gazettes of Commonwealth universities (back numbers also). 11 Yes, for ref only. 12 Mon-Fri 9.30-17.30. 13 (a) c.6,000; (b) c.400. 15 (a) 1 (c) 1.

AUSTRALIAN REFERENCE LIBRARY, Australian High Commission, Australia House, Strand, London, WC2B 4LA (Tel 01-836 2435).
6 Australian Govt, Dept of Foreign Affairs. 8 Australiana. 11 Yes. 12 Mon-Fri 9.00-17.15. 13 (a) 15,000; (b) 1,500. 15 (a) 5 (c) 2.

AUSTRIAN INSTITUTE LIBRARY, 28 Rutland Gate, London, SW7 1PQ (Tel 01-584 8653/4) Inf Officer: Ms Hannelore Schmidt.
6 Austrian Ministry of Foreign Affairs. 8 Austrian his-

LONDON—*continued*

tory, art, music, literature, periodicals & papers; films, slides & records.   **10** BLL.   **11** Yes.   **12** Mon-Fri 9.00-12.00, 15.00-18.00.   **13** (b) 80.   **15** (a) 1.

BABCOCK AND WILCOX (OPERATIONS) LTD, LONDON LIBRARY, 165 Great Dover St, London SE1 4YB (Tel 01-407 8383; Telex 884151/2/3) Libn: Mr. J. B. P. Stirling.
8 Mechanical engineering (particularly design & manufacture of conventional & nuclear steam-raising plants).   **11** No.
13 (a) over 3,000; (b) c. 100.   **15** (a) 1.

BANK OF ENGLAND LIBRARIES: REFERENCE LIBRARY; LIBRARY LITERARY ASSOCIATION, Threadneedle St, London EC2R 8AH (Tel 01-601 4444) Libn: Mr T. I. Bell FLA; Dep Libn: Mrs C. V. Harland BA, FLA.
8 Ref Lib: monetary economics & central bank publications. Lib & Literary Assoc: fiction & non-fiction.   **9** UK economic tracts & pamphlets (17th-19th cent); government reports on banking & finance (19th cent).   **11** No, but specific requests in writing considered.   **13** (a) Ref Lib: c. 50,000, Lib & Lit Assoc: 30,000; (b) c. 4,000.   **15** Joint Staff: (a) 19; (b) 1; (c) 6.

BARNET COLLEGE LIBRARY, Wood St, Barnet, Hertfordshire, EN5 4AZ (Tel 01-449 9191) Tutor-Libn: Miss M. F. Adams ALA; Asst Libn: Mrs A. E. Morgan ALA.
6 London Borough of Barnet.   **8** General; science; mechanical & electrical engineering; commerce; art; sociology; history; geography; & literature.   **10** BLL.   **11** Yes, for ref only, on application to Libn.   **12** Term: Mon-Thurs 8.45-20.45, Fri 8.45-19.00; vac: Mon-Fri 9.00-12.30, 13.30-17.00.   **13** (a) 22,000; (b) 200.   **14** £5,200.   **15** (a) 6 (c) 2.

BATTERSEA COLLEGE OF EDUCATION LIBRARY (will merge with the Polytechnic of the South Bank), Home Economics Teachers, Manor House, 58 North Side, Clapham Common, London, SW4 9RZ (Tel 01-288 2015/6) Chief Libn: Miss B. R. Graves ALA; Dep Libn: Mrs A. Lerwill ALA.
6 ILEA.   **7** Primary Teachers, Manresa House, Holybourne Ave, London SW15 (01-788 7771/5), Dep Libn: Miss A. Davis ALA.   **8** General; education; Home Economics.   **9** Education; home economics; nutrition; children's literature.
10 WANDPETLS.   **11** No.   **12** College hours.   **13** (a) 53,000; (b) 300; (c) audiovisual software (exc films).
14 c. £9,000.   **15** (a) 7½ (b) 1 (c) 4.

BERMANS AND NATHANS LTD, RESEARCH SERVICES LIBRARY, 40 Camden St, London, NW1 ODH (Tel 01-387 0999 ext 226) Research Libn: Ms Renata Veness.
8 Costume; theatre; films; entertainment.   **9** Rare costume books; 19th cent magazines ('Illustrated London News' complete); film stills; fashion.   **11** No.   **12** Mon-Fri 9.00-17.30.   **13** (a) 2,100; (b) 7, (c) cuttings; costumes; social history.   **15** (a) 2.

BICC RESEARCH AND ENGINEERING LTD LIBRARY, 38 Wood Lane, Shepherds Bush, London, W12 7DX (Tel 01-743 1212 ext 134; Telex 933724) Libn: Miss M. G. Kingston BSc, ARIC, MInstInfSc; Asst: Mrs E. C. King.
8 Electrical engineering; high voltage transmission; related topics.   **10** CICRIS.   **11** No.   **12** Mon-Fri 9.00-17.30.
13 (a) 10,000; (b) 130; (c) patents; standards; microfiche.
15 (a) 2 (b) 1.

BISHOPSGATE INSTITUTE LIBRARY, 230 Bishopsgate, London, EC2M 4QH (Tel 01-247 6844)   Ref. Libn: Mr D. R. Webb BA, FLA; Asst Ref Libn: Miss A. E. Carpenter ALA.
6 Board of Governors of Bishopsgate Foundation.
8 General; reference.   **9** London history (emphasis on City area, c. 30,000 books & pamphlets); George Howell colln (early history of Trade Unionism & Labour movement inc many mss); G. J. Holyoake colln (early Co-operative movement, inc many mss); London & Middlesex Archaeological Society Library.   **11** Yes.   **12** Mon-Fri 9.30-17.30
13 (a) c. 30,000 (exc special collns); (b) 150; (c) London prints, watercolours, maps etc.   **14** £7,000.   **15** (a) 2 (b) 1 (c) 2.

BOROUGH ROAD COLLEGE LIBRARY (proposed merger with Maria Grey College & part of Chiswick Polytechnic, Sept 1976, to form West London Institute of Higher Educa-

tion), Borough Rd, Isleworth, Middlesex, TW7 5DU (Tel 01-560 5991 ext 27) Coll Libn: Mr L. F. Preston BA, ALA; Dep Coll Libn: Miss H. M. Midgelow ALA.
6 British and Foreign School Society.   **8** Education & educational psychology; philosophy; English language & literature, French language & literature; history; sciences (biology, chemistry, physics); maths; geography & geology; art; music; physical education.   **9** History of British & Foreign School Society.   **10** BLL; CICRIS.   **11** No.   **12** Term: Mon-Fri 9.00-21.00, Sat 9.00-13.00; vac: Mon-Fri 9.00-17.00.   **13** (a) 56,000; (b) 325; (c) College archives.
14 £11,000.   **15** (a) 6 (b) 1 (c) 2.

BRITISH AIRWAYS, EUROPEAN DIVISION, LIBRARY, Engineering Base, London (Heathrow) Airport, Hounslow, Middlesex, TW6 2JR (Tel 01-759 3131 ext 4459/4303; Telex 22133) Libn: C. P. Robertson ALA; Dep: Mrs R. R Parker ALA.
8 Air transport engineering & economics.   **10** CICRIS.
11 No, except in special circumstances with prior permission of Libn.   **12** Mon-Fri 8.30-16.45.   **13** (a) 40,000; (b) 320.   **15** (a) 7 (c) 3.

BRITISH AND FOREIGN BIBLE SOCIETY LIBRARY, 146 Queen Victoria St, London EC4V 4BX (Tel 01-248 4751) Libn: Miss G. E. Coldham FLA.
8 Christian scriptures in over 1,700 languages; library contains only Bibles or parts of Bibles.   **9** Francis Fry colln (English Bibles); Christian Ginsburg colln (Hebrew, Latin, German & other Bibles).   **11** Yes, to view; to study a letter of introduction & prior arrangement preferred.   **12** Mon-Fri 9.00-17.00.   **13** (a) c. 26,000; (b) 46; (c) archives of Society (from 1804).   **15** (a) 2 (b) 1 (c) 1.

British Broadcasting Corporation, see also Radio Times

BBC CENTRAL MUSIC LIBRARY, 156 Great Portland St, London, W1A 6AJ (Tel 01-580 4468 ext 3598) Music Libn: Miss Miriam Miller MA, FLA, LRAM; Asst Music Libn: Mr Clifford Bartlett MA.
8 Music.   **11** No, only for broadcasting purposes.
12 Mon-Fri 9.30-17.30.   **13** (a) 3,000; (b) 20; (c) 31,000 sets of orchestral parts; 61,000 choral sets; 36,000 songs; 72,000 sets of chamber music etc.   **15** (a) 43 (b) 2 (c) 15.

BBC REFERENCE LIBRARY, Broadcasting House, London, W1A 1AA (Tel 01-580 4468 ext 3747; Telex 265781) Ref Libn: Mr G. L. Higgens FLA; Dep: Mr David Lee.
7 Television Service Lib, Television Centre, Wood Lane, W12 TRJ (01-743 8000 ext 2540) Libn: Mr A. J. Holt ALA; External Services Lib, Bush House, Aldwych, WC2B 4PH (01-240 3456 ext 2280) Libn: Mrs M. Welch BA, ALA; Monitoring Service Lib, Caversham Court, Reading (0734-472742) Libn: Miss J. Pollard; Engineering Research Dept Lib, Kingswood Warren, Tadworth, Surrey (073783-2361) Libn: Mrs A. Peters BCom, Dip NZLS.   **8** General.
9 British Broadcasting; drama & film; music (not scores).
10 BLL; LASER.   **11** No.   **12** Mon-Fri 9.30-20.00, Sat 9.30-17.00; Branches vary.   **13** (a) 133,000; (b) 1,400; (c) 150,000 illustrations; 4,200 maps; 1,700 microfilm spools; 1,500 microfiches.

British Council, see also Language Teaching Laboratory

CENTRAL LIBRARY, 10 Spring Gardens, London SW1A 2BN (Tel 01-930 8466; Telex 916522) Libn, Central Library: Mr Bernard P. F. Adams MBE, FLA; Dep: Mr Roy Mayo ALA.
8 Reference books & periodicals on most subjects, viewed from a British standpoint.   **9** Bibliographies & bibliographic guides; librarianship; comparative education; Overseas Colln (countries in which British Council operates); cultural relations.   **10** BLL; LASER.   **11** No.
12 Mon-Fri 9.30-17.30 (Fri 17.00).   **13** (a) 30,000; (b) 250.   **14** £4,000.   **15** (a) 8 (b) 4 (c) 5.

EDUCATION AND SCIENCE DIVISION LIBRARY, 10 Spring Gardens, London, SW1A 2BN (Tel 01-930 8466) Libn: Mr J. Duffy BSc, ALA.
8 Education & science.   **9** Science education at school level; British material on education & science for overseas use.   **10** BLL; UK Overseas British Scientific Informa-

CODE: **1** Name of Library. **2** Address. **3** Telephone & Telex. **4** Officer in charge. **5** Deputy. **6** Governing body. **7** Branches. **8** Main Subjects. **9** Special Collections. **10** Co-operative Schemes. **11** Open to public? **12** Hours. **13** Stock: (a) books (b) periodicals (c) other. **14** Finance. **15** Staff: (a) non-manual (b) graduate (c) chartered librarians.

LONDON—*continued*

tion Services. **11** Yes, by appointment. **12** 9.30-17.00. **13** (a) 4,000; (b) 500. **14** £7,000. **15** (a) 16 (b) 8 (c) 2.

FINE ART LIBRARY, 97-99 Park St, London W1Y 4NJ (Tel 01-408 1200) Libn: Ms Judith Collins MA.
8 Ref lib & archive of British art & artists (especially 20th cent). **11** Yes, by appointment. **15** (b) 1.

MEDICAL INFORMATION SERVICE, 10 Spring Gardens, London SW1A 2BN (Tel 01-930 8466) Head of Medical Inf Service: Miss J. F. Hall.
8 Medicine (inc ancilary subjects); psychology. **11** No. **12** Mon-Fri 9.15-17.30. **13** (a) 11,000; (b) 350. **15** (a) 13 (b) 2 (c) 2.

BRITISH DENTAL ASSOCIATION LIBRARY, 64 Wimpole St, London, W1M 8AL (Tel 01-935 0875; Telex Bridention, London W1) Libn: Miss E. M. Spencer BA, ALA.
8 Dentistry. **9** Rare books. **10** BLL. **11** Yes, for scientific research in dental subjects. **12** Mon-Fri 9.30-17.30. **13** (a) 8,000; (b) 220; (c) 3000 pamphlets; 30 films; 5 tapes. **14** £2,000. **15** (a) 3 (b) 1.

BRITISH GAS CORPORATION LIBRARY, Watson House, Peterborough Rd, London, SW6 3HN (Tel 01-890 3092) Head of Scientific Information Group: Mr R. Cooke MIInfSc; Libn: Miss B. M. Sanger ALA.
8 Gas utilisation, domestic. **9** BSI. **10** CICRIS. **11** Yes, by prior arrangement with Libn. **12** Mon-Fri 8.45-17.15. **13** (a) 2,870; (b) 310; (c) patent specifications; microfiche. **14** £12,500. **15** (a) 4 (b) 2 (c) 1.

BRITISH INSTITUTE OF MANAGEMENT LIBRARY, Management House, Parker St, London, WC2B 5PT (Tel 01-405 3456) Libn & Head of Inf: Miss G. A. Dare BA, ALA, DipLib; Dep Libn: Miss Julia Juttke BSc, MSc.
8 Management; accounting; taxation; commercial & industrial law; management of specific types of organisation. **9** Unpublished material; company internal documentation; case studies; management games; participative exercises; index to management training films. **10** BLL. **11** Yes, for ref only. **12** Mon-Fri 9.30-17.15. **13** (a) 60,000; (b) 300. **14** c. £8,000. **15** (a) 19 (b) 4 (c) 5.

BRITISH INSTITUTE OF RECORDED SOUND LIBRARY, 29 Exhibition Rd, London, SW7 2AS (Tel 01-589 6603/4) Libn: Miss Pat Howard BA, DipLib; Inf Officer: Mr Eric Hughes.
8 Recorded sound; music; history of sound recording (not scientific material). **9** Archive of sound recordings (all types of music, plays, animal noises). **11** Yes, for ref & listening only. **12** Mon-Fri 10.00-13.30, 14.30-17.45. **13** (a) c. 4,500; (b) 109; (c) trade catalogues; microfilm; c. 125,000,000 recorded items. **15** (a) 1 (b) 1 (c) 1.

BRITISH INTERPLANETARY SOCIETY LIBRARY, 12 Bessborough Gardens, London, SW1V 2JJ. (Tel 01-828 9371) Libn: Mr. L. J. Carter ACIS.
8 Space research & technology; rocket engineering; astronomy; electronics. **9** Technical reports on all aspects of space research & technology; space film library. **10** BLL. **11** No. **13** (a) 3,000; (b) 40; (c) 2,000 technical reports. **15** (a) 1.

BRITISH MEDICAL ASSOCIATION, NUFFIELD LIBRARY, BMA House, Tavistock Sq, London, WC1H 9JP (Tel 01-387 4499) Libn: Mr F. M. Sutherland MA, FLA; Dep Libn: Mr T. J. Salt.
8 Medicine. **9** Paris MD theses. **11** No. **12** Mon-Fri 9.00-17.30 (Wed 21.00). **13** (a) c. 85,000; (b) c. 1,000. **15** (a) 12 (b) 1 (c) 3.

BRITISH NUMISMATIC SOCIETY LIBRARY, (with Royal Numismatic Society Library), Warburg Institute, Woburn Sq, London, WC1H 0AB. Hon Libn: Mr R. H. Thompson ALA.

8 Coins & currency, medals, tokens, etc, of Great Britain, the Commonwealth, & the English-speaking world (from earliest times). **9** Sale catalogues (c. 500 vols). **11** No, except at discretion of Warburg Institute. **12** None (regularly open only at meetings of the society). **13** (a) c. 4,500; (b) 29. **14** £25.

BRITISH OPTICAL ASSOCIATION LIBRARY, 65 Brook St, London W1Y 2DT (Tel 01-629 3382/3/4) Libn: Miss J. M. Taylor BA.
8 Ophthalmic optics; ophthalmology; optics. **9** Works on the eye & vision (from 16th cent); Contact Lens Society Library (Keith Clifford Hall colln). **10** BLL. **11** Yes, for ref only, by arrangement with Libn. **12** Mon-Fri 9.15-12.30, 13.30-17.00. **13** (a) 10,000; (b) 92. **15** (a) 1 (b) 1.

BROMLEY COLLEGE OF TECHNOLOGY LIBRARY (will merge with Ravensbourne College of Art and Design and Stockwell College of Education, to form Bromley Institute of Higher Education), Rookery Lane, Bromley, Kent, BR2 8HE (Tel 01-462 6331) Libn: Mr F. B. Merret ALA; Dep Libn: Mrs Sandra Spalding ALA.
6 London Borough of Bromley. **8** Applied biology; business & social studies; engineering. **10** BLL; LASER. **11** Yes. **12** Term: Mon-Fri 9.00-21.00; vac: Mon-Fri 9.00-17.00. **13** (a) 21,370; (b) 236. **14** £10,714.

BRUNEL UNIVERSITY LIBRARY, Kingston Lane, Uxbridge, Middlesex, UB8 3PH (Tel 0895-37188; Telex 261173) Univ Libn: Mr C. E. N. Childs BA; Dep Libn: Mr R. W. P. Wyatt MA, FLA.
8 Science; technology; social sciences. **9** Photographs relating to I. K. Brunel (500). **10** CICRIS; LASER. **11** Yes, for ref only. **12** Term: Mon-Fri 9.00-21.00, Sat 9.30-21.00; vac: Mon-Fri 9.00-17.00. **13** (a) 120,000; (b) 2,200; (c) 800 videocassettes; 1,000 other audio-visual items. **14** £130,000. **15** (a) 32 (b) 9 (c) 8.

CAMBERWELL SCHOOL OF ART AND CRAFTS LIBRARY, Peckham Rd, London, SE5 8UF (Tel 01-703 0987) Libn: Mr Matthew T. Maxwell BA, ALA.
6 ILEA. **8** Art; design; crafts; graphics; printing **9** Walter Crane Colln. **10** BNBC. **11** No. **12** Mon-Thurs 9.30-19.00, Fri 9.30-18.30. **13** (a) 18,000; (b) 110. **15** (a) 2⅔ (b) 1 (c) 1.

CANNING HOUSE LIBRARY, 2 Belgrave Sq, London SW1 8PJ (Tel 01-2303/7) Libn: G. H. Green BA.
6 Hispanic & Luso-Brazilian Council. **8** All subjects (not highly technical) relating to parts of world where Portuguese & Spanish are spoken. **9** Technical dictionaries in Portuguese & Spanish; W. H. Hudson colln. **10** BLL. **11** Yes. **12** Mon-Fri 9.30-17.30. **13** (a) 50,000; (b) 200; (c) discs; film-strips. **15** (a) 3 (b) 2 (c) 1.

CATHOLIC CENTRAL LIBRARY, 47 Francis St, London, SW1P 1QR (Tel 01-834 6128) Administrator: Br Alan LeMay SA; Libn: Mrs Mary Buck.
6 Franciscan Friars of the Atonement, Graymoor, Garrison, NY, USA, 10524. **8** Scripture; theology; church history; ecumenism; Catholic biography. **9** Post-reformation catholic history; papal documents & magisterial statements; Vatican Council II; ecumenism. **10** BLL. **11** Yes, subscription for home reading (from £1.50). **12** Mon-Fri 10.30-18.30, Sat 10.30-16.30. **13** (a) over 50,000; (b) 150; (c) pamphlets; tracts; documentation. **14** £3,500. **15** (a) 3.

CENTRAL ELECTRICITY GENERATING BOARD, CENTRAL LIBRARY, Sudbury House, 15 Newgate St, London, EC1A 7AU (Tel 01-248 1202; Telex 883141) Libn: Miss G. G. Terry ALA; Principal Asst: Mr B. E. Collins ALA.
7 9 regional libs. **8** Electrical & mechanical engineering; power generation (all types & aspects); management; industrial relations. **9** Historical colln; students textbook colln (for students within the industry). **11** Yes, by written

LONDON—*continued*

application only.   **12** 8.30-16.50.   **13** (a) 70,000;
(b) 1,200.   **14** £54,000.   **15** (a) 16 (c) 6.

CENTRAL PUBLIC HEALTH LABORATORY LIBRARY,
Colindale Ave, London, NW9 5HT (Tel 01-205 7041) Libn:
Miss B. H. Whyte MA, ALA.
6 Public Health Laboratory Service Board.   **8** Medical
microbiology.   **11** No.   **12** Mon-Fri 9.30-17.30.
13 (a) 20,000; (b) 500.   **15** (a) 5 (b) 3 (c) 3.

CENTRAL SCHOOL OF ART AND DESIGN LIBRARY, Southampton Rd, London WC1B 4AP (Tel 01-405 1825 ext 39)
Tutor-Libn: Mr Donald Watts BA, MIL; Asst Libn: Mr
Maxwell A. Proctor.
6 ILEA.   **8** Art & design in ceramics, textiles, engineering,
industrial design, furniture, jewellery, theatre, graphics.
10 BLL.   **11** Yes, by appointment only.   **12** Term: Mon-
Thurs 9.30-19.00, Fri 9.30-17.30; Easter vac: Mon-Fri 9.30-
16.30.   **13** (a) 22,000; (b) 230; (c) c.6,000 pamphlets;
10,000 slides.   **14** £6,800.   **15** (a) 5 (b) 1.

CENTRE FOR OVERSEAS PEST RESEARCH LIBRARY,
College House, Wrights Lane, London, W8 5SJ (Tel 01-937
8191) Senior Scientific Officer: Miss P. J. Wortley BSc,
MIBiol, MIInfSc, DipLib.
6 Ministry of Overseas Development.   **8** Pest research in
agriculture & public health (particularly migratory pests of
regional or international importance, especially in the
tropics); research on environmental effects of pesticides.
9 Unique colln of literature on locusts & grasshoppers from
earliest records to present; locust & bird pest (Quelea)
archives; trade literature on spraying equipment & pesticides;
photographs.   **11** Yes, to accredited enquirers on prior
application to Libn.   **12** Mon-Fri 10.00-16.00.   **13** (a)
8165; (b) 860; (c) 10,000 photographs, slides, films; 17,000
maps; 7,000 charts; 300,000 mss; c.100 microforms;
c.50,000 reprints; records & tapes.   **15** (a) 10; (b) 7.

CHARTERED INSTITUTE OF TRANSPORT LIBRARY,
80 Portland Pl, London, W1N 4DP (Tel 01-580 5216) Libn:
Mrs J. F. O. Southgate BA, ALA.
6 Council of the Institute.   **8** Economics administration &
operation of all forms of transport (road, rail, sea & air), less
emphasis on engineering & scientific aspects.   **9** Reinohl
Colln of tickets.   **11** Yes, for ref only.   **12** Mon-Fri
10.00-17.00.   **13** (a) 15,000; (b) 300; (c) slides; filmstrips.
14 £2,000.   **15** (a) 1 (b) 1 (c) 1.

CHARTERED INSURANCE INSTITUTE LIBRARY, 20 Aldermanbury, London, EC2V 7HY (Tel 01-606 3835) Libn: Mr
Adrian J Lee BA, ALA; Dep Libn: Ms Margaret J. Saunders
BA, DipLib.
8 Insurance.   **9** Old insurance policies.   **11** Yes, for
bona-fide researchers only.   **12** Mon-Fri 10.00-18.00.
13 (a) 15,000; (b) 600; (c) cuttings; annual reports.
15 (a) 5 (b) 4 (c) 4.

CHELSEA SCHOOL OF ART LIBRARY, Manresa Rd, London,
SW3 6LS (Tel 01-352 4846 ext 8) Libn: Mr Clive Phillpot ALA.
6 ILEA.   **7** Lime Grove, (shared with Hammersmith &
West London College) W12 8EB (01-743 3321 ext 52).
8 General art history & closely related subjects. (Lime
Grove: art & design).   **9** Painting, sculpture & graphic arts
since 1800 (mainly Western); exhibition catalogues & foreign-
language material.   **10** ARLIS.   **11** No.   **12** 9.30-17.00.
(later during term).   **13** (a) 17,000 (+c.6,000 at Lime
Grove); (b) 100 (+c.100 at Lime Grove).

CHEMICAL SOCIETY LIBRARY, Burlington House, London,
W1V 0BN (Tel 01-734 9971; Telex 268001) Libn: Mr R. G.
Griffin, FLA; Senior Asst: Mr J. Kennedy, BA.
8 Chemistry.   **9** Historical (alchemy & early chemistry);
Nathan (explosives & gunnery).   **11** Yes, corporate bodies
may subscribe.   **12** Mon-Fri 9.00-18.00 (Thurs 21.00),
Sat 9.00-17.00.   **13** (a) 70,000; (b) 750.   **14** £24,000.
15 (a) 7 (b) 2 (c) 1.

CHISWICK POLYTECHNIC LIBRARY, (proposed merger with
Borough College & Maria Grey College, Sept 1976, to form
West London Institute of Higher Education, also with Isleworth
Polytechnic to form Hounslow Borough College), Bath Rd,

Chiswick, London, W4 2EN (Tel 01-995-3801 ext 11) Libn:
Miss M. W. Power ALA; Dep: Mrs J. Yeoh BA.
6 London Borough of Hounslow.   **7** Belmont Music Centre.
8 Health & social studies; business; fashion; general; music.
10 CICRIS.   **11** Yes, for ref only.   **12** Mon-Fri 8.45-
19.30 (Fri 17.30).   **13** (a) 26,000; (b) 230; (c) gramophone
records; microtexts.   **14** £9,000.   **15** (a) 3½ (b) 1 (c) 1.

CHURCH MISSIONARY SOCIETY LIBRARY, 157 Waterloo Rd,
London, SE1 8UU (Tel 01-928 8681) Libn: Miss J. M. Woods
ALA.
8 Missionary work; comparative religion; church overseas;
ecumenical movement.   **10** BLL.   **11** Yes.   **12** Mon-
Fri 9.30-17.00.   **13** (a) 20,000; (b) 56; (c) separate
Archives Dept, Archivist: Miss R. A. Keen BA.   **14** £400.
15 (a) 1½ (c) 1.

**CIDEC (INTERNATIONAL COPPER DEVELOPMENT
COUNCIL) LIBRARY,** Orchard House, Mutton Lane, Potters
Bar, Hertfordshire (Tel 0707-50711; Telex 27711) Libn: Miss
Renee Cross; Dep: Miss Susanne Mainzer.
8 Metallurgy; chemical, mechanical, electrical & marine
engineering; finishing & plating; metalworking; building &
plumbing; statistics (on copper).   **10** BLL; Aslib.   **11** Yes,
to bona-fide enquirers.   **12** Mon-Fri 9.30-17.00.
13 (a) 3,000; (b) 140.   **15** (a) 4 (b) 1 (c) 1.

CITY LITERARY INSTITUTE LIBRARY, Stukeley St, London,
WC2B 5LJ (Tel 01-242 6971) Mrs S. Mullner ALA.
6 ILEA.   **8** Humanities for adult education; ref.   **10** BLL;
ILEA.   **11** No.   **13** (a) 17,000; (b) 50.   **15** (a) 3 (c) 2.

**CITY OF LONDON POLYTECHNIC LIBRARY AND
LEARNING RESOURCES SERVICE,** Calcutta House, Old Castle
St, London, E1 7NT (Tel 01-283 1030; Telex 8812073) Dep
Chief Libn: Mr Alan Pritchard ALA, AIInfSc, MBCS.
7 84 Moorgate, EC2M 6SQ (01-283 1030), Libn: Mr C. Lindsey
ALA; Calcutta House, Old Castle St, E1 7NT (01-283 1030),
Libn: Miss M. Coppack BA, DipLib; Central House, 59/63
Whitechapel High St, E1 7PF (01-283 1030), Libn: Miss I.
Sutton BA, DipLib; 100 Minories, EC3N 1JY (01-283 1030),
Libn: Mrs A. Houghton BA, ALA.   **8** Business; science;
art; navigation.   **11** Yes, on application to site libns.
12 Term: 9.00-21.00; vac: 9.00-17.00.   **13** (a) 75,000;
(b) 1,600; (c) archives; microfiche; microfilm; videotapes;
audiotapes; slides; films; transparencies; filmstrips; wallcharts.   **14** £90,000.   **15** (a) 59 (b) 21 (c) 20.

CITY UNIVERSITY LIBRARY, St John St, London EC1V 4PB
(Tel 01-253 4399) Libn: Mr S. J. Teague BSc, FLA, FRSA;
Dep: Mr R. V. Fox ALA.
7 Ophthalmic Optics Lib, Cranwood Annexe, Cranwood St,
EC1V 9HH; Graduate Business Centre Lib, Lionel Denny
House, 23 Goswell Rd, EC1M 7BB.   **8** Engineering; applied
science; social science.   **9** British Computer Society
Library.   **10** BLL.   **11** Yes, for ref only, by application
to Libn.   **12** Term: Mon-Fri 9.00-21.00 (Fri 20.00), Sat
9.30-12.30; vac: Mon-Fri 9.00-17.00.   **13** (a) 100,000;
(b) 1,300; (c) several thousand microtexts; 10,000 slides;
30 Tape-slide programmes; video & audio tapes.
14 £104,100.   **15** (a) 30 (b) 11 (c) 8.

**CIVIL SERVICE DEPARTMENT, CENTRAL MANAGEMENT
LIBRARY,** Old Admiralty Building, Whitehall, London, SW1A
2AZ (Tel 01-839-7733 (ext 496)) Libn: Mrs B. M. Howard.
8 Management; policy sciences; public adminstration; computer applications.   **9** Published & semi-published material
of Treasury O & M Division 1945-68; Civil Service Department (from 1968).   **11** No, but applications from bona-fide
researchers considered.   **12** Mon-Fri 9.00-17.00.
13 (a) 20,000; (b) 300; (c) microfiche; microfilm; cassette
tapes.   **15** (a) 12 (c) 8.

CLOCKMAKERS' COMPANY LIBRARY, Guildhall Library,
Aldermanbury, London EC2P 2EJ (Tel 01-606 3030) Hon Libn:
Mr Godfrey Thompson FLA.
6 Worshipful Company of Clockmakers.   **8** Mainly histori-
cal horology.   **11** Yes.   **12** Mon-Sat 9.30-17.00.
13 (a) 950; (b) 8; (c) card index of clockmakers (mainly
British, but some foreign); 75 pictures; c.1,500 watchpapers;
Company's records.

COATES BROS & CO LTD, CENTRAL LIBRARY, St Mary

CODE: 1 Name of Library. **2** Address. **3** Telephone & Telex. **4** Officer in charge. **5** Deputy. **6** Governing body.
7 Branches. **8** Main Subjects. **9** Special Collections. **10** Co-operative Schemes. **11** Open to public? **12** Hours.
13 Stock: (a) books (b) periodicals (c) other. **14** Finance. **15** Staff: (a) non-manual (b) graduate (c) chartered librarians.

LONDON—*continued*

Cray, Orpington, Kent, BR5 3PP (Tel 0689-32545)
Senior Inf Officer: Mr John L. Orpwood BSc, BA, ARIC,
AIInfSc, ATSC.
8 Surface coatings technology (paints, printing inks, low
molecular weight polymers, adhesives). **9** BSI (500).
11 No. **12** 8.30-17.00. **13** (a) 2,500;(b) 180;(c)
c. 5,000 British patent specifications (from Group C3);
c. 2,000 foreign patent specifications (Europe & USA); c. 100
shelf feet trade literature; 200 other national standards;
raw materials; competititive products. **14** £3,500.
15 (a) 3 (b) 3.

COLLEGE FOR THE DISTRIBUTIVE TRADES LIBRARY,
30 Leicester Sq, London WC2H 7LE (Tel 01-839 1547) Libn:
Mr P. H. Gaze MSc, BSc, ALA; Dep: Mr J D. Bogue ALA.
6 ILEA. **7** Dept of Display, 107 Charing Cross Rd, WC2H
0DX; Dept of Food Commodities, 90 Briset House, 6-9 Briset
St, EC1M 5SL. **8** Retailing; marketing; advertising; textiles;
display techniques; meat sciences. **11** Yes, for ref only.
12 Term: 9.00-19.00; vac: 9.30-12.30, 13.30-16.30.
Branches vary. **13** (a) 14,000;(b) 180. **14** £6,900.

COLLEGE OF ALL SAINTS LIBRARY, London, N17 8HR
(Tel 01-808 2842) Tutor-Libn: Miss M. E. Edmondston BA,
FLA; Dep Libn: Mr C. P. Yates MA, ALA.
6 College of All Saints Foundation Ltd. **8** Education;
general (inc home economics). **10** BLL. **11** Yes, by
special permission. **12** Term: 8.50-21.00; vac: 9.00-
12.00, 13.00-17.00. **13** (a) c. 60,000;(b) c. 200;(c) 110
gramophone records. **14** £7,657. **15** (a) 4 (b) 2 (c) 2.

COLOMA COLLEGE OF EDUCATION LIBRARY, Wickham
Court, Layhams Rd, West Wickham, Kent, BR4 9HH (Tel
01-777 8321 ext 15) Coll Libn: Miss S. J. Winterburn ALA;
Dep: Sister Mary Bernardine.
6 Board of Governors of Coloma College. **8** General;
education; child psychology. **11** Yes, for ref only, at Libn's
discretion, by prior arrangement. **12** Term: Mon-Fri
9.30-18.30 (ref only, 22.00), Sat 10.00-12.15; vac: irregular,
but usually Mon-Fri 9.30-16.30. **13** (a) 47,000;(b) 207;
(c) gramophone records, films, tapes, charts etc in separate
resource centre. **14** £7,600. **15** (a) 4½ (c) 1.

COMMONWEALTH INSTITUTE LIBRARY AND RESOURCE
CENTRE, Kensington High St, London, W8 6NO (Tel 01-602
3252, ext 13) Libn: Mr Michael Foster FLA; Dep Libn: Mrs
C. Keane ALA.
8 People, culture, geographical description, economic &
political background of the contemporary Commonwealth
inc its 34 independant countries & their dependencies; education; race relations; immigration; aid & development.
9 Audio-visual materials on the Commonwealth; Commonwealth literature colln (imaginative literature, texts &
criticism in English); Commonwealth telephone directory
colln (all available telephone directories of Commonwealth
territories); newscuttings on the Commonwealth.
10 SCOLMA; Association of Commonwealth Literature &
Language Studies; Working Party on Library Holdings of
Commonwealth Literature. **11** Yes, loans on proof of
address. **12** Mon-Sat 10.00-17.30. **13** (a) over 40,000;
(b) 555;(c) over 10,000 audio-visual materials: tape recordings; discs; filmstrips; slides; ohp transparencies; illustrations; maps; pamphlets; periodical articles; portfolios (printed
materials); wallcharts; study kits; samples of products.
14 £16,256.

COMMONWEALTH SECRETARIAT LIBRARY, 10 Carlton
House Terrace, London, SW1Y 5AH (Tel 01-839 3411) Libn:
Miss Eileen H. Murtagh ALA.
8 Official statistics on economy of Commonwealth countries;
economics; development in Commonwealth; education; youth;
international affairs. **11** Yes, by appointment with Libn.

12 Mon-Fri 9.15-17.15. **13** (a) c.3,500;(b) c.3,200.
14 £5,500. **15** (a) 3 (c) 1.

CONFEDERATION OF BRITISH INDUSTRY LIBRARY, 21
Tothill St, London, SW1H 9LP (Tel 01-930 6711; Telex 21332
Cobustry London) Libn: Mr J. A. Hyde, ALA.
8 Industry & government relations; international affairs &
trade; economic situation; taxation; regional policy; prices &
incomes; industrial relations; social security; safety; company
law & practice; energy policy; industrial wastes & water
supply; education, training & manpower; research, development & standards; international representation of British
industry. **11** No, but help offered where possible.
12 9.30-17.30. **13** (a) 5,000;(b) 550;(c) newspapers;
company reports on microfilm; EEC & ILO publications.
15 (a) 6 (b) 2 (c) 2.

CONSUMERS' ASSOCIATION LIBRARY, 14 Buckingham St,
London, WC2N 6DS (Tel 01-839 1222; Telex 918197) Chief
Libn: Mr Peter A. Thomas FLA; Dep Libn: Mr Chris Lamb ALA.
8 Consumerism; product testing & standards; domestic
science; economics; engineering; travel & holidays; transport;
law. **9** Overseas consumer magazines (50); UK local consumer group magazines (70); cuttings on items of consumer
interest (1,800 files). **11** No. **12** Mon-Fri 10.00-18.00.
13 (a) 7,000; (b) 500; (c) 8,000 microfiche. **14** £6,000.
15 (a) 9 (b) 2 (c) 3.

COUNCIL FOR PLACES OF WORSHIP LIBRARY, (formerly
the Council for the Care of Churches), 83 London Wall,
London, EC2M 5NA (Tel 01-638 0971/2) Libn: Mr David
Michael Williams.
6 General Synod of the Church of England. **8** Ecclesiastical art & architecture (inc furnishings); ecclesiology & conservation (especially Church of England); liturgiology; heraldry; ecclesiastical law; church music; bibliography.
9 Illustrations, press cuttings, guide books on most of
churches and chapels of Church of England; information on
artists & craftsmen involved in church work; files on construction & conservation, inc records of recent conservation
work; mss work on spires; illustrations of sculptured
crosses. **10** Inter-library loans. **11** Yes, preferably
by prior arrangement. **12** Mon-Fri 10.00-18.00, Sat by
arrangement. **13** (a) c. 8,000; (b) 112; (c) 4,500 slides
(lending colln, catalogue available); archives; c. 14,000 survey
files. **15** (a) 1½ (b) 1 (c) 1.

COUNCIL FOR SMALL INDUSTRIES IN RURAL AREAS
LIBRARY, 35 Camp Rd, Wimbledon Common, London SW19
4UP (Tel 01-947 6761; Telex 21185) Libn: Miss J. A. Elliott.
6 Development Commission. **8** Business management &
technical subjects, with particular ref to small firms.
11 No. **13** (a) 3,500;(b) 150. **14** £2,500. **15** (a) 1.

CROYDON COLLEGE OF DESIGN AND TECHNOLOGY
LIBRARY, Fairfield, Croydon, Surrey, CR9 1DX (Tel 01-688
9271 ext 129) Coll Libn: Mr Peter Stracey ALA; Dep Libn:
Mrs M. F. Lawrence FLA.
6 London Borough of Croydon, Education Dept. **7** School
of Art & Design Annexe, Barclay Rd, Croydon, Surrey, CR9
1AX. **8** General; electrical & mechanical engineering;
building; business & management; printing; art history; costume; ceramics; social work; science. **10** BLL. **11** Yes,
for ref only. **12** Term: 9.00-21.00; vac: 9.00-17.00.
13 (a) 44,000; (b) 476. **14** £8,500. **15** (a) 6 (c) 3.

CRUISING ASSOCIATION LIBRARY, Ivory House, St
Katharine Dock, London, E1 9AT (Tel 01-481 0881) Asst Hon
Libn: Ms P. J. Boyland ALA.
6 Cruising Association Council. **8** Sailing; cruising; boat
design; maritime history; all aspects of boats & boating.
9 Cruise planning section (ie charts, port inf, harbour
details); atlases (old atlases & maps). **11** No, exc for visiting yachtsmen & students of naval history. **12** Mon-Fri
9.30-17.30. **13** (a) over 10,000; (b) 15; (c) c. 12 albums of
photographs of sailing craft. **14** c. £250.

LONDON—*continued*

CUSTOMS AND EXCISE, MUSEUM AND LIBRARY, King's
Beam House, Mark Lane, London EC3R 7HE (Tel 01-626
1515) Head of Lib Services: Mr S. R. Prestidge; Libn: Mr
T. G. Smith.
6 HM Honourable Commissioners of Customs and Excise.
7 Alexander House, 21 Victoria Ave, Southend-on-Sea.
8 Law & administration of indirect taxes, historical & current; trade, historical & current.   **9** Printed & ms material
relating to duties of Customs & Excise.   **10** BLL; Aslib.
11 Yes, by special permission.   **12** 9.00-17.00.   **13** (a)
33, 000; (b) 780.   **14** £26, 000.   **15** (a) 32 (b) 11 (c) 1;
translators 10.

DEPARTMENT OF EMPLOYMENT HEADQUARTERS
LIBRARY, 12 St James's Sq, London SW1Y 4LL (Tel 01-214
6734) Chief Libn: Mr H. E. Brooks FLA; Dep: Mrs E. C. Law
BA, ALA.
8 Industrial relations; management; trades unions; employment & unemployment; all labour topics; incomes; statistics
of these subjects.   **10** Inter-library loans.   **11** Yes, for
ref only, to researchers on application to Libn.   **12** Mon-
Fri 9.00-17.00.   **13** (a) c. 80, 000; (b) c. 450.   **15** (a) 23
(b) 3 (c) 4.

DEPARTMENT OF ENERGY LIBRARY, Thames House
South, Millbank, London SW1P 4QJ (Tel 01-211 4679; Telex
918777) Libn: Miss C. D. Carrington ALA.
8 All aspects of energy industries & energy policy; offshore
industry; minerals; iron & steel.   **11** Yes, by prior appointment only.   **12** Mon-Fri 9.00-17.00.   **13** (a) 20, 000;
(c) 2, 000 serials.   **15** (a) $9\frac{1}{2}$ (b) 1 (c) 3.

DEPARTMENT OF HEALTH AND SOCIAL SECURITY
LIBRARY, Alexander Fleming House, Elephant & Castle,
London SE1 6BY (Tel 01-407 5522 ext 6363; Telex 883669)
Chief Libn: Miss A. M. C. Kahn MBE, BA, FLA; Dep Libn:
Mr K. W. Best MBE, FLA.
7 Health Building Lib, Euston Tower, 286 Euston Rd, NW1
3DN (01-388 1188 ext 206), Libn: Miss I. M. M. Cameron MA,
ALA; Medicines Lib, Finsbury Sq, EC2A 1PP (01-638 6020
ext 328), Libn: Mr E. D. Dua ALA; Social Security Lib, 10
John Adam St, WC2N 6AB (01-217 3318), Libn: Mr D. W.
Whitehead ALA; Supplies Lib, 14 Russell Sq, WC1 5EP (01-
636 6811 ext 3258), Libn: Mrs E. K. Forshaw DipLib.
8 Health; personal social services; social security.
9 Poor Law history; public health history.   **11** Yes, for ref
only, for accredited researchers.   **12** Mon-Fri 9.00-17.00.
13 (a) 200, 000; (b) 1, 300.   **15** (a) 51 (b) 10 (c) 17.

DEPARTMENT OF INDUSTRY LIBRARY SERVICES, Central
Library, 1 Victoria St, London SW1H 0ET (Tel 01-215 3031;
Telex 918779) Head of Lib Services: K. A. Mallaber FLA;
Dep Libn: P. M. de Paris FLA.
7 Marine Lib, Sunley House, 90 High Holborn, WC1V 6LP,
Libn: Mr T. J. Marriott BA, ALA; Solicitor's Lib, Kingsgate
House, 66-74 Victoria St, SW1E 6SJ, Libn: Mr N. Hasker LLB,
ALA; Technology Lib, Abell House, John Islip St, SW1P 4LN,
Libn: Mrs V. E. Brown ALA.   **8** Economics & economic
conditions; industrial & commercial organisation; merchant
shipping; marine safety; oil pollution; law; science, technology & research administration.   **9** UK Parliamentary
papers (Lords & Commons) from 1801; UK local acts (from
1831, 1831-55 imperfect).   **10** BLL.   **11** Yes, by prior
appointment only.   **12** Mon-Thurs 9.00-17.30, Fri 9.00-
17.00.   **13** (b) 3, 000.   **15** (a) 77 (b) 22 (c) 32.

DEPARTMENT OF INLAND REVENUE, BOARD'S LIBRARY,
New Wing, Somerset House, London WC2R 1LB (Tel 01-438
6325) Libn: A. G. Cumbers; Dep Libn: R. B. Shoebridge.
8 Taxation; economics; law; financial statistics.   **9** Foreign
direct tax legislation.   **11** Yes, on application in writing to
Libn.   **12** Mon-Fri 9.00-17.30.   **13** (a) 45, 000; (b) 350;
(c) cuttings on fiscal topics.   **15** (a) 13.

DEPARTMENT OF THE ENVIRONMENT LIBRARY, 2
Marsham St, London SW1P 3EB (Tel 01-212 4847; Telex
22801) Chief Libn: Mr W. Pearson MBE, BSc, ALA.
7 Architects Sub-Lib, Becket House, Lambeth Palace Rd,
London SE17ER; Countryside Commission Lib, John Dower
House, Crescent Pl, Cheltenham, Gloucestershire, GL50 3RA

(0242-21381), Libn: Mr D. Kestell ALA; Directorate of
Ancient Monuments & Historic Buildings Lib, Fortress House,
23 Savile Row, London W1X 2AA (01-734 6010 ext 230) Libn:
Miss D. Parsons AALA; St Christopher House Sub-Lib (Transport Engineering), Room G/44, Southwark St, SE1 0TE (01-
928 7999 ext 2891), Libn: Mr R. Lymbery ALA; Central Water
Planning Unit Lib, Reading Bridge House, Reading, Berkshire, RG1 8PS (0734-57551), Libn: Mrs L. C. Dixon BA,
FLA.   **8** Housing; local government; regional planning;
town & country planning; new and expanded towns; roads;
traffic; transport (road, railway, inland waterways etc);
environmental pollution (clean air; coastal waters; noise;
refuse; radioactivity; water); water supply; sewage; countryside; sport & recreation; ports.   **9** Development & structure
plans; local acts (from 1780); Ministry of Housing & Local
Govt circulars (from 1848); Mayson Beeton Colln (books &
topographical prints of London & Home Counties); House of
Commons Sessional Papers (from 1818).   **10** BLL.
11 No, except to accredited researchers & professional staff
of local authorities & of new towns, by appointment on written
application.   **12** Mon-Fri 10.00-16.30.   **13** (a) 250, 000;
(b) 2, 500; (c) c. 12, 500 microforms; Census Data & Environmental Protection Agency (U.S.) deposit library.
14 £180, 000.   **15** (a) 80 (b) 18 (c) 34.

DESIGN COUNCIL PHOTOGRAPHIC LIBRARY, Design
Centre, 28 Haymarket, London SW1Y 4U (Tel 01-839 8000;
Telex 8812963) Libn: Miss Rita Exner BA; Clerk/Asst Ms
Helen Wilkes.
6 Council of the Design Council.   **8** All aspects of design,
architecture; consumer goods; crafts; furniture; graphics;
interior design; lighting; street furniture; tableware; textiles;
toys; transport; wallpaper.   **9** Black & white photographs
of Festival of Britain, Britain Can Make It Exhibition, Utility
Furniture etc.   **11** Yes.   **12** 9.30-17.00.   **13** (c)
c. 15, 000 ref 35 mm colour transparencies; black & white
historical collns.   **15** (a) 2 (b) 1.

DICKENS HOUSE LIBRARY, 48 Doughty St, London WC1N
2LT (Tel 01-405 2127) Museum Curator & Libn: Miss
Marjorie E. Pillers.
6 Trustees of Dickens House.   **8** Dickens: his life & works;
critical works.   **9** 1st editions.   **11** No, but genuine
researchers by appointment, £2 fee.   **12** Mon-Fri 10.00-
17.00.   **13** (a) c. 5, 000; (c) c. 4, 000 photographs; grama-
phone records & tapes; press cuttings.

DIRECTORATE OF OVERSEAS SURVEYS, TECHNICAL
SERVICES LIBRARY, Kingston Rd, Tolworth, Surbiton, Surrey
KT5 9NS (Tel 01-337 8661) Senior Map Officer:Mrs I. C.
Meux MA.
6 Ministry of Overseas Development.   **7** Map Lib, (ext
241), Libn: Mrs E. V. Kenworthy BSc; Survey Data Lib, (ext
242), Libn: Mr R. T. Porter BA; Air Photo Lib, (ext 290),
Libn: Miss L. E. Parker BSc; Book Lib, (ext 235), Libn: Mr
A. J. Gillies BSc.   **8** Production of topographical maps by
photogrammetric methods.   **10** BLL.   **11** Yes, for ref
only, by appointment.   **12** Mon-Fri 9.30-16.00.
13 (a) c. 14, 000; (b) c. 550; (c) 80, 000 maps; 2, 000, 000 air
photographs.   **14** £850.   **15** (b) 7.

DULWICH COLLEGE LIBRARY, London SE21 7LD.
6 Governors of Dulwich College.   **8** Theology; classics;
law; English literature; history.   **9** Manor of Dulwich
archives; Henslowe-Alleyn mss (Elizabethan theatre);
Reading mss (18th cent music); Dulwich College archives.
11 Yes, for scholarly work, after written application.
12 Term: Mon-Sat 9.00-16.00 (Wed & Sat 12.00).
13 (a) 65, 000; (b) 40; (c) archives; records.   **15** (a) 10 (b)
1 (c) 1.

EALING TECHNICAL COLLEGE LIBRARY, St Mary's Rd,
Ealing, London W5 5RF (Tel 01-579 4111) Coll Libn: Mr
R. A. Thomas FLA, DMA; Dep Coll Libn: Mrs I. Hurst ALA.
6 London Borough of Ealing.   **7** Woodlands Ave, Acton
W3 9DN, Libn: Miss M. W. Robinson BA, ALA.   **8** Business;
economics; languages (Chinese, French, German, Russian &
Spanish); art; photography; law; librarianship; hotel & catering
trades.   **10** CICRIS.   **11** Yes, for ref only.   **12** Term:
Mon-Fri 9.15-21.00, Sat 10.00-16.00; vac: Mon-Fri 9.30-
16.30.   **13** (a) 68, 280; (b) 884; (c) 1, 600 slides; 400 tapes;
112 filmstrips; 82 microtexts.   **15** (a) 16 (b) 3 (c) 7.

CODE: 1 Name of Library. **2** Address. **3** Telephone & Telex. **4** Officer in charge. **5** Deputy. **6** Governing body.
7 Branches. **8** Main Subjects. **9** Special Collections. **10** Co-operative Schemes. **11** Open to public? **12** Hours.
13 Stock: (a) books (b) periodicals (c) other. **14** Finance. **15** Staff: (a) non-manual (b) graduate (c) chartered librarians.

LONDON—*continued*

EAST HAM COLLEGE OF TECHNOLOGY LIBRARY, High St
South, East Ham, London E6 4ER (Tel 01-472 1480) Libn:
Mr L. W. Plumstead BA, ALA; Dep Libn: Miss C. Watkins BA.
6 London Borough of Newham.   **8** Art; building; business;
electrical & mechanical engineering; gas technology; liberal
studies; science.   **10** LASER.   **11** Yes, with Libn's consent.   **12** Term: Mon-Fri 9.00-20.30; vac: Mon-Fri 9.00-
17.00.   **13** (a) 27,000; (b) 170.   **14** £7,000.   **15** (a) 4
(b) 2 (c) 1.

ELECTRICITY COUNCIL LIBRARY, 30 Millbank, London
SW1P 4RD (Tel 01-834 2333) Libn: Mrs I. Elsom ALA; Dep:
Miss A. Milroy ALA.
8 Electricity supply; administrative, commercial & economic
aspects; distribution engineering.   **9** Electricity supply
industry annual reports (from 1921).   **10** BLL.   **11** Yes,
at Libn's discretion.   **12** Mon-Fri 8.45-17.15.   **13** (a)
18,000; (b) 600.   **14** £25,300.   **15** (a) 6 (c) 2.

ENGLISH-SPEAKING UNION, WALTER HINES PAGE
MEMORIAL LIBRARY, AND BOOKS ACROSS THE SEA,
Dartmouth House, 37 Charles St, London W1X 8AB (Tel 01-
629 0104).
6 National Committee of England & Wales, English-Speaking
Union.   **8** American life, literature & history; small sections on Australia, Canada, New Zealand & India.   **10** Inter-
library loans.   **11** No, exc at Libn's discretion.   **12** Mon-
Fri 9.30-17.30.   **13** (a) c. 11,500.   **15** (a) 1 (b) 2.

EUGENICS SOCIETY LIBRARY, 69 Eccleston Sq, London
SW1V 1PJ (Tel 01-834 2091) Hon Libn: Prof B. Benjamin;
Gen Sec: Miss S. E. Waters.
8 Eugenics; population; biology; genetics; sociology; sexual
sociology.   **10** BLL.   **11** Yes, by appointment only.
12 9.30-17.30.   **13** (a) c. 5,000; (b) c. 45; (c) heredity
charts suitable for colleges & schools.   **14** c. £350.
15 (a) ½.

EVANGELICAL LIBRARY, 78A Chiltern St, London W1M 2HB
(Tel 01-935 6997) Libn & Secretary: Mr Gordon R. Sayer.
8 Theology; church history.   **10** BLL.   **11** Yes, by sub-
scription/donation.   **12** Mon-Sat 10.00-17.00.   **13** (a)
250,000; (b) 130; (c) portraits; printers blocks of portraits &
illustrations.   **15** (a) 3½.

FAWCETT LIBRARY, 27 Wilfred St, London SW1E 6PR (Tel
01-828 4966) Libn: Miss M. Surry ALA.
6 Fawcett Library Trust.   **8** Social, legal & economic
position of women everywhere; all topics dealt with in respect
of women (eg sport, art, etc).   **9** Archives of women's
organisations; photographic colln.   **10** BLL.   **11** Yes,
with £3.50 (max.) membership fee.   **12** Mon-Fri 10.30-
17.00.   **13** (a) 20,000; (c) newspaper cuttings.

FLETCHERS' COMPANY LIBRARY, Guildhall Library,
Aldermanbury, London EC2P 2EJ (Tel 01-606 3030) Libn of
Guildhall Library: Mr Godfrey Thompson FLA.
6 The Worshipful Company of Fletchers.   **8** Archery.
11 Yes.   **12** Mon-Sat 9.00-17.00.   **13** (a) 112; (b) 2; (c)
archives of the Company on deposit.   **15** Served by the
staff of Guildhall Library.

FOREIGN AND COMMONWEALTH OFFICE/MINISTRY OF
OVERSEAS DEVELOPMENT JOINT LIBRARY, Sanctuary
Buildings, Great Smith St, London SW1P 3BZ (Tel 01-212
6568) Libn: Miss E. C. Blayney ALA.
7 Downing St, SW1 (01-930 2323); Cornwall House, Stamford
St, SE1 (01-928 7511); Eland House, Stag Pl, SW1.   **8** International relations & diplomacy; history, economy, politics &
law of foreign & Commonwealth countries; early travel;
diplomatic memoirs; treaty collns, overseas development &
technical assistance.   **9** Official publications of all
Commonwealth countries & territories inc a comprehensive
colln of Commonwealth legislation; map colln (current maps,

charts, atlases & gazeteers).   **10** BLL.   **11** Yes, for ref
only.   **12** Mon-Fri 9.30-17.30.

FRENCH INSTITUTE LIBRARY, 15 Queensberry Pl, London
SW7 2DT (Tel 01-589 6211 ext 33).
6 Institut Français.   **8** French literature, history, sciences,
language, philosophy, arts.   **11** Yes, for ref only.   **12** Mon-
Fri 10.00-18.00 (Tues & Fri 20.00).   **13** (a) 62,000; (b)
250.   **15** (a) 4½ (c) 1.

FURZEDOWN COLLEGE LIBRARY (will merge with Phillipa
Fawcett College), Welham Rd, London SW17 9BU (Tel 01-672
0131) Chief Libn: Mr Brian Wiltshire BA, ALA; Dep Libn:
Ms Kathleen Furnham ALA.
6 ILEA.   **8** Education; sociology; English & American
literature; linguistics; French; history; geography; science;
music; dance; maths; religion.   **9** Teaching practice
library; model school library; media resources colln.
10 BLL; WANDPETLS.   **11** No.   **12** Term: Mon-Fri
8.45-20.00 (Fri 18.00); vac: Mon-Fri 9.00-16.30.   **13** (a)
60,000; (b) 300; (c) 3,500 gramophone records; 10,000 slides,
tapes etc.   **14** £9,000.   **15** (a) 8 (b) 3 (c) 4.

GARDENERS' COMPANY LIBRARY, Guildhall Library,
Aldermanbury, London EC2P 2EJ (Tel 01-606 3030) Hon Libn:
Mr Godfrey Thompson FLA.
6 The Worshipful Company of Gardeners.   **8** Historical
works on gardens & gardening.   **11** Yes.   **12** Mon-Sat
9.30-17.00.   **13** (a) 469; (b) 1.

GARNETT COLLEGE LIBRARY, Downshire House,
Roehampton Lane, London SW15 4HR (Tel 01-788 2586)
Libn: Mrs R. J. Lovell FLA; Dep Libn: Mrs A. E. Frogatt
ALA.
6 ILEA.   **7** Central London Annexe, West Sq, SE1, Libn:
Miss B. Larkum ALA.   **8** Psychology; philosophy; sociology;
education.   **10** BLL; WANDPETLS; ILEA.   **11** No, exc for
ref.   **12** Term: 9.00-18.30; vac: 9.00-17.00.   **13** (a)
30,000; (b) 240; (c) gramophone records; video tapes; audio
tapes; film loops; slides; ohp transparencies.   **15** (a)
6½ (b) 2 (c) 4.

GARRATT GREEN SCHOOL LIBRARY, Burntwood Lane,
London SW17 0AQ (Tel 01-946 6201) Libn: Mrs A. S. Richards
ALA.
6 GLC; ILEA.   **8** General.   **10** WANDPETLS.   **11** No.
12 During school time.   **13** (a) 20,000; (b) 65; (c) tapes;
slides; multi-media kits; film loops; discs; wallcharts; film
strips; ohp transparencies; illustrations.   **15** (a) 1.

GEOLOGICAL SOCIETY OF LONDON LIBRARY, Burlington
House, Piccadilly, London, W1V 0JU (Tel 01-734 5673).
8 Geology & allied sciences.   **9** Sir Roderick Murchison's
mss & journals.   **11** Yes, for a small fee.   **12** Tues,
Thurs & Fri 10.00-17.30, Mon 13.00-17.30, Wed 10.00-20.00.
13 (a) 300,000; (b) 702; (c) 32,000 geological maps & sections
(current and rare); 3,700 rare books.   **15** (a) 2 (b) 2.

GLAZIERS' COMPANY LIBRARY, Guildhall Library,
Aldermanbury, London, EC2P 2EJ (Tel 01-606 3030)
Libn of Guildhall Lib: Mr Godfrey Thompson FLA.
6 Worshipful Company of Glaziers.   **8** Historical works
on decorative & stained glass.   **11** Yes.   **12** Mon-Sat.
9.30-17.00.   **13** (a) 175; (c) Company's records.

GOETHE-INSTITUTE LONDON, LIBRARY, 50-51 Princes
Gate, Exhibition Rd, London, SW7 2PG (Tel 01-589 3648/9)
Libn: Mrs Inge Niemöller DipBibl; Dep: Miss Luise von Löw
DipBibl.
8 Literature; history; art; music; philosophy; religion;
geography; economics; politics; sociology; pedagogics;
folklore; theatre.   **9** Modern literature; contemporary
history; languages.   **10** Inter-library loans.   **11** Yes.
12 Mon, Tues, Thur, Fri 15.00-20.00, Wed & Sat 10.00-13.00.
13 (a) 20,000; (b) 125; (c) 17 daily papers.   **15** (a) 4 (c) 2.

LONDON—*continued*

GOLDSMITHS' HALL LIBRARY, Foster Lane, London,
EC2V 6BN (Tel 01-606 8971) Miss S. M. Hare BA.
6 Worshipful Company of Goldsmiths. **8** Gold & silver
wares; jewellery; hall-marking; related subjects; city livery
companies. **9** Twining colln (books, pamphlets & photographs of Crown Jewels & Regalia); c. 10,000 colour slides
of antique & modern silver & jewellery; 9 colour films.
11 Yes, by appointment. **12** Mon-Fri 10.00-17.30.
13 (a) c. 6,500; (b) 25; (c) c. 450 vols of company records
(from 14th cent); display index of c. 10,000 photographs of
jewellery & silver. **14** £650. **15** (a) 2 (b) 1.

GRAND LODGE LIBRARY, Freemasons' Hall, Great Queen
St, London, WC2B 5AZ (Tel 01-405 3633) Libn & Curator of
Museum: Mr T. O. Haunch MA; Asst Libn: Mr J. M. Hamill
BA, ALA.
6 United Grand Lodge of England. **8** History & development of Freemasonry. **9** Commonwealth & foreign
material. **11** No. **13** (a) 33,000. **15** (a) 5. (b) 2 (c) 1.

GRAY'S INN LIBRARY, South Sq, Gray's Inn, London,
WC1R 5EU (Tel 01-242 8592) Libn: P. C. Beddingham.
6 Honourable Society of Gray's Inn. **8** Law. **9** Works
of Francis Bacon. **11** No. **12** 9.00-20.00.
13 (a) 38,000. **15** (a) 4.

Greater London Council

MEMBERS' LIBRARY, Room 114, County Hall, London,
SE1 7PB (Tel 01-633 7132/6759) Libn: Mr H. O. Wilson
ALA; Dep Libn: Miss E. J. Cobb ALA.
8 London history & topography; local government &
related subjects. **9** Prints, drawings & maps; photo-
graph library (London, LCC & GLC services); run in
conjunction with the Greater London Record Office which
contains records of the GLC and its predecessors,
manorial, ecclesiastical, business, estate & private
records relating to the London area. **10** BLL; Aslib.
11 Yes, for ref only. **12** Mon-Fri 9.15-17.00.
13 (a) 90,000; (b) 320; (c) 30,000 prints & drawings;
200,000 photographs. **15** (a) 9 (b) 1 (c) 3.

RESEARCH LIBRARY, Director General's Dept, Room 514,
County Hall, London, SE1 7PB (Tel 01-633 6061) Head of
Research Lib: Mr A. Gonasall MSc, BSc, MIInfSc; Dep: Mr W.
Thom ALA.
7 Civil Engineering Lib, Room 609, Broadway Buildings,
WC1, Libn: Mrs P. Hamlyn ALA. **8** Local government
management, finance, transportation, planning, social
services, housing, tourism & recreation. **9** National &
local statistical series; 35 mm slides on London
(especially transportation & planning); complete Greater
London Development Plans. **11** Yes, by prior arrangement. **12** 8.00-17.30. **13** (a) 12,000; (b) 500;
(c) over 2,000 reports, periodicals & pamphlets on
microfiche; 10,000 pamphlets & reports. **14** £15,000.
15 (a) 23; (b) 4; (c) 8.

HACKNEY COLLEGE LIBRARY, Hackney Centre, 89-115
Mare St, London E8 3RH (Tel 01-985 8484) Coll Libn: Miss
P. A. Trevett FLA; Assoc Libn: Mr A. Gardner ALA.
6 Hackney College Board of Governors; ILEA. **7** Poplar
Centre, High St, E14 (01-987 4205) Libn: Mr A. Gardner;
Stoke Newington Centre, Ayrsome Rd, N16, Libn: Mr A.
Thomas BA, ALA; Dalston Lane, Triangle House, Cassland
Rd Annexe, E8. **8** Science; engineering; horology; building;
marine, electrical & motor vehicle engineering.
9 Horology. **11** No. **12** Term: 9.00-19.00; vac: 9.30-
16.30. **13** (a) 45,000; (b) 200; (c) c. 500 nonbook materials.
14 £13,600. **15** (a) 13 (b) 1 (c) 7.

HAMMERSMITH AND WEST LONDON COLLEGE LIBRARY,
Greyhound Rd, London W14 9SE (Tel 01-385 7183) Chief Libn:
Mrs N. J. Venshou ALA; Dep Libn: Mrs P. Trenaman MA,
ALA.
6 ILEA. **7** Brook Green, W6 (01-602 3771) Libn: Miss B.
Martins ALA; Macbeth St, W6 (01-748 7422); Hugon Rd, SW6
(01-736 0181); Lime Grove (shared with Chelsea School of
Art), W12 (01-743 3321). **8** General; business; professional
studies (eg banking, accountancy); building management &

building craft studies; English as a foreign language.
10 CICRIS. **11** Yes, for ref only. **12** Mon-Fri 8.45-
20.30. branches vary. **13** (a) 50,000; (b) 390; (c) slides;
tapes; cassettes; records; ohp transparencies; filmstrips.
14 £15,000. **15** (a) 12 (b) 3 (c) 7.

HARROW COLLEGE OF TECHNOLOGY AND ART LIBRARY,
Watford Rd, Northwick Park, Harrow, Middlesex, HA1 3TP
(Tel 01-864 4411) Libn: Mr G. A. Beech ALA, Cert Ed; Asst
Libns: Mrs J. McFarlane BA, ALA; Mr J. Priestley BA.
6 London Borough of Harrow. **8** Art; photography;
management; hairdressing; science; health & community
studies; engineering. **10** CICRIS. **11** Yes. **12** 8.45-
20.30. **13** (a) 22,000; (b) 300; (c) 12,000 slides.
14 £10,000. **15** (a) 7 (b) 3 (c) 2.

HARROW SCHOOL, VAUGHAN LIBRARY, Harrow-on-the-
Hill, Middlesex, HA1 3HW, Vaughan Libn: Mr J. H. W.
Morwood MA.
8 General. **9** Part of 'Framley Parsonage' ms (only
Trollope ms in England). **11** No. **13** (c) Harrow school
archives (inc some Byron documents).

HAVERING TECHNICAL COLLEGE LIBRARY, 42 Ardleigh
Green Rd, Hornchurch, Essex, RM11 2LL (Tel 040 24-55011)
Tutor-Libn: Mr Michael J. Rees BA, ALA, Cert Ed; Asst
Libn: Mr David Hare BSc.
6 London Borough of Havering. **8** Mechanical, automobile,
electrical & electronic engineering; science; radio & TV
engineering; accountancy; banking; health service administration; business; law; management; social work; teacher-
education; art; crafts; design; display; hairdressing; beauty;
languages; mental handicaps. **11** Yes, for ref only.
12 Mon-Thurs 9.00-20.00, Fri 9.00-17.00.
13 (a) 26,750; (b) 175; (c) 740 wall charts; 120 gramophone
records; 50 (8 mm) filmloops; 475 filmstrips; 15 learning
programmes; 2 (16 mm) films; 45 multi-media kits; 200
overhead transparencies; 150 audio tapes; 100 video tapes;
21 microfilms. **14** £4,500. **15** (a) 3½ (b) 2 (c) 1.

HEALTH AND SAFETY EXECUTIVE LIBRARY, Baynards
House, 1 Chepstow Place, Westbourne Grove, London
W2 4TG (Tel 01-229 3456 ext 497) Libn: Mrs M. K. Mailes
MA, BSc, ALA, MIInfSc; Dep Libn: Miss O. Jesuvant BSc,
ALA.
7 Industrial Health and Safety Laboratories Lib, Cricklewood. **8** Occupational health & safety in all aspects of
industry & working life. **11** Yes, upon formal application
to Libn. **12** 9.00-17.00. **13** (a) 4,000; (b) 400;
(c) slides; pamphlets. **15** (a) 8; (b) 4; (c) 2.
(c) 2.

HIGHGATE LITERARY AND SCIENTIFIC INSTITUTION,
11 South Grove, Highgate Village, London, N6 6BS (Tel
01-340 3343) Libn: Mrs Gwynydd E. Gosling.
6 Committee of Management of Highgate Literary &
Scientific Institution. **8** General. **9** Local history;
London; Coleridge. **11** No, except for ref to local collns.
12 Reading Room: Mon-Sat 10.00-18.00 (Wed & Sat 13.00);
Library: Mon-Sat 10.00-13.00, 15.00-18.00 (Wed & Sat
13.00). **13** (a) c. 30,000; (b) 25; (c) archives; photographs;
prints. **14** £600. **15** (a) 1.

HISTORICAL ASSOCIATION LIBRARY, 59A Kennington Park
Rd, London, SE11 4JH (Tel 01-735 3901/2974) Dep Libn:
Miss Veronica Dodson.
6 Council of Historical Association. **8** History & allied
subjects. **9** School textbook colln (history only).
11 No. **12** Mon-Fri 10.00-17.30, Sat 10.00-12.00.
13 (a) c. 720; (b) c. 25. **15** (a) 1.

HOME OFFICE LIBRARY, Romney House, Marsham St,
London, SW1P 3DY (Tel 01-212 5945; Telex 916024)
Home Office Libn: Mr D. B. Gibson FLA; Dep Libn: Miss
K. M. Suddaby ALA.
7 Legal & Political Lib, Whitehall, SW1A 2AP (01-930 8100
ext 145) Libn: Miss A. J. Ezard ALA; Construction Lib,
30 Orange St, WC2H 7HT (01-930 8499 ext 33), Branch Libn:
Mr. J. Baldwin BSc, DipLib. **8** Sociology; law; politics.
11 Yes, upon prior application for material not readily
obtainable elsewhere. **12** 9.30-17.30. **13** (a) 50,000;
(b) 700; (c) 144 reels of microfilm. **14** £87,726.
15 (a) 20½ (b) 6 (c) 5.

CODE: **1** Name of Library. **2** Address. **3** Telephone & Telex. **4** Officer in charge. **5** Deputy. **6** Governing body.
7 Branches. **8** Main Subjects. **9** Special Collections. **10** Co-operative Schemes. **11** Open to public? **12** Hours.
13 Stock: (a) books (b) periodicals (c) other. **14** Finance. **15** Staff: (a) non-manual (b) graduate (c) chartered librarians.

LONDON—*continued*

HONG KONG GOVERNMENT OFFICE LIBRARY, 6 Grafton
St, London W1X 3LB (Tel 01-499 9821; Telex 28404 Hongaid
London) Libn: Mr John Owston ALA.
8 Hong Kong government publications; all aspects of Hong
Kong life & affairs (especially commerce, industry & trade).
9 Over 12, 000 photographs; films & slides. **11** Yes, at
Libn's discretion. **12** Mon-Fri 9.30-17.30.
13 (a) 2, 500; (b) 80 (inc 6 H.K. newspapers). **15** (a) 3;
(c) 1.

HORNIMAN MUSEUM AND LIBRARY, London Rd, Forest
Hill, London, SE23 3PQ (Tel 01-699 2339) Libn: Mr D. W.
Allen BSc, ALA; Asst Libn: Miss H. A. Wheeler ALA.
6 ILEA. **8** Anthropology; ethnography; musicology;
zoology. **11** Yes, for ref only. **12** Tues-Sat 10.30-
17.45, Sun 14.00-17.45. **13** (a) 20, 000; (b) 150; (c) illustrations, cuttings & slides. **14** £1, 500. **15** (a) 2 (b) 1
(c) 2.

HOTEL CATERING AND INSTITUTIONAL MANAGEMENT
ASSOCIATION LIBRARY, 191 Trinity Rd, London SW17 7HN
(Tel 01-672 4251) Inf Officer: Ms Pamela Shillito BSc.
8 Management; catering; food service hygiene; design.
11 Yes, but only for ref. **12** Mon-Fri 9.00-12.30, 13.30-
17.00. **13** (a) c. 1, 500; (b) 32. **14** £650. **15** (a) 1½
(b) 1.

HOUSE OF COMMONS LIBRARY, London, SW1A 0AA (Tel
01-219 3666; Telex 916318) Mr D. C. L. Holland CB, MA;
Dep: Dr D. Menhennet MA, DPhil, FRSA.
8 Parliament; law; modern history; social sciences; biography;
research services. **9** Parliamentary papers (British)
(from 1801); statistical & scientific collns; government, EEC
& UN publications. **11** No, except in certain special circumstances when the House is not sitting; apply to Libn.
13 (a) 125, 000; (b) 1, 500; (c) press cuttings. **15** (a) 72
(b) 29 (c) 11.

HOUSE OF LORDS LIBRARY, Old Palace Yard, Westminster,
London SW1A 0PW (Tel 01-219 5242) Libn: Mr C. S. A.
Dobson CBE, BA, FSA; Asst Libn: Mr R. H. V. C. Morgan BA.
8 Law; parliament; history; general; literature.
9 Sessional papers of both houses (from 1801); peerage
cases & peerage law; Peel colln (Irish tracts, c. 1600-1810).
11 Yes, to researchers through written application to
Libn for specific printed works not readily accessible
elsewhere. **12** 10.30-16.30 if House is not sitting for
public business. **13** (a) c. 90, 000. **15** (a) 8 (b) 2.

HOUSING CENTRE LIBRARY, 62 Chandos Pl, London
WC2N 4HG (Tel 01-240 3424) Inf Officer: Miss Marjorie
Cleaver AIHM.
6 Housing Centre Trust. **8** Housing; planning; architecture; design; building; history. **11** Yes, for ref only.
12 9.30-17.00.

HUGUENOT LIBRARY, c/o University College, Gower St,
London WC1E 6BT (Tel 01-387 7050 ext 245) Hon Libn:
C. F. A. Marmoy FLA.
6 French Protestant Hospital & Huguenot Society of London.
8 History; biography; genealogy; theology; (in relation to
Huguenots & their dispersion). **9** Archives of French
Protestant Hospital (founded 1718, now at Rochester);
Wagner colln of pedigrees; 'Royal Bounty' Archives.
11 No; academic information through Libn, but individual
genealogical information from Huguenot Society's research
asst, Mrs J. Wheatley FLA, 177 Hampstead Way, NW11 7YA.
12 As Univ Coll Lib's Rare Books Room. **13** (a) c. 4, 000;
(b) 12. **14** £35. **15** (c) 1.

IBM TECHNICAL INFORMATION CENTRE LIBRARY, 17
Addiscombe Rd, Croydon, Surrey, CR9 6HS (Tel 01-686 0621;
Telex Inbusmac Crydn 264873)
6 International Business Machines, UK Ltd. **8** Data

Processing & its applications; management theory &
techniques. **9** IBM manuals. **10** BLL; SASLIC.
11 Yes, for ref only. **12** Mon-Fri 9.00-17.30 (Fri 17.00).

IMPERIAL WAR MUSEUM, DEPARTMENT OF PRINTED
BOOKS, Lambeth Rd, London SE1 6HZ (Tel 01-735 8922)
Keeper of the Dept: Dr G. M. Bayliss ALA; Dep Head of Dept:
Mr D. B. Nash.
6 Trustees of Imperial War Museum. **8** All aspects of
the two World Wars & of other military operations involving
Britain & the Commonwealth since 1914. **11** Yes, by
appointment only. **12** Mon-Fri 10.00-17.00. Closed last
two weeks of Oct. **13** (a) c. 115, 000; (b) 350; (c) 15, 000
maps & technical drawings; 25, 000 pamphlets. **15** (a) 12
(b) 4 (c) 2.

INDEPENDENT BROADCASTING AUTHORITY LIBRARY,
70 Brompton Rd, London SW3 1EY (Tel 01-584 7011)
Chief Libn: Mrs Linda Gill-Roberts ALA; Dep Libn: Miss
Jacqueline Pearce ALA.
7 Crawley Court, Winchester, Hampshire, Libn-in-charge:
Mrs L. S. Roberts BA, ALA. **8** World broadcasting;
electrical & electronic engineering. **9** Press cuttings on
broadcasting (from 1950). **10** BLL; HATRICS. **11** Yes,
for ref only. **12** Mon-Fri 9.30-17.30. **13** (a) c. 6, 000;
(b) c. 200; (c) TV Times, Radio Times on microfilm.
15 (a) 6 (c) 2.

INDIA HOUSE LIBRARY, High Commission of India, Aldwych,
London WC2B 4NA (Tel 01-836 8484; Telex HICOMIND LDN
267166) Inf Officer: Miss M. Travis.
6 Gov of India. **8** Most subjects of Indian interest (in
English). **9** Mahatma Gandhi; Govt of India official publications: Central Govt (from 1920), State Govt (less well
covered). **10** BLL; inter-library loans. **11** Yes.
12 Mon-Fri 9.00-13.00, 14.00-17.00. **13** (a) c. 55, 185;
(b) 92. **15** (a) 1.

INDIA OFFICE LIBRARY AND RECORDS, Orbit House, 197
Blackfriars Rd, London SE1 8NG (Tel 01-928 9531) Dir:
Miss J. C. Lancaster MA, FSA, FRHistS, ALA; Dep Libn:
Mr R. G. C. Desmond MA, FLA; Dep Archivist: Mr Martin I.
Moir MA.
6 Foreign & Commonwealth Office. **7** Newspaper
Reading Room, Bush House, Aldwych, London WC2.
8 South Asian studies. **9** Oriental mss, prints, drawings
& photographs (printed catalogue); archives of East India Co
(1600-1858), Board of Control (1784-1858), India Office
(1858-1947) & Burma Office (1937-1948). **11** Yes, by
written application on a form obtainable from Director.
12 Mon-Fri 9.30-18.00, Sat 9.30-13.00; Newspaper Reading
Room: Tues & Thurs 10.00-17.00. **13** (a) 100, 000
(Western languages) & 200, 000 (Oriental languages);
(b) 600 (Western) & 80 (Oriental); (c) 20, 000 Oriental mss;
25, 000 prints, drawings & miniatures; 120, 000 photographs;
20, 000 maps. **15** (a) 66; (b) 17; (c) 7.

INNER LONDON EDUCATION AUTHORITY LIBRARY,
County Hall, London SE1 7PP (Tel 01-633 6990) Libn: Mr H. R
Mainwood OBE, FLA; Dep: Mrs K. Pearce ALA.
8 General; education; psychology; child study. **10** BLL.
11 No, except for ref. **12** Term: Mon-Fri 9.00-18.00,
Sat 9.00-12.00; vac: Mon-Fri 9.00-16.30. **13** (a) 280, 000;
(b) 13.

INNER TEMPLE LIBRARY, London EC4Y 7DA (Tel 01-353
2959) Libn: Mr W. W. S. Breem; Sub-Libn: Miss D. A. Parnham.
6 Honourable Society of the Inner Temple. **8** English
& Commonwealth law; Scots, Irish & South African law;
Roman law; canon & ecclesiastical law; jurisprudence.
9 English legal history; topography; geneaology & heraldry.
10 BIALL. **11** No. **12** Oct-July: Mon-Fri 9.30-19.00;
Aug-Sept: Mon-Fri 10.00-17.00. **13** (a) 85, 000; (b) 340;
(c) 10, 000 mss. **15** (a) 6 (b) 3 (c) 2.

LONDON—*continued*

INSTITUTE OF ACTUARIES LIBRARY, Staple Inn Hall,
High Holborn, London WC1V 7QJ (Tel 01-242 0106) Hon Libn:
Mr Peter Norton FIA; Asst Hon Libn: Mr Rodger William
Scadden BSc, FIA.
8 Actuarial science & its applications; maths; statistics;
insurance & superannuation; economics; demography; law.
10 Inter-library loans.   **11** No, except to suitable non-
members.   **12** 1 Oct-30 April: Mon-Fri 9.30-17.30;
1 May-30 Sept: Mon-Fri 9.30-17.00.   **13** (a) 10,000;
(b) 153.   **14** £1,200.   **15** (a) 1 (c) 1.

INSTITUTE OF CHARTERED ACCOUNTANTS IN ENGLAND
AND WALES, MEMBERS' LIBRARY, Moorgate Pl, London
EC2R 6EQ (Tel 01-628 7060) Libn: Mrs K.M.Morris MA,
MIL, ALA; Dep Libn: Mr M.F.Bywater BSc, ALA.
6 Council of Institute of Chartered Accountants in England
& Wales.   **8** Accountancy; management; taxation; company
law; finance.   **9** Bookkeeping & accounting (3,000 vols pre-
1900) (printed catalogue).   **10** BLL; Aslib.   **11** Yes, to
bona-fide researchers, on recommendation of a member.
12 Mon-Fri 9.30-17.30.   **13** (a) 28,000; (b) 250; (c) company information services.   **14** c.£12,000.   **15** (b) 4
(c) 4.

INSTITUTE OF CHARTERED SECRETARIES AND ADMINI-
STRATORS LIBRARY, 16 Park Crescent, London W1N 4AH
(Tel 01-580 4741) Libn & Inf Officer: Miss M.Skipp ALA.
8 Company law; company secretarial practice; commercial
law; economics; management; accountancy & law.   **9** Company histories.   **10** BLL.   **11** No.   **12** Mon-Fri 9.30-
17.15.   **13** (a) 6,000; (b) 200.   **14** £2,000.   **15** (a) 3
(c) 1.

INSTITUTE OF COST AND MANAGEMENT ACCOUNTANTS
LIBRARY, 63 Portland Pl, London W1N 4AB (Tel 01-637
4716) Libn & Inf Officer: Miss S.Maluty; Asst Libn: Miss
N.G.Soot Hung.
8 Accountancy; management; economics; statistics.   **11** No.
12 Mon-Fri 10.00-17.00.   **13** (a) 7,500; (b) 196.
14 £3,500.   **15** (a) 3 (b) 1 (c) 1.

INSTITUTE OF GEOLOGICAL SCIENCES, REFERENCE
LIBRARY OF GEOLOGY, Geological Museum, Exhibition Rd,
South Kensington, London SW7 2DE (Tel 01-589 3444 ext
257) Chief Libn: Mr K.J.Spencer FLA; Dep Chief Libn: Miss
J.M.Fitch ALA.
6 Natural Environment Research Council.   **7** Scotland
Regional Office Lib, Murchison House, West Mains Rd, Edinburgh, EH9 (031-667 1000), Libn: Mr C.D.Will BA, ALA;
Northern England & Wales Regional Office Lib, Ring Rd,
Halton, Leeds, LS15 8TQ (0532-649161 ext 51), Libn: Miss
J.V.Bacon BSc, MSc, InfSc, ALA.   **8** Earth sciences.
9 Photographs of British scenery & geology.   **11** Yes, for
ref.only.   **12** Mon-Fri 10.00-16.30, Sat 10.00-13.00,
14.00-16.30.   **13** (a) 120,000; (b) 3,300; (c) 70,000 maps;
40,000 pamphlets; 20,000 photographs; archives; microtexts.
15 (a) 20 (b) 6 (c) 10.

INSTITUTE OF LINGUISTS LIBRARY, Lloyds Bank Chambers,
91 Newington Causeway, London SE1 6BN (Tel 01-407 4755/
3871) Inf Officer & Libn: Miss S.D.Beaumont.
8 Technical, polyglot & foreign language dictionaries.
11 Yes, by prior arrangement.   **12** Mon-Fri 10.00-17.00.
13 (a) c.6,000; (b) 30; (c) language tapes & records.
14 £600.   **15** (a) ¼.

INSTITUTE OF MASTERS OF WINE (formerly Wine Trade
Club) LIBRARY, Guildhall Library, Aldermanbury, London
EC2P 2EJ (Tel 01-606 3030) Libn of Guildhall Library: Mr
Godfrey Thompson FLA.
8 Wine & allied subjects (mainly historical).   **9** George
Delaforce bequest.   **10** BLL; inter-library loans.
11 Yes.   **12** Mon-Sat 9.30-17.00.   **13** (a) 1,090; (b) 1.

INSTITUTE OF PERSONNEL MANAGEMENT, Central
House, Upper Woburn Pl, London WC1H 0HX (Tel 01-387
2844) Manager, Inf Services: Mrs D.Rockingham-Gill; Libn:
Miss M.A.Arnott, BA, BLS.
8 Personnel management; general management; industrial
relations; education & training; behavioural sciences; labour
economics & manpower studies; law.   **9** Company publications (eg policy manuals, staff handbooks, agreements,
personnel forms & a periodicals index of over 3,000 items).
11 No.   **12** Mon-Fri 9.00-17.00.   **13** (a) 10,000; (b)
120.   **14** £22,000.   **15** (a) 9½ (b) 5½ (c) 2½.

INSTITUTE OF PETROLEUM LIBRARY, 61 New Cavendish
St, London W1M 8AR (Tel 01-636 1004) Libn: Miss P.M.
Duffett MA.
8 Petroleum technology.   **10** BLL; Aslib.   **11** Yes, for
ref only.   **12** Mon-Fri 9.30-17.00.   **13** (a) 10,000;
(b) 100.   **15** (a) 2 (b) 1.

INSTITUTE OF QUANTITY SURVEYORS LIBRARY, 98
Gloucester Pl, London W1H 4AT (Tel 01-935 4048) Asst
Sec: Mr D.G.C.Stevens BA, ACIS.
8 Quantity surveying & building economics.   **11** No.
12 9.00-13.00, 14.00-17.00.   **13** (a) 2,000; (b) 30.
14 £400.   **15** (b) ¼.

INSTITUTION OF CIVIL ENGINEERS LIBRARY, Great George
St, London SW1P 3AA (Tel 01-839 3611) Libn: Mr H.C.
Richardson ALA; Dep Libn: Miss D.J.Bayley BA, ALA.
8 Civil engineering & related theoretical & applied sciences.
9 Vulliamy colln (horology).   **10** CEIL.   **11** No.
12 Mon-Fri 9.15-17.30.   **13** (a) 80,000; (b) 2,000; (c)
50 films; 2,000 slides.   **14** £8,000.   **15** (a) 6 (b) 2 (c) 2.

INSTITUTION OF ELECTRICAL ENGINEERS LIBRARY,
Savoy Pl, London WC2R 0BL (Tel 01-240 1871) Head of
Lib & Inf Services: Mr H.Wilman MIInfSc; Libn: Mr J.
Gurnsey ALA, AIInfSc.
8 Electrical engineering; electronics; related pure science.
9 Sir Francis Ronalds colln; Michael Faraday papers; John
Watkins Brett & Jacob Brett papers; Oliver Heaviside papers;
Silvanus P.Thompson library; Cooke & Wheatsone papers.
11 Yes.   **12** Mon-Fri 9.00-17.00 (Tues & Thurs 19.00,
May-Oct).   **13** (a) 35,000; (b) 600.   **15** (a) 11 (b) 3 (c) 3.

INSTITUTION OF ELECTRONIC AND RADIO ENGINEERS
LIBRARY, 8-9 Bedford Sq, London WC1B 3RG (Tel 01-637
2771).
6 Council of Institution of Electronic & Radio Engineers.
8 Electronics & radio engineering; telecommunications.
10 CEIL.   **11** No, but enquiries dealt with whenever possible.   **12** Mon-Fri 9.15-17.15.   **13** (a) 5,500; (b) 300.
15 (a) 1½ (c) 1.

INSTITUTION OF GAS ENGINEERS LIBRARY, 17 Grosvenor
Crescent, London SW1X 7ES (Tel 01-245 9811) Libn: Miss
Barbara P.J.Evans ALA; Asst: Mrs Anne Jarrett.
8 Gas engineering; science; research & development.
9 Early books on gas works, lighting etc, largely uncata-
logued as yet.   **10** CEIL.   **11** Yes.   **12** Mon-Fri 9.15-
17.15.   **13** (a) c.6,000; (b) c.200; (c) c.1,500 archives;
c.500 pamphlets.   **14** c.£1,000.   **15** (a) 2 (c) 1.

INSTITUTION OF HEATING AND VENTILATING ENGINEERS
LIBRARY (temporarily closed), 49 Cadogan Sq, London
SW1X 0JB (Tel 01-235 7671).
8 Heating; ventilating; air conditioning.

INSTITUTION OF MECHANICAL ENGINEERS LIBRARY,
1 Birdcage Walk, London SW1H 9JJ (Tel 01-839 1211; Telex
917944) Libn: Mr R.T.Everett; Dep: Mr S.G.Morrison.
8 Mechanical engineering.   **9** George Stephenson letters
& mss.   **10** CEIL.   **11** No.   **12** Mon-Fri 9.30-17.30.
13 (a) 140,000 (inc pamphlets); (b) 1,000.   **15** (a) 12 (c) 1.

INSTITUTION OF MINING AND METALLURGY LIBRARY,
44 Portland Pl, London W1N 4BR (Tel 01-580 3802) Libn:
Miss R.Oblatt.
8 Economic geology; mining & mineral processing (exc
coal & non-ferrous extractive metallurgy); allied subjects.
10 BLL; CEIL.   **11** Yes.   **12** Mon-Fri 9.45-17.00 (Wed
19.00).   **13** (a) 10,000; (b) 450; (c) 1,000 geological maps.
15 (a) 4.

INSTITUTION OF MUNICIPAL ENGINEERS LIBRARY,
25 Eccleston Sq, London SW1V 1NX (Tel 01-834 5082/3)
Sec: A.Banister OBE, BSc, CEng, FICE, FIMunE.
6 Council of the Institution.   **8** Local government, management & organisation in local authorities, water authorities &
other public undertakings.   **10** CEIL.   **11** No.

CODE: 1 Name of Library. **2** Address. **3** Telephone & Telex. **4** Officer in charge. **5** Deputy. **6** Governing body.
7 Branches. **8** Main Subjects. **9** Special Collections. **10** Co-operative Schemes. **11** Open to public? **12** Hours.
13 Stock: (a) books (b) periodicals (c) other. **14** Finance. **15** Staff: (a) non-manual (b) graduate (c) chartered librarians.

LONDON—*continued*

12 Mon-Fri 9.30-16.30. **13** (a) 2,500; (b) 200.
14 £50.

INTERNATIONAL COOPERATIVE ALLIANCE LIBRARY,
11 Upper Grosvenor St, London W1X 9PA (Tel 01-499 5991)
Libn: Ms Anne Lamming; Asst to Libn: Ms Mila Martinez.
8 Co-operative movements in all countries. **10** BLL.
11 Yes, prior notification is desirable. **12** Mon-Fri
8.45-16.45. **13** (a) 15,000; (b) 400. **15** (a) 3.

INTERNATIONAL PLANNED PARENTHOOD FEDERATION
LIBRARY AND DOCUMENTATION SERVICE, 18-20 Lower
Regent St, London SW1Y 4PW (Tel 01-839 2911; Telex
919573) Head of Lib & Documentation Service: Mme J.P.
Forget; Libn: Mrs R.A.Ward ALA.
8 Family planning & population; related fields of health, welfare, education & development. **9** Complete set of international conferences on family planning & population, large
colln of UN documents: UNFPA, Population Commission,
Status of Women Commission etc. **10** Association of
Population Libraries and Information Centers. **11** Yes,
for bona-fide students, researchers, teachers etc. **12** Mon-
Fri 10.00-17.00. **13** (a) 6,000; (b) 300; (c) 1,600 documentation files of pamphlets, press cuttings etc; 500 conference proceedings; 2,500 UN documents. **14** £5,700.
15 (a) 8 (b) 2 (c) 3.

INTERNATIONAL WOOL SECRETARIAT ECONOMICS LI-
BRARY, 6/7 Carlton Gardens, London SW1Y 5AE (Tel 01-930
7300) Economics Libn: Mrs Susan Morrell BSc, MA, ALA;
Inf Asst: Miss S.Keyes.
7 Technical Centre, Valley Dr, Ilkley, Yorkshire, (09433-
5555), Libn: Mrs C.Williams. **8** Wool; wool textile economics & statistics; general textiles. **11** Yes, but only by
prior appointment with Libn. **12** Mon-Fri 9.00-17.00.
13 (a) 5,000; (b) 450; (c) 8,000 pamphlets. **14** £6,000.
15 (a) 2 (b) 1 (c) 1.

ISLEWORTH POLYTECHNIC LIBRARY (proposed merger
with part of Chiswick Polytechnic, Sept 1976, to form Hounslow Borough College), London Rd, Isleworth, Middlesex,
TW7 4HS (Tel 01-568 0244) Libn: Mrs Audrey Good; Senior
Asst Libn: Mr R.M.Dobbing BA, ALA.
6 London Borough of Hounslow. **7** Science & Electrical
Lib, St Johns Rd, Isleworth (01-568 0244). **8** Psychology;
sociology; education; pure science; mechanical & electrical
engineering; languages; art; photography; literature;
geography; history; fiction; hairdressing; catering & domestic
science. **9** Art books. **10** CICRIS; GLGCL. **11** Yes,
at Libn's discretion. **12** Term: Mon-Fri 9.00-19.30.
13 (a) 21,000; (b) 162; (c) 150 records; illustrations.
14 £5,000. **15** (a) 5 (b) 1 (c) 1.

ITALIAN INSTITUTE LIBRARY, 39 Belgrave Sq, London
SW1X 8NX (Tel 01-235 1461/2/3; Telex Italcultur) Libn: A.F.
Spallone.
6 Italian Institute of Culture. **8** History; art; fiction;
poetry; Italian classics; essays on Italian literature; theatre;
music; tourism; religion; philosophy; economics; folklore (in
Italian & English). **9** Dante Alighieri. **10** BLL.
11 Yes. **12** Mon-Fri 10.00-13.00, 14.30-17.30.
13 (a) c.23,000; (b) 123; (c) slides; gramophone records;
films. **15** (a) 1.

JEWS' COLLEGE LIBRARY, 11 Montagu Pl, London W1H
2BA (Tel 01-723 9974) Libn: Mrs E.Zimmels. **8** Hebraica
& Judaica. **9** Montefiore colln (mss). **11** Yes, for ref
only. **12** Mon-Thurs 10.00-13.00, 14.00-17.00, Fri 10.00-
13.00. **13** (a) 60,000; (c) 700 mss; 8 incunabula. **15** (a) 1.

J.WALTER THOMPSON INFORMATION CENTRE, 40 Berkeley Sq, London W1X 6AD (Tel 01-629 9496; Telex 22871)
Acting Head Libn: Ms Carolyn Okill.
8 Advertising; marketing. **10** BLL. **11** Yes, but only

for educational or research purposes. **12** Mon-Fri 9.30-
17.30. **13** (a) c.4,500; (b) 200; (c) press cuttings & company information; 'Times' & 'Financial Times' on microfilm
(from 1969). **15** (a) 10 (b) 1 (c) 5.

KILBURN POLYTECHNIC LIBRARY, Priory Park Rd,
London NW6 7UJ (Tel 01-624 0022 ext 7) Coll Libn: Mr E.E.
Ghansah ALA.
6 Local authority. **7** Colindale branch, 373 Edgware Rd,
NW9 (01-205 2517) Libn: Mrs C.Tyler; Police College
B Lib, Metropolitan Police Cadet Training School, Aerodrome
Rd, NW9 (01-205 1125) Libn: Miss G.P.Wells. **8** General
education; languages; business; science & technology; fashion;
home economics; community studies. **11** No. **12** Mon-
Fri 9.00-20.00 (Fri 17.00). **13** (a) 26,000; (b) 204; (c)
190 gramophone records. **14** £5,100. **15** (a) 5 (c) 1.

KING'S FUND CENTRE LIBRARY, 24 Nutford Pl, London
W1H 6AN (Tel 01-262 2641) Libn: Mrs J.M.B.White ALA;
Inf Officer: Mr R.G.Bennett.
6 King Edward's Hospital Fund for London. **8** Health care
planning & organisation. **10** BLL. **11** Yes. **12** Mon-
Sat 9.30-17.30. **13** (a) 12,000; (b) c.200. **14** £3,750.
15 (a) 7 (b) 1 (c) 2.

KINGSTON POLYTECHNIC LIBRARY, Penrhyn Rd, Kingston
upon Thames, Surrey, KT1 2EE (Tel 01-549 1366; Telex
928530) Libn: Mr H.A.Chesshyre FLA; Dep Libns: (Staff &
Administration) Mrs E.A.L.Esteve-Coll ALA; (Resources)
Mr.P.R.Brunning ALA.
7 Campus Libraries: Knights Park, Kingston upon Thames
(01-549 0063 ext 31), Libn: Mrs G.Varley BA, DipLib, ALA;
Canbury Park Rd, Kingston upon Thames (01-549 0151 ext
207), Libn: Mrs J.Hunter MA, MLibSc; Gypsy Hill, Kenry
House, Kingston Hill, Kingston upon Thames (01-549 1141),
Tutor-Libn: Miss M.Hammond FLA; New Malden (from
Sept 1976), 41-44 Coombe Rd, New Malden, Libn: Mr R.D.
Gee.FLA. **8** Arts & languages; law; economics; chemistry;
geology; geography; sociology; management; engineering;
quantity surveying; estate management; art & design; architecture; town planning. **9** HMSO SSS. **11** Yes, after
signing visitors' book. **12** Mon-Fri 9.00-22.00, Sat 9.00-
17.00. Branches vary. **13** (a) 131,945; (b) 1,978; (c)
71,204 slides; 7,572 microfilms; 12,960 illustrations; 2,388
gramophone records. **14** £165,000. **15** (a) 47 (b) 18
(c) 18.

LABORATORY OF THE GOVERNMENT CHEMIST
LIBRARY, Cornwall House, Stamford St, London SE1 9NQ
(Tel 01-928 7900) Libn: Mrs Maureen MacKenzie MIInstSc;
Asst Libn: Mr H.Baxter MIInstSc, LRIC.
6 Dept of Industry. **8** Analytical chemistry. **9** 'Chemical
Abstracts'; 'Analyst'; analytical abstracts journals on analytical
chemistry. **10** LINK. **11** Yes, but only by special
arrangement. **12** 8.30-17.30. **13** (a) 6,200; (b) 500; (c)
9,000 pamphlets. **14** £12,000. **15** (a) 5 (b) 2.

LABOUR PARTY LIBRARY, Transport House, Smith Sq,
London SW1P 3JA (Tel 01-834 9434 ext 31) Libn: Mrs.I.
Wagner DPhil; Dep Libn: Mrs J.Samuel.
8 Politics (socialism); economics; social sciences.
9 Press cuttings (from 1918); photographs; posters; Party
archives. **10** International Association of Labour History
Institutions. **11** Yes, members of the Labour Party &
academic researchers. **12** 9.30-17.15. **13** (a) 8,500;
(b) 256; (c) 14,000 photographs; 400 posters; archives; 5,000
microfiches; press cuttings; 5,000 press releases.
14 £9,600. **15** (a) 10 (b) 3 (c) 2.

LAMBETH PALACE LIBRARY, London SE1 7JU (Tel 01-
928 6222) Libn: Mr E.G.W.Bill MA; Dep: Miss M.Barber BA.
6 Trustees of Lambeth Palace Library. **8** Ecclesiastical
& some general history, bibliography, palaeography, early
printing, topography, genealogy, theology (to 1900). **9** 700
medieval mss; 2,500 STC vols; 150 incunabula; records of
Court of Arches, Faculty Office, Archbishops of Canterbury,

LONDON—*continued*

Convocation.   **11** Yes, with introduction, at Libn's discretion.   **12** Mon-Fri 10.00-17.00.   **15** (a) 5 (b) 5 (c) 3.

LANGUAGE TEACHING LIBRARY, 20 Carlton House Terrace, London SW1Y 5AP (Tel 01-839 2626 ext 13 or 01-930 8466 ext 2782) Libn: Mrs J.O. Howard BA, FLA; Dep Libn: Miss J. Price BA, DipLib.
6 Centre for Information on Language Teaching and Research, and English Teaching Information Centre, British Council.   **8** Linguistics; teaching of English as a foreign language; French; German; Italian; Russian; Spanish; (inc textbooks & audio-visual courses); selective coverage of other languages.   **11** Yes, to anyone professionally concerned with language or language teaching.   **12** Mon-Fri 9.30-17.30 (Fri 17.00).   **13** (a) 23,000 books; (b) 380; (c) theses; syllabuses; microfiches; microfilms; news cuttings; 650 audio-visual courses; 2,000 tapes; 700 gramophone records; 700 filmstrips; 1,000 slides; wallcharts.   **14** £8,000.   **15** (a) 8 (b) 3 (c) 2.

LAW SOCIETY LIBRARY, 113 Chancery Lane, London WC2A 1PL (Tel 01-242 1222; Telex 261203) Libn: Mr F.P. Richardson FLA; Dep Libn: Mr A.J. Darby.
8 Comprehensive ref library in all branches of English law & selected branches of other jurisdictions (e.g. Scottish, Irish, European communities law).   **10** Inter-library loans.
11 No.   **12** Mon-Fri 9.00-17.00.   **13** (a) 65,000; (b) 300.
15 (a) 4 (c) 3.

LEWIS'S MEDICAL, SCIENTIFIC AND TECHNICAL LENDING LIBRARY, H.K. Lewis & Co Ltd, 136 Gower St, London, WC1E 6BS (Tel 01-387 4282)
8 Medical scientific; technical.   **11** Yes, annual subscription £4.00.   **12** Mon-Fri 9.00-17.30; Sat 9.00-13.00.
13 (a) 50,000.   **15** (a) 8.

LINCOLN'S INN LIBRARY, London WC2A 3TN (Tel 01-242 4371) Libn: Mr Roderick Walker.
6 Honourable Society of Lincoln's Inn.   **8** Law.
12. 9.30-15.00.   **13** (a) 120,000.   **15** (a) 5.

LINNEAN SOCIETY OF LONDON LIBRARY, Burlington House, Piccadilly, London W1V OLQ (Tel 01-734 1040) Libn & Archivist: Mr Gavin D.R. Bridson.
8 Natural history from earliest times to present (especially taxonomy, evolution, Linnaeana, fauna & flora of the Paleoarctic Region, history of biology).   **9** Library & mss of Carl Linnaeus, Sir James Edward Smith & others; extensive mss colln; engraved & photographic portraits of naturalists to 1900; early herbals; medals & other personal relics of fellows.
10 BLL.   **11** Yes, on written application to Libn.
12 Mon-Fri 10.00 (Wed 14.00)-17.00.   **13** (a) over 90,000; (b) c.650.   **15** (a) 1½.

LONDON CHAMBER OF COMMERCE AND INDUSTRY, RESEARCH AND INFORMATION DEPARTMENT, LIBRARY, 69 Cannon St, London EC4N 5AB (Tel 01-248 4444; Telex 888941) Head of Research & Inf Dept: W.H. Lovelock ALA; Dep: J. Padget.
8 UK internal & external trade; UK & overseas industry & commerce & related subjects; customs, tariffs, regulations relating to commerce & industry.   **11** No.   **12** 9.30-17.30.   **13** (a) 4,000; (b) 1,500; (c) 210 customs tariffs; 150,000 newspaper cuttings.   **15** (a) 19 (b) 6 (c) 2.

LONDON COLLEGE OF FASHION LIBRARY, 20 John Prince's St, London WC1M 9HE (Tel 01-493 8341/5 ext 63) Chief Libn: Mrs Muriel Ross ALA.
6 ILEA.   **7** 100 Curtain Rd, EC2A 4BA (01-739 4002) Libn: Mrs H. Lancaster ALA; Golden Lane, Baltic St, EC1Y OTB (01-253 9898).   **8** Hairdressing; beauty therapy; costume & clothing design; textiles & clothing technology.   **10** BLL.
11 No.   **12** Term: 9.00-19.00; vac: 9.00-17.00.   **13** (a) 30,000; (b) 220; (c) fashion photographs; fashion press cuttings.   **15** (a) 11 (b) 3 (c) 4.

LONDON COLLEGE OF FURNITURE LIBRARY, 41 Commercial Rd, London E1 1LA (Tel 01-247 1953) Libn: Miss N. Irvine ALA; Dep Libns: Miss J. Williamson BA; Mr R.C. Farr ALA.
6 ILEA.   **8** Furniture industry & history; cabinet making; upholstery; finishing; wood machining; materials science; timber; textiles; environment; architecture; interior design; industrial design; art history; musical instruments; handicrafts; toymaking & design; anthropometrics; building theory; display design.   **10** BLL; ILEA.   **11** Yes, for serious enquiries.   **12** Term: Mon-Thurs 8.45-19.15, Fri 8.45-17.00; vac: by arrangement.   **13** (a) c.17,000; (b) 270; (c) slides & other teaching aids.   **15** (a) 5½ (b) 1 (c) 3.

LONDON COLLEGE OF PRINTING LIBRARY, Elephant & Castle, London SE1 6SB (Tel 01-735 8484) Libn: Miss P.J. Batley ALA; Dep Libn: Miss A. Hutchinson ALA.
6 ILEA.   **7** Clerkenwell Branch, Back Hill, SE1.
8 Printing; graphic arts; management; fine arts; general.
9 Early printed books; illustrated books; examples of modern printing.   **10** BLL; LASER; WANDPETLS; GLGCL.
11 Yes, with Libn's permission.   **12** Term: 9.00-19.15; vac: 9.30-16.30 (unless otherwise announced).   **13** (a) 50,000; (b) 800; (c) 5,000 microfiche; 25,000 slides; 150 videotapes; 50 tapes; 400 audio-visual kits.   **15** (a) 14 (b) 2 (c) 9.

LONDON GRADUATE SCHOOL OF BUSINESS STUDIES LIBRARY, Sussex Pl, Regents Park, London NW1 4SA (Tel 01-262 5050) Libn: Mr K.D.C. Vernon FLA; Senior Asst Libn: Miss V.F. Oldland ALA.
8 Management & business.   **9** Company reports; discussion papers issued by business schools in UK, Europe & USA; statistical publications; information files; reserved collection.   **10** BLL.   **11** Yes.   **12** Term: Mon-Fri 9.00-21.30, Sat 9.30-12.30; vac: Mon-Fri 9.00-17.00.
13 (a) 24,000; (b) 550.   **14** £15,500.   **15** (a) 9 (b) 3 (c) 4.

LONDON HOSPITAL PATIENTS' LIBRARY, Whitechapel, London E1 1BB (Tel 01-247 5454 ext 44) Libn: Mrs H.P. Raimes; Dep: Mrs J. Abdon Jones.
6 Special Trustees of London Hospital.   **8** General.
11 No.   **12** Daily 9.00-17.00 (exc Wed).   **13** (a) c.25,000.   **15** (a) 2½.

LONDON LIBRARY, 14 St James's Sq, London SW1Y 4LG (Tel 01-930 7705/6) Libn: Mr Stanley Gillam BLitt, MA; Dep: Mr Douglas Matthews BA, FLA.
6 Committee of Management.   **8** Arts; humanities; social sciences (not law, medicine, science or technology).
9 Higginson colln (hunting & field sports); Heron-Allen colln (Omar Kháyýam).   **10** BLL.   **11** No.   **12** Mon-Sat 9.30-17.30 (Thurs 19.30).   **13** (a) c.1,000,000; (b) 400.
14 £35,000.   **15** (a) 35 (b) 7 (c) 5.

LOUGHTON COLLEGE OF FURTHER EDUCATION LIBRARY, Borders Lane, Loughton, Essex, IG1D 35A (Tel 01-508 8311)
6 Essex Education Committee.   **8** Sociology; sciences; applied sciences; language; literature; arts; history; geography; careers.   **10** LASER.   **12** Term: Mon-Thurs 8.45-21.30, Fri 8.45-17.30, Sat 8.45-12.00.
13 (a) 15,000; (b) 150; (c) gramophone records; cassette tapes; slides; OHP transparencies; viewing & listening facilities; charts; games & models.

MARIA GREY COLLEGE LIBRARY (proposed to merge with Borough Rd College & part of Chiswick Polytechnic, Sept 1976, to form the West London Institute of Higher Education), 300 St Margaret's Rd, Twickenham, Middlesex TW1 1PT (Tel 01-891 0121)   Libn: Mrs D.E. Jones ALA; Asst Libn: Mrs J.E. Wood ALA.
6 London Borough of Hounslow.   **8** Psychology; education; children's literature.   **9** Murray Library (Victorian children's books).   **10** BLL.   **11** Yes, but only with written permission.   **12** Term: Mon-Fri 9.00-21.00, Sat 10.00-12.00; vac: Mon-Fri 9.00-17.00.   **13** (a) 55,000; (b) 240.   **14** £8,640.   **15** (a) 5 (c) 2.

MARYLEBONE CRICKET CLUB LIBRARY, Lord's Ground, London, NW8 8QN (Tel 01-289 1611)   Curator: Mr Stephen E.A. Green MA, DipArchAdmin.
8 Cricket.   **11** Yes, by appointment only.   **12** Mon-Fri 9.30-17.30; Summer: Sat (if cricket in progress) 9.30-17.00.
13 (a) c.15,000; (b) c.20; (c) archives; gramophone records; microfilms.   **15** (a) 2½ (b) 1.

CODE: 1 Name of Library. **2** Address. **3** Telephone & Telex. **4** Officer in charge. **5** Deputy. **6** Governing body.
7 Branches. **8** Main Subjects. **9** Special Collections. **10** Co-operative Schemes. **11** Open to public? **12** Hours.
13 Stock: (a) books (b) periodicals (c) other. **14** Finance. **15** Staff: (a) non-manual (b) graduate (c) chartered librarians.

LONDON—*continued*

MARX MEMORIAL LIBRARY, 37a Clerkenwell Green,
London EC1R ODU (Tel 01-253 1485) Libn: Mrs Margaret
Kentfield; Sec: Mr H. Watson.
6 Elected committee. **8** Social & political theory; economics; political science; labour & trade union history.
9 Spanish war; J.D. Bernal Peace Library; John Williamsons
Library (American labour movement). **11** No. **12** Mon-
Fri 16.00-21.00, Sat 11.00-13.00. **13** (a) 17,000; (b) 150;
(c) 28,000 pamphlets; microfilm; archives. **14** £50.
15 (a) 2½.

MERCHANT NAVY COLLEGE LIBRARY, Greenhithe, Kent,
DA9 9NZ (Tel 0322-84 2039).
6 ILEA. **8** Nautical; general. **10** Inter-library loans.
11 Yes, to bona-fide enquirers. **12** Term: 9.00-17.15.
13 (a) c.6,000; (b) c.50. **14** £2,500.

MERTON TECHNICAL COLLEGE LIBRARY, London Rd,
Morden, Surrey, SM4 5QX (Tel 01-640 3001) Libn: Mr D.J.
Fawcett ALA, FInstPet, DipTL.
6 London Borough of Merton. **7** Annexe, Gladstone Rd,
Wimbledon, SW19 1QP (01-542 2442). **8** Electrical, mechanical & production engineering; computers; sociology.
Annexe Lib: Business; management; catering; domestic
science. **10** SASLIC. **11** Yes, for ref only, by arrangement. **12** Term: 9.15-19.00. **13** (a) 18,000; (b) 160;
(c) various resource materials. **14** £4,500. **15** (a) 4
(c) 1.

MIDDLESEX POLYTECHNIC LIBRARY (Hendon), The
Burroughs, London, NW4 BT (Tel 01-202 6545 ext 42) Site
Libn (Hendon): Miss M.A. Browne ALA.
7 Site Libraries: Hornsey, Libn: Mr D Cheshire; Enfield,
Libn: Mr L. Kiibey; Trent Park, Libn: Mrs M. Lane; New
College. **8** Accountancy; air pollution; physics; art history;
business; catering; chemistry; computers; education; engineering; English; geography; history; law; linguistics; science.
10 BLL; Aslib; CICRIS. **11** Yes, for ref only. **12** Term:
Mon-Fri 9.00-21.00; vac: Mon-Fri 9.00-17.00. **13** (a)
70,000; (b) over 900; (c) gramophone records; microtexts.
15 (a) 12 (b) 6 (c) 5.

MIDDLE TEMPLE LIBRARY, Middle Temple Lane, London,
EC4Y 9BT (Tel 01-353 4303) Libn & Keeper of Records:
Miss E. McNeill BA, DLS, ATCL, ALA.
6 Honourable Society of the Middle Temple. **8** Law:
English; Scottish; Irish; European; Commonwealth; public
international; American. **9** European communities colln
(financed by all 4 Inns of Court, maintained by Middle Temple
Libn); American law. **10** BIALL. **11** Yes, if material
not easily available elsewhere. **12** Mon-Fri 9.30-19.00
13 (a) 140,000; (b) 200. **14** £18,500. **15** (a) 10 (b) 7
(c) 5.

MINISTRY OF AGRICULTURE, FISHERIES AND FOOD,
MAIN LIBRARY, 3 Whitehall Pl, London SW1A 2HH (Tel 01-
839 7711; Telex 22124) Chief Libn: Mr F.C. Hurst FLA;
Dep: Mr E.A.R. Bush BA, ALA.
7 Great Westminster House, Horseferry Rd, SW1H 2AE,
Libn: Mr M. Tither BA, ALA; Government Buildings (Toby
Jug Site), Tolworth, Surbiton, Surrey, Libn: Mrs S.M.D.
Fitzgerald ALA. **8** Agriculture, fisheries, food)all aspects, inc statistics, economics, pure & applied science,
especially biology). Food nutrition & animal health covered
by the branch libraries. **9** Cowan & Cotton (apiculture);
Punnett (poultry genetics). **10** BLL; Aslib. **11** Yes, for
ref. **12** Mon-Fri 9.30-17.00. **13** (a) 193,300; (b)
2,850; (c) some microfilm & microfiche. **15** (a) 36 (b) 10
(c) 13.

Ministry of Defence

ADASTRAL HOUSE LIBRARY, Theobalds Rd, London,

WC1X 8RU (Tel 01-405 3434 ext 7515/7109) Libn: Mr
L.H. Miller ALA; Dep: Mr B.S. Cheal BA, ALA.
8 Aviation; aeronautics; history of flight; R.A.F. (historical); foreign air forces; world affairs; general biographical. **9** Air Ministry Orders. **11** Yes, by special
appointment. **12** 8.30-17.30. **13** (a) 64,000; (b) 130;
(c) 'Times' on microfilm. **15** (a) 5 (b) 1 (c) 2.

ST GILES COURT LIBRARY, 1-13 St Giles High St,
London WC2H 8LD (Tel 01-632 3772) Libn: Mr K.N. Musk
ALA; Dep: Miss P.P. Payne ALA.
7 St Christopher House, Southwark St, SE1 (01-928 3947),
Libn: Miss M.P. Pochin ALA; Strand Lib, 73-75 The
Strand, WC2R ODT (01-217 4498). **8** Aerospace engineering; military aviation; electronics; mechanical engineering; computers & telecommunications; economics;
government; management. **11** No. **12** Mon-Thurs
8.45-17.15, Fri 8.00-16.30. **13** (a) 40,000; (b) 1,500.
15 (a) 35 (b) 1 (c) 8.

WHITEHALL LIBRARY, Old War Office Building, Whitehall, London SW1A 2EU (Tel 01-218 0015/16) Libn: Mr
J.C. Andrews FLA; Dep Libn & Head of Scientific & Technical Services: Mr G.A. Barnes FLA.
8 Scientific & technical; managerial; general; political;
economic; biographical; military. **9** Royal United Services Military Library. **11** Yes, but only by special
application & appointment. **12** 9.00-17.00. **13** (a)
900,000; (b) 1,100. **15** (a) 47 (b) 6 (c) 17.

MORLEY COLLEGE LIBRARY, 61 Westminster Bridge Rd,
London SE1 7HT (01-928 8501) Libn: Miss E.M. Slack BA,
ALA.
6 Council of Morley College. **8** Music; art; languages;
social studies; humanities; science. **11** No. **12** Term:
Mon-Fri 11.00-21.15. **13** (a) 22,000 (inc musical scores);
(c) 1,100 gramophone records; 45 language cassettes.
14 £2,750. **15** (a) 3½ (b) 3 (c) 1.

MUSEUM OF MANKIND LIBRARY, Ethnography Dept of
British Museum, 6 Burlington Gardens, London W1X 2EX
(Tel 01-437 2224 ext 53) Libn: Ms Audrey Stephen BA.
6 British Museum. **8** Anthropology with emphasis on
material culture; travel outside Europe; archaeology of the
New World, Africa & Oceania. **9** Christy library (mainly
19th cent travel books). **11** Yes, for ref only. **12** Mon-
Fri 10.00-13.00, 14.00-16.45. **13** (a) c.14,000; (b)
c.100; (c) c.1,400 pamphlets; archive photographs (anthropology); prints & drawings; dept archives; a few gramophone
records & microfilms. **14** £2,700 plus binding. **15** (a)
3 (b) 1.

NATIONAL BOOK LEAGUE, MARK LONGMAN LIBRARY,
7 Albemarle St, London W1X 4BB (Tel 01-493 9001) Libn:
Mrs S. Anne Clarke ALA.
8 Books about books (book production, bibliography, book
trade, reading). **9** Linder colln (works & original drawings
by Beatrix Potter); Harriet Shaw Weaver colln (James
Joyce); Perez colln (British bookplates). **10** BLL.
11 Yes. **12** Mon-Fri 9.30-17.30. **13** (a) 10,000; (b)
c.100. **15** (a) 1.

NATIONAL FARMERS' UNION LIBRARY, Agriculture
House, Knightsbridge, London SW1X 7NJ (Tel 01-235 5077;
ext 129; Telex 919669) Libn: Mrs V. Beale; Asst Libn:
Mrs J.E. Singleton BA.
8 Agriculture & horticulture: policies; politics; economics;
marketing; history; general & technical aspects; land use;
trade in agricultural produce. **9** National Farmers Union
history. **10** BLL; Aslib. **11** Yes, for ref only.
12 9.45-17.15. **13** (a) 12,000; (b) 300. **14** c.£12,000.
15 (a) 7 (b) 3 (c) 1.

NATIONAL GALLERY LIBRARY, Trafalgar Sq, London,
WC2N SDN (Tel 01-839 3321) Dep Keeper & Libn: Mr Allan
Braham; Research Asst: Ms Ann Trinder. **8** Information
relevant to paintings colln. **9** Eastlake library. **11** No.

LONDON—*continued*

NATIONAL HOSPITAL FOR NERVOUS DISEASES, GOWERS LIBRARY, Queen Sq, London, WC1N 3BG (Tel 01-837 3611 ext 311) Hospital Libn: S. E. A. Kenchington ALA.
7 Maida Vale Hospital, Maida Vale, W9; East Finchley Convalescent Home, Bishops Ave, N2. **8** General. **11** Yes, for patients. **12** Mon-Fri 10.00-18.00. **13** (a) 10,000; (b) 50. **14** £2,000. **15** (a) 2 (c) 1.

NATIONAL INSTITUTE OF ADULT EDUCATION LIBRARY, 35 Queen Anne St, London W1M OBL (Tel 01-637 4241) Libn: Miss Y. I. Soliva.
8 Adult education (literacy, community development, correspondence). **10** BLL. **11** Yes. **12** Mon-Fri 9.30-17.15. **13** (a) 4,430; (b) 150; (c) pamphlets; press cuttings. **14** c. £500. **15** (a) 1.

NATIONAL INSTITUTE OF ECONOMIC AND SOCIAL RESEARCH, GARION LIBRARY, 2 Dean Trench St, Smith Sq, London, SW1P 3HE (Tel 01-222 7665) Libn: Miss C. Moore BA, ALA; Asst Libn: Miss L. Sanderson ALA.
8 Economics. **9** International statistical series (economic). **11** Yes, with Libn's permission. **12** 10.00-18.00. **13** (a) 20,000; (b) 700. **15** (a) 2 (b) 1 (c) 2.

NATIONAL LIBRARY FOR THE BLIND, 35 Great Smith St, London, SW1 3BU (Tel 01-222 2725) Libn & Dir General: Dr W. A. Munford MBE, NSc, PhD, FLA.
6 Council of National Library for the Blind. **7** Northern branch, 5 St John St, Manchester, M3 4DL. **8** General (embossed & enlarged types). **11** Yes. **12** Mon-Fri 9.00-17.00. **13** (a) 400,000. **14** £70,000. **15** (a) 78 (b) 2 (c) 5.

NATIONAL MARITIME MUSEUM LIBRARY, Romney Rd, Greenwich, London SE10 9NF (Tel 01-858 4422) Libn: Dr M. W. B. Sanderson MA, PhD; Mrs M. Patrick BA.
6 Trustees of National Maritime Museum. **8** Maritime history, naval & mercantile; history of navigation & nautical astronomy; voyages & travel; atlases & cartography; development, construction & uses of all types of ships & watercraft, of all countries & periods; fisheries; piracy; maritime trade & law. **9** A. G. H. Macpherson colln (books & atlases); Sir James Caird colln; Philip Gosse (pirate) library; H. H. Brindley colln; Basil Lubbock colln; Reynolds' (polar) library; C. N. Robinson colln; Capt Henry Daniel colln. **11** Yes, for students of maritime research on issue of a reader's ticket. **12** Mon-Sat 10.00-13.00, 14.00-17.00. **13** (a) 65,000; (b) 400. **14** £20,000. **15** (a) 5 (b) 2.

NATIONAL OPERATIC AND DRAMATIC ASSOCIATION LIBRARY, 1 Crestfield St, London WC1H 8AU (Tel 01-837 5655) Libn: Mr B. Dunn.
8 Vocal scores; libretti; musical plays; Gilbert & Sullivan; one-act plays; three-act plays. **11** Yes, on payment of hire charges. **12** 9.30-17.15. **15** (a) 3.

NATIONAL PHILATELIC SOCIETY LIBRARY, 44 Fleet St, London EC4Y 1BN (Tel 01-353 7210) Hon Libn: Mr A. J. Brown.
8 Philately. **9** China Philatelic Society's Library; Travelling Post Office & Seapost Society's Library. **11** No. **12** 9.30-14.00, 15.00-17.30.

NATIONAL PHYSICAL LABORATORY LIBRARY, Teddington, Middlesex, TW11 0LW (Tel 01-977 3222; Telex 262344) Chief Libn: Miss P. M. Udy BA, ALA; Dep Libn: Miss G. P. Davis ALA.
6 Dept of Industry. **8** Physics & chemistry; maths; computer science; materials science; metrology; ship building. **9** History of science & technology; works of famous scientists. **10** BLL. **11** No. **13** (a) 60,000; (b) 1,800. **15** (a) 9 (b) 2 (c) 3.

NATIONAL UNION OF TEACHERS LIBRARY, Hamilton House, Mabledon Pl, London WC1H 9BD (Tel 01-387 2442 ext 133) Libn: Mrs V. A. Brinkley-Willsher ALA.
8 Education; child welfare; child psychology. **9** NUT publications; govt publications on education. **10** BLL; BNBC; inter-library loans. **11** Yes, for ref only. **12** Mon-Fri 9.00-17.15. **13** (a) 15,000; (b) 250; (c) 3,000 govt publications; 15,000 pamphlets. **15** (a) 4¾ (c) 2.

NATURE CONSERVANCY COUNCIL LIBRARY SERVICE, 19-20 Belgrave Sq, London SW1X 8PY (Tel 01-235 3241) Chief Libn: Miss S. M. Penny FLA; Dep Libn: Mr M. J. Rush MA, ALA.
7 Nature Conservancy Council, Scottish HQ Library, 12 Hope Terrace, Edinburgh, EH9 2AS (031-447 4784), Libn: Miss M. Peters. **8** Nature conservation; protection of countryside; natural history; land use planning; outdoor recreation. **11** Yes, to bona-fide students & researchers on application. **12** 9.30-17.00. **13** (a) 35,000; (b) 1,400. **15** (a) 12 (b) 3 (c) 4.

OFFICE OF POPULATION CENSUSES AND SURVEYS LIBRARY, St Catherines House, 10 Kingsway, London WC2B 6JP (Tel 01-242 0262) Libn: Miss B. D. Chater; Dep Libn: Mr T. Norfolk.
6 Director and Registrar General. **7** Segensworth Rd, Titchfield, Fareham, Hampshire (032-94 42511). Libn: Miss M. C. Conlan. **8** Law & administration of birth, death & marriage registration; demography, epidemiology, public health, social & preventive medicine; sociology; psychology; statistical & social survey methodology. **9** Population censuses & vital statistics reports (complete for UK, reasonably complete for commonwealth & many foreign countries); social survey reports. **11** Yes, by arrangement, for ref only. **12** Mon-Fri 9.30-16.30. **13** (a) 20,000; (b) 270. **15** (a) 6 (b) 2.

ORDER OF ST JOHN LIBRARY, St John's Gate, Clerkenwell, London EC1M 4DA (Tel 01-253 6644) Libn: Dr Lionel Butler MA, PhD, FRHistS; Curator: Miss Pamela Willie MA.
8 History of Order of St John; crusades; heraldry; military religious order. **11** Yes, by arrangement. **12** Mon-Fri 10.00-17.00. **13** (a) over 6,000; (c) 1,000 mss. **15** (a) 2 (b) 2.

OXFORD UNIVERSITY PRESS, LONDON, LIBRARY, Ely House, 37 Dover St, London W1X 4AH (Tel 01-629 8494) Libn: Miss Anne Harden BA; Dep: Mr Barry Marshall.
6 Oxford University. **8** Showroom of Oxford University Press, inc virtually all books, now in print, published by OUP & its branches, also some other reference books & a few interesting old books. **11** Yes, for ref only. **12** Mon-Fri 9.00-17.30. **13** (a) c. 10,000; (b) c. 30. **15** (a) 2 (b) 1, or 2.

PADDINGTON COLLEGE, Paddington Green, London W2 1NB (Tel 01-402 6221 ext 38) Coll Libn: Mrs F. Norris ALA; Dep Libn: Miss J. Wood BA, ALA.
6 ILEA. **7** Saltram Crescent, W9 3HW (01-969 2391) Libn: Miss J. Allen ALA; Beethoven St, W10 4LP (01-969 4655) Libn: Miss J. Allen ALA. **8** Engineering (mechanical, electrical, electronic, motor vehicle, gas, welding, heating & ventilating); medical laboratory science; animal technology; prosthetics; chiropody; physics; maths; photography; glasswork; business. **11** Yes, for ref only, on application to Libn. **12** Term: Mon-Fri 9.00-21.00; vac: hours vary. Branches vary. **13** (a) 30,000; (b) 278; (c) gramophone records; tapes; slides. **14** £13,830. **15** (a) 10½ (b) 1 (c) 4.

PAINT RESEARCH ASSOCIATION LIBRARY, Waldegrave Rd, Teddington, Middlesex TW11 8LD (Tel 01-977 4427; Telex 928720) Libn: Miss S. C. Haworth BSc, MA, DipLib; Asst Libn: Mrs B. Faulkner.
8 Paints; surface coatings; corrosion; associated aspects of chemistry (especially polymer & analytical chemistry); physics (colour physics & measurement); microbiology. **11** Yes, by special arrangement (a fee is usually charged). **12** Mon-Fri 8.45-17.15. **13** (a) 20,000; (b) 350; (c) microfilms; standards & specifications. **15** (a) 10 (b) 2 (c) 1.

PASSMORE EDWARDS MUSEUM LIBRARY, Romford Rd, Stratford, London E15 4LZ (Tel 01-534 4545 ext 376) Curator: Ian G. Robertson MA, AMA.
8 Archaeology; history; biology; geology. **9** Essex topographical collns (inc much material from Essex Field Club). **10** Union List of Periodicals; Newham Library Service. **11** No, but books may be seen by appointment; loans at Curator's discretion. **13** (a) 10,000; (b) 71. **14** £800.

CODE: **1** Name of Library. **2** Address. **3** Telephone & Telex. **4** Officer in charge. **5** Deputy. **6** Governing body. **7** Branches. **8** Main Subjects. **9** Special Collections. **10** Co-operative Schemes. **11** Open to public? **12** Hours. **13** Stock: (a) books (b) periodicals (c) other. **14** Finance. **15** Staff: (a) non-manual (b) graduate (c) chartered librarians.

LONDON—*continued*

PHARMACEUTICAL SOCIETY OF GREAT BRITAIN LIBRARY, 17 Bloomsbury Sq, London WC1A 2NN (Tel 01-405 8967) Libn: R. G. Todd FPS.
6 Council of Society. **7** Scottish Dept Lib, 36 York Pl, Edinburgh, EH1 3HU (031-556 4386), Libn: Miss Linda Cameron BSc. **8** Pharmacy; materia medica; pharmacology; chemistry; botany. **9** Historical colln (inc many foreign pharmacopoeias); English & foreign herbals (inc Latin 'Herbarius' of 1485); London pharmacopoeias (from 1618); Hanbury Library (550 vols of rare illustrated botanical works). **10** BLL. **11** Yes, for ref only, to bona-fide enquirers. **12** Mon-Fri 9.00-17.00. **13** (a) 43,100; (b) 500; (c) 12,375 pamphlets. **15** (a) 7 (b) 2.

PHILIPPA FAWCETT COLLEGE OF EDUCATION (will merge with Furzedown College), Leigham Court Rd, London SW16 2QD (Tel 01-677 9641) Coll Libn: Miss N. M. Morgan MA, FLA; Dep Libn: Miss H. Ellisdon BA, ALA.
6 ILEA. **8** Education. **10** WANDPETLS. **11** No. **12** Mon-Fri 9.00-18.00 (Fri 17.00). **13** (a) 50,300; (b) 240; (c) 2,500 records; c. 30,000 slides; 450 audiotapes; 400 videotapes. **14** £11,000. **15** (a) 5 (b) 2 (c) 2.

POETRY SOCIETY LIBRARY, National Poetry Centre, 21 Earls Court Sq, London W5 (Tel 01-373 7861/2) General Sec: Mr M. Mackenzie.
8 Poetry in all its aspects, history & criticism; anthologies: art of poetry; speaking; American poets. **9** 'Poetry Review' (from beginning). **11** Yes, by previous arrangement. **12** Mon-Fri 9.30-17.00 (Tues 22.00).

POLISH LIBRARY, 9 Princes Gardens, London SW7 1NB (Tel 01-589 2154) Libn: Dr Zdzislaw Jagodziński PhD; Dep Libn: Mrs Jadwiga Nowak.
6 Polish Library Council, Polish Social & Cultural Assoc. **8** Polish history, culture, literature, geography, law, economics, politics, sociology, folklore & general Polish affairs (in Polish & other languages). **9** Lanckoroński colln (old Polish books & prints); Polish emigré publications; Conradiana (works by & concerning Joseph Conrad), colln of bookplates. **10** BLL; inter-library loans. **11** Yes, but majority of books may be consulted in Reading Room only. **12** Mon & Thurs 10.00-17.00, Tues & Fri 10.00-20.00, Wed & Sat 10.00-13.00. **13** (a) 90,000; (b) 400; (c) 38,000 photographs; 500 mss; 11,000 bookplates, maps, music, prints, drawings; c. 2,600 old periodical titles. **14** £1,000. **15** (a) 5 (b) 1.

POLYTECHNIC OF CENTRAL LONDON LIBRARY, 309 Regent St, London W1R 8AL (Tel 01-580 2020) Chief Libn: Prof Wilfred Ashworth BSc, FLA, ARPS, FInstInfSc, DipLib; Lib Devt Officer: Miss Ann Caro MA, ALA, DipLib; Bibliographic Services Officer: Miss W. Abbott BA, ALA.
7 Photography & Communication Studies, 18-20 Riding House St, W1 (01-486 5811), Libn: Miss J. Sheppard BA, ALA; Engineering & Science, 115 New Cavendish St, W1M 8JS (01-486 5811), Libn: Mrs K. Jesch BSc, MSc; Management & Environment, 35 Marylebone Rd, NW1 5LS (01-486 511), Management Libn: Mrs A. Dolitzscher MA, FLA; Environment Libn: Miss J. Beardwood BSc, DipLib, ALA; Languages, Red Lion Sq, Holborn, WC1R 4SR (01-405 3144), Libn: Miss T. Czerniewska BA, ALA; DipLib; Law, 235-238 High Holborn, WC1V 7DN (01-405 3144), Libn: Miss P. Sherlock ALA; Social Sciences & Business Studies, 32-38 Wells St, W1P 3FG (01-486 5811), Libn: Miss M. Coghlan BA, ALA; Education, Sidney Webb College, 9-12 Barrett St, W1M 6DE (01-487 5911), Libn: Miss B. Williams ALA. **11** Yes, for ref only, by arrangement. **13** (a) 120,000; (b) 1,500. **14** £90,000. **15** (a) 48 (b) 32 (c) 20.

POLYTECHNIC OF NORTH LONDON, LIBRARY AND INFORMATION SERVICE, Holloway, London N7 8DB (Tel 01-607 6767; Telex 25228) Chief Libn: Mr John Cowley BA, FLA.
6 ILEA. **7** Camden High St (01-267 1107), Libn: Miss M. White ALA; 205-225 Essex Rd, N1 (01-226 0131), Libn: Mr G. Fitzmaurice BA, ALA; Holloway Rd, N7 (01-607 6767), Libn: Mr E. R. Yescombe MBE, FLA; Prince of Wales Rd, Kentish Town, NW5 (01-485 0101), Libn: Miss A. Winser BA, ALA; 62-66 Highbury Green N7 (01-359 0941) Libn: Miss R. Melling BA, ALA; Marlborough Building, 383 Holloway Rd, N7, Libn: Miss P. Bater BA, ALA. **8** General. **9** National College of Rubber Technology; librarianship. **10** LASER. **11** Yes, on application to Chief Libn. **12** Term: 9.00-20.00; vac: 9.00-17.00. **13** (a) 200,000; (b) 1,500; (c) 200 discs; 1,000 microforms; 2,500 slides; 200 sound tapes. **14** £130,000.

POLYTECHNIC OF THE SOUTH BANK LIBRARY, (will merge with Battersea College of Education & Rachel McMillan Annexe), Borough Rd, London SE1 0AA (Tel 01-928 8989) Chief Libn: Mr G. J. Broadis MA, FLA, FRSA; D. F. W. Hawes FLA, FRSA.
7 Built Environment Faculty Lib, Wandsworth Rd, London SW8 2JY, Libn: K. G. Turner ALA; Environmental Sciences & Technology Lib, Borough Rd, SE1 OAA, Libn: Miss A. M. Brown MA, DipLib, ALA. **8** Maths; physics; chemistry; chemical engineering; polymer technology; metals science; applied biology; food science; electrical, electronic, mechanical & production engineering; social sciences; nursing (with Westminster Hospital); accountancy & management; law; languages (European); construction science; environmental engineering; architecture; town planning & estate management. **9** Building materials colln. **10** LINK. **11** Yes, for ref only. **12** Term: Mon-Fri 9.00-21.00; vac: Mon-Fri 9.30-17.00. **13** (a) 172,130; (b) 2,310; (c) 300 microfilms; 10,000 photographic slides; other microforms & audio-visual materials. **14** £150,000. **15** (a) 41½ (b) 23 (c) 20.

PORT OF LONDON AUTHORITY LIBRARY, London Dock House (South), Thomas More St, London E1 9AZ (Tel 01-476 6900 ext 93/242) Libn & Archivist: Mr Richard Brown; Mr William Upsher JP.
8 Port administration; transport; docks; London (local history). **9** Dock Company minutes (complete from 1799); River & Port Committee of City of London (1770-1908); Thames Commissioner Minutes (to amalgamation with PLA, 1908). **11** Yes, for ref by prior arrangement only. **12** 9.00-17.00. **13** (a) c. 5,000; (c) c. 3,000 unframed prints & graphics; 800 framed pictures; artifacts & tools of the associated trades from Roman times. **14** £6,000. **15** (a) 2 (b) 1.

PROPERTY SERVICES AGENCY LIBRARY, Lambeth Bridge House, London SE1 7SB (Tel 01-211 7236; Telex 22221/2/3) Principal Libn: C. D. Overton MA, FLA; Senior Libn: C. E. Rogers ALA.
7 64 libraries in Britain & Western Europe. Principal branches: Argyle House, Edinburgh (031-229 9191), Libn: Mr McVittie ALA; Government Buildings, Cardiff (0222-62131), Libn: Mrs Llewellyn; Chessington (01-397 5266), Libn: Mr T. Voy; Whitgift Centre, Croydon (01-686 8710), Libn: Miss J. Hocking; Apollo House, Croydon (01-686 5622), Libn: Mr J. H. Chapman; Lunar House, Croydon (01-686 3499), Libn: Mr H. J. Field; St Christopher House, Southwark St (01-928 7999), Libn: Mr E. E. Leake; Southbridge House, Southwark Bridge Rd, (01-928 2044), Libn: Mr J. Underwood. **8** Construction industry; supplies; training; ancient monuments of Scotland & Wales. **9** Major collns of product information on construction industry (Whitgift, Chessington libraries); photographs (Hannibal House, London & Argyle House, Edinburgh). **10** LINK; FIND; SASLIC; HULTIS. **11** Yes, if inf is otherwise unavailable. **12** Mon-Fri 9.00-17.00. **13** (a) c. 100,000; (b) 1,000; (c) microtexts of all

LONDON—*continued*

significant construction industry periodical articles on a
world basis (since July 1972).   **14** £120,000.   **15** (a) 130,
(b) 11 (c) 22.

PUBLIC RECORD OFFICE LIBRARY, Chancery Lane, London
WC2A 1LR (Tel 01-405 0741 ext 20) Libn: C.D. Chalmers MA;
Dep Libn: R.V. Weygang.
8 English history; European history; colonial history; American history; archives; public records & record publications.
11 Yes, for ref only.   **12** Mon-Fri 9.30-17.00, Sat 9.30-
13.00.   **13** (a) 90,000; (b) 190.   **15** (a) 4 (b) 1.

RADIO TIMES, HULTON PICTURE LIBRARY, 35 Marylebone
High St, London W1M 4AA (Tel 01-580 5577 ext 4621; Telex
265781) Libn: Mrs C. Sergides BSc, ALA; Dep Libn: Mrs
E.K. Moreland.
6 British Broadcasting Corporation.   **8** Photographs,
drawings, engravings, mss, colour transparencies & maps,
(over 6,000,000) covering a wide range of historical subjects, personalities & people; arts; sciences & life in all its
aspects.   **9** Rischgitz colln (1,000,000 historical prints);
Sasha London Theatre colln (1920's-1940); Gordon Anthony-
De Marney colln (1930's-1950's); Baron photo colln (1935-
1956).   **11** Yes, for pictures for commercial reproduction.
12 Mon-Fri 9.30-17.30.   **15** (a) 27 (b) 6 (c) 3.

RAVENSBOURNE COLLEGE OF ART & DESIGN LIBRARY,
(will merge with Bromley College of Technology & Stockwell College of Education to form the Bromley Institute of
Higher Education), Walden Rd, Chislehurst, Kent (Tel 01-468
7071) Libn: Mr Richard Bird ALA.
6 London Borough of Bromley.   **8** Fine & applied arts;
design.   **11** Yes.   **12** Term: Mon-Thurs 9.30-19.30,
Fri 9.30-17.00; vac: 9.30-16.30.   **13** (a) 17,500; (b) 140;
(c) 35,000 slides.   **15** (a) 3½ (c) 2.

RECKITT AND COLMAN LTD, LIBRARY AND INFORMATION
SERVICE, PO Box 26, Burlington Lane, Chiswick, London
W4 2RW (Tel 01-994 6464 ext 155; Telex 21268) Libn: Mr
R.M. Williamson AIInfSci; Asst Libn: Miss D.M. Scarbrow.
8 Economics; law; applied sciences; management; commercial.   **10** CICRIS.   **11** Yes, for ref only.   **12** Mon-Fri
8.45-16.25.   **13** (a) 5,000; (b) 200.   **14** £6,000.
15 (a) 2.

RELIGIOUS SOCIETY OF FRIENDS LIBRARY, Friends House,
Euston Rd, London NW1 2BJ (Tel 01-387 3601) Libn: Mr
Edward H. Milligan.
6 London Yearly Meeting.   **8** Quaker history, thought &
practice; other subjects of Quaker interest (e.g. anti-slavery,
peace).   **11** Yes, identification and/or introduction required.   **12** Mon-Fri 9.30-17.30.   **13** (a) 25,000; (b) 150;
(c) archives; mss collns; microfilms; pictures.   **15** (a) 5.

REMPLOY TECHNICAL LIBRARY, 415 Edgware Rd, Cricklewood, London NW2 6LR (Tel 01-452 8020; Telex 23178)
Technical Libn: Miss K. Campbell.
8 Technical & commercial information (books, journals, press
cuttings) relevant to Company's manufactures; management;
employment of disabled.   **10** CICRIS.   **11** No, but literature on employment of the disabled available at discretion of
Libn.   **12** Mon-Fri 9.30-17.00.   **13** (a) 3,000; (b) 100.
15 1.

REUTERS LIBRARY, 85 Fleet St, London EC4P 4AJ (Tel
01-353 6060 ext 226)   **4** Chief Libn: Mr Endre Somjen.
8 Overseas news of all kinds (UK not covered).   **11** Yes,
usually by appointment & payment of a minimum fee (at
present £5).   **12** Mostly 24 hours a day.   **13** (a) 3,500;
(b) very few; (c) teleprinter tape, filed according to subject;
some archival material.   **15** (a) 19 (b) 6 (c) 2.

ROEHAMPTON INSTITUTE OF FURTHER EDUCATION
LIBRARY, c/o Grove House, Roehampton Lane, London SW15
5PJ. Chairman of Resources for Learning Committee
(rotated among Site Librarians).
7 Site Libraries: Southlands College of Education, 65 Wimbledon Parkside, SW19 5NN (01-946 2234), Libn: Mr J.F.
Clarke BA, ALA, DipEd; Froebel Institute College of Education, Grove House, Roehampton Lane, SW15 5PJ (01-876 2242),
Libn: Mr J.O. Chislett BA, ALA; Whitelands College of

Education, West Hill, Putney, SW15 3SN (01-788 8268), Libn:
Miss C.S. Ker BA, FLA; Digby Stuart College, Roehampton
(01-876 8273), Libn: Miss Solmonsz.   **8** Maths; geography;
natural history; movement & dance; psychology; education;
divinity; history; sociology; arts & crafts; music; English;
French; drama; physical & biological sciences; music; general.
9 Froebel & Froebelian movement; education; religious
studies; Sharpe colln (190 early children's books); John
Ruskin (works & some biographical material); a Bishop's
Bible; a 19th cent illuminated Koran ms; a Nuremberg
Chronicle; Gould's 'Birds of New Guinea'; early botanical
works (inc hand copy of 'Herbario Rinio').   **10** BLL;
WANDPETLS.   **11** Yes, for ref only, on prior application to
Libn: **12** Term: Mon-Fri 9.00-20.00; vac: Mon-Fri 9.00-
17.00.   **13** (a) c. 200,000; (b) c. 350; (c) microtexts; archives;
gramophone records; cassettes & tapes; filmstrips.

ROYAL ACADEMY OF ARTS LIBRARY, Burlington House,
Piccadilly, London W1V 0DS (Tel 01-734 9052) Libn: Miss
Constance-Anne Parker.
8 Fine arts.   **9** History of Royal Academy & English art.
11 Yes, by arrangement with Libn.   **12** Mon-Fri 10.00-
13.00, 14.00-17.00.   **13** (a) 20,000.   **15** (a) 1½ (b) 2.

ROYAL ACADEMY OF MUSIC LIBRARY, Marylebone Rd,
London NW1 5HT (Tel 01-935 5461) Libn: Miss M.J.
Harington BA, LRAM.
8 Music.   **9** Henry Wood Orchestral Library;
Otto Klemperer archive.   **11** Yes, for ref only.   **12** Term:
Mon-Fri 9.00-18.30; vac: 9.30-17.00.   **13** (a) 10,000;
(b) 40; (c) 80,000 music scores; 1,100 gramophone records;
18 microfilms; some archive material, programmes etc.
15 (a) 6 (b) 2 (c) 3.

ROYAL AERONAUTICAL SOCIETY LIBRARY, 4 Hamilton
Pl, London W1V OBQ (Tel 01-499 3515) Libn & Inf Officer:
Mr A.W.L. Nayler DInstM, AMRAS; Dep: Mrs E. Dane.
8 Aerospace.   **9** Cuthbert Hodgeson & Poynton colln
(ballooning).   **10** BLL.   **11** Yes, on application to Libn.
12 Mon-Fri 9.30-16.30.   **13** (a) c. 25,000; (b) 420; (c)
Photos; slides; prints; technical reports.   **15** (a) 3 (b) 1
(c) 1.

ROYAL AIR FORCE MUSEUM LIBRARY, Aerodrome Rd,
Hendon, London NW9 5LL (Tel 01-205 2266 ext 11) Libn: Mr
R.F. Barker MA, LLB.
6 MoD(Air).   **8** Aviation history; aerospace affairs.
11 Yes, by appointment only.   **12** Mon-Fri 10.00-12,00,
13.00-16.30.   **13** Manuals; programmes; scale drawings;
photocopying facilities.   **15** (a) 2 (b) 2.

ROYAL ANTHROPOLOGICAL INSTITUTE LIBRARY, 6
6 Burlington Gardens, London W1X 2EX (Tel 01-734 6370)
Libn: Miss B.J. Kirkpatrick MBE, FLA; Dep: Mr R.E.
McNaughton MA, ALA.
8 Anthropology.   **9** Sir Richard Burton's library.
10 BLL.   **12** Mon-Fri 10.00-16.45.   **13** (a) 65,000;
(b) 671; (c) archive & mss colln.   **15** (a) 4 (b) 2 (c) 2.

ROYAL ARMY MEDICAL COLLEGE LIBRARY, Millbank,
London SW1P 4RJ (Tel 01-834 9060 ext 390) Libn: Mrs
Mary A. Dunsford ALA.
6 MoD.   **8** Medicine.   **9** Fayrer, Home, Johnston, Spiller,
Macpherson & Waring collns; works & diaries of RAMC
officers.   **11** No.   **12** 9.30-17.30.   **13** (a) 29,000; (b)
180; (c) archives.   **15** (a) 1 (c) 1.

ROYAL ASTRONOMICAL SOCIETY LIBRARY, Burlington
House, Piccadilly, London W1V 0NL (Tel 01-734 4582) Libn:
Dr R.E.W. Maddison FLA.
6 Council of the Royal Astronomical Society.   **8** Astronomy
& geophysics.   **9** Grove-Hills colln (rare books).
11 No, except with letter of introduction from a Fellow.
12 Mon-Fri 10.00-17.00.   **13** (a) 25,000; (b) c.300;
(c) archives (not indexed); correspondence of Sir William
Herschel.   **14** £4,500.   **15** (a) 2 (b) 2.

ROYAL BOTANIC GARDENS LIBRARY, Kew, Richmond,
Surrey, TW9 3AB (Tel 01-940 1171) Chief Libn & Archivist:
Mr V.T.H. Parry MA, FLA; Dep Libn: Mrs D.C. Scott ALA.
6 MAFF.   **7** Jodrell Laboratory, Kew; Museums Dept, Kew;
Gardens Lib, Kew; Wakehurst Pl (044-488 435).   **8** Botany;
plant taxonomy & geography; anatomy; physiology; cyto-

CODE: 1 Name of Library. 2 Address. 3 Telephone & Telex. 4 Officer in charge. 5 Deputy. 6 Governing body. 7 Branches. 8 Main Subjects. 9 Special Collections. 10 Co-operative Schemes. 11 Open to public? 12 Hours. 13 Stock: (a) books (b) periodicals (c) other. 14 Finance. 15 Staff: (a) non-manual (b) graduate (c) chartered librarians.

LONDON—*continued*

genetics, economic botany; horticulture. **9** Kewensia colln (local history); Linnean colln; Pre-Linnean colln; plant illustrations (170,000); Portrait colln; Darlington Reprint colln. **10** Inter-library loans. **11** No. **12** Mon-Thurs 9.00-17.30, Fri 9.00-17.00, Sat 9.00-16.30. **13** (a) over 100,000; (b) 1,500; (c) extensive archives (inc 250,000 letters); statutory place of deposit under the Public Records Acts. **14** £13,000 purchase grant (plus binding & exchange agreements). **15** (a) 14 (b) 2 (c) 6.

ROYAL COLLEGE OF ART LIBRARY, Kensington Gore, London SW7 2EU (Tel 01-584 5020) Libn: Mr Hans Brill MA; Asst Libn: Ms Joan Walden ALA.
6 Council of Royal College of Art. **7** Technical Information Office, (01-584 5020 ext 350); Technical Inf Officer: Ms Margaret Pope. **8** Visual arts; history & criticism of other arts; literature in English; foreign literature in translation; history; religion; philosophy; psychology; science. **10** BLL. **11** Yes, for ref only. **12** Term: Mon-Fri 10.00-19.00 (Tues 21.00); vac: Mon-Fri 10.00-17.00. **13** (a) 26,000; (b) c.160; (c) microfilm. **14** £12,000. **15** (a) 6½ (b) 4 (c) 2.

Royal College of Music

> LIBRARY, Prince Consort Rd, London SW7 2BS.
> **8** Music. **11** No, except by written application for otherwise unavailable inf.

> PARRY ROOM LIBRARY, Prince Consort Rd, London SW7 2BS
> **8** Music. **11** Yes, for information unavailable elsewhere, by application in writing for reader's ticket. **12** Term: Mon-Fri 10.00-17.00.

ROYAL COLLEGE OF OBSTETRICIANS AND GYNAECOLOGISTS, MARKLAND LIBRARY, 27 Sussex Pl, Regent's Park, London NW1 4RG (Tel 01-262 5425) Libn: Miss Patricia C. Want ALA; Miss Mary Evans ALA.
8 Obstetrics, gynaecology & closely related subjects only. **11** No. **12** Mon-Fri 10.00-17.00. **13** (a) 10,000; (b) 120. **14** £3,470. **15** (a) 2 (c) 2.

ROYAL COLLEGE OF PHYSICIANS OF LONDON LIBRARY, 11 St Andrew's Place, Regent's Park, London NW1 4LE (Tel 01-935 1174; Telex Medicorum London NW1) Harveian Libn: Dr C. E. Newman CBE, MD, FRCP; Libn: Mr L. M. Payne MBE, FLA; Asst Libn: Mr G. Davenport BA, ALA.
8 History & biography of medicine; books by Fellows (& Licentiates up to 1825); medical education. **9** Library of Marquis of Dorchester (original catalogue, c.3,000 vols); 108 incunabula (mostly medical); Evan Bedford Library of Cardiology (c.1,000 vols). **10** BLL; LAMedSectExch. **11** Yes, at discretion of, & on application to, the Harveian Libn. **12** Mon-Fri 10.00-17.00. **13** (a) 43,000; (b) 108; (c) 2,000 bookplates & 10,000 portraits of medical men; lantern slides; tape-recordings; 5,000 autograph letters; Oriental & Western mss. **15** (a) 7 (b) 3 (c) 3.

ROYAL COLLEGE OF PSYCHIATRISTS LIBRARY (temporarily closed), 17 Belgrave Sq, London SW1X 8PG (Tel 01-235 2351) Hon Libn: Dr H. R. Rollin FRCPsych.
8 Psychiatry. **9** Historical books on psychiatry. **11** No. **12** Probably 9.30-16.30, but library temporarily in store pending building renovation. **13** (a) c.2,000; (b) c.40.

ROYAL COLLEGE OF SURGEONS OF ENGLAND LIBRARY, 35-43 Lincoln's Inn Fields, London WC2A 3PN (Tel 01-405 3474) Libn: Mr E. H. Cornelius MA, DipLib, ALA; Senior Asst Libn: Mr I. F. Lyle ALA.
8 Surgery & its specialities (inc anaesthesia, dental surgery, anatomy, pathology, physiology); history of medicine. **9** Hunter Baillie Papers (letters, documents, etc., of the Hunter Baillie & Denman families); Lister Papers (case books, letters & documents of Lord Lister); Owen Papers (mss of, & letters to, Sir Richard Owen). **10** MLA of USA; LA Med Sect Exch. **11** No except at discretion of Libn, on recommendation, & for specific purposes. **12** Mon-Fri 10.00-18.00, Sat 10.00-12.30. **13** (a) 140,000; (b) 650; (c) 3,000 engraved portraits; 1,000 bookplates; c.3,000 mss. **14** c.£10,500. **15** (a) 7 (b) 2 (c) 3.

ROYAL COLLEGE OF VETERINARY SURGEONS, WELLCOME LIBRARY, 32 Belgrave Sq, London SW1X 8QP (Tel 01-235 6568) Libn: Miss Benita Horder BA, ALA.
6 Royal College of Veterinary Surgeons' Trust Fund. **8** Veterinary science. **10** BLL; Aslib. **11** Yes, on introduction by member. **12** Mon-Fri 10.00-17.00. **13** (a) 25,000; (b) 250. **15** (a) 5 (b) 2 (c) 2.

ROYAL COMMONWEALTH SOCIETY LIBRARY, Northumberland Ave, London WC2N 5BJ (Tel 01-930 6733) Libn & Dir of Studies: Mr Donald H. Simpson MA, FLA, FRGS; Dep Libn: Mrs E. Hammerton BA.
8 The Commonwealth & its members, past & present. **9** Offical publications; Canadian books. **10** BLL; SCOLMA (Nigeria). **11** Yes, subject to Libn's permission. **12** Mon-Fri 9.00-19.00, Sat 10.00-13.00, 13.45-18.00. **13** (a) c.150,000; (b) 600; (c) archives of RCS; over 600 mss; reports; pamphlets; 30,000 photographs; 5,500 maps. **15** (a) 9 (b) 4 (c) 3.

ROYAL ENTOMOLOGICAL SOCIETY LIBRARY, 41 Queens Gate, London SW7 5HU (Tel 01-584 8361) Libn: Mrs Jane Backhouse BSc, ALA.
8 Entomology. **9** Correspondence & diaries; photographs of entomologists (indexed but not catalogued); records of the society's predecessors. **10** BLL. **11** Yes, by special arrangement only. **12** Mon-Fri 9.30-17.00. **13** (a) 9,000; (b) 245; (c) 45,000 reprints. **15** (a) 1 (b) 1 (c) 1.

Royal Geographical Society

> LIBRARY, Kensington Gore, London SW7 2AR, (Tel 01-589 5466) Libn: Mr G. S. Dugdale MA, FLA; Dep Libn: Mr D. Wileman BA, ALA.
> **8** Geography (all branches); travel & exploration; cartography. **10** BLL. **11** No. **12** Mon-Fri 9.30-17.30. **13** (a) c.90,000; (b) c.700. **15** (a) 3½ (b) 2 (c) 2.

> MAP ROOM, 1 Kensington Gore, London SW7 2AR (Tel 01-589 5466) Keeper of the Map Room: Brig R. A. Gardiner, MBE, FSA; Map Curator: Mr H. G. Bilcliffe.
> **8** World-wide & extraterrestrial maps, atlases, charts, (aeronautical & marine), globes, gazetteers & carto-bibliographies, (both old & current). **10** Bibliographie Cartographique Internationale (Centre National de la Recherche Scientifique, Paris); Union Catalog of Maps (Berkeley Documentation Center, California). **11** Yes, for ref only. **12** Mon-Fri 9.30-17.30. **13** (a) 600,000 maps; 4,000 atlases. **15** (a) 4 (b) 1.

ROYAL HORTICULTURAL SOCIETY, LINDLEY LIBRARY, PO Box 31, Vincent Sq, London SW1P 2PE (Tel 01-834 4333) Libn & Archivist: P. F. Stageman.
6 Council of Royal Horticultural Society. **8** Horticulture; arboriculture; botany. **11** Yes, by prior application to Sec. **12** Mon-Fri 9.30-17.30. **13** (a) 36,700. **15** (a) 2.

ROYAL INSTITUTE OF BRITISH ARCHITECTS, SIR BANISTER FLETCHER LIBRARY, 66 Portland Pl, London W1N 4AD (Tel 01-580 5533) Libn: Mr David E. Dean MA, DipEd, ALA; Dep Libn: Mr Jan F. van der Wateren MA, DipLib, ALA.
7 Drawings Colln, 21 Portman Sq, W1H 9HF (01-580 5533 ext 245, or 487 5441), Curator: Mr John Harris.

LONDON—*continued*

8 Architecture.   **9** Handley-Read colln (Victorian decorative arts); mss colln (12,000 19th cent. mss); drawings colln (250,000 architectural drawings from Tudor times onwards); photographic colln (c. 40,000, of 20th cent. European architecture.   **11** Yes for ref only.   **12** Mon-Fri 10.00-20.00 (Mon 17.00), Sat 10.00-13.30. Closed for 4 weeks prior to Aug Bank Holiday.   **13** (a) 100,000; (b) 650.   **14** £14,000.   **15** (a) 20 (b) 12 (c) 9.

ROYAL INSTITUTE OF INTERNATIONAL AFFAIRS LIBRARY, Chatham House, St James's Sq, London SW1 4LE (Tel 01-930 2233) Libn: Miss Dorothy Hamerton MA, ALA; Dep Libn: Mrs June Wells BA, ALAA.
8 International politics; economics; jurisprudence.   **9** UN depository library; documents from EEC & other international organizations.   **10** BLL; SCOLMA.   **11** Yes, postgraduate research students & certain overseas visitors with suitable introduction.   **12** Mon-Fri 10.00-18.00.   **13** c. 139,000 (inc pamphlets); (b) 650.   **15** (a) 9 (b) 7 (c) 6.

ROYAL INSTITUTION LIBRARY, 21 Albemarle St, London W1X 4BS (Tel 01-493 0669) Libn & Inf Officer: Mrs I. M. McCabe BSc, MSc, DipLib, AIInfSc; Archivist: Mr J. R. Friday BA; Asst Libn: Miss J. Lloyd Thomas.
6 Royal Institution of Great Britain.   **8** Science; history & philosophy of science.   **9** 19th & 20th cent scientific archives.   **11** Yes, by application to libn.   **12** Mon-Fri 10.00-17.30.   **13** (c) Photo copying service.

ROYAL INSTITUTION OF CHARTERED SURVEYORS LIBRARY, 12 Great George St, London SW1P 3AD (Tel 01-839 5600) Libn: Miss Pauline J. Lane.
8 Agriculture; building & construction; landlord & tenant; land law; planning law; land surveying.   **9** Early surveying books & topography; law reports series.   **11** Yes, if introduced by a member.   **12** Mon-Fri 9.30-17.30.   **13** (a) 30,000; (b) 280.   **14** £10,500.   **15** (b) 2 (c) 7.

ROYAL INSTITUTION OF NAVAL ARCHITECTS, DENNY LIBRARY, 10 Upper Belgrave St, London SW1X 8BQ (Tel 01-235 4622) Libn: Miss Lindsay M. Duncan.
6 Council of RINA.   **8** Naval architecture; marine engineering; historical ref books.   **9** Scott colln (naval architecture from 17th cent).   **10** BLL; inter-library loans.   **11** Yes, for ref only.   **12** Mon-Fri 9.30-13.00, 14.00-17.00.   **14** £500.   **15** (a) 1.

ROYAL NATIONAL INSTITUTE FOR THE BLIND, REFERENCE LIBRARY, 224 Great Portland St, London W1N 6AA (Tel 01-388 1266 ext 209) Ref Libn: Ms Christine S. Chin.
6 Executive Council.   **8** Blindness & welfare of the blind.   **10** BLL.   **11** Yes.   **12** 10.00-17.00.   **13** (b) 150.   **15** (a) 2 (b) 1 (c) 1.

ROYAL NAVAL COLLEGE LIBRARY, Greenwich, London SE10 9NN (Tel 01-858 2154) Libn: Miss J. M. Webster ALA.
6 MoD (Navy).   **7** Staff College Lib, Libn: Miss M. Stewart MA, MLitt; Nuclear Dept Lib, Libn: Mr S. R. B. Williams MINucE.   **8** Naval history; politics; defence; international affairs; nuclear science & technology.   **10** Inter-library loans.   **11** No.   **13** (a) 30,000; (b) 200.   **15** (a) 5 (b) 1 (c) 1.

ROYAL SOCIETY OF ARTS LIBRARY, 8 John Adam St, London WC2N 6EZ (Tel 01-839 2366 ext 48) Curator-Libn: Mr D. G. C. Allan MSc, FSA, FRHistS; Dep: Miss Susan Blundell.
8 Encouragement of arts, manufactures & commerce.   **9** Society's early archives; international exhibitions (1850-1900).   **10** BLL; Aslib.   **11** No.   **13** (a) 5,500; (b) 73.

ROYAL SOCIETY OF MEDICINE LIBRARY, 1 Wimpole St, London W1M 8AC (Tel 01-580 2070) Libn: Mr Philip Wade BA, FLA; Dep Libn: Mr David W Stewart BA, ALA.
8 All aspects of medicine.   **11** Yes, only on introduction by a fellow of the society.   **12** Mon-Fri 9.30-21.30, Sat 9.30-17.30.   **13** (a) c. 400,000; (b) 2,300.   **15** (a) 22 (b) 11 (c) 12.

ROYAL STATISTICAL SOCIETY LIBRARY, 25 Enford St, London W1H 2BH (Tel 01-723 5882) Libn: Mrs M. Snaith.
8 Statistics.   **9** Yule library (early works on statistics).   **11** No.   **12** Mon-Fri 10.00-17.00.   **13** (a) 40,000; (b) 300; (c) 20,000 vols early UK & foreign trade statistics & monographs.

ROYAL TOWN PLANNING INSTITUTE LIBRARY, 26 Portland Pl, London W1N 4BE (Tel 01-636 9107) Libn: Mr J. L. Barrick ALA; Dep: Ms Louisa Stephens TPTC(Aus).
6 Council of Royal Town Planning Institute.   **8** Town & country planning; transportation; housing; conservation; recreation.   **11** Yes, for ref only.   **12** Mon-Fri 9.00-17.00 (Fri 16.30).   **13** (a) 11,000; (b) 112.   **14** £800.   **15** (a) 2 (c) 1.

ST MARTIN'S SCHOOL OF ART LIBRARY, 109 Charing Cross Rd, London WC2H 0DU (Tel 01-437 0058 ext 29) Libn: Miss Catriona Robertson ALA; Dep: Miss Katherine Baird ALA.
6 ILEA.   **8** Fine arts; graphic design; fashion & textiles; cinema; photography; psychology; sociology; literature.   **9** Photographs on all subjects; exhibition catalogues; posters.   **10** ILEA; ARLIS; inter-library loans.   **11** Yes, for ref only, by special arrangement.   **12** 9.00-19.00.   **13** (a) 17,000; (b) 170; (c) microfilm; cassette tapes; gramophone records.   **15** (a) 4 (b) 1 (c) 2.

ST MARY'S COLLEGE LIBRARY, Strawberry Hill, Twickenham, TW1 4SX (Tel 01-892 0051 ext 252) Tutorlibn: Mr Robert J. Hoare ACP, DIP Adv Ed; Libn: Miss S. F. Kent ALA.
6 Catholic education council.   **8** Education; physical education; history; geography; art; English; biology; chemistry; classics; French; handicraft; music; physics; philosophy; psychology; religious study; sociology; children's books.   **10** Physical education association.   **11** No.   **12** Term: Mon-Fri 9.00-21.00; Vac: Mon-Fri 9.00-17.00.   **13** (a) 73,000; (b) 310; (c) microfilm; microcards; microfiches; audio-tapes.   **14** £16,000.   **15** (a) 8 (b) 1 (c) 3.

ST PAUL'S SCHOOL LIBRARY, Lonsdale Rd, Barnes, London SW13 9JT (Tel 01-748 9162) Libn: Mr A. H. Mead MA, B Litt; Asst Libn: Miss M. E. Newton BA, ALA.
6 Mercers' Company.   **8** English literature; history; geography; classics; modern languages & literature; maths; music; arts; religion; economics; science; sport.   **9** Rare books & mss, (inc first editions of Old Paulines, eg, John Milton, G. K. Chesterton, Compton Mackenzie, Edward Thomas, Ernest Raymond, Montgomery of Alamein); 16th, 17th, 18th cent classics books; small Aldine collection.   **11** No.   **12** Mon-Fri 8.45-17.15.   **13** (a) c. 20,000; (b) 44; (c) archives.   **14** c. £2,000.   **15** (a) 2½ (b) 2 (c) 1.

SCIENCE MUSEUM LIBRARY, South Kensington, London SW7 5NH (Tel 01-589 6371; Telex 21200) Keeper: Dr J. A. Chaldecott PhD, MSc, FInstP; Dep Keeper: Miss H. J. Parker BSc.
6 Dept of Education & Science.   **8** Science & technology (at post-graduate level); source material on history of science & technology.   **9** Comprehensive colln. of national & subject bibliographies; British patent specifications, abridgments & indexes; extensive colln of atomic-energy reports.   **10** BLL.   **11** Yes.   **12** Mon-Sat 10.00-17.30.   **13** (a) 440,000; (b) 5,600; (c) photocopying service; archives, microtexts.   **15** (a) 76 (b) 19 (c) 1.

SEAFARERS EDUCATION SERVICE AND COLLEGE OF THE SEA LIBRARY, Mansbridge House, 207 Balham High St, London SW17 7BH (Tel 01-673 8866/7) Libn: Mr F. J. Bryan ALA.   **7** College of the Sea, Kingston House, James St, Liverpool.   **8** Seafarers' books; general.   **9** Merchant Navy.   **10** BLL; Wandpetls.   **11** No.   **13** (a) 250,000; (b) 6; (c) 3,000 films (16 mm sound).   **14** £50,000.

SERVICES CENTRAL LIBRARY, Kimber Rd, London SW18 4PQ (Tel 01-874 8111) Chief Libn: Mr R. A. Wafer ALA; Libn-in-charge, lending dept: Miss M. M. Simpson ALA.
6 Institute of Army Education.   **8** General; military science; military history; psychology; management; languages.   **9** Regimental histories; playsets.   **10** BLL; BNBC.

CODE: 1 Name of Library. **2** Address. **3** Telephone & Telex. **4** Officer in charge. **5** Deputy. **6** Governing body.
7 Branches. **8** Main Subjects. **9** Special Collections. **10** Co-operative Schemes. **11** Open to public? **12** Hours.
13 Stock: (a) books (b) periodicals (c) other. **14** Finance. **15** Staff: (a) non-manual (b) graduate (c) chartered librarians.

LONDON—*continued*

11 Yes, by appointment only, to accredited students.
12 Mon Tues 8.30-17.00, Wed-Fri 8.30-16.30.
13 (a) over 100,000; (b) 30. **15** (a) 17 (c) 4.

SHELL INTERNATIONAL PETROLEUM COMPANY
LIBRARY, Shell Centre, York Rd, London SE1 7NA
(Tel 01-934 5367; Telex 919651) Libn: Mr M. Scoones FLA;
Inf officer: Mrs J. Sandison BSc.
8 Petroleum & chemical industries; economics & management. **10** BLL; Aslib. **11** Yes on special application.
13 (a) 40,000; (b) 814. **15** (a) 32 (b) 5 (c) 6.

SION COLLEGE LIBRARY, Victoria Embankment, London
EC4Y 0DN (Tel 01-353 7983) Libn: Miss J. M. Owen BA,
ALA.
6 President & Court of Governors of Sion College.
8 Current: theology, church history (especially Anglican) &
allied subject; past: the above plus humanities in general.
9 Sion College Port Royal Library (c. 400 vols by or about
member of Abbey of Port Royal); Bishop Edmund Gibson's
pamphlet colln (c. 400 cols, late 18th-early 19th cent);
Rev W. Scott's pamphlet colln (c. 200 vols, 19th cent
ecclesiastical). **10** BLL; Association of British Theological
& Philosophical libraries. **11** Yes, for ref only.
12 Mon-Fri 10.00-17.00. **13** (a) 100,000; (b) 50.
15 (c) 2.

SOCIETY FOR CULTURAL RELATIONS WITH THE USSR
LIBRARY, 320 Brixton Rd, London SW9 6AB (Tel 01-274
2282) Libn & Inf Officer: Mr Bruce Hamilton BSc.
8 All aspects of soviet culture, history & life. **9** Art
& history books (mostly in Russian). **10** Inter-library
loans. **11** Yes, for ref only. **12** 10.00-17.00.
13 (a) 16,000; (b) many; (c) records; photographs; slides.
15 (a) 6 (b) 3.

SOCIETY OF CHIROPODISTS LIBRARY, 8 Wimpole St,
London W1M 8BX (Tel 01-580 3228) Libn: Mrs J. Shanks
MChS.
8 Chiropody, podology & associated topics (e.g. footwear).
9 Historical section (Seelig colln). **11** No, except by
special arrangement with Sec of the society. **12** Mon-
Fri 9.30-16.45. **13** (a) c. 600; (b) c. 40. **14** £20.

SOCIETY OF GENEALOGISTS' LIBRARY, 37 Harrington
Gardens, London SW7 4JX (Tel 01-373 7054) Libn: L. W.
Lawson Edwards; Asst Libn: Dr M. L. Bierbrier PhD.
8 Genealogy; heraldry; topography. **9** Boyd's marriage
index (covers 10% of marriages in England prior to 1837);
great slip index (card index of 3 million individual names);
document colln (800 box files of family notes & pedigrees);
apprentices of Great Britain (abstracts of indentures in
public record office 1710-1772). **10** BLL. **11** Yes,
on payment of daily fee. **12** Tues-Fri 10.00-18.00
(Wed & Thurs 20.00), Sat 10.00-17.00. **13** (a) 40,000;
(b) 115; (c) 1,550 microfilms. **15** (a) 3 (b) 1.

SOUTHALL COLLEGE OF TECHNOLOGY LIBRARY AND
RESOURCES CENTRE, Beaconsfield Rd, Southall, Middlesex,
UB1 1DP. (Tel 01-571 1740) Tutor Libn: Mrs M. E. Hinton
BA, ALA; Asst Libn: Mr A. F. D. Tucker ALA, AMIRT.
6 London Borough of Ealing. **8** Science & technology;
general. **9** History of commercial aviation (c. 800 books
& pamphlets). **10** CICRIS; Aslib. **11** No. **12** Term:
Mon-Thurs 9.00-19.30, Fri 9.00-17.30; vac: by arrangement. **13** (a) c. 35,000; (b) 300. **15** (a) 6½ (c) 2.

SOUTH EAST LONDON COLLEGE LIBRARY, Lewisham
Way, London SE4 1UT (Tel 01-692 7296 ext 38) Coll Libn:
Miss E. L. Taylor ALA; Dep Libns: Mrs G. S. Lewis BSC,
ALA; Mrs C. B. Sheehan ALA.
6 ILEA. **7** Wickham B Lib, Lewisham Way, (01-692 6319
ext. 27); Downham B Lib, Goud-Hurst Road, (01-698 1720
ext 27); Lower Sydenham B Lib, Worsley Bridge Rd, SE26

(01-650 8227); Plassy Road B Lib, Catford, SE6 (01-698
7311). **8** General. **10** BLL; MSC. **11** No.
12 9.00-20.00. Branches vary. **13** (a) 30,000; (b) 300;
(c) audio-visual materials. **14** £16,500.

SOUTHGATE TECHNICAL COLLEGE LIBRARY, High St,
Southgate, London N14 6BS (Tel 01-886 6521) Chief Coll
Libn & Senior Tutor-Libn: Mr R. S. Jones ALA. Main Coll
Libn: Mrs H. A. Clarke ALA; Tutor-Libn: Miss S. Drury ALA.
6 London Borough of Enfield. **7** Montagu Annexe,
Montagu Rd, London N18 2LY, Libn: Mr R. McIlveen.
8 Arts; business; catering; clothing; education; engineering
(electrical, mechanical & motor vehicle); sciences; general.
9 Radio & TV circuit diagrams; careers & higher education
information, audio-visual resources. **10** BLL; inter-
library loans. **11** Yes, for ref only. **12** Term: Mon-
Fri 8.45-20.00 (Fri 18.30); vac: 9.30-17.00. **13** (a) 33,000;
(b) 206; (c) 443 records; 339 tapes; 260 films & strips; 87
loops & progammes; 10 multi-media kits. **14** £17,550.
15 (a) 11 (b) 2 (c) 5.

SOUTH LONDON COLLEGE LIBRARY, Knight's Hill, London
SE27 0TX (Tel 01-670 4488) Coll Libn: Mr Norman I.
Lancashire ALA.
7 Tower Bridge Branch, Tooley St, SE1 2RJ (01-407 1831)
Libn: Mrs E. Redfern BA, ALA. **8** Maths; physics;
chemistry; biology; geology; business; food technology; dental
technology; telecommunications; general. **10** LINK.
11 No. **12** Term: Mon-Fri 9.00-20.00. **13** (a) 15,000;
(b) 120. **15** (a) 4²⁄₃ (b) 2 (c) 3.

SOUTHWARK COLLEGE LIBRARY, The Cut, London SE1
8LE (Tel 01-928 9561) Libn: Mr Donald W. Wendon ALA
FRSA; Dep Libn: Miss J. P. Macrae ALA.
7 Tanner St, SE1 (01-237 8178/9), Libn in charge: Miss J. P.
MacRae ALA; 209/215 Blackfriars Rd, SE1 (01-928 9441)
Libn in charge: Mr N. Ahmad BA, DipLibSc, ALA; West Sq,
St George's Rd, SE11. **8** Arts; humanities; business;
English; general; English as a foreign language; sciences
(inc fire brigade); social work; ref. **9** Slides (20th cent
arts, over 1,000 slides); fire brigade studies (over 1,500
items). **10** Inter-library loans; ILEA. **11** No.
12 Term: Mon-Thurs 9.00-19.00, Fri 9.00-17.00.
Branches vary. **13** (a) 30,000; (b) 185; (c) slides; filmstrips; tapes. **14** £9,500. **15** (a) 8 (b) 2 (c) 3.

SOUTH WEST LONDON COLLEGE LIBRARY, Tooting
Broadway, London SW17 0TQ (Tel 01-672 2441) Libn: F. D.
Staples ALA, Dep: Miss E. Williams ALA.
6 ILEA. **7** Accountancy Lib, 196 Garratt Lane SW18
(01-874 2145/6680); Business & Professional Studies Lib,
10 Wiseton Rd, SW17 (01-672 9535). **8** Accountancy;
banking; business & office management; economics; geography; industrial relations; law; marketing; personnel
management; statistics. **9** Newspaper clippings on current
business & financial topics ref only). **10** Wandpetls.
11 No. **13** (a) 16,000; (b) 275.

STATISTICS AND MARKET INTELLIGENCE LIBRARY,
Export House, 50 Ludgate Hill, London EC4M 7HU
(Tel 01-248 5757 ext 368; Telex 886143) Libn: Mr Lewis
Foreman MLib, FLA; Dep Libn: Miss M. H. Wilson ALA.
6 Dept of Industry. **8** UK statistics; statistics of overseas countries & international compilations; trade & telephone
directories of overseas countries; market surveys & development plans. **11** Yes. **12** Mon-Fri 9.00-17.30.
13 (a) 6,500 statistical serials; 3,000 directories; (c) 300
foot-runs of other publications. **15** (a) 17 (b) 5 (c) 6.

STOCKWELL COLLEGE OF EDUCATION LIBRARY (will
merge with Bromley College of Technology & Ravensbourne
College of Art and Design to form the Bromley Institute of
Higher Education), The Old Palace, Rochester Ave, Bromley,

LONDON—*continued*

Kent, BR1 3DH (Tel 01-460 9944) Chief Libn: Mr Eric
Winter BA, FLA; Dep: Miss M. Clayton BA, ALA.
6 Joint Education Committee of Bromley-Kent. **8** Art
& design; education; English; drama; French; geography;
history; film; TV; music; physical education; religion; natural
sciences. **9** Films, video-tapes, slides, sound tapes on
education. **11** No. **12** Term: Mon-Fri 9.00-21.00,
Sat 9.30-11.30; vac: Mon-Fri 9.30-16.15. **13** (a) 55,000;
(b) 284; (c) c.20,000 non-book materials: microforms-film
strips; film-loops; slides; video-cassettes; records; mounted
illustrations, audio-tapes. **14** £16,000. **15** (a) 11 (b) 3
(c) 5.

SWEDENBORG SOCIETY LIBRARY, 20-21 Bloomsbury
Way, London WC1A 2TH (Tel 01-405 7986) Libn: Mr A.S.
Wainscot.
8 Life & works of Emanuel Swedenborg; philosophy; theology.
9 Swedenborg's works; photo-reproductions of his mss (50
folio vols); New-Church (Swedenborgian) literature; archive
material. **11** Yes. **12** Mon-Fri 9.30-17.00 **13** (a)
c.5,000; (b) 20; (c) 111 microfilms of Swedenborgiana; 600
3" × 3" lantern slides; c 3,200 pamphlets. **15** (a) ½.

SWEDISH EMBASSY LIBRARY, 23 North Row, London
W1R 2DN (Tel 01-499 9500; Telex 28 249).
8 Swedish history, geography, politics, economics, culture
& institutions. **11** Yes. **12** 10.00-12.00, 14.00-16.00.
13 (c) gramophone records.

TATE GALLERY LIBRARY, Millbank, London SW1P 4RG
(Tel 01-828 1212 ext 255) Libn: Mr Antony Symons BA, FLA.
6 Tate Gallery trustees. **8** British painting; modern art.
9 Over 46,000 temporary exhibition catalogues. **11** No.
13 (a) c.12,000; (b) c.200 (inc museum & gallery bulletins);
(c) microfilm (446 reels). **15** (a) 3 (b) 2 (c) 1.

TAVISTOCK INSTITUTE OF HUMAN RELATIONS AND
TAVISTOCK CLINIC JOINT LIBRARY, Tavistock Centre,
Belsize Lane, London NW3 5BA (Tel 01-435 7111) Libn:
Mrs Margaret Walker, ALA.
8 Psychology, psychiatry; psychoanalysis; sociology;
organizational studies. **10** BLL; Aslib; inter-library loans.
11 No. **12** Mon-Fri 9.30-17.30. **13** (a) c.15,000
(inc pamphlets); (b) 215. **14** c.£5,000. **15** (a) 3 (c) 2.

THAMES POLYTECHNIC LIBRARY, (will merge with
Dartford College of Education), Wellington St, London SE18
6PF (Tel 01-854 2030) Chief Libn: Mr J.M. Allford BSc,
ALA; Dep: Mr D. Dickson FLA.
6 Court of Governors of Thames Polytechnic. **7** Vencourt
House, King St, W6 9LU, Libn-in-charge: Miss H. Saxby
BA, ALA. **8** Accounting; architecture; biology; building;
surveying; chemistry; civil engineering; computing; economics; English; estate management; French; geography;
German; history; landscape architecture; law; management;
materials science; maths; mechanical & electrical engineering; philosophy; physics; politics; quantity surveying; sociology; Spanish. **11** No. **12** vac: Mon-Fri 9.00-17.00
(longer hours & Sat opening during term). **13** (a) 95,000;
(b) 900; (c) sound & video recordings; slides. **14** £63,000.
15 (a) 22 (b) 9 (c) 11.

3M LIBRARY & INFORMATION SERVICE, 3M House,
Wigmore St, London W1A 1ET (Tel 01-486 5522; Telex 28155)
Libn: Mrs A.A. Jordan ALA; Asst Libn: Mrs A. Mallach.
6 3M United Kingdom Ltd. **7** Market Intelligence Lib,
380-384 Harrow Rd, W9 2HU (01-286 6044), Libn: Miss S.
Bell. **8** Management; marketing; other commercial subjects; 3M product technologies (e.g. printing, photography,
plastics, adhesives, microfilm etc). **11** No. **12** 8.45-
17.00. **13** (a) c.1,000; (b) 500; (c) sales training films;
films on company history, products etc. **14** £14,000.
15 (a) 3 (b) 1 (c) 1.

TIMES NEWSPAPERS LTD, INFORMATION AND MARKET-
ING INTELLIGENCE UNITS, New Printing House Sq, London
WC1X 8EZ (Tel 01-837 1234) Manager: Ms Christine Hull
BA, MIInfSc; Senior Inf Officer: Ms Margaret Curtis.
8 Marketing; economic & business conditions; management;
industry; services; demographic & social conditions; the
press; advertising; (UK & overseas). **9** 'British Rate
& Data' (from 1954); 'Advertisers Aid' (from 1938); 'National
Readership Survey' (from 1956); 'Board of Trade Journal'
(from 1962); 'Household Food Consumption' (from 1953); 'IPC
Cosmetics Survey' (from 1953); 'Family Expenditure Survey'
(from 1957); other long runs of statistics. **11** Yes, by
subscription. **12** 9.30-17.30. **13** (a) c.1,200; (b) 250;
(c) clippings. **14** £6,000. **15** (a) 11 (b) 4 (c) 2.

TOTTENHAM COLLEGE OF TECHNOLOGY LIBRARY,
High Rd, London N15 4RU (Tel 01-802 3111 ext 64) Coll
Libn: Mrs S. Gilbert ALA. Senior Asst Libn: Miss A.
Smedley ALA.
6 London Borough of Haringey. **8** Public health; building;
hairdressing & wigmaking; business. **10** GLGCL.
11 No. **12** Mon-Fri 9.00-19.30 (Fri 17.00). **13** (a)
17,350; (b) 145; (c) filmstrips (35 mm). **14** £9,000.
15 (a) 5½ (c) 3.

TRAINING SERVICES AGENCY LIBRARY, Room 403, 168
Regent St, London W1 6DE (Tel 01-214 6360) Libn: Mr A.
Rath ALA.
8 Training & related topics. **10** ITB Library Group.
11 No. **12** 9.00-17.00. **13** (a) 900; (b) 100; (c) research
reports. **14** £5,500. **15** (a) 4; (b) 1; (c) 1.

TRINITY COLLEGE OF MUSIC, BRIDGE MEMORIAL
LIBRARY, Mandeville Pl, London W1M 6AQ (Tel 01-935
5773 ext 16) Libn: Mr David Toplis ARCM.
8 Music. **11** No. **12** Mon-Fri 9.00-18.00 (Fri 17.00).
13 (a) 50,000 (inc performance material); (c) 800 records.
14 over £1,000. **15** (a) 2½.

TROPICAL PRODUCTS INSTITUTE LIBRARY, 56-62 Gray's
Inn Rd, London WC1X 8LU (Tel 01-242 5412) Libn: Mr John
A. Wright; Dep Libn: Mr John P. Flanagan.
6 Ministry of Overseas Development. **7** Industrial
Development Dept, Culham, Abingdon, Oxfordshire,
OX14 3DA (086-730551). **8** Tropical agriculture (particularly production, processing, preservation, storage,
transportation, quality control, marketing & utilisation of
plant & animal products of the tropics and sub-tropics).
9 US Dept of Agriculture publications. **11** Yes, for ref
only by researchers. **12** Mon-Fri 9.00-17.30.
13 (a) 150,000; (b) 1,250; (c) over 1,000 annual reports.
15 (a) 8 (b) 1 (c) 4.

TWICKENHAM COLLEGE OF TECHNOLOGY LIBRARY,
Egerton Rd, Twickenham, Middlesex, TW2 7SJ (Tel 01-892
6656 ext 13) Tutor-Libn: Mr Brian L. Pearce FLA, FRSA;
Asst Tutor-Libn: Mrs H.M. Nelson ALA.
6 London Borough of Richmond upon Thames. **7** Lib
Annexe, (01-892 6656 ext 44), Libn: Mrs H.M. Nelson ALA.
8 Electrical, electronic & control engineering; mechanical
& production engineering; building & civil engineering;
printing, photography, fine art & graphic design; economics
& management; computing; maths & science; languages;
humanities; general. **9** HND projects & essays; BSI; maps
& town plans. **10** BLL; CICRIS. **11** Yes, but loans at
Libn's discretion. **12** Term: Mon-Fri 9.30-20.30 (Fri
19.00); vac: Mon-Fri 9.30-16.30. Branch varies.
13 (a) 36,000; (b) 325; (c) 18,500 slides & filmstrips; 2,000
illustrations, wallcharts, prints & reproductions; 56 filmloops; 65 microfilms; 543 audiotapes; 86 records.
14 c.£15,600. **15** (a) 6 (c) 4.

UNITED NATIONS INFORMATION CENTRE LIBRARY,
14-15 Stratford Pl, London W1N 9AF (Tel 01-629 3816) Libn:
Miss M.A. McAfee.
7 None, but list of UN depository libraries in UK supplied
on request. **8** Activities of UN & its agencies; regular
published surveys & international statistics on economic &
social subjects; special studies on social sciences, art &
literature, libraries & museums, agriculture, international
law, international trade & industrialization, human rights,
population, refugees, environmental problems, etc.

CODE: 1 Name of Library. **2** Address. **3** Telephone & Telex. **4** Officer in charge. **5** Deputy. **6** Governing body.
7 Branches. **8** Main Subjects. **9** Special Collections. **10** Co-operative Schemes. **11** Open to public? **12** Hours.
13 Stock: (a) books (b) periodicals (c) other. **14** Finance. **15** Staff: (a) non-manual (b) graduate (c) chartered librarians.

LONDON—*continued*

11 Yes.   **12** Mon, Wed & Thurs 10.00-17.00.   **13** (c) UN
material (printed publications & mimeographed documents;
older materials on microfilm).   **15** (a) 2.

UNITED SOCIETY FOR THE PROPAGATION OF THE
GOSPEL LIBRARY, 15 Tufton St, London SW1P 3QQ (Tel 01-
222 4222) Libn: Mrs D. Brewster.
8 Anglican communion; Africa; India; USA; ex-British
colonies.   **10** BLL.   **11** Yes, small charge.
12 Mon-Fri 10.00-17.30.   **13** (a) 28,000; (b) c.50;
(c) separate archives dept; records of former SPG & UMCA.
15 (a) 1 (c) 1.

University of London

UNIVERSITY LIBRARY, Senate House, Malet St, London
WC1E 7HU (Tel 01-636 4514; Telex 269400, (Unilibsen Ldn)
Dir of Central Lib Services & Goldsmiths' Libn: Mrs K.
Garside MA; Associate Libn: Miss B. Burton MA, FLA.
8 General.   **9** Goldsmiths' Library (early works on
economics, inc railways, slavery, temperance; 65,000
vols); Sterling Library (early & rare editions of English
literature; 4,000 vols); De Morgan Library (early maths &
astronomy; 4,000 vols); Durning-Lawrence Library, (Francis
Bacon & Shakespeare; 6,000 vols); Harry Price Library
(psychical research & magic, 15,000 vols); Quick
Memorial Library (early education; 1,000 vols;
Bromhead Library, (early works on London; 4,000 vols);
United States Library (23,000 vols); Belgian Library
(4,500 vols); palaeography & archives (8,000 vols).
10 BLL.   **11** Yes, for ref on written application, at
Director's discretion.   **12** Term: Mon-Fri 9.30-21.00,
Sat 9.30-17.30; summer vac: 9.30-17.30.
13 (a) c.1,000,000; (b) c.6,000; (c) 42,000 maps; 7,500
gramophone records; 270,000 slides; microfilms,
microcards; university archives; mss.   **14** £165,000.
15 (a) 95; (b) 38; (c) 32.

University of London Senate Institutes

COURTAULD INSTITUTE OF ART, BOOK LIBRARY,
20 Portman Sq, London W1H 0BE (Tel 01-935 9292)
Libn: Mr P.M. Doran BA, ALA.
8 History of European art & architecture.   **11** No.
12 Term: Mon-Fri 9.30-19.00; vac: Mon-Fri 10.00-
18.00.   **13** (a) 37,000; (b) 271; (c) 38,000 unbound
pamphlets, off-prints & exhibition catalogues; some
microfiche.   **15** (a) 6 (b) 4 (c) 2.

INSTITUTE OF ADVANCED LEGAL STUDIES LIBRARY,
25 Russell Sq, London WC1B 5DR (Tel 01-580 4868)
Libn: Mr W.A.F.P. Steiner LLM, MA, ALA, barrister-at-
law; Dep Libn: Miss M. Anderson BA, ALA.
8 Law.   **10** SCOLMA.   **11** No.   **12** Mon-Fri 10.00-
20.00 (Fri 17.30), Sat 10.00-12.30.   **13** (a) 120,000;
(b) c.1,950; (c) a few microtexts.   **15** (a) 13; (b) 12;
(c) 8.

INSTITUTE OF ARCHAEOLOGY LIBRARY, 31-34 Gordon
Sq, London WC1H 0PY (Tel 01-387 6052) Libn: Miss H.M.
Bell BA.
8 Archaeology.   **9** Latin American archaeology;
underwater archaeology; eastern European archaeology;
Middle Eastern archaeology.   **10** Standing Conference
of Librarians of Libraries of Univ of London.   **11** Yes,
by day ticket, for special research.   **12** Term: Mon-Fri
10.00-18.30, Sat 10.00-16.30; vac: Mon-Fri 10.00-17.30,
Sat 10.00-16.30 (exc summer vac).   **13** (a) 30,000;
(b) 581; (c) some excavation records.   **14** £7,000.
15 (a) 4 (b) 3 (c) 1.

INSTITUTE OF CLASSICAL STUDIES AND THE
HELLENIC AND ROMAN SOCIETIES LIBRARY, 31-34
Gordon Sq, London WC1H 0PY (Tel 01-387 7697) Libn:
Miss A.E. Healey BA, ALA.
8 Classical antiquity (archaeology; art; epigraphy; history;
language; literature; papyrology; philosophy; religion;
science, etc.).   **10** BLL (Hellenic & Roman Societies
only).   **11** No, but postal & telephone enquiries accepted.
12 Mon-Fri 9.30-18.00, Sat 10.00-17.00.
13 (a) 45,000; (b) 380; (c) 40 microfilms; 1,000 maps.
15 (a) 5 (b) 4 (c) 2.

INSTITUTE OF COMMONWEALTH STUDIES LIBRARY,
27 Russell Sq, London WC1B 5DS (Tel 01-580 5876)
Libn: Mrs P.M. Larby MA, FLA; Senior Asst Libn:
Mrs C. Travis BA, ALA.
8 Commonwealth history (from 1850); Commonwealth
politics, social studies & economics.   **9** Documents of
Commonwealth political parties; Commonwealth bibliography.   **10** SCOLMA (Sierra Leone & Gambia).
11 No.   **12** Term: Mon-Fri 9.30-19.00 (Thurs & Fri
18.00); vac: Mon-Fri 9.30-17.30.   **13** (a) 70,000;
(b) 700.   **14** £8,000.   **15** (a) 5 (b) 4 (c) 3.

INSTITUTE OF EDUCATION LIBRARY, 11-13 Ridgmount
St, London WC1E 7AH (Tel 01-637 0846) Libn: D.J.
Foskett MA, FLA; Dep Libn: Ms Margaret E. Couch FLA.
8 Education in all aspects.   **10** LASER; LISE.
11 Yes, by written application to Libn.   **12** Term: Mon-
Fri 9.30-21.00, Sat 9.30-12.30; vac: 9.30-19.30.
13 (a) 160,000; (b) 1,700.   **14** £41,500.   **15** (a) 26
(b) 15 (c) 12.

INSTITUTE OF GERMANIC STUDIES LIBRARY, 29
Russell Sq, London WC1B 5DP (Tel 01-580 2711/3480)
Libn-in-charge: Mr V.J. Riley MA, ALA.
8 German language & literature.   **9** Priebsch-Closs
colln (17th & 18th cent editions); English Goethe Society
Library (works by & on Goethe); Gundolf colln of mss,
letters, etc, relating to the George circle.   **11** Yes, to
consult books not available elsewhere.   **12** Mon-Fri
9.30-18.00.   **13** (a) 39,000; (b) 300.   **14** £7,000.
15 (a) 3 (b) 2 (c) 2.

INSTITUTE OF HISTORICAL RESEARCH LIBRARY,
Senate House, Malet St, London WC1E 7HU (Tel 01-636
0272/3) Sec & Libn: Mr William Kellaway MA, FLA, FSA.
6 Committee of Management.   **8** History of the
peoples of Western Europe & their expansion overseas.
10 BUCOP; union catalogues of Latin American studies,
United States studies, and Byzantine studies.   **11** No.
13 (a) 112,000; (b) 500.   **15** (a) 8 (b) 7 (c) 8.

INSTITUTE OF LATIN AMERICAN STUDIES LIBRARY,
31 Tavistock Sq, London WC1H 9HA (Tel 01-387 5671/2)
Bibliographer/Libn: Ms Brigid M. Harrington BA,
DipLib, ALA; Asst Libn: Miss E.M. Long MA, BPhil, MA.
8 Bibliographies, ref works & guides in the Latin
American field.   **10** Organiser of National Union
Catalogue of Latin Americana.   **11** Yes, for ref only.
12 Mon-Fri 9.30-17.30.   **13** (a) c.2,000; (b) c.56;
(c) microfilm of 'La Nacion' (Argentinian newspaper)
(from 1951).   **15** (a) 3 (+ one part time) (b) 3 (c) 2.

INSTITUTE OF UNITED STATES STUDIES LIBRARY,
31 Tavistock Sq, London WC1H 9EZ (Tel 01-387 5534)
Libn: Mrs Angela Smith BA, ALA; Asst Libn: Miss Alison
Cowden MA, ALA.
6 Committee of Management.   **8** Bibliographies &
other reference books covering all aspects of American
studies.   **9** American Studies Union Catalogue (for 20
London libraries).   **11** Yes, at Libn's discretion, to
consult the Union Catalogue & material not readily
available elsewhere.   **12** Mon-Fri 9.30-17.30.
13 (a) 1,000; (b) 30.   **14** £2,000.   **15** (a) 2½ (b) 2
(c) 2.

University of London Senate Institutes—*continued*

SCHOOL OF SLAVONIC AND EAST EUROPEAN STUDIES
LIBRARY, Senate House, Malet St, London WC1E 7HU
(Tel 01-637 4934/40) Libn: Mr J. E. O. Screen MA, ALA;
First Asst Libn: Mr A. Helliwell BA, FLA.
8 History, language & literature of Russia, Ukraine,
Belorussia, Poland, Czechoslovakia, Yugoslavia, Bulgaria,
Rumania, Albania, Hungary, Finland, Estonia, Latvia &
Lithuania. 9 Ivanyi colln (books in English, on Hungary);
Gaster colln (Rumanian literature). 10 Slavonic Union
Catalogue. 11 Yes, by application to Libn. 12 Mon-
Fri 10.00-19.00, Sat 10.00-13.00; long vac: Mon-Fri
10.00-18.00. 13 (a) 180,000; (b) 1,000. 14 £21,000.
15 (a) 13 (b) 11 (c) 3.

WARBURG INSTITUTE LIBRARY, Woburn Sq, London
WC1H 0AB (Tel 01-580 9663) Libn: Mr J. B. Trapp MA;
Dep: Dr C. Ligota MA, PhD.
8 Survival & influence of Greek & Roman civilization;
history of the classical tradition. 10 BLL.
11 No, except in special circumstances, by permission
of Dir of Institute. 12 Mon-Fri 10.00-18.00, Sat 10.00-
13.00 (closed Sats Aug & Sept). 13 (a) c. 200,000;
(b) c. 900. 15 (a) 8 (b) 6 (c) 1.

University of London Colleges

BEDFORD COLLEGE LIBRARY, Inner Circle, Regent's
Park, London NW1 4NS (Tel 01-486 4400) Libn: Mr G. M.
Paterson BA, ALA; Sub-Libns: Miss J. Sherlock BA, DipLib;
Mr R. M. Shrigley BA, ALA.
8 Humanities; social sciences; biochemistry; botany;
chemistry; Dutch; English; French; geography; geology;
German; Greek; history; Italian; Latin; maths; philosophy;
physics; physiology; psychology; sociology; zoology.
9 Dutch language & literature; medical sociology.
10 BLL. 11 Yes, on application to Libn. 12 Term:
Mon-Fri 9.00-21.00, Sat 9.00-13.00; vac: Mon-Fri 9.00-
17.00. 13 (a) c. 200,000; (b) c. 1,000. 14 c. £55,000.
15 (a) 21 (b) 9 (c) 8.

BIRKBECK COLLEGE LIBRARY, Malet St, London
WC1E 7HX (Tel 01-580 6622) Libn: Mr A. P. Howse MA,
FLA; Dep Libn: Mr R. F. E. Knight MA, FLA.
7 (Social Sciences) 7-15 Gresse St, W1; Ormond House,
Queen Sq, WC1. 8 Arts; biological, physical & social
sciences. 9 J. D. Bernal working papers. 10 BLL.
11 Yes, with written application showing special need.
12 Term: Mon-Fri 10.00-22.30, Sat 10.00-17.00; vac:
Mon-Fri 10.00-20.00. 13 (a) 145,000; (b) 1,100.
14 £42,000.

CHELSEA COLLEGE LIBRARY, Manresa Rd, London
SW3 6LX (Tel 01-352 6421) Coll Libn: Mr A. G. Quinsee
BA, ALA; Dep Libn: Miss J. E. Hardy BA, MSc, ALA.
7 Centre for Science Education, Bridges Pl, SW6 4HR
(01-736 3401); Biological Sciences Group, Hortensia Rd,
SW10 0QX (01-352 5778); Geology Annexe, 271 King St,
W6 9LZ (01-748 8322); Physics, Electronics, Computer-
centre Annexe, Pulton Pl, SW6 5PR (01-736 1244).
8 Botany; biochemistry; chemistry; electronics; geology;
history & philosophy of science; maths; pharmacology;
physics; physiology; zoology; graduate science teacher
training 9 Darwin colln of 1st editions. 10 BLL.
11 Yes, for ref only 12 Term: Mon-Fri 9.00-21.00,
Sat 9.00-13.00; vac: Mon-Fri 9.00-17.00 13 (a) 94,000;
(b) 900 (c) microcard, microfiche & microfilm of some
journals. 14 £55,000 15 (a) 19 (b) 12 (c) 13.

GOLDSMITHS' COLLEGE LIBRARY, Lewisham Way, New
Cross, London SE14 6NW (Tel 01-692 0211) Coll Libn:
Miss E. M. Moys BA, FLA; Dep Libn: Mr M. J. Taylor BA,
ALA.
6 College Library Committee. 8 General (exc agriculture, business, engineering, medicine). 10 BNBC.
11 Yes, for ref only, letter of introduction required.
12 Term: Mon-Fri 9.15-21.00, Sat 9.15-12.00; vac: Mon-
Fri 9.15-17.00. 13 (a) 128,000; (b) 920; (a) 12,000
items of audio-visual materials. 14 £30,000. 15 (a)
24 (b) 8 (c) 10.

HEYTHROP COLLEGE LIBRARY, 11-13 Cavendish Sq,
London W1M 0AN (Tel 01-580 6941) Libn: Mr Michael J.
Walsh MA, ALA; Asst Libn: Mr J. Stephen Poole BA.
8 Theology; scripture; patristics; canon law; church history;
philosophy; Semitic languages; sociology. 11 Yes, by
prior arrangement with Libn. 12 Term: Mon-Fri 9.00-
21.00, Sat 9.00-13.00; vac: Mon-Fri 9.00-13.00.
13 (a) c. 150,000; (b) c. 260; (c) 5,000 microfiche.
14 c. £6,000. 15 (a) 3 (b) 3 (c) 1.

IMPERIAL COLLEGE OF SCIENCE AND TECHNOLOGY,
LYON PLAYFAIR LIBRARY, South Kensington, London
SW7 2AZ (Tel 01-589 5111 ext 2100; Telex 261503)
Coll Libn: Mr A. Whitworth MA; 2 sub-libns, in charge of
Reader's Services & of Acquisitions.
8 Science & technology (exc medicine, veterinary science,
agriculture, astronomy); industrial sociology; manage-
ment science. 9 College archives, inc T. H. Huxley
papers; Haldane Library (general humanities & recreation-
al literature); Annan Colln (history of mining); Operational
Research Society Library; Tensor Society of Great Britain
Library; Computing & Control colln; London Natural
History Society Library. 10 BLL; Aslib; BNBC;
SCONUL. 11 Yes, for ref only at Libn's discretion.
12 Term: Mon-Fri 9.30-21.00, Sat 9.30-17.30; vac: Mon-
Fri 9.30-17.30. 13 (a) 150,000; (b) 950; (c) videotapes;
archives; gramophone records; microtexts. 14 £90,000.
15 (a) 42 (b) 14 (c) 14.

KING'S COLLEGE LONDON LIBRARY, Strand, London
WC2R 2LS (Tel 01-836 5454) Libn: Mr I. Angus MA, DipLib;
Dep: Mr R. W. Pound MA, ALA.
8 Classics; English; French; German; modern Greek;
Portuguese, Spanish (inc Latin American studies); history (inc imperial history); philosophy; war studies; education; music; theology & ecclesiastical history; laws;
biophysics; chemistry; geography; geology; maths; physics;
plant sciences; zoology; anatomy; biochemistry; pharmacology; physiology; engineering (civil, electrial & mechanical). 9 Marsden Library (philology, early Bibles,
travel); Box Library (Hebrew & Old Testament studies);
Enk Library (classics); Wheatstone Library (electricity
& kindred subjects up to 1865). 10 BLL; BUCOP;
SCOLMA. 11 Yes, on application to Libn with recommendation. 12 Term: Mon-Fri 9.30-20.45, Sat 9.30-
12.45; Christmas & Easter vac: Mon-Fri 9.30-17.45,
Sat 9.30-12.00; long vac : Mon-Fri 9.30-16.30.
13 350,000; (b) 2,250; (c) Liddell Hart Centre (military
archives); 2,000 gramophone records; microforms.
14 £100,000. 15 (a) 44 (b) 16 (c) 10.

LONDON SCHOOL OF ECONOMICS & POLITICAL
SCIENCE, BRITISH LIBRARY OF POLITICAL & ECONO-
MIC SCIENCE, Houghton St, London WC2A 2AE (Tel 01-405
7686) Libn: Dr D. A. Clarke MA, ALA; Dep Libn: Mr C. P.
Corney BLitt, MA, ALA.
8 Economics; politics; sociology; history; law. 9 Edward
Fry Library (international law); Shuster Library (comparative legislation); Passfield papers. 10 SCOLMA.
11 Yes, on application to Libn. 12 Mon-Fri 10.00-
21.20 (17.00 in Aug); Sat (term) 10.00-17.00. 13 (a)
670,000; (b) 12,000; (c) archives. 15 (a) 63 (b) 25
(c) 18.

NEW COLLEGE, LONDON LIBRARY, 527 Finchley Rd,
London NW3 7BE (Tel 01-435 3719) Hon Libn: Rev G. F.
Nuttall MA, DD.
6 London Board of Governors. 8 Theology.
9 Works formerly in libraries of dissenting academies;
Puritan & dissenting history & theology; Philip Doddridge
(1702-51) correspondance (11 vols). 11 No.
13 (a) 32,000; (b) 10. 14 £275.

QUEEN ELIZABETH COLLEGE LIBRARY, Campden Hill
Rd, London W8 7AH (Tel 01-937 5411) Libn: Mr P. M. O.
Stonham BA, ALA.
6 College Council. 8 Pure & life sciences; nutrition;
food & management sciences. 9 Historical works on
nutrition & food science. 10 BLL. 11 Yes, for ref
only, by permission of Libn. 12 Mon-Fri 9.30-21.00.

CODE: 1 Name of Library. **2** Address. **3** Telephone & Telex. **4** Officer in charge. **5** Deputy. **6** Governing body.
7 Branches. **8** Main Subjects. **9** Special Collections. **10** Co-operative Schemes. **11** Open to public? **12** Hours.
13 Stock: (a) books (b) periodicals (c) other. **14** Finance. **15** Staff: (a) non-manual (b) graduate (c) chartered librarians.

University of London Colleges—*continued*

13 (a) 38,000; (b) 480.   **14** c. £32,000.   **15** (a) 10
(b) 7 (c) 6.

QUEEN MARY COLLEGE LIBRARY, Mile End Rd,
London E1 4NS (Tel 01-980 4811 ext 472/452) Libn: Mr
T. H. Bowyer BSc, FLA; Dep Libn: Miss B. Burton MA, FLA.
7 Law Library, Faculty of Laws, Mile End Rd, E1 4NS.
8 Science; engineering, humanities; law; economics.
9 EDC.   **11** Yes, on application to Libn.   **12** Term
& Easter vac: Mon-Fri 9.15-21.30, Sat (term only)
10.00-18.00; other vacs: Mon-Fri 9.15-17.00.   **13** (a)
200,000; (b) 2,055.   **15** (a) 27 (b) 8 (c) 11.

ROYAL VETERINARY COLLEGE LIBRARY, Royal College
St, London NW1 0TU (Tel 01-387 2898 ext 231) Coll Libn:
Mr R.Catton BA, ALA.
6 College Council.   **7** Field Station, Hawkshead House,
Hawkshead Lane, North Mimms, Hatfield, Hertfordshire
(0707-55486).   **8** Veterinary sciences.   **9** Historical
colln.   **10** LAMedSectExch.   **11** Yes, for ref only.
12 Mon-Fri 9.30-17.20.   **13** (a) 26,000; (b) 400.
15 (a) 4 (b) 2 (c) 2.

SCHOOL OF ORIENTAL AND AFRICAN STUDIES
LIBRARY, Malet St, London WC1E 7HP (Tel 01-637 2388)
Libn: B. C. Bloomfield MA, FLA; Dep: A. C. Butler BA, FLA.
8 Africa & Asia (humanities & social sciences only) in all
languages.   **10** SCOLMA; Middle East Libraries Committee; ULG.   **11** Yes, on written application.
12 Term & Easter vac: Mon-Fri 9.00-20.30, Sat 9.30-
12.30; other vacs: Mon-Fri 9.00-17.00, Sat 9.30-12.30.
13 (a) 450,000; (b) 3,000; (c) 2,180 mss; 14,000 sheets
maps; 5,000 reels microfilm; 35,000 sheets microfiche;
20,000 photographs; 25,000 slides; 500 tapes & discs;
800 prints & drawings.   **14** £160,000.   **15** (a) 56
(b) 15.

SCHOOL OF PHARMACY LIBRARY, 29-39 Brunswick
Sq, London WC1N 1AX (Tel 01-837 7651) Libn: Mrs
Linda L. R. Lisgarten ALA; Dep: Mrs B. A. Thornber ALA.
8 Pharmaceutics; pharmacognosy; pharmacology; chemistry; engineering science; allied subjects.   **11** Yes, for
ref only.   **12** Term: 9.00-21.00; vac: 9.00-17.00.
13 (a) c. 10,500; (b) c. 160.   **15** (a) 3 (b) 1 (c) 3.

UNIVERSITY COLLEGE LIBRARY, Gower St, London
WC1E 6BT (Tel 01-387 7050) Univ Libn: Mr Joseph W.
Scott BA, ALA.
8 Arts; laws; science; engineering; medical sciences;
environmental studies; history (U.S.& Latin America);
Egyptology; Roman law; Scandinavian studies; history of
London.   **9** Special collns: Barlow Dante library;
Graves (early science) library; Johnston Lavis (vulcano-
logy) library; Whitely Stokes (Celtic) library; C. K. Ogden
Library; Sir John Rotton Library; Hume tracts; Lansdowne
& Halifax tracts; James Joyce colln; George Orwell
archive; Little Magazines colln; Parliamentary Papers
(1735-1850). **Mss:** Jeremy Bentham; Henry Peter; Sir
Edwin Chadwick; Moses Gaster; Latin-American business
archives; Society for Diffusion of Useful Knowledge; Uni-
versity College & its members. **Deposited libraries:**
Bibliographical Soc, Folk-Lore Soc, Gaelic Soc of London,
Geologists' Assoc, Hertfordshire Natural History Soc &
Field Club, Huguenot Soc, London Mathematical Soc,
Malacological Soc, Mocatta Library of Anglo-Judaica,
Norwegian Embassy, Royal Historical Soc, Viking Soc for
Northern Research.   **10** Inter-library loans.   **11** Yes,
on written application, at Libn's discretion.   **12** Term:
9.30-21.00; Christmas & Easter vacs; 9.30-19.00; Long
vac: 9.30-17.00.   **13** (a) 804,000; (b) 8,150; (c) 1,200
maps; c.150,000 mss (mainly early 19th cent letters).
14 £150,000.   **15** (a) 77 (b) 25 (c) 16.

WESTFIELD COLLEGE, CAROLINE SKEEL LIBRARY,
Kidderpore Ave, London NW3 7ST (Tel 01-435 7141)
Libn: Dr P. Revell BA, MA, PhD, FLA.
6 Council.   **8** Classics; English; French; German; history;
history of art; Spanish; botany & biochemistry; chemistry;
computer science; maths; physics; zoology.   **9** c.3,000
Lyttleton family mss letters (19th-20th cent).   **10** BLL.
11 Yes, for ref only.   **12** Term: Mon-Fri 9.00-21.00, Sat
9.00-17.00; vac: Mon-Fri 9.00-17.00.   **13** (a) 112,500; (b)
700.   **14** c. £36,000.   **15** (a) 17 (b) 11 (c) 2.

University of London Medical Schools and Institutes

CHARING CROSS HOSPITAL MEDICAL SCHOOL
LIBRARY, Brandenburgh House, Fulham Palace Rd, London
W6 8RF (Tel 01-748 2050 ext 2826) Libn: Mrs L. S.
Godbolt BA, ALA; Dep: Mr P. Morrell ALA.
8 Anatomy; physiology; biochemistry; medicine.   **11** No.
12 Mon-Fri 9.00-21.00, Sat 9.00-12.00.   **13** (a) 20,000;
(b) 400.   **15** (a) 7 (b) 2 (c) 4.

GUYS HOSPITAL MEDICAL SCHOOL, WILLS LIBRARY,
London Bridge, London SE1 9RT (Tel 01-407 7600 ext 3374)
Libn: Miss J.M. Farmer FLA; Dep Libn: Miss P. Gale MA.
8 Biomedicine.   **9** Historical colln; colln of works by
Guy's men; Physical Society & Davies-Colley memorial
collns.   **11** Yes, for ref with Libn's prior permission.
12 Mon-Fri 9.00-22.00, Sat 9.00-13.00.   **13** (a) 27,000;
(b) 260.   **14** £15,000.   **15** (a) 6 (b) 4 (c) 2.

INSTITUTE OF CANCER RESEARCH LIBRARY, Royal
Cancer Hospital, Chester Beatty Research Institute,
Fulham Rd, London SW3 6JB (Tel 01-352 5946) Libn: Mr
D. A. Brunning ALA. Dep: Mrs Oliver Severn ALA.
6 Committee of Management.   **8** Cancer research,
experimental & clinical; chemistry; biochemistry; cytology;
genetics; clinical medicine; medical radiology.   **9** Thurs-
tan Holland colln (early radiological literature); small
historical colln on cancer.   **10** BLL; BNBC; Aslib;
MLA of USA.   **11** No.   **12** Mon-Fri 9.00-17.45.
13 (a) 25,000; (b) 700; (c) 25 microtexts.   **15** (a) 7
(c) 3.

INSTITUTE OF CHILD HEALTH LIBRARY, 30 Guilford
St, London WC1N 1EH (Tel 01-242 9789 ext 122) Libn:
Miss E. S. Brooke ALA; Asst Libn: Miss J.I.Moat BA,
ALA.
8 Paediatrics.   **9** Charles West colln (library of founder
of Great Ormond Street Hospital).   **11** No.   **12** Mon-
Fri 9.00-18.00.   **13** (a) 5,825; (b) 105.   **15** (a) 2 (b) 1
(c) 2.

INSTITUTE OF DENTAL SURGERY LIBRARY, Eastman
Dental Hospital, Grays Inn Rd, London WC1X 8LD (Tel
01-837 7251) Libn: Mrs M. A. Cowperthwaite ALA.
6 British Postgraduate Medical Federation.   **8** Dentistry.   **11** No.   **12** Mon-Fri 9.00-17.30.   **13** (a)
4,800; (b) 75.   **15** (a) $1\frac{3}{4}$ (c) 1.

INSTITUTE OF NEUROLOGY, ROCKEFELLER MEDICAL
LIBRARY, National Hospital, Queen Sq, London WC1N
3BG (Tel 01-837 3611) Medical Libn: Mrs M. B. Bailey
AIInfSc; Dep: Mrs B. Travers.
7 Maida Vale Hospital, Maida Vale, W6.   **8** All branches
of neurology; psychiatry; psychology; general medicine;
biomedical subjects.   **9** Historical neurological works;
works by Queen Sq staff.   **10** Duplicates exchanged.
11 Yes, for ref only on application.   **12** Mon-Fri 9.00-
18.00.   **13** (a) 15,000; (b) 250; (c) reprints.
14 £5,500.   **15** (a) 2 (c) 1.

INSTITUTE OF OPHTHALMOLOGY LIBRARY, Judd St,
London WC1H 9QS (Tel 01-387 9621) Libn: Mrs E. A.
Probert BA.
8 Ophthalmology; basic sciences in cognate subjects.
9 Main international journals on ophthalmology.

University of London Medical Schools—*continued*

11 Yes, by prior arrangement, in special circumstances, for ref only.   **12** Mon-Fri 9.30-17.30 (Tues & Fri 19.00).   **13** (a) 11,914; (b) 220.   **14** £2,000.   **15** (a) 3 (b) 1.

INSTITUTE OF ORTHOPAEDICS LIBRARY, Royal National Orthopaedic Hospital, 234 Great Portland St, London W1N 6AD (Tel 01-387 5070 ext 17) Libn: Mr C. Davenport BSc, ARCS.
7 Royal National Orthopaedic Hospital, Brockley Hill, Stanmore, Middlesex, HA7 4LP (01-954 2300).   **8** Orthopaedics.   **11** No.   **12** Mon-Fri 9.30-17.30.
13 (a) 8,000; (b) 200.   **14** £6,000.   **15** (a) 1½ (b) 1.

INSTITUTE OF PSYCHIATRY LIBRARY, De Crespigny Park, Denmark Hill, London SE5 8AF (Tel 01-703 5411) Libn: Miss H. Marshall MA, ALA; Asst Libn: Mr P. Grey BA, ALA.
8 Psychiatry; psychoanalysis; psychology; neuroscience; biochemistry; sociology; biometrics.   **9** Guttman-Maclay colln (books & pictures on art & psychopathology); historical colln.   **10** BLL; LAMedSectExch.   **11** No.
12 Mon-Thurs 9.00-21.00, Fri 9.00-19.00; Sat 9.00-12.45.   **13** (a) 29,000; (b) 350; (c) 27,000 reprints; 700 theses & dissertations.   **14** £16,000.   **15** (a) 5 (b) 4 (c) 5.

INSTITUTE OF UROLOGY LIBRARY, 172 Shaftesbury Ave, London WC2H 8JE (Tel 01-836 5361) Libn: Miss Anthea Minchom BA, ALA.
8 Urology; nephrology.   **9** Winsbury-White reprint colln.   **10** Periodical Exchange (Wellcome Library).
11 No.   **12** Mon-Fri 9.30-17.30.   **13** (a) 2,000; (b) 30.   **14** c. £1,200. **15** (a) 1 (b) 1 (c) 1.

KING'S COLLEGE HOSPITAL MEDICAL SCHOOL LIBRARY, Denmark Hill, London SE5 89X (Tel 01-274 6222 ext 2028/9) Libn: Miss G. M. Pentelow ALA; Dep Libn: Miss C. N. Rea BA, MLS.
7 Normanby College, King's College Hospital, Denmark Hill, London SE5 (01-274 6222 ext 2681); Belgrave Hospital for Children; Dulwich Hospital; St Giles Hospital; St Francis Hospital.   **8** Medicine; surgery; medical sciences; dentistry; medical history; biography; nursing; midwifery; physiotherapy.   **9** King's colln of books, pamphlets, reprints & tape recordings; Literiana (books, photographs, apparatus & other mementoes of Lord Lister), colln of early works (mainly 16th, 17th & 18th cent).   **10** BLL; inter-library loans.   **11** No.   **12** Mon-Thurs 9.00-19.00, Fri & Sat 9.30-12.30 (exc Aug).   **13** (a) 18,500; (b) 300.   **15** (a) 7½ (b) 2 (c) 2.

LONDON HOSPITAL MEDICAL COLLEGE LIBRARY, Turner St, London E1 2AD (Tel 01-247 0644 ext 17) Libn: Mr J. P. Entract ALA, DipHist.
6 Academic Board.   **8** Medicine & allied sciences.
9 Classical authors & works on history of medicine; bibliography & other records of London Hospital alumni; Thompson-Yates Research Library (journals).
10 BLL, interloans between medical schools & postgraduate colleges.   **11** Yes, by prior written arrangement with Dean or Libn.   **12** Mon-Fri 9.00-22.30, Sat 9.00-14.00.   **13** (a) 23,000; (b) 360; (c) archives (from foundation of Hospital in 1740).   **14** £13,500.   **15** (a) 3 (b) 1 (c) 2.

LONDON SCHOOL OF HYGIENE AND TROPICAL MEDICINE LIBRARY, Keppel St, London WC1E 7HT (Tel 01-636 8636) Libn: Mr Victor J. Glanville ALA; Dep: Mrs M. C. Downes ALA.
8 Tropical medicine; public health; community medicine; epidemiology & medical statistics; communicable diseases; parasitology; medical entomology.   **9** Reece colln (smallpox & vaccination); Ross archives (personal papers of Sir Ronald Ross).   **11** Yes, to bona-fide enquirers.
12 Oct-July: Mon-Fri 9.00-20.00, Sat 9.30-12.00; Aug & Sept: Mon-Fri 9.30-17.00.   **13** (a) 60,000; (b) 1,200; (c) c. 100 sets of tape-slides.   **15** (a) 10 (c) 4.

MIDDLESEX HOSPITAL MEDICAL SCHOOL LIBRARY, Riding House St, London W1P 7PN (Tel 01-636 8333 ext 248) Libn: Ms Jean Hickling FLA.
8 Medicine & ancillary sciences.   **10** LAMedSectExch.
11 No.   **12** Term: Mon-Fri 9.30-21.00, Sat 9.30-12.30; vac: Mon-Fri 9.30-18.00, Sat 9.30-12.30.   **13** (a) 12,000; (b) 300.   **14** £14,000.   **15** (a) 3 (b) 2 (c) 2.

ROYAL DENTAL HOSPITAL OF LONDON, SCHOOL OF DENTAL SURGERY, STOBIE MEMORIAL LIBRARY, 32 Leicester Sq, London WC2H 7LJ (Tel 01-930 8831) Hon Libn: Prof H. J. J. Blackwood; Libn: Mrs R. J. Locker.
8 Dentistry; general medicine.   **11** No.   **12** Mon-Fri 9.30-17.30.   **13** (a) 4,500; (b) 76.   **14** £5,500.
15 (a) 1.

ROYAL POSTGRADUATE MEDICAL SCHOOL, WELLCOME LIBRARY, Hammersmith Hospital, DuCane Rd, London W12 0HS (Tel 01 743 2030) Libn: Ms Eileen M. Read BA, ALA; Dep Libn: J. F. Hewlett ALA.
8 Medicine & medical sciences.   **10** CICRIS.   **11** No.
12 Mon-Fri 9.00-21.00 (Aug 18.00), Sat 9.30-12.30.
13 (a) 22,000; (b) 620; (c) 100 slide/tape programmes.
14 £21,000.   **15** (a) 9 (b) 3 (c) 3.

ST BARTHOLOMEW'S HOSPITAL MEDICAL COLLEGE LIBRARY, West Smithfield, London EC1A 7BE (Tel 01-606 7777 ext 315) Libn: Mr John L. Thornton FLA; Senior Asst: Miss Gaynor M. Davies ALA.
7 Medical College Lib, St Bart's Hospital, Charterhouse Sq, EC1M 6BQ (01-253 0661 ext 105) Libn-in-charge: Mrs Barbara Bulger.   **8** Medicine clinical & pre-medical).
9 Athenae colln (writings by Bart's men).   **11** No.
12 Mon-Fri 9.00-18.00 (Aug 10.00-17.00). Branches vary.
13 (a) 36,000; (b) 300.   **14** £15,000.   **15** (a) 8 (c) 2.

ST GEORGE'S HOSPITAL MEDICAL SCHOOL LIBRARY, Hyde Park Corner, London SW1X 7NA (Tel 01-235 4343) Libn: Ms Fiona Mackay Picken ALA; Dep: Ms Marina Hudson BA, ALA.
7 Tooting Branch, c/o Students Centre, St George's Hospital Medical School, Bleckshaw Rd, SW17, B Libn: Ms Susan Brady; Medical School Lib, Atkinson Morley's Hospital, SW20.
8 Clinical medicine & related topics.   **9** Sir Benjamin Brodie (mss) colln; St George's history colln.   **10** London Medical Schools Union List of Periodicals; LAMedSectExch.
11 Yes, to bona-fide enquirers.   **12** Mon-Fri 9.30-18.00 (Thurs 17.00), Sat 9.30-12.30 (exc Aug).   **13** (a) c. 17,000; (b) 350.   **14** c. £20,000.   **15** (a) 5 (b) 1 (c) 2.

ST MARY'S HOSPITAL MEDICAL SCHOOL LIBRARY, Paddington, London W2 1PG (Tel 01-723 1252 ext 17) Libn: Mr N. D. Palmer BA, ALA; Asst Libn: Miss A. T. Prendergast ALA.
8 Medicine.   **9** Publications by former students & staff of St Mary's.   **11** No.   **12** Mon-Fri 9.00-19.00 (Wed 17.00).
13 (a) 23,000; (b) 350.   **11** £11,000.   **15** (a) 3½ (b) 1 (c) 2.

ST THOMAS'S HOSPITAL MEDICAL SCHOOL LIBRARY, London SE1 7EH (Tel 01-928 9292 ext 2367) Libn: Mr Frederick A. Tubbs DipLit.
6 Council.   **7** Lambeth Hospital Medical Lib, Brook Dr, SE11 4TH, Libn: Mrs E. Mamman; South Western Hospital, Lander Rd, Stockwell SW9 9NU; 56 departmental libraries.
8 General medicine & surgery.   **9** Students' lists & notebooks (18th & 19th cent).   **11** No.   **12** Mon-Fri 9.00-21.00 (exc Aug).   **13** (a) 19,707 & 13,175 in depts; (b) 108 & 308 in depts.   **14** £7,000 (exc depts).   **15** (a) 7.

WESTMINSTER MEDICAL SCHOOL LIBRARY, 17 Horseferry Rd, London SW1P 2AR (Tel 01-828 9811 ext 2318) Libn: Mr W. J. Robertson MA, DipLib.
8 Medicine, surgery.   **11** No.   **12** 24 hours a day.
13 (a) over 10,000; (b) 240.   **15** (a) 2 (b) 1 (c) 1.

UXBRIDGE TECHNICAL COLLEGE LIBRARY, Park Rd, Uxbridge, Middlesex, UB8 1NQ (Tel 0895-30411) Libn: Mr A. J. Shelley ALA.
6 Hillingdon Borough Council.   **8** Commerce & technology.
10 BLL; CICRIS.   **11** No.   **12** Term: 9.15-17.15.
13 (a) c. 14,000; (b) c. 100.   **15** (a) 2; (c) 1.

CODE: 1 Name of Library. **2** Address. **3** Telephone & Telex. **4** Officer in charge. **5** Deputy. **6** Governing body.
7 Branches. **8** Main Subjects. **9** Special Collections. **10** Co-operative Schemes. **11** Open to public? **12** Hours.
13 Stock: (a) books (b) periodicals (c) other. **14** Finance. **15** Staff: (a) non-manual (b) graduate (c) chartered librarians.

LONDON—*continued*

VAUGHAN WILLIAMS MEMORIAL LIBRARY, Cecil Sharp
House, 2 Regent's Park Rd, London NW1 7AY (Tel 01-485
2206) Libn: Ms Barbara Newlin BA, MALS; Lib Asst: Mr
David Armitage.
6 English Folk Dance & Song Society. **8** Folk song, folk
dance & folk music (mostly British, but some foreign);
folklore, customs, folk instruments. **9** Mss of early folk
song & dance collectors (eg Hammond, Gardiner, Butterworth,
Broadwood, Gilchrist, Sharp [on microfilm], Vaughan Williams
[hand-written copy]); 17th & 18th cent books on country dance.
11 Yes. **12** Mon-Fri 9.30-17.30, Sat 10.00-13.00, 14.00-
17.00. **13** (a) 8,000; (b) 80; (c) 4,000 records & tapes of
British & foreign folk music; 10,000 photographs; 500 colour
slides; 100 films; original broadsheets of customs, singers,
folk dancers etc. **15** (a) 2; (b) 1; (c) 1.

VICTORIA AND ALBERT MUSEUM LIBRARY, South Kensington London SW7 2RL (Tel 01-589 6371) Keeper of Lib: Mr J.P.
Harthan MA; Dep Keeper of Lib: Mr R.W. Lightbown MA.
6 Dept of Education & Science. **8** Fine & applied arts of
all periods & countries (inc early books & technical
treatises on art); aesthetics; art of the book (illuminated &
calligraphic mss, fine printing, illustration & binding).
9 Dyce & Forster collns (general literature, especially
19th cent England); bookbindings (historical styles); Clements
colln (armorial bookbindings); Guy Little & Renier colln
(children's books). **11** Yes, for ref on single visits;
regular readers & access to special collns only by application
for reader's ticket. **12** Mon-Sat 10.00-17.45 (Sat closed
13.00-14.00). **13** (a) 400,000 books; (b) 1,500; (c) photographs. **15** (a) 35 (b) 12 (c) 10.

VINYL PRODUCTS LTD, LIBRARY, Mill Lane, Carshalton,
Surrey, SM5 2JU (Tel 01-669 4422; Telex 266264) Technical
Inf Officer Libn: Miss Joan Cullen BSc, MIInfSci; Asst Inf
Officer: Mr D.A. Spender BSc.
8 Polymer technology. **9** Polymer technology & applications in paints, paper coating, textiles, building, adhesives etc.
11 No. **12** 9.00-17.30. **13** (b) c.100. **15** (a) 2 (b) 2.

Waltham Forest College

   LIBRARY, Forest Rd, London E17 4JB (Tel 01-527 2272)
Tutor-Libn: Mr B. Payne BSc, ALA; Dep Libn: Miss H.
Puckette BA, ALA.
6 London Borough of Waltham Forest. **7** Walthamstow
Annexe, 398 Hoe St, E17 9AA (01-520 1875); Chingford
Annexe, 156 Chingford Mount Rd, E4 9BS (01-529 0728);
Lloyd Park Annexe, Fleeming Rd, E17 5ET (01-527 8537).
8 Health education; food; fashion; business administration;
general; sciences; technology. **10** BLL. **11** Yes.
12 Term: Mon & Thurs 9.00-19.00, Tues, Wed & Fri
9.00-17.00; vac: Mon & Thurs 9.00-17.00. Branches
vary. **13** (a) 20,000; (b) 250. **14** £12,000.
15 (a) 8 (b) 2 (c) 2.

NATIONAL INSTITUTE OF INDUSTRIAL PSYCHOLOGY,
CHARLES MYERS LIBRARY, c/o North-East London
Polytechnic, Livingstone House, Livingstone Rd, London
E15 2LJ (Tel 01-534 7825) Libn: Mr H.S. Chahal BA, ALA.
6 Library temporarily in care of Waltham Forest College
(North-East London Polytechnic). **8** Occupational
psychology; vocational guidance. **9** Probably most
comprehensive library in its field in UK; some journals
from 1920; comprehensive colln of papers by founder,
Dr C.S. Myers. **10** BLL. **11** Yes, for ref only.
12 Mon-Fri 9.00-17.00. **13** (a) 15,000; (b) 103.
15 (a) 1 (b) 1½ (c) 1.

WANDSWORTH TECHNICAL COLLEGE LIBRARY,
Wandsworth High St, London SW18 2PP (Tel 01-870 2241
ext 208) Libn: Mr C.J. Fellows ALA; Dep: Miss E.P. Harmer
ALA.
6 ILEA. **8** Electrical, electronic & mechanical engineering; computers; educational technology; economics & business;
social sciences. **10** WANDPETLS. **11** Yes, with prior
permission from Principal (applications in writing).
12 Term: 9.00-20.00; vac: 9.00-17.00. **13** (a) 30,000;
(b) 272; (c) 204 audio tapes; 595 gramophone records; 114
video tapes; 13 films; 259 filmloops; 300 slide sets & filmstrips. **14** £11,000. **15** (a) 6; (c) 2.

WATER INFORMATION CENTRE, 1 Queen Anne's Gate,
London SW1H 9BT (Tel 01-930 3100; Telex 918518)
Inf Officer: Mr Norman Day ALA; Dep Inf Officer: Mr
Gordon Plumb BA, ALA.
6 National Water Council. **8** All aspects of water, with
emphasis on organisation & administration of water industry
in England & Wales. **9** Comprehensive colln of publications of water industry (from April 1974). **10** Water
Industry Library Information Group. **11** Yes, by appointment. **12** Mon-Fri 9.15 to 17.00. **13** (a) 3,000;
(b) 230; (c) Archives of British Waterworks Association,
Association of River Authorities, & National Water Council.
14 £4,000. **15** (a) 7 (b) 2 (c) 3.

WELLCOME INSTITUTE FOR THE HISTORY OF
MEDICINE LIBRARY, 183 Euston Rd, London NW1 2BP
(Tel 01-387 4477) Libn: Mr Eric J. Freeman BA, ALA;
Dep Libn: Mr Robin M. Price MA, ALA.
6 Wellcome Trustees. **8** History of medicine & allied
sciences. **9** Spanish-American & Oriental collns.
10 BLL; LA Med Sect Exch. **11** Yes, at Libn's discretion. **12** Mon-Fri 9.45-17.15. **13** (a) c.400,000;
(b) c.350; (c) 100,000 autograph letters; microfilms;
archives. **14** £19,800. **15** (a) 22 (b) 8 (c) 9.

WELLCOME RESEARCH LABORATORIES LIBRARY,
Langley Court, Beckenham, Kent, BR3 3BS (Tel 01-658 2211)
Principal Libn: Mrs S. Elmes.
6 Wellcome Foundation. **8** Pharmaceutical science &
allied subjects. **11** No. **12** Mon-Fri 8.45-17.15.
13 (a) 50,000; (b) 600. **15** (a) 13 (b) 1 (c) 1.

WESTMINSTER ABBEY, CHAPTER LIBRARY, London
SW1P 3PA (Tel 01-222 4233) Libn: Mr Howard M. Nixon
MA, FSA.
6 Dean & Chapter. **8** History of Westminster Abbey;
17th & 18th cent general ref library. **9** 16th & 17th cent
music; books from library of William Camden. **11** Yes,
on written request. **12** Mon-Fri 10.00-13.00, 14.00-16.45.
13 (a) 14,000. **15** (a) 2 (b) 1 (c) 1.

WESTMINSTER COLLEGE LIBRARY, Vincent Sq, London
SW1P 2PD (Tel 01-828 6951 ext 38) Coll Libn: Miss J.O.
Brown FLA.
6 ILEA. **7** Kensington Div, 1 St Alban's Grove, W8 5PN
(01-937 8458), Libn: Miss E.D. Warren ALA; Pulteney Div,
Peter St, Wardour St, W1V 4HS (01-437 3924); Castle Lane,
SW1E 6DR (01-834 5738), Libn: Miss J. Rowe BA, ALA.
8 Food & catering; hotel administration; home economics;
civil engineering; English for foreigners. **10** BLL.
11 Yes, at Vincent Sq for ref only. **12** Term: 8.45-18.15.
Branches vary. **13** (a) 27,000; (b) 235; (c) 550 tapes.
14 c.£9,000. **15** (a) 7⅔; (b) 1; (c) 3.

WIENER LIBRARY, 4 Devonshire St, London W1N 2BH
(Tel 01-636 7247) Libn: Mrs C.S. Wichmann; Cataloguer:
Miss J.B. Langmaid.
6 Executive Committee of Institute of Contemporary History
& Wiener Library Ltd. **8** German Jewry; National
Socialism; Europe between the wars; German history (20th
cent); Palestine & Israel. **9** Nuremburg documents (40,000
indexed transcripts, trial records, etc, many unpublished);
press cuttings (8 indexed archives). **11** Yes, at Libn's
discretion, with letter of introduction. **12** Mon-Fri 10.00-
17.30. **13** (a) c.80,000; (b) c.130; (c) documents & press
cuttings; 220 microfilms. **15** (a) 5; (b) 2.

LONDON—*continued*

WILLESDEN COLLEGE OF TECHNOLOGY LIBRARY,
Denzil Rd, London NW10 2XD (Tel 01-459 0147) Coll Libn:
Miss K. M. Hancock ALA; Dep Libn: Miss A. C. Challiner ALA.
6 London Borough of Brent. **8** Automobile engineering;
building; education; electrical, mechanical & production
engineering. **10** CICRIS. **11** No, except by special
arrangement. **12** Term: Mon-Fri 9.00-20.00 (Fri 17.00);
vac: Mon-Fri 10.00-16.00. **13** (a) 30,500; (b) 150.

WILLIAM BOOTH MEMORIAL COLLEGE LIBRARY,
Denmark Hill, London SE5 8BQ (Tel 01-733 1191) Libn: Capt R.
Trotman.
6 Salvation Army. **8** Theology; Salvation Army history.
9 'Christian Mission' magazines (1870s); other S. A. periodicals of historical interest. **11** Yes, for serious researchers.
12 9.00-21.45. **13** (a) c.8,000; (b) c.20. **15** (a) 1.

WIMBLEDON SCHOOL OF ART LIBRARY, Merton Hall Rd,
London SW19 3QA (Tel 01-540 0231) Libn: Ms Patricia A.
Harrison ALA.
6 London Borough of Merton. **8** Fine arts; literature
(particularly drama); philosophy; history. **9** Costumes;
plays. **10** BLL; British Theatre Association (formerly
British Drama League); ARLIS. **11** Yes, on written
application to the Libn, for ref only. **12** Term: Mon-Thurs
9.00-20.30, Fri 9.00-18.00; vac: Mon-Fri 9.00-16.30.
13 (a) 15,472; (b) 76; (c) 20,000 slides; 305 gramophone
records. **14** £3,700. **15** (a) 2½; (c) 1.

WIMPEY LABORATORIES LTD LIBRARY, Beaconsfield Rd,
Hayes, Middlesex, UB4 0LS (Tel 01-573 7744 ext 130; Telex
935797) Libn: Mr C. Lowther FLA; Lib Asst: Mrs P. Fidler.
8 Building; civil & mechanical engineering; metallurgy;
chemistry. **9** Internal reports colln; BSI; trade literature.
10 CICRIS; Aslib. **11** No. **12** Mon-Fri 8.45-17.15.
13 (a) c.20,000; (b) c.200; (c) slides; photographs.
15 (a) 2 (c) 1.

ZOOLOGICAL SOCIETY OF LONDON LIBRARY, Regents
Park, London NW1 4RY (Tel 01-722 3333) Libn: Mr R. Fish
FLA; Asst Libn: Miss F. Hamilton ALA.
8 Zoology. **11** No. **12** Mon-Fri 9.30-17.30.
13 (a) 120,000; (b) 1,200; (c) archives; c.12,000 photographs.
15 (a) 5; (b) 1; (c) 3.

LONDONDERRY, Co. Derry

DU PONT LTD, TECHNICAL LIBRARY, PO Box 15,
Londonderry, BT47 1TU (Tel 0504-65123) Technical Libn:
Mr Gordon C. Whiteside.
8 Analytical chemistry; polymer science; organic chemistry;
textile technology. **11** No, but will assist with requests
from libraries. **12** Mon-Fri 8.00-16.30. **13** (a) 1,500;
(b) 90; (c) 5,000 company reports; 7,000 microfiche &
microfilm reports. **15** (a) 1.

LOUGHBOROUGH, Leicestershire

LOUGHBOROUGH COLLEGE OF EDUCATION LIBRARY,
(will merge with Loughborough University of Technology),
Ashby Rd, Loughborough, LE11 3TN (Tel 05093-5752)
Tutor-Libn: Miss M. I. McKay MA, ALA.
6 Leicestershire CC. **8** General. **9** Physical education; crafts. **10** BLL; SCOPELC. **11** No. **12** Term:
Mon-Fri 9.00-21.30; Sat 9.00-12.30; vac: Mon-Fri 9.00-
12.30, 13.30-17.30. **13** (a) 70,000; (b) 450; (c) c.1,000
microtexts; c.500 gramophone records. **14** £20,000.
15 (a) 7½ (b) 2 (c) 4.

LOUGHBOROUGH TECHNICAL COLLEGE LIBRARY,
Radmoor, Loughborough, LE11 3BT (Tel 05093-5831) Tutor-
Libn: Mr E. Sheard, ALA.
6 Leicestershire CC, Education Committee. **8** Mechanical, electrical & automobile engineering; catering &
domestic science; business; building; science; general;
education; fine art history; painting; sculpture; furniture;
textiles; graphics; embroidery; silversmithing; jewellery;
ceramics. **9** Bibliography & librarianship.
10 EMRLB. **11** No. **12** Term: 9.00-21.00; vac: 9.00-
12.30, 14.00-17.30. **13** (a) 43,000; (b) 680; (c) micro-

texts; filmstrips; maps; exhibition catalogues.
14 £12,500. **15** (a) 8 (b) 2 (c) 3.

LOUGHBOROUGH UNIVERSITY OF TECHNOLOGY
LIBRARY, (will merge with Loughborough College of
Education), Loughborough, LE11 3TU (Tel 0509-63171;
Telex 34319) Univ Libn: Prof A. J. Evans BPharm, PhD,
FLA, MIInfSc; Dep Libn: Dr R. A. Wall PhD, FLA.
8 Pure & applied science; engineering; social sciences;
education. **10** LETIS. **11** Yes, with Libn's written
approval. **12** Term: Mon-Fri 9.00-22.00, Sat 9.00-17.00,
Sun 10.00-21.00 (Sat afternoon & Sun for ref only); vac:
Mon-Fri 9.00-17.30, Sat 9.00-12.30. **13** (a) 115,000;
(b) 2,900; (c) 65,000 reports, microforms, etc.
14 £120,000. **15** (a) 45 (b) 11 (c) 13.

MINNESOTA 3M LABORATORIES LIBRARY, Morley St,
Loughborough, LE11 1EP (Tel 0509-68181; Telex 34587)
Libn: Mrs J. B. Chapman ALA; Asst Libn: Mrs C. A. Trevis.
8 Medicine; pharmacy; chemistry. **9** Lists of medical
preparations available in different countries. **10** LETIS;
NANTIS. **11** No. **12** Mon-Fri 9.00-17.30.
13 (a) 6,607; (b) 213. **14** £11,000. **15** (a) 4½ (c) 1.

LOWESTOFT, Suffolk

LOWESTOFT COLLEGE OF FURTHER EDUCATION
LIBRARY, St Peter's St, Lowestoft, NR32 2NB (Tel 0502-
4177) Libn: Mr M. H. Canham MA.
6 Suffolk CC. **8** General technical subjects, inc engineering (electrical & mechanical), construction & nautical subjects; commerce; art; sociology; general. **10** NINES.
11 Yes, for ref only. **12** Term: Mon-Fri 9.00-21.00
(Fri 17.30); vac: Mon-Fri 9.00-17.00. **13** (a) 15,000;
(b) 177; (c) filmstrips; slides; sound tapes; gramophone
records; multi-media packs. **14** £5,200. **15** (a) 3½ (b) 1.

LUTON, Bedfordshire

BARNFIELD COLLEGE LEARNING RESOURCES CENTRE
& LIBRARY, New Bedford Rd, Luton, LU3 2AX (Tel 0582-
57531) Tutor-Libn: Mr Graham Bulpitt BA, ALA, CertEd;
Asst Tutor-Libn: Mr Peter D. Kewley BA, ALA.
6 Bedfordshire CC. **8** General; arts; humanities; crafts
& design; fashion; social science. **10** ARLIS; inter-
library loans. **11** Yes. **12** Term: Mon-Fri 9.00-19.00
(Fri 17.45); vac: Mon-Fri 9.00-12.00, 14.00-17.00.
13 (a) 9,000; (b) 175; (c) 8,000 slides (mainly art history);
filmstrips; records; sound & videotapes. **14** £6,500.
15 (a) 5 (b) 2 (c) 2.

LUTON COLLEGE OF TECHNOLOGY LIBRARY, (will
merge with Putteridge Bury College of Education), Park Sq,
Luton, LU1 3JU (Tel 0582-34111 ext 236; Telex 825995)
Libn: Mr Alan R. Geeson ALA; Dep: Mr M. Shoolbred BA, ALA.
6 Bedfordshire CC. **8** Business; management; economics;
sociology; industrial relations; law; electrical, automotive &
mechanical engineering; maths; physics; chemistry; geology;
biology; geography; building. **11** Yes, for ref only.
12 Term: Mon-Fri 9.00-20.00; vac: Mon-Fri 9.00-13.00,
14.00-17.00. **13** (a) 33,000; (b) 300; (c) 60 rolls microfilm. **14** £20,000. **15** (a) 5 (b) 1 (c) 2.

MACCLESFIELD, Cheshire

MACCLESFIELD COLLEGE OF FURTHER EDUCATION
RESOURCE CENTRE & LIBRARY, Park Lane, Macclesfield
SK11 8LF (Tel 0625-27744) Tutor-Libn: Mrs J. M. Howle
ALA.
6 Cheshire CC. **7** College Annexe, Park Green,
Macclesfield. **8** General; nursing; social welfare; arts;
business; European studies; engineering. **10** NWRLB.
11 No. **12** Mon-Thurs 8.45-20.00, Fri 8.45-17.00.
13 (a) 10,200; (b) 136; (c) film strips; slides; multi-media;
tapes; records; ohp transparencies. **14** £5,000. **15** (a)
3 (c) 2.

MAIDENHEAD, Berkshire

BERKSHIRE COLLEGE OF ART LIBRARY, Marlow Rd,
Maidenhead, SL6 7AF (Tel 0628-24302) Libn: Mr Ken Potter
BA; Dep: Ms Judith Begg BA.
6 Berkshire Education Authority. **8** Art; architecture;

CODE: **1** Name of Library. **2** Address. **3** Telephone & Telex. **4** Officer in charge. **5** Deputy. **6** Governing body. **7** Branches. **8** Main Subjects. **9** Special Collections. **10** Co-operative Schemes. **11** Open to public? **12** Hours. **13** Stock: (a) books (b) periodicals (c) other. **14** Finance. **15** Staff: (a) non-manual (b) graduate (c) chartered librarians.

MAIDENHEAD, Berkshire—*continued*

printing. **10** Inter-library loans. **11** No. **12** Mon-Fri 9.30-18.00. **13** (a) 2,600; (b) 41; (c) 50 gramophone records. **14** £880. **15** (a) 1 (b) 1.

WYETH LABORATORIES LIBRARY, Huntercombe Lane South, Taplow, Maidenhead, SL6 OPH (Tel 0753-28311; Telex 847640) Libn: Mrs M. J. Williams. **8** Chemistry; medicine; pharmacy; pharmacology; toxicology. **11** No. **12** 8.45-17.00. **13** (a) 4,750; (b) 198; (c) 8,000 reprints/photocopies. **14** £11,000. **15** (a) 3.

MANCHESTER

ANCHOR CHEMICAL CO INFORMATION SERVICE & LIBRARY, Clayton Lane, Clayton, Manchester, M11 4SR (Tel 061-223 2461 ext 147; Telex 667829) Libn & Inf Officer: Ms Silvia Gilroy. **7** Birch Vale, Via Stockport, SK12 5AH (0663-43233), Libn: Mrs Packett. **8** Rubber & plastics technology; production & marketing. **11** No, but telephone enquiries favourably considered. **12** 8.30-17.00. **13** (a) c. 2,000 books; (b) c. 250; (c) 1,000 patents; trade literature; 150 boxes conference papers; 1,000 standards; 25,000 periodicals. **14** c. £3,000. **15** (a) 1.

ASHBURNE HALL LIBRARY, Old Hall Lane, Manchester, M14 6HA (Tel 061-224 3394). **6** Ashburne Hall Committee. **8** General. **9** Morley colln (private library of John, Lord Morley) (5,640 vols). **11** Yes, with authorisation of Manchester Univ Libn. **13** (a) 14,680. **15** (b) 1.

CARBORUNDUM COMPANY LTD, TECHNICAL LIBRARY, Trafford Park, Manchester, M17 1HP (Tel 061-872 2381 ext 93; Telex 66-344) Libn: Mrs Kathleen Poplawska AIInfSc. **8** Abrasives; refractories; technical ceramics; resins; coated materials; high temperature materials. **9** American Ceramic Society journal, bulletin & abstracts (from 1st issue to date); British Ceramic Society transactions & abstracts (from 1st issue to date). **11** No. **12** 8.30-16.30. **13** (a) 5,500; (b) 100; (c) patents (British, US & others); standards (British, US, ISO etc); company confidential reports. **15** (a) 1.

CHETHAM'S LIBRARY, Long Millgate, Manchester, M3 1SB (Tel 061-834 7961) Libn: Miss A. C. Swape MA; Asst Libn: Miss G. Groocock ALA. **6** The Feoffees, Chetham's Hospital School of Music. **8** History. **9** Halliwell-Phillipps broadsides; 16th-18th cent books; 17th cent printed books; local history of North West England. **11** Yes, over 18 years, for ref only. **12** Mon-Fri 9.00-17.00, Sat by appointment only. **13** (a) c. 85,000; (b) 59; (c) mss; c. 90 incunabula. **15** (a) 2 (b) 1; (c) 1.

CO-OPERATIVE UNION LIBRARY, Holyoake House, Hanover St, Manchester, M60 OAS (Tel 061-834 0975) Inf Officer & Libn: Mr T. R. Garratt. **8** Cooperative history, economics, politics, trade union history, distributive trades, international cooperative affairs. **9** Robert Owen correspondence, from 1820 (3,000 letters); G. J. Holyoake correspondence, 1835-1903 (4,000 letters). **11** Yes, by appointment. **12** Mon-Fri 10.00-17.00. **15** (a) 1 (b) 1.

CO-OPERATIVE WHOLESALE SOCIETY LTD. LABORATORIES, LIBRARY, 28 Knowsley St, Cheetham, Manchester, M8 8JU (Tel 061-8321 6246 ext 12) Libn: Mr N. Dellar BA. **8** Food technology; analytical chemistry. **10** NWRLB. **11** No, unless information unobtainable elsewhere. **12** 8.30-16.45. **13** (a) 4,000. **15** (a) 2 (b) 1.

DIDSBURY COLLEGE OF EDUCATION LIBRARY, (will merge with Manchester Polytechnic & Hollings College), 799 Wilmslow Rd, Didsbury, Manchester, M20 8RR (Tel 061-445 7871) Tutor-Libn: Mr W. H. Shercliff MA, FLA, DipArchAdmin, CertEd; Dep: Mr A. G. Neil BA, FLA. **6** Manchester Education Committee. **8** General, except commercial & technical. **9** Morten-Dandy colln (children's books, textbooks & educational books up to 1949); John Seymour Memorial colln (Brontes). **10** Manchester University Area Training Organisation; Library Board of Studies cooperative schemes, e. g. Joint Union List of Periodicals. **11** No. **12** Term: Mon-Thurs 9.00-20.30, Fri 9.00-16.45; vac: Mon-Fri 9.00-16.45; occasional Sats 9.00-12.30. **13** (a) 85,000; (b) 800; (c) pictures; slides; filmstrips; tapes; records; film loops; models; specimens; (c. 30,000). **14** £36,000. **15** (a) 16 (b) 3 (c) 6.

ELIZABETH GASKELL COLLEGE OF EDUCATION LIBRARY, (will merge with Manchester College & Mather College, Sept 1976), Hathersage Rd, Manchester, M13 0JA (Tel 061-225 9054) Tutor-Libn: Mrs Andrena M. Dobbin MA, ALA; Dep: Mr Stephen Pearson, BA. **6** Manchester Education Committee. **8** Home economics; history; geography; sociology; English; French; art; education; speech therapy; institutional management. **9** Early cookery books; Art Nouveau pattern books; colln on war-time food. **11** No. **13** (a) 51,000; (b) 205; (c) slides; filmstrips; microfiche; microfilms; audio-visual material. **14** £13,500. **15** (b) 3 (c) 3.

Granada Television

FILM LIBRARY, Quay St, Manchester, M60 9EA (Tel 061-832 7211; Telex 66 88 59) Film Lib Supervisor: Ms Monica M. Ford BA, ALA; Film Libn: Ms Sylvia Cowling BA, ALA. **8** Granada TV film productions, completed programmes & stock shots, (sale only). **9** Zoology; anthropology. **11** No, but enquiries about film material accepted. **12** 9.30-13.00, 14.00-18.00. **13** (c) films (sound & mute). **15** (a) 6 (b) 3 (c) 3.

LIBRARY, Quay St, Manchester, M60 9EA (Tel 061-832 7211; Telex 668859 Television Mchr) Libn: Mr Gerald Hagan BA, ALA; Dep Libn: Mr John Stretch BA. **8** General. **9** Black & white prints & colour transparencies for press & programme use; newspaper & periodical cuttings; programme & company archives. **11** Yes, with special permission. **12** 9.30-18.00. **13** (a) 8,000; (b) 60. **15** (a) 6 (b) 3 (c) 3.

MANCHESTER BUSINESS SCHOOL LIBRARY, Booth St West, Manchester, M15 6PB (Tel 061-273 8228; Telex 668354 MBSMNCHR) Libn: Mr J. D. Dews MA, FLA. **8** Business & management. **10** BLL; NWRLB. **11** Yes, for ref only. **12** Mon-Fri 9.00-20.30; Sat 9.00-12.30. **13** (a) 30,000; (b) 700; (c) company reports; working papers; newspapers; microfilms; clippings; extel; McCarthy information service. **14** £14,000. **15** (a) 12 (b) 4 (c) 6.

MANCHESTER EDUCATION COMMITTEE LIBRARY, Teachers Centre, Southern Hey, 137 Barlow Moor Rd, West Didsbury, Manchester, M20 8PW (Tel 061-434 3421/2/3 ext 8) Libn: Miss P. M. Owen ALA. **6** Library Sub-Committee of Management Committee of Teachers Centre. **8** Education & related subjects. **9** Textbooks; reading schemes. **11** No. **12** Term: Mon-Fri 9.30-20.00 (Wed & Fri 17.00); vac: Mon-Fri 9.30-17.00. **13** (a) 41,767; (b) c. 80; (c) gramophone records. **14** £3,600. **15** (a) 3 (b) 1 (c) 1.

MANCHESTER POLYTECHNIC LIBRARY, (will merge with Didsbury College of Education & Hollings College), All Saints, Manchester, M15 6BX (Tel 061-228 2351; Telex 667915) Poly Libn: Mr I. Rogerson ALA; Dep Libns: Mr P. F.

MANCHESTER—*continued*

Jackson ALA (Reader Services); Mr G. E. Maxim FLA
(Technical Services).
7 Art & Design Lib, All Saints, (061-273 2715); Aytoun Lib,
Chorlton St, 1 (061-236 7702); John Dalton Lib, Chester St, 1
(061-236 7784); Hilton House Lib, Hilton St, 1 (061-236
9831); Piccadilly Lib, Piccadilly, 1 (061-236 2552); Didsbury
Lib, School Lane, Didsbury (061-434 3331).   **8** General.
9 Local colln of material on Manchester area; Manchester
Architects library; junior library; comprehensive colln of
children's books (1850-1914); 19th-20th cent printing &
illustration.   **10** NWRLB; BLCMP.   **11** Yes, by prior
written application to Libn.   **12** Term: Mon-Fri 9.00-
21.00; vac: Mon-Fri 9.00-16.30. Branches vary.   **13** (a)
180,000; (b) 2,000; (c) 800 gramophone records; 500 reels
microfilm; 800 filmstrips; 400 filmloops; 400 cassettes; 4,000
slides.   **14** £144,000.   **15** (a) 51 (b) 20 (c) 25.

Manchester University

JOHN RYLANDS UNIVERSITY LIBRARY, Oxford Rd,
Manchester, M13 9PP (Tel 061-273 3333; Telex 668932)
Univ Libn & Dir: Dr F.W.Ratcliffe JP, MA, PhD; Dep
Dirs: S.Roberts MA, Admin; Dr F.Taylor MA, PhD, FSA,
(Principal Keeper).
6 Victoria University of Manchester.   **7** Christie
Science Lib, Libn: F.Y.Abel BA; Medical Lib, Libn: D.
Cook MA; Special Collns Division, Deansgate (061-834
5343), Libn: Dr F.Taylor.   **8** General.   **9** c.300
collns. Althorp library (c.40,000 vols early & rare
printed books); Bullock colln (Italian 16th cent); Christie
library (mss & renaissance); Manchester museum,
Manchester Medical Society & Partington library (history of science & medicine); 'Manchester Geographical';
Crawford colln (oriental & western mss); 'Manchester
Guardian'archives; Spencer colln. Printed catalogues.
10 BLL; SKELLEM; Manchester Educational Precinct;
NWRLB.   **11** Yes, to view exhibitions & buildings;
bona-fide scholars admitted for research.   **12** Term
& Easter vac: Mon-Fri 9.00-21.30, Sat 9.00-13.00
(13.00-18.00 for ref only); other vacs: Mon-Fri 9.30-
17.30, Sat 9.30-13.00.   **13** (a) Over 2,500,000;
(b) c.8,000; (c) 17,000 mss; c.500,000 deeds, charters,
family muniments etc; over 400,000 titles in microform;
over 400,000 archival items.   **14** c.£400,000.
15 (a) c.140 (b) 39.

SCHOOL OF EDUCATION LIBRARY, Humanities Building,
University of Manchester, Manchester, M13 9PL
(Tel 061-273 3333 ext 2) Libn-in-Charge: Mr R.P.Carr
BA, MA; Lib Asst: Miss A.Blackshaw.
6 University Council.   **8** Education; psychology;
linguistics.   **9** Educational & psychological test colln
(restricted access).   **10** BLL; LISE.   **11** Yes, at
Libn's discretion.   **12** Term: Mon-Fri 9.30-12.30,
13.30-20.00 (summer term 19.00); vac: Mon-Fri 9.30-
12.30, 13.30-17.00.   **13** (a) 21,958; (b) 120; (c) c.2,000
theses in education; c.200 filmstrips.   **15** (a) 2 (b) 1.

SCIENCE AND TECHNOLOGY INSTITUTE LIBRARY,
Sackville St, Manchester, M60 1QD (Tel 061-236 3311)
Libn: Mr E.D.G.Robinson JP, MA, ALA; Dep Libn:
Mr W.A.Price BA, FLA.
8 Science & technology; management; european studies.
9 Joule colln (1818-1889).   **10** NWRLB.   **11** Yes.
12 Term & Easter vac: Mon-Fri 9.00-21.00, Sat 9.00-
12.00 (summer term 17.00); other vacs: Mon-Fri 9.00-
17.00.   **13** (a) 108,000; (b) 1,750; (c) 28,000 microforms.   **14** £84,000.   **15** (a) 30 (b) 12 (c) 6.

MATHER COLLEGE OF EDUCATION LIBRARY, (will
merge with Manchester College & Elizabeth Gaskell College
of Education, Sept 1976), 34 Whitworth St, Manchester,
M1 3HA (Tel 061-236 9873) Tutor-Libn: Miss J.Simmons;
Dep: Mrs M.Woodhouse.
6 LEA Manchester.   **8** Education; general.   **9** Thomas
Hardy.   **10** BLL.   **11** No.   **12** Term: 9.00-19.30;
vac: 9.00-16.45.   **13** (a) 40,500; (b) 240; (c) charts;
slides; audio tapes; postcards; illustrations.   **15** (a) 6
(b) 1 (c) 3.

NORTHERN BAPTIST COLLEGE WITH HARTLEY-
VICTORIA METHODIST COLLEGE, LIBRARY, Brighton
Grove, Manchester, M16 8GH (Tel 061-224 2214) Libn:
Mr David Goodbourn BA, DipAE.
8 Theology; biblical studies; ethics; pastoral studies;
church history.   **9** Baptist historical material.   **11** Yes,
borrowing only by arrangement.   **12** 9.00-21.30.
13 (b) 15.   **14** £600.

NORTH TRAFFORD COLLEGE LIBRARY, Talbot Rd,
Stretford, Manchester, M32 0XH (Tel 061-872 3731) Senior
Tutor-Libn: Mrs D.Wood ALA; Libn: Mr G.W.Anderson
ALA.
6 Trafford MDC.   **7** Annexe, Moss Rd, Stretford, M32 0XH.
8 General; mechanical engineering; natural sciences;
business management; chemical plant technology.
10 NWRLB.   **11** Yes.   **12** Term: Mon-Thurs 8.45-
20.00, Fri 8.45-16.30; vac: Mon-Fri 9.00-12.30.
13 (a) 22,000; (b) 200; (c) 70 gramophone records; 400 filmstrips.   **14** £6,000.   **15** (a) 7 (c) 3.

PORTICO LIBRARY & NEWSROOM, 57 Mosley St, Manchester, M2 3HY (Tel 061-236 6785) Libn: Ms Rachel
Horsfield.
6 Trustees & General Committee of Proprietary Library.
8 General.   **11** No, except on application, for special
reasons.   **12** Mon-Fri 9.30-17.00 (Thurs 19.00).
13 (a) c.30,000.   **15** (a) 1.

RENOLD LTD, CENTRAL LIBRARY, Renold House,
Wythenshawe, Manchester, M22 5WL (Tel 061-437 5221;
Telex 669052) Central Libn & Archivist: Mr C.D.Hughes
BA.
6 Renold Group.   **7** Libraries of industrial establish-
ments, centrally catalogued, with central book acquisitions.
8 Industrial technology; applicational science; research &
development; materials research; commercial & industrial
law; economics & corporate planning; personnel; stock
market & financial planning.   **9** Industrial history
(especially early history of Precision Chain Industry): carto-
graphic material (primarily economic); company reports
& accounts.   **11** Yes, but only for approved research.
12 Mon-Fri 9.00-13.00, 14.00-17.00 (Fri 16.00).
13 (a) 6,000; (b) 150.   **14** £5,000.

ROYAL NORTHERN COLLEGE OF MUSIC LIBRARY,
124 Oxford Rd, Manchester, M13 9RD (Tel 061-273 6283)
Libn: Mr Anthony Hodges GTCL, FTCL, ARCM; Dep: Miss
W.L.Birchall ARMCM, FLA.
6 Manchester Corporation (Joint committee from Manchester, Salford, Cheshire, Lancashire).   **8** Music.
9 Henry Watson historical instruments; Horenstein bequest;
Brodskiana (letters from & to famous musicians); Barbirolli
scores.   **10** BLL.   **11** Yes, for ref only.   **12** Term:
Mon-Fri 9.30-21.00, Sat 9.30-15.00; vac: Mon-Fri 9.30-
17.00.   **13** (a) 35,000 (inc music); (b) 80; (c) 5,000
gramophone records; 500 cassettes.   **14** £11,000.
15 (a) 7 (b) 2 (c) 2.

SEDGLEY PARK COLLEGE OF EDUCATION LIBRARY,
Prestwich, Manchester, M25 8JT (Tel 061-773 4001) Tutor-
Libn: Mr D.Grady ALA.
8 General; education; history; geography; French; English;
religion.   **9** Teaching practice.   **11** Yes, for ref.
12 Term: Mon-Fri 9.00-19.00; vac: Mon-Fri 9.00-17.00.
13 (a) c.45,000; (b) c.150; (c) audio-visual materials;
records; tapes; slides; charts.   **14** £8,000.   **15** (a) 4½
(b) 2 (c) 2.

SHIRLEY INSTITUTE LIBRARY, Didsbury, Manchester,
M20 8RX (Tel 061-445 2062) Editor & Libn: J.H.Black BSc,
FTI.
6 Cotton, Silk & Man-Made Fibres Research Association.
8 Textile technology.   **10** BLL.   **11** No.   **13** (b) 250.
15 (a) 2½.

TEXTILE INSTITUTE LIBRARY, 10 Blackfriars St,
Manchester, M3 5DR (Tel 061-834 8457; Telex Chamcom.
Mchr 667822 prefixed Tex.Inst) Inf Asst: Ms C.A.Farn-
field BSc, MSc, AIInfSc.
8 Textiles.   **9** Historical books (1700-1850).   **11** Yes,
by arrangement with Inf Asst.   **12** Mon-Fri 9.00-17.00.

CODE: 1 Name of Library. 2 Address. 3 Telephone & Telex. 4 Officer in charge. 5 Deputy. 6 Governing body.
7 Branches. 8 Main Subjects. 9 Special Collections. 10 Co-operative Schemes. 11 Open to public? 12 Hours.
13 Stock: (a) books (b) periodicals (c) other. 14 Finance. 15 Staff: (a) non-manual (b) graduate (c) chartered librarians.

MANCHESTER—*continued*

13 (a) 4, 000; (b) 57; (c) Textile Institute archives.
15 (a) 1 (b) 1.

UNITARIAN COLLEGE, McLACHLAN LIBRARY, Daisy
Bank Rd, Victoria Park, Manchester, M60 5QL (Tel 061-
224 2849) Univ Libn: Dr F. W. Ratcliffe MA, PhD; Principal
Warden: Rev A. J. Long MA.
6 Unitarian College General Committee. **8** English
literature; biography; theology & philosophy; history of non-
conformity. **9** History of dissent (records of Unitarianism
& non-conformity generally, especially in the North of
England). **11** No, but access can be arranged through
Manchester Univ Libn. **13** (a) c. 30, 000; (c) mss &
archives on history of dissent. **14** £75.

MANSFIELD, Nottinghamshire

WEST NOTTINGHAMSHIRE TECHNICAL COLLEGE
LIBRARY, Derby Rd, Mansfield, NG18 5BH (Tel 0623-27191)
6 Nottinghamshire CC. **8** Construction; engineering;
food & fashion; business. **10** EMRLB; NANTIS. **11** Yes,
subject to approval of Principal. **12** Term: Mon-Fri
9. 00-17. 00 (Fri 18. 00); vac: hours vary. **13** (a) 22, 114;
(b) 176; (c) slides; tapes. **14** £5, 500. **15** (a) 2½ (c) 1.

MIDDLESBROUGH, Cleveland

TEESSIDE COLLEGE OF ART LIBRARY, Green Lane,
Linthorpe, Middlesbrough, TS5 7RJ (Tel 0642-821441 ext 32)
Tutor-Libn: Mr Adrian D. Bull BSc.
6 Governors of Teesside College of Art. **8** Fine arts;
aesthetics; art history; painting; sculpture; architecture;
ceramics; drawing; design; textiles; print making; human
engineering; advertising; typography; photography; film/TV;
visual psychology/perception/optics; interior design; colour
science. **9** 'The Railway and the Artist' (reproductions
& slides; index of artists under compilation). **10** ARLIS;
Aslib; LIST; Fine Arts Resource North. **11** Yes, for ref
only. **12** Term: Mon-Thurs 9. 00-20. 00, Fri 9. 00-17. 00;
vac: 9. 00-12. 30, 13. 45-17. 00. **13** (a) 12, 000; (b) 150;
(c) 65, 000 slides; 200 records; 200 tapes & cassettes; 500
pamphlets; 20 videocassettes; 50 films (16 mm).
14 £9, 000. **15** (a) 5 (b) 2.

TEESSIDE POLYTECHNIC LIBRARY, Borough Rd,
Middlesbrough, TS1 3BA (Tel 0642-44176) Chief Libn:
R. Moss BA, FLA.
6 Cleveland CC. **8** Science; technology; social sciences;
arts; humanities. **10** LIST. **11** No. **12** Term:
8. 45-21. 00; vac: 8. 45-17. 00. **13** (a) 70, 000; (b) 1, 200;
(c) audio-visual material. **15** (a) 22 (b) 7 (c) 6.

MILLPORT, Cumbrae

UNIVERSITY MARINE BIOLOGICAL STATION LIBRARY,
Millport, Cumbrae, KA28 OEG (Tel 047553-581)
6 Universities of London & Glasgow. **8** Marine biology.
11 No. **12** Mon-Fri 8. 45-17. 00. **13** (a) 2, 200; (b) 18;
(c) reprints of scientific papers. **14** £600.

MILTON KEYNES, Buckinghamshire

OPEN UNIVERSITY LIBRARY, Walton Hall, Milton Keynes,
MK7 6AA (Tel 0908-74066; Telex 826739) Univ Libn:
Mr D. J. Simpson BSc, FLA.
8 General. **9** Educational technology. **11** Yes, for
ref only. **12** Mon-Fri 9. 00-17. 30 (Fri 17. 00).
13 (a) 52, 000; (b) 1, 300; (c) films; videotapes; audiotapes;
audiocassettes; gramophone records; slide/tapes; slides;
filmstrips; transparencies; photographs; illustrations; wall
charts. **14** £93, 000. **15** (a) 29 (b) 13 (c) 15.

MIRFIELD, West Yorkshire

COMMUNITY OF THE RESURRECTION LIBRARY, House of
the Resurrection, Stocks Bank Rd, Mirfield, WF14 0BN
(Tel 0924-4318) Community Libn: Rev R. G. Arkell, CR.
8 Theology; religious life. **9** c. 2, 000 mss & books
printed before 1800 (on permanent loan at York University).
11 No, resident guests only. **13** (a) 55, 000; (b) 45;
(c) gramophone records. **14** £550.

NEWBURY, Berkshire

NEWBURY COLLEGE OF FURTHER EDUCATION LIBRARY,
Oxford Rd, Newbury (Tel 0635-42824) Libn: Mrs M. Kirkham
MA, ALA.
6 Berkshire CC. **8** Business; economics & sociology;
history & geography; languages inc English; science &
technology. **11** No except for bona-fide students.
12 Term: Mon-Thurs 9. 00-19. 30, Fri 9. 00-17. 15; vac:
Mon-Fri 9. 00-17. 00. **13** (a) 12, 000; (b) 110. **14** £2, 860.
15 (a) 2¾ (b) 1 (c) 1.

NEWCASTLE UPON TYNE, Tyne & Wear

INTERNATIONAL RESEARCH AND DEVELOPMENT CO
LTD LIBRARY, Fossway, Newcastle upon Tyne, NE6 2YD
(Tel 0632-650451; Telex 53-7086).
8 Mechanical & electrical engineering; applied sciences.
10 NRLB. **11** No. **12** Company working hours.
13 (a) c. 3, 500; (b) c. 220. **14** c. £6, 000. **15** (a) 3
(b) 1.

NATURAL HISTORY SOCIETY OF NORTHUMBRIA
LIBRARY, Hancock Museum, Newcastle upon Tyne, NE2 4PT
(Tel 0632-26386) Honorary Secretary: Mrs Grace Hickling
MBE, MA.
8 Botany; geology; zoology; general natural history.
9 Thomas Bewick drawings. **11** No. **12** By arrangement. **13** (a) c. 10, 000. **14** £300.

NEWCASTLE UPON TYNE COLLEGE OF ARTS AND
TECHNOLOGY LIBRARY, Maple Terrace, Newcastle upon
Tyne, NE4 7SA (Tel 0632-30216) Senior Libn: Mrs L.
Morgan ALA; Asst Libn: Miss S. M. Dowse ALA.
6 Newcastle upon Tyne Education Committee. **7** Dept of
Visual Studies, Bath Lane, & Sandyford Rd, Newcastle upon
Tyne, 1; Catering Dept, Sandyford Rd, Newcastle upon Tyne, 1.
8 Building construction; civil, mechanical, electrical &
electronic engineering; general; art & design, printing;
bakery & catering; business; science; hairdressing.
9 Barbour Index; BSI. **10** NRLB; TALIC. **11** Yes, on
application. **12** 9. 00-19. 00. **13** (a) 50, 000; (b) 250.
14 £22, 000. **15** (a) 8 (c) 3.

NEWCASTLE UPON TYNE POLYTECHNIC LIBRARY, Ellison
Building, Ellison Pl, Newcastle upon Tyne, NE1 8ST (Tel
0632-26002) Poly Libn: Mr K. G. E. Harris MA, FLA; Dep: Mr
I. R. Winkworth BA, ALA.
6 Polytechnic Council. **8** General. **10** TALIC; NRLB;
NEMROC; Newcastle upon Tyne Libraries Joint Working
Party. **11** Yes, by arrangement. **12** Term: Mon-Fri
9. 00-21. 00 (Fri 17. 00), Sat 9. 30-17. 00; vac: Mon-Fri 9. 00-
17. 00. **13** (a) 175, 000; (b) 3, 200; (c) 600 microforms;
teaching practice resources; tapes; discs; tape/slide programmes; slides; films; filmloops. **14** £218, 500.
15 (a) 60 (b) 20 (c) 29.

NEWCASTLE UPON TYNE UNIVERSITY LIBRARY, New-
castle upon Tyne, NE1 7RU (Tel 0632-28511; Telex 53654)
Libn & Keeper of the Pybus Colln: Dr B. J. Enright MA,
DPhil; Dep Libn: Mr J. M. Wood MA, FLA.
7 Dept of Fine Art Lib, The University, Newcastle upon
Tyne, NE1 7RU (0632-28511 ext 204), Libn: Miss G. E. Rogers
MA, ALA; School of Education Lib, St Thomas St, Newcastle
upon Tyne, NE1 7RU (0632-28511 ext 2575), Libn: Mr A. G.

NEWCASTLE UPON TYNE, Tyne and Wear—*continued*

Howard MA, FLA.　**8**　Arts; pure & applied sciences; medicine; dentistry.　**9**　Gertrude Bell colln (Middle East); Burman colln (Alnwick); Charlton colln (brass rubbings); Gilchrist colln (agriculture); Heslop colln (dictionaries); Hindson-Reid colln (engraved wood blocks); Merz colln (maths); Pybus colln (history of medicine); Runciman & Trevelyan papers; Robert White colln (English literature, ballads & chapbooks); early Northern school libraries.　**10**　BLL; NRLB; LISE; NEMROC.　**11**　No.　**12**　Term & Easter vac: Mon-Fri 9.00-21.00, Sat 9.00-16.30; Christmas & Summer vac: Mon-Fri 9.00-17.00, Sat 9.00-13.00.　**13**　(a) 475,000; (b) 4,440; (c) audio & video tapes; slides; microforms.　**14**　c. £237,000.　**15**　(a) 70 (b) 25 (c) 15.

NORTH EAST COAST INSTITUTION OF ENGINEERS AND SHIPBUILDERS LIBRARY, Bolbec Hall, Newcastle upon Tyne, NE1 1TB (Tel 0632-20289) Libn: Capt H. G. S. Brownbill DSC, BA, RN.
6　Council of North East Coast Institution of Engineers & Shipbuilders.　**8**　Naval architecture; shipbuilding; marine & mechanical engineering.　**10**　BLL.　**11**　No, but bona-fide students welcome.　**12**　Mon-Fri 9.30-13.00, 14.00-17.00.　**13**　(a) 10,000; (b) 40.　**14**　£500.　**15**　(b) 1.

NORTHERN COUNTIES COLLEGE OF EDUCATION LIBRARY, Coach Lane, Newcastle upon Tyne, NE7 7XA (Tel 0632-666241) Tutor-Libn: Mr Hugh Hedley BA, ALA; Dep: Miss Ann Bowman MA, DipEd, ALA.
6　Northumberland CC.　**8**　Education; home economics; English language & literature; geography; history; social sciences; art; religion; music; physical education; biology; psychology.　**10**　BLL; NRLB; UCISE.　**11**　Yes.
12　Term: Mon-Fri 8.30-20.00; vac: Mon-Fri 8.30-12.00, 13.00-17.00.　**13**　(a) 46,000; (b) 350; (c) museum (especially costumes & household equipment); audio-visual materials.　**14**　£23,450.　**15**　(a) 9 (b) 3 (c) 3.

NORTH OF ENGLAND INSTITUTE OF MINING AND MECHANICAL ENGINEERS LIBRARY, Neville Hall, Westgate Rd, Newcastle upon Tyne, NE1 1TD (Tel 0632-22201) Libn: Mrs S. Corn.
8　Mining engineering.　**9**　Buddle colln (mss reports on mining, early 1800's); Bell colln (22 vols newspaper cuttings on mining, early 1800's); Watson colln (115 vols early mining reports); London Lead Co (Court Minute's books & maps).　**10**　NRLB.　**11**　Yes, to students & researchers, by appointment.　**12**　Mon-Fri 9.30-16.00.　**13**　(a) 35,000; (b) 10; (c) geological & ordnance maps.　**15**　(a) 2.

NORTHUMBRIAN WATER AUTHORITY LIBRARY, Northumbria House, Regent Centre, Gosforth, Newcastle upon Tyne, NE3 3PX (Tel 0632-843151; Telefacsimile 843151 (0632) Libn: Mr Robert Workman ALA; Asst Libn: Mrs Susan Banketell MA.
8　Water; management; planning; civil engineering; law.　**10**　TALIC; Water Industry Library & Information Group.
11　Yes.　**12**　Mon-Fri 8.45-17.06 (Fri 16.06).
13　(a) 1,000; (b) 200; (c) 2,000 reports.　**14**　£12,250.
15　(a) 3 (c) 2.

NEWPORT, Gwent

BUSINESS STATISTICS OFFICE LIBRARY, Cardiff Rd, Newport, NPT 1XG (Tel 0633-56111 ext 2973; Telex 497121) Libn: M. I. J. Lain ALA.
6　Dept of Industry.　**8**　UK official statistics; statistical methodology.　**11**　Yes.　**12**　Mon-Fri 9.00-17.00 (Fri 16.30).　**15**　(a) 5; (c) 2.

GWENT COLLEGE OF HIGHER EDUCATION LIBRARY, College Crescent, Caerleon, Newport, NP6 1NS (Tel 0633-421292 ext 270/275) Senior Tutor-Libn: Mr L. C. Pugh MA, ALA; Dep Miss M. J. Maggs ALA, ATI.
6　Gwent Education Authority.　**7**　Faculty of Art & Design, Clarence Pl, Newport (0633-59984), Libn: Mrs J. Nash; Faculty of Management & Administration, & Faculty of Science & Technology, Allt-yr-yn Ave, Newport (0633-51525), Libn: Miss M. J. Maggs ALA, ATI.　**8**　Education; humanities; science & technology; social sciences; management.

10　WRLS.　**11**　No, except on application to Senior Tutor-Libn.　**12**　Term: Mon-Fri 9.30-20.00 (Fri 17.15); vac: Mon-Fri 9.30-17.15.　**13**　(a) 70,000; (b) 600; (c) audio-visual material.　**14**　£27,000.　**15**　(a) 14 (b) 4 (c) 5.

NEWPORT, Shropshire

HARPER ADAMS AGRICULTURAL COLLEGE LIBRARY, Newport, TF10 8NB (Tel 0952-811280) Libn: Miss T. James ALA.
6　College Governors.　**8**　Agriculture; science; economics.
10　BLL.　**11**　No.　**13**　(a) 6,000; (b) 150.　**14**　£1,675.
15　(a) 1 (c) 1.

NORTHAMPTON, Northamptonshire

BRITISH TIMKEN TECHNICAL AND COMMERCIAL INFORMATION SERVICES LIBRARY, Duston, Northampton, NN5 6UL (Tel 0604-52311; Telex 31620) Libn: W. T. Eales.
6　The Timken Company.　**8**　Bearing technology; tribology; industrial & commercial management.　**9**　National Engineering Laboratory reports; ASLE, ASME, SAE, Papers, BSI.　**10**　CADIG.　**11**　No, except with permission of company management.　**12**　8.00-16.30.　**13**　(a) 3,000; (b) 160; (c) technical indexes system (microfilm) components & material.　**15**　(a) 3.

NENE COLLEGE LIBRARY, Moulton Park, Northampton, NN2 7AL (Tel 0604-715000) Park Campus Libn: Mr David Powell BA, FLA; Avenue Campus Libn: Mr Victor H. Hatley BA, ALA.
6　Northampton CC.　**7**　Corby Annexe, Rockingham Rd, Croby (05366-9126 4521), Libn: Mrs Patricia Thomson BA.
8　Education; humanities; social sciences; pure & applied sciences; maths; religion; philosophy.　**9**　Leather technology.　**10**　BLL; EMRLS.　**11**　Yes, by application to Libns.
12　Term: Mon-Fri 9.00-20.00, Sat 9.00-12.00; vac: Mon-Fri 9.00-17.00.　**13**　(a) c. 80,000; (b) c. 350.　**14**　£35,000.

NORTHAMPTONSHIRE COLLEGE OF AGRICULTURE LIBRARY, Moulton, Northampton, NN3 1RR (Tel 0604-491131).
6　Local Authority.　**8**　Agriculture & horticulture.
11　No.　**12**　Mon-Sat 11.00-17.00.　**13**　(a) 3,000; (b) 30.
14　£400.　**15**　(a) ½.

NORTHWICH, Cheshire

MID CHESHIRE COLLEGE LIBRARY, Chester Rd, Hartford, Northwich, CW8 1LJ (Tel 0606-75281) Tutor-Libn: Mr S. Foster MIMunE, CEng; Asst Libn: Mrs M. Watson BSc, ALA.
6　Cheshire CC Education Committee.　**8**　Economics; business management.　**11**　No.　**12**　Mon-Fri 9.00-19.00 (Fri 17.00).　**13**　(a) 18,000; (b) 120; (c) 200 gramophone records.　**14**　£7,000.　**15**　(a) 3 (b) 1 (c) 1.

NORWICH, Norfolk

JOHN INNES INSTITUTE LIBRARY, Colney Lane, Norwich, NR4 7UH (Tel 0603-52571).
6　Agricultural Research Council.　**8**　Genetics; plant breeding; virology; ultrastructural studies; horticulture.
9　900 rare books on horticulture (16th-18th cent); William Bateson papers (genetics).　**10**　BLL.　**11**　Yes, by appointment only.　**12**　9.00-17.30.　**13**　(b) 210; (c) 20,000 catalogued reprints.　**14**　£10,000.　**15**　(a) 2.

KESWICK HALL COLLEGE OF EDUCATION LIBRARY, Norwich, NR4 6TL (Tel 0603-56841) Libn: Mr S. Tillyard MA, ALA.
6　Church of England Voluntary College.　**8**　Education; general.　**9**　Local colln of material on East Anglia.
11　Yes, on application, for ref only.　**12**　Term: Mon-Thurs 9.00-21.00, Fri 9.00-18.00, Sat 9.15-12.00; vac: hours vary.　**13**　(a) 48,000; (b) 200.　**14**　£8,775.
15　(a) 4½ (b) 2 (c) 2.

NORFOLK AND NORWICH LIBRARY, Guildhall Hill, Norwich, (Tel 0603-21193) Libn: Mrs Hazel Mary Bacon; Asst Libn: Mrs Phyllis Baker.
6　Honorary Committee.　**8**　Local history; general.
10　BLL; inter-library loans.　**11**　Yes, for lectures or exhibitions.　**12**　Mon-Fri 10.00-17.00 (Thurs 13.00), Sat 10.00-13.00.　**13**　(a) 37,000; (b) 20.　**15**　(a) 3.

CODE: 1 Name of Library. **2** Address. **3** Telephone & Telex. **4** Officer in charge. **5** Deputy. **6** Governing body.
7 Branches. **8** Main Subjects. **9** Special Collections. **10** Co-operative Schemes. **11** Open to public? **12** Hours.
13 Stock: (a) books (b) periodicals (c) other. **14** Finance. **15** Staff: (a) non-manual (b) graduate (c) chartered librarians.

NORWICH, Norfolk—*continued*

NORFOLK COLLEGE OF AGRICULTURE AND HORTICUL-
TURE LIBRARY, Easton, Norwich, NR9 5DX (Tel 0603-
742105) Libn: G. M. Reynolds BSc, CertEd.
6 Local authority. **8** Agriculture; horticulture.
9 Agricultural surveys & husbandry books (from c. 1700).
11 Yes, but only by previous appointment. **12** Always
open to students but not always supervised. **13** (a) 2,000;
(b) 12. **14** £400. **15** (b) ½.

NORWICH CITY COLLEGE LIBRARY, Ipswich Rd, Norwich,
NR2 2LJ (Tel 0603-60011 ext 74) Coll Libn: B. Derbyshire
ALA; Dep Coll Libn: C. Storey BA, ALA.
6 Local authority. **7** Library Resources & Careers
Centre, Media/Resources Libn: Mrs L. Webb ALA.
8 Humanities; social sciences; business management;
science; technology. **9** Business management; audio-
visual materials. **10** BLL; EMRLB; Aslib; NINES.
11 Yes, for ref. **12** Term: Mon-Fri 8.45-21.00, Sat 9.00-
12.00; vac: Mon-Fri 9.00-17.00. **13** (a) 35,000; (b) 500;
(c) 2,000 gramophone records; 2,000 other audio visual
items (tapes, slide programmes, filmstrips, videotapes).
14 £18,000. **15** (a) 10½ (b) 2 (c) 4.

UNIVERSITY OF EAST ANGLIA LIBRARY, University Plain,
Norwich, NR4 7TJ (Tel 0603-56161; Telex 97154) Univ Libn:
Mr W. L. Guttsman; Dep Libn: Miss E. Fudakowska.
8 Humanities; social sciences; pure sciences. **9** Military
history; Abbott (English literature); Ketton-Cremer (local
history). **11** Yes. **12** Mon-Fri 9.00-22.00, Sat 9.00-
17.00, Sun 14.00-19.00; vac: (normally) Mon-Fri 9.00-
18.00. **13** (c) gramophone records; microforms; audio-
visual material. **14** c. £197,000. **15** (a) 52 (b) 12 (c) 8.

NOTTINGHAM, Nottinghamshire

BOOTS COMPANY LTD, RESEARCH LIBRARY, Nottingham,
NG2 3AA (Tel 0602-56255 ext 308/9/10; Telex 37/128/9)
Chief Research Libn: Mr T. M. Smyth ALA; Dep Research
Libn: Mrs E. G. Fletcher ALA.
7 Chemical Sciences Lib, Pennyfoot St; Plant Sciences Lib,
Lenton Research Station; Animal Sciences Lib, Thurgarton
Research Station; Development Lib, Beeston; Quality Control
Lib, Beeston. **8** Medicine; biology; biochemistry;
chemistry; pharmacy; chemical engineering; agriculture;
horticulture; pharmacology; economics; management; retailing; cosmetics; food science; company archives.
10 EMRLB; NANTIS. **11** Yes, with recommendation.
12 Mon-Fri 8.30-17.00. **13** (b) over 1,200; (c) archives.
15 (a) 4 (c) 4.

HATRA LIBRARY (FORMERLY HOSIERY AND ALLIED
TRADES RESEARCH ASSOCIATION LIBRARY & LACE
RESEARCH ASSOCIATION LIBRARY), 7 Gregory Boulevard,
Nottingham, NG7 6LD (Tel 0602-63311) Librarian & Inf
Officer: J. A. Smirfitt MSc, ATI; Miss C. C. Singleton BSc,
MIInfSc.
8 Textiles, particularly knitting & lace; textile dyeing;
clothing manufacture. **9** British & foreign books on
knitting & lace manufacture; British & U.S. knitting patents;
foreign standard specifications for knitted goods.
10 NANTIS; LETIS; Aslib. **11** Yes, by appointment.
12 Mon-Fri 9.00-17.00. **13** (a) 5,000; (b) 300; (c) 10,000
patents; 500 standards specifications. **15** (a) 4 (b) 3.

NOTTINGHAM UNIVERSITY LIBRARY, Nottingham, NG7 2RD
(Tel 0602-50101) Univ Libn: Dr R. S. Smith BA, PhD, FLA;
Dep Libn Humanities: Miss D. A. Clarke BA, FLA; Dep Libn
Sciences: Mr G. L. Hayhurst BA, FLA.
7 Science Lib; Medical Lib; Law Lib; School of Agriculture
Lib, Sutton Bonington, near Loughborough, LE12 5RD
(05097-2386), Libn: Miss N. W. Rhodes BA, ALA. **8** Arts;
social sciences; education; pure & applied sciences; medicine;
agriculture. **9** Briggs Colln (early educational literature);

D. H. Lawrence; French Revolution; English drama (late 18th
& early 19th cents). **10** EMRLB; NANTIS. **11** Yes,
upon written application. **12** Term: Mon-Fri 9.00-22.00,
Sat 9.00-17.00; vac: Mon-Fri 9.00-21.00, Sat 9.00-17.00.
13 (a) 480,000; (b) 5,600; (c) 143,000 pamphlets; 87,000
microforms, tapes, films etc. **15** (a) 96 (b) 33 (c) 40.

TRENT POLYTECHNIC, Burton St, Nottingham, NG1 4BU
(Tel 0602-48248) Libn: Mr D. Daintree MA, FLA; Dep Libn:
Miss P. Footitt ALA.
6 Nottinghamshire CC. **7** Clifton Lib, Clifton, Nottingham,
NG11 8NJ (0602-211181), Libn: Mr Alan Hopkinson BA, ALA;
York House Lib, Mansfield Rd, Nottingham; Bonington Lib,
Dryden St, Nottingham; Chaucer Lib, Shakespeare St, Nottingham. **8** General (exc medicine). **10** NANTIS.
11 Yes, for ref only. **12** Term: Mon-Fri 8.45-21.00, Sat
8.45-12.00; vac: Mon-Fri 8.45-17.15. **13** (a) 130,000;
(b) 1,700; (c) slides; audio & visual tapes; films; filmstrips;
microtexts; gramophone records. **14** £140,000.
15 (a) 44½ (b) 6 (c) 18.

ORMSKIRK, Lancashire

EDGE HILL COLLEGE LIBRARY, St Helen's Rd, Ormskirk,
L39 4QP (Tel 0695-75171) Dir of Learning Resources: Mr
P. J. Pack BA, ALA.
6 Lancashire CC. **8** Education (pre-service & in-service);
English; social sciences; geography; general. **11** No.
13 (a) 85,000; (b) 400; (c) gramophone records; tapes; slides;
filmstrips; illustrations. **15** (a) 14 (b) 4 (c) 4.

OXFORD, Oxfordshire

CO-OPERATIVE REFERENCE LIBRARY, 31 St Giles, Oxford,
OX1 3LF (Tel 0865-53960/1)
6 Plunkett Foundation for Co-operative Studies. **8** All
types of co-operative activity (especially agricultural).
9 Letters & diaries of Sir Horace Plunkett (1881-1932);
Co-operative Independent Commission papers (1958).
10 Inter-library loans. **11** Yes. **12** Mon-Fri 9.00-
17.00. **13** (a) 12,000; (b) 140; (c) 12,000 pamphlets.
15 (a) 1 (b) 1.

MAISON FRANCAISE LIBRARY, Norham Rd, Oxford, OX2
6SF (Tel 0865-54576/7) Libn: Mrs C. Morris; Asst Libn:
Mrs A. Brock.
6 Ministere Des Affaires Etrangeres (Paris). **8** Arts;
literature; history; geography; politics; sociology; law;
economics; philosophy; theology; (all in French). Not sciences.
11 Yes, by subscription of 50 pence per year. **12** Mon-
Fri 10.00-13.00, 14.00-18.30, Sat 10.00-12.00. Closed Aug.
13 (a) 28,800; (b) 110; (c) 2,000 gramophone records; slides.
15 (a) 2 (b) 2 (c) 1.

MANCHESTER COLLEGE LIBRARY, Mansfield Rd, Oxford,
OX1 3TD (Tel 0865-41514/5) Principal & Libn: Rev Bruce
Findlow BA; Asst Libn: Mrs Barbara Smith BA.
6 Council of Governors. **8** Theology; comparative
religion; history of dissent. **9** Books from libraries of
dissenting academies (published before 1800); Martineau
family mss; Shepherd papers; Joseph Priestley. **10** Inter-
library loans; BUCOP. **11** Yes, on production of accredi-
tation. **12** Term: Mon-Fri 10.00-16.00; vac: Mon-Fri
10.00-13.00. **13** (a) 65,000; (b) 72. **15** (a) 2 (b) 2.

OXFORD CENTRE FOR MANAGEMENT STUDIES LIBRARY,
Kennington, Oxford, OX1 5NY (Tel 0865-735422) Libn: Mrs
K. P. Hilton MA; Dep: Mrs W. Daw.
6 Centre's Council of Management. **8** Management
studies. **11** No, except with consent of Libn, in exceptional
circumstances. **12** 9.00-17.30. **13** (a) 9,000; (b) 160;
(c) 500 UK & 100 foreign company reports & accounts; 150
cuttings files of press comment; subject catalogue of periodical articles. **14** c. £6,000. **15** (a) 2 (b) 1.

OXFORD, Oxfordshire—*continued*

OXFORD COLLEGE OF FURTHER EDUCATION LIBRARY,
Oxpens Rd, Oxford, OX1 1SA (Tel 0865-45871) Tutor-Libn:
Mr R. S. Sephton BA, FLA, LTCL; Asst Libn: Miss J. M.
Setterfield.
6 Oxfordshire County Education Committee. **7** Cowley
Rd, Oxford, OX4 1UF. **8** Business; mechanical & electrical
engineering; building; domestic subjects; English as a foreign
language; teaching in further education; general.
10 BLL. **11** Yes. **12** Term: Mon-Fri 9.00-20.00
(Fri 17.00); vac: Mon-Fri 9.00-17.00. **13** (a) 22,000;
(b) 162; (c) 900 slides; 450 filmstrips; 222 reel tapes; 40
cassettes; 400 language cassettes; 220 gramophone records;
190 wallcharts. **14** £7,200. **15** (a) 4½ (b) 1 (c) 2.

OXFORD POLYTECHNIC LIBRARY (merging with Lady
Spencer Churchill College of Education Jan 1976), Headington, Oxford, OX3 0BP (Tel 0865-64777) Libn: Mr D. L. Smith
MA, FLA; Dep: Mr G. S. Gilmour BA, ALA.
7 Lady Spencer Churchill College of Education Lib, Holton
Park, Wheatley, OX9 1HX (08677-2691), Libn: Miss J. I. Webb
ALA. **8** Architecture; planning; art; science; engineering;
social studies; management; catering; English; languages;
history; geography; education; children's books. **9** BSI.
11 Yes. **12** Term: Mon-Fri 9.00-22.00 (Fri 21.00), Sat
9.00-13.00; vac: Mon-Fri 9.00-17.00. **13** (a) 70,000;
(b) 1,000; (c) microtexts; maps; slides. **14** £75,400.
15 (a) 21 (b) 7 (c) 8.

OXFORD UNIVERSITY

BODLEIAN LIBRARY, Oxford, OX1 3BG (Tel 0865-44675;
Telex 83656) Bodley's Libn: Dr R. Shackleton MA, DLitt,
FBA, FSA, FRSL; Dep Libn: I. G. Philip MA, FSA.
6 Curators of Bodleian Library. **7** Radcliffe Science
Lib, South Parks Rd (0865-54161), Keeper of Scientific
Books & Superintendent: D. H. Boalch MA, FSA; Bodleian
Law Lib, St Cross Rd (0865-49631), Libn: E. H. Cordeaux
MA; Rhodes House Lib, South Parks Rd (0865-55762),
Libn: F. E. Leese BLitt, MA; Indian Institute Lib, New
Bodleian, Parks Rd (0865-44675 ext 245), Libn: H. J. Stooke
MA. **8** As a national copyright library, all subjects are
covered. **9** UN Deposit Library. **10** BLL; SCONUL;
MEDLARS. **11** Yes, by recommendation only.
12 Mon-Fri 9.00-22.00 (vac 19.00), Sat 9.00-13.00.
13 (a) c. 3,356,400; (b) 31,220; (c) microtexts; mss
(papyri, illuminated mss, contemporary archives & autographs). **14** c. £363,000. **15** (a) c. 250 (b) c. 78 (c)
15.

AGRICULTURAL ECONOMICS INSTITUTE LIBRARY,
Dartington House, Little Clarendon St, Oxford, OX1 2HP
(Tel 0865-52921) Libn: Miss S. F. Brown ALA.
8 Agricultural economics, history & statistics; land economics; population (with ref to food supply); regional planning; rural sociology; statistical theory & method.
9 Small colln on agriculture (1770-1870); complete agricultural statistics for Great Britain; press cuttings on
agriculture & agricultural policy (1930s); press notices of
Ministry of Agriculture (from 1940). **10** BLL.
11 Yes, by special arrangement. **12** Term: Mon-Fri
9.00-18.00; vac: Mon-Fri 9.00-13.00, 14.00-17.30.
13 (a) 16,498; (b) 756; (c) 18,000 pamphlets.
15 (a) 1½.

ASHMOLEAN LIBRARY, Oxford, OX1 2PH (Tel 0865-
57522/55768/511117) Libn: Mr Clifford Currie BCL, MA,
LLB, FLA.
6 Committee for the Ashmolean Library. **7** Bibliographical, Mr P. Bartholomew BA; Griffith Institute Lib,
Libn: Miss S. Hönigsberg MA; Heberden Coin Room Lib
& Main Lib, Libn: Mr B. McGregor MA, MPhil; Sir John
Beazley Archive, Libn: Dr D. Kurtz DPhil; Western Art
Lib, Libn: Miss M. Miller MA. **8** Archaeology; Egyptology; papyrology; ancient Near Eastern studies; classical
languages & literature; ancient history; patristics & Byzantine studies; numismatics; Western art & architecture.
9 Important notes, diaries & personal collns: Sir Arthur
Evans (Knossos etc), Howard Carter (tomb of Tut'an-
khamun); F. J. Haverfield & Sir Ian Richmond (Roman

British papers); A. H. Sayce, Sir Alan Gardiner, F. L.
Griffith, Nina & Norman de Garis Davies, Sir John Beazley;
Grenfell & Hunt papyrological library. **11** No.
12 Mon-Fri 9.00-21.00 (vac 17.00), Sat 9.00-13.00.
Branches vary. **13** (a) c. 200,000 (inc archival mater-
ial); (b) 1,208. **14** £26,572. **15** (a) 21 (b) 19 (c) 1.

BOTANY SCHOOL LIBRARY, South Parks Rd, Oxford,
OX1 3RA (Tel 0865-53391) Libn: Mrs H. J. McArdle.
8 Biochemistry; physiology; genetics; cytology; ecology;
morphology; taxonomy. **9** Sherard colln (printed books
& mss). **10** Union List of Serials in the Science Area,
University of Oxford. **11** No. **12** Term: 9.00-19.00;
vac: 9.00-17.15. **13** (a) 26,600; (b) 281; (c) colln of
Druce mss. **15** (a) 1.

COMMONWEALTH STUDIES INSTITUTE LIBRARY, 21 St
Giles, Oxford, OX1 3LA (Tel 0865-52952/4) Libn: Mr R. J.
Townsend.
6 Committee for Commonwealth Studies. **8** Political,
economic & social development of developing countries.
9 Poetry, plays, short stories & novels of Afro-Carrib-
bean authors; press clippings. **10** Oxford Univ Modern
Middle-Eastern Studies Committee (for North African
material). **11** Yes, for loans only. **12** Term: Mon-
Fri 9.00-13.00, 14.00-19.00, Sat 9.00-12.30; vac: Mon-
Fri 9.00-13.00, 14.00-17.00. **13** (a) c. 10,000; (b)
c. 325; (c) c. 18,000 pamphlets & reports. **15** (a) 2.

ECONOMICS AND STATISTICS (INSTITUTE OF)
LIBRARY, St Cross Building, Manor Rd, Oxford (Tel 0865-
49631).
8 Economics & statistics. **11** No.

EDUCATIONAL STUDIES DEPARTMENT LIBRARY, 15
Norham Gardens, Oxford, OX2 6PY (Tel 0865-54121)
Libn: Miss G. M. Ledger BA, FLA; Lib Asst: Mrs B. E.
Savage.
8 Education; psychology; sociology. **9** Government
publications (pre-1918); school textbooks (until 1968).
10 BLL; LISE. **11** Yes, for ref only. **12** Term: 9.00-
19.00; vac: 9.30-18.00. **13** (a) 25,000; (b) 200; (c)
microtexts. **14** £5,000. **15** (a) 2 (b) 1 (c) 1.

ENGINEERING SCIENCE DEPARTMENT LIBRARY, Parks
Rd, Oxford, OX1 3PJ (Tel 0865-59988) Libn: Mrs E. Rose.
8 Engineering science. **11** Yes, on request to Libn.
12 9.00-17.00. **13** (a) 12,000; (b) 100. **15** (a) 1 (c) 1.

ENGLISH FACULTY LIBRARY, St Cross Building, Manor
Rd, Oxford, OX1 3UQ (Tel 0865-49631 ext 268) Libn: Miss
M. J. P. Weedon BA, MA, DipLib; Dep: Miss E. C. Davies MA,
FLA.
6 Standing Committee of English Faculty Board.
8 English language & literature of all periods; bibliography; old Icelandic. **9** F. York Powell colln (old
Icelandic books on loan from Christ Church); E. H. W.
Meyerstein's published works & mss; Wilfred Owen's
personal library & some mss & relics. **11** No.
12 Full term: Mon-Fri 9.30-19.00, Sat 9.30-12.30; vac:
Mon-Fri 9.30-13.00, 14.00-16.00. **13** (a) c. 55,000
(inc pamphlets); (b) c. 150; (c) c. 600 gramophone records.
15 (a) 3 (b) 3 (c) 2.

ETHNOLOGY AND PREHISTORY DEPARTMENT,
BALFOUR LIBRARY, Pitt Rivers Museum, Parks Rd,
Oxford, OX1 3PP (Tel 0865-54979) Libn: Mr H. P. G.
Unsworth; Admin Sec: Miss E. Torr.
8 Ethnology; archaeology; anthropology; non-industrialized
technologies of ancient & modern simpler societies;
religion; travel; music; art. **9** Mss collns (mainly
ethnological papers & correspondence) of Henry Balfour,
Sir Edward Burnett Tylor, Sir Francis Knowles & Sir
Baldwin Spencer. **11** No. **12** Mon-Fri 9.00-12.30,
14.00-17.00 (vac 16.00). **13** (a) 9,500; (b) 250.
14 £2,500. **15** (a) 1½.

EXTERNAL STUDIES DEPARTMENT LIBRARY, Rewley
House, 3-7 Wellington Sq, Oxford, OX1 2JA (Tel 0865-
52901) Libn: A. J. Trump BA.
8 Archaeology; art; literature; music; economics; history;
philosophy; politics. **11** No. **13** (a) 167,000; (b) 127;
(c) archives (from 1885). **15** (a) 2 (b) 1.

CODE: 1 Name of Library. 2 Address. 3 Telephone & Telex. 4 Officer in charge. 5 Deputy. 6 Governing body.
7 Branches. 8 Main Subjects. 9 Special Collections. 10 Co-operative Schemes. 11 Open to public? 12 Hours.
13 Stock: (a) books (b) periodicals (c) other. 14 Finance. 15 Staff: (a) non-manual (b) graduate (c) chartered librarians.

OXFORD UNIVERSITY—*continued*

FORESTRY LIBRARY, Commonwealth Forestry Institute,
South Parks Rd, Oxford, OX1 3RB (Tel 0865-57891) Libn:
E. F. Hemmings; Dep: Miss J. S. Howse ALA.
8 Forestry; plant science & related subjects. 9 World
coverage, chief forestry library of the Commonwealth.
10 SCOLMA. 11 No. 12 Term: Mon-Fri 9.00-
19.00, Sat 9.00-12.00; vac: Mon-Fri 9.00-13.00, 14.15-
17.00. 13 (a) 14,000; (b) 800; (c) c. $\frac{1}{3}$ of library
material is on 3,000 boxes of 35mm microfilm. 15 (a)
4 (c) 1.

GEOGRAPHY (SCHOOL OF) LIBRARY, Mansfield Rd,
Oxford, OX1 3TB (Tel 0865-46134) Libn & Map Curator:
Miss E. M. Buxton MA, FLA; Asst Libn: Miss C. M. Gidley
BA, ALA.
8 Geography & related subjects. 10 BLL. 11 No.
12 Full term: Mon-Fri 9.00-13.00, 14.15-19.00, Sat
9.00-13.00; vac: Mon-Fri 9.00-13.00, 14.30-17.00.
13 (a) over 55,000 (inc govt publications & pamphlets);
(b) 210; (c) over 49,000 maps; microfilms; microfiche.
15 (a) 4 (b) 3 (c) 2.

HISTORY FACULTY LIBRARY, Merton St, Oxford, OX1 4JG
(Tel 0865-43395) Libn: Miss M. A. Abley.
6 Board of Faculty of Modern History. 8 Medieval &
modern history. 9 Main printed sources for English
medieval history; copies of all set texts for history
schools. 11 No. 12 Hours vary. 13 (a) c. 31,000;
(b) c. 80. 15 (a) 3 (b) 2 (c) 2.

MODERN LANGUAGES FACULTY LIBRARY, Taylor
Institution, Oxford, OX1 3NA (Tel 0865-56303) Libn: Mr
G. L. Robson MA, DipLib, ALA.
7 Slavonic Section: Taylor Institution Annexe, 67 St Giles,
Oxford, Libn: Mr D. L. Howells MA; Spanish & Portuguese
Section: Taylor Institution Annexe, 65 St Giles, Oxford,
Libn: Mr A. Seldon. 8 Medieval & modern European
languages (exc English) & their literatures (mainly
French, German, Italian, Russian, Spanish & Portuguese).
9 European newspapers & weeklies. 10 SCONUL.
11 No. 12 Full term: Mon-Fri 9.00-18.00, Sat 9.00-
13.00; vac: Mon-Fri 9.00-13.00, 14.00-17.00. Branches
vary. 13 (a) 51,000; (b) 40. 14 £9,000. 15 (a) 4½
(b) 3½ (c) 1.

MUSEUM OF THE HISTORY OF SCIENCE LIBRARY,
Broad St, Oxford, OX1 3AZ (Tel 0865-43997) Libn: Dr
J. D. North; Dep: Mrs Anne Prince.
8 Historic scientific instruments. 9 Lewis Evans
colln (books & mss on scientific instruments); several
mss collns on cognate subjects; Gunther loan colln of
printed books. 10 Inter-library loans. 11 Yes, by
prior application to Curator. 12 Mon-Fri 10.30-13.00,
14.30-17.00. 13 (a) c. 8,600; (b) 32; (c) microfilms;
early recorded cylinders; 439 mss. 14 £650.

MUSIC FACULTY LIBRARY, 32 Holywell, Oxford, OX1
3SL (Tel 0865-47069) Libn: Mrs V. M. Elliott-Leach
MusB.
8 Music (textbooks & scores; especially Byzantine &
Mediaeval). 10 Inter-library loans. 11 Yes, for ref
only. 12 Term: Mon-Fri 9.30-13.00, 14.00-17.30, Sat
10.00-13.00; vac: Mon-Fri 10.00-13.00, 14.00-16.30.
13 (a) 16,400; (b) 52; (c) c. 5,000 gramophone records.
14 £4,416. 15 (a) 3 (b) 3.

ORIENTAL INSTITUTE LIBRARY, Pusey Lane, Oxford,
OX1 2LE (Tel 0865-59272) Libn: Mr A. D. Hyder MA;
Asst Libn: Mr M. J. Minty MA, ALA.
8 Jewish, Islamic, South Asian, Chinese & Japanese
Studies. 9 Dept of Eastern Art Library (Ashmolean
Museum) is administered by Oriental Institute Library.
10 Union Catalogue of Asian Periodicals; Union Catalogue

of modern Middle Eastern material (for Oxford libraries
only); JLG joint acquisition scheme. 11 Yes, at Libn's
discretion. 12 Term: Mon-Fri 9.15-21.00, Sat 9.15-
17.00; vac: Mon-Sat 9.15-13.00 (closed Sats in long vac);
Eastern Art Lib: Mon-Fri 10.00-13.00, 14.00-16.00, Sat
10.00-12.30. 13 (a) 60,000; (b) 225; (c) 150 rolls microfilm; 300 reels tape. 15 (a) 5 (b) 2 (c) 1.

PUSEY HOUSE LIBRARY, St Giles, Oxford, OX1 3LZ
(Tel 0865-59519) Custodian of Lib: Rev Dr K. W. Noakes.
8 Theology; philosophy; church history. 9 Pamphlets
& mss (19th cent especially Oxford movement). 11 Yes,
on written application to Custodian. 12 Full term:
9.00-22.00; vac 9.00-19.00. 13 (a) 45,000; (b) 50.

SOCIAL STUDIES LIBRARY, 45 Wellington Sq, Oxford,
OX1 2JF (Tel 0865-55935) Libn: Mr Derek Day MA, ALA.
8 Economics; economic history; politics; sociology; social
work; philosophy; social psychology. 11 No. 12 Full
term: Mon-Fri 9.30-18.30, Sat 9.30-13.00; rest of year:
Mon-Fri 10.00-12.30, 14.00-17.00. 13 (a) 37,000;
(b) 72; (c) Oxford BPhil theses in social sciences.
14 £7,000. 15 (a) 4 (b) 4 (c) 3.

TAYLOR INSTITUTION LIBRARY, St Giles, Oxford, OX1
3NA (Tel 0865-57917) Libn: Giles G. Barber BLitt, MA,
FSA.
6 Curators of the Taylor Institution. 8 Languages &
literatures of modern continental Europe. 9 Finch
colln (early editions of principal European writers);
Fiedler colln (German literary philological & historical
works); Dante colln (formed by Canon Edward Moore);
Martin & Butler Clarke collns (Spanish & Portuguese);
Morfill & Nevill Forbes collns (Slavonic); W. P. Ker colln
(Icelandic & Scandinavian); Afrikaans, Basque & Albanian
collns; colln of Lutheran tracts & pamphlets; Voltaire &
major 18th cent French authors. 11 No, except with
written permission of Curators. 12 1 Oct-30 June:
Mon-Fri 9.00-19.00, Sat 9.00-13.00; 1 July-30 Sept: Mon-
Fri 10.00-13.00, 14.00-17.00, Sat 10.00-13.00. 13 (a)
260,713; (b) 740; (c) microfilms; facsimiles; mss & autograph material.

THEOLOGY FACULTY LIBRARY, Pusey House, St Giles,
Oxford, OX1 3LZ (Tel 0865-57117) Hon Libn: Rev P. W.
Bide; Lib Asst: Miss J. Sheldon-Williams.
8 Theology; philosophy; history; ethics. 9 Corpus
Christianorum (all series); Luther's complete works
(Philadelphia). 11 No. 12 Term: Mon-Sat 9.00-
22.00; vac: Mon-Sat 9.00-19.00. 13 (a) 9,000; (b) 20.
15 (a) 1 (b) 1.

ZOOLOGY DEPARTMENT, ALEXANDER LIBRARY,
EDWARD GREY INSTITUTE OF FIELD ORNITHOLOGY,
South Parks Rd, Oxford, OX1 3PS (Tel 0865-56789 ext 299)
Libn: Miss D. F. Vincent BA, ALA.
8 Ornithology. 11 Yes, by arrangement. 12 Mon-
Fri 9.00-13.00, 14.15-17.30. 13 (a) 7,500; (b) 320;
(c) 750 boxes of reprints; theses of members of Institute;
mss, field notes, diaries (many by distinguished ornithol-
ogists). 14 £700. 15 (a) 1 (b) 1 (c) 1.

Oxford University Colleges

ALL SOULS COLLEGE, CODRINGTON LIBRARY, Oxford,
OX1 4AL (Tel 0865-22251) Libn: Mr J. S. G. Simmons
MBE, MA, FLA; Dep: Mr B. J. T. Britton MA.
8 History & law; political science. 9 Military history;
'Letters of Junius'; peerage cases 11 No. 12 Mon-
Fri 9.30-18.30 (vac 16.30), Sat 9.30-12.30 (closed Aug &
Sept). 13 (a) 120,000; (b) 271; (c) college archives;
microfilms. 14 £8,000. 15 (a) 3 (b) 2 (c) 1.

BALLIOL COLLEGE LIBRARY, Oxford, OX1 3BJ (Tel
0865-49601) Libn: Mr E. V. Quinn MA.
6 Master & Fellows. 8 General. 9 Mss colln (printed

OXFORD, UNIVERSITY—*continued*

catalogue); early printed books.   **11** No, but scholars may examine particular material by appointment. **13** (a) 70,000; (b) c. 85.

BLACKFRIARS LIBRARY, St Giles, Oxford, OX1 3LY (Tel 0865 57607) Libn: Rev Osmund Lewry OP, STL; Asst Libn: Rev Robert Ombres OP, LLB, LLM.
6 English Dominican Studium.   **8** Scripture; theology; church history; philosophy.   **9** Early printed editions of Dominican authors; works by Walter Pater, François Mauriac, etc, from library of André Raffalovich; St Dominic's Press, Ditchling, Sussex; private presses; William Beckford; autograph letters of George Tyrell SJ. **10** Inter-library loans.   **11** Yes.   **12** Mon-Fri 9.00-18.00.   **13** (a) 24,000; (b) 110; (c) 1 papyrus; 5 mss; cuneiform tablets.   **14** £1,200.   **15** (b) 2.

CAMPION HALL LIBRARY, Oxford, OX1 1QS (Tel 0865-40861) Lib Fellow: Mr V. Bywater.
8 General.   **9** None—no Gerard Manley Hopkins mss. **11** No.   **13** (a) c. 20,000.   **15** (a) ½ (b) 1.

CHRIST CHURCH LIBRARY, Oxford, OX1 1DP (Tel 0865-43957) Libn: Dr J. F. A. Mason MA, DPhil, FSA, FRHistS; Asst Libn: Mr H. J. R. Wing MA, ALA.
8 General; classics; history; philosophy; politics; economics; geography; English language & literature; French; German; Spanish; maths; natural science.   **9** Theology & patristics (16th-18th cent); music (printed & ms, 16th-17th cent); pamphlets (17th-18th cent).   **10** BLL. **11** No.   **13** (a) c. 110,000; (b) 160.   **15** (a) 3 (b) 2 (c) 1.

CORPUS CHRISTI COLLEGE LIBRARY, Merton St, Oxford, OX1 4JF (Tel 0865-49431) Libn: T. H. Aston MA; Asst Libn: Dr D. G. Cooper.
8 General; classical languages & literature; philosophy; history; English language & literature.   **9** Incunabula (258); early printed books (STC 1,931); Coleraine colln (16th-18th cent Italian books); mss (565).   **11** No. **13** (a) c. 55,000; (b) c. 150.   **15** (a) 2½ (b) 2 (c) 1.

EXETER COLLEGE LIBRARY, Oxford, OX1 3DP (Tel 0865-44681) Libn & Archivist: Dr J. R. Maddicott MA, DPhil; Dep Miss A. V. Greasley BA
6 Rector & Fellows.   **8** History; law; English literature; French; German; classics; theology; physics; chemistry; maths; biological sciences.   **9** Medieval & later mss; early printed books.   **11** No, except scholars, on written application to Libn.   **12** 9.00-17.00.   **13** (a) c. 70,000; (b) c. 90.   **15** (a) 1 (b) 1.

JESUS COLLEGE LIBRARY, Oxford, OX1 3DW (Tel 0865-49511) Libn: Dr A. E. Pilkington MA, DPhil; Sub-Libn: Mrs H. Carr ALA.
8 General.   **9** Celtic colln; 16th-18th cent colln housed in the Fellows' Library.   **10** BLL.   **11** No, except by special arrangement.   **12** Term: 8.00-24.00; vac: limited hours.   **13** (a) 13,000; (b) 70; (c) mss in Fellows Library.   **14** £3,000   **15** (a) 1 (c) 1.

KEBLE COLLEGE LIBRARY, Oxford, OX1 3PG (Tel 0865-511904).
8 Classics; theology; liturgy; sciences; general.   **9** Port-Royal; 80 medieval & 98 incunabula; Brooke, Millard, & Hatchett-Jackson collns; Keble & Liddon archive material. **11** No.   **13** (a) c. 60,000; (b) 90; (c) some gramophone records of Chaucer & mediaeval material.   **15** (a) 1.

LINCOLN COLLEGE LIBRARY, Oxford, OX1 3DR. Fellow Libn: N. Wilson MA; Asst Libn: Mrs J. Wynne.
8 General.   **9** Old books; incunabula, mss.   **11** No, except individuals on application.   **12** Term: 8.00-23.30; vac: 9.00-22.00.   **13** (a) c. 26,000; (b) c. 70. **14** c. £4,500.   **15** (a) 1.

MAGDALEN COLLEGE LIBRARY, High St, Oxford, OX1 4AU (Tel 0865-41781 ext 67) Libn: Dr G. L. Harriss PhD; Dep Libn: Mr F. W. J. Scovil MA, ALA.
6 President & Fellows.   **8** All academic subjects except geography & geology.   **9** Gerrans mathematical library; McFarlane medieval colln.   **11** No.   **13** (a)

c. 85,000; (b) 171; (c) archives (college estates & accounts). **14** £5,700.   **15** (a) 2 (c) 1.

MANSFIELD COLLEGE LIBRARY, Oxford, OX1 3TF (Tel 0865-43507) Libn: Rev G.W.Trowell MSc; Dep: Mrs V.Brown.
6 Council.   **8** Theology.   **11** Yes, if introduced; prior application desirable.   **12** Term: 24 hours a day (staffed only 9.30-14.00).   **13** (a) 12,500; (b) 25. **14** c. £1,200.   **15** (a) ⅔ (b) ⅓

MERTON COLLEGE LIBRARY, Oxford, OX1 4JD (Tel 0865-49651) Libn: R. Highfield; Asst Libn: J. Burgass ALA.
8 General.   **11** No.   **12** Hours vary.   **13** c. 40,000. **15** (a) 2 (b) 2 (c) 1.

NEW COLLEGE LIBRARY, Oxford, OX1 3BN (Tel 0865-48451 ext 270) Libn: Dr G. V. Bennett MA, DPhil; Asst Libn: Mrs Sandra J. K. M. Feneley BEd.
6 Warden & Fellows.   **8** History; classics; law; English; philosophy; modern languages; maths; biochemistry; physiology; chemistry; economics; engineering; music; physics; psychology; politics; theology; zoology.   **9** mss & Alfred Milner papers (on deposit in Bodleian Library); Sydney Smith letters.   **11** No, except by written application to Libn, at least 1 week in advance.   **12** 9.00-13.00, 14.15-17.15.   **13** (a) 70,000; (b) 120; (c) archives (printed catalogue; inquiries to F. W. Steer, Consultant Archivist).   **15** (a) 1 (b) 2.

NUFFIELD COLLEGE LIBRARY, Oxford, OX1 1NF (Tel 0865-48014) Fellow Libn: Dr R. M. Hartwell MA, DPhil.
8 Social sciences.   **9** Cobbett mss; cherwell papers; modern political papers.   **11** No, except to suitably accredited researchers.   **12** Mon-Fri 9.30-13.00, 14.00-18.00, Sat 9.30-13.00 (exc Aug).   **13** (a) 50,000; (b) 1,158; (c) mss; archives.

ORIEL COLLEGE LIBRARY, Oxford, OX1 4EW (Tel 0865-21752) Coll Libn: Dr W. E. Parry, MA, DPhil; Asst Libn: Miss J. Macdonald.
6 Provost & Fellows.   **8** General.   **9** Lord Leigh's Library (18th century gentleman's library); parts of medieval college library; works & letters of college members (Newman, Kibb, Hawkins etc).   **11** No, except for individuals by special arrangement.   **12** 9.00-17.00. **13** (a) 50,000; (b) 60; (c) 1,000 letters.   **14** £6,000. **15** (a) 1⅔ (b) 1⅔.

PEMBROKE COLLEGE LIBRARY, Oxford, OX1 1DW (Tel 0865-42271) Libn: Dr J. D. Fleeman; Asst Libn: Mrs J. K. Cordy MA.
8 General.   **9** Chandler colln (Aristotelia & other philosophy).   **11** No, but scholars may see particular items by arrangement.   **12** Term: 9.00-midnight; vac: shorter hours.   **13** (a) c. 30,000; (b) c. 60; (c) college archives. **14** £3,000.   **15** (a) 1 (b) 1.

QUEEN'S COLLEGE LIBRARY, Oxford, OX1 4AW (Tel 0865-48411) Asst Libn: Miss H. Powell BLitt, MA.
8 Classics; philosophy; history (ancient & modern); politics; economics; law; maths; chemistry; physics; physiology; psychology; theology; topography; language & literature (English, French, German, Spanish & Russian). **9** American history; Egyptology; substantial antiquarian holdings.   **10** BLL.   **11** No.   **12** Term: Mon-Fri 9.30-13.00, 14.00-22.00, Sat 9.30-13.00; vac: 9.30-13.00, 14.30-17.00, Sat 9.30-13.00.   **13** (a) c. 130,000; (b) 132; (c) 545 mss.   **15** (a) 3 (b) 2.

REGENT'S PARK COLLEGE LIBRARY, Pusey St, Oxford, OX1 2LB (Tel 0865-59887) Libn: Rev P. S. Fiddes MA; Student Libn: Mr R. J. Draycott BA.
8 Theology (biblical studies, Christian doctrine, church history, Puritanism).   **9** Angus Library colln (17th-20th cent Baptist writings), finest colln in this country, inc important mss.   **11** No, except with Libn's direct permission.   **12** 9.00-16.00.   **13** (a) 20,000; (b) 12. **14** £1,400.   **15** (b) 1.

ST ANNE'S COLLEGE LIBRARY, Oxford, OX2 6HS (Tel 0865-57417) Libn: Mrs A. K. Swift BA, ALA, MLS; Asst Libn: Mrs E. M. E. Wood MA.
7 Geldart Law Library.   **8** Psychology; philosophy;

CODE: **1** Name of Library. **2** Address. **3** Telephone & Telex. **4** Officer in charge. **5** Deputy. **6** Governing body.
7 Branches. **8** Main Subjects. **9** Special Collections. **10** Co-operative Schemes. **11** Open to public? **12** Hours.
13 Stock: (a) books (b) periodicals (c) other. **14** Finance. **15** Staff: (a) non-manual (b) graduate (c) chartered librarians.

OXFORD UNIVERSITY—*continued*

politics; economics; maths; natural sciences; medicine; art; classics; history; modern languages; English literature; law. **9** Bibliography & typography (bequest 1974, by Miss P. M. Handover). **11** No. **12** Term: 24 hours a day; vac: 9.00-midnight. **13** (a) 50,000; (b) 90; (c) college archives. **14** £6,500. **15** (a) 2 (b) 2 (c) 1.

ST ANTONY'S COLLEGE LIBRARY, Woodstock Rd, Oxford, OX2 6JF (Tel 0865-59651) Libn: Miss M. Kendall MA, ALA.
7 Middle East Centre Lib, 137 Banbury Rd, (0865-59896), Bibliographer: Dr D. Hopwood MA, DPhil. **8** Modern European history. **9** Russian colln; Far East colln; Latin American colln. **11** No. **13** (a) 70,000; (b) 424; (c) microfilms. **15** (a) 4 (b) 3 (c) 2.

ST EDMUND HALL LIBRARY, Queen's Lane, Oxford, OX1 4AR (Tel 0865-45511) Fellow Libn: Mr C. J. Wells MA; Libn: Mrs S. E. Wernberg-Møller MA.
6 Principal & Fellows. **8** General. **9** Aularian colln (books & articles written by past & present members of college). **11** No. **12** Term: 8.00-23.45; vac: as required. **13** (a) c.25,000; (b) 80; (c) college archives. **14** £5,000. **15** (a) 1 (b) 1.

ST HILDA'S COLLEGE LIBRARY, Oxford, OX4 1DY (Tel 0865-41821) Libn: Mrs G. I. Hampshire MA, BLit.
8 General. **11** No. **12** 24 hours a day. **13** (a) c.35,000; (b) 63; (c) college archives. **15** (a) 2½ (b) 1.

ST HUGH'S COLLEGE LIBRARY, St Margaret's Rd, Oxford, OX2 6LE (Tel 0865-5734) Fellow & Tutor-Libn: Dr J. G. Russell MA, DPhil, FRHistS; Dep: Mrs H. Edbury MA, ALA.
8 General. **9** Oxford movement colln; French & Italian literature & history; ornithology & natural history; some early printed books. **10** BLL; inter-library loans.
11 No, individual inquiries dealt with at discretion.
12 Term: all day; vac: by arrangement. **13** (a) c.42,000; (b) c.60. **15** (a) 1½ (b) 2 (c) 1.

ST JOHN'S COLLEGE LIBRARY, Oxford, OX1 3JP (Tel 0865-47671) Libn: H. M. Colvin; Asst Libn: Mr C. Morgenstern.
8 General. **9** A. E. Housman colln (his classical texts, many annotated by him); early science, especially medicine. **11** No, except by appointment for bona-fide researchers. **12** Term: 9.00-23.00, Sun 10.00-23.00; vac: hours vary. **13** (a) 100,000; (b) c.120; (c) college muniments (large colln, card-indexed). **15** (a) 3 (b) 1.

SOMERVILLE COLLEGE LIBRARY, Oxford, OX2 6HD (Tel 0865-57595 ext 35) Libn: Miss P. A. Adams BA, DipLibInfSt; Senior Asst Libn: Mrs C. Kirwan BA, DipLibInfSt.
8 English; history; classics; modern languages; philosophy; physical & biological sciences; maths; economics; politics; law; theology. **9** Library of J. S. Mill; Library of Amelia B. Edwards (exc Egyptological material, but inc letters, papers, mss & drawings). **11** No, except for properly accredited researchers. **12** College hours. **13** (a) 80,000; (b) 65. **14** £5,000. **15** (a) 2 (b) 3.

UNIVERSITY COLLEGE LIBRARY, Oxford, OX1 4BH (Tel 0865-41661) Libn: Dr Roy Park MA, PhD; Dep: Miss A. M. Cowles ALA.
8 Arts; sciences; law. **9** Attlee papers (41 boxes miscellaneous material, 1939-1951. **11** No. **12** 8.15-midnight. **13** (a) c.24,000; (b) 101. **14** £5,500. **15** (a) 1½ (c) 1.

WADHAM COLLEGE LIBRARY, Oxford, OX1 3PN (Tel 0865-42564) Libn: Mr R. S. Dawson MA.
6 Warden, Fellows & Scholars. **8** General. **9** Bisse colln (16th cent theology); Wiffen colln (16th cent Spanish

Protestant theology); Godolphin colln (17th cent Spanish).
11 No, except for academic research, with advance notice. **15** (a) 1.

WESTMINSTER COLLEGE LIBRARY, North Hinksey, Oxford, OX2 9AT (Tel 0865-47644) Tutor-Libn: E. J. C. Sackett MA, DipEd, ALA; Dep: J. Warmington MA, ALA.
6 Methodist Education Committee (Committee for Education & Youth). **8** Drama; French; geography; history; maths; music; sciences; English; religion; education; art; physical education; children's books; teachers books.
11 No. **13** (a) 60,000; (b) 200; (c) 2,600 pictures; 4,000 slides; 1,000 filmstrips; 400 gramophone records; 100 sound tapes; 160 microfilms; 36 filmloops. **14** £9,000. **15** (a) 4½ (b) 2½ (c) 2.

WORCESTER COLLEGE LIBRARY, Oxford, OX1 2HB (Tel 0865-47251) Libn: R. A. Sayce; Dep: Miss L. Montgomery MA.
8 General; literature; history; architecture. **9** Clarke colln (Civil War documents & pamphlets); English poetry & drama; architectural books & drawings; Pottinger colln (19th cent pamphlets). **11** Yes, on application by serious students only. **12** By arrangement.
13 (a) 80,000.

OXFORD UNIVERSITY PRESS LIBRARIES, The University Press, 1 Walton St, Oxford, OX2 6AB (Tel 0865-57565).
6 Delegates to the University Press, Oxford. **8** Typography; printing technology; English Bibles; Oxford printed books. **9** Typographical museum. **11** No. **15** (a) 1¼ (b) ¼.

RUSKIN COLLEGE LIBRARY, Oxford, OX1 2HE (Tel 0865-54331) Libn: Mr D. F. M. Horsfield MA.
8 Social sciences; history; industrial relations; literature.
9 Abe Lazarus Memorial library & archive (history of labour movement in 20th cent, particularly 1930-1950).
11 No, except researchers on written application to Libn.
12 Term: Mon-Fri 9.00-13.00, 14.00-17.00; vac: by arrangement. **13** (a) 15,000; (b) 100; (c) 3,000 pamphlets.
14 £4,350. **15** (a) 2 (b) 1.

PAISLEY, Renfrewshire

PAISLEY COLLEGE LIBRARY, High St, Paisley, PA1 2BE (Tel 041-887 1241; Telex 778951) Head Libn: Mr Hamish C. Maclachlan MA, FLA.
6 College Governors. **8** Social sciences; natural sciences; mechanical, electrical, civil & chemical engineering; management; computing. **9** Land economics (especially Scotland); BSI; Scottish Railway plans & documents.
11 Yes, by application to Libn. **12** Term: Mon-Fri 9.10-20.50, Sat 9.30-12.30; vac: Mon-Fri 9.10-16.50.
13 (a) 58,000; (b) 1,108; (c) 250 gramophone records; 500 accessioned microforms plus c.2,500 unaccessioned.
14 £65,000. **15** (a) 19 (b) 5 (c) 5.

PERSHORE, Hereford & Worcester

PERSHORE COLLEGE OF HORTICULTURE LIBRARY, Pershore, WR10 3JP (Tel 038-65 2227) Coll Libn: Mrs D. B. Paynter ALA.
6 Local Authority Education Dept. **8** Horticulture; pollution; landscaping; botany; beekeeping. **9** Annual reports of horticultural research stations; Soil Survey records & maps; all horticultural journals of note.
10 WATL; WESLINK; GTIS. **11** Yes, by appointment.
12 Term: Mon-Fri 9.00-21.00; vac: Mon-Fri 9.00-17.00; weekends by arrangement. **13** (a) 3,700; (b) 45; (c) ministry publications, all MAFF leaflets & bulletins; 60 soil maps. **14** £1,000. **15** (c) 1.

PERTH, Perthshire

PERTH ACADEMY, LADY MACKENZIE LIBRARY, Murray
Pl, Perth (Tel 0738-23491) Principal, Library & Careers: Mr
Frank J. Russell MA; Dep: Mrs McCorkindale ALA.
6 Perth/Tayside Regional Council.   **9** Some very early
school texts & bound exercises (from 1777); copies of
Mairs Arithmetic, first edition; early books on Perth & area.
11 No.   **12** Mon-Fri 9.00-15.30.   **13** (a) 6,653; (b) 14;
14 £400.   **15** (a) 2 (b) 1 (c) 1.

PETERBOROUGH, Cambridgeshire

PETERBOROUGH TECHNICAL COLLEGE LIBRARY, Park
Crescent, Peterborough, PE1 4DZ (Tel 0733-67366) Tutor-
Libn: B. P. Engler BA, FLA:CertEd; Dep: Mrs C. Rowat ALA.
6 Cambridgeshire CC.   **8** Technology; science; social
sciences; humanities.   **11** No.   **12** Term: Mon-Thurs
8.45-19.15, Fri 9.00-17.00; vac: Mon-Fri 9.00-17.00.
13 (a) 28,000; (b) 350.   **14** £7,500.   **15** (a) 5 (b) 2 (c) 2.

PETERLEE, Co. Durham

EASINGTON TECHNICAL COLLEGE LIBRARY, Peterlee,
SR8 1NU (Tel 078-323 2225) Libn: Mrs H. Yeaman ALA.
6 Durham CC.   **8** Engineering; coal-mining; business.
11 Yes, for ref only.   **12** Term: Mon-Fri 9.00-18.45 (Fri
16.15); vac: Mon-Fri 9.00-16.15.   **13** (a) 9,015; (b) 44.
15 (a) 2 (c) 1.

PLYMOUTH, Devon

COLLEGE OF ST MARK AND ST JOHN LIBRARY, Derriford
Rd, Plymouth, PL6 8BH (Tel 0752-777188) Libn: Miss Mary
Strutt ALA; Dep Libn: Lindesay Burton BA, ALA.
6 Council of Management.   **8** Education; history of
education.   **10** BLL.   **11** Yes, for ref only.   **12** Term:
Mon-Fri 9.00-20.00 (Fri 17.00), Sat 9.30-12.30; vac: Mon-
Fri 9.00-17.00.   **13** (a) 62,000; (b) 540; (c) 3,000 non-book
items.   **14** £10,000.

MARINE BIOLOGICAL ASSOCIATION OF THE UNITED
KINGDOM LIBRARY, Citadel Hill, Plymouth, PL1 2PB
(Tel 0752-21761) Libn: Mr Allen Varley FLA.
8 Marine biology; oceanography; fisheries.   **9** Marine
Pollution Information Centre.   **11** No, open to research
scientists only.   **12** Mon-Fri 9.00-13.00, 14.15-17.15.
13 (a) 60,000; (b) 1,500; (c) archives; films; charts;
microfiche; slides.   **15** (a) 7½ (b) 3 (c) 1.

PLYMOUTH COLLEGE OF ART AND DESIGN LIBRARY,
Tavistock Pl, Plymouth, PL4 8AT (Tel 0752-68000 ext 3066)
Coll Libn: Mrs E. Lee; Asst Coll Libn: Mrs A. Billman BA.
6 Devon County Education Authority.   **8** Education;
fashion; fine art; graphic design; literature; painting &
decorating; photography; printing, sociology; three-dimensional
design.   **11** Yes, for ref, by appointment only.   **12** Term:
Mon-Fri 9.00-18.30 (Fri 17.00).   **13** (a) 1,200; (b) 100;
(c) 80 gramophone records; 13,000 art slides; 2,000 mounted
illustrations.   **15** (a) 2 (b) 1.

PLYMOUTH POLYTECHNIC LEARNING RESOURCES
CENTRE, Drake Circus, Plymouth, PL4 8AA (Tel 0752-
21312 ext 219; Telex 45423) Head of Learning Resources
Centre: Miss M. Lattimore MA, FLA; Dep: Mr R. Oldroyd
BA, DipLib.
8 Architecture; behavioural sciences; management &
business; maths; physical sciences; geosciences; biosciences;
maritime studies; electrical, communications & civil
engineering.   **10** Inter-library loans.   **11** Yes, on
written application, for ref only.   **12** Term: Mon-Fri
8.30-21.00, Sat 8.30-12.00; vac: Mon-Fri 8.30-17.00.
13 (a) c.70,000; (b) c.1,300; (c) microtext; audio & video
cassettes; tape/slides.   **14** £94,000.   **15** (a) 29 (b) 10
(c) 10.

ROYAL NAVAL ENGINEERING COLLEGE LIBRARY,
Manadon, Plymouth, PL5 3AQ (Tel 0752-53740 ext
Manadon 310/404/419) Libn: Mr D. N. Allum BA, ALA; Dep
Libn: Mrs E. T. Mason ALA.
6 MoD (Navy).   **8** Engineering (control, electrical,

electronic, mechanical, materials, marine & aeronautical);
maths; liberal studies (current affairs, defence policy).
11 Yes, by prior arrangement only.   **12** Mon-Fri 8.00-
16.30 (Fri 16.00), Sat 8.00-11.30.   **13** (a) c.32,000;
(b) 450; (c) 1,000 reports.   **15** (a) 6 (b) 1 (c) 2.

PONTYPRIDD, Mid-Glamorgan

POLYTECHNIC OF WALES LIBRARY, Llantwit Rd, Treforest,
Pontypridd, CF37 1DL (Tel 0443-405133) Poly Libn: Mr
G. W. F. Ewins BSc, ALA; Sub-Libn: Mr R. T. W. Denning BA,
FLA.
7 Buttrills Rd, Barry (04462-3101) Campus Libn: Mr C. J. W.
Newman.   **8** Science (mathematics, physics & chemistry);
engineering (chemical, civil, electrical, mechanical & mining);
business studies; management; social studies; languages; arts;
education.   **9** Local photographs.   **10** BLL; WRLS.
11 Yes.   **12** Term: Mon-Fri 9.00-21.00, Sat 9.00-17.00;
vac: Mon-Fri 9.00-17.00 (Fri 16.30).   **13** (a) 130,000;
(b) 1,750; (c) 300 slides; 120 records & tapes; 2,700 microtexts.   **14** £89,750.   **15** (a) 23 (b) 7 (c) 8.

PORT ERIN, Isle of Man

MARINE BIOLOGY DEPARTMENT LIBRARY, Port Erin,
Isle of Man (Tel 0624-83 2027) Sub-Libn Science: Mr W. E.
Wilkes MA, FLA (based in Liverpool); Dep: Mrs A. M. Barton
MA.
6 University of Liverpool.   **8** Marine biology.   **11** No.
12 Always available to staff.   **13** (a) 8,000; (b) 430.
14 £3,250.

PORTSMOUTH, Hampshire

HIGHBURY TECHNICAL COLLEGE LIBRARY, Cosham,
Portsmouth, PO6 2SA (Tel 07018-83131) Libn: R. F. Gibbs
ALA.
6 Hampshire CC.   **8** Business; construction; general;
health, home & fashion; hotel-keeping & catering; management;
electrical, marine & mechanical engineering; maths; science.
10 SWRLB; HATRICS.   **11** Yes, for ref only; loans at
discretion of Libn.   **12** Term: Mon-Thurs 8.30-20.00,
Fri 8.30-18.30; vac: Mon-Fri 9.00-17.00.   **13** (a) 29,500;
(b) 350; (c) 500 microforms; 650 audio tapes.   **14** £10,000.
15 (a) 8 (c) 3.

PORTSMOUTH COLLEGE OF ART AND DESIGN LIBRARY,
Winston Churchill Ave, Portsmouth, PO1 2DJ (Tel 0705-
26435) Coll Libn: Miss Muriel Ruth Manns BA, ALA.
8 Fine arts.   **9** Some William Blake facsimile editions.
10 BLL.   **11** Yes, for ref only.   **12** Term: Mon-Fri
9.00-20.30 (Weds & Thurs 18.00, Fri 16.30); vac: Mon-Fri
9.30-12.30, 13.30-17.00 (Fri 16.30).   **13** (a) 11,000; (b) 92;
(c) c.400 gramophone records; 11,000 slides.   **14** £3,200.
15 (a) 2 (b) 1 (c) 1.

PORTSMOUTH COLLEGE OF EDUCATION LIBRARY,
(will merge with Portsmouth Polytechnic, April 1976, to form
the Faculty of Educational Studies), Locksway Rd, Portsmouth,
PO4 8JF (Tel 0705-35241) Libn-Tutor: Mr E. O. Cunningham
MA, ALA; Dep Miss M. P. Gilham ALA.
6 Hampshire Local Education Authority.   **8** Education;
psychology.   **9** Local history; children's books.
10 BLCMP (planned).   **11** Yes, for ref only.   **12** Mon-
Fri 9.00-21.00 (Fri 20.00), Sat 9.30-12.30.   **13** (a) 70,000;
(b) 400; (c) 200 microfilms; 600 slides; 300 filmstrips.
14 £16,000.   **15** (a) 8 (b) 1 (c) 3.

PORTSMOUTH POLYTECHNIC LIBRARY, (will merge with
Portsmouth College of Education, April 1976), Hampshire
Terrace, Portsmouth, PO1 2EG (Tel 0705-27681 ext 248)
Libn: Mr W. G. Gale BA, ALA; Dep Libn: Mr D. Jackson BSc,
DipLib.
6 Hampshire CC.   **7** Science Lib, Libn: Mr D. R. King
BSc, MSc; Engineering Lib, J Block, Burnaby Rd, Portsmouth,
Libn: K. W. Mildren BSc, ALA, AIInfSc; Geography Lib, Lion
Terrace, Portsmouth, Libn: Mr J. Peters; Humanities Lib,
Drill Hall, Hampshire Terrace, Portsmouth, Libn: D. F.
Francis BA, ALA; Social Sciences Lib, Libn: D. A. Taylor
BA, ALA.   **8** Humanities; social sciences; natural sciences;

CODE: **1** Name of Library. **2** Address. **3** Telephone & Telex. **4** Officer in charge. **5** Deputy. **6** Governing body.
7 Branches. **8** Main Subjects. **9** Special Collections. **10** Co-operative Schemes. **11** Open to public? **12** Hours.
13 Stock: (a) books (b) periodicals (c) other. **14** Finance. **15** Staff: (a) non-manual (b) graduate (c) chartered librarians.

PORTSMOUTH, Hampshire—*continued*

engineering; environmental studies. **9** EDC; Bolton colln
(architecture books). **10** SWRLB; HATRICS. **11** Yes,
with letter of introduction. **12** Term: Mon-Fri 9.00-22.00
(Fri 21.00), Sat 9.00-17.30, Sun 14.00-18.00; vac: Mon-Fri
9.00-17.00. Branches vary. **13** (a) 222,000; (b) 2,900;
(c) 350 microforms; 50 tapes. **14** c. £150,000.
15 (a) 36 (b) 22 (c) 8.

PRESTON, Lancashire

LANCASHIRE RECORD OFFICE, Bow Lane, Preston,
PR1 2RE (Tel 0772-51905) County Archivist: R. Sharpe
France MA; Dep County Archivist: D. J. H. Smith BA.
6 Lancashire CC. **8** Lancashire history. **11** Yes.
12 Mon-Fri 9.00-17.00. **13** (a) c. 12,000; (b) 40;
(c) c. 7,000,000 documents; microfilms. **15** (a) 15 (b) 6.

PRESTON POLYTECHNIC LIBRARY, Corporation St,
Preston, PR1 2TQ (Tel 0772-51831 ext 215) Poly Libn:
Mr J. R. Edgar, MA, FLA; Sub-Libns: Mr M. P. Day BSc, MSc
(Planning); Mr A. Lawrence ALA (Technical Services);
Mr B. M. Shimmon FLA (Services).
6 Polytechnic Council. **7** Marshall House Sectional Lib,
Ringway, Preston (0772-51831 ext 271/2), Libn: Mr R. M.
Campbell BA, ALA; Chorley Campus Lib, Union St, Chorley
(02572-5811) Libn: Miss J. B. Smith BA, ALA; Poulton-le-
Fylde Campus Lib, Breck Rd, Poulton-le-Fylde, Blackpool,
FY6 7AW (039 12-4651), Libn: Miss A. Bradley BA, ALA,
Lancaster Campus Lib, Meeting House Lane, Lancaster,
Libn: Mr J. M. Harrison ALA. **8** General. **9** Illustrated
books colln; Preston Incorporated Law Society colln; local
history collns. **10** NWRLB. **11** Yes, for ref only, by
arrangement. **12** Term: Mon-Fri 9.00-21.00 (Fri 20.00);
vac: Mon-Fri 9.00-17.00. Branches vary. **13** (a) 150,000;
(b) c. 1,200; (c) 704 video tapes; 286 teaching programmes;
2131 microrecords; 380 programmed learning texts; 166
charts; 754 gramophone records; 52 films; 289 filmstrips;
12 photographs; 232 audio cassette tapes; 12,000 slides;
27 tape-slide programmes. **14** £150,000. **15** (a) 36
(b) 14 (c) 19.

PRINCES RISBOROUGH, Buckinghamshire

PRINCES RISBOROUGH LABORATORY LIBRARY, Princes
Risborough, Aylesbury, HP17 9PX (Tel 08444-3101; Telex
83559) Libn: Mrs Clare Abbott BSc, DipLib; Dep: Mrs Ann
Cooper ALA.
6 Building Research Establishment. **8** Timber & its
uses, with special ref to building. **10** BLL; Aslib.
11 Yes, by appointment. **12** Mon-Fri 8.00-17.00 (Fri
16.30). **13** (a) 3,400; (b) 342; (c) 175 slides; 13 journals on
microfilm; 20,070 microfiche; 8,000 pamphlets. **15** Staff
total 4; graduate 1; chart libns 1.

READING, Berkshire

ATOMIC WEAPONS RESEARCH ESTABLISHMENT
LIBRARY, Aldermaston, Reading, RG7 4PR (Tel 07356-4111)
Libn: Mr P. D. Friend GM, BSc, MIInfSc; Dep: Mr D. V. Wilson
FLA.
6 MoD (Procurement Executive). **8** Nuclear science &
engineering. **11** No. **13** (a) 50,000; (b) 1,300; (c) reports,
inc microfiches.

BULMERSHE COLLEGE OF HIGHER EDUCATION, Woodlands
Ave, Earley, Reading, RG6 1HY (Tel 0734-663387) Coll Libn:
Mr J. H. Merrick; Dep Libn: Mr J. G. Cox BA, ALA.
6 Governors of the College. **8** Education; educational
psychology; sociology; physical education; religious education;
history; geography; art; English literature; French; German;
music; maths; environmental studies; children's literature.
9 World War I; historical mss; film & TV; urban & regional

planning. **11** Yes, for ref only. **12** Term: Mon-Fri
9.00-21.00 (Fri 17.00), Sat 9.30-12.30; vac: Mon-Fri 9.00-
12.00, 13.00-17.00. **13** (a) 80,000; (b) 400; (c) 650
gramophone records; 850 slides; 350 cassettes; 650 filmstrips;
170 miscellaneous audio-visual items. **14** £40,000.
15 (a) 13 (b) 5 (c) 6.

CENTRAL WATER PLANNING UNIT LIBRARY, Reading
Bridge House, Reading, RG1 8PS (Tel 0734-57551)
6 Dept of Environment. **8** Hydrology; hydrogeology;
water supply; related subjects. **11** Yes, for bona fide
enquiries. **12** Mon-Fri 9.00-17.00. **13** (a) 5,000;
(b) 60.

NATIONAL INSTITUTE FOR RESEARCH IN DAIRYING,
STENHOUSE WILLIAMS MEMORIAL LIBRARY, Shinfield,
Reading, RG2 9AT (Tel 0734-883103) Libn: Mr Brian F. Bone
BA, ALA, AIInfSc; Technical Inf Officer: Mr Norman W.
Briggs BSc, AIInfSc.
6 Agricultural Research Council. **8** Dairying; agriculture;
biochemistry; endocrinology; statistical analysis; nutrition;
microbiology. **11** Yes. **12** Mon-Fri 9.00-17.30 (Fri
17.00). **13** (a) 19,000; (b) 450; (c) 32,000 pamphlets.
14 £12,000. **15** (a) 6 (b) 3 (c) 1.

READING COLLEGE OF TECHNOLOGY, P. S. TAYLOR
LIBRARY, Kuys Rd, Reading, RG1 4HJ (Tel 0734-583501)
Libn: Mrs S. M. Bowtell ALA; Asst Libn: Miss R. Keeble
ALA.
6 Berkshire CC. **8** Art; biology; building; catering;
chemistry; civil engineering; economic history; economics;
electrical, mechanical & electronic engineering; home
economics; management; metal working; photography;
physics; woodworking; workshop technology; sociology;
history. **9** Complete BSI. **10** BLL; BLG. **11** Yes,
for ref only. **12** Term: 9.00-20.00; vac: 9.00-12.30,
14.00-17.00. **13** (a) 28,000; (b) 200. **14** £7,400.
15 (a) 4 (c) 2.

READING SCHOOL LIBRARY, Reading, RG1 5LW (Tel
0734-61406)
8 General. **9** History of Reading school; mss; registers;
books. **11** Yes, by appointment. **12** Term: all day;
vac: by appointment. **13** (a) c. 6,000.

READING UNIVERSITY LIBRARY, Whiteknights, Reading,
RG6 2AE (Tel 0734-84331; Telex 847813) Univ Libn: Mr
James Thompson BA, FLA; Dep Libn: Ms Edith M. Cairns
MA, FLA.
6 Curators of the Library. **7** Education Lib, London Road
Site, The University, Reading, RG1 5AQ (0734-85234), Libn:
G. W. Geoghegan BA, ALA; Music Lib, 35 Upper Redlands Rd,
Reading, RG1 5JE (0734-83584), Libn: Dr A. Margaret Laurie
MA, BMus, PhD, ARCM. **8** General. **9** Overstone
Library (8,000 vols, mainly 18th & 19th cent economics,
political & religious thought, travel, literature & history);
Cole Library (8,000 vols, early medicine & history of zoology);
Stenton Library (4,700 vols, mainly mediaeval history);
Finzi Poetry Colln (5,000 vols); Henley Parish Library (500
vols); Turner Colln (French Revolution). **10** BLL; LISE.
11 Yes, with permission. **12** Term: Mon-Fri 9.00-22.15
(Fri 19.00), Sat 9.00-18.00, Sun 14.00-18.00; vac: Mon-Fri
9.00-17.00, Sat 9.00-13.00. **13** (a) 424,766; (b) 4,201;
(c) 48,026 pamphlets; 1,362 mss (collns of letters etc
counted as one item); 4,388 microforms (microfilm reels,
microcards & microfiches); 1,932 sound recordings.
15 (a) 63 (b) 41 (c) 30.

REDDITCH, Hereford & Worcester

REDDITCH DEVELOPMENT CORPORATION TECHNICAL
LIBRARY, Holmwood, Plymouth Rd, Redditch, B97 4PD
(Tel 0527-64200 ext 213) Technical Libn: K. A. Small ALA;
Asst Libn: D. P. Russell ALA.
8 New towns; architecture; planning; engineering; finance;

REDDITCH, Hereford & Worcester—*continued*

legal; estates; management.   **9** BSI.   **10** WESLINK;
WMRLB; SWMLS; WATL; Construction Industry Information
Group.   **11** Yes.   **12** 8.30-17.30 (flexible).
13 (a) 10,000; (b) 130; (c) reports; government publications;
trade literature; photographs; slides; press cuttings; samples;
computer programmes; microfiche.   **14** £3,000.
15 (a) 2 (c) 2.

REDRUTH, Cornwall

CORNWALL TECHNICAL COLLEGE LIBRARY, Trevenson,
Pool, Redruth, TR15 3RD (Tel 02092-2911) Coll Libn: Mr
K.D.Staite ALA; Dep: Ms P.Orient ALA.
6 Local Authority.   **7** Art & Design Lib, Libn: Ms V.
Moyle ALA.   **8** Education; engineering; English; geography;
history; sociology.   **9** Children's literature (model
teaching practice colln, 3,000 vols); BSI; environmental
studies.   **10** Cornwall information service (co-ordinating
centre).   **11** Yes, by arrangement.   **12** 8.45-21.00.
13 (a) 34,000; (b) 300; (c) 500 gramophone records;
complete set of Open University course units.   **14** £14,000.
15 (a) 8 (b) 1 (c) 4.

RETFORD, Nottinghamshire

EATON HALL COLLEGE OF EDUCATION LIBRARY,
Retford, DN22 0PR (Tel 0777-6441 ext 30) Tutor-Libn: Mr
S.T.Lucas FRSA, FLA; Asst Libn: Miss B.Dixon BA, ALA.
6 Nottinghamshire CC.   **8** General.   **10** BLL;
Nottingham University School of Education & Area Training
Organization Libraries; EMRLB.   **11** Yes, for ref only.
12 Term: Mon 9.00-21.00, Tues-Thurs 9.00-19.00, Fri
9.00-17.00, Sat 9.00-11.30; vac: Mon-Fri 9.00-12.15,
13.15-17.00.   **13** (a) c.65,000; (b) c.350; (c) c.450 slides,
microfilms, filmstrips, tape recordings (reel & cassette),
portfolios.   **14** £15,590.   **15** (a) 6 (b) 1 (c) 2.

RIPON, North Yorkshire

RIPON CATHEDRAL LIBRARY, Ripon, HG4 (Tel 0765-2072)
Canon Libn: Rev James G.B.Ashworth; Archivist: Ms Jean
Mortimer.
6 Dean & Chapter.   **8** Theology; philosophy; history; bible;
liturgy.   **9** Mediaeval mss; a 9th cent fragment; Carolingian
miniscule; 13th cent bible of 535 leaves; historiated capitals;
14th cent Anselmiana; late 12th cent copy of Jeremiah &
the Lamentations with commentary, & Revelation, both
written at St Mary's Priory, Bridlington; 'Bonaventura'
of Nicholas Love, written at Mount Grace Priory; Ripon
Psalter of 1418; 2 incunabula from Fountains Abbey, late 15th
cent; a Caxton, Boethius 'De Consolatione Philosophiae'.
11 Yes, by previous application to Canon Libn.   **12** 10.00-
17.00.   **13** (a) c.3,000; (c) Most archives transferred to
Brotherton Library, Leeds; microtext of 'Leeds Crockford'
by Rev Canon R.J.Wood.   **14** £100.   **15** (b) 1.

ROCHDALE, Lancashire

ROCHDALE TECHNICAL COLLEGE LIBRARY, St Marys
Gate, Rochdale, OL12 6RY (Tel 0706-40421 ext 39) Tutor-
Libn: Mr A.Ashworth BA, ALA; Asst Libn: Miss C.M.
Greenwood BA, ALA.
6 Rochdale MDC.   **8** Mechanical & electrical engineering;
spring-making; sociology; economics & commerce; catering;
English & Western European languages & literature;
costume; child care.   **9** Rochdale College of Art Library
(inc history of art, painting, photography, printmaking,
sculpture, pottery & ceramics, advertising).   **10** BLL;
NWRLB.   **11** Yes, for ref only.   **12** Term: Mon-Fri
9.00-20.00 (Fri 19.30); vac: Mon-Fri 9.00-16.30.
13 (a) 29,000; (b) 90.   **14** £5,820.   **15** (a) 4 (b) 2 (c) 2.

ROCHESTER, Kent

ROCHESTER CATHEDRAL LIBRARY, Minor Canon Row,
Rochester, ME1 1ST.
6 Dean & Chapter.   **8** Theology; ecclesiastical history;
biography.   **11** No.   **12** By arrangement.

ROTHERHAM, South Yorkshire

BRITISH STEEL CORPORATION SPECIAL STEELS
DIVISION LIBRARY, Swinden Laboratories, Moorgate,
Rotherham, S60 3AR (Tel 0709-4901; Telex 54472) Libn:
Miss Joyce Spurr ALA; Asst Libn: Miss C.E.Blowers ALA.
8 Research & development for special steels; physics;
chemistry; metallurgy; engineering; industrial hygiene.
9 Foreign standard specifications for steels; steelmakers
trade brochures; translations of foreign scientific &
technical journal articles.   **10** SINTO; Aslib.   **11** No.
13 (b) 540; (c) 27,000 pamphlets & externally published
reports; 3,000 steelmakers trade catalogues; 17,000
standard specifications (British & foreign); 11,000
translations.   **15** (a) 9 (b) 2 (c) 3.

ROTHERHAM COLLEGE OF TECHNOLOGY LIBRARY,
Howard St, Rotherham, S65 1JJ (Tel 0709-65015 ext 29)
Libn: Miss B.C.Lim ALA; Lib Asst: Mrs E.Thorpe.
6 Rotherham BC.   **7** Annexe Lib, Park St; Annexe Lib,
Clough Bank.   **8** Mechanical; electrical; metallurgy;
maths; commerce; social welfare; cookery; nursing.
11 Yes.   **12** Mon-Thurs 9.00-19.30, Fri 9.00-17.00.
13 (a) 14,000; (b) 80.   **14** £2,100.   **15** (a) 2 (c) 1.

RUGBY, Warwickshire

ASSOCIATED ENGINEERING DEVELOPMENTS LTD
LIBRARY, Cawston House, Cawston, Rugby, CV22 7SA
Libn: Mr T.M.Jones.
8 Engine dynamics & component design; materials engineering; powder metallurgy; foundry technology; heat
transfer; mechanical & production engineering; lubrication
& wear; special machine tools; control system.
9 ASTM standards.   **10** CADIG; NANTIS.   **11** No.
12 Mon-Fri 8.00-16.30.   **13** (a) 3,500; (b) 200.
14 £10,000.   **15** (a) 2.

RUGBY SCHOOL, TEMPLE READING ROOM, Barby Rd,
Rugby (Tel 0788-73959)
8 General.   **11** Yes, on application to Libn.   **12** Winter
8.30-18.00; summer 8.30-19.00.   **13** (a) 21,000.
14 £1,000.

SAFFRON WALDEN, Essex

FISONS AGROCHEMICAL DIVISION LIBRARIES, Chesterford
Park, Saffron Walden, CB10 1XL (Tel 0799-23542; Telex
817300) Libn: Mrs J.Hartley.
6 Fisons Agrochemical Division.   **7** Applied Biology &
Organic Libraries, Chesterford Park, Saffron Walden;
Chemical Development & Commercial Library, Harston.
8 Botany; zoology; mycology; applied chemistry & biology;
pesticides; agricultural chemicals; associated subjects
relevant to a manufacturing company.   **9** Colln of international flora; identification of insect, plant & fungus species.
10 HASL; inter-library loans.   **11** No, not under any
circumstances.   **13** (a) over 4,000; (b) c.250.

ST ALBANS, Hertfordshire

ST ALBANS COLLEGE OF FURTHER EDUCATION, DONALD
NEWMAN LIBRARY, 29 Hatfield Rd, St Albans, AL1 3RJ
(Tel 0727-60423; Telex 263208) Head of Lib Dept: Mr R.H.
Nichols ALA; Miss D.E.Walker BA, ALA.
6 Hertfordshire CC.   **8** Mechanical, electrical & aeronautical engineering; home economics; business; law; computer science; maths; chemistry; physics; biology; sociology;
economics; politics; languages; literature; arts & crafts;
child care; careers.   **9** Further education; audio-visual
materials.   **10** BLL; HERTIS; LASER.   **11** Yes, on
application to Libn.   **12** Term: Mon-Fri 8.45-20.00
(Fri 17.00); vac: 9.00-12.30, 14.00-17.00.   **13** (a) 15,000;
(b) 200; (c) archives; 100 film loops; 280 filmstrips; 160
gramophone records; 55 audio tapes; 2,500 slides; 29 ohp
transparency sets; 88 multi-media kits; 91 poster charts.
15 (a) 7½ (b) 2 (c) 4.

CODE: 1 Name of Library. **2** Address. **3** Telephone & Telex. **4** Officer in charge. **5** Deputy. **6** Governing body.
7 Branches. **8** Main Subjects. **9** Special Collections. **10** Co-operative Schemes. **11** Open to public? **12** Hours.
13 Stock: (a) books (b) periodicals (c) other. **14** Finance. **15** Staff: (a) non-manual (b) graduate (c) chartered librarians.

ST ALBANS, Hertfordshire—*continued*

UNITED GLASS LTD LIBRARY, Porters Wood, St Albans, AL3
6NY (Tel 0727-59261; Telex 22770) Libn & Inf Officer: Mr D.
A. Curtis ALA, AIInfSc; Asst Libn & Inf Officer: Ms Ann
Steel ALA.
8 Glass; plastics; packaging. **10** HERTIS. **11** No.
12 Mon-Fri 9.00-17.00. **13** (a) 3,000; (b) 200;
(c) microforms (fiche & open reel). **15** (a) 4 (c) 2.

ST ANDREWS, Fife

UNIVERSITY OF ST ANDREWS LIBRARY, St Andrews,
KY16 9TR (Tel 033481-4333; Telex 76213) Univ Libn: Mr
D. MacArthur MA, BSc, FLA; Dep Libn: Mr D.W. Doughty
MA, FLA.
6 Library Committee, appointed by University Court &
Senate. **7** St Mary's College (Divinity); Divisional
libraries in Chemistry, Mathematics & Physics Institutes,
administered by Main Library. **8** General. **9** von
Hügel (philology); J.D. Forbes (science, separate catalogue);
G.H. Forbes (theology); Bishop Low (theology); Donaldson
(classics); early printed books; local colln. **10** BLL; NSL.
11 Yes. **12** Term: 9.00-22.00. **13** (a) 650,000
(estimate); (b) c.4,000; (c) microfilm; microfiche; etc.; mss;
archives. **14** £94,900. **15** (a) 40 (b) 24 (c) 12.

ST HELENS, Merseyside

ST HELENS COLLEGE OF TECHNOLOGY LIBRARY, St
Helens, WA10 1PZ (Tel 0744-20831) Tutor-Libn: Mr B.D.
Layland.
6 College Governors. **8** Economics; politics; public &
social administration; physical sciences; electrical,
mechanical & mining engineering; history & geography.
9 Management studies (inc sociology, economics &
statistics). **10** LADSIRLAC. **11** Yes, for ref (loans
in special cases). **12** Term: Mon-Fri 8.45-21.00
(Fri 17.30); vac: Mon-Fri 8.45-17.30. **13** (a) 25,000;
(b) 160. **14** £7,000. **15** (a) 5 (c) 2.

ST LEONARDS-ON-SEA, Sussex

HASTINGS COLLEGE OF FURTHER EDUCATION LIBRARY,
Archery Rd, St Leonards-on-Sea, TN38 0HX (Tel 0424-
423847) Tutor-Libn: Mr R.M. Thomas MA, ALA.
6 East Sussex CC. **8** General. **10** BLL. **11** Yes, for
ref only. **12** 9.00-18.30. **13** (a) 13,980; (b) 150;
(c) 480 tapes; 120 filmstrips. **14** £3,700. **15** (a) 2½
(b) 1½ (c) 1½.

SALFORD, Lancashire

SALFORD COLLEGE OF TECHNOLOGY LIBRARY, Frederick
Rd, Salford M6 6PU (Tel 061-736 6541) Tutor-Libn: Miss
S.J. Lowe MA, ALA.
8 Salford MDC. **8** Art & industrial design; building &
environmental control; business; engineering; food & home
economics; chiropody; radiography; textiles. **10** NWRLB.
11 Yes. **12** Term: Mon-Fri 9.00-20.30 (Fri 19.00);
vac: Mon-Fri 9.00-16.30. **15** (a) 40,000; (b) 400;
(c) 10,000 slides; 150 film strips; 350 gramophone records;
750 illustrations; 50 teaching units. **14** £10,000.
15 (a) 6 (b) 3 (c) 3.

UNIVERSITY OF SALFORD LIBRARY, Salford, M5 4WT (Tel
061-736 5843; Telex 668680 (Univ Salford)) Univ Libn: Mr
A.C. Bubb BA, FLA; Dept Univ Libn: Miss A.E. Lumb MA,
FLA.
8 Social sciences; natural sciences; technology; humanities.
10 NWRLB. **11** Yes, for ref only, on application.
12 Term: Mon-Fri 9.00-21.00, Sat 9.00-12.00; vac: Mon-
Fri 9.00-17.00. **13** (a) 180,000; (b) 2,000; (c) microtexts;
maps; photographs; films; sound tapes; (3,500 items).
14 £100,000. **15** (a) 46 (b) 13 (c) 13.

SALISBURY, Wiltshire

SALISBURY AND WELLS THEOLOGICAL COLLEGE
LIBRARY, 19 The Close, Salisbury, SP1 2EB (Tel 0722-4856)
Libn: Mrs N.M. Hill.
8 Theology; history; ethics. **9** 19th cent sermons.
10 Inter-library loans. **11** No. **12** Term: 24 hours a
day. **13** (a) 27,000 (b) 16. **14** £1,000. **15** (a) ½.

SALISBURY CATHEDRAL LIBRARY, The Close, Salisbury
SP1 2EF (Tel 0722-4081) Cathedral Libn: Rev Stanley C.
Dedman ALA.
6 Dean and Chapter. **8** Early mss; incunabula; history of
cathedral & see; theology. **9** Personal libraries of Izaak
Walton, Bishop Seth Ward, Dean Hamilton, etc; display items:
one of the 4 extant original copies of Magna Carta; 10th cent
Latin psalter with Anglo-Saxon glosses; 10th cent Latin
psalter in two versions, Gallican & Hebrew. **11** Yes, but
only to display area; main library restricted to visiting
students & researchers after introduction & authentication.
12 Oct-May: Mon, Wed, Fri 10.00-12.00, 14.00-15.30;
May-Oct: Mon-Sat 10.00-12.00, 14.00-15.30. **13** (a)
c.10,000; (c) archives; microfilm of mss held at Southampton
Univ Library. **15** (c) 1.

SALISBURY COLLEGE OF TECHNOLOGY LIBRARY,
Southampton Rd, Salisbury, SP1 2LW (Tel 0722 23711) Tutor-
Libn: L.A. Halsey FLA.
6 Wiltshire CC. **8** Building; engineering; science; (biology
& microbiology); social sciences; home economics; hotel &
catering; business; management. **9** BSI. **10** BLL;
HATRICS; SWRLB. **11** Yes. **12** Term: Mon-Fri 9.00-
20.00; vac: Mon-Fri 9.00-17.00. **13** (a) 17,000; (b) 240.
14 £2,350. **15** (a) 2½ (c) 1.

SHEFFIELD, South Yorkshire

GEOGRAPHICAL ASSOCIATION, FLEURE LIBRARY, 343
Fulwood Rd, Sheffield, S10 3BP (Tel 0742-661666).
8 Geography & related subjects. **9** Large colln of
school textbooks; geography journals & periodicals.
11 Yes for ref only. **12** Mon-Fri 9.00-17.00. **13** (a)
16,000; (b) 202; (c) 200 filmstrips. **15** (a) 1 (b) 1.

GLASS TECHNOLOGY JOINT LIBRARY, 'Elmfield', Northumberland Rd, Sheffield S10 2TZ (Tel 0742-78555 ext 131)
Libn: Mrs L.M. Whitehead ALA; Dep: Mrs D. Shekelton FLA.
6 University of Sheffield. **8** Ceramics; glasses & polymers. **10** SINTO. **11** Yes, with Libn's permission.
12 Mon-Fri 8.30-22.00. **13** (a) 9,000; (b) 140; (c) photographs. **14** £3,000. **15** (a) 1½ (c) 2.

GRANVILLE COLLEGE OF FURTHER EDUCATION
LIBRARY, Granville Rd, Sheffield S2 2RL (Tel 0742-70271
ext 232) Tutor-Libn: Mr J. Roberts BA, ALA; Dep: Mrs D.M.
Hopkinson ALA.
6 City of Sheffield MDC Education Dept. **8** Art & design;
food & fashion; general; liberal studies; health & welfare;
mechanical & electrical engineering; motor vehicle engineering. **11** Yes, for ref only. **12** Term: Mon-Fri 8.45-
19.30 (Mon, Thurs & Fri 18.30); vac: 8.45-17.15. **13** (a)
18,231; (b) 101; (c) 32 audio-tapes; 120 video tapes; 16 film
loops; 281 film strips; 500 slides; 124 gramophone records;
tapes. **14** £3,500. **15** (a) 3 (b) 1 (c) 2.

JOSEPH LIVESEY LIBRARY, Livesey-Clegg House, 44 Union
St, Sheffield, S1 2JP (tel 0742-22770) Sec: Miss Muriel Daniel.
6 British National Temperance League. **8** Temperance
reform. **9** Joseph Livesey's & William E. Moss's collns.
11 Yes, by appointment. **12** 9.30-17.00. **13** (a) c.5,000;
(c) various tract leaflets. **14** £150. **15** (a) 1.

SAFETY IN MINES RESEARCH ESTABLISHMENT LIBRARY,
Red Hill, off Broad Lane, Sheffield, S3 7HQ (Tel 0742-78141)
Libn: Miss E.E. Rodgers; Dep Miss J.M. Matkin BSc, ALA.
6 Health & Safety Executive. **7** Field Laboratories,

SHEFFIELD, South Yorkshire—*continued*

Harpur Hill; Buxton, Derbyshire (0298-2664) Libn: Mrs P. J. Sproulle BA, ALA. **8** Research & testing of safety & health in mines & other industries; use of electrical equipment in hazardous areas. **9** Mine incident reports; mine regulations; specifications for electrical equipment in hazardous areas. **10** BLL; SINTO. **11** Yes, bona-fide enquirers by arrangement. **12** 9.00-17.00. **13** (a) 20,000; (b) 450; (c) translations; microfiches. **15** (a) 13 (b) 5 (c) 4.

SHEFFIELD POLYTECHNIC LIBRARY, (will merge with Sheffield City & Totley-Thornbridge Colleges of Education, April 1976), Pond St, Sheffield S1 1WB (Tel 0742-20911 ext 331; Telex 54680) Poly Libn: Mr L. G. Tootell FLA; Dep Poly Libn: Mr K. B. Swallow ALA.
7 School of Art & Design Lib, Psalter Lane, Sheffield, Asst Libn: G. W. Smith BA. **8** Business & management; engineering; science; social studies; art & design. **9** EDC. **10** SINTO. **11** Yes, for ref only. **12** Term: Mon-Fri 8.45-21.00; vac: Mon-Fri 9.00-17.00. **13** (a) 160,000; (b) 1,473. **14** £143,000. **15** (a) 33 (b) 8 (c) 14.

SHIRECLIFFE COLLEGE OF FURTHER EDUCATION LIBRARY, Shirecliffe Rd, Sheffield S5 8XZ (Tel 0742-78301 ext 36) Resources Libn: Mr J. M. Stanbra MA, BA, ALA; Asst Libn: Mrs C. Markham ALA.
6 Sheffield MDC. **8** Building; civil engineering; valuation & estate management; social health & welfare. **9** Complete BSI; large colln on building materials. **10** SINTO. **11** Yes, but loans by arrangement with Libn. **12** Term: 9.00-19.00; vac: 9.00-17.00. **13** (a) 12,000; (b) 120; (c) video tapes; slides; film strips; audio tapes; other audiovisual teaching aids. **14** £5,000. **15** (a) $2\frac{1}{2}$ (b) 1 (c) 2.

UNIVERSITY OF SHEFFIELD LIBRARY, Western Bank, Sheffield, S10 2TN (Tel 0742-78555; telex 54348) Univ Libn: Mr C. K. Balmforth MA, FLA; Dep Libn: Mr W. J. Hitchens MA.
7 Applied Science Lib, St George's Sq, Sheffield, S1 3JD (0742-7855 ext 41); Institute of Education Lib (0742-22087), Libn: Mr C. K. Balmforth MA, FLA; Edward Bramley Law Lib, Shearwood Rd, Sheffield, 10; Dept of Music Lib, (0742-667234), Libn: T. McCanna BA, ALA. **8** General. **9** Firth colln (Civil War Tracts); Japanese studies (economics, politics, sociology). **10** SINTO; YHJLS; JLG. **11** Yes, on application, at Libn's discretion. **12** Term & Easter vac: Mon-Fri 9.00-21.30, Sat 9.00-13.00; other vacs: Mon-Fri 9.00-17.00, Sat 9.00-12.30. **13** (a) c.580,000; (b) c.5000; (c) pamphlets (64,000); archives; microtexts; gramophone records; audio-visual materials. **14** £250,000. **15** (a) 85 (b) 35 (c) 29.

SHERBORNE, Dorset

SHERBORNE SCHOOL LIBRARY, Abbey Rd, Sherborne, DT9 3AP Libn: A. DChilds FLA.
6 Governors of Sherborne School. **8** General. **9** c.900 printed books of 16th-18th cent (classics, theology, history, topography, some early Bibles). **11** No. **12** Term: 8.00-23.00; vac: by arrangement. **13** (a) 20,000; (b) 25; (c) school archives.

SHREWSBURY, Shropshire

SHREWSBURY TECHNICAL COLLEGE LIBRARY, London Rd, Shrewsbury SY2 6PR (Tel 0743-51544) Asst Libn: Ms Barbara A. Sansom BA, DipLib.
6 Salop CC. **7** School of Art Lib, Abbey Foregate, Shrewsbury, SY2 6AA (0743-53077). **8** Science; technology; commerce; professional studies. **9** Complete BSI. **10** WMRLB. **11** Yes, by arrangement. **12** Term: Mon-Thurs 9.00-21.15 (under review), Fri 9.00-17.00; vac: Mon-Fri 9.00-17.00. **13** (a) 12,000; (b) 120. **14** £2,000. **15** (a) 4 (b) 2 (c) 2.

SLOUGH, Berkshire

CEMENT AND CONCRETE ASSOCIATION LIBRARY, Wexham Springs, Slough, SL3 6PL (Tel 02816-2727; Telex 848352) Head of Dept: Mr H. A. Stoddart MIInfSc, FISTC, MInstAM; Senior Inf Officer: Mr J. C. N. Russell LRIC, AIInfSc.
8 Concrete technology. **11** Yes, by appointment. **12** Mon-Fri 9.00-17.00. **13** (b) c.480; (c) concrete product data literature. **15** (a) $14\frac{1}{2}$ (b) 5 (c) 2.

PEST INFESTATION CONTROL LABORATORY LIBRARY, Ministry of Agriculture, Fisheries & Food, London Rd, Slough, SL3 7HJ (Tel 0753-34626 ext 143/144) Libn & Inf Officer: Miss H. C. N. Turnbull MA.
6 MAFF. **8** Stored products (raw, agricultural, non-perishable); insects, mites & microorganisms which attack stored products; chemical, biological & physiological means of control. **10** inter-library loans. **11** No. **13** (a) 7,200; (b) 350 (periodicals & serials); (c) 20,000 pamphlets. **15** (a) 5 (b) 3 (c) 1.

SLOUGH COLLEGE OF TECHNOLOGY LIBRARY, Wellington St, Slough, SL1 1YG (Tel 0753-34585) Tutor-Libn: Mr N. F. Dawson BA, ALA; Dep: Miss J. E. Pollard BSc, DipLib, ALA
6 Berkshire CC. **8** Catering; engineering; building; maths; computing; science; business; management; liberal & general studies. **10** BLL; LASER. **11** Yes. **12** Term: Mon-Fri 9.00-21.00 (Fri 19.00); vac: Mon-Fri 9.00-17.00. **13** (a) 40,000; (b) 450; (c) 132 microtexts; 240 gramophone records. **14** £19,000. **15** (a) 4 (b) 2 (c) 2.

SOLIHULL, West Midlands

SOLIHULL TECHNICAL COLLEGE LIBRARY, Blossomfield Rd, Solihull B91 1SB (Tel 021-705 6376) Mrs J. Condon BA, ALA; Dep: Mrs P. Singleton.
6 Solihull MB. **8** Social sciences; home economics; art; business. **11** Yes, for ref; Open University & National Extension College students may borrow. **12** Term: Mon-Thurs 9.00-20.00, Fri 9.00-17.00; vac: Mon-Fri 9.00-16.00. **13** (a) 15,600; (b) 96; (c) newscuttings from 1970. **15** (a) 3 (b) 1 (c) 2.

SOUTHAMPTON, Hampshire

ORDNANCE SURVEY LIBRARY, Romsey Rd, Maybush, Southampton, SO9 4DH (Tel 0703-775555 ext 334/691; Telex 47103) Technical Libn: Mr R. F. Thornton; Lib Asst: Miss S. Staley City & Guilds Lib Asst.
6 Government Dept. **7** Archaeology Division; Air Survey Branch. **8** Geodesy; survey; cartography; archaeology; photogrammetry; electronic computers; astrogeodesy; printing; satellite geodesy. **9** Ordnance survey archival material. **10** HATRICS; SWRLB; inter-governmental library cooperation. **11** No, research students on application to Libn. **12** Mon-Fri 8.30-17.00 (Fri 16.30). **13** (a) 40,000; (b) 200; (c) archives; films; filmstrips; microfilm; microfiche. **14** £4,000. **15** (a) 4 (c) 1.

SOUTHAMPTON COLLEGE OF ART LIBRARY, East Park Terrace, Southampton, SO9 4WU (Tel 0703-27666 ext 40) Libn: Mrs M. Stubbs BA, ALA.
6 Hampshire CC. **8** Fine arts; printing; painting & decorating; fashion; general visual ref. **11** Yes, for ref only. **12** Term: Mon-Fri 9.00-21.00 (Fri 16.30); vac: Mon-Fri 9.00-17.00. **13** (a) 11,000; (b) 100; (c) 16,000 slides; 100 filmstrips; 50 records; 31 tapes. **14** £4,000. **15** (a) 3 (b) 1 (c) 1.

SOUTHAMPTON COLLEGE OF TECHNOLOGY LIBRARY, East Park Terrace, Southampton, SO9 4WW (Tel 04895-29381) Coll Libn: Mr R. C. Corlett FLA; Dep Coll Libn: Mrs N. M. Shepherd BA.
6 Hampshire CC. **8** Engineering (civil, electrical, electronic, mechanical, production, marine, chemical); business; management; town & country planning; social work; public administration; marine electronics. **10** HATRICS. **11** Yes, for ref. **12** Term: 9.00-21.00; vac: 9.00-17.00. **13** (a) 23,500; (b) 400; (c) 200 microtexts; 35 films. **14** £13,500. **15** (a) 5 (b) 1 (c) 2.

CODE: **1** Name of Library. **2** Address. **3** Telephone & Telex. **4** Officer in charge. **5** Deputy. **6** Governing body.
7 Branches. **8** Main Subjects. **9** Special Collections. **10** Co-operative Schemes. **11** Open to public? **12** Hours.
13 Stock: (a) books (b) periodicals (c) other. **14** Finance. **15** Staff: (a) non-manual (b) graduate (c) chartered librarians.

SOUTHAMPTON, Hampshire—*continued*

SOUTHAMPTON SCHOOL OF NAVIGATION LIBRARY,
Warsash, Southampton, SO3 6ZL (Tel 04895-6161).
6 Hampshire CC. **8** Navigation; seamanship; safety at
sea; marine law; naval architecture; oceanography; meteorology; small boat handling & building. **9** Old navigation &
seamanship books from 1700; pamphlets inc Admiralty
notices to mariners; statutory instruments concerning merchant shipping; Dept of Trade 'M' notices. **10** HATRICS;
SWRLB; Aslib; Marine Librarians' Association. **11** Yes,
for ref, borrowing with special permission only. **12** Term:
Mon-Fri 9.00-21.30, Sat 9.00-12.30; vac: Mon- Fri 9.00-
17.00. **13** (a) 12,500; (b) 200. **14** £5,500. **15** (a) 2½
(c) 1.

UNIVERSITY OF SOUTHAMPTON LIBRARY, Southampton,
SO9 5NH (Tel 0703-559122; Telex 47661) Univ Libn: Mr
B.M. Bland MCom; Dep: Mr R.G. Woods MA, DipLib.
7 School of Education Lib, Libn: Mrs J.V. Marder BA;
Wessex Medical Lib, Medical Sub-Libn: Mr T.A. King BA,
ALA. **8** Medicine; arts; law; social sciences; education;
science & engineering (inc oceanography, electronics, aeronautics & sound & vibration research). **9** Cope colln of
Hampshire materials; Perkins agricultural library; Parkes
library on relations between the Jewish & non-Jewish world;
Hampshire Field Club library; Ford colln of parliamentary
papers. **10** BLL; SWRLB; HATRICS; S3RB. **11** Yes, for
ref, external membership, inc borrowing, for approved appli-
cants. **12** Term: Mon-Fri 9.00-22.00, Sat 9.00-17.00,
Sun 14.00-18.00. **13** (a) 480,000; (b) 6,154; (c) 593 mss;
10,569 microforms (original vols); 2,530 microfilms.
14 c.£211,000. **15** (a) 87 (b&c) 39.

SOUTHEND-ON-SEA, Essex

SOUTHEND-ON-SEA COLLEGE OF TECHNOLOGY LIBRARY,
Carnarvon Rd, Southend-on-Sea SS2 6LS (Tel 0702-353931)
Coll Libn: Mrs E.A. Harper ALA.
6 Essex CC. **8** General; art; technical. **9** BSI.
10 Inter-library loans. **11** No. **12** Term: 9.00-19.00;
vac: 9.00-17.00. **13** (a) c.22,000; (b) c,300. **14** £6,750.
15 (a) 4 (c) 1.

SOUTH SHIELDS, Tyne & Wear

SOUTH SHIELDS MARINE AND TECHNICAL COLLEGE
LIBRARY, St George's Ave, South Shields, NE36 6ET (Tel
08943-60403 ext 7) Coll Libn: Miss E.M. Oxley ALA; Dep:
Miss A. Gibson BA, ALA.
8 Marine engineering; nautical science; radio; shipbuilding;
other technical & academic subjects. **10** NRLB. **11** Yes,
for ref only. **12** Term: 9.00-20.00; vac: 9.00-17.00.
13 (a) c.20,000; (b) 166; (c) college archival material; microfiche. **14** £8,500. **15** (a) 5 (b) 1 (c) 3.

STAFFORD, Staffordshire

STAFFORD COLLEGE OF FURTHER EDUCATION LIBRARY,
Earl St, Stafford, ST16 2QR (Tel 0785-2361) Coll Libn: M.T.
Sleightholm ALA, MIL; Dep Libn: J.P. Riley BA, DipEd.
6 Staffordshire Education Committee. **7** Oval Annexe Lib,
The Oval, Stafford, Libn: P.R. Thompson ATD. **8** Building;
business; catering & domestic studies; design; engineering;
fashion; fine art; liberal studies; maths; science; computing.
10 LINOSCO; MISLIC. **11** Yes. **12** Term: Mon-Fri
8.45-21.00 (Fri 17.30); vac: Mon-Fri 8.45-17.15 (Fri 16.45).
Branch varies. **13** (a) 17,750; (b) 590; (c) 7,800 slides;
486 filmstrips; 31 films; 301 ohp transparencies; 4 multi-
media kits. **15** (a) 9 (b) 2 (c) 3.

WILLIAM SALT LIBRARY, Eastgate St, Stafford, (Tel 0785-
52276) Libn: Mr F.B. Stitt BA, BLitt, FRHistS.
6 Trustees of William Salt Library. **8** Local history.
9 18th-19th cent Staffordshire views; transcripts of parish
registers; mss. **11** Yes, but small children not admitted.
12 Tues-Sat 10-00-12.45, 13.45-17.00. **13** (c) archives;
pictures.

STEVENAGE, Hertfordshire

FURNITURE INDUSTRY RESEARCH ASSOCIATION LIBRARY,
Maxwell Rd, Stevenage, SG1 2EW (Tel 0438-3433) Libn: Mrs
P.A. Bristow ALA.
8 Furniture; plastics; woodworking machinery; finishing;
adhesives; textiles. **11** No. **12** 8.30-17.00. **13** (a)
c.4,500; (b) c.400. **15** (a) 2½ (c) 1.

WATER RESEARCH CENTRE (STEVENAGE LABORATORY)
LIBRARY, Elder Way, Stevenage, SG1 1TH (Tel 0438-2444)
Head of Lib Services: Miss I.M. Lamont BSc; Libn: Mrs G.
Cox ALA.
8 Water resources; treatment of sewage & industrial waste
waters; pollution of water. **9** Information service on
toxicity & biodegradability (INSTAB), available for a large
number of compounds (list available on request). **10** Inter-
library loans. **11** No. **12** 8.30-17.00. **13** (a) c.6,000;
(b) 256; (c) c.17,000 pamphlets. **14** c.£4,500. **15** (a) 4
(b) 1 (c) 1.

STIRLING, Stirlingshire

STIRLING UNIVERSITY LIBRARY, Stirling, FK9 4LA
(Tel 0786-3171; Telex 778874) Univ Libn: Mr P.G. Peacock
BA; Mr L. Corbett FIInfSc, ALA.
7 Resources Centre, Pathfoot Building, University of
Stirling (0786-3171 ext 2195), Libn: Miss J. Cochrane.
8 General. **9** Early editions of Scott; Watson colln (labour
history, the left). **11** Yes, on application to Libn.
12 Term: 9.00-22.30. **13** (a) 210,000; (b) 2,000; (c)
slides; records; microtexts. **14** £110,000. **15** (a) 37 (b)
15.

STOCKPORT, Cheshire

SIMON ENGINEERING LTD LIBRARY, Cheadle Heath, Stockport, SK3 0RT (Tel 061-428 3600) Head Inf & Lib Services:
Miss J.M. Forsyth BSc ALA.
8 Chemical, civil & food engineering. **10** NWRLB.
11 No. **12** 8.30-13.00, 14.00-17.00. **13** (a) 10,000;
(b) 300. **15** (a) 4 (b) 1 (c) 1.

STOCKPORT COLLEGE OF TECHNOLOGY LIBRARY,
Wellington Rd South, Stockport, SK1 3UQ (Tel 061-480 7331
ext 29) Coll Libn: Mr F.J. Chirgwin BA, FLA, AMBIM, FRSA;
Senior Asst Libn: Mrs I. Jackson ALA.
6 Stockport MB. **8** Applied social sciences; art & design;
building & civil engineering; electrical, mechanical &
production engineering; general education; management &
business; science. **9** Chemistry; mechanical engineering
(inc aeronautics); child care; graphic design; complete sets:
BSI, Ordnance Survey (1 inch & 1 : 50,000 series) Beilstein,
British Humanities Index (from 1915 on microfilm),
'Chemical Society Journal' (from 1880); 'Journal of Institute
of Brewing' (from 1906). **10** BLL; NWRLB. **11** Yes.
12 Term: Mon-Fri 9.00-21.00; vac: Mon-Fri 9.00-17.30.
13 (a) 25,000; (b) 350; (c) college archives; microtexts.
14 £10,000. **15** (a) 10 (b) 6 (c) 5.

STOKE-ON-TRENT, Staffordshire

BRITISH CERAMIC RESEARCH ASSOCIATION, MELLOR
MEMORIAL LIBRARY, Queens Rd, Penkhull, Stoke-on-Trent,
ST4 7LQ (Tel 0782-45431) Inf Officer: Mr D. Murfin BSc,
PhD; Libn: Miss A. Cooper.
8 Ceramics & allied subjects. **10** LINOSCO. **11** No.

STOKE-ON-TRENT, Staffordshire—*continued*

12 8.45-17.30.   **13** (a) 13,000; (b) c.200; (c) 35,000 reports, standards & other unbound pamphlets; 7,000 lantern slides.   **15** (a) 8½ (b) 2.

CONCOURSE LIBRARY, Stoke Rd, Shelton, Stoke-on-Trent, ST11 9JX (Tel 0782-24651) Tutor-Libn: Mr Geoffrey Charles Otter FLA, FRSA; Asst Libn: Ms Hazel Stockdale ALA.
6 Staffordshire Education Committee.   **8** Social sciences; domestic science; office skills; management; building construction.   **10** LINOSCO; WMRLB.   **11** Yes, by arrangement with Libn.   **12** Term: Mon-Fri 9.00-21.00:(Fri 19.00); vac: Mon-Fri 9.00-16.30.   **13** (a) c.24,500; (b) 148; (c) 350 audio-visual materials.   **14** £5,700.   **15** (a) 5 (c) 2.

NORTH STAFFORDSHIRE POLYTECHNIC LIBRARY, College Rd, Stoke-on-Trent, ST4 2DE (Tel 0782-45531) Polytechnic Libn: Mr E.S.Waterson MA, FLA; Dep Tutor-Libn: Mr H.R.Astall FLA.
6 Staffordshire CC.   **7** Beaconside, Stafford (0785-52331), Libn: Mr H.R.Astall FLA.   **8** Engineering (electrical, mechanical, mining); ceramics; computing; international relations; art; management; economics.   **10** MISLIC; LINOSCO.
11 Yes, on application to Libn.   **12** Term: Mon-Fri 9.00-21.00, Sat 9.00-12.00; vac: Mon-Fri 9.00-17.15.   **13** (a) 80,000; (b) 1,000.   **14** £92,500.   **15** (a) 32 (b) 7 (c) 11.

STOKE POGES, Buckinghamshire

FULMER RESEARCH INSTITUTE LTD LIBRARY, Hollybush Hill, Stoke Poges, Slough, SL2 4QD (Tel 02816-2181; Telex 848314 Fulmer) Libn: Mr R.F.Flint ALA.
8 Metals; polymer & plastics; corrosion; chemistry & physics.   **9** BSI.   **11** Yes, with special permission.
12 Mon-Fri 9.00-17.00.   **13** (a) 10,000; (b) 400; (c) pamphlets.   **14** £10,000.

STRATFORD-UPON-AVON, Warwickshire

SHAKESPEARE CENTRE LIBRARY, Henley St, Stratford-upon-Avon, CV37 6QW (Tel 0789 4016) Dir: Dr Levi Fox OBE, MA, FSA; Senior Libn: Miss Marian J.Horn BA, DipLibn, ALA, Senior Archivist: Mr Robert Bearman BA.
6 Shakespeare Birthplace Trust.   **8** Life, work & times of Shakespeare; English drama & theatrical history & biography, with associated pictorial collns; local history, topography & geneaology.   **9** Royal Shakespeare Theatre records: prompt books, press cuttings, photographs, music, programmes, posters; Stoker colln (Henry Irving); Wheler & Saunders collns (Warwickshire documents & drawings); Bloom colln (local genealogy).   **10** WMRLB.   **11** Yes, for ref; applications for readers tickets to Dir; temporary tickets on personal application to Senior Libn or Archivist.   **12** Reading Room: Mon-Fri 10.00-17.00 (Records Office closed 13.00-14.00), Sat 9.30-12.30.   **13** (a) c.25,000; (b) 40; (c) 50,000 deeds & documents inc c.6,000 manorial documents; 4,000 prints & drawings; 250 gramophone records.   **15** (a) 5 (b) 4 (c) 2.

STROUD, Gloucestershire

MID-GLOUCESTERSHIRE TECHNICAL COLLEGE LIBRARY, Stratford Rd, Stroud, GL5 4AH (Tel 045-36 3424) Libn: Mr B.A R.Newson ALA.
6 Gloucestershire Education Committee.   **10** GTIS; SWRLB.   **11** Yes, by prior arrangement.   **12** Mon-Fri 9.00-17.00 (Fri 16.15), (term: 9.00-19.00, 3 days per week).
13 (a) 8,926; (b) 120.   **15** (a) 2 (c) 1.

SUNDERLAND, Tyne & Wear

MONKWEARMOUTH COLLEGE OF FURTHER EDUCATION LIBRARY, Swan St, Sunderland, SR5 1EB (Tel 0783-71193) Coll Libn: Ms Jean Hornsey ALA; Asst Libn: Ms Susan Cameron MA.
6 Local Authority.   **7** Stansfield St, Sunderland. (0783-70445) Libn: Ms Gladys Sheriff.   **8** Catering; domestic science; science; economics; sociology; history; geography; maths; nursery nursing.   **10** BLL; NRLB.   **11** Yes, on application to Libn.   **12** Term: Mon-Wed 8.45-19.00 (Thurs & Fri 17.00); vac: 9.00-12.00, 13.15-17.15.   **13** (a) 16,000; (b) 80; (c) 120 gramophone records.   **14** £4,991.   **15** (a) 4 (b) 1 (c) 1.

SUNDERLAND POLYTECHNIC, SIR JOHN PRIESTMAN LIBRARY, Green Terrace, Sunderland, SR1 3SD (Tel 0783-76191) Poly Libn: Mr David T.Lewis ALA, DipAdEd, CertEd.
6 Sunderland Polytechnic Board of Governors.   **7** Faculty of Education, Langham Tower, Ryhope Rd, Sunderland (0783-71217), Libn: Mr N.West BA; Social Sciences Lib, Benedict Building St George's Way, Stockton Rd, Sunderland (0783-79316), Site Libn: Mr W.F.Mason BA, ALA; Faculty of Art & Design, Backhouse Building, Ryhope Rd, Sunderland (0783-41211) Libn: Mrs C.Bagnall MA, ALA.   **8** Science & technology; language & literature; education; psychology; philosophy; sociology & social work; politics; economics; law & public administration; management; geography & town planning; history; English literature & drama; music & religion; art & design.   **9** Audio-visual; teaching practice; Open University publications; British government publications; complete BSI; complete set of O.S. one-inch maps; slide colln (16,000) on painting, sculpture, architecture.   **10** NRLB; TALIC.
11 Yes, for ref only.   **12** Term: Mon-Fri 9.00-21.00 (Fri 17.30), Sat 9.00-12.30; vac: Mon-Fri 9.00-17.30.
13 (a) c.150,600; (b) 1,354.   **14** £115,000.   **15** (a) 46 (b) 11 (c) 23.

SWAFFHAM, Norfolk

SWAFFHAM PARISH CHURCH LIBRARY, The Vicarage, Swaffham (Tel 0760-21373) Vicar of Swaffham.
6 Parochial Church Council.   **8** Medieval theology.
9 16th & 17th cent works of theology.   **11** No, scholars only.   **12** Special arrangement.

SWANSEA, West Glamorgan

SWANSEA COLLEGE OF TECHNOLOGY LIBRARY, Mount Pleasant, Swansea, SA1 6ED (Tel 0792-51881) Tutor-Libn: R.L.B.Morse BA, DipEd.
6 West Glamorgan Education Committee.   **8** Commercial management; production, mechanical & electrical engineering; building; mining; sciences.   **10** BLL.   **11** No.   **12** Mon-Fri 9.00-19.00.   **13** (a) 15,000; (b) 103.   **14** £6,000.
15 (a) 2 (b) 1 (c) ½.

SWANSEA MEMORIAL COLLEGE LIBRARY (LLYFRGELL COLEG COFFA ABERTAWE), Memorial College, Ffynone, Swansea (Tel 0792-59260) Libn: Prof D.Elwyn Davies MA, BD, PhD.
8 Bible; theology; philosophy; church history; religions; biography; sociology; psychology; religious literature (especially in Welsh & English).   **9** Pre-1800 religious works in Latin, Welsh & English.   **11** Yes, by arrangement with Libn.   **13** (a) 18,000; (b) 40.

UNIVERSITY COLLEGE OF SWANSEA LIBRARY, Singleton Park, Swansea, SA2 8PP (Tel 0792-25678; Telex 48358) Libn: F.J.W.Harding MA, BLitt, FSA, ALA; Dep: D.M.Ellis BA, FLA.
7 Education Lib, Hendrefoilan, Gower Rd, Swansea, SA2 7NB (21231 ext 62), Libn: Miss E.F.Wood BA, ALA.   **8** Arts; economic & social sciences; education; pure & applied sciences.   **9** Celtic (primarily Welsh) books & periodicals; archives & printed works relating to coalfields & industries of South Wales.   **10** BLL; WRLB.   **11** Yes, for special ref by prior arrangement.   **12** Term: Mon-Fri 9.00-22.00, Sat 9.00-17.00, Sun 14.00-18.00; vac: Mon-Fri 9.00-17.00, Sat 9.00-12.00.   **13** (a) 350,000; (b) 3,600; (c) 30,000 archive records & mss; 320 microform titles.   **14** £196,000.
15 (a) 47 (b) 20 (c) 15.

SWINDON, Wiltshire

COLLEGE LIBRARY, Regent Circus, Swindon, SN1 1PT (Tel 0793-29141) Tutor-Libn: Mr L.E.Milton MA, DipLib, ALA; Site Libns: (Regent Circus) Mrs B.E.Porter ALA; (North Star Ave), Mr D.J.McCann MA, DipLib, ALA.
6 Wiltshire CC.   **7** The College, North Star Ave, Swindon,

CODE: 1 Name of Library. **2** Address. **3** Telephone & Telex. **4** Officer in charge. **5** Deputy. **6** Governing body.
7 Branches. **8** Main Subjects. **9** Special Collections. **10** Co-operative Schemes. **11** Open to public? **12** Hours.
13 Stock: (a) books (b) periodicals (c) other. **14** Finance. **15** Staff: (a) non-manual (b) graduate (c) chartered librarians.

SWINDON, Wiltshire—*continued*

SN2 1DY. **8** Engineering; management; home economics
& catering. **10** SWRLB; Swindon Area Association of
Libraries for Industry & Commerce. **11** Yes, at Libn's
discretion. **12** Term: Mon-Fri 9.00-20.00 (Fri 17.00);
vac: variable. **13** (a) c.24,000; (b) 270; (c) newspaper
cuttings. **14** £4,300. **15** (a) 6 (b) 3 (c) 3.

TADWORTH, Surrey

BEECHAM PHARMACEUTICALS, WALTON OAKS LIBRARY,
Beecham Pharmaceuticals Research Division, Walton Oaks,
Dorking Rd, Tadworth, KT20 7NT (Tel 07378-244) Libn:
Mrs Muriel Forward.
8 Nutrition & diseases associated with nutritional disorders,
eg. diabetes & obesity; animal nutrition; animal husbandry.
11 No. **12** 9.00-17.15. **13** (a) c.8,500; (b) 150.
14 £6,000. **15** (a) 2.

TAUNTON, Somerset

SOMERSET ARCHAEOLOGICAL AND NATURAL HISTORY
SOCIETY'S LIBRARY, Taunton Castle, Taunton, TA1 4AD
(Tel 0823 88871) Sec of the Society: Mr H. L. M. Patten.
8 History; archaeology; natural history & literature of
Somerset. **11** Yes, for ref only. **12** Tues-Sat 9.30-
12.30, 14.00-17.30. **13** (a) 25,000; (b) 90; (c) drawings;
prints & photographs.

SOMERSET COLLEGE OF ARTS AND TECHNOLOGY,
LEARNING RESOURCE CENTRE AND LIBRARY, Wellington
Rd, Taunton, TA1 5AX (Tel 0823-83403 ext 236) Tutor-Libn:
Mr C. E. Bond FLA; Dep: Mrs A. Totterdell BA, ALA.
6 Somerset CC, Education Committee. **8** General; art &
design; business; building & surveying; catering; engineering.
10 SWRLB. **11** Yes, by arrangement with Libn. **12** Mon-
Fri 9.00-20.30 (Fri 17.00). **13** (a) 15,100; (b) 320.
14 £14,000. **15** (a) 4 (b) 1 (c) 2.

TENBURY WELLS, Hereford & Worcester

ST MICHAEL'S COLLEGE LIBRARY, Tenbury Wells,
WR15 8PH.
8 Antiquarian musical source material only. **11** No.
12 Yes, but only by written appointment after written
application giving references. **13** (a) c.4,500; (c) over
1,500 mss.

THURSO, Caithness

DOUNREAY EXPERIMENTAL REACTOR ESTABLISHMENT
TECHNICAL INFORMATION SERVICE LIBRARY, Thurso,
KW14 7TZ (Tel 0847-2121; Telex 7597) Libn: Mrs R. C.
James MA, ALA. Senior Inf Officer: Mr H. J. C. Paterson
ALA.
6 United Kingdom Atomic Energy Authority, Reactor Group.
8 Nuclear chemistry; nuclear physics; metallurgy;
engineering; maths. **9** US atomic energy commission
reports on microfiche (64,000). **10** BLL; NLS. **11** No,
but written enquiries answered. **12** Mon-Fri 8.20-16.55
(Fri 16.00). **13** (a) 33,000; (b) 320; (c) 80 films; 5,500
slides; 100,000 microfiche reports. **14** £12,500.
15 (a) 7 (b) 1 (c) 2.

TORQUAY, Devon

SOUTH DEVON TECHNICAL COLLEGE LIBRARY, Newton
Rd, Torquay, TQ 25BY (Tel 0803-35711) Coll Libn: Mr E. J.
Salholm BA, ALA; Asst Libn: Mrs G. Mercer, BA, ALA.
6 Devon CC. **8** Business; engineering; building; construction; hotel & catering; domestic science; science; art.
11 Yes, for ref. **12** Term: Mon-Fri 8.45-20.00 (Fri.
17.00); vac: Mon-Fri 8.45-17.00 (Fri 16.30). **13** (a)
21,000; (b) 300; (c) teaching programmes; slides; film
strips; tapes; records; ohp transparencies; (c.400 items in
all). **14** £6,500. **15** (a) 4 (b) 2 (c) 2.

TROWBRIDGE, Wiltshire

TROWBRIDGE TECHNICAL COLLEGE LIBRARY, College
Rd, Trowbridge, BA14 0ES (Tel 02214-4081) Tutor-Libn:
Mr K. W. Pepper JP, ALA.
6 Wiltshire CC. **8** General. **11** Yes. **12** Term:
Mon-Fri 8.45-19.00 (Fri 17.00). **13** (a) 14,000; (b) 100.
15 (a) 2 (c) 1.

TRURO, Cornwall

BISHOP PHILLPOTTS' LIBRARY, Quay St, Truro (Tel 0872-
2771) Canon Libn: Ven P. C. Young, MA, BLitt.
6 Truro Diocesan Board of Finance. **8** Theology;
classics; chronology. **9** Incunabula; polyglot & other
early Bibles; Concilia; Acta Sanctorum; patristics. **11** No.
12 Mon-Fri 9.00-17.00 (Thurs 13.00). **13** (a) 12,000;
(b) 9. **14** £175.

WAKEFIELD, West Yorkshire

H. M. PRISON SERVICE STAFF COLLEGE LIBRARY,
Love Lane, Wakefield, WF2 9AQ (Tel 0924-71291 ext 47)
Libn: Mr Richard Turbet BA, ALA; Clerical Asst: Mrs
Brunt.
6 Home Office. **7** Officers Training School, Aberford
Rd, Wakefield, Libn: Mrs A. Rawlinson; Officers' Training
School, Leyhill, Wotton-under-Edge, GL12 8HL, Asst
Governor: Mr R. J. May BA. **8** Penology; criminology;
sociology; psychology; management. **9** Prison history.
11 No. **12** Mon-Fri 8.30 (Wed 9.00)-17.00 (Wed 20.00,
Fri 16.30). **13** (a) 15,000; (b) 100. **14** £4,000.
15 (a) 1½ (b) 1 (c) 1.

WAKEFIELD COLLEGE OF TECHNOLOGY AND ARTS
LIBRARY, Margaret St, Wakefield, WF1 2DH (Tel 0924-
70501) Tutor-Libn: Miss M. Fovargue BA, ALA; Asst Libn:
Mrs J. M. Cockshott ALA.
6 Wakefield MDC. **8** Science; engineering & building;
sociology; politics & government; economics; business &
management; catering & home economics; education; history
& geography; literature; art. **9** Complete BSI.
10 YHJLS. **11** Yes, for ref only. **12** Mon-Fri 9.00-
21.00 (Fri 17.00). **13** (a) 15,000; (b) 200; (c) examination papers (AEB, City & Guilds); college prospectuses;
filmstrips; teaching machine programmes. **14** £3,200.
15 (a) 3 (b) 1 (c) 2.

WALLINGFORD, Oxfordshire

HYDRAULICS RESEARCH STATION LIBRARY, Wallingford,
OX10 8BA (Tel 04913-2381 ext 342/3) Libn: Mr L. M. Manley
BA, ALA.
8 Civil engineering hydraulics; hydraulic structures;
rivers; estuaries; harbours & ports; sediment transport;
hydrology; ground water; irrigation. Not hydraulics of
machines. **11** Yes, for researchers, by arrangement.

WALLINGFORD, Oxfordshire—*continued*

12 Mon-Fri 8.30-17.00 (Fri 16.30).　**13** (a) 2, 500; (b) 200; (c) 3, 000 technical reports; various microfiches & microfilms.　**15** (a) 3 (c) 1.

WALLSEND, Tyne & Wear

SOUTH EAST NORTHUMBERLAND TECHNICAL COLLEGE LIBRARY, Embleton Ave, Willington Sq, Wallsend, NE28 9NJ (Tel 0632-624081) Libn: Miss J.M.Smeaton ALA.
6 North Tyneside MBC.　**8** Engineering; business; social services; general.　**10** NRLB.　**11** Yes, for ref only.　**12** Mon-Fri 9.00-17.30.　**13** (a) 17, 500; (b) 109.
14 £5, 000.　**15** (a) 2 (c) 1.

WALSALL, West Midlands

WALSALL COLLEGE OF TECHNOLOGY LIBRARY, St Paul's St, Walsall WS1 1XN (Tel 0922-25124) Tutor-Libn: Miss M.E.W.Chattell ALA; Dep: Mrs W.Ewen ALA.
6 Walsall Education Committee.　**8** Technology; business; food; science.　**10** MISLIC; SOSCOL; WESLINK.　**11** Yes, for ref only.　**12** Term: 9.15-19.00; vac: 9.00-17.00.
13 (a) 20, 000; (b) 130.　**15** (a) 5 (c) 2.

WEST MIDLANDS COLLEGE LIBRARY, Gorway, Walsall, WS1 3BD (Tel 09227-29141 ext 29) Libn: Mr I.D.Sidgreaves BA, ALA; Dep: Miss V.McNeil BA, ALA.
6 Walsall MBC.　**10** WMRLB; University of Birmingham Board of College Libraries.　**11** Yes, for bona-fide students, by prior written application.　**12** Term: Mon-Fri 8.30-21.00, Sat 9.00-12.00, Sun 14.00-17.00; vac: Mon-Fri 9.00-12.30, 13.30-17.00 (Fri 16.30).　**13** (a) 70, 000; (b) 500; (c) 5, 000 assorted audio-visual items.
14 £31, 000.　**15** (a) 14 (b) 3 (c) 5.

WANTAGE, Oxfordshire

BNF METALS TECHNOLOGY CENTRE LIBRARY, Grove Laboratories, Denchworth Rd, Wantage, OX12 9BJ (Tel 023-57 2992; Telex 837 166) Head of Inf Dept: Mr J.J.McGlynn VRD, MA; Libn: Miss B.J.Walgrave ALA.
8 Non-ferrous metallurgy & related subjects.　**11** No.

WARLEY, West Midlands

WARLEY COLLEGE OF TECHNOLOGY LIBRARY, Crocketts Lane, Smethwick, Warley, B66 3BU (Tel 021-558 4121) Tutor-Libn: T.Hildred BA, ALA.
6 Sandwell MBC.　**8** Technical (engineering; chemistry; construction technology etc).　**10** SOSCOL.　**11** No.
12 Term: Mon-Fri 9.00-20.30; vac: Mon-Fri 9.00-17.00.
13 (a) 22, 000; (b) c.140.　**14** £6, 000.　**15** (a) 4 (c) 1.

WARRINGTON, Cheshire

PADGATE COLLEGE OF HIGHER EDUCATION LIBRARY, Fearnhead, Warrington, WA2 ODB (Tel 0925-33571) Tutor-Libn: Miss M.M.Tye BA, ALA.
6 Cheshire Education Authority.　**8** General; education; children's books.　**9** Lewis Carroll colln.　**10** BLL.
11 Yes, for ref only.　**12** Term: Mon-Fri 9.00-21.00; vac: Mon-Fri 9.00-17.00.　**13** (a) 60, 000; (b) 550; (c) 400 gramophone records.　**14** £10, 000.　**15** (a) 7½ (b) 3 (c) 2.

U.K.ATOMIC ENERGY AUTHORITY, INFORMATION DEPARTMENT AND LIBRARY, Risley, Warrington, WA3 6AT (Tel 0925-31244; Telex 62301) Chief of Lib & Inf Services: Mr J.Roland Smith FLA.
6 UKAEA, Reactor Group.　**8** Nuclear power engineering.
9 British & foreign atomic energy reports (340, 000).
10 LADSIRLAC; INIS (IAEA).　**11** No, written enquiries accepted.　**13** (a) 25, 000; (b) 750; (c) 40% of current report accessions are in microfiche.　**14** £21, 000.
15 (a) 24 (b) 4 (c) 6.

WATFORD, Hertfordshire

BUILDING RESEARCH STATION LIBRARY, Bucknall's Lane, Garston, Watford, WD2 7JR (Tel 09273-74040; Telex 923220) Libn: Dr H.H.Neville MA, BSc, PhD; Dep Libn: Mr P.J.Elvin BSc.
6 Building Research Establishment.　**8** Building science.
10 HASL.　**11** Yes, by prior arrangement.　**12** Mon-Fri 8.45-16.15 (Fri 16.00).　**13** (a) 10, 000; (b) 900; (c) 150, 000 reports, mainly on building science (c.10, 000 on microfiche).　**15** (a) 26 (b) 14 (c) 2.

CASSIO COLLEGE OF FURTHER EDUCATION LIBRARY, Langley Rd, Watford, WD1 3RH (Tel 0923-24362 ext 44) Head of Lib Resources & Inf Service: Mr A.D.Jones MA, LesL, FLA; Tutor-Libn: Mrs C.Melling ALA.
6 College Governors.　**7** Callowland Adult Education Centre, Watford (0923-22900), Libn: G.Swinscoe FRHS.
8 Economics; economic history; geography; languages; retailing; food industries; domestic science; business.
10 HERTIS.　**11** Yes, for ref; loans by arrangement.
12 8.45-21.00.　**13** (a) c.26, 000; (b) c.200.　**14** £4, 000.
15 (a) 10 (b) 3 (c) 3.

WATFORD COLLEGE OF TECHNOLOGY LIBRARY, Hempstead Rd, Watford, WD1 3EZ (Tel 0923-41211; Telex 262461)
7 Art Lib, Alexandra Annexe, Ridge St, North Watford (0923-32268) Libn: Mrs H.Bren MA.　**8** Business; marketing; management; communication; printing; packaging; science; computing & engineering.　**10** HERTIS.
11 Yes.　**12** Term: Mon-Thurs 8.45-21.00, Fri 8.45-18.00; vac: Mon-Fri 9.00-17.00.　**13** (a) 30, 000; (b) 450; (c) microtexts; audio tapes; film strips; fine print specimens.
14 £10, 000.　**15** (a) 8 (b) 4 (c) 3.

WEDNESBURY, West Midlands

WEST BROMWICH COLLEGE OF COMMERCE AND TECHNOLOGY LIBRARY, Woden Rd South, Wednesbury, WS10 OPE (Tel 021-569-4695) Chief Libn: Mr K.Blakeman BA, ALA; Senior Tutor-Libn: Mr D.Jennings ALA.
6 Sandwell MDC.　**7** Management Services Divn, Wood Green, Wednesbury (021-569 4635), Libn: Mr D.Jennings ALA; General Studies Divn, Kendrick St, Wednesbury (021-569 4680), Libn: Mrs J.Mackenzie BA, ALA; Engineering Divn, High St, West Bromwich (021-569 2509), Libn: Mrs K.Muskett ALA.　**8** Accountancy; management; metallurgy; foundry technology; engineering; humanities.
9 Complete BSI; Diecasting Society Library colln.
10 MISLIC; WESLINK.　**11** Yes.　**12** 9.00-21.00; Branches 9.00-19.00.　**13** (a) 40, 000; (b) 300; (c) 1, 000 items non-book material.　**14** £12, 000.　**15** (a) 10½ (b) 3 (c) 4.

WELLESBOURNE, West Midlands

NATIONAL VEGETABLE RESEARCH STATION LIBRARY, Wellesbourne, Warwick, CV35 9EF (Tel 0789-840382) Libn: Mr D.A.Woodroffe BSc; Asst Libn: Mrs J.Keegan.
6 British Society for the Promotion of Vegetable Research.
8 Horticulture & agriculture; botany & chemistry.
10 WMRLB.　**11** Yes, on prior application to Libn.
12 Mon-Fri 8.45-17.00.　**13** (a) 4, 500; (b) 400; (c) circulars; bulletins; memoirs & reprints from horticultural & agricultural research stations throughout the world.
14 £4, 750.　**15** (a) 3 (b) 1.

WELLINGBOROUGH, Northamptonshire

WELLINGBOROUGH TECHNICAL COLLEGE LIBRARY, Church St, Wellingborough, NN8 4PD (Tel 09333-4165) Libn: Miss Hilda M.Bradley, BA, DipEd.
6 Northamptonshire CC.　**8** General; commerce; production engineering; metal fabrication; boot & shoe technology; automobile & electrical engineering; building.　**10** Interlibrary loans.　**11** Yes, by arrangement.　**12** Mon-Fri 9.00-21.00 (Fri 17.00).　**13** (a) 9, 400; (b) 63.
14 £1, 750.　**15** (a) 1 (b) 1.

CODE: 1 Name of Library. **2** Address. **3** Telephone & Telex. **4** Officer in charge. **5** Deputy. **6** Governing body.
7 Branches. **8** Main Subjects. **9** Special Collections. **10** Co-operative Schemes. **11** Open to public? **12** Hours.
13 Stock: (a) books (b) periodicals (c) other. **14** Finance. **15** Staff: (a) non-manual (b) graduate (c) chartered librarians.

WELLS, Somerset

WELLS CATHEDRAL LIBRARY, Wells (Tel 0749-78763)
Rev Canon P. M. Martin, Chancellor of Wells.
6 Dean & Chapter. **8** General (15th-18th cent).
9 Charters from 958; Chapter records & muniments from
c.1240; Orientalia, bequeathed by Bishop G. Hooper 1727;
450 vols bequeathed by Bishop T. Ken 1711. **11** Yes, to
exhibitions in vestibule only; students admitted to library
by special arrangement. **12** Easter-Sept: Tues, Thurs
& Bank Holidays 14.30-16.00. **13** (a) c.5,000; (b) 3.
14 £1,000. **15** (b) ½.

WELWYN GARDEN CITY, Hertfordshire

MID HERTFORDSHIRE COLLEGE LIBRARY, The Campus,
Welwyn Garden City, AL8 6AH (Tel 07073-26318) Head of
Lib Dept: B. C. Willgoss ALA; Tutor-Libn: H. Sepany BA,
ALA.
6 Hertfordshire CC. **8** Engineering (automobile, electrical); radio; TV; sociology; science. **9** Workshop
manuals. **10** HERTIS. **11** Yes, for ref & loans.
12 Term: Mon-Fri 9.00-21.00 (Fri 19.00); vac: Mon-Fri
9.00-17.00. **13** (a) 25,000; (b) 170; (c) microtexts;
gramophone records; visual aids; film strips; slides; tapes.
14 £4,500. **15** (a) 6 (b) 1 (c) 4.

WEYBRIDGE, Surrey

CENTRAL VETERINARY LABORATORY LIBRARY,
Woodham Lane, New Haw, Weybridge, KT15 3NB (Tel 09323-
41111 ext 313; Telex 262318) Libn: Mr D. E. Gray FLA;
Dep Libn: Mr R. M. Park MA, ALA.
6 MAFF. **8** Veterinary medicine & allied science; causes,
epizootiology, diagnosis & control of diseases of farm live-
stoke, inc poultry & rabbits. **11** Yes, on written application
to Libn. **12** Mon-Fri 8.30-17.00 (Fri 16.30) **13** (a)
27,000; (b) 800; (c) microfiches & microfilms; 3,500 pamphlets; 6,500 reports; 10,000 theses; 7,500 reprints.
15 (a) 10 (b) 3 (c) 4.

NATIONAL COLLEGE OF FOOD TECHNOLOGY LIBRARY,
St Georges Ave, Weybridge, KT13 ODE (Tel 0932-43991)
Libn: Mr S. Green FLA.
6 University of Reading. **8** Food science & technology;
chemistry; biology; microbiology; biochemistry; management. **10** SASLIC. **11** No. **12** Mon-Fri 9.00-17.00.
13 (a) 12,000; (b) 120. **14** £6,000. **15** (a) 3 (c) 1.

WEYMOUTH, Dorset

SOUTH DORSET TECHNICAL COLLEGE LIBRARY,
Newstead Rd, Weymouth, DT4 ODX (Tel 03057-3133/4)
Tutor-Libn: Mr J. M. Yarker ALA.
8 Social sciences; maths & science; engineering (mechanical
& electrical); construction; home economics & catering;
general; management & business. **10** SWRLB; inter-
library loans. **11** Yes, local residents etc. may borrow
on recommendation of County Libn. **12** Term: Mon-Fri
8.45-20.00 (Fri 18.00); vac: Mon-Fri 9.30-12.30, 14.00-
16.30. **13** (a) 18,000; (b) 100; (c) audio-visual aids.
14 £3,400. **15** (a) 3 (c) 1.

WEYMOUTH COLLEGE OF EDUCATION (will merge with
Bournemouth College of Technology), Cranford Ave, Weymouth, DT4 7LQ (Tel 03057-72311) Tutor-Libn: Miss M.
Benham BA.
8 Education, art, physical education. **13** (a) c.46,000;
(b) c.300. **14** c.£11,000.

WHITEHAVEN, Cumbria, see WORKINGTON

WIDNES, Cheshire

LAPORTE INDUSTRIES LTD, GENERAL CHEMICALS
DIVISION LIBRARY, Moorfield Rd, Widnes, Halton, WA8 OH8
(Tel 051-424 5555) Divisional Libn: Miss J. Littler ALA,
LRIC, AIInfSc.
8 Chemical, relating to manufactured products.
10 LADSIRLAC. **12** 8.30-17.00. **13** (a) 7,000; (b) 80.
15 (a) 2 (b) 1 (c) 1.

WIGAN, Lancashire

WIGAN COLLEGE OF TECHNOLOGY LIBRARY, Parson's
Walk, Wigan, WN1 1RU (Tel 0942-41711 ext 14) Chief Libn:
M. M. Hadcroft, MA, ALA, AIInfSc.
8 Social sciences; law; education; science & technology;
mechanical, electrical & civil engineering; geology; art.
9 Manchester Geological Society colln (early geology &
mining books & journals). **10** NWRLB; LADSIRLAC.
11 Yes, borrowing only through 'associate reader' scheme.
12 Term: Mon-Fri 9.00-21.00 (Fri 17.00); vac: Mon-Fri
9.00-17.00. **13** (a) 43,000; (b) 450; (c) 300 audio-visual
items. **14** £12,000. **15** (a) 7 (b) 4 (c) 3.

WINCHESTER, Hampshire

IBM UNITED KINGDOM LABORATORIES LTD, INFORMA-
TION SERVICE & LIBRARY, Hursley Park, Winchester,
SO21 2JN (Tel 0962-4433; Telex 47645) Manager Lib &
Inf Services: Mr J. J. Kalb.
8 Computers & data processing; programming; electronic
& mechanical engineering; physics; chemistry.
10 HATRICS. **11** Yes, to bona-fide enquiries, by appointment. **12** Mon-Fri 8.00-16.25 (Fri 15.05). **13** (a)
12,000; (b) 376; (c) 141,000 microforms; machine manuals;
language records. **15** (a) 6 (c) 2.

SCHOOL OF ART LIBRARY, Park Av, Winchester, SO23
8DL (Tel 0962-61891) Libn: Mrs S. L. Morgan BA; Dep: Mrs
M. Jenkins.
6 Hampshire Education Committee. **8** History of art,
painting, sculpture, drawing, print-making, textiles. **11** No,
except by special arrangement. **12** Term: 9.00-20.30;
vac: mainly mornings. **13** (a) 10,000; (b) 75; (c) 17,000
slides; 300 records. **14** £3,800. **15** (a) 1¼ (b) 1.

THOROLD AND LYTTELTON LIBRARY, Basement, 11 The
Close, Winchester, SO23 9LS Chairman of Management
Committee: Rev Canon T. G. King OBE, MA; Sec & Libn:
Mrs E. G. A. Prior.
6 Management Committee. **8** Theology. **11** No.
12 Mon-Fri 9.00-17.00. **13** (a) c.20,000. **14** £300.

WINCHESTER COLLEGE, WARDEN AND FELLOWS'
LIBRARY, College St, Winchester, SO23 9NA (Tel 0962-
64242 ext 37) Fellows' Libn: Mr Paul Yeats-Edwards FLA.
8 Religion; religious history; literature; classics; geography;
science; mathcs; topography; 18th cent satire; Reformation
literature; architecture; music. **9** Box colln (early maps
& road-books, topography); Turner colln (early Bibles inc
Erasmus's Greek Testaments); Thistlethwayte, Atcheson,
Jackson Bequests (incunabula & early printed books).
11 Yes, by appointment only. **12** Mon-Fri 9.00-16.30,
Sat by arrangement only. **13** (a) c.20,000 printed items;
(c) mss c.200 mss, inc music, (8th-20th cent). **14** £500.
15 (a) 1 (c) 1.

WINDSOR, Berkshire

ETON COLLEGE LIBRARY, (Keeper's Office) Penzance,
Windsor, SL4 6DB (Tel 07535-69991 ext 38) Keeper of Coll
Lib & Collns: Mr P. L. Strong MA, DAA.
6 Provost & Fellows of Eton College. **8** General for
Collegiate Library to 1800; later additions mainly in biblio-
graphy, history, theology, literature & Etoniana (authors &

WINDSOR, Berkshire—*continued*

subjects); 17th-19th cent school texts printed at Eton.
9 Western & Oriental mss (Pote colln of Oriental mss
now in Cambridge U.L.); incunabula; Aldines; Elzeviers;
17th cent pamphlets, etc; pre-Restoration plays; fine bindings; modern presses (complete Kelmscott set). **11** No,
except by written appointment. **12** By appointment.
13 (a) c.30,000; (b) 7. **15** (a) 2 (b) 1.

WISBECH, Cambridgeshire

ISLE OF ELY COLLEGE OF FURTHER EDUCATION
INFORMATION CENTRE AND LIBRARY, Ramnolh Rd,
Wisbech, PE13 2JE (Tel 0945-2561) Libn & Inf Officer:
M. Lender DipCSSD, DipEd.
6 Cambridgeshire CC. **7** Media resources in Education
Technology Section. **8** Education; art history; printing;
construction; horticulture. **9** Old books on bee-keeping.
11 Yes. **12** Mon-Fri 9.00-21.00. **13** (a) 11,500;
(b) 200; (c) video tapes; slides (art & history); gramophone
records. **14** £7,000. **15** (a) 5 (c) 1.

WOLVERHAMPTON, West Midlands

GUEST KEEN AND NETTLEFOLDS LTD, GROUP TECHNO-
LOGICAL CENTRE, Birmingham New Rd, Wolverhampton,
WV4 6BW (Tel 0902-34361; Telex 339724) Chief Inf Officer:
H. H. Goom ALA, FIInfSc; Dep Chief Inf Officer: B. H.
Vickery BSc, ALA.
8 Engineering; metallurgy; management. **10** WMRLB;
WESLINK; MISLIC. **11** No. **12** Mon-Fri 8.30-17.15
(Fri 16.00). **13** (a) 30,000; (b) 500. **14** £12,000.
15 (a) 16 (b) 6 (c) 4.

WOLVERHAMPTON TECHNICAL TEACHERS COLLEGE,
Compton Rd West, Wolverhampton, WV3 9DX (Tel 0902-
24286) Tutor-Libn: M. J. Freeman BA, ALA, ACP; Asst
Libn: Mrs D. M. Arthur BA, ALA, DipLib.
6 Wolverhampton Local Education Authority. **8** Education; training; agriculture; horticulture; business; technology;
educational technology; nursing; science; maths. **9** Agri-
culture/horticulture (particularly teaching of these subjects, inc overseas teaching); adult literacy tutor's colln;
large colln of FE & HE prospectuses. **10** BLL; MISLIC;
SOSCOL; WESLINK. **11** Yes, for ref only. **12** Mon-Fri
9.00-18.00. **13** (a) 16,000; (b) 200; (c) 300 items non-
book media. **14** £7,400. **15** (a) 3 (b) 2 (c) 2.

WORCESTER, Hereford & Worcester

WORCESTER COLLEGE OF EDUCATION LIBRARY,
Henwick Grove, Worcester (Tel 0905-422131) Libn: M. A.
Moore MA, DipLib, FLA; Dep Libn: J. W. Lloyd BA, ALA.
8 General; education. **10** Inter-library loans. **11** Yes,
for ref only. **12** Term: Mon-Fri 9.00-21.00 (Fri 18.00),
Sat 9.00-12.30; vac: Mon-Fri 9.00-17.30. **13** (a) 77,500;
(b) 450; (c) non-book materials. **14** £24,500. **15** (a) 10
(b) 5 (c) 3.

WORCESTER TECHNICAL COLLEGE LIBRARY, Deansway,
Worcester, WR1 2JF (Tel 0905-28383) Tutor-Libn: Mr H. M.
Jones MSc, DipEd; Asst Libn: Mr P. M. James ALA.
6 Hereford and Worcester CC. **8** Building; business;
catering; engineering; general; science. **10** WATL;
WESLINK. **11** No. **12** Term: Mon-Fri 9.00-19.00
(Fri 17.00); vac: Mon-Fri 9.30-12.30, 14.00-18.00.
13 (a) c.22,000; (b) 285; (c) microfilm; non-book materials.
15 (a) 4½ (b) 2 (c) 2.

WORKINGTON, Cumbria

WEST CUMBRIA COLLEGE LIBRARY, Park Lane,
Workington CA14 2RW; Flatt Walks, Whitehaven CA28 7RN
(Tel 0900-3527) Tutor-Libn: Mr David E. Laskey ALA.
6 Cumbria CC. **8** Electrical & mechanical engineering;
catering; business & management; law; construction; social
sciences; chemistry; physics; education. **9** Law (All
England Law Reports); Halsbury's Statutes and Laws.
10 BLL; NRLB. **11** Yes. **12** Term: Mon-Fri 9.00-

20.00; vac: Mon-Fri 9.00-17.00. **13** (a) 20,000; (b) 400;
(c) filmstrips & slides. **14** £6,500.

WORKSOP, Nottinghamshire

G.R. STEIN REFRACTORIES LTD, CENTRAL RESEARCH
LABORATORIES, LIBRARY AND INFORMATION DEPART-
MENT, Sandy Lane, Worksop, S80 3EU (Tel 0909-2291;
Telex 54585) Technical Administrator: Mrs K. Morgan;
Asst to Technical Administrator: Mrs J. M. Froggatt.
8 Refractories technology & associated subjects.
10 BLL; Aslib; SINTO. **11** No. **12** 9.00-17.00.
13 (a) c.950; (b) 57.

WORSLEY, Manchester

WORSLEY COLLEGE OF FURTHER EDUCATION LIBRARY,
Walkden Rd, Worsley, Manchester, M28 4QD (Tel 061-
790 2730/5080) Tutor-Libn: Mr H. Hunt BA, HNC, TCERT;
Asst Libns: Mrs R. Dalton, Mrs K. Groarke.
6 Salford Education Committee. **8** Engineering;
science; literature; history; art; hairdressing. **9** Lancashire & local history. **10** NWRLB. **11** No. **12** Mon-
Fri 8.45-19.15. **13** (a) 17,000; (b) 110; (c) 4,000
archives (illustrations & cuttings); 250 gramophone records;
150 film strips & loops. **14** £1,000. **15** (a) 2½ (b) 1.

WORTHING, Sussex

WORTHING COLLEGE OF FURTHER EDUCATION
LIBRARY, Broadwater Rd, Worthing, BN14 8HJ (Tel 0903-
31445) Libn: Mr R. E. M. Wright ALA, DipHum; Asst Libn:
Miss J. Vince ALA.
6 West Sussex CC. **8** Commerce; general; English;
modern languages & literature; history; geography; science;
engineering (mechanical & electrical); joinery; commerce
inc secretarial studies, accounting & business. **9** Major
banking journals & reviews kept for 5 years. **10** SASLIC.
11 Yes, if engaged in local industry & commerce, or have
bona-fide enquiry. **12** Term: Mon-Fri 8.45-19.15
(Fri 17.15); vac: 8.45-17.15. **13** (a) 18,000; (b) 212;
(c) 60 jackdaws; maps; videotapes; gramophone records;
newspaper supplements (classified); pamphlets.
14 £2,750. **15** (c) 2.

WREXHAM, Clwyd

NORTH EAST WALES INSTITUTE OF HIGHER EDUCATION
LIBRARY, Wrexham, LL11 2AW (Tel 0978-3551) Head of
Learning Resources: Dr J. O. Clarke.
6 Local Authority. **7** Cartrefle College of Education,
Wrexham, Libn: Miss Olive Jones BA; Kelsterton College of
Technology, Connah's Quay, Deeside, Clwyd, Libn: Mr B.
Campbell ALA, Aston College, Wrexham, Libn: Mr P. W.
Curtis BA, ALA. **8** Science; engineering; business;
building; art; general; education. **9** Complete BSI; audio-
visual materials (Cartrefle). **11** Yes, for specific enquiries. **12** Term: Mon-Fri 9.00-20.00 (Fri 16.30);
vac: Mon-Fri 9.00-17.00 (Fri 16.30). **14** £5,000.
15 (a) 2 (b) 1 (c) 1.

WRITTLE, Essex

WRITTLE AGRICULTURAL COLLEGE LIBRARY, Writtle,
Chelmsford, CM1 3RR (Tel 0245-420705)
6 Essex CC. **8** Agriculture; horticulture; land use;
economics; botany; zoology; engineering. **10** Inter-
library loans. **11** Yes, by arrangement. **12** Mon-Fri
9.00-17.00. **13** (a) c.20,000; (b) 195; (c) tape/slide
packages. **14** £4,000. **15** (a) 3 (c) 1.

YORK, North Yorkshire

ASKHAM BRYAN COLLEGE OF AGRICULTURE AND
HORTICULTURE LIBRARY, Askham Bryan, YO2 3PR
(Tel 0904-66232) Tutor-Libn: Mr G. A. Howitt BA, DipEd,
ALA.
6 North Yorkshire CC. **8** Agriculture; horticulture;
landscape technology; agricultural engineering. **11** Yes,

CODE: **1** Name of Library. **2** Address. **3** Telephone & Telex. **4** Officer in charge. **5** Deputy. **6** Governing body. **7** Branches. **8** Main Subjects. **9** Special Collections. **10** Co-operative Schemes. **11** Open to public? **12** Hours. **13** Stock: (a) books (b) periodicals (c) other. **14** Finance. **15** Staff: (a) non-manual (b) graduate (c) chartered librarians.

YORK, North Yorkshire—*continued*

on individual application. **12** Term: Mon-Fri 9.00-21.00; vac: Mon-Fri 9.00-17.00. **13** (a) 10,500; (b) 118. **14** £3,500. **15** (a) 1 (b) 1 (c) 1.

COLLEGE OF RIPON AND YORK ST JOHN LIBRARY AND RESOURCE CENTRE, Lord Mayor's Walk, York, YO3 7EX (Tel 0904-5677) Tutor-Libn: Mr J.M.O.Rees-Williams. **6** Church of England. **7** Ripon Campus, College Rd, Ripon HG4 2QX (0765-2691) Tutor-Libn: Mr Geoffrey Frank Willett MA. **8** Education; arts; sciences. **9** Victorian children's books; school textbooks. **10** BLL; YRLB; Physical Education Association. **11** Yes. **12** Term: Mon-Fri 8.30-21.00, Sat 8.30-12.00; vac: Mon-Fri 9.00-17.00. Branch varies. **13** (a) 100,000; (b) 450; (c) film strips; wall charts; illustrations; teaching kits; samples. **14** £24,000.

UNIVERSITY OF YORK, J.B.MORRELL LIBRARY, Heslington, York, YO1 5DD (Tel 0904-59861; Telex 57933) Univ Libn: Mr Harry Fairhurst MA; Dep: Miss Margaret Evans BA. **7** Inst of Advanced Architectural Studies Library, King's Manor, York, Asst Libn in Charge: K.V.Parker BA. **8** General. **9** Mirfield colln (2,500 vols pre-1800 printed books); Halifax Parish library; Slaithwaite Parish library; Wormald colln; Dyson colln (17th-18th cent English literature). **10** YRLB. **11** Yes. **12** Term: Mon-Fri 9.00-22.00, Sat 9.00-17.15; vac: Mon-Fri 9.00-21.00 (July & Aug 17.15). **13** (a) 220,000; (b) 2,100; (c) microtexts; slides; tapes; tape-slide presentations; gramophone records; films; film-strips. **14** £127,000. **15** (a) 45 (b) 17 (c) 18.

YORK COLLEGE OF ARTS AND TECHNOLOGY LIBRARY, Tadcaster Rd, York, YO2 1UA (Tel 0904-67161) Tutor-Libn: W.Kitchen FLA, CertEd; Asst Tutor-Libn: J.S.Brown ALA. **6** North Yorkshire Education Committee. **8** Building; science; maths; engineering; business (inc management); art; general. **11** Yes, for ref only. **12** Term: Mon-Fri 8.45-21.00 (Fri 17.30). **13** (a) 30,000; (b) 300. **14** £5,000. **15** (a) 4 (c) 2.

YORK MINSTER LIBRARY, Dean's Park, York, YO1 2JD (Tel 0904-25308) Libn: Canon R.Cant MA; Sub-Libn: C.B.L.Barr MA, ALA. **6** Dean & Chapter. **8** Middle Ages; religious history; religious literature; theology; art history; early printed books. **9** Yorkshire local history (10,000 vols, plus maps, engravings, archives); Dean & Chapter archives; early mss & printed music; York printing; Civil War tracts. **11** Yes. **12** Mon-Fri 9.00-17.00. **13** (a) 60,000; (b) 10; (c) archives; maps & plans; prints & drawings. **15** (a) 4 (b) 2½ (c) 2.

MUSEUMS, ART GALLERIES AND STATELY HOMES

The entries are arranged alphabetically by town. The whole of the Greater London area is included under 'London'.

Prices of admission and hours of opening were correct for 1975, but should not be regarded as accurate for 1976 and later years. The dates of opening given are inclusive. Museums should be assumed to be closed on all bank holidays unless either bank holiday hours are specifically given, or the museum is stated to be closed on certain bank holidays, in which case it can be assumed to be open on all others.

Commercial art galleries and art galleries which have no permanent collections were, in general, omitted. Stately homes with important collections of furniture, paintings, memorabilia etc were generally included, but the dividing lines were often difficult to establish.

MUSEUMS AND ART GALLERIES: QUESTIONNAIRE

1. Official name of Museum, Art Gallery, Stately
Home etc   2. Full postal address   3. Telephone
number; Telex number   4. Name of governing
body where applicable   5. Name, designation
and qualifications of officer in charge
6. Committee responsible for museum, Art
Gallery, Stately Home etc   7. If the Museum,
Art Gallery, Stately Home etc is part of a larger
department, indicate name of that department
and give name, designation and qualifications of the
chief officer   (Note: questions 6 and 7 apply
only to Museums etc provided by local authorities)
8. Is the Museum, Art Gallery, Stately Home etc
open to the public   9. Hours of opening:
Weekdays, Saturdays, Sundays, Bank Holidays.
Is admission free, if not give charges   10. Scope
of Museum, Art Gallery, Stately Home etc
11. Special exhibits or facilities   12. Number
of full-time staff: (a) Professionally qualified
(b) Other non-manual; (c) Manual.

MUSEUMS, ART GALLERIES AND STATELY HOMES

ABERDEEN, Aberdeenshire

ABERDEEN ART GALLERY AND MUSEUMS, Schoolhill,
Aberdeen, AB9 1FQ (Tel 0224-23942).   4 City of Aberdeen
DC.   5 Dir: Mr Ian McKenzie Smith DA, ARSA, ASIA,
FRSA, FSA(Scot).   6 Art Gallery & Museums.   8 Open to
the public.   9 Mon-Sat (inc bank hols) 10.00-17.00 (Thurs
20.00), Sun 14.00-17.00. Free.   10 Scottish painting;
20th cent British & 19th cent French painting; English watercolour, sculpture, prints & drawing library. Annex 1 James
Dun's House, 61 Schoolhill; Annex 2 Provost Skene's House,
Guestrow.   11 Temporary exhibitions; events; recitals;
film shows; drama; poetry; lectures, etc. Gallery shop;
monthly calendar; coffee shop.   12 (a) 5 (b) 4 (c) 17.

Aberdeen University

ANTHROPOLOGICAL MUSEUM, Aberdeen, AB9 1AS
(Tel 0224-40241).   4 University Court.   5 Officer-
in-Charge: Prof R. D. Lockhart MD, ChM, LLD, FRSE,
FSA(Scot).   8 Open to the public.   9 Mon-Fri 9.00-
17.00. Free.   10 Ethnographic colln; Egyptian colln;
classical vases; local antiquities; Chinese bronzes & ceramics.   11 Urns (or beakers) & skeletal remains of short
stone cist, (or beaker) people.   12 (a) 1; (b) 2; (c) 4.

ZOOLOGY DEPARTMENT MUSEUM, Tillydrone Ave, Old
Aberdeen, AB9 2TN (Tel 0224-40241). 5 Hon Curator:
Prof G. M. Dunnet; Lecturer-in-charge; Dr. S. Symmons.
8 Open, by appointment.   9 Mon-Fri 9.00-17.30. Free.
10 Essentially a university teaching museum, but exhibits
suitably arranged for school parties, colleges etc; comprehensive colln of British birds; skulls, skeletons, skins
etc of all vertebrate groups; invertebrates (especially
shells).   11 Fenton colln (British birds eggs in complete clutches with data); Duncan colln (British lepidoptera); wild cat skins; blue mountain hares; study skins of
birds & mammals prepared for research & ref throughout
the year.   12 (a) 1; (c) 3 (inc taxidermist).

GORDON HIGHLANDERS REGIMENTAL MUSEUM, Viewfield
Rd, Aberdeen, AB1 7XH (Tel 0224-38174).   4 Gordon Highlanders Regimental Trust.   5 Officer-in-Charge: Major
C. R. D'I. Kenworthy.   8 Open to the public.   9 Wed &
Sun 14.00-17.00. 5p.   10 Regimental uniforms, medals &
military insignia.   11 Very fine medal colln.
12 (c) 1.

ABERDOUR, Fife

INCHCOLM ABBEY, Aberdour.   4 Dept of Environment.
5 Information Officer, Argyle House, 3 Lady Lawson St,
Edinburgh.   9 Mon-Sat 9.30-19.00, Sun 14.00-19.00.
Oct-March: closes 16.00 daily. Adults 5p, children 2½p.
10 Remains of an Augustinian monastery on an island in
the Firth of Forth (founded 1123).   11 13th cent octagonal
chapter house, wall painting of funeral procession of clerics.
12 (c) 1.

ABERFORD, West Yorkshire

LOTHERTON HALL, Aberford, Leeds, LS25 3EB (Tel 097
332-259).   4 Leeds MDC.   5 Dir of Art Galleries:
Mr Robert Rowe CBE, MA, FMA.   7 Leisure Services
Dept. Dir: M. J. Palmer-Jones MA.   8 Open to the public.
9 Daily 10.30-18.15 (or dusk). Closed Dec 25 & 26.
10 Small country house (core 18th cent, most of rest Edwardian). Gascoigne family collns of paintings, furniture,
silver & porcelain; 19th & 20th cent decorative arts; English
costume.   11 Study facilities for ceramics; fashion; medieval chapel.   12 (a) Served from Temple Newsam.

ABERGAVENNY, Gwent

ABVERGAVENNY AND DISTRICT MUSEUM, The Castle,
Castle St, Abergavenny, NP7 5EE (Tel 0873-4282).
4 Monmouth DC.   5 Curator: Mr R. P. Davies MA.
6 Leisure & Recreation.   8 Open to the public.   9 Mon-
Sat 11.00-17.00, Sun 14.30-17.00. Closed Dec 25 & 26.
Adults 10p, children & OAPs 5p.   10 Local history; folk
life.   11 Welsh border kitchen.   12 (a) 1 (b) 2.

ABERYSTWYTH, Dyfed

CEREDIGION MUSEUM, 14 Vulcan St, Aberystwyth, SY23 1JH
(Tel 0970-2924).   4 Ceredigion DC.   5 Curator: Dr J.D.
Owen BSc, PhD.   6 Amenities & Leisure.   8 Open to the
public.   9 Mon-Sat (inc bank hols) 14.00-18.00. Closed
Dec 25, 26 & Good Friday. Free at present, 5p charge under
consideration.   10 Life of man in Ceredigion (Cardigan-
shire) throughout the ages; folk material; furniture; agricultural & craft implements; seafaring material; industrial
archaeology; archaeological section being built up.
11 Welsh furniture; lead mining; craft objects.   12 (a) 1
(c) 1.

ORIEL GALLERY, CANOLFAN Y CELFYDDYDAU,
ABERYSTWYTH ARTS CENTRE, Penglais, Aberystwyth,
SY23 3DE (Tel 0970-4277).   4 University College of Wales.
5 Arts Centre Manager: Mr Roger Tomlinson BA.   6 Arts
Centre (Gallery Sub-Committee).   8 Open to the public.
9 Mon-Sat 10.00-17.00. Free.   10 Exhibitions, (changed
c. 3 weekly intervals).   11 Integral screen & track lighting
system.   12 (a) 1 (c) 1.

ABINGDON, Oxfordshire

PENDON MUSEUM OF MINIATURE LANDSCAPE AND
TRANSPORT, Long Wittenham, Abingdon. (Tel 086730-7365).
4 Pendon Museum Trust Ltd.   8 Open to the public.
9 Sat, Sun & bank hols (summer only) 14.00-18.00. Other
times by arrangement. Adults 30p, children & OAPs 20p.
10 Miniature English countryside of the 1930s, accurately
detailed; model of one of Brunel's timber viaducts in Dart-
moor with representative trains; fully detailed models of
cottages & farm buildings in thatched village of the Vale of
the White Horse; early 19th cent railway relics; John Ahern's
famous Madder Valley railway layout; small shop; refreshments; toilets; small car park.

ACCRINGTON, Lancashire

HAWORTH ART GALLERY, Manchester Rd, Accrington,
BB5 2JS (Tel 0254-33782).   4 Hyndburn BC.
6 Recreation & Amenities.   7 Amenities & Recreation
Dept, Mr J. Knowles DLC, MARM.   8 Open to the public.
9 Daily (inc bank hols) 14.00-17.00 (plus April-Sept: Sun
18.00-20.00). Free.   11 Temporary exhibitions (all
media, mostly living artists); largest colln in Europe of 19th
cent Tiffany glass; oil & water colour painting.   12 (a) 1
(b) 1 (c) 1.

AIKERNESS, Orkney Isles

AIKERNESS BROCH, Aikerness, Evie, Orkney, KW17 2NH
4 Dept of Environment.   5 Information Officer, Argyle
House, 3 Lady Lawson St, Edinburgh.   8 Open to the public.
9 April-Sept: Mon-Sat 9.30-19.00; Oct-March: Mon-Fri
9.30-16.00; Sun (all year) 14.00-16.00. Adults 5p, children
2½p.   10 Iron Age Broch tower over 10 ft high.
11 Complex of secondary huts & other buildings, all
surrounded by a deep rock cut ditch.

AIRDRIE, Lanarkshire

AIRDRIE PUBLIC LIBRARY MUSEUM (temporarily closed),
Wellwynd, Airdrie, ML6 0AG (Tel 02366-63221). **4** Monklands DC. **5** Libn: M. A. Black ALA. **6** Leisure &
Recreation. **7** Chief Libn: Mr John Fox. **8** Closed
during renovations. **10** General; some articles of local
interest.

ALCESTER, Warwickshire

COUGHTON COURT, Coughton, Alcester, B49 5JA
(Tel 078971-2435). **4** National Trust. **5** Custodian:
Miss Mary Thompson. **8** Open to the public. **9** April-
Oct: Sat & Sun 14.00-18.00. Parties other times by arrange-
ment. Adults 50p, children 25p, group rates. **11** Shop; tea
rooms. **12** (a) 3 (b) 5.

RAGLEY HALL, Alcester, B49 5NJ (Tel 078971-2845/2455).
4 Owner: the Marquess of Hertford. **8** Open to the public.
9 Easter-Oct: Tues-Thurs, Sat, Sun & bank hols 14.00-17.30.
Park: daily 11.00-19.00. House & grounds: Adults 80p,
children 40p. Grounds only: adults 40p, children 20p.
10 17th cent Palladian house (designed by Robert Hook in
1680), recently restored; baroque plasterwork; 400 acre park
laid out by Capability Brown (1750). **11** Adventure Wood
in park for children (10-16 years); country trail; picnic
places.

ALDEBURGH, Suffolk

ALDEBURGH MUSEUM, Moot Hall, Aldeburgh. **4** Trustees.
5 Hon Sec to Trustees: Rt Rev Falkner Allinson MA.
8 Open to the public. **9** Sat & Sun (Easter-mid June),
daily (mid June-Aug): 11.00-12.00, 14.00-16.30. Adults
10p, children free, OAPs 5p. **10** Elizabethan building;
local fishing & brick works; local dignitaries (George Crabbe
poet etc); Roman remains; sea birds; railway; lifeboat;
pictures; photographic history of town; flints; fossils.
11 Snape burial ship; Claw Beaker; copy of ring burial urns;
early maps of Aldeburgh. **12** (b) 3.

ALDERNEY, Channel Islands

ALDERNEY SOCIETY MUSEUM, The Old School, High St,
Alderney (Tel 048 182-2539). **4** Alderney Society.
5 Hon Dir: Mr Kenneth Wilson. **8** Open to the public.
9 Mon-Sat (inc bank hols) 10.00-12.30, Sun by arrangement for parties. adults 10p, children 5p. **10** Archaeology
(Iron Age 'A' material excavated on island); German occupation 1940-45; folk life in Alderney; geology of Alderney;
ship wrecks off Alderney. **11** Archival material available
for students.

ALDERSHOT, Hampshire

AIRBORNE FORCES MUSEUM, Browning Barracks, Aldershot,
GU11 2DS (Tel 0252-24431, ext 619). **4** Airborne Forces
Museum Trustees. **5** Officer-in-charge: Major H. M.
McRitchie MC. **8** Open to the public. **9** Mon-Fri 9.00-
12.30, 14.00-17.00, Sat 9.30-12.30, 14.00-17.00, Sun (& bank
hols) 10.00-12.30, 14.00-16.30. adults 10p, serving & ex-
members of Airobrne Forces & families 5p, children 2½p.
10 History of Airborne Forces. **11** Weapons; equipment;
uniforms; medals; models; research library (by special
arrangement). **12** (a) 1 (b) 2.

QUEEN ALEXANDRA'S ROYAL ARMY NURSING CORPS
MUSEUM, Royal Pavilion, Farnborough Rd, Aldershot,
GU11 1PZ (Tel 0252-24431 ext 301). **4** MoD. **5** Officer-
in-charge: Major J. Battersby RO III. **8** Open to the public. **9** Mon-Fri 9.00-12.30, 14.00-16.30. Free.
10 History of the Corps. **12** (b) 2.

ROYAL ARMY DENTAL CORPS HISTORICAL MUSEUM,
Headquarters & Training Centre RADC, Evelyn Woods Rd,
Aldershot, GU11 2LS (Tel 0252-24431 ext 3470). **4** MoD
(Army). **5** Curator: Major H. W. Loveday. **7** Comman-
dant Headquarters & Training Centre RADC. **8** Open to
the public. **9** Mon-Fri 9.00-16.00. Free. **10** Connec-

tions between dentistry & the British Army (from 1660 to
present). **11** Uniforms; prisoner of war exhibits; early
instruments.

ROYAL ARMY MEDICAL CORPS HISTORICAL MUSEUM,
Keogh Barracks, Ash Vale, Aldershot, GU12 5RQ (Tel 0252-
24431 ext 292). **4** Trustees & Executive Committee.
5 Curator & Sec: Major Gen A. MacLennan (Retd) MB, CHB.
8 Open to the public. **9** Mon-Fri 9.00-16.00. Free.
10 History of the Army Medical Service (from 1660).
11 Relics of Wellington, Napoleon, Florence Nightingale,
2 double VC's etc. **12** (a) 1 (c) 1.

ROYAL ARMY VETERINARY CORPS MUSEUM, RAVC
School and Stores, Gallwey Rd, Aldershot, GU11 2DQ
(Tel 0252-24431 ext 2261/2). **8** Open to the public.
9 Mon-Fri 9.00-12.30, 14.00-16.30. Free. **10** Military
veterinary services, & equipment.

ROYAL CORPS OF TRANSPORT MUSEUM, RHQ RCT,
Buller Barracks, Aldershot, GU11 2BX (Tel 0252-24431
ext 2417). **4** Institution of the Royal Corps of Transport.
5 Officer-in-Charge: Lt Col K. Capel-Cure AFC. **8** Open
to the public. **9** Mon-Fri 9.30-12.00, 14.00-16.00. Free.
10 History of RCT & its predecessors (from 1794); uniforms;
models, artefacts; pictures & photographs. **11** Uniform
jacket of Royal Wagon Train Officer at time of Waterloo; full
dress uniform of Commissariat General; Army Services
Corps badges. **12** (b) 1 (c) 1.

ALEXANDRIA, Dunbartonshire

CAMERON HOUSE, Alexandria, G83 8QZ (Tel 0389-56226/7).
5 Comptroller: K. Thune-Larsen. **8** Open to the public.
9 Easter-Sept: daily (inc bank hols) 11.00-18.00. Adults
25p, children 10p. **10** Home of Mr & Mrs P. Telfer
Smollett; historic house; porcelain; silver; Staffordshire pottery animals; armour & weapons; Victorian nursery with 4
generations of toys; whisky bottles. **11** Tobias Smollett
literary museum. **12** (b) 2 (c) 3.

ALFORD, Lincolnshire

MANOR HOUSE FOLK MUSEUM, The Manor House, West St,
Alford. **4** Alford & District Civic Trust Ltd. **5** Hon
Sec: Mr A. S. Hackett BSc, MRSH, LRIC, LIBiol.
8 Open to the public. **9** July & Aug: Tues 10.30-12.30,
Tues & Sun 14.30-17.00. Other times by appointment.
Adults 10p, children 2p. **10** Local history & social life.
11 Craft shops; sweet factory; agricultural gallery; chemist
shop; Victoriana; schoolroom.

ALLOWAY, Ayrshire

AYRSHIRE (ECO) YEOMANRY MUSEUM, Rozelle, Monument
Rd, Alloway, KA7 4NQ (Tel 0465-3119). **5** Curator: Major
J. C. K. Young TD. **8 & 9** Opening March 1976; daily (exc
Thurs) 10.00-16.00. Free. **10** History of the Ayrshire
Yeomanry. **11** Uniforms, medals, weapons etc belonging
to the Regiment.

BURNS COTTAGE & MUSEUM, Alloway (Tel 0292-41321).
4 Burns Monument Trustees. **5** Hon Sec & Treasurer:
Mr W. H. Dunlop CA. **8** Open to the public. **9** April-
Oct: Mon-Sat (inc bank hols) 9.00-19.00; Sun 14.00-19.00
(July & Aug: 10.00-19.00); Nov-March: Mon-Sat (inc bank
hols) 10.00-16.00. Adults 10p, OAPs & children 5p.
10 Birthplace of Burns; his letters poems, songs & other
relics. **11** 1st (Kilmarnock) edition of the Bible; Scots
musical museum. **12** (b) 4½.

BURNS MONUMENT, Alloway (Tel 0292-41215) **4** Burns
Monument Trustees. **5** Hon Sec & Treasurer: Mr W.H.
Dunlop CA. **8** Open to the public. **9** April-Oct: Mon-
Sat (inc bank hols) 9.00-19.00, Sun 14.00-19.00 (July & Aug
10.00-19.00); Nov-March: Mon-Sat (inc bank hols) 10.00-
16.00. Adults 10p, children & OAPs 5p. **10** Monument;
statue house; gardens. **11** Statues by Thom of Tam
O'Shanter & Souter Johnnie. **12** (b) 4.

CODE: 1 Name of Museum, Art Gallery or Stately Home. 2 Address. 3 Telephone & telex. 4 Governing body. 5 Officer in charge. 6 Committee responsible. 7 Larger department, chief officer. 8 Open to public. 9 Hours; admission charges. 10 Scope. 11 Special exhibits or facilities. 12 Staff (a) professionally qualified (b) other non-manual (c) manual.

ALNWICK, Northumberland

ALNWICK CASTLE, Alnwick, NE66 1NG (Tel 0665-2207). **4** Owner: Duke of Northumberland. **5** Agent: W. F. P. Hugonin FRICS. **8** Open to the public. **9** Mid May-Sept: daily (exc Fri) 13.00-17.00. Adults 40p, children 20p; party rates. **10** 11th cent castle, restored 1854-65; armoury; guard chamber; library; dungeon; state coach; pictures (Titian, Canaletto, Van Dyck etc); fine furniture; Meissen china; landscape by Capability Brown. **11** Museum of early British & Roman relics.

'THE FIFTH', or ROYAL NORTHUMBERLAND FUSILIERS, REGIMENTAL MUSEUM, The Abbots Tower, Alnwick Castle, Alnwick, NE66 1NG (Tel 0665-2152/0632-29670. **4** Regimental Trustees. **5** Officer-in-Charge: Lt Col R. M. Pratt DSO, DL. **8** Open to the public. **9** May-Sept: Sat-Thurs 13.30-16.30. Winter by arrangement. 10p. **10** Regimental history (300 years). **11** Uniforms; weapons; medals; pictures. **12** (c) 1.

ALTON, Hampshire

ALLEN GALLERY, 10-12 Church St, Alton, GU34 2BW (Tel 0420-82802). **4** Hampshire CC. **5** Curator: Mr S. R. Dowey MA, AMA, MIBiol. **6** Recreation. **7** Hampshire County Museum Service, Chilcomb House, Chilcomb Lane, Bar End, Winchester, SO23 8RD (0962-66242/3), Dir: Miss Margaret C. MacFarlane. **8** Open to the public. **9** Mon-Sat 10.00-13.00, 14.00-17.00. Free. **10** Paintings from the W. H. Allen colln & loan exhibitions.

CURTIS MUSEUM, High St, Alton, GU34 1BA (Tel 0420-82802). **4** Hampshire CC. **5** Dir: Miss Margaret C. Macfarlane BA, AMA; Curator: Mr S. R. Dowey MA, AMA, MIBiol. **6** Recreation. **7** Hampshire County Museum Service, Chilcomb House, Chilcomb Lane, Bar End, Winchester SO23 8RD (0962-66242/3), Dir: Miss Margaret C. Macfarlane. **8** Open to the public. **9** Mon-Sat 10.00-13.00, 14.00-17.00. Free. **10** Local geology, botany, zoology, archaeology & history; domestic life; craft tools; pottery; dolls; toys; games. **11** Sporting firearms (in Annexe). **12** (a) 1 (b) 5.

ALTRINCHAM, Cheshire

ALTRINCHAM MUSEUM AND ART GALLERY (in store), Borough Librarian, Birch House, Talbot Rd, Old Trafford, Manchester, M16 0GH (Tel 061-872 6133). **4** Trafford BC. **5** Borough Libn: Mr J. W. H. Watters ALA. **9** Exhibition space planned in new library (open 1978). **10** Paintings; local history; temporary exhibitions.

ALYTH, Perthshire

ALYTH FOLK MUSEUM, Commercial St, Alyth, PH11 8EG (Tel 08283-594). **4** Loyal Alyth Library Trust. **5** Hon Sec: Mr J. O. S. Alexander. **8** Open to the public. **9** Sat, Sun & bank hols 14.30-16.30. Other times by arrangement. Free. **10** Folk life; farm & domestic implements, utensils & appliances; saddler's tools; blacksmith's bellows & horse-shoeing equipment. **11** Velocipede bicycle (1868); precision tools made by David Low (a local man).

AMBLESIDE, Cumbria

RYDAL MOUNT, Ambleside, NA22 9LU (Tel 09663-3002). **5** Joint Curators: Lt Comm & Mrs P. P. R. Dane. **8** Open to the public. **9** March-mid Jan: daily (inc bank hols) 10.00-17.30 (16.00 Nov-mid Jan); mid Jan-Feb: Sun 10.00-16.00. Adults 30p, children 15p; group rates. **10** Elizabethan cottage, home of William Wordsworth (1813-1850). 4½ acre garden largely landscaped by the poet with views of Windermere & Rydal Water. **11** Light refreshments (May-Oct). **12** (a) 2.

ANNAN, Dumfriesshire

ANNAN BURGH MUSEUM, Moat House, Annan (Tel 04612-2456). **4** Annan & Eskdale Regional Council. **5** Curator: Mr Alexander Inglis Milton. **8** Open to the public. **9** Mon-Fri 10.00-12.00, 14.00-16.00. Other times by arrangement. Free. **10** General folk museum & hall of fame. **11** Relics of Thomas Carlyle & Archibald Arnott (Napoleon's physician). **12** (a) 1.

ANSTRUTHER, Fife

SCOTTISH FISHERIES MUSEUM, St Ayles, Harbourhead, Anstruther, KY10 3AB (Tel 0333-310628). **4** Scottish Fisheries Museum Trust Ltd. **5** Curator & Sec: Mr Gordon Thomas Clarkson. **8** Open to the public. **9** April-Oct: Mon-Sat (inc bank hols) 14.00-18.00, Sun 14.00-17.00; Nov-March: Wed-Mon (inc bank hols) 14.30-16.30. Adults 20p, children & OAPs 10p, parties (10 or more) ½ price. **10** Artifacts, models, paintings & photographs illustrating history of Scottish industrial fishing, inc related fisherfolk life; open courtyard containing actual fishing yawls. **11** Marine aquarium; simulated fishing-boat wheelhouse; small dual-purpose lecture/temporary exhibition hall, ref library, shop. **12** (a) 1 (c) 2.

ARBROATH, Angus

ARBROATH ABBEY MUSEUM, Arbroath, Angus. **4** Dept of Environment. **5** Information Officer, Room J 728, Argyle House, 3 Lady Lawson St, Edinburgh, EH3 9SD. **8** Open to the public. **9** Mon-Sat 9.30-19.00, Sun 14.00-19.00. Closed 16.00 daily Oct-Mar. Adults 15p, children 5p.

ARBROATH ART GALLERY, Public Library, Hill Terrace, Arbroath, DD11 1EJ (Tel 02414-2248). **4** Angus DC. **5** Libn & Curator: Mr G. Moore BA, ALA. **6** Leisure & Recreation. **7** Libraries & Museums, Dir: Mr Gavin Drummond, ALA. **8** Open to the public. **9** Mon-Fri (exc Thurs) (inc bank hols) 9.30-18.00, Sat 9.30-17.00. Free. **10** Work by local artists or of local landscapes. **11** Occasional visiting exhibitions. **12** (a) 1.

ST VIGEANS MUSEUM, 2-4 Kirkstile, St. Vigeans, Arbroath. **4** Dept of Environment on behalf of Sec of State for Scotland. **5** Key-Keeper: Mrs Laura Dunbar. **8** Open to the public. **9** Mon-Sat (inc bank hols) 9.30-17.00 (16.00, Oct-March). Adults 5p, children 2½p. **10** Pictish & early Christian sculptured stones. (Museum is being expanded). **11** The Drostan Stone. **12** (b) 1.

SIGNAL TOWER MUSEUM, Ladyloan, Arbroath, DD11 1PU (Tel 02414-5598). **4** Angus DC. **5** Curator: Mrs Kathryn L. Moore BSc, AMA, FSA (Scot). **6** Leisure & Recreation. **7** Libraries & Museums Dept, Dir: Mr Gavin Drummond ALA. **8** Open to the public. **9** Mon-Sat 9.30-13.00, 14.00-17.00 (closed Thurs). Closed on some local hols. Free. **10** History & development of Arbroath & district. **11** The building of Bell Rock Lighthouse; local industries (inc Shanks lawnmowers & hand-made shoes); fishing industry & the sea; Arbroath silver; guild books; weights & measures, etc. **12** (a) 1 (c) 1.

ARMAGH, Co. Armagh, Northern Ireland

ARMAGH COUNTY MUSEUM, The Mall East, Armagh, BT61 9BE. **4** Armagh County Museum Management Committee of Ulster Museum Trustees. **5** Curator: Mr D. R. M. Weatherup FMA. **8** Open to the public. **9** Mon-Sat (inc some bank hols). 10.00-13.00, 14.00-17.00. Free. **10** Natural history; history & folklife of County Armagh; Irish paintings. **11** Regular winter art exhibitions (local & national); schools service. **12** (a) 1 (b) 1 (c) 4.

ROYAL IRISH FUSILIERS, REGIMENTAL MUSEUM, Sovereign's House, The Mall, Armagh, BT61 9DL (Tel 0861-522911). **5** Officer-in-Charge: Major G. A. N. Boyne JP. **8** Open to the public. **9** Mon-Fri 10.00-12.30, 14.00-

ARMAGH, Co. Armagh—*continued*

16.30; other days by prior arrangement. Free.   **10** Uniforms; medals; badges; pictures illustrating history of Regiment; ref library.   **11** Flag of 8th French Regt, (only flag in existence captured in an invasion of the British Isles, 1798). **12** (a) 1 (b) 1 (c) 1.

ARRAN, ISLE OF, Buteshire

BRODICK CASTLE, Brodick Castle, Isle of Arran, KA27 8HY (Tel 0770-2202).   **4** National Trust for Scotland. **5** Officer-in-Charge: Mr J.M. Frogie.   **8** Open to the public.   **9** Easter-Sept 1: Mon-Sat 13.00-17.00, Sun 14.00-17.00. Gardens: daily 10.00-17.00. Castle & gardens: Adults 40p, children 20p; gardens only: adults 20p, children 10p; car park 10p.   **10** Silver, porcelain & paintings from collns of the Dukes of Hamilton, William Beckford, & Earls of Rochford.   **11** Gardens & Goatfell.

ARRETON, Isle of Wight

ARRETON MANOR, Arreton, Isle of Wight, PO30 3AA. **5** Owner: Count Slade De Pomeroy.   **8** Open to the public. **9** Easter-early Nov: Mon-Sat (inc bank hols) 10.00-18.00, Sun 14.00-18.00. Winter by appointment. Manor House 25p, Pomeroy Museum 25p, children half price.   **10** Period furniture, fine oak carved Jacobean panelling, King Charles I snuff box (authenticated); Echoes of Childhood Museum (dolls, toys, doll's houses, children's & baby prams etc.); Folk Museum (inc farm implements).   **11** Pomeroy Museum (5' 9" square doll's house built & furnished in the Regency style); National Wireless Museum (inc items from WWI). **12** (c) 3.

ARUNDEL, Sussex

ARUNDEL CASTLE, Arundel, BN18 9LH (Tel 0903-882173). **5** Castle Manager: Mr R.W. Puttock.   **8** Open to the public. **9** At present, March-mid June: Mon-Thurs 13.00-16.00; mid June-Sept: Mon-Fri (& Sun in Aug) 12.00-16.00. Adults 50p, children & OAPs 25p. Ceremonial robes: adults 6p, children 3p (extra). Proceeds given to charity.   **10** 11th cent keep; castle restored 1700-1900; home of Dukes of Norfolk since 13th cent; portraits (Holbein, van Dyck, Gainsborough etc); furniture (from 15th cent); armoury. **11** Ceremonial robes & mantles inc personal possessions of Mary, Queen of Scots. Car park, tea room.

POTTERS MUSEUM OF CURIOSITY, 6 High St, Arundel, BN18 9AB (Tel 0903-882420 (evns).   **5** Owner & Curator: Mr James Cartland.   **8** Open to the public.   **9** Mon-Sun (inc bank hols): summer 10.30-17.30, winter most afternoons. Adults 20p, children & OAP's 10p, special rates for parties. **10** Works of Walter Potter, the Victorian taxidermist (1835-1918). Animal tableaux (eg Kittens Tea Party; Rabbits School; Death of Cock Robin; Guinea Pigs Cricket Match) & curiosities from all over the world).

ASHBURTON, Devon

ASHBURTON MUSEUM, 1 West St, Ashburton, Newton Abbot, TQ13 7DT (Tel 0364-52298).   **4** Ashburton Museum Trust. **5** Hon Asst Curator: W.R. Hatch BA.   **8** Open to the public.   **9** mid May-Sept: Tues & Thurs-Sat 14.30-17.00. Free.   **10** Local antiquities; weapons; period costumes; lace; implements; American Indian antiques; bygones. **11** Local geological specimens.

ASHBURY, Berkshire

ASHDOWN, Ashbury, Lambourn.   **4** National Trust. **8** Open to the public.   **9** Wed (April-Sept), 1st & 3rd Sat each month (May-Sept): 14.00-18.00. Grounds & roof top 30p. Grounds only: 15p. No reductions.   **10** 4 storey chalk block house built (1665) for Elizabeth of Bohemia; portraits.

ASHFORD, Kent

GODINTON PARK, Ashford, TN23 3BP (Tel 0233-26773). **5** Owner: Mr Alan Wyndham Green.   **8** Open to the public. **9** June-Sept: Sun & bank hols 14.00-17.00. Other times by appointment. Adults 30p, children 15p; party rates. **10** Jacobean house; elaborate panelling; fine furniture (17th & 18th cent); English & European porcelain; portraits (17th & 18th cent); formal gardens.   **12** (c) 2.

INTELLIGENCE CORPS MUSEUM, Templer Barracks, Ashford, TN23 3HH (Tel 0233-25251, ext 206).   **5** Curator: Lt Col (Rtd) W.W. Leary BEM; Asst Curator: Mr H.A. Hunter.   **8** Open to the public.   **9** Mon-Fri: 10.00-12.00, 14.00-16.00; other times by prior arrangement. Free. **10** All aspects of military intelligence (from the time of Elizabeth I).   **12** (b) 2.

ASHWELL, Hertfordshire

ASHWELL VILLAGE MUSEUM, Swan St, Ashwell, Baldock. **4** Ashwell Village Museum Trustees.   **5** Hon Curator: Mr Albert W. Sheldrick.   **8** Open to the public.   **9** Sun 15.00-17.30; other times by prior arrangement. Free. **10** Folk museum, stone age to present.

ASTON MUNSLOW, Shropshire

WHITE HOUSE MUSEUM OF BUILDINGS & COUNTRY LIFE, Aston Munslow, Craven Arms, SY7 9ER.   **5** Owner & Dir: Miss J. Constance Purser.   **8** Open to the public. **9** April-Oct: Wed 14.00-18.00; July & Aug: Tues-Thurs 14.00-18.00, Sat 11.00-18.00; bank hol weeks: daily (exc Fri & Sun) 11.00-18.00. House 30p, museum 25p, combined 50p.   **10** Homestead & surrounding buildings (13th cent with 15th, 17th & 19th cent additions); domestic & dairy utensils in position.   **11** Cider house (17th cent); stable (1680); kitchen; dairies; washhouse; nursery.

AVEBURY, Wiltshire

ALEXANDER KEILLER MUSEUM, Avebury, Marlborough (Tel 06723-250).   **4** Dept of Environment.   **5** Curator: Mrs F.J. de M. Vatcher FSA.   **8** Open to the public. **9** March, April & Oct: Mon-Sat 9.30-17.30, Sun 14.00-17.30 (April: Sun 9.30-17.30); May-Sept: daily 9.30-19.30; Nov-Feb: Mon-Sat 9.30-16.00, Sun 14.00-16.00. Closed Dec 24-26 & Jan 1. Adults 10p, OAPs & children 5p; party rates. Monuments complex free.   **10** Information about, & objects from, Avebury Neolithic & Bronze Age monuments; objects from medieval occupation.   **12** (a) 1 (b) 2.

AVEBURY MANOR, Avebury, Marlborough, SN8 1RF (Tel 06723-203).   **5** Owner: Lady Knowles.   **8** Open to the public.   **9** May-Aug: daily (exc Tues) 14.00-18.00; April & Sept: Sat & Sun 14.00-18.00. Bank hols 10.00-18.00. Adults 40p, children 20p.   **10** 16th cent manor house; fine panelling; decorative plaster-work; state rooms in which Queen Anne was entertained; topiary gardens; herb garden; animals in park (Soay sheep) & llamas.

AXBRIDGE, Somerset

ASHTON WINDMILL, Chapel Allerton, Axbridge.   **4** Bristol DC.   **5** Dir, City Museum: Mr N. Thomas MA, FMA, FSA. **6** Arts & Leisure.   **8** Open only by arrangement with Dir of City Museum.   **10** Last windmill in the region complete with sails & machinery.

AXBRIDGE MUSEUM, KING JOHN'S HUNTING LODGE, The Square, Axbridge (Tel 093473-812).   **4** Sedgemoor DC. **5** County Museums Officer: P.A. Stevens MA, FMA. **6** Leisure & Amenities.   **7** Dir: P. Fisher.   **8** Open to the public.   **9** Daily (inc bank hols) 14.00-17.00. Free. **10** Medieval timber framed shop (3 stories); local history & archaeology; bygones; some natural history.   **11** Axbridge nail-like Bristol nails; Axbridge mint coins.

CODE: 1 Name of Museum, Art Gallery or Stately Home. 2 Address. 3 Telephone & telex. 4 Governing body. 5 Officer in charge. 6 Committee responsible. 7 Larger department, chief officer. 8 Open to public. 9 Hours; admission charges. 10 Scope. 11 Special exhibits or facilities. 12 Staff (a) professionally qualified (b) other non-manual (c) manual.

AYLESBURY, Buckinghamshire

BUCKINGHAMSHIRE COUNTY MUSEUM, Church St, Aylesbury, HP20 2QP (Tel 0296-82158/88849). 4 Buckinghamshire CC. 5 Curator: Mr C.N. Gowing MA, FMA. 6 Education (Library & Museum Sub-Committee). 7 Education Dept, Chief Education Officer: Mr R.P. Harding BSc, FIMA, DPA, AKC. 8 Open to the public. 9 Mon-Fri 9.30-17.00, Sat 9.30-12.30, 13.30-17.00. Closed Dec, 25, 26 & Good Friday. Free. 10 Geology, natural history, archaeology & history of Buckinghamshire; local crafts & agriculture; small art colln. 11 Education room. 12 (a) 6 (b) 3 (c) 4.

WADDESDON MANOR, Waddesdon, Aylesbury (Tel 029 665-211/282). 4 National Trust. 5 Administrator: Col A.R. Waller MBE, MC. 8 Open to the public. 9 April-Oct: Wed-Sun 14.00-18.00; bank hols 11.00-18.00 (closed following Wed). 55p, Fri 75p. Grounds & aviary only: adults 25p, children 10p. 10 House built 1874-89 by Baron Ferdinand de Rothschild for his art colln. Extensive grounds inc aviary & herd of Sikka deer. 11 17th & 18th cent French paintings & furniture; Dutch paintings; Gainsborough & Reynolds portraits; Sèvres porcelain; Savonnerie carpets, etc. Restaurant; home-grown produce stall.

AYOT ST LAWRENCE, Hertfordshire

SHAW'S CORNER, Ayot St Lawrence, Welwyn, AL6 9BX. 4 National Trust. 8 Open to the public. 9 March-Nov: Wed-Sun & bank hol Mon 11.00-13.00, 14.00-18.00 (or sunset if earlier). Adults 40p, children 20p. 10 Home of George Bernard Shaw (1906-1950), exactly as he left it; personal paraphernalia; literary relics.

AYR, Ayrshire

CENTRAL ART GALLERY & MUSEUM, 12 Main St, Ayr, KA8 8ED (Tel 0292-69141). 4 Kyle & Carrick DC. 5 Organiser of Museums & Galleries: Miss M. McKellar MA. 6 Leisure & Recreation. 7 Libraries & Museums, Dir of Library Services: Mr Allan Leach BA, DPA, FLA. 8 Open to the public. 9 Mon-Sat 10.00-13.00, 14.00-19.30. Free. 10 Museum: principally local history (Ayrshire). Gallery: permanent colln of paintings, drawings & prints; temporary exhibitions. 12 (b) 3 (c) $\frac{1}{2}$.

BACUP, Lancashire

BACUP NATURAL HISTORY SOCIETY AND FOLK MUSEUM, 24 Yorkshire St, Bacup, OL13 5EG (Tel 070683-4621). 5 Hon Curator: C. Read. 8 Open to the public. 9 Thurs 19.30-21.30. Other times by appointment. Free, but contributions welcome. 10 Natural history & local history; flint colln (mainly local); Victoriana with local connections; birds in glass cases (many local).

BADMINTON, Avon

BADMINTON HOUSE, Badminton, GL9 1DB (Tel 045421-202). 4 Owner: His Grace, The Duke of Beaufort KG. 8 Open to the public. 9 May 29-31 & June-Sept: Wed 14.30-17.00. Adults 30p, OAPs 25p, children 10p. 10 Home of the Dukes of Beaufort since the 17th cent, fine example of the Palladian style; paintings (Italian, Dutch & English Schools); carvings & furniture. 12 (b) 3.

BAGSHOT, Surrey

ROYAL ARMY CHAPLAINS' DEPARTMENT MUSEUM, Bagshot Park, Bagshot, GU19 5HS (Tel 0276-73172). 4 MoD (Army), Royal Army Chaplains' Dept Museum Trustees. 5 Curator: Lt Col G.C.E. Crew BA, MInstP&S, MCIT, AMBIM. 8 Open by appointment only. 9 Mon-Fri 10.00-12.30, 14.30-16.00. Other days by special arrangement only. Free. 10 Residence of Duke of Connaught & Strashearn (1878-1942). Museum illustrates story of Chaplaincy services in British Army (1796-1976). 12 (a) 1.

BAKEWELL, Derbyshire

CHATSWORTH, Bakewell, DE4 1PN (Tel 0246-882204). 5 Comptroller: D.A. Fisher; Libn & Keeper of Collns: Mr Thomas S. Wragg MBE. 8 Open to the public. 9 April-mid Oct: Wed-Fri 11.30-16.00, Sat & Sun 13.30-17.00, bank hol Mon & Tues 11.00-17.00. Adults £1.00, children 30p. Gardens only: adults 30p, children 15p. Car park 20p. 10 Home of the Dukes of Devonshire; built 1687-1707, additions 1820-30; wood carvings by Samuel Watson; ironwork by Tijou; painted walls & ceilings by Verrio & Laguerre; fine furniture; tapestry; paintings; china; State Apartments; sculpture; books; mss; archives; gardens. 11 Farmyard (live farming & forestry exhibitions); Stand Wood walks.

OLD HOUSE MUSEUM, Cunningham Place, Bakewell, DE4 1DD (Tel 062 981-2378). 4 Bakewell & District Historical Society. 5 Chairman: J.T. Brighton MA. 8 Open to the public. 9 Easter-Sept: daily (inc bank hols) 14.30-17.00. Adults 20p, children 10p. 10 Restored parsonage house (1534 with 17th & 18th cent additions), once belonging to the Dean & Chapter of Lichfield; tools & crafts of the Peak District (inc lead mining & farming); 19th cent costume. 11 Wattle & daub screens; garderobe; fireplaces; children's room (shop, toys etc of the past); tools & trades; costumes.

BAMBURGH, Northumberland

GRACE DARLING MUSEUM, Bamburgh, NE69 7AE. 4 Royal National Lifeboat Institution. 5 Officer-in-Charge: Comm B.H. Dunn, FCA, RN. 8 Open to the public. 9 April-mid Oct: daily (inc bank hols) 11.00-19.00. Free. 10 Relics of Grace Darling, members of her family & of the wrecked S.S. Forfarshire. 11 Coble in which Forfarshire survivors were rescued by Grace Darling & her father, William Darling, Keeper of Longstone Lighthouse on the Outer Farnes. 12 (b) 4.

BANBURY, Oxfordshire

BANBURY MUSEUM, Marlborough Rd, Banbury, OX16 8DF (Tel 0295-2282). 4 Oxfordshire CC. 5 Museum Dir: Mr Crispin Paine MA, AMA; Keeper of Branch Museum Services: Miss F.M. Stanton. 6 Libraries, Museums & Archives. 7 Museum Services Dept, Mr Richard Foster MA, AMA. 8 Open to the public. 9 May-Sat (exc Tues) 10.00-13.00, 14.00-17.00. Free. 10 Local history, folk life, archaeology & natural history. 11 A Scrapbook of Victorian Banbury exhibition; regular temporary exhibitions. 12 (a) 1 (b) 1.

BROUGHTON CASTLE, Banbury, OX15 5EF (Tel 0295-2624). 5 Owner: Lord Saye & Sele. 8 Open to the public. 9 April-Sept: Wed; June-Aug: Sun; bank hol Sun & Mon. Adults 45p, children 20p. 10 Moated castle (built 1300 & 1550); Civil War connections; fine fireplaces, panelling etc.

UPTON HOUSE, Banbury, OX15 6HT (Tel 029587-266). 4 National Trust. 5 Officer-in-Charge Lt Col T.B.G. Slessor. 8 Open to the public. 9 Wed 14.00-18.00, Sat (May-Sept) 14.00-18.00. house & gardens: 35p, gardens only: 15p. 10 Late 17th cent house, (remodelled); Lord Bearsted's works of art; terraced garden descends very steeply from lawn to lake & valley. 11 Brussels tapestries; Sèvres porcelain; Chelsea figures; 18th cent furniture; over 150 pictures representing practically every European school. 12 (b) 2 (c) 2.

BANGOR, Gwynedd

PENRHYN CASTLE, Bangor, LL57 4HN (Tel 0248-53084).
4 National Trust.   **5** Administrator: Air Commodore A.D.
Panton CB, OBE, DFC, RAF (Ret'd).   **8** Open to the public.
9 April-Oct: daily 14.00-17.00, (June-Sept: Mon-Fri 11.00-
17.00); bank hols 11.00-17.00. Adults 60p, children 30p.
10 Castle, rebuilt 1840 on 8th cent site, inc part of 15th cent
fortified building; much original furniture; 45 acres of parkland, inc walled garden.   **11** Industrial Railway Museum;
doll colln; stuffed birds, animals & insects; natural history;
refreshments; shop.   **12** (b) 3 (c) 10.

University College of North Wales

DEPARTMENT OF ZOOLOGY MUSEUM, Brambell Laboratories, Deiniol Rd, Bangor, LL57 2UW (Tel 0248-51151 ext.
518).   **8** Open to the public.   **9** term: Mon-Fri 9.00-
17.30. Free.   **10** Undergraduate zoology.

MUSEUM OF WELSH ANTIQUITIES, Old Canonry, Gwynedd Rd, Bangor (Tel 0248-51151, ext 437).   **5** Hon
Curator: Prof A.H. Dodd MA, DLitt.   **8** Open to the public.   **9** Mon-Sat 10.30-16.30. Free.   **10** Archaeology;
folk life; separate art gallery.   **12** (a) 2 (b) 1 (c) 1.

ORIEL BANGOR ART GALLERY, Oriel Bangor Ffordd
Gwynnodd, Bangor (Tel 0248-53368).   **5** Curator: Mr
Michael Cullimore.   **8** Open to the public.   **9** Mon-
Sat 10.30-17.00. Free.   **10** 12 Exhibitions per year
of Old Master, mainstream & avante garde works.
12 (a) 1 (b) 2.

BANNOCKBURN, Stirlingshire

BANNOCKBURN MONUMENT, Visitor Centre, Bannockburn,
FK7 OLJ (Tel 0786-2664).   **4** National Trust for Scotland.
5 Resident Warden: Mr H.P. Owens.   **9** Apr-mid Oct:
Mon-Fri 10.00-18.00 (19.00, July & Aug), Sun 11.00-19.00.
Adults 30p, children 5p; car park 10p.   **10** Site of battle
where Robert the Bruce defeated the English; Borestone
statue of Robert the Bruce; auditorium & information centre.
11 Audio-visual presentation of wars of independence.

BARLASTON, Staffordshire

WEDGWOOD MUSEUM, Josiah Wedgwood & Sons Ltd, Barlaston, Stoke-on-Trent, ST12 9ES (Tel 078139-2141).   **4** Trustees of Wedgwood Museum.   **5** Officer-in-Charge: Mr.
Bruce Tattersall MA, AMA.   **9** Mon-Fri 9.00-17.00. Free.
10 Comprehensive colln of works of Josiah Wedgwood (1760
to present); related material (family portraits & Wedgwood
archives).   **12** (a) 1 (b) 2 (c) 1

BARNARD CASTLE, Co. Durham

BOWES MUSEUM, Barnard Castle, DL12 8NP (Tel 08333-
2139).   **4** Durham CC.   **5** Curator: Mr Michael H.
Kirkby MA, FMA.   **6** Museums Sub-Committee.   **7** Education Dept; Dir: Mr Douglas Curry MA.   **8** Open to the
public.   **9** Mon-Sat 10.00-17.30 (17.00 March, Apr & Oct)
(16.00 Nov-Feb), Sun 10.00-17.00 (winter 14.00-16.00).
Closed Dec 25, 26 & Jan 1. Adults 20p, children & OAPs 5p.
10 Old master & 19th cent paintings of most European
schools; varied English & continental ceramics; textiles &
costumes; sculpture & carving; French & English period rooms;
archaeology, social & natural history of region.   **11** Silver
Swan (famous automaton); paintings by El Greco, Goya,
Tiepolo, Canaletto, Boucher etc; sculpture by Houdon, Clodion
& 15th cent. Netherlandish & German schools; furniture by
Thomas Hope, style of Chippendale, Hepplewhite etc; bureau-
toilette which belonged to Marie Antoinette; Café & restaurant.   **12** (a) 8; (b) 10; (c) 15.

BARNSLEY, South Yorkshire

CANNON HALL MUSEUM, Cawthorne, Barnsley, S75 4AT
(Tel 022 679-8270).   **4** Barnsley MBC.   **5** Curator: Mr
Brian Murray BA.   **7** Education Dept, Chief Officer:
T. Brooks BSc.   **8** Open to the public.   **9** Mon-Sat 10.30-
17.00, Sun 14.30-17.00. Closed Dec 25 & Good Friday. Free.
10 Decorative arts; fine furniture; glassware; silver etc.

11 William Harvey colln of Dutch & Flemish paintings (formerly known as The National Loan Colln) on permanent
display. Regimental museum of the 13th/18th Royal Hussars
(Queen Mary's Own).   **12** (a) 1 (b) 1 (c) 3 + part-time staff.

COOPER ART GALLERY, Church St, Barnsley, S70 2AH.
4 Cooper Trust.   **5** Hon Dir: Mr L.H.H. Glover ARCA,
ATD.   **8** Open to the public.   **9** Mon-Sat 11.30-17.00.
Free.   **10** 19th & 20th cent painting; Sir Michael Sadler
colln (English drawing & watercolours); visiting exhibitions.
12 (b) 2.

BARNSTAPLE, Devon

ARLINGTON COURT, Barnstaple, EX31 4LP (Tel 027182-
296).   **4** National Trust.   **5** Administrator: Mr J.E.
Brunner.   **8** Open to the public.   **9** April-Oct: daily (inc
bank hols, exc Good Friday) 11.00-12.30, 14.00-15.30.
Adults 80p, children 40p. Garden, grounds & stables only:
50p.   **10** Regency house; Miss Rosalie Chichester colln
(shells, pewter, costumes, model ships) 19th cent furnishings;
park grazed by Shetland ponies & Jacob's sheep; nature trail.
11 19th cent horse-drawn vehicles in stables; shop.

NORTH DEVON ATHENAEUM LIBRARY AND MUSEUM, The
Square, Barnstable, EX32 8LN (Tel 0271-2174).   **4** Trustees of North Devon Athenaeum (Rock Trust).   **5** Libn
& Curator Mr G.A. Morris.   **8** Open to the public.
9 Mon-Fri 10.00-13.00, 14.15-18.00, Sat 10.00-13.00.
Free, but children under 14 must be accompanied by adult.
10 Local antiques; North Devon pottery; ceremonial spoons;
geological fossil specimens; Roman pottery & coins excavated
at Signal Station Martinhoe & Old Barrow; butterfly & coin
colln; maps, etc.   **11** Detailed history of North Devon,
books & ms records.   **12** (b) 2.

BARROW-IN-FURNESS, Cumbria

FURNESS MUSEUM, Ramsden Square, Barrow-in-Furness,
LA14 1LL (Tel 0229-20650).   **4** Barrow & Dalton DC.
5 Curator: D.J. Hughes.   **6** Public Amenities.   **8** Open
to the public.   **9** Mon-Sat 10.00-17.00. Free.   **10** Pre-
dominantly local history.   **11** Vickers ship models &
Victorian ship models; prehistoric Furness; 18th & 19th
cent Furness domestic & agricultural equipment.   **12** (a) 1
(b) 1.

BASINGSTOKE, Hampshire

WILLIS MUSEUM AND ART GALLERY, New St, Basingstoke,
RG21 1DP (Tel 0256-65902).   **4** Hampshire CC.
5 Curator-in-charge: Mr A.M. Burchard MA, AMA.
6 Recreation.   **7** Hampshire County Museum Service,
Chilcomb House, Chilcomb Lane, Bar End, Winchester SO23
8RD (0962-66242/3) Dir: Miss M.C. Macfarlane.   **8** Open
to the public.   **9** Mon 13.30-17.30; Tues-Sat 10.00-12.30,
13.30-17.30. Free.   **10** Local archaeology, natural
history & geology; Basingstoke Canal; horology; watch &
clockmakers' tools; pottery; recent accessions & temporary
exhibitions in Art Gallery. A new town history gallery to be
opened shortly.   **12** (a) 1 (b) 2.

BATH, Avon

AMERICAN MUSEUM IN BRITAIN, Claverton Manor, Bath,
BA2 7BD (Tel 0225-60503).   **5** Dir: Mr Ian McCallum
ARIBA.   **8** Open to the public.   **9** April-Oct: Tues-Sun
14.00-17.00; bank hols 12.00-17.00. Educational tours all
year round (by prior arrangement). Adults 50p, children &
OAPs 40p. Grounds only: 15p.   **10** American decorative &
fine arts (17th-19th cent) in period rooms & galleries
emphasising domestic life; open-air exhibits (inc Folk Art
Gallery, transportation exhibits, herb garden & shop,
replica of George Washington's Mount Vernon garden); library
of 3,000 vols American history & arts, open for research.
11 Gallery of maritime history with replica of whaleship
captain's cabin; 18th cent. tavern; American Indian exhibit;
opening of the West exhibit; fine American furniture (1680-
1880).   **12** (a) 11 (b) 7.

CODE: 1 Name of Museum, Art Gallery or Stately Home. 2 Address. 3 Telephone & telex. 4 Governing body. 5 Officer in charge. 6 Committee responsible. 7 Larger department, chief officer. 8 Open to public. 9 Hours; admission charges. 10 Scope. 11 Special exhibits or facilities. 12 Staff (a) professionally qualified (b) other non-manual (c) manual.

BATH, Avon—*continued*

COSTUME AND FASHION RESEARCH CENTRE, 4 The Circus, Bath, BA1 2EW (Tel 0225-28411 ext 429). **4** Bath City Council. **5** Research Officer: Miss P.C. Byrde MA. **6** SPA **7** Dept of Leisure & Tourist Services, Dir: Mr Ray Barratt ACCA, AMBIM. **8** Open to the public. **9** Mon-Fri 14.00-17.00. Free. **10** An extension to the Museum of Costume in Bath; research facilities in the history of costume. **11** Library; study colln of costume; textiles & embroidery; periodic exhibitions & lectures. **12** (a) 1

GEORGIAN HOUSE, 1 Royal Crescent, Bath, BA1 2LR (Tel 0225-28126). **4** Bath Preservation Trust. **5** House Manager: Ms von Haeften. **8** Open to the public. **9** Tues-Sat 11.00-17.00, Sun & bank hols 14.00-17.00. Adults 30p, students, children & OAPs 15p. **10** Restored & furnished Georgian house.

HOLBURNE OF MENSTRIE MUSEUM, Great Pulteney St, Bath, BA2 4DB (Tel 0225-66669). **4** University of Bath. **5** Curator: Dr Mary Olive Holbrook BA, PhD. **8** Open to the public. **9** Mon-Sat (inc bank hols) 11.00-17.00, Sun 14.30-18.00. Adults 15p, students & children 5p. **10** Fine & decorative arts (mainly 16th-early 19th cent); silver & porcelain; paintings (Stubbs, Ramsay, Gainsborough, Guardi etc); furniture; miniatures; maiolica. **11** Temporary exhibitions. **12** (a) 1 (b) 1 (c) 3.

MUSEUM OF COSTUME, Assembly Rooms, Alfred St, Bath, BA1 1LZ (Tel 0225-28411, ext 298). **4** Bath City Council. **5** Chief Costume Asst: Mrs Myra Mines. **6** Spa Com- **7** Dept of Leisure & Tourist Services, Dir: Mr Ray Barratt ACCA, AMBIM. **8** Open to the public. **9** March-Oct: Mon-Sat 9.30-18.00, Sun 10.00-18.00; Nov-Feb: Mon-Sat 10.00-17.00, Sun 11.00-17.00. Closed Dec 25. Adults 40p; children 20p; party rates. **10** Fashion (c 1580-1976) in an Underwear Room. **11** Royal clothes (Queens Victoria, Alexandra, Mary & the Queen Mother); Lord Byron's Albanian outfit; Lady Byron's wedding dress, Lawrence of Arabia's robes & suit worn as a child. **12** (a) 5 (b) 10 (c) 5.

ROMAN BATHS AND MUSEUM, Pump Room, Bath, BA1 1LZ (Tel 0225-28411). **4** Bath City Council. **5** Curator: M.B. Owen BA. **6** SPA. **7** Leisure & Tourist Services, Dir: Mr Ray Barratt ACCA, AMBIM. **8** Open to the public. **9** Daily (inc bank hols) 9.00-18.00 (Nov-Feb 17.00), Sun 11.00-17.00. Adults 40p, children 20p. **10** Roman baths remains *in situ;* prehistoric, Roman, medieval, post-medieval archaeology. **12** (a) 1 (b) 7 (c) 1.

VICTORIA ART GALLERY & MUSEUM, Bridge St, (& Exhibition Rooms, 18 Queen Sq), Bath BA1 2HP (Tel 0225-28144). **4** Bath City Council **5** Acting Curator: Miss Jill Knight NDD. **7** Dept of Leisure & Tourist Services, Dir: Mr Ray Barratt ACCA, AMBIM. **8** Open to the public. **9** Mon-Sat 10.00-18.00; bank hols 10.00-13.00, 14.00-17.00. Free. **10** Fine arts, paintings, prints & drawings; local topography; ceramics & glass; coins & tokens; watches; bygones; geology. **11** Temporary exhibitions (local & national). **12** (a) 1 (b) 1 (c) 8.

BATLEY, West Yorkshire

BAGSHAW ART GALLERY, Market Place, Batley, WF17 5DA; c/o Libraries, Museums & Art Galleries Headquarters, Princess Alexandra Walk, Huddersfield, HD1 2SU (Tel 0484-21356; Telex 517463). **4** Kirklees MBC. **5** Chief Curator & Libn: Mr Stanley T. Dibnab FLA, AMBIM. **6** Education. **7** Dir of Education Services: Mr Ernest T. Butcher MA. **8** Open to the public. **9** Mon-Fri 10.00-18.00, Sat 10.00-17.00. Free. **12** (a) served from Huddersfield Art Gallery.

BAGSHAW MUSEUM, Wilton Park, Batley, WF17 0AS; c/o Libraries, Museums & Art Galleries Headquarters, Princess Alexandra Walk, Huddersfield, HD1 2SU (Tel 0484-21356; Telex 517463). **4** Kirklees MBC. **5** Chief Curator & Libn: Mr Stanley T. Dibnab FLA, AMBIM; Curator: Mr Phillip C. Cruttendon BA, AMA, FGS. **6** Education. **7** Dir of Educational Services: Mr Ernest T. Butcher MA. **8** Open to the public. **9** Mon-Fri (inc bank hols) 10.00-18.00, Sat 10.00-17.00, Sun 14.00-17.00. Free. **10** Local history; natural history (Chinese jades, ivories & hard stones). **12** (a) Served from Huddersfield Art Gallery.

BATTLE, Sussex

BATTLE AND DISTRICT HISTORICAL SOCIETY MUSEUM, Langton House, Abbey Green, Battle, TN33 0AG. **4** Battle & District Historical Society Museum Trust. **5** Hon Curator: Mr D.H. Beaty-Pownall. **8** Open to the public. Easter-early Oct. **9** Mon-Sat (inc bank hols) 10.00-13.00, 14.00-17.00, Sun 14.30-17.30. Adults 5p, children 3p. **10** Local history; Romano-British ironwork; gunpowder industry; local bygones; Battle of Hastings. **11** Diorama of Battle of Hastings; Stothard reproduction (1816) of Bayeux Tapestry. **12** (b) 2.

BEAMISH, Co Durham

BEAMISH (NORTH OF ENGLAND OPEN AIR MUSEUM), Beamish Hall, Beamish, Stanley, DH9 0RG (Tel 02073-3580/3586). **4** Joint Committee (representing the four North-Eastern County Councils). **5** Museum Director: Mr Frank Atkinson MA, BSc, FSA, FMA. **8** Open to the public. **9** Easter-Sept: Tues-Sun & bank hols 10.00-18.00. Shorter hours in winter. Adults 20p, children & OAPs 5p. **10** Open air museum of buildings, machinery, objects & information illustrating development of industry & way of life in North East England; colliery; railway; farm; all working condition. **11** 1925 electric tramcar from Gateshead operates a regular summer service on $\frac{1}{2}$ mile of track; steam industrial locomotives; 1822 Hetton Colliery loco-motive by George Stephenson; replica of 1825 'Locomotion' (S & DR) by George Stephenson, demonstrated in steam; restored 1900's farm; rebuilt 1867 Rawley railway station; ref library (inc photographs & oral recordings). **12** (a) 5 (b) 5 (c) 21.

BEAULIEU, Hampshire

BUCKLER'S HARD MARITIME MUSEUM, Buckler's Hard, Beaulieu, Brockenhurst (Tel 059063-203). **5** Gen Manager: Mr K.G. Robinson; Curator: Mr A.J. Holland. **8** Open to the public. **9** Daily (inc bank hols) 10.00-21.00 (Easter-Spring bank hol 10.00-18.00), (Oct-Easter 10.00-16.30). Not free. **10** 18th cent shipbuilding village.

NATIONAL MOTOR MUSEUM; PALACE HOUSE AND GARDENS; BEAULIEU ABBEY RUINS, Beaulieu, Brocken-hurst, SO4 7ZN (Tel 0590-612345). **4** National Motor Museum Trust. **5** Gen Manager: Mr K.G. Robinson; Curator: Mr M.E. Ware. **8** Open to the public. **9** Daily (inc bank hols) 10.00-18.30 (Aug 20.30), (Oct-Easter 17.00). Not free, children half price. **10** Palace House, the former gatehouse of Beaulieu Abbey; Abbey ruins; National Motor Museum (story of motoring from 1895 onwards). **11** Temporary exhibitions, festivals & other special events (mostly connected with motoring); restaurants.

BEBINGTON, Merseyside

BEBINGTON CIVIC CENTRE, Civic Way, Bebington, L65 0AX (Tel 051-645 2080). **4** Wirral MBC. **5** Chief Libn & Arts Officer: H.H.G. Arthur FLA, FRSA, MBIM. **7** Leisure Services Dept, Dir: Mr B.J. Barnes MInstBM,

BEBINGTON, Merseyside—*continued*

ARM, MInstRM.   **8** Open to the public.   **9** Mon-Fri 10.00-
20.00 (Thurs 13.00), Sat 10.00-16.30. Free.   **10** Local
history, paintings, photographs & antiquities.   **11** Temporary exhibitions; Saxon Cross.   **12** (a) 1 (c) 2.

BEDFORD, Bedfordshire

BEDFORD MUSEUM, The Embankment, Bedford, MK40 3NY
(Tel 0234-53323).   **4** North Bedfordshire BC.
5 Officer-in-Charge: H. J. Turner AMA.   **6** Amenities.
7 Amenities Dir: D. R. Knapp BSc, ARCS.   **8** Open to the
public.   **9** Tues-Sat 11.00-17.00, Sun 14.00-17.00.
Closed Dec 25, 26 & Good Friday. Free.   **10** Local archaeology; social & rural life history; some Mediterranean
archaeology.   **11** Temporary exhibitions.   **12** (a) 2
(b) 1 (c) 2.

CECIL HIGGINS ART GALLERY (temporarily closed),
Castle Close, Bedford, MK40 3NY (Tel 0234-53791).
4 Bedford DC.   **5** Curator: Miss Halina Grubert BA.
6 Trustees & Amenities.   **7** Amenities, Dir: Mr D. R.
Knapp BSc, ARCS.   **8** Yes, but closed until mid 1976.
Free.   **10** Fine & decorative arts.   **12** (a) 4 (b) 3 (c) 3.

ELSTOW MOOT HALL, Elstow Green, Elstow, Bedford
(Tel 0234-66889).   **4** Bedfordshire CC.   **5** Curator:
Mr E. Cotton.   **6** Leisure.   **7** Arts & Recreation Dept,
Chief Officer: Mr Peter Smith AMA, FGS.   **8** Open to the
public.   **9** Tues-Sat 10.00-13.00, 14.00-17.00, Sun 14.00-
17.30. Closes at dusk in winter. Adults 5p, OAPs,
children & school parties free.   **10** Life & times of John
Bunyan.   **12** (b) 1.

BELFAST, Northern Ireland

ROYAL ULSTER RIFLES REGIMENTAL MUSEUM, 5
Waring St, Belfast, BT1 2EW (Tel 0232-32086).   **5** Curator:
Lt Col W. R. H. Charley.   **8** Open by arrangement.
9 Mon-Fri 9.00-16.00, Sat 10.00-12.00. Free.   **10** Medals,
uniforms & trophies of 83rd, 86th Regiments, Royal Irish
Rifles & Royal Ulster Rifles (1793-1968).   **12** (b) 1 (c) 1.

ULSTER MUSEUM, Botanic Gardens, Belfast, BT9 5AB
(Tel 0232-668251).   **4** Board of Trustees.   **5** Dir: Mr
Alan Warhurst BA, FSA, FMA.   **8** Open to the public.
9 Mon-Sat 11.00-18.00, Sun 14.30-17.30. Closed Dec 25,
26, Jan 1 & July 12. Free.   **10** Antiquities; art; botany &
zoology; geology, technology & local history; design & production dept.   **11** Treasure from the Spanish Armada
galleass 'Girona'; pictures by Turner, Gainsborough,
Reynolds; Irish gold ornaments; British, Irish & foreign
coins; Coelacanth from Madagascar; world-wide gem colln.
12 (a) 45 (b) 33 (c) 95.

BEMBRIDGE, Isle of Wight

RUSKIN GALLERIES, Bembridge School, Bembridge, Isle
of Wight (Tel 098 387-2101).   **4** Ruskin Gallery Trust.
5 Curator: Mr J. S. Dearden.   **8** Open to the public.
9 Open by appointment only. Free.   **10** Pictures, mss &
books relating to John Ruskin & his circle.

BERKELEY, Gloucestershire

BERKELEY CASTLE, Berkeley, GL13 9BQ (Tel 045 381-332).
8 Open to the public.   **9** April-Sept: Tues-Sat 14.00-17.00
(May-Aug: 11.00-17.00), April-Oct: Sun 14.00-17.00, bank
hols 11.00-17.00. Adults 40p, children 20p.   **10** Norman
castle where Edward II was murdered; family colln of
furniture, tapestries, paintings, silver, china & carved
timber work.

BERWICK-UPON-TWEED, Northumberland

BERWICK-UPON-TWEED ART GALLERY AND MUSEUM,
Marygate, Berwick-upon-Tweed, TD15 1BT (Tel 0289-7320).
4 Berwick-upon-Tweed BC.   **5** Area Libn & Curator:
Miss M. H. Simpson ALA.   **6** Amenities.   **7** Environment

Dept, Dir: A. R. Field MAPHI, MSH.   **8** Open to the public.
9 Art Gallery, Mon-Wed & Fri 10.00-20.00, Thurs 14.00-
17.00, Sat (June-Sept only) 10.00-17.00. Museum, June-Sept:
Mon-Sat 14.00-17.00. Free.   **10** Art gallery: part of
Burrell colln. Museum: local history.

KING'S OWN SCOTTISH BORDERERS REGIMENTAL
MUSEUM, The Barracks, The Parade, Berwick-Upon-Tweed,
TD15 1DG (Tel 0289-7426/7).   **4** Regimental Trustees.
5 Regimental Sec & Museum Curator: Lt Col W. M. B. Dunn
TD.   **8** Open to the public.   **9** Mon-Fri 9.30-12.00,
13.15-16.00, Sat 9.30-12.00. Other times by arrangement.
Adults 5p, children 3p.   **10** Medals, weapons, uniforms,
badges, flags, trophies, etc connected with the Regiment.
11 Some items loaned for exhibitions.   **12** (c) 1.

BEVERLEY, North Humberside

BEVERLEY MUSEUM AND ART GALLERY, Champney Rd,
Beverley, HU17 9BQ (Tel 0482-882255).   **5** Chief Admin
Officer: Mr Roy Gregory LLB, DMA, Solicitor.
6 Recreational Services.   **8** Open to the public.
9 Mon-Sat 10.00-17.00. Free.   **10** Local history; art
gallery (mainly paintings by Elwell family).

PRINCE OF WALES'S OWN REGIMENT OF YORKSHIRE,
THE EAST YORKSHIRE REGIMENT SECTION MUSEUM,
11 Butcher Row, Beverley, HU17 0AA (Tel 0482-882157).
5 Officer-in-Charge: Lt Col C. J. Robinson MBE.   **8** Open
to the public.   **9** Tues-Fri 14.00-16.30, or by appointment.
Free.   **10** Regimental silver, medals, portraits, uniforms,
library, etc, in a domestic setting.   **12** (b) 2 (c) 1.

BEWDLEY, Worcestershire

BEWDLEY MUSEUM, Load St, Bewdley (Tel 0299-403573).
4 Wyre Forest DC.   **5** Curator: Miss Susanna Davis BA.
7 Recreation & Amenities Dept, Chief Officer: Mr B.
Onions MRIM.   **8** Open to the public.   **9** Tues-Sat
& bank hols 11.00-13.00, 14.00-17.30, Sun 14.00-17.30.
Adults 10p, children 5p.   **10** Local history (inc crafts &
industries).   **11** Craftsmen sometimes work in studios
within the museum.   **12** (a) 1 (b) 1 (c) 2.

BEXHILL-ON-SEA, East Sussex

BEXHILL MUSEUM, Egerton Rd, Bexhill-on-Sea, TN39 3HL
(Tel 0424-211769).   **4** Bexhill Museum Association.
5 Curator: Mr H. J. Sargent FMA.   **8** Open to the public.
9 Mon-Sat (inc bank hols) 10.00-13.00, 14.30-16.30. Free.
10 Natural history, geology, archaeology, & history of the
district; some material of a wider scope, mainly for school
use.   **11** Temporary exhibitions.   **12** (a) 1.

BIBURY, Gloucester

ARLINGTON MILL MUSEUM, Bibury, Cirencester, GL7 5NL
(Tel 028 574-368).   **5** Officer-in-Charge: Mr David Verey
FSA, MA, ARIBA.   **8** Open to the public.   **9** Daily (inc
bank hols) 11.00-13.00, 14.00-19.00. Adults 20p, students
15p, children 10p.   **10** Country museum (arts & crafts,
agriculture, Victoriana, corn mill machinery).   **12** (a) 1
(b) 1 (c) 1.

BIDEFORD, North Devon

BIDEFORD MUSEUM, Bideford Divisional Library, New Rd,
Bideford, EX39 4LN (Tel 023 72-6075).   **4** Devon CC.
5 Acting Divisional Libn: Mr G. S. C. Green.   **6** Countryside & Amenities.   **7** Bideford Divisional Library.
8 Open to the public.   **9** Mon & Wed 9.30-17.00, Tues,
Thurs & Fri 9.30-18.45, Sat 9.30-12.45. Free.   **10** Local
history.

BURTON ART GALLERY, Kingsley Rd, Bideford, EX39 2QQ.
4 Torridge DC.   **5** Curator: Mr R. Baldry.   **8** Open to
the public.   **9** Mon-Fri 9.00-13.00, 14.00-17.00, Sat 9.00-
13.00. Free.   **10** Silver; pewter; porcelain; paintings.

CODE: **1** Name of Museum, Art Gallery or Stately Home. **2** Address **3** Telephone & telex. **4** Governing body. **5** Officer in charge. **6** Committee responsible. **7** Larger department, chief officer. **8** Open to public. **9** Hours; admission charges. **10** Scope. **11** Special exhibits or facilities. **12** Staff (a) professionally qualified (b) other non-manual (c) manual.

BIGGAR, Lanarkshire

GLADSTONE COURT, Biggar, ML12 6DN (Tel 0899-20005). **4** Biggar Museum Trust. **5** Officer-in-Charge: Mr Brian A. Lambie. **8** Open to the public. **9** Mon-Sat 10.00-12.30, 14.00-17.00 (Closed Wed pm), Sun 14.00-17.00. Closed local hols. Adults 10p, children 5p. **10** Small street museum of shops, offices & windows; open-air museum complex just begun. **12** (a) 1.

BIGGLESWADE, Bedfordshire

SHUTTLEWORTH COLLECTION, Old Warden Aerodrome, Biggleswade, SG18 9EP (Tel 076727-288). **4** Richard Ormonde Shuttleworth Remembrance Trust. **5** Trustee: Air Commodore A.H. Wheeler CBE, MA, FRAeS; Gen Manager: Mr D.F. Ogilvy ARAeS. **8** Open to the public. **9** Daily (inc bank hols) 10.00-17.00. Adults 50p, children 25p. Special prices on flying days. **10** Veteran & vintage aircraft; veteran cars. **11** Aircraft fly at various times during summer; library & research dept; restaurant, picnic area & shop. **12** (a) 20 (c) 5.

BIGNOR, Sussex

ROMAN VILLA, Bignor, Pulborough, RH20 1PH (Tel 07987-259). **5** Curator: Mr J. Morgan; Owner: Capt H. Tupper MC, DL. **8** Open to the public. **9** Tues-Sun 10.00-17.00, (April-Sept, & bank hols 10.00-18.30). Not free. **10** Site of 4th cent Roman villa; Roman artifacts found on site (inc fine mosaic floors in situ). **11** Model of villa; drawings & diagrams of hypocaust & baths; wall plaster, pottery, tiles etc; question papers available.

BILLERICAY, Essex

CATER MUSEUM, 74 High St, Billericay, CM12 9AS (Tel 02774-22023). **8** Open to the public. **9** Mon-Fri 12.30-17.00, Sat 11.30-17.00. Free. **10** Local history & social life. **11** Model fire-engines & appliances (1666-1957). **12** (b) 2.

BILLINGHAM, Cleveland

BILLINGHAM ART GALLERY, Town Centre, Billingham (Tel 0642-555443). **4** Stockton BC. **5** Officer-in-Charge: J.P. Warbrook. **7** Leisure & Amenities, Chief Officer: Mr B.M. Connolly. **8** Open to the public. **9** Mon-Sat 10.00-18.00. Free. **10** Modern Works. **12** (a) 1 (c) 3.

BIRCHINGTON, Kent

POWELL-COTTON MUSEUM, Quex Park, Birchington, CT7 0BH (Tel 0843-42168). **4** Powell-Cotton Museum Trust. **5** Dir: Mr C. Powell-Cotton CMG, MBE, MC, BA; Curator & Zoology Officer: Mr R.A. Barton. **8** Open to the public. **9** Thurs 14.30-18.00; Spring bank hol-Sept: Sun, Wed & Thurs 14.30-18.00; mid July-mid Sept: daily (exc Mon & Sat) 14.30-18.00. Furnished rooms in Quex house, & gardens, open only in summer. Adults: summer 20p, winter 10p; children ½ price. **10** African & Asian animals in large dioramas showing natural habitat; ethnographic & native art from Africa, Asia & Pacific; local archaeology; weapons. **11** Special arrangements for schools & parties. Free car park. **12** (a) 2 (b) 3 (c)3.

BIRKENHEAD, Merseyside

BIRKENHEAD PRIORY, Priory St, Birkenhead. **4** Wirral BC. **5** Curator (Asst Dir of Leisure Services): Mr H.H.G. Arthur FLA, FRSA, MBIM. **7** Leisure Services, Dir: Mr Brian J. Barnes MInstBM, ARM(M), MInstRM. **8** Open to the public. **9** Tues-Fri 10.00-12.00, 14.00-16.00, (Oct-April 10.00-13.00), Sat 10.00-12.00. Free. **10** Priory ruins dating from 1150. **11** Colln of objects excavated from site. **12** (b) 1 guide.

WILLIAMSON ART GALLERY AND MUSEUM, Slatey Rd, Birkenhead, L43 4UE (Tel 051-652 4177: Telex 628136). **4** Wirral BC. **5** Curator (Asst Dir of Leisure Services): Mr H.H.G. Arthur FLA, FRSA, MBIM. **6** Leisure Services; **7** Dir of Leisure Services: Mr Brian J. Barnes MInstBM, ARM(M), MInstRM. **8** Open to the public. **9** Mon-Sat 10.00-17.00 (Thurs 10.00-21.00), Sun 14.00-19.00. Closed Easter, Spring & Summer bank hols. Free. **10** Paintings; sculptures; etchings; pottery & porcelain; glass; silver; furniture; local history (inc shipping). **11** English water colours; Knowles Boney colln (Liverpool porcelain); Birkenhead colln (Della Robbia); Seacombe ware; Maritime Museum (ship builders' models & Port of Merseyside); Philip Wilson Steer, OM, colln. **12** (a) 4 (b) 1 (c) 7.

BIRMINGHAM

ASTON HALL, Aston, Birmingham, B6 7JD (Tel 021-327 0062). **4** City of Birmingham DC. **5** Dir: Mr Dennis Farr, MA, FRSA, FSA. **6** Leisure Services. **8** Open to the public. **9** Mon-Sat 10.00-17.00, Sun (April-Sept only) 14.00-17.00. Adults 6p, children 3p, family tickets 13p. **10** Fine Jacobean house (1618-1635) in its own park in heart of the City; grand balustraded staircase & exceptional long gallery.

BIRMINGHAM MUSEUM AND ART GALLERY, Congreve St, Birmingham, B3 3DH (Tel 021-235 2834). **4** City of Birmingham DC. **5** Dir: Mr Dennis Farr MA, FRSA, FSA. **6** Leisure Services. **8** Open to the public. **9** Mon-Sat 10.00-18.00, Sun 14.00-17.30. Closed Good Friday, Dec 25 & 26. Free. **10** Ceramics; painting; sculpture; applied arts; archaeology (inc Near & Far East & South America); zoology; botany; geology; human biology. **11** 17th cent Italian paintings; 19th cent English & European paintings; silver; coins; stamps; fossils; animal, reptile & bird exhibits.

Birmingham University

BARBER INSTITUTE OF FINE ARTS, Birmingham, B15 2TS (Tel 021-472 0962). **4** Trustees of the Barber Institute of Fine Arts. **5** Dir: Prof H.A.D. Miles. **9** Normally open, term: Mon-Fri 10.00-17.00, Sat 10.00-13.00. Free. **10** European art, chiefly painting (14th-19th cent); Byzantine & Roman imperial coins.

CHAMBERLAIN MUSEUM, The Medical School, Edgbaston, Birmingham, B15 2TT (Tel 021-472 1301). **4** Faculty of Medicine & Dentistry. **8** Not open to cine & Dentistry. **10** For the instruction & education of undergraduate & postgraduate medical & dental students. **11** Demonstrations by the Dept of Pathology; Humphries Odontological Colln; self-instruction area administered by educational services unit.

DEPARTMENT OF GEOLOGICAL SCIENCES, PO Box 363, Birmingham, B15 2TT (Tel 021-472 1301). **5** Curator: Mr P.J. Osborne BSc. **8** Open to the public. **9** Mon-Fri 9.00-17.00, Sat by arrangement. Free. **10** All branches of geological science (at present in process of rearrangement.) **12** (a) 1.

BISHOP ASBURY COTTAGE, Newton Rd, Great Barr, Birmingham (correspondence to: Curator, Art Gallery & Museum, Holyhead Rd, Wednesbury, West Midlands, WS10 7DF) (Tel 021-556 0683). **4** Sandwell MBC. **5** Curator: Mr A.J. Tibbles MA. **6** Libraries & Museums Sub-Committee. **7** Borough Libn: R.B. Ludgate ALA. **8** Open to the public. **9** Open by appointment only. Free. **10** Childhood home of Francis Asbury (1745-1816) 1st Methodist Bishop of America & pioneer of Methodist movement in US; mid-17th cent cottage with inglenook fireplace, furnished in period style.

BIRMINGHAM—*continued*

cent cottage with inglenook fireplace, furnished in period style.

BLAKESLEY HALL, Blakesley Rd, Yardley, Birmingham, B25 8RN (Tel 021-783 2193).　**4** City of Birmingham DC.　**5** Dir: Mr Dennis Farr MA, FRSA, FSA.　**6** Leisure Services.　**8** Open to the public.　**9** Mon-Sat 9.30-18.00, Sun 14.00-17.00. Free.　**10** 16th cent timber-framed yeoman's house with displays from Pinto colln of wooden objects; local history.

CANNON HILL MUSEUM, Pershore Rd, Birmingham, B5 7RL (Tel 021-472 7775).　**4** City of Birmingham DC.　**5** Dir: Mr Dennis Farr MA, FRSA, FSA.　**6** Leisure Services.　**8** Open to the public.　**9** Mon-Sat 10.00-20.00 (Oct-March 10.00-17.00), Sun 14.00-17.00. Free.　**10** Natural history; wildlife (European animals).

CITY OF BIRMINGHAM MUSEUM OF SCIENCE AND IN-DUSTRY, Newhall St, Birmingham, B3 1RZ (Tel 021-236 1022).　**4** City of Birmingham DC.　**5** Dir: Mr N.W. Bertenshaw BScTech, CEng, MIEE, FIMechE, FMA.　**6** Leisure Services.　**7** Museums & Art Gallery, Dir: Mr D. Farr MA, FMA, FRSA.　**8** Open to the public.　**9** Mon-Fri 10.00-17.00 (1st Wed each month 10.00-21.00), Sat 10.00-17.30, Sun 14.00-17.30. Closed Dec 25, 26 & Good Friday. Free.　**10** Varied engineering exhibits inc comprehensive selection of vehicles; items from City Arms colln of scientific equipment; aeroplanes; bicycles; locomotives; fire arms.　**11** Mechanical musical instruments, ornamental lathes & their products; Charles Thomas colln of pens, writing equipment & samples of writing, (European & Oriental); captions, tape units & museographs.　**12** (a) 4 (b) 14 (c) 52.

SAREHOLE MILL, Cole Bank Rd, Birmingham, B13 0BD (Tel 021-777 6612).　**4** City of Birmingham DC.　**5** Dir: Mr Dennis Farr MA, FRSA, FSA.　**6** Leisure Services.　**8** Open to the public.　**9** April-Nov: Sun-Fri 14.00-19.00, Sat 11.00-19.00. Adults 10p; children 5p (must be accompanied by an adult).　**10** 18th cent water-powered corn mill restored to working order; milling & English rural pursuits.

WEOLEY CASTLE ARCHAEOLOGICAL SITE, 150 Alwold Rd, Birmingham, B29 5RX (Tel 021-427 4270).　**4** City Museums & Art Gallery.　**5** Dep Keeper, (Dept of Archaeology): Mrs Ruth Taylor BA, AMA.　**6** Leisure Services.　**7** Dir of City Museums & Art Gallery: Mr Dennis Farr MA, FRSA, FSA.　**8** Open to the public.　**9** Wed 14.00-20.00, Thurs, Fri & Sun 14.00-17.00, Sat 10.00-17.00. Adults 2½p, children 1p.　**10** Ruins of a medieval fortified manor-house (late 13th cent) with evidence for earlier buildings on the site revealed by excavations.　**11** Small site museum displaying material from the excavations.　**12** (c) 2.

BIRSTALL, West Yorkshire

OAKWELL HALL FARM MUSEUM, Nova Lane, Birstall, WF17 9LG; c/o Libraries, Museums & Art Galleries Headquarters, Princess Alexandra Walk, Huddersfield, HD1 2SU (Tel 0484-21356; Telex 517463).　**4** Kirklees MBC.　**5** Chief Curator & Libn: Mr Stanley T. Dibnab FLA, AMBIM. Curator: Mr John R. Lidster.　**6** Education.　**7** Dir of Educational Services: Mr Edward T. Butcher MA.　**9** Tues-Fri (inc bank hols) 10.00-18.00, Sat 10.00-17.00, Sun 14.00-17.00. Free.　**10** Elizabethan house; c. 1720 furnishings; Brontë associations.　**12** (a) Served from Huddersfield Art Gallery.

BISHOPS STORTFORD, Hertfordshire

RHODES MUSEUM & COMMONWEALTH CENTRE, South Rd, Bishops Stortford, CM23 3JG (Tel 0279-51746).　**4** Rhodes Centre Management Committee.　**5** Chairman: Lt Col R.J. Venn TD, DL.　**8** Open to the public.　**9** Mon-Sat 10.00-16.00. Free.　**10** Birthplace of Cecil Rhodes; diamond & gold mining; Matabele War; Jameson Raid; Boer War.　**11** Birth room furnished as in 1853; personal mementos of Rhodes & family; mining machinery.　**12** (b) 2.

BLACKBURN, Lancashire

BLACKBURN MUSEUM AND ART GALLERY, Library St, Blackburn, BB1 7AJ (Tel 0254-55201).　**4** Blackburn BC.　**5** Asst Dir of Recreation (Arts): Mr Adrian Lewis BA, MSc, AMA.　**7** Recreation Dept, Dir: Mr Paul Sykes DMA, FLA, MIRM.　**8** Open to the public.　**9** Mon-Fri 9.30-20.00, Sat 9.30-18.00. Free.　**10** Local history; Egyptology; ceramics; East Lancashire Regimental Museum.　**11** Mediaeval illuminated mss; coins; Japanese prints; icons; 18th-19th cent watercolours. Also Tuxtan Tower (near Bolton).　**12** (a) 1 (b) 5 (c) 12.

LEWIS TEXTILE MUSEUM, 3 Exchange St, Blackburn, BB1 7JN (Tel 0254-59511).　**4** Blackburn BC.　**5** Asst Dir of Recreation (Arts): Mr Adrian Lewis BA, MSc, AMA.　**7** Recreation Dept, Dir: Mr Paul Sykes DMA, FLA, MIRM.　**8** Open to the public.　**9** Mon-Sat 10.00-17.00 (Wed & Fri 19.30). Free.　**10** Mechanical history of the cotton industry, from wooden handlooms to steel power loom, & from spinning wheel to Crompton's Spinning Mule; Kay's fly-shuttle (c. 1775); Lancashire loom (c. 1860).　**11** Exhibits can be operated for visiting parties booked in advance.　**12** (b) 1 (c) 2.

BLACKPOOL, Lancashire

GRUNDY ART GALLERY, Queen St, Blackpool, FY1 1PX (Tel 0253-23977/8).　**4** Blackpool BC.　**5** Officer-in-Charge: Mr P. Dunnderdale FLA.　**6** Attractions & Leisure.　**8** Open to the public.　**9** Mon-Sat 10.00-17.00. Free.　**10** Contemporary oil & watercolours; ivories; china; 19th cent paintings.　**12** (a) 1 (c) 1.

BLAIR ATHOLL, Perthshire

BLAIR CASTLE, c/o Mr T.P. Stewart, Estate Office, Blair Atholl, Pitlochry, PH18 5TH (Tel 079 681-355).　**4** Atholl Estates.　**5** Officer-in-Charge: Mr T.P. Stewart, TD, FRICS, JP.　**9** Easter & April: Sun & Mon 10.00-18.00, Sun 14.00-18.00. Adults 50p, children & OAPs 25p; educational parties 20p.　**10** 13th cent castle; 32 rooms containing furniture, pictures, china, arms, armoury, Jacobite relics etc, depicting Scottish history over 400 years.　**11** Restaurant; caravan site.　**12** (a) 4.

CLAN DONNACHAIDH MUSEUM, Bruar Falls, Blair Atholl, PH18 5PW (Tel 079 683-264).　**4** Clan Donnachaidh Society.　**5** Hon Sec: Mrs Una Shaw; Curator: A.M. McRae FSA(Scot).　**8** Open to the public.　**9** Mon-Sat (inc bank hols) 10.00-17.30, Sun 14.00-17.30. Free.　**10** History of the clan in peace & war; characteristics of its homeland; lives & work of the men & women who compose it.　**11** Stone of the Standard (Clach-Na-Brataich), a spherical ball of rock crystal (from 1314).　**12** (b) 1.

BLANDFORD CAMP, Dorset

ROYAL CORPS OF SIGNALS MUSEUM, Blandford Camp, Blandford, DT11 8RF (Tel 025 82-2581, ext 248).　**4** Royal Signals Institution.　**5** Dir: Lt Col E.G. Day OBE, TD; Curator: Mr W.F. Bailey.　**8** Open to the public.　**9** Mon-Fri 10.00-13.00, 14.00-17.00, Sat 10.00-12.00. Free.　**10** History & development of military communications, & of Royal Signals Corps.　**11** Many unique pieces of communication equipment.　**12** (a) 1 (b) 1 (c) 1.

BLANTYRE, Lanarkshire

DAVID LIVINGSTONE MEMORIAL, Blantyre, Glasgow, G7Z 9BT (Tel 0698-823140).　**4** Scottish National Memorial to David Livingstone Trust.　**5** Warden: Mr William Cunningham.　**8** Open to the public.　**9** Mon-Sat (inc bank hols) 10.00-18.00, Sun 14.00-18.00. Adults 20p, children 5p.　**10** Birthplace of David Livingstone.　**12** (b) 1 (c) 1.

CODE: 1 Name of Museum, Art Gallery or Stately Home. **2** Address. **3** Telephone & telex. **4** Governing body. **5** Officer in charge. **6** Committee responsible. **7** Larger department, chief officer. **8** Open to public. **9** Hours; admission charges. **10** Scope. **11** Special exhibits or facilities. **12** Staff (a) professionally qualified (b) other non-manual (c) manual.

BLICKLING, Norfolk

BLICKLING HALL, Blickling, Norwich, NR11 6NF (Tel 026 373-3471). **4** National Trust. **5** Administrator: Major-Gen P. T. Tower CB, DSO, MBE; Custodian: Mr H. Denis Mead. **8** Open to the public. **9** Daily: Easter to Spring bank hol 14.00-18.00, Spring bank hol to Sept 11.00-18.00. Adults 50p, children 25p. **10** Jacobean house, tapestries, pictures, furniture, print room & 12,000 book library. Gardens both formal & landscaped, park & lake. **11** Tearooms, shop & information centre; free car park; free picnic area in old walled orchard. **12** (b) 1 (c) 4.

BODMIN, Cornwall

BODMIN MUSEUM, 13 Rock Lane, Bodmin, PL31 1NR (Tel 0208-4159). **4** Bodmin Town Council. **5** Hon Curator: Mr L. E. Long. **8** Not open to public; open to genuine students for ref only. **10** Chiefly local history; some geological & natural history specimens. **11** Photographs on local history subjects. **12** (b) 1.

DUKE OF CORNWALL'S LIGHT INFANTRY REGIMENTAL MUSEUM, The Keep, Bodmin, PL31 1EG (Tel 0208-2810). **5** Curator: Lt Col J. E. E. Fry MC, DL. **8** Open to the public. **9** Mon-Fri 9.00-12.30, 14.00-16.45. Free. **12** (b) 2 (c) 2.

BOLTON, Lancashire

CENTRAL MUSEUM AND ART GALLERY, Le Mans Crescent, Bolton, BL1 1SA (Tel 0204-22311; Telex 635001). **4** Bolton MBC. **7** Arts Dept, Dir: Miss D. N. Pearce FLA, FRSA. **8** Open to the public. **9** Mon-Fri 10.00-18.00, Sat 10.00-17.30. Free. **10** Natural history, archaeology & local history; Egyptology; early English watercolours; general, fine & applied art collns; aquarium. **11** British bird skins; geology (coal measure fossils); Mason coleoptera; herbaria; Egyptology (Badarian & textile collns); sculpture (British school: Epstein, Moore, Hepworth, etc), Samuel Crompton papers; costume. **12** (a) 12 (b) 9 (c) 11.

HALL I'TH'WOOD, Off Green Way, Off Crompton Way, Bolton (Tel 0204-51159). **4** Bolton MBC **5** Senior Keeper of Local History: R. J. Bradbury BSc. **7** Arts Dept, Dir: Miss D. N. Pearce FLA, FRSA. **8** Open to the public. **9** Mon-Sat (April-Sept) 10.00-18.00, (Oct-March) 10.00-17.00, closed Thurs all year, Sun (April-Sept) 14.00-18.00. Closed Dec 25, 26 & Jan 1. Free. **10** Furnished manor house (from 1483-1648), birthplace of Samuel Crompton, inventor of the cotton "mule"; Crompton relics; period furnishings; folk life. **11** Cafe, open April-Sept. **12** (b) 1 (c) 1.

SMITHILLS HALL, Off Smithills Dean Rd, Bolton, BL1 7NP (Tel 0204-41265). **4** Bolton MBC. **5** Senior Keeper of Local History: R. J. Bradbury BSc. **7** Arts Dept, Dir: Miss D. N. Pearce FLA, FRSA. **8** Open to the public. **9** Mon-Sat (exc Thurs) 10.00-18.00 (17.00 Oct-March), Sun (April-Sept) 14.00-17.00. Closed Dec 25, 26 & Jan 1. Free. **10** 15th & early 16th cent timbered hall, furnished. **11** Nature trail. **12** (b) 1 (c) 2.

TEXTILE MACHINERY MUSEUM, Branch Library, Tonge Moor Rd, Bolton, BL2 2LE (Tel 0204-21394). **4** Bolton MBC. **5** Senior Keeper of Local History: R. J. Bradbury BSc. **7** Arts Dept, Dir: Miss D. N. Pearce FLA, FRSA. **8** Open to the public. **9** Mon, Tues & Thurs 9.30-19.30, Wed 9.30-13.00, Sat 9.30-12.30. Free. **10** Early cotton machinery. **11** Samuel Crompton's "mule": Hargreave's "jenny"; Arkwright's water frame.

BOOTLE, Merseyside

BOOTLE MUSEUM AND ART GALLERY, Bootle Library, Oriel Rd, Bootle, L20 7AG (Tel 051-922 4040). **4** Sefton MDC. **5** Museums & Arts Officer: H. B. Ratcliffe ARCA.

7 Libraries & Arts Dept, Libn & Arts Services Officer: A. R. Hardman FLA, FRSA. **8** Open to the public. **9** Mon-Fri 9.00-19.00, Sat 9.00-13.00. Free. **10** Paintings, drawings & ceramics. **11** Ceramics (inc Liverpool & other English porcelain). **12** (a) 1 (c) 1.

BOROUGHBRIDGE, North Yorkshire

ALDBOROUGH ROMAN TOWN, Boroughbridge, York, YO5 9ES (Tel 090 12-2768). **4** Dept of Environment, Ancient Monuments, Duncombe Place, York, YO1 2ED. **8** Open to the public. **9** Sun-Fri (inc bank hols) 9.30-19.00 (Oct-Feb 16.00) (March-April 17.30). Adults 5p, children 2½p; 10% discount for party (11 or more). **10** Roman finds.

BOSTON, Lincolnshire

BOSTON GUILDHALL, South St, Boston, PE21 6HT (Tel 0205-4601). **4** Boston BC. **5** Dir of Planning & Technical Services: Mr Ivan C. Stimson CEng, MICE, FIMunE, FIPHE, FInstHE. **6** Amenity. **7** Planning & Technical Services. **8** Open to the public. **10** Local interest. **11** Cells used to imprison Pilgrim Fathers; medieval kitchen. **12** (b) 1 (c) 1.

BOURNEMOUTH, Dorset

ROTHESAY MUSEUM, 8 Bath Rd, Bournemouth, BH1 2ER (Tel 0202-21009). **4** Bournemouth BC. **5** Curator: Mr Graham Teasdill FMA, FRSA, FRNS, FZS. **6** Amenities (Art Gallery & Museums Sub-Committee). **8** Open to the public. Mon-Sat 10.30-17.00 (April-Oct 18.00), Sun 14.30-17.00 . Closed Dec 25, 26, Jan 1 & Good Friday (& usually 2 more days at Xmas). Free, except on Thurs & daily June-Sept: Adults 10p, children 5p. **10** Arms & armour; ethnography; marine history; local history & archaeology; butterflies & moths; ceramics; period furniture & Victorian bygones. **12** (a) 1 (b) 7 (c) 16.

RUSSELL-COTES ART GALLERY AND MUSEUM, East Cliff, Bournemouth, BH1 3AA (Tel 0202-21009). **4** Bournemouth BC. **5** Curator: Mr Graham Teasdill FMA, FRSA, FRNS, FZS. **6** Amenities (Art Gallery & Museums Sub-Committee). **8** Open to the public. Mon-Sat 10.30-17.00 (April-Oct 18.00), Sun 14.30-17.00. Closed Good Friday, Dec 25, 26, Jan 1 (& usually 2 more days at Xmas). Free except on Thurs & daily June-Sept: Adults 10p, children 5p. **10** Period rooms, theatrical colln (mainly associated with Sir Henry Irving); paintings; ceramics; Oriental antiquities; geological terrace. **11** Frequent temporary exhibitions; send stamped addressed envelope for details. **12** (a) 1 (b) 7 (c) 16.

BOVINGTON CAMP, Dorset

CLOUD'S HILL, Bovington Camp, Wareham. **4** National Trust. **9** April-Sept: Wed, Thurs, Sun & bank hol Mon 14.00-18.00; Oct-March: Sun 12.00-16.00. Charges: 20p; HM forces 15p. **10** Home of T. E. Lawrence (Lawrence of Arabia) after leaving RAF; personal possessions & mementoes.

BRADFORD, West Yorkshire

BOLLING HALL MUSEUM, Bolling Hall Rd, Bradford, BD4 7LP (Tel 0274-23057). **4** City of Bradford Metropolitan Council. **5** Chief Officer: Mr John M. A. Thompson MA, AMA. **6** Cultural Activities Panel. **7** Dir of Educational Services: W. R. Knight MA. **8** Open to the public. **9** Daily (May-Aug) 10.00-20.00, (April & Sept) 10.00-19.00, (Oct-March) 10.00-17.00. Closed Dec 25 & Good Friday. Free. **10** Local history; 15th cent house with 18th cent wing designed by Robert Carr & furnished according to period, fine plaster ceilings. **11** "Ghost Room";

BRADFORD, West Yorkshire—*continued*

Polyphon Heraldic Glass; costume & pottery. Car Park. Recorded guide available.   12 (a) 2 (b) 1 (c) 6.

BRADFORD INDUSTRIAL MUSEUM, Moorside Mills, Moorside Rd, Eccleshill, Bradford, BD2 3HP (Tel 0274-631756/638068).   4 Bradford MDC.   5 Chief Officer: Mr John M. A. Thompson MA, AMA.   6 Cultural Activities Panel.   7 Educational Services Division, Dir: W. R. Knight MA.   8 Open to the public.   9 Daily 10.00-17.00. Closed Dec 25 & Good Friday. Free.   10 Former spinning mill complex; industrial archaeology especially growth of the local worsted industry.   11 Textile galleries; motive power gallery, working machinery inc water wheel; transport gallery, vintage & veteran cars, locomotive; tram & trolley shed; mill manager's house (furnished as early 1900); Gavioli organ; temporary exhibitions.   12 (a) 6 (b) 8 (c) 16.

CARTWRIGHT HALL ART GALLERY AND MUSEUM, Lister Park, Bradford, BD9 4NS (Tel 0274-493313).   4 City of Bradford Metropolitan Council.   5 Chief Officer: Mr John M. A. Thompson MA, AMA.   6 Cultural Activities Panel.   7 Dir of Educational Services: W. R. Knight MA.   8 Open to the public.   9 Daily 10.00-20.00, (April & Sept 19.00), (Oct-March 17.00). Closed Dec 25 & Good Friday. Free.   10 English paintings, drawings & water-colours (from 18th cent); works from 10th cent Italian schools; international print colln.   11 British International Print Biennale (next exhibition 1976); McAlpine loan colln of prints; temporary exhibitions of art & natural sciences. Cafe.   12 (a) 4 (b) 7 (c) 10.

BRADING, Isle of Wight

OSBORN-SMITH'S WAX MUSEUM, Brading, Isle of Wight, PO36 0DQ (Tel 098 372-286).   4 Osborn-Smith Ltd.   5 Curator: Mr Graham Osborn-Smith FSA(Scot).   8 Open to the public.   9 Daily (inc bank hols) 10.00-17.00 (May-Sept 22.00).   Adults 45p, children 28p; party rate: adults 40p, children 22p.   10 Cameos of Island history, with authentic costume, wax figures, period furniture & harmonious settings, inc sound, light & motion. Island's oldest house (c. 1228).   11 Some of the instruments of torture from the Royal Castle of Nuremberg; cafeteria.

ROMAN VILLA, Brading, Isle of Wight, PO36 0AB; c/o Pink & Arnold, Staple Chambers, Winchester, Hampshire, SO23 8SS (Tel 0962-3374).   4 Nunwell Enterprises.   5 Custodian: Mrs. Rosemary Goodyer.   8 Open to the public.   9 Easter-Sept: Mon-Sat (inc bank hols) 10.00-dusk, Sun 14.30-dusk. Oct-Easter: by arrangement only. Adults 20p, children 15p. School parties 10p each (teacher free).   10 Remains of a 3rd cent Roman villa; domestic implements & pottery found on site.   11 Painted wall plaster; floor mosaics; hypocaust.

BRAMHALL, Cheshire

BRAMALL HALL, Bramhall Park, Bramhall, Stockport, SK7 3NX (Tel 061-485 3708).   4 Stockport MBC.   5 Asst Dir (Culture): R. E. G. Smith FLA.   7 Recreation & Culture Division, Dir: H. Hitchcock IPFA, FRVA, MInstRM.   8 Open to the public.   9 Daily (exc Thurs) 10.00-13.00, 14.00-19.00 (16.00 Oct-March). Adults 20p, children 10p, children in parties 5p.   10 Elizabethan (black & white) manor house; period furniture & paintings.   12 (b) 2 (c) ½.

BREAMORE, Hampshire

BREAMORE CARRIAGE MUSEUM, Breamore, Fordingbridge, SP6 2DE (Tel 07257-233/270).   4 Breamore Estate Co Ltd.   5 Sir Westrow Hulse Bart; Mr White.   8 Open to the public.   9 April-Sept: daily (exc Mon & Fri) (inc bank hols) 14.00-17.30. Adults 45p, combined ticket 90p, children ½ price; parties ⅓ discount in April, May & Sept.   10 17th cent stables of Breamore House, containing the "Red Rover" last stage coach from London to Southampton, & many other coaches & carts, inc harnesses & lamps.   12 (b) 1.

BREAMORE COUNTRYSIDE MUSEUM, Breamore, Fordingbridge, SP6 2DE (Tel 07257-468).   4 Breamore Estate Co Ltd.   5 Sir Westrow Hulse Bart; Agricultural exhibits: Mr P. Wale.   8 Open to the public.   9 April-Sept: daily (exc Mon & Fri) (inc bank hols) 14.00-17.30. Adults 45p, combined ticket 90p, children ½ price; parties ⅓ discount in April, May & Sept.   10 History of farm implements & techniques; blacksmith's shop; wheelwright's shop; dairy; brewery; tractors.   12 (b) 2.

BREAMORE HOUSE, Breamore, Fordingbridge, SP6 2DE (Tel 07257-233/270; Telex Countryside Museum Breamore 468).   4 Breamore Estate Co Ltd.   5 Sir Westrow Hulse Bart. Agricultural exhibits: Mr P. Wale.   8 Open to the public.   9 April-Sept: daily (exc Mon & Fri) 14.00-17.30. Adults 45p, combined tickets 90p, children half.   10 Elizabethan manor house (1583); paintings (17th, 18th & 19th cent); tapestries (2 by De Teniers); porcelain (Oriental & English); furniture (oak, walnut & mahogany).

BRECHIN, Angus

BRECHIN MUSEUM, St Ninian's Square, Brechin, DD9 7AA (Tel 03562-2687).   4 Angus DC.   6 Leisure & Recreation.   7 Libraries & Museums Service, Dir: G. N. Drummond ALA.   8 Open to the public.   9 Mon-Fri 9.30-18.00, Sat 9.30-17.00.   10 History of Brechin & district.

BRECON, Powys

BRECKNOCK MUSEUM, Captain's Walk, Brecon, LD3 7DS (Tel 0874 4121/2).   4 Powys CC.   5 Curator: Mrs Hilary K. Bulmer MA, AMA.   6 Libraries & Museums.   7 County Libn: Mr George Llewellyn ALA.   8 Open to the public.   9 Mon-Sat (inc bank hols) 10.00-17.00 (Thurs 18.00). Free.   10 Human & natural history of Breconshire.   11 18th & 19th cent lovespoons; early Christian monuments (6th-10th cent).   12 (a) 1 (b) 5.

SOUTH WALES BORDERERS AND MONMOUTHSHIRE REGIMENT MUSEUM, The Barracks, Brecon (Tel 0874-3111 ext 263).   5 Curator: Major G. J. B. Egerton DL.   8 Open to the public.   9 Daily 9.00-12.30, 14.00-17.00. Closed Dec 25 & 26. Free.   10 Regimental history (inc captured enemy items; arms; uniforms; pictures; prints & photographs; medals; many sporting trophies; silver; documents).   11 13 of the 23 Victoria Crosses awarded to the Regiment.   12 (b) 1.

BRIDLINGTON, North Humberside

SEWERBY HALL ART GALLERY & MUSEUM, Sewerby Park, Bridlington, YO15 1EA (Tel 0262-77874).   4 North Wolds BC.   5 Officer-in-Charge: Mr John Frederick Grainger FInstPRA(Dip).   6 Tourism & Recreation.   8 Open to the public.   9 Easter-Sept: Sun-Fri 10.00-12.30, 13.30-18.00, Sat 13.30-18.00. Free, except for admission to Park.   10 Local archaeology, history & military; Amy Johnson Trophy colln; small permanent colln in Art Gallery.   11 Local artists exhibitions; display of pictures owned by local authority.   12 (b) 1 (c) 2.

BRIDPORT, Dorset

MUSEUM AND ART GALLERY, South St, Bridport, DT6 3NR (Tel 03082-2116).   4 West Dorset DC.   5 Curator: Mr John Sales.   6 Recreation & Amenities.   7 Area Officer: Mr F. Greenslade.   8 Open to the public.   9 Mon-Sat (inc most bank hols) 10.30-13.00. Adults 5p, children 2p.   10 Local exhibitions, especially local net, twine & rope industry with working looms. Romano/British excavation finds. Dr Donald Omand's colln of dolls wearing national or historical costumes.   11 One man exhibitions by local artists.   12 (a) 1 (b) 2 (c) 1.

BRIGHOUSE, West Yorkshire

BRIGHOUSE ART GALLERY, Halifax Rd, Brighouse (Tel 04847-4740).   4 Calderdale MBC.   5 Museums Dir: Mr R. A. Innes.   6 Recreation & Amenities.   8 Open

CODE: 1 Name of Museum, Art Gallery or Stately Home.   2 Address.   3 Telephone & telex.   4 Governing body.   5 Officer in charge.   6 Committee responsible.   7 Larger department, chief officer.   8 Open to public.   9 Hours; admission charges. 10 Scope.   11 Special exhibits or facilities.   12 Staff (a) professionally qualified (b) other non-manual (c) manual.

BRIGHOUSE, West Yorkshire—*continued*

to the public.   9 Mon-Sat 11.00-19.00 (Oct-March 17.00), Sun 14.30-17.00. Free.   10 Temporary exhibitions; c. 400 pictures; English water-colours; wood carvings.   12 (a) Served from Clay House, Greetland, Halifax.

BRIGHTON, Sussex

BARLOW COLLECTION OF CHINESE CERAMICS, BRONZES & JADES, University of Sussex, Falmer, Brighton, BN1 9RH (Tel 0273-66755).   4 Trustees of Barlow Collection. 5 Curator: Dr John Sweetman AMA, Dept of Fine Art, The University, Southampton, SO9 5NH.   8 Open to the public. 9 Tues & Thurs 10.00-12.00, 14.00-16.00. Other times by arrangement. Free.   10 Early ceramics (c. 2nd cent BC-18th cent AD), especially T'ang & Sung periods; early bronzes (from 11th cent BC) & jades (from 1st cent AD). 12 (a) 1 (b) 1.

BOOTH MUSEUM OF NATURAL HISTORY, Dyke Rd, Brighton, BN1 5AA (Tel 0273-63005/552586).   4 Brighton BC. 5 Principal Keeper Natural Sciences: Mr C.A.B. Steel BSc, AMA, FLA.   6 Amenities.   7 Royal Pavilion, Art Gallery & Museums, Dir: Mr J.H. Morley, MA, FMA.   8 Open to the public.   9 Oct-March: Mon-Sat 10.00-17.00, Sun 14.00-17.00; April-Sept: Mon-Sat 10.00-18.00, Sun 14.00-18.00. Closed Dec 25, 26 & Good Friday. Free.   10 Natural history; insects; birds; mammalian osteology; palaeontology & minerals.   11 Temporary exhibitions; ornithological & entomological library.   12 (a) 3 (b) 1 (c) 2.

BRIGHTON ART GALLERY AND MUSEUM, Church St, Brighton, BN1 1UE (Tel 0273-63005).   4 Brighton BC. 5 Dir, Royal Pavilion, Art Gallery & Museums: Mr J.H. Morley MA, FMA.   6 Amenities.   8 Open to the public. 9 Mon-Fri 10.00-19.00 (Oct-March 18.00), Sat 10.00-17.00, Sun 10.00-18.00 (Oct-March 17.00). Closed Dec 25, 26 & Good Friday. Free.   10 Old master paintings, water-colours, prints & fine furniture; Willett Colln of English pottery & porcelain; Edward James Colln of Surrealist, fine & applied art of Art Nouveau & Art Deco periods; ethnography; archaeology; musical instruments. Building originally stables for the Royal Pavilion.   11 Frequent special exhibitions; balcony cafe.   12 (a) 9 (b) 8 (c) 21.

NATIONAL TOY MUSEUM, Rottingdean Grange, Rottingdean, Brighton, BN2 7HA (Tel 0273-31004).   4 Brighton BC. 5 Keeper: Miss M. Waller MA.   6 Amenities.   7 Royal Pavilion, Art Gallery & Museums, Dir: Mr J.H. Morley MA, FMA.   8 Open to the public.   9 Mon-Fri 10.00-19.00 (18.00 winter), Sat 10.00-17.00, Sun 14.00-18.00 (17.00 winter). Closed Dec 25, 26 & Good Friday. Free. 10 Antique toys.   12 (a) 1.

PRESTON MANOR (THOMAS-STANFORD MUSEUM), Preston Park, Brighton, BN1 6SD (Tel 0273-552101). 4 Brighton BC.   5 Keeper: Miss Marion Waller MA. 6 Amenities.   7 Royal Pavilion, Art Gallery & Museums, Dir: Mr John Morley MA, FMA.   8 Open to the public. 9 Mon-Sat 10.00-17.00, Sun 14.00-17.00. Closed Dec 25, 26 & Good Friday. Adults 15p, OAPs & students 8p, children 5p, parties 13p.   10 Georgian & Edwardian house on 13th cent foundation; period furniture, paintings, silver, glass etc (majority left by Sir Charles & Lady Thomas-Stanford); Macquoid bequest of furniture, paintings & silver (16th-19th cent).   11 Occasional special exhibitions.   12 (a) 1 (c) 3.

ROTTINGDEAN GRANGE ART GALLERY AND MUSEUM, The Grange, The Green, Rottingdean, BN2 7HA (Tel 0273-31004).   4 Brighton BC.   5 Keeper: Miss M. Waller MA. 6 Amenities.   7 Royal Pavilion, Art Gallery & Museums, Dir: Mr John Morley MA, FMA.   8 Open to the public. 9 Mon-Fri 10.00-19.00 (winter 18.00), Sat 10.00-17.00,

Sun 14.00-18.00 (winter 17.00). Closed Dec 25, 26 & Good Friday. Free.   10 Toys from National Toy Museum; local history (inc books by Rudyard Kipling).   11 Exhibitions by local and national artists.   12 (a) 1 (c) 1.

ROYAL PAVILION, Brighton, BN1 1UE (Tel 0273-63005). 4 Brighton BC.   5 Dir, Royal Pavilion, Art Gallery & Museums: Mr J.H. Morley MA, FMA.   6 Amenities. 8 Open to the public.   9 Winter: daily 10.00-17.00; summer: daily 10.00-20.00. Closed Dec 25 & 26. Not free. 10 Former royal palace (built in 1787 by Henry Holland, rebuilt 1815-22 by John Nash, in a variety of exotic styles); interiors, inc much of the furniture, are of Chinese inspiration; important Regency furniture & objets d'art.   11 Many pieces of original furniture returned on loan from Her Majesty the Queen. Tea Room: open March-Sept. 12 (a) 6 (b) 9 (c) 21.

BRISTOL, Avon

BLAISE CASTLE HOUSE MUSEUM OF SOCIAL HISTORY, Henbury Rd, Bristol, BS10 7QS (Tel 0272-625378). 4 Bristol DC.   5 Curator: Mr J.W. Griffin BA, AMA. 6 Arts & Leisure.   7 City Museum & Art Gallery, Dir City Museum: Mr Nicholas Thomas MA, FSA, FMA. 8 Open to the public.   9 Mon-Sat 14.00-17.00 (May-Sept 17.30), March-Nov: Sun 15.00-17.00. Free.   10 English, & in particular local, social & agricultural history; costume; toys & games; domestic life; corporate life.   12 (a) 1 (b) 2 (c) 2½.

CHATTERTON HOUSE, Redcliffe Way, Bristol, BS1 6NL (Tel 0272-299771).   4 Bristol DC.   5 Dir, City Museum: Mr N. Thomas MA, FMA, FSA.   6 Arts & Leisure. 8 Open only by arrangement with Dir of City Museum. 10 Birthplace of the poet, Thomas Chatterton.

CITY OF BRISTOL MUSEUM AND ART GALLERY, Queens Rd, Clifton, Bristol, BS8 1RL (Tel 0272-299771).   4 Bristol DC.   5 Dir, City Art Gallery: Mr A.D.P. Wilson MA, FSA, FMA; Dir, City Museum: Mr N. de L'E.W. Thomas MA, FSA, FMA.   6 Arts & Leisure.   8 Open to the public. 9 Mon-Sat (inc some bank hols) 10.00-17.30. Free. 10 Local archaeology, geology, history, natural history, technology; the arts, especially glass, porcelain, pottery & the Bristol School of artists; Egyptology; ethnography; European painting; Oriental art.   11 Oriental glass; Assyrian reliefs from Nimrud; Bristol Delftware; BBC's colln of historic broadcasting equipment; temporary exhibitions etc; schools teaching & loan service.   12 (a) 19 (b) 38 (c) 30.

GEORGIAN HOUSE, 7 Great George St, Bristol, BS1 5RR (Tel 0272-299771).   4 Bristol DC.   5 Dir, City Art Gallery: Mr A.D.P. Wilson MA, FMA, FSA.   6 Arts & Leisure.   8 Open to the public.   9 Mon-Sat (inc bank hols exc Spring) 11.00-17.00. Free.   10 Late 18th cent house furnished in style of the period.   11 Collector's cabinet by John Channon (c. 1745); harpsichord by Jacob Kirckman (1757); armchair (1786) & secretaire bookcase (1787) by Bristol cabinet-makers.   12 (a) Served from City Art Gallery (c) 2.

HARVEYS WINE MUSEUM, Harvey House, 12 Denmark St, Bristol, BS99 7JE (Tel 0272-298011).   4 John Harvey & Sons Ltd.   5 Senior Public Relations Asst: Mrs J.M. Hudd. 8 Open, by appointment.   9 Mon-Fri 9.00-17.30. Charges: according to nature of visit, generally 60p.   10 Countries of origin & styles of wine; basic viniculture; silver, glass, artifacts related to wine; shown in original cellars. 11 Tastings & lectures.   12 (a) 4.

KINGS WESTON ROMAN VILLA, Long Cross, Lawrence Weston, Bristol.   4 Bristol DC.   5 Dir, City Museum: Mr N. Thomas MA, FSA, FMA.   6 Arts & Leisure. 8 Open to the public.   9 Key obtainable from Caretaker:

BRISTOL, Avon—*continued*

Mr J. Stewart, 17 Hopewell Gardens, Lawrence Weston. Free.
10 Walls & mosaic pavement of a Romano-British villa.

RED LODGE, Park Row, Bristol, BS1 5LJ (Tel 0272-299771).
4 Bristol DC. **5** Dir, City Art Gallery: Mr A. D. P. Wilson
MA, FMA. **6** Arts & Leisure. **8** Open to the public.
9 Mon-Sat (inc some bank hols) 13.00-17.00. Free.
10 Late 16th cent house; early 18th cent staircase; 16th &
18th cent furnishings; fine plaster ceilings, fireplaces & oak
panelling. **12** (c) 3.

ST NICHOLAS CHURCH AND CITY MUSEUM, St Nicholas St,
Bristol, BS1 (Tel 0272-299771). **4** Bristol DC.
5 Curator-in-charge: D. P. Dawson BA, AMA. **6** Arts &
Leisure. **7** City Museum & Art Gallery, Dirs: Mr N.
Thomas MA, FSA, FMA & Mr A. D. P. Wilson MA, FMA, FSA.
8 Open to the public. **9** Mon-Sat (inc some bank hols)
10.00-17.30. Free. **10** Local church plate, vestments &
paintings (inc Triptych by Hogarth for St Mary Redcliffe);
local mediaeval antiquities. Shell of mid-18th cent church
designed by J. Bridges & W. Paty ('neat & truly Gothic',
Walpole), 14th cent lower church. **12** (a) Served from
City Museum & Art Gallery.

BRIXHAM, Devon

BRIXHAM MUSEUM AND H.M. COASTGUARD NATIONAL
MUSEUM, Bolton Cross, Brixham; correspondence to: 13
Lindthorpe Way, Brixham, TQ5 8NY (Tel 08045-2937).
4 Brixham Museum & History Society. **5** Hon Curator:
Mr John E. Horsley; Hon Sec & Treasurer: Mr Reginald
Edwin Taylor. **8** Open to the public. **9** Week before
spring bank hol-Sept: Mon-Sat (inc bank hols) 10.00-13.00,
14.30-17.30, 19.15-21.00, Sun 14.30-17.30; Oct & Easter-
week before spring bank hol: Wed & Sun 14.30-17.00. Adults
20p, children 5p; school parties by arrangement free.
10 Maritime; Brixham fishing vessels; 2 master trading
ships; top sail schooners; brigantines; hookers; half models;
local folk museum; HM Coastguard National Museum.

BROADSTAIRS, Kent

BLEAK HOUSE, Bleak House, Broadstairs, (Tel 0843-62224).
5 Curator: Mr F. Lee. **8** Open to the public. **9** May-
Oct: daily. Adults 20p, children 15p. **10** Home for some
years of Charles Dickens & his family; he wrote letters &
magazine articles about it & also wrote 'David Copperfield'
& planned 'Bleak House' there. **11** Charles Dickens'
dining room, bedroom & study with his original desk chair;
bed which he used in Rochester is in bedroom; a rare page
proof corrected in his own hand together with his penknife.
12 (a) 3 (c) 2.

BROADWAY, Hereford & Worcester

SNOWSHILL MANOR, Broadway, WR12 7JU (Tel 038 681-
2410). **4** National Trust. **5** Administrator: Mr A. J. De
La Mare. **8** Open to the public. **9** May-Sept: Wed-Thurs
& bank hols 11.00-13.00, 14.00-18.00, Fri 14.00-18.00;
April-Oct: Sat & Sun 11.00-13.00, 14.00-18.00. Adults 40p,
children 20p; parties of 15 or more 30p. **10** 16th cent
manor house with 17th & 18th cent additions; Chinese &
Japanese objects; nautical instruments; costumes; Samurai &
European armour; musical instruments; clocks; spinning &
weaving tools; toys; bicycles; perambulators; model waggons;
coaches & ships.

BROKERSWOOD, Wiltshire

PHILLIPS COUNTRYSIDE MUSEUM OF NATURAL HISTORY
& FORESTRY, Brokerswood, Westbury, BA13 4EH (Tel 0373-
2238). **4** Trustees of Phillips Countryside Museum.
5 Curator: Miss Eunice Overend BSc. **8** Open to the
public. **9** Daily (inc bank hols) 10.00 to dusk. Charges: 30p.
10 Natural history & forestry; 80 acres of forest with
extensive labelling of natural history exhibits in situ.
11 Barber colln of birds eggs (c.2,000 species);
Leightons lichens (c.400 types of lichen & moss). **12** (a)
1.

BROMSGROVE, Hereford & Worcester

AVONCROFT MUSEUM OF BUILDINGS, Stoke Heath, Bromsgrove, B60 4JR (Tel 0527-31886). **4** Council of Management. **5** Dir: Mr M. G. L. Thomas MA. **8** Open to the
public. **9** March-Nov: daily (inc bank hols) 11.00-18.00
parties by arrangement. Adults 30p, OAPs, students & children 15p. **10** Open-air museum where vernacular buildings
threatened with destruction have been rescued & re-erected.
11 Windmill; granary; barn; timber-framed houses; chain &
nail making workshops, shop & cafe. **12** (a) 2 (b) 2 (c) 6.

BUDLEIGH SALTERTON, Devon

BICTON GARDENS COUNTRYSIDE MUSEUM, Bicton Gardens, East Budleigh, Budleigh Salterton, EX9 7BQ (Tel 039 56-
465). **4** Privately owned, adminstered by Clinton Devon
Estates, Rolle Estate Office, East Budleigh. **8** Open to the
public. **9** Daily (inc bank hols): 24 March-24 May, & 1 Oct-
15 Oct: 14.00-18.00; 25 May-15 Sept: 10.00-18.00; 16 Sept-
30 Sept: 11.00-18.00. Adults: 12p; children 5p. **10** Old
farm implements; waggons; tractors; steam & stationary
engines; barn & dairy equipment; tools of various rural
trades (cider-making equipment, household items, etc).
11 Divided into seedtime, harvest, the dairy, the blacksmith
etc; large wooden cider press (c.1800); Marshall traction
engine (1894); Titan Tractor (1918); many 19th cent waggons
& carts.

FAIRLYNCH ARTS CENTRE AND MUSEUM, 27 Fore St,
Budleigh Salterton, EX9 6NP (Tel 03954-2666). **4** Committee
of Management. **5** Chairman: Mrs P. M. L. Hull JP.
8 Open to the public. **9** Easter-Oct & Xmas-Jan: daily
14.30-17.00 & July- Sept: Mon-Sat 10.30-12.30. Adults
12p, students 5p, children 2p. **10** Local history, arts &
crafts, geology, ecology; costume; Honiton lace & lacemaking.
11 Xmas exhibition; local artists; lacemaking demonstrations (weekends).

BUNGAY, Suffolk

BUNGAY MUSEUM, Council Offices, Earsham St, Bungay
(Tel 0986-2780). **5** Officer-in-charge: Dr L. H. Cane MB.
8 Open to the public. **9** Mon-Fri 9.00-13.00, 14.00-17.00.
Key at Council Office or at weekends from Curator, 19
Trinity St, Bungay. Free. **10** Local history.

BURFORD, Oxfordshire

TOLSEY MUSEUM, High St, Burford. **4** Tolsey Museum
Committee. **5** Hon Sec: Mrs E. F. Wise, The Welsh Shop,
Burford. **8** Open to the public. **9** Easter-Oct: daily
(inc bank hols) 14.30-17.30. Adults 10p, Children 5p.
10 Maces, seals, charters belonging to the ancient Corporation of Burford, & other objects illustrating local history,
buildings & occupations.

BURNLEY, Lancashire

MUSEUM OF LOCAL CRAFTS AND INDUSTRIES, Towneley
Hall Art Gallery and Museums, Towneley Hall, Burnley
BB11 3RQ (Tel 0282-24213). **4** Burnley BC. **5** Curator:
Mr Hubert R. Rigg FRSA, FSA(Scot). **6** Arts Sub-
Committee. **7** Recreation & Leisure Services Dept,
Borough Recreation Officer: Mr J. Mattocks LInstPRA,
MInstBCA. **8** Open to the public. **9** Mon-Sat (inc bank
hols) 10.00-17.30 (17.00 winter), Sat 13.00-17.00 (14.00-
17.00 winter). Free. **10** Local crafts & industries inc
mining, textiles, basket-making, clogging, woodcarving,
cooperage, Cliviger pottery, etc. **12** (a) 3 (b) 4 (c) 7.

TOWNELEY HALL ART GALLERY & MUSEUMS, Towneley
Hall, Burnley, BB11 3RQ (Tel 0282-24213). **4** Burnley BC.
5 Curator: Mr H. R. Rigg FRSA, FSA(Scot). **6** Arts Sub-
Committee. **7** Recreation & Leisure Dept; Borough Recreation Officer: Mr J. Mattocks LInstPRA, MInstBCA. **8** Open
to the public. **9** Mon-Sat, 10.00-17.30 (17.00 winter),
Sun 13.00-17.00 (14.00-17.00 winter). Closed Dec 25, 26 &
Jan 1. Free. **10** Furnished rooms inc an Elizabethan
long gallery and an entrance hall with plaster-work by

CODE: 1 Name of Museum, Art Gallery or Stately Home. 2 Address. 3 Telephone & telex. 4 Governing body. 5 Officer in charge. 6 Committee responsible. 7 Larger department, chief officer. 8 Open to public. 9 Hours; admission charges. 10 Scope. 11 Special exhibits or facilities. 12 Staff (a) professionally qualified (b) other non-manual (c) manual.

BURNLEY, Lancashire—*continued*

Vassali (completed in 1729). Collns inc oak furniture, 18th & 19th cent paintings & Zoffany's painting of Charles Towneley; early English watercolours; glass; ceramics; natural history; military items. A museum of local crafts & industries is housed in the former brew house nearby. 11 Temporary exhibitions Easter-Sept. 12 (a) 3 (b) 4 (c) 7.

BURTON UPON TRENT, Staffordshire

BURTON UPON TRENT MUSEUM AND ART GALLERY, Guild St, Burton upon Trent, DE14 1NA (Tel 0283-3042). 4 East Staffordshire DC. 6 Libraries, Records & Museums. 7 Staffordshire County Library; Principal Area Libn (East): Mr K. F. Stanesby FLA; County Archivist: F. B. Stitt BA, BLitt. 8 Open to the public. 9 Mon-Fri 11.00-18.00, Sat 11.00-17.00. Free. 10 Local history. 11 Temporary exhibitions; Gallery of British Birds (opened 1975). 12 (c) 2.

HOAR CROSS HALL, Hoar Cross, Burton upon Trent, DE13 8QS (Tel 928 375-224). 5 Owners: Mr & Mrs W. A. Bickerton-Jones. 8 Open to the public. 9 Spring bank hol-Aug bank hol: Sun 14.30-17.30, bank hol Mon 12.30-18.00, bank hol Tues 14.30-18.00. Other days by appointment. Adults 40p, children 15p. 10 Hall contains one of the largest private collns of arms & armour (European & Eastern); Victorian costumes, paintings & furnishings. 11 Medieval banquets (Sats in winter). 12 (b) 2.

BURWASH, Sussex

RUDYARD KIPLING'S HOME, Bateman's, Burwash, TN19 7DS (Tel 04354-882302). 4 National Trust. 5 Administrator: Mrs B. A. Sutherland. 8 Open to the public. 9 Daily (exc Fri) (inc some bank hols) 14.00-17.30 (& June-Sept: Mon-Thurs 11.00-12.30). Free to National Trust members, House, garden & mill: adults 40p, children 25p; garden & mill: adults 25p, children 10p; garden: adults 15p, children 10p. 10 Ironmaster's house (built 1634), Rudyard Kipling's home (1902-1936). 11 Kipling colln (photographs & mss); old watermill recently restored to working order, with turbine used by Kipling to generate electricity for Bateman's for 25 years (one of oldest of its kind). Tea room.

BURY, Lancashire

BURY ART GALLERY AND MUSEUM, Manchester Rd, Bury, BL9 0DG. (Tel 061-764 4110/4021). 4 Bury MDC. 5 Keeper of Art: Mr M. A. E. Millward MA, AMA; Keeper of Social History: Mr D. Janes MA. 6 Recreation & Amenities. 7 Libraries & Arts Dir: Mr P. Chadwick FLA. 8 Open to the public. 9 Mon-Fri 10.00-18.00, Sat 10.00-17.00. Free. 10 **Art Gallery:** Victorian pictures & drawings, inc an important Turner painting & works by Constable, Maclise, Crome, etc. **Museum:** local history, archaeology, natural history & geology. 11 Temporary exhibitions. 12 (a) 2 (b) 1 (c) 4.

BURY TRANSPORT MUSEUM, Castlecroft Rd, Bury, BL9 0LN (Tel 061-764 7790). 4 East Lancashire Light Railway Co Ltd & East Lancashire Railway Preservation Society. 5 Curator: H. Hatcher. 8 Open to the public. 9 Sat, Sun & bank hols (exc Dec 25) 11.00-17.00. Adults 20p, children 10p, family 50p. 10 Steam locomotives; buses; fire engines; steam roller; working model railway. 11 Locomotive in steam (last Sun each month & bank hol Sun & Mon). Souvenir shop; refreshments.

LANCASHIRE FUSILIERS REGIMENTAL MUSEUM, Wellington Barracks, Bury (Tel 061-764 2208). 5 Officer-in-Charge: Major T. P. Shaw MBE. 8 Open to the public. 9 Mon-Sat 9.00-17.00 (closed Thurs). Adults 5p, children 2p. 10 History of Regiment & British Army (1688-1975); regimental relics of all kinds; period uniforms; medals; antique weapons; silver plate; pictures. 11 Relics of Napoleon Bonaparte & Duke of Wellington; relics of Major-General James Wolfe of Quebec; Victoria Crosses; dioramas of battles of Minden & Omdurman. 12 (c) 1.

BURY ST EDMUNDS, Suffolk

GERSHOM PARKINGTON MEMORIAL COLLECTION OF CLOCKS AND WATCHES, 8 Angel Corner, Bury St Edmunds (Tel 0284-2375). 4 St Edmundsbury BC. 6 Recreation & Amenities. 8 Open to the public. 9 Mon-Sat 10.00-13.00, 14.00-17.00, (Nov-Feb 16.00). Closes Dec 25, Jan 1 & Good Friday. Free. 10 Time-keeping instruments. 12 (a) 1 (b) 2.

ICKWORTH HOUSE, The Rotunda, Ickworth, Bury St Edmunds, IP29 5QE (Tel 028 488-270). 4 National Trust. 5 Curator: Mr Edward T. Joy MA, BSc, FSA. 8 Open to the public. 9 Easter-mid Oct: Wed, Thurs, Sat, Sun & bank hols 14.00-18.00. Adults 40p, children 20p. 10 Elliptical rotunda connected by curved corridors to wings, built by 4th Earl of Bristol to his own design (1794-1834). 11 Silver; family portraits (from 16th cent); French & English furniture (especially late Regency c. 1830). 12 (a) 2 (c) 3.

MOYSE'S HALL MUSEUM, Cornhill, Bury St Edmunds, IP33 1DX (Tel 0284-2375 ext 67). 4 St Edmundsbury BC. 5 Officer-in-Charge: Miss Elizabeth Owles BA, FSA. 6 Recreation & Amenities. 7 Borough Secretary's Dept; Mr John E. Vaughan DMA. 8 Open to the public. 9 Mon-Sat 10.00-13.00, 14.00-17.00 (Nov-Feb 16.00). Closed Dec 25, Jan 1 & Good Friday. Charges: 10p. 10 Late 12th cent building; archaeology; natural history; bygones; porcelain. 11 Philip Corder relics.

SUFFOLK REGIMENT MUSEUM, The Keep, Gibraltar Barracks, Bury St Edmunds, IP33 3RN (Tel 0284-5371) 4 Suffolk Regiment Association. 5 Officer-in-Charge: Col W. A. Heal OBE. 8 Open to the public. 9 Mon-Fri 10.00-13.00, 14.00-16.30. Free. 10 Suffolk Regiment uniforms, insignia, medals, historical documents, photographs. 12 (a) 1 (b) 2 (c) 1.

BUSCOT PARK, Oxfordshire

BUSCOT, Buscot Park, Farringdon, SN7 8BU. 4 National Trust. 8 Open to the public. 9 Wed (Oct-March) & 1st Sat & Sun each month (April-Sept) 14.00-18.00. Adults 60p, children 30p. Grounds only: adults 20p, children 15p. 10 18th cent house in Adam style; Faringdon colln (paintings, inc some Rembrandts); fine furniture; 55 acre park with water gardens. 11 Buscot weir & most of village also owned by National Trust.

BUXTON, Derbyshire

BUXTON MUSEUM, Terrace Rd, Buxton, SK17 6DU (Tel 0298-4658). 4 Derbyshire CC. 5 Officer-in-Charge: Mr I. E. Burton ALA. 6 Education. 8 Open to the public. 9 Mon-Fri 9.30-18.00, Sat & bank hols 9.30-17.00. Free. 10 Pleistocene & later animal remains from local caves; local rocks, minerals, fossils & stones; Blue John & Ashford Marble ornaments; paintings, prints, pottery, glass.

CAERLEON, Gwent

LEGIONARY MUSEUM, Caerleon. 4 National Museum of Wales, Cardiff. 8 Open to the public. 9 Mon-Sat 9.30-19.00 (17.30 March, April & Oct) (16.00 Nov-Feb), Sun 14.00-19.00 (17.00 March, April & Oct) (16.00 Nov-Feb). Closed gallery of the National Museum of Wales; objects found on site of Roman legionary fortress of Isca. 12 (b) 2.

CAERNARVON, Gwynedd

ROYAL WELCH FUSILIERS REGIMENTAL MUSEUM,
The Queen's Tower, Caernarvon Castle, Caernarvon,
LL55 2AY (Tel 0286-3362). **4** Trustees. **5** Officer-
in-Charge: Major E. L. Kirby MC, TD, DL. **8** Open to the
public. **9** Oct-April: Mon-Sat 9.30-17.30, Sun 14.00-17.30
(Nov-Feb: closes 16.00 daily); May-Sept: daily 9.30-19.00.
Closed Dec 24-26. Not free. **10** History of the Regiment
from its foundation in 1689. **11** Russian 16 pounder field
gun captured at battle of Alma (1854); medals (inc 8 Victoria
Crosses & Peninsular War Gold Crosses); uniforms; weapons;
trophies; royal & other portraits; library. **12** (a) 1 (b) 1
(c) 3.

SEGONTIUM, Caernarvon. **4** National Trust & Dept of
Environment, on behalf of Secretary of State for Wales.
8 Open to the public. **9** Mon-Dat 9.30-19.00, Sun 14.00-
19.00. Closes 17.30 daily March, April & Oct; 16.00 daily
Nov-Feb. Closed Dec 25 & 26. Adults 10p, children & OAPs
5p; group rates. **10** Remains of Roman fort; museum of
relics found on site.

CAMBERLEY, Surrey

CAMBERLEY MUSEUM, Knoll Rd, Camberley, GU15 3SY
(Tel 0276-64483). **4** Surrey Heath BC. **5** Curator:
Mrs M. Rendell. **6** Recreations & Amenities. **8** Open
to the public. **9** Tues-Sat 14.00-17.00. Free.
10 Archaeology; history; natural history; costume.
11 Temporary exhibitions (occasionally). **12** (a) 1 (b) 1
(c) 1.

ROYAL ARMY ORDNANCE CORPS MUSEUM, Blackdown
Barracks, Deepcut, Camberley, GU16 6RN (Tel 04867-4511
ext 650). **5** Curator: Lt Col W. B. Saunders (Retd).
8 Open to the public. **9** Mon-Fri 9.30-16.30 (Fri 16.00).
Free. **10** Background history of the Royal Army Ordnance
Corps. **12** (b) 2 (c) 1.

ROYAL MILITARY ACADEMY SANDHURST COLLECTION,
Camberley, GU15 4PQ (Tel 0276-63344 ext 489).
5 Curator: Dr T. A. Heathcote BA, PhD, FRAS. **8** Open
to the public. **9** Daily 10.00-16.30. Free. **10** History
of RMAS & officer training unit. **11** Lecture tours by
arrangement. **12** (a) 2 (b) 1 (c) 5.

CAMBO, Northumberland

WALLINGTON HALL, Wallington, Cambo, Morpeth, NE61 4AR
(Tel 067 074-283). **4** National Trust. **5** Administrator:
Mr H. B. Swainson. **8** Open to the public. **9** April-Sept:
daily (exc Tues) (inc bank hols) 14.00-18.00; Oct: Sat & Sun
14.00-17.00. Not free. **10** Large mansion house.
11 Fine porcelain, furniture & pictures; dolls' houses &
museum; exceptional rococo plasterwork by the Francini
brothers. **12** (b) 1.

CAMBORNE, Cornwall

CAMBORNE MUSEUM, Public Library, The Cross, Camborne,
TR14 8HA. **4** Kerrier DC. **6** Amenities. **7** Sec to
Council: S. G. Stevens. **8** Open to the public. **9** Mon-
Wed & Fri 15.00-17.00, Sat 14.00-16.00. Free. **10** Local
exhibits. **11** Tin mining industry; minerals.

HOLMAN MINING MUSEUM, Trevenson St, Camborne,
TR14 8DS (Tel 0209-712750; Telex 45501). **4** CompAir
Construction & Mining Ltd. **5** Curator: Mr R. Thomas.
8 Open to the public. **9** Mon-Fri 9.00-12.00, 13.00-16.30.
Free. **10** History of mining equipment used in Cornish
tin mining industry; geological specimens. **11** Working
Cornish Rotative Beam Engine (built 1851, now owned by
National Trust).

CAMBRIDGE, Cambridgeshire

CAMBRIDGE AND COUNTY FOLK MUSEUM, 2/3 Castle St,
Cambridge, CB3 0AQ (Tel 0223-55159). **4** Council of
Management. **5** Officer-in-Charge: Miss Enid M. Porter
MA. **8** Open to the public. **9** Tues-Sat (& bank hols)
10.30-13.00, 14.00-17.00, Sun 14.30-16.30. Adults 10p,
OAPs, students & children 5p. **10** Former White Horse
Inn (16th cent); life, work & leisure of people of Cambridge
& Cambridgeshire from 17th cent to present. **11** Trades
& occupations; history of Cambridge & the university; folk-
lore; children's toys; nursery furniture; domestic crafts;
rural life; pictures & photographs of old Cambridgeshire.
12 (a) 1 (c) 1.

Cambridge University

FITZWILLIAM MUSEUM, Trumpington St, Cambridge,
CB2 1RB (Tel 0223-69501/3). **5** Dir: Prof A. M. Jaffé
8 Open to the public. **9** Tues-Sat: 10.00-17.00, Sun
14.15-17.00. Closed Dec 23-26, Jan 1 & Good Friday.
Free. **10** West Asiatic, Egyptian, Greek & Roman
antiquities; coins & medals; European ceramics & glass,
arms & armour, ivories, enamels, metalwork, bronzes,
furniture & textiles; Islamic & Far Eastern art (Chinese
& Korean); paintings, drawings & miniatures; prints; mss;
early printed books; music & literary autographs.
11 New Exhibition Gallery. **12** (a) 11 (b) 22 (c) 19.

KETTLE'S YARD, Northampton St, Cambridge, CB3 0AQ
(Tel 0223-52124). **5** Resident: E. R. P. Clough BA.
8 Open to the public. **9** Daily (inc bank hols) 14.00-
16.00. Exhibition gallery: Mon-Sat (inc bank hols) 12.00-
18.00, Sun 14.00-18.00. Free. **10** Formerly the
private colln of H. S. Ede (inc works by Ben Nicholson,
David Jones, Christopher Wood, Gaudier-Brzeska,
Miró, Brancusi & others 20th cent artists); exhibitions of
20th cent art in adjoining gallery. **12** (a) 2.

MINERALOGICAL MUSEUM, Department of Mineralogy &
Petrology, Downing Place, Cambridge, CB2 3EW (Tel
0223-64131). **5** Officer-in-Charge Dr S. O. Agrell PhD.
8 Open to the public. **9** Mon-Fri 9.30-13.00, 14.30-17.00,
Sat 9.30-12.00. Free. **10** Minerals, crystal, gem-stones
etc. **12** (a) 1 (b) 1.

MUSEUM OF ARCHAEOLOGY AND ETHNOLOGY,
Downing St, Cambridge, CB2 3DZ (Tel 0223-59714).
5 Curator: Mr Peter W. Gathercole MA, AMA. **8** Open
to the public. **9** Mon-Sat (& Spring bank hol) 14.00-
18.00. Free. **10** Archaeological collns (palaeolithic
material from Europe, Asia & Africa; later material from
Europe, Near East, other parts of Asia & America; local
collns of various periods); ethnological collns (Africa,
Asia, the Americas & Pacific). **11** Some facilities for
research (by appointment). **12** (a) 4.

MUSEUM OF CLASSICAL ARCHAEOLOGY, Little St
Mary's Lane, Cambridge, CB2 1RR (Tel 0223-65621 ext
204). **5** Curator: Prof R. M. Cook. **8** Open to the
public. **9** Mon-Fri & bank hols 9.00-13.00, 14.15-
17.00, Sat 9.00-13.00. Closed Dec 26 & Easter Monday.
Free. **10** Casts of Greek & Roman sculpture.
12 (b) 2½ (c) 1.

MUSEUM OF ZOOLOGY, Downing St, Cambridge, CB2 3EJ
(Tel 0223-58717). **5** Dir: Dr K. A. Joysey BSc, MA, PhD.
8 Open to the public. **9** Mon-Fri 14.15-17.15. Closed
1 week at Xmas & Easter. Free. **10** Material used in
teaching & research in zoology. **11** Research collns
for comparative osteology & vertebrate palaeontology.
12 (a) 6 (b) 4 (c) 1.

SCOTT POLAR RESEARCH INSTITUTE MUSEUM,
Lensfield Rd, Cambridge, OB2 1ER (Tel 0223-66499).
5 Curator: Mr C. A. Holland MA. **8** Open to the public.
9 Mon-Sat 14.30-18.00. Free. **10** Polar exploration &
research (past & present); Eskimo & general polar art;
polar transportation (sledges, kayaks, model ships, etc);
polar wildlife.

SEDGWICK MUSEUM OF GEOLOGY, Downing St,
Cambridge, CB2 3EQ (Tel 0223-51585). **5** Officer-in-
Charge: Prof H. B. Whittington DSc, FRS. **8** Open to
the public. **9** Mon-Fri 9.00-13.00, 14.15-17.00, Sat
(full term only) 9.00-13.00. Free. **10** Fossils of
world wide provenance & all ages with subordinate collns
of building stones, etc. **12** (a) 3 (c) 3.

CODE: 1 Name of Museum, Art Gallery or Stately Home. **2** Address **3** Telephone & telex. **4** Governing body. **5** Officer in charge. **6** Committee responsible. **7** Larger department, chief officer. **8** Open to public. **9** Hours; admission charges. **10** Scope. **11** Special exhibits or facilities. **12** Staff (a) professionally qualified (b) other non-manual (c) manual.

Cambridge University—*continued*

WHIPPLE MUSEUM OF THE HISTORY OF SCIENCE, Free School Lane, Cambridge CB2 3RH (Tel 0223-54481). **4** History & Philosophy of Science Syndicate. **5** Curator: Mr D. J. Bryden MA, BSc, DipHist&PhilSc. **8** Open to the public. **9** Mon-Fri 14.00-17.00. Free. **10** Scientific instruments from middle ages to early 20th cent.

CULTURE CENTRE OF ALGAE AND PROTOZOA, 36 Storey's Way, Cambridge, CB3 0DT (Tel 0223-61378). **4** Natural Environment Research Council. **5** Dir: E. A. George MA. **8** Not open to public. **10** Maintenance & supply of cultures of algae (other than seaweeds) & free-living protozoa, mainly for teaching & research; c. $\frac{1}{4}$ of the cultures are of taxonomic type material. **12** (a) 10 (b) 3 (c) 5.

SELF HELP BUILDING MUSEUM, 15 Hale St, Cambridge, CB4 3BZ (Tel 0223-54414). **5** Officer-in-Charge: Mr Peter A. Clegg MA, MED. **8** Open by appointment only. **9** Sat & Sun: 10.00-11.30, 12.00-13.30, 14.30-16.30, 17.00-18.30. Free. **10** Do-it-yourself renovation; demolition; plastering; plumbing; maintenance & repairs. **11** Solar energy; conservatories; Agas; plywood technology; architectural designs & consultancy. **12** (b) 2.

CANTERBURY, Kent

BUFFS REGIMENTAL MUSEUM, c/o The Royal Museum, The Beaney, 18 High St, Canterbury, CT1 2JF (Tel 0227-64081). **4** Canterbury City Council & Regimental Trustees. **5** Curator of City Museums: Mr K. G. H. Reedie MA, FSA(Scot), AMA. **7** Amenities & Recreation Dept, City Amenities Officer: Mr W. H. S. Preston. **8** Open to the public. **9** Mon-Sat (inc Easter Mon) 10.00-13.00, 14.00-17.00, (Oct-March 14.00-16.00 only). Adults 6p, children 2p. School parties free on application to Curator. **10** Regimental history; uniforms; medals; silver; pictures; weapons. **11** Medieval building (Poor Priests' Hospital). **12** (c) 1.

QUEEN'S REGIMENTAL MUSEUM, Howe Barracks, Canterbury, CT1 1JU (Tel 0227-65281). **5** Officer-in-Charge: Major E. A. McCarthy (Retd). **8** Open to the public. **9** Mon-Fri 9.00-12.30, 14.00-16.30. Free. **10** Uniforms; medals; weapons; militaria; history of the Queens Royal Surrey Regt, The Queens Own Buffs Regt, The Royal Sussex Regt & The Middlesex Regt. **12** (c) 1.

ROMAN PAVEMENT, c/o The Royal Museum, The Beaney, 18 High St, Canterbury, CT1 2JF (Tel 0227-52747). **4** Canterbury City Council. **5** Curator of City Museums: Mr K. G. H. Reedie MA, FSA(Scot), AMA. **7** Amenities & Recreation Dept, City Amenities Officer: Mr W. H. S. Preston. **8** Open to the public. **9** Mon-Sat (inc Easter Monday) 10.00-13.00, 14.00-17.00, (Oct-Mch 13.00-16.00 only). Adults 6p, children 2p, school parties free on application to Curator. **10** Excavations after 1942 bombings revealed Roman town house, part incorporated as a basement to new buildings & opened as a museum of Roman Canterbury. **11** Roman mosaic panels & hypocaust. **12** (c) 1.

ROYAL MUSEUM, The Beaney, 18 High St, Canterbury, CT1 2JF (Tel 0227-52747). **4** Canterbury City Council. **5** Curator of City Museums: Mr K. G. H. Reedie, MA, FSA(Scot), AMA. **7** Amenities & Recreation Dept, City Amenities Officer: Mr W. H. S. Preston. **8** Open to the public. **9** Mon-Sat (inc Easter Monday) 9.30-17.30. Free. **10** Archaeology of East Kent; local history & bygones; oils, watercolours & prints; English, Continental & Eastern china & porcelain; Greek pottery; natural sciences colln. Invicta steam engine in Dane John Gardens. **11** Anglo Saxon & Roman glass; Roman silver spoons; the Canterbury Cross (Anglo Saxon); Sidney Cooper paintings. **12** (a) 2 (b) 2 (c) 4.

WESTGATE TOWER, c/o The Royal Museum, The Beaney, 18 High St, Canterbury, CT1 2JF (Tel 0227-52747). **4** Canterbury City Council. **5** Curator of City Museums: Mr K. G. H. Reedie MA, FSA(Scot), AMA. **7** Amenities & Recreation Dept, City Amenities Officer: Mr W. H. S. Preston. **8** Open to the public. **9** Mon-Sat (inc Easter Monday) 10.00-13.00, 14.00-18.00 (Oct-March 14.00-18.00 only). Adults 6p, children 2p, school parties free on application to Curator. **10** 14th cent gatehouse containing arms & armour; history of the tower & city fortifications, later used as gaol. **12** (c) 1.

CARDIFF, South Glamorgan

NATIONAL MUSEUM OF WALES, Cathays Park, Cardiff, CF1 3NP (Tel 0222-26241). **4** Council of National Museum of Wales. **5** Dir: Dr G. O. Jones MA, DSc, PhD. **8** Open to the public. **9** Mon-Sat & bank hols 10.00-18.00 (Oct-March 17.00), Sun 14.30-17.00. Free. **10** Fine art; applied art; botany; geology; industry; zoology; archaeology. **11** Special exhibitions; lunchtime lectures, concerts, reading; library; Reardon Smith Lecture theatre. **12** (a) 100 (b) 60 (c) 26.

WELSH FOLK MUSEUM, St Fagans, Cardiff, CF5 6XB (Tel o222-561357). **4** Court of National Museum of Wales. **5** Curator: Mr Trefor M. Owen MA, FSA. **8** Open to the public. **9** Mon-Sat 10.00-17.00, Sun 14.30-17.00 (April-June & Sept: closes 18.00 daily), (July, Aug & all bank hols closes 19.00 daily). Adults 10p, children under 16 & OAPs 5p, pre-arranged educational parties free. **10** Exhibit & research centre in Welsh folk study. **11** Gallery of material culture; agricultural gallery; costume gallery; St Fagans Castle; 13 re-erected buildings; exhibiting craftsmen; gardens. **12** (a) 19 (b) 71 (c) 59.

CARLISLE, Cumbria

BORDER REGIMENT AND KING'S OWN ROYAL BORDER REGIMENT MUSEUM, Queen Mary's Tower, The Castle, Carlisle, CA3 8UR (Tel 0228-32774). **4** Trustees of the Regimental Museum. **5** Officer-in-Charge: Lt Col R. K. May. **8** Open to the public. **9** Mon-Sat 9.30-17.30 (May-Sept 19.30) (Nov-Feb 16.00), Sun: March & Oct 14.00-17.30, April 9.30-17.30, May-Sept 9.30-19.00 Nov-Feb 14.00-16.00. Closed Dec 25, 26 & Jan 1. Adults summer 20p, winter 10p, children 5p, (inc museum & castle). **10** The Border Regt, King's Own Royal Border Regt, Cumbria Militia, Territorials, Volunteers & Yeomanry; pictures; prints; silver; uniforms; arms; trophies; dioramas. **11** Schools free on request from Dept of Environment. **12** (a) 1 (c) 2.

MUSEUM AND ART GALLERY, Tullie House, Castle St, Carlisle, CA3 8TP (Tel 0228-34781). **4** Carlisle City Council. **5** Curator: Mr Robert Hogg BSc, FMA. **6** Recreation & Amenities. **8** Open to the public. **9** Mon-Fri 9.00-20.00 Sat 9.00-19.00, (Oct-March closes 19.00 daily); bank hols & Sun (June-Aug only) 14.30-17.00. Free. **10** Local human & natural history, fine & decorative arts. **11** Centre of study for Hadrian's wall; comprehensive colln of British birds; Williamson bequest (English porcelain); Bottomley bequest (19th cent British paintings). **12** (a) 6½ (b) 1 (c) 6.

CARMARTHEN, Dyfed

COUNTY MUSEUM, Quay St, Carmarthen, SA31 3JT (Tel 0267-6754). **4** Dyfed CC. **6** Education (Museums Sub-Committee). **8** Open to the public. **9** Mon-Fri 9.30-12.30, 13.15-17.00. Free. **10** Collns of archeological objects from the county, & some small foreign collns (eg Egyptiana); costume (inc military costume & arms); ceramics (especially Llanelli & other S. Wales ware); folk objects (eg love spoons made in the county); books (especially good archaeological colln). **11** Roman gold chain;

CARMARTHEN, Dyfed—*continued*

Salisbury first Welsh Testament; occasional small temporary exhibitions.   **12** (a) 2 (b) 1 (c) 1.

CASTLE ASHBY, Northamptonshire

CASTLE ASHBY, Estate Office, Castle Ashby, NN7 1LJ (Tel 060 129-233).   **5** Agent for Compton Estates: J. G. Pearson FRICS.   **8** Open to the public.   **9** April-Sept: Sun & bank hols 14.00-17.30, June-Aug: Thurs, Sat, Sun & bank hols 14.00-17.30. Adults 50p, children 25p; gardens & terraces only: 20p.   **10** Earliest part of building 1574, South wing by Inigo Jones (1635); terraces & gardens laid out 1860; parkland with 3½ mile tree-lined avenue; plaster ceilings; oak panelling; stair-cases & chimney-pieces (1600-1635); tapestries & furniture (1660-1700).
11 Pictures: English school (Reynolds, Romney, Lawrence, Hoppner, Gainsborough, Raeburn), Italian Renaissance (1480-1520) (Mantegna, Bellini, Sebastiano del Piombo, Botticini, Dosso Dossi); Also works by Guardi, Van Dyck, Jan Steen etc.

CASTLE CORNET, Guernsey, Channel Islands

GUERNSEY MUSEUM AND ART GALLERY, Castle Cornet, Guernsey (Tel 0481-21657).   **4** States of Guernsey.
5 Curator: Mrs H. R. Cole MA; Administrator: Mr B. D. White.   **6** Ancient Monuments.   **8** Open to the public.
9 Daily (inc bank hols) 10.00-18.00. Adults 20p, children 5p.   **10** Historic castle; RAF, maritime & military museums.   **11** Guernsey Militia uniforms & badges; armoury; local paintings; maritime exhibits; German occupation room. New museum (opening 1977) at Candie Gardens, St Peter Port.   **12** (a) 1 (b) 3 (c) 5.

CASTLE HOWARD, North Yorkshire

CASTLE HOWARD COSTUME GALLERIES, Castle Howard, York, YO6 7BZ (Tel 965384-333).   **4** Castle Howard Estate Ltd.   **5** Curator: Mr Richard A. Robson.
8 Open to the public.   **9** Easter-1st Sun in Oct: daily (exc Mon & Fri) 13.30-17.00 (bank hols 11.30-17.30). Adults 60p, children 30p.   **10** 18th-20th cent costumes, in appropriately created settings, showing British social life.   **11** Special arrangements for schools, by appointment; restaurant.   **12** (a) 1 (b) 1.

CAWTHORNE, South Yorkshire

VICTORIA JUBILEE MUSEUM, Taylor Hill, Cawthorne, Barnsley, S75 4HQ (Tel 022 679-8336).   **4** Museum Trustees.   **5** Chairman of Trust: Mr A. H. Park, 11 Five Acres, Cawthorne S75 4HZ; Hon Sec: M. Moxon.   **8** Open to the public.   **9** Sat, Sun & bank hols: 14.30-17.00. Parties only by arrangement. Adults 3p; children 1p.
10 Swords; arms; coal fossils; flat irons; stuffed birds; sewing machines; gamekeepers' gear; china; glass; pottery; birds eggs; works by local artists; clocks, etc.

CERES, Fife

FIFE FOLK MUSEUM, The Weigh House, Ceres, Cupar (Tel 03373-410).   **4** Central & North Fife Preservation Society.   **5** Hon Curator: Mrs Margaret L. Mercer MA.
8 Open to the public.   **9** April-Oct: Mon-Sat (exc Tues) (inc bank hols) 14.00-17.00, Sun 15.00-18.00. Adults 10p, children 5p.   **10** Local history & social life.
11 Agriculture; trade tools; weights & measures; costume.

CHALFONT ST GILES, Buckinghamshire

MILTON'S COTTAGE MUSEUM, Deanway, Chalfont St Giles, HP8 4JH (Tel 024-07-2313).   **4** Milton's Cottage Trust.   **5** Curator: Mr K. L. Jeffery.   **8** Open to the public.   **9** Mon-Sat inc bank hols (closed Tues): 10.00-13.00, 14.15-18.00, Sun 14.15-18.00. Adults 15p, children 5p, parties of 20 or more 10p each.   **10** 16th cent house where Milton finished 'Paradise Lost'; colln of Milton relics.

11 1st, 2nd, 4th & 6th editions of 'Paradise Lost'; 1st edition of 'Paradise Regained'; portraits & documents relating to Milton & his period.   **12** (a) 2.

CHARD, Somerset

FORDE ABBEY, Chard, TA20 4LU (Tel 04602-231).
5 Owner: M. Roper.   **8** Open to the public.   **9** May-Sept: Sun & Wed 14.00-18.00. 60p.   **10** 12th cent Cistercian monastery (modernised 1650); 30 acres of gardens.

CHATHAM, Kent.

CORPS OF ROYAL ENGINEERS MUSEUM, Brompton Barracks, Chatham, ME4 4UG (Tel 0634-44555 ext 312).
4 Institution of Royal Engineers.   **5** Officer-in-Charge: Lt Col C. T. P. Holland MBE, (Retd).   **9** Mon-Fri 10.00-12.30, 14.30-16.30. Other times by prior arrangement. Free.
10 History of the Corps of Royal Engineers; development of military engineering science.   **11** Relics of Major General Charles George Gordon & of Field Marshal Lord Kitchener.   **12** (a) 2 (c) 2.

CHAWTON, Hampshire.

JANE AUSTEN'S HOME, Chawton, Alton, GU34 1SG (Tel 0420-83262).   **4** Jane Austen Memorial Trust.
5 Curator: Mrs E. M. Rose.   **8** Open to the public.
9 Daily (exc Mon & Tues, Nov-March) 11.00-16.30. Closed Dec 25 & 26. Adults 20p, children 5p.   **10** Jane Austen's home from 1809-1817; personal relics of Jane Austen & family.   **11** Old bake house.   **12** (b) 3.

CHEDDAR, Somerset

CHEDDAR VETERAN & VINTAGE CAR MUSEUM, The Cliffs, Cheddar, BS27 3QA (Tel 0934-742446).   **5** Manager: Mr G. N. Bibby.   **8** Open to the public.   **9** Daily (inc bank hols) 10.00-19.00 (winter 16.30), closed Dec 25. Adults 25p, children 12p, party rates.   **10** Veteran & vintage cars; motorcycles & motoring miscellany.
11 1903 White Steam Car; 1913 Lion-Peugeot.   **12** (b) 1 (c) 1.

GOUGH'S CAVE, Cheddar Caves, Cheddar, BS27 3QF (Tel 0934-742343).   **5** General Manager: Mr L. W. Say.
8 Open to the public.   **9** Daily (inc bank hols) 10.00-17.30 (winter 16.30). Charges: 5p.   **10** Archaeological remains found in & around Gough's Cave (inc 'Cheddar Man'); pictorial & dioramic display of Cheddar from 10,000 years ago to present.   **11** Cheddar man; Baton-de-Commandement; dioramas.   **12** (b) 1.

CHEDDLETON, Staffordshire

CHEDDLETON FLINT MILL, Leek Rd, Cheddleton, Leek.
4 Cheddleton Flint Mill Industrial Heritage Trust.
5 Officer-in-Charge: Mr Robert Copeland, Briton House, Tittensor, Stoke-on-Trent, ST12 9HH.   **8** Open to the public.   **9** Sat, Sun & bank hols 13.00-17.30. Other times by prior arrangement. Free, but donations welcome.
10 Two restored water-driven flint-grinding mills supplying flint to the pottery industry; old machinery & artifacts used in the preparation of raw materials for the pottery industry.
11 Model Newcomen pumping engine pumping water to overshot waterwheel, & 100 HP Robey reciprocating steam engine; restored horse-drawn narrow boat 'VIENNA' moored on the Caldon Canal; one-ton Staffordshire miller's cart; plate way with waggon.

CHELMSFORD, Essex

CHELMSFORD AND ESSEX MUSEUM, Oaklands Park, Moulsham St, Chelmsford, CM2 9AQ (Tel 0245-53066/60614).
4 Chelmsford DC.   **5** Curator: Mr D. L. Jones.   **6** Arts.
7 Recreation Dept, Recreation Manager: Mr B. L. Hammond CEng, MICE, MIMunE, AMBIM, MInstRM.   **8** Open to the public.   **9** Mon-Sat (inc bank hols) 10.00-17.00, Sun

CODE: 1 Name of Museum, Art Gallery or Stately Home. 2 Address. 3 Telephone & telex. 4 Governing body. 5 Officer in charge. 6 Committee responsible. 7 Larger department, chief officer. 8 Open to public. 9 Hours; admission charges. 10 Scope. 11 Special exhibits or facilities. 12 Staff (a) professionally qualified (b) other non-manual (c) manual.

CHELMSFORD, Essex—*continued*

14.00-17.00. Free. 10 Roman Essex; bygones; coins; costumes; paintings; British birds; geology; shells; Victorian Room; Tunstill colln of glass. 11 Essex Regiment Museum, temporary exhibitions (programmes on request). 12 (a) 1; (b) 2 (c) 3.

CHELTENHAM, Gloucestershire

CHELTENHAM BOROUGH COUNCIL ART GALLERY AND MUSEUM SERVICE, Clarence St, Cheltenham, GL50 3JT (Tel 0242-37431/2). 4 Cheltenham BC. 5 Dir: Mr David Addison BA, DipEd, AMA. 6 Arts Sub-Committee. 8 Open to the public. 9 Mon-Sat 10.00-18.00. Free. 10 & 11 Ceramics (British, European & Oriental); furniture (17th-20th cent, inc Gimson); good costume; paintings; prints; drawings; glass, temporary exhibition programme concentrates on art, particularly 20th cent. Lectures & films, particularly on art. Reserve collns available by prior arrangement. Fine art (paintings, drawings & prints); applied art (ceramics, glass, metalwork, furniture & costume); archaeology (British, Egyptian, Roman & Greek); social history (craft & domestic items, local history); geology & natural history (particularly Gloucestershire); personalia of Edward Wilson. 12 (a) 5 (b) 5 (c) 5.

HOLST BIRTHPLACE MUSEUM, Clarence Rd, Cheltenham, GL50 3JT (Tel 0242-37431). 4 Cheltenham BC. 5 Dir: Mr David Addison BA, DipEd, AMA. 6 Arts. 7 Art Gallery & Museum Service. 8 Open to the public. 9 Mon-Sat 13.30-17.30. Free. 10 Gustav Holst personalia; period house. 12 Served from Cheltenham Art Gallery & Museum.

SKYFAME AIRCRAFT MUSEUM, Staverton Airport, Cheltenham, GL51 6SP (Tel 0452-713109). 4 Skyfame Ltd. 5 Founder, Managing Dir & Curator: Mr Peter Malcolm Thomas. 8 Open to the public. 9 Daily 11.00-17.00 bank hols (exc Xmas) 10.00-18.00. Adults 40p, children 20p, group rates. 10 WW II British aircraft historical information service; air show. 11 15 famous aircraft (inc 1st jet flying-boat ever built; an early autogiro; WW II fighters, bombers, trainers, transports) over 700 models, oldest model powered aircraft in Britain; picture gallery, Supporters Society (organises lectures, film shows). 12 (a) 1 (b) 2 (c) 6.

CHEPSTOW, Gwent

CHEPSTOW MUSEUM, Bridge St, Chepstow, (all communications to: 41 Hardwick Ave, Chepstow, NP6 5DS). 4 Chepstow Society, Museum Section. 5 Hon Sec & Curator: Mrs M. Waters. 8 Open to the public. 9 May-Sept: daily. Adults 5p, children 2p. 11 Local history.

CHERTSEY, Surrey

CHERTSEY MUSEUM, The Cedars, Windsor St, Chertsey, KT16 8AT (Tel 09328-65764). 4 Runnymede District Council. 5 Curator: Miss J. L. Bentley BA. 6 Leisure & Public Services. 7 Clerk & Chief Executives Dept, Clerk & Chief Executive: Mr L. W. Way. 8 Open to the public. 9 Tues-Fri & bank hols 14.00-17.00, Sat 10.00-13.00, 14.00-17.00. Free. 10 18th & 19th cent costume & furniture; ceramics; local history & archaeology. 12 (a) 1 (b) 1 (c) 1.

CHESTER, Cheshire

CHESHIRE MILITARY MUSEUM, The Castle, Chester (Tel 0244-43552). 4 Committee of the Cheshire Military Museum. 5 Regimental Sec: Brig B. L. Rigby CBE. 8 Open to the public. 9 Daily (inc bank hols) 9.30-17.00

(19.30 April-Sept). adults 10p, children 5p. 10 Military history of all regiments connected with Cheshire. 12 (c) 2.

GROSVENOR MUSEUM, 27 Grosvenor St, Chester, CH1 2DD (Tel 0244-21616). 4 City of Chester DC. 5 Curator: Mr C. N. Moore MA, FMA. 6 Civic Amenities. 8 Open to the public. 9 Mon-Sat 10.00-17.00, Sun 14.00-17.00. Closed Dec 25, 26, Jan 1 & Good Friday. Free. 10 Archaeology (especially Roman), local history; costumes; natural history; local topographical paintings. 11 Early 18th cent recorders. 12 (a) 17 (b) 8 (c) 14.

KING CHARLES' TOWER, c/o Grosvenor Museum, 27 Grosvenor St, Chester, CH1 2DD (Tel 0244-21616). 4 City of Chester DC. 5 Curator of Grosvenor Museum: Mr C. N. Moore MA, FMA. 6 Civic Amenities. 8 Open to the public. 9 Easter & May-Sept: Mon-Fri 10.00-18.30, Sat 10.00-19.00, Sun 14.30-18.30. Adults 6p, children 3p; school parties free. 10 17th cent tower on site of Roman & medieval towers; dioramas & material about Civil War Chester. 12 Served from Grosvenor Museum.

WATER TOWER, c/o Grosvenor Museum, 27 Grosvenor St, Chester, CH1 2DD. 4 City of Chester DC. 5 Curator of Grosvenor Museum: Mr C. N. Moore MA, FMA. 6 Civic Amenities. 8 Open to the public. 9 Easter & May-Sept: Mon-Fri 10.00-18.30, Sat 10.00-19.00, Sun 14.30-18.30. Adults 6p, children 3p; school parties free. 10 Tower in city wall built for defence of medieval city, dioramas & material on medieval Chester.

CHESTERFIELD, Derbyshire

HARDWICK HALL, Doe Lea, Chesterfield, S44 5QJ (Tel 0246-850430). 4 National Trust. 8 Open to the public. 9 Easter-Oct: Wed, Thurs, Sat, Sun & bank hols 13.00-17.00 (sunset if earlier). Gardens: Easter-Oct: daily 12.00-17.30. Adults 50p, children 25p. Gardens only: adults 25p, children 10p. 10 Hall built (1591-7) by Bess of Hardwick; contemporary furniture; tapestries & needlework. 11 Tea in Great Kitchen.

LECTURE HALL, New Square, Chesterfield, S40 1AH (Tel 0246-34378). 4 Chesterfield BC. 5 Chief Recreation & Leisure Officer: Mr R. B. Rogers FInstPRADip, MInstBM, MInstRM, MInstBCA. 6 Recreation & Leisure. 8 Open to the public. 9 Mon-Sat 10.00-17.00. Free. 10 Art exhibitions. 12 (a) 1 (c) 3.

REVOLUTION HOUSE, Old Whittington, Chesterfield. 4 Chesterfield BC. 5 Chief Recreation & Leisure Officer: Mr R. B. Rogers FInstPRADip, MInstBM, MInstRM, MInstBCA. 6 Recreation & Leisure. 8 Open to the public. 9 Good Friday-Sept: daily (inc bank hols) 11.00-12.30, 14.00-17.00, 18.00-dusk. Free. 10 Inn connected with plotting of the 1688 revolution; 17th cent furnishings. 11 Handford colln of local documents relating to Samuel Pegge, Revolution House & parish of Whittington; rare Whittington glass. 12 (b) 2.

CHICHESTER, Sussex

CHICHESTER DISTRICT MUSEUM, 29 Little London, Chichester, PO19 1PB (Tel 0243-84683). 4 Chichester DC. 5 Curator: Mr Andrew G. Woodcock BSc, MA, AMA. 6 Amenities & Recreations. 8 Open to the public. 9 Tues-Sat (inc bank hols): 10.00-18.00 (Oct-Mch 17.00). Free. 10 Archaeology & local history. 11 Temporary exhibitions. 12 (a) 3 (c) 1.

CORPS OF ROYAL MILITARY POLICE MUSEUM, Roussillon Barracks, Broyle Rd, Chichester (Tel 0243-86311, ext 37). 5 Officer-in-Charge: Major R. J. R. Whistler RMP (Retd). 8 Open to the public. 9 Mon-Fri 9.30-18.00; other days by appointment only. Free. 10 Exhibits; trophies; records; archives; medals; weapons; badges; uniforms; equipment.

CHICHESTER, Sussex—*continued*

GOODWOOD HOUSE, Goodwood, Chichester, PO18 0PX
(Tel 0243-527107).   **4** Goodwood Estate Co Ltd.   **5** House
Manager: Mr D. Legg-Willis.   **8** Open to the public.
9 Tour with lunch: Sun (Jan-Dec) 11.15, Wed (April-Oct)
11.15; Tour with tea: Sun & Wed (April-Oct) 15.00; tour only:
6 days per year (write for dates) 14.30-17.00. Tour with
lunch: £3.75; tour with tea: £1.25; tour only: adults 40p,
children & OAPs 10p.   **10** Family portraits (Van Dyck,
Lely, Reynolds, Romney, Lawrence etc); French & English
furniture; Sevres.

GUILDHALL MUSEUM, c/o Chichester District Museum,
29 Little London, Chichester, PO19 1PB (Tel 0243-84683).
4 Chichester DC.   **5** Curator: Mr Andrew G. Woodcock
BSc, MA, AMA.   **6** Amenities & Recreations.   **8** Open to
the public.   **9** June-Sept: Tues-Sat 12.45-16.45. Free.
10 Archaeology & geology; history of the building (a 13th
cent Franciscan church).   **12** (a) served from Chichester
District Museum.

ROYAL SUSSEX REGIMENT MUSEUM, 29 Little London,
Chichester, PO19 1PB (Tel 0243-84683).   **4** Trustees.
5 Officer-in-Charge: Major J. Ainsworth.   **8** Open to the
public.   **9** Tues-Sat (inc bank hols): 10.00-18.00 (Oct-
Mch 17.00). Free.   **12** Served by Chichester District
Museum.

WEALD AND DOWNLAND OPEN AIR MUSEUM, Singleton,
Chichester (Tel 024363-348).   **4** Weald & Downland Open
Air Museum Ltd.   **5** Dir: Mr Christopher S. H. Zeuner.
8 Open to the public.   **9** Tues-Sat (inc bank hols) 11.00-
18.00 (Oct-March 11.00-dusk). Adults 30p, children 15p.
10 Vernacular architecture.   **11** Buildings saved from
demoltion & re-erected on museum site.   **12** (b) 3 (c) 4.

CHIDDINGSTONE, Kent

CHIDDINGSTONE CASTLE, Chiddingstone, Edenbridge, TN8
7AD (Tel 089284-347).   **5** Owner: Mr Denys Eyre Bower.
8 Open to the public.   **9** Tues-Fri 14.00-17.30, Sat, Sun
& bank hols 11.30-17.30. Adults 35p, children 15p.
10 Portraits, mss, letters, medals & relics of royal house of
Stuart; (inc miniatures by Samuel Cooper of Charles II &
James, Duke of York; Lely's portrait of Nell Gwynne in the
nude; Monmouth's last letter to James II the night before his
execution); Japanese lacquer (inc Beckford cabinet from
Fonthill; c.300 inro & tobacco boxes), metalwork, swords &
netsuke; Egyptian colln (c.4,000 BC—Roman times, inc
stoneheads & ushabti); Buddhistic images & paintings.

CHILHAM, Kent

BATTLE OF BRITAIN (KENT) MUSEUM, Chilham Castle,
Chilham, Canterbury, CT4 8DB (Tel 022776-292/692-2241
ext 1).   **5** Officer-in-Charge of Museum: R. Windrow.
8 Open to the public   **9** Daily (exc Mon & Fri) (inc bank
hols) 14.00-18.00. Museum: free, Grounds: adults 40p,
children 25p.   **10** Records of air battles over Kent during
WWII; all types of planes, firearms, bombs, uniforms, logs,
maps, records, newspaper cuttings.   **11** Display of free-
flying eagles & hawks; 25 acres Jacobean gardens; waterfowl,
deer, exotic sheep, wild boar, pony rides for children. Cafe
& shop; free car park.   **12** (a) 2 (c) 8

CHIPPENHAM, Wiltshire

DYRHAM PARK, Chippenham, SN14 8ER (Tel 027582-2501).
4 National Trust.   **5** Administrator: Mr Owen V. S. Justice.
8 Open to the public.   **9** Wed-Fri (April-Sept), Sat & Sun
(March-Nov): 14.00-18.00; bank hol Mon 12.00-18.00
Adults 50p, children 25p, group rates.   **10** William & Mary
house (rebuilt 1692-1704); period furniture; paintings, furnishings & ceramics show a marked Dutch influence.
11 Delftware; tea in Orangery (April-Sept).

CHIRK, Clwyd

CHIRK CASTLE, Chirk, Wrexham, LI4 5AF (Tel 069186-
2460).   **5** Owner: Lt Col R. Myddelton.   **8** Open to the

public.   **9** Easter-Oct: Tues, Thurs, Sat & Sun 14.00-17.00,
bank hols 11.00-17.00. Adults 50p, children 15p.   **10** Early
14th cent castle, exterior unchanged; 16th-19th cent interiors;
paintings; 18th cent gates; gardens.   **11** Tea rooms;
souvenir shop.

CHORLEY, Lancashire

ASTLEY HALL, Astley Park, Chorley PR7 1NP (Tel 02572-
2166).   **4** Chorley BC.   **5** Amenities Officer: Mr Gordon
Haworth MIBMDip, MIMEnt, MIRM, LInstPRA.   **7** Amenities
Dept.   **8** Open to the public.   **9** Daily (inc bank hols):
(April-Sept) 14.00-20.00, (Oct-Mch) 12.00-17.00. Charges:
5p; organised parties free.   **10** 17th cent house; museum &
art gallery.   **11** Temporary exhibitions.   **12** (b) 3 (c) 3.

CHRISTCHURCH, Dorset

RED HOUSE MUSEUM AND ART GALLERY, 2 Quay Rd,
Christchurch, BH23 1BU (Tel 02015-2860).   **4** Hampshire
CC.   **5** Officer-in-Charge: Mr J. H. Lavendar BSc, ARCS.
6 Recreation.   **7** Hampshire County Museum Service,
Chilcomb House, Chilcomb Lane, Bar End, Winchester,
SO23 8RD (0962-66242/3); Dir: Miss Margaret C. Macfarlane
BA, MA.   **8** Open to the public.   **9** Tues-Sat (& bank hols)
10.00-12.30, 13.30-17.30, Sun 14.00-17.30. Adults $5\frac{1}{2}$p,
children $2\frac{1}{2}$p.   **10** Local archaeology & natural history;
domestic life; costumes; dolls; 19th cent fashion plates; agricultural equipment; local prints, drawings, tokens, documents,
photographs & industrial relics.   **11** Herb garden; temporary exhibitions.   **12** (a) 1 (b) 2.

CHURCH STRETTON, Shropshire

ACTON SCOTT WORKING FARM MUSEUM, Wenlock Lodge,
Acton Scott, Church Stretton, SY6 6QN (Tel 06946-322).
4 Shropshire CC.   **5** Keeper of Agrarian History: Mr
Andrew Morrey BSc.   **6** Leisure Activities.   **7** County
Museum Curator: G. I. McCabe MA, AMA.   **8** Open to the
public.   **9** Mon-Fri 13.00-17.00, Sat, Sun & bank hols
10.00-18.00. Other times by appointment. Adults 20p,
children 10p, season tickets available.   **10** Shropshire
farm (c.1900); people actively encouraged to participate in
jobs to be done around farm.   **11** Special facilities for
handicapped people.   **12** (a) 3 (b) 2 (c) 10 seasonal.

CIRENCESTER, Gloucestershire

CORINIUM MUSEUM, Park St, Cirencester, GL7 2BX (Tel
0285-5611).   **4** Cotswold DC.   **5** Curator: Mr D. J. Viner
BA.   **6** Technical Services.   **8** Open to the public.
9 Mon-Sat (inc bank hols) 10.00-18.00; Sun 14.00-18.00.
Adults 10p; children free; OAPs & students 5p.   **10** Archaeology & history of Cirencester & the Cotswolds, collected
locally from Corinium, 2nd largest town in Roman Britain.
11 Enlarged & re-designed museum opened in 1974; temporary exhibitions.   **12** (a) 2 (b) 3.

COALVILLE, Leicestershire

OLD MANOR HOUSE, Donington-le-Heath, Coalville (Tel
(0533-539111).   **4** Leicestershire CC.   **5** Dir: Mr Patrick
J. Boylan BSc, FGS, AMA.   **6** Libraries & Museums.
8 Open to the public.   **9** Easter-Sept: Wed-Sun 14.00-
18.00. Free.   **10** Medieval manor house, 16th & 17th cent
alterations.   **11** Cafe in adjacent barn.   **12** Served from
Leicestershire Museum.

COATBRIDGE, Lanarkshire

COATBRIDGE PUBLIC LIBRARY MUSEUM, 25 Academy St,
Coatbridge, ML5 3AT (Tel 0236-24150).   **4** Monklands DC.
5 Libn: G. Carter ALA.   **6** Leisure & Recreation.
7 Chief Libn: Mr John Fox.   **8** Open to the public.
9 Tues & Fri 19.00-21.00. Free.   **10** Local history.

COCKERMOUTH, Cumbria

WORDSWORTH HOUSE, Main St, Cockermouth, CA13 9RX
(Tel 090082-2413).   **4** National Trust.   **5** Custodian: Mrs

CODE: 1 Name of Museum, Art Gallery or Stately Home. **2** Address. **3** Telephone & telex. **4** Governing body. **5** Officer in charge. **6** Committee responsible. **7** Larger department, chief officer. **8** Open to public. **9** Hours; admission charges. **10** Scope. **11** Special exhibits or facilities. **12** Staff (a) professionally qualified (b) other non-manual (c) manual.

COCKERMOUTH, Cumbria—*continued*

M.L.Smith. **8** Open to the public. **9** Mon-Sat (inc bank hols) 10.30-12.30, 14.00-17.00 (closed Thurs afternoon). Adults 30p, children 15p; National Trust members free. **10** Georgian house (built 1745); birthplace of William Wordsworth; Georgian furnishings, inc some of Wordsworth's belongings, in 2 rooms.

COLCHESTER, Essex

COLCHESTER AND ESSEX MUSEUM, The Castle, Colchester CO1 1TJ (Tel 0206-77475/76071 ext 346). **4** Colchester BC. **5** Curator: Mr D.T.D.Clarke MA, FMA, FSA, FRNS. **6** Cultural Activities. **7** Environmental Dept, Borough Environmental Officer: Mr G.A.Graves CEng, FIMunE. **8** Open to the public. **9** Mon-Sat 10.00-17.00 (16.00 Oct-March), Sun (April-Sept only) 14.30-17.00. Closed Dec 25-27 & Good Friday. Oct-March: free; April-Sept: adults 12p, children & OAPs free. **10** Norman castle (c.1080) built over vaults of Roman Temple of Claudius (c.AD 50); archaeology (especially Roman). **11** Tours of vaults & prisons by appointment (adults 11p, children 5p); schools service. **12** (a) 7 (b) 2 (c) 13.

HOLLYTREES, High St, Colchester (Tel 0206-76071 ext 345). **4** Colchester BC. **5** Curator: Mr D.T.D.Clarke MA, FMA, FSA, FRNS. **6** Cultural Activities. **7** Environmental Dept, Borough Environmental Officer: Mr G.A.Graves CEng, FIMunE. **8** Open to the public. **9** Mon-Sat 10.00-17.00 (16.00 Oct-March). Closed Dec 25-27 & Good Friday. Free. **10** Georgian house (1718); local social history; costumes; toys; domestic & agricultural items. **12** Serviced from Colchester & Essex Museum.

MINORIES GALLERY, 74 High St, Colchester, CO1 1UE (Tel 0206-77067). **4** Trustees of the Victor Batte-Lay Trust, **5** Curator: A.C.H.Dunlop BA. **8** Open to the public. **9** Tues-Sat (& most bank hols) 11.00-17.00, Sun 14.00-18.00. Adults 10p; students & children 2½p, Sat all free. **10** Georgian town house & garden with a small permanent colln; some paintings & drawings by Constable on loan from Borough of Colchester. **11** Temporary exhibitions. **12** (a) 1 (b) 1 (c) 2.

MUSEUM OF SOCIAL HISTORY, Holy Trinity Church, Trinity St, Colchester, CO1 1JN (Tel 0206-76071 ext 347). **4** Colchester BC. **5** Curator: Mr D.T.D.Clarke MA, FMA, FSA, FRNS. **6** Cultural Activities. **7** Environmental Dept, Borough Environmental Officer: Mr G.A.Graves CEng, FIMunE. **8** Open to the public. **9** Mon-Sat 10.00-17.00 (16.00 Oct-March). Closed Dec 25-27 & Good Friday. Free. **10** 14th cent church with 11th cent tower; local social history; country life & crafts. **12** Served from Colchester & Essex Museum.

NATURAL HISTORY MUSEUM, All Saints Church, High St, Colchester, CO1 1DN (Tel 0206-76071 ext 344) **4** Colchester BC **5** Curator: Mr D.T.D.Clarke MA, FMA, FSA, FRNS. **6** Cultural Activities. **7** Environmental Dept, Borough Environmental Officer: Mr G.A.Graves CEng, FIMunE. **9** Mon-Sat 10.00-17.00 (16.00 Oct-March). Closed Dec 25-27 & Good Friday. Free. **10** 13th cent church with 15th cent tower, nave rebuilt 1855; local natural history (dioramas & aquarium). **12** Served from Colchester & Essex Museum.

COLNE, Lancashire

BRITISH IN INDIA MUSEUM, Sun St, Colne, BB8 0JJ (Tel 0282-63129). **4** Owner: Hendon Mill Co Ltd. **5** Officer-in-Charge: H.J.H.Nelson. **8** Open to the public. **9** May-Sept: Sat & Sun 14.00-17.00. Adults 20p, children & OAPs 5p. **10** British rule in India until partition. **11** Model railway (Kalka-Simla line); diorama (last stand of the 44th at Ganda-

mak); various articles relating to Mermanjan (an adventurous Afghan princess); postage stamps. **12** (c) 1.

COMRIE, Perthshire

COMRIE MUSEUM, Dunira St, Comrie, PH6 2LJ (Tel 07647-350). **5** Owner: Ms Elizabeth May Wilson LLB, NP. **8** Open to the public. **9** April-Oct: Sat 10.00-12.00, 14.30-16.00. Free. **10** 18th cent smiddy house & crofter's kitchen; Victorian mixter-maxter; Scottish agricultural & heritage photographs; blacksmiths implements; domestic utensils. **12** (b) 4.

CONWY, Gwynedd

ROYAL CAMBRIAN ACADEMY OF ART, 'Plas Mawr', High St, Conwy, LL32 8DE (Tel 049 263-3413). **5** Curator/Sec: Mr Leonard Mercer. **8** Open to the public. **9** Mon-Sat (inc bank hols) 10.00-17.30, Sun 10.30-17.00. Adults 10p, children 5p; parties of 14 or more: adults 7p, children 4p. **10** 'Plas Mawr', unique example of Elizabethan architecture. **11** 'Victoria Gallery', largest gallery in North Wales available for hire. Temporary art exhibitions. **12** (a) 1.

COOKHAM-ON-THAMES, Berkshire

STANLEY SPENCER GALLERY, Kings Hall, Cookham-on-Thames, Maidenhead. (Tel 06285-23533). **4** Sir Stanley Spencer Memorial Trust. **5** Chairman of Trustees: Mr Geoffrey Robinson; Hon Sec to Trustees & Committee: Mrs Joan George. **8** Open to the public. **9** Summer: Mon-Fri 10.30-13.00, 14.00-18.00; Sat, Sun (& bank hols) 10.30-13.00, 14.00-19.00; Winter: Sat, Sun (& bank hols) 11.00-13.00, 14.00-17.00. Adults 15p, students & parties 10p, children 5p. **10** Permanent exhibition of c.20 paintings, some pen & wash studies, sketches & portrait drawings by Stanley Spencer. **11** Gallery's most-discussed exhibit is the large unfinished canvas, 'Christ Preaching at Cookham Regatta'. Colln of books; temporary exhibitions; one of the Trustees, the artist's daughter or the Hon Sec will attend, by appointment, to talk about artist's work. **12** (b) 2 (c) 1.

CORRIS, Powys

CORRIS RAILWAY MUSEUM, Station Yard, Corris, Machynlleth, SY20 9R. **4** Corris Railway Society. **8** Open to the public. **9** Mid July-Aug: Tues-Fri. Hours under review. Free. **10** Corris Railway (1850-1948); industries served by railway; local history. **11** Photographs; remains of coach (c.1898); various waggons.

CORSHAM, Wiltshire

CORSHAM COURT, Corsham, Chippenham SN13 0BZ (Tel 0249-712214). **5** Owner: Hon A.J.Methuen ARICS. **8** Open to the public. **9** Wed & Thurs (April-Oct), daily (mid July-mid Sept), Sun (all year), bank hols & during Bath Festival: 11.00-12.30, 14.00-18.00 (16.30 in winter). Adults 40p, children 15p, parties (over 10) 25p. **10** Elizabethan & Georgian house; Chippendale furniture; Italian & other Old Masters; English portraits (Reynolds, Romney etc); gardens by Capability Brown. **12** (b) 2.

COVENTRY, West Midlands

HERBERT ART GALLERY AND MUSEUMS, Earl St, Coventry, CV1 5RG (Tel 0203-25555; Telex 31469). **4** Coventry DC, West Midland Metropolitan County. **5** Dep Dir (Arts & Museums): Dr Thomas Werner. **6** Libraries, Arts & Leisure. **7** Libraries, Arts & Museums Dept; Dir: Mr Anthony Davis ALA. **8** Open to the public. **9** Mon, Thurs, Fri & Sat 10.00-18.00, Tues & Wed 10.00-20.00, Sun 14.00-17.00. Closed Dec 25 &

COVENTRY, West Midlands—*continued*

Good Friday. Free. **10** Industry & transport: folk life & social history (inc archaeology); natural history; visual arts, arts services. **11** Temporary exhibitions especially of visual arts. **12** (a) 14 (b) 3 (c) 19.

LUNT ROMAN FORT AND INTERPRETIVE CENTRE, Herbert Art Gallery & Museum, Bayley Lane, Coventry, CV1 5RG (Tel 0203-25555 ext 2417; Telex 31469). **4** Coventry City Council. **5** Senior Keeper of Social History: Mr D. Janes MA. **6** Libraries, Arts & Leisure. **7** Libraries, Arts & Museums Dept, Dir: Mr A. Davis ALA. **8** Open to the public. **9** Mon-Sat 10.00-17.00, Sun & bank hols 14.00-18.00. Adults 30p, children, students & OAPs 15p, group rates. **10** 1st cent excavated timber gateway & 2 sections of turf rampart reconstructed *in situ;* timber granary serves as a site museum & interpretive centre; the Gyrus (cavalry training ring) will be reconstructed in May 1976. **11** Life-size models of a Roman legionary & auxiliary cavalryman; objects found during excavation; various items of simulated Roman military equipment; back-projection unit in continual operation. **12** (c) 5.

COWES, Isle of Wight.

COWES MARITIME MUSEUM, Cowes Library, Beckford Rd, Cowes, PO31 7SG (Tel 098 382-3341). **4** Isle of Wight CC. **5** Chief Asst Libn: Mr R. G. Futter ALA. **6** Amenities & Leisure Services. **7** Dir of Cultural Services: Mr L. J. Mitchell BA, FLA. **8** Open to the public. **9** Mon-Sat 9.30-17.30. Free. **10** Maritime history. **11** Models, photographs, books relating to J. S. Whites, shipbuilders of Cowes.

CRATHES, Kincardineshire

CRATHES CASTLE & GARDENS, Crathes, Banchory, AB3 3QJ (Tel 033044-525). **4** National Trust for Scotland. **8** Open to the public. **9** April & Oct: Wed 11.00-13.00, 14.00-17.30, Sat & Sun 14.00-17.30; May-Sept: Mon-Fri 11.00-17.30, Sun 14.00-17.30. Gardens: daily 9.30-17.30. Castle only: adults 35p, children 15p; garden only: adults 20p, children 10p. **11** 16th cent painted ceilings; restaurant.

CREETOWN, Wigtownshire

CREETOWN GEM ROCK MUSEUM, Old School, Creetown, Newton Stewart, DG8 7HP (Tel 067182-357). **5** Owner: Mr Joe Craig BSc. **8** Open to the public. **9** Mon-Sat 9.30-18.00, Sun 14.00-18.00. Oct-May: closed 13.00-14.00. Adults 10p, children 5p. **10** Largest colln of gem rocks in Britain, rocks, minerals & semi-precious gem stones. **11** Souvenir shops. **12** (a) 3.

CRICKHOWELL, Powys

WELSH BRIGADE MUSEUM, Welsh Depot, Cwrt-y-Gollen, Crickhowell, NP8 1TH (Tel 0873-810386). **5** Curator: Major J. Harry (Retd). **8** Open to the public. **9** Mon, Thurs & Fri 9.00-16.30, Tues 9.00-12.00. Free. **12** (b) 1.

CROMARTY, Ross-shire

HUGH MILLER COTT MUSEUM, Church St, Cromarty (Tel 03817-245). **4** National Trust for Scotland. **5** Custodian: Mrs K. Morrison. **8** Open to the public. **9** Mon-Sat 10.00-12.00, 13.00-17.00, Sun 14.00-17.00. Adults 15p, coach parties 10p, OAPs free. **10** Geology; old newspapers, letters etc; 1 set (12 vols) of Hugh Miller's writings on geology & local history. **12** (a) 1.

CULROSS, Fife

CULROSS PALACE, Culross, Dunfermline. **4** Dept of Environment on behalf of the Sec of State for Scotland. **8** Open to the public. **9** April-Sept: Mon-Sat (inc bank hols) 9.30-19.00, Sun 14.00-19.00; Oct-Mar: Mon-Sat (inc bank hols) 10.00-16.00, Sun 14.00-16.00. Charges: 5p. **10** Jacobean architecture, wood panelling & ceilings with tempera paintings.

ERSKINE OF TORRIE INSTITUTE, Dunimarle Castle, Culross, Dunfermline, KY12 8JN (Tel 038 388-229). **4** Trustees of the late Mrs M. S. Erskine. **5** Custodian: Mr T. N. Grant. **8** Open to the public. **9** April-Oct: Wed, Thurs, Sat & Sun (& some bank hols) 14.00-18.00. Other times by arrangement. Adults 20p, children 10p; advance bookings (10 or more) 10% discount. **10** Empire furniture; paintings; glass; china; books; antiques; weapons; gardens & grounds; guided tours & historical background. **12** (b) 1.

DARLINGTON, Co. Durham

DARLINGTON ART GALLERY, Crown St, Darlington, DL1 1ND (Tel 0325-2034). **4** Darlington BC. **5** District Libn: Miss S. I. Cairns ALA. **6** Recreation. **8** Open to the public. **9** Mon-Fri 10.00-20.00, Sat 10.00-17.30. Free. **10** General.

DARLINGTON MUSEUM, Tubwell Row, Darlington, DL1 1PD (Tel 0325-3795). **4** Darlington BC. **5** Curator: A. Suddes BA. **6** Recreation. **8** Open to the public. **9** Mon (inc bank hols)-Wed & Fri 10.00-13.00, 14.00-18.00, Thurs 10.00-13.00, Sat 10.00-13.00, 14.00-17.30. Closed Dec 25, 26 & Jan 1. Free. **10** Local social & natural history; history of railways & the Stockton & Darlington & North Eastern Railway Companies. **11** Model locomotives: Locomotion 1, LNER No. 10,000; John Dobbin's Watercolour "The Opening of the Stockton & Darlington Railway, 1825." Observation beehive during summer months. **12** (a) 1 (b) 1 (c) 2.

DARLINGTON NORTH ROAD STATION MUSEUM, Hopetown Lane, Darlington (Tel 0325-60532). **4** Darlington North Road Station Museum Trust. **5** Manager: Mr J. Noddings. **8** Open to the public. **9** Mon-Sat (inc bank hols) 10.00-17.00. Adults 20p, children 10p. **10** Restored railroad station (1842) housing full-size locomotives & rolling stock & small exhibits. **11** Some station rooms restored in period style. **12** (b) 4.

DARTFORD, Kent

DARTFORD DISTRICT MUSEUM, Market St, Dartford, DA1 1EU (Tel 0322-21325). **4** Dartford DC. **6** Recreations & Amenities. **7** Recreation & Amenities Officer: Mr J. B. Dyer AInstPRA(Dip). **8** Open to the public. **9** Mon, Tues, Thurs & Fri 12.30-17.30, Sat 9.00-17.00. Free. **10** Local geological & Roman, Saxon & natural history. **11** School loan service. **12** (a) 1 (b) 2.

DARTMOUTH, Devon

DARTMOUTH MUSEUM & NEWCOMEN ENGINE HOUSE, The Butterwalk, Dartmouth, TQ6 9PZ (Tel 08043-2923). **4** Friends of Dartmouth Museum Association (Managers); structure owned by Dartmouth Town Council. **5** Hon Curator: R. Cawthorne. **8** Open to the public. **9** Mon-Sat (inc bank hols): May-Oct 11.00-19.00, Nov-April 14.15-18.00. Closed Dec 25 & Good Friday. Adults 6p, children 3p. **10** Local & maritime history; over 100 ship models; seascapes; local photographs; an original Newcomen engine may be seen working in nearby engine house. **12** (b) 2.

DAWLISH, Devon

DAWLISH MUSEUM, The Knowle, Barton Terrace, Dawlish, EX7 9QH. **4** Dawlish Museum Society. **5** Chairman: H. G. Morgan MA. **8** Open to the public. **9** May-Sept: Mon-Sat (inc bank hols) 10.00-12.30, 14.00-17.00, Sun 14.00-17.00. Adults 10p, children 5p. **10** Late 18th cent house; 19th & 20th cent local history; Victorian drawing room, kitchen, shop. **11** Temporary exhibitions; ref library, facilities for study & research.

DEAL, Kent

DEAL CASTLE MUSEUM, Victoria Rd, Deal, CT14 7BA. **4** Kent County Library. **5** Custodian of Castle: Mr F. W. Huxtable. **6** Education. **7** Kent County Library, Library & Museums Officer: Miss L. Millard. **8** Open to

CODE: 1 Name of Museum, Art Gallery or Stately Home. 2 Address. 3 Telephone & telex. 4 Governing body. 5 Officer in charge. 6 Committee responsible. 7 Larger department, chief officer. 8 Open to public. 9 Hours; admission charges. 10 Scope. 11 Special exhibits or facilities. 12 Staff (a) professionally qualified (b) other non-manual (c) manual.

DEAL, Kent—*continued*

the public. 9 Mon-Sat: 9.30-17.30 (May-Sept 19.00), (Nov-Feb 16.00); Sun: 14.00-17.30, (Nov-Feb 9.30-16.00). Free. 10 Local archaeology.

MARITIME AND LOCAL HISTORY MUSEUM, 22 St George's Rd, Deal, CT14 6BA (Tel 03045-4869). 4 Trustees. 5 Dir: Mr W. H. Honey. 8 Open to the public. 9 Daily (inc bank hols) 14.00-17.00 (+ Thurs 18.00-20.00). Adults 5p, children 3p. 10 Local history of Deal, Walmer, Kingsdown & district, (especially maritime history). 11 Locally built boats (galley & punts); research into preservation of timber & metal objects affected by sea water (eg items from wrecks or found in sea sand).

DEDHAM, Essex

SIR ALFRED MUNNINGS ART MUSEUM, Castle House, Dedham, Colchester, CO7 6AZ (Tel 0206-3222127). 8 Open to the public. 9 Mid May-mid Oct: Sun, Wed (+ Sat in Aug) & bank hols 14.00-17.00. Organised parties other times by arrangement. Adults 15p, children 5p. 10 House, 2 studios & other galleries contain many paintings, drawings, sketches & other works by Sir Alfred Munnings, KCVO, President of the Royal Academy 1944-1949.

DERBY, Derbyshire

DERBY INDUSTRIAL MUSEUM, The Silk Mill, Silk Mill Lane, off Full St, Derby, DE1 3AR (Tel 0332-31111 ext 740). 8 Open to the public. 9 Tues-Fri 10.00-17.45, Sat 10.00-16.45. Closed Dec 25, 26 & Good Friday. Free. 10 Silk mill (built 1702, extended 1717-1720), first full-scale factory in England; local industries (textiles, lead, coal, iron, limestone, ceramics & bricks). 11 Development of Rolls Royce aero engines.

DERBY MUSEUMS AND ART GALLERY, The Strand, Derby, DE1 1HS (Tel 0332-31111 ext 781). 4 Derby BC. 5 Chief Museums Officer: Mr Bryan P. Blake BA, AMA. 6 Leisure. 8 Open to the public. 9 Mon-Fri 10.00-18.00. Closed Dec 25, 26 & Good Friday. Free. 10 Antiquities; social history; ethnography; coins & medals; militaria; zoology; geology & botany; paintings by Joseph Wright (1734-1797); porcelain; costume. 11 Prince Charles Edward room (1745 rebellion); scale model layout of Midland Railway. School service & holiday activities for children. 12 (a) 12 (b) 9 (c) 15.

ELVASTON CASTLE COUNTRYSIDE PARK MUSEUM, Borrowash Rd, Elvaston, Derby (Tel 0332-74241). 4 Derbyshire CC. 5 Museum Officer: Mr Michael Tong BSc. 6 County Leisure. 7 Planning Dept, County Planning Officer: Mr H. Cowley BA, FRTPI. 8 Open to the public. 9 Mon-Sat 12.00-17.00, Sun 12.00-18.00. Free. 10 Rural crafts & agriculture; local natural history & geology. 11 Horse-drawn vehicles; 15th cent tithe barn (under reconstruction); access for disabled visitors. 12 (a) 2 (b) 2.

KEDLESTON HALL, Derby, DE6 4JN (Tel 0332-840386). 4 Owner: Viscount Scarsdale. 5 Hon Curator: Commodore J. Whayman CBE, DSC, RD. 8 Open to the public. 9 Easter-Sept: Sun & bank hol Mon, Hall & Museum 14.00-18.00, park, gardens & church 12.30-19.00. Open weekdays by private arrangement only, to parties of 30 or more. Adults 40p, children 20p, Indian Museum 5p extra. 10 Robert Adam house (1757-65) on site of 12th cent manor house; marble hall; state rooms; old master paintings; contemporary furnishings; 500 acre park (Canada goose sanctuary) & gardens; 12th cent church; Indian Museum (silver, ivories, ancient spears, poisoned arrows & works of art presented to Lord Curzon when Viceroy of India, 1898-1905; Robert Adam's signed drawings of house).

ROYAL CROWN DERBY WORKS MUSEUM, Osmaston Rd, Derby, DE3 8JZ (Tel 0332-47051). 5 Museum Curator: Mr John Twitchett; Resident Asst Museum Curator: Miss Betty Bailey. 8 Open to the public. 9 First Tues of each month: 10.00-16.00. Free. 10 Display of china made in Derby since 1750.

DEVIZES, Wiltshire

WILTSHIRE ARCHAEOLOGICAL AND NATURAL HISTORY SOCIETY, DEVIZES MUSEUM, 41 Long St, Devizes, SN10 1NS (Tel 0380-2765). 4 Wiltshire Archaeological & Natural History Society. 5 Officer-in-Charge: F. K. Annable BA, FSA, FMA. 6 Council of Museum. 8 Open to the public. 9 Tues-Sat 11.00-17.00. Adults 15p, students 5p, OAPs & children 2½p. 10 Palaeolithic, mesolithic, neolithic, bronze age, iron age, Roman, mediaeval & some recent history; natural history. 11 Prehistoric collns relating to southern history. 11 Prehistoric collns relating to southern Britain, Stourhead colln of bronze age grave groups recovered in early 19th cent by Sir Richard Colt Hoare & William Cunnington. 12 (a) 3 (b) 2 (c) 2.

WILTSHIRE REGIMENT MUSEUM, Le Marchant Barracks, London Rd, Devizes, SN10 2ER (Tel 0380-2241 ext 339). 4 Wiltshire Regiment Museum Trust (administered by RHQ The Duke of Edinburgh's Royal Regt). 5 Major (Retd) A. D. Parsons MBE, MC, BA. 8 Open to the public. 9 Mon-Fri 10.00-12.30, 14.00-16.30. Free, but donations welcome. 10 The Wiltshire Regiment (1756-1959). 12 (b) 1 (c) 1.

DEWSBURY, West Yorkshire

CROW'S NEST MUSEUM AND ART GALLERY, Dewsbury. c/o Libraries, Museums & Art Galleries Headquarters, Princess Alexandra Walk, Huddersfield, HD1 2SU (Tel 0484-21356; Telex 517463). 4 Kirklees MBC. 5 Chief Curator & Libn: Mr Stanley T. Dibnab FLA, AMBIM. 6 Education. 7 Dir of Education Services: Mr Ernest T. Butcher MA. 8 Open to the public. 9 Tues-Fri (inc bank hols) 10.00-18.00, Sat 10.00-17.00, Sun 14.00. Free. 10 Local & natural history. 12 (a) Served from Huddersfield Art Gallery.

DIRLETON, East Lothian

DIRLETON CASTLE, Dirleton. 4 Dept of Environment. 5 Information Officer, Argyle House, 3 Lady Lawson St, Edinburgh. 8 Open to the public. 9 Mon-Sat 9.30-19.00, Sun 14.00-19.00. Oct-March: closes 16.00 daily. Adults 10p, children 5p. 10 One of the most beautiful ruins in Scotland; ancient stronghold of the De Vaux. 11 Group of towers (13th cent); flower garden; buildings from 14th-16th cent.

DISLEY, Cheshire

LYME HALL, Lyme Park, Disley, Stockport, SK12 2NX (Tel 06632-2023). 4 Stockport MBC, & National Trust. 5 Country Parks Officer: Mr J. G. Turner. 6 Recreation & Culture Division jointly with National Trust. 7 Dir of Recreation & Culture: Mr Harry Hitchcock IPFA, FRVA. 8 Open to the public. 9 Tues-Sun (inc bank hols) 13.00-17.30 (Oct & March 16.00). Adults 20p, children 10p, booked parties of children 5p. 10 Stately home situated in 1,230 acres of parkland, woods & moorland; designated a Country Park. 11 Period furniture, tapestries & Grinling Gibbons carvings. 12 (b) 3 (c) 5.

DISS, Norfolk

BRESSINGHAM STEAM MUSEUM AND GARDENS, Bressingham, Diss, IP22 2AB (Tel 037 988-386). 4 Bressingham Steam Trust. 5 Dir: Mr Alan H. V.

DISS, Norfolk—*continued*

Bloom; Chief Mechanical Engineer: Mr G. E. Saunders.
8 Open to the public.   **9** Mid May-Sept: Thurs (& Wed in
Aug) 13.30-17.30, Sun (& bank hols) 13.30-18.00. Adults
25p, children 15p.   **10** 39 wheeled, rail & road locomotives;
5 miles of tracks for steam-hauled rides; 6 acres informal
gardens, containing over 5,000 species & varieties of
hardy plants.   **12** (a) 6 (b) 1 (c) 4.

DODINGTON, Avon

DODINGTON CARRIAGE MUSEUM, Dodington, Chipping
Sodbury, BS17 6SG (Tel 0454-318899).   **5** Curator: Mr
Gordon J. Offord.   **8** Open to the public.   **9** Late March-
Sept; daily (inc bank hols) 11.00-18.00. Not free.
10 c.40 vehicles; miniatures models; diorama; 200 coach-
coachbuilders drawings.   **11** Comet stage coach; Offord
Coronation Landau; Opie colln (30 models of royal carriages).
12 (b) 2 (c) 2.

DODINGTON HOUSE, Dodington, Chipping Sodbury, BS17 6SF
(Tel 0454-318899).   **5** General Manager: Mr J. Cairns
Boston.   **8** Open to the public.   **9** Late March-Sept:
daily (inc bank hols) 11.00-18.00. Not free.   **10** Stately
home.   **11** Children's adventureland; children's farm;
exhibition of British model soldier society; agricultural
implements.   **12** (a) 1 (b) 5 (c) 8.

DONCASTER, South Yorkshire

BENTLEY MUSEUM, Bentley Public Library, Doncaster
(Tel 0302-62095).   **4** Doncaster MBC.   **6** Education.
7 Dir of Museums & Arts Services: Mr John Barwick FMA.
8 Open to the public.   **9** Mon-Fri 9.00-19.00, Sat 9.00-
17.00. Free.   **10** Local history & environment; historical
exhibitions.   **12** (c) 1.

CUSWORTH HALL MUSEUM, Cusworth, Doncaster, DN4 7TU.
4 Doncaster MBC.   **5** Officer-in-Charge: Mr John Good-
child.   **6** Education.   **7** Dir of Museums & Arts Service:
Mr John Barwick FMA.   **8** Open to the public.   **9** Mon-
Sat (inc bank hols) 11.00-17.00, Sun 12.00-17.00 (closes
daily 16.00, Nov-Feb).   Free.   **10** Museum of South Yorkshire industrial life.   **11** Publications; research facilities;
study base for school parties.   **12** (a) 2 (b) 4 (c) 11.

DONCASTER MUSEUM AND ART GALLERY, Chequer Rd,
Doncaster DN1 2AE (Tel 0302-62095/60814).   **4** Doncaster
MBC.   **5** Curator: Mr T. G. Manby MA, AMA.
6 Education.   **7** Dir of Museums & Arts Service: Mr John
Barwick FMA.   **8** Open to the public.   **9** Mon-Sat (inc
bank hols) 10.00-17.30, Sun 14.00-17.00.   Free.
10 Historical, environmental collns; fine & applied art;
Romano-British & horseracing collns.   **11** Frequent
special exhibitions, publications, lectures, concerts; facilities
for school parties; loan service for local schools; refreshment room & car park.   **12** (a) 7 (b) 8 (c) 7.

DORCHESTER, Dorset

ATHELHAMPTON HALL, Dorchester, DT2 7LG (Tel 030 584-
363).   **5** Sec: Miss P. Wilkinson.   **8** Open to the public.
9 Wed, Thurs, Sun & bank hols 14.00-18.00. Adults 40p,
children 30p; house only: 20p.   **10** Medieval house.
11 10 acres formal & landscape gardens; plants & antiques
for sale; childrens playground.   **12** (b) 1 (c) 3.

DORSET COUNTY MUSEUM, High West St, Dorchester,
DT1 1XA (Tel 0305-2735).   **4** Dorset Natural History &
Archaeological Society.   **5** Curator: Mr R. N. R. Peers MA,
AMA, FSA.   **8** Open to the public.   **9** Mon-Sat (inc bank
hols) 10.00-17.00. Closed Dec 25, 26 & Good Friday. Adults
15p, children 5p (free under 10).   **10** Archaeology, local
history & natural history of Dorset.   **11** Reconstruction
of Thomas Hardy's study & other material relating to him,
temporary exhibitions.   **12** (a) 3 (b) 1 (c) 2.

DORSET MILITARY MUSEUM, The Keep, Dorchester,
DT1 1RN (Tel 0305-4066).   **5** Curator: Lt Col D. V. W.
Wakely MC.   **8** Open to the public.   **9** Mon-Fri (& Sat,
July-Sept) 9.00-13.00, 14.00-17.00; Sat (Oct-June) 9.00-
12.00. Adults 10p, children 5p.   **10** Dorset Regiment,
Militia & Volunteers, Queens Own Dorset Yeomanry (Devonshire & Dorset Regiment from 1958), uniforms, weapons,
medals, pictures, miscellaneous militaria & personal items.
12 (b) 2.

DORKING, Surrey

POLESDEN LACEY, Polesden Lacey, Dorking, RH5 6BD
(Tel 0372-52048).   **4** National Trust.   **5** Agent: Mr J. W.
Simson ARICS; Custodian: Mr L. Villanis.   **8** Open to the
public.   **9** March-Oct: Tues (not following bank hol), Wed,
Thurs, 14.00-17.30; March-Nov: Sat, Sun & bank hols 14.00-
17.30. Closes at sunset if earlier. Free to National Trust
members; adults 50p, children 22p.   **10** Regency villa built
in 1823.   **11** Greville colln (pictures, tapestries, furniture
& other works of art). Restaurant.   **12** (b) 1 (c) 6.

DOUGLAS, Isle of Man

MANX MUSEUM, AND ART GALLERY, Douglas, Isle of Man
(Tel 0624-5522).   **4** Manx Museum & National Trust.
5 Dir: A. M. Cubbon OBE, BA, FSA, FMA.   **8** Open to the
public.   **9** Mon-Sat 10.00-17.00. Closed Dec 25, 26, Good
Friday & Tynewald Day. Free.   **10** Archaeology, folk life,
natural history & art related to Isle of Man.   **11** Calf of
Man crucifixion carving (8th cent); finds from Viking ship
burials etc; pre-reformation silver chalice from Jurby;
Van Dyke portraits of James, 7th Earl of Derby & his
Countess Charlotte; reconstruction of Manx farm kitchen &
bedroom, etc.   **12** (a) 2 (b) 6 (c) 2.

MANX VILLAGE FOLK MUSEUM, Cregneash; c/o Manx
Museum, Douglas, Isle of Man.   **4** Trustees of the Manx
Museum.   **5** Dir of Manx Museum: A. M. Cubbon OBE, BA,
FSA, FMA.   **8** Open to the public.   **9** Mid May-Sept:
Mon-Sat (& bank hols) 10.00-13.00, 14.00-17.00. Adults 3p,
children 1p.   **10** Traditional life & crafts of a Manx upland
crofting community.   **11** Thatched home of crofter-fisher-
man; weaver's shed with hand-loom; turner's shed with
treadle-lathe; smithy.   **12** (a) Served from Manx Museum.

NAUTICAL MUSEUM, Correspondence to The Manx Museum,
Douglas, Isle of Man.   **4** Trustees of the Manx Museum.
5 Dir, Manx Museum: A. M. Cubbon OBE, BA, FSA, FMA.
8 Open to the public.   **9** Mid May-Sept: Mon-Sat (inc bank
hols) 10.00-13.00, 14.00-17.00. Adults 3p, children 1p.
10 Manx maritime life & trade in the days of sail.   **11** 18th-
cent armed schooner-rigged yacht built in Castletown (1791)
housed in her contemporary boat cellar, with cabin room
above in style of the Nelson period; late 19th cent punt (small
boat) of Manx 'Nickle' fishing boat.   **12** (a) Served from
Manx Museum.

DOUNE, Perthshire

DOUNE MOTOR MUSEUM AND DOUNE CASTLE, Estates
Office, Doune, FK16 6HB (Tel 0786 84-203).   **4** Earl of
Moray.   **5** Manager: Mr Robert Reid.   **8** Open to the
public.   **9** April-Oct: daily (inc bank hols) 10.00-18.00.
Adults 30p, children 10p, party rates.   **10** 14th cent
medieval castle renovated in 1883; 30 vintage & post vintage
thoroughbred motor cars.   **12** (b) 3 (c) 2.

DOVER, Kent

CRABBLE WATERMILL, River, Dover.   **4** Dover DC.
5 Curator, Dover Museum: Ms Erica R. Coveney.   **8** Open
9 Summer: Sat & Sun. Other times by arrangement. Adults
10p, at present no children under 14 admitted.   **10** 1812
watermill, restored.   **12** (b) 1.

DOVER MUSEUM, Ladywell, Dover, CT16 1DQ (Tel 0304-
201066).   **4** Dover DC.   **5** Curator: Ms Erica R. Coveney.
7 Leisure & Recreation Dept, Dir: Mr B. L. J. Woods DMA,
FIMEnt, MInstRM.   **8** Open to the public.   **9** Mon-Sat
(inc bank hols) 10.00-16.45 (Oct-March 10.00-12.00, 14.00-
16.30). Free.   **10** Local history; militaria; ceramics;
archaeology; geology; horology; art; Victoriana; stitchcraft;
butterflies & moths; coins; chairs; diorama; George Took
colln of Oology (bird's eggs).   **11** Dover Treasure Trove

CODE: **1** Name of Museum, Art Gallery or Stately Home. **2** Address **3** Telephone & telex. **4** Governing body. **5** Officer in charge. **6** Committee responsible. **7** Larger department, chief officer. **8** Open to public. **9** Hours; admission charges. **10** Scope. **11** Special exhibits or facilities. **12** Staff (a) professionally qualified (b) other non-manual (c) manual.

DOVER, Kent—*continued*

discovered Market Square 1955 (Archaeologia Cantiana, Vol. LXIX, 1955 & British Numismatic Journal, Vol. XXVIII, 1956); birds eggs & butterflies on view 10.00-11.30, or by arrangement. **12** (b) 1 (c) 1.

DOWNE, Kent.

DOWN HOUSE, Luxted Rd, Downe, Orpington, BR6 7JT (Tel 0689-59119). **4** Royal College of Surgeons of England. **5** Officer-in-Charge: Sir Hedley Atkins, KBE, PPRCS; Custodian Mr P. Titheradge. **8** Open to the public. **9** Daily (exc Mon & Fri) 13.00-17.30. Closed Dec 25 & 26. Adults 40p, children 15p. **10** Memorial to Charles Darwin; his old study & drawing room; exhibition of history of evolution. **12** (b) 1 (c) 1.

DRIFFIELD, North Humberside

BURTON AGNES HALL, Burton Agnes, Driffield, YO25 0NB (Tel 026289-324). **5** Officer-in-Charge: Mr M.W. Wickham-Boynton. **8** Open to the public. **9** May-mid Oct: Mon-Fri (inc bank hols) 13.45-17.00, Sun 13.45-18.00. Adults 35p, children & OAPs 20p. **10** Stately home (built 1598). **11** Furniture; fine china & tapestries; paintings.

SLEDMERE HOUSE, Sledmere, Driffield, YO25 0XG (Tel 0377-86208). **5** House Sec: Mrs N. Lambert. **8** Open to the public. **9** Easter-early Oct: Tues-Thurs, Sat, Sun & bank hols 13.30-17.30. Adults 40p, children 20p. Ground only: adults 25p, children 15p. **10** Georgian house (built 1751, enlarged 1787); plasterwork by Joseph Rose; Chippendale, Sheraton & French furnishings; paintings; porcelain; antique statuary; room of Turkish tiles; gardens & park by Capability Brown. **11** Cafeteria & restaurant; children's playground; vintage motor cycle rallies. **12** (b) 6 (c) 6.

DUDLEY, West Midlands

DUDLEY MUSEUM AND ART GALLERY, 3 St James's Rd, Dudley, DY1 1HP (Tel 0384-56321). **4** Dudley MBC. **7** Leisure & Recreation Services, Dir: Mr John Hoyle FLA. **8** Open to the public. **9** Mon-Sat 10.00-18.00. Free. **10** Fine art (inc modern prints & sculpture); English & foreign glass (Brierley Hill Glass Museum & Stourbridge Glass colln); geology; Black Country Museum (social history & industrial archaeology). **11** Temporary exhibitions. **12** (a) 3 (b) 5 (c) 6.

DUMFRIES, Dumfrieshire

DUMFRIES MUSEUM, Corbelly Hill, Dumfries, DG2 7SW (Tel 0387-3374). **4** Nithsdale DC. **5** Officer-in-Charge: Mr A.E. Truckell MBE, MA, FSA(Scot), FMA. **6** Leisure & Recreation. **8** Open to the public. **9** Mon-Sat 10.00-13.00, 14.00-17.00, Sun (summer only) 14.00-17.00. Free except for Camera Obscura adults 5p, children 3p. **10** Natural & human history (inc archaeology) of Dumfries & Galloway; local archives. **11** Burns colln; local fossil footprint colln. Old Bridge House Museum nearby (1662 house, built into medieval stone bridge) social history. **12** (a) 1 (b) 1 (c) 2.

DUNBAR, East Lothian

PRESTON MILL & PHANTASSIE DOOCOT, East Linton, Dunbar (Tel 062086-426). **4** National Trust for Scotland. **5** Warden: Mr Travis Hunter. **8** Open to the public. **9** Mon-Sat 10.00-12.30, 14.00-19.30, Sun 14.00-19.30 (Oct-Feb: closes 16.30 daily). Adults 20p, children 10p. **10** One of few mills of its kind in Scotland in working order; machinery renovated by Rank Hovis McDougall Ltd; old dovecot nearby.

DUNBEATH, Caithness

LHAIDHAY CROFT MUSEUM, Dunbeath, KW6 6EH. **4** Lhaidhay Preservation Trust. **5** Officer-in-Charge: Mrs E. Cameron. **8** Open to the public. **9** May-Sept: daily (inc bank hols) 9.00-20.00. Charges: 10p. **10** Typical Caithness croft complex (mid 19th cent); stable, dwelling house & byre under 1 roof; thatched winnowing barn with crux rafters. **11** Farm implements. **12** (b) 2.

DUNBLANE, Perthshire

CATHEDRAL MUSEUM, Cathedral Sq, Dunblane (Tel 078682-3123/3179). **4** Society of Friends of Dunblane Cathedral. **5** Hon Curators: Ms Helen A. Lamb DA & Mr James MacIntyre FRICS, FSA(Scot). **6** Council of Society of Friends of Dunblane Cathedral. **8** Open to the public. **9** Late May-Oct: Mon-Sat (inc bank hols) 10.30-12.30, 14.30-16.30. Free but contributions welcome. **11** Medieval carvings; ancient documents & prints; colln of communion tokens.

DUNDEE, Angus

BARRACK STREET MUSEUM, Barrack St, Dundee, DD1 1PG (Tel 0382-25492/3). **4** Dundee DC. **5** Dir: Mr James D. Boyd DA, FMA, FRSA, FSA(Scot). **6** Civic Amenities (Art Galleries & Museums Sub-Committee). **8** Open to the public. **9** Mon-Sat 10.00-17.00. Closed Dec 25 & Jan 1. Free. **10** Shipping & industry; local history. **11** Ship models built or owned in or by Dundee; touring exhibitions, topics of local & regional interest. **12** (a) 3 (c) 2.

BROUGHTY CASTLE MUSEUM, Broughty Ferry, Dundee, DD5 2BE (Tel 0382-76121). **4** Dundee DC. **5** Dir: Mr James D. Boyd DA, FMA, FRSA, FSA (Scot). **6** Civic Amenities (Art Galleries & Museums Sub-Committee). **8** Open to the public. **9** Mon-Thurs, Sat 10.00-13.00, 14.00-17.00; Sun (summer only) 14.00-17.00. Closed Dec 25 & Jan 1. Free. **10** History of castle & former Burgh of Broughty Ferry; whaling; arms & armour; ecology of the Tay. Castle is under care of Dept. of Environment & is being restored as an example of a mid-19th cent estuary fort. **11** Dundee whaling; Arctic & Antarctic material & exploration; Eskimo material; arms, armour & military associations. **12** (a) 1 (b) 1 (c) 3.

CAMPERDOWN HOUSE, Camperdown Park, Dundee DD2 4TF. **4** Dundee DC. **6** Civic Amenities (Art Galleries & Museums Sub-Committee). **8** Open to the public. **9** Mon-Sat 10.00-17.00, Sun (summer only) 14.00-17.00. Free. **10** House built 1824-29 by Earl of Camperdown (designed by William Burns); furniture, pictures, costume, personalia of the Duncan family. **11** J.S. Copley painting of Admiral Adam Duncan; Simpson colln of Keyboard Instruments, Costume etc. **12** (a) 2 (b) 1 (c) 4.

CITY ART GALLERY & MUSEUM, Albert Sq, Dundee, DD1 1DA (Tel 0382-25492/3). **4** Dundee DC. **5** Dir: Mr James D. Boyd DA, FMA, FRSA, FSA(Scot); Depute: Mr William R. Hardie MA. **6** Civic Amenities (Art Galleries & Museums Sub-Committee). **8** Open to the public. **9** Mon-Sat 10.00-17.30. Closed Dec 25 & Jan 1. Free. **10** 17th & 18th cent Italian, Dutch, Flemish, British art; 19th & 20th cent British art; Brangwyn colln; applied art; archaeology; history; ethnology; natural history. **11** Scottish silver; archaeology & natural history of Tayside region; applied art.

JAMES GUTHRIE ORCHAR ART GALLERY, 31 Beach Crescent, Broughty Ferry, Dundee (Tel 0382-77337). **4** Trustees. **5** Curator: Mr Joseph McIntyre DA. **8** Open to the public. **9** Sat & Sun 14.00-17.00. Free. **10** 19th cent Scottish paintings (principally Scott Lauder School). **11** Turner (watercolour); Cox; de Wint; Fielding; over 30 etchings by J.M. Whistler.

DUNDEE, Angus—*continued*

ST MARY'S TOWER, Kirk Style, Nethergate, Dundee, DD1 4DG
(Tel 0382-25492/3).   **4** Dundee DC.   **5** Dir: Mr James D.
Boyd DA, FMA, FRSA, FSA(Scot).   **6** Civic Amenities (Art
Galleries & Museums Sub-Committee).   **8** Open to the
public.   **9** Open daily. Free.   **10** Tower built (late 15th
cent) by town council to complete St Mary's Church (late
12th cent). 3 independent churches in one building. Displays
history of churches on site, & of ancient Dundee royalty.
11 Medieval sculptured church monuments; stained glass by
Burne-Jones; ecclesiastic relics; a peal of 8 bells.   **12** (c)
2.

SPALDING GOLF MUSEUM, Camperdown Park, Dundee,
DD2 4JF.   **4** City of Dundee DC.   **5** Dir: Mr James D.
Boyd DA, FMA, FRSA, FSA(Scot.).   **6** Civic Amenities
(Art Galleries & Museums Sub-Committee).   **8** Open to the
public.   **9** Mon-Sat (inc bank hols) 10.00-17.00. Free.
10 History of golf, early golf clubs etc.   **12** Served from
City Art Gallery & Museums.

DUNFERMLINE, Fife

ANDREW CARNEGIE BIRTHPLACE MEMORIAL, Moodie St,
Dunfermline, KY12 7PL (Tel 0383-24302).   **4** Carnegie
Dunfermline Trust, Abbey Park House, Dunfermline, KY12
7PB.   **8** Open to the public.   **9** Mon-Sat (May-Aug)
11.00-13.00, 14.00-19.00 (winter 17.00), Sun 14.00-18.00.
Free.   **10** Weaver's cottage; birthplace of Andrew
Carnegie; associated Memorial Hall illustrating his life
& philanthropies.   **12** (c) 2.

DUNFERMLINE MUSEUM, Viewfield, Dunfermline, Y12 7HY
(Tel 0383-21814).   **4** Dunfermline DC.   **6** Leisure &
Recreation.   **7** Dir of Libs, Museums & Art Galleries: Mr
James K. Sharp FLA.   **8** Open to the public.   **9** Wed-
Sun 11.00-13.00, 14.00-17.30 (later in summer). Free.
10 Local history, with emphasis on linen.   **11** Temporary
exhibitions.   **12** (a) 1 (c) 1.

PITTENCRIEFF HOUSE, Pittencrieff Park, Dunfermline,
KY12 8QH (Tel 0383-22935).   **4** Carnegie Dunfermline
Trust, Abbey Park House, Dunfermline, KY12 7PB.   **8** Open
to the public.   **9** Summer: Mon-Sat 11.00-19.00; Sun 14.00-
18.00. Free.   **10** Costume gallery & temporary exhibition
gallery.   **11** Visitor centre & craft shop.

DURHAM, Co. Durham

DURHAM LIGHT INFANTRY MUSEUM AND ARTS CENTRE,
Aykley Heads, Durham City, DH1 5TU (Tel 0385-2214/ 67798).
4 Durham CC.   **5** Keeper-in-charge: Miss Nerys A.
Johnson BA, DipEd.   **6** Museums & Libraries Sub-Committee.   **7** Education Dept, Dir: Mr D.H. Curry MA.   **8** Open
to the public.   **9** Tues-Sat (& bank hols) 10.00-17.00, Sun
14.00-17.00. Adults 10p, children & OAPs 5p.   **10** Historical collns of Durham Light Infantry Regiment (1758-1968)
inc medals, weapons, uniforms, documents & photographs.
11 Arts centre: changing programme of exhibitions, events
workshops, concerts films etc; coffee bar & free car park.
12 (a) 3 (b) 2 (c) 4.

DURHAM UNIVERSITY GULBENKIAN MUSEUM OF ORIEN-
TAL ART, Elvet Hill, Durham, DH1 3TH (Tel 0385-66711).
5 Curator: Mr Philip S. Rawson MA.   **8** Open to the public.
9 Mon-Fri (inc bank hols) 9.30-13.00, 14.15-17.00, Sat
9.30-12.00; Easter-Xmas: Sat & Sun 14.15-17.00. Charges:
25p.   **10** Art of China, Japan, India, Tibet, Southeast Asia,
Muslim Western area, ancient Middle East, Central Asia.
11 Occasional temporary exhibitions.   **12** (a) 2 (b) 4 (c) 2.

MONKS' DORMITORY MUSEUM, The College, Durham, DH1
3EH (Tel 0385-62489).   **4** Dean & Chapter.   **5** Chapter
Libn: Rev Canon Ronald L. Coppin BA; Asst Libn: Mr Roger
C. Norris MA.   **8** Open to the public.   **9** Mon-Sat 10.00-
16.30, Sun & bank hols 13.00-16.30. Adults 10, children 5p.
10 Monastic dormitory (built 1398-1404) with original timber roof; Anglo-Saxon sculptured stones; Saxon & mediaeval
mss from monastic library; early printed books & fine bindings; mediaeval episcopal regalia; mediaeval seals & char-

ters; embroidered copes; engravings & pictures; coins; Roman
antiquities.   **11** Original wooden coffin St Cuthbert (d. 687)
with its bold contemporary incised designs; 7th cent personal
cross of gold & garnet stone; 10th cent stole & maniple placed
in coffin by Queen Aelflaed.   **12** (a) 1 (b) 1.

DURSLEY, Gloucestershire

LISTER MUSEUM, Dursley, GL11 4HS (Tel 0453-4141).
4 R.A. Lister & Co Ltd.   **5** Publicity Manager: Mr Don
Asher.   **9** Open by appointment only. Free.
10 Engineering machinery (petrol & diesel engines,
agricultural machinery) manufactured by R.A. Lister &
Co (from c. 1900).

EARDISLAND, Hereford & Worcester

BURTON COURT, Eardisland, Leominster (Tel 05447-231).
5 Owners: Lt Cdr & Mrs R.M. Simpson.   **8** Open to the
public.   **9** Spring bank hol-mid Sept: Wed, Thurs, Sat,
Sun & bank hol Mons 14.30-18.00. Adults 20p, children 10p,
coach parties 15p.   **10** 14th cent Great Hall; tour of house
& gardens; curios; European & Oriental costumes; art;
embroidery.   **11** Teas; pick your own soft fruit in season.
12 (a) 1.

EASTBOURNE, Sussex

TOWER 73 (The Wish Tower), King Edward's Parade,
Eastbourne (Tel 0323 35809/21635).   **4** Eastbourne BC.
5 Curator: Mr Philip Dutton MA, BSc.   **6** Tourism &
Leisure.   **7** Art Gallery & Museums Dept, Dir: Mr David
Galer.   **8** Open to the public.   **9** Easter-Sept: daily
(inc bank hols) 10.00-17.30. Adults 9p, children, students
& OAPs 6p; school parties reduced rate.   **10** Restored
Martello Tower built during Napoleonic Wars; historical
background & details of building, manning & armament.
12 (a) 2 (b) 1 (c) 1.

TOWNER ART GALLERY, Borough Lane, Eastbourne,
BN20 8BB (Tel 0323-21635).   **4** Eastbourne BC.
5 Dir: Mr David Galer.   **6** Tourism & Leisure.
8 Open to the public.   **9** Mon-Sat (inc bank hols) 10.00-
17.00, Sun 14.00-17.00 (April-Sept closes 18.00). Free.
10 Permanent colln of 19th & 20th cent British artists;
original artists' prints; Georgian caricatures; topographical
colln of pictures of Old Eastbourne.   **11** Lectures, film
shows, recitals as advertised frequently throughout the
year; about ten special exhibitions p.a.   **12** (a) 1 (b) 1½
(c) 3.

ECCLES, Lancashire

MONKS HALL MUSEUM, 42 Wellington Rd, Eccles,
Manchester, M30 0NP (Tel 061-789 4372).   **4** Salford
City Council.   **5** Curator: S. Shaw FMA.   **7** Cultural
Services Dept; Manager: M.W. Devereux FLA.   **8** Open to
the public.   **9** Mon-Fri (inc bank hols) 10.00-18.00, Sat
10.00-17.00. Free.   **10** Paintings; prints; pottery; local
bygones.   **11** Nasmyth machinery (inc steam hammer);
temporary exhibitions.   **12** (a) 1 (c) 2.

EDINBURGH

BRAIDWOOD AND RUSHBROOK MUSEUM, Fire Station,
McDonald Rd, Edinburgh (Tel 031-229 7222).   **4** Lothian &
Borders Fire Brigade.   **5** Divisional Commander: I. Mc-
Murtrie AMIFireE; Firemaster: J. Anderson MIFireE.
8 Open to the public.   **9** Hours under review. Free.
10 History of the Fire Brigade, equipment, organisation,
badges etc; British & foreign brigades.   **11** Fire Engines
(1800-1939); historical records & early equipment.

CANONGATE TOLBOOTH, 163 Canongate, Edinburgh,
EH8 8BN (Tel 031-556 5813).   **4** City of Edinburgh DC.
5 City Curator: Mr Herbert Coutts AMA, FSA(Scot).
7 Dept of Recreation & Leisure, Officer-in-Charge: Mr
William Bell MA, LLB.   **8** Open to the public.   **9** Mon-
Sat 10.00-17.00 (18.00 June-Sept), Sun (during Edinburgh
Festival only) 14.00-17.00. Closed Dec 25 & Jan 1. Free.

CODE: 1 Name of Museum, Art Gallery or Stately Home. **2** Address. **3** Telephone & telex. **4** Governing body. **5** Officer in charge. **6** Committee responsible. **7** Larger department, chief officer. **8** Open to public. **9** Hours; admission charges. **10** Scope. **11** Special exhibits or facilities. **12** Staff (a) professionally qualified (b) other non-manual (c) manual.

EDINBURGH—*continued*

10 Historic courthouse of old burgh of Canongate.
11 Temporary exhibitions, Telfer Dunbar Colln (Tartan).
12 (c) 4.

CHARLOTTE SQUARE, 5, 6 & 7 Charlotte Sq, Edinburgh,
EH2 4DU (Tel 031-226 5922). **4** National Trust for
Scotland. **8** Open to the public. **9** Mon-Sat 10.00-17.00,
Sun 14.00-17.00. Adults 25p, children 10p. **10** Row of
Robert Adam houses; No. 7, lower floors, typical Georgian
house, furnished in period showing domestic surroundings
& reflecting social conditions. **11** Audio-visual display.

CITY OF EDINBURGH ARTS CENTRE, Old Royal High
School, Regent Rd, Edinburgh, EH7 5BL (Tel 031-556 9917).
4 City of Edinburgh DC. **5** Asst Keeper: Mrs M. Sharp
DA. **7** Dept of Recreation & Leisure, Mr William Bell
MA, LLB. **8** Open to the public. **9** Mon-Sat (inc bank
hols) 10.00-17.00, Sun 14.00-17.00. Free. **10** Paintings
by Scottish artists. **11** Temporary exhibitions; studio
facilities for young artists. **12** (a) 2 (b) 1.

EDINBURGH CASTLE, Edinburgh. **4** Dept of Environment.
5 Information Officer, Argyle House, 3 Lady Lawson St,
Edinburgh. **8** Open to the public. **9** May-Oct: Mon-Sat
9.30-18.00, Sun 11.00-18.00; Nov-April: Mon-Sat 9.30-
17.15, Sun 12.30-16.30. April-Sept: adults 25p, children 10p;
Oct-March: adults 10p, children 5p; OAPs 5p all year.
10 Famous Scottish castle. **11** Mons Meg cannon; Scottish
National War Memorial; St Margarets Chapel; Argyll
Battery; Half Moon Battery; the Great Hall; Scottish regalia.

FRUIT MARKET GALLERY, 29 Market St, Edinburgh,
EH1 1DF (Tel 031-226 5781). **4** Scottish Arts Council.
5 Art Dir: Mr William Buchanan; Exhibitions Officer:
Mr Robert Breen. **8** Open to the public. **9** Open during
exhibitions: Mon-Sat 10.00-17.30. Usually free. **10** Mainly
exhibitions of living artists (from Britain & abroad).
12 (a) 3 (b) 4 (c) 2.

HUNTLY HOUSE MUSEUM, 142 Canongate, Edinburgh,
EH8 8DD (Tel 031-556 5813). **4** City of Edinburgh DC.
5 City Curator: Mr Herbert Coutts AMA, FSA(Scot).
7 Dept of Recreation & Leisure, Mr William Bell MA, LLB.
8 Open to the public. **9** Mon-Sat 10.00-17.00 (18.00
June-Sept), Sun (during Edinburgh Festival only) 14.00-17.00.
Closed Dec 25 & Jan 1. Free. **10** Local history; Edinburgh
silver; glass; Scottish pottery. **12** (a) 5 (b) 6 (c) 8.

JOHN KNOX MUSEUM, 45 High Street, Edinburgh, EH1 1SR
(Tel 031-556 3300). **4** Church of Scotland. **5** Officer-
in-Charge: Mr H. G. Lindley. **8** Open to the public.
9 Mon-Sat (inc some bank hols) 10.00-17.00. Adults 11p,
children 5p; parties (over 20) ½ price. **10** Home of
Scottish Reformist, John Knox, for last nine years of his
life; items related to Reformation & John Knox. **12** (b) 3.

LADY STAIR'S HOUSE, Lawnmarket, Edinburgh, EH1 2PA
(Tel 031-225 8160). **4** City of Edinburgh DC. **5** City
Curator: Mr Herbert Coutts AMA, FSA(Scot). **7** Dept of
Recreation & Leisure, Mr William Bell MA, LLB. **8** Open
to the public. **9** Mon-Sat 10.00-17.00 (18.00 June-Sept),
Sun (during Edinburgh Festival only) 14.00-17.00. Closed
Dec 25 & Jan 1. Free. **10** Restored 17th cent town house.
11 Personalia of Robert Burns, Sir Walter Scott & Robert
Louis Stevenson. **12** (c) 3.

LAURISTON CASTLE, 2a Cramond Rd South, Edinburgh,
EH4 5QD (Tel 031-336 2060). **4** Lauriston Castle Trust,
administered by City of Edinburgh DC. **5** City Curator:
Mr H. Coutts AMA, FSA(Scot); Resident Custodian: Mr
Charles Angus. **6** Museums & Libraries. **7** City
Curator: Mr Herbert Coutts. **8** Open to the public.
9 April-Oct: Sat-Thurs (inc bank hols) 11.00-13.00, 14.00-
17.00; Nov-Mch: Sat & Sun 14.00-16.00. Free. **10** 16th
cent tower-house with 19th cent additions; Edwardian

furnishings; fine furniture. **11** Blue John (Derbyshire
Spar); Crossley wool mosaics; furniture; porcelain; silver;
tapestries etc. **12** (b) 1 (c) 5.

MR PURVES' LAMP EMPORIUM AND MUSEUM SHOP,
59 St Stephen St, Edinburgh 3 (Tel 031-556 4503).
5 Officer-in-Charge: Mr William Mackay Purves ACII,
BA, FSA(Scot). **8** Open to the public. **9** Sat 10.00-
18.00. Other times by arrangement. Free. **10** Oil &
gas lighting equipment. **11** Paraffin pressure lamps; gas
& oil lamp incandescent mantles. **12** (a) 1.

MUSEUM OF CHILDHOOD, Hyndford's Close, 38 High St,
Edinburgh EH1 1TG (Tel 031-556 5447). **4** City of
Edinburgh DC. **5** Keeper of Childhood Collns: Mr R. T.
Hutchings MA. **7** Dept of Recreation & Leisure, Mr
William Bell MA, LLB. **8** Open to the public. **9** Oct-
May: Mon-Sat (inc bank hols) 10.00-17.00, Sun (during
Edinburgh Festival only) 14.00-17.00. Adults 5p, children
2½p. **10** The artifacts of childhood inc toys, dolls, books,
costume & nursery equipment. **12** (a) 1 (b) 2 (c) 3.

NATIONAL GALLERY OF SCOTLAND, The Mound,
Edinburgh, EH2 2EL (Tel 031-556 8921). **5** Dir: Mr Hugh
Scrutton CBE. **8** Open to the public. **9** Mon-Sat
10.00-17.00, Sun 14.00-17.00. Closes at 20.00 during
Edinburgh Festival. Free. **10** European & Scottish paint-
ing (14th-20th cents).

NATIONAL MUSEUM OF ANTIQUITIES OF SCOTLAND,
1 Queen St, Edinburgh, EH2 1JB (Tel 031-556 8921).
4 Board of Trustees. **5** Keeper: Mr Robert B. K.
Stevenson MA, FSA. **8** Open to the public. **9** Mon-Sat
10.00-17.00, Sun 14.00-17.00. Closed Dec 25 & Jan 1.
Free. **10** Prehistoric, Roman, early medieval archaeology;
later social history; applied arts; numismatics; also agricultural history, country crafts & domestic life; scientific research & conservation laboratories, (not open to public at
present). **12** (a) 14 (b) 12 (c) 15.

OUTLOOK TOWER (under repair), Castlehill, Edinburgh.
4 University of Edinburgh. **5** Project's Officer: Miss L.
Paterova. **8** Open to the public. **9** Easter & mid June-
Oct: Mon-Sat 10.00-18.00, Sun 12.30-18.00. Adults 15p,
children 10p. **10** Camera obscura.

PALACE OF HOLYROODHOUSE, Edinburgh. **4** Dept of the
Environment. **5** Information Officer, Argyle House, 3 Lady
Lawson St, Edinburgh. **8** Open to the public. **9** May-
Oct: Mon-Sat 9.30-18.00, Sun 11.00-18.00; Nov-April: Mon-
Sat 9.30-17.15, Sun 12.30-16.30. Closed mid May-mid July.
April-Sept: adults 25p, children 10p; Oct-March: adults 10p,
children 5p; OAPs 5p. **10** Official residence in Scotland, of
the Queen. **11** Queen Mary's bedchamber; the kings bed-
room of 1675; picture gallery; historic apartments.

PRESTONGRANGE MINING MUSEUM AND HISTORICAL
SITE, c/o 2 Woodlands Grove, Edinburgh, 15 (Tel 031-661 2718).
4 East Lothian DC. **5** Hon Curator: Mr David Spence.
6 Leisure & Recreation. **8** Open to the public. **9** Mon-
Fri 9.00-16.30, Sun 10.30-15.30. Free, but donations
welcome. **10** Cornish beam pumping engine; colliery winding engine (to be rebuilt) No 7 Grant Ritchie Locomotive 042.
11 Excavations in progress. **12** (b) 1.

PRINTMAKERS WORKSHOP LTD, 29 Market St, Edinburgh,
EH1 1DF (Tel 031-225 1098). **5** Managing Sec: Mr Kenneth
Duffy DA. **8** Open to the public. **9** Mon-Sat 10.00-17.00
Free. **10** Etching, lithography, silk-screen printing, photo-
graphy & other related printmaking facilities. **11** Print
Gallery exhibits work by members & contemporary print-
makers. **12** (a) 1 (b) 3.

RICHARD DEMARCO GALLERY LTD, Monteith House,
61 High St, Edinburgh, EH1 1SR (Tel 031-557 0707).
4 Board of Directors. **5** Gallery Dir: Mr Richard
Demarco RSW. **8** Open to the public. **9** Tues-Fri

EDINBURGH—*continued*

10.00-17.30, Sat 11.00-17.00. Free.   **10** Contemporary art in all its forms; contemporary Scottish art; bringing foreign artists to Scotland.   **11** Play readings; video (hopefully); seminars; dance workshops; 'Edinburgh Arts' a summer school run by The Demarco Gallery, involving 25 artists in a European journey, culminating at the Edinburgh Festival in a major exhibition.   **12** (a) 1 (b) 2.

ROYAL BOTANIC GARDEN EXHIBITION HALL, Inverleith Row, Edinburgh, EH3 5LR. (Tel 031-552 7171 ext 271).
4 MAFF for Scotland.   **5** Education Officer: Dr C.C. Wood BSc, PhD, FLS.   **7** Royal Botanic Garden, Chief Officer & Regius Keeper: D.M. Henderson BSc, FRSE.   **8** Open to the public.   **9** Mon-Sat 10.00-17.00, Sun 11.00-17.00 (10.00-17.00 during Edinburgh Festival). Closed Jan.1. Free.
10 Botany.   **11** Temporary exhibits; diorama windows; audio visual units; living plants; plant growth & pollination; the Cairngorms; Scottish pinewoods; economic plants.
12 (a) 1 (b) 1.

ROYAL COLLEGE OF SURGEONS OF EDINBURGH MUSEUM, 18 Nicolson St, Edinburgh, EH8 9DW (Tel 031-556 6206).
5 Officer-in-Charge: Dr Andrew A. Shivas TD, MD, FRCSE, DPH, FRCPath.   **8** Open only by application in writing.
9 Mon-Fri 9.00-17.00. Free.   **10** Surgical pathological material; X-ray & microscopic material; historical medical instruments, equipment & paintings; antique & obsolescent dental equipment; medical & surgical items.   **12** (a) 2 (b) 6 (c) 1.

ROYAL SCOTS REGIMENTAL MUSEUM, Regimental Headquarters, The Castle, Edinburgh, EH1 2YT (Tel 031-336 1761 ext 7265).   **4** Royal Scots Museum Trust.   **5** Dir: Col B.A. Fargus OBE.   **8** Open to the public.   **9** Oct-May: Mon-Fri 9.30-16.00; June-Sept: Mon-Sat 9.30-17.30, Sun 11.00-17.30. Free.   **10** Regimental regalia, colours, uniforms, medals, silver, weapons etc.   **11** Souvenir shop.
12 (b) 1 (c) 2.

ROYAL SCOTTISH ACADEMY, The Mound, Edinburgh, EH2 2EL (Tel 031-225 6671).   **4** Council.   **5** President: Mr Robin Philipson PRSA, HRA, ARA.   **8&9** Open during exhibitions: Mon-Sat 10.00-21.00, Sun 14.00-17.00. Charges: 25p.   **10** Temporary exhibitions.   **12** (a) 1 (b) 3 (c) 2.

ROYAL SCOTTISH MUSEUM, Chambers St, Edinburgh, EH1 1JF (Tel 031-225 7534).   **4** Scottish Education Dept.
5 Dir: Dr Norman Tebble DSc, FIBiol.   **8** Open to the public.   **9** Mon-Sat 10.00-17.00, Sun 14.00-17.00. Closed Dec 25 & 26, Jan 1 & 2. Free.   **10** Decorative arts of the world; Egyptology & ethnography; animals; fossils & minerals of the world; science & technology.   **11** Temporary exhibitions; lectures, films, gallery talks; holiday activities for children & young people; club for young people.   **12** Total c. 162.

SCOTTISH ARTS COUNCIL GALLERY, 19 Charlotte Square, Edinburgh, EH2 4DF (Tel 031-226 6051).   **4** Scottish Arts Council.   **5** Art Dir: Mr William Buchanan; Exhibitions Officer: Mr Robert Breen.   **8** Open to the public.
9 Mon-Sat 10.00-18.00, Sun 14.00-18.00. Closed 1 week in 4, between exhibitions. Usually free.   **10** Temporary exhibitions of all aspects of fine arts.   **11** Housed in Charlotte Square, designed by Robert Adam in 1791.
12 (a) 3 (b) 4 (c) 2.

SCOTTISH NATIONAL GALLERY OF MODERN ART, Royal Botanic Garden, Edinburgh, EH3 5LR (Tel 031-332 3754).
4 National Galleries of Scotland, Trustees.   **5** Keeper: Mr Douglas Hall BA, FMA.   **8** Open to the public.   **9** Mon-Sat 10.00-18.00 or dusk, Sun 14.00-18.00 or dusk. Closed Dec 25, 26, & Jan 1, 2. Free.   **10** 20th cent paintings, drawings, prints & sculpture.   **11** Temporary exhibitions.
12 (a) 2 (b) 2 (c) 19.

SCOTTISH NATIONAL PORTRAIT GALLERY, 1 Queen St, Edinburgh, EH2 1JD (Tel 031-556 8921).   **4** Board of Trustees for the National Galleries of Scotland.   **5** Keeper: R.E. Hutchison.   **7** National Galleries of Scotland, Dir: Mr Hugh Scrutton.   **8** Open to the public.   **9** Mon-Sat (inc bank hols) 10.00-17.00 (20.00 during Edinburgh Festival),

Sun 14.00-17.00. Free.   **10** Portraits of men & women who played a prominent part in Scottish history (16th-20th cent).   **11** Over 20,000 engraved portraits; c.30,000 photographs illustrating portraiture in Scotland; over 3,000 items of the work of D.O. Hill & Robert Adamson, pioneer photographers.   **12** (a) 5 (b) 5.

SCOTTISH UNITED SERVICES MUSEUM, The Castle, Edinburgh, EH1 2NG (Tel 031-226 6907).   **4** Scottish Education Dept.   **5** Keeper: Mr William A. Thorburn FSA(Scot).
8 Open to the public.   **9** Mon-Sat 9.30-18.00 (Oct-May 16.00); June-Oct: Sun 11.00-18.00. Closed Dec 25, 26 & Jan 1, 2. Free to students, by appointment; otherwise included in Edinburgh Castle entrance charge.   **10** History of Navy, Army, & Air Force, at all periods; extensive & comprehensive displays of costume, weapons, & related material; 30,000 catalogued items, inc the oldest established colln of military costume in UK.   **11** Substantial pictorial & written archives on all aspects of British armed forces history, with emphasis on Scottish elements; research facilities available to students by appointment.   **12** (a) 4 (b) 1.

EGHAM, Surrey

EGHAM MUSEUM, Literary Institute, High St, Egham.
4 Egham by Runnymede Historical Society.   **8** Open to the public.   **9** Sat 10.30-12.30, 14.30-16.30.   Free   **10** Local history & archaeological finds.

ROYAL HOLLOWAY COLLEGE (UNIVERSITY OF LONDON), PICTURE GALLERY, Egham Hill, Egham, TW20 0EX (Tel 078 43-4455).   **4** College Council.   **5** Communications should be addressed to Sec of the College.   **8** Open by appointment or on Open Days advertised in the press. Free.
10 Colln of paintings, mostly Victorian.

ELGIN, Morayshire

ELGIN MUSEUM, 1 High St, Elgin, IV30 1EQ (Tel 0343-3675).
4 Elgin Society.   **8** Open to the public.   **9** Mon & Wed-Sat 10.00-12.30, 14.00-17.00, Tues 10.00-13.00. Adults 10p, child 3p.   **10** District museum with some general & foreign exhibits.   **11** Old Red Permian & Triassic fossils; neolithic & Bronze Age artifacts etc.

ENNISKILLEN, Co Fermanagh

ROYAL INNISKILLING FUSILIERS REGIMENTAL MUSEUM, The Castle, Enniskillen, BT74 7HL (Tel 0365-3142).
4 Trustees.   **5** Curator: Major H.E.P.F. Thrupp.
8 Open to the public.   **9** Mon-Fri 10.30-12.30, 14.00-16.30 (Fri 16.00). Other days by arrangement. Adults 10p, children 5p; parties of 20 or more ½ price.   **10** History of the Regiment (1688-1968).   **12** (b) 1 (c) 1.

EPSOM, Surrey

BOURNE HALL MUSEUM, Bournehall, Ewell, Epsom (Tel 01-393 9573).   **4** Epsom & Ewell Corporation.   **5** Curator: Mr G. Hunter DFC, MA, FMA.   **6** Amenities.   **7** Entertainments.   **8** Open to the public.   **9** Mon-Sat 10.00-17.00. Free.   **10** Local history; archaeology; early photography; 20th cent costume; dolls & toys.   **11** Large art gallery, temporary exhibitions.   **12** (a) 1 (b) 1 (c) 1.

EVESHAM, Hereford & Worcester

ALMONRY MUSEUM, Vine St, Evesham (Tel 0386-6944).
4 Vale of Evesham Historical Society; owned by Evesham Town Council.   **5** Hon Curator; Mr B.G. Cox.   **8** Open to the public.   **9** Tues, Thurs-Sun, & bank hols 14.30-18.30. Adults 10p, children free.   **10** Local history.   **11** Civic exhibits (Governing Charter etc); monastic remains from Evesham Abbey; agricultural exhibits from Vale of Evesham; Victoriana; Simon de Montfort memorial room (Battle of Evesham).

EXETER, Devon

DEVONSHIRE REGIMENT MUSEUM, Wyvern Barracks, Exeter EX2 6AF (Tel 0392-76581).   **4** Trustees.

CODE: 1 Name of Museum, Art Gallery or Stately Home. 2 Address. 3 Telephone & telex. 4 Governing body. 5 Officer in charge. 6 Committee responsible. 7 Larger department, chief officer. 8 Open to public. 9 Hours; admission charges. 10 Scope. 11 Special exhibits or facilities. 12 Staff (a) professionally qualified (b) other non-manual (c) manual.

EXETER, Devon—*continued*

5 Officer-in-Charge: Lt Col (Retd) G. W. B. Spencer. 8 Open to the public. 9 Mon-Fri 9.00-16.30. Other days by special arrangement. Free. 10 General militaria directly connected with the Devonshire Regiment. 12 (c) 1.

EXETER CITY GUILDHALL, High St, Exeter EX4 3EB (Tel 0392-72979) 4 Exeter City Council. 5 Dir of Museums: Mr Stephen Locke, BSc, AMA, FGS. 6 Leisure. 8 Open to the public. 9 Mon-Sat 10.00-17.30 (subject to civic functions). Closed Dec 25 & Jan 1. Free. 10 Mediaeval guildhall, at one time court & still used as Exeter City Council Chamber, the oldest surviving municipal building in the country. 11 Elizabethan frontage; fine timber roof; city silver & regalia. 12 Served by Exeter City Museums.

EXETER MARITIME MUSEUM, The Quay, Exeter, EX2 4AN (Tel 0392-58075). 4 International Sailing Craft Association. 5 Dir: Major D. R. Goddard MA. 8 Open to the public. 9 Daily (inc bank hols) 10.00-18.00 (Winter 17.00). Adults 50p, children 20p; party rates: adults 40p, children 15p. 10 More than 70 boats (from Britain, Europe, the Middle & Far East, the Pacific islands, & America), whenever possible, maintained in working condition. 11 Larger craft afloat on the Exeter Canal; 2 indoor displays in period warehouses which formed part of the old Port of Exeter. 12 (a) 1 (b) 2 (c) 3.

ROUGEMONT HOUSE MUSEUM, Castle St, Exeter EX4 3PU (Tel 0392-56724). 4 Exeter City Council. 5 Dir of Museums: Mr Stephen Locke BSc, AMA, FGS. 6 Leisure. 8 Open to the public. 9 Mon-Sat 10.00-13.00, 14.00-17.30. Closed Dec 25 & Jan 1. Free. 10 Local history & archaeology; Devon militaria. 11 Recent Exeter excavations; coin display & study colln. 12 (a) Served from Royal Albert Memorial Museum.

ROYAL ALBERT MEMORIAL MUSEUM AND ART GALLERY, Queen St, Exeter, EX4 3RX (Tel 0392-56724). 4 Exeter City Council. 5 Dir of Museums: Mr Stephen Locke, BSc, AMA, FGS. 6 Leisure. 8 Open to the public. 9 Mon-Sat 10.00-17.30. Closed Dec 25 & Jan 1. Free. 10 Paintings, sculpture, ceramics, costume, glass, silver, horology, ethnography, natural history (British & foreign); foreign archaeology. 11 Exeter silver; North Devon pottery; American natural history & ethnography; early Devon artists; study colln of worldwide butterflies; temporary exhibitions; education service; archaeological field unit. 12 (a) 11 (b) 5 (c) 12.

ST NICHOLAS PRIORY, The Mint, Exeter EX4 3BL (Tel 0392-56724). 4 Exeter City Council. 5 Dir of Museums: Mr Stephen Locke BSc, AMA, FGS. 6 Leisure. 8 Open to the public. 9 Mon-Sat 10.00-13.00, 14.00-17.30. Closed Dec 25 & Jan 1. Adults 17p, children 10p. 10 Restored guest house (11th cent) of Benedictine Priory with adaptations (16th & 17th cent). 11 Fine Norman undercroft; small displays of mediaeval stonework, woodwork & pewter. 12 (a) Served by Exeter Museum Service.

TOPSHAM MUSEUM, 25 The Strand, Topsham, Exeter. 4 Exeter City Council in association with private owner. 5 Dir of Museums: Mr Stephen Locke, BSc, AMA, FGS, in association with private owner. 6 Leisure. 8 Open to the public. 9 Mon, Wed & Sat 14.00-17.00. Closed Dec 25 & Jan 1. Free. 10 History of the port & trade of Topsham. 12 (a) Served by Exeter Museum Service.

FALKIRK, Stirlingshire

FALKIRK MUSEUM, 15 Orchard St, Falkirk, FK1 1RF (Tel 0324-27703). 4 Falkirk DC. 5 Curator: J. M. Sanderson FLS, FSA(Scot). 6 Amenity & Recreation. 7 Dept of Libraries Museums & Art Galleries, District Chief Libn: A. H. Howson ALA. 8 Open to the public.

9 Mon-Sat 10.00-17.00. Free. 10 Local history & natural history. 11 Education Service. 12 (a) 3 (c) 2.

SCOTTISH PRISON SERVICE COLLEGE MUSEUM, Newlands Rd, Brightons, Falkirk, FK2 0DE (Tel 0324-711727). 4 Scottish Prison Service, Scottish Home & Health Dept. 5 Principal, Scottish Prison Service College: Mr George Dingwall. 9 Open only by arrangement, Mon-Fri 9.00-17.00. 10 Display of photographs, equipment, records, staff accoutrements & other objects of historical interest in development of Scottish Prison Service. 12 Served by college instructing staff.

FALKLAND, Fife

ROYAL PALACE OF FALKLAND, Falkland, Kirkcaldy, KY7 7BY (Tel 03375-397). 4 National Trust for Scotland. 5 Principal Guide: Mr Norman Lothian. 8 Open to the public. 9 Mon-Sat 10.00-18.00, Sun (April-mid Oct) 14.00-18.00. Palace & Gardens: 50p, child 20p; gardens: 25p, child 10p; car park 10p; school parties 10p; Scots Guards free. 10 16th cent palace, with Chapel Royal Grounds inc part of the old Burgh with town houses (inc many Little Houses). 11 Burgh regalia & history; reception & visitor centre.

FARNHAM, Surrey

FARNHAM MUSEUM, Willmer House, 38 West St, Farnham, GU9 7DX. 4 Waverley DC. 5 Officer-in-Charge: Mr Ashton Booth NDD, ATD, AMA. 6 Leisure & Culture. 7 Mr John Birch. 8 Open to the public. 9 Tues-Sat 11.00-17.00, Sun (& bank hols) 14.30-17.00. Closed Dec 25. Free. 10 Decorative & fine art; local & agricultural history; local archaeology. 11 Personalia of William Cobbett, author of 'Rural Rides' etc; hops, pubs & brewing. 12 (a) 1 (b) 2.

FOLKESTONE, Kent

FOLKESTONE MUSEUM, Grace Hill, Folkestone (Tel 0303-57583). 4 Kent CC. 5 County Museums Officer: Miss L. Millard BA. 6 Libraries Museums & Archives Sub-Committee. 7 County Library, County Libn: Mr Dean Harrison MA, FLA. 8 Open to the public. 9 Mon-Sat 10.00-13.00, 14.30-17.30. Free. 10 Local archaeology, history, geology & natural history. 11 Temporary art exhibitions. 12 (c) 1.

FORFAR, Angus

MEFFAN MUSEUM, 20 West High St, Forfar, DD8 1BB (Tel 0307-3468). 4 Angus DC. 5 Officer-in-Charge: Mr Ernest Mann. 7 Forfar Public Library. 8 Open to the public. 9 Mon-Fri 9.00-19.00, Sat 9.00-18.00. Free. 10 Local archaeology; regalia of Forfar Town Council.

FORT GEORGE, Inverness-shire

SEAFORTH HIGHLANDERS, THE QUEEN'S OWN CAMERON HIGHLANDERS AND QUEEN'S OWN HIGHLANDERS (SEAFORTH AND CAMERONS), REGIMENTAL MUSEUM, Fort George, Inverness, IV1 2TD (Tel 06676-278). 4 Regimental Trustees, Queen's Own Highlanders. 5 Curator: Major H. Barker MBE. 8 Open to the public. 9 April-Sept: Mon-Sat 10.00-18.30, Sun 14.00-18.00; Oct-Mch: Mon-Fri 10.00-16.00. Closed Good Friday, Easter, August bank hol & last two weeks in June. Free. 10 Uniforms, medals, silver, pictures of all three Regiments with items of interest from Lovat Scouts & Caithness Artillery. 12 (c) 2.

FORT WILLIAM, Inverness-shire

WEST HIGHLAND MUSEUM, Cameron Sq, Fort William, PH33 6AJ (Tel 0397-2169). 4 Private. 5 Sec &

FORT WILLIAM, Inverness-shire—*continued*

Curator: Miss S. Archibald.   **8** Open to the public.
9 Mon-Sat, 9.30-13.00, 14.15-17.00 (mid June-mid Sept
9.30-21.00). Closed Dec 25 & Jan 1. Adult 10p, children 5p.
10 General, local history, natural history, tartans, Jacobite
items, etc.   **11** "Secret portrait" of Bonnie Prince Charlie.
12 (b) 1.

GAINSBOROUGH, Lincolnshire

MANOR HOUSE, The Old Hall, Parnell St, Gainsborough,
DN21 2NB (Tel 0427-2669).   **5** Belongs to Dept of Environment, administered by Friends of The Old Hall Association.
8 Open to the public.   **9** Daily 14.00-17.00. Closed Dec
25, 26 & Sun in winter, but organised parties at any time by
prior arrangement with Sec. Not free.   **10** 15th cent half-
timbered manor house containing period rooms & furniture,
mediaeval kitchen, great hall etc; associations with Richard
III, Henry VIII & Catharine Parr; early meeting place for the
Pilgrim Fathers; John Wesley preached in the Hall on
several occasions; Guided tour (c. 2 hours).

GATESHEAD, Tyne & Wear

SHIPLEY ART GALLERY, Prince Consort Rd South, Gateshead, NE8 4JB (Tel 0632-771495).   **4** Tyne & Wear CC.
5 Curator: Miss Marilyn Carr MA.   **6** Leisure.
7 Museums & Art Galleries, Dir: Mr K. J. Barton MPhil,
FSA, FMA.   **8** Open to the public.   **9** Mon-Sat (inc bank
hols) 10.00-18.00, Sun 15.00-17.00. Free.   **10** 16th & 17th
cent North European paintings (David Teniers, Ricci, Canaletto, Balten, Schauffelein etc); local gallery (applied arts &
wood carving by Gerrard Robinson); craft centre (inc
ceramics, batiks, Northumbrian small pipes & embroidery;
crafts on sale).   **11** Temporary exhibitions (some on
crafts).   **12** (a) 2 (b) 1 (c) 5.

GERRARDS CROSS, Buckinghamshire

BEE RESEARCH ASSOCIATION COLLECTION OF HISTORI-
CAL AND CONTEMPORARY BEEKEEPING EQUIPMENT,
Hill House, Chalfont St Peter, Gerrards Cross, SL9 0NR
(Tel 028 13-85011).   **8** Open to the public.   **9** Mon-Fri
9.00-17.30.   **10** Beekeeping & honey-hunting equipment,
world-wide, all periods. Related items to do with honey,
beeswax etc.

GLAMIS, Angus

ANGUS FOLK MUSEUM, Kirkwynd Cottages, Glamis, Forfar,
DD8 1RT.   **4** National Trust for Scotland.   **5** Caretaker:
Mrs Jean Irons.   **9** Easter-Sept: daily 13.00-18.00. Other
times by arrangement. Adults 20p, children 10p.   **10** Six
17th cent cottages with stone-slabbed roofs; Lady Maitland's
colln of folk material.

GLANDFORD, Norfolk

GLANDFORD SHELL MUSEUM, Glandford, Holt, NR25 7JP
(Tel 026 374-349).   **4** Managing Trustees.   **5** Caretakers:
Mr & Mrs L. Page.   **8** Open to the public.   **9** Mon-Sat
9.00-13.00, 14.00-17.00 (16.00 in winter), Sun (summer only)
14.00-17.00. Closed for 2 weeks before Xmas. Charges:
2½p.   **10** Sea shells (worldwide).   **11** A tapestry; bits
of old Pompeii; coral.   **12** (b) 2.

GLASGOW

GLASGOW ART GALLERY AND MUSEUM, Kelvingrove,
Glasgow, G3 8AG (Tel 041-334 1134).   **4** City of Glasgow
DC.   **5** Dir: Mr Trevor A. Walden CBE, MSc, FMA; Dep Dir:
Mr George Buchanan DFM, BA, DA, AMA.   **6** Museums &
Art Galleries.   **8** Open to the public.   **9** Mon-Sat 10.00-
17.00, Sun 14.00-17.00. Closed Dec 25 & Jan 1. Free.
10 Italian, Flemish, Dutch, French & British paintings
(perhaps the finest civic art colln in Great Britain); archaeology; ethnography; natural history; sculpture; silver; pottery
& porcelain; connoisseur's colln of arms & armour; wildlife; the story of man in Scotland.   **11** Selections from the

Burrell colln (paintings, stained glass, sculptures); temporary
exhibitions; museum education dept with staff of 8 qualified
teachers.   **12** (a) 42 (b) 30 (c) 151.

GLASGOW UNIVERSITY, HUNTERIAN MUSEUM AND
GALLERY, Glasgow, G12 8QQ (Tel 041-339 8855).
4 University of Glasgow.   **5** Acting Dir: Prof Leslie
Alcock MA, FSA, FRSE, FRHistS; Dir Designate: Prof Frank
Willett, MA, DipAnthropology, FRAI; Hon Keeper of Zoo-
logical Collns: Dr P. E. P. Norton; Hon Keeper of Anatomical
Colln: Prof R. J. Scothorne BSc, MD, FRSE.   **8** Open to the
public (except for Hunterian Coin Cabinet & Anatomical
Colln).   **9** Mon-Fri 9.00-17.00, Sat 9.00-12.00 (Zoological
collns 11.00). Free.   **10 & 11** Cultural Collns (anthropology & archaeology: prehistoric Europe & Africa; Romans in
Scotland; ancient Mediterranean & Near East; ethnography;
Hunterian Coin Cabinet, not open to the public; Olduvai Gorge,
early man; carved Roman stones from Antonine wall; finds
from Roman & from Hebridean Iron Age sites; Australian
aborigine & Pacific islands material). Geology (minerals,
rocks & fossils, especially Scottish geology; evolution of
selected mammal groups; reptilian footprints in cretaceous
limestone from Dorset; geological models of Arran &
Glasgow area). Fine Art (16th-20th cent European painting,
drawing & sculpture; 15th-20th cent European & American
prints; paintings, drawings, pastels & prints by James McNeill
Whistler; furniture & drawings by Charles Rennie Mackintosh;
15th-17th cent Italian prints; history of print making).
Zoology (zoological displays mainly intended for undergraduate teaching; considerable collns of insect material
available for research). Anatomy, not open to public (William
Hunter anatomical collns; teaching displays).   **12** (a) 6
(b) 11.

MUSEUM OF TRANSPORT, 25 Albert Dr, Glasgow, G41 2PE
(Tel 041-423 8000).   **4** City of Glasgow DC.   **5** Keeper:
A. S. E. Browning CENg, MRINA, MIES; Dir: T. A. Walden
CBE, MSc, FMA.   **6** Civic Amenities.   **7** Museums & Art
Galleries.   **8** Open to the public.   **9** Mon-Sat 10.00-17.00,
Sun 14.00-17.00. Closed Dec 25 & Jan 1. Free.
10 Scottish & other cars; commercial vehicles: rollers, fire
engines, traction engine trams, buses, trolley bus; bicycles &
motor cycles; horse drawn vehicles; locomotives & other
railway exhibits.   **11** Glasgow tramcars of all ages, comprehensive colln of Scottish-built cars, oldest extant pedal
cycle in world, locomotives built in Scotland for Scottish
railway companies.   **12** (a) 2 (b) 5 (c) 20.

PEOPLE'S PALACE MUSEUM, Glasgow Green, Glasgow,
G40 1AT (Tel 041-554 0223).   **4** City of Glasgow DC.
5 Asst Keeper, Local History: Ms Elspeth King MA,
FSA(Scot).   **6** Civic Amenities.   **7** Glasgow Museums &
Art Galleries, Dir: T. A. Walden CBE, MSc, FMA.   **8** Open
to the public.   **9** Mon-Sat (inc bank hols) 10.00-17.00,
Sun 14.00-17.00. Free.   **10** Glasgow history (from
earliest times to present); mediaeval sculpture; early guilds;
the tobacco trade; textile, ceramic & glass industry; trade
union & suffragette colln.   **12** (a) 1 (b) 1 (c) 1.

POLLOK HOUSE, 2060 Pollokshaws Rd, Glasgow, G43 1AT
(Tel 041-632 0274).   **4** City of Glasgow DC.   **5** Keeper
of Decorative Arts: Mr Brian J. R. Blench MA, FRGS,
FSA(Scot).   **6** Museums & Art Galleries.   **7** Dir: Mr
T. A. Walden CBE, MSc, FMA.   **8** Open to the public.
9 Mon-Sat 10.00-17.00 (summer 21.00). Closed Dec 25 &
Jan 1. Free.   **10** 18th cent house suitably furnished;
British & European decorative art material of 18th & early
19th cent; Stirling Maxwell colln of paintings; Spanish Glass.
11 Restaurant.   **12** (c) 5.

REGIMENTAL HEADQUARTERS AND MUSEUM, 518
Sauchiehall St, Glasgow, G2 3LT (Tel 041-332 5634).
4 Regimental Council.   **5** Officer-in-Charge: Capt (Retd)
A. J. Wilson.   **8** Open to the public.   **9** Mon-Fri 9.00-
17.00. Free.   **10** Regimental relics of Royal Scots
Fusiliers, Highland Light Infantry & Royal Highland
Fusiliers.   **12** (b) 1 (c) 1.

THIRD EYE CENTRE, 350 Sauchiehall St, Glasgow G2 3JD
(Tel 041-332 7521).   **4** Board of Management.   **5** Dir:
Mr Tom McGrath; Administrator: Mr Andrew Porter.
8 Open to the public.   **9** Tues-Sat 11.00-23.00, Sun 14.00-

CODE: 1 Name of Museum, Art Gallery or Stately Home. 2 Address. 3 Telephone & telex. 4 Governing body. 5 Officer in charge. 6 Committee responsible. 7 Larger department, chief officer. 8 Open to public. 9 Hours; admission charges. 10 Scope. 11 Special exhibits or facilities. 12 Staff (a) professionally qualified (b) other non-manual (c) manual.

GLASGOW—*continued*

19.00 (sometimes close earlier). Free. 10 Visual arts centre. 11 Plays; concerts; events; café; bar. 12 (b) 8.

UNIVERSITY OF STRATHCLYDE, Collins Exhibition Hall, Richmond St, Glasgow, G1 1XQ (Tel 041-552 4400 ext 2197). 5 Officer-in-Charge: Mr Martin Warren BSc. 8 Open to the public. 9 Mon-Sat (during exhibitions) 10.00-17.00. Closed Aug. Free. 10 Temporary exhibitions (mainly arts, & history of Strathclyde region). 12 (a) 1 (c) 1.

GLASTONBURY, Somerset

GLASTONBURY ANTIQUARIAN SOCIETY MUSEUM, The Tribunal, High St, Glastonbury, BA6 9DP (Tel 0458-32949). 4 Glastonbury Antiquarian Society. 8 Open to the public. 9 Daily (inc bank hols): 9.30-17.00 (March, April & Oct 17.30) (Nov-Feb 16.00), Sun: opens 14.00 closes as weekday. Adults 5p, OAP's & children 2½p. 10 Local antiquities (inc finds from the Iron Age lake village). 12 (a) Served by Somerset County Museum; (c) 1.

GLENCOE, Argyll

GLENCOE AND NORTH LORN FOLK MUSEUM, Ballaculish, Glencoe. 4 Local committee. 5 President: Mrs Eley Appin; Sec: Miss Fairweather, Invercoe House, Glencoe (Tel 08552 332). 8 Open to the public. 9 Mon-Sat (inc bank hols) 10.00-17.30 or after. Adults 10p, children 5p. 10 Domestic bygones; costume; agricultural tools; Jacobite & other historic items; guns, swords, etc; old photographs; wild flower studies; some natural history. 11 Local slate quarry (now closed).

GLENLUCE, Wigtownshire

GLENLUCE ABBEY, Glenluce, Newton Stewart. 4 Dept of Environment. 5 Information Officer, Argyle House, 3 Lady Lawson St, Edinburgh. 8 Open to the public. 9 Mon-Sat 9.00-19.00, Sun 14.00-19.00. Oct-March: closes 16.00 daily. Adults 5p, children 2½p. 10 Cistercian house (founded 1192 by Roland, Earl of Galloway) now in a ruinous state. 11 Vaulted chapter house, interesting tombstones.

GLOUCESTER, Gloucestershire

BISHOP HOOPER'S LODGING, 99/103 Westgate St, Gloucester GL1 2PG (Tel 0452-24131). 4 Gloucester Corporation. 5 Curator: J. F. Rhodes, MA, AMA. 6 Leisure. 7 Museums Dept. 8 Open to the public. 9 Mon-Sat 10.00-17.30. Closed Dec 25, 26 & Good Friday. Free. 10 Gloucestershire folk life; history of Gloucestershire Regiment. 11 Regimental medals & silver. 12 (a) 1 (c) 5.

CITY MUSEUM AND ART GALLERY, Brunswick Rd, Gloucester, GL1 1HP (Tel 0452-24131). 4 Gloucester Corporation. 5 Curator: J. F. Rhodes. MA, AMA. 6 Leisure. 7 Museums Dept. 8 Open to the public. 9 Mon-Sat 10.00-17.30. Closed Dec 25, 26 & Good Friday. Free. 10 Archaeology; natural history; numismatics; furniture; glass; silver; ceramics; temporary art exhibitions. 11 Local Roman finds; silver pennies from Gloucester & Gloucestershire mints (Anglo-Saxon & Norman); English barometers. 12 (a) 4 (b) 4 (c) 8.

GODALMING, Surrey

GODALMING MUSEUM, Old Town Hall, High St, Godalming; correspondence to: 38 West St, Farnham GU9 7DX. 4 Waverley DC. 5 Officer-in-Charge: Mr H. G. A. Booth ATD, AMA. 7 Dept of Leisure & Culture, Mr John Birch.

8 Open to the public. 9 Tues, Fri & Sat 15.00-17.00. Free. 10 Local history. 11 Local Romano-British & wool trade exhibits. 12 (c) 1.

GOLSPIE, Sutherland

DUNROBIN CASTLE MUSEUM, Dunrobin Castle, Golspie, KW10 6SF (Tel 04083-377). 4 Dunrobin Castle Ltd. 5 Custodian: P. G. Banks. 8 Open to the public. 9 May-Sept: Mon-Fri (inc bank hols) 11.00-12.30, 13.15-18.00, Sun 13.00-18.00. Adults 5p, children free. 10 Castle (1275); world wide colln of trophies; local antiquities & archaeological remains; fine paintings; period furniture; family silver; formal gardens being restored. 11 Car park; tea room; gift shop. 12 (b) 11 (c) 1.

GOMERSAL, West Yorkshire

RED HOUSE MUSEUM, Oxford Rd, Gomersal. c/o Libraries Museums & Art Galleries Headquarters, Princess Alexandra Walk, Huddersfield, HD1 2SU (Tel 0484-21356; Telex 517463). 4 Kirklees MBC. 5 Chief Curator & Libn: Mr Stanley T. Dibnab FLA, AMBIM; Asst Curator: Mr Derek Copley AMISM. 6 Education. 7 Dir of Educational Services: Mr Ernest T. Butcher MA. 8 Open to the public. 9 Tues-Fri (inc bank hols) 10.00-18.00, Sat 10.00-17.00, Sun 10.00-17.00. Free. 10 1820 house mentioned by Charlotte Brontë in 'Shirley'. 12 (a) Served from Huddersfield Art Gallery.

GOOLE, North Humberside

GOOLE MUSEUM AND ART GALLERY, Carlisle St, Goole, DN14 5AA (Tel 0405-3784). 4 Humberside CC. 5 Area Libn: Mrs M. E. Miles. 7 Humberside Leisure Services, Dir: Mr R. G. Roberts DMS, FLA, AIMEnt. 8 Open to the public. 9 Mon-Fri 9.30-19.00, Sat 9.30-17.00. Free. 10 Reuben Chappell paintings & Garside colln.

GORDON, Berwickshire

MELLERSTAIN, Gordon TD3 6LG (Tel 057381-225). 4 Owner: Lord Binning. 5 Curator: Ms Marion Naismith. 8 Open to the public. 9 May-Sept: Sun-Fri 14.00-17.30. Charges: 35p (subject to revision). 10 Mansion by William & Robert Adam (1725-65); interiors by Robert Adam; magnificent ceilings; old master paintings; antique furniture; library; gardens.

GOSPORT, Hampshire

SUBMARINE MUSEUM, HMS Dolphin, Gosport, PO12 2AB (Tel 0705-22351 ext 41250). 4 Trustees of the Submarine Museum. 5 Curator: Commander P. R. Compton-Hall MBE, RN (Retd). 8 Open only on application 14 days beforehand to the Visits Officer HMS Dolphin, Gosport, (Tel: 22351 ext 41868). 9 Free. 10 Submarine history, development & achievement from earliest times to the present. 11 A post WWII Submarine, HMS Alliance, is open to viewing close to the museum. 12 (a) 1 (b) 2 (c) 1.

GRANGEMOUTH, Stirlingshire

GRANGEMOUTH MUSEUM, Grangemouth Public Library, Bo'ness Rd, Grangemouth (Tel 03244-3291). 4 Falkirk DC. 6 Leisure & Recreation. 7 Falkirk District Libraries, District Chief Libn: Mr Alex H. Howson, ALA. 8 Open to the public. 9 Mon, Tues & Thurs 9.30-20.00, Wed, Fri & Sun 9.30-17.00. Free. 10 Local history.

GRANTHAM, Lincolnshire

BELTON HOUSE, Belton, Grantham, NG32 2LS (Tel 0476-66116). 5 House Superintendent: Mr P. W. Elmer.

GRANTHAM, Lincolnshire—*continued*

8 Open to the public. 9 Tues, Wed, Thurs, Sat & bank hols 12.00-18.00. Adults 40p, children 20p. Gardens only: adults 25p, children 15p. 10 House built 1685 (Sir Christopher Wren?); 600 acre park. 11 Duke of Windsor souvenirs; fine furniture; silver; porcelain; carvings by Grinling Gibbons; Aubusson carpets; Gobelin tapestries; paintings (inc family portraits from Joshua Reynolds to Frank Salisbury & a da Vinci 'Mona Lisa'). 12 (b) 5.

BELVOIR CASTLE, Estate Office, Belvoir Castle, Grantham, NG32 1PD (Tel 047682-262). 5 Controller to the Duke of Rutland: Mr A.R. Meek. 8 Open to the public. 9 Wed, Thurs, Sat & bank hol Tues 12.00-18.00, bank hol Mon 11.00-19.00, Sun 14.00-19.00 (Oct 18.00). Adults 50p, children 25p, party rates. 10 Castle overlooking Vale of Belvoir; works of art; historical objects. 11 Military museum of the 17th/21st Lancers.

GRANTHAM MUSEUM, St Peter's Hill, Grantham; correspondence to: Director, Lincolnshire Museums, Old Barracks, Burton Rd, Lincoln. 4 Lincolnshire CC. 6 Museums Sub-Committee. 7 Lincolnshire Museums, Dir: Mr Antony Gunstone BA, FSA, FMA. 8 Open to the public. 9 Mon-Sat 10.00-17.00. Free. 10 History of Grantham & district. 11 Important colln of local prehistoric material & of relics associated with Sir Isaac Newton.

GRAYS, Essex

THURROCK LOCAL HISTORY MUSEUM, Central Library, Orsett Rd, Grays, RM17 5DX (Tel 0375-76827). 4 Thurrock BC. 5 Curator: Mr D.A. Wickham FLA. 6 Recreations. 8 Open to the public. 9 Mon-Sat 10.00-20.00. Free. 10 Archaeology; social, craft & agricultural development of Thurrock. 11 School & club parties; outside lectures to organisations; services to educational courses; excavations. 12 (a) 1 (b) 2.

GREAT YARMOUTH, Norfolk

ELIZABETHAN HOUSE MUSEUM, 4 South Quay, Great Yarmouth NR30 2QH (Tel 0493-55746). 4 Norfolk CC. 5 Curator: Mr C.H. Lewis MA, AMA. 7 Norfolk Museums Service, Dir: Mr F.W. Cheetham BA, FMA. 8 Open to the public. 9 Mon-Fri (inc bank hols) & Sun (June-Sept only) 10.00-13.00, 14.00-17.30. Free. 10 Merchants house (c.1596); furnished rooms; domestic life. 12 (a) 2 shared by all Gt Yarmouth museums (c) 1.

EXHIBITION GALLERIES, Central Library, Tolhouse St, Great Yarmouth NR30 2SH (Tel 0493-4551/2279). 4 Norfolk CC. 5 Curator: C.H. Lewis MA, AMA. 7 Norfolk Museums Service, Dir: F.W. Cheetham BA, FMA. 8 Open to the public. 9 Mon-Sat (inc bank hols) 9.00-18.00. Free. 12 (a) 2 shared by all Gt Yarmouth museums.

'LYDIA EVA', STEAM DRIFTER, mored near Town Hall, South Quay, Great Yarmouth. 4 Norfolk CC (owned by Maritime Trust). 5 Curator: C.H. Lewis MA, AMA. 7 Norfolk Museums Service, Dir: F.W. Cheetham BA, FMA. 8 Open to the public. 9 June-Sept: Sun-Fri (inc bank hols) 10.00-13.00, 14.00-18.00. Adults 10p, children 5p. 10 The last steam berring drifter (built 1930); fisheries. 12 (a) 2 shared by Gt Yarmouth museums.

MARITIME MUSEUM FOR EAST ANGLIA, Marine Parade, Great Yarmouth (Tel 0493-2267). 4 Norfolk CC. 5 Curator: C.H. Lewis MA, AMA. 7 Norfolk Museums Service, Dir: F.W. Cheetham BA, FMA. 8 Open to the public. 9 June-Sept: daily (inc bank hols) 10.00-13.00, 14.00-20.00; Oct-May: Mon-Fri (inc bank hols) 10.00-13.00, 14.00-17.30. Adults 15p, OAPs & accompanied children free, unaccompanied children 5p. 10 Maritime history; fisheries (especially herring); lifesaving; ship models; the Norfolk wherry etc. 12 (a) 2 shared by all Gt Yarmouth museums. (c) 1.

TOLHOUSE MUSEUM, Tolhouse St, Great Yarmouth (Tel 0493-58900). 4 Norfolk CC. 5 Curator: C.H. Lewis MA, AMA. 7 Norfolk Museums Service, Dir:

F.W. Cheetham BA, FMA. 8 Open to the public. 9 Mon-Fri (inc bank hols) & Sun (June-Sept only) 10.00-13.00, 14.00-17.30. Free. 10 Mediaeval building with dungeons; local history. 12 (a) 2 shared by all Gt Yarmouth museums (c) 1.

GREENOCK, Renfrewshire

McLEAN MUSEUM AND GREENOCK ART GALLERY, 9 Union St, Greenock PA16 8JH (Tel 0475-23741). 4 McLean Museum Trust. 5 Hon Sec & Treasurer: Mr J. Cairns Christie VRD, AIB(Scot). 8 Open to the public. 9 Mon-Sat (inc bank hols) 10.00-12.30, 14.00-17.00 (16.30 in winter). Free. 10 Shipping; rocks; animals; birds; natural history; large art gallery. 11 Caird art colln. 12 (b) 3.

GRESSENHALL, Norfolk

NORFOLK RURAL LIFE MUSEUM, (not yet open), Beech House, Gressenhall, Dereham (Tel 036286-563). 4 Norfolk CC. 5 Curator: Miss Bridget Yates MA, AMA. 6 Museums. 7 Norfolk Museums Service, Dir: Mr Francis W. Cheetham, BA, FMA. 9 Not yet open. 10 Agricultural implements & items relating to the history of agriculture in Norfolk; Norfolk rural crafts tools & finished products.

GRIMSBY, South Humberside

DOUGHTY MUSEUM, Town Hall Sq, Grimsby, DN31 1HG (Tel 0472-59161). 4 Grimsby BC. 5 Dir of Administration: R.J.B. Morris MA, LLM. 6 Services & Amenities. 8 Open to the public. 9 Tues-Sat 10.00-12.30, 14.00-17.30. Free. 10 Ship models; china etc. 12 (c) 1.

GUILDFORD, Surrey

CLANDON PARK, Guildford (Tel 048636-432). 4 National Trust. 5 Administrator: Mr A.H. Parnell. 8 Open to the public. 9 April-mid Oct: Tues-Thurs, Sat, Sun & bank hol Mon 14.00-17.30. Free to National Trust members. 10 House, built c.1735 by Giacomo Leoni for the 2nd Lord Onslow, contains very fine plaster decoration. 11 Colln of furniture, needlework & china bequeathed by Mrs Hannah Gubbay.

GUILDFORD HOUSE GALLERY, 155 High St, Guildford GU1 3AJ (Tel 0483-32133). 4 Guildford BC. 5 Exhibitions Officer: Miss I.C. Rhodes AMA. 6 Arts & Recreation. 7 Leisure & Recreation Dept, Dir: J. Fairclough FInst PRA(Dip), DHE. 8 Open to the public. 9 Mon-Sat 10.30-17.00. Free. 10 17th cent building; varied programme of temporary exhibitions; small permanent colln. 11 Picture loan service; open for evening meetings as an arts centre; Friends of Guildford House (monthly winter meetings, visits to other galleries, opera, ballet, theatre etc). 12 (a) 1 (b) 7 (c) 3.

GUILDFORD MUSEUM, Castle Arch, Guildford, GU1 3SX (Tel 0483-66551). 4 Guildford BC. 5 Curator: Mr Felix Holling BA, AMA, FSA. 6 Arts & Recreation. 7 Leisure & Recreation Dept, Leisure & Recreation Officer: Mr John Fairclough FInstPRA(Dip), DHE. 8 Open to the public. 9 Mon-Sat 11.00-17.00, Closed Dec 25, 26 & Good Friday. Free. 10 Local history & archaeology; needlework. 11 Lewis Carroll items; Wealden ironwork. 12 (a) 3 (b) 2.

LOSELEY HOUSE, Loseley Park, Guildford, GU3 1HS (Tel 0483-66090). 5 Owner: J.R. More-Molyneux. 8 Open to the public. 9 Wed-Sat (& Spring & Summer bank hols) 14.00-17.00. Adults 35p, children 20p; party rates. 10 Elizabethan house (1562); panelling from Henry VIII's Nonsuch Palace; period furniture; paintings; magnificent ceilings & chimney pieces. 11 House shop & farm shop. 12 (b) 3.

WOMENS ROYAL ARMY CORPS REGIMENTAL MUSEUM, WRAC Centre, Queen Elizabeth Park, Guildford, GU2 6QH (Tel 0483-71201 ext 383). 4 MoD. 5 Curator: Major P.R. Wyndham Tate WRAC (Retd). 8 Open to the public. 9 Mon-Fri 9.00-16.00. Free. 10 Military uniforms of

CODE: 1 Name of Museum, Art Gallery or Stately Home. 2 Address 3 Telephone & telex. 4 Governing body. 5 Officer in charge. 6 Committee responsible. 7 Larger department, chief officer. 8 Open to public. 9 Hours; admission charges. 10 Scope. 11 Special exhibits or facilities. 12 Staff (a) professionally qualified (b) other non-manual (c) manual.

GUILDFORD, Surrey—*continued*

QMAAC, ATS & WRAC; medals; photographs; models; military insignia.

HAILES, Gloucestershire

HAILES ABBEY SITE MUSEUM, Hailes Abbey, Winchcombe (Tel 0242-602398). 4 Dept of Environment, for the National Trust. 5 Custodian: E. N. Greenhalf. 8 Open to the public. 9 Mon-Sat (inc bank hols) May-Sept 9.30-19.00, Mch, April & Oct 9.30-17.30, Nov-Feb 9.30-16.00; Sun opens 14.00, closes as weekday. Adults 5p, children & OAP's 2½p, free to members of The National Trust. 10 Cistercian Abbey of Hailes. 12 (b) 2.

HAILSHAM, Sussex

MICHELHAM PRIORY, Upper Dicker, Hailsham, BN27 3QS (Tel 03216-224). 4 Sussex Archaeological Trust. 5 Sec & Curator: G. W. R. Harrison RN(retd). 8 Open to the public. 9 Easter-mid Oct: daily (inc bank hols) 11.00-17.30. Grounds & house: adults 30p, children 5p; grounds only: ½ price. 10 13th cent monastic buildings; 16th cent Tudor buildings & great barn; 14th cent gatehouse & moat (7 acres); extensive gardens; 15th-17th cent furniture; tapestries; ironwork; stained glass; brass rubbings; samplers; seals. 11 Musical instruments (folk, 17-20th cent); doll's house; forge & wheelwright's museum; wagons & ploughs; crafts shop; picture gallery. 12 (b) 1 (c) 3.

HALESWORTH, Suffolk

HEVENINGHAM HALL, Halesworth IP19 0EA (Tel 098683-355). 4 Dept of Environment, administered by National Trust. 5 Curator: C. E. Sheppard. 8 Open to the public. 9 April-Oct: Weds, Thurs, Sat, Sun & bank hols 14.00-17.30. Adults 30p, children 15p. 10 18th cent mansion in Palladian style by Sir Robert Taylor; interior decoration in neo-classical style by James Wyatt with detailed decoration painted by Biagio Robecca. 11 Furniture designed by Wyatt; plans of the park by Capability Brown on view, also some designs (rejected) by Wyatt; orangery designed by Wyatt; stable yard designed by Brown. 12 (b) 1 (c) 6.

HALIFAX, West Yorkshire

BANKFIELD MUSEUM, Ackroyd Park, Haley Hill, Halifax, HX3 6HG (Tel 0422-54823). 4 Calderdale MBC. 5 Museums Dir: Mr R. A. Innes. 6 Recreation & Amenities. 8 Open to the public. 9 Mon-Sat 11.00-19.00 (Oct-March 17.00), Sun 14.30-17.00. Free. 10 Textiles; textile machinery; costume. 11 Duke of Wellington's Regimental Museum; 4th/7th Royal Dragoon Guards Regimental Museum. 12 Served from Clay House, Greetland, Halifax.

SHIBDEN HALL FOLK MUSEUM, Shibden Hall, Halifax, HX3 6XG (Tel 0422-52246). 4 Calderdale MBC. 5 Museum Dir: Mr R. A. Innes. 6 Recreation & Amenities. 9 Mon-Sat 11.00-19.00 (Oct-March 17.00), Sun 14.30-17.00. Adults 8p, children 4p. 10 15th cent house; 17th & 18th cent furnishings; barns & outbuildings with vehicles, farm implements, & craft workshops. 12 Served from Clay House, Greetland, Halifax.

HAMILTON, Lanarkshire

HAMILTON DISTRICT MUSEUM, 129 Muir St, Hamilton, ML3 6BJ (Tel 06984-24230). 4 Hamilton DC. 5 Curator: Mr Gavin Walker. 6 Leisure & Recreation. 7 Libraries & Museum Dept. 8 Open to the public. 9 Mon-Fri (exc Wed) 10.00-12.00, 13.00-15.00, Sat 10.00-17.00, Sun & bank hols 14.00-17.00. Free. 10 Coaching inn (1696); local history; transport; costume; weaving; natural history; industrial archaeology; period kitchen; municipal history; mining; Sir Harry Lauder colln. 12 (a) 3 (b) 2 (c) 1.

HAREWOOD, West Yorkshire

HAREWOOD HOUSE, Harewood, Leeds, LS17 9LQ (Tel 097336-225). 4 Owner: Earl of Harewood. 5 House Opening Manager: Mr David P. S. Wrench. 8 Open to the public. 9 April-mid Oct: daily. Adults 35p, children 20p. 10 House built by Carr of York & Robert Adam in 1759, enlarged by Charles Barry in 1843; Chippendale furniture; Sèvres & Chinese porcelain; Italian paintings. 12 (b) 2 (c) 2.

HARLOW, Essex

HARLOW MUSEUM, Third Ave, Harlow, CM18 6YL (Tel 0279-34431). 4 Harlow DC. 5 Museum Officer: Ms Katharine Davison BA. 6 Museum Executive. 7 Leisure Services Dept, Mr Alan Jackson FInstPRA(Dip), MInstrum. 8 Open to the public. 9 Fri-Mon & Wed (inc bank hols) 10.00-18.00 (winter 17.00), Tues & Thurs 10.00-21.00. Closed Dec 25 & 26. Free. 10 Local archaeology, history, folk life & natural history; general & local geology. 11 Lecture room, seats 60; library; education service; butterfly garden; continuing changing displays. 12 (a) 3 (b) 1 (c) 3.

HARROGATE, North Yorkshire

HARROGATE ART GALLERY, Public Library, Victoria Ave, Harrogate. Museum Service, c/o Council Offices, Harrogate, HG1 2SG (Tel 0423-3340). 4 Harrogate DC. 5 Museums Curator: K. W. Brown FGS. 6 Recreation & Amenities. 7 Dept of Administration, Chief Executive: J. Neville Knox, Solicitor. 8 Open to the public. 9 Mon-Fri 9.30-19.00, Sat 9.30-17.00, Sun 14.00-17.00. Closed between exhibitions. Free. 10 English oils, watercolours, drawings, (mainly 19th-20th cent). 11 Temporary exhibitions (local & national). 12 (a) 1 (c) ½.

ROYAL PUMP ROOM MUSEUM, Royal Parade, Harrogate. Museum Service, c/o Council Offices, Harrogate, HG1 2SG (Tel 0423-3340). 4 Harrogate DC. 5 Museums Curator: K. W. Brown FGS. 6 Recreation & Amenities. 7 Dept of Administration, Chief Executive: J. Neville Knox, Solicitor. 8 Open to the public. 9 Mon-Sat 11.00-19.00 (17.00 Oct-March), Sun 14.00-17.00. Closed February, Dec 25, 26 & Jan 1. Free. 10 Local history; archaeology; bygones; ceramics; costume. 11 Sulphur well. 12 (a) 1 (b) ½ (c) 2.

HARTLEPOOL, Cleveland

GRAY ART GALLERY & MUSEUM, Clarence Rd, Hartlepool, TS24 8BT (Tel 0429-68916). 4 Hartlepool BC. 5 Curator: Mr H. S. Middleton, BSc, AMA. 6 Museums & Libraries. 7 Leisure & Amenities Dept; Dir: Mr J. B. A. Sharples AIMEnt, MHCIMA, MInstRM. 8 Open to the public. 9 Mon-Sat 10.00-17.30, Sun 15.00-17.00. Closed Dec 25, 26, Jan 1 & Good Friday. Free. 10 19th & 20th cent oil paintings & watercolours; local artists & topography; local archaeology & history; natural history; applied art; Oriental ceramics & idols; Japanese netsukes. 11 Temporary exhibitions; reconstructed local blacksmith's shop. 12 (a) 4 (b) 2 (c) 5.

MARITIME MUSEUM, Northgate, Hartlepool (Tel 0429-72814). Hartlepool BC. 5 Curator: Mr H. S. Middleton BSc, AMA. 6 Museums & Libraries. 7 Leisure & Amenities Dept, Dir: Mr J. B. A. Sharples AIMEnt, MHCIMA, MInstRM. 8 Open to the public. 9 Mon-Sat (inc bank hols) 10.00-17.00. Closed Dec 25, 26 & Jan 1 & Good Friday. Free.

HARTLEPOOL, Cleveland—*continued*

10 Local maritime history; ship models; reconstructed fisherman's cottage & ship's bridge; lantern of one of first gas lit lighthouse in Britain.

HASTINGS, East Sussex

MUSEUM AND ART GALLERY, Cambridge Rd, Hastings, TN34 1ET (Tel 0424-435952). **4** Hastings BC. **5** Curator: Mr David C. Devenish BA, AMA. **6** Museum Advisory. **7** Tourism & Recreation Dept; Tourism & Recreation Officer: Mr John Taylor NDH, FInstPRADip, DARB, RFS. **8** Open to the public. **9** Mon-Sat 10.00-13.00, 14.00-17.00, Sun 15.00-17.00. Closed Dec 24-26 & Good Friday. Free. **10** Local geology; zoology; archaeology & history; Wealden pottery & ironwork; British, European & Oriental ceramics; pictures, local & general; Oriental & primitive art (especially oceanic); Durbar Hall (Indian Palace). **11** Temporary exhibitions. **12** (a) 2 (b) 1 (c) 2.

MUSEUM OF LOCAL HISTORY, Old Town Hall, High St, Hastings TN34 3ET (Tel 0424-425855). **4** Hastings BC. **5** Curator: Mr David C. Devenish BA, AMA. **6** Museum Advisory. **7** Tourism & Recreation, Officer: Mr John Taylor NDH, FInstPRADip, DARB, RFS. **8** Open to the public. **9** Easter-Oct: Mon-Sat (inc bank hols) 10.00-12.30, 14.30-17.30. Free. **10** Local archaeology & history especially maritime & Cinque Ports. **12** (a) 2 (b) 1 (c) 1.

HATFIELD, Hertfordshire

HATFIELD HOUSE, Hatfield, AL9 5NF (Tel 07072-62823/65159). **4** The Marquess of Salisbury. **5** Curator & Administrator: Mrs Margaret Guilliland. **8** Open to the public. **9** March 25-Oct 7: Tues-Sat 12.00-17.00, Sun 14.00-17.00, bank hol Mon 11.00-17.00. Closed Good Friday. Adults 70p, children 30p. **10** Jacobean house built (1607-1611) by Robert Cecil, 1st Earl of Salisbury; family home of the Cecils ever since; staterooms; paintings; fine furniture; rare tapestries; historic armour; original stained glass in chapel; surviving wing of the Royal Palace of Hatfield (1497) where Elizabeth 1 spent much of her girlhood & held her first Council of State in November 1558, with William Cecil, Lord Burghley, as her Chief Minister. **11** Special exhibits. Restaurant & cafeteria; Elizabethan banquets in Old Palace (Tues, Fri & Sat).

HAWICK, Roxburghshire

HAWICK MUSEUM & ART GALLERY, Wilton Lodge Park, Hawick, TD9 7JL (Tel 0450-3457). **4** Roxburgh DC. **6** Technical Services. **7** Leisure & Recreation Dept, Dir: Mr Herbison Boyd. **8** Open to the public. **9** Mon-Sat (inc bank hols) 10.00-17.00 (Nov-Mch 16.00); Sun (April-Oct) 14.00-17.00. Adults 4p, children 2p. **10** Scottish border way of life; natural history; geology; coins; war medals; communion tokens; maps & mss. **11** Knitwear & machinery. **12** (b) 2.

HAWORTH, West Yorkshire

BRONTË PARSONAGE MUSEUM, Church St, Haworth, Keighley, BD22 8DR (Tel 0535-42323). **4** Brontë Society. **5** Custodian: Mr Norman Raistrick. **8** Open to the public. **9** Mon-Sat (inc bank hols) 11.00-17.30 (Oct-Mch 16.30), Sun 14.00-17.30 (Oct-Mch 16.30). Adults 15p, children 5p. **10** Brontëana. **12** (a) ½ (b) 2 (c) 1½.

HELSTON, Cornwall

HELSTON MUSEUM, Old Butter Market, Church St, Helston, TR13 8ST. **4** Kerrier DC. **5** Hon Curator: Mr G. A. Banks. **6** Amenities. **8** Open to the public. **9** Mon-Sat 10.30-12.30, 14.00-16.30. Free. **10** Local folk life. **11** Old farm implements; horse-drawn cider press; Henry Trengrouse's life-saving apparatus (invented locally); Cornish kitchen; horse-drawn fire engines; Marconi exhibits re 1st wireless message sent to US; military uniforms; minerals. **12** (b) 1 (c) 1.

HENLEY-ON-THAMES, Oxfordshire

GREY'S COURT, Rotherfield Greys, Henley-on-Thames. **4** National Trust. **8** Open to the public. **9** April-Sept: Mon, Wed & Fri 14.15-18.00; grounds & Carlisle colln only: Mon-Sat 14.15-18.00. House & garden 40p. Garden only: adults 30p, children 15p. Carlisle colln: adults 15p, children 7½p. **10** 17th cent house amid ruins of 13th cent manor, fortified in 14th cent (keep & towers); fine plasterwork. **11** Carlisle colln of miniature houses.

HEPTONSTALL, West Yorkshire

GRAMMAR SCHOOL MUSEUM, Hebden Bridge, Heptonstall (Tel 042284-3738). **4** Calderdale MBC **5** Museums Dir: Mr R. A. Innes. **6** Recreation & Amenities. **8** Open to the public. **9** Mon-Sat 11.00-19.00 (Oct-March 17.00), Sun 14.30-17.00. Free. **10** Folk life. **12** (c) Served from Clay House, Greetland, Halifax.

HEREFORD, Hereford & Worcester

CHURCHILL GARDENS MUSEUM, Venns Lane, Hereford (Tel 0432-67409). **4** Hereford DC. **5** Curator: N. R. Dove BSc, AMA. **6** Leisure & Recreation. **7** Hereford City Museums. **8** Open to the public. **9** Daily (inc summer bank hols) 14.00-17.00. Free. **10** Costume 1700-1950s (expanding); furniture 18th-19th cent; paintings (local oils & water colours); Brian Hatton Art Gallery—colln of work of local artist; pottery; porcelain. **11** School service; sessions by arrangement; public print loan service. **12** (a) 2 (b) 4.

HEREFORD CITY MUSEUMS AND ART GALLERY, Broad St, Hereford, HR4 9AU (Tel 0432-2456/56081). **4** Hereford DC. **5** Curator: N. R. Dove BSc, AMA. **6** Leisure & Recreation. **8** Open to the public. **9** Mon-Wed & Fri (inc summer bank hols) 10.00-18.00, Thurs & Sat 10.00-17.00. Free. **10** Local geology & archaeology; natural history; folk life; fine & applied arts. **11** School parties by arrangement; school loans service; inquiries service. **12** (a) 2 (b) 4.

THE OLD HOUSE, High Town, Hereford, HR1 2AA. **4** Hereford DC. **5** Curator: N. R. Dove BSc, AMA. **6** Leisure & Recreation. **7** Hereford City Museums. **8** Open to the public. **9** Summer: Mon-Sat (inc bank hols) 10.00-13.00, 14.00-17.30, Sun 14.00-17.30; Winter: Mon-Sat 14.00-17.30. Adults 6p, children 2p. **10** 17th cent furniture & fittings. **11** Schools service, sessions by arrangement. **12** (a) 2 (b) 4.

HERNE BAY, Kent

HERNE BAY MUSEUM, Herne Bay Library, 124 High St, Herne Bay, CT6 5JY (Tel 02273-4896). **4** Kent CC. **5** Kent County Museums Officer: Miss L. Millard. **6** Education (Libraries & Museum Sub-Committee). **7** Kent County Library, Dean Harrison MA, FLA. **8** Open to the public. **9** Mon-Fri 9.30-19.00 (Wed 13.00), Sat 9.30-17.00. Free. **10** Local history & natural history; stone, bronze & early iron age specimens; Roman material from Reculver. **11** J. Gilchrist Wilson colln of stone age material.

HERTFORD, Hertfordshire

HERTFORD MUSEUM, 18 Bull Plain, Hertford, SG14 1DT. **4** Hertford Town Council. **5** Curator: A. G. Davies, BA, AMA. **6** Museum. **8** Open to the public. **9** Mon-Sat (inc Easter, spring & bank hols) 10.00-17.00. Free. **10** Local (ie East Herts) history. **11** Reference library. **12** (a) 2 (b) ½ (c) 2.

HIGHER BOCKHAMPTON, Dorset

HARDY'S COTTAGE, Higher Bockhampton, Dorchester, DT2 8QJ (Tel 0305-2366). **4** National Trust. **5** Tenant of Cottage: Mrs A. D. Winchcombe MA. **8** Open to the public. **9** Interior: by appointment with tenant; exterior: March-Oct: daily 11.00-18.00. Interior 20p; garden free. **10** Thatched cottage, birthplace of Thomas Hardy, his home

CODE: 1 Name of Museum, Art Gallery or Stately Home. **2** Address **3** Telephone & telex. **4** Governing body. **5** Officer in charge. **6** Committee responsible. **7** Larger department, chief officer. **8** Open to public. **9** Hours; admission charges. **10** Scope. **11** Special exhibits or facilities. **12** Staff (a) professionally qualified (b) other non-manual (c) manual.

HIGHER BOCKHAMPTON, Dorset—*continued*

for 34 years; built by his great grandfather; most rooms can be seen. **11** Two original letters; photos; foreign translations of Hardy's works.

HIGH WYCOMBE, Buckinghamshire

HUGHENDEN MANOR, Hughenden Valley, High Wycombe, HP14 4LA (Tel 0494-28051/32580). **4** National Trust. **5** Custodian: Mr F. McArdell. **8** Open to the public. **9** Feb-Nov: Wed-Fri (& bank hol Mon) 14.00-18.00, Sat & Sun 12.30-18.00. Adults 50p, children 25p. **10** Home of Benjamin Disraeli, Earl of Beaconsfield, (1848-1881); late 18th cent house, much altered by the Disraelis in 1862/3, typical of country gentleman's house of that period. **11** Disraeli furniture, pictures, books & many presents from Queen Victoria. Tea & biscuits; shop. **12** (b) 2.

WYCOMBE CHAIR AND LOCAL HISTORY MUSEUM, Castle Hill House, Priory Ave, High Wycombe, HP13 6PX (Tel 0494-23879). **4** Wycombe DC. **5** Curator: I. G. Sparkes FLA, ARHistS. **7** Technical Services Dept. **8** Open to the public. **9** Mon, Tues, Thurs-Sat 10.00-13.00, 14.00-17.00. Free. **10** Furniture, especially chairmaking & the Windsor Chair; other crafts (eg caning & lacemaking); local history. **11** Reconstructed Bodger's hut & Benchman's workshop. **12** (a) 1 (b) 1.

HITCHIN, Hertfordshire.

HITCHIN MUSEUM & ART GALLERY, Paynes Park, Hitchin, SG5 1EQ (Tel 0462-4476). **4** North Hertfordshire DC. **5** Dir: Miss F. M. Gadd BA, AMA. **6** Recreation & Amenities (Museum & Sub-Committee). **7** Sec: Mr F. W. Hammond. **8** Open to the public. **9** Mon-Sat 10.00-17.00. Free. **10** Local history; R. L. Hine's colln of archives; paintings by Samuel Lucas Sr (1805-1870), & other local artists; costume; natural history; regimental museum of Herts Yeomanry Trust. **11** Temporary exhibitions; schools service for educational visits & loans. **12** (a) 9 (b) 2 (c) 4.

HOLKHAM, Norfolk

HOLKHAM HALL, Holkham, Wells-Next-The-Sea, NR23 1AB (Tel 032871-227). **5** Agent: I. H. Whitworth TD, FRICS. **8** Open to the public. **9** Thurs (June-Sept) & Mon (July-Aug) 11.30-17.00. Adults 40p, OAPs & children 20p. **10** Pictures; tapestries; statuary; furnishings.

HOLLINGBOURNE, Kent.

EYHORNE MANOR, Hollingbourne. **8** Open to the public. **9** May-Aug: Sat, Sun & bank hols 14.30-18.00. Other times by appointment. Charges: 20p. **10** Early 15th cent manor house with 17th cent additions; domestic irons, early laundry equipment & herbs connected with the industry.

HOLYWOOD, Co. Down, Northern Ireland

ULSTER FOLK AND TRANSPORT MUSEUM, Cultra Manor, Holywood, BT18 0EU (Tel 02317-5411). **4** Board of Trustees. **5** Dir: Mr George B. Thompson MSc, FMA. **8** Open to the public. **9** Mon-Sat 11.00-19.00, Sun 14.00-19.00 (May & June: Tues & Weds 11.00-21.00), (Oct-April closes daily 17.00). Closed Dec 24-26. Adults 15p, children & OAPs 5p; pre-arranged group visits half-price. **10** Open-air folk park; dialect, oral tradition, folk music, custom, belief; horse-drawn & motorised vehicles; aviation history, trams; buses; broad & narrow gauge rail vehicles; maritime section. **11** Education service; ref library of local social history, Irish & comparative ethnology, transport history. **12** (a) 19 (b) 17 (c) 86.

HONITON, Devon

HONITON AND ALLHALLOWS MUSEUM, High St, Honiton. **5** Hon Curator: H. J. Yallop OBE, MA, BSc, FRIC. **8** Open to the public. **9** May-Sept: Mon-Sat 10.00-16.00. Charges: 5p. **10** Local history. **11** Honiton lace.

HORSHAM, Sussex

HORSHAM MUSEUM, Causeway House, 9 The Causeway, Horsham, RH12 1HE (Tel 0403 4959). **4** Horsham DC. **6** Leisure & Recreation (Museum Sub-Committee). **7** Dir of Community Services: G. S. Adams MAPHI, FRSH. **8** Open to the public. **9** Tues-Sat 13.00-17.00. Free. **10** 16th cent timbered building, with displays of local & regional interest; Sussex kitchen; blacksmith; saddler; dairy; wheelwright; room of toys; temporary exhibitions. **11** 17th cent dated slipware drug jar. **12** (a) 2.

HOVE, Sussex

HOVE MUSEUM OF ART, 19 New Church Rd, Hove, BN3 4AB (Tel 0273-779410). **4** Hove BC. **5** Curator: Mr John Boyden BA. **6** Recreation & Amenities. **8** Open to the public. **9** Mon-Sat 10.00-17.00. Free. **10** English fine & decorative art (18th & 19th cent); temporary exhibitions. **11** Pocock colln of ceramics. **12** (a) 1 (b) 1 (c) 3.

HUDDERSFIELD, West Yorkshire

ART GALLERY, c/o Libraries, Museums & Art Galleries Headquarters, Princess Alexandra Walk, Huddersfield, HD1 2SU (Tel 0484-21356; Telex 517463). **4** Kirklees MBC. **5** Chief Curator & Libn: Mr Stanley T. Dibnab FLA, AMBIM. **6** Education. **7** Dir of Educational Services: Mr Ernest T. Butcher MA. **8** Open to the public. **9** Mon-Fri 10.00-18.00, Sat 10.00-17.00. Free. **10** Local collns; modern British artists; travelling exhibitions. **11** Schools service; photographic service for research; publications on archaeology & special collns (eg toys). **12** (a) 16 (b) 8 (c) 12.

TOLSON MUSEUM, Ravensknowle Park, Huddersfield. c/o Libraries, Museums & Art Galleries Headquarters, Princess Alexandra Walk, Huddersfield, HD1 2SU (Tel 0484-21356 Telex 517463) **4** Kirklees MBC. **5** Chief Curator & Libn: Mr Stanley T. Dibnab FLA, AMBIM. Curator: E. W. Aubrook FMA. **6** Education, **7** Dir of Educational Services: Mr Ernest T. Butcher MA. **8** Open to the public. **9** Mon-Fri (inc bank hols) 10.00-18.00, Sat 10.00-17.00, Sun 14.00-17.00. Adults 5p, children 2½p. **10** Local history; natural history; toys; glass; aquarium; industry; transport. **12** (a) served from Art Gallery.

HULL, *see* **Kingston-upon-Hull**

HUNTINGDON, Cambridgeshire

CROMWELL MUSEUM, Grammar School Lane, Huntingdon PE18 6LF (Tel 0480-52181). **4** Cambridgeshire CC. **6** Leisure & Amenities. **7** Libraries, County Libn: Mr Royston Brown FLA, AMBIM. **8** Open to the public. **9** Tues-Fri 11.00-13.00, 14.00-17.00, Sat 11.00-13.00, 14.00-16.00, Sun 14.00-16.00. Free. **10** Documents relating to Cromwellian era, inc signed documents by Oliver Cromwell; portraits (inc Oliver Cromwell & his family); personal articles which belonged to Oliver Cromwell.

HUNTLY, Aberdeenshire

ADAMSTON AGRICULTURAL MUSEUM, Adamston, Huntly, AB5 6AL (Tel 046684-231). **5** Owner: Hew McCall-Smith. **8** Open to the public. **9** Daily at reasonable

HUNTLY, Aberdeenshire—*continued*

times. Free but collection taken for Royal Scottish Agricultural Benevolent Institution. **10** Agricultural implements; hand tools; butter & cheesemaking equipment;
horse harness; veterinary instruments; corn dollies; household equipment; grain sowing & threshing equipment; farm
life in N. E. Scotland.

HUTTON LE HOLE, North Yorkshire

RYEDALE FOLK MUSEUM, Hutton Le Hole, York, YO6 6UD
(Tel 07515-367). **4** Crosland Foundation Trustees.
5 Curator: Mr Bertram Frank. **8** Open to the public.
9 April-Oct: daily 14.00-18.00. Holiday seasons & bank
hols 11.00-18.00. Adults 20p, children 10p. **10** Work,
crafts domestic life, pastimes, superstitions & origins of
people of Ryedale. **11** Reconstructed buildings (cottages, manor house) & Elizabethan glass furnace; craft-
shops. **12** (a) 1.

HYTHE, Kent

HYTHE LOCAL HISTORY ROOM, 'Oaklands', Stade St,
Hythe (Tel 0303-66152/3). **4** Hythe Town Council.
5 Town Clerk: G. A. Hagedorn. **6** Finance & General
Purposes. **8** Open to the public. **9** Mon, Wed-Fri
10.00-12.00, 14.00-17.00 (18.00 Mon & Fri), Tues 10.00-
12.00, Sat 10.00-12.00, 14.00-16.30. Free. **10** Archaeological material (Stone Age-Saxon) local history; maps
& furniture; 17th cent set of drawings by Baker-Clack.

ICKWORTH, *see* **Bury St Edmunds**

ILFRACOMBE, Devon

ILFRACOMBE MUSEUM, Wilder Rd, Ilfracombe, EX34 8AF
(Tel 02716-63541). **4** Private trust. **5** Hon Curator:
Mr John Longhurst. **8** Open to the pubic. **9** daily
10.00-19.00 (winter 12.30). Adults 5p, children 3p.
10 Items of local interest; natural history; Victoriana.
12 (a) 1.

ILKLEY, West Yorkshire

MANOR HOUSE MUSEUM AND ART GALLERY, Castle
Yard, Ilkley, LS29 9DS (Tel 09433-66228). **4** City of
Bradford MC. **5** Chief Officer: Mr John M. A. Thompson
MA, AMA. **6** Cultural Activities Panel. **7** Educational
Services; Dir: W. R. Knight MA. **8** Open to the public.
9 Daily 10.00-20.00 (April & Sept 19.00), Oct-March 17.00).
Closed Dec 25 & Good Friday. Free. **10** Small Tudor
manor house on site of Roman fort with exposed Roman wall
in grounds; changing exhibitions of work by contemporary
artists. **11** Roman & pre-historic archaeological material.
12 (b) 2 (c) 3.

INGATESTONE, Essex.

INGATESTONE HALL, Ingatestone, CM4 9NP (Tel 02775-
3340). **4** Essex CC. **5** County Archivist: Mr K. C.
Newton, MA, FRHistS. **6** Library, Museum & Records.
7 Essex Record Office. **8** Open to the public.
9 Easter Sat-1st Sat in Oct: Mon-Sat (& bank hols) 10.00-
12.30, 14.00-16.30. Free. **10** Annual exhibitions of
archives, pictures & photographs on history of Essex.
11 Period furniture & armorial china. **12** (a) 2 (b) 1.

INVERARAY, Argyll

INVERARAY CASTLE (partially closed for restoration),
Inveraray, Argyll, PA32 8XT (Tel 0499-2275). **5** Chamberlain of Argyll: J. T. Kennedy Short, Argyll Estates Office,
Cherry Park, Inveraray, PA32 8XE. **8** Open to the public,
partially closed for renovations due to fire damage.
9 April (May 1976)-June: Sat-Thurs 10.00-12.00, 14.00-
18.00; July-mid Oct: daily 10.00-18.00; bank hols: 14.00-
18.00. Not free. **10** Mid 18th cent castle designed by
Roger Morris; built of local stone & lime; home of Dukes
of Argyll; headquarters of Clan Campbell (from 15th cent);

armoury (inc Rob Roy's dirk handle & sporran); French
tapestries (c.1770); portraits (inc Gainsborough); Victorian
room. **11** Shop.

INVERKEITHING, Fife

INVERKEITHING MUSEUM, The Friary, Inverkeithing.
4 Dunfermline DC. **6** Leisure & Recreation. **7** Dir of
Libs, Museums & Art Galleries: Mr James K. Sharp FLA.
8 Open to the public. **9** Wed-Sun 10.00-12.30, 14.30-
17.00. Free. **10** History of Inverkeithing. **12** (b) 1
(c) 1.

INVERNESS, Inverness-shire

INVERNESS MUSEUM & ART GALLERY, Castle Wynd,
Inverness, IV2 3ED (Tel 0463-31138). **4** Inverness DC.
6 Leisure & Recreation. **8** Open to the public.
9 Mon-Sat 9.00-17.00. Free. **10** Scottish Highland
region.

INVERURIE, Aberdeenshire.

INVERURIE MUSEUM, Town House, Inverurie (Tel 04672-
21619). **4** Combined District Councils of Gordon, Banff &
Buchan, Deeside & Kincardine. **5** Hon Curator: Dr Anthony
A. Woodham BSc, PhD, FRIC, FSA(Scot). **8** Open to the
public. **9** Mon-Fri 9.00-12.00, 15.00-17.00, Sat 9.00-
12.00. Free. **10** Local prehistory; geology (mainly
Scottish minerals & fossils); natural history (local & foreign
shells & lepidoptera); stuffed birds (local); coins; byegones;
early toys & games; N. American Eskimo relics.
11 Recent excavations (Beakers & an urn cemetery);
temporary exhibitions. **12** (b) 1.

IONA, Argyll

MUSEUM OF THE CATHEDRAL, The Abbey, Isle of Iona,
PA76 6SN (Tel 06817-214). **4** Trustees of Iona Cathedral.
8 Open to the public. **9** Mon-Sat 9.30-21.00, Sun 14.00-
20.00. Free. **10** Carved & sculptured stones (from Irish
times to medieval) mostly from Relig Odhrain, burial place
of the kings & chieftains on Iona from the 6th cent.
12 (b) 1.

IPSWICH, Suffolk

CHRISTCHURCH MUSEUM, c/o The Museum, High St,
Ipswich, IP1 3QH (Tel 0473-213761/2). **4** Borough of
Ipswich. **5** Curator: Ms Patricia M. Butler MA, FSA,
FMA. **6** Recreation & Amenities (Entertainments Sub-
Committee). **7** Dir of Recreation & Amenities: Mr Bert
Sharples MHCIMA, MIMEnt. **8** Open to the public.
9 Mon-Sat (inc bank hols) 10.00-17.00, Sun 14.30-16.30.
Closed Dec 24, 25 & Good Friday. Free. **10** 1548 country
house furnished in period to Victorian; good collns English
ceramics & glass; 19th cent Suffolk artists; costume colln in
store; art gallery attached. **11** Art gallery: Gainsboroughs, Constables, Wilson Steers, Camden Town; modern
prints (Pissaro to Riley); some modern sculpture. Schools
service; group tours (adults). **12** Served from Ipswich
Museum.
THE MUSEUM, High St, Ipswich, IP1 3QH (Tel 0473-213761/2).
4 Borough of Ipswich. **5** Curator: Ms Patricia M. Butler
MA, FSA, FMA. **6** Recreation & Amenities (Entertainments Sub-Committee). **7** Recreation & Amenities;
Dir: Mr Bert Sharples MHCIMA, MIMEnt. **8** Open to the
public. **9** Mon-Sat (inc bank hols) 10.00-17.00, Sun 14.30-
16.30. Closed Dec 24, 25 & Good Fri. Free. **10** Suffolk
geology & archaeology (especially paleolithic); 250 small
habitat cases of British birds & mammals; British insects;
ethnography; art gallery attached. **11** Replicas of Mildenhall Treasure, Sutton Hoo finds & Ipswich torcs; 19th cent
Suffolk artists. Schools service. **12** (a) 7 (b) 6 (c) 13.

IRONBRIDGE, Shropshire.

IRONBRIDGE GORGE MUSEUM, Church Hill, Ironbridge,
Telford, TF8 7RE (Tel 095-245-3522). **4** Ironbridge
Gorge Museum Trust. **5** Dir: Mr Neil Cossons MA, FSA,

CODE: 1 Name of Museum, Art Gallery or Stately Home. 2 Address. 3 Telephone & telex. 4 Governing body. 5 Officer in charge. 6 Committee responsible. 7 Larger department, chief officer. 8 Open to public. 9 Hours; admission charges. 10 Scope. 11 Special exhibits or facilities. 12 Staff (a) professionally qualified (b) other non-manual (c) manual.

IRONBRIDGE, Shropshire—*continued*

FMA. **8** Open to the public. **9** Daily 10.00-18.00 (Nov-Mch 17.00). Closed Dec 25. Adults 25p, children, OAPs & students 15p. **10** Historic relics of the Shropshire coal field; *in-situ* conservation of industrial & social buildings & monuments in Ironbridge Gorge. Also an Open Air Museum at Blists Hill. **11** Working machinery, inc potter, black-smith, local mine winding engine & Victorian printing shop; toll keeper's cottage; cast-iron ware; wall & floor tiles; Coalport China; pictures; technical library. **12** (a) 5 (b) 36 (c) 10.

IRVINE, Ayrshire

IRVINE BURNS CLUB, 28 Eglinton St, Irvine KA12 8AS (Tel 0294-78126). **4** Irvine Burns Club Directors. **5** Stewards: Mr & Mrs John McCandlish. **8** Open to the public. **9** Sat 14.30-17.00. Other times by appointment. Free. **10** Murals depicting Burns in Irvine; pictures; original mss; holograph letters from hon members library; Burns, Galt, Montgomery, Poe & Scottish literature. **12** (c) 2.

JODRELL BANK, Cheshire

CONCOURSE BUILDING AND PLANETARIUM, University of Manchester, Jodrell Bank, Macclesfield, SK11 9DL (Tel 04777-339). **4** University of Manchester. **5** Manager: R. G. Lascelles JP, BA, FRAS. **8** Open to the public. **9** Good Friday-Oct: daily (inc bank hols) 14.00-18.00; Nov-Easter: Sat & Sun 14.00-17.00. Adults 40p, children & OAPs 20p. Planetarium extra: Adults 30p, children 15p. **10** Science of radio astronomy; situated alongside 250 ft radio telescope. **11** Small radio telescope (25 ft) can be operated by public; planetarium.

KEIGHLEY, West Yorkshire

CLIFFE CASTLE ART GALLERY AND MUSEUM, Keighley, Yorkshire BD20 3HP (Tel 05352-64184). **4** City of Brad-ford Metropolitan Council. **5** Chief Officer: Mr John M. A. Thompson MA, AMA. **6** Cultural Activities Panel. **7** Dir of Educational Services: Mr W. R. Knight MA. **8** Open to the public. **9** Daily 10.00-20.00 (April-Sept 19.00) (Oct-March 17.00). Closed Dec 25 & Good Friday. Free. **10** Victorian mansion; archaeology; local geology; social & natural history. **11** Reconstructed workshops; toys & musical instruments; Bracewell Smith Hall houses temporary art exhibitions. Cafe in adjacent parkland. **12** (a) 6 (b) 5 (c) 11.

KENDAL, Cumbria

ABBOT HALL ART GALLERY, Abbot Hall, Kendal, LA9 5AL (Tel 0539-22464). **4** Lake District Art Gallery Trust. **5** Dir: Miss M. E. Burkett BA. **8** Open to the public. **9** Mon-Fri: 10.30-17.30, Sat & Sun 14.00-17.00. Closed Good Friday. Adults 20p, children 5p. **10** 18th cent period rooms & Gillow furniture; Romney paintings; china; glass; silver; changing exhibitions; contemporary pictures, sculp-tures, prints, ceramics etc. **11** Northern Arts Exhibition Service. **12** (a) 6 (b) 4 (c) 2.

KENDAL MUSEUM, Station Rd, Kendal LA9 6BT (Tel 0539-21374). **4** South Lakeland DC. **5** Curator: A. J. Turner. SMA. **6** Museum & Arts. **7** Tourism & Recreation Dept, Chief Officer: A. Haycock DMA. **8** Open to the public. **9** Mon-Sat (inc bank hols) 10.30-16.30. Adults 5p, children 3p. **10** Natural history; archaeology; local interest. **12** (a) 1 (c) 2.

LEVENS HALL, Kendal, LA8 0PB (Tel 04486-321). **5** Officer-in-Charge: C. H. Bagot ARICS. **8** Open to the

public. **9** Tues-Thurs, Sun & bank hols 14.00-17.00. Gardens open daily April-Oct. Not free. **10** House (13.00 1570); furniture (1690-1710); Gillow (18th cent) furniture; topiary garden (1690-1730). **11** Full size traction engines; steam models (1820-1920); garden centre. **12** (a) 2 (b) 2 (c) 10.

MUSEUM OF LAKELAND LIFE AND INDUSTRY, Kendal, LA9 5AL (Tel 0539-22464). **4** Lake District Museum Trust. **5** Dir: Miss M. E. Burkett BA. **8** Open to the public. **9** Mon-Fri 10.30-12.30, 14.00-17.00, Sat & Sun 14.00-17.00. Closed Good Friday & 2 weeks at Xmas. Adults 20p, children 5p. **10** Social & economic history of Lake District; period rooms; costume; agriculture; coppice trades; mining & quarrying; wool trade; blacksmithing. **12** (a) 6 (b) 4 (c) 4.

SIZERGH CASTLE, Kendal, LA8 8AE (Tel 04486-60285). **4** National Trust. **5** Co-Donor: Lt Cdr T. Hornyold-Strickland. **8** Open to the public. **9** April-Sept: Wed & Sun, Thurs (July & Aug only) 14.00-17.45. Adults 40p, children 20p, group rates. **10** Large 14th cent pele tower, Tudor great hall & Elizabethan wings with Georgian & Victorian alterations; fine panelling & ceilings. **11** Stuart & Jacobite relics.

KENNETHMONT, Aberdeenshire

LEITH HALL, Kennethmont, Huntly AB5 4NQ (Tel 04643-216). **4** National Trust for Scotland. **5** Trust Rep: Miss M. M. Hunter. **8** Open to the public. **9** House (May-Sept only) Mon-Sat 11.00-13.00, 14.00-17.30, Sun 14.00-17.30. Gardens 10.00-dusk. Adults 35p, children 15p; gardens only: adults 15p, children 5p. **10** House built around courtyard; family & Jacobite relics; military items.

KESWICK, Cumbria

FITZ PARK MUSEUM & ART GALLERY, Fitz Park, Keswick, CA12 4NF (Tel 0596-73263). **4** Fitz Park Trust. **5** Curator: Mr Norman Gandy. **8** Open to the public. **9** Mon-Sat (inc bank hols) April-Oct 10.00-12.00, 14.00-17.00, July-Aug 10.00-12.00, 14.00-19.00. Adults 10p, children 5p; school parties 2½p. **10** Robert Southey mss; some mss of William Wordsworth, Hartley Coleridge & others; Sir Hugh Walpole mss; minerals & rocks of the district; natural history. **11** Model of Lake District (c.1834); musical stones; study facilities. **12** (b) 1.

KETTERING, Northamptonshire

ALFRED EAST ART GALLERY, Sheep St, Kettering, NN16 0AN (Tel 0536-85215). **4** Kettering BC. **7** Amenity & Recreation Dept; Borough Amenities Officer: Mr J. Pemble DHE, AInstPRA. **8** Open to the public. **9** Mon-Sat 10.00-20.00, bank hols 14.00-18.00. Free. **10** Permanent colln of paintings by local & other artists. **11** Whole gallery given to special exhibitions as and when required. **12** (b) 1.

WESTFIELD MUSEUM, West St, Kettering, NN16 0AR (Tel 0536-85213). **4** Kettering BC. **5** Officer-in-Charge: Mr F. V. Lyall MA, Post Graduate Academic Dip European Prehistoric Archaeology. **7** Amenity & Recrea-tion Dept; Borough Amenities Officer: Mr J. Pemble DHE, AInstPRA. **8** Open to the public. **9** Mon-Sat 10.00-17.00 (Wed & Fri in summer 10.00-20.00), bank hols 14.00-1 00. Free. **10** Local archaeology, history & geology; f twear & shoe machinery. **11** Special exhibitions. **12** (a) 1 (c) 3.

KIDDERMINSTER, Hereford & Worcester

HEREFORD & WORCESTER COUNTY MUSEUM, Hartlebury Castle, Kidderminster, DY11 7XZ (Tel 02996-416).
4 Hereford & Worcester CC. **5** County Museum Officer: Mr George L. Shearer. **6** Education. **8** Open to the public. **9** Mon-Fri 10.00-18.00, Sat & Sun 14.00-18.00. Adults 10p, children, students & OAPs 2½p. **10** Archaeology; folk life; recent history; local crafts & industries; costume, toys & social life material; gypsy caravans; horse drawn carts & waggons & other transport items.
11 Exhibition of work by local schoolchildren in connection with museum education service; ample free parking, picnic area. **12** (a) 6 (b) 5 (c) 9.

KIDDERMINSTER ART GALLERY & MUSEUM, Market St, Kidderminster, DY10 1AD (Tel 0562-66610). **4** Wyre Forest DC. **5** Curator: Mr David Jones ATD, AMA.
7 Recreation & Amenities Dept; Chief Recreation & Amenities Officer: N. B. Onions MIRM. **8** Open to the public.
9 Mon-Fri 9.30-18.00, Sat 9.30-16.00. Free.
10 Etchings by Frank Brangwyn; drawings, paintings & objects connected with local history. **11** Continuous programme of temporary exhibitions, some showing work of local artists. **12** (a) 1 (b) 1 (c) 2.

KILBARCHAN, Renfrewshire

WEAVER'S COTTAGE, Kilbarchan PA10 2JZ. **4** National Trust for Scotland. **5** Trust Representative: Mrs A. Hallifax-Crawford; Custodian: Mrs H. Munro. **8** Open to the public. **9** Sun (May-Oct only), Tues, Thurs & Sat 14.00-17.00. Adults 20p, children 10p. **10** Typical cottage of 18th cent handloom weaver; weaving equipment & domestic utensils. **12** (b) 1.

KILMARNOCK, Ayrshire

BURNS MONUMENT & MUSEUM, Kay Park, Kilmarnock, (Tel 0563-26401). **4** Kilmarnock & Loudoun DC.
6 Leisure. **7** Cultural Services Dept; Manager: J. F. T. Thomson MA, FLA. **8** Open to the public. **9** Wed-Mon (inc bank hols): April-Sept 12.30-20.30, Oct-Mch 10.00-17.00. Charges: 3p. **11** Original Burns mss: first Kilmarnock edition of published works; paintings, etchings, illustrations & relics connected with Burns & his contemporaries. **12** (a) 2 (b) 1.

DICK INSTITUTE, Elmbank Ave, Kilmarnock, KA1 3BU (Tel 0563-26401). **4** Kilmarnock & Loudoun DC.
5 Manager, Cultural Services Dept: J. F. T. Thomson MA, FLA. **6** Leisure. **8** Open to the public. **9** Mon-Fri 10.00-20.00 (winter 17.00), Sat 10.00-17.00. Free.
10 Geology; archaeology; ornithology; ethnography; arms & armour; early printed books; art gallery general but has good Glasgow School colln. **11** Thomson Geological colln; paperweights; Scottish basket-hilted swords; Ferguson colln of early photographic (magic lantern) slides. **12** (a) 4 (b) 1 (c) 1.

KINGSBRIDGE, Devon

COOKWORTHY MUSEUM, The Old Grammar School, 108 Fore St, Kingsbridge TQ7 1AW (Tel 0548-3235). **4** William Cookworthy Museum Society. **5** Curator: Miss Kathy Gee BA. **8** Open to the public. **9** Easter-Oct: Mon-Sat (inc bank hols) 10.00-17.00. Adults 15p, children 5p. **10** Local history; old photographs; costume; Victorian kitchen & dairy; craft & farming history; story of William Cookworthy (born in Kingsbridge) who discovered china clay. **12** (a) 1 (c) 1.

KINGS LYNN, Norfolk

LYNN MUSUEM, Old Market St, Kings Lynn PE30 1NL (Tel 0553-5001). **4** Norfolk CC. **5** Curator: Mr R. Trett BA, AMA. **7** Norfolk Museums Service; Dir: Mr Francis W. Cheetham BA, FMA. **8** Open to the public. **9** Mon-Sat 10.00-17.00. Adults 5p; children & OAPs free.
10 Local history; natural history & archaeology of N.W.

Norfolk. **11** Temporary exhibitions. **12** (a) 3 (b) 1 (c) 4.

MUSEUM OF SOCIAL HISTORY, 27 King St, King's Lynn PE30 1ET (Tel 0553-5001). **4** Norfolk CC. **5** Curator: Mr Robert Trett BA, AMA. **6** Museums Joint Committee.
8 Open to the public. **9** Tues, Thurs & Fri 14.00-17.00. Free. **10** Social history; domestic life & dress (inc dolls, toys & local colln of glass). **11** Taylor colln of glass, (18th & 19th cent, inc the so-called 'Lynn glass' & coloured glass). **12** (a) 1 (c) 1.

KINGSTON UPON HULL, North Humberside

FERENS ART GALLERY, Queen Victoria Sq, Hull, HU1 3RA (Tel 0482-224316). **4** Kingston upon Hull City Council.
5 Curator: Mr John Bradshaw MA. **6** Cultural Services.
7 Dir of Leisure Services: J. A. Milne FInstPRA. **8** Open to the public. **9** Mon-Fri 10.00-17.30, Sun 14.30-16.30. Closed Dec 25, 26 & Good Friday. **10** Old Master paintings; Humberside marine paintings; modern paintings & sculpture.
11 Temporary exhibitions; cafe (Mon-Sat 10.00-16.45).
12 Served from Town Docks Museum.

MARITIME MUSEUM (closed indefinitely) Pickering Park, Hessle Rd, Hull JUL 6RY **4** Kingston upon Hull City Council. **5** Curator: Mr John Bradshaw MA. **6** Cultural Services. **7** Dir of Leisure Services: J. A. Milne FInstPRA.
8 Closed indefinitely. **10** Maritime life & history.

SPRINGHEAD PUMPING STATION, The Director, Yorkshire Water Authority, Eastern Division, Essex House, Manor St, Kingston upon Hull, HU1 1YU (Tel 0482-28591).
8 & 9 Open by arrangement only. Free. **10** Part of working pumping station; exhibits of waterworks interest (17th cent to present). **11** Single-acting, Cornish beam engine erected in 1876, now not working, but in position.

TOWN DOCKS MUSEUM, Queen Victoria Square, Hull, HU1 3RA (Tel 0482-29548). **4** Kingston upon Hull City Council.
5 Curator: Mr J. Bradshaw MA. **6** Cultural Services.
7 Dir of Leisure Services: J. A. Milne FInstPRA. **8** Open to the public. **9** Mon-Sat 10.00-17.30, Sun 14.30-16.30. Closed Dec 25, 26 & Good Friday. **10** Whales & whaling; fishing & trawling (from late Summer 1976). **12** (a) 10 (b) 4 (c) 18.

TRANSPORT AND ARCHAEOLOGY MUSEUM, 36 High St, Hull, HU1 1NQ (Tel 0482-27625). **4** Kingston upon Hull City Council. **5** Curator: Mr John Bradshaw MA.
6 Cultural Services. **7** Dir of Leisure Services: J. A. Milne FInstPRA. **8** Open to the public. **9** Mon-Sat 10.00-17.00, Sun 14.30-16.30. Closed Dec 25, 26 & Good Friday. **10** Historic coaching & motoring vehicles, bicycles; local archaeology inc Roman mosaics & Garton slack chariot burial. **12** Served from Town Docks Museum.

UNIVERSITY OF HULL COLLECTION OF SOUTH-EAST ASIAN ART AND TRADITIONAL CRAFTSMANSHIP, Centre for South-East Asian Studies, University of Hull, Hull, HU6 7RX (Tel 0482-46311 ext 7758). **5** Lecturer in South-East Asian Social Anthropology: Mr L. G. Hill MA, BLitt.
8 Not open to the public except by appointment. **10** S.E. Asian wood carvings, metalware, cloth etc.

WILBERFORCE HOUSE AND GEORGIAN HOUSES, 23-25 High St, Hull, HU1 1NQ (Tel 0482-27625). **4** Kingston upon Hull City Council. **5** Curator: Mr John Bradshaw MA.
6 Cultural Services. **7** Dir of Leisure Services: J. A. Milne FInstPRA. **8** Open to the public. **9** Mon-Fri 10.00-17.00, Sun 14.30-16.30. Closed Dec 25, 26 & Good Friday. **10** Birthplace of slavery abolitionist, William Wilberforce, slavery relics; Jacobean & Georgian rooms with period furniture, Hull silver, costumes, ceramics, dolls etc. **12** Served from Town Docks Museum.

KINLOCHEIL, Inverness-shire

GLENFINNAN MONUMENT, Kinlocheil, Fort William, (Tel 039 783-250). **4** National Trust for Scotland. **5** Warden: Mr R. Mackellaig. **8** Open to the public. **9** April-Oct:

CODE: 1 Name of Museum, Art Gallery or Stately Home. 2 Address. 3 Telephone & telex. 4 Governing body. 5 Officer in charge. 6 Committee responsible. 7 Larger department, chief officer. 8 Open to public. 9 Hours; admission charges. 10 Scope. 11 Special exhibits or facilities. 12 Staff (a) professionally qualified (b) other non-manual (c) manual.

KINLOCHEIL, Inverness-shire—*continued*

daily 9.30-18.00 (June-Aug 20.00). Adults 15p, children 5p. 10 Monument erected 1815 to commemorate clansmen who fought for Prince Charles Edward. 11 Visitor's centre.

KINNESSWOOD, Kinross-shire

MICHAEL BRUCE COTTAGE MUSEUM, The Loan, Kinness-wood. 4 Michael Bruce Memorial Trust. 5 Sec to the Trustees: Mr David Dyer FRSA. 8 & 9 Open by arrangement with Mr T. Buchan, The Garage, Drummond Place, Kinnesswood. Free. 10 Cottage where Michael Bruce, the Gentle Poet of Loch Leven, was born in 1746 & where his father worked a handloom; period furnishings. 11 The poet's Bible; examples of handwoven linen; Communion tokens, also publications inc 'The Life and Works of Michael Bruce'.

KIRKCALDY, Fife

INDUSTRIAL MUSEUM, Forth House, Abbotshall Rd, Kirk-caldy, KY1 1YG (Tel 0592-60732). 4 Kirkcaldy DC. 5 Officer-in-Charge: Mr Alexander Hidalgo BA, FSA(Scot). 6 Leisure & Recreation. 7 Dir: A. Sneddon LLB. 8 Open to the public. 9 May-Sept: Mon-Sat 14.00-19.00. Free. 10 Local industries (linoleum, coal); wheelwrights shop, horse-drawn vehicles; drapers shop. 12 (a) 2.

KIRKCALDY MUSEUMS & ART GALLERY, War Memorial Gardens, Kirkcaldy, KY1 1YG (Tel 0592-60732). 4 Kirk-caldy DC. 5 Curator: Mr Alexander Hidalgo BA, FSA(Scot). 6 Leisure & Recreation; 7 Dir of Leisure & Recreation: A. Sneddon LLB. 8 Open to the public. 9 Mon-Sat 11.00-17.00, Sun 14.00-17.00. Free. 10 Local archaeology, social & natural history, industry. Art gallery: mainly Scottish & Camden Town group. 12 (a) 2 (b) 1 (c) 6.

KIRKCUDBRIGHT, Kirkcudbrightshire

BROUGHTON HOUSE, High St, Kirkcudbright (Tel 0557-30437). 4 E.A. Hornell Trustees. 5 Officer-in-Charge: J.K. Welsh, Hewats (Solicitors), Castle Douglas, Kirkcudbright-shire. 8 Open to the public. 9 Summer: Mon-Fri 11.00-13.00, 14.00-18.00; Winter: Tues & Thurs 14.00-18.00. Free. 10 E.A. Hornell paintings; library of S.W. Scotland items, Scottish ballads & Burns. 12 (a) ½ (c) 2.

STEWARTRY MUSEUM, St Mary St, Kirkcudbright. 4 Stewartry Museum Assoc. 5 Hon Curator: Mr Thomas R. Collin FSA(Scot). 8 Open to the public. 9 Summer: Mon-Sat (inc bank hols) 10.00-12.00, 13.00-17.00; winter: by arrangement. Adults 10p, children 5p. 10 Local affairs.

KIRKINTILLOCH, Dunbartonshire

AULD KIRK MUSEUM, Cowgate, Kirkintilloch, Glasgow. 4 Strathkelvin DC. 6 Leisure & Recreation. 7 Chief Libn: Mrs A. Mackenzie FLA. 8 Open to the public. 9 Hours under review. Free. 10 Local history.

KIRKOSWALD, Ayrshire

CULZEAN CASTLE, Kirkoswald, Maybole (Tel 06566-236/274). 4 National Trust for Scotland. 5 Trust Rep-resentatives: Capt & Mrs John Mott; Custodian: Mr J. Letham Connell JP. 8 Open to the public. 9 March-Oct: daily 10.00-16.00 (April-June 10.00-18.00). Other months by prior arrangement. Park open all year (free). Adults 50p, children 20p; party rates (exc July & Aug). 10 Castle & farm buildings (1772-1792) by Robert Adam. 11 Reception complex (restaurant, exhibitions, shop etc.).

KIRKWALL, Orkney Isles

TANKERNESS HOUSE MUSEUM, Broad St, Kirkwall. (Tel 0856-3218 ext 10). 4 Orkney Islands Council. 8 Open to the public. 9 Mon-Sat (inc bank hols) 10.30-13.00, 14.00-17.00. Free. 10 Archaeology; folklore; crafts. 12 (c) 1.

KIRRIEMUIR, Angus

BARRIE'S BIRTHPLACE, 9 Brechin Rd, Kirriemuir, DD8 4BX (Tel 05752-2646). 4 National Trust for Scotland. 5 Trust Representative: Miss O. A. G. Bennell. 8 Open to the public. 9 April-Oct: Mon-Sat 10.00-12.30, 14.00-18.00, Sun 14.00-18.00. Other times by arrangement. Adults 15p, children 5p. 10 Barrie's life; original mss, corrected proofs etc; his writing desk; his portrait by Sir John Lavery.

KNUTSFORD, Cheshire

TATTON HALL, Tatton Park, Knutsford, WA16 6QL (Tel 0565-3155). 4 Cheshire CC. 5 Dir: Commander P.A.C. Neate. 6 Tatton Park Sub-Committee. 7 Countryside & Recreation Division; Dir: Major P.V. Moore. 8 Open to the public. 9 Daily (inc bank hols) 14.00-17.15. Adults 25p, children 10p. 10 Regency mansion containing silver, paintings, furniture (mainly by Gillow of Lancaster); trophies, vehicles & world-wide curiosities belonging to Egerton family. 11 Horn Book; Canaletto, Van Dyke & De Heem paintings; Wyatt drawings. 12 (b) 1 (c) 8.

LACOCK, Wiltshire

FOX TALBOT MUSEUM, Lacock, Chippenham, SN15 2LG (Tel 024 973-459). 4 National Trust. 5 Curator: Mr Robert Lassam. 8 Open to the public. 9 Feb-Oct: daily (inc bank hols) 11.00-18.00. Adults 30p, children 15p. 10 History of William Henry Fox Talbot, (inventor of photography); archive of letters & original material; audio-visual theatre; 'Pencil of Nature' exhibition; photographs of Fox Talbot's calotypes. 12 (c) 1.

LACKHAM AGRICULTURAL MUSEUM, Lackham College of Agriculture, Lacock, Chippenham, SN15 2NY (Tel 0249-3251). 4 Wiltshire CC. 5 Warden (part-time Curator): Mr G.H. Owen. 7 Libraries & Museums Service. 8 Open to the public. 9 Occasional Sundays & other open days. Free. 10 Agricultural implements, tools & machines. 11 Early milking machines; tractors.

LACOCK ABBEY, High St, Lacock, Chippenham, SN15 2LG. 4 National Trust. 8 Open to the public. 9 April-Oct: daily (exc Mon & Tues in April, May & Oct) 14.00-18.00. Adults 50p, children 25p. 10 Parts of 13th cent nunnery; abbey converted into Tudor mansion; octagonal tower; timbered courtyard; 16th cent brewery; 18th cent Gothic alterations. 11 Medieval village nearby (mostly owned by National Trust).

LANARK, Lanarkshire

CRAIGNETNAN CASTLE, Lanark. 4 Dept of Environment. 5 Information Officer, Argyle House, 3 Lady Lawson St, Edinburgh. 8 Open to the public. 9 Mon-Sat 9.30-19.00, Sun 14.00-19.00. Oct-March: closes 16.00 daily. Adults 5p, children 2½p. 10 History of the castle. 11 Photographs & plans; gargoyle & fish's head.

LANCASTER, Lancashire

CITY MUSEUM, Old Town Hall, Market Sq, Lancaster, LA1 1HT (Tel 0524-64637). 4 Lancaster City Council. 5 Curator: Ms Edith Tyson FMA. 6 Leisure. 8 Open to the public. 9 Mon-Sat (inc bank hols) 10.00-17.30.

LANCASTER, Lancashire—*continued*

Free. **10** Local history & archaeology; decorative arts.
11 King's Own Regiment Museum; temporary exhibitions.
12 (a) 3 (b) 3 (c) 3.

LAPWORTH, West Midlands

PACKWOOD HOUSE, Lapworth, Solihull, B94 6AT (Tel 05643-
2024). **4** National Trust. **5** Curator: Major C.B.
Grundy MC. **8** Open to the public. **9** April-Sept: Wed-
Sun 14.00-19.00; Oct-March: Wed, Sat & Sun 14.00-17.00.
Closed Dec 25 & Good Friday. Not free. **10** Tudor &
Carolean house; contemporary furniture, tapestries & needle-
work. **11** Yew topiary of Sermon on the Mount (c.1650).
12 (b) 2 (c) 3.

LARGS, Ayrshire

KIRKGATE HOUSE, Manse Court, Largs, KA30 8AW.
4 Largs & District Historical Society. **8** Open to the
public. **9** June-Sept: Mon-Sat 14.00-17.00. Other times
by arrangement. Free, but donations welcome. **10** Local
history (inc pictures, papers, books & bygones).

LEAMINGTON SPA, Warwickshire

LEAMINGTON SPA ART GALLERY AND MUSEUM, Avenue
Rd, Leamington Spa, CV31 3PP.(Tel 0926-26559). **4** Warwick DC. **5** Curator: Mrs Margaret A.Slater. **6** Re-
creation & Amenities. **7** Amenities Dept; Mr Alan Pedley
FInstPRA(Dip). **8** Open to the public. **9** Mon, Tues,
Thurs-Sat (inc bank hols) 10.45-12.45, 14.30-17.00 (+Thurs
18.00-20.00), Sun (April-Dec only) 14.30-17.00. Closed
Xmas, Boxing Day & Good Friday. Free. **10** Paintings by
Dutch & Flemish masters; 20th cent oils & water colours,
mainly English; 16th & 19th cent pottery & porcelain.
11 18th cent English drinking glasses (Jahn Colln); modern
English Glass; Thomas Baker paintings. **12** (b) 2 (c) 1.

LECHLADE, Gloucestershire

KELMSCOTT MANOR, Lechlade, GL7 3HJ (Tel 03675-486).
4 Society of Antiquaries of London. **5** Hon Curator:
A.R.Dufty CBE, ARIBA, FSA. **8** Open to the public.
9 April-Sept: 1st Wed of each month 11.00-16.00. Adults
50p, children 25p. **10** Summer home of William Morris;
many original furnishings & furniture; unique colln of
Kelmscott Press books.

LEDBURY, Hereford & Worcester

EASTNOR CASTLE, Ledbury, HR8 1RD (Tel 0531-2304).
5 Joint Owner: Hon Mrs Hervey-Bathurst. **8** Open to the
public. **9** Open, by appointment only, from Spring bank
holiday-Sept. Adults 30p, children 15p. **10** Neo-Gothic
castle (1812); 6 rooms open; pictures; tapestries; armour.
11 Pugin drawing room; arboretum. **12** (b) 1 (c) 2.

LEEDS, West Yorkshire

ABBEY HOUSE MUSEUM, Abbey Rd, Leeds, LS5 3EH
(Tel 0532-755821). **4** Leeds MDC. **5** Dir, City Museum:
Mr C.Maynard Mitchell FSA, FMA. **7** Leisure Services;
Dir: M.Palmer-Jones MA. **8** Open to the public.
9 Mon-Sat (April-Sept) 10.00-18.00, (Oct-March) 10.00-
17.00, Sun & bank hols (April-Sept) 14.00-18.00, (Oct-
March) 14.00-17.00. Adults 10p, children 2½p; parties of
20 or more 2½p. **10** Folk museum covering life &
work of people of Yorkshire over last 200 years. **11** Three
'streets' of rebuilt houses, shops & workshops taken from
various parts of Yorkshire, rebuilt & furnished as they would
have been c.1850. **12** (a) 3 (b) 1 (c) 8.

CITY ART GALLERY, The Headrow, Leeds, LS1 3AA (Tel
0532-31301 ext 395). **4** Leeds MDC. **5** Dir, Art Galleries: Mr Robert Rowe CBE, MA, FMA. **7** Leisure
Services Dept; Dir: M.J.Palmer-Jones MA. **8** Open to
the public. **9** Mon-Sat 10.30-18.30, Sun 14.30-17.00.
Closed Dec 25 & 26. Free. **10** English & Continental
paintings, sculpture, watercolours & prints. **11** Picture
loan scheme; Prints & watercolours. **12** Served from
Temple Newsam.

LEEDS CITY MUSEUM, Municipal Buildings, Leeds, LS1 3AA
(Tel 0532-31301, ext 539). **4** Leeds MDC. **5** Dir: Mr
C.Maynard Mitchell FSA, FMA. **7** Leisure Services;
Dir: M.Palmer-Jones MA. **8** Open to the public.
9 Mon-Sat 10.00-18.30. Free. **10** Natural history;
archaeology; ethnography & numismatics. **11** Dioramas
of natural history; Aquarium; Roman material from Lanuvia;
outstanding numismatic collns. **12** (a) 5 (b) 6 (c) 8.

Leeds University

DEPARTMENT OF SEMITIC STUDIES MUSEUM, Leeds,
LS2 9JT (Tel 0532-31751, ext 6268). **5** Head of Dept: Dr
B.S.J.Isserlin MA, BLitt, DPhLI. **8** Open to the public.
9 Term: Mon-Fri 10.00-16.00. Free. **10** Ancient
Near-Eastern (especially Palestinian, Biblical) archaeo-
logy; Middle Eastern (especially Palestinian) folk lore;
Jewish art & ceremonial objects; ancient Near-Eastern
writing & inscriptions; mss (some illuminated) in Arabic,
Persian, Hebrew, Samaritan, Syriac. **11** Palestinian
Bronze Age finds; Palestinian & Jewish textiles & em-
broideries; illuminated mss.

MUSEUM OF THE HISTORY OF EDUCATION, Leeds,
LS2 9JT (Tel 0532-31751 ext 6159). **5** Joint Curators:
Dr P.H.J.H.Gosden MA, PhD; Dr W.B.Stephens MA,
PhD, FSA. **8 & 9** Open to the public in term time by prior
appointment only. Free. **10** Textbooks; exercise books;
scientific apparatus; school records; physical objects.

MUSEUM OF INDUSTRY AND SCIENCE, Armley Mills,
Canal Rd, Leeds, LS12 2QF (Tel 0532-637861). **4** Leeds
City Council. **5** Curator: Mr P.J.Kelley. **6** Leisure
Services. **7** Dept of Leisure Services; Dir: Mr M.C.
Palmer-Jones MA. **9** Expected opening 1977.
10 Illustrates rise of factory system in West Riding with
particular ref to traditional industries of the district (e.g.
textiles, tanning, tailoring & clothing manufacture, engineering & locomotive building). Museum is housed in a water-
powered textile mill, developed from an earlier fulling,
scribbling & corn mill. **11** Water wheels; water turbines;
several large steam engines. **12** (a) 3 (b) 1 (c) 2.

TEMPLE NEWSAM HOUSE, Temple Newsam House, Leeds,
LS15 0AE (Tel 0532-647321). **4** Leeds MDC. **5** Dir
of Art Galleries: Mr Robert Rowe CBE, MA, FMA.
7 Leisure Services Dept; Dir: M.J.Palmer-Jones MA.
8 Open to the public. **9** Daily 10.30-18.15 (or dusk).
Closed Dec 25 & 26. Adults 15p, accompanied children 5p,
OAPs free. **10** Tudor house inc 18th & late 19th cent
rooms; English furniture, silver, ceramics, sculpture &
painting; Oriental ceramics; needlework & gilt suite made
for house c.1743. **11** Study facilities for ceramics; lacture
rooms. **12** (a) 10 (b) 9 (c) 42.

LEEK, Staffordshire

LEEK ART GALLERY, Nicholson Institute, Leek, ST13 6DW
(Tel 0538-382615). **4** Staffordshire Moorlands DC.
5 Dep Area Libn: Ms Edith Jerram ALA. **6** Libraries,
Records & Museums. **8** Open to the public. **9** Mon-Fri
10.00-21.00, Sat 9.30-17.30. Free. **10** Temporary exhibitions; small permanent colln. **11** Work of Leek Embroidery Society.

LEICESTER, Leicestershire

BELGRAVE HALL, Church Rd, Belgrave, Leicester, LE4 5PE
(Tel 0533-539111). **4** Leicestershire CC. **5** Dir: Mr
Patrick J.Boylan BSc, FGS, AMA. **6** Libraries & Museums.
8 Open to the public. **9** Mon-Sat 10.00-17.30, Sun 14.00-
17.30. Closed Dec 25, 26 & Good Friday. Free. **10** Queen
Anne house (1709-1713), 18th-19th cent furnishings. Stable
block with coaches, harness room & agricultural implements;
botanical gardens. **12** (a) Served from Leicestershire
Museum.

GUILDHALL, Guildhall Lane, Leicester, LE1 5FQ (Tel 0533-
539111). **4** Leicestershire CC. **5** Dir: Mr Patrick J.
Boylan BSc, FGS, AMA. **6** Libraries & Museums.

CODE: 1 Name of Museum, Art Gallery or Stately Home. 2 Address. 3 Telephone & telex. 4 Governing body. 5 Officer in charge. 6 Committee responsible. 7 Larger department, chief officer. 8 Open to public. 9 Hours; admission charges. 10 Scope. 11 Special exhibits or facilities. 12 Staff (a) professionally qualified (b) other non-manual (c) manual.

LEICESTER, Leicestershire —*continued*

8 Open to the public. 9 Mon-Sat 10.00-17.30, Sun 14.00-17.30. Closed Dec 25, 26 & Good Friday. Free. 10 Early medieval hall of Corpus Christi Guild, used as town hall from late 15th cent-1876; police cells; old town library (c.1633). 12 (a) Served from Leicestershire Museum.

JEWRY WALL MUSEUM & SITE, St Nicholas Circle, Leicester (Tel 0533-539111). 4 Leicestershire CC. 5 Dir: Mr Patrick J. Boylan BSc, FGS, AMA. 6 Libraries & Museums. 8 Open to the public. 9 Mon-Sat 10.00-17.30, Sun 14.00-17.30. Closed Dec 25, 26 & Good Friday. Free. 10 Local archaeology to 1500; next to 2nd cent Roman Jewry Wall & baths. 11 Bronze age Welby hoard; Roman milestone; Romano-British mosaics; wall plaster; Moutsorrel bucket; Glen Parva Anglo-Saxon skeleton; late medieval stained glass. 12 (a) Served from Leicestershire Museum.

LEICESTERSHIRE MUSEUM AND ART GALLERY, New Walk, Leicester, LE1 6TD (Tel 0533-539111). 4 Leicestershire CC. 5 Dir: Mr Patrick J. Boylan BSc, FGS, AMA. 6 Libraries & Museums. 8 Open to the public. 9 Mon-Sat 10.00-17.30, Sun 14.00-17.30. Closed Dec 25, 26 & Good Friday. Free. 10 18th, 19th & 20th cent English paintings, drawings & watercolours; German Expressionist paintings, drawings & prints; 19th & 20th cent French paintings; old master prints & some paintings; modern prints; 17th-20th cent English ceramics; some Oriental & Near Eastern ceramics; 16th-19th cent English silver; Egyptology; British mammals & birds; local geology; freshwater aquarium. 11 Lunch-time concerts (Oct-March: Thurs). 12 (a) 59 (b) 17 (c) 51.

LEICESTERSHIRE MUSEUM OF TECHNOLOGY, Abbey Pumping Station, Corporation Rd, Abbey Lane, Leicester, LE4 5PW (Tel 0533-539111). 4 Leicestershire CC. 5 Dir: Mr Patrick J. Boylan BSc, FGS, AMA. 6 Libraries & Museums. 8 Open to the public. 9 Mon-Sat 10.00-17.30, Sun 14.00-17.30. Closed Dec 25, 26 & Good Friday. Free except for special events: adults 25p, children 10p. 10 Giant beam engines of old sewerage pumping station; power transport & hosiery industry galleries being developed. 12 (a) Served from Leicestershire Museum.

NEWARKE HOUSES MUSEUM, The Newarke, Leicester, LE2 7BY (Tel 0533-539111). 4 Leicestershire CC. 5 Dir: Mr Patrick J. Boylan BSc, FGS, AMA. 6 Libraries & Museums. 8 Open to the public. 9 Mon-Sat 10.00-17.30, Sun 14.00-17.30. Closed Dec 25, 26 & Good Friday. Free. 10 Local social history (15th cent to present); 17th cent room; local clockmaker's workshop; 19th cent street scene; local clocks; musical instruments; Daniel Lambert. 12 (a) Served from Leicestershire Museum.

ROYAL LEICESTERSHIRE REGIMENT MUSEUM, The Magazine, Oxford St, Leicester (Tel 0533-539111). 4 Leicestershire CC. 5 Dir: Mr Patrick J. Boylan BSc, FGS, AMA. 6 Libraries & Museums. 8 Open to the public. 9 Mon-Sat 10.00-17.30, Sun 14.00-17.30. Closed Dec 25, 26 & Good Friday. Free. 10 Regimental history, mementoes, battle trophies & relics. Early 15th cent gatehouse to the Newarke. 12 (a) Served from Leicestershire Museum.

WYGSTON'S HOUSE AND MUSEUM OF COSTUME, St Nicholas Circle, Leicester (Tel 0533-539111). 4 Leicestershire CC. 5 Dir: Mr Patrick J. Boylan BSc, FGS, AMA. 6 Libraries & Museums. 8 Open to the public. 9 Mon-Sat 10.00-17.30, Sun 14.00-17.30. Closed Dec 25, 26 & Good Friday. Free. 10 Late medieval building with later additions; 18th-20th cent costumes; reconstructions of draper's, milliner's & shoe shops of 1920's. 12 (a) Served from Leicestershire Museum.

LEIGH, Lancashire

TURNPIKE GALLERY, Leigh Library, Leigh, WN7 1EB (Tel 05235-4131). 4 Wigan MBC. 5 Officer-in-Charge: Mrs M. Buchanan BA, AMA. 6 Recreation & Amenities. 7 Dept of Leisure, Dir: Mr Gil Swift BA. 8 Open to the public. 9 Tues-Fri 10.00-18.00, Sat 10.00-15.30. Free. 10 Temporary exhibitions; picture loan service. 12 (a) 1 (c) 2.

LEIGHTON BUZZARD, Bedfordshire.

ASCOTT, Wing, Leighton Buzzard (Tel 029 668-242). 4 National Trust. 8 Open to the public. 9 April-Sept: Wed, Sat, Sun (July-Aug only) & bank hols 14.00-18.00. House & gardens: 80p. Gardens only: adults 40p, children 20p. 10 Anthony de Rothschild colln of French & Chippendale furniture (original needlework), paintings (Rubens, Gainsborough, Hogarth etc), Oriental porcelain; unusual gardens.

LEOMINSTER, Hereford & Worcester

EYE MANOR, Leominster, HR6 0DT (Tel 0568 85-244). 5 Owner: Mr C. Sandford. 8 Open to the public. 9 April-June: Wed, Thurs, Sat, Sun & bank hols (& following Tues) 14.30-17.30; July-Sept: daily 14.30-17.30. Adults 30p, children 10p. 10 17th-cent manor-house with nine plasterwork ceilings. 11 Family treasures & examples of craftwork (inc Mr Sandford's Golden Cockerel Press books & Mrs Sandford's corn dollies, paper sculpture, etc), historical costume dolls ("Beck Colln") at a small extra charge.

LEOMINSTER FOLK MUSEUM, Etnam St, Leominster (Tel 0568-2567). 4 Trustees of Leominster Museum. 5 Hon Curator: N.C. Reeves BA; Hon Sec: Mr Norman Davis. 8 Open to the public. 9 Nov-March: Fri & Sat 10.00-13.00, 14.00-16.30; April-Nov: Mon-Sat (inc bank hols) 10.00-13.00, 14.00-17.00, Sun 14.00-17.00. Adults 5p, children 2p. 10 Local life (iron age-present); costumes; swords; pictures (John Scarlet Davis). 11 School parties & organizations welcome.

LERWICK, Shetland Isles

SHETLAND COUNTY MUSEUM, Lower Hillhead, Lerwick, Shetland, ZE1 0EL (Tel 0595-3868). 4 Shetland Islands Council. 5 Curator: T. Henderson FSA(Scot). 6 Education. 8 Open to the public. 9 Mon-Sat 10.00-13.00, 14.00-17.00 (& Mon, Wed & Fri 18.00-20.00). Free. 10 Shetland life (pre-history to present); ship models; fishing; sailing; archaeology; relics from wrecks (inc 4 bronze cannon, one from the Armada ship 'El Gran Grifon'). 11 Temporary art exhibitions (local & national). 12 (a) 2.

LETCHWORTH, Hertfordshire

LETCHWORTH, FIRST GARDEN CITY MUSEUM (not yet open), 296 Norton Way South, Letchworth, SG6 1SU. 4 North Hertfordshire DC. 5 Dir: Miss F.M. Gadd BA, AMA. 6 Recreation & Amenities (Museum Sub-Committee). 7 Sec: Mr F.W. Hammond. 9 Will open late 1976. Free. 10 Original office of Parker & Unwin, architects, designers of Letchworth; development of Letchworth, the first garden city; history of garden city movement.

LETCHWORTH MUSEUM & ART GALLERY, Broadway, Letchworth, SG6 3PD (Tel 04626-5647). 4 North Hertfordshire DC. 5 Dir: Miss F.M. Gadd BA, AMA. 6 Recreation & Amenities (Museum Sub-Committee). 7 Sec: Mr F.W. Hammond. 8 Open to the public. 9 Mon-Sat 10.00-17.00. Free. 10 Natural history; archaeology of North Herts; art gallery. 11 Temporary exhibitions; schools service.

LEWES, Sussex

ANNE OF CLEVES HOUSE MUSEUM, Southover High St, Lewes (Tel 07916-4610). 4 Sussex Archaeological Society. 5 Curator: Ms Fiona Marsden MA, AMA. 8 Open to the public. 9 Feb-Nov: Mon-Sat (inc bank hols) 10.30-13.00,

LEWES, Sussex—*continued*

14.00-17.00; April-Oct: Sun 14.00-17.00. Adults 15p, parties & students 10p, children 5p.   **10** Traditional Sussex industries (iron work, pottery etc); furnished rooms; bygones; history of Lewes Gallery.   **12** (a) As for Barbican House Museum; (b) 1.

BARBICAN HOUSE MUSEUM, Barbican House, High St, Lewes, BN7 1YE (Tel 07916-4379).   **4** Sussex Archaeological Society.   **5** Curator: Ms Fiona Marsden MA, AMA.   **8** Open to the public.   **9** Mon-Sat (inc bank hols) 10.00-13.00, 14.00-17.00, Sun (April-Oct) 14.00-17.00. Adults 15p, students & parties 10p, children 5p.   **10** Sussex archaeology (Stone Age, Bronze Age, Iron Age, Roman, Saxon & Medieval); Sussex prints & watercolours.   **12** (a) 1 (b) 1 (c) 1.

FIRLE PLACE, Firle Place, Firle, Lewes, BN8 6LP (Tel 079 159-256).   **5** Owner: Viscount Gage KCVO; Sec: Miss M.F. Bellamy.   **8** Open to the public.   **9** June-Sept: Wed & Thurs: 14.15-17.30, Sun & bank hols 15.00-18.00. Adults 40p, children 10p.   **10** House built 1487, most rebuilt 1730; European & British Old Master paintings; furniture; porcelain (especially Sèvres).   **12** (c) 12.

GLYNDE PLACE, Glynde, Lewes, BN8 6SX (Tel 079 159-229/ 07916-2957).   **5** Owner: Mrs Humphrey Brand; Administrator: Mrs K.C. Stewart.   **8** Open to the public.   **9** May-mid Oct: Thurs, Sat, Sun & bank hols 14.15-17.30. Adults 30p, parties (over 20) 15p, children 10p.   **10** Early Elizabethan architecture; portraits by Hoppner, Lely & Zoffany; bronzes by Francesco Bertos; Rubens sketch; documents from 12th cent; needlework & pottery.

LEWIS, ISLE OF, Ross & Cromarty

BLACK HOUSE, 42 Arnol, Lewis, PA86 9DB.   **4** Dept of Environment.   **5** Information Officer, Argyle House, 3 Lady Lawson St, Edinburgh.   **8** Open to the public.   **9** Mon-Sat (inc bank hols) 9.30-19.00 (Oct-March 16.00). Adults 5p, children 2½p.   **11** House contains many of its original furnishings, inc box beds, dresser etc.

LICHFIELD, Staffordshire.

SAMUEL JOHNSON BIRTHPLACE MUSEUM, Breadmarket St, Lichfield, WS13 6LG (Tel 05432-24972).   **4** Lichfield DC.   **5** Officer-in-Charge: Dr Graham Nicholls BA, PhD.   **6** Leisure & Recreation.   **7** Dept of Administration; Dir: K.D. Brownlow DPA, MILGA.   **8** Open to the public.   **9** Mon-Sat 10.00-13.00, 14.00-17.00 (16.00 Nov-March), Sun (June-Sept) 14.30-17.00. Adults 10p, children 5p.   **10** Life & writing of Samuel Johnson; furniture, paintings, mss, personal possessions; extensive library of Johnsoniana.   **12** (a) 1 (b) 1 (c) 1.

STAFFORDSHIRE REGIMENTAL MUSEUM, Whittington Barracks, Lichfield, WS14 9PY (Tel 054 32-22971).   **5** Curator: Col H.C.B. Cook OBE (Retd).   **8** Open to the public.   **9** Mon-Fri 9.30-16.30. Other times by arrangement. Free.   **10** Historical record of former North & South Staffordshire Regiments inc Militia, Volunteers & Territorials; medals, uniforms, weapons, battle relics & historical documents connected with the Regiments.

LINBY, Nottinghamshire.

NEWSTEAD ABBEY, Linby, Nottingham, NG15 8GE (Tel 06234-2822).   **4** Nottingham City Council.   **5** Chief Museums Officer: Mr Brian Loughborough MA, AMA.   **7** Leisure Services Dept, Dir: Mr Hugh McD. Lawson.   **8** Open to the public.   **9** Good Friday-Sept: Sun & bank hols 14.00-18.30, Mon-Sat 14.00-17.00 (tours on the hour). Abbey: adults 11p, children 5p. Grounds: adults 22p, children 8p. Carpark: 14p.   **10** 16th cent mansion built on remains of 12th cent priory church (19th cent neo-Gothic restoration); many of Lord Byron's possessions (pictures, furniture, mss, first editions); 300 acre park with Japanese water garden & tropical garden.

LINCOLN, Lincolnshire.

CITY AND COUNTY MUSEUM, Broadgate, Lincoln, LN2 1EZ (Tel 0522-30401).   **4** Lincolnshire CC.   **6** Museums Sub-Committee.   **7** Lincolnshire Museums, Old Barracks, Burton Rd, Lincoln; Dir: Mr Antony J.H. Gunstone BA, FSA, FMA.   **8** Open to the public.   **9** Mon-Sat (inc bank hols) 10.00-17.30, Sun 14.30-17.00. Free.   **10** County colln of archaeology & natural history; history of Lincoln.   **11** Prehistoric & roman collns.   **12** (a) 3 (b) 1 (c) 4.

LINCOLN CATHEDRAL TREASURY, The Cathedral, Lincoln.   **4** Dean & Chapter.   **5** Officer-in-Charge: Rev P.C. Hawker FSA.   **8** Open to the public.   **9** Mon-Sat (inc bank hols) 14.30-16.30, Sun 14.15-15.15. Charges: 5p.   **10** Silver from Diocese of Lincoln; foundation charter (William I); Magna Carta (1215).

MUSEUM OF LINCOLNSHIRE LIFE, Old Barracks, Burton Rd, Lincoln, LN1 3LY (Tel 0522-28448/29864).   **4** Lincolnshire CC.   **5** Keeper of Lincolnshire History: Mrs C.M. Wilson AMA.   **6** Museums Sub-Committee.   **7** Lincolnshire Museums, Dir: Mr Antony J.H. Gunstone BA, FSA, FMA.   **8** Open to the public.   **9** Tues-Sun (inc bank hols) 11.00-17.00. Adults 10p, children 5p; party rates.   **10** History of Lincolnshire (past 300 years) with emphasis on local agriculture, crafts, industries & technology.   **12** (a) 3 (b) 1 (c) 4.

ROYAL LINCOLNSHIRE REGIMENTAL MUSEUM, Sobraon Barracks, Burton Rd, Lincoln, LN1 3PY (Tel 0522-25444).   **4** Museum Trust, Royal Lincolnshire Regiment.   **5** Curator: Major E. Jessup.   **8** Open to the public.   **9** Mon-Fri 9.30-12.30, 14.00-17.00. Free.   **11** Uniforms, arms, equipment, silver & medals; reference library of histories, documents etc connected with Royal Lincolnshire Regiment.   **12** (b) 1.

USHER GALLERY, Lindum Rd, Lincoln, LN2 1NN (Tel 0522-27980).   **4** Lincolnshire CC.   **5** Keeper of Art: Mr Richard Wood DipAD.   **6** Museums Sub-Committee.   **7** Lincolnshire Museums, Old Barracks, Burton Rd, Lincoln; Dir: Mr Antony J.H. Gunstone BA, FSA, FMA.   **8** Open to the public.   **9** Mon-Sat (inc bank hols) 10.30-17.30, Sun 14.30-17.00. Free.   **10** Fine & decorative art; Peter De Wint paintings & archive; local topographical views; Usher watch colln; Hill Anglo-Saxon & Norman coinage of Lincolnshire.   **11** Temporary exhibitions.   **12** (a) 2 (b) 1 (c) 6.

LINDISFARNE, Northumberland

LINDISFARNE CASTLE, Holy Island, Berwick-upon-Tweed, TD15 2RX (Tel 028 989-244).   **4** National Trust.   **5** Custodians: Mr & Mrs C. Harrison.   **8** Open to the public.   **9** April, May & June 21-Sept: daily (exc Tues) 13.00-17.00. June 1-June 20: Wed 13.00-17.00. Not free.   **10** A tiny fort converted into a private house.   **11** 17th cent English & Flemish oak furniture; Ridinger & other prints.

LINLITHGOW, West Lothian.

HOUSE OF THE BINNS, Linlithgow.   **4** National Trust for Scotland.   **8** Open to the public.   **9** Easter-Sept: daily (exc Fri) (inc bank hols) 14.00-17.30. Grounds 10.00-19.30. Adults 30p, children 15p; Royal Scots Dragoon Guards & 'The Greys' in uniform, free.   **10** Reflects early 17th cent transition in Scottish architecture from fortified stronghold to more gracious mansion; magnificent moulded ceilings; home of the Dalyells.

LINLITHGOW PALACE, Linlithgow.   **4** Dept of Environment.   **5** Information Officer, Argyle House, 3 Lady Lawson St, Edinburgh.   **8** Open to the public.   **9** Mon-Sat 9.30-19.00, Sun 14.00-19.00. Oct-March: closes 16.00 daily. Adults 10p, children 5p.   **10** Birthplace of Mary, Queen of Scots, burnt by Hawleys Dragoons in 1746, north wing reconstructed in neo-classical style; Parish Church of St Michael nearby.

LITTLEHAMPTON, Sussex

LITTLEHAMPTON MUSEUM, 12 River Rd, Littlehampton, BN17 5BN (Tel 090 64-5149).   **4** Arun DC.   **5** Officer-in-Charge: C.E. Powell FIMEnt.   **6** Recreation, Amenities &

CODE: 1 Name of Museum, Art Gallery or Stately Home. 2 Address 3 Telephone & telex. 4 Governing body. 5 Officer in charge. 6 Committee responsible. 7 Larger department, chief officer. 8 Open to public. 9 Hours; admission charges. 10 Scope. 11 Special exhibits or facilities. 12 Staff (a) professionally qualified (b) other non-manual (c) manual.

LITTLEHAMPTON, Sussex—*continued*

Community Services. 7 Amenities & Recreation Dept, Amenities & Recreation Officer: N.J.Westgate FIMEnt. 8 Open to the public. 9 Sat (Summer only), Mon, Wed & Fri, (inc bank hols) 10.30-13.00, 14.15-16.30. Free. 10 Local history & topography, nautical & maritime items.

LIVERPOOL, Merseyside

CROXTETH HALL AND PARK, Croxteth, Liverpool, L12 0HB. (Tel 051-228 5311). 4 Merseyside CC. 5 Dir: Mr Geoffrey D.Lewis MA, FSA, FMA. 6 Arts & Culture. 8 No, museum facilities at present under development with a view to first-phase opening in 1976. 12 (b) 3 (c) 27.

MERSEYSIDE COUNTY MUSEUMS, William Brown St, Liverpool, L3 8EN (Tel 051-207 0001). 4 Merseyside CC. 5 Dir: Mr Geoffrey D.Lewis MA, FSA, FMA. 6 Arts & Culture. 8 Open to the public. 9 Mon-Sat (inc bank hols) 10.00-17.00, Sun 14.00-17.00. Closed Dec 25, 26 & Good Friday. Free except planetarium: adults 22p, children 11p. 10 Antiquities; decorative arts; ethnology; social & industrial history; maritime history; land transport; geology; botany; zoology (inc aquarium & vivarium); physical sciences; archives. 11 King's Regiment colln; Museum Education Service; temporary exhibitions; planetarium. 12 (a) 46 (b) 37 (c) 101.

SPEKE HALL, The Walk, Liverpool, L24 1XD (Tel 051-427 7231). 4 Merseyside CC. 5 Dir: Mr Geoffrey D.Lewis MA, FSA, FMA. 6 Arts & Culture. 8 Open to the public. 9 Mon-Sat 10.00-17.00; Sun: April-Sept 14.00-19.00, Oct-March 14.00-17.00. Adults 25p, children 10p; special rates for block bookings & educational parties. 10 Historic house & furniture. 12 (a) 1 (b) 2 (c) 6.

SUDLEY ART GALLERY, Mossley Hill Rd, Liverpool, L18 8BX (Tel 051-724 3245). 4 Merseyside CC. 5 Dir: Mr Timothy Stevens MA. 6 Arts & Culture. 8 Open to the public. 9 Mon-Sat 10.00-17.00, Sun 14.00-17.00. Closed Dec 24-26 & Good Friday. Free. 10 Victorian paintings. 11 Emma Holt bequest of British 19th cent paintings, some 18th & 19th cent foreign paintings; displays from Merseyside County Museums. 12 (a) as Walker Art Gallery (b) 1 (c) 12.

UNIVERSITY OF LIVERPOOL SCHOOL OF DENTAL SURGERY MUSEUM, Pembroke Place, Liverpool. 5 Curator: J.Hopper LDS, DORTH, RCS. 8 Not open to public; except for study & research, on request. 10 History of dental surgery; displays of current clinical methods; pathological material. 12 (a) 1.

WALKER ART GALLERY, William Brown St, Liverpool, L3 8EL (Tel 051-207 1371). 4 Merseyside CC. 5 Dir: Mr Timothy Stevens MA. 6 Arts & Culture. 8 Open to the public. 9 Mon-Sat 10.00-17.00, Sun 14.00-17.00. Closed Dec 24-26 & Good Friday. Free. 10 European paintings, sculpture, drawings, watercolours, prints (from 1300). 11 Early Italian & Netherlandish painting, British painting (1750-1914); also loan exhibitions inc John Moore's Liverpool exhibitions & Peter Moore's Liverpool projects. 12 (a) 8 (b) 13 (c) 43.

LLANBERIS, Gwynedd.

NORTH WALES QUARRYING MUSEUM, Llanberis, Caernarvon. (Tel 028682-630). 4 National Museum of Wales, Cardiff. 8 Open to the public. 9 Easter-Sept: daily (inc bank hols) 9.30-19.00. Adults 20p, children & OAPs 5p. 10 Machinery & equipment associated with the local slate-quarrying industry. 12 (b&c) 3 (plus 5 during summer).

LLANDRINDOD WELLS, Powys

LLANDRINDOD WELLS MUSEUM, Temple St, Llandrindod Wells, LD1 5LD (Tel 0597-2212). 4 Powys CC. 5 Officer-in-Charge: C.Newman BA, FLA. 7 County Libraries & Museums Dept; Chief Officer: G.Llewellyn FLA. 8 Open to the public. 9 Mon-Sat 10.00-12.30, 14.00-17.00. Free. 10 Archaeology; a site museum for Castell Collen Excavations. 11 Costume dolls; local history. 12 (a) 1.

TOM NORTON'S COLLECTION OF OLD CYCLES AND TRICYCLES, The Automobile Palace, Temple St, Llandrindod Wells, (Tel 05917-2214; Telex 35137). 5 Managing Dir: Mr T.Norton. 8 Open to the public. 9 Mon-Sat 8.00-18.00. Free, illustrated catalogue available (price 20p). 10 History of bicycles. 11 Hegdes English Boneshaker (1869); Ariel or Spider (1870); Rover (c.1886); Crypto (c.1888); 2 penny-farthings.

LLANELLI, Dyfed

ART GALLERY, Central Library, Vaughan St, Llanelli, SA15 3TY (Tel 05542-3538). 4 Llanelli BC. 5 Borough Libn & Curator: Mr H.A.Prescott FLA. 6 Development & Leisure. 8 Open to the public. 9 Mon-Sat (inc bank hols) 9.30-19.00. Free. 10 Works of local interest.

MANSION HOUSE, Parc Howard, Llanelli, Dyfed. SA15 3LJ (Tel 05542-3538). 4 Llanelli BC. 5 Borough Libn & Curator: Mr H.A.Prescott FLA. 6 Development & Leisure. 8 Open to the public. 9 Mon-Sat (inc bank hols) 10.00-20.00. Free. 10 Works of local interest. 11 Paintings by James Dickson Innes; Llanelli Pottery. 12 (a) 2 (b) 1 (c) 2.

LLANFAIRPWLL, Gwynedd.

PLAS NEWYDD, Llanfairpwll, Isle of Anglesey, LL61 6DQ. 4 National Trust. 5 Administrator: Mr Hugo Houghton. 8 Open to the public. 9 July-Oct: Sun-Fri 14.00-17.30. Adults 60p, children 30p. 10 18th cent house by James Wyatt; 18th & 19th cent furniture; 16th-20th cent pictures; views of Snowdonia; spring garden; Rex Whistler's largest wall painting; military museum. 11 Teas.

LLANGOLLEN, Clwyd.

PLAS NEWYDD, Llangollen, LL20 2AW. 4 Glyndwr DC. 5 Officer-in-Charge: H.G.Fawcett. 8 Open to the public. 9 Mon-Sat (inc bank hols) 10.00-19.00, Sun 11.00-16.00. Adults 10p, children 5p. Gardens free. 11 Carved oak; antiques; stained glass; Cordovan leather; picturesque gardens. 12 (b) 2.

LLANIDLOES, Powys

LLANIDLOES MUSEUM OF LOCAL HISTORY AND INDUSTRY, Market Hall, Llanidloes. 4 Powys CC. 5 Hon Curator: C.E.Vaughan Owen FSA. 7 County Libraries & Museums Dept; Chief Officer: G.Llewellyn FLA. 8 Open to the public. 9 Easter, then Whitsun-Sept: Mon-Sat (inc bank hols) 11.00-13.00, 14.00-17.00. Free. 10 Life & work of Llanidloes & surroundings. 11 Relics connected with Chartist outbreak in 1839 & some fragments from excavations of Roman fort at Caersws.

LLANYSTUMDWY, Gwynedd

LLOYD GEORGE MEMORIAL MUSEUM, Llanystumdwy, Criccieth, LL52 0SH (Tel 076671-2654). 8 Open to the public. 9 Mon-Fri (inc bank hols) 10.00-17.00. Adults 15p, OAPs 10p, children 5p. 10 Caskets, deeds of freedom, documents, scrolls & mementoes of the late David, First Earl Lloyd George of Dwyfor. 12 (b) 1.

LODE, Cambridgeshire

ANGLESEY ABBEY, Lode, Cambridge, CB5 9EJ (Tel 0223-811200).   **4** National Trust.   **8** Open to the public.
9 April-mid Oct: Tues-Thurs, Sat, Sun & bank hols 14.00-18.00. Gardens: daily 14.00-18.00. Adults 60p, children 30p. Gardens only (Mon & Fri) adults 30p, children 15p.
10 13th cent abbey (Elizabethan & early 20th cent alterations); Fairhaven colln (paintings; statues; furniture; jade; clocks; tapestries).   **11** 100 acres magnificent gardens; Windsor colln of paintings.   **12** (c) 9.

LONDON (GLC AREA)

ARMOURIES, Tower of London, London EC3 4AB (Tel 01-709 0765). **5** Master of the Armouries: Mr A.R.Dufty CBE, FSA. **8** Open to the public. **9** Mon-Sat (inc bank hols) 9.30-18.00, Sun 14.30-18.00 (winter: closes 16.30 daily). Adults 40p, children 20p, winter ½ price. **10** National colln of arms & armour. **11** Royal armour; British military arms; cannon; hunting weapons. **12** (a) **13** (b) 4 (c) 40.

ARMY MUSEUMS OGILBY TRUST, 85 Whitehall, London SW1A 2EL (Tel 01-839 1979). **5** Sec: Col P.S.Newton MBE. **8 & 9** Ref library open to genuine researchers Mon-Fri 9.30-17.00. Free unless research is for commercial gain. **10** Trust gives technical & financial aid to all (130) Army regimental/corps/service museums; data on all aspects of army post-1660. **11** Spencer Wilkinson papers; source index on British military costume prints. **12** (a) 5.

ARTILLERY MUSEUM, The Rotunda, Woolwich, SE18 4JJ (Tel 01-854 2424 ext 385). **4** Royal Artillery Institution. **5** Senior Museum Asst: Mr S.C.Walter. **8** Open to the public. **9** Mon-Fri (inc bank hols) 10.00-12.45, 14.00-17.00, Sat 10.00-12.30, Sun 14.00-17.00. Winter: Sun-Fri closes 16.00. Free. **10** Development of British ordnance (Crecy—1945). **11** 'Crecy Bombard' in moat of Bodiam Castle, Sussex (13 pounder gun served by 'L' Battery RHA at Nery 1 Sept 1914).

BADEN-POWELL STORY, Baden-Powell House, Queensgate, London, SW7 5JS (Tel 01-584 0671; Telex 913755). **4** Scout Association. **8** Open to the public. **9** Daily 9.00-18.00. Closed Dec 25. Free. **10** Memorial to Robert Baden-Powell.

BARNET MUSEUM, 31 Wood St, Barnet, Hertfordshire (Tel 01449-54150). **4** Barnet BC. **5** Curator: W.S.Taylor. **6** Barnet & District Local History Society. **8** Open to the public. **9** Tues & Thurs 14.30-16.30, Sat 10.00-12.30, 14.30-16.30. Free. **10** Temporary exhibitions (mostly local). **12** (b) 12.

BEAR GARDENS MUSEUM, Bankside, Southwark, London, SE1 (Tel 01-928 6342). **4** World Centre For Shakespeare Studies. **5** Dir: Mr Colin Mabberley BA. **8** Open to the public. **9** Mon-Fri 10.00-17.00, Sat & Sun 13.00-17.00. Adults 10p, students & OAPs 5p. **10** Elizabethan & Jacobean theatre colln; temporary exhibitions (theatrical or local interest). **11** Models of Elizabethan & Jacobean playhouses. **12** (a) 2 (b) 1 (c) 1.

BETHLEM ROYAL HOSPITAL MUSEUM AND ARCHIVES, Monks Orchard Rd, Beckenham, Kent, BR3 3BX (01-777 6611). **4** Bethlem Royal Hospital & Maudsley Hospital Board of Governors. **5** Archivist: Ms Patricia H.Allderidge MA, DipArchAdmin. **7** Archives Dept. **8** Open to the public. **9** Mon-Fri 9.30-17.00. Archives by appointment only. Free. **10** History of Bethlem Royal Hospital (the original 'Bedlam') & Maudsley Hospital; their place in the history of psychiatry & treatment of the insane (from 1247). **11** Archives of the hospital available for research, to bona-fide students; various historical aspects of insanity & treatment; pictures by & material on the painter Richard Dadd; early almsboxes; iron manacles; relics from earlier buildings. **12** (a) 1 (b) 1.

BETHNAL GREEN MUSEUM, Cambridge Heath Rd, London E2 9PA (Tel 01-980 2415/3204). **4** Victoria & Albert Museum. **5** Officer-in-Charge: Miss Elizabeth Aslin. **8** Open to the public. **9** Mon-Sat 10.00-18.00, Sun 14.30-18.00. Closed Dec 24-26, Jan 1 & Good Friday. Free. **10** Toys; dolls; dolls houses; model & toy theatres; Spitalfields silk. 19th cent continental decorative arts & sculpture (inc Rodin); wedding dresses & childrens clothes. **11** Temporary exhibitions.

BRITISH DENTAL ASSOCIATION MUSEUM, 64 Wimpole St, London W1M 8AL (Tel 01-935 0875). **5** Hon Curator: J.A. Donaldson BA, FDS, RCS. **8** Open by appointment only. **10** History of dental surgery.

BRITISH MUSEUM, Great Russell St, London WC1 3DG (Tel 01-636 1555: Telex Britmus Liblon). **4** British Museum, Trustees. **5** Dir: Sir John Pope-Hennessy CBE, FBA, FSA, FRSL. **8** Open to the public. **9** Mon-Fri (inc bank hols) 10.00-17.00, Sat 14.30-18.00. Free. **10** Greek, Roman, western Asiatic, Oriental, Egyptian, mediaeval, prehistoric & Romano-British & later antiquities; coins & medals; prints & drawings; ethnography. **11** Parthenon friezes ('Elgin Marbles'); royal gold cup of the kings of England & France; Sutton Hoo ship burial; Rosetta Stone; Portland vases; treasures from death pits at Ur of Chaldees. **12** (a) 302 (b) 502 (c) 56.

BRITISH MUSEUM, *see also* Museum of Mankind

BRITISH MUSEUM (NATURAL HISTORY), Cromwell Rd, London SW7 5BD (Tel 01-589 6323). **4** Trustees of the British Museum (Natural History). **5** Dir: Dr G.F. Claringbull PhD. **8** Open to the public. **9** Mon-Sat 10.00-18.00. Sun 14.30-18.00. Closed Dec 24-26, Jan 1 & Good Friday. Free. **10** National colln of animals & plants (both recent & fossil) & of rocks, minerals & meteorites; special exhibits on natural selection, insect pests, neolithic man, & the formation of fossils. **11** Free gallery tours, lectures & films most weekdays; free educational service for parties of schoolchildren & students. **12** (a) c.365 (b) c.280 (c) 81.

BRITISH MUSEUM (NATURAL HISTORY) *see also* Tring, Hertfordshire

BROADCASTING GALLERY, Independent Broadcasting Authority, 70 Brompton Rd, London SW3 1EY (Tel 01-584 7011; Telex 24345). **4** Independent Broadcasting Authority. **5** Publicity & Broadcasting Gallery Manager: M.Hallett MIPR. **8** Open to the public. **9** Mon-Fri 10.00-11.30, 14.30-15.30. Free. **10** All aspects of broadcasting (past & present, international & British). **11** Audio-visual techniques. **12** (b) 3.

BROMLEY BOROUGH MUSEUM, The Priory, Church Hill, Orpington, Kent, BR6 0HH (Tel 31551; Telex 896712). **4** Bromley BC. **5** Curator: Mrs Susann Palmer MPhil, AMA, FRAI, DipArch. **6** General Purposes. **7** Libraries,

LONDON—*continued*

Borough Libn: Mr D. M. Laverick FLA.   **8** Open to the
public.   **9** Mon-Fri 9.00-18.00, Sat 9.00-17.00. Free.
10 General archaeology of all periods (emphasis on local
finds), some geology & ethnography.   **11** Local Roman &
pagan Saxon excavations; temporary exhibitions; museum
club for children.   **12** (a) 1 (c) 2.

BROOMFIELD MUSEUM, Broomfield Park, Broomfield Lane,
London N13 4HE (Tel 01-882 1354).   **4** Enfield BC.
5 Local History & Museums Officer: D. O. Pam FLA.
6 Leisure & Amenities.   **7** Libraries, Museums, Arts &
Entertainments Dept, Dir: Mr A. E. Brown FLA.   **8** Open
to the public.   **9** Easter-Sept: Tues-Fri 10.00-20.00,
Sat & Sun 10.00-18.00; Oct-Easter: daily (exc Mon) 10.00-
17.00. Free.   **10** Paintings & drawings (mainly by local
artists); small permanent colln.   **11** Temporary exhibitions
(especially local history); Close co-operation with local art,
historical, archaeological & civic societies; conducted visits
for schools; lectures.   **12** (a) 1 (b) 3 (c) 6.

BRUCE CASTLE MUSEUM, Lordship Lane, London, N17 8NU
(Tel 01-808 8772).   **4** Haringey BC.   **5** Controller of
Libs Museum & Arts: W. S. H. Ashmore FLA.   **6** Civic
Amenities (Library, Museum & Arts Panel).   **8** Open to the
public.   **9** Mon-Fri (exc Wed) 10.00-17.00, Sat 10.00-
12.30, 13.30-17.00. Free.   **10** Local history & archives;
British postal history. **11** Middlesex Regimental Museum;
art exhibitions.   **12** (a) 3 (b) 2 (c) 2.

CAMDEN ARTS CENTRE, Arkwright Rd, London NW3 6DG
(Tel 01-435 2643/5224).   **4** Arkwright Arts Trust.
5 Administrator: Ms Zuleika Dobson.   **7** Leisure Services.
8 Open to the public.   **9** Mon-Sat 11.00-18.00 (20.00
Fri), Sun 14.00-18.00. Free.   **10** Temporary exhibitions.
11 Art classes, activities & events.   **12** (a) 1 (b) 9 (c) 3.

CARLYSLE'S HOUSE, 24 Cheyne Row, London SW3 5HL
(Tel 01-352 7087).   **4** National Trust.   **5** Custodian:
Mrs E. Hay.   **8** Open to the public.   **9** Jan-Nov: Wed-
Sat & bank hols 11.00-13.00, 14.00-18.00, Sun 14.00-18.00.
Closes sunset if earlier. Adults 40p, students 20p.
10 Early 18th cent terraced house; home of Thomas &
Jane Carlyle (1834-their deaths); their furniture, books,
letters, personal relics & portraits; strong Victorian
atmosphere.   **11** Students may study Carlyle's papers &
documents by appointment in writing with Custodian or
through the National Trust.   **12** (b) 1.

CHARTERED INSURANCE INSTITUTE MUSEUM, The Hall,
20 Aldermanbury, London EC2V 7HY (Tel 01-606 3835).
5 Asst Sec: P. V. Saxton FCII, MITO, AMBIM.   **8** Open
to the public.   **9** Mon-Fri 9.15-17.15 (Fri 17.00).
Free.   **10** Fire marks; insurance fire-fighting equipment;
other insurance bygones.   **11** Comprehensive colln of
British fire marks.   **12** (a) 1 (c) 4.

CHURCH FARM HOUSE MUSEUM, Greyhound Hill, Hendon,
London NW4 4JR (Tel 01-203 0130).   **4** Barnet BC.
5 Libn in Charge, Ref & Museum Services: Miss M.
McDerby ALA.   **6** Libraries & Arts.   **7** Borough
Libn: Mr S. J. Butcher FLA, FRSA.   **8** Open to the public.
9 Mon-Sat 10.00-12.30, 13.30-17.30 (Tues 10.00-13.00),
Sun (& bank hols) 14.30-18.00. Free.   **10** Some period
rooms.   **11** Temporary exhibitions.   **12** (b) 1.

CLOCKMAKER'S COMPANY MUSEUM, Guildhall Library,
Aldermanbury, London EC2P 2EJ (Tel 01-606 3030).
4 Worshipful Company of Clockmakers, administered by
the Library Committee, Guildhall, London.   **5** Hon Curator:
Mr Godfrey Thompson FLA.   **8** Open to the public.
9 Mon-Sat 9.30-17.00. Free.   **10** Development of clocks
& watches (inc many by London makers).   **11** Examples
by East, Tompion, Graham, Knibb, Quare; Harrison's
prototype of his marine chronometers, unique colln of
watch keys.

COMMONWEALTH ART GALLERY, Kensington High St,
London W8 6NQ (Tel 01-602 3252).   **4** Commonwealth
Institute Board of Governors.   **5** Curator: Mr Donald
Bowen NDD, FRSA.   **8** Open to the public.   **9** During
exhibitions: Mon-Sat (inc bank hols) 10.00-17.30, Sun
14.30-18.00. Free.   **10** Temporary exhibitions only of
the work of Commonwealth (inc British) painters, sculptors
& craftsmen.   **12** (a) 2 (c) 1.

CRICKET MEMORIAL GALLERY, Lord's Ground, London
NW8 8QN (Tel 01-289 1611).   **4** Marylebone Cricket
Club.   **5** Curator: Mr Stephen E. A. Green MA, DipArch
Admin.   **6** Arts & Literary Sub-Committee.   **8** Open
to the public.   **9** Summer: Mon-Sat 10.30-17.00, winter:
by appointment, Mon-Fri 10.00-16.30. Bank hols: only if
cricket is being played. Adults 11p, children 5p.
10 History of cricket.   **11** Cricket paintings, trophies,
bygones & objects of art.   **12** (a) 1 (b) 1 (c) 1.

CUMING MUSEUM, 155-157 Walworth Rd, London SE17 1RS
(Tel 01-703 3324/6514/5529).   **4** Southwark BC.
5 Keeper: M. R. Maitland Muller BA, AMA.   **6** Libraries
& Amenities.   **7** Libraries Dept, Borough Libn & Curator:
K. A. Doughty FLA.   **8** Open to the public.   **9** Mon-
Fri 10.00-17.30 (Thurs 19.00), Sat 10.00-17.00. Free.
10 Archaeology & history of Southwark area.   **11** London
supersititions; an 18th cent performing bear; Dickensiana;
products of ceramic designer George Tinworth; evolution
of local milk distribution methods; free information leaflets;
enquiry & identification service; assistance to teachers &
their classes; facilities for study of original source
material (by appointment).   **12** (a) 2 (c) 1.

CUTTY SARK CLIPPER SHIP, King William Walk, Greenwich, London SE10 9HT (Tel 01-858 3445).   **4** Cutty
Sark Society.   **5** Master: Capt D. M. Reid.   **8** Open to the
public.   **9** Mon-Sat 11.00-18.00, Sun 14.30-18.00. Close
17.00 daily in winter. Closed Dec 26 & Jan 1. Adults 30p,
children 15p; group rates.   **10** Last of the clipper ships;
yacht 'Gipsy Moth IV'.   **11** Ship figureheads.   **12** (a) 4
(c) 16.

DICKENS HOUSE MUSEUM, 48 Doughty St, London WC1N
2LF (Tel 01-405 2127).   **4** Dickens House Trustees.
5 Curator: Miss Marjorie E. Phillers.   **8** Open to the public.
9 Mon-Sat 10.00-17.00. Adults 25p, Students 15p, children 10p
groups by prior arrangements.   **10** House where Charles
Dickens lived (1837-1839) when he finished 'Pickwick
Papers', wrote 'Oliver Twist' & 'Nicholas Nickleby'; relics;
furniture; first editions; mss; reading desk.   **11** Suzannet
Rooms (Dickensiana); ref lib & research room (by appointment).   **12** (b) 3 (c) 2.

Dr JOHNSON'S HOUSE, 17 Gough Square, London EC4A 3DE
(Tel 01-353 3745).   **4** Dr Johnson's House Trust.
5 Curator: Miss M. Eliot.   **8** Open to the public.
9 Mon-Sat 10.30-17.00 (Oct-April 16.30). Adults 11p,
students & children 5½p.   **10** Relics of Dr Johnson;
portraits; 18th cent prints.

EPPING FOREST MUSEUM, *see* Queen Elizabeth's Hunting
Lodge

FENTON HOUSE, Windmill Hill, London NW3 6RT (Tel
01-435 3471).   **4** National Trust.   **5** Custodians:
Monica & Richard Usborne.   **8** Open to the public.
9 Wed-Sat 11.00-17.00, Sun 14.00-17.00. Closed all Dec,
Jan 1 & Good Friday. Adults 50p, children 25p, garden free.
10 House (1693); porcelain (English, continental & Chinese);
furniture & pictures; tapestry; 1½ acre garden.   **11** Early
keyboard instruments (Benton-Fletcher Committee).
12 (b) 2 (c) 2.

FORTY HALL MUSEUM, Forty Hill, Enfield, Middlesex,
EN2 9HA (Tel 01-363 8196).   **4** Enfield BC.   **5** Curator:
M. H. O. Paterson BA, FRSA, FMA.   **6** Leisure &
Amenities.   **7** Libraries, Arts & Entertainments, Dir:
Mr A. E. Brown FLA.   **8** Open to the public.   **9** Easter-
Sept: Tues-Fri & bank hols 10.00-20.00, Sat & Sun 10.00-
18.00; Oct-Easter Tues-Sun & bank hols 10.00-17.00.
Free.   **10** 17th & 18th cent furniture, pictures, ceramics,
glass, metalwork & needlework, chiefly English; local history
(prints, maps & other documents); some local antiquities.
11 Furniture & electrotypes of English silver lent by
Victoria & Albert Museum; material from Enfield Archaeological Society's excavations at Elsynge 1963-66; temporary
exhibitions.   **12** (a) 1 (b) 1 (c) 5.

CODE: 1 Name of Museum, Art Gallery or Stately Home. 2 Address. 3 Telephone & telex. 4 Governing body. 5 Officer in charge. 6 Committee responsible. 7 Larger department, chief officer. 8 Open to public. 9 Hours; admission charges. 10 Scope. 11 Special exhibits or facilities. 12 Staff (a) professionally qualified (b) other non-manual (c) manual.

LONDON—*continued*

GEFFRYE MUSEUM, Kingsland Rd, London, E2 8EA (Tel 01-739 8368). **4** ILEA. **5** Curator: Mr Jeffery Daniels MA. **6** Geffrye Museum Advisory Committee. **7** Education Officer: Dr E.W. Briault. **8** Open to the public. **9** Tues-Sat & bank hols 10.00-17.00, Sun 14.00-17.00. Free. **10** English furniture & woodwork (c.1600-1939) arranged as period rooms in former almshouses of the Ironmongers' Company (1715). **11** Education dept: special arrangements for school visits (must be booked in advance & for children visiting in their own time. **12** (a) 5 (b) 1 (c) 6.

GEOLOGICAL MUSEUM, Exhibition Rd, South Kensington, London SW7 2DE (Tel 01-589 3444). **4** National Environment Research Council. **5** Dir: Sir Kingsley Dunham DSc, SD, ScD, FRS, FRSE, CEng, HonFIMM; Curator: Mr F.W. Dunning, OBE, BSc, FGS. **8** Open to the public. **9** Mon-Sat 10.00-18.00, Sun 14.30-18.00. Closed Good Friday, Dec 24-25 & Jan 1. Free. **10** History & evolution of the earth; principles of physical geology (especially regional geology of Great Britain & economic geology & mineralogy of the world; & study colln of rocks, fossils & minerals. **11** Sound & multi-slide presentation on Britain's energy resources; gemstones in their parent rock association, in natural & crystal form, & in their final cut state; talks, demonstrations & films; field excursions; bookshop. **12** (a) 12 (b) 7 (c) 1.

GIPSY MOTH IV, *see* Cutty Sark

GOLDSMITH'S HALL, *see* Worshipful Company of Goldsmiths

GORDON MUSEUM, Guy's Hospital Medical School, London SE1 9RT (Tel 01-407 7600 ext 3372). **4** Guy's Hospital Medical School. **5** Curator: J.D. Maynard MS, FRCS. **8** No, open to medical personnel only, by appointment. **9** Mon-Fri 9.00-17.00. **11** Anatomical, dermatological & pathological specimens. **12** (b) 3.

GRAND LODGE MUSEUM, Freemasons' Hall, Great Queen St, London WC2B 5AZ (Tel 01-405 3633). **4** United Grand Lodge of England. **5** Officer-in-Charge: Mr T.O. Haunch MA. **8** Not open to public. **10** History & development of Freemasonry. **12** (a) 2 (b) 3.

GREENWICH BOROUGH MUSEUM, Plumstead Library, 232 Plumstead High St, London SE18 1JL (Tel 01-854 1728). **4** Greenwich BC. **5** Borough Libn & Curator: Mr H. Davis FLA; Keeper: Mr R.G. Rigden AMA. **7** Directorate of Recreational Services, Dir: Mr C.J.C. Field. **8** Open to the public. **9** Mon & Thurs-Sat 10.00-13.00, 14.00-17.00, Tues 14.00-20.00. Free. **10** Pre-history, history & natural history of Greenwich. **11** Dawson colln of butterflies; school loans service; lectures by request. **12** (a) 2 (b) 1 (c) 1.

GREENWICH NATURAL HISTORY MUSEUM, New Eltham Library, Southwood Rd, London SE9 (Tel 01-850 2322). **4** Greenwich BC. **5** Borough Libn & Curator: Mr H. Davis FLA. **7** Directorate of Recreational Services, Dir: Mr C.J. Field. **8** Open to the public. **9** Mon-Fri 9.00-17.00. Free. **10** Natural history

GUARDS MUSEUM, Wellington Barracks, London SW1 (Tel 01-930 4466 ext 2270). **4** HQ Household Division, Horse Guards, Whitehall, SW1. **5** Officer-in-Charge: Lt Col P.R. Adair. **8** Open to the public. **9** Mon-Sat 10.00-17.00 (16.00 winter), Sun & bank hols 11.30-13.30, 14.30-17.00. Charges: 5p. **10** History of the 5 Regiments of Foot Guards. **12** (b) 2.

GUILDHALL ART GALLERY, King St, Cheapside, London EC2P 2EJ (Tel 01-606 3030 ext 2864). **4** Corporation of London. **5** Dir: Mr Godfrey Thompson FLA. **6** Library. **8** Open to the public. **9** Mon-Sat 10.00-17.00. Free. **10** Paintings, drawings, sculpture of London interest; English British school 17th-20th cent. **12** (a) 3 (b) 1 (c) 2.

GUILDHALL MUSEUM, *see* Museum of London

GUNNERSBURY PARK MUSEUM, Gunnersbury Park, London W3 8LQ (Tel 01-992 1612/2247). **4** Ealing & Hounslow BC joint owners, administered by Hounslow BC. **5** Curator: Miss Bridget Goshawk AMA. **6** Gunnersbury Park. **7** Libraries Dept, Chief Libn: Miss Florence M. Green FLA. **8** Open to the public. **9** Mon-Fri 14.00-17.00, Sat, Sun & bank hols 14.00-18.00. Oct-March: closes 16.00 daily. Closed Dec 24-26 & Good Friday. Free. **10** Rothschild's early 19th cent mansion; local history, social history, & topography. **11** Transport (coaches, Hansom cab, early bicycles); 19th & 20th cent costume; Sadler colln of flint implements; Chiswick Press; early maps & views of the locality. **12** (a) 1 (b) 1 (c) 1.

HALL PLACE, Bourne Rd, Bexley, Kent, DA5 1PQ (Tel 03225-26574; Telex 846119). **4** Bexley BC. **5** Local Studies Officer: J.C.M. Shaw BA. **6** Civic Amenities. **7** Libraries; Borough Libn: P.E. Morris FLA. **8** Open to the public. **9** Mon-Sat 10.00-17.00 (dusk in winter); Sun (summer only) 14.00-18.00. Free. **10** 16th-17th cent house; temporary exhibitions (local & general). **11** Local studies dept; enquiries & study centre. Also local history, archaeology & natural history at Walnut Tree Rd, Erith, Kent. **12** (a) 3 (b) 2.

HAM HOUSE, Richmond, Surrey, TW10 7RS (Tel 01-940 1950). **4** National Trust, administered by Victoria & Albert Museum. **5** Keeper, Dept of Furniture & Woodwork, Victoria & Albert Museum: Mr P.K. Thornton. **8** Open to the public. **9** April-Sept: Tues-Sun & bank hols 14.00-18.00; Oct-March: Tues-Sun & bank hols 12.00-16.00. Closed Good Friday, Dec 24-26 & Jan 1. Adults 20p, children, OAPs, students 10p; school parties sometimes free. **10** Early 17th cent house; furniture & paintings mostly late 17th cent. **12** (a) Staffed by Victoria & Albert Museum.

HAMPTON COURT PALACE, East Molesey, Surrey, KT8 9AU (Tel 01-977 8441). **4** Lord Chamberlain's Office, Dept of Environment. **5** District Works Office for Dept of Environment: C.M. Goode; Superintendent of The Royal Colln for Lord Chamberlain: Mr Wm. Watson. **8** Open to the public. **9** Mon-Sat 9.30-18.00 (Oct. March & April 17.00) (Nov-Feb 16.00), Sun 11.00-18.00 (winter 14.00-16.00). Closed Dec 24-26, Jan 1 & Good Friday. Winter: adults 10p, children 5p. Summer: adults 30p, children 10p. **10** State apartments; paintings in the Royal Colln; period furniture; Tudor kitchens, cellars & tennis court. **11** Carriages etc from the Royal Mews at Buckingham Palace (April-Sept: Tues-Sun 10.00-17.00. Admission 5p).

HAYES & HARLINGTON MUSEUM, Public Library, Golden Crescent, Hayes, UB3 1AQ (Tel 01-573 2855). **4** Hayes & Harlington Local History Society (premises owned by Hillington BC). **5** Hon Curator: B.T. White. **7** Premises only: Libraries Dept; Borough Libn. **8** Open to the public. **9** Mon-Fri 9.00-20.00 (Wed 13.00), Sat 9.00-17.00. Free. **10** Local history of Hayes, Harlington & Cranford (West of River Crane).

HAYWARD GALLERY, Belvedere Rd, South Bank, London SE1 8XZ (Tel 01-928 3144). **4** Arts Council of Great Britain. **5** Administrator: Mr Francis Ward. **7** Art Dept of Arts Council of Great Britain, Art Dir: Mr Robin Campbell. **8** Open to the public. **9** Mon-Fri 10.00-20.00, Sat 10.00-18.00; Sun 12.00-18.00. Not free, charges vary according to exhibition. **10** Temporary exhibitions of art, photography, sculpture. **12** (b) 18 (c) 42.

LONDON—*continued*

HMS BELFAST, Symons Wharf, Vine Lane, London SE1 2JH
(Tel 01-407 6434).   **4** HMS Belfast Trust Ltd.   **5** Dir:
Rear Admiral P. R. C. Higham CB.   **8** Open to the public.
9 Daily (exc Dec 24 & 25) 11.00-dusk. Not free.   **10** Last
of the British gunned cruisers; 7 Decks; how the ship's company lived & fought.   **12** (b) 15 (c) 36.

HOGARTH'S HOUSE, Hogarth Lane, Great West Rd, Chiswick,
W4 2QN (Tel 01-994 6757). Correspondence to: Chief Libn,
Civic Centre, Lampton Rd, Hounslow, TW3 4DN (Tel 01-570
7728).   **4** Hounslow BC.   **5** Resident Caretaker: Mrs S.
Brook.   **6** Libraries Sub-Committee.   **7** Libraries Dept,
Chief Officer: Miss F. M. Green FLA.   **8** Open to the
public.   **9** Mon-Sat 11.00-18.00, Sun 14.00-18.00. Closes
all day Tues & 16.00 other days in winter. Closed Dec 25,
26 & Good Friday. Adults 10p, children 5p, parties by
arrangement.   **10** Narrow 3-storeyed brick & tiled house
(c. 1700) with original panelled walls & hanging bay window
overlooking garden where mulberry tree still fruits annually;
Hogarth's summer residence from 1749; no contemporary
furnishings; over 150 framed prints from Hogarth's engravings, copper plates for 'Hudibras' books & other artefacts
illustrating the artist's life & times.   **11** Brochure (12p
plus postage); photographs; postcards; transparencies.
12 (c) 1.

HORNIMAN MUSEUM AND LIBRARY, London Rd, Forest Hill,
London SE3 3PQ (Tel 01-699 1872/2339/4911).   **4** GLC &
ILEA.   **5** Curator: Mr David M. Boston MA, OBE.
6 Horniman Museum Advisory.   **7** ILEA External Relations
Branch, M. Lightfoot.   **8** Open to the public.   **9** Mon-Sat
(inc bank hols) 10.30-18.00, Sun 14.00-18.00. Free.
10 Ethnography; musical instruments; archaeology; zoology;
palaeontology; aquarium.   **11** Navaho sand painting;
animals; Carse colln of wind instruments; evolution; education
centre.   **12** (a) 19 (b) 30.

HUNTERIAN MUSEUM, Royal College of Surgeons of England,
Lincoln's Inn Fields, London WC2A 3PN (Tel 01-405 3474).
4 Hunterian Trustees.   **5** Curator: Miss E. Allen.
8 Open by written application only, parties must make an
appointment.   **9** Mon-Fri 10.00-17.00, Sat 10.00-13.00.
Free.   **10** Based on the colln founded by John Hunter (1728-
1793), the famous surgeon/anatomist, to illustrate his views
& theories on comparative anatomy, physiology & pathology.
Not a natural history colln.   **11** Odontological Museum:
development, structure & pathology of teeth & jaws; colln of
historical surgical instruments.

IMPERIAL WAR MUSEUM, Lambeth Rd, London SE1 6HZ.
(Tel 01-735 8922).   **4** Imperial War Museum Trustees.
5 Dir: Dr Noble Frankland DFC.   **8** Open to the public.
9 Mon-Sat 10.00-18.00, Sun 14.00-18.00. Closed Dec 24-26,
Jan 1 & Good Friday. Free.   **10** All aspects of military
operations involving Britain & the Commonwealth since 1914;
weapons & equipment; works of art; books; documents; films &
photographs.   **11** Two 15-inch guns from the battleships
Ramillies & Resolution; a Mark V tank; a German V2 rocket;
a Battle of Britain Spitfire; the Victoria Cross won by Boy
Jack Cornwell at the Battle of Jutland & the original German
surrender document signed by Field Marshal Montgomery
in 1945.   **12** (a) 157 (b) 62.

INDEPENDENT BROADCASTING AUTHORITY, *see* Broadcasting Gallery

INDUSTRIAL HEALTH AND SAFETY CENTRE, 97 Horseferry Rd, London SW1P 2DY (Tel 01-828 9255).   **4** Health
& Safety Executive.   **5** Dir: Mr J. W. Hobson.   **8** Open to
the public.   **9** Mon-Fri 10.00-16.30. Free.   **10** Methods
& applications for promoting industrial health & safety.
11 Temporary exhibitions (usually 6 months).   **12** (a) 7
(b) 3 (c) 14.

IVEAGH BEQUEST, KENWOOD, Hampstead Lane, London
NW3 7JR (Tel 01-348 1286/7).   **4** GLC.   **5** Curator:
Mr John Jacob MA.   **6** Arts & Recreation.   **7** Historic
Buildings Division) Surveyor of Historic Buildings: Mr Ashley

Barker OBE, FRIBA) of the Architect's Dept, Architect: Sir
Roger Walters KBE, FRIBA.   **8** Open to the public.
9 Daily 10.00-19.00 (Oct, Feb & March 17.00) Nov-Jan
16.00). Closed Dec 24, 25 & Good Friday. Free.   .
10 Iveagh Bequest of Old Master paintings (Vermeer,
Rembrandt, Frans Hals etc) & English 18th cent portraits
(Reynolds, Gainsborough, Romney, etc); housed in Robert
Adam mansion, noted for its magnificent library.
11 Summer exhibition on 18th cent & modern art; Maufe colln
of Georgian shoebuckles.   **12** (a) 3 (b) 6 (c) 28.

JEWISH MUSEUM, Woburn House, Upper Woburn Place,
London WC1H 0EP (Tel 01-387 3081).   **4** Jewish Museum
Committee.   **5** Joint Secs: Mr David Hackner & Mr Phineas
L. May; Curator: Mrs Carole Mendleson BA.   **8** Open to the
public.   **9** Mon-Thurs 14.30-17.00, Fri & Sun 10.30-12.45.
Closed bank hols & Jewish hols. Free.   **10** Comprehensive
colln of ritual objects & antiquities illustrating Jewish life &
worship.

JOHN EVELYN SOCIETY WIMBLEDON MUSEUM, Village
Club, 26 Lingfield Rd, Wimbledon, London SW19 4QD (Tel
01-946 0764).   **5** Officer-in-Charge: Mr C. G. Parsloe MA,
FRHistSoc.   **8** Open to the public.   **9** Sat 14.30-17.00.
School parties or for research, other times by appointment.
Free.   **10** Local history of Wimbledon & surrounding
areas.   **11** Photographic survey of area at turn of century;
Nelson/Hamilton deeds of Merton Place.   **12** (a) 1 (b)
Committee of 10.

JOHN WESLEY'S HOUSE AND MUSEUM, 47 City Rd, London
EC1Y 1AU (Tel 01-253 2262).   **4** Wesley's Chapel Trustees.
5 Curator: Mr S. Cole.   **8** Open to the public.   **9** Mon-
Sat 10.00-13.00, 14.00-16.00. Charges: 10p.   **10** 18th
cent house in which John Wesley lived & died; his personal
possessions & much of his furniture.   **12** (b) 1.

KEATS HOUSE, Wentworth Place, Keats Grove, Hampstead,
London NW3 2RR (Tel 01-435 2062; Telex 24323).
4 Camden BC.   **5** Dir of Libs & Arts, & Curator of Keats
House: Mr Wm R. Maidment OBE, FLA; Asst Curator: Mrs
C. M. Gee ALA.   **6** Leisure Services.   **8** Open to the
public.   **9** Mon-Sat (inc bank hols) 10.00-18.00, Sun: hours
under review. Free.   **10** John Keats lived in this house
(1818-1820); mss; letters, relics of Keats & his circle; Keats
Memorial Library (over 6,000 vols on Keats & the Roman-
tics).   **11** Keats's annotated copies of Shakespeare & Milton; microfilm reader.   **12** (a) 1 (b) 3 (c) 2.

KENSINGTON PALACE STATE APARTMENTS, London
W8 4PX (Tel 01-937 9561).   **4** Dept of Environment,
Directorate of Ancient Monuments & Historic Buildings.
5 Manager: Mr C. H. L. Purver.   **8** Open to the public.
9 Mon-Sat 10.00-18.00, Sun 14.00-18.00 (close 17.00
daily Oct & Feb, 16.00 daily Nov-Jan). Closed Dec 24-26,
Jan 1 & Good Friday. Adults 15p, children & OAPs 5p; party
rates.   **10** State apartments of the palace used by William
III & Mary II, Anne, George I & George II; birthplace of Queen
Victoria & Queen Mary.

KEW PALACE, Kew Gardens, Richmond, Surrey TW9 3AQ.
4 Dept of Environment.   **8** Open to the public.   **9** April-
Sept: Mon-Sat 11.00-17.30, Sun 14.00-18.00. Closed Good
Friday. Adults 5p, children & OAPs 2½p.   **10** Items from
Royal colln.

KINGSTON UPON THAMES MUSEUM AND ART GALLERY,
Fairfield Rd, Kingston upon Thames (Tel 01-546 5386).
4 Kingston upon Thames BC.   **5** Borough Libn & Curator:
Mr W. G. B. Brown FLA; Asst Curator: Mrs M. P. Smith BA,
AMA.   **6** Arts & Recreation.   **8** Open to the public.
9 Mon-Sat 9.00-17.00. Art Gallery: hours vary according
to exhibitions. Free.   **10** Prehistory & natural history of
Kingston upon Thames, Surrey & the nearer Thames Valley.
Art Gallery: circulating & local society exhibitions.
11 Martin Brothers' salt glaze stoneware; zoopraxiscope,
slides etc. illustrating the work of Eadweard Muybridge,
motion picture pioneer.   **12** (a) 1 (b) 1 (c) 2.

KNELLER HALL MUSEUM, Royal Military School of Music,
Kneller Hall, Twickenham, Middlesex, TW2 7DU (Tel 01-898
5533).   **4** MOD (Army).   **5** Officer-in-Charge: Lt Col
R. Bashford OBE (Rtd).   **8** Open to the public.   **9** May-

CODE: 1 Name of Museum, Art Gallery or Stately Home. 2 Address. 3 Telephone & telex. 4 Governing body. 5 Officer in charge. 6 Committee responsible. 7 Larger department, chief officer. 8 Open to public. 9 Hours; admission charges. 10 Scope. 11 Special exhibits or facilities. 12 Staff (a) professionally qualified (b) other non-manual (c) manual.

LONDON—*continued*

Sept: Wed (when concerts being given) 18.30-20.00. Organized parties: other times by arrangement. Free. 10 Musical instruments.

KODAK MUSEUM, Kodak Ltd, Headstone Drive, Harrow, Middlesex, HA1 4TY (Tel 01-427 4380; Telex 21925). 5 Curator: Mr Brian W. Coe FBKS. 8 & 9 Open by appointment only; Mon-Fri 9.30-16.30. Free. 10 History of photography & allied processes. 12 (a) 3.

LEIGHTON HOUSE, ART GALLERY AND MUSEUM, 12 Holland Park Rd, London W14 8LZ (Tel 01-602 3316). 4 Kensington BC. 5 Officer-in-Charge: D. Hart DA, FRSA. 6 Libraries & Amenities. 7 Libraries Dept, Borough Libn: Mr M. Barnes DMA, ALA, AMBIM, MILGA. 8 Open to the public. 9 Mon-Sat 11.00-17.00 (18.00 during temporary exhibitions). Free. 10 Victorian house designed & lived in by Lord Leighton; ceramics; pottery by William de Morgan; 15th, 16th, & 17th cent Persian tiles (part of interior applied decoration); 19th cent British painting & furniture; temporary exhibitions of fine & applied art. 11 Art lecture courses; concerts & recitals. 12 (a) 1 (c) 4.

LIVESEY MUSEUM, 682 Old Kent Rd, London SE15 1JF (Tel 01-639 5604). 4 Southwark BC. 5 Officer-in-Charge: Miss J. P. Slaney BA, AMA. 6 Libraries & Amenities. 7 Libraries Dept, Borough Libn & Curator: K. A. Doughty FLA. 8 Open to the public. 9 Open during exhibitions only; Mon-Sat 10.00-17.00. Free. 10 Temporary exhibitions (mainly local); outside exhibition area with large permanent exhibits of street furniture (tollgate, bollard, etc). 12 (a) 1 (b) 3.

LLOYD'S NELSON COLLECTION, Lloyd's, Lime St, London, EC3M 7HA (Tel 01-623 7100). 4 Corporation of Lloyd's. 5 Officer-in-Charge: Mr T. A. F. Atkins. 7 Lloyd's Inf & Publicity Dept, Manager: Mr Douglas Greenall. 8 Open by appointment only. 9 Mon-Fri 10.00-16.30. Free. 10 Lloyd's presentation silver swords & letters (especially of Lord Nelson & his circle); artefacts & objets d'art relating to Nelson. 11 H.M.S. Euryalus: Master's rough logbook covering Trafalgar campaign; Lord Nelson's portrait (full length) by Lemuel Abbott; John Julius Angerstein portrait by Thomas Lawrence; Lloyd's patriotic fund swords & vases.

LONDON MUSEUM, *see* Museum of London

LONDON SCOTTISH REGIMENTAL MUSEUM, 59 Buckingham Gate, London SW1E 6AL (Tel 01-828 0234). 5 Hon Curator: T. I. Bulpin. 8 Open to the public. 9 Open by appointment only. Free. 10 Arms, uniforms etc, pertaining to the Regiment.

LONDON TRANSPORT COLLECTION, Syon Park, Brentford, Middlesex TW8 8JF (Tel 01-560 0882). 4 London Transport Executive. 5 Manager: Mr John R. Day MCIT, AssocIRSE. 8 Open to the public. 9 Daily 10.00-19.00 (Oct-March 17.00). Closed Dec 25 & 26. Adults 25p, children & OAPs 15p; party rates. 10 Historic vehicles (from 1829 onwards): horse & motor buses; trams; trolleybuses; locomotives & railway rolling stock from London Transport & its predecessors; posters; signs; tickets; models. 11 Souvenir shop; Schools 'PROJECT' book, can be used in conjunction with a visit, as basis of a course in transport, mechanical engineering & social studies for 8-12 year olds. 12 (a) 1 (b) 4 (c) 1.

MALL GALLERIES, The Mall, London SW1 (Tel 01-930 6844). 4 Federation of British Artists. 5 Sec General: Mr Maurice Bernard Bradshaw. 8 Open to the public. 9 Mon-Fri 10.00-13.00, Sat 10.00-13.00. Charges: 20-40p. 10 Current exhibitions of the London Art Socities.

MARBLE HILL HOUSE, Richmond Rd, Twickenham, Middlesex TW1 2NL (Tel 01-892 5115). 4 GLC. 5 Curator: Mr John Jacob MA. 6 Arts & Recreation. 7 Historic Buildings Division (Surveyor of Historic Buildings: Mr Ashley Barker OBE, FRIBA) of the GLC Architect's Dept, Architect: Sir Roger Walters KBE, FRIBA. 8 Open to the public. 9 Sat-Thurs 10.00-17.00 (Nov-March 16.00). Closed Dec 24 & 25. Free. 10 Palladian villa, built 1724-29 for Henrietta Howard, Countess of Suffolk; early 18th cent paintings & furniture. 11 Summer exhibitions on 18th cent & modern art. 12 (a) 3 (shared with the Iveagh Bequest, Kenwood) (b) 4 (c) 12.

MOCATTA MUSEUM (temporarily closed), University College, Gower St, London WC1E 6BT (Tel 01-387 7050 ext 240). 4 Jewish Historical Society of England. 9 In store & inaccessible pending a decision as to possibilities of display. 10 Synagogue ware, mainly silver; Anglo-Jewish historical material.

MUSEUM OF LONDON (not open yet), London Wall, London EC2. 4 Museum of London Board of Governors. 5 Dir: T. A. Hume BA, FSA, FMA. 9 Due to open late 1976. 10 Combined collns of the former London Museum & the Guildhall Museum; history & topography of London from prehistoric times to the present. 11 Paintings, prints & drawings; costume; library; temporary exhibitions; education service. 12 (a) 41 (b) 9.

MUSEUM OF MANKIND (Ethnography Department of the British Museum), 6 Burlington Gardens, London W1X 2EX (Tel 01-437 2224). 4 Trustees of the British Museum. 5 Keeper of Ethnography, British Museum: M. D. McLeod MA, BLitt. 8 Open to the public. 9 Mon-Sat 10.00-17.00, Sun 14.30-18.00. Free. 10 Ethnographic & anthropological collns of the British Museum; regular exhibitions (eg African pottery, Solomon Islands, Hawaii, Australian Aborigines); permanent colln of some of the Museum's most important & famous pieces; access to reserve collns by appointment. 11 Regular film shows; special films for schools or visiting parties by prior appointment; very large anthropological & archaeological library can be used by the public; comprehensive service for schools & colleges. 12 (a) c.17 (b) c.10 (c) c.35.

MUSICAL MUSEUM, 368 High St, Brentford, Middlesex, TW8 0BD (Tel 01-560 8108). 4 British Piano Museum Charitable Trust. 5 Founder & Dir: Mr Frank Walter Holland FIMIT. 8 Open to the public. 9 April-Oct: Sat & Sun 11.00-17.00. Adults 50p, children 30p. 10 Mainly automatic musical instruments worked by paper music rolls, pinned barrels, discs etc; reproducing piano & reproducing pipe organ which play music from music rolls recorded earlier in this century; orchestrions; music boxes; street barrel pianos. 11 Steinway Duo-Art Grand Piano (once owned by Princess Beatrice, youngest daughter of Queen Victoria); Welte Philharmonic Reproducing Pipe Organ; Wurlitzer Theatre Organ; Stodart piano (upon which Mendelssohn played). 12 (a) 2.

NATIONAL ARMY MUSEUM, Royal Hospital Rd, London SW3 4HT (Tel 01-730 0717/9). 5 Dir: Mr William Reid. 8 Open to the public. 9 Mon-Sat 10.00-17.30, Sun 14.00-17.30. Closed Dec 24-26, Jan 1 & Good Friday. Free. 10 Story of British, Indian & Colonial Land Forces 1485-1914; paintings & prints; silver & ceramics; early photographs, relics, uniforms & medals; weapons. 11 Reading room. 12 (a) 30 (b) 36.

NATIONAL FILM ARCHIVE, 81 Dean St, London W1V 6AA (Tel 01-437 4355 Telex 27624). 4 British Film Institute. 5 Curator: Mr David Francis BSc. 8 Open only for enquiries or access to Stills Dept. 9 Mon-Fri 9.30-18.00. 10 National colln of cinematograph films & television programmes of artistic & historic importance (all countries, but especially British); stills, posters & other related

LONDON—*continued*

material.   **11** Stills Dept sells copy-stills to authors, publishers, researchers etc; viewing service for study of Archive films on Archive's premises; production library for sale of film extracts to film & TV producers etc.   **12** (b) 51.

NATIONAL GALLERY, Trafalgar Square, London WC2N 5DN (Tel 01-839 3321).   **4** Trustees of the National Gallery. **5** Dir: Mr Michael Levey (resigning Dec 1976); Keeper: Mr Cecil Gould.   **8** Open to the public.   **9** Mon-Sat 10.00-18.00 (21.00 Tues & Thurs, June-Sept only), Sun 14.00-18.00. Closed Dec 24-26, Jan 1 & Good Friday. Free. **10** Western European art (paintings) (c.1300-c.1900). **11** Restaurant; Seminar Room; Smoking Room; Reading Room; public lavatories (inc paraplegic accommodation). **12** (a) 22 (b) 28 (c) 211.

NATIONAL MARITIME MUSEUM, Romney Rd, Greenwich, SE10 9NF (Tel 01-858 4422).   **4** Trustees.   **5** Dir: Mr Basil Greenhill CMG, BA, FSA, FRHistS.   **8** Open to the public.   **9** Mon-Sat 10.00-18.00 (17.00 in winter), Sun 14.30-18.00. Closed Dec 24-26, Jan 1 & Good Friday. Free. **10** British maritime history in historic buildings at Royal Greenwich; Old Royal Observatory; the Queen's House; pictures & paintings; Caird Library; archives; actual craft & ship models; uniforms; swords; medals; personal relics; silver; china; glass; furniture; astronomical & navigation instruments; ships' draughts; historic photographs. **11** Nelson's Trafalgar coat; Harrison chronometers 1-4; Franklin relics; contemporary dockyard ship models; lecture theatre; draught room; boat-building workshop.   **12** (a, b & c) c.250.

NATIONAL MONUMENTS RECORD, Fortress House, 23 Savile Row, London, W1X 1AB (Tel 01-734 6010).   **4** Royal Commission on Historical Monuments.   **5** Curator: Mr Cecil Farthing OBE, BA, FSA.   **8** Open to the public. **9** Mon-Fri 10.00-17.30. Free.   **10** English historic architecture (c.1,000,000 photographs & measured drawings); c.250,000 air photographs of English archeological sites.   **12** (a) 7 (b) 10 (c) 2.

NATIONAL MUSEUM OF LABOUR HISTORY, Limehouse Town Hall, Commercial Rd, London E14 7HA (Tel 01-515 3229).   **4** Trade Union, Labour, Co-operative Democratic History Society Trustees.   **5** Sec: Mr Henry Fry. **8** Open to the public.   **9** Tues-Fri 11.00-16.30 (Wed 18.30). Parties by arrangement. Free.   **10** Social history of last 200 years; Thomas Paine; London Corresponding Society; Mary Wollstonecraft; Robert Owen; trade unions; Socialism. **11** Lectures, if required.   **12** (b) 3 (c) 2.

NATIONAL PORTRAIT GALLERY, St Martin's Place, London WC2H 0HE (Tel 01-930 8511).   **4** Trustees of the National Portrait Gallery.   **5** Dir: Dr John Hayes, MA, PhD, FSA. **8** Open to the public.   **9** Mon-Fri 10.00-17.00, Sat 10.00-18.00, Sun 14.00-18.00. Closed Dec 24-26, Jan 1 & Good Friday. Free (except for some special exhibitions). **10** Britain's history through portraits of her famous men & women (from early Tudors to the present); primarily a historical colln, but inc great works of art by well-known artists; paintings; drawings; sculpture; engravings; miniatures; photographs.   **11** Temporary exhibitions; annexe at 15 Carlton House Terrace, SW1; Education Dept (public lectures; visits & activities for children, students & adults).   **12** (a) 21 (b) 12 (c) 58.

NATIONAL POSTAL MUSEUM, King Edward Building, King Edward St, London EC1. (Tel 01-432 3851).   **4** The Post Office.   **5** Curator: Mr A.G. Rigo de Righi FRPS. **8** Open to the public.   **9** Mon-Fri 10.00-16.30, Sat 10.00-16.00. Free.   **10** Postage stamps & philatelic archives of Great Britain etc; Post Office colln; R.M. Phillips colln (19th cent British stamps); World (UPU) colln (c.1850-present); philatelic colln & archives of Thomas De La Rue & Co (1855-1965).   **11** Temporary exhibitions (on stamps & postal history); special facilities (inc films) for visits by schools & societies.   **12** (a) 2 (b) 2 (c) 7.

NATURAL HISTORY MUSEUM, *see* British Museum (Natural History)

ORDER OF ST JOHN MUSEUM, St John's Gate, Clerkenwell, London EC1M 4DA (Tel 01-253 6644).   **5** Curator: Ms Pamela Willis MA.   **8** Open to the public.   **9** Mon-Fri 10.00-17.00. Sat afternoons by arrangement. Free. **10** History of the Knights of St John of Jerusalem, of Rhodes & of Malta, & of the St. John Ambulance Brigade; coins, furniture; porcelain; silver; paintings; armour.   **11** St. John's Gate, 16th cent archway.   **12** (a) 2.

ORLEANS HOUSE GALLERY, Riverside, Twickenham, TW1 3DJ (Tel 01-940 0031; Telex 917174).   **4** London Borough of Richmond upon Thames.   **6** Amenities.   **7** Libraries Dept, Borough Libn: Mr Derek Jones MA, FLA.   **8** Open to the public.   **9** Tues-Sat 13.00-17.30, Sun & bank hols 14.00-17.30. Oct-March: closes 16.30 daily. Free. **10** Ionides colln of topographical paintings, watercolours & engravings of Richmond & Twickenham; special exhibitions on local history.   **11** James Gibbs' baroque Octagon Room, 1720.   **12** (b) 1 (c) 1.

OSTERLEY PARK, Isleworth, Middlesex, TW7 4RB (Tel 01-560 3918).   **4** National Trust, administered by Victoria & Albert Museum.   **5** Keeper, Dept of Furniture & Woodworks, Victoria & Albert Museum: Mr Peter K. Thornton. **8** Open to the public.   **9** April-Sept: Tues-Sun & bank hols 14.00-18.00; Oct-March: Tues-Sun & bank hols 12.00-16.00. Closed Dec 24-26, Jan 1 & Good Friday. Park: daily 10.00-20.00 (or sunset). Adults 20p, children & OAPs 10p, National Trust members free. Car park 10p. **10** Elizabethan house remodelled by Robert Adam; original furnishings; Elizabethan stable.   **11** Refreshments (summer only).   **12** Administered from V. & A. Museum (b) 1 (c) 6.

PASSMORE EDWARDS MUSEUM, Romford Rd, Stratford, London E15 4LZ (Tel 01-534 4545 ext 376).   **4** Governors of the Passmore Edwards Museum (appointed by London Borough of Newham, Museums Association, Essex Field Club & Newham Teachers Association).   **5** Curator: Mr Ian G. Robertson MA, AMA.   **6** Further Education Sub-Committee, London Borough of Newham.   **7** Education Dept, London Borough of Newham, Dir: Dr J.S. Wilkie MA, PhD.   **8** Open to the public.   **9** Mon-Fri 10.00-18.00 (20.00 Thurs), Sat 10.00-13.00, 14.00-17.00. Free. **10** Archaeology; folklife; geology; local & natural history of Essex, especially West Essex & Eastern Greater London. **11** Bow porcelain & Essex military collns; extension services section (loans, talks, projects for schools & local educational bodies).   **12** (a) 5 (b) 7 (c) 1.

PHARMACEUTICAL SOCIETY OF GREAT BRITAIN MUSEUM, 17 Bloomsbury Sq, London, WC1A 2NN (Tel 01-405 8967).   **4** Council of Society.   **5** Officer-in-Charge: Mr R.G. Todd FPS.   **8** Open to bona-fide enquirers only. **9** Mon-Fri 9.30-17.00. Free.   **10** Materials of historical pharmaceutical interest.   **11** 17th & 18th cent drugs; English delft drug jars; bell-metal mortars; dispensing apparatus; medicine chests; microscopes.   **12** (a) 1.

POLISH INSTITUTE & SIKORSKI MUSEUM, 20 Princes Gate, London SW7 1QA (Tel 01-589 9249).   **5** Hon Curator: Capt Ryszard S.J. Dembinski.   **8** Open to the public.   **9** Mon-Fri 14.00-16.00, 1st Sat each month 10.00-17.00. Free. **10** Polish regimental standards, orders, medals, uniforms, numismatics; personal effects of General Sikorski; archives (Polish wartime government in exile & Free Polish Forces). **11** Some 17th cent Polish armour; Turkish tent (captured 1621); 18th cent miniatures; paintings; 18th & 19th cent Polish noblemen's saschas (belts).

POLLOCK'S TOY MUSEUM, 1 Scala St, London W1P 1LT (01-636 3452).   **4** Trustees of Pollock's Toy Museum, Management Committee.   **5** Consultant & Founder: Mrs Marguerite Fawdry.   **8** Open to the public.   **9** Mon-Sat 10.00-17.00. Adults 20p, children, students, OAPs 10p. **10** Toy theatres, dolls, folk toys (from China, Russia, Africa, India, Europe, Japan, South-America etc).   **11** Toy theatre performances; toy shop.

PUBLIC RECORD OFFICE, Chancery Lane, London WC2A 1LR (Tel 01-405 0741).   **5** Keeper of Public Records: J.R. Ede.   **8** Open to the public.   **9** Search Rooms: Mon-

CODE: 1 Name of Museum, Art Gallery or Stately Home. 2 Address. 3 Telephone & telex. 4 Governing body. 5 Officer in charge. 6 Committee responsible. 7 Larger department, chief officer. 8 Open to public. 9 Hours; admission charges. 10 Scope. 11 Special exhibits or facilities. 12 Staff (a) professionally qualified (b) other non-manual (c) manual.

LONDON—*continued*

Fri 9.30-17.00, Sat 9.30-13.00. Museum: Mon-Fri 13.00-16.00. Free. **10** Records of central government & courts of law (from 11th cent-present). **11** Domesday Book; Gunpowder Plot papers; Log of HMS Victory; various royal autographs etc.

QUEEN ELIZABETH'S HUNTING LODGE AND EPPING FOREST MUSEUM, Rangers Rd, Chingford, London E4 7QH (Tel 01-529 6681). **4** Corporation of London, Conservators of Epping Forest. **5** Curator: J. P. Seddon BSc. **6** Epping Forest Committee of the Corporation of London. **7** Conservators of Epping Forest, Mr A. Qvist FRICS. **8** Open to the public. **9** Wed-Sun & bank hols 14.00-18.00 (dusk in winter). Parties other times by arrangement. Adults 5p, children free. **10** Hunting lodge built for the use of Henry VIII and his court; antiquities relating to Epping Forest; natural history of the area. **12** (a) 1 (c) 1.

QUEEN'S GALLERY, Buckingham Palace, London SW1A 1AA Correspondence to: Lord Chamberlain's Office, St James Palace, London SW1. **8** Open to the public. **9** Tues-Sat & bank hols 11.00-17-00, Sun 14-00-17-00. Adults 30p, students, OAPs & children 10p. **10** Pictures, works of art, etc from the Royal colln. **11** Small bookstall (postcards, slides, catalogues etc of current exhibition).

QUEEN'S ROYAL SURREY REGIMENTAL MUSEUM, Portsmouth Rd, Kingston upon Thames, Surrey, KT1 2NB (entrance in: Surbiton Rd, Kingston upon Thames) (Tel 01-546 6248). **4** RHQ The Queen's Regiment (Queen's Surreys Office). **5** Regimental Sec: Major F. J. Reed (Retd). **8** Open to the public. **9** Mon-Fri 9.30-12.30, 13.30-16.30. Free. **10** Regimental relics of the former Queen's Royal Regiment (West Surrey), the former East Surrey Regiment & the former Queen's Royal Surrey Regiment. **11** Old uniforms, plate, pictures, weapons & military exhibits of a general nature, inc photographs of the 1860's. **12** (c) 1.

RANGER'S HOUSE, Chesterfield Walk, Blackheath, London SE10 8QX (Tel 01-853 0035). **4** GLC. **5** Curator: Mr John Jacob MA. **6** Arts & Recreation. **7** Historic buildings Division (Surveyor of Historic Buildings: Mr Ashley Barker OBE, FRIBA) of the Architect's Dept, Architect: Sir Roger Walters KBE, FRIBA. **8** Open to the public. **9** Daily 10.00-17.00 (16.00 Nov-Jan). Closed Dec 24, 25 & Good Friday. Free. **10** Suffolk colln of Jacobean full-length & later Stuart portraits & Old Master paintings. **12** (a) 3 (shared with Iveagh Bequest, Kenwood) (b) 4 (c) 14.

ROYAL ACADEMY OF ARTS, Piccadilly, W1V 0DS (Tel 01-734 9052). **4** President & Council. **5** President: Sir Hugh Casson RIBA; Sec: Mr Sidney C. Hutchison MVO, FSA, FMA. **8** Open to the public. **9** Mon-Sat (inc bank hols) 10.00-18.00, Sun 14.00-18.00. Not free. **10** Summer exhibition of contemporary paintings, engravings, sculpture & architecture; loan exhibitions of the Old Masters etc; RA's own colln on display in its private rooms. **11** The Taddei Tondo by Michelangelo (marble relief); art schools.

ROYAL AIR FORCE MUSEUM, RAF Hendon, Aerodrome Rd, London NW9 5LL (Tel 01-205 2266). **4** Trustees of RAF Museum. **5** Officer-in-Charge: Dr J. I. Tanner MA, PhD, FRHistS, FRAeS, FSA. **8** Open to the public. **9** Mon-Sat 10.00-18.00, Sun 14.00-18.00. Closed Dec 25, 26 & Good Friday. Free. **10** 100 years of military aviation history from military ballooning in the 1870's to the current & future activities of the RAF. **11** Restaurant; cinema/lecture hall; facilities for disabled (wheel chair, lift etc). **12** (a) 15 (b) 63 (c) 18.

ROYAL BOTANIC GARDENS, Kew, Richmond TW9 3AE (Tel 01-940 1171). **4** MAFF. **5** Dir: Prof J. Heslop-Harrison MSc, PhD, DSc, FRS, FRSE, MRIA, FLS, FIBiol; Officer-in-Charge, Museums: Miss R. C. R. Angel BSc,

DipHortSci, FLS. **8** Open to the public. **9** Mon-Sat 10.00-16.50, Sun & bank hols, 10.00-17.50. Closes earlier in winter. 1p (to Gardens, no extra charge for museum). **10** Economic botany; picture gallery of flower paintings. **11** Orientation area in the gardens; temporary exhibits in Orangery. **12** (a) 6 (b) 3 (c) 1.

Royal College of Music

DEPARTMENT OF PORTRAITS AND EPHEMERA, Prince Consort Rd, London SW7 2BS (Tel 01-589 3643). **5** Keeper of Portraits: Mr Oliver Davies. **8 & 9** Open by appointment; Mon-Fri 10.00-17.00. Free. **10** Portraits of musicians (150 originals, 5,000-6,000 engravings, photographs etc); concert programmes; ephemeral music; ref library on musical iconography. **12** (a) 1.

MUSEUM OF INSTRUMENTS, Prince Consort Rd, London SW7 2BS (Tel 01-589 3643). Curator: Mrs E. P. Wells ARCM. **8 & 9** Open by appointment; term: Mon & Wed 10.30-16.30. Charges: 10p. **10** Donaldson, Hipkins & Ridley collns; c.450 exhibits, mostly European keyboard, stringed & wind instruments (16th-19th cent); small ethnological section. **122** (a) 2.

ROYAL HOSPITAL, CHELSEA, Royal Hospital Rd, Chelsea, London SW3 4SR (Tel 730-0161 ext 28). **5** Officer-in-Charge: Major R. A. C. Wellesley PSC. **8** Open to the public. **9** Mon-Sat 10.00-12.00, 14.00-16.30, Sun 14.00-16.30. Free. **10** Facets of Royal Hospital. **11** Uniforms, medals & badges; historical pictures & charts of Christopher Wren's original conception of the Royal Hospital; 'Wellington Hall' devoted to the Duke of Wellington & his battles. **12** (b) 3 (c) 1.

ROYAL INSTITUTE OF BRITISH ARCHITECTS DRAWINGS COLLECTION AND HEINZ GALLERY, 21 Portman Sq, London W1H 9HF (Tel 01-487 5441). **5** Curator: Mr John Harris FSA, HonFRIBA. **8** Open to the public. **9** Open, but hours under review. Free. **10** c.250,000 architectural drawings (ie. design & topographical drawings) mostly British (16th cent onwards). **11** Photography service; temporary exhibitions. **12** (a) 3 (b) 2.

ROYAL MEWS, Buckingham Palace, London SW1A 1AA (Tel 01-930 4832). **4** The Crown Equerry. **8** Open to the public. **9** Wed & Thurs 14.00-16.00. Closed during Ascot & various other times. Adults 15p, children 5p. **10** Working stables. **11** State harness, horses, carriages, early royal cars.

ROYAL SOCIETY OF PAINTERS IN WATERCOLOURS GALLERY, 26 Conduit St, London W1R 9TA (Tel 01-629 8300). **4** Royal Society of Painters in Water Colours. **5** Officer-in-Charge: Mr Malcolm Fry FRSA, HonRWS. **8** Open during exhibitions only. **9** Mon-Fri 10.00-17.00, Sat 9.30-12.30. Charges: 20p. **10** Annual exhibitions: Royal Society of Painters in Water Colours (April & Sept); Royal Society of Painter-Etchers & Engravers (March); Society of Miniaturists (Aug); RWS Art Club (Aug). **12** (a) 1 (b) 1 (c) 1.

ST BRIDE'S CRYPT MUSEUM, St Bride's Church, Fleet St, London EC4Y 8AU (Tel 01-353 1301). **4** Rector & Churchwardens of St Bride's. **5** Officer-in-Charge: Rector of St. Bride's: Rev. Dewi Morgan BA. **8** Open to the public. **9** Mon-Sat (inc bank hols) 9.00-17.00 (or later), Sun 9.00-19.30. Free. **10** 2,000 years of the history of this site & personalities connected with it; history of printing & communications. **11** Line of a 12th cent Roman ditch; remains of a 2nd cent Roman pavement; masonry remains of churches from 6th, 9th, 12th, 15th & 17th cent; related artefacts, illustrations, etc.

SCIENCE MUSEUM, Exhibition Rd, London SW7 2DD (Tel 01-589 6371). **4** Dept of Education & Science. **5** Dir: Dr M. K. Weston. **8** Open to the public. **9** Mon-Sat 10.00-18.00, Sun 14.30-18.00. Closed Dec 24-26, Jan 1

LONDON—*continued*

& Good Friday. Free.   **10** History & development of the physical sciences, industry & technology; instruments, equipment & machinery; precise scale models.   **11** 1829 rocket locomotive; 1903 Wright Flyer (replica); 1888 Benz motor car.

SERPENTINE GALLERY, Kensington Gardens, London W2 3XA (Tel 01-402 6075).   **4** Arts Council of Great Britain.   **5** Gallery Organiser: Ms Sue Grayson.   **8** Open to the public.   **9** During exhibitions: daily (May-July) 11.00-20.00, (April & Aug) 10.00-17.00, (March, Sept & Oct) 10.00-18.00, (Nov-Feb) 10.00-16.00. Closed Dec 24-26, Jan 1 & Good Friday. Free.   **10** One-man & group shows of contemporary art (monthly).   **12** (a) 5.

SIR JOHN SOANE'S MUSEUM, 13 Lincolns Inn Fields, London WC2 3BP (Tel 01-405 2107).   **4** Trustees of Sir John Soane's Museum.   **5** Officer-in-Charge: Sir John Summerson CBE, FBA, DLitt.   **8** Open to the public.   **9** Tues-Sat 10.00-17.00. Free.   **10** House & Museum of Sir John Soane (1753-1837); his antiquities, paintings, sculptures, drawings, mss & library of 8,000 titles; also adjoining house in which Soane lived before he built the museum.   **11** 'Rake's Progress' & 'Election' cycles by William Hogarth; sarcophagus of Pharoah Seti I; drawings of Robert & James Adam; lecture tours (Sat 14.30).   **12** (a) 2 (b) c. 8 (c) c. 4.

SOUTH LONDON ART GALLERY, Peckham Rd, London SE5 8UH (Tel 01-703 6120).   **4** Southwark BC.   **5** Keeper: Mr Kenneth Sharpe BA, DipEd.   **6** Libraries & Amenities.   **7** Libraries Dept, Borough Libn & Curator: K.A. Doughty FLA.   **8 & 9** Open during exhibitions; Mon-Sat 10.00-18.00, Sun 15.00-18.00. Free.   **10** British drawings & paintings (mostly Victorian); contemporary paintings; London Borough of Southwark Topographical colln drawings & paintings.   **11** Temporary exhibitions; 20th cent print colln (available for ref Mon-Fri 10.00-17.00).   **12** (a) 1 (b) 2.

SYON HOUSE, Brentford, Middlesex, TW8 8JG (Tel 01-560 0884).   **4** Duke of Northumberland KG, PC.   **8** Open to the public.   **9** May-Sept: Mon-Thurs 13.00-17.00; Aug & Sept: Sun 13.00-17.00; Easter, Spring & Autumn bank hols: 13.00-17.00. Adults 35p, OAPs & children 20p; party rates.   **10** Historic Tudor mansion; interior re-decorated & furnished by Robert Adam; royal & family portraits; Old Masters; antique statuary; park laid out by Capability Brown.   **11** Free car park; cafeteria; bars; restaurant.   **12** See also Alnwick Castle.

TATE GALLERY, Millbank, London SW1P 4RG (Tel 01-828 1212).   **4** Trustees.   **5** Dir: Sir Norman Reid DA, FMA, FIIC.   **8** Open to the public.   **9** Mon-Sat (inc bank hols) 10.00-18.00, Sun 14.00-18.00. Free, except for special loan exhibitions.   **10** National collns of British painting of all periods; modern foreign painting; modern sculpture.   **11** Education Dept; Gallery Shop (books, prints, postcards etc); restaurant; coffee shop.   **12** (a) 33 (b) 46 (c) 161.

THEATRE MUSEUM, Victoria & Albert Museum, South Kensington, London SW7 2RL; and Leighton House, Kensington High St. Planning to move to Covent Garden Flower Market in 2-3 years. (Tel 01-589 6371).   **4** Dept of Education & Science.   **5** Curator: Mr Alexander Schouvaloff.   **8** Open to the public.   **9** Mon-Sat 10.00-18.00, Sun & bank hols 14.00-18.00. Study Room: Mon-Fri 10.00-16.50. Closed Dec 25 & Good Friday. Free.   **10** Comprehensive colln on all performing arts (inc theatre, ballet, opera, music hall, pantomime, circus, puppets).   **11** Gabrielle Enthoven, Harry Beard & Hinkins collns of toy theatres; Guy Little colln of photographs.   **12** (a) 14.

THOMAS CORAM FOUNDATION FOR CHILDREN (FOUNDLING HOSPITAL), 40 Brunswick Square, London WC1N 1AZ (Tel 01-278-2424).   **5** Curator: J.G.B. Swinley.   **8** Open to the public.   **9** Mon-Fri 10.00-16.00. Adults 20p, children 10p.   **10** Mainly 18th cent paintings & sculptures in replicas of original rooms of the Foundling Hospital to which the works were given by the artists; works by Hogarth

(3); Reynolds; Gainsborough; Roubilliac; Rysbrack; Copley; West; Hudson. Handel relics & Foundling Hospital mementoes.   **11** Guided tour by prior arrangement.   **12** (b) 1.

TOWER OF LONDON, London EC3N 4AB (Tel 01-709 0765).   **4** Dept of Environment.   **5** Resident Governor & Keeper of the Jewel House: Major Gen W.D.M. Raeburn CB, DSO, MBE, MA.   **8** Open to the public.   **9** Mon-Sat 9.30-17.00 (16.00 Nov-Feb), Sun (Mar-Oct only) 14.00-17.00. Closed Dec 24-26, Jan 1 & Good Friday. Mar-Oct: adults 80p, OAPs & children 30p, Nov-Feb: adults 20p, OAPs & children 10p.   **10** Royal palace & fortress.   **11** Crown Jewels.

TUDOR BARN ART GALLERY, Well Hall Pleasaunce, Well Hall Rd, Eltham, London SE9 (Tel 01-850 2340).   **4** Greenwich BC.   **5** Borough Libn & Curator: Mr H. Davis FLA; Keeper: Mr J. Bunston BA, AMA.   **6** Recreational Services Committee.   **7** Directorate of Recreational Services, Dir: Mr C.J.C. Field.   **8** Open to the public.   **9** Sun-Fri (inc bank hols) 11.00-20.00 (Sept-March: dusk). Free.   **10** Restored 16th cent building; temporary exhibitions (mainly contemporary local art, some local history).   **12** (a) 1 (b) 1 (c) 2.

University of London

COURTAULD INSTITUTE GALLERIES, Woburn Square, London WC1H 0AA (Tel 01-580 1015).   **5** Curator of Collns: Mr Philip Troutman.   **8** Open to the public.   **9** Mon-Sat 10.00-17.00, Sun 14.00-17.00. Closed Dec 25, 26 & Good Friday. Free.   **10** Paintings by Impressionist & post-Impressionist masters; Old Master paintings, sculptures, drawings & other works of art (ivories, majolica, etc).   **11** Masterpieces by Manet, Monet, Renoir, Degas, Sisley, Pissarro, Seurat, Van Gogh, Gauguin, Toulouse-Lautrec, Cezanne.   **12** (a) 2 (b) 10.

KING'S COLLEGE, DEPARTMENT OF GEOLOGY MUSEUM, Strand, London WC2R 2LS (Tel 01-836 5454).   **5** Curator: Mr John D.R. Fryer BSc, FLS, FGS.   **8** Not open to public.   **10** Undergraduate teaching material & postgraduate research material.   **12** (a) 1.

LONDON HOSPITAL MEDICAL COLLEGE MUSEUM, Turner St, London E1 2AD (Tel 01-247 0644).   **4** London University.   **5** Officer-in-Charge: E.C.B. Butler MB, FRCS.   **8** Not open to public, medical students only. Free.   **10** Pathological specimens; history of medicine.   **12** (a) 4 (b) 1.

PERCIVAL DAVID FOUNDATION OF CHINESE ART, 53 Gordon Square, London WC1H 0PD (Tel 01-387 3909).   **4** School of Oriental & African Studies.   **5** Curator: Miss Margaret Medley BA, FSA.   **8** Open to the public.   **9** Mon 14.00-17.00, Tues-Fri 10.30-17.00. Free.   **10** Chinese porcelains (10th-18th cent) collected by the late Sir Percival David.   **12** (a) 1 (b) 3 (c) 4.

QUEEN MARY COLLEGE, DEPARTMENT OF GEOLOGY MUSEUM, Mile End Rd, London E1 4NS (Tel 01-980 4811 ext 3058).   **5** Curator: J.N. Carreck MPhil, FMA, FGS.   **7** Dept of Geology, Head of Dept: Prof W.W. Bishop PhD, FGS.   **8** Not open to public; professional & amateur geologists & teachers on application.   **9** Mon-Fri 9.30-18.00. Free.   **10** All rocks, minerals & fossils required for teaching & research (graduate & post-graduate).   **11** A specimen loan service is available to local schools teaching geology.   **12** (a) 2.

UNIVERSITY COLLEGE, DEPARTMENT OF EGYPTOLOGY, PETRIE MUSEUM, Gower St, London WC1E 6BT (Tel 01-387 7050).   **5** Officer-in-Charge: Dr D.M. Dixon.   **8 & 9** Open by appointment; Mon-Fri 11.00-16.30. Free.   **10** Egyptian civilization.   **12** (a) 2 (c) 1.

UNIVERSITY COLLEGE, ZOOLOGY AND COMPARATIVE ANATOMY MUSEUM, Gower St, London WC1E 6BT (Tel 01-387 7050 ext 426).   **8** Not open to public.   **9** Mon-Fri 9.00-17.30. Free.   **10** Specialised teaching colln of zoological material.   **12** (a) 1 (b) 1 (c) 1.

VALENCE HOUSE MUSEUM, Valence House, Becontree Ave, Dagenham, Essex, RM8 3HT (Tel 01-592 2211).   **4** Barking BC.   **5** Curator & Archivist: Mr James Howson.

CODE: 1 Name of Museum, Art Gallery or Stately Home. **2** Address **3** Telephone & telex. **4** Governing body. **5** Officer in charge. **6** Committee responsible. **7** Larger department, chief officer. **8** Open to public. **9** Hours; admission charges. **10** Scope. **11** Special exhibits or facilities. **12** Staff (a) professionally qualified (b) other non-manual (c) manual.

LONDON—*continued*

7 Libraries, Borough Libn: E. W. McManus FLA. **8** Open to the public. **9** Open by appointment only until further notice. Free. **10** Local history (inc Fanshawe family portraits) in 17th-cent manor house.

VESTRY HOUSE MUSEUM OF LOCAL HISTORY, Vestry Rd, Walthamstow E17 9NH (Tel 01-527 5544 ext 391). **4** Waltham Forest BC. **5** Asst-in-Charge: A. D. Law AMA. **6** Further Education & Libraries. **7** Dept of Libraries & Arts, Borough Libn & Curator: H. L. Chambers FLA. **8** Open to the public. **9** Mon-Sat 10.00-17.00 (20.00 Mon & Wed). Free. **10** Material relating to London Borough of Waltham Forest, inc local archives, photographs, paintings, three-dimensional objects etc. **11** The Bremer car, probably the first British motor car, made by Fred Bremer at Walthamstow 1892-4. **12** (a) 4 (c) 1½.

VICTORIA AND ALBERT MUSEUM, South Kensington, SW7 2RL (Tel 01-589 6371). **4** Dept of Education & Science. **5** Dir: Dr Roy Strong FSA. **8** Open to the public. **9** Mon-Sat 10.00-17.50, Sun 14.30-17.50. Free. **10** Ceramics; furniture & woodwork; textiles; metalwork; jewellery; glass; prints & drawings; paintings; Oriental & Indian objects; architecture & sculpture. **11** Temporary exhibitions; opinions given (Tues & Thurs 14.30-16.30); National Art Library; lectures & gallery talks; restaurant. **12** (a) 204 (b) 400 (c) 46.

WALLACE COLLECTION, Manchester Sq, London W1M 6BN (Tel 01-935 0687/0688). **4** Trustees of the Wallace Collection. **5** Dir: T. W. I. Hodgkinson CBE, FMA. **8** Open to the public. **9** Mon-Fri 10.00-17.00, Sun 14.00-17.00. Free. **10** Paintings (Titian, Rubens, Van Dyck, Rembrandt, Hals, Velazquez, Murillo, Reynolds, Gainsborough & Delacroix); 18th cent French arts: paintings (Watteau, Boucher, Fragonard etc), sculpture, goldsmith work, Sèvres porcelain; maiolica; European & Oriental armour & arms. **12** (a) 6 (b) 12 (c) 53.

WELLCOME INSTITUTE FOR THE HISTORY OF MEDICINE MUSEUM, 183 Euston Rd, London NW1 2BP (Tel 01-387 4477; Telex Welmuseum London). **4** Wellcome Trust. **5** Dir: Dr Edwin S. Clarke MD, FRCS; Curator: Mr Colin A. Sizer BSc, FMA. **8** Open to the public. **9** Mon-Fri 10.00-17.00. Free. **10** History of medicine & allied sciences from prehistoric times to present (inc non-Western medicine). **12** (a) 2 (c) 3.

WELLCOME MUSEUM OF MEDICAL SCIENCE, PO Box 129, 183 Euston Rd, London NW1 2BP (Tel 01-387 4688). **4** Wellcome Foundation. **5** Officer-in-Charge: Dr A. J. Duggan MD, DTM, FMA. **8** Open only to members of medical & para-medical professions. **9** Mon-Fri 9.00-17.00. Free. **10** Communicable & non-communicable diseases of man (with particular ref to the practice of medicine in hot countries). **11** Temporary exhibits (topical medical subjects). **12** (a) 2 (b) 4 (c) 5.

WELLINGTON MUSEUM (APSLEY HOUSE), 149 Piccadilly, London W1V 9FA (Tel 01-499 5676). **4** Victoria & Albert Museum; Dept of Education & Science. **5** Officer-in-Charge: H. V. T. Percival. **8** Open to the public. **9** Mon-Sat (inc bank hols) 10.00-18.00, Sun 14.30-18.00. Free. **10** Colln of the first Duke of Wellington's works of art & personal relics; paintings; porcelain; silver plate; furniture; sculpture; swords; medals; orders; batons etc.

WHITECHAPEL ART GALLERY, Whitechapel High St, London E1 7QX (Tel 01-247 1492). **4** Trustees of the Charity. **5** Dir: Ms Jasia Reichardt; Chairman of the Trust: Mr Pat Matthews. **8** Open to the public. **9** Open Tues-Sun during exhibitions. Free. **10** Temporary exhibitions (several concurrently). **11** Coffee bar. **12** (a) 3 (b) 1 (c) 4.

WILLIAM MORRIS GALLERY AND BRANGWYN GIFT, Water House, Lloyd Park, Forest Rd, London E17 4PP (Tel 01-527 5544 ext 390). **4** Waltham Forest BC. **5** Asst-in-Charge: Ms Norah C. Gillow MA. **6** Education. **7** Libraries & the Arts, Borough Libn & Curator: H. L. Chambers FLA. **8** Open to the public. **9** Mon-Sat 10.00-17.00, 1st Sun each month 10.00-12.00, 14.00-17.00. Free. **10** All aspects of the work of William Morris & the firm of Morris & Co; the Brangwyn Gift, (19th & 20th cent paintings, drawings, prints, sculpture, several works by Brangwyn himself); Mackmurdo Bequest (work by the Century Guild & ceramics by William de Morgan); small colln of Martinware. **11** Ref Library (by appointment); publications, catalogues, postcards, slides & photographs. **12** (a) 3 (c) 4.

WIMBLEDON LAWN TENNIS MUSEUM (not yet open), The All England Lawn Tennis and Croquet Club, Church Rd, Wimbledon, London SW19 5AE (Tel 01-946 2244). **4** Committee of Management of the Championships. **5** Curator: A. B. Cooper. **9** Due to open in 1977.

WOODLANDS ART GALLERY, 90 Mycenae Rd, Blackheath, London SE3 7SE (Tel 01-858 4631). **4** Greenwich BC. **5** Borough Libn & Curator: Mr H. Davis FLA; Keeper of Art Galleries: Mr John Bunston BA, AMA. **7** Directorate of Recreational Services, Dir: Mr C. J. C. Field. **8** Open to the public. **9** Mon-Fri (exc Wed) (inc bank hols) 10.00-19.30, Sat 10.00-18.00, Sun 14.00-18.00. Free. **10** House built 1774 for founder of Lloyds; local topographical watercolours & drawings. **11** Temporary exhibitions (local history, contemporary local art & special loan exhibitions). **12** (a) 1 (b) 1 (c) 2.

WORSHIPFUL COMPANY OF GOLDSMITHS MUSEUM, Goldsmiths Hall, Foster Lane, London EC2 6BN (Tel 01-606 8971). **4** Wardens of the Goldsmiths Company. **5** Clerk: Mr Peter Jenkins, MBE, MC. **8** Not open to public except on Open Days (enquire from St Paul's information centre). Free. **10** Antique & modern silver, jewellery & medals. **11** Public exhibitions of modern goldsmiths' work.

LONDON COLNEY, Hertfordshire.

SALISBURY HALL, AND THE DE HAVILLAND MOSQUITO AIRCRAFT MUSEUM, London Colney, St Albans, AL2 1BU (Tel 0727-23274). **5** Owner, Salisbury Hall, & Hon Sec, Mosquito Aircraft Museum: Mr W. J. Goldsmith. **8** Open to the public. **9** Easter-Sept: Thurs (July-Sept only) & Sun 14.00-16.00; bank hols 10.30-17.30. Hall & Gardens: adults 40p, children 15p. Mosquito Aircraft Museum: adults 20p, children 5p. **10** 17th cent manor house; wood panelling; early English stone portrait medallions of Roman emperors; house surrounded by medieval moat. **11** Prototype Mosquito (designed & built here, 1940); Vampire; Venom; White colln (500 scale model aircraft).

LONGLEAT, Wiltshire

LONGLEAT HOUSE AND GROUNDS, Longleat, Warminster, BA12 7NN (Tel 09853-303). **4** Marquess of Bath. **5** Comptroller to the Marquess of Bath: Mr James Dwerryhouse. **8** Open to the public. **9** Easter-Oct: daily 10.00-18.00; Nov-Easter 10.00-16.00. Closed Xmas Day. Private apartments open summer: daily 11.00-18.00. Adults 50p, children 25p. Murals 25p extra. **10** Elizabethan house (built by Sir John Thynne 1566-1580) in park landscaped by Capability Brown; altered by Sir Jeffrey Wyatville & decorated in ornate Italian style (19th cent); fine private library; ceilings moulded in the Venetian manner; 18th & 19th cent furniture; paintings by Titian, Reynolds, Lawrence, Eworth, Graham Sutherland & a fine set of Woottons. **11** Lord Weymouth's murals in private apartments.

LOOE, Cornwall

CORNISH MUSEUM, Lower St, East Looe, PL13 1DA (Tel 05036-2423).   **5** Curator: Mr W. H. Paynter.   **8** Open to the public.   **9** Daily (inc bank hols) May-Sept. Adults 10p, children 5p.   **10** Life & culture of Cornwall; arts & crafts, local history, folklore, mining, fishing, early travel, lighting; games & pastimes.   **11** Unique colln of relics dealing with Cornish witchcraft, charms & superstitions.   **12** (a) 1 (b) 1.

LOWESTOFT, Suffolk

EAST ANGLIA TRANSPORT MUSEUM, Chapel Rd, Carlton, Colville, Lowestoft, NR33 8BL.   **4** East Anglia Transport Museum Society.   **5** Sec: Mr M. L. Carr.   **8** Open to the public.   **9** Spring bank hol-Sept: Sat 14.00-16.00, Sun & bank hols 11.00-18.00; Aug: Mon-Fri 11.00-18.00. Adults 15p, children 5p; party rates.   **10** Land transport (railways trams, buses, trolleybuses, lorries, cars, cycles etc).
11 Ride on trams (Sun & bank hols); rides on narrow gauge railway.

LOWESTOFT MARITIME MUSEUM, Bowling Green Cottage, Sparrow's Nest, Whapload Rd, Lowestoft. Correspondence to Hon Sec, L. & E. S. Maritime Society, 22 Pakefield Rd, Lowestoft, NR33 0HS (Tel 0502-67157).   **4** Lowestoft East Suffolk Maritime Society.   **5** Chairman of Maritime Museum Management Committee: Mr W. Soloman RNR.
8 Open to the public.   **9** May-Oct: daily (inc bank hols) 10.00-12.30, 14.00-17.00, 18.00-dusk. Adults 10p, children 5p; party rates.   **10** Maritime items; history of port of Lowestoft & its fishing industry.   **11** Models of local boats; fishing gear. Royal Naval Patrol Service items.

SOMERLEYTON HALL, Lowestoft (Tel 0502-730224).
5 Administrator: Lord Somerleyton.   **8** Open to the public.   **9** Easter-mid Oct: Sun & Thurs 14.00-18.00; July & Aug: Tues, Weds & bank hols 14.00-18.00. Adults 50p, children & OAPs 25p; group rates; season tickets.   **10** 16th cent hall with 19th cent additions; antique furnishings & paintings; gardens; maze (designed 1846).   **11** Children's farm; miniature railway; garden trail; aviary; information centre; gift shop; tearoom.

LUDLOW, Shropshire

LUDLOW MUSEUM, Butter Cross (display area) & Old St, (ref collns, laboratories & offices), Ludlow (Tel 0584-3857/ 2474).   **4** Shropshire CC.   **5** Curator: Mr John Norton MBE, FGS, FRES.   **6** Leisure Activities.   **7** County Museum Curator: G. I. McCabe MA, AMA.   **8** Open to the public.   **9** Mon-Sat 10.30-12.30, 14.00-17.00, Sun (June-Aug only) 10.00-13.00, 14.00-17.00. Closed Good Friday & Xmas time. Adults 10p, children & students free.   **10** Local history (prehistoric-Victorian); geology of Welsh Borderland; local zoology & botany.   **11** Extensive geological & other ref collns available for study; lecture room; publications.
12 (b) 3 (c) 2.

READERS HOUSE, Ludlow.   **4** Owned by King Edward VI Ludlow Municipal Charities; rented by Ludlow Parochial Church Council.   **8** Open to the public.   **9** Mon-Fri 9.00-12.45, 14.15-17.00. Other times by prior arrangement. Charges: 2½p.   **10** 17th cent house.

LUSS, Dunbartonshire

ROSSDHU, Luss (Tel 043686-231).   **9** Easter-Sept: Wed-Mon.   **10** Stately home (1773); ruins of 16th cent castle & chapel; paintings; stuffed native animals & birds.
11 Refreshments; craft shop.

LUTON, Bedfordshire

LUTON MUSEUM AND ART GALLERY, Wardown Park, Luton, LU2 7HA (Tel 0582-36941).   **4** Luton DC.
5 Asst Recreation Services Manager, Museum: Mr Frank Hackett FGS, AMA.   **7** Recreation Services Dept; Recreation Services Officer: J. A. Maddox AInstPRA, MIRM, MIBCA.
8 Open to the public.   **9** Feb-Nov: Mon-Sat 10.00-18.00,

Sun 14.00-18.00; Oct-March: closes at 17.00 daily. Closed Dec 24, 25 & Jan 1. Free.   **10** Bedfordshire archaeology & history; rural trades & crafts, particularly straw hat & pillow lace industries, social & domestic life; furniture; woodwork; decorative & fine art; costume; needlework accessories; doll & toy colln; natural history & Bedfordshire herbarium in reserve.   **11** Lacemaker's bobbins in silver, brass & bone for sale to craftsmen.   **12** (a) 3 (b) 5 (c) 5.

WERNHER COLLECTION, Luton Hoo, Luton, LU1 3TZ (Tel 0582-22955).   **5** Curator: Mr Michael Urwick Smith MA, AMA.   **8** Open to the public.   **9** Easter-Sept: Mon, Wed, Thurs, Sat & bank hols 11.00-18.00, Sun 14.00-18.00. Adults 35p, children 20p.   **10** Old Master paintings; English & French furniture; Flemish & French tapestries; German Renaissance silver-gilt; English silver-gilt; English & Sèvres porcelain; medieval ivories; Limoges enamels; Renaissance bronzes & jewellery; Russian Fabergé jewels & portraits & personal mementoes of Russian Imperial Family.   **11** Bermejo 'St. Michael'; Altdorfer 'Christ Taking Leave of His Mother'.
12 (a) 1 (b) 12 (c) 6.

LUTTERWORTH, Leicestershire

STANFORD HALL MOTOR-CYCLE AND CAR MUSEUM, Lutterworth, LE17 6DH (Tel 078 885-250).   **8** Open to the public.   **9** Easter-Sept: Thurs, Sat & Sun 14.30-18.00; bank hols & following Mon & Tues 12.00-18.00. House: adults 40p, children 20p; grounds or motorcycle museum: adults 15p, children 5p.   **10** William & Mary House (1690); antique furniture, pictures, mss; costumes & kitchen utensils; Percy Pilcher's flying machine; racing motor cycles & vintage cars.   **11** Cafeteria.

LYME REGIS, Dorset

PHILPOT MUSEUM, Bridge St, Lyme Regis, DT7 3QA (Tel 02974-3127).   **4** Trustees on behalf of Lyme Regis Town Council.   **5** Hon Curator: Mr Henry Chessell BA.
8 Open to the public.   **9** Open Easter-Sept: daily; Nov-Easter: Tues, Thurs, Sat & Sun. Adults 10p, children 5p.
10 Local history, geology & fossils; old lace, prints.
12 (b) 2 (c) 1.

MACCLESFIELD, Cheshire

CAPESTHORNE HALL, Macclesfield, SK11 9JY (Tel 062583-221).   **5** Hall Manager: Mr Frederick C. Stevens.
8 Open to the public.   **9** Mon-Fri (May-Sept), Sun (March-Sept) & bank hols: 14.00-17.30, Sat (May-Sept) 14.00-16.00. Adults 40p, children 20p; party rates.   **10** Family residence; fine paintings; furniture; marbles; Greek vases; silver; family muniments from 1153; Georgian chapel; nature walk.

MACCLESFIELD MUSEUM, West Park, Prestbury Rd, Macclesfield, SK10 3BJ (Tel 0625-24067).   **4** Macclesfield BC.   **5** Hon Curator: Col C. D. F. Phillips Brocklehurst.
7 Amenities & Recreation Dept; Chief Officer: Mr A. Collins.   **8** Open to the public.   **9** Summer: Mon-Sat 9.30-17.30, Sun 14.00-17.00; winter: Mon-Sat 9.30-16.30. Closed Dec 25, 26 & Good Friday. Free.   **10** Egyptian antiquities; Victorian paintings (inc Sir Edwin Landseer PRA & Rosa Bonheur); pictures by C. F. Tunnicliffe RA, a native of Macclesfield; drawings & prints of topographical interest; silk; stuffed giant panda.   **11** Travelling exhibitions from Victoria & Albert Museum, & North Western Museum & Art Gallery Service; exhibitions of local artists.
12 (a) 1 (c) 2.

MAIDENHEAD, Berkshire

CLIVEDEN, Maidenhead (Tel 06286-5069).   **4** National Trust.   **8** Open to the public.   **9** April-Oct: Wed, Sat & Sun 14.30-17.00. Gardens, April-Oct: Wed-Sun & bank hols 11.00-18.30. House 10p. Gardens: adults 60p, children 30p, (Fri ½ price).   **10** House built by Sir Charles Barry (1850); fine tapestry & furniture; formal gardens with 18th cent temples; wooded walks.   **11** Restaurant; shop.

CODE: 1 Name of Museum, Art Gallery or Stately Home. 2 Address. 3 Telephone & telex. 4 Governing body. 5 Officer in charge. 6 Committee responsible. 7 Larger department, chief officer. 8 Open to public. 9 Hours; admission charges. 10 Scope. 11 Special exhibits or facilities. 12 Staff (a) professionally qualified (b) other non-manual (c) manual.

MAIDENHEAD, Berkshire—*continued*

HENRY REITLINGER BEQUEST, Oldfield, Riverside, Guard's Club Rd, Maidenhead, SL6 8DN (Tel 0628-21313). 4 Trustees. 5 Curator: Mrs Marjorie Cocke. 8 Open to the public. 9 Tues & Thurs 10.00-12.30, 14.15-16.30, 1st Sun each month 14.30-16.30. Free. 10 Paintings; drawings, sculpture; Italian, Persian & Chinese ceramics; Chelsea & Dresden pottery. 12 (c) 2.

MAIDSTONE, Kent

BOUGHTON MONCHELSEA PLACE, Boughton Monchelsea, Maidstone (Tel 0622-43120). 5 Owner: Mr M.B. Winch. 8 Open to the public. 9 Easter-Oct: Sat, Sun & bank hols & Wed (Aug only): 14.15-18.00. Adults 30p, children 15p. 10 Battlemented Elizabethan manor (1567), Regency alterations; costumes; old vehicles & farm implements; Tudor Kitchen.

MUSEUM AND ART GALLERY, St Faith's St, Maidstone ME14 1LH (Tel 0622-54497). 4 Maidstone BC. 5 Curator: Mr L.R.A. Grove BA, FMA, FSA, FRES. 6 Arts & Recreation. 7 Chief Officer: Mr Trevor Dobinson MIRM, FCEOA. 8 Open to the public. 9 Mon-Sat 9.00-17.00 (April-Sept: 18.00). Free. 10 Tudor building; art, archaeology & natural history of Kent; oil paintings (British, Dutch, Italian, 16th cent onwards); British watercolours; ethnography (mainly Pacific); sculpture; pottery & porcelain (Europe & Far East); British birds & mammals; Japanese colln; musical instruments; costumes. 11 12th cent Bible; Handel's portable clavichord; Henry VIII's Kissing chair; William Hazlitt portraits & miniatures; Anglo-Saxon glass & jewellery. 12 (a) 6 (b) 1 (c) 6.

QUEENS OWN ROYAL WEST KENT REGIMENTAL MUSEUM, Saint Faith's St, Maidstone, ME14 1LH (Tel 0622-54497). 4 Maidstone BC. 5 Officer-in-Charge: Mr Kenneth J. Collins MA. 6 Arts & Recreation. 8 Open to the public. 9 Mon-Sat 10.00-18.00 (winter 17.00). Free. 10 Items from West Kent Militia, 50th Regiment of Foot, 97th Regiment of Foot & The Queen's Own Royal West Kent Regiment. 11 Medals; uniforms; weapons; pictures, silver, accoutrements. 12 (a) Served by Maidstone Museum.

TYRWHITT-DRAKE, MUSEUM OF CARRIAGES, Mill St, Maidstone (Tel 0622-54497). 4 Maidstone BC. 5 Curator: Mr L.R.A. Grove BA, FMA, FSA, FRES. 6 Arts & Recreation. 7 Chief Officer: Mr Trevor Dobinson MIRM, FCEOA. 8 Open to the public. 9 Mon-Sat 10.00-13.00, 14.00-17.00. Adults 3p, children 1p; organized parties (arranged in advance) free. 10 15th cent stables of Archbishop of Canterbury; art of coach-building; c. 50 horse-drawn vehicles; coach accessories, harness, models, prints; prams & children's carts. 12 (b) 1½.

MALMESBURY, Wiltshire

ATHELSTAN MUSEUM, 20 Bristol Rd, Malmesbury. 4 North Wiltshire DC. 6 Community Services. 7 Chief Technical Officer: M. Croker MIMUNE, ARICE. 8 Open to the public. 9 Mon-Sat & bank hols 10.00-12.00, 14.00-16.00. Free. 10 Small town & country museum; local history & life. 12 (b) 1.

MANCHESTER

CITY ART GALLERY, Mosley St, Manchester, M2 3JL (Tel 061-236 2391). 4 City of Manchester. 5 Dir of Art Galleries: Mr G.L. Conran MA, FMA. 7 Cultural Services Dept, Dir: Mr L.G. Lovell FLA. 8 Open to the public. 9 Mon-Sat 10.00-18.00, Sun 14.30-17.00. Closed Dec 25 & Good Friday. Free. 10 British & foreign paintings; applied arts; sculpture; miniatures; Assheton-

Bennett colln (silver & 17th cent Dutch paintings); Thomas Greg colln (English pottery). 11 Temporary exhibitions. Athenaeum Annexe (museum of ceramics), schools service. 12 (a) 23 (b) 8 (c) 70.

FLETCHER MOSS MUSEUM, The Old Parsonage, Wilmslow Rd, Didsbury, Manchester, M20 8AU (Tel 061-445 1109). 4 City of Manchester. 5 Dir of Art Galleries: Mr G.L. Conran MA, FMA. 7 Cultural Services Dept, Dir: Mr L.G. Lovell FLA. 8 Open to the public. 9 Nov-Feb: Mon-Sat 10.00 (Sun 14.00)-16.00; March, April, Sept, Oct: Mon-Sat 10.00 (Sun 14.00)-18.00, May-Aug: Mon-Sat 10.00 (Sun 14.00)-20.00. Free. 10 English watercolours (18th cent onwards) inc Turners; prints in summer. 12 Served from City Art Gallery.

GALLERY OF ENGLISH COSTUME, Platt Hall, Rusholme, Manchester, M14 5LL (Tel 061-224 5217). 4 Manchester Corporation Art Galleries. 5 Dir Art Galleries: Mr G.L. Conran MA, FMA. Keeper: Mrs C.M. Walkley MA, BPhil. 7 Cultural Services, Dir: Mr L.G. Lovell FLA. 8 Open to the public. 9 Mon-Sat 10.00-18.00, Sun 14.00-18.00. Closes 16.00 daily Nov-April. Closed Dec 25 & Good Friday. Free. 10 Former seat of Worsley family (c. 1764); English costume (from 1700-present). 12 (a) 3.

HEATON HALL, Heaton Park, Prestwich, Manchester, M25 5SW (Tel 061-7731231). 4 City of Manchester. 5 Dir of Art Galleries: Mr G.L. Conran MA, FMA. 7 Cultural Services Dept, Dir: Mr L.G. Lovell FLA. 9 Nov-Feb: Mon-Sat 10.00-16.00, Sun 14.00-16.00; March, April, Sept, Oct: Mon-Sat 10.00-18.00, Sun 14.00-18.00; May-Aug: Mon-Sat 10.00-20.00, Sun 14.00-20.00. 10 Designed by James Wyatt (1772) for 1st Earl of Wilton. Many original decorative features; 18th cent furniture & pictures. 11 Organ recitals. 12 Served from City Art Gallery.

Manchester University

MANCHESTER MUSEUM, The University, Oxford Rd, Manchester, M13 9PL (Tel 061-273 3333). 5 Dir: Dr David E. Owen CBE. 8 Open to the public. 9 Mon-Sat 10.00-17.00 (Wed 21.00). Closed Dec 25, 26 & Good Friday. Free. 10 Archaeology; botany; entomology; ethnology; geology; numismatics; zoology; aquarium & vivarium. 11 Temporary exhibitions. 12 (a) 19 (b) 17 (c) 15.

WHITWORTH ART GALLERY, Whitworth Park, Manchester, M15 6ER (Tel 061-273 1880). 5 Dir: Prof C.R. Dodwell MA, PhD, LittD, FBA, FRHistS, FSA; Keeper: Francis W. Hawcroft BA, FMA. 8 Open to the public. 9 Mon-Sat 10.00-17.00. Closed Xmas week, Jan 1 & Good Friday. Free. 10 Old Master paintings, prints & drawings; English drawings & watercolours; textiles; Japanese colour woodcuts; contemporary paintings, prints & drawings. 11 Turner watercolours; Pre-Raphaelite drawings; Post-Impressionist watercolours; Dürer & Italian Renaissance prints; Morris tapestries; British 19th & 20th cent fabrics; Coptic textiles; European vestments & embroideries; Islamic textiles; costume & carpets. 12 (a) 6 (b) 4 (c) 17.

MANCHESTER SHIP CANAL MUSEUM, Ship Canal House, King St, Manchester M2 4WX (Tel 061-872 2411). 5 Officer-in-Charge: Mrs E. Butler. 8 & 9 Not open to general public; open to students & researchers by appointment only. Free. 10 History & development of the Manchester ship canal. 11 Documents & correspondence relating to forming of company, progress of Parliamentary bills & construction work.

NORTH WESTERN MUSEUM OF SCIENCE AND INDUSTRY, 97 Grosvenor St, Manchester, M1 7HF (Tel 061-273 6636). 4 Joint Committee (City of Manchester, University, UMIST,

MANCHESTER—*continued*

local industry & commerce).   **5** Dir: Dr Richard L.
Hills MA, PhD, DIC.   **8** Open to the public.   **9** Mon-Sat
10.00-17.00 Closed Dec 25 & Good Friday. Free.
10 Cotton textile industry (preparation, carding, spinning;
weaving & knitting; dyeing & bleaching; calico printing);
calculating machines; power generation, transmission &
use (animals; steam; hot air; internal combustion; electricity;
hydraulics; electronics; domestic equipment); machine tools;
railway locomotives, track & signals; papermaking &
printing; physical sciences; photography.   **11** Education
service (061-273 1955). 1/3-scale working model of
Newcomen's Atmospheric Steam Engine (1712); only-
surviving Royce (pre-Rolls Royce) motor-car engine/gear-
box; only working roller-drafting cotton-spinning mule in a
museum; Joule colln (apparatus of famous Manchester
scientist); National Paper Museum colln (making paper by
hand & machine).   **12** (a) 3 (b) 8 (c) 7.

QUEEN'S PARK ART GALLERY, Queen's Park, Rochdale
Rd, Harpurhey, Manchester, M9 1SH (Tel 061-205 2121).
4 City of Manchester.   **5** Dir of Art Galleries: Mr G. L.
Conran MA, FMA; Keeper of Military History: Mr P. R.
Russell-Jones.   **7** Cultural Services Dept, Dir: Mr L. G.
Lovell FLA.   **8** Open to the public.   **9** Nov-Feb: Mon-
Sat 10.00 (Sun 14.00)-16.00; March, April, Sept, Oct; Mon-
Sat 10.00 (Sun 14.00)-18.00; May-Aug: Mon-Sat 10.00 (Sun
14.00)-20.00. Closed Dec 25 & Good Friday. Free.
10 Victorian & later paintings; Rutherston loan colln of
modern art. Museum of Manchester Regiment & 14th/20th
King's Hussars.   **12** Served from City Art Gallery.

WYTHENSHAWE HALL, Wythenshawe Park, Northenden,
Manchester, M23 0AB (Tel 061-998 2331).   **4** City of
Manchester.   **5** Dir of Art Galleries: Mr G. L. Conran
MA, FMA.   **7** Cultural Services Dept, Dir: Mr L. G. Lovell
FLA.   **9** Nov-Feb: Mon-Sat 10.00 (Sun 14.00)-16.00;
March, April, Sept, Oct: Mon-Sat 10.00 (Sun 14.00)-18.00;
May-Aug: Mon-Sat 10.00 (Sun 14.00)-20.00. Free.
10 Timber manor house; 17th cent furniture & pictures;
local history.   **12** (a) Served from City Art Gallery.

MANSFIELD, Nottinghamshire

MANSFIELD DISTRICT COUNCIL MUSEUM AND ART
GALLERY, Leeming St, Mansfield, NG18 1NG (Tel 0623-
22561 ext 264).   **4** Mansfield DC.   **5** Curator: Ms
Susan A. Griffiths BA.   **6** Recreation & Amenities.
7 Central Administration & Legal Services; Dir: B. K. E.
Harman, Solicitor.   **8** Open to the public.   **9** Mon-Sat
10.00-18.00 (Oct-April: Sat 10.00-17.00). Free.
10 Natural history; bygones; ceramics; art; archaeology.
11 Temporary exhibitions; water-colours of old Mansfield
by Albert S. Buxton; Manners colln of lustre ware; Wedgwood
& Rockingham.   **12** (a) 1 (b) 1 (c) 3½.

MARKET HARBOROUGH, Leicestershire

ROCKINGHAM CASTLE, Market Harborough, LE16 8TH
(Tel 053 670-240).   **5** Owner: Commander Michael Watson.
8 Open to the public.   **9** Easter-Sept: Sun, Thurs, bank
hol Mon & Tues 14.00-18.00. Other times by appointment.
Adults 40p, children 20p.   **10** Elizabethan house within
walls of Norman castle; 18th-20th cent pictures; 20 acres
gardens; associations with Charles Dickens.   **11** Home-
made teas.

MATLOCK, Derbyshire

HEATHCOTE MUSEUM, Birchover, Matlock, DE4 2BN
(Tel 062988-313).   **5** Proprietor: Mr J. P. Heathcote MA,
FSA.   **8** Open to the public.   **9** Open on application,
preferably by prior arrangement. Free.   **10** Archaeological finds from Bronze Age barrows on Stanton Moor.

TRAMWAY MUSEUM, Crich, Matlock, DE4 5DP (Tel 077
385-2565).   **4** Tramway Museum Society.   **5** Sec: G. B.
Claydon LLB, MInstTA.   **8** Open to the public.   **9** Easter-
Oct: Sat, Sun & bank hols 11.00-18.00; June-Aug: Tues-Thurs

10.00-17.00. Not free.   **10** Trams, tramways & related
equipment; Victorian/Edwardian street.   **11** Working
tramway on which visitors can ride; Derbyshire lead mining.

MEIGLE, Perthshire

MEIGLE MUSEUM, Meigle, PH12 8SB.   **4** Dept of Environment, on behalf of Sec of State for Scotland.   **8** Open to the
public.   **9** Mon-Sat (inc bank hols): April-Sept 9.30-19.00,
Oct-Mar 10.00-16.00. Charges: 5p.   **10** Early Christian
sculptured stones.   **12** (b) 1.

MELBOURNE, Derbyshire

MELBOURNE HALL, Melbourne, Derby, DE7 1EN (Tel
03316-2502).   **4** Owner: Marquess of Lothian.   **5** Sec:
Mrs L. M. Leech.   **8** Open to the public.   **9** Easter-
Oct: Tues-Thurs, Sat & Sun 14.00-18.00. Bank hols 11.00-
18.00. Adults 50p, children 20p. Gardens only: adults 20p,
children 10p.   **10** 12th cent house, restored 17th cent;
pictures; antique furniture; works of art.   **11** Famous
formal gardens; 18th cent wrought iron pergola by Robert
Bakewell; tea rooms; gift shop; guided tours.

MELROSE, Roxburghshire

ABBOTSFORD HOUSE, Melrose, TD6 9BQ (Tel 0896-2043).
4 Sec of State for Scotland.   **8** Open to the public.
9 Mon-Sat (inc bank hols) 10.00-17.00, Sun 14.00-17.00.
Adults 30p, children 15p.   **10** House built & lived in by
Sir Walter Scott, contains his library & historical relics.
12 (b) 1.

MELROSE ABBEY MUSEUM, Melrose TD6 9LG (Tel 0896-
82 262).   **4** Dept of Environment, on behalf of the Sec of
State for Scotland.   **8** Open to the public.   **9** Mon-Sat
(inc bank hols): April-Sept 9.30-19.00, Oct-Mar 10.00-16.00;
Sun: April-Sept 14.00-19.00, Oct-Mar 14.00-16.00.
Charges: 5p.   **10** Pottery; floor tiles; sculptured stonework
& other material related to Melrose Abbey.   **12** (b) 1.

MELTON MOWBRAY, Leicestershire

NATIONAL TRUST COLLECTION OF STAFFORDSHIRE
PORTRAIT FIGURES, Stapleford Park, Melton Mowbray,
LE14 2SF (Tel 0664-245).   **4** National Trust.   **5** Officer-
in-Charge: Lord Gretton.   **8** Open to the public.   **9** May-
Sept: Sun, Wed, Thurs & bank hols 14.30-18.30. House &
grounds: adults 65p, children 32p; Portrait Figures: adults
15p, children 6p, additional, free to National Trust members.
10 Mansion (built 1500, restored 1633), stone decorations
from history & legend. Pictures; tapestries; furniture; over
400 Victorian Staffordshire figures.   **11** Miniature, pas-
senger-carrying, steam railway; miniature liners on lake;
18th cent Georgian church.   **12** (c) 1.

MENAI BRIDGE, Gwynedd

MUSEUM OF CHILDHOOD, Water St, Menai Bridge, Anglesey,
LL59 5DD (Tel 0248-712001).   **5** Owner & Dir: Mr Robert
Brown CEng.   **8** Open to the public.   **9** Easter-Oct:
Mon-Sat (inc bank hols) 9.00-18.00, Sun 13.00-17.00. Other
times by appointment. Adults 25p, children, students & OAPs
15p.   **10** Toys & children's playthings; furniture, pictures,
paintings, pottery depicting children's interests throughout
the ages.   **12** (b) 2.

MENSTRIE, Clackmannanshire

MENSTRIE CASTLE, Menstrie, FK11 7AH.   **4** National
Trust for Scotland & Clackmannanshire CC.   **8** Open to
the public.   **9** May-Sept: Wed, Sat & Sun 14.30-17.00.
Other times by prior arrangement.   **10** Commemoration
rooms for Sir William Alexander; coat of arms of Nova
Scotian baronetcies.

MERTHYR TYDFIL, Mid Glamorgan

CYFARTHFA CASTLE, ART GALLERY AND MUSEUM,
Cyfarthfa Park, Merthyr Tydfil, CF47 8RE (Tel 0685-3112).
8 Open to the public.   **10** Paintings; ceramics; silver;
glass; natural history; geology; fossils; Welsh folk life; local
history; Welsh kitchen.

CODE: 1 Name of Museum, Art Gallery or Stately Home. 2 Address. 3 Telephone & telex. 4 Governing body. 5 Officer in charge. 6 Committee responsible. 7 Larger department, chief officer. 8 Open to public. 9 Hours; admission charges. 10 Scope. 11 Special exhibits or facilities. 12 Staff (a) professionally qualified (b) other non-manual (c) manual.

MIDDLE CLAYDEN, Buckinghamshire

CLAYDEN HOUSE, Middle Clayden, Buckingham, MK18 2EX. 4 National Trust. 8 Open to the public. 9 April-Oct: Tues-Thurs, Sat, Sun & bank hol Mon (closed following Tues) 14.00-18.00. Adults 50p, children 25p. 10 18th cent house; rococco rooms; Chinese room; Florence Nightingale's sitting room & bedroom. 11 Teas.

MIDDLESBROUGH, Cleveland

CAPTAIN COOK BIRTHPLACE MUSEUM, Stewarts Park Lodge, Marton, Middlesbrough, TS7 8AS (Tel 0642-37168). 4 Middlesbrough BC. 5 Leisure Officer (Museums): Mr C.E. Thornton. 7 Recreation & Amenities Dept; Recreation & Amenities Officer: Mr G.G. Watson. 8 Open to the public. 9 Tues-Sat 10.00-13.00, 14.00-18.00, Summer: Sun afternoons; most bank hols 10.00-18.00. Free. 10 Life of Captain Cook. 12 (c) 1.

DORMAN MEMORIAL MUSEUM, Linthorpe Rd, Middlesbrough, TS5 6LA (Tel 0642-83781). 4 Middlesbrough BC. 5 Leisure Officer (Museums): Mr C.E. Thornton. 7 Recreation & Amenities Dept; Recreation & Amenities Officer: Mr G.G. Watson. 8 Open to the public. 9 Mon-Fri (inc most hols) 10.00-18.00, Sat 10.00-17.00. Free. 10 Local history; social & industrial history; local geology & natural history; photography; commercial equipment; Linthorpe pottery. 12 (a) 2 (b) 2 (c) 6.

MIDDLESBROUGH ART GALLERY, 320 Linthorpe Rd, Middlesbrough, TS1 3QY (Tel 0642-47445). 4 Middlesbrough BC. 5 Leisure Officer (Museums): Mr C.E. Thornton. 7 Recreation & Amenities Dept; Recreation & Amenities Officer: Mr G.G. Watson. 8 Open to the public. 9 Mon-Fri (& most hols) 10.00-18.00, Sat 10.00-17.00. Free. 10 Temporary exhibitions, local & national. 12 (a) 1 (c) 4.

MILLOM, Cumbria

MILLOM FOLK MUSEUM, St Georges Rd, Millom, LA18 4DD (Tel 0657-2555). 4 Millom Folk Museum Society. 5 Sec: Mr E. James. 8 Open to the public. 9 Easter-Sept: Mon-Fri 14.00-17.00, bank hol weekends 10.00-17.00. Adults 10p, children 5p; party rates. 10 Local life & industry, agriculture (mainly iron ore mining & ironworks 1850-1968). 11 Full-scale replica of iron ore mine drift & shaft bottom; miner's cottage.

MILLPORT, Isle of Cumbrae

UNIVERSITY MARINE BIOLOGICAL STATION MUSEUM AND AQUARIUM, Millport, Isle of Cumbrae, KA28 0EG (Tel 047-553581). 4 Universities of London & Glasgow. 5 Dir: Prof N. Millott. 8 Open to the public. 9 Mon-Fri (& Sat May-Sept) (inc bank hols): 9.30-12.30, 14.00-17.00. Adults 10p, children 5p; institutional parties: adults 5p, children 2p. 10 Marine life of Clyde area; aquarium shows living fish & invertebrates of area.

MILNGAVIE, Dunbartonshire

LILLIE ART GALLERY, Station Rd, Milngavie, Glasgow G62 8BZ. 4 Milngavie & Bearsden DC. 5 Curator: Ms Elizabeth M. Dent MA, AMA. 6 Leisure & Recreation. 8 Open to the public. 9 Tues-Fri (inc most bank hols) 14.00-17.00, 19.00-21.00, Sat & Sun 14.00-17.00. Free. 10 Mainly contemporary Scottish paintings, some Glasgow school paintings; small sculpture colln. 11 Temporary exhibitions of contemporary artists; loan exhibitions. 12 (a) 1 (c) 1.

MONMOUTH, Gwent

MONMOUTH MUSEUM, Priory St, Monmouth, NP5 3NX (Tel 0600-3519). 4 Monmouth DC. 5 Curator: K.E. Kissack. 6 Developments & Leisure (Museums Sub-Committee). 7 Administrative & Legal Services: S.C. Davis FCIS. 8 Open to the public. 9 April-Oct: Mon-Fri 10.30-13.00, 14.15-17.15 (July & Aug: 10.00-18.00); July & Aug: Sun 14.30-17.30; bank hols 10.00-18.00. Adults 5p, children 2p. 10 Local history; Nelson. 12 (a) 1 (b) 1 (c) 3.

MONTACUTE, Somerset

MONTACUTE HOUSE, Montacute, TA15 6XP (Tel 093 582-3289). 4 National Trust. 5 Administrator: Wing Commander D.H. Wood RAF (Rtd). 8 Open to the public. 9 April-Sept: Wed-Sun (& bank hols) 12.30-18.00; March, Oct & Nov: Wed, Sat & Sun 14.00-18.00. Adults 70p, children 35p; group rates. 10 Elizabethan great house (1588-1601), longest gallery in England; heraldic glass; plasterwork; panelling; tapestries. 11 Late 16th & 17th cent portraits from National Portrait Gallery. Teas (April-Sept). 12 (a) 1 (b) 1.

MORETON-IN-MARSH, Gloucestershire

CHASLETON HOUSE, Moreton-in-Marsh, GL56 0SU (Tel 060 874-355). 5 Owner: Mr Alan Clutton Brock. 8 Open to the public. 9 Mon, Tues, Thurs-Sat 10.30-13.00, 14.00-17.30, Sun 14.00-17.00 (dusk in winter). Adults 35p, children 15p. 10 Jacobean mansion (1603-1612) original interiors; fine plasterwork & panelling; original furniture & tapestries, ceramics; embroideries; topiary garden. 11 Tearoom (summers only).

MORWELLHAM, Devon

MORWELLHAM CENTRE, Morwellham, Tavistock, PL19 8JH (Tel 0822-832766). 4 Dartington Amenity Research Trust. 8 Open to the public. 9 Mon-Sat 10.00-18.00 (dusk in winter). Adults 40p, children 20p. 10 Visitor centre based on historic River Tamar copper port. 11 Audio-visual 'Introduction To Morwellham'; museum of local industry & mining; 3 waterwheels on site; limekilns; quays; docks; canal & tunnel; remains of inclined railways; 2 trails; wayside exhibits; hydro-electric station; farm exhibit. 12 (a) 1 (b) 2 (c) 6.

MUCH WENLOCK, Shropshire

MUCH WENLOCK MUSEUM, Much Wenlock (Tel 095 285-582). 4 Shropshire CC. 5 Custodian: Mrs O. Childs. 6 Leisure Activities. 7 County Museum Curator: G.I. McCabe MA, AMA. 8 Open to the public. 9 Mon-Sat (inc bank hols) 11.00-12.30, 14.00-17.00, Sun 14.00-18.00. Adults 10p, children free. 10 Local history. 12 (b) 1.

NAIRN, Nairnshire

NAIRN LITERARY INSTITUTE MUSEUM, Viewfield House, King St, Nairn IV12 4EE. 5 Hon Curator: Miss Isobel Rae MA. 8 Open to the public. 9 Sat (June-Sept) & Wed (July): 14.00-16.00. Free, but donations welcome. 10 Victoriana; local history (inc agricultural & domestic exhibits). 11 Weapons (inc early Australian & African); early Peruvian pottery; local fossils. 12 (b) 1.

NETHER ALDERLEY, Cheshire

NETHER ALDERLEY MILL, Congleton Rd, Nether Alderley, Macclesfield SK10 4TW. 4 National Trust. 8 Open to the public. 9 April-Oct: Wed & Sun 14.00-17.00. Adults 20p, children 10p.

NETHER ALDERLEY, Cheshire—*continued*

10 Water-powered corn mill (built 1581), working till 1939, restored 1970; wheat ground, when available, otherwise mill runs idly for visitors. **11** Illustrated talks on water-mills, development of stone-grinding with hand-mills etc.

NETHER STOWEY, Somerset

COLERIDGE COTTAGE, Lime St, Nether Stowey. **4** National Trust. **5** Caretaker: Mrs Dinham. **8** Open to the public. **9** April-Sept: Sun-Thurs 14.00-18.00. Charges: 10p, no reductions. **10** Home of Samuel Taylor Coleridge (1797-1800), where he wrote 'The Ancient Mariner' &'Kubla Khan'.

NEWARK, Nottinghamshire

NEWARK D.C. MUSEUM, Appleton Cote, Newark, NG24 1JY (Tel 0636-2358). **4** Newark DC. **5** Museum Curator: Mr H.V. Radcliffe. **6** (Recreation & Amenities Museum Sub-Committee). **7** Officer-in-Charge: Mr D. Dudley. **8** Open to the public. **9** Mon-Sat 10.00-13.00, 14.00-17.00, April-Sept: Sun 14.00-17.00. Free. **10** Local. **11** Temporary exhibitions. **12** (a) 1 (b) 1 (c) 2.

NEWBURY, Berkshire

NEWBURY DISTRICT MUSEUM, The Wharf, Newbury, RG14 5AN (Tel 0635-42400 ext 212). **4** Newbury DC. **5** Curator Emeritus: H.H. Coghlan FSA, FRAnthI. **6** Recreations & Amenities. **7** Technical Dept: Chief Technical Officer: Mr J.M.C. Turner. **8** Open to the public. **9** Mon-Sat 10.00-12.30, 13.30-16.00 (April-Sept 17.00). Closed Wed afternoon. Free. **10** Prehistory (Roman & Saxon, especially local); history of Newbury; local natural history. **11** Technology of ferrous & non-ferrous metals. **12** (a) ½ (b) 2 (c) 1½.

NEWCASTLE, Staffordshire

BOROUGH MUSEUM, Brampton Park, Newcastle ST5 0QP (Tel 0632-619705). **4** Borough Council. **5** Curator: Mr Paul J. Bemrose MA, FIMEnt. **7** Recreation & Amenities Dept; P.W.C. Davies FInstPA, MInstBCA. **8** Open to the public. **9** Mon-Sat 9.30-13.00, 14.00-18.00 (Sat 17.30), May-Sept: Sun 14.00-17.30. Free. **10** Fine & decorative arts; weapons; natural, local & geological history; toys; dolls; horology. **11** Temporary exhibitions; lectures; research facilities. **12** (a) 1 (b) 5.

HOBBERGATE ART GALLERY, The Brampton, Newcastle (Tel 0632-611962). **4** Borough Council. **5** Curator: Mr Paul J. Bemrose MA, FIMEnt. **7** Recreation & Amenities Dept; P.W.C. Davies FInstPA, MInstBCA. **8** Open to the public. **9** Mon-Sat 9.30-13.00, 14.00-18.00 (Sat 17.30), May-Sept: Sun 14.00-17.30. Free. **10** Fine & decorative arts; weapons; natural, local & geological history; toys; dolls; horology. **11** Temporary exhibitions; lectures; research facilities.

NEWCASTLE UPON TYNE, Tyne & Wear

GIBSIDE CHAPEL, Gibside, Burnopfield, Newcastle upon Tyne NE16 6BG (Tel 020 74-2255). **4** National Trust. **5** Caretaker: Mrs S.H. Cheeseman. **8** Open to the public. **9** Wed-Sun (April-Oct), Wed (March & Oct), Sat (March-Oct), Sun (all year) & bank hols: 14.00-16.00. Free but collection box in Chapel. **10** Mausoleum of Bowes family. **11** Georgian church with delicate plasterwork, panelled pews of cherry-wood & a rare mahogany three-tier pulpit; terrace with oak avenue.

JOHN GEORGE JOICEY MUSEUM, Holy Jesus Hospital, City Rd, Newcastle NE1 2AS (Tel 0632-24562). **4** Tyne & Wear CC. **5** Curator & Keeper of Social History: Mr W.W. Wake. **6** Leisure. **7** Museums & Art Galleries Services; Dir: Mr K.J. Barton MPhil, FSA, FMA. **8** Open to the public. **9** Mon-Sat (inc bank hols) 10.00-18.00. Free. **10** History of Newcastle upon Tyne; armoury museum; period rooms (1600-1910); museum of 15th & 19th Kings Royal Hussars & the Northumberland

Hussars. **11** Work of Thomas Bewick, engraver, & Gerrard Robinson, woodcarver. **12** (a) 1 (c) 9.

LAING ART GALLERY AND MUSEUM, Higham Pl, Newcastle NE1 8AG (Tel 0632-27732/26989. **4** Tyne & Wear CC. **5** Dir: B. Collingwood Stevenson MA, FMA, FRSA. **6** Leisure. **7** Museum Service Dir of Museums & Art Galleries: Mr K.J. Barton MPhil, FSA, FMA. **8** Open to the public. **9** Mon-Sat 10.00-18.00 (Tues & Thurs 20.00), Sun 14.30-17.30. Closed Dec 25, Jan 1, Good Friday. Free. **10** Paintings (British School); sculpture; applied arts: silver, glass, pottery, porcelain, pewter, costume, etc. **11** Temporary exhibitions; lunchtime lectures; concerts. **12** (a) 6 (c) 10.

MUSEUM OF SCIENCE AND ENGINEERING, Exhibition Park, Town Moor, Newcastle NE2 4PZ (Tel 0632-815129). **4** Tyne & Wear CC. **6** Leisure. **7** Museums & Art Galleries Services; Dir: Mr K.J. Barton MPhil, FSA, FMA. **8** Open to the public. **9** Summer: Mon-Sat 10.00-18.00 (Tues & Thurs 20.00), Sun 14.30-17.30; winter: Mon-Sat 10.00-16.00, Sun 13.30-16.30. Free. **10** Early railway material, inc George Stephenson's locomotive for Killingworth colliery; early electrical equipment; ship models, marine engineering, inc the original 'Torbinia', 1st turbine-powered ship. **12** (c) 4.

University of Newcastle upon Tyne

HANCOCK MUSEUM, Barras Bridge, Newcastle NE2 4PT (Tel 0632-23599). **5** Curator: A.M. Tynan BSc, FMA. **8** Open to the public. **9** Mon-Sat 10.00-17.00, April-Sept: Sun 14.00-17.00. Closed Dec 25, 26, 31, Jan 1 & Good Friday. Adults 10p, children 5p. **10** Natural history: zoology, birds, geology, botany, some ethnography, tropical & freshwater aquaria. **11** Egyptian mummy unwrapped; family of grey seals of the Farne Islands; family of Chillingham white cattle. **12** (a) 4 (b) 6 (c) 6.

HATTON GALLERY, Newcastle NE1 7RU (Tel 0632-28511 ext 2049). **5** Officer-in-Charge: Prof Kenneth Rowntree. **8** Open to the public. **9** Mon-Fri 10.00-18.00, Sat 10.00-17.00. Free. **10** Paintings (16th-18th cent); small colln of contemporary English paintings & drawings; temporary exhibitions. **11** Only remaining Merzbau by Kurt Schwitters.

MUSEUM OF ANTIQUITIES OF THE UNIVERSITY AND THE SOCIETY OF ANTIQUARIES OF NEWCASTLE UPON TYNE, Dept of Archaeology, The University, Newcastle upon Tyne NE1 7RU (Tel 0632-28511). **5** Keeper: Dr D.J. Smith PhD, FSA. **8** Open to the public. **9** Mon-Sat 10.00-17.00. Closed Dec 24-26, Jan 1 & Good Friday. Free. **10** Regional prehistoric, Roman, Anglo-Saxon, Viking, & medieval antiquities; also some Mediterranean. **11** Scale models of Hadrian's wall; reconstruction of a temple of Mithras & of Roman armour & weapons. **12** (b) 1 (c) 1.

PLUMMER TOWER MUSEUM, Croft St, Newcastle NE1 6NQ (Tel 0632-22204). **4** Tyne & Wear CC. **5** Officer-in-Charge: B. Collingwood Stevenson MA, FMA, FRSA. **6** Leisure. **7** Museum Service; Dir of Museums & Art Galleries: Mr K.J. Barton MPhil, FSA, FMA. **8** Open to the public. **9** Mon-Sat 10.00-13.00, 14.30-18.00. Closed Dec 25, Jan 1 & Good Friday. Free. **10** 18th & 19th cent period rooms; furniture; pottery; glass; silver; pictures. **12** (a) 1 (c) 1.

NEWENT, Gloucestershire

FALCONRY CENTRE, Newent, GL18 1JJ (Tel 0531 820286). **5** Officer-in-Charge: Phillip Glasier. **8** Open to the public. **9** Wed-Mon 10.30-17.30 (or dusk if earlier). Closed Dec 22-28. Adults 50p, children 25p. **10** Only museum in the world devoted entirely to raptors & falconry; live colln; breeding aviaries; pictures, photographs & equipment of falconry; trained birds; flying demonstrations. **11** Lectures, courses. **12** (a) 3.

CODE: 1 Name of Museum, Art Gallery or Stately Home. **2** Address. **3** Telephone & telex. **4** Governing body. **5** Officer in charge. **6** Committee responsible. **7** Larger department, chief officer. **8** Open to public. **9** Hours; admission charges. **10** Scope. **11** Special exhibits or facilities. **12** Staff (a) professionally qualified (b) other non-manual (c) manual.

NEWPORT, Gwent

NEWPORT MUSEUM & ART GALLERY, John Frost Sq, Newport, Gwent NPT 1PA (Tel 0633-65781). **4** Newport BC. **5** Curator: Cefni Barnett FSA, FMA. **7** Leisure services; Dir: W.M.Morrish. **8** Open to the public. **9** Mon-Sat 10.00-17.30. Free. **10** Natural history; geology; county archaeology & social history (material from Romano-British town of Caerwent); British & Welsh paintings; early English water colours. **11** Schools service; public lectures; picture loan scheme. **12** (a) 6 (b) 2 (c) 8.

NEWPORT, Isle of Wight

ARRETON MANOR, *see* Arreton

CARISBROOKE CASTLE MUSEUM, Newport, Isle of Wight PO30 1XY (Tel 098-581 3112). **4** Dept of Environment; and Trustees. **5** Curator: Mr J.D.Jones MA, FSA(Scot), FMA. **8** Open to the public. **9** Mon-Sat 9.30-19.30, Sun 14.00-17.30. March, April & Oct: closes 17.30 daily. Nov-Feb: closes 16.00 daily. Summer: 20p, winter: 10p; OAPs & children 5p. **10** Medieval castle; local history & archaeology. **11** Personal relics of Charles I (imprisoned here 1647-8); Princess Elizabeth organ (1602); Carisbrooke Falcon (bronze cannon of 1549); Newtown mace (c.1490); Moon's Hill hoard of Bronze Age weapons.

ROMAN VILLA, SHIDE, 48 Avondale Rd, Newport, Isle of Wight. Correspondence to: County Library HQ, Parkhurst Rd, Newport, Isle of Wight, PO30 IUD (Tel 098-2324). **4** Isle of Wight CC. **5** Chief Asst Libn: R.G.Futter ALA. **6** Amenities & leisure. **7** Dir of Cultural Services: L.J.Mitchell BA, FLA. **8** Open to the public. **9** June-Sept: Sun-Fri (inc bank hols) 10.30-17.30. Adults 10p, children free, school parties £1.00. **10** Remains of Roman villa with tessellated & mosaic floors, well preserved hypocaust & bath system, complete outline of villa visible, fire place. **11** Site finds. **12** (b) 1.

NEWTOWN, Powys

NEWTOWN TEXTILE MUSEUM, 5-7 Commercial St, Newtown, SY16 2BL (Tel 0686-26243). **5** Chairman: Mr Peter Lewis BA, DL; Caretaker: Mrs R.Rees. **8** Open to the public. **9** Tues-Fri & bank hols 14.00-16.30. Other times by arrangement. Free. **10** Early 19th cent wool-weaving factory & cottages; local 19th cent history & social life. **11** Original exhibits on loan from National Folk Museum of Wales.

ROBERT OWEN MEMORIAL MUSEUM, Broad St, Newtown, SY16 2NZ. **4** Robert Owen Memorial Museum Council of Management. **5** Sec: Mr Edgar Spooner. **8** Open to the public. **9** Mon-Sat (inc bank hols) 10.30-12.30, 14.30-16.30. Free. **10** Robert Owen's papers & some belongings; library of books on Robert Owen.

NORTHAMPTON, Northamptonshire

ABINGTON MUSEUM, Abington Park, Northampton (Tel 0604-31454). **4** Northampton BC. **5** Curator: W.N. Terry FRGS, FRNS, FMA. **7** Leisure & Recreation; Chief Officer: G.G.Bott DipPE. **8** Open to the public. **9** Mon-Sat (inc bank hols) 10.00-12.30, 14.00-18.00, April-Sept: Sun 14.30-17.00. Free.

CENTRAL MUSEUM AND ART GALLERY, Guildhall Rd, Northampton, NN1 1OP (Tel 0604-34881). **4** Northampton BC. **5** Curator: W.N.Terry FRGS, FRNS, FMA. **7** Leisure & Recreation; Chief Officer: G.G.Bott DipPE. **8** Open to the public. **9** Mon-Sat (inc bank hols) 10.00-18.00 (Thurs & Sat 20.00). Free. **12** (a) 7 (b) 3 (c) 11.

NORTHAMPTONSHIRE REGIMENT MUSEUM, Abington Park, Northampton (Tel 0604-31454). **5** Curator: Major (Retd) D.Baxter. **8** Open to the public. **9** Mon-Sat (inc bank hols) 10.00-12.30, 14.00-18.00, April-Sept: Sun 14.30-17.00. Free. **10** History of the Northamptonshire Regiment (1744-1960).

ROYAL PIONEER CORPS MUSEUM, Simpson Barracks, Wootton, Northampton, NN4 0HX (Tel 0604-62742 ext 34). **4** Museums Ogilby Trust. **5** Curator: Major C.M. Cusack (Ret'd). **8** Open to the public. **9** Mon-Fri 9.00-12.30, 14.00-17.00. Weekends & bank hols by special arrangement. Free. **10** Royal Pioneer Corps history & items of military interest.

NORTH BERWICK, East Lothian

NORTH BERWICK MUSEUM, School Rd, North Berwick (Tel 0620-3470). **4** East Lothian DC. **7** Leisure, Recreation & Tourism Dept, Dir: Mr R.A.P.Mellor. **8** Open to the public. **9** Easter-Sept: Mon-Sat 10.00-13.00, 14.00-17.00, Sun 14.00-17.00. Free. **10** Local history & natural history.

NORWICH, Norfolk

BRIDEWELL MUSEUM OF LOCAL INDUSTRIES, Bridewell Alley, Norwich, NR2 1AQ (Tel 0603-22233 ext 700). **4** Norfolk CC. **7** Norfolk Museums Service, Dir: Mr Francis W.Cheetham BA, FMA. **8** Open to the public. **9** Mon-Sat 10.00-17.00. Closed Dec 25, 26 & Jan 1. Free. **10** Mediaeval merchants house, (north wall squared & split Norfolk flintwork), used as a Bridewell (1583-1828) to imprison beggars & tramps; life & culture of Norfolk people (18th-20th cent). **11** Norwich-made textiles, shoes & decorative iron-work; Norfolk building materials & techniques.

CASTLE MUSEUM, Norwich, NR1 3JU (Tel 0603-22233). **4** Norfolk CC. **5** Dir, Norfolk Museums Service: Mr Francis W.Cheetham BA, FMA. **7** Norfolk Museums Service. **8** Open to the public. **9** Mon-Sat 10.00-17.00 (July & Aug 17.30), Sun 14.00-17.00. Closed Dec 25, 26 & Jan 1. Adults 10p (June-Sept: 25p), children & OAPs free. **10** Norman keep (1130) with cellars & dungeons containing relics from use as a county gaol; natural, social, cultural & archaeological history of Norfolk (inc 6 dioramas of characteristic Norfolk scenes); Norwich School paintings; modern art. **11** Temporary exhibitions; tours of battlements & dungeons (school parties & groups must book in advance); Norfolk ecology gallery; exotic invertebrates; buttery & coffee bar; sales counter (souvenirs, books, craft-work); crafts display area.

ROYAL NORFOLK REGIMENT MUSEUM, Britannia Barracks, Norwich, NR1 4HJ (Tel 0603-28455). **5** Officer-in-Charge: Lt Col A.Joanny MBE (Retd). **8** Open to the public. **9** Weekdays 9.00-12.30, 14.00-16.30. Free. **10** Militaria, arms, medals, paintings, uniforms of 9th Regiment of Foot, Norfolk Regiment & Royal Norfolk Regiment. **11** Small military library; regimental silver; regimental trophies from Tibet, Burma & Japan (19th cent); Victoria Cross. **12** (b) 1 (c) 1.

ST PETER HUNGATE CHURCH MUSEUM, Princes St, Norwich (Tel 0603-22233). **4** Norfolk CC. **7** Norfolk Museums Service, Dir: Mr Francis W.Cheetham BA, FMA. **8** Open to the public. **9** Mon-Sat 10.00-17.00. **10** 15th cent church; church furnishings & religious objects (from 12th cent) church plate; musical instruments formerly used in local churches. **11** Illuminated mss (inc part of a Wycliffe bible).

NORWICH, Norfolk–*continued*

STRANGERS HALL MUSEUM OF DOMESTIC LIFE, Charing
Cross, Norwich, NR2 4AL (Tel 0603-22233 ext 645).
4 Norfolk CC.   **7** Norfolk Museums Service, Dir: Mr
Francis W. Cheetham BA, FMA.   **8** Open to the public.
9 Mon-Sat 10.00-17.00. Closed Dec 25, 26 & Jan 1. Free
(except June-Sept adults 10p).   **10** Medieval house (many
period additions); 16th-19th cent furnishings; costumes.
11 15th cent tapestries, 18th cent Irish glass chandelier;
Norwich shop signs; an early Panhard-Levassor car; toys
& playthings.

NOSTELL, West Yorkshire

NOSTELL PRIORY, Doncaster Rd, Nostell, Wakefield
(Tel 0924-862221).   **4** National Trust.   **5** Agent:
G.M.V. Winn.   **8** Open to the public.   **9** Aug-mid Sept:
daily 14.00-18.00; Easter-Aug & mid Sept-mid Oct: Wed,
Sat & Sun 14.00-18.00. Bank hol Sun & Mon 11.00-18.00.
Adults 40p, children 20p.   **10** House built in 1733, addition
by Robert Adam in 1766, fine 18th cent decoration; Chippendale furniture designed for the house.   **11** Vintage &
veteran motor cycles; fishing & boating; tea rooms.
12 (c) 5.

NOTTINGHAM, Nottinghamshire

BREWHOUSE YARD FOLK MUSEUM, Brewhouse Yard,
Nottingham, NG7 1FB (Tel 0602-49599).   **4** Nottingham
City Council.   **5** Senior Keeper of Human History: A.G.
MacCormick BA, AMA.   **7** Leisure Services Dept.
8 Hope to open 1976/77.   **10** Local social history;
17th & 18th cent brewhouse yard cottages (being restored).
12 (a) 3 (b) 1 (c) 1.

COSTUME AND TEXTILE MUSEUM, 43-51 Castlegate,
Nottingham, NG1 6AG (Tel 0602-411579).   **5** Chief Museums
Officer: Mr B. Loughbrough MA, AMA.   **7** Leisure Services.   **8** Not yet open.   **10** Row of Georgian terraced
houses; costume (17th cent to present); lace (especially
Nottingham machine made); English & foreign textiles;
dolls; lace-making equipment.

NOTTINGHAM CASTLE MUSEUM, Museum & Art Gallery,
The Castle, Nottingham, NG1 6EL (Tel 0602-43615).
4 Nottingham City Council.   **5** Chief Museums Officer:
Mr Brian Loughbrough MA, AMA.   **7** Leisure Services
Dept, Museums Division; Dir of Leisure Services: Mr Hugh
McD. Lawson.   **8** Open to the public.   **9** Oct-March:
daily (inc bank hols) 10.00-16.45; April-Sept: Mon-Sat (inc
bank hols) 10.00-18.45 (Fri 17.45), Sun 10.00-16.45. Free,
except Sun & bank hols 4p.   **10** 17th cent house; ceramics;
silver; glass; medieval Nottingham alabaster carvings; local
history & archaeology; classical Oriental & ethnographical
antiquities; art gallery.   **11** Works by Nottingham born
artists R.P. Bonington, Paul & Thomas Sandby; Sherwood
Foresters Regimental Museum (MoD); early 20th cent
chemist's shop; 2 temporary exhibition galleries.   **12** (a) 8
(b) 8 (c) 18.

NOTTINGHAM INDUSTRIAL MUSEUM, Courtyard Buildings,
Wollaton Park, Nottingham, NG8 2AE (Tel 0602-284602).
4 Nottingham City Council.   **5** Senior Keeper (Technology)
& Curator of Industrial Museum: Mr Philip Broomhead BA.
7 Leisure Services, Dir: Mr Hugh McD. Lawson; Museums
Division, Chief Museums Officer: Mr Brian Loughbrough MA,
AMA.   **8** Open to the public.   **9** Thurs, Sat & bank hols
10.00-19.00 (Oct-March: closes at dusk); Sun (March-Oct)
14.00-17.00, (Nov-Feb) 13.30-dusk. Closed Dec 25 & Good
Friday. Other times by arrangement (for parties). Free.
10 18th cent stables; history of Nottingham's industries
(especially hosiery & lace-making); transport; general
engineering; street furniture; agricultural material (hopefully
1975/6).   **11** 1858 beam pumping engine; mid 19th cent
horse gin.   **12** (a) 1 (b) 1 (c) 3.

NOTTINGHAM NATURAL HISTORY MUSEUM, Wollaton Hall,
Wollaton Park, Nottingham, NG8 2AE (Tel 0602-281333).
4 Nottingham City Council.   **5** Chief Museums Officer:

Mr Brian Loughbrough MA, AMA.   **7** Leisure Services
Dept, Museums Division; Dir of Leisure Services: Mr Hugh
McD. Lawson.   **8** Open to the public.   **9** April-Sept:
Mon-Sat 10.00-19.00, Sun 14.00-17.00; Nov-Feb: Mon-Sat
10.00-16.30, Sun 13.30-16.30; Oct & March: Mon-Sat 10.00-
17.30, 13.30-16.30. Closed Dec 25 only. Free.   **10** Ref
collns of natural history; local, foreign & general natural
history; botany; vertebrate & invertebrate zoology; geology;
British & foreign herbaria; insects; 19th cent camellia house.
11 Temporary exhibitions schools activities room for school
parties; adventure playground; cafeteria; nature trail; conducted tours of areas not open to public by appointment.
12 (a) 7 (b) 2 (c) 8.

Nottingham University

UNIVERSITY ART GALLERY, University Park, Nottingham, NG7 2RD (Tel 0602-56101 ext 2253).   **5** Officer-
in-Charge: Prof Alastair Smart MA, DA, FRSA.
7 Department of Fine Art.   **8** Open to the public.
9 Term: Mon-Fri 11.00-20.30, Sat 11.00-17.00. Free.
10 Temporary exhibitions (Old Masters & contemporary
art).   **12** (a) 6 (b) 6 (c) 2.

UNIVERSITY MUSEUM, University Park, Nottingham,
NG7 2RD (Tel 0602-56101 ext 2983/2564).   **5** Officer-
in-Charge: Mr Jeffrey May MA, FSA.   **8** Open to the
public.   **9** Mon-Fri 9.00-17.00. Other times by
appointment. Free.   **10** Archaeology of Britain & Europe
in prehistoric, Roman & medieval times.   **11** Oswald
colln of Roman Samian pottery, moulds & kiln; furniture;
ref colln of Romano-British & medieval coarse pottery;
medieval building materials; Iron Age salt-making material from Lincolnshire coast sites.

NUNEATON, Warwickshire

CADEBY LIGHT RAILWAY MUSEUM, Cadeby Rectory,
Nuneaton (Tel 0455-290462).   **5** Officer-in-Charge: Rev
E.R. Boston MA.   **8** 2nd Sat each month: 14.00-18.00.
Other times by arrangement. Free, but voluntary gifts for
church funds appreciated.   **10** 2 ft gauge light railway
Bagnal 0-4-0 ST No 2090 'Pixie', Ornstein & Koppell 0-4-0
WT; Nunslet & Kerr Stuart locomotives under restoration;
Foster agricultural traction engine No 14593 (1927); Avling
steam rollers No 5163 (1903) & No 7856 (1912) & No 11520
(1926); Robey tandem steam roller No 41593 (1921). Model
of part of Great Western Railway in South Devon c. 1925 with
c. 40 4 mm scale locomotives in regular use.

MUSEUM AND ART GALLERY, Riversley Park, Nuneaton,
CV11 5TU (Tel 0682-2683).   **4** Nuneaton BC.   **5** Curator:
Mr Leonard James Struebig FRAI.   **6** Recreation &
Amenities.   **7** Leisure & Recreation; Officer: B.J. Rowland
DPE, MInst, GradISM, ARMM, FBAPT.   **8** Open to the
public.   **9** Mon-Fri 12.00-19.00, Sat & Sun 10.00-19.00;
Winter: closes at 17.00. Closed Dec 25 & Good Friday. Free.
10 Local history (prehistory to medieval); anthropology &
ethnography; paintings & engravings.   **11** George Eliot
colln, May B. Lee (Lady Stott) colln of miniatures.

OAKHAM, Leicestershire.

OAKHAM CASTLE, Oakham (Tel 0533-539111).
4 Leicestershire CC.   **5** Dir: Mr Patrick J. Boylan BSc,
FGS, AMA.   **6** Libraries & Museums.   **8** Open to the
public.   **9** Summer: daily 9.30-19.00; winter: daily 9.30-
16.00. Free.   **10** Great hall of late Norman castle; unique
colln of horseshoes presented by visiting peers of the realm.
12 Served from Leicestershire Museum.

RUTLAND COUNTY MUSEUM, Catmos St, Oakham, LE15 6HW
(Tel 0206-3654).   **4** Leicestershire CC.   **5** Dir: Mr
Patrick J. Boylan BSc, FGS, AMA. Keeper: T.H. McK. Clough
MA, AMA.   **6** Libraries & Museums.   **8** Open to the
public.   **9** Mon-Sat 10.00-13.00, 14.00-17.00, Sun (summer
only) 14.00-17.00. Closed Dec 25, 26 & Good Friday. Free.
10 Former 18th cent riding school; local geology, archaeology, social history, agricultural implements, carts, craft
tools.   **12** Served from Leicestershire Museum.

CODE: 1 Name of Museum, Art Gallery or Stately Home. **2** Address **3** Telephone & telex. **4** Governing body. **5** Officer in charge. **6** Committee responsible. **7** Larger department, chief officer. **8** Open to public. **9** Hours; admission charges. **10** Scope. **11** Special exhibits or facilities. **12** Staff (a) professionally qualified (b) other non-manual (c) manual.

OLDHAM, Lancashire

OLDHAM ART GALLERY. Union St, Oldham, OL1 1DN (Tel 061-624 0505; Telex 667779). **4** Oldham MBC. **5** Dir: J. W. Carter FLA. **6** Arts & Recreation. **8** Open to the public. **9** Mon & Wed-Fri 10.00-19.00, Tues & Sat 10.00-13.00. Closed Easter, Xmas & local holidays. Free. **11** Temporary exhibitions; British 19th & 20th cent painting; British watercolours; Oriental objets d'art; ceramics & glass; contemporary glass. Local Interest Centre, Greaves St, Oldham (local ephemera, archives & environmental material). **12** (a) 7 (b) 5 (c) 2.

OLLERTON, Nottinghamshire

THORESBY HALL, Near Ollerton, Newark, NG22 9EJ (Tel 0623-823210). **5** Comptroller: Mr. N. J. Thorpe. **8** Open to the public. **9** Wed, Thurs & Sat 14.30-18.00, Sun 14.00-18.00; bank hol: Sun & Mon 12.30-18.00, Tues 14.30-18.00. Adults 40p, children 20p. **10** Victorian mansion (1864); public entertainment (Sun in summer). **11** Frank Bradley colln (model & toy theatres); Vina Cook colln Victorian dolls. **12** (c) 2.

OLNEY, Buckinghamshire

COWPER AND NEWTON MUSEUM, 'Orchard Side', Market Place, Olney, MK46 4AJ (Tel 0234-711516). **4** Belongs to town of Olney, governed by a board of trustees. **8** Open to the public. **9** Mon-Sat (inc bank hols) 10.00-12.00, 14.00-17.00 (Nov-Easter: 14.30-16.30 only). Adults 20p, OAP's & children 10p. **10** Personal belongings, furnishings, paintings of William Cowper: 18th cent items; local lace trade; archaeology. **11** Literary library, opened on request. **12** (a) 1.

OXFORD, Oxfordshire

CHRIST CHURCH PICTURE GALLERY, Christ Church, Oxford, OX1 1DP (Tel 0865-42102). **5** Curator: Mr David Pears. **8** Open to the public. **9** Mon-Sat 14.00-16.30. Closed Dec 24-Jan 1 & week before Easter. Adults 15p, children 7½p; free on Thurs & to members of Oxford University. **10** Old Master paintings & drawings (1300-1750). **12** (a) 1 (c) 3.

MUSEUM OF MODERN ART, 30 Pembroke St, Oxford, OX1 1BP (Tel 0865-722733). **4** Modern Art Oxford, Ltd. **5** Officer-in-Charge: Mr Nick Serota MA. **8** Open to the public. **9** Tues-Sat 10.00-17.00, Sun 14.00-17.00. Free. **10** Changing exhibitions of contemporary artists from England & abroad, usually 4 exhibitions every 6 weeks (group shows, one-man retrospectives, recent work & didactic). **11** Coffee bar; bookstall. **12** (a) 3 (b) 2 (c) 1.

MUSEUM OF OXFORD, St Aldate's, Oxford, OX1 1DZ (Tel 0865-21970). **4** Oxfordshire CC. **5** Dir of Museum Services: Mr R. A. Foster MA, AMA; Senior Asst Keeper (Oxford): Mr Martyn Heithon MA. **7** Dept of Museum Services. **8** Open to the public. **9** Tues-Sat (inc bank hols exc Mon) 10.00-17.00. Free. **10** History of the city of Oxford. **11** Temporary exhibitions; classroom/lecture room. **12** (a) 2 (b) 4.

Oxford University

ASHMOLEAN MUSEUM, Beaumont St, Oxford, OX1 2PH (Tel 0865-57522). **5** Dir: D. T. Piper, CBE, MA, FSA, FRSL. **8** Open to the public. **9** Mon-Fri 10.00-16.00, Sat 10.00-17.00, Sun 14.00-16.00. Closed Dec 24-26, Good Friday-Easter Sunday, Mon & Tues after 1st Sun in Sept. Free. **10** Art & archaeological collns of the University; British, European, Mediterranean, Egyptian & Near Eastern archaeology; Italian, Dutch, Flemish, French & English oil paintings; old master drawings, watercolours & prints; miniatures; European ceramics; sculpture & bronzes; English silver; applied art; Hope colln of engraved portraits; coins & medals; Chinese & Japanese porcelain, paintings & lacquer; Chinese bronzes; Tibetan art; Indian sculpture & painting; Islamic pottery & metalwork. **11** Minoan, Mycenean & Cycladic objects mostly collected & presented by Sir Arthur Evans (former Keeper), from Knossos; the 'Alfred Jewel' (late 9th cent); Guy Fawkes' lantern; gold from the Persian treasury; Pre-Raphaelite paintings & drawings; Uccello's 'Hunt in a Forest at Night'; di Cosimo's 'Forest Fire'; Claude Lorrain's 'Landscape with Ascanius Shooting the Stag of Sylvia'; drawings by Michelangelo, Raphael, Rembrandt, Watteau, Gainsborough, Rowlandson, Samuel Palmer, Turner (watercolours), Ruskin, etc. **12** (a) 32 (b) 39 (c) 48.

CHRIST CHURCH PICTURE GALLERY, *see* under Oxford

MUSEUM OF THE HISTORY OF SCIENCE, Broad St, Oxford, OX1 3AZ (Tel 0865-43997). **4** Committee of the Museum of the History of Science. **5** Curator: F. R. Maddison MA. **8** Open to the public. **9** Mon-Fri (inc bank hols) 10.30-13.00, 14.30-16.00. Free. **10** Old Ashmolean Building (17th cent); early astronomical & mathematical instruments, microscopes, photographic apparatus; clocks & watches; air pumps; early X-ray apparatus; chemical apparatus (inc early 19th cent chemical glassware); surgical & dental instruments; history of pharmacy. **11** Lewis Evans colln (scientific instruments). **12** (a) 5 (b) 3 (c) 1.

PITT RIVERS MUSEUM, Parks Rd, Oxford OX1 3PP (Tel 0865-54979). **8** Open to the public. **9** Mon-Sat 14.00-16.00. Schools by appointment in mornings. Free. **10** Ethnology & archaeology: world coverage, especially in ethnology. **12** (a) 5 (b) 6 (c) 8.

UNIVERSITY MUSEUM, Parks Rd, Oxford OX1 3PW (Tel 0865-57467). **4** Committee for the Scientific Collections in the University Museum (for the University of Oxford). **5** Curator of the University Museum (1974-7) & of the Zoological Collns: Dr T. S. Kemp MA, PhD. **8** Open to the public. **9** Mon-Sat 10.00-16.00. Closed several days at Xmas & Easter. Free. **10** Contains the entomological, zoological, geological & mineralogical collns of the University, inc much type material (emphasis on undergraduate teaching). **12** (a) 6 (b) 7½ (c) 6.

ROTUNDA MUSEUM OF ANTIQUE DOLLS' HOUSES, (Grove House), 44 Iffley Turn, Oxford, OX4 7DU. **8** Open to the public. **9** May-mid Sept: Sun 14.15-17.15. Adults 10p. Children under 16 not admitted. **10** Period dolls' houses (1700-1900) & their contents (furnishings, silver, china, books, food etc); display cabinets; in garden of private house. **12** (b) 1.

PADIHAM, Lancashire

GAWTHORPE HALL, Padiham, Burnley (Tel 0282-72177). Management Committee (National Trust, Lancashire Education Committee, Nelson & Colne College). **5** Principal, Nelson & Colne College: Mr David J. Moore BA, MA. **8** Open to the public. **9** Easter-Sept: Mon, Wed & Sat 14.00-18.00. Adults 20p, children 10p. **10** Jacobean house (1603); fine panelling & moulded ceilings. **11** Courses; concerts; Rachel Kay-Shuttleworth colln (needlework, embroidery, lace, costume & textiles).

PAIGNTON, Devon

TORBAY AIRCRAFT MUSEUM, Higher Blagdon, Paignton, TQ3 3YG (Tel 0803-53540). **5** Curator: Mr Keith Fordyce MA. **8** Open to the public. **9** Daily 10.00-18.00 (winter 16.00). Closed Dec 25 & 26. Adults 45p, children 25p; party-

PAIGNTON, Devon—*continued*

raters. **10** Preservation & restoration of vintage aircraft; aviation memorabilia: items relating to history of aviation in the West Country. **11** Aviation shop; licensed cafeteria (peak summer season only). **12** (a) 2 (b) 1 (c) 1.

PAISLEY, Renfrewshire

MUSEUM, ART GALLERIES, AND COATS OBSERVATORY, High St, Paisley, PA1 2BA (Tel 041-889 3151). **4** Renfrew DC. **5** Chief Curator of Museums & Art Galleries: Mr David R. Shearer AMA, FSA(Scot). **6** Arts. **8** Open to the public. **9** Mon-Fri 10.00-17.00 (Thurs 20.00), Sat 10.00-18.00. Free. **10** Art, natural history, local history, ceramics; textiles. **11** Paisley shawls in 19th cent social history. **12** (a) 6 (b) 8 (c) 13.

PEMBROKE DOCK, Dyfed

PEMBROKESHIRE MOTOR MUSEUM, Pembroke Dock (Tel 06463-3279). **5** Proprietor: C. Chester Smith. **8** Open to the public. **9** Easter-Sept: Sun-Fri (inc bank hols) 10.00-18.00. Adults 30p, children 15p. **10** Cycles, motor cycles & vehicles (from 1860); costumes, pumps & garage equipment; toys & working models.

PENARTH, South Glamorgan

TURNER HOUSE, Plymouth Rd, Penarth. **4** National Museum of Wales, Cardiff. **8** Open to the public. **9** Tues-Sat (& bank hols) 11.00-12.45, 14.00-17.00, Sun 14.00-17.00. Closed Dec 24-26 & Good Friday. Free. **10** Branch art gallery of the National Museum of Wales, Cardiff. Temporary exhibitions. **12** (b) 1.

PENSHURST, Kent.

PENSHURST PLACE, Penshurst, Tonbridge, TN11 8DH (Tel 089 284-307). **4** Owner: Lord de L'Isle VC, KG. **5** Administrator: W.C. Hall, **8** Open to the public. **9** April-Sept: Tues-Thurs, Sat & Sun 14.00 (July-Sept 13.00)-17.30, bank hols 11.30-17.30. Adults 60p, children 25p. Toy museum 10p. **10** Medieval house & great hall (c.1340); state apartments & picture gallery (15th-17th cent); vaulted stone crypt, now an armoury; china; silver; portraits; fine furniture; Tudor gardens & orchard. **11** Toy museum. Restaurant. **12** (a) 3 (c) 4.

PENZANCE, Cornwall

NEWLYN ART GALLERY, Newlyn, Penzance (Tel 0736-3715). **4** Newlyn Orion Galleries. **5** Dir: Mr John Halkes. **8** Open to the public. **9** Mon-Sat 10.00-17.00. Closed Good Friday. Free. **10** Contemporary painting & sculpture. **11** Temporary exhibitions; early Newlyn School; works by Albert Reuss (1889-1975), picnic area by seashore. **12** (a) 2.

PENLEE HOUSE MUSEUM, Penlee House, Penlee Gardens, Murrab Rd, Penzance (Tel 0736-3625). **4** Penwith DC. **5** District Museums Officer: Gaynor Coles BA, DipMusStuds. **6** Recreation & Amenities. **7** District Sec: D.H. Hosken DMA, FInstLEx. **8** Open to the public. **9** Mon-Sat 12.30-16.30. Free. **10** Local archaeology, folk life, social history & environment. **11** Temporary exhibitions. **12** (a) 1.

ROYAL GEOLOGICAL SOCIETY OF CORNWALL MUSEUM, Alverton St, Penzance, TR18 2QR. **5** Curator: G.J. Shrimpton BSc, ACSM, CEng, FIMM, FGS. **8** Open to the public. **9** May-Sept: Mon-Sat (inc bank hols) 9.30-12.30. Free. **10** Rocks; minerals; fossils.

PERTH, Perthshire

BLACK WATCH REGIMENTAL MUSEUM, Balhousie Castle, Hay St, Perth, PH1 5H3 (Tel 0738-26287 ext 1) **4** Regimental Trustees of the Black Watch (Royal Highland Regiment) **5** Hon Dir: Col George A. Rusk, DSO, MC, FSA(Scot);

Curator: Mr James E.R. Macmillan FSA(Scot). **8** Open to the public. **9** Mon-Fri 10.00-12.00, 14.00-15.30 (May-Oct 16.30). Free, but barrel for donations. **10** Historic descent of The Black Watch (RHR) & its Allied Regiments, (from 1740); paintings; prints; uniforms; colours; weapons; silver. **11** Relics of F.M. Earl Wavell; uniforms of King George V as Col-in-Chief. **12** (a) 1 (c) 1.

PERTH MUSEUM AND ART GALLERY, 78 George St, Perth, PH1 5LB (Tel 0738-32488). **4** Perth & Kinross DC. **5** Curator: Mr James A. Blair. **6** Leisure & Recreation. **8** Open to the public. **9** Mon-Sat (inc bank hols) 10.00-13.00, 14.00-17.00, Sun 14.00-16.00. Free. **10** Art (mainly Scottish academic); applied art (silver, costume, furniture etc); local history; archaeology; natural history. **11** Temporary exhibitions; lecture facilities; school loans. **12** (a) 2 (b) 1 (c) 6.

SCONE PALACE, Perth, PH2 6BD (Tel 0738-51416) **5** Curator: Miss Helen Fairbank. **8** Open to the public. **9** Mon-Sat 10.00-18.00, Sun 14.00-18.00. Not free. **10** Ancient coronation site of Scottish Kings; stately home; 17th & 18th cent European ivories; 18th & 19th cent French furniture, 18th & 19th cent porcelain; French & English clocks in working order; 16th cent needlework; Vernis Martin vases etc.

PETERBOROUGH, Cambridgeshire

PETERBOROUGH CITY MUSEUM AND ART GALLERY, Priestgate, Peterborough, PE1 1LF (Tel 0733-3329) **4** Peterborough City Council. **5** Curator: Miss Judith A. Levin BA, AMA. **7** Dept of Leisure & Amenities; Leisure & Amenities Officer: D.J. Constant. **8** Open to the public. **9** Tues-Sat 12.00-17.00. Closed Dec 25, 26 & Good Friday. Free. **10** Local archaeology, history, geology & natural history; ceramics & glass; paintings (mostly local topography & portraits); Napoleonic prisoner-of-war work in bone & straw; marquetry made at Norman Cross prison. **11** Temporary exhibitions. **12** (a) 4 (b) 1 (c) 5.

PETERSFIELD, Hampshire

UPPARK HOUSE, South Harting, Petersfield, GU31 5QR (Tel 073085-317/458). **4** National Trust. **5** Custodian: Mr N.D. Miles. **8** Open to the public. **9** April-Sept: Wed, Thurs, Sun & bank hols 14.00-18.00. Adults 50p, children 25p; parties (over 15) by prior arrangement 40p. **10** 18th cent house; fine furniture & plaster work; Grand Tour pictures; marble chimney pieces; 18th cent kitchen; Victorian kitchen; vaulted beer cellar; housekeeper's room (H.G. Wells's mother lived here). **11** Dolls house (Queen Anne period, fully furnished); shop. **12** (a) 2 (c) 2.

PETWORTH, West Sussex

PETWORTH HOUSE, Petworth, GU28 0AE. **4** National Trust. **8** Open to the public. **9** April-Oct: Wed, Thur, Sat & bank hols 14.00-18.00. Park open daily year round. Adults 50p, children 25p, pre-booked parties (15 or more) 35p. Park: free. **10** House rebuilt 1688-96; furniture; paintings (inc Van Dykes & Turners); park by Capability Brown; 13th cent chapel.

PICKERING, North Yorkshire

BECK ISLE MUSEUM OF RURAL LIFE, Bridge St, Pickering, YO18 8DT. **5** Hon Curator: Mr G. Clitheroe. **8** Open to the public. **9** Easter-Oct: Daily 10.30-12.30, 14.00-17.00. Adults 15p, children 5p. **10** Folk museum, (house was first agricultural institute in England). **11** Colombian printing press c.1854 (demonstrated by prior arrangement); costumes; wheelwrights shop; public house; ironmongers shop; photography room with colln of cameras; large-scale model of a natural gas plant; Victorian room; natural history; farming tools & machinery. Shops.

CODE: 1 Name of Museum, Art Gallery or Stately Home. 2 Address. 3 Telephone & telex. 4 Governing body. 5 Officer in charge. 6 Committee responsible. 7 Larger department, chief officer. 8 Open to public. 9 Hours; admission charges. 10 Scope. 11 Special exhibits or facilities. 12 Staff (a) professionally qualified (b) other non-manual (c) manual.

PLYMOUTH, Devon

CITY MUSEUM & ART GALLERY, Drake Circus, Plymouth, PL4 8AJ (Tel 0752-68000 ext 3092). 4 City of Plymouth. 5 Dir: Mr A.A. Cumming OBE, FMA. 6 Leisure Services. 8 Open to the public. 9 Mon-Sat 10.00-18.00 (Fri 20.00), Sun 15.00-17.00. Closed Dec 25, 26 & Jan 1. Free. 10 Fine art; applied art; local history; archaeology; natural history. 11 Cottonian colln (paintings, drawings, prints & early printed books, 18th cent); Clarendon colln (16th & 17th cent portraits); Plymouth & Bristol porcelain. 12 (a) 9 (b) 6 (c) 21.

ELIZABETHAN HOUSE, 32 New St, Plymouth, PL1 2NA (Tel 0752-68000 ext 3092). 4 City of Plymouth. 5 Dir, City Museums: Mr A.A. Cumming OBE, FMA. 6 Leisure Services. 8 Open to the public. 9 Mon-Sat 10.00-13.00, 14.15-18.00 (dusk in winter), Sun (summer only) 15.00-17.00. Closed Dec 25, 26 & Jan 1. Free. 10 16th cent house in Plymouth's historic quarter, furnished according to period. 12 (a) Served from City Museum & Art Gallery (c) 1.

WARLEIGH WOOD NATURE RESERVE AND TRAIL MUSEUM, c/o City Museum & Art Gallery, Drake Circus, Plymouth, PL4 8AJ (Tel 0752-68000). 4 City of Plymouth. 5 Dir, City Museums: Mr A.A. Cummings OBE, FMA. 6 Leisure Services. 8 Open by appointment only. Apply to Natural History Asst, City Museum & Art Gallery, Plymouth. 10 30 acre nature reserve, flanked by River Tavy; former railway station, now Trail Museum. 12 (a) Served from City Museum & Art Gallery (c) 1.

PONTEFRACT, West Yorkshire

KING'S OWN YORKSHIRE LIGHT INFANTRY REGIMENTAL MUSEUM, Wakefield Rd, Pontefract, WF8 4ES (Tel 0977-3181). 5 Curator & Regimental Sec: Col N.S. Pope DSO, MBE. 8 Open to the public. 9 Mon-Fri 9.00-16.30. Free. 10 Regimental history. 11 Medals & small arms.

POOL, Cornwall

CAMBORNE SCHOOL OF MINES MUSEUM, Trevenson, Pool, Redruth, TR15 3SE (Tel 02092-714866). 4 Cornwall CC. 5 Museum Curator: Dr Rosa Leslie Atkinson BSc, PhD. 6 Education. 8 Open to the public. 9 Mon-Fri 9.00-16.30. Free. 10 Geological & mineralogical exhibition. 12 (a) 1

POOLE, Dorset

GUILDHALL MUSEUM, Market St, Poole, BH15 1NP (Tel 02013-5323). 4 Poole BC. 5 Curator of Museums: Mr J.R. Dockerill MA, AMA. 6 Amenities & Recreation. 8 Open to the public. 9 Mon-Sat 10.00-17.00, Sun 14.00-17.00. Closed Dec 25, 26 & Good Friday. Adults 5p, children 2p. 11 18th cent ceramics, glassware; changing exhibitions on local themes. 12 (a) 6 (b) 4 (c) 5-15.

SCAPLEN'S COURT (OLD TOWN HOUSE), High St, Poole. 4 Poole BC. 5 Curator: Mr J.R. Dockerill MA, AMA. 6 Amenities & Recreation. 8 Open to the public. 9 Mon-Sat 10.00-17.00, Sun 14.00-17.00. Closed Dec 25, 26 & Good Friday. Adults 5p, children 2p. 10 15th cent Guildhall, restored. 11 Archaeology; local history; industrial archaeology (inc scientific conservation of an Iron Age dugout canoe found in Poole Harbour).

PORTLAND, Dorset

PORTLAND MUSEUM, Wakeham, Portland, DT5 1HS. 4 Weymouth & Portland BC. 5 Officer-in-Charge: J.A.C. West ALA. 6 Leisure & Recreation (Museums Sub-Committee). 7 Dept of Leisure Activities; Dir: Mr Peter Maddock FIMEnts. 8 Open to the public. 9 Easter-Sept: Mon-Wed & Fri 10.00-20.00, Thurs & Sat 10.00-17.00, Sun 14.00-17.00; Oct-Easter: daily (except Tues) 10.00-13.00, 14.00-17.00. Adults 5p; OAPs students & children free. 10 Illustrations & relics of old Portland, inc the stone industry. 11 Relics of Portland Prison; reproductions of prints for sale. 12 (b) 2.

PORTSMOUTH, Hampshire

CHARLES DICKENS BIRTHPLACE MUSEUM, 393 Commercial Rd, Portsmouth, PO1 4QL (Tel 0705-26155). 4 Portsmouth City Council. 5 Dir of Portsmouth City Museums: R.F. Harrison FMA. 6 Libraries Museums & Arts. 8 Open to the public. 9 Daily: 10.30-17.30. Adults 10p, children 5p. 10 House (built 1805) where Dickens was born & briefly lived; early 19th cent middle class furnishing; Dickensiana. 12 Served from Portsmouth City Museum.

CITY MUSEUM & ART GALLERY, Museum Rd, Old Portsmouth, PO1 2LJ (Tel 0705-811527). 4 Portsmouth City Council. 5 Dir of Portsmouth City Museums: R.F. Harrison FMA. 6 Libraries, Museums & Arts. 8 Open to the public. 9 Daily 10.30-17.30. Adults 10p, children 5p. 10 Displays of social & domestic artefacts (from 1750); pictorial display of Portsmouth history; furniture; pottery; glass; local paintings & modern art. 11 Temporary exhibitions; licensed bar & refreshments. 12 (a) 5 (b) 3 (c) 12.

CUMBERLAND HOUSE MUSEUM & AQUARIUM, Eastern Parade, Portsmouth, PO4 9RF (Tel 0705-32654). 4 Portsmouth City Council. 5 Dir of Portsmouth City Museums: R.F. Harrison FMA. 6 Libraries, Museums & Arts. 8 Open to the public. 9 Daily 10.30-17.30. Adults 10p, children 5p. 10 Natural history of Portsmouth region with special ref to Farlington Marshes; mammals; birds; insects; geology; freshwater aquarium. 12 (a) 3 (c) 3.

EASTNEY PUMPING STATION AND GAS ENGINE HOUSE, Henderson Rd, Eastney, Portsmouth, PO4 9JF (Tel 0705-32203). 4 Portsmouth City Council. 5 Dir of Portsmouth City Museums: R.F. Harrison FMA. 6 Libraries, Museums & Arts. 9 April-mid Sept: Sat, Sun & bank hols 10.30-17.30. Adults 10p, children & OAPs 5p. 10 Boulton & Watt reciprocal steam pumps (1887); Crossley gas engines; tangye pumps. 12 Served from Portsmouth City Museum.

FORT WIDLEY, Portsdown Hill Rd, Portsmouth, PO6 3LS (Tel 0705-811527). 4 Portsmouth City Council. 5 Dir of Portsmouth City Museums: R.F. Harrison FMA. 6 Libraries, Museums & Arts. 8 Open to the public. 9 April-mid Sept: daily (inc bank hols) 14.00-18.00. Adults 10p, children & OAPs 5p. 10 Fort built by Lord Palmerston (1860s), labyrinth of underground passages, magazines & gun emplacements. 12 Served from Portsmouth City Museum.

PORTSMOUTH ROYAL NAVAL MUSEUM, HM Naval Base, Portsmouth, PO1 3LR (Tel 0705-22351 ext 22868/23869). 4 Board of Trustees. 5 Dir: Capt A.J. Pack RN (retd); Curator: Comm S.G. Clark MBE, AMBIM, BA, RN (retd). 8 Open to the public. 9 Mon-Sat 10.30-17.30, Sun 13.00-17.00 (Nov-Feb: closes 16.30 daily), Closed Dec 25. Adults 10p, OAPs, children & school parties 5p; service personnel in uniform free. 10 Lord Nelson's flagship, HMS Victory; museum houses relics of Nelson & Trafalgar, ships models & figureheads; Nelson McCarthy colln (prints, paintings, ceramics, medallions etc, commemorating Nelson). 11 Bookstall, souvenir centre; refreshments. 12 (a) 5 (b) 14 (c) 2.

ROUND TOWER AND POINT BATTERY, Broad St, Portsmouth Point, Portsmouth. 4 Portsmouth City Council. 5 Dir of Portsmouth City Museums: R.F. Harrison FMA. 6 Libraries, Museums & Arts. 8 Open to the public.

PORTSMOUTH, Hampshire—*continued*

9 April-Sept: daily 10.00-18.00 (May-Aug 20.00). Free.
10 Elizabethan artillery military fortification.
12 (a) Serviced from Portsmouth City Museum.

ROYAL MARINES MUSEUM, Royal Marines Barracks,
Eastney, Southsea, Portsmouth, PO4 9PX (Tel 0705-22351
ext 6135). **4** Royal Marines Board of Trustees, MoD
(Navy). **5** Officer-in-Charge: Major A.G. Brown RM
(retd), MBE; Dep Curator: Major A.J. Donald RM. **8** Open
to the public. **9** Mon-Fri 10.00-16.00, Sat, Sun & bank
hols 10.00-12.00. Free. **10** Royal Marines history (from
1664); dioramas & audio visual exhibits; in original RM
officers' mess (1865). **11** 10 RM Victoria Crosses; uniforms (from 1664); souvenir shop; research facilities on
application to Dep Curator. **12** (a) 7 (b) 13 (c) 3.

SOUTHSEA CASTLE AND MUSEUM, Clarence Esplanade,
Southsea, Portsmouth, PO5 3PA (Tel 0705-24584).
4 Portsmouth City Council. **5** Dir of Portsmouth City
Museums: R.F. Harrison FMA. **6** Libraries Museums &
Arts. **8** Open to the public. **9** May-Aug: daily 10.30-
21.00; Sept-April: 10.30-17.30. Adults 10p, children 5p.
10 Fort built by Henry VIII as part of his national coastal
defences; Naval & military history, development of the
fortifications; local archaeology; finds from wreck of the
Tudor warship 'Mary Rose'. **12** (a) 5 (b) 2 (c) 9.

PORT SUNLIGHT, Merseyside

LADY LEVER ART GALLERY, Port Sunlight, Wirral,
L62 5EQ (Tel 051-645 3623). **4** Trustees. **5** Curator:
Mr R.W. Fastnedge DFC, BA. **8** Open to the public.
9 Mon-Sat 10.00-17.00, Sun 14.00-17.00. Closed Dec 25,
26 & Good Friday. Free. **10** Paintings & water colours
(mainly British); sculpture; Chinese pottery & porcelain;
Wedgwood wares; English furniture (mainly 18th cent).
11 Guide Lecturer available by appointment. **12** (a) 1
(b) 2 (c) 11.

PORT TALBOT, West Glamorgan

MUSEUM OF STONES, Margam Museum, Margam Abbey,
Margam, Port Talbot. **4** Dept of Environment.
5 Superintendant: Mr J. Roberts. **8** Open to the public.
9 Wed, Sat, Sun & bank hols 14.00-17.00 (16.00 Oct-March).
Adults 10p, children & OAPs 5p.

PRESTON, Lancashire

HARRIS MUSEUM AND ART GALLERY, Market Square,
Preston, PR1 2PP (Tel 0772-58248). **4** Preston BC.
5 Asst Dir of Leisure & Amenities (Museum & Art Gallery):
Miss G. Tresidder ARCA. **7** Leisure & Amenities Dept,
Dir: Mr W. Sheryn. **8** Open to the public. **9** Mon-Sat
10.00-17.00. Free. **10** Fine art; decorative art; social
history; archaeology; natural history; local history (inc
Preston Guild). **11** 19th cent British paintings & water
colours; paintings by Devis family; 18th-20th cent costume
& textiles; ceramics (inc all major English factories); 18th
cent drinking glasses; 18th-20th cent toys & games; mesolithic elk (from Poulton-le-Fylde); Frohawk study skins.
12 (a) 3 (b) 4 (c) 11.

QUEEN'S LANCASHIRE REGIMENT (incorporating THE
LOYAL REGIMENT) MUSEUM, Fulwood Barracks, Preston,
PR2 4AA (Tel 0772-700161). **4** Regimental Council of
The Queen's Lancashire Regiment. **5** Officer-in-Charge:
Major P.A. Mauldon (retd). **8** Open to the public.
9 Mon-Fri 8.30-12.30, 14.00-16.30. Other times by
appointment. Free. **10** Silver; medals; swords; badges;
buttons; uniforms; weapons; equipment; paintings; pictures.
Library of military publications & Army lists (from 1791).
12 (a) 1 (c) 1.

SAMLESBURY HALL, Preston New Rd, Samlesbury, Preston,
PR5 0IP (Tel 025 481-2010/2229). **4** Council for the
Protection of Rural England & Samlesbury Hall Trust.
5 Dir: Mr Stanley Jeeves. **8** Open to the public.
9 Tues-Sat 11.30-17.00. Charges: 25p. **10** 14th cent

manor house; antiques; changing exhibitions of crafts, pottery,
paintings. **11** Lectures & films on the environment.
12 (b) 9 (c) 1.

PULBOROUGH, West Sussex ·

PARHAM PARK, Pulborough, RH20 4HS (Tel 090 66-2021).
4 Owner: Mr & Mrs P.A. Tritton. **8** Open to the public.
9 Easter-Oct: Weds, Thurs, Sun & bank hols 14.00-17.30.
Gardens 13.00-18.00. House & Gardens: adults 50p, OAPs
& children 30p. Gardens only: 10p. **10** Elizabethan house;
furniture; needlework; china; Elizabethan, Stuart & Georgian
portraits. **11** Walled garden & pleasure grounds; free
car park; teas in Big Kitchen; shop.

RAVENGLASS, Cumbria

MUNCASTER CASTLE & BIRD GARDENS, Ravenglass,
CA18 1RQ (Tel 06577 614). **5** Curator: Mr P. Denham-
Cookes MRAC. **8** Open to the public. **9** Tues-Thurs,
Sun & bank hols: 14.00-17.00. Grounds open Easter-Sept:
daily 13.00-18.00. Grounds: Adults 30p, children 10p.
Castle (extra): Adults 20p, children 10p. **10** 16th & 17th
cent furniture; over 500 varieties of rhododendrons; azaleas;
ornamental & tropical birds. **11** Temporary exhibitions.
12 (a) 5 (c) 7.

READING, Berkshire

READING MUSEUM & ART GALLERY, Blagrave St, Reading,
RG1 1QL (Tel 0734-55911 ext 478). **4** Reading BC.
5 Dir: Mr T.L. Gwatkin MA, FMA. **6** Leisure.
8 Open to the public. **9** Mon-Fri 10.00-17.30, Sat 10.00-
17.00. Free. **10** Local archaeology & natural history.
11 Temporary art exhibitions; Duke of Wellington's loan
colln of Roman antiquities from Silchester; Thames Conservancy colln of prehistoric & medieval metalwork.
12 (a) 11 (b) 8 (c) 7.

Reading University

COLE MUSEUM OF ZOOLOGY, Zoology Dept, Whiteknights, Reading, RG6 2AJ (Tel 0734-85123). **5** Hon
Curator: M.G. Hardy MA. **8** Open to the public.
9 Mon-Fri 9.00-17.00. Other times by arrangement.
Free. **10** Illustrates the relationship between form
& function in animals.

INSTITUTE OF AGRICULTURAL HISTORY AND MUSEUM
OF ENGLISH RURAL LIFE, Whiteknights, Reading,
RG6 2AG (Tel 0734-85123 ext 475). **5** Keeper: C.A.
Jewell BSc. **10** History of agriculture & rural life.
11 Library, archives & records may be consulted on
application to the Keeper. **12** (a) 6 (b) 5 (c) 3.

MUSEUM OF GREEK ARCHAEOLOGY, Faculty of Letters,
Whiteknights, Reading, RG6 2AA (Tel 0734-85123).
5 Curator: Mrs A.D. Ure BA. **8 & 9** Open to the public
by appointment; term: Mon-Fri 9.00-17.00. Free. **10** A
teaching colln of classics & archaeology; Greek vases;
c.200 Egyptian objects. **11** Boeotian & South Italian
vases. **12** (a) ½.

STRATFIELD SAYE HOUSE, Reading, RG7 2BZ (Tel 025 684-
602). **4** Stratfield Saye Estates Management Co. Ltd.
5 Chief Agent: C. Scott FRICS. **8** Open to the public.
9 Daily (exc Fri) (inc bank hols) 11.30-17.30. Adults 50p,
children 25p. **10** Home of Dukes of Wellington since
1817; Duke of Wellington memorabilia. **12** (a) 2 (b) 19
(c) 6.

REDCAR, Cleveland

REDCAR MUSEUM OF SHIPPING AND FISHING, King St,
Redcar (Tel 064 93-71921). **4** Langbaurgh BC.
5 Curator: R.J. Colori BA. **6** Recreation & Amenities
(Museums Sub-Committee). **7** Recreation & Amenities
Officer: A.D. Dodds. **8** Open to the public. **9** Mon-Sat
(inc bank hols) 10.00-18.00. Free. **10** Local fishing,
shipping & sea rescue. **11** The 'Zetland', oldest existing
lifeboat in the world. **12** (a) 2 (b) 1 (c) 3.

CODE: 1 Name of Museum, Art Gallery or Stately Home. **2** Address. **3** Telephone & telex. **4** Governing body. **5** Officer in charge. **6** Committee responsible. **7** Larger department, chief officer. **8** Open to public. **9** Hours; admission charges. **10** Scope. **11** Special exhibits or facilities. **12** Staff (a) professionally qualified (b) other non-manual (c) manual.

RETFORD, Nottinghamshire

LOUND HALL MINING MUSEUM, Houghton, Bothamsall, Retford, DN22 8DF (Tel 0623-860728). **4** National Coal Board. **5** Officer-in-Charge: Dr A. R. Griffin BA, PhD, MBIM. **8 & 9** Open to the public only by prior arrangement. Adults 10p, children free. **10** Coal-mining artefacts. **11** Brinsley Tandem headgear; Worsley underground canal barge; locomotives. **12** (b) 1.

RIBCHESTER, Lancashire

MUSEUM OF ROMAN ANTIQUITIES, Riverside, Ribchester, Preston, PR3 3XS (Tel 025-484-261). **4** National Trust. **5** Curator: Mrs Nancy M. Dixon. **8** Open to the public. **9** Feb-Nov: daily (exc Fri) (inc bank hols) 14.00-17.00 (May-Sept 17.30); Dec-Jan: Sat only 14.00-17.00. Adults 10p, children 5p; National Trust members free. **10** Artefacts from Roman Ribchester cavalry fort; models of Roman buildings etc; local artefacts; foundation of granaries. **11** Book, map, etc, Stall. **12** (a) 1 (c) 1.

RICHMOND, North Yorkshire

GREEN HOWARDS REGIMENTAL MUSEUM, Trinity Church Sq, Richmond (Tel 0748-2133). **4** Trustees of the Green Howards Museum. **5** Officer-in-Charge: Col J. M. Forbes DL, JP. **8** Open to the public. **9** Mon-Sat 10.00-18.00 (Nov-March 17.00); April-Oct: Sun 14.00-17.00. Closed Whit Monday. Adults 10p, children 5p. **10** Uniforms, headdress, battle relics, medals & prints of The Green Howards from 1688, inc North York Militia & North York Rifle Volunteers. **12** (a) ½ (b) ½.

RIPLEY, North Yorkshire

RIPLEY CASTLE, Ripley, Harrogate, HG3 3AY (Tel 0423-770186). **5** Owner: Sir Thomas Ingilby, Bart. **8** Open to the public. **9** May-Sept: Sun (& Easter, Spring & Aug bank hols) 14.00-18.00. Adults 40p, children 30p; group rates. **10** 14th cent castle; library (several thousand books, mainly c. 1700, with many more books & documents stored in county archives in Leeds). **11** Priest's hole; 16-lock treasure chest; 16th cent panelling; Civil War royal Greenwich armour & other weapons; a Roman pig of lead; floor made from the deck of a British man-o-war; chandeliers; paintings; furniture. **12** (b) 2.

ROCHDALE, Lancashire

ROCHDALE MUSEUM AND ART GALLERY, Sparrow Hill, Rochdale, OL16 1AF (Tel 0706-47474 ext 769). **4** Rochdale MBC. **5** Museum Curator: Mr A. Page. **6** Recreation & Amenities. **7** Libraries & Arts Services, Dir: G. Thornber ALA. **8** Open to the public. **9** Tues-Sat 10.00-17.00 (18.00 Sat, April-Sept only). Free. **10** Local history & archaeology; folk collns; John Bright Room; vivarium; furniture; costume; industry; natural history; geology; Egyptology. **11** Temporary exhibitions; educational area. **12** (a) 2 (b) 1 (c) 1½.

TOAD LANE STORE AND CO-OPERATIVE MUSEUM, Toad Lane, Rochdale, OL16 1AY (Tel 061-834 0975). **4** Co-operative Union Ltd. **5** Inf Officer & Libn: T.R. Garratt. **9** Open by prior arrangement only. **10** History of Rochdale Pioneers Equitable Society, inc original store (opened 1844); documents & personal effects of founder members & Robert Owen & G.J. Holyoake.

ROCHESTER, Kent

EASTGATE HOUSE MUSEUM, High St, Rochester, ME1 1EW (Tel 0634-44176). **4** Medway BC. **5** Curator: Mr M. Moad. **6** Tourism & Entertainments. **7** Dir of Recreation: Mr T. Hogarth. **8** Open to the public. **9** Mon-Thurs, Sat, Sun & bank hols 14.00-17.30. Free. **10** Local history & archaeology; relics of Charles Dickens; models of local sailing craft; costume; Victoriana, arms & armour etc. **11** Local archive collns & conducted parties by appointment. **12** (a) 3 (c) 2.

ROSSENDALE, Lancashire

ROSSENDALE MUSEUM, Whitaker Park, Rawtenstall, Rossendale (Tel 07062-7777). **4** Rossendale BC. **5** Curator: Mr Jon Elliott ALA. **6** Leisure, Recreation & Amenities. **8** Open to the public. **9** April-Sept: Mon-Fri (inc bank hols) 14.00-17.00, 18.00-19.30, Sat 10.00-12.00, 14.00-17.00, Sun 15.00-17.00; Oct-March: Mon-Fri 14.00-17.00, Sat 10.00-12.00, 14.00-17.00. Free. **10** Rossendale bygones; fine arts; natural history. **11** Exhibition gallery; lecture/tea room. **12** (b) ½ (c) 1.

ROTHERHAM, South Yorkshire

MUNICIPAL MUSEUM AND ART GALLERY, Clifton Park, Clifton Lane, Rotherham, S65 2AA (Tel 0709-65481; Telex 54483). **4** Rotherham BC. **5** Principal Officer (Museum & Exhibitions): M. Densley NDD, ATD. **7** Libraries, Museum & Arts; Dir: L. G. Lovell FLA. **8** Open to the public. **9** Mon-Sat (exc Fri) 10.00-17.00 (April-Sept: 18.00, Thurs 20.00); Sun 14.30-16.30 (April-Sept 17.00). Free. **10** Rockingham porcelain; some other South Yorkshire pottery; English glass; local church silver; Roman antiquities from Templebrough; natural history. **11** Rockingham rhinoceros vase; new galleries & educational facilities. **12** (a) 5 (b) 5 (c) 7.

ROTHESAY, Buteshire

BUTE MUSEUM, Stuart St, Rothesay, PA20 0EP. **4** Buteshire Natural History Society. **8** Open to the public. **9** April-Sept: Mon-Sat (inc bank hols) 10.30-12.30, 14.30-16.30; mid June-mid Sept: Sun 14.30-16.30; Oct-March: Tues-Sat 14.30-16.30. Adults 5p, children 2p. **10** All exhibits from Bute County; archeology; history; recent bygones; geology; natural history; wild flowers in summer. **12** (b) 1.

RUDDINGTON, Nottinghamshire

RUDDINGTON FRAMEWORK KNITTERS' SHOPS MUSEUM, Chapel St, Ruddington, Nottingham, NG11 6HE (Tel 0602-212116). **4** Ruddington Framework Knitters' Shops Preservation Trust. **5** Joint Secs: Mrs D. E. Beardall; (Custodian) Mrs D. M. Shrimpton. **8 & 9** Open to the public by appointment only. Charges: 10p; school parties 5p. **10** 2 frame shops; 2 through cottages & back-to-back outhouses (1828); only known extant example of transition from early domestic industry to later power-driven machines in large factories. **11** Reconstructed 'stockingers' shop' with 7 hand frames (1 in working order); local handframe knitted garments; 19th cent photographs, documents etc; miscellaneous hosiery equipment. Cottages in process of restoration.

RUDDINGTON VILLAGE MUSEUM, The Hermitage, Wilford Rd, Ruddington, NG11 6EL (Tel 0602-212116). **4** Ruddington & District Local History Society. **5** Sec: Mrs D. M. Shrimpton; Bookings Sec: Mrs B. Pizzey (0602-211096). **8** Open to the public. **9** Tues 10.30-12.00, Fri 19.30-21.00. Other times by appointment. Free but donations welcomed. **10** Archaeological finds (pre-history, Roman, Saxon, Norman etc) from Society's excavation on site of early Mother Church (demolished 1773); costume; china; Victoriana; juniors' village scale model; photographs; samplers; craft tools etc; local archives (source material, maps, documents, records); topical exhibitions.

RUGBY, Warwickshire

RUGBY LIBRARY EXHIBITION GALLERY AND MUSEUM,
St Matthew's Street, Rugby, CV21 3BZ (Tel 0788-2687;
Telex 31488). **4** Warwickshire CC & Rugby Corporation.
5 Curator: J.H.Haiste FLA. **8** Open to the public.
9 Mon-Fri 10.00-20.00, Sat 10.00-16.00. Free. **10** Loan
exhibitions; local items; contemporary paintings.

RUGELEY, Staffordshire

BLITHFIELD HALL, Rugeley, WS15 3NL (Tel 088921-249).
5 Manager: F.Harrison. **8** Open to the public. **9** Good
Friday-mid Sept: Wed, Thurs, Sat, Sun, bank hol Mon & Tues
14.30-18.00. Adults 40p, children 25p; reduction for parties.
10 Museum of childhood in historic house occupied by same
family for over 800 years; great hall; carved oak staircase
(17th cent); Georgian costumes. **11** Lilian Lunn exhibition
of miniature figures; Frank Bradley colln of toy theatres;
Harley colln of steam-driven toys; children's playground in
garden; unique herd of black & white goats descended from
some given by King Richard II. **12** (b) 1 (c) 1.

RUNCORN, Cheshire

NORTON PRIORY MUSEUM, Norton Priory, Warrington Rd,
Runcorn, WA7 1RE (Tel 09285-69895). **4** Norton Priory
Museum Trust. **5** Archaeology & Museum Officer:
Mr J.Patrick Greene AMA. **8** Open to the public.
9 Wed-Sun & bank hols 14.00-18.00 (June-Aug 20.00).
Adults 15p, children, students & OAPs 5p; reduced rate for
parties. **10** Archaeology & history of Norton Priory, fully
excavated site (occupied for 800 years); mosaic tile floor
(c.1300). 12th cent undercroft; Georgian woodlands.
11 Schools service; free car park. **12** (a) 3 (b) 5.

RUTHWELL, Dumfries-shire

DUNCAN SAVINGS BANK MUSEUM, Ruthwell. **4** Trustee
Savings Banks Association Ltd (Scottish Area). **5** Officer-
in-Charge: Leslie M.W.Reid. **8** Open to the public.
9 Open throughout the year at reasonable hours. Free.
10 Trustee Savings Banks history; the original Savings
Bank opened by Rev Dr Henry Duncan DD in 1810 now
houses the official museum of the movement. **11** Records
of early accounts; correspondence between Dr Duncan &
Edinburgh Savings Bank at the time his Bill was before
Parliament; multi-lock box used to hold cash, home safes
from various parts of the world etc.

RYHOPE, Tyne & Wear

RYHOPE ENGINES MUSEUM, Ryhope Pumping Station,
Ryhope, Sunderland, SR2 0ND (Tel 0783-210235). **4** Ryhope
Engines Trust. **5** Hon Sec: S.A.Staddon FRICS. **8** Open
to the public. **9** Sat & bank hols 11.00-18.00, Sun 14.00-
18.00. Adults 15p, children 5p, but when in steam charges
are doubled. **10** 2 *in situ* beam engines (built 1868);
water supply & use; working waterwheel driven pump.
11 One engine is steamed on several weekends each year.

SAFFRON WALDEN, Essex

SAFFRON WALDEN MUSEUM, Museum St, Saffron Walden
(Tel 0799-22494). **4** Uttlesford DC (building & collections
owned by Museum Society). **5** Curator: Mr L.M.Pole
BSc, DipSocAnthrop, AMA. **6** Recreation & Amenities.
7 Chief Executive's Dept; Chief Executive Officer: Mr J.F.
Vernon MA, Solicitor. **8** Open to the public. **9** Mon-Sat:
winter 11.00-16.00, summer 11.00-17.00. Sun & bank hols
14.30-17.00. Free. **10** Local archaeology; ceramics;
ethnology; geology; glass; costumes; natural history & folk
life. **11** Colln of vehicles at Audley End House Stable
Block; lectures to school parties by arrangement. **12** (a) 2;
(c) 1.

ST ALBANS, Hertfordshire

CITY MUSEUM, Hatfield Rd, St Albans, AL1 3RR (Tel 0727-
56679). **4** St Albans City & District Council. **5** Dir:
Mr D.Gareth Davies BA, AMA. **6** Recreation (Museums
& Libraries Sub-Commitee). **7** Recreation Dept; Chief
Officer: R.E.H.Pringle IPFA. **8** Open to the public.
9 Mon-Sat 10.00-17.00. Free. **10** Social history; folk
life; natural history (especially geology & lepidoptera).
11 Salaman colln (craft tools). **12** (a) 10 (b) 7 (c) 3.

CLOCK TOWER, Market Place, St Albans, AL3 5DR (Tel
0727-60984). **4** St Albans City & District Council.
5 Officer-in-Charge: Mr D.Gareth Davies BA, AMA.
6 Recreation (Museums & Library Sub-Committee).
7 Recreation Dept, Chief Recreation Officer: R.E.H.
Pringle IPFA. **8** Open to the public. **9** Spring bank hol-
mid Sept: Mon-Fri (exc Thurs afternoon) & Sat (from
Easter): 10.00-17.30; Easter-mid Sept: Sun 11.00-17.30.
Adults 6p, children 3p. **10** Curfew tower (built 1402-11).
12 (a) 12 (b) 3 (c) 5.

VERULAMIUM MUSEUM, St Michaels, St Albans, AL3 4SW
(Tel 0727-54659/59919). **4** St Albans City & District
Council. **5** Dir: D.Gareth Davies BA, AMA. **6** Recreation (Museums & Libraries Sub-Committee). **7** Recreation
Dept, Chief Recreation Officer: R.E.H.Pringle IPFA.
8 Open to the public. **9** Mon-Sat 10.00-17.30, Sun 14.00-
17.30 (Nov-March: closes 16.00 daily). Closed Dec 25, 26 &
Jan 1. Adults 15p, students & children 5p; residents & school
parties free. **10** Archaeology, particularly of the Roman
town & its environs; bath wing of Roman townhouse with
hypocaust. **11** School service. **12** (a) 10 (b) 7 (c) 3.

ST ANDREWS, Fife

ST ANDREWS CATHEDRAL MUSEUM, St Andrews (Tel 033
481-2563). **4** Dept of Environment on behalf of Sec of
State for Scotland. **8** Open to the public. **9** Mon-Sat
(inc bank hols) April-Sept 9.30-19.00, Oct-Mar 10.00-16.00,
April-Sept 14.00-19.00, Oct-Mar 14.00-16.00. Charges: 5p.
10 Early Christian crosses; medieval material relating to
cathedral & priory; post-Reformation gravestones. **11** 10th
cent sarcophagus. **12** (b) 1.

UNIVERSITY OF ST ANDREWS KRAZY KAT ARKIVE
OF 20TH CENTURY POPULAR CULTURE, Dept of Fine Arts,
University of St Andrews, KY16 9AL (Tel 033 481-4610).
4 Committee of Management. **5** Dir: Mr Robin Spencer
BA, MA. **8 & 9** Open to students weekdays, by arrangement. Free. **10** Science fiction; models; ephemera etc.
12 (a) 1.

ST HELENS, Merseyside

PILKINGTON GLASS MUSEUM, Prescot Rd, St Helens,
WA10 3TT (Tel 0744-28882 ext 2499; Telex 62-417).
4 Pilkington Brothers Ltd. **5** Acting Admin Asst: Mrs
Jennifer Metcalfe. **8** Open to the public. **9** Mon-Fri
10.00-17.00 (March-Oct: Wed 10.00-21.00), Sat, Sun & bank
hols 14.00-16.30. Closed Xmas. Free. **10** History of
glassmaking techniques. **11** Temporary exhibitions.
12 (b) 2 (c) 1.

ST HELENS MUSEUM AND ART GALLERY, Gamble Institute,
Victoria Sq, St Helens, WA10 1DY (Tel 0744-24061 ext 247).
4 St Helens BC. **5** Officer-in-Charge: Miss D.P.
Hillhouse BA, Postgraduate Certificate in Museum Studies.
6 Libraries, Museum & Arts. **7** Libraries, Museum &
Arts Dept; Dir: Mr G.K.Senior FLA. **8** Open to the
public. **9** Mon-Sat 10.00-17.00. Free. **10** Local
history & industries (glass, chemical, coalmining); ceramics;
natural history; geology; costume; watercolours; archaeology;
Egyptology. **11** Pilkington colln of watercolours.
12 (a) 1 (b) 1 (c) 2.

ST HELIER, Jersey, Channel Islands

MUSEUMS AND ART GALLERY OF LA SOCIÉTÉ
JERSIAISE, 9 Pier Rd, St Helier, Jersey; and La Hougue
Bie, Grouville, Jersey (Tel 0534-22133). **4** La Société
Jersiaise. **5** Curator: Dr J.T.Renouf BSc, PhD, FRGS.
6 Executive. **7** La Société Jersiaise; President: Mr J.G.
Speer BA; Hon Sec: Mrs W.E.Macready. **8** Open to the
public. **9** Mon-Sat (inc most bank hols) 10.00-17.00.

CODE: 1 Name of Museum, Art Gallery or Stately Home. 2 Address. 3 Telephone & telex. 4 Governing body. 5 Officer in charge. 6 Committee responsible. 7 Larger department, chief officer. 8 Open to public. 9 Hours; admission charges. 10 Scope. 11 Special exhibits or facilities. 12 Staff (a) professionally qualified (b) other non-manual (c) manual.

ST HELIER, Jersey, Channel Islands—*continued*

Adults 20p, children 10p; school parties half-price.
10 Geology, archaeology, history, natural history, agriculture of Jersey. Art Gallery of paintings by Jersey artists or of Jersey subjects. Library relating to all aspects of the Société's work, inc many rare French books. **11** Old silver made by Jersey silversmiths. Life of Lily Langtry (the 'Jersey Lily') with her possessions, photographs etc; La Hougue Bie, one of finest neolithic tombs in Western Europe, with original 40 foot capping of earth; 2 medieval chapels.
12 (a) 1 (b) 6 (c) 2.

ST IVES, Cambridgeshire

NORRIS LIBRARY AND MUSEUM, The Broadway, St Ives, Huntingdon, PE17 4BX (Tel 0480-65101). **4** St Ives Town Council. **5** Curator: Christopher Ian Morris MA.
6 Norris Library & Museum Committee. **8** Open to the public. **9** Mon 10.00-13.00, Tues-Fri 10.00-13.00, 14.00-17.00, Sat 10.00-12.00. Free. **10** Archaeology (prehistoric-17th cent, especially good Roman pottery; 19th cent guns & pistols; ice-skates; pattens; 14th & 15th cent swords, spurs etc; bygones (fen implements, cooper's tools, domestic utensils); clay-pipes; pipkins, porringers & witch bottles; medieval tiles; straw & bone work by French prisoners of war at Norman Cross; rush work; pillow-lace tools; Victoriana; silver-ware; 19th cent surgical instruments; local paintings & photographs. **11** Ice-skates (inc very early bone runners, photos of Victorian skaters; advertisements for skates, a poster for a match); land surveyor's measuring wheel; 200 year old fire pump (4 wheeled cart) from Earith; Abbot's chair (stone object shaped like a chair, said to be the meeting place of Hurstingstone Handred). **12** (a) 1.

ST IVES, Cornwall

BARBARA HEPWORTH MUSEUM, Trewyn Studio, St Ives (Tel 073670-6226). **4** Executors of Dame Barbara Hepworth. **5** Curator: Mr Brian Smith. **8** Open to the public. **9** Provisional hours: Mon-Fri (inc bank hols) 10.00-17.30. Probably adults 50p, with reductions.
10 Barbara Hepworth's home & garden, with working studios as at her death; group of her sculptures. **11** Probably informal talks about Dame Barbara's work.

BARNES MUSEUM OF CINEMATOGRAPHY, 44 Fore St, St Ives, TR26 1HE. **5** Curator: Mr John Barnes.
8 Open to the public. **9** April-Sept: daily 11.00-13.00, 14.30-17.00. Winter months by appointment only. Adults 10p, children 5p. **10** History of moving pictures & the photographic image.

PENWITH GALLERY, Back Road West, St Ives, TR26 1NL (Tel 073670-5579). **4** Penwith Society of Arts.
5 Curator: Mrs Kathleen Watkins. **8** Open to the public.
9 Mon-Sat 10.00-13.00, 14.30-17.00 (Wed closes 12.30).
Charges: 5p. **10** Modern art; paintings; sculpture; pottery; prints. **12** (a) 1.

ST NEOTS, Cambridgeshire

LONGSANDS MUSEUM, Longsands Rd, St Neots, PE19 1LQ (Tel 0480-72740). **4** Longsands Museum Association.
5 Hon Curator: Mr Granville T. Rudd. **8** Open to the public. **9** Tues & Thurs 13.30-17.00. Other times by appointment. Free. **10** Local archaeology, crafts, rural life, agriculture, militaria; some costumes, ethnography, coins & medals. **11** Loans service to schools & colleges; lecture service.

ST OSYTH, Essex

ST OSYTH PRIORY, St Osyth, Clacton-on-Sea (Tel 0255-820492). **8** Open to the public. **9** Aug: daily 14.30-16.30. Charges: 40p. **10** Chinese jade & other works of art.

ST PETER PORT, Guernsey, Channel Islands

HAUTEVILLE HOUSE, MAISON DE VICTOR HUGO, 38 Hauteville, St Peter Port, Guernsey (Tel 0481-21911).
4 La Ville de Paris, Direction de L'Action Culturelle.
5 Administrator: Mr R. Martin. **8** Open to the public.
9 Mon-Sat 10.00-12.00, 14.00-16.30 (closed Thurs afternoons). Adults 20p, children, students, groups of more than 10, 10p. **10** House lived in & decorated by Victor Hugo (1856-1870). **11** Tapestries; china; carvings in wood (some by Victor Hugo); drawings of the poet. **12** (a) 1 (b) 2.

ST PETER'S, Jersey, Channel Islands

JERSEY MOTOR MUSEUM, St Peter's, Jersey (Tel 0534-33825). **5** Dir: Mr Richard Mayne. **8** Open to the public. **9** Mid March-Nov: daily 10.00-17.00. Adults 25p, children 10p. **10** Cars (from 1900); motorcycles; railway carriage (1870); military vehicles; boneshaker bicycle; engines; aircraft engines. **12** (b) 4 (c) 2.

ST PETER'S BUNKER WAR MUSEUM, St Peter's, Jersey (Tel 0534-33825). **5** Dir: Mr Richard Mayne. **8** Open to the public. **9** Mid March-Nov: daily 10.00-17.00.
Adults 20p, children 10p. **10** WWII German equipment; uniforms; weapons; models; optics; radio; civilian occupation, photographs etc. **12** (b) 4 (c) 2.

SALFORD, Lancashire

ORDSALL HALL MUSEUM, Taylorson St, Salford, M5 3EX (Tel 061-872 0251). **4** Salford City Council. **5** Curator & Asst Cultural Services Manager: S. Shaw FMA.
7 Cultural Services Dept; Manager: M. W. Devereux FLA.
8 Open to the public. **9** Mon-Sat 10.00-17.00, Sun 14.00-17.00. Closed Dec 24, 25, Jan 1 & Good Friday. Free.
10 Tudor manor house, period rooms (great hall, star chamber & Victorian farmhouse kitchen); social history.
11 Occasional temporary exhibitions. **12** (a) 2 (c) 3.
SALFORD ART GALLERY AND MUSEUM, Peel Park, Salford, M5 4WU (Tel 061-736 2649/737 7692). **4** Salford City Council. **5** Curator: S. Shaw FMA. **6** Cultural Services. **7** Cultural Services Dept; Manager: M. W. Devereux FLA. **8** Open to the public. **9** Mon-Sat 10.00-18.00 (Oct-March 17.00), Sun 14.00-17.00. Closed Dec 24, 25 & Good Friday. Free. **10** Largest public colln of paintings & drawings by L. S. Lowry; 19th cent oil paintings; ceramics; social history (period street of 19th & 20th cent).
11 Temporary art exhibitions. **12** (a) 5 (b) 2 (c) 7.

SALFORD SCIENCE MUSEUM, Buile Hill Park, Eccles Old Rd, Salford, M6 8GL (Tel 061-736 1832). **4** Salford Corporation. **5** Officer-in-Charge: Mr S. Shaw FRES, FMA.
7 Cultural Services Dept; Manager: Mr M. W. Devereux FLA.
8 Closed for repairs at present. **10** Coal mining.
12 (a) 2 (c) 2.

SALISBURY, Wiltshire

SALISBURY AND SOUTH WILTSHIRE MUSEUM, 42 St Ann St, Salisbury, SP1 2DT (Tel 0722-4465). **4** Museum Chairman & Council. **5** Curator: Hugh de S. Shortt MA, FSA, FMA, FAMS, FRNS. **8** Open to the public. **9** Mon-Sat 10.00-16.00 (May-Sept 17.00). Closed Dec 24-Jan 1 & Good Friday. Free to members, OAPs, students & children; adults 15p; parties of 10 or more booked in advance 10p.
10 English pottery & porcelain; local prehistory, archaeology,

SALISBURY, Wiltshire—*continued*

history, bygones, costumes, coins, city & guild relics (inc the Giant & Hob-nob); natural history.   **11** Temporary exhibitions.   **12** (a) 3 (b) 3 (c) 2.

SANDOWN, Isle of Wight

MUSEUM OF ISLE OF WIGHT GEOLOGY, Sandown Branch Library, High St, Sandown, Isle of Wight (Tel 098 384-2748).   **4** Isle of Wight CC.   **5** Officer-in-Charge: Dr. A. Insole BSc, PhD.   **6** Amenities & Leisure Services.   **7** Dir of Cultural Services: Mr L. J. Mitchell BA, FLA.   **8** Open to the public.   **9** Mon-Fri 9.30-17.30, Sat 9.30-17.00. Free.   **10** Local geology & palaeontology.   **12** (a) 1.

SANDTOFT, South Yorkshire

SANDTOFT TRANSPORT CENTRE, Sandtoft, near Doncaster. Correspondence to: P. A. Goddard, 20 Selkirk Ave, Warmsworth, Doncaster, DN4 9PH.   **4** Management Committee.   **5** Chairman: M. J. C. Dare, 14 Ilkley Rd, Caversham, Reading, Berkshire, RG4 7BB.   **8** Open to the public.   **9** Sun & bank hols: afternoon, Sat by appointment. Trolleybuses operate bank hols & last Sun each month (April-Sept). Free, except on operating days: adults 10p, children & OAPs 5p; Open Day: 30p.   **10** Britain's largest colln of preserved trolleybuses & motorbuses; working trolleybus system; vehicles from Britain, Belgium & Germany.

SCARBOROUGH, North Yorkshire

MUSEUM OF LOCAL HISTORY, Londesborough Lodge, The Crescent, Scarborough, YO11 2PW (Tel 0723-67326).   **4** Scarborough BC.   **5** Officer-in-Charge: Miss N. C. Shatz BA, AMA.   **6** Leisure & Amenities.   **7** Dept of Tourism & Amenities, Dir: D. J. Waterman FIMEnt.   **8 & 9** Not open yet, museum in preparation. Not free.   **10** History & development of Scarborough.   **12** (a) 1 (c) 2.

ROTUNDA, Vernon Rd, Scarborough (Tel 0723-67326).   **4** Scarborough BC.   **5** Officer-in-Charge: Miss N. C. Shatz BA, AMA.   **6** Leisure & Amenities.   **7** Dept of Tourism & Amenities, Dir: D. J. Waterman FIMEnt.   **8** Open to the public.   **9** Mon-Sat (inc bank hols) 10.00-13.00, 14.00-17.00, Sun 14.00-17.00. Free.   **10** Local archaeology; shipping; folk life.   **11** Coin colln; Bronze Age trunk burial.   **12** (a) 1 (c) 1.

SCARBOROUGH ART GALLERY, The Crescent, Scarborough, YO11 2PW (Tel 0723-67326).   **4** Scarborough BC.   **5** Arts & Museums Officer: R. K. Dunham AMA.   **7** Dept of Tourism & Amenities; Dir: D. J. Waterman FIMEnt.   **8** Open to the public.   **9** Mon-Sat 10.00-13.00, 14.00-17.00; spring bank hol-Sept: Sun 14.00-17.00. Free.   **10** Local watercolours (18th-early 20th cent); modern prints; Laughton bequest (18th & 19th cent paintings).   **12** (a) 1 (c) 2.

WOOD END MUSEUM OF NATURAL HISTORY, The Crescent, Scarborough, YO11 2PW (Tel 0723-67326 ext 5).   **4** Scarborough BC.   **5** Curator: C. I. Massey AMA.   **7** Tourism & Amenities Dept; Dir: D. J. Waterman FIMEnt.   **8** Open to the public.   **9** Mon-Sat 10.00-13.00, 14.00-17.00, Sun (Spring bank hol-Sept only) 14.00-17.00. Closed Dec 25, 26, Jan 1 & Good Friday. Free in winter; Spring bank hol-Sept: adults 5p, children 3p.   **10** Local natural history & geology; aquarium (tropical, freshwater & saltwater).   **11** Former home of Sitwell family; Sitwell books, drawings etc.   **12** (a) 1 (b) 1 (c) 3.

SCUNTHORPE, South Humberside

NORMANBY HALL, Normanby, Scunthorpe (Tel 0724-720215).   **4** Scunthorpe BC.   **5** Curator: G. C. Knowles MA, AMA.   **7** Leisure & Recreation Dept; Chief Officer: M. T. Lucas.   **8** Open to the public.   **9** Mon-Fri 10.00-17.00, Sat (in summer), Sun & bank hols 14.00-17.00. Closed Good Friday. Adults 10p, children 5p.   **10** Regency mansion refurnished & redecorated in period.   **11** Costume galleries.   **12** (a) 1 (c) 1.

SCUNTHORPE MUSEUM & ART GALLERY, Oswald Rd, Scunthorpe, DN15 7BD (Tel 0724-3533).   **4** Scunthorpe BC.   **5** Curator: G. C. Knowles MA, AMA.   **7** Leisure & Recreation Dept; Chief Officer: M. T. Lucas.   **8** Open to the public.   **9** Mon-Sat 10.00-17.00, Sun & bank hols 14.00-17.00. Closed Dec 26 & Good Friday. Free, except Sat & Sun afternoons: Adults 5p, children 2½p.   **10** Local archaeology, history, natural history & geology; period rooms.   **11** Temporary exhibitions.   **12** (a) 2 (b) 2 (c) 2.

SELBORNE, Hampshire

GILBERT WHITE MUSEUM & OATES MEMORIAL MUSEUM 'The Wakes', Selborne, Alton, GU34 3JH (Tel 042050-275).   **4** Oates Memorial Trust.   **5** Curator: Mr Clifford Cross BSc.   **8** Open to the public.   **9** April-Oct: Mon-Sat (exc Fri, but inc bank hols) 10.30-12.30, 14.00-17.00, Sun 14.00-17.00; Nov-March: Sat & Sun 14.00-17.00. Closed Xmas & Boxing Days. Adults 20p, children 5p.   **10** Former home of Gilbert White, pioneer naturalist; extensive gardens; history & natural history of Selborne. Oates Memorial Museum: Capt Lawrence Oates, history & natural history of Antarctica; Frank Oates, exploration of Southern Africa.   **11** Gilbert White Environmental Studies Centre in grounds; day field study courses can be arranged for organised groups, by appointment.   **12** (a) 3 (b) 1 (c) 2.

SELKIRK, Selkirkshire

BOWHILL HOUSE, Selkirk.   **8** Open to the public.   **9** Mid April-Sept: Sat-Thurs 14.00-17.15. Not free.   **10** Paintings (Reynolds, Gainsborough, Canoletto etc); 17th cent French furniture; porcelain; brocade & Chinese hand-painted wall coverings; relics of Duke of Monmouth & Sir Walter Scott.

SEVENOAKS, Kent

KNOLE, Sevenoaks, TN15 0RP.   **4** National Trust.   **8** Open to the public.   **9** March-Nov: Wed-Sat & bank hols 10.00-12.00, 14.00-17.00 (March & Nov: closes 15.30). April-Oct: parties on Tues afternoon by prior arrangement. Adults 50p, children 25p; National Trust members free.   **10** One of largest private houses in England (begun 1456, extended c. 1603); Jacobean interior; 17th & 18th cent furniture, rugs & tapestries; Sackville family portraits.

SHAFTESBURY, Dorset

ABBEY RUINS, Park Walk, Shaftesbury, SP7 8JR (Tel 0747-2910).   **4** Owner: Miss Phyllis Mary Carter.   **8** Open to the public.   **9** Tues-Sat & bank hols 10.00-12.30, 14.00-19.00, Sat 13.00-19.00. Adults 15p, children 5p; OAPs & students 10p; parties over 12: adults 10p, children 3p.   **10** Finds from excavations on site; model of town with abbey standing; model of church of abbey.   **11** Carved stones; mediaeval tiles; site excavations exposed; mediaeval stone cross.   **12** (a) 1 (b) 2 (c) 2.

GALLERY 24, Bimport, Shaftesbury (Tel 0747-2931).   **5** Owners: Roy & Sheila Sanford.   **8** Open to the public.   **9** Tues-Sun 10.00-18.00. Closed Feb. Free.   **10** Both new & internationally known artists; domestic & ceramic pottery by leading craftsmen; jewellery.   **12** (a) Owners only.

LOCAL HISTORY MUSEUM, Gold Hill, Shaftesbury (Tel 0747-2157).   **4** Shaftesbury & District Historical Society.   **5** Hon Curator: Miss W. M. Segger.   **8** Open to the public.   **9** Easter-Sept: Mon-Sat (inc bank hols) 11.00-17.00, Sun 15.00-17.00. Adults 10p, children 3p.   **10** Local history.   **11** Bygones; fans; needlework; domestic & small agricultural items; fire-engine (1744); pottery, flints & tools from local excavations.

SHAWBOST, Isle of Lewis, Ross & Cromarty

WEST SIDE MUSEUM, Shawbost, Isle of Lewis PA86 9BJ (Tel 085171-213).   **4** Shawbost Secondary School.

CODE: 1 Name of Museum, Art Gallery or Stately Home. 2 Address 3 Telephone & telex. 4 Governing body. 5 Officer in charge. 6 Committee responsible. 7 Larger department, chief officer. 8 Open to public. 9 Hours; admission charges. 10 Scope. 11 Special exhibits or facilities. 12 Staff (a) professionally qualified (b) other non-manual (c) manual.

SHAWBOST, Isle of Lewis—*continued*

5 Headmaster: Mr Charles MacLeod MA. **8** Open to the public. **9** Mon-Sat (inc bank hols) 10.00-18.00. Voluntary contributions. **10** Crofting & fishing life in the Hebrides. **11** Nearby, thatched Norse corn-grinding mill restored by pupils of Shawbost secondary school. **12** (c) 1.

SHEFFIELD, South Yorkshire

ABBEYDALE INDUSTRIAL HAMLET, Abbeydale Rd, South Sheffield, S7 2QW (Tel 0742-367731). **5** Dir of Museums: Mr J.E. Bartlett MA, FMA, FSA. **6** Libraries & Arts. **8** Open to the public. **9** Daily (inc bank hols) 10.00-17.00 (spring bank hol-Aug bank hol 20.00). Adults 20p, children 10p, pre-booked parties over 20 10p, OAPs free. **10** Restored steel & scythe works (late 18th-early 19th cent) with associated housing. **12** Served from City Museum.

BISHOPS' HOUSE, Norton Lees Lane, Meersbrook Park, Sheffield S8 9BE (Tel 0742-57701). **4** City of Sheffield MDC. **5** Dir, City Museums: Mr J.E. Bartlett MA, FSA, FMA. **6** Libraries & Arts. **8 & 9** Open from May 1976; Wed-Sat (inc bank hols) 10.00-17.00, Sun 11.00-17.00. Not free. **10** Small historic timber-framed house (15th cent with substantial 16th & 17th cent alterations); furnished; local history. **11** Temporary exhibitions; childrens activities room. **12** (a) 1 (c) 2.

CITY MUSEUM, Weston Park, Sheffield, S10 2TP (Tel 0742-27226). **4** Sheffield MDC. **5** Dir of Museums: Mr J.E. Bartlett MA, FMA, FSA. **6** Libraries & Arts. **8** Open to the public. **9** Daily (inc bank hols) 10.00-17.00 (spring bank hol-Aug bank hol 20.00). Free. **10** Decorative art; antiquities; geology; ethnography; natural history; archaeology. **11** Temporary exhibitions. **12** (a) 11 (b) 6 (c) 15.

GRAVES ART GALLERY AND HAYS GALLERY, Surrey St, Sheffield, S1 1XZ (Tel 0742-734781/2). **5** Dir, Sheffield City Art Galleries: Mr H.F. Constantine FMA, FIIC. **6** Libraries & Arts. **7** Sheffield City Art Galleries. **8** Open to the public. **9** Mon-Sat 10.00-20.00, Sun 14.00-17.00. Free. **10** Pictures; prints; sculpture; applied art; Oriental art. **11** British, Chinese, Oriental & Mediterranean art; picture lending service; coffee bar. **12** (a) 8 (b) 6 (c) 18.

MAPPIN ART GALLERY, Weston Park, Sheffield, S10 2TP (Tel 0742-26281). **4** Sheffield MDC. **5** Keeper: Mr Julian Spalding BA, AMA. **6** Libraries & Arts. **7** Sheffield City Art Galleries; Dir: H.F. Constantine FMA, FIIC. **8** Open to the public. **9** Mon-Sat 10.00-17.00 (June-Aug 20.00), Sun 14.00-17.00. Closed Dec 25 & 26. Free. **10** 18th & 19th cent British landscape painting (inc works by Wilson, Turner, Constable, Crome & Danby); Victorian art (inc works by Landseer, Hunt, Millais, Collinson, Burne-Jones & Tissot); modern British paintings, prints & sculpture. **11** Changing exhibitions of Victorian & 20th cent British art & artists (inc contemporary shows & events); films; lunch time lectures; children's activities; exhibitions by local artists. **12** (a) 1 (b) 1 (c) 7.

YORK AND LANCASTER REGIMENTAL MUSEUM, Regimental Headquarters, Endcliffe Hall, Endcliffe Vale Rd, Sheffield, S10 3EU (Tel 0742-662734). **4** Trustees of the York and Lancaster Regimental Museum. **5** Officer-in-Charge: Lt Col. A.W. Stansfeld MBE. **8** Open to the public. **9** Mon-Fri 10.00-12.30, 14.00-16.00. Other times by appointment only. Free but donations welcome. **10** History of York & Lancaster Regiment (from 1758); uniforms, medals etc. **12** (b) 3 (c) 1.

SHERBORNE, Dorset

SHERBORNE CASTLE, Correspondence to: Sherborne Castle Estates, Digby Estate Office, Cheap St, Sherborne, DT9 3PY (Tel 093581-3182). **4** Owner: Mr Simon Wingfield Digby. **5** Controller: P.A. Howe. **8** Open to the public. **9** Easter-Sept: Thurs, Sat, Sun & bank hols 14.00-18.00. Adults 50p, children 30p. **10** An Elizabethan/Jacobean mansion with Georgian & Victorian additions; built by Sir Walter Raleigh in 1594; home of the Digby family since 1617; fine furniture; paintings; porcelain; books; Lakeside grounds & old castle (12th cent) ruins adjacent. **11** Tearoom. **12** (b) 1 (c) 4.

SHERBORNE MUSEUM, Abbey Gate House, Church Lane, Sherborne, DT9 3BP (Tel 093581-2252). **4** Sherborne Museum Association. **5** Hon Curator: Miss D.M. Rogers BA. **8** Open to the public. **9** April-Oct: Tues-Sat (& some bank hols) 10.30-12.30, 15.00-16.30; Nov-March: Tues & Sat only 10.00-12.30, 15.00-16.30; Sun 15.00-17.00. Adults 5p, children 3p, schools free. **10** Local history (prehistory, Roman medieval etc); almshouses; Victorian dolls house; agricultural & domestic bygones; three 19th cent steam engines; silk industry; natural history. **11** Temporary exhibitions (pottery, costumes, bibles, etc).

SHERBORNE ST JOHN, Hampshire

THE VYNE, Sherborne St John, Basingstoke, RG26 5DX (Tel 025 686-337). **4** National Trust. **5** Officer-in-Charge: Maj Gen E.N.K. Estcourt DSO, OBE. **8** Open to the public. **9** Wed & bank hols 11.00-13.00, 14.00-18.00, Thurs, Sat & Sun 14.00-18.00. Charges: 35p; parties over 15 25p. **10** Tudor house; fine panelling; Renaissance chapel with 1520 glass; 17th & 18th cent furniture.

SHIFNAL, Shropshire

WESTON PARK, Shifnal (Tel 095276-207). **5** Curator: M.L. Tebbutt. **8** Open to the public. **9** Park: April-Sept: Tues-Thurs, Sat 12.00-19.30; Sun & bank hols 11.00-19.00. House: Tues-Thurs, Sat & Sun 14.00-18.00. House & grounds: Adults 55p, children 35p, school parties 30p, OAPs 45p; Grounds: adults 30p, children 20p, OAPs 25p, school parties 25p. **10** House built 1671; tapestries (Aubusson & Gobelin); paintings (Holbein, Van Dyck, Reynolds, Gainsborough etc); furniture; books; silver. **11** Adventure playground; aquarium; pottery studio; garden shop; refreshments; nature trails; park & gardens.

SHOREHAM-BY-SEA, Sussex

MARLIPINS MUSEUM, 36 High St, Shoreham-by-Sea, BN4 5DA. **4** Sussex Archaeological Trust. **8** Open to the public. **9** Easter & May-Sept: Mon-Sat (inc bank hols) 10.00-12.30, 14.00-17.00, Sun 14.00-17.00. Free. **10** 12th cent buildings; local history, particularly maritime. **11** Ship models & paintings.

SHREWSBURY, Shropshire

CLIVE HOUSE MUSEUM, College Hill, Shrewbury, SY1 1LZ (Tel 0743-54811). **4** Shrewsbury & Atcham BC. **5** Curator: Mr R.E. James. **6** Recreation & Leisure. **7** Chief Executives Dept, L.C.W. Beesley BA, MA, FCIS, AMBIM. **8** Open to the public. **9** Mon-Sat 10.00-13.00, 14.00-18.00 (opens 12.00 Mon) (closes 16.30 daily Nov-April). Free. **10** Shropshire pottery & porcelain; industrial archaeology; costume (in progress); paintings; old English drinking glasses. **11** Museum of the Queen's Dragoon Guards (Curator: Mr B. Thirkell). Caughley & Coalport porcelain. **12** (a) 2 (c) 1.

SHREWSBURY, Shropshire—*continued*

COLEHAM PUMPING STATION, Longden Coleham,
Shrewsbury; correspondence to: Clive House, College Hill,
Shrewsbury SY1 1LZ (Tel 0743-54811).   **4** Shrewsbury &
Atcham DC.   **5** Curator: Mr R. E. James.   **6** Recreation
& Leisure.   **7** Chief Executive's Dept, L. C. W. Beesley BA,
MA, FCIS, AMBIM.   **8** Open to the public.   **9** Wed
& Fri 14.00-17.00. Other times by appointment. Free.
10 2 house-built, compound rotative, steam engines (built
1900, in use till 1969).   **12** (a) Served from Clive House
Museum, (c) 1.

KING'S SHROPSHIRE LIGHT INFANTRY REGIMENTAL
MUSEUM, Sir John Moore Barracks, Copthorne, Shrewsbury,
SY3 8LZ (Tel 0743-4427).   **5** Curator: Mr Maurice E.
Jones.   **8** Open to the public.   **9** Mon-Fri 10.00-12.00,
14.00-16.00. Other times by appointment. Free.
10 Military colours, medals, weapons, uniforms, etc, of the
KSLI; captured items (inc Regimental Colour of James City
Light Infantry of US Army, a lock of hair of Emperor
Napoleon I & a replica of the Koh-i-Noor diamond, the
original being captured by the Regiment).   **12** (a) 1.

ROWLEY'S HOUSE MUSEUM, Barker St, Shrewsbury, SY1 1QH
(Tel 0743-61193).   **4** Shrewsbury & Atcham BC.
5 Curator: Mr R. E. James.   **6** Recreation & Leisure.
7 Chief Executive's Dept, L. C. W. Beesley BA, MA, FCIS,
AMBIM.   **8** Open to the public.   **9** Mon-Sat 10.00-13.00,
14.00-17.00. Free.   **10** Local prehistory, local Roman
(Uriconium) & medieval history; byegones; natural history.
11 Facsimile of Roman silver mirror; Hadrian's inscrip-
tion; Roman soldier's discharge certificate; six-sided
copper axe mould.   **12** (a) Served from Clive House.
(c) 1.

SHREWSBURY BOROUGH ART GALLERY (closed during
repairs), Castle Gates, Shrewsbury, SY1 2AS (Tel 0743-54811).
4 Shrewsbury & Atcham BC.   **5** Curator: Mr R. E. James.
6 Recreation & Leisure.   **7** Chief Executive's Dept,
L. C. W. Beesley BA, MA, FCIS, AMBIM.   **8 & 9** Temporarily closed for structural repairs. Free.   **10** Travelling
exhibitions (local & national); early English water-colours.
12 (a) Served from Clive House.

SHROPSHIRE YEOMANRY AND SHROPSHIRE R. H. A.
MUSEUM, Territorial House, Sundorne Rd, Shrewsbury,
SY1 4RL (Tel 0743-50605).   **4** Board of Trustees.
5 Officer-in-Charge: G. Archer Parfitt FCII.   **8** Open
to the public.   **9** Mon-Fri 9.00-17.00. Other days when
the Drill Hall is open for training purposes.   Free.
10 Uniforms, guidons, weapons & relics of the Regiment
(from 1795).   **11** Relics of Sgt H. Whitfield VC; mss &
photographic records of the Regiment.

SHUGBOROUGH, Staffordshire

MUSEUM OF STAFFORDSHIRE LIFE, Shugborough House,
Shugborough, Great Haywood, Stafford, ST17 0XB (Tel 0889-
388).   **4** Staffordshire CC.   **5** Curator: Mrs Pamela
Murray BA, AMA.   **6** Libraries, Records & Museums.
7 County Record Dept; County Archivist: F. B. Stitt.
8 Open to the public. **9** Tues-Fri 10.30-17.30, Sat & bank
hols 11.00-17.30, Sun 14.00-17.30. Free.   **10** Service
areas of large country house (laundry, stables, brewhouse,
coachhouse); natural & manmade environment of Staffordshire
(natural history, geology, agricultural, domestic, crafts,
costume etc).   **12** (a) 5 (b) 15 (c) 3.

SHUGBOROUGH HOUSE, Shugborough, Great Haywood,
Stafford, ST17 0XB (Tel 0889-388).   **4** Staffordshire CC &
National Trust.   **5** Curator: Mrs Pamela Murray BA, AMA.
6 Libraries, Records & Museums.   **7** Staffordshire County
Museum Service.   **8** Open to the public.   **9** Tues-Fri
10.30-17.30, Sat 14.00-17.30, Sun 14.00-18.30, bank hols
11.00-17.30. Adults 30p, children 10p; group rates.   **10** 18th
cent French furniture; paintings; porcelain; silver; late 17th
cent house, home of Earl of Lichfield; fine neo-classical
park monuments.   **11** Cafe.   **12** (a) 2 (b) 18 (c) 9.

SIDMOUTH, Devon

SIDMOUTH MUSEUM, Sidmouth (Tel 03955-6139).   **4** Sid
Vale Association.   **5** Hon Curator: Mr Gerald Gibbens MB,
BS.   **8** Open to the public.   **9** Mon-Sat (inc bank hols)
10.30-12.30, 14.30-16.30, Sun 14.30-16.30. Adults 10p,
children 5p.   **10** Local history (particularly 240 prints of
the Regency period); lace; wild flowers.   **12** (c) 2.

SILCHESTER, Buckinghamshire

CALLEVA MUSEUM, The Rectory, Silchester. (Tel 0734-
700362).   **4** Trustees of Calleva Museum.   **5** Chairman:
A. P. D. Smyth.   **8** Open to the public.   **9** Daily (inc
bank hols) 9.00-dusk. Free.   **10** Roman life in Calleva
Atrebatum (some models).

SKIDBY, North Humberside

SKIDBY WINDMILL, Skidby, Cottingham.   **5** Chief Admin
Officer: Mr Roy Gregory LLB, DMA, Solicitor.   **6** Recreational Services.   **8** Open to the public.   **9** May-Sept:
Sat 10.00-16.00; Sun 13.00-16.30. Parties other times by
arrangement. Charges: 10p.   **10** Last surviving windmill
in working order, in Northeast.   **12** (c) 1.

SKIPTON, North Yorkshire

CRAVEN MUSEUM, PO Box 13, Town Hall, High St, Skipton
BD23 A1H (Tel 0756-4079).   **4** Craven DC.   **5** Curator:
Miss P. J. Harding, BA, AMA.   **6** Recreation & Amenities.
7 Finance Dept; Chief Financial Officer: Mr G. Murray
IPFA, ARVA.   **8** Open to the public.   **9** Oct-March: Mon-
Fri (exc Tues) & Sun 14.00-17.00, Sat 10.00-12.00, 13.30-
16.30; April-Sept: Mon-Fri (exc Tues) 11.00-17.00, Sat
10.00-12.00, 13.00-17.00, Sun 14.00-17.00. Free.
10 Archaeology, history, geology & natural history of Craven.
11 Lead mining; Brigantian bronze sword in scabbard; finds
from Elbolton Cave; Craven & North of England minerals.
12 (a) 2.

SOUTHAMPTON, Hampshire

BARGATE GUILDHALL MUSEUM, Bargate, Southampton,
SO1 0DA (Tel 0703-22544).   **4** Southampton City Council.
5 Curator: A. J. Howarth.   **6** Leisure.   **7** Leisure
Services Dept, J. D. J. Bullock FIMEnt, FCEDA, MIPR,
MIRM.   **8** Open to the public.   **9** Mon-Sat (inc bank
hols) 10.00-17.00, Sun 14.30-16.30. Free.   **10** 13th-14th
cent guildhall; local history; temporary exhibitions.   **12** (c)
2.

GODS HOUSE TOWER MUSEUM, Tower House, Town Quay,
Southampton, SO1 1LX (Tel 0703-20007).   **4** Southampton
City Council.   **5** Curator: A. J. Howarth.   **6** Leisure.
7 Leisure Services Dept, J. D. J. Bullock FIMEnt, FCEDA,
MIPR, MIRM.   **8** Open to the public.   **9** Mon-Sat (inc
bank hols) 10.00-17.00, Sun 14.30-16.30. Free.
10 Archaeology of Southampton; imported ceramics.
11 Post-medieval ceramics; Roman, Saxon, medieval & post-
medieval archaeology; administrative HQ for museum services.   **12** (a) 2 (b) 2 (c) 2.

MARITIME MUSEUM, Woolhouse, Bugle St, Southampton (Tel
0703-23941).   **4** Southampton City Council.   **5** Curator:
A. J. Howarth.   **6** Leisure.   **7** Leisure Services Dept,
J. D. J. Bullock FIMEnt, FCEDA, MIPR, MIRM.   **8** Open to
the public.   **9** Mon-Sat (inc bank hols) 10.00-17.00, Sun
14.30-16.30. Free.   **10** Maritime history only.   **11** Ship
models; port models; marine steam & other engines.
12 (c) 2.

SOUTHAMPTON ART GALLERY, Civic Centre, Southampton,
SO9 4XL (Tel 0703-23855 ext 464/5).   **4** Southampton City
Council.   **5** Asst Dir of Leisure Services (Museums &
Art Gallery): Mr Tony Howarth.   **6** Leisure (Arts & Enter-
tainments Sub-Committee).   **7** Dir of Leisure Services:
Mr John Bullock FIMEnt, FCEDA, MIPR.   **8** Open to the

CODE: 1 Name of Museum, Art Gallery or Stately Home. 2 Address. 3 Telephone & telex. 4 Governing body. 5 Officer in charge. 6 Committee responsible. 7 Larger department, chief officer. 8 Open to public. 9 Hours; admission charges. 10 Scope. 11 Special exhibits or facilities. 12 Staff (a) professionally qualified (b) other non-manual (c) manual.

SOUTHAMPTON, Hampshire—*continued*

public. 9 Mon-Sat 10.00-19.00, Sun 14.00-17.00. Closed Dec 25 & Good Friday. Free. 10 Italian, French, Dutch & Flemish old masters; European paintings (19th-20th cent); British paintings (18th-20th cent); some sculpture & ceramics. 11 Temporary exhibitions; art gallery shop; cafe planned. 12 (a) 7 (b) 3 (c) 7.

TUDOR HOUSE MUSEUM, Bugle St, Southampton (Tel 0703-24216/23855 ext 768) 4 Southampton City Council. 5 Curator: A. J. Howarth. 6 Leisure. 7 Leisure Services Dept, J. D. J. Bullock FIMEnt, FCEDA, MIPR, MIRM. 8 Open to the public. 9 Mon-Sat (inc bank hols) 10.00-17.00, Sun 14.30-16.30. Free. 10 16th-19th cent social domestic life; local history & topography; decorative arts (especially costume & jewellery). 11 Education service & galleries (Sandell Rooms); enquiry & sales service; technical services; curator's headquarters. 12 (a) 5 (c) 4.

TUDOR MERCHANTS HALL, Westgate St, Southampton, SO1 0AY. 4 Southampton City Council. 5 Curator: A. J. Howarth. 6 Leisure. 7 Leisure Services Dept, J. D. J. Bullock FIMEnt, FCEDA, MIPR, MIRM. 9 Not open to public. 10 Ancient (fish) market hall, restored 1974/5. 11 Education service activities centre; lecture & performance hall; community use hall. 12 (c) 1.

SOUTHEND-ON-SEA, Essex

PRITTLEWELL PRIORY MUSEUM, Priory Park, Victoria Ave, Southend-on-Sea SS2 6NB (Tel 0702-42878). 4 Southend-on-Sea BC. 5 Borough Libn & Curator: L. Helliwell FLA, MBE. 6 Amenities (Libraries & Museums Sub-Committee). 8 Open to the public. 9 Mon-Sat 11.00-18.00 (Oct-March 16.30), Sun (April-Sept only) 14.30-18.00. Closed Dec 25, 26 & Good Friday. Free. 10 Local archaeology, history, social life & natural history, housed in 19th cent wing of restored Cluniac Priory (founded c. 1110), of which the Refectory and Prior's Chamber remain. 12 (a) Served by Southend-on-Sea Museums Service.

SOUTHCHURCH HALL MUSEUM, Southchurch Hall Close, Southend-on-Sea, SS1 2TE (Tel 0702-67671). 4 Southend-on-Sea BC. 5 Borough Libn & Curator: L. Helliwell FLA, MBE. 6 Amenities (Libraries & Museums Sub-Committee). 8 Open to the public. 9 Mon-Fri: 14.00-17.30, Sat 11.00-17.30, Sun (April-Sept only) 14.30-17.30. Organised parties by appointment Mon-Fri 10.00-12.30. Closed Dec 25, 26 & Good Friday. Free. 10 Early 14th cent timber-framed manor house, central hall open to roof; restored, equipped & furnished as a medieval manor house; small Tudor wing & exhibition room. 12 (a) Served by Southend-on-Sea Museums Service.

SOUTH MOLTON, Devon

SOUTH MOLTON MUSEUM, Town Hall, South Molton (Tel 07695-2501). 4 Friends of the Museum, South Molton. 5 Sec: R. H. Dallorzo. 8 Open to the public. 9 Mon-Sat (inc Easter, spring & Aug bank hols) 11.00-12.30, 14.30-16.30 (closed Sat mornings in winter). Free. 10 Borough history; industrial farming implements; local geology; pewter. 11 Temporary local art & craft exhibitions; town charters 1300, 1600, 1670 & deeds; fire engine (1735-1868); 10ft wooden cider press; photographic records (from 1860); borough weights & measures (from 1800). 12 (a) 1.

SOUTHPORT, Merseyside

ATKINSON ART GALLERY, Lord St, Southport, PR8 1DH (Tel 0704-33133 ext 149). 4 Sefton MDC. 5 Museums & Arts Officer: Mr H. B. Ratcliffe ARCA. 7 Libraries & Arts Dept; Libn & Arts Services Officer: A. R. Hardman FLA, FRSA. 8 Open to the public. 9 Mon-Fri 10.00-17.00.

Free. 10 Paintings; sculpture; drawings; prints; glass; china. 11 Temporary exhibitions, (inc groups & one-man shows); facilities for concerts, lectures, meetings of local societies; link with new Arts Centre, adjacent. 12 (a) 1 (b) 3 (c) 3.

BOTANIC GARDENS MUSEUM, Churchtown, Southport, PR9 7NB (Tel 0704-27547). 4 Sefton MDC. 5 Museums & Arts Officer: Mr H. B. Ratcliffe ARCA. 7 Libraries & Arts Dept; Libn & Arts Services Officer: A. R. Hardman FLA, FRSA. 8 Open to the public. 9 Mon-Sat 10.00-18.00 (Oct-April 17.00), Sun 14.00-17.00 (closes at dusk in winter). Free. 10 Local & natural history; ceramics; silver. 11 Victorian period room; Ainsdale nature reserve; early 'dug-out' canoe. 12 (a) 1 (c) 4.

SOUTH QUEENSFERRY, West Lothian

HOPETOUN HOUSE, South Queensferry, EH30 9SL (Tel 031-331 1348/1546) 4 Hopetown House Preservation Trust. 5 Factor: J. N. Douglas-Menzies FRICS. 8 Open to the public. 9 May-Sept: Sat-Wed (inc bank hols) 13.30-17.30. House, museum & grounds: adults 50p, children 20p. Grounds only: adults 25p, children 10p. 10 Adam mansion; extensive 18th cent pleasure grounds & deer parks; mid 18th cent interiors with fine rococo plaster ceilings & period furniture; paintings (inc Van Dyck, Rubens, Canaletto, Gainsborough, Raeburn). 11 Teas; gift shop. 12 (a) 1 (b) 7 (c) 4.

QUEENSFERRY MUSEUM, Council Chambers, 53 High St, South Queensferry, EH30 9HP (Tel 031-331 1590). 4 City of Edinburgh DC. 5 City Curator: Mr Herbert Coutts AMA, FSA(Scot). 7 Recreation & Leisure Dept, Mr William Bell MA, LLB. 8 Open to the public. 9 Mon-Fri (inc bank hols) 10.00-17.00, Sat & Sun (hours to be arranged). Free. 10 Local authority & trade in the old Royal Burgh of Queensferry (charters etc). 12 (c) 1.

SOUTH SHIELDS, Tyne & Wear

ROMAN FORT AND MUSEUM, Baring St, South Shields (Tel 08943-61369). 4 Tyne & Wear CC. 5 Principal Keeper: J. H. Wilson BA, FMA. 6 Leisure. 7 Museums & Art Galleries Services; Dir: Mr K. J. Barton, MPhil, FSA, FMA. 8 Open to the public. 9 May-Sept: Mon-Sat (inc bank hols) 10.00-19.30, Sun 11.00-19.30; Oct-April: Mon-Fri (inc bank hols) 10.00-16.00, Sat 10.00-12.00. Free. 10 Domestic, military & personal items found in Roman fort; altars; tombstones; sculptures. 11 Memorial stones found in South Shields. 12 (c) 2.

SOUTH SHIELDS MUSEUM, Ocean Rd, South Shields (Tel 08943-4321). 4 Tyne & Wear CC. 6 Leisure. 7 Museums & Art Galleries Services; Dir: Mr K. J. Barton MPhil, FSA, FMA. 8 Open to the public. 9 Mon-Fri 10.00-19.00, Sat 10.00-17.00. Free. 10 Natural history; local glass; local history. 11 Original model of 1st lifeboat, invented in South Shields by W. Wouldhave (1789). 12 (c) 1.

SPALDING, Lincolnshire

SPALDING GENTLEMEN'S SOCIETY MUSEUM, Broad St, Spalding, PE11 1TB (Tel 0775-4658). 4 Council of the Society. 5 Hon Curator: Mr Norman Leveritt. 8 Open only by previous application to Hon Curator. Free. 10 Local bygones; ceramics; glass; coins; library. 11 Loewental colln (Chinese glass, ceramics, hardstone carvings & vessels, Meissen porcelain). 12 (c) 1.

STAFFORD, Staffordshire

IZAAK WALTON COTTAGE, Shallowford, Stafford (Tel 078577-278). 4 Staffordshire CC. 5 Keeper: Mr John

STAFFORD, Staffordshire—*continued*

Rhodes.   **6** Libraries, Museums & Records.   **7** County Record Office; County Archivist: Mr F. B. Stitt.   **8** Open to the public.   **9** Daily (exc Tues) (inc bank hols) 10.00-12.00, 14.30-16.30. Adults 5p, children 3p.   **10** Izaak Walton's restored country cottage.   **12** (b) 1.

STAFFORD MUSEUM & ART GALLERY, The Green, Stafford, ST17 4BJ (Tel 0785-2151).   **4** Staffordshire CC. **5** Keeper: Mr John Rhodes.   **6** Libraries, Museums & Records.   **7** County Record Office; County Archivist: Mr F. B. Stitt.   **8** Open to the public.   **9** Mon-Fri 10.00-19.00, Sat 10.00-17.00. Free.   **10** Local social & industrial history; art gallery shows loan exhibitions & work by local artists.   **12** (b) 1 (c) 2.

STAINDROP, Co Durham

RABY CASTLE, Staindrop, Darlington, DL2 3AH (Tel 08336-202).   **5** Curator: Mrs E. A. Steele.   **8** Open to the public. **9** May-Sept: daily 14.00-17.00. Castle: adults 35p, children 15p; gardens & coach houses: adults 20p, children 10p. **10** Mediaeval fortified house (restored 18th & 19th cent); Dutch, Flemish & English paintings; fine furniture (English & French); European & Oriental porcelain; state coaches of Dukes of Cleveland; horse-drawn vehicles, inc small fire-engines; walled gardens (18th cent) noted for sweet peas. **12** (a) 1 (c) 1.

STALYBRIDGE, Cheshire

ASTLEY CHEETHAM ART GALLERY (temporarily closed). Trinity St, Stalybridge, SK15 2BN (Tel 061-338-2708). **4** Tameside MDC.   **5** Museums Officer: Mrs H. C. Caffrey BA, AMA.   **7** Libraries & Arts, Chief Libn & Arts Officer: Mr T. M. Featherstone BA, FLA.   **8 & 9** Reopening Autumn 1976; hours under review. Free.   **10** Medieval-early renaissance, 18th-19th cent & local paintings; some antiquities.   **11** Exhibitions in local studies centre at Stalybridge Library, & other places in Tameside.   **12** (a) 1 (c) 2.

STAMFORD, Lincolnshire

STAMFORD MUSEUM, Public Library, High St, Stamford, PE9 2BB; Correspondence To: Director, Lincolnshire Museums, Old Barracks, Burton Rd, Lincoln, LN1 3LY (Tel 0780-3442).   **4** Lincolnshire CC.   **6** Museums Sub-Committee.   **7** Dir: Mr Antony Gunstone BA, FSA, FMA. **8** Open to the public.   **9** Mon & Wed 10.00-19.00, Tues 10.00-18.00, Fri 9.00-18.00, Sat 10.00-16.00. Free. **10** History of Stamford & district.

STEEPLE ASTON, Oxfordshire

ROUSHAM HOUSE, Steeple Aston, Oxford (Tel 0869-47110). **8** Open to the public.   **9** April-Sept: Wed, Sun & bank hols. 14.00-17.30. Gardens: Daily 10.00-18.00. Not free. **10** House (built 1635); Royalist garrison in Civil War; paintings; contemporary furniture; interiors by William Kent (1738) & Roberts of Oxford (1765).   **11** 30 acre garden, Kent's only surviving landscape design.

STEVENAGE, Hertfordshire

STEVENAGE MUSEUM, Lytton Way, Stevenage, SG1 1XR (Tel 0438-54100).   **4** Stevenage BC.   **5** Curator: Mr Colin V. Dawes BSc, AMA.   **7** Leisure Services Dept; Leisure Services Officer: M. L. Banks BA, DipPhysEd. **8** Open to the public.   **9** Mon-Sat 9.30-17.30, Sun 14.00-18.00. Free.   **10** Local history & folk life; natural history; local archaeology.   **11** Temporary exhibitions (local & national); childrens activities; Museum Club; audio-visual presentations; educational facilities.   **12** (a) 3 (b) 2 (c) 1.

STICKLEPATH, Devon

FINCH FOUNDRY TRUST, AND STICKLEPATH MUSEUM OF RURAL INDUSTRY, Sticklepath, Okehampton, EX20 2NW. (Tel 083 784-352).   **5** Dir: Mr R. A. Barron.   **8** Open to the

public.   **9** Daily (inc bank hols) 11.00-18.00. Adults 15p, children 10p.   **10** Water-powered edge-tool factory with 3 working water wheels; water turbine generating electricity for heating & lighting; hand tools made or used at factory; other bygones; gallery of water power.   **11** Water-powered blower for forges; water-powered tilt hammers & metal cutting shears; water-powered grindstone for sharpening tools.   **12** (b) 1.

STIRLING, Stirlingshire

ARGYLL AND SUTHERLAND HIGHLANDERS REGIMENTAL MUSEUM, The Castle, Stirling, FK8 1EJ (Tel 0786-2356). **5** Curator: Lt Col G. P. Wood MC, A & SH.   **8** Open to the public.   **9** April-Sept: Mon-Fri (inc bank hols) 10.00-18.00, Sat & Sun 11.00-18.00. Free.   **10** Pictures, silver, medals, uniforms of the Argyll & Sutherland Highlanders. **12** (b) 2 (c) 2.

MacROBERT ART GALLERY, MacRobert Arts Centre, University of Stirling, Stirling, (Tel 0786-3171 ext 2549). **5** Administrator: Mrs Deborah G. Butler BA.   **7** MacRobert Arts Centre, Dir: Mr J. Dodgson.   **8** Open to the public. **9** Hours under review. Free.   **10** Temporary exhibitions of all visual arts.   **12** (a) 1.

SMITH ART GALLERY AND MUSEUM (temporarily closed). Albert Place, Stirling, FK8 2RQ; Correspondence to: c/o Old High School Academy Rd, Stirling. (Tel 0786-2849). **4** Stirling Region & District Smith Art Gallery & Museum Joint Committee.   **5** Curator: Mr James K. Thomson AMA, FSA(Scot).   **8** Closed for renovations.   **10** Archaeology, ethnology; local domestic history; geology; art.   **12** (a) 1 (c) 1.

STOCKPORT, Cheshire

VERNON PARK MUSEUM, Turncroft Lane, Stockport, SK1 4AR (Tel 061-480 3668).   **4** Stockport MBC. **6** Recreation & Culture.   **7** Dept of Culture, Asst Dir (Culture): R. E. G. Smith FLA; Recreation & Culture Division, Dir: H. Hitchcock IPFA, FRVA, MInstRM.   **8** Open to the public.   **9** Mon-Sat 10.00-18.00 (Nov-Feb 17.00), Sun 14.00-17.00. Free.   **10** General.   **11** Blue John window. **12** (a) 1 (b) 3 (c) 2.

WAR MEMORIAL AND ART GALLERY, Greek St, Stockport (Tel 061-480 9433).   **4** Stockport MBC.   **5** Asst Dir (Culture): R. E. G. Smith FLA.   **7** Recreation & Culture Division; Dir: H. Hitchcock IPFA, FRVA, MInstRM.   **8** Open to the public.   **9** Mon-Fri 12.00-18.00, Sat 10.00-16.00. Free.   **10** Oils & water colours.   **11** Open exhibition & temporary loan collns.   **12** (a) 1 (c) $1\frac{1}{2}$.

STOCKTON-ON-TEES, Cleveland

PRESTON HALL MUSEUM, Yarm Road, Stockton-on-Tees, (Tel 0642-781184).   **4** Stockton BC.   **5** Officer-in-Charge: J. P. Warbrook, BSc, FGS, FZS, AMA.   **7** Leisure & Amenities, Chief Officer: Mr B. M. Connolly.   **8** Open to the public. **9** Mon-Sat 10.00-18.00, Sun 14.00-18.00. Free.   **10** Social history.   **11** Spence colln of arms & armour; 'Dice Players' by George de La Tour.   **12** (a) 1 (b) 1 (c) 12.

STOCKTON AND DARLINGTON RAILWAY MUSEUM, Bridge Rd, Stockton-on-Tees, (Tel 0642-62803).   **4** Stockton BC. **5** Officer-in-Charge: J. P. Warbrook.   **7** Leisure & Amenities, Chief Officer: Mr B. M. Connolly.   **8** Open to the public. **9** Mon-Sat 10.00-18.00. Free.   **10** History of the Stockton & Darlington Railway.   **12** (a) 1 (c) 1.

STOKE BRUERNE, Northamptonshire

WATERWAYS MUSEUM, Stoke Bruerne, Towcester, NN12 7SE (Tel 0604-862229).   **4** British Waterways Board. **5** Curator: R. J. Hutchings.   **8** Open to the public. **9** Summer: daily 10.00-18.00; winter: Tues-Sun 10.00-16.00. Closed Dec 25 & 26. Adults 15p, children 5p.   **10** History of canals; traditional clothing, cabinware, implements; paintings, photographs & documents; reconstruction of butty boat cabin.   **11** Early traditional narrow boat; boat weighing machine; cast iron lock gates.   **12** (b) 4 (c) 2.

CODE: 1 Name of Museum, Art Gallery or Stately Home. **2** Address. **3** Telephone & telex. **4** Governing body. **5** Officer in charge. **6** Committee responsible. **7** Larger department, chief officer. **8** Open to public. **9** Hours; admission charges. **10** Scope. **11** Special exhibits or facilities. **12** Staff (a) professionally qualified (b) other non-manual (c) manual.

STOKE-ON-TRENT, Staffordshire

BENNETT HOUSE, 205 Waterloo Rd, Cobridge, Stoke-on-Trent, ST6 2HS (Tel 0782-25426). **4** Stoke-on-Trent DC. **5** Dir: A. R. Mountford MA, FMA, FSA. **6** Museums. **8** Open to the public. **9** Mon, Wed, Thur & Sat (inc bank hols) 14.00-17.00. Free. **10** Arnold Bennett's house as a young man. **11** Personal effects of Arnold Bennett. **12** (b) 1.

CITY OF STOKE-ON-TRENT MUSEUM AND ART GALLERY, Hanley, Stoke-on-Trent, ST1 4HS (Tel 0782-22714/5). **4** Stoke-on-Trent DC. **5** Dir: A. R. Mountford MA, FMA, FSA. **6** Museums. **8** Open to the public. **9** Mon-Sat (inc bank hols) 10.00-18.00, Sun 14.30-17.00. Closed Dec 25 & Good Friday. Free. **10** Staffordshire pottery & porcelain; continental, South American, Near Eastern & Oriental pottery; 18th cent English water-colours; English painting since 1900; sculpture; costumes; samplers; dolls; Staffordshire archaeology; natural history (inc Staffordshire birds & mammals). **12** (a) 3 (b) 8 (c) 3.

FORD GREEN HALL, Smallthorne, Stoke-on-Trent. (Tel 0782-534771). **4** Stoke-on-Trent DC. **5** Dir City Museum: A. R. Mountford MA, FSA, FMA. **6** Museums. **8** Open to the public. **9** Mon, Wed, Thurs & Sat 10.00-12.30, 14.00-18.00 (winter 16.30), Sun 14.00-17.00. Closed Dec 25, 26 & Jan 1. Free. **10** Oldest house in city; 16th-18th cent furniture. **11** Fire-arms; coats-of-arms; glass; pottery; silver. **12** (b) 1.

SPITFIRE MUSEUM, Bethesda St, Hanley, Stoke-on-Trent. **4** Stoke-on-Trent DC. **5** Dir, City Museum: A. R. Mountford MA, FSA, FMA. **6** Museums. **8** Open to the public. **9** Mon-Sat 9.00-17.30. Closed Dec 25, 26 & Jan 1. Free. **10** Spitfire Aircraft RW 388 Mk LF I6e with a Rolls Royce Packard Merlin 266 engine built in 1944; associated RAF material, photographs etc. **12** (b) 1.

SPODE LIMITED, MUSEUM, Spode Works, Stoke-on-Trent, **ST4 1BX** (Tel 0782-46011; Telex 36420). **5** Art Dir, Spode Ltd, & Curator of Works Museum: Mr Harold Holdway. **8 & 9** Open Mon-Fri by appointment. Free. **10** Spode, Copeland & Garrett, & Copeland wares in dry bodies, earthenware, stone china, bone china & parian. **11** Blue Room devoted to underglaze prints, especially Blue prints on earthenware.

STOURTON, Wiltshire

STOURHEAD HOUSE, Stourton, Warminster, BA12 6QH (Tel 074 784-348). **4** National Trust. **8** Open to the public. **9** April-Sept: daily (exc Mon & Tues in April & Sept) 14.00-18.00; March, Oct & Nov: Sat & Sun 14.00-18.00. Gardens: daily year round 8.00-19.00 (or sunset if earlier). House 60p, gardens 60p, reduced rates for children & groups. **10** Palladian house (1772); furnished by the younger Thomas Chippendale; Regency interiors; romantic 18th cent landscape gardens.

STOWMARKET, Suffolk

MUSEUM OF EAST ANGLIAN LIFE, Abbot's Hall, Stowmarket, IP14 1DL (Tel 04492-2229). **4** Trustees of the Museum. **5** Dir: Mr Geoffrey Wilding BSc, CEng, MIMechE, AMA. **8** Open to the public. **9** April-Oct: Mon-Sat (inc bank hols) 11.00-17.00, Sun 14.00-17.00. Adults 20p, children 10p. **10** 16th cent barn; wheeled vehicles; re-erected 14th cent aisled hall; smithy; watermill; mill house; cart lodge; agricultural tools & equipment; craft tools & domestic items. **12** (a) 4.

STRANRAER, Wigtownshire

TIDEMARK SHELLCRAFTS, Arndald House, 1 Charlotte St, Stranraer. **5** Owner: Mr Joe Craig BSc. **8** Open to the public. **9** Mon-Sat (exc Wed) 9.30-13.30, 14.30-17.30. **10** Worldwide & local seashells. **11** Souvenir shop.

WIGTOWN DISTRICT MUSEUM, London Rd, Stranraer DG9 8ES (Tel 0776-2151 ext 277). **4** Wigtown DC. **5** Curator: Mr Stanley Pilling. **8** Open to the public. **9** Mon-Fri 9.30-17.00, Sat 9.30-13.00. Free. **10** Local geology, natural history, archaeology & social history. **11** Sir John Ross colln (Arctic explorer); old Scots wooden plough (c. 1790). **12** (b) 1 (c) 1.

STRATFORD-UPON-AVON, Warwickshire

ANNE HATHAWAY'S COTTAGE, Shottery, Stratford-upon-Avon (Tel 0789-2100). **4** Shakespeare Birthplace Trust. **5** Dir: Dr Levi Fox OBE, MA, FSA. **8** Open to the public. **9** Nov-March: Mon-Sat 9.00-16.00, Sun 13.30-16.30; April-Oct: Mon-Sat 9.00-19.00 (April, May & Oct 18.00), Sun 10.00-18.00. Adults 30p, children 10p. **10** Tudor yeoman's house with timber-framed walls & thatched roof where Anne Hathaway lived before her marriage to Shakespeare; period furniture (from 16th cent on); kitchen bread-oven still *in situ;* late-Tudor bedstead of the Hathaway family; English cottage-style garden.

HALL'S CROFT, Old Town, Stratford-upon-Avon, CV37 6BG (Tel 0789-2107). **4** Shakespeare Birthplace Trust. **5** Dir: Dr Levi Fox OBE, MA, FSA. **8** Open to the public. **9** Nov-March: Mon-Sat 9.00-12.45, 14.00-16.00; April-Oct: Mon-Sat 9.00-18.00, Sun 14.00-18.00. Adults 20p, children 10p. **10** Home of Shakespeare's daughter Susanna, wife of Dr John Hall; middle-class Tudor domestic architecture with late Tudor & Jacobean furniture; 16th & 17th cent medicine.

HARVARD HOUSE MEMORIAL TRUST, High St, Stratford-upon-Avon, CV37 6AU (Tel 0789-4507). **5** Local Trustee: Dr Levi Fox OBE, DL, MA, FSA, FRHistS, FRSL; Custodian: Mrs J. Dvoran. **8** Open to the public. **9** April-Oct: Mon-Sat (inc bank hols) 9.00-13.00, 14.00-18.00, Sun 14.00-18.00; Nov-March: Mon-Sat 9.00-13.00, 14.00-16.00. Adults 15p, children 7p. **10** Period house associated with family of John Harvard, founder of the American university. **12** (b) 1.

MARY ARDEN'S HOUSE, Wilmcote, near Stratford-upon-Avon, CV37 9UN (Tel 0789-3455). **4** Shakespeare Birthplace Trust. **5** Dir: Dr Levi Fox OBE, MA, FSA. **8** Open to the public. **9** Nov-March: Mon-Sat 9.00-12.45, 14.00-16.00; April-Oct: Mon-Sat 9.00-18.00, Sun 14.00-18.00. Adults 20p, children 10p. **10** Tudor farmhouse (3 miles from Stratford) where Shakespeare's mother lived; period furnishings; museum of Warwickshire rural life in barns; stone dovecote; village stocks; cider mill.

NEW PLACE, Chapel St, Stratford-upon-Avon, CV37 6EP (Tel 0789-2325). **4** Shakespeare Birthplace Trust. **5** Dir: Dr Levi Fox OBE, MA, FSA. **8** Open to the public. **9** Nov-March: Mon-Sat 9.00-12.45, 14.00-16.00; April-Oct: Mon-Sat 9.00-18.00, Sun 14.00-18.00. Adults 20p, children 10p. **10** Foundations of Shakespeare's last home in garden. Thomas Nash's house adjoining, contains Tudor period furnishings, local history & archaeology; Anglo-Saxon jewellery; medieval chest of the Gild of the Holy Cross; Elizabethan-style knot garden.

ROYAL SHAKESPEARE THEATRE PICTURE GALLERY AND MUSEUM, Waterside, Stratford-upon-Avon, CV37 6BB (Tel 0789-3693). **4** Governors of the Royal Shakespeare Theatre. **8** Open to the public. **9** Mon-Sat 10.00-13.00, 14.00-18.00, Sun 14.00-18.00; Nov-March: closes at 16.00 daily. Closed Dec 25 & Good Friday. Adults 20p, children 10p. **10** Shakespearean portraits; paintings of scenes from plays; portraits & sculpture of actors; relics of celebrated players; scenery & costume designs. **12** (b) 2 (c) 1.

SHAKESPEARE'S BIRTHPLACE, Henley St, Stratford-upon-Avon, CV37 6QW (Tel 0789-4016). **4** Shakespeare Birthplace Trust. **5** Dir: Dr Levi Fox OBE, MA, FSA. **8** Open to the public. **9** Nov-March: Mon-Sat 9.00-

STRATFORD-UPON-AVON, Warwickshire—*continued*

16-00, Sun 13.30-16.30; April-Oct: Mon-Sat 9.00-19.00
(April, May & Oct 18.00), Sun 10.00-18.00. Adults 30p,
children 10p.   **10** 16th cent half-timbered house where
Shakespeare was born; period furnishings; shakespeareana
(inc pictures, prints, ceramics, coins & medals, books &
documents); a 1st folio & some quartos of Shakespeare's
plays; original Shakespearean documents; 2 early silver-
gilt maces of Stratford-upon-Avon Corporation; early 17th
cent 'baby-minder'.   **11** Library & records repository;
bookshop.

WARWICKSHIRE YEOMANRY MUSEUM, Tavr Centre, New
Broad St, Stratford-upon-Avon, CV37 6HW (will be moving
to the Warwick County Museum) (Tel 0789-2266).
5 Acting Curator: Major R. Neal MBE, 18 Newfield Ave,
Kenilworth, CV8 2AU.   **8** Open to the public.   **9** Mon-Fri
9.00-16.30. Other days by arrangement. Free.   **10** Silver
& uniforms (from 1850); dispatches; diaries; other militaria.
11 Lady Butler painting of the Battle of Huj; several
Schnaffles paintings.

STRATHAVEN, Lanarkshire

JOHN HASTIE MUSEUM, Lethame Rd, Strathaven, ML10 6EF
(Tel 0357-21257).   **4** East Kilbride DC.   **6** Halls, Enter-
tainments & Libraries.   **7** Libraries Dept; Chief Libn:
Mr D. E. Harrison FLA.   **8** Open to the public.   **9** May-
Sept: Mon-Fri (inc bank hols) 14.00-17.00, Sat 14.00-19.00.
Free.   **10** Local history.   **11** John Hastie gun colln;
Burnbrae colln (china, inc Aynsley china plates depicting
local scenes).

STREET, Somerset

STREET SHOE MUSEUM, C & J Clark, Street, BA16 0YA
(Tel 04584-3131).   **5** Officer-in-Charge: Ms Elaine Dyer
BA, DipHistArt.   **8** Open to the public.   **9** April-Oct:
Mon-Sat 10.00-13.00, 14.00-16.45. Free.   **10** Shoes from
Roman times to present; 19th cent shoe making machinery;
history of Clarks through 19th cent documents; engravings
of shoemakers.   **12** (a) 1 (b) 1 (c) 1.

STROMNESS, Orkney Isles

SKARA BRAE PREHISTORIC VILLAGE, Bay of Skail,
Stromness, Orkney.   **4** Dept of Environment.   **5** Information Officer, Argyle House, 3 Lady Lawson St, Edinburgh.
8 Open to the public.   **9** Mon-Sat 9.30-19.00, Sun 14.00-
19.00. Oct-March: closes 16.00 daily. Adults 10p, children
5p.   **10** Cluster of dwellings in drift sand (1600-1400 BC);
stone furniture; hearths, drains; rectangular rooms with
round corners.   **12** (c) 1.

STROMNESS MUSEUM, 52 Alfred St, Stromness, Orkney
Isles, KW16 3DF (Tel 085 685-246).   **4** Orkney Natural
History Society.   **5** Hon Curator: Bryce S. Wilson DipArt.
8 Open to the public.   **9** Mon-Sat 11.00-12.30, 13.30-
17.00 (July & Aug: opens 10.30). Adults 10p, children 2½p.
10 Maritime; local history; natural history; archaeology.
11 Hugh Miller's key fossil, Asterolepis of Stromness;
Robert Rendall's colln of Orkney shells; album of newspaper
cuttings & photographs of the salving of WWI German Fleet
at Scapa Flow.   **12** (c) 1.

STROUD, Gloucestershire

STROUD AND DISTRICT MUSEUM, Lansdown, Stroud,
GL5 1BB (Tel 045 36-3394).   **4** Stroud Museum Management Committee.   **5** Curator: Mr Lionel F. J. Walrond
AMA.   **8** Open to the public.   **9** Mon-Fri 10.30-17.00,
Sat 10.30-13.00, 14.00-17.00. Closed Dec 25, Jan 1 & Good
Friday. Free.   **10** Local archaeology, geology & folk life;
industries; buildings; pottery; dolls; numismatics.
11 Roman altars; dinosaur bones & 20 ft model reconstruction; mammoth remains from local gravels; pictures etc
relating to local cloth industry; early lawn mowers invented
at Stroud.   **12** (a) 1 (b) 1.

SUDBURY, Derbyshire

SUDBURY HALL AND MUSEUM, Sudbury, Derby, DE6 5HT
(Tel 028 378-305).   **4** National Trust.   **5** Curator: Mr
John Hodgson AMA.   **8** Open to the public.   **9** April-Oct:
Wed-Sun (inc bank hols). Museum free. Hall: adults 40p,
children 20p, National Trust members free.   **10** Furnished
Charles II house with outstanding plasterwork & woodcarving; county museum with permanent exhibition about childhood; art gallery; studios for craftsmen.   **11** Summer programme of international concerts, lectures, films etc;
educational facilities (inc art, dance & drama studios &
library).   **12** (a) 1 (b) 8 (c) 2.

SUDBURY, Suffolk

GAINSBOROUGH'S HOUSE, Gainsborough St, Sudbury,
CO10 6EU (Tel 078 73-72958).   **4** Gainsborough House
Society.   **5** Curator: Mr Robert McPherson BA.   **8** Open
to the public.   **9** Mon-Sat (inc bank hols) 10.00-12.30,
14.00-17.00, Sun 14.00-17.00. Adults 10p, children, students
& OAPs 5p.   **10** Gainsboroughs; 18th cent paintings &
furniture.   **11** Temporary exhibitions; library (inc
Gainsborough letters).   **12** (a) 1 (b) 2.

SUMBURGH HEAD, Shetland Isles

JARLSHOF, Sumburgh Head, Shetland.   **4** Dept of Environment.   **5** Information Officer, Argyle House, 3 Lady
Lawson St, Edinburgh.   **8** Open to the public.   **9** Mon-
Sat 9.30-19.00, Sun 14.00-14.00-19.00, Oct-March: closes
16.00 daily. Adults 10p, children 5p.   **10** Remains of
3 extensive village settlements occupied from Bronze Age;
complete Viking settlement.   **11** Ovalstone-built huts,
stone-built wheelhouses.

SUNDERLAND, Tyne & Wear

GRINDON CLOSE BRANCH MUSEUM, Grindon Lane,
Sunderland SR4 0JZ (Tel 0783-284042).   **4** Tyne & Wear
CC.   **5** Keeper of Social History: Mr W. W. Wake.
6 Leisure.   **7** Museums & Art Galleries Services, Dir:
Mr. K. J. Barton MPhil, FSA, FMA.   **8** Open to the public.
9 Mon-Fri 9.30-19.30 (Thurs 17.00), Sat 9.30-16.00.
Free.   **10** Edwardian period rooms; chemist's shop;
dentist's surgery; cobbler's & general dealer's & post office
shops.   **12** (c) 1.

MONKWEARMOUTH STATION MUSEUM, North Bridge St,
Sunderland, SR5 1AP (Tel 0783-77075).   **4** Tyne & Wear CC.
5 Curator & Keeper of Land Transport: Mr Neil T. Sinclair
MA, AMA.   **6** Leisure.   **7** Museums & Art Galleries
Services, Dir: Mr K. J. Barton MPhil, FSA, FMA.   **8** Open
to the public.   **9** Mon-Fri 9.30-17.30, Sat 9.30-16.00,
bank hols 10.00-17.00. Free.   **10** History of local land
transport; Monkwearmouth history (inc St Peter's church,
built 674).   **11** Restored booking office; picture lending.
12 (a) 1 (b) 2 (c) 2.

NATIONAL MUSEUM OF MUSIC HALL, Garden Place,
Sunderland, SR1 3HA (Tel 0783-41835).   **4** Tyne & Wear CC.
5 Keeper of Theatre History: Mr J. Ging.   **6** Leisure.
7 Museums & Art Gallery Services, Dir: Mr K. J. Barton
MPhil, FSA, FMA.   **8** Open to the public.   **9** Mon-Sat
10.00-19.00, bank hols 10.00-17.00. Free.   **10** History of
music hall & theatre; personalia; costumes.   **12** (a) 1 (b) 1
(c) 2.

SUNDERLAND MUSEUM AND ART GALLERY, Borough Rd,
Sunderland, SR1 1PP (Tel 0783-41235/8).   **4** Tyne & Wear
CC.   **5** Dir & Principal Keeper of Human History: Mr
James H. Wilson BA, FMA.   **6** Leisure.   **7** Museums &
Art Galleries Services, Dir: Mr. K. J. Barton MPhil, FSA,
FMA.   **8** Open to the public.   **9** Mon-Fri 9.30-18.00,
Sat 9.30-16.00, Sun 15.00-17.00, bank hols 10.00-17.00.
Free.   **10** Art gallery: 18-20th cent paintings, water-
colours & graphic art. Museum: local pottery & glass;
shipping; silver; local antiquities & printed material; natural
history; archaeology.   **11** Marine & ship paintings & drawings by local artists; Sunderland pottery & glass.   **12** (a) 4
(b) 3 (c) 11.

CODE: 1 Name of Museum, Art Gallery or Stately Home. 2 Address. 3 Telephone & telex. 4 Governing body. 5 Officer in charge. 6 Committee responsible. 7 Larger department, chief officer. 8 Open to public. 9 Hours; admission charges. 10 Scope. 11 Special exhibits or facilities. 12 Staff (a) professionally qualified (b) other non-manual (c) manual.

SWANSEA, West Glamorgan

GLYNN VIVIAN ART GALLERY AND MUSEUM, Alexandra Rd, Swansea, SA1 5DZ (Tel 0792-55006). 4 Swansea City Council. 5 Curator: Mr John S. Bunt. 6 Arts. 7 Chief Executive & Town Clerk's Dept. 8 Open to the public. 9 Mon-Sat (inc bank hols) 10.30-17.30. Free. 10 Ceramics (inc Swansea & Nantgarw pottery & porcelain & some fine 18th cent Continental ware); Eustace Calland colln of British glass; old master drawings & paintings; 20th cent British art (inc contemporary painting & sculpture). 11 Temporary exhibitions. 12 (a) 1 (b) 3 (c) 6.

UNIVERSITY COLLEGE OF SWANSEA AND ROYAL INSTITUTION OF SOUTH WALES MUSEUM, Victoria Rd, Swansea, SA1 1SN (Tel 0792-53763). 4 Joint Management Committee. 5 Superintendent: Dr Michael John Isaac MA, PhD. 8 Open to the public. 9 Mon-Sat 10.00-17.00. Closed Dec 25, 26, Jan 1 & Good Friday. Adults 10p, children 5p. 10 Industrial archaeology; ceramics; geology; archaeology; ornithology; Welsh kitchen; local interests. 11 Swansea & Nantgarw pottery; local archaeology. 12 (a) 1 (b) 2 (c) 2½.

SWINDON, Wiltshire

GREAT WESTERN RAILWAY MUSEUM, Faringdon Rd, Swindon, SN1 5BJ (Tel 0793-26161 ext 562). 4 Thamesdown BC. 5 Curator: S. J. Woodward BA. 7 Arts & Recreation Dept, Dir: D. F. Hodson MA. 8 Open to the public. 9 Mon-Sat (inc bank hols) 10.00-17.00, Sun 14.00-17.00. Adults 20p, children 10p, party discount. 10 History of Great Western Railway; models; prints; photography, etc. 12 (a) 2 (shared with Bath Rd); (b) 1; (c) 4.

LYDIARD HOUSE, Lydiard Tregoze, Swindon, SN5 9PA (Tel 0793-770401). 4 Thamesdown BC. 5 Curator: S. J. Woodward BA. 7 Arts & Recreation Dept; Dir: D. F. Hodson MA. 8 Open to the public. 9 Mon-Sat (inc bank hols) 10.00-13.00, 14.00-17.30, Sun 14.00-17.30. Adults 15p, children 7p, party discounts. 10 Georgian stately home; 7 state rooms; adjoining parish church of St Mary's. 11 Temporary exhibitions. 12 (a) 2 (shared with Bath Rd); (b) 1 (c) 1.

MUSEUM AND ART GALLERY, Bath Rd, Swindon, SN1 4BA (Tel 0793-26161 ext 560). 4 Thamesdown BC. 5 Curator: S. J. Woodward BA. 7 Arts & Recreation Dept, Dir: D. F. Hodson MA. 8 Open to the public. 9 Mon-Sat (inc bank hols) 10.00-18.00, Sun 14.00-17.00. Free. 10 Swindon colln of modern British paintings & ceramics; coins; musical instruments; local geology, natural history & bygones; Manners colln of pot lids & ware. 11 Temporary exhibitions; museum education service (school loans, quizzes, junior museum club). 12 (a) 2 (b) 1 (c) 3.

RICHARD JEFFERIES MUSEUM, Coate, Swindon, SN3 6AA (Tel 0793-26161 ext 563). 4 Thamesdown BC. 5 Curator: S. J. Woodward BA. 7 Arts & Recreation Dept, Dir: D. F. Hodson MA. 8 Open to the public. 9 Wed, Sat & Sun 14.00-17.00. Free. 10 Life of Richard Jefferies & Alfred Williams through personalia, photographs, 1st editions, etc. 12 (a) 2 (b) 1 (c) 1. All shared with Bath Rd.

TAMWORTH, Staffordshire

TAMWORTH CASTLE MUSEUM, Tamworth (Tel 0827-3561, ext 294). 4 Tamworth BC. 5 Curator: Miss Claire F. Tarjan BA. 6 Leisure Activities. 7 Recreation & Amenities Dept; Borough Recreation & Amenities; Officer: Mr B. H. Moore. 8 Open to the public. 9 March-Oct: Mon-Thurs & Sat (inc bank hols) 10.00-20.00, Sun 14.00-20.00; Nov-Feb: Mon-Thurs & Sat (inc bank hols) 10.00-17.00, Sun 14.00-17.00. Closes 1 hour before sunset, if earlier. Closed Xmas day. Adults 20p, OAPs 10p, children 5p, accompanied children free, parties (20 or more) 10p. 10 Norman Shell Keep with medieval, Tudor & Jacobean additions; local history. 11 17th cent panelled rooms; drawing room has important heraldic frieze; early English coins of the Tamworth Mint; local archaeology; schools service with special facilities for children. 12 (a) 3 (c) 4.

TARBOLTON, Ayrshire

BACHELORS' CLUB, Sandgate, Tarbolton, Mauchline, KA5 5RB (Tel 09254-424). 4 National Trust for Scotland. 5 Guide & Custodian: Mr Samuel Hay. 8 Open to the public. 9 No fixed hours as guide lives nearby; best to telephone before arrival. Adults 15p, children 5p; free to members of National Trust. 10 Robert Burns. 11 Farm kitchen scene (c. 1825); alehouse where Robert Burns visited. 12 (a) 1.

TAUNTON, Somerset

POST OFFICE TELECOMMUNICATIONS MUSEUM, 38 North St, Taunton, TA1 1LY (Tel 0823-3391; Telex 46193). 5 Officer-in-Charge: Mr Peter John Povey BEM. 8 Open to the public. 9 Sat 13.30-17.00. Other times by arrangement. Free. 10 Historic telegraph, telephone & other telecommunications equipment; related books, documents, pictures etc; working exhibits. 11 Special services for teachers. 12 (a) 1.

SOMERSET COUNTY MUSEUM, Taunton Castle, Castle Green, Taunton, TA1 4AA (Tel 0823-3451 ext 374). 4 Somerset CC. 5 County Museums Officer: Mr Philip A. Stevens MA, FMA. 6 Education & Cultural Services (Museums Sub-Committee). 8 Open to the public. 9 Mon-Sat 10.00-17.30. Closed Dec 25 & Good Friday. Adults 10p, children 5p, school parties free. 10 Local antiquities; geology; natural history & military relics; pottery; glassware; silver; costume gallery. 12 (a) 5 (b) 3 (c) 3.

TENBY, Dyfed

TENBY MUSEUM, Castle Hill, Tenby, SA70 7BP (Tel 0834-2809). 5 Officer-in-Charge: Mr Wilfred Harrison MBE, MA. 8 Open to the public. 9 Winter: Mon-Sat 10.00-13.00, 14.00-16.00 (Fri 10.00-13.00 only); Summer: daily 10.00-18.00. Closed Dec 25, 26 & Good Friday. Adults 10p, children 3p, school parties free. 10 Local geology; natural history; archaeology; history & art; paintings by local artists. 11 Tenby Corporation muniments & other records (by appointment); school & other parties (by prior arrangement). 12 (b) 2.

TUDOR MERCHANTS HOUSE, Quay Hill, Tenby, SA70 7BX. 4 National Trust. 8 Open to the public. 9 Easter-Oct: Mon-Fri 10.00-13.00, 14.30-18.00, Sun 14.00-18.00. Adults 20p, children 10p. 10 15th cent merchant's house. 11 Shop.

TENTERDEN, Kent

ELLEN TERRY MEMORIAL MUSEUM, Smallhythe Place, Tenterden, TN30 7NG (Tel 07977-2334). 4 National Trust. 5 Curator: Mrs Anthony Thomas. 8 Open to the public. 9 March-Oct: daily (exc Tues & Fri) (inc bank hols) 14.00-18.00 (or dusk if earlier). Adults 30p, children 15p, free to National Trust members. 10 Late 15th cent timbered house owned by Ellen Terry (1899-1928, when she died there); her furniture; personal & theatrical possessions of Miss Terry, Sir Henry Irving, Mrs Siddons, Garrick, Kean and others. 11 Miss Terry's theatrical costumes; some costumes of William Terris, Sir Henry Irving & Fred Terry; Miss Terry's library inc working scripts (may be consulted by students on appointment with Curator). 12 (b) 1.

TEWKESBURY, Gloucestershire

TEWKESBURY MUSEUM, Barton St, Tewkesbury, GL20 5PX
(Tel 0684-292367).   **4** Tewkesbury BC.   **5** Curator: Mr
John E. Cockcroft BA.   **6** Recreation & Cultural.
7 Amenities & Leisure Officer.   **8** Open to the public.
9 March-Oct: daily (inc bank hols) 10.00-17.00. Free.
10 Local history; applied arts; social & industrial history;
archaeology.   **11** Large diorama of Battle of Tewkesbury
(1471); Jacobean furnished rooms.   **12** (a) 1 (c) 1.

THETFORD, Norfolk

ANCIENT HOUSE MUSEUM, 21 White Hart St, Thetford,
IP24 1AA (Tel 0842-2599).   **4** Norfolk CC.   **5** Curator:
Miss A. J. Maddock MA, AMA.   **6** Museums.   **7** Norfolk
Museums Service, Dir: Mr F. W. Cheetham BA, FMA.
8 Open to the public.   **9** Mon-Sat 10.00-17.00 (closed
Mon 13.00-14.00), Sun 14.00-17.00. Closed Dec 25 & Good
Friday. Free.   **10** 15th cent timber-framed house (carved
& moulded woodwork); local history, natural history (inc
archaeology), & antiquities.   **12** (a) 1 (c) 1.

ART GALLERY, The Guildhall, Market Place, Thetford
(Tel 0842-4247).   **4** Norfolk CC & Thetford Town Council.
5 Curator: Miss A. J. Maddock MA.   **6** Museums.
7 Norfolk Museums Service, Dir: F. W. Cheetham BA, FMA.
8 Open to the public.   **9** Open by appointment only. Free.
10 Duleep Singh colln (Norfolk & Suffolk portraits).

EUSTON HALL, Euston, Thetford, IP24 2QW (Tel 0842-3281).
4 His Grace, The Duke of Grafton.   **5** Agent Euston
Estate: R. G. E. Starling BSc.   **8** Open to the public.
9 May-Sept: Thurs. Adults 35p, children & OAPs 20p.
10 Stately home; 17th cent parish church, Wren style.
11 Paintings, mainly portraits by Van Dyck, Lely, Reynolds
& Stubbs; pleasure grounds by John Evelyn; landscaping by
William Kent & Capability Brown.   **12** (b) 8.

THORNHILL, Dumfriesshire

DRUMLANRIG CASTLE, Thornhill.   **8** Open to the public.
9 Mid April-mid Aug: Sat-Thurs 14.00-17.15.   **10** Late
17th cent castle; paintings (Rembrandt, Holbein, Leonardo da
Vinci); Louis XIV cabinets; silver chandelier (1680); Bonnie
Prince Charlie's money box; gardens.

THURSO, Caithness

ROBERT DICK MUSEUM, Thurso Public Library, Thurso,
KW14 7AF (Tel 0847-3237).   **4** Highland Regional Council.
5 Div Libn: Mr David Morrison ALA.   **7** Dept of Leisure
& Recreation.   **8** Open to the public.   **9** July & Aug: Mon-
Sat 10.00-13.00, 14.00-17.00. Other times by arrangement.
Free.   **10** Robert Dick herbarium; geology; palaeontology.

TILFORD, Surrey

OLD KILN AGRICULTURAL MUSEUM, The Reeds Rd, Tilford,
Farnham, GU10 2DL (Tel 025 125-2300).   **5** Owner: Mr
Henry Jackson.   **8** Open to the public.   **9** April-Sept:
Wed, Sat, Sun & bank hols 12.00-18.00. Adults 30p, children
15p; 10% discount for parties.   **10** Agriculture & allied
crafts (since 1750); farm implements, mainly horse-drawn.
11 Wheelwright's shop; blacksmith's forge; arboretum;
picnic area; free parking.   **12** (a) 2.

TIVERTON, Devon

TIVERTON MUSEUM, St Andrew St, Tiverton (Tel 08842-
56298).   **4** Tiverton Museum Society.   **5** Chairman &
Hon Curator: Mr W. P. Authers MBE.   **8** Open to the
public.   **9** Mon-Sat 10.30-12.30, 14.30-16.30. Free.
10 Local history & life.   **11** Waggons & agricultural
equipment; Victorian laundry; loan exhibitions.

TORPHICHEN, West Lothian

CAIRNPAPPLE HILL, Torphichen (Tel 0506-53733).
4 Dept of Environment.   **5** Information Officer, Argyle

House, 3 Lady Lawson St, Edinburgh.   **8** Open to the public.
9 April-Sept: Mon-Sat 9.30-19.00, Sun 14.00-19.00. Oct-
March: Sat 9.30-16.00, Sun 14.00-16.00, Mon-Fri by appointment with Custodian. Adults 5p, children 2½p.   **10** Sanctuary & burial cairns.

TORQUAY, Devon

TORQUAY NATURAL HISTORY SOCIETY MUSEUM, 529
Babbacombe Rd, Torquay, TQ1 1HG (Tel 0803-23975).
4 Executive Committee.   **5** Curator: Norman Harris
BSc PhD.   **8** Open to the public.   **9** Mon-Sat 10.00-
17.00. Closed Xmas week & Good Friday. Adults 15p,
children & OAPs 5p.   **10** Natural history of Devon
(inc geology & archaeology); folk-life of Devon; Victoriana.
11 Finds from Kents Cavern & other caves of S. Devon;
story of a Devon river; Laycock Gallery of Folk-life.
12 (a) 1 (b) 1½ (c) 2.

TORRE ABBEY MANSION HOUSE, The Kings Drive,
Torquay, TQ2 5JX (Tel 0803-23593).   **4** Torbay BC.
5 Entertainments Officer: Mr Paul E. Clifford.   **6** Recreation.   **7** Dept of Leisure Services, Trevor J. Durbidge
DLC, MInstRM, AMBIM.   **8** Open to the public.
9 Easter-Oct: daily (inc bank hols) 10.00-13.00, 14.00-
17.30. Charges: 10p.   **10** Art gallery & monastic ruins.
11 Temporary exhibitions.   **12** (b) 3.

TOTNES, Devon

ELIZABETHAN HOUSE, 70 Fore St, Totnes, TQ9 5RU
(Tel 0803-863821).   **4** Totnes Town Council.   **5** Hon
Curator & Chairman: Mr D. W. Mitchell.   **6** 70 Fore St Joint
Management Committee.   **8** Open to the public.
9 Mon-Sat (inc bank hols) 10.30-13.00, 14.00-17.30.
Adults 10p, children 5p.   **10** Merchants house (c. 1575);
folk material; archaeology; period furniture & costumes;
toys, domestic articles.   **11** Local ref library; computer
exhibition.   **12** (b) 2 (c) 1.

TOWYN, Clwyd

NARROW GAUGE RAILWAY MUSEUM, Towyn, Abergele.
4 Narrow Gauge Railway Museum Trust.   **5** Chairman
of Trustees: Lt Col T. M. Simmons MA; Hon Sec to Trustees:
Mrs H. W. Clarey BA.   **8** Open to the public.   **9** Easter-
Oct: daily (inc bank hols) 10.00-17.00 (whenever the Talyllyn
Railway is operational. Adults 10p, children 5p.   **10** Relics
of British narrow gauge railways; locomotives; rolling stock;
track; signals etc.

TREFECCA, Powys

HOWEL HARRIS MUSEUM, Trefecca, Brecon (Tel 087481-
241).   **4** Presbyterian Church of Wales.   **5** Warden:
Rev A. Meirion Roberts; Curator: Mrs Olwen Davies.
8 Open to the public.   **9** Mon-Fri (inc bank hols) 11.00-
17.00. Other times by appointment. Free.   **10** Social
& religious history of Wales in the 18th cent.   **11** Rare
books (Trevecka Press); furniture; prints & articles associated with Howel Harris's 18th cent religio-industrial settlement at Trevecka.

TRESCO, Isles of Scilly

VALHALLA MARITIME MUSEUM, Tresco, Isles of Scilly
(Tel 07204-876).   **5** Owner & Hon Curator: R. A. Dorrien
Smith.   **8** Open to the public.   **9** Mon-Sat (inc bank
hols) 10.00-16.00. Charges: 10p.   **10** 58 figureheads;
signboards, cannons etc recovered from wrecks on Isles of
Scilly.

TRING, Hertfordshire

ZOOLOGICAL MUSEUM AND SUB-DEPARTMENT OF
ORNITHOLOGY, BRITISH MUSEUM (NATURAL HISTORY),
Akeman St, Tring, HP23 6AP (Tel 044282-4181).
5 Officer-in-Charge: Mr A. P. Coleman; Head of Sub-Dept
of Ornithology: Dr D. W. Snow.   **8** Open to the public.
9 Mon-Sat 10.00-17.00, Sun 14.00-17.00. Closed Dec

CODE: **1** Name of Museum, Art Gallery or Stately Home. **2** Address **3** Telephone & telex. **4** Governing body. **5** Officer in charge. **6** Committee responsible. **7** Larger department, chief officer. **8** Open to public. **9** Hours; admission charges. **10** Scope. **11** Special exhibits or facilities. **12** Staff (a) professionally qualified (b) other non-manual (c) manual.

TRING, Hertfordshire—*continued*

24-26, Jan 1 & Good Friday. Free. **10** Mounted specimens of animals from all parts of the world; British butterflies, moths, shells, birds & birds' eggs. **12** (a) 12 (b) 10 (c) 7.

TRURO, Cornwall

COUNTY MUSEUM, River St, Truro, TR1 2SJ (Tel 0872-2205). **4** Royal Institution of Cornwall. **5** Officer-in-Charge: H. L. Douch BA. **8** Open to the public. **9** Mon-Sat 9.00-13.00, 14.00-17.00. Free. **10** Museum: history of Cornwall; Rashleigh colln of minerals; pewter; ceramics; Japanese ivories & lacquer. Art-Galleries: De Pass Colln of master drawings; works of John Opie. **11** Library on Cornish & museum subjects. **12** (b) 2 (c) 2.

TUNBRIDGE WELLS, Kent

BROADWATER COLLECTION (closed at present), Broadwater Court, Tunbridge Wells TN2 5PB (Tel 0892-28984). **4** Broadwater Collection Trust. **5** Officer-in-Charge: Mr Brian Jewell. **8** Not open at present. **10** Typewriters; sewing machines; transport. **11** Industrial & social historical research.

TUNBRIDGE WELLS ART GALLERY & MUSEUM, Civic Centre, Tunbridge Wells, TN2 4RN (Tel 0892-26121 ext 79). **4** Tunbridge Wells DC. **5** Curator: R. G. E. Sandbach MA, AMA. **7** Amenities Dept; D. McGuffog FInstPra (Dip). **8** Open to the public. **9** Mon-Sat 10.00-17.30. Free. **10** Art Gallery: Ashton Bequest (Victorian paintings); temporary exhibitions. Museum: local arts & crafts (inc Tunbridge ware), history geology, bygones, archaeology, costume, dolls & toys. **12** (a) 2 (c) 3.

TURRIFF, Aberdeenshire

DELGATIE CASTLE, Turriff, AB5 7TD (Tel 08882-3479). **5** Officer-in-Charge: Capt Hay of Hayfield. **8** Open to the public. **9** Wed & Sun 14.30-17.00. Adults 50p, children 25p.

TYSOE, Warwickshire

COMPTON WYNYATES, Tysoe, CV35 0UD (Tel 029588-229). **5** Agent for Compton Estates: J. G. Pearson FRICS. **8** Open to the public. **9** April-Sept: Wed, Sat, Sun (& bank hol Mon & Tues) 14.00-17.30. Adults 50p, children 25p; gardens only: 20p. **10** Earliest building 1480; battlemented towers & turrets (added 1512-1520); porch dedicated to Henry VIII bears Royal Arms & those of Katherine of Aragon; room where he slept; much of interior little changed since 1520; pink brick house with twisted chimneys.

WAKEFIELD, West Yorkshire

WAKEFIELD CITY ART GALLERY, Wentworth Terrace, Wakefield, WF1 3QW (Tel 0924-75402). **4** Wakefield MDC. **5** Museums & Art Galleries Officer: Mrs Gillian Spencer MA. **6** Education (Libraries & Museums Sub-Committee). **7** Education Dept, Chief Education Officer: Mr R. Eyles BSc. **8** Open to the public. **9** Mon-Sat 12.30-17.30, Sun 14.30-17.30. Free. **10** English 20th cent paintings, sculptures, drawings & prints (Henry Moore, Barbara Hepworth, Graham Sutherland, L. S. Lowry, Alan Davie, Bryan Kneale, Reg Butler); some old master oil paintings, drawings & watercolours. **11** Print loan scheme. **12** (a) 2 (b) 2 (c) 3.

WAKEFIELD CITY MUSEUM, Wood St, Wakefield (Tel 0924-61767). **4** Wakefield MDC. **5** Museums & Art Galleries Officer: Mrs Gillian Spencer MA. **6** Education (Libraries & Museums Sub-Committee). **7** Education Dept; Chief Education Officer: Mr R. Eyles BSc. **8** Open to the public. **9** Mon-Sat 12.30-17.30, Sun 14.30-17.30. Free. **10** Local social history; ceramics; glass; jewellery; silver. **11** Charles Waterton Natural History Colln. **12** (a) 2 (c) 2.

WALKERBURN, Peeblesshire

SCOTTISH MUSEUM OF WOOL TEXTILES, Tweedvale Mill, Walkerburn (Tel 089 687-208; Telex 72155). **4** Scottish Museum of Wool Textiles Trust. **5** Officer-in-Charge: Mr Colin John Ballantyne, former Pres of National Association of Scottish Woollen Manufacturers. **8** Open to the public. **9** Mon-Fri (inc bank hols) 9.00-17.00; summer: Sat & Sun 14.00-16.00. Adults 10p, children 5p. **10** Machinery etc connected with woollen textile industry.

WALL, Staffordshire

LETOCETUM, Wall Roman Site, Watling St, Wall, Lichfield, WS14 0AN (Tel 0543-480768). **4** Dept of Environment. **5** Custodian: Mr F. H. Linney. **8** Open to the public. **9** Mon-Sat (inc bank hols) 9.30-17.00, Sun 14.00-17.00. Adults 5p, children 2½p. **10** Pottery; coins; brooches etc. **11** Adjoins Roman bathhouse. **12** (a) 1 (b) 2.

WALLASEY, Merseyside

WALLASEY MUSEUM AND EXHIBITION HALL, Wallasey Library, Earlston Rd, Wallasey, L45 5DX (Tel 051-639 2334/5). **5** Chief Libn & Arts Officer: H. H. G. Arthur FLA, FRSA, MBIM. **7** Leisure Services Dept, Dir: Mr B. J. Barnes MInstBM, ARM(M), MInstRM. **8** Open to the public. **9** Mon-Fri 9.30-20.00 (Tues 13.00), Sat 9.30-17.00. Free. **10** Paintings; local pictures; ship models; archaelogy. **11** Temporary exhibitions; models of Wallasey ferry boats. **12** (a) 1 (c) 2.

WALSALL, West Midlands

WALSALL MUSEUM AND ART GALLERY, Lichfield St, Walsall, WS1 1TR (Tel 0922 21244 ext 241). **4** Walsall MBC. **5** Curator: M. A. Mosesson BA. **6** Recreation. **7** Library & Museum Services, Dir: F. H. Lamb ALA. **8** Open to the public. **9** Mon-Fri 10.00-18.00, Sat 10.00-17.30. Free. **10** Fine & applied art; lorinery (bits & spurs) & saddlers' ironmongery; local material (inc memorabilia of Jerome K. Jerome, Sister Dora etc). **11** Garman-Ryan colln (fine art, antiquities & ethnography inc largest colln of works by Sir Jacob Epstein in Europe); Museum of Leathercraft colln. **12** (a) 3 (b) 2 (c) 4.

WALSINGHAM, Norfolk

SHIREHALL MUSEUM, Walsingham, NR22 6BP. **4** Norfolk CC. **6** Museums. **7** Norfolk Museums Service, Dir: Mr Francis W. Cheetham BA, FMA. **8** Open to the public. **9** Mon-Fri (June-Sept only) & Sat (May-Oct only): 10.00-12.00, 14.00-16.00. **10** Almost perfect 18th cent courtroom with original fittings & a prisoner's Lock Up; history of Walsingham; small information centre on the area.

WARLEY, West Midlands

AVERY HISTORICAL MUSEUM, W. & T. Avery Ltd, Foundry Lane, Smethwick, Warley, B66 2LP (Tel 021-558 1112 ext 23; Telex 336490). **5** Curator: Mr D. W. Ellis. **8** Open to the public. **9** Mon-Fri 9.30-16.00. Free. **10** History of weighing; scales; weights; instruments; records etc. **12** (b) 1 (c) 1.

WARRINGTON, Cheshire

MUSEUM AND ART GALLERY, Bold St, Warrington, WA1 1JG (Tel 0925-30550). **4** Warrington BC. **5** Dir: J.R.Rimmer BEM, FMA. **6** Recreation & Amenities. **8** Open to the public. **9** Mon-Fri 10.00-19.00, Sat 10.00-17.00. Free. **10** Ethnographic & ethnological collns; zoology; botany; geology; archaeology; bygones; ceramics; glass; numismatics; applied art. **11** Local artists; early English watercolours. **12** (a) 5 (b) 3 (c) 5.

SOUTH LANCASHIRE REGIMENT (PWV) AND THE LANCASHIRE REGIMENT (PWV) MUSEUM, Peninsula Barracks, Warrington, WA2 7BR (Tel 0925-33563). **4** Regimental Council. **5** Officer-in-Charge: Major (Retd) J. Kenny MBE. **8** Open to the public. **9** Mon-Fri 9.00-12.00, 14.00-16.15. Other days by previous arrangement. Free. **10** Military exhibits from 1717 onwards; uniforms; accoutrements; badges; medals; limited arms; historical records; military library; photographs. **12** (b) 1 (c) 1.

WARWICK, Warwickshire

LORD LEYCESTER HOSPITAL, 60 High St, Warwick, CV34 4BH (Tel 0926-42035/41422). **5** Master of the Hospital: Capt E.H. Lee DSC, RN. **7** Curator & Regimental Sec: Major J.S. Sutherland MBE (Retd). **8** Open to the public. **9** Mon-Sat (inc bank hols) 10.00-17.30 (winter 16.00). Adults 20p, children 10p. **10** Medieval buildings (c.1400); Great Hall of King James I; Guildhall; Brethren's Kitchen; Chapel of St James; Guildhall Museum (history of the Hospital). **11** Queen's Own Hussars Regimental Museum, (regimental colln of old uniforms, guidons, pictures, medals etc). Afternoon teas (Easter-Sept); Great Hall can be hired for private functions; catering. **12** (b) 1 (c) 1.

WARWICK CASTLE, Warwick, CV34 4QU (Tel 0926-45421). **5** General Manager: Mr M.W.R.Corp; Curator: Mr F.H.P. Barker. **8** Open to the public. **9** Daily (inc bank hols) 10.30-17.30 (shorter hours Oct-Feb). Not free. **10** Late 14th cent castle; pictures; furniture; armour & weapons.

WASHINGTON, Tyne & Wear

WASHINGTON OLD HALL, Washington Village (Tel 0632-466879). **4** National Trust. **5** Custodian: Mr C. Dickens. **8** Open to the public. **9** Daily (exc Fri) (inc bank hols) 10.00-13.00, 14.00-18.00. Not free. **10** Seat of George Washington's ancestors, rebuilt as a small manor house. **11** Period furniture; Delft ware; Washington relics.

WEDNESBURY, West Midlands

SANDWELL ART GALLERY & MUSEUM, Holyhead Rd, Wednesbury, WS10 7DF (Tel 021-556 0683). **4** Sandwell MBC. **5** Curator: Mr A.J.Tibbles MA. **6** Libraries & Museums Sub-Committee. **7** Borough Libn: R.B.Ludgate ALA. **8** Open to the public. **9** Mon-Sat 10.00-17.00. Free. **10** Edwin Richards colln (Victorian oil paintings, watercolours & drawings); local history; applied arts; temporary exhibitions (local & national). **12** (a) 1 (b) 1 (c) 1.

WELLS, Somerset

WELLS MUSEUM, 8 Cathedral Green, Wells, BA5 2UE (Tel 0749-73477). **5** Hon Curator: Mr Norman Cook BA, FSA, FMA. **8** Open to the public. **9** April-Sept: Mon-Sat (inc bank hols) 10.00-18.00; Oct-March: Mon-Sat 14.00-16.30; June-Sept: Sun 14.30-17.30. Adults 10p, children 5p. **10** Local archaeology (especially caves); folk life; natural history; geology; samplers. **12** (a) 2 (c) 2.

WELSHPOOL, Powys

POWIS CASTLE, Welshpool, SY21 8RF. **4** National Trust. **8** Open to the public. **9** Easter & May-Sept: Wed-Sun 14.00-17.30; Spring & late summer bank hols: 11.30-17.30. Castle & gardens: 60p; gardens only: 40p; castle only: 40p. Children ½ price. **10** Medieval castle (reconstructed 17th cent); fine plaster work; murals; paintings; tapestries;

early Georgian furniture; historic terraced garden (before 1722); topiary; rare trees & shrubs. **11** Relics of Clive of Inaida; refreshments; shop.

POWYSLAND MUSEUM, Salop Rd, Welshpool, SY21 7DX. **4** Powys CC. **5** Hon Curator: Mr J.Elwyn Davies. **7** Libraries & Museums Dept, Chief Officer: G.Llewellyn FLA. **8** Open to the public. **9** Mon, Tues & Sat 14.00-16.30, Thurs & Fri 11.00-13.00, 14.00-16.30 (& 18.00-19.00 April-Sept). Free. **10** Folk-life; local archaeology. **11** Local domestic dairying & agricultural material; bronze age colln. **12** (b) 1

WEST BROMWICH, West Midlands

OAK HOUSE, Oak Rd, West Bromwich, B70 8HJ (Tel 021-553 0759). **4** Sandwell MBC. **5** Curator: Mr A.J. Tibbles MA. **6** Libraries & Museum Sub-Committee. **7** Borough Libn: R.B.Ludgate ALA. **8** Open to the public. **9** Mon-Wed, Fri & Sat 10.00-16.00 (May-Sept 17.00), Thurs 10.00-13.00, Sun (May-Sept only) 14.30-17.00. Closed Dec 25, Jan 1, Good Friday, Easter Sat & Sun. Free. **10** Tudor yeoman's house in half-timbered style with 16th-early 18th cent furniture & fine Jacobean panelling & carving.

WESTCLIFF-ON-SEA, Essex

BEECROFT ART GALLERY, Station Rd, Westcliff-on-Sea, SS0 7RA (Tel 0702-47418). **4** Southend-on-Sea BC. **5** Borough Libn & Curator: Mr L.Helliwell FLA. **6** Amenities (Libraries & Museums Sub Committee). **8** Open to the public. **9** Mon-Sat 10.30-17.30, Sun 14.30-17.30. Closed Dec 25, 26 & Good Friday. Free. **10** British & Continental paintings; British contemporary art; paintings, drawings & prints illustrating growth of Southend, also the Thames Estuary. **11** Temporary exhibitions monthly. **12** (a) Served by Southend-on-Sea Museums Service.

WESTERHAM, Kent

CHARTWELL, Chartwell, Westerham, TN16 1PS (Tel 073278-368). **4** National Trust. **5** Administrator: Mrs D.J.Broome. **8** Open to the public. **9** Wed & Thurs 14.00-18.00, Sat, Sun & bank hols 11.00-18.00. House & garden 50p, garden only 20p. **10** Sir Winston Churchill's home. **11** Car park; coach park; self-service restaurant.

SQUERRYES COURT, Westerham, TN16 1SJ (Tel 0959-62345). **5** Curator: Mr C.H. Langton. **8** Open to the public. **9** March-Oct: Wed, Sat, Sun & bank hol Mon 14.00-17.30. Adults 30p, children 15p. **10** William & Mary manor house (1681); old master paintings; Soho tapestries; period furniture & china; General Wolfe memorabilia. **11** Kent & County of London Yeomanry (Sharpshooters) Regimental Museum (uniforms medals, photographs etc).

WEST HOATHLY, West Sussex

PRIESTS HOUSE, West Hoathly, East Grinstead, RH19 4PP (Tel 034289-479). **4** Sussex Archaeological Society. **5** Custodian: Ms Dora Arnold. **8** Open to the public. **9** April-Sept. **10** Early 15th cent house, wattle & daub; Horsham slab roof; old furniture & needlework. **12** (b) 1.

WESTON-SUPER-MARE, Avon

WOODSPRING MUSEUM AND GALLERY, Burlington St, Weston-Super-Mare, BS23 1PR (Tel 0934-21028). **4** Woodspring DC. **5** Curator: Miss K.J.Evans BA, AMA. **6** Leisure Services. **7** Dir of Leisure Services: B.H. Flavell FHCIMA, FIMEnt. **8** Open to the public. **9** Mon-Sat 10.00-18.00 (17.00 Oct-Easter) Closed Dec 25 & 26. Free. **10** Local history & natural history. **11** Temporary exhibitions (monthly); Victorian seaside holiday; old chemist shop; dairy (cheese & butter-making); cider-making; costumes; toys & dolls; early domestic appliances; firearms; coins; Smyth-Pigott portraits; Weston base for island of Steepholm; archaeology. Refreshments; shop. **12** (a) 2. (b) 1 (c) 2.

CODE: 1 Name of Museum, Art Gallery or Stately Home. 2 Address. 3 Telephone & telex. 4 Governing body. 5 Officer in charge. 6 Committee responsible. 7 Larger department, chief officer. 8 Open to public. 9 Hours; admission charges. 10 Scope. 11 Special exhibits or facilities. 12 Staff (a) professionally qualified (b) other non-manual (c) manual.

WEYBRIDGE, Surrey

WEYBRIDGE MUSEUM, Church St, Weybridge, KT13 8DE (Tel 0932-43573). 4 Elmbridge BC. 5 Museum Curator: Mrs Avril Lansdell AMA. 6 Recreation & Amenities. 7 Mr Alwyn Bowen. 8 Open to the public. 9 Mon-Fri 14.00-17.00, Sat 10.00-13.00, 14.00-17.00. Free. 10 Local history, geology, archaeology & costume. 11 Excavated material from Oatlands Palace (Henry VIII); local costumes; papers & photographic material of Brooklands Track. 12 (a) 2 (b) 2 (c) 2.

WEYMOUTH, Dorset

WEYMOUTH MUSEUM OF LOCAL HISTORY, Westham Rd, Weymouth, DT4 8NF (Tel 03057-74246). 4 Weymouth & Portland BC. 5 Officer-in-Charge: J.A.C. West ALA. 6 Leisure & Recreation (Museums Sub-Committee). 7 Dept of Leisure Activities, Dir: Mr Peter Maddock FIMEnts. 8 Open to the public. 9 Easter-Sept: Mon-Wed & Fri 10.00-20.00, Thurs & Sat 10.00-17.00; Oct-Easter: daily (exc Tues) 10.00-13.00, 14.00-17.00. Adults 5p, OAPs, students & children free. 10 Illustrations & relics of old Weymouth & Portland; household bygones; local transport. 11 Local shipwrecks; reproductions of prints for sale. 12 (b) 3 (c) 1.

WHITBY, North Yorkshire

WHITBY MUSEUM, Pannett Park, Whitby, YO21 1RE (Tel 0947-2908). 4 Whitby Literary & Philosophical Society. 5 Hon Keeper: J.G. Graham MA. 8 Open to the public. 9 May-Sept: Mon-Sat 9.00-17.30, Sun 14.00-17.00; Oct-April: Mon-Fri 10.30-13.00, Sat 10.30-16.00, Sun 14.00-16.00. Closed Dec 25, 26 & Jan 1. Adults 10p, children 5p, school parties 4p. 10 Local history & topography. 11 Geology (Whitby 'Type' Ammonites); Captain Cook exhibits; Whitby Abbey; shipping wing. 12 (a) 7.

WHITEHAVEN, Cumbria

WHITEHAVEN MUSEUM AND ART GALLERY, Market Place, Whitehaven, CA28 7JG (Tel 0946-5678). 4 Copeland BC. 5 Curator: Mr Harry Fancy AMA. 7 Recreation & Amenities, Dir: C. Wesley Park BSc. 8 Open to the public. 9 Mon-Sat (inc bank hols) 10.00-18.00. Free. 10 Natural, social & economic history of Borough of Copeland. 11 Geology; marine paintings; mining; Whitehaven pottery. 12 (a) 2 (b) 1 (c) 1.

WICK, Caithness

WICK MUSEUM (WICK SOCIETY MUSEUM), Carnegie Public Library, Wick, KW1 5AB (Tel 0955-2864). 4 Owned by Highland Regional Council, run by Wick Society. 5 Div Libn: Mr David Morrison ALA. 7 Dept of Leisure & Recreation. 8 Open to the public. 9 July & Aug: Mon-Sat 10.00-13.00, 14.00-17.00. Other times by arrangement. Free. 10 Herring industry.

WIGAN, Lancashire

WIGAN MUSEUM AND ART GALLERY, Station Rd, Wigan (Tel 0942-41387) 4 Wigan MBC. 5 Museums Officer: Mrs M. Buchanan BA, AMA. 6 Recreation & Amenities. 7 Dept of Leisure, Mr Gil Swift BA. 8 Open to the public. 9 Mon-Sat 10.00-17.00. Free. 10 Local history; local art; musical instruments; natural history. 11 Wigan pewter; Rimmer colln of musical instruments. 12 (a) 4, (b) 1.

WILLENHALL, West Midlands

WILLENHALL LOCK MUSEUM, Willenhall Regional Library, Walsall St, Willenhall, WV13 2EX (Tel 0922-21244 ext 241). 4 Walsall MBC. 5 Curator: Mr Michael A. Mosesson BA.

6 Recreation & Leisure. 7 Libraries & Museum Services, Dir: F.H. Lamb ALA. 8 Open to the public. 9 Mon-Fri 10.00-18.00, Sat 10.00-17.30. Free. 10 History of the lock; colln of locks (especially 19th cent English). 12 (a) Served from Walsall Museum.

WILTON, Wiltshire

WILTON HOUSE, Wilton, Salisbury, SP2 0BJ (Tel 072274-3115). 4 Trustees of the Wilton Estate. 5 Agent to the Earl of Pembroke: R.H. Mellish BA, FRICS; Private Sec: Mrs Dora Boulton. 8 Open to the public. 9 Easter-Sept: Tues-Sat & bank hols 11.00-18.00, Sun 14.00-18.00. Adults 40p, children 20p, party rates. 10 16th cent house, home of Earl of Pembroke; art colln (Rembrandt, Rubens, Van Dyck etc); Chippendale & Kent furniture; Inigo Jones state apartments (inc single & double cube rooms); historic marbles. 11 7,000 miniature model soldiers.

WIMBORNE, Dorset

PRIEST'S HOUSE MUSEUM, 23 High St, Wimborne, BH21 1HR (Tel 020125-2533). 4 Priest's House Museum Association. 5 President: Lt Col G.E. Gray CEng, MIMechE, AIIC; Acting Hon Curator: Miss H.M. Coles. 8 Open to the public. 9 Easter-Sept & 3 weeks at Xmas: Mon-Sat (inc bank hols) 10.30-12.30, 14.30-16.30. Adults 10p, school children 3p. 10 Archaeology; local history & rural life equipment.

WINCHCOMBE, Gloucestershire

SUDELEY CASTLE, Winchcombe, GL54 5JD (Tel 0242-602308). 5 General Manager: Mr A.E. Salmon. 8 Open to the public. 9 March-Oct: daily 12.00-17.30, Grounds 11.00-19.00. Not free. 10 12th cent building (restored 19th cent); tomb & relics of Queen Katherine Parr; Tudor furnishings, stained glass, needlework; Art colln (inc Constable, Turner, Rubens, Van Dyke); 'Emma Dent' colln of Victoriana. 11 'Royal Sudeley', light & sound re-creation of castle's history. 12 (a) 1 (b) 5 (c) 8.

WINCHELSEA, Sussex

THE MUSEUM, Court Hall, Winchelsea. 4 Mayor & Corporation of Winchelsea. 5 Curator: Mr A. Satow. 8 Open to the public. 9 Mid May-Sept: Mon-Sat (inc bank hols) 11.00-13.00, 15.00-18.00, Sun 15.00-18.00. Adults 15p, children 5p. 10 Local & Cinque Ports history.

WINCHESTER, Hampshire

GUILDHALL PICTURE GALLERY, Broadway, Winchester SO23 9BE (Tel 0962-68166 ext 289). 4 Winchester City Council. 5 Curator: Miss E.R. Lewis BA, AMA. 6 Amenities. 8 Open to the public. 9 Tues-Thurs 11.00-16.00, Fri & Sat 11.00-17.00, Sun 14.00-17.00. Free. 10 Temporary exhibitions (local & national).

ROYAL HAMPSHIRE REGIMENT MUSEUM AND MEMORIAL GARDEN, Serle's House, Southgate St, Winchester, SO23 9EG (Tel 0962-61781 ext 261/262). 4 Regimental Trustees. 8 Open to the public. 9 Mon-Fri 10.30-12.30, 14.00-16.00. Free. 10 Uniforms; old weapons; awards.

WESTGATE, High St, Winchester (Tel 0962-68166 ext 269). 4 Winchester City Council. 5 Curator: Miss E.R. Lewis BA, AMA. 6 Amenities. 8 Open to the public. 9 Mon-Sat 10.00-18.00 (or 16.00, or 17.00, according to season), Sat 14.00-16.30. Adults 5p, children 2½p. 10 Medieval gateway to the City. 11 Exhibition of arms & armour.

WINCHESTER CITY MUSEUM, The Square, Winchester (0962-68166, ext 269) 4 City of Winchester. 5 Curator: Miss E.R. Lewis BA, AMA. 6 Amenities. 8 Open to the public. 9 Mon-Sat (inc bank hols) 10.00-16.00 (or 18.00

WINCHESTER, Hampshire —*continued*

according to season). Sun 14.00-16.30. Free. **10** Archaeology & history of Winchester & area.

WINDSOR, Berkshire

Eton College
MYERS MUSEUM, Eton College, Windsor, SL4 6DW (Tel 075 35-66230). **4** Provost & Fellows of Eton College. **5** Curator: Dr M.H. Ballance MA, PhD. **8** Open to the public. **9** Sun 14.30-16.30. Free, at present. **10** Archaeology, principally Egyptian, some Greek, Roman & other ancient cultures. NATURAL HISTORY SOCIETY MUSEUM, Queen's Schools, Eton College, Windsor, SL4 6DW. **5** Hon Curator: R. Fisher BSc. **8** Open to the public. **9** Mon-Fri 14.00-1st school of afternoon, Sun 14.30-17.30. Free. **10** Taxonomic display of animals; fossils; British birds, eggs & lepidoptera. **12** (c) 1.

GUILDHALL EXHIBITION, The Guildhall, High St, Windsor, SL4 1LR. **4** Royal Borough of Windsor & Maidenhead. **5** Amenities & Leisure Officer: K.M. McGarry DPE, DMS(Rec). **6** Amenities & Leisure. **8** Open to the public. **9** Daily (inc bank hols) 13.30-16.30. Not free. **10** Building completed by Sir Christopher Wren (1690); Borough insignia & plate; paintings of English sovereigns; Royal Windsor uniform worn at court & state occasions; objects depicting history of Royal Windsor. **12** (a) 1 (b) 2.

HOUSEHOLD CAVALRY MUSEUM, Combermere Barracks, Windsor, SL4 3DN (Tel 075 35-68222). **4** RHQ Household Cavalry. **5** Officer-in-Charge: Lt Col A.D. Meakin MInstAM. **8** Open to the public. **9** Mon-Fri 9.00-17.00. Free. **10** Equipment, uniforms, weapons, horse furniture.

WINDSOR CASTLE, Windsor (Tel 075 35-68286). **5** Officer-in-Charge: Lord Chamberlain, St James's Palace, London SW1; local: superintendent, Windsor Castle. **8** Open to the public. **9** Precincts: daily (inc bank hols) 10.00-16.00 (or dusk). State apartments, Queen Mary's dolls' house, exhibitions etc: mid Oct-mid March: Mon-Sat 10.30-15.00; mid March-mid Oct: Mon-Sat 10.30-17.00, Sun 13.30-17.00. State apartments closed for state visits (Easter, June & Xmas). State apartments: adults 20p, children 10p; dolls' house & exhibitions 10p each. **10** Precincts; state apartments. **11** Paintings & works of art from the royal colln; Queen Mary's dolls' house.

WOBURN, Bedfordshire

WOBURN ABBEY ARTS CENTRE (Inc The Russell Room, The Bedford Room & The Howland Room), Woburn MK17 9PX (Tel 052 525-666). **4** Trustees of Bedford Estates. **5** Exhibitions Organiser: Ms Johanna Brown BA. **8** Open to the public. **9** Daily (inc bank hols) 13.30-18.00. Free. **10** 18th cent buildings (designed by Flitcroft); contemporary & traditional art; paintings & sculpture; crafts (batik dye, jewellery & ceramics, embroidery & prints).

WOLVERHAMPTON, West Midlands

BANTOCK HOUSE MUSEUM, Bantock Park, Merridale Rd, Wolverhampton WV3 9LQ (Tel 0902-24548). **4** Wolverhampton MBC. **5** Curator: Mr David Rodgers MA. **6** Leisure & Amenities. **7** Art Gallery & Museums Dept; Chairman: Councillor H.E. Lane. **8** Open to the public. **9** Weekdays (inc bank hols) 10.00-19.00, Sat 10.00-18.00, Sun 14.00-17.00. Free. **10** 18th & 19th cent decorative arts; English enamels & West Midland Japanned ware; English pottery; first period Worcester porcelain; 18th & 19th cent dolls; local history.

BILSTON MUSEUM AND ART GALLERY, Mount Pleasant, Bilston, Wolverhampton, WV14 7LS (Tel 0902-42097). **4** Wolverhampton BC. **5** Officer-in-Charge: P.J. Neeld BA. **6** Leisure & Amenities. **8** Open to the public. **9** Mon-Sat 10.00-18.00. Free. **10** Local history & industry; English 18th cent painted enamels (many made in Bilston); art. **11** Temporary exhibitions. **12** (a) 2 (c) 1.

WIGHTWICK MANOR, Wightwick Bank, Wolverhampton, WV6 8EE (Tel 0902-761025). **4** National Trust. **5** Curator: Miss M.L. Davidson. **8** Open to the public. **9** March-Jan: Thurs & Sat (& bank hol Sun & Mon) 14.30-17.30; May-Sept: Wed 14.00-18.00. Charges: 30p, Sat 40p. Gardens: 20p (students 15p). **10** William Morris, pre-Raphaelite house (built 1887-93).

WOLVERHAMPTON ART GALLERY, Lichfield St, Wolverhampton, WV1 1DU (Tel 0902-24549). **4** Wolverhampton MBC. **5** Curator: Mr David Rodgers MA. **6** Leisure & Amenities. **8** Open to the public. **9** Mon-Sat (inc bank hols) 10.00-18.00. Free. **10** 18th & 19th cent English oil paintings & watercolours; Old Master drawings; modern English & American paintings & prints; Oriental colln (inc Japanese swords & netsuke, Chinese ivory carving etc). **12** (a) 3 (b) 4 (c) 2.

WOODSTOCK, Oxfordshire

OXFORDSHIRE COUNTY MUSEUM, Fletcher's House, Park St, Woodstock, OX7 1SN (Tel 0993-811456). **4** Oxfordshire CC. **5** Dir of Museum Services: Mr R.A. Foster MA, AMA. **6** Libraries, Museums & Archives. **8** Open to the public. **9** Mon-Fri 10.00-17.00; May-Sept: Sat 10.00-18.00, Sun 14.00-18.00; Oct-April: Sat 10.00-17.00. Free. **10** History of the County of Oxfordshire. **12** (a) 15 (b) 28.

WOOKEY HOLE, Somerset

WOOKEY HOLE CAVES AND MILL, Wookey Hole, Wells, BA5 1BB (Tel 0749-72243). **4** Madame Tussaud's Ltd. **5** Manager: Mr C. Hunt. **8** Open to the public. **9** Daily (inc bank hols) 10.00-18.00 (16.30 winter). Adults 85p, children & OAPs 50p. **10** Caves (source of the River Axe); relics of prehistoric & Roman inhabitants of caves; paper-making mill. **11** Lady Bangor's colln (fairground relics); Mme Tussaud's store room (moulds, costumes etc), restaurant & cafeteria. **12** (b) 12 (c) 8.

WORCESTER, Hereford & Worcester

DYSON PERRINS MUSEUM OF WORCESTER PORCELAIN, Royal Porcelain Works, Severn St, Worcester (Tel 0905-23221). **4** Trustees of Dyson Perrins Museum. **5** Curator: Mr Henry Sandon. **8** Open to the public. **9** Mon-Sat 10.00-13.00, 14.00-17.00 (Oct-March: closed Sat). Free. **10** Worcester porcelain **11** Dr. Wall period wares; examples of all the Royal services made by Worcester; American birds modelled by Dorothy Doughty. **12** (a) 1.

TUDOR HOUSE MUSEUM, Friar St, Worcester WR1 2NA. (Tel 0905-22154 (at present)). **4** Worcester City Council. **5** Principal Curator: Mrs G.K. Owen BA, AMA. **6** Amenities & Recreation. **7** City Architect & Planning Officer's Dept, Mr A.G. Arnold RIBA, DipTP, MRTPI. **8** Open to the public. **9** Mon-Sat (exc Thurs) 10.30-17.00. Closed Dec 25, Jan 1 & Good Friday. Free. **10** Social & domestic history of Worcester. **12** Served from City Museum.

WORCESTER CITY MUSEUM AND ART GALLERY, Foregate St, Worcester, WR1 1DT (Tel 0905-22154 (at present)). **4** Worcester City Council. **5** Principal Curator: Mrs G.K. Owen BA, AMA. **6** Amenities & Recreation. **7** City Architect & Planning Officer's Dept, Mr A.G. Arnold RIBA, DipTP, MRTPI. **8** Open to the public. **9** Mon-Sat 9.30-18.00 (Thurs & Sat 17.00). Closed Dec 25, Jan 1 & Good Friday. Free. **10** Art Galleries: monthly exhibitions (local & national); permanent colln of local prints, drawings & watercolours & works by local artists. **11** Museum: local geology, natural history, archaeology & local history; museums of the Worcestershire Regiment & of the Worcestershire Yeomanry. **12** (a) 3 (b) 4 (c) 7.

WORTHING, Sussex

WORTHING MUSEUM AND ART GALLERY, Chapel Rd, Worthing, BN11 1HD (Tel 0903-39189). **4** Worthing BC. **5** Curator: J.F.L. Norwood BA, AMA. **6** Leisure & Recreation. **7** Amenities Dept, Borough Amenities Officer: R.P. Caldicott FIMEnt. **8** Open to the public. **9** Mon-Sat 10.00-19.00 (Oct-March 17.00). Closed Dec 25, 26 &

CODE: **1** Name of Museum, Art Gallery or Stately Home. **2** Address. **3** Telephone & telex. **4** Governing body. **5** Officer in charge. **6** Committee responsible. **7** Larger department, chief officer. **8** Open to public. **9** Hours; admission charges. **10** Scope. **11** Special exhibits or facilities. **12** Staff (a) professionally qualified (b) other non-manual (c) manual.

WORCESTER, Hereford & Worcester

Good Friday. Free. **10** Regional geology & archaeology; costume; dolls & toys; pictures; ceramics; glass. **11** Anglo-Saxon glass & jewellery from Highdown Hill. **12** (a) 3 (b) 2 (c) 4.

WROXETER, Shropshire

WROXETER ROMAN SITE, Wroxeter, Shrewsbury SY5 6PH (Tel 074 375-330). **4** Dept of Environment (Ancient Monuments). **8** Open to the public. **9** May-Sept: daily 9.30-19.00; Oct-March: Mon-Sat 9.30-17.30, Sun 14.00-17.30, (Nov-Feb closes daily at 16.00). Closed Dec 25 & 26. Adults 5p, OAPs & children 2½p, school parties free. **10** Findings from the site, supplementing Rowleys Mansion & Clive House Museums in Shrewsbury. **11** Pottery; iron tools; military equipment; personal ornaments; tomb stone.

WYE, Kent

WYE COLLEGE MUSEUM OF AGRICULTURE, Wye College, Wye, Ashford, TN25 5AH (Tel 0233-812401). **5** Hon Curators: F.C. Thompson & R.F. Farrar. **8** Open to the public. **9** June-Sept: Wed & Sun (Aug only) 14.00-17.00, other times by prior arrangement. Free. **10** Agricultural implements; waggons; horse-drawn implements; hand tools. Housed in 14th-cent barn & early 19th cent oast house. **11** Many specialised items connected with hop growing.

YANWORTH, Gloucestershire

CHEDWORTH ROMAN VILLA AND MUSEUM, The Roman Villa, Yanworth, Cheltenham, GL54 3LJ (Tel 024 289-256). **4** National Trust. **5** Custodian: A.N. Irvine. **8** Open to the public. **9** Tues-Sun (& bank hol Mon): 10.00-13.00, 14.00-18.00 (or sunset if earlier). Adults 25p, children 10p. **10** Villa site & finds.

YELVERTON, Devon

BUCKLAND ABBEY, Yelverton, PL20 6EY (Tel 075269-3607). **4** City of Plymouth. **5** Dir, Plymouth City Museums: Mr A.A. Cumming OBE, FMA. **6** Leisure Services. **8** Open to the public. **9** Summer: Mon-Sat 11.00-18.00; Sun 14.00-18.00; Winter: Wed, Sat & Sun 15.00-17.00. Closed Dec 25, 26 & Jan 1. Adults 40p, children 20p. **10** 13th cent Cistercian Abbey converted to secular use by Sir Richard Grenville in 1576; bought by Sir Francis Drake in 1581; Drake's drum & other personal relics. **11** West Country folk colln; Elizabethan portraits; maritime colln ('From Sail to Steam'); colln of silver associated with the West Country; tithe barn (built in 1300) houses a colln of carriages & farming equipment. **12** Served from City Museum & Art Gallery Plymouth. (c) 4.

YEOVIL, Somerset

BRYMPTON d'EVERCY, Yeovil (Tel 093 586-2528). **5** Owner: Mr Charles E.B. Clive-Ponsonby-Fane DOe. **8** Open to the public. **9** Sat-Wed: 12.00-18.00. 65p. Charges: 65p. **10** Historic house; country life museum. **12** (a) 1 (b) 2.

YEOVIL MUSEUM, Hendford Manor Hall, Hendford, Yeovil, BA20 1UN (Tel 0935-5171 (Sat 0935-24774)). **4** Yeovil DC. **5** Officer-in-Charge: A Heal CEng, FIMunE, FIHE. **6** Amenities. **7** Chief Technical Officer's Dept. **8** Open to the public. **9** Mon-Sat (exc Thurs) 10.30-13.00, 14.15-17.00. Free. **10** Local history & archaeology. **11** Stiby colln of firearms; Pinney glass colln; Ballwood costume colln; finds from the Romano-British villas of Lufton, Westlands & Ilchester Mead. **12** (c) 1.

YORK, North Yorkshire

CASTLE MUSEUM, Tower St, York. (Tel 0904-53611). **4** York City Council. **5** Officer-in-Charge: Mr Peter C.D. Brears DipAD, AMA. **6** Castle Museum. **8** Open to the public. **9** Mon-Fri 9.30-18.30, Sat 9.30-20.00, Sun 10.00-20.00 (Oct-March closes daily at 17.00). Closed Dec 25, 26 & Jan 1. **10** Yorkshire folk life. **11** Period Victorian & Edwardian streets & rooms, military collns; armoury; costumes; agricultural collns; musical instruments; fine furniture; pottery; decorative arts. **12** (a) 3 (b) 8 (c) 20.

MERCHANT ADVENTURERS' HALL, Fossgate, York, YO1 2XD (Tel 0904-54818). **4** Company of Merchant Adventurers of the City of York. **5** Clerk to the Company: Mr David C. Stewart CA, Abbotsford, 16 Lang Road, Bishopthorpe, York, YO2 1QL; Custodian: Mrs W.K. Armstrong. **8** Open to the public. **9** Mon-Sat 10.00-12.30, 14.00-17.30 (16.00 Nov-March). Adults 10p, children & OAPs 5p, school parties 3p. **10** 14th-16th cent guildhall; chapel & undercroft used for the fraternity (religious & social purposes), upper hall used for the mistery (trade). **12** (b) 1½.

NATIONAL RAILWAY MUSEUM, Leeman Rd, York, YO2 4XJ. (Tel 0904-21261). **4** Dept of Education & Science; outstation of Science Museum, London. **5** Keeper: Dr J.A. Coiley MA, PhD. **8** Open to the public. **9** Mon-Sat 10.00-18.00, Sun 14.30-18.00. Closed Dec 24-26, Jan 1 & Good Friday. Free. **10** Over 20 full-sized locomotives; c.20 carriages; technical, economic, & social development of railways. **11** Temporary exhibitions about railways; steam locomotives occasionally on special excursions over British Railways' tracks; refreshment facilities; shop. **12** (a) 11.

TREASURER'S HOUSE, Minster Yard, York, YO1 2JH (Tel 0904-24247). **4** National Trust. **5** Administrator: E. Bunting. **8** Open to the public. **9** April-Oct: daily (inc bank hols) 10.30-18.00. Adults 40p, parties 30p, children 20p. **10** Town house built for the Treasurers of York Minster in 12th cent & largely restored in 17th & 18th cents, antique furniture; early English china & pottery; 17th & 18th cent glass. **11** Worksheets for children. **12** (b) 4 (c) 2.

YORK CITY ART GALLERY, Exhibition Square, York, YO1 2EW (Tel 0904-23839). **4** York DC. **5** Curator: Mr John Ingamells. **6** Museum & Art Gallery. **8** Open to the public. **9** Mon-Sat 10.00-17.00, Sun 14.30-17.00. Closed Dec 25, 26 & Good Friday. Free. **10** English & European paintings (from 14th cent); modern stoneware pottery; drawings & prints (primarily local topography).

YORKSHIRE MUSEUM, Museum Gardens, York, YO1 2DR (Tel 0904-29745). **4** North Yorkshire CC. **5** Curator: T.M. Clegg FMA, MBOU. **6** Libraries, Archives & Museums (Museum Sub-Committee). **8** Open to the public. **9** Mon-Sat (inc bank hols) 10.00-17.00, Sun 13.00-17.00. Adults 11p, children 5p. **10** Local archaeology, geology, natural history & decorative arts; ancient monuments (St. Mary's Abbey, Multangular Tower etc) in gardens. **11** Roman collns; Ormside bowl & other Anglo-Saxon art objects; Viking finds; medieval alabasters; cave bones; fossils; extinct birds (inc great auk). **12** (a) 7 (b) 2 & 5 (c) 7.

ZENNOR, Cornwall

WAYSIDE MUSEUM, Old Mill House, Zennor, St Ives, TR26 3DA. (Tel 073670-6945). **5** Hon Curator: Mr E.J. Wigley. **8** Open to the public. **9** Daily (inc bank hols) 10.00-dusk. Free. **10** West Cornwall folk life; mining; domestic life; crafts; mill; archaeology; smithy; models; cottage kitchen with open hearth. **12** (a) 1.

REPUBLIC OF IRELAND

Entries for the Republic of Ireland are grouped into Public Libraries, Special Libraries and Museums, Art Galleries etc. The public libraries are arranged alphabetically under the name of the local authority. The special libraries and the museums are arranged alphabetically by town.

Hours of opening and, where relevant, prices of admission were correct for 1975, but should not be regarded as accurate for 1976 and later years. The dates of opening given are inclusive. Libraries and museums should be assumed to be closed on bank holidays unless stated otherwise.

Information on libraries and museums in the Republic of Ireland was difficult to obtain, and as a result many had to be omitted. No information was available about the public libraries of four local authorities (Limerick City Council, County Monaghan, County Sligo and Waterford City Council).

PUBLIC LIBRARIES: QUESTIONNAIRE

1. Name of Local Authority   2. Population served
3. Full postal address of Central Library or Administrative Headquarters   4. Telephone number of above; Telex number
5. Name of Chief Librarian, with designation and qualifications (if responsible for a wider service than libraries alone, please state)
6. Name of deputy to (5) with designation and qualifications
7. Committee responsible for libraries   8. If the officer named in (5) is subordinate to some other officer, state designation of the latter together with name and qualifications   9. Opening hours of main libraries: Monday to Friday: adult lending, reference, children's; Saturday: adult lending, reference, children's
10. Basis of organisation   11. Names, addresses and telephone numbers of Regional or District Libraries within the system, together with name and qualifications of Librarian in charge
12. Names and addresses of full-time Branch Libraries (excluding question 11) open at least 30 hours per week   13. Number of part-time libraries; number of mobiles
14. List any Special Collections of significance other than those which are regional or national commitments (exclude collections covered in questions 15 to 17)   15. Gramophone records: number of Record Libraries; Issues 1974/75: (a) Records, (b) Cassettes etc; Stock: (c) Records, (d) Cassettes etc; (e) Loan charges or subscription, if any; (f) Scale of fines   16. Picture loan collection: Stock; Charges, if any   17. Does the Library provide any of the following services? Schools, Housebound, Prisons, Hospitals, Old People's Homes, other extramural services   18. Is the Library, or the department of which it is part, responsible for: Cultural activities? Entertainments? (Give total estimated expenditure on cultural activities and entertainments for 1975/76, including salaries, wages and administration; designation of officer directly in charge of these activities; number of staff employed in this field (a) officer; (b) manual)   19. Name issue methods employed for adult lending other than Browne
20. Lending Library loan period if other than 2 weeks
21. Lending Library fine scales: (a) Adult; (b) Children; (c) Old Age Pensioners   22. Local co-operation: name any purely local co-operative scheme in which Library participates   23. Stock: (a) Adult Lending; (b) Adult Reference; (c) Children's (excluding schools); (d) Schools; (e) Number of individual periodical titles taken   24. Issues 1974/75 (issues from mobiles and to housebound to be included as appropriate): (a) Adult Lending (excluding institutions); (b) Junior Lending (excluding schools); (c) Schools; (d) Institutions
25. Staff (figures given should relate to established posts including vacancies, if any; where part-time staff are employed their total weekly working hours should be divided by the hours normally worked by full-time members of staff, usually 35 or 36, and thus converted to the equivalent of full-time staff): (a) Total officers; (b) Total manual; (c) Number of chartered librarians actually employed (including graduate chartered librarians); (d) Number of graduates actually employed   26. Finance (based on annual estimates for 1975/76): (a) Total expenditure (including cultural activities if part of Library budget); (b) Total income other than from rate; (c) Expenditure per head of population (total expenditure divided by population served); (d) Expenditure on books, binding and periodicals; (e) Total expenditure on gramophone records and allied material; (f) Total expenditure on salaries and wages (including superannuation and national insurance but excluding Town Hall establishment charges)   27. Capital Projects approved for start in 1975 or 1976 and costing more than £250,000.

SPECIAL LIBRARIES: QUESTIONNAIRE

1. Official title of Library   2. Full postal address
3. Telephone number; Telex number   4. Name, designation and qualifications of officer in charge   5. Name, designation and qualifications of deputy to (4)
6. Name of governing body   7. Branch Libraries, if any, with brief address and telephone number, and name of officer in charge with qualifications   8. Main subjects covered by Library   9. Special Collections of significance
10. Co-operative schemes in which Library participates   11. Is the general public allowed access to the Library (state any special conditions)   12. Hours of opening   13. Stock: (a) Books and bound periodicals, number of volumes; (b) Number of individual periodical titles taken; (c) Other materials in the Library, with number of items if possible
14. Finance: estimated expenditure 1975/76 for books, binding, periodicals and all similar materials such as records, microtexts etc
15. Staff (hours worked by part-time staff per week should be totalled and divided by the number of normal working hours of a full-time member of staff to give the equivalent of full-time working): (a) Total number of full-time staff (excluding manual employees); (b) Number of graduate staff; (c) Number of chartered librarians (including graduates).

MUSEUMS AND ART GALLERIES: QUESTIONNAIRE

1. Official name of Museum, Art Gallery, Stately Home etc
2. Full postal address   3. Telephone number; Telex number
4. Name of governing body where applicable   5. Name, designation and qualifications of officer in charge
6. Committee responsible for Museum, Art Gallery Stately Home etc   7. If the Museum, Art Gallery, Stately Home etc is part of a larger department indicate name of that department and give name, designation and qualifications of the chief officer (Note: questions 6 and 7 apply only to Museums etc provided by local authorities)   8. Is the Museum, Art Gallery, Stately Home etc open to the public   9. Hours of opening: Weekdays, Saturdays, Sundays, Bank Holidays. Is admission free, if not give charges   10. Scope of the Museum, Art Gallery, Stately Home etc   11. Special exhibits or facilities   12. Number of full-time staff: (a) Professionally qualified; (b) Other non-manual; (c) Manual.

REPUBLIC OF IRELAND

PUBLIC LIBRARIES

BRAY URBAN DISTRICT COUNCIL (pop 14,467) Public Library, Florence Rd, Bray, Co. Wicklow (0001-862600). Chief Libn: Miss Eileen Murray FLAI; Senior Asst: Ms Carol Hughes. **7** Library Advisory. **9** Mon-Sat: ad ldg & ref 10.00-13.00, 14.30-18.00, 19.00-21.00, children Thurs 16.00-18.00, Tues & Sat 15.00-18.00. **17** Schools, ref libs in primary schools. **20** 3 weeks. **21** (a) 1p pw; (b&c) no fines. **23** (a) 30,041; (b) 1,264; (c) 12,211; (d) 3,200; (e) 7. **24** (a) 110,597; (b) 38,372. **25** (a) 4; (b) 1; (c) 1. **26** (a) £17,804; (b) £533 (Government grant for schools) + £300 (subscriptions from members); (c) £1.23; (d) £4,400; (f) £8,729.

CARLOW COUNTY COUNCIL (pop 34,025) Carlow County Library Headquarters, Dublin St, Carlow, (0503-41181). County Libn: Muiris Ō Raghaill ALA. **8** County Manager. **9** Mon-Sat 10.00-13.00, 14.00-17.30 (plus Tues & Thurs 18.30-20.30, ad ldg & children only). **10** HQ; Branch. **12** Carlow Town B Lib, Dublin St, Carlow. **13** P-t 3; mobiles 1. **14** Local history colln. **17** Schools, hospitals, old people's homes. **20** 3 weeks. **21** (a, b&c) Fines not being charged (trial period). **23** (a) 33,207; (b) 1,353; (c) 9,167; (d) 8,856; (e) 46. **24** (a) 86,485; (b) 47,787. **25** (a) 10; (b) 1; (c) 3. **26** (a) £54,582; (b) £1,720; (c) £1.60; (d) £18,000; (f) £19,876.

CAVAN COUNTY COUNCIL (pop 52,618) Cavan County Library, Casement St, Cavan (049-31799). Chief Libn: Miss Brid Sheridan FLAI; Dep: Miss Sara Cullen FLAI. **9** Mon-Fri: ad ldg & ref 20 hours, children 13 hours. **13** P-t 10. **14** Cavan local colln. **17** Schools **20** 3 weeks for non-fiction. **21** (a&b) 2p pw; (c) no fines. **25** (a) 6; (b) 2. **26** (b) £27,850; (c) £0.542; (d) £10,098. 67; (f) £15,485.09.

CLARE COUNTY COUNCIL Clare County Libraries, Mill Rd, Ennis, Co. Clare (065-21732). County Libn: Noel Crowley FLAI. **9** Mon-Fri: 11.00-13.00, 14.15-17.30, 19.00-21.00.

CORK CORPORATION (pop 130,000) City Library, Grand Parade, Cork (0021-21053/25641). City Libn: Mr Sean Bohan BA, FLAI, DipLib; Dep: Miss Mary Collins FLAI. **7** Library. **9** Mon-Fri: ad ldg & ref 10.00-13.00, 14.30-20.00 (18.00 Wed), children 14.30-18.00; Sat: 10.00-13.00, 14.30-18.00. **10** HQ; Branch. **11** St Mary's Rd, Cork (52380), Libn: Miss I.P. Quinn ALA; Tory Top Rd, Cork (56648), Libn: Miss J. Powell DipLib. **13** P-t 2; mobiles 1. **17** Schools, prisons hospitals, old people's homes. **21** (a) 1p pd; (b) 1p pw; (c) free membership, but fines charged. **22** Cork Archives Council. **23** (a) 95,857; (b) 19,820; (c) 25,260; (d) 68,640; (e) 60. **24** (a) 568,998; (b) 209,639. **25** (a) 35; (b) 5; (c) 7; (d) 3. **26** (a) £164,000; (b) £44,035; (c) £1.26; (d) £60,000; (f) £66,000. **27** Extension & rebuilding of Central City Library (£442,000; commenced 1 April 1975).

CORK COUNTY COUNCIL (pop 224,238) Courthouse, Cork (0021-25189). Chief Libn: Mr Padraig O'Maidin FLAI. **7** Library. **9** Mon-Fri: ad ldg 9.30-18.30, ref & children 9.30-17.30; Sat: ad ldg & children 9.30-17.30. **10** HQ; District; Branch. **11** District Libraries: Bantry Library, Libn: Miss Hanna O'Sullivan FLAI; Fermoy Library, Libn: Mr Timothy Cadogan FLAI. **12** Cobh; Cork; Mallow; Millstreet. **13** P-t 15; mobiles 5. **14** Cork Archives Centre (Archivist: Miss Ann Barry BA). **17** Schools, housebound, hospitals. **21** (a&b) 1p pw; (c) no fines. **23** Adult non-fiction 149,790; Adult fiction 145,950; (c&d) 258,901. **24** (a) 1,023,591; (b&c) 734,474. **25** (a) 27; (b) 15; (c) 5; (d) 6. **26** (a) £221,310; (b) £41,595; (c) £0.98; (d) £68,500; (f) £91,100.

DONEGAL COUNTY COUNCIL The Courthouse, Lifford, Co. Donegal (008481-5). Chief Libn: Mr Edward MacIntyre. **14** Local. **17** Schools. **21** (a&b) 2p pw.

DUBLIN CORPORATION AND DUBLIN COUNTY COUNCIL (pop 798,384) Central Public Library, Pearse St, Dublin 2 (0001-777662/5; telex 4838 LBRY EI). City & County Libn: Mairin O'Byrne Dip Lib, FLAI; Dep City & County Libn: Robert J. Casey DipLib, FLAI. **7** Cultural. **9** Mon-Wed & Fri: 10.00-13.00, 14.30-21.00; Thurs & Sat: 10.00-13.00, 14.30-18.00. **10** HQ; Branch. **11** Special Services: Information Centre for Commerce & Technology, 106 Capel St, Dublin 1; College of Technology, Bolton St, Dublin 1; College of Technology, Kevin St, Dublin 8; College of Technology, Cathal Brugha St, Dublin 1; Music & Gramophone Record Lib, 18 Lr Kevin St, Dublin 8; Schools Libraries Headquarters, 1 Wellington Quay, Dublin 2. **12** Ballyfermot (Adult) Lib, Kylemore Rd, Dublin 10; Ballyfermot (Junior) Lib, Drumfin Park, Dublin 10; Cabinteely Lib, Bray Rd, Co Dublin; 106 Chapel St, Dublin 1; Charleville Mall Lib, North Strand, Dublin 1; Monastery Rd, Clondalkin, Co Dublin; Dolphin's Barn Lib, Parnell Rd, Dublin 8; Drumcondra Lib, Millmount Ave, Dublin 9; Dundrum, Co Dublin; Main St, Howth; Inchicore Lib, 34 Emmet Rd, Dublin 8; Marino Mart, Dublin 3; 138-142 Pearse St, Dublin 2; Pembroke Lib, Anglesea Rd, Dublin 4; Phibsborough Lib, Blackquire Bridge, Dublin 7; Raheny Lib, Howth Rd, Dublin 5; 167 Rathmines Rd, Dublin 6; Ringsend Lib, 2-16 Fitzwilliam St, Dublin 4; Stillorgan, Co Dublin; Tallaght, Co Dublin; Terenure Lib, Templeogue Rd, Dublin 6; 22 Thomas St, Dublin 8; Walkinstown Lib, Percy French Rd, Dublin 12. **13** P-t 1; mobiles 4. **14** Dix, Gilbert, Yeats & general Irish collns. **15** 1; (c) 3,000; (d) 1,000; (e) £3.00 pa; (f) as books. **17** Schools, prisons, old people's homes, lightships, psychiatric post-graduate training units. **21** (a, b&c) 1p 1st week, 2p 2nd week, 3p pw thereafter. **22** Joint Book Storage with Trinity College, Dublin; with Dun Laoghaire Corp for School Libraries. **23** (a) 982,803; (c) 536,353; (d) 262,304; (e) 1,180. **24** (a) 23,092,720; (b&c) 6,203,158; (d) 139,272 **25** (a) 253; (b) 57; (c) 56; (d) 22. **26** (a) £821,292; (b) £162,002; (c) £1.02; (d) £255,879; (e) £9,000; (f) £385,473.

DUN LAOGHAIRE CORPORATION (pop 54,000) Dun Laoghaire Public Library, Lower Georges St, Dun Laoghaire, Co. Dublin (0001-801254). Chief Libn: Mr Patrick J. White DLT, DPA, FLAI; Dep: Miss Agnes Doyle; Chief Asst: Ms Una O'Connor DLT, FLAI. **8** Borough Manager: Mr Herbert Byrne MA. **9** Tues-Fri: ad ldg & ref 10.00-13.00, 14.00-18.00, 19.00-20.30, children 14.30-18.00; Sat: 10.00-13.00, 14.00-18.00. **10** HQ; Branch. **12** Blackrock; Dalkey; Dun Laoghaire. **14** Art (painting & sculpture); boat-building; sailing; yachting; fishing; Irish history; Irish literature (drama, poetry in English). **17** Secondary schools. **21** (a&b) 1p pw or part; (c) no fines. **23** (a) 140,000; (b) 1,000; (c) 28,000; (e) 30. **24** (9 months only) (a) 331,748; (b) 98,991. **25** (a) 16; (b) 3; (c) 3; (d) 2. **26** (a) £90,500; (b) £4,250; (c) £1.70; (d) £26,000; (f) £38,390.

GALWAY COUNTY COUNCIL (pop 149,223) County Library Headquarters, Courthouse, Galway (0091-62471). Sec & County Libn: Mr Thomas Sharkey. **7** Libraries (Advisory only). **8** County Manager: Mr Peter Kearns. **9** Mon-Fri: ad ldg & ref 10.30-13.00, 14.30-20.30, children 15.00-18.00; Sat: ad ldg & ref 10.30-13.00, 14.30-17.30, children 10.30-13.00. **10** HQ. **13** P-t 28; mobiles 3. **17** Schools, old people's homes, mental hospital. **21** (a&c) 2p pw or part; (b) no fines. **23** (a&b) 113,323; (c) 35,853; (d) 107,442. **24** (9 months only) (a) 232,921;

GALWAY COUNTY COUNCIL —*continued*

(b) 130, 905; (c) c. 516, 000.
25 (a) 14; (b) 3; (c) 1.   **26** (a) £126, 450; (b) £21, 890;
(c) £0. 70; (d) £40, 120; (f) c. £55, 700.

KERRY COUNTY COUNCIL (pop 112, 772) County Library
Headquarters, Tralee, Co. Kerry (066- 21200). County Libn:
Mrs Kathleen Browne FLAI.   **7** Library.   **9** Tralee
Branch: Mon-Fri 11. 00-20. 30, Sat 11. 00-18. 00. Other
Branches: Tues-Sat 11. 00-13. 00, 14. 00-18. 00, 19. 00-20. 30.
10 HQ; Branch.   **12** Caherciveen; Castleisland; Dingle;
Kenmare; Killarney; Listowel; Tralee.   **13** P-t 3; mobiles 2.
14 Local history (at HQ).   **17** Schools, housebound, hospitals.   **21** (a, b&c) 1p pw.   **22** IJFR.   **23** (a&b) 76, 846;
(c) 28, 418; (d) 49, 854; (e) 83.   **24** (a) 235, 000; (b) 120, 090;
(c) 149, 562.
25 (a) 20; (b) 3; (c) 1; (d) 1.   **26** (a) £112, 490; (b) £13, 950;
(c) c. £1. 00; (d&e) £35, 300; (f) £50, 940.

KILDARE COUNTY COUNCIL (pop 71, 977) Kildare County
Library, Athgarvan Rd, Droichead Nua, Co. Kildare (045-
31486). County Libn: Mr Seamus S. O'Conchubhair BA, DLT,
FLAI; Dep: Mr Michael V. Kavanagh FLAI.   **7** Library.
9 Mon-Fri: ad ldg & ref 11. 00-13. 00, 14. 00-17. 00, 18. 00-
20. 30, children 15. 00-17. 30; Sat: ad ldg & ref 11. 00-13. 00,
15. 00-17. 00, children 11. 00-13. 00.
10 HQ; Branch.   **12** Athgarvan Rd, Droichead Nua;
Courthouse, Athy; Town Hall, Naas; Main St, Leixlip.   **13** P-t
11; mobiles 1.   **16** Building up colln of pictures & sculptures by Irish artists under Arts Council Scheme.
17 Schools, housebound, hospitals, old people's homes,
courses & seminars for teachers.   **20** 3 weeks on mobile.
21 (a&b) ½p pw; (c) no fines.   **22** IJFR.   **23** (a) 101, 561;
(b) 5, 884; (c) 38, 723; (d) 10, 738; (e) 44.   **24** (a) 106, 188;
(b&c) 173, 626.
25 (a) 22; (b) 4; (c) 4; (d) 1.   **26** (a) £102, 861; (b) £5, 432;
(c) £1. 43; (d) £31, 500; (f) £44, 296.

KILKENNY COUNTY COUNCIL (pop 61, 500) John St,
Kilkenny (056- 22021). Chief Libn: Mr John C. McTernan,
FLAI.   **7** Library.   **9** Mon-Fri: ad ldg & ref 10. 30-
13. 00, 14. 30-17. 00, 19. 00- 21. 00, children 10. 30-13. 00,
14. 30-17. 00.
10 HQ; Branch.   **12** City Lib, John's Quay, Kilkenny.
13 P-t 2; mobiles 1.
14 Local history & archives (c. 1, 500 items).   **17** Schools
hospitals, old people's homes.   **21** (a&b) 1p pw.
23 (a) 53, 000; (b) 3, 500; (c) 24, 000; (d) 16, 000; (e) 10.
24 (a) 140, 000; (b) 20, 000; (c) 35, 500.
25 (a) 10; (b) 3; (c) 2; (d) 1.   **26** (a) £50, 500; (b) £5, 000;
(c) £0. 82; (d) £18, 000; (f) £21, 500.

LAOIS COUNTY COUNCIL (pop 45, 259) Laois County Library, Church St, Portlaoise (0502-21482). County Libn: Mr
Edwin Phelan ACIS.   **9** Mon-Fri: ad ldg & ref 10. 00-12. 30,
14-17. 00 (&Wed & Thurs 19. 00-20. 30), children 14. 00-17. 00
(closed Mon); Sat: ad ldg & ref 10. 00-13. 00.
10 HQ; Branch.   **12** Main St, Abbey Leix; Pearse St,
Mountmellick; Shannon Rd, Mountrath; Main St, Portartington;
Mill St, Rathdowney; Court Square, Stradbally.   **13** P-t 10.
14 Local history.   **17** Schools, prison, hospitals.   **20** 3
weeks.   **21** (a) 1p pw; (b) no fines.   **23** (a&b) 52, 919;
(c) 25, 952; (d) 31, 447.   **24** (a&d) 108, 278; (b) 87, 326;
(c) 192, 100.
25 (a) 11; (b) 1; (c) 2.   **26** (a) £68, 133; (b) £10, 270;
(c) £1. 505; (d) £23, 760; (f) £22, 948.

LEITRIM COUNTY COUNCIL (pop 28, 360) County Library,
Courthouse, Ballinamore, Co. Leitrim (008041-12). Acting
County Libn: Ms Rosaleen Comfrey.   **7** Library Advisory.
9 Mon-Fri: ad ldg & ref 36½ hours, children 28½ hours;
Sat: ad ldg & ref 2½ hours; children 3 hours.
10 HQ; Branch.   **12** Ballinamore; Carrick-on-Shannon.
13 P-t 5.
17 schools, prisons, hospitals, old people's homes.
20 Students-4 weeks.   **21** (a&b) 1p pw.   **24** (a) 77, 440;
(b) 97, 695.
25 (a) 3; (b) 2.   **26** (a) £15, 653. 84; (b) £1, 285; (c) £0. 49;
(d) £6, 989. 81; (f) £7, 371. 56.

LIMERICK COUNTY COUNCIL (pop 81, 389) 58 O'Connell St,
Limerick (0061-48477/48692). County Libn: Ms Roisin De
Nais FLAI; Dep: Miss Mary Berkery.   **8** County Manager.
9 Mon-Fri: 10. 30-13. 30, 15. 00-18. 00; Sat: ad ldg 10. 30-
13. 30, 15. 00-18. 00.
10 HQ.   **12** Newcastle West; Rathkeale.   **13** P-t 30;
mobiles 2.
14 Anglo-Irish fiction.   **15** 1; (a) 2, 000; (c) 500; (e) 50p
per 6 months; (f) 2p pw.   **17** Schools, hospitals, old people's
homes.   **18** Cultural activities with children, (Asst Libn,
Schools service).   **21** (a, b&c) 2p pw.   **23** (a&b) 126, 359;
(c&d) 128, 813 (e) c. 20.   **24** (a) 362, 467; (b&c) 633, 634.
25 (a) 10; (b) 2; (c) 2.   **26** (a) £73, 938; (c) £0. 887;
(d) £22, 500; (f) £26, 800.

**LONGFORD AND WESTMEATH JOINT LIBRARY
COMMITTEE** (pop 81, 784) County Library Headquarters,
Dublin Rd, Mullingar, Co. Westmeath (044-8416). County
Libn & Sec: Ms Marian Keaney FLAI.   **7** Joint Library.
9 Mon-Fri: ad ldg & ref 11. 00-13. 00, 15. 00-18. 00,
18. 30-20. 00, children 15. 30-17. 30.
10 HQ; Branch; Centre.   **12** Fr. Mathew Hall, Athlone,
Co. Westmeath; Market Sq, Mullingar, Co. Westmeath;
Church St, Longford; Regional Technical College Lib, Athlone,
Co. Westmeath.   **13** P-t 22; mobiles 1 + 1 exhibition
exchange delivery van.
14 Kirby Colln (illustrated editions of 'The Vicar of Wakefield'; Howard Bury Papers (on deposit).   **16** Paintings by
20th cent Irish artists & prints & photographs of local
interest (not for loan).   **17** Schools, housebound, hospitals,
old people's homes, mobile library service to rural areas.
18 Cultural activities, mainly exhibitions & lectures.
20 Students 6 weeks.   **21** (a, b&c) 1p pw.   **23** (a, b, c&d)
265, 429; (e) 25.   **24** 1973-4 (a&b) 253, 313; (c) 465, 619;
(d) 7, 234.
25 (a) 18; (b) 3; (c) 5; (d) 1.   **26** (a) £97, 290; (b) £11, 068;
(c) £1. 19; (d) £32, 120; (f) £43, 813.   **27** New County Library
Headquarters, Clonard, Mullingar.

LOUTH COUNTY COUNCIL (pop 75, 000) Louth County
Library, Chapel St, Dundalk, Co. Louth (042-5457). Chief
Libn: Mr Patrick J. Moynagh DLT, FLAI; Dep: Miss Ann J.
Ward BA, DLT.   **9** Mon-Fri: ad ldg 11. 00-17. 00, 18. 00-
20. 00, ref 11. 00-17. 00, children 15. 00-17. 00; Sat: ad ldg &
ref 11. 00-17. 00; children 10. 30-12. 30.
10 HQ.   **12** Fair St, Drogheda; Bridge St, Ardee.   **13** P-t
1; mobiles 2.
16 67 paintings (property of Drogheda Municipal Art
Gallery Committee).   **17** Schools.   **21** (a) 10p; (b) 5p.
23 (a) 40, 000; (b) 740; (c) 24, 000.   **24** (a) 130, 000;
(b) 140, 000.
25 (a) 15; (b) 2; (c) 4; (d) 3.   **26** (a) £71, 423; (b) £3, 500;
(c) c. £0. 91; (d) £18, 000; (f) £42, 000.   **27** Approval for new
Headquarters & Branch in Dundalk.

MAYO COUNTY COUNCIL (pop 109, 525) County Library
Headquarters, Castlebar, Co. Mayo (008107-70). Acting
County Libn: Miss Mary O'Grady, DLT.   **9** Mon-Fri:
10. 00-13. 00, 14. 00-17. 30, 19. 00-21. 00 (some nights): Sat:
10. 00-13. 00, 14. 00-18. 00.
10 HQ; Branch.   **12** Castlebar, Co. Mayo; Lillala Rd,
Ballina, Co. Mayo.   **13** P-t 12; mobiles 1.
17 Schools, old people's homes.   **23** (a&b) 66, 646; (c)
47, 622; (d) 36, 384; (e) 25.   **24** (a) 179, 000; (b) 134, 665;
(d) 2, 000.
25 (a) 15; (b) 3.   **26** (a) £119, 000; (c) c. £1. 00; (d) £39, 000;
(f) c. £40, 000.   **27** New Library Headquarters (should
commence 1976).

MEATH COUNTY COUNCIL (pop 71, 616) County Library,
Railway St, Navan, Co. Meath (046-21134). County Libn:
Mr William P. Smith DipinLibTr; Asst Libn: Mr Patrick J.
Daly.   **8** County Manager.   **9** Mon-Fri: ad ldg 10. 30-
12. 30, 14. 30-17. 00, 19. 00-20. 30, ref 9. 30-13. 00, 14. 00-
17. 00, 19. 00-20. 30, children 14. 30-17. 00; Sat: 10. 00-12. 30.
10 HQ; Branch; Rural Centre.   **12** Laytown; Main St,
Dunshaughlin; Main St, Dunboyne; Courthouse, Trim; Court-
house, Kells; Main St, Athboy; Castle St, Oldcastle; Old Church,
Kilmessan; Courthouse, Duleek.   **13** P-t 10.

CODE: 1 Local authority. 2 Population. 3 Postal address of HQ. 4 Telephone & telex. 5 Chief Libn. 6 Deputy.
7 Committee responsible. 8 Officer to whom Libn is responsible (if any). 9 Hours. 10 Organisation. 11 Area libraries.
12 Branches. 13 Part-time libraries; mobiles. 14 Special collections. 15 Gramophone records: number of libraries,
(a) record issues (b) cassette issues (c) record stock (d) cassette stock (e) loan charges (f) fines. 16 Pictures: stock; .
charges. 17 Other services. 18 Cultural activities (expenditure, officer in charge, staff: (a) officers (b) manual). 19 Issue
method (if not Browne). 20 Loan period (if not 2 weeks). 21 Fines: (a) adult (b) children (c) OAPs. 22 Co-operative
schemes. 23 Stock: (a) adult lending (b) adult reference (c) children (d) schools (e) current periodical titles. 24 Issues:
(a) adult (b) children (c) schools (d) institutions. 25 Staff: (a) officers (b) manual (c) chartered libns (d) graduates.
26 Finance: (a) total expenditure (b) non-rate income (c) per capita expenditure (d) expenditure for books (e) expenditure
for records etc (f) salaries & wages. 27 Capital projects.

MEATH COUNTY COUNCIL—*continued*

14 Local history.   17 Schools, old people's homes.
21 (a, b&c) 1p pw or part.   22 ICLS; IJFR.
23 (a) 95,000; (b) 5,000; (c) 10,300; (d) 46,440; (e) 45.
24 (a) 193,975; (b) 67,590; (c) 577,757.
25 (a) 12; (b) 2; (c) 2; (d) 1.   26 (a) £98,610; (b) £2,500;
(c) £1.38; (d) £34,000; (f) £27,515.

OFFALY COUNTY COUNCIL (pop 51,829) County Library
Headquarters, Tullamore, Co. Offaly (0506-21113). Acting
County Libn: A. M. Coughlan DipinLibTr; Acting Asst County
Libn: Miss B. Lynam.   9 Mon-Fri: 10.00-13.00, 14.00-
17.00, 19.00-21.00; Sat: 10.00-13.00.
10 HQ; Branch; Centre.   13 P-t 9.
17 Schools, old people's homes.   20 4 weeks.
21 (a, b&c) 2p pw.   23 (a, b, c&d) 73,000; (e) 13.
25 (a) 8; (b) 1; (c) 1.   26 (a) £45,015; (b) £2,600; (c) £0.90;
(d) £21,000; (f) £20,000.

ROSCOMMON COUNTY COUNCIL (pop 53,519) County
Library, Abbey St, Roscommon (0903-6203). County Libn:
Ms Helen Maher FLAI.   9 Mon-Sat: 3 hours daily.
10 HQ; Branch.   13 Mobiles 1.
14 Irish interest & local colln (c. 4,000 items).
17 Schools, old people's homes.   20 Mobile-4 weeks.
21 (a&b) 1p pw.   23 (a) 46,370; (b) 683; (c) 7,235;
(d) 18,500; (e) 37.   24 (a) 101,529; (b&c) 266,744.
25 (a) 13; (b) 2; (c) 1.   26 (a) £73,552; (b) £7,740;
(c) £1.37; (d) £25,875; (e) (microfilm) £1,050; (f) £26,500.

TIPPERARY COUNTY JOINT LIBRARIES COMMITTEE
Castle Ave, Thurles, Co. Tipperary. (008652-153).
Chief Libn: Mr Daniel J. Kinnane; Asst. Libn: Miss Anne
Corridan.   9 Mon-Fri: ad ldg 14.00-15.00, 1830-20.30
(plus 11.00-12.30 Tues & Thurs), ref 930-17.30; children
15.30-17.00; Sat: ad ldg & children 11.00-12.30, 14.30-16.30.
10 HQ; Branch.   13 P-t 288 (inc schools); mobiles 2.
17 schools, hospitals, old people's homes.   21 (a&b) 1p pw.
22 BLL.
25 (a) 12; (b) 2; (c) 17.   26 (a) £106,180; (b) £11,155;
(c) £0.85; (d) £35,380; (f) £47,340.

WATERFORD COUNTY COUNCIL County Library, Lismore,
Co Waterford (008487-15) County Libn: Ms Catherine Hayes
BA, HDipinEd, DipinLibTr; Dep: Mr Matthew V. Gough.
7 Library.   9 Mon-Fri: ad ldg & ref 9.00-17.00, 19.00-
21.00, children 15.30-17.30; Sat: ad ldg 19.00-21.30, children
15.00-17.00.
10 HQ; Branch.   12 Ballyduff; Cappoquin; Dungarvan;
Dunmore; Filmacthomas; Lismore; Portlaw; Stradbally;
Tallow; Tramore.   13 P-t 10; mobiles 1 & 1 exchange van.
17 schools, old people's homes.   21 (a&b) 1p pw.
23 (a&b) 64,339.   24 9 months only (a) 95,448; (b&c)
152,320.
25 (c) 1; (d) 1.   26 (a) £57,712; (b) Dept of Education
grant £3,800; (d) £13,250; (f) c. £27,500.

WESTMEATH COUNTY, *see* **Longford**

WEXFORD COUNTY COUNCIL (pop 85,892) County Library
Headquarters, County Hall, Wexford (053-22211). Chief
Libn: Miss Catherine T. O'Rourke FLAI; Dep: Miss Anna
Drury.   8 County Manager: T. F. Broe BComm.   9 Mon-
Fri: 11.00-13.00, 14.15-17.30 (20.00 Wed).
10 HQ; Branch.   12 Enniscorthy; Gorey; New Ross.
13 1 delivery van.
17 Schools, housebound, hospitals, old people's homes.
21 (a&b) 10p per month.   23 (a) 431,850; (b) 2,285;
(c) 33,152; (d) 22,163; (e) 32.   24 9 months only (a) 180,669;
(b) 23,334; (c) 265,800; (d) 7,804.
25 (a) 8; (b) 3; (c) 1.   26 (a) £50,000; (b) £4,400; Dept of
Education grant £4,000; fines & receipts £400; (c) £0.58;
(d) £28,000; (f) £20,000.

WICKLOW COUNTY COUNCIL (pop 51,828) County
Library, Greystones, Co. Wicklow (0001-874387). Chief Libn:
Mr Joseph Hayes FLAI; Dep: Ms Margaret McCrea DLT.
7 Library Advisory.   9 Mon-Fri: 9.00-17.00 (21.00
Tues & Thurs); Sat: 10.00-13.00.
10 HQ; Branch.   13 P-t 3.
14 Irish colln.   17 Schools, housebound, hospitals, old
people's homes.   21 (a&b) 1p pw.   23 (a) 66,421;
(b) 4,935; (d) 34,363; (e) 22.   24 (a) 83,360; (b&c) 41,117.
25 (a) 4; (b) 4; (c) 2.   26 (a) £34,754; (b) £2,634; (c) £0.50;
(d) £10,500; (f) £17,500.

SPECIAL LIBRARIES

CASHEL, Co. Tipperary

CASHEL DIOCESAN LIBRARY, Cashel (Tel 008196-43)
Custodian of the Library: Very Rev D. G. A. Clarke.
6 Chapter of Cashel Cathedral.   8 Incunabula (c. 20); 16th
& 17th cent books (religious, legal & geographical).
9 Part of Chaucer's 'House of Fame'; Rolewinck's
'Chronicle of the Times'; 'The Nuremberg Chronicle',
11   12 Mon-Fri: 9.00-15.00.   13 (a) 20,000.

CASTLEKNOCK, Co. Dublin

DUNSINK OBSERVATORY LIBRARY, Dunsink Observatory,
Castleknock, (Tel 0001-383887/383544) Sec: Miss A. M.
Callanan.
6 School of Cosmic Physics, Dublin Institute for Advanced
Studies.   8 Astronomy.   9 'Nature' (from 1877); 'Philo-
sophical Transactions of the Royal Society' (1829-1932);
'Astrophysical Journal' (complete).   10 Dublin Libraries
Information Service.   11 Not open to public.   12 Mon-
Fri: 9.99-17.00.   13 (a) 5,000; (b) 80; (c) Astronomical
charts.   14 £2,500.   15 (a) ½.

CORK, Co. Cork

UNIVERSITY COLLEGE, CORK, LIBRARY, Cork (Tel 0021-
26871; Telex 6050) Univ Libn: Mr Patrick Quigg BSc, ALA.
7 Medical Lib (ext 492); Science Lib (ext 284); Dairy Science
Lib (ext 389); Music Lib (ext 240).   8 Humanities; social
sciences; biological sciences; physical sciences; medicine;
dairy science.   9 Bax Memorial (music); Gulbenkian
Foundation (music & records); Lloyd (music); Sexton (Anglo-
Indian); Sperrin-Johnson (music); Hawtin Bequest (general);
Richard Caulfield mss; Fermoy papers; Lyons mss; Bishop
Murphy mss; William O'Brien mss.   10 BLL; ICLS.
11 Open, with special permission from Libn.   12 9.00-
20.30 (23.00 for ref only).   13 (a) 260,000 (b) 1,400.
14 £100,000.   15 (a) 31; (b) 10; (c) 8.

DUBLIN, Co. Dublin

ARCHBISHOP MARSH'S LIBRARY, St Patrick's Close,
Dublin 8 (Tel 0001-753917) Keeper: Dr John Gerald Simms
MA, PHD, FTCD; Dep Keeper: Mr Cecil Robert James Bradley
MA.
6 Governors & Guardians of Marsh's Library.   8 Theology
& religious controversy; medicine; law; science; travel;
classical literature. 1st public library in Ireland (1707).
9 Library of Edward Stillingfleet (1635-1699, Bishop of
Worcester).   11 Open for research only.   12 Mon 14.00-
16.00, Wed-Fri 10.30-12.30, 14.00-16.00, Sat 10.30-12.30.
13 (a) 25,000.   14 £20.   15 (a) 3; (b) 2.

CHESTER BEATTY LIBRARY, *see* Museums section

INCORPORATED LAW SOCIETY OF IRELAND LIBRARY,
Solicitors Buildings, Four Courts, Dublin 7 (Tel 0001-784533)
Libn: Mr Colum Gavan Duffy MA, LLB, FLAI, solicitor;
Asst Libn: Miss Margaret Byrne BA, DipLibTr.
6 Council of Incorporated Law Society of Ireland.   8 All
aspects of law.   9 None (the old library was destroyed by
fire in 1922).   10 ICLS.   11 Open with Libn's permission
only.   12 Mon-Fri 9.00-17.30 (vac: closed 12.45-14.00).
13 (a) 10,000; (b) 25; (c) Irish unreported judgments.
14 £2,500.

INSTITUTE FOR INDUSTRIAL RESEARCH AND STANDARDS
LIBRARY, Technical Information Division, Ballymun Road,
Dublin 9 (Tel 0001-370101; Telex 5449) Dir: G. P. Sweeney,
FLA, AIInfSc; Libn: J. McCluskey, ALA.
8 Science & technology, excluding medicine & agriculture.

9 Complete BSI (housed separately).   11   .   12 Min-
Fri 9.15-13.00, 14.00-17.15.   13 (a) 24,000; (b) 850.
14 £35,000.

IRISH CENTRAL LIBRARY FOR STUDENTS, 53-4 Upper
Mount St, Dublin 2 (Tel 0001-761167/761963; Telex 5733)
Dir: Mr Tom Armitage BA, DLT, FLAI; Asst Libns: Ms
Therese Hall FLAI; Ms Mary Grogan FLAI.
6 Library Council.   8 Irish writers; Irish subjects;
librarianship.   9 Evie Hone donation (art, stained glass,
c. 2,000 vols); Dr Maguire donation (school texts, c. 3,000
vols); RCB donation (classics).   10 BLL; LASER; NWRLB;
most international co-ops.   11 Not open to public.
12 Mon-Fri 9.30-13.00, 14.15-17.00 (17.30 Mon).
13 (a) 60,000; (b) 179; (c) films on libraries.

NATIONAL LIBRARY OF IRELAND, Kildare St, Dublin 2
(Tel 0001-765521) Dir: Dr Patrick Henchy; Keeper of Printed
Books: Mr Alf MacLochlainn.
6 Council of Trustees.   8 All aspects of Irish studies.
9 Joly colln (Library's foundation colln, especially strong in
French material & music); Dix colln (Irish local printing);
Ormonde papers (mss of the Butlers, Earls of Ormonde, etc,
12th-19th cent).   10 Acts as Secretariat for Irish Association for Documentation & Information Services; edits IADIS
Union List of Serials.   11   .   12 Mon-Fri 10.00-22.00,
Sat 10.00-13.00.   13 (a) 500,000; (b) 1,000; (c) 40,000
numbered mss; many collns of mss in process.
14 £35,000.   15 (a) 56; (b) 17.

REPRESENTATIVE CHURCH BODY LIBRARY, Braemor
Park, Rathgar, Dublin 14 (Tel 0001-979979) Libn: Miss H. G.
Willis ALA.
6 Representative Body of the Church of Ireland.   8 Religion; theology; history; biography.   9 Mss relating to
Church of Ireland; biographical material about clergy of
Church of Ireland Watson Colln of prayer books.   10 BLL
(through ICLS).   11 Open for ref; members may borrow
12 Mon-Fri 10.00-13.00, 13.45-17.00.   13 (a) 21,000;
(b) 65; (c) archives (Church of Ireland).   15 (a) 2; (c) 1.

ROYAL COLLEGE OF SURGEONS IN IRELAND LIBRARY,
123 St Stephen's Green, Dublin 2 (Tel 0001-751254/758171)
Libn & Coll Historian: Dr J. B. Lyons FRCPI; Exec Libn:
Mrs K. M. Bishop BA.
6 Council of the Royal College of Surgeons in Ireland.
8 General medicine; surgery; obstetrics; related subjects.
9 Arthur Jacob library of 1876; Butcher Wheeler library;
William Doolin historical colln.   10 Inter-library loans;
ICLS; (Photocopies of material not available for loan supplied).
11 Not open to public.   12 Postgraduate Lib: Mon-Fri.
9.30-17.30; Undergraduate Reading Room: Mon-Fri 9.30-
22.00.   13 (a) Over 30,000; (b) 292; (c) medical pamphlets
(17th cent).   14 c. £3,500.   15 (a) 3; (b) 2.

ROYAL DUBLIN SOCIETY LIBRARY, Ballsbridge, Dublin 4
(Tel 0001-680645; Telex 4409 ALRTEI) Libn: Mr Alan Robert
Eager FLA, FLAI.
8 General scientific & technical library; periodical literature;
agriculture; fine arts; Irish colln.   9 Early agricultural
works; 17th cent printing; 18th cent science colln.   10 BLL;
ICLS.   11 Open for consultation by appointment.
12 10.00-19.00.   13 (a) 210,000; (b) 1,200; (c) microfilm.
15 (a) 12; (b) 2; (c) 1.

ROYAL IRISH ACADEMY LIBRARY, 19 Dawson St, Dublin 2.
(Tel 0001-762570) Libn: Mrs Brigid Dolan MA, DipLibTr;
Dep: Miss Maire Ni Dhomhnallain MA, DiPLibrTr.
8 Books of Irish interest (history, biography, archaeology,
linguistics & literature); periodicals in humanities & sciences
(inc maths & natural history).   9 Haliday pamphlets
(1682-1859), 2,209 vols; Haliday tracts (1578-1859), 536 boxes;
colln of early scientific books (1654-1850); library of Thomas

CODE: **1** Name of Library. **2** Address. **3** Telephone & Telex. **4** Officer in charge. **5** Deputy. **6** Governing body.
7 Branches. **8** Main Subjects. **9** Special Collections. **10** Co-operative Schemes. **11** Open to public? **12** Hours.
13 Stock: (a) books (b) periodicals (c) other. **14** Finance. **15** Staff: (a) non-manual (b) graduate (c) chartered librarians.

Moore. **10** ICLS. **11** Open on the recommendation of members. **12** Mon-Fri 9.30-17.30, Sat 9.30-13.00. Closed last 3 weeks in Aug. **13** (a) 32,500; (b) c.2,000; (c) 2,500 mss (inc 60 vellum mss); 31,075 vols pamphlets. **15** (a) 5; (b) 5; (c) 3.

ST PATRICK'S COLLEGE OF EDUCATION LIBRARY, Drumcondra, Dublin 9 (Tel 0001-376191) Chief Libn: Mr George Byrne.
8 General; education (especially primary); practical education & teaching practice (or curriculum) library. **9** Textbooks for special education (handicapped children, physical, mental, deprived, teaching of reading, etc). **10** BLL.
11 Not open to public. **12** Mon-Fri 10.00-22.00; Sat 10.00-12.30. **13** (a) c.38,000; (b) c.150; (c) films; film loops; tapes; slides; other audio-visual material & ausio-visual teaching laboratory. **15** (a) 6; (b) 3; (c) 1.

TRINITY COLLEGE LIBRARY, College St, Dublin 2 (Tel 0001-772941; Telex 5442) College Libn & Archivist: Mr Peter Brown MA; Dep: Mr Sean Phillips BA, DipLibStud.
7 Dept of Mss, Keeper: Mr W. O'Sullivan MA; Dept of Older Printed Books, Sub-Libn: Miss M. Pollard MA, FLA.
8 British & Irish copyright library, all subjects covered; university library. **9** Large collns of mss & older printed books. **10** BLL, ICLS. **11** Open only to researchers for works not obtainable elsewhere. **12** Oct-June: term 9.30-22.30, vac 10.00-22.30; July-Sept: 10.00-17.00. **13** (a) 1,500,000; (b) 6,372; (c) archives (large colln). **14** £95,000 (plus Belfield, British & Irish copyright acquisitions). **15** (a) 113; (b) 45; (c) 23.

UNIVERSITY COLLEGE, DUBLIN, LIBRARY, Dublin 4 (Tel 0001-693244; Telex 4114) Libn: Mr Henry J. Heaney, MA, FLA; Dep Libn: Miss Mary E. Semple BA, DipLib, ALA.
7 Science Lib, Belfield (0001-693244), Sub-Libn: Miss E. Glynn MA, DipLib; Medical Lib, Earlsfort Terrace, Dublin 2 (0001-752116), Sub Libn: Miss S. Nevin BSc, DipLib; Engineering Lib, Upper Merrion St, Dublin 2 (0001-761584), Sub Libn: Miss U. Lavelle BA, DipLib; Agriculture Lib, Ballymun Rd, Glasnevin, Dublin 9 (0001-373631); Veterinary Lib, Hume House, Ballsbridge, Dublin 4, Sub Libn: Miss M. Hayes BComm, DipLib; Architecture Lib, Earlsfort Terrace, Dublin 2 (0001-752116), Asst Libn in charge: Mrs M. Kelly BA, DipLib. **8** General **9** Zimmer colln (Celtic philology); O Lochlainn & O'Kelly collns (early & modern Irish printing); Baron Palles colln (legal literature); C.P.Curran colln (Joyceana); colln of Newmaniana; deposit library for US Atomic Energy Commission. **10** ICLS; IADIS; Union Catalogue of Periodicals in Irish Libraries. **11** Open for ref only. **12** 9.30-22.30. **13** (a) 666,600; (b) 5,500; (c) gramophone records; microtexts; mss; slides; tapes. **14** £220,000. **15** (a) 49; (b) 47; (c) 39.

WORTH LIBRARY, Steevens' Hospital, Steevens' Lane, Dublin 8 (Tel 0001-772606) Keeper: Very Rev Dr Victor G. Griffin MA, DTh; Dep: J.B.Prenderville FRCSI.
6 Governors of Dr Steevens' Hospital. **8** Medicine; some interesting editions of the classics; fine bindings. **11** Not open, except by special arrangement, for research only. **13** (a) 4,500.

GALWAY, Co. Galway

UNIVERSITY COLLEGE, GALWAY, LIBRARY, Galway (Tel 091-7611; Telex 33203 UNIG E1) Libn: Mr Christopher J. Townley BA, BComm.
8 General; arts; science; medicine; law; commerce; engineering; agriculture (partly). **9** Aims to collect all works published in the Irish language; mss colln of Douglas Hyde; local newspapers. **10** BLL; ICLS. **11** Open mainly for ref. **12** Term: Mon-Fri 9.00-11.00, Sat 9.00-18.00, Sun 10.00-18.00. **13** (a) 130,000; (b) 1,400; (c) c.100 items microfilm; mss. **14** c.£80,000. **15** (a) 29; (b) 9; (c) 7.

KILKEE, Co. Clare

DOCTOR SWEENEY MEMORIAL LIBRARY, O'Connell St, Kilkee (Tel 008413-34) Libn: Miss Mary Teresa Hynes.
6 Commissioners of Charitable Bequests & Donations.
8 History; travel; arts; crafts; sociology; nature study; literature; religion; applied sciences; recreation; politics.
9 Local mss (from 1800's); local history; Begley's Irish-English Dictionary (compiled by a Co. Clare man, published in Paris in 1732). **11** . **12** Mon-Fri 9.30-12.30, 13.30-17.00. **13** (a) 8,400; (c) periodicals & newspapers. **14** £1,490.

KILKENNY, Co. Kilkenny

OSSORY DIOCESAN LIBRARY, St Canices Library, Kilkenny (Tel 056-21633).
8 Theology (17th & 18th cent). **11** Open for ref only. **12** Open by arrangement. **13** (a) c.2,000.

MAYNOOTH, Co. Kildare

ST PATRICK'S COLLEGE LIBRARY, Maynooth (Tel 0001-286261) Dep Libn: Mrs Mary Connolly BA, ALA.
8 Theology; philosophy; classics; English; French; German; Celtic studies; geography; maths; chemistry; physics; biology. **9** O'Curry mss; Irish mss. **11** **12** Term: Mon-Sat 9.00-21.30, Sun 14.00-21.30; vac: Mon-Fri 10.00-17.00. **13** (a) c.100,000. **15** (a) 6; (b) 3; (c) 2.

MUSEUMS, ART GALLERIES AND STATELY HOMES

DUBLIN, Co. Dublin

CHESTER BEATTY LIBRARY AND GALLERY OF ORIENTAL
ART, 20 Shrewsbury Rd, Dublin 4 (Tel 0001-692386).
4 Chester Beatty Library Trustees.   **5** Libn: Dr Patrick
Henchy LLD; Dep: Mr David L. James MA.   **9** Mon-Fri
10.00-13.00, 14.30-17.00.   **10** Arabic & Islamic mss;
Islamic, Indian & Far Eastern Art; Armenian & Ethiopian
paintings; Islamic & Far Eastern art; Armenian & Ethiopian
of Persian & Indian Moghul paintings in Europe; Arabic
mss; biblical papyri; photos, slides & microfilms on request

DUBLIN CIVIC MUSEUM, 58 South William St, Dublin 2.
4 Corporation of Dublin.   **5** Acting Curator: Miss Maura
Tallon FLAI.   **6** Cultural.   **7** Public Libraries Dept,
City of County Libn: Miss Mairin O'Byrne DipLib, FLAI.
8 Open to the public.   **9** Tues-Sat 10.00-18.00, Sun &
bank hols 11.00-14.00. Free.   **10** History of Dublin.
12 (a) 1 (c) 2.

GUINNESS MUSEUM, Arthur Guinness Son & Co (Dublin) Ltd.
St James's Gate, Dublin 8 (Tel 0001-756701).   **5** Curator:
Mr R. H. Sheil MA, MITO, MIITM.   **8** Open to the public.
9 Mon-Fri 10.00-16.00. Free.   **10** Brewing & allied
trades in Ireland.   **11** Coopers' tools; transport; bottles;
labels; advertising.   **12** (a) 1 (b) 1.

HUGH LANE MUNICIPAL GALLERY OF MODERN ART,
Charlemont House, Parnell Sq, Dublin 1 (Tel 0001-741903).
4 Dublin Corporation.   **5** Curator: Ethna Waldron.
8 Open to the public.   **9** Tues-Sat 10.00-18.00, Sun 11.00-
14.00. Free.   **10** Modern paintings & sculpture of
Irish & European schools.   **11** Frequent temporary
exhibitions; Lane colln (19th cent French); stained glass
room.   **12** (a) 1 (b) 1 (c) 6.

MUSEUM OF BIBLICAL ANTIQUITIES, East Chapel, Trinity
College, Dublin 2 (Tel 0001-772914 ext 448).   **4** University
of Dublin.   **5** Dir: Prof J. Weingreen.   **8** Open to the
public.   **9** Open by appointment only. Free.   **10** Mainly
pottery objects from various archaeological sites in Israel
& Jordan (biblical & post-biblical periods); background
display of Babylonian & Egyptian objects of these periods.
11 Israelite royal stamped jar handles from Lachish (7th
cent BC); Punic monkey jug (6th cent BC); sequence of lamps
from 2000 BC to Byzantine period; casts of the Lachish
Ivories & the Gezer Calendar; Egyptian figurines, scarabs,
beads & canopic jars.

NATIONAL GALLERY OF IRELAND, Merrion Sq, Dublin 2
(Tel 0001-767571).   **4** Board of Governors & Guardians.
5 Dir: Dr James White LLD.   **8** Open to the public.
9 Mon-Sat (inc bank hols) 10.00-18.00 (21.00 Thurs), Sun
14.00-17.00. Free.   **10** All European & American
schools of painting (1300-1900).   **11** Temporary exhibitions; art reference library; lecture theatre; sales shop;
restaurant.   **12** (a) 10 (b) 6 (c) 32.

NATIONAL MUSEUM OF IRELAND, Kildare St, Dublin 2
(Tel 0001-765521).   **4** Dept of Education.   **5** Dir: Dr
A. T. Lucas MA, DLitt.   **8** Open to the public.   **9** Tues-
Fri (& bank hols) 10.00-17.00, Sun 14.00-17.00. Free.
10 National collns of antiquities, fine arts (exc painting
& sculpture), history, folk life, zoology & geology.
11 Prehistoric gold ornaments; early Christian period:
Ardagh Chalice, Tara Brooch, shrines & other art metalwork.   **12** (a) 17 (b) 10 (c) 52.

DUN LAOGHAIRE, Co. Dublin

JAMES JOYCE TOWER, Moran Park, Sandycove, Dun
Laoghaire (Tel 0001-809265; Telex 4846).   **4** Eastern
Regional Tourism Organisation Ltd.   **5** Officer-in-Charge:

Mr P. J. Long MEcon.   **8** Open to the public.   **9** May-
Sept: Mon-Sat (inc bank hols) 10.00-13.00, 14.00-17.15, Sun
14.30-18.00. Adults 15p, students 10p, children 5p.
10 Mainly personal belongings & photographs of James
Joyce.   **11** Copies of correspondence, clothing, etc.

GORT, Co. Galway

THOOR BALLYLEE (YEATS'S TOWER), Ballylee, Gort,
(Tel 008568-8)   **4** Western Regional Tourism Organization, Aras Failte, Victoria Place, Galway.   **5** Curator:
Miss M. Frances MacNally.   **8** Open to the public.
9 March-Oct: daily (inc bank hols) 10.00-18.00 (July &
Aug 21.00). Adults 25p, students & large groups 15p, children
10p & 5p.   **10** W. B. Yeats; also Lady Gregory of Coole
Park & Edward Martyn of Tullira Castle.   **11** 1st editions
of Yeats; Dun Emer embroideries; Elkin Mathews broadsheets; lectures & talks on the poet; sound guides in English,
French, German & Spanish; tea rooms & car-parks.
12 (a) 1 (b) 6.

KILKENNY, Co. Kilkenny

ROTHE HOUSE MUSEUM, Parliament St, Kilkenny (Tel 056-
22893).   **4** Kilkenny Archaeological Society.   **5** Hon
Curator: Mrs Sheila M. Lane.   **8** Open to the public.
9 Adults 30p, students 15p, children 5p; group rates.
10 Restored Elizabethan merchant's town house; period
furniture; archaeological & historical material; original
courtyard & well.

KILLARNEY, Co. Kerry

MUCKROSS HOUSE, Killarney, (Tel 064-31440).   **4** Trustees
of Muckross House (Killarney) Ltd.   **5** Manager: Mr
Edmond F. Myers BA.   **8** Open to the public.   **9** Easter-
Oct: daily 10.00-19.00; Nov-Easter: Tues-Sun 11.00-17.00.
Adults 35p, children 15p.   **10** 19th cent manor; natural
& social history of Co. Kerry; folk life; period furniture,
prints, maps etc.   **11** 4 craft-workers; refreshment room;
craft shop.   **12** (a) 1 (b) 8 (c) 9.

MONAGHAN, Co. Monaghan

MONAGHAN COUNTY MUSEUM, The Courthouse, Monaghan
(Tel 008518-82211).   **4** Monaghan CC.   **5** Curator:
Mr Aidan Walsh BA.   **7** County Manager.   **8** Open to the
public.   **9** Tues-Sat 10.00-13.00, 14.00-17.00. Free.
10 Archaeology; folk life; local history; industrial
archaeology. (For the future: natural history, costume,
paintings & prints of local interest).   **11** 14th cent metal-
plated wooden altar-cross known as Cross of Clogher; selection of prehistoric & historic archaeological material lent by
National Museum of Ireland, Dublin.   **12** (a) 1 (b) 1 (c) 1.

STRADBALLY, Co. Laois

IRISH STEAM PRESERVATION MUSEUM, Stradbally
(Tel 0502-25136).   **4** Irish Steam Preservation Society
Ltd.   **8** Open to the public.   **9** Open all year, by
appointment only. Charges: 25p.   **10** Items of the steam
era.   **11** Steam traction engines, rollers & models.

WATERFORD, Co. Waterford

REGINALD'S TOWER MUSEUM, The Quay, Waterford.
4 Waterford Corporation.   **5** Curator: Mrs June Glosten.
8 Open to the public.   **9** Mon-Fri (inc bank hols) 10.00-
18.00, Sat 10.00-12.30. Adults 10p, children free.   **10** City
charters; Danish relics.

WATERFORD ART GALLERY, 5 O'Connell St, Waterford
(Tel 0051-4233).   **4** Waterford Corporation.   **6** Waterford Art Advisory Committee.   **8** Open to the public.
9 Mon-Fri 13.00-17.30, 19.00-21.00, Sat 11.00-13.00,
14.30-17.30. Free.   **10** Paintings & sculpture.

INDEX

This is a combined index for all five sections of the book. It includes general subjects, special collections and the names of individual institutions, all shown in capital letters. The entries under these headings are listed alphabetically by town within each section, and the sections follow the order of the text: British Library, Public Libraries, Special Libraries, Museums. The sections are indicated by the letters BL, P, S and M immediately preceding or following the name of the town. Entries from the Republic of Ireland have been integrated into these sections for the purposes of indexing and are differentiated by the word Eire appearing after the name of the town; in the text, Ireland follows the Museums section. Special collections are indexed both under the name of the collection and, where possible, under subject. Very broad subjects included in most libraries and museums, such as archives, local history, manuscripts etc, have not been indexed. The normal academic subjects of educational institutions (ie economics, English, French, geography, German, history, Italian, mathematics, science and sociology) have not been indexed unless a special collection or department was mentioned in the entry.

Abbreviations used in the index are listed below:

Acad - Academy	Coll - College	Gall - Gallery	Mem - Memorial
Agric - Agriculture	Colln - Collection	Geo - Geology	Mil - Military
Anthrop - Anthropology	Comm - Commerce	Govt - Government	Min - Ministry
Antiq - Antiquities	Confed - Confederation	GWR - Great Western Railway	Mss - Manuscripts
Arch - Archaeology	C'wealth - Commonwealth	HE - Higher Education	Mus - Museum
Assoc - Association	Dept - Department	Hist - History	Nat - National
Astron - Astronomy	Dev - Development	Ho - House	P - Public Libraries Section
Auth - Authority	Dist - District	Horti - Horticulture	PE - Physical Education
BC - Borough Council	Div - Division	Hosp - Hospital	Poly - Polytechnic
Bio - Biology	Ed - Education	Indust - Industry /Industrial	Ref - Reference
BL - British Library Section	Eng - Engineering	Inf - Information	Reg - Regiment
Bld - Building	Est - Establishemnt	Inst - Institute /Institution	S - Special Libraries Section
Brit - British	Fac - Faculty	Int - International	Soc - Society
Cath - Cathedral	FE - Further Education	Lab - Laboratory	Stat - Station
Co - County /Company	Fed - Federation	Lib - Library	Tech - Technical /Technology
		M - Museums Section	Univ - University
		Med - Medical	

ABBEYDALE INDUSTRIAL
  HAMLET: Sheffield M
ABBEY HOUSE MUSEUM:
  Leeds M
ABBEY MUSEUM: Arbroath M
ABBOT COLLN (English lit)
S Norwich: Univ of East Anglia
ABBOT HALL ART GALLERY:
  Kendal M
ABBOTSFORD HOUSE:
  Melrose M
ABBOTT, LEMUEL
M London: Lloyd's Nelson colln
ABINGTON MUSEUM:
  Northampton M
ABRAHAM COLLN (Hebrew)
S Cambridge: C Univ, Oriental
ACCOUNTANCY
S Aberdeen: A Coll of Comm
S Bristol: B Poly
S Coventry: Lanchester Poly
S Darlington: D Tech Coll
S Dundee: D Coll of Tech
S Edinburgh: Inst of Chartered
    Accountants
S Glasgow: Central Coll of Comm
S   Inst of Chartered
    Accountants
S Hornchurch: Havering Tech
S Leeds: L Poly
S Liverpool: L Poly
S London: Anbar Tear Sheet
S   Association of Cert
    Accountants
S   British Inst of Management
S   Hammersmith & West L
S   Havering Tech Coll
S   Institute of Chartered
    Accountants
S   Institute of Chartered Secs
S   Institute of Cost &
    Management
S   Middlesex Poly
S   Poly of South Bank
S   South West L Coll
S   Thames Poly
S Wednesbury: W Bromwich
    Coll of Comm
S Worthing: W Coll of FE
ACTON LIBRARY (history)
S Cambridge: C Univ, Univ Lib
ACTON SCOTT WORKING
  FARM: Church Stretton M
ACTON TECHNICAL COLLEGE:
  London S
ACTUARIES, FACULTY OF:
  Edinburgh S
ACTUARIES, INSTITUTE OF:
  London S
ADAM, ROBERT
M Buscot Park: Buscot
M Derby: Kedleston Hall
M Edinburgh: Charlotte Square
M   Scottish Arts Council
M Gordon: Mellerstain

M Harewood: H House
M Kirkoswald: Culzean Castle
M London: Iveagh Bequest
M   Osterley Park
M   Sir John Soane's Mus
M   Syon House
M Nostell: N Priory
M South Queensferry:
    Hopetoun House
ADAMSON, ROBERT
M Edinburgh: Scottish Nat
    Portrait Gallery
ADAMSTON AGRICULTURAL
  MUSEUM: Huntly M
ADASTRAL HOUSE
S London: Ministry of Defence
ADDENBROOKE, JOHN
S Cambridge: C Univ Colls,
    St Catherine's
ADHESIVES
S London: Coates Bros
S   3M Lib
S   Vinyl Products
S Stevenage: Furniture Indust
ADULT EDUCATION,
  NAT INST OF: London S
ADVERTISING
S London: Advertising Assoc
S   Coll for Distrib Trades
S   J. Walter Thompson
S   Times Newspapers Ltd
S Middlesbrough:
    Teesside Coll of Art
S Rochdale: R Tech
    see also BUSINESS;
    MARKETING
ADVERTISING ASSOCIATION:
  London S
ADVOCATES LIBRARY:
  Edinburgh S
AERONAUTICAL RESEARCH
  COUNCIL: London S
AERONAUTICS, see
  AIRCRAFT; AVIATION;
  ENGINEERING, AERO
AFRICA
BL Ref Div, Dept of Oriental Mss
S Birmingham: B Univ
S   Cadbury Schweppes
S Brighton: Univ of Sussex
S Cambridge: C Univ,
    African Studies
S Canterbury: Univ of Kent
S Edinburgh: E Univ
S Exeter: E Univ
S Liverpool: Univ of L
S London: Commonwealth Inst
S   Mus of Mankind
S   Royal Inst of Int Affairs
S   United Soc for Propagation
    of Gospel
S   Univ of L, Inst of
    Commonwealth
S   Univ of L Colls, King's
    School of Oriental

S Oxford: O Univ,
    Commonwealth Studies
M Birchington: Powell-Cotton Mus
M Nairn: N Literary Inst
AFRIKAANS
S Oxford: O Univ, Taylor Inst
AGRICULTURAL ECONOMICS
  INSTITUTE
S Oxford: O Univ
AGRICULTURAL HISTORY,
  INSTITUTE OF
M Reading: R Univ
AGRICULTURAL RESEARCH
  COUNCIL, MEAT
  RESEARCH: Bristol S
AGRICULTURE &
  HORTICULTURE
P Hereford & Worcester
P Lincolnshire
P Wiltshire
S Aberdeen: A Univ
S   Macaulay Inst
    Rowett Research Inst
S Aberystwyth: Univ Coll
S   Welsh Plant Breeding Stat
S Bangor: Univ Coll
S Bedford: Mander Coll
S   Nat Inst of Agric Eng
S Belfast: Queen's Univ
S Bracknell: ICI
S Bristol: Long Ashton
S Cambridge: C Univ,
S   Applied Bio Dept
S   Clinical Vet Med Dept
S   Land Econ Dept
S   Nat Inst of Agric Botany
S Dublin, Eire: Royal D Soc
S   Univ Coll
S Dundee: Scottish Horti Inst
S East Malling: E M Research
S Edinburgh: Royal Bot Garden
S   Scottish Office
S Galway, Eire: Univ Coll
S Ipswich: Fisons Ltd
S Littlehampton:
    Glasshouse Crops
S London: Centre for Overseas
    Pest Research
S   Ministry of Agric
S   Nat Farmers' Union
S   Royal Botanic Gardens
S   Royal Horti Soc
S   Royal Inst of Chartered
    Surveyors
S   Tropical Products Inst
S   United Nations Inf Centre
S Newcastle upon Tyne:
    NuT Univ
S Norwich: John Innes Inst
S Nottingham: Boots Co
S   N Univ
S Oxford: Co-op Ref Lib
S   O Univ, Agric Econ Inst
S Reading: Nat Inst for Research
    in Dairying

S Saffron Walden: Fisons
S Southampton: Univ of S
S Wellesbourne: Nat Veg Stat
S Wisbech: Isle of Ely Coll of FE
S Wolverhampton: W Tech
    Teachers Coll
M Aberystwyth: Ceredigion Mus
M Alford: Manor House Folk
M Arreton: A Manor
M Aston Munslow: White House
M Aylesbury: Bucks Co Mus
M Bakewell: Old House Mus
M Barrow in Furness: F Mus
M Beamish: B Mus
M Birmingham: Sarehole Mill
M Breamore: B Countryside Mus
M Bristol: Blaise Castle
M Budleigh Salterton: Bicton
M Cardiff: Welsh Folk Mus
M Ceres: Fife Folk Mus
M Christchurch: Red House Mus
M Church Stretton: Acton Scott
M Colchester: Hollytrees
M Comrie: C Mus
M Derby: Elvaston Castle
M Dodington: D House
M Dunbeath: Lhaidhay Croft Mus
M Dursley: Lister Mus
M Edinburgh: Nat Mus of Antiq
M Evesham: Almonry Mus
M Farnham: F Mus
M Glencoe: G & N Lorn Folk Mus
M Grays: Thurrock Local Hist
M Gressenhall: Norfolk Rural Life
M Hailsham: Michelham Priory
M Halifax: Shibden Hall Folk
M Helston: H Mus
M Huntly: Adamston Agric
M Kendal: Lakeland Life
M Kingsbridge: Cookworthy Mus
M Lacock: Lackham Agric Mus
M Leicester: Belgrave Hall
M Lincoln: Mus of Lincs Life
M Maidstone:
    Boughton Monchelsea
M Millom: M Folk Mus
M Morwellham: M Centre
M Nairn: N Literary Inst
M Nottingham: N Indust Mus
M Nuneaton: Cadeby Railway
M Oakham: Rutland Co Mus
M Pickering: Beck Isle Mus
M Reading: R Univ,
    Inst of Agric
M St Helier: Mus & Art Gallery
M St Neots: Longsands Mus
M Shaftesbury: Local Hist Mus
M Sherborne: S Mus
M Shugborough: Staffs Life
M South Molton: S M Mus
M Stowmarket: E Anglian Life
M Stranraer: Wigton Dist Mus
M Tilford: Old Kiln Agric
M Tiverton: T Mus
M Welshpool: Powysland Mus

C

C

D

E

EAST LANCASHIRE RAILWAY PRESERVATION SOCIETY:
M Bury: B Transport Mus
EAST LANCASHIRE REGIMENTAL MUSEUM
M Blackburn: B Mus
EASTNEY PUMPING STATION & GAS ENGINE HOUSE: Portsmouth M
EASTNOR CASTLE: Ledbury M
EAST OF SCOTLAND COLLEGE OF AGRICULTURE
S Edinburgh: E School of Agric
EAST SURREY REGIMENT
M London: Queen's Royal Surrey Reg Mus
EAST YORKSHIRE REGIMENT MUSEUM: Beverley M
EATON HALL COLLEGE OF EDUCATION: Retford S
ECHOES OF CHILDHOOD MUSEUM:
M Arreton: A Manor
ECOLOGY, see ENVIRONMENTAL STUDIES
ECONOMICS
S Belfast: Parliament Blds Lib
S London: Bank of Eng Lib
S Confed of Brit Indust
S Consumers' Assoc
S Dept of Industry
S Dept of Inland Revenue
S Goethe Institut
S Institute of Actuaries
S Institute of Chartered Secs
S Institute of Cost & Management Accounts
S Labour Party Lib
S Marx Mem Lib
S Nat Inst of Economics
S Polish Lib
S Reckitt & Coleman
S Royal Inst of Int Affairs
S Shell Int
S United Nations
S Univ of L, Univ Lib
S Univ of L Colls, LSE
S Manchester: Co-op Union
EDGE HILL COLLEGE: Ormskirk S
EDGEWORTH, MARIA
S Birmingham: B Univ
EDINGTON COLLN (engravings)
P North Tyneside
EDUCATION
P London, Lewisham
P Midlothian
S Basildon: B Coll of FE
S Bath: B Univ
S Belfast: Parliament Blds Lib
S Queen's Univ
S Birmingham: City of B Poly
S Bradford: B Coll
S Brighton: B Poly
S Bristol: B Univ
S Brunel Tech Coll
S Filton Tech Coll
S Redland Coll
S Cambridge: C Univ Colls,
S   Girton
S   Hughes Hall
S Cardiff: Univ Coll
S Chatham: Medway & Maidstone Coll
S Chesterfield: C Coll of Art
S Coleraine: New Univ
S Darlington: D Coll of Tech
S Derby: Bishop Lonsdale Coll
S Eastbourne: Chelsea Coll
S Edinburgh: Dunfermline Coll
S Educational Inst
S Scottish Office
S Egham: Shoreditch Coll
S Ewell: E Co Tech Coll
S Glasgow: Cardonald Coll
S Langside Coll of FE
S Grays: Thurrock Tech
S Harlow: H Tech Coll
S Hatfield: H Poly
S Hornchurch: Havering Tech
S Leeds: City of L & Carnegie
S L Poly
S L Univ
S Trinity & All Saints' Coll
S Leicester: L Univ
S Letchworth: Coll of Tech
S Lincoln: Bishop Grosseteste
S Liverpool: St Katharine's
S Univ of L
S London: Acton Tech Coll
S Assoc of C'wealth Univs
S Borough Rd Coll
S Brit Council
S City Literary Inst
S Coll of All Saints
S C'wealth Inst
S C'wealth Secretariat
S Confed of Brit Indust
S Furzedown Coll
S Garnett Coll
S Goethe Institut
S Havering Tech Coll
S Inner L Ed Authority
S Institute of Personnel Management
S International Planned Parenthood
S Isleworth Poly
S Kilburn Poly
S Maria Grey Coll
S Middlesex Poly
S Nat Inst of Adult Ed
S Nat Union of Teachers
S Poly of Central L
S St Mary's Coll
S Southgate Tech Coll
S Univ of L, Univ Lib
S   Inst of Ed
S Univ of L Colls, King's
S Wandsworth Tech
S Willesden Coll
S Loughborough: L Univ
S Manchester: M Ed Committee
S Newport: Gwent Coll
S Northampton: Nene Coll
S Nottingham: N Univ
S Ormskirk: Edge Hill Coll
S Oxford: O Poly
S O Univ, Ed Studies Dept
S O Univ Colls, Westminster
S Plymouth: P Coll of Art
S Redruth: Cornwall Tech
S Southampton: Univ of S
S Sunderland: S Poly
S Swansea: Univ Coll
S Wakefield: W Coll of Tech
S Warrington: Padgate Coll
S Wigan: W Coll of Tech
S Wisbech: Isle of Ely Coll
S Wolverhampton: W Tech Coll
S Workington: W Cumbria Coll
S Wrexham: NE Wales Inst
S York: Coll of Ripon & York
M Leeds: L Univ, Mus of Hist of Ed
  see also COLLEGES OF EDUCATION
EDUCATION, SPECIAL
S Bristol: Redland Coll
S Dublin, Eire: St Patrick's
S Edinburgh: E Ed Inst
S Leeds: L Poly
S London: Havering Tech
  see also SPEECH THERAPY
EDWARDS, AMELIA B.
S Oxford: O Univ Colls, Somerville
EDWARDS, BETHAN
P East Sussex
EEC, see EUROPEAN ECONOMIC COMMUNITY
EGYPTOLOGY
S Aberystwyth: Nat Lib of Wales
S Cambridge: C Univ, Oriental
S Durham: D Univ
S London: Univ of L Colls, Univ
S Oxford: O Univ, Ashmolean
S O Univ Colls, Queen's
M Aberdeen: A Univ, Anthrop
M Blackburn: B Mus
M Bolton: Central Mus
M Bristol: City of B Mus
M Cambridge: C Univ, Fitzwilliam
M Camarthen: Co Mus
M Cheltenham: C BC Art Gall
M Chiddingstone: C Castle
M Dublin, Eire: Mus of Biblical Antiquities
M Edinburgh: Royal Scottish
M Leicester: L Mus & Art Gall
M London: Brit Mus
M Sir John Soane's Mus
M Univ of L Colls, Univ
M Macclesfield: M Mus
M Newcastle upon Tyne: NuT Univ, Hancock Mus
M Oxford: O Univ, Ashmolean
M Reading: R Univ, Mus of Greek Arch
M Rochdale: R Mus
M St Helens: St H Mus
M Windsor: Eton Coll, Myers Mus
  see also ISLAM; MIDDLE EAST
ELECTRICAL ENGINEERING, see ENGINEERING, ELECTRICAL
ELECTRICITY
S Leatherhead: Central Electricity Generating
S London: Central Electricity Generating
S Electricity Council
S Univ of L Colls, King's
M Looe: Cornish Mus
M Manchester: North Western
M Morwhellam: M Centre
M Newcastle upon Tyne: Mus of Science
M Sticklepath: Finch Foundry
ELECTRICITY COUNCIL: London S
ELECTRONIC ENGINEERING, see ENGINEERING, ELECTRICAL
ELGIN MARBLES
M London: Brit Mus
EL GRECO
M Barnard Castle: Bowes Mus
ELIOT, GEORGE
P Coventry
P Warwickshire
M Nuneaton: Mus & Art Gall
ELIOT, T.S.
S Cambridge: C Univ Colls, King's
ELIZABETHAN HOUSE: Plymouth M
ELIZABETHAN HOUSE: Totnes M
ELIZABETHAN HOUSE MUSEUM: Great Yarmouth M
ELIZABETH GASKELL COLLEGE OF EDUCATION: Manchester S
ELLEN TERRY MEMORIAL MUSEUM: Tenterden M
ELLIOT COLLN (theology)
P East Sussex
ELLIS, RICHARD (mss)
S Aberystwyth: Univ Coll
ELSTOW MOOT HALL: Bedford M
ELVASTON CASTLE COUNTRYSIDE PARK MUSEUM: Derby M
ELWELL FAMILY
M Beverley: B Mus
EMBROIDERY, see NEEDLEWORK
EMERSON, PETER, COLLN
P Norfolk
EMMANUEL COLLEGE: Cambridge, C Univ Colls S
ENAMELS
M Cambridge: C Univ, Fitzwilliam Mus
M Luton: Wernher Colln
M Wolverhampton: Bantock Ho
M Bilston Mus
ENDSLEIGH COLLEGE OF FURTHER EDUCATION: Kingston upon Hull S
ENERGY, see DEPT OF ENERGY; ELECTRICITY; GAS; NUCLEAR FUEL; PETROLEUM
ENGINEERING
BL Ref Div, Science Ref Lib
S Banbury: Alcan
S Bradford: Univ of B
S Bristol: B Univ
S Imperial Tobacco
S Cambridge: C Univ,
S   Engineering Fac
S   C Univ Colls,
S   Girton
S Chatham: Royal Eng Corp
S Chester: C Coll of FE
S Cinderford: W Glos Coll
S Coventry: Lanchester Poly
S Cranwell: RAF Coll
S Dartmouth: Brit Royal Naval
S Dublin: Univ Coll
S Dundee: Univ of D
S Edinburgh: Heriot Watt Univ
S Property Services Agency
S Telford Coll of FE
S Exeter: E Coll
S Gateshead: Clarke Chapman
S Galway, Eire: Univ Coll
S Glasgow: Barmulloch Coll
S Cardonald Coll
S G Univ
S Langside Coll of FE
S Nat Engineering Lab
S Stow Coll
S Halifax: Percival Whitley
S Harwell: Atomic Energy Est
S Ilkeston: SE Derbyshire
S Leicester: L Univ
S Liverpool: Univ of L
S London: Brit Broadcasting
S Central School of Art
S City Univ
S Consumers' Assoc
S Hackney Coll
S Poly of Central L
S Univ of L Colls, School of Pharmacy
S Macclesfield: M Coll of FE
S Oxford: O Univ, Eng Fac
S Rotherham: Brit Steel
S Stafford: S Coll of FE
S Thurso: Dounreay Reactor
S Wolverhampton: Guest Keen
S Worsley: W Coll of FE
S Worthing: W Coll of FE
S Wrexham: NE Wales Inst
S Writtle: W Agric Coll
M Birmingham: City of B Mus
M Dursley: Lister Mus
M Leeds: Mus of Ind & Science
M Manchester: North Western
M Nottingham: N Indust Mus
  see also COLLEGES OF TECHNOLOGY; INDUST ARCHAEOLOGY; POLYS; TECHNOLOGY
ENGINEERING, AERONAUTICAL
S Bedford: Aircraft Research
S Cranwell: RAF Coll
S Derby: Rolls Royce
S Farnborough: Royal Aircraft
S Hatfield: H Poly
S London: Aero Research
S Brit Airways
S Brit Interplanetary Soc
S Min of Defence
S Plymouth: Royal Naval Eng
S St Albans: St A Coll of FE
S Southampton: Univ of S
S Stockport: S Coll of Tech
  see also AIRCRAFT; AVIATION
ENGINEERING, AGRICULTURAL
S Bedford: Nat Coll of Agric Eng
S Nat Inst of Agric Eng
S York: Askham Bryan Coll
  see also AGRICULTURE; COLLEGES OF AGRIC
ENGINEERING, AUTOMOTIVE
S Birmingham: Austin Morris
S Bradford: Hepworth & Grandage
S Bromsgrove: B Coll of FE
S Cinderford: W Glos Coll of FE
S Cleckheaton: BBA
S Darlaston: Rubery Owen
S Edinburgh: Stevenson Coll
S London: Hackney Coll
S Paddington Coll
S Sheffield: Granville Coll
  see also MOTOR VEHICLES
ENGINEERING, CHEMICAL
S Belfast: Min of Commerce
S Cambridge: C Univ, Chem Eng
S Chester: Brit Nuclear Fuels
S Colchester: Univ of Essex
S Harwell: Atomic Energy Est
S Ipswich: Fisons
S London: CIDEC
S Poly of S Bank
S Nottingham: Boots Co
S Stockport: Simon Eng Ltd
  see also CHEMISTRY
ENGINEERING, CIVIL
S Borehamwood: John Laing
S Coventry: Lanchester Poly
S Edinburgh: Property Services
S Scottish Office
S Leeds: Yorks Water Auth
S Liverpool: L Poly
S London: Greater L Council
S Institution of Civil Engs
S Thames Poly
S Wimpey Labs
S Newcastle upon Tyne: Northumbrian Water Auth
S Paisley: P Coll
S Pontypridd: Poly of Wales
S Reading: R Coll of Tech
S Sheffield: Shirecliffe Coll
S Stockport: Simon Eng Ltd
ENGINEERING, ELECTRICAL
S Bedford: Aircraft Research
S Birmingham: Tube Investments
S Bracknell: B Coll of FE
S Brighton: ITT
S Chester: Brit Nuclear Fuels
S Colchester: Univ of Essex
S Cranwell: RAF Coll
S Edinburgh: Ferranti
S Royal Observatory
S Stevenson Coll
S Farnborough: Royal Aircraft
S Harlow: Std Telecomm

E

S Leicester: English Electric Co
S London: Barnet Coll
S   BICC Research
S   Brit Interplanetary Soc
S   Central Elec Generating
S   CIDEC
S   Hackney Coll
S   Indep Broadcasting Auth
S   Institution of Elec Engs
S   Institution of Electronic
    & Radio Engineers
S   Isleworth Poly
S   Min of Defence
S Lowestoft: L Coll of FE
S Newcastle upon Tyne:
    Int Research
S Oxford: O Coll of FE
S Plymouth: Royal Naval Eng
S Sheffield: Granville Coll
S Winchester: IBM
S Workington: West Cumbria Coll
S Worthing: W Coll of FE
ENGINEERING, FOUNDRY
S Chesterfield: C Coll of Art
S Falkirk: F Coll of Tech
S Ilkeston: SE Derbyshire Coll
S Rugby: Assoc Engineering
S Wednesbury: West Bromwich
ENGINEERING, HEATING &
   VENTILATING, see HEATING
ENGINEERING, MARINE
P Sunderland
P Wirral
S Glasgow: Anniesland Coll
S Hebburn: H Tech Coll
S Liverpool: L Poly
S London: CIDEC
S   Hackney Coll
S   Nat Physical Lab
S   Royal Inst of Naval
    Architects
S Newcastle upon Tyne:
    NE Coast Inst of Engs
S Plymouth: Royal Naval Eng
S Portsmouth: Highbury Tech
S Southampton: S Coll of Tech
S South Shields: S S Marine Coll
M Newcastle upon Tyne:
    Mus of Science
   see also ARCHITECTURE,
   NAVAL
ENGINEERING, MECHANICAL
S Birmingham: Tube Investments
S Bracknell: B Coll of FE
S Brighton: ITT
S Chester: Brit Nuclear Fuels
S Cranwell: RAF Coll
S Glasgow: Weir Pumps
S Leicester: English Electric Co
S Lincoln: Ruston-Paxman
    Diesels
S London: Babcock & Wilcox
S   Barnet Coll
S   Central Elec Generating
S   CIDEC
S   Institution of Mech Eng
S   Min of Defence
S   Wimpey Labs
S Lowestoft: L Coll of FE
S Newcastle upon Tyne:
    Int Research
S   NE Coast Inst of Engs
S   North of England Inst
S Plymouth: Royal Naval Eng
S Sheffield: Granville Coll
S Rugby: Assoc Engineering
S Winchester: IBM
S Workington: West Cumbria
S Worthing: W Coll of FE
ENGINEERING, MINING, see
   MINING
ENGINEERING, PRODUCTION
S Birmingham: Tube Investments
S Coventry: Lanchester Poly
S Rugby: Assoc Engineering
ENGINEERING, TV & RADIO
S London: Havering Tech Coll
S   Institution of Electronic
    & Radio Engineers
S   Southgate Tech Coll
S Welwyn Garden City:
    Mid Herts Coll
   see also BROADCASTING;
   TELECOMMUNICATIONS
ENGINES
S Derby: Rolls Royce
S Lincoln: Ruston-Paxman
S Rugby: Assoc Engineering
M Dartmouth: D Mus
M Camborne: Holman Mining
M Canterbury: Royal Mus
M Cheddleton: C Flint Mill
M Derby: D Indust Mus
M Edinburgh: Prestongrange Mus
M Kingston upon Hull:
    Springhead Pumping Stat
M Leicester: L Mus of Tech
M Manchester: N Western Mus
M Newcastle upon Tyne:
    Mus of Science
M Portsmouth: Eastney Stat
M Ryhope: R Engines Mus
M St Peter's: Jersey Motor Mus
M Southampton: Maritime Mus
   see also STEAM ENGINES
ENGINES MUSEUM: Ryhope M
ENGLISH AS A FOREIGN
   LANGUAGE
S London: Hammersmith &
    West L Coll
S   Language Teaching Lib
S   Southwark Coll
S   Westminster Coll
S Oxford: O Coll of FE
ENGLISH ELECTRIC CO:
   Leicester S
ENGLISH GOETHE SOCIETY
   LIB:
S London: Univ of L, Inst of
    Germanic Studies
ENGLISH SPEAKING UNION:
   London S
ENGRAVINGS, see ETCHINGS
   & ENGRAVINGS
ENK LIB (classics)
S London: Univ of L Colls,
    King's
ENTOMOLOGY
S Cambridge: C Univ,
    Applied Bio Dept
S Edinburgh: Scottish
    Beekeepers
S Liverpool: L School of
    Tropical Med
S London: Royal Ent Soc
S   Univ of L Med Schools,
    L School of Hygiene
M Bangor: Penrhyn Castle
M Brighton: Booth Mus
M Ipswich: The Mus
M London: Brit Mus (Nat Hist)
M Manchester: M Univ, M Mus
M Nottingham: N Nat Hist Mus
M Oxford: O Univ, Univ Mus
M Portsmouth: Cumberland Ho
   see also BEEKEEPING;
   COLEOPTERA;
   LEPIDOPTERA; PESTS
ENVIRONMENTAL STUDIES
S Aberdeen: Marine Lab
S Ashford: Wye Coll
S Bedford: Nat Coll of Ag Eng
S Belfast: Min of Commerce
S Birmingham: Westhill Coll
S Bognor Regis: B R Coll
S Bracknell: ICI
S Brecon: Welsh Nat Water Dev
S Brighton: B Tech Coll
S Cambridge: C Univ,
    Applied Bio Dept
S Coleraine: New Univ
S Dundee: Univ of D
S Leatherhead: Central
    Electricity Generating
S Liverpool: Univ of L
S London: Centre for Overseas
    Pest Research
S   Nature Conservancy Council
S   Poly of Central L
S   Poly of S Bank
S   United Nations
S Oxford: O Univ, Botany
S Portsmouth: P Poly
S Reading: Bulmershe Coll
S Redruth: Cornwall Tech
S Salford: S Tech Coll
M Budleigh Salterton: Fairlynch
    Arts Centre
M Doncaster: D Mus
M Dundee: Broughty Castle
M Norwich: Castle Mus
M Penzance: Penlee House
M Selborne: Gilbert White Mus
   see also CONSERVATION
EPPING FOREST MUSEUM
M London: Queen Elizabeth's
    Hunting Lodge
EPSTEIN, JACOB
M Bolton: Central Mus
M Walsall: W Mus
ERSKINE OF TORRIE
   INSTITUTE: Culross M
ESKIMOS
M Cambridge: C Univ, Scott
    Polar Inst
M Dundee: Broughty Castle
M Inverurie: I Mus
ESPERANTO
P Stafford
ESSEX ARCHAEOLOGICAL
   SOCIETY: Colchester S
ESSEX REGIMENT MUSEUM:
M Chelmsford: C & Essex Mus
ESTATE MANAGEMENT
S Cirencester: Royal Agric Coll
S London: Kingston Poly
S   Poly of S Bank
S   Thames Poly
S Redditch: R Dev Corp
S Sheffield: Shirecliffe Coll
ETCHINGS & ENGRAVINGS
P Edinburgh
P London, City
P North Tyneside
M Birkenhead: Williamson Gall
M Durham: Monks' Dormitory
M London: Nat Portrait Gallery
M   Orleans House Gallery
M   Royal Academy
M   Royal Coll of Music
M   Royal Soc of Painters
M Newcastle upon Tyne:
    John George Joicey Mus
M Nuneaton: Mus & Art Gall
M Oxford: O Univ, Ashmolean
ETHICS, see PHILOSOPHY
ETHNOGRAPHY, see
   ANTHROPOLOGY
ETON COLLEGE: Windsor S
EUGENICS SOCIETY: London S
EUING COLLN
S Glasgow: G Univ
EUROPEAN DOCUMENTATION
   CENTRES
BL Ref Div, Dept of Printed
    Books
S Birmingham: City of B Poly
S Coventry: Lanchester Poly
S Leeds: L Poly
S Leicester: L Univ
S London: L Univ Colls,
    Queen Mary
S Portsmouth: P Poly
S Sheffield: S Poly
EUROPEAN ECONOMIC
   COMMUNITY
S Brighton: Univ of Sussex
S London: Confed of Brit Indust
S   House of Commons
S   Law Soc
S   Middle Temple
S   Royal Inst of Int Affairs
EUSTON HALL: Thetford M
EVANGELICAL LIBRARY:
   London S
EVANS, SIR ARTHUR
SM Oxford: O Univ, Ashmolean
EVANS MEDICAL LTD:
   Liverpool S
EVOLUTION
S London: Linnaean Soc
M Downe: Down House
M London: Brit Mus (Nat Hist)
M   Horniman Mus
   see also GENETICS
EWART COLLN (textiles)
S Belfast: B Lib
EWORTH, HANS
M Longleat: L House
EXETER COLLEGE:
   Oxford, O Univ Colls S
EXHIBITION GALLERIES:
   Great Yarmouth M
EYE MANOR: Leominster M
EYHORNE MANOR:
    Hollingbourne M
EYRES PRESS
P Cheshire

F

FABERGE
M Luton: Wernher Colln
FACTORIES
M Alford: Manor House Folk
M Derby: D Indust Mus
M Newtown: N Textile Mus
M Ruddington: R Framework
    Knitters Shop
   see also INDUSTRIAL
   ARCHAEOLOGY; MILLS
FACULTY OF ACTUARIES:
   Edinburgh S
FAIRBANK COLLN (surveying)
P Sheffield
FAIRFAX RHODES LIB
S Cambridge: C Union Soc
FAIRHAVEN COLLN
M Lode: Anglesey Abbey
FAIRLYNCH ARTS CENTRE
   & MUSEUM: Budleigh
    Salterton M
FALCONRY CENTRE: Newent M
FARADAY, MICHAEL
S London: Institution of
    Electrical Engineers
FAR EAST, see ORIENTAL
   STUDIES
FARINGDON COLLN
M Buscot Park: Buscot
FARJEON, ELEANOR
P London, Camden
FARMING, see AGRICULTURE
FAROESE COLLN
P Shetland
FASHION
S Ashington: Northumberland
    Co Tech Coll
S Birmingham: City of B Poly
S Cheltenham: Glos Coll of Art
S Clacton on Sea: St Osyth's
S Leicester: L Poly
S   South Fields Coll of FE
S Liverpool: L Poly
S   Mabel Fletcher Tech
S   Bermans & Nathans
S   Chiswick Poly
S   Kilburn Poly
S   L Coll of Fashion
S   St Martin's School of Art
S   Waltham Forest Coll
S Luton: Barnfield Coll
S Mansfield: West Notts Tech
S Plymouth: P Coll of Art
S Portsmouth: Highbury Tech
S Sheffield: Granville Coll
S Southampton: S Coll of Art
S Stafford: S Coll of FE
   see also COSTUME
FAWCETT LIBRARY: London S
FAYRER COLLN
S London: Royal Army Med Coll
FEDERATION OF BRITISH
   ARTISTS
M London: Mall Galleries
FEDERER COLLN
P Bradford
FENTON COLLN (birds' eggs)
M Aberdeen: A Univ, Zoology
FENTON HOUSE: London M
FERENS ART GALLERY:
    Kingston upon Hull M
FERGUSON COLLN
S Glasgow: G Univ
FERMOY PAPERS
S Cork, Eire: Univ Coll
FERRANTI LTD: Edinburgh S
FERRARI COLLN
S Cambridge: C Univ Colls,
    St John's
FERRIER'S MEDICAL LIBRARY:
    Edinburgh S
FIBREGLASS, see GLASS,
   FIBRE
FIEDLER COLLN (German)
S Oxford: O Univ, Taylor Inst
FIELDING, ANTONY
M Dundee: James Guthrie
    Orchar Gallery
FIFE FOLK MUSEUM: Ceres M
FILTON TECHNICAL COLLEGE:
    Bristol S
FINCH COLLN
S Oxford: O Univ, Taylor Inst
FINCH FOUNDRY TRUST:
    Sticklepath M
FINE EDITIONS, see
   BOOKBINDING
FINE PRESSES, see
   PRIVATE PRESSES
FINZI COLLN (poetry)
S Reading: R Univ
FIRE
S Abinger: Fire Service Coll
S Borehamwood: Building
    Research Est
S London: Southwark Coll
FIRE-ENGINES
M Billericay: Cater Mus
M Bury: B Transport Mus
M Edinburgh: Braidwood &
    Rushbrook Mus
M Glasgow: Mus of Transport
M Helston: H Mus
M London: Chartered Insurance
    Inst Mus
M St Ives: Norris Lib
M Shaftesbury: Local Hist Mus
M South Molton: S M Mus
M Staindrop: Raby Castle
FIREPLACES
M Bakewell: Old House Mus
M Banbury: Broughton Castle

L

LHAIDHAY CROFT MUSEUM:
Dunbeath M
LIBERAL PARTY
S Buckingham: Univ Coll at B
LIBRARIANSHIP
BL Ref Div, Dept of Printed
Books
S Aberdeen: Robert Gordon
S Aberystwyth: Coll of
Librarianship
S Birmingham: City of B Poly
S Bristol: Brunel Tech Coll
S Edinburgh: Napier Coll
S Leeds: L Poly, Dept of
Librarianship
S Liverpool: L Poly
S London: Aslib
S   Brit Council
S   Ealing Tech Coll
S   Poly of North L
S Loughborough: L Tech Coll
LIBRARY ASSOCIATION LIB
BL Ref Div, Dept of Printed
Books
LICHEN
M Brokerswood: Phillips
Countryside Mus
LIGHTFOOT, BISHOP J.B
S Cambridge: C Univ,
Divinity Fac
LILLIE ART GALLERY:
Milngavie M
LINCOLN COLLEGE:
Oxford, O Univ Colls S
LINCOLN'S INN: London S
LINDER COLLN
S London: Nat Book League
LINDISFARNE GOSPELS
BL Ref Div: Dept of Mss
LINDSEY COLLEGE OF
AGRICULTURE: Lincoln S
LINGUISTICS
S Bangor: Univ Coll
S Birmingham: B Univ
S   Westhill Coll
S Cambridge: C Univ,
S   Classical Fac Lib
S   Mod & Med Languages
S   Tyndale Lib
S Cardiff: Welsh Folk Mus
S Colchester: Univ of Essex
S Coleraine: New Univ
S Dublin, Eire: Royal Irish Acad
S   Univ Coll
S Glasgow: Notre Dame Coll
S London: Furzedown Coll
S   Language Teaching Lib
S   Middlesex Poly
S   Univ of L Colls, King's
S Manchester: M Univ,
School of Ed
S St Andrew's: Univ of St A
LINGUISTS, INSTITUTE OF:
London S
LINNAEUS, CARL
S London: Linnaean Soc
S   Royal Botanic Gardens
LISTER, LORD
S London: Royal Coll
of Surgeons
S   Univ of L Med Schools,
King's
LISTER MUSEUM: Dursley M
LITTLE & RENIER COLLN
S London: Victoria & Albert
LITTLE, GUY, COLLN
M London: Theatre Mus
LITTLE MAGAZINES COLLN
S London: Univ of L Colls, Univ
LIVERPOOL PORCELAIN
M Birkenhead: Williamson Gall
M Bootle: B Mus
LIVESEY MUSEUM: London M
LIVINGSTONE, DAVID,
MEMORIAL: Blantyre M
LLANDAFF COLLEGE OF
TECHNOLOGY: Cardiff S
LLANDRILLO TECHNICAL
COLLEGE: Colwyn Bay S
LLOYD COLLN (music)
S Cork, Eire: Univ Coll
LLOYD, DAVID DE (mss)
S Aberystwyth: Univ Coll
LLOYD GEORGE, DAVID
P Gwynedd
M Llanystumdwy:
Lloyd George Mem Mus
LLOYD, H.A., COLLN
S London: Antiquarian
Horological Soc
LLOYD'S NELSON COLLN:
London M
LOCOMOTIVES
M Beamish: B Mus
M Birmingham: City of B Mus

M Bradford: B Indust Mus
M Bury: B Transport Mus
M Darlington: D Mus
M   D North Rd Stat Mus
M Diss: Bressingham Steam Mus
M Edinburgh: Prestongrange
M Glasgow: Mus of Transport
M Leeds: Mus of Ind & Science
M London: L Transport Colln
M   Science Mus
M Manchester: North Western
M Newcastle upon Tyne:
Mus of Science
M Nuneaton: Cadeby Light
Railway
M Retford: Lound Hall Mining
M Towyn: Narrow Gauge
Railway Mus
M York: Nat Railway Mus
see also RAILWAYS
LODGE, SIR OLIVER
S Birmingham: B Univ
LOEWENTAL COLLN
M Spalding: S Gentlemen's Soc
LONDON
P London, City
S Cambridge: C Univ Colls,
Magdalene
S London: Armouries Lib
S   Bishopsgate Inst
S   Dept of Environment
S   Greater L Council
S   Highgate Literary
& Scientific Inst
S   Port of L Auth
S   Univ of L, Univ Lib
S   Univ of L Colls, Univ
M London: Mus of L
LONDON CORRESPONDING
SOCIETY
M London: Nat Mus of
Labour Hist
LONDON HOSPITAL
S London Univ of L Med Schools
M London: Univ of L
LONDON LEAD COMPANY
S Newcastle upon Tyne:
North of Eng Inst of Mining
LONDON MATHEMATICAL
SOCIETY LIB
S London: Univ of L Colls, Univ
LONDON NATURAL HISTORY
SOCEITY LIB
S London: Univ of L Colls,
Imperial
LONDON SCHOOL OF
ECONOMICS & POLITICAL
SCIENCE:
London, Univ of L Colls
LONDON SCHOOL OF
HYGIENE & TROPICAL
MEDICINE:
London, Univ of L Med S
LONDON SCOTTISH
REGIMENTAL MUSEUM:
London M
LONG ASHTON RESEARCH
STATION: Bristol S
LONG COLLN (classics)
P East Sussex
LONGSANDS MUSEUM:
St Neots M
LORD BRASSEY'S LIB
P East Sussex
LORD LEYCESTER
HOSPITAL: Warwick M
LORRAINE, CLAUDE
M Oxford: O Univ, Ashmolean
LOSELEY HOUSE: Guildford M
LOTHERTON HALL:
Aberford M
LOTHIAN DISTRICT LIBS
P East Lothian
P Mid Lothian
P West Lothian
LOUDOUN DISTRICT LIBS
P Kilmarnock & Loudoun
LOUGHTON COLLEGE OF
FURTHER EDUCATION:
London S
LOUND HALL MINING
MUSEUM: Retford M
LOVAT SCOUTS
M Fort George: Seaforth
Highlanders Reg Mus
LOVESPOONS
M Brecon: Brecknock Mus
M Carmarthen: Co Mus
LOW, BISHOP, COLLN
S St Andrew's: Univ of St A
LOWRY, L.S.
P Salford
M Salford: S Art Gallery
M Wakefield: W City Art Gall
LOYAL REGIMENT

M Preston: Queen's Lancs Reg
LUBBOCK, BASIL, COLLN
S London: Nat Maritime Mus
LUCAS, SAMUEL
M Hitchin: H Mus
LUNN, LILLIAN, COLLN
M Rugeley: Blithfield Hall
LUNT ROMAN FORT &
INTERPRETIVE CENTRE:
Coventry M
LUTHER, MARTIN
S Oxford: O Univ, Taylor Inst
S   Theology Fac
LUTTRELL PSALTER
BL Ref Div, Dept of Mss
'LYDIA EVA', STEAM
DRIFTER: Gt Yarmouth M
LYDIARD HOUSE: Swindon M
LYME HALL: Disley M
LYNN MUSEUM: King's Lynn M
LYONS MSS
S Cork, Eire: Univ Coll
LYTTLETON FAMILY PAPERS
S London: Univ of L Colls

M

MABEL FLETCHER
TECHNICAL COLLEGE:
Liverpool S
MacANDREW, R.A., COLLN
S Cambridge: C Univ, Zoology
MACAULEY, T.B., COLLN
P Western Isles
MACBEAN COLLN
S Aberdeen: A Univ
MacCULLUM SCOTT PAPERS
S Buckingham: Univ Coll at B
MACCURDY LIB
S Cambridge: C Univ,
Psychological Lab
MACDONALD, GEORGE
P North East Scotland
MACEWEN COLLN
S Glasgow: Royal Coll of
Physicians
MACHEN, ARTHUR, COLLN
P Gwent
MACKENZIE COLLN
S Glasgow: Royal Coll of
Physicians
MACKENZIE, COMPTON
S London: St Paul's School
MACKENZIE, WILLIAM LYON
S Dundee: Univ of D
MACKINTOSH, RENNIE
M Glasgow: G Univ, Hunterian
MACKINTOSH COLLN
P Perth & Kinross
MACKMURDO BEQUEST
M London: William Morris Gall
MACLISE, DANIEL
M Bury: B Art Gallery
MACPHERSON, A.G.H., COLLN
S London: Nat Maritime Mus
MacPHERSON COLLN
S London: Royal Army Med
MACQUOID BEQUEST
M Brighton: Preston Manor
MacROBERT ART GALLERY:
Stirling M
MAGDALEN COLLEGE:
Oxford, O Univ Colls S
MAGDALENE COLLEGE:
Cambridge, C Univ Colls S
MAGIC & WITCHCRAFT
S Glasgow: G Univ
S London: Univ of L, Univ Lib
M Looe: Cornish Mus
MAGNA CARTA
BL Ref Div, Dept of Mss
S Salisbury: S Cath
M Lincoln: L Cath Treasury
MAGUIRE DONATION
S Dublin, Eire: Irish Central Lib
MAISON DE VICTOR HUGO:
St Peter Port M
MAISON FRANCAISE
LIBRARY: Oxford S
MAJOLICA
M Bath: Holburne of Menstrie
M London: Univ of L,
Courtauld Inst
M   Wallace Colln
MALACOLOGICAL SOC LIB
S London: Univ of L Colls, Univ
MALAYSIAN RUBBER
PRODUCERS RESEARCH
ASSOCIATION: Hertford S
MALL GALLERIES: London M
MALTHUS
S Cambridge: C Univ Colls,
Jesus

MANAGEMENT
S Aberdeen: Robert Gordon
S Ashford: Wye Coll
S Basingstoke: B Tech Coll
S Bath: B Univ
S Birmingham: Austin Morris
S   City of B Poly
S   Univ of Aston
S Bishop Auckland: B A Tech
S Blackburn: Coll of Tech
S Bournemouth: B Coll of Tech
S Bradford: Univ of B
S Brighton: B Poly
S Bristol: B Poly
S   Filton Tech Coll
S Bromsgrove: B Coll of FE
S Cambridge: C Univ,
Engineering Fac
S Cardiff: Wales Gas Lib
S Chatham: Medway &
Maidstone Coll
S Chesham: Nat Defence Coll
S Chesterfield: Coll of Art
S Cranfield: C Inst of Tech
S Cranwell: RAF Coll
S Darlaston: Rubery Owen Group
S Darlington: D Coll of Tech
S Derby: Rolls Royce
S Doncaster: D Coll of Tech
S Eastleigh: William R. Warner
S Ewell: E Co Tech Coll
S Galashiels: Scottish Coll
S Glasgow: Inst of Chartered
Accountants
S   Queen's Coll
S   Stow Coll
S Gloucester: G City Coll
S Grays: Thurrock Tech
S Harlow: H Tech Coll
S Hatfield: H Poly
S Hitchin: H Coll
S Hornchurch: Havering Tech
S Kincardine: Scottish Police
S Leeds: L Poly
S Letchworth: Coll of Tech
S Liverpool: L Poly
S London: Anbar Tear Sheet
S   Assoc of Certified
Accountants
S   Brit Inst of Management
S   Central Electric Generating
S   Civil Service Dept
S   Confed of Brit Industry
S   Council for Small Inds
S   Croydon Coll
S   Dept of Employment
S   Greater L Council,
Research Lib
S   Hammersmith & West L
S   Harrow Coll of Tech
S   Havering Tech Coll
S   Hotel Catering & Inst
Management
S   IBM Tech Inf Centre
S   Institute of Chartered
Accountants
S   Institute of Chartered Secs
S   Institute of Cost &
Management
S   Institute of Personnel
S   J. Walter Thompson
S   Kingston Poly
S   L Coll of Printing
S   L Grad School of Business
S   Merton Tech Coll
S   Ministry of Defence,
St Giles Court
Whitehall Lib
S   Poly of Central L
S   Poly of S Bank
S   Reckitt & Colman
S   Remploy Technicals
S   Services Central Lib
S   Shell Int
S   Thames Poly
S   3M Lib & Inf Service
S   Times Newspapers
S   Twickenham Coll
S   Univ of L Colls,
Imperial
Queen Eliz
S Luton: L Coll of Tech
S Manchester: Eliz Gaskell Coll
S   M Univ, Science & Tech
S   North Trafford Coll
S   Renold
S Newcastle upon Tyne:
Northumbrian Water Auth
S Newport: Gwent Coll of HE
S Northampton: Brit Timken
S Norwich: N City Coll
S Nottingham: Boots Co Lib
S Oxford: O Poly
S Paisley: P Coll
S Plymouth: P Poly

M Skipton: Craven Mus
M Truro: Co Mus
MINGANA COLLN (mss)
S Birmingham: Selly Oaks Colls
MINIATURE LANDSCAPE &
    TRANSPORT MUSEUM:
    Abingdon M
MINIATURES
S London: India Office
M Bath: Holburne of Menstrie
M Cambridge: C Univ,
    Fitzwilliam Mus
M Dodington: D Carriage Mus
M London: Nat Portrait Gallery
M   Polish Inst
M   Royal Soc of Painters
M Maidstone: Mus & Art Gallery
M Manchester: City Art Gallery
M Nuneaton: Mus & Art Gallery
M Oxford: O Univ, Ashmolean
MINING
P Doncaster
S Ashington: Northumberland
    Co Tech Coll
S Cannock: C Chase Tech Coll
S Canterbury: C Coll of Tech
S Doncaster: Coll of Tech
S Falkirk: F Coll of Tech
S Hebburn: H Tech Coll
S Ilkeston: SE Derbyshire Coll
S Leicester: NW Leics Tech
S London: Institution of
    Mining & Met
S   Univ of L Colls,
    Imperial
S Newcastle upon Tyne:
    North of Eng Inst of
    Mining
S Peterlee: Easington Te ch
S Pontypridd: Poly of Wales
S St Helens: St H Coll
S Sheffield: Safety in Mines
S Stoke on Trent:
    N Staffs Poly
S Swansea: S Coll of Tech
S   Univ Coll
M Aberystwyth: Ceredigion
M Bakewell: Old House Mus
M Beamish: B Mus
M Bishops Stortford: Rhodes
M Burnley: Mus of Local Crafts
M Camborne: C Mus
M   Holman Mining Mus
M Edinburgh: Prestongrange
M Glencoe: G & N Lorn Folk
M Hamilton: H Dist Mus
M Ironbridge: I Gorge Mus
M Kendal: Mus of Lakeland
    Life
M Llanberis: N Wales Quarrying
M Looe: Cornish Mus
M Matlock: Tramway Mus
M Millom: M Folk Mus
M Morwellham: M Centre
M Newcastle upon Tyne:
    Mus of Science
M Pool: Camborne School of
    Mines Mus
M Portland: P Mus
M Retford: Lound Hall Mining
M St Helens: St H Mus
M Salford: S Science Mus
M Skipton: Craven Mus
M Whitehaven: W Mus
M Zennor: Wayside Mus
MINISTRY OF
    AGRICULTURE, FISHERIES
    & FOOD: London S
MINISTRY OF COMMERCE,
    DEPT OF INDUSTRIAL
    & FORENSIC SCIENCE:
    Belfast S
MINSITRY OF DEFENCE:
    London S
MINISTRY OF OVERSEAS
    DEVELOPMENT, see
    FOREIGN &
    COMMONWEALTH OFFICE
MINORIES GALLERY:
    Colchester M
MINS COLLN (palaeography)
S Cambridge: C Univ,
    Classical Fac
MIRFIELD COLLN (books)
S York: Univ of Y
MIRO, JOAN
M Cambridge: C Univ,
    Kettle's Yard
MISSIONS
S Birmingham: Selly Oaks Colls
S London: Church Missionary
S   William Booth Coll
M Blantyre: David Livingstone
MOCATTA LIB
S London: Univ of L Colls, Univ

MOCATTA MUSEUM: London M
MOIR LIB (beekeeping)
P Edinburgh
MOLLUSCS
S Cardiff: Nat Mus of Wales
S London: Univ of L Colls, Univ
MONET, CLAUDE
M London: Univ of L,
    Courtauld Inst
MONKS' DORMITORY
    MUSEUM: Durham M
MONKS HALL MUSEUM:
    Eccles M
MONKWEARMOUTH COLLEGE
    OF FURTHER EDUCATION:
    Sunderland S
MONKWEARMOUTH STATION
    MUSEUM: Sunderland M
MONMOUTHSHIRE REGIMENT
    MUSEUM: Brecon M
MONTEFIORE COLLN (mss)
S London: Jews' Coll
MONTGOMERY OF ALAMEIN
S London: St Paul's School
MOORE, HENRY
M Bolton: Central Mus & Art Gall
M Wakefield: W City Art Gallery
MOORE, THOMAS
S Dublin, Eire: Royal Irish Acad
MORAY HOUSE COLLEGE OF
    EDUCATION: Edinburgh S
MORE, SIR THOMAS
P London, City
MORFILL COLLN
S Oxford: O Univ, Taylor Inst
MORGAN LIBRARY, DE
S London: Univ of L, Univ Lib
MORGAN, WILLIAM DE
P London, Kensington &
    Chelsea
M London: Leighton House
M   William Morris Gallery
MORLEY COLLEGE: London S
MORLEY, LORD JOHN, COLLN
S Manchester: Ashburne Hall
MORRIS, HENRY, COLLN
S Coleraine: New Univ
MORRIS, ROGER
M Inveraray: I Castle
MORRIS, WILLIAM
M Lechlade: Kelmscott Manor
M London: William Morris Gall
M Manchester: M Univ,
    Whitworth Gallery
M Wolverhampton: Wightwick
MORRISON MSS
P Western Isles
MORTEN-DANDY COLLN
S Manchester: Didsbury Coll
MOSAICS
M Bignor: Roman Villa
M Brading: Roman Villa
M Bristol: Kings Weston Roman
    Villa
M Canterbury: Roman Pavement
M Edinburgh: Lauriston Castle
M Kingston upon Hull:
    Transport & Arch Mus
M Leicester: Jewry Wall Mus
M Newport: Roman Villa
M Runcorn: Norton Priory Mus
MOSS, WILLIAM E.
S Sheffield: Joseph Livesey Lib
MOTOR MANUALS
P Sefton
MOTOR VEHICLES
S Beaulieu: Nat Motor Mus
S Birmingham: Austin Morris
S Cinderford: West Glos Coll
S Coventry: Lanchester Poly
M Beaulieu: Nat Motor Mus
M Biggleswade: Shuttleworth
M Bradford: B Indust Mus
M Cheddar: C Veteran &
    Vintage Car Mus
M Doune: D Motor Mus
M Glasgow: Mus of Transport
M Holywood: Ulster Folk Mus
M Kingston upon Hull:
    Transport & Arch Mus
M London: Royal Mews
M   Science Mus
M   Vestry House Mus
M Lowestoft: E Anglia Transport
M Lutterworth: Stanford Hall
M Manchester: North Western
M Norwich: Strangers Hall Mus
M Nostell: N Priory
M Pembroke Dock:
    Pembrokeshire Motor Mus
M St Peter's: Jersey Motor Mus
    see also ENGINEERING,
    AUTOMOTIVE; TRANSPORT
MOTT HARRISON LIB
P Bedfordshire

MOUNT ST BERNARD ABBEY:
    Leicester S
MOUNTAINEERING
P Leeds
S Edinburgh: Nat Lib of Scot
S Lancaster: Univ of L
MOVEMENT, see DANCE
MOYSE'S HALL MUSEUM:
    Bury St Edmonds M
MR PURVES' LAMP
    EMPORIUM: Edinburgh M
MUCKROSS HOUSE:
    Killarney, Eire M
MUNCASTER CASTLE:
    Ravenglass M
MUNICIPAL ENGINEERS,
    INSTITUTION OF:
    London S
MUNNINGS, SIR ALFRED,
    ART GALLERY: Dedham M
MURCHISON, RODERICK
S London: Geological Soc
MURILLO, BARTOLOME
M London: Wallace Colln
MURISON BURNS COLLN
P Dumfermline
MURPHY, BISHOP, MSS
S Cork, Eire: Univ Coll
MURRAY, DAVID, COLLN
S Glasgow: G Univ
MURRAY LIB
S London: Maria Grey Coll
MUSIC
BL Ref Div, Dept of Printed
    Books
BL   Dept of Mss
P Avon
P Berkshire
P Buckinghamshire
P Clackmannan
P Dundee
P East Sussex
P Edinburgh
P Essex
P Glasgow
P Hampshire
P Hertfordshire
P Kent
P Lancashire
P Leeds
P Lincolnshire
P London, City
P   Redbridge
P   Westminster
P Manchester
P Northern Ireland, Belfast
P Perth & Kinross
P Rhondda
P Shropshire
P Stafford
P Surrey
P Isle of Man
S Bangor: Univ Coll
S Bedford: B Coll of Ed
S Belfast: Queen's Univ
S Birmingham: B Univ
S   B Univ, Extramural Lib
S   City of B Poly
S   Westhill Coll
S Bognor Regis: B R Coll
S Bristol: Filton Tech Coll
S Cambridge: Cambs Coll of Art
S   C Union Soc
S   C Univ, Univ Lib
S   Extramural Studies
S   Fitzwilliam Mus
S   Music Faculty
S   C Univ Colls, Clare
S   Girton
S   Gonville & Caius
S   King's
S   Magdalene
S Chelmsford: Mid Essex Tech
S Clacton on Sea: St Osyth Coll
S Colchester: NE Essex Tech
S Cork, Eire: Univ Coll
S Dartford: D Coll of Ed
S Derby: Bishop Lonsdale
S Dublin, Eire: Nat Lib of
    Ireland
S Dudley: D Coll of Ed
S Durham: Dean & Chapter Lib
S Eastbourne: Chelsea Coll
S Edinburgh: E Univ
S   Nat Lib of Scotland
S   Scottish United Services
S Egham: Royal Holloway Coll
S Glasgow: G Univ Lib
S   Notre Dame Coll of Ed
S   Royal Scottish Acad of
    Music & Drama
S Hereford: H Cath Lib
S   H Coll of Ed
S Lancaster: Univ of L
S Leeds: Trinity & All Saints'

S Lincoln: Bishop Grosseteste
S Liverpool: Mabel Fletcher
S   Notre Dame Coll of Ed
S   Univ of L
S London: Austrian Inst Lib
S   Borough Rd Coll
S   BBC Music Lib
S   BBC Ref Lib
S   Brit Inst Recorded Sound
S   Chiswick Poly
S   Council for Places
    of Worship
S   Dulwich Coll
S   Furzedown Coll
S   Furzedown Coll
S   Goethe Institut
S   Horniman Mus
S   Italian Inst
S   Morley Coll
S   Nat Operatic & Dramatic
S   Polish Lib
S   Roehampton Inst of FE
S   Royal Academy of Music
S   Royal Coll of Music
S   St Mary's Coll
S   St Paul's School
S   Stockwell Coll of Ed
S   Trinity Coll of Music
S   Univ of L Colls, King's
S   Vaughan Williams Lib
S   Westminster Abbey
S Manchester: Royal Northern
    Coll of Music
S Newcastle upon Tyne:
    Northern Co Coll
S Oxford: O Univ,
S   Ethnology Dept
S   External Studies Dept
S   Music Faculty
S   O Univ Colls,
S   Christ Church
S   Westminster
S Stratford upon Avon:
    Shakespeare Centre
S Sunderland: S Poly
S Tenbury Wells: St Michael's
S Winchester: W Coll
S York: Y Minster
M Alloway: Burns' Cottage
M Cambridge: C Univ,
    Fitzwilliam Mus
M London: Royal Coll of Music
MUSICAL INSTRUMENTS
S Cambridge: C Univ, Music Fac
S London: L Coll of Furniture
S   Vaughan Williams Lib
S Manchester: Royal Northern
    Coll of Music
M Alloway: Burns' Cottage
M Birmingham: City of B Mus
M Brighton: B Art Gallery
M Bristol: Georgian House
M Broadway: Snowshill Manor
M Chester: Grosvenor Mus
M Dundee: Camperdown House
M Hailsham: Michelham Priory
M Keighley: Cliffe Castle Gall
M Keswick: Fitz Park Mus
M Leicester: Newarke Houses
M London: Fenton House
M   Horniman Mus
M   Kneller Hall Mus
M   Musical Mus
M   Royal Coll of Music
M Maidstone: Mus & Art Gall
M Newport: Carisbrooke Castle
M Norfolk: St Peter Hungate
M Swindon: Mus & Art Gallery
M Wigan: W Mus
M York: Castle Mus
MUSIC HALL, NATIONAL
    MUSEUM OF: Sunderland M
MUYBRIDGE, EADWEARD
M London: Kingston upon
    Thames Mus
MYERS MUSEUM:
    Windsor, Eton Coll M

N

NAPIER COLLEGE OF
    COMMERCE &
    TECHNOLOGY: Edinburgh S
NAPIER SHAW LIB
S Cambridge: C Univ, Physics
NAPOLEON BONAPARTE
P Avon
P Humberside
M Aldershot: Royal Army Med
    Corps Hist Mus
M Annan: A Burgh Mus
M Bury: Lancs Fusiliers Reg

P

S Royal Coll of Psychiatrists
S St Martin's School of Art
S Services Central Lib
S St Mary's Coll
S Tavistock Institute
S Univ of L Med Schools,
     Inst of Neurology
S   Inst of Psychiatry
S Waltham Forest, Nat Inst
     of Indust Psychology
S Manchester: M Univ,
     School of Ed
S Newcastle upon Tyne:
     Northern Co Coll
S Oxford: O Univ, Ed Studies
S   Social Studies Lib
S Portsmouth: P Coll of Ed
S Sunderland: S Poly
S Wakefield: HM Prison Service
PUBLIC ADMINISTRATION
S Edinburgh: Scottish Office
S Gloucester: City of Tech
S Leeds: Trinity & All Saints'
S London: Civil Service Dept
S   Greater L Council
S   Institution of Municipal Engs
S St Helens: St H Coll of Tech
S Southampton: S Coll of Tech
S Sunderland: S Poly
PUBLIC HEALTH
S Chelmsford: Med Recording
S Edinburgh: Scottish Health
     Service Centre
S   Scottish Office
S Hamilton: Bell Coll
S Liverpool: Mabel Fletcher
S London: Central Public Health
S   Dept of Health
S   Harrow Coll of Tech
S   Havering Tech Coll
S   King's Fund Centre
S   Office of Pop Censuses
S   Tottenham Coll of Tech
S   Univ of L Med Schools,
     L School of Hygiene
S   Waltham Forest Coll
S Portsmouth: Highbury Tech
S Sheffield: Granville Coll
S   Shirecliffe Coll
     see also INDUSTRIAL HEALTH
PUBLIC RECORD OFFICE:
    London S,M
PUBLISHING
S Edinburgh: Napier Coll
S London: Nat Book League
S Oxford Univ Press
PUGIN, AUGUSTUS WELBY
M Ledbury: Eastnor Castle
PUMPING STATION,
    COLEHAM: Shrewsbury M
PUMPING STATION,
    EASTNEY: Portsmouth M
PUNJABI
P Kirklees
P London, Tower Hamlets
P Sandwell
PUNNETT COLLN
S London: Min of Agric
PUSEY HOUSE LIBRARY:
    Oxford, O Univ S
PYBUS COLLN (medicine)
S Newcastle upon Tyne:
     NuT Univ

Q

QUAKERS
P Cheshire
P Gwent
P Kildare, Eire
S Lancaster: Univ of L
S London: Religious Soc
QUANTITY SURVEYING
S London: Institute of
     Quantity Surveyors
S   Kingston Poly
S   Thames Poly
     see also SURVEYING
QUARRYING, see MINING
QUEEN ALEXANDRA'S
    ROYAL ARMY NURSING
    CORPS MUSEUM:
    Aldershot M
QUEEN ELIZABETH COLLEGE:
    London, Univ of L Colls S
QUEEN ELIZABETH'S
    HUNTING LODGE:
    London M
QUEEN MARY COLLEGE:
    London, Univ of L S,M,
QUEEN MARY'S OWN
    13th/18th ROYAL HUSSARS
    MUSEUM: Barnsley M

QUEENS' COLLEGE:
    Cambridge, C Univ Colls S
QUEEN'S COLLEGE: Glasgow S
QUEEN'S COLLEGE:
    Oxford, O Univ Colls S
QUEEN'S COLLEGE AT
    BIRMINGHAM: Birmingham S
QUEEN'S DRAGOON GUARDS
M Shrewsbury: Clive House Mus
QUEEN'S GALLERY: London M
QUEEN'S LANCASHIRE
    REGIMENT: Preston M
QUEEN'S OWN BUFFS REG
M Canterbury: Queen's Reg
QUEEN'S OWN CAMERON
    HIGHLANDERS: Fort George M
QUEEN'S OWN DORSET
    YEOMANRY
M Dorchester: Dorset Mil Mus
QUEEN'S OWN
    HIGHLANDERS: Fort George M
QUEEN'S OWN HUSSARS
M Warwick: Lord Leycester Hosp
QUEEN'S OWN ROYAL WEST
    KENT: Maidstone M
QUEEN'S PARK ART GALLERY:
    Manchester M
QUEEN'S REGIMENTAL
    MUSEUM: Canterbury M
QUEEN'S ROYAL SURREY
    REGIMENT
M London: QRS Reg Mus
M Canterbury: Queen's Reg Mus
QUEEN'S UNIVERSITY:
    Belfast S
QUICK MEMORIAL LIB
S London: Univ of L, Univ Lib

R

RABELAIS
S Cambridge: C Univ Colls,
     St John's
RABY CASTLE: Staindrop M
RADIO, see BROADCASTING
RADIOCHEMICAL CENTRE:
    Amersham S
RADIO TIMES: London S
RAEBURN, SIR HENRY
M Castle Ashby
M South Queensferry:
     Hopetoun House
RAFFALOVICH, ANDRE
S Oxford: O Univ Colls,
     Blackfriars
RAGLEY HALL: Alcester M
RAILWAYS
P Doncaster
P Durham
P Gateshead
P Hampshire
P London, Brent
P Wiltshire
S Derby: Brit Rail Research
S Lancaster: Univ of L
S Leicester: L Univ
S London: Chartered Inst
     of Transport
S   Univ of L, Univ Lib
S Paisley: P Coll
M Abingdon: Pendon Mus
M Aldeburgh: A Mus
M Bangor: Penrhyn Castle
M Beamish: B Mus
M Bury: B Transport Mus
M Corris: C Railway Mus
M Darlington: D Mus
M   D North Rd Stat Mus
M Derby: D Mus
M Diss: Bressingham Steam Mus
M Glasgow: Mus of Transport
M Holywood: Ulster Folk Mus
M London: L Transport Collns
M Lowestoft: E Anglia Transport
M Manchester: N Western Mus
M Melton Mowbray: Nat Trust
M Morwellham: M Centre
M Newcastle upon Tyne:
     Mus of Science
M Nuneaton: Cadeby Light
     Railway Mus
M St Peter's: Jersey Motor Mus
M Stockton on Tees:
     Darlington Railway Mus
M Swindon: GWR Mus
M Towyn: Narrow Gauge Mus
M York: Nat Railway Mus
     see also LOCOMOTIVES;
     STEAM ENGINES;
     TRANSPORT
RAMSAY, ALLAN
M Bath: Holburne of Menstrie
RANGER'S HOUSE: London M

RAPHAEL
M Oxford: O Univ, Ashmolean
RASHLEIGH COLLN
M Truro: Co Mus
RAVENSBOURNE COLLEGE OF
    ART & DESIGN: London S
RAYMOND, ERNEST
S London: St Paul's School
READERS HOUSE: Ludlow M
READING MSS
S London: Dulwich Coll
RECKITT & COLMAN LTD:
    London S
RECORDED SOUND, BRITISH
    INSTITUTE OF: London S
RECREATION, see SPORT
RECUSANCY
S Kingston upon Hull:
     Endsleigh Coll of Ed
RED HOUSE MUSUEM:
    Gomersal M
RED HOUSE MUSEUM & ART
    GALLERY: Christchurch M
REDLAND COLLEGE:
    Bristol S
REDLICH, HANS, COLLN
S Lancaster: Univ of L
RED LODGE: Bristol M
REECE COLLN
S London: Univ of L Med,
     L School of Hygiene
REFRACTORIES
S Manchester: Carborundum Co
S Worksop: G.R. Stein
REGENT'S PARK COLLEGE:
    Oxford: O Univ Colls S
REGIMENT OF FOOT, 9th
M Norwich: Royal Norfolk Reg
REGIMENT OF FOOT,
    50th & 97th
M Maidstone: Queen's Own
     Royal West Kent Mus
REGIMENTAL HISTORY, see
    MILITARY HISTORY
REGINALD'S TOWER MUSEUM:
    Waterford, Eire M
REID, GEORGE, COLLN
P Dunfermline
REID, R.C., COLLN
P Dumfries
REITH, CHARLES, COLLN
S Kincardine: Scottish Police
REITLINGER, HENRY,
    BEQUEST: Maidenhead M
RELIGION, see THEOLOGY
RELIGIOUS LIFE
S Leicester: Mount St Bernard
S London: Sion Coll
S Mirfield: Community of the
     Resurrection
S Oxford: O Univ Colls,
S   Blackfriars
S   Keble
RELIGIOUS MILITARY
    ORDERS
S Cambridge: C Univ Colls,
     Corpus
S M London: Order of St John
RELIGIOUS SOCIETY OF
    FRIENDS: London S
REMBRANDT
M Buscot Park: Buscot
M London: Iveagh Bequest
M   Wallace Colln
M Oxford: O Univ, Ashmolean
M Thornhill: Drumlanrig Castle
M Wilton: W House
REMPLOY: London S
RENDALL, ROBERT, COLLN
M Stromness: S Mus
RENDEL-HARRIS COLLN
S Birmingham: B Univ
RENOIR, PIERRE AUGUSTE
M London: Univ of L,
     Courtauld Inst
RENOLD LTD: Manchester S
REPRESENTATIVE CHURCH
    BODY LIBRARY:
    Dublin, Eire S
RETAILING
S Aberdeen: A Coll of Comm
S Hitchin: H Coll
S London: Coll for Distrib Trades
S Nottingham: Boots Co
S Watford: Cassio Coll
     see also MARKETING
REUSS, ALBERT
M Penzance: Newlyn Art Gallery
REUTERS: London S
REVOLUTION HOUSE:
    Chesterfield M
REYNOLDS, SIR JOSHUA
M Aylesbury: Waddesdon Manor
M Belfast: Ulster Mus
M Castle Ashby

M Chichester: Goodwood House
M Corsham: C Court
M Grantham: Belton House
M London: Iveagh Bequest
M   Thomas Coram Foundation
M   Wallace Colln
M Longleat: L House
M Selkirk: Bowhill House
M Shifnal: Weston Park
M Thetford: Euston Hall
REYNOLDS LIB
S London: Nat Maritime Mus
RHODES MUSEUM &
    COMMONWEALTH CENTRE:
    Bishops Stortford M
RICARD, PAUL, COLLN
S Coleraine: New Univ
RICCI, SEBASTIANO
M Gateshead: Shipley Art Gallery
RICHARD DEMARCO GALLERY
    Edinburgh M
RICHARD JEFFERIES MUSUEM:
    Swindon M
RICHARDS, EDWIN, COLLN
M Wednesbury: Sandwell Art Gall
RICHMOND, SIR IAN
S Oxford: O Univ, Ashmolean
RIDINGER, JOHAN ELIAS
M Lindisfarne: L Castle
RIDLEY COLLN
M London: Royal Coll of Music
RILEY, BRIDGET
M Ipswich: Christchurch Mus
RIMMER COLLN
M Wigan: W Mus
RISCHGITZ COLLN (prints)
S London: Radio Times
ROBERT DICK MUSEUM:
    Thurso M
ROBERT GORDON'S
    INSTITUTE OF
    TECHNOLOGY: Aberdeen S
ROBERT OWEN MEMORIAL
    MUSEUM: Newtown M
ROBERT THE BRUCE
M Bannockburn: B Monument
ROBERTS, CECIL
P Nottinghamshire
ROBERTS OF OXFORD
M Steeple Aston: Rousham Ho
ROBERTSON SMITH COLLN
S Cambridge: C Univ Colls,
     Christ's
ROBES, see COSTUME
ROBINSON, C.N., COLLN
S London: Nat Maritime Mus
ROBINSON, GERRARD
M Gateshead: Shipley Art Gall
M Newcastle upon Tyne:
     John George Joicey Mus
ROCHFORD, EARLS OF
M Arran: Brodick Castle
ROCK-CLIMBING, see
    MOUNTAINEERING
ROCKINGHAM CASTLE:
    Market Harborough M
ROCKINGHAM CHINA
M Mansfield: M Dist Council Mus
M Rotherham: Municipal Mus
RODDAM COLLN (playbills)
P North Tyneside
RODIN, AUGUSTE
M London: Bethnal Green Mus
ROEHAMPTON INSTITUTE
    OF FURTHER
    EDUCATION: London S
ROLLE COLLEGE OF
    EDUCATION: Exmouth S
ROLLS ROYCE
S Derby: Rolls Royce
S   D Industrial Mus
M Manchester: N Western Mus
M Stoke on Trent: Spitfire Mus
     see also MOTOR VEHICLES
ROMAN ARCHAEOLOGY
M Aldeburgh: A Mus
M Alnwick: A Castle
M Barnstaple: North Devon
     Athenaeum
M Bath: Roman Baths & Mus
M Battle: B & Dist Hist Soc
M Bignor: Roman Villa
M Borough Bridge: Aldborough
     Roman Town
M Brading: Roman Villa
M Bridport: Mus & Art Gallery
M Bristol: Kings Weston Roman
     Villa
M Caerleon: Legionary Mus
M Caernarvon: Segontium
M Cambridge: C Univ,
M   Fitzwilliam
M   Mus of Classical Arch
M Canterbury: Roman Pavement
M   Royal Mus

U

UCCELLO, PAOLO
M Oxford: O Univ, Ashmolean
UKAEA
S Abingdon: Culham Lab
S Harwell: Atomic Energy Est
S Thurso: Dounreay Reactor
S Warrington: UK Atomic
      Energy Authority
ULSTER FOLK & TRANSPORT
   MUSEUM: Holywood M
ULSTER MUSEUM: Belfast M
UN, see UNITED NATIONS
UNITARIAN COLLEGE:
   Manchester S
UNITED GLASS LTD:
   St Albans S
UNITED NATIONS
BL Ref Div, Dept of Printed
      Books, Official Pub Lib
S Aberystwyth: Univ Coll
S Brighton: Univ of Sussex
S London: House of Commons
S   Int Planned Parenthood
S   Royal Inst of Int Affairs
S   United Nations Inf Centre
S Oxford: O Univ, Bodleian
UNITED SOCIETY FOR THE
   PROPAGATION OF THE
   GOSPEL: London S
UNITED STATES
P Gloucestershire
P Wirral
S Aberystwyth: Univ Coll
S Derby: Bishop Lonsdale Coll
S Lincoln: Bishop Grosseteste
S Liverpool: St Katharine's
S London: Eng-Speaking Union
S   Furzedown Coll
S   Marx Mem Lib
S   Middle Temple Lib
S   Public Record Office
S   United Soc for
          Propagation of Gospel
S   Univ of L, Univ Lib
S   Inst of Hist Research
S   Inst of US Studies
S   Univ of L Colls, Univ
S Oxford: O Univ Colls, Queen's
M Bath: American Mus
M Birmingham: Bishop Asbury
      Cottage
UNIVERSITY COLLEGE:
   Oxford, O Univ Colls S
UNIVERSITY MARINE
   BIOLOGICAL STATION:
   Millport S,M
UNIVERSITY OF LIVERPOOL
   SCHOOL OF DENTAL
   SURGERY MUSEUM:
   Liverpool M
UPPARK HOUSE: Petersfield M
UPTON HOUSE: Banbury M
URDU
P Humberside
P Kirklees
P London, Tower Hamlets
P Sandwell
UROLOGY, INSTITUTE OF:
   London, Univ of L Med S
US, see UNITED STATES
USHAW COLLEGE: Durham S
USHER COLLN (watches)
M Lincoln: Usher Gallery
USHER GALLERY: Lincoln M
USSR, see SOVIET STUDIES
UXBRIDGE TECHNICAL
   COLLEGE: London S

V

VALENCE HOUSE MUSEUM:
   London M
VALHALLA MARITIME
   MUSEUM: Tresco M
VANCOUVER, CAPTAIN, COLLN
P London, Richmond
VAN DYCK, SIR ANTHONY
M Alnwick: A Castle
M Arundel: A Castle
M Castle Ashby
M Chichester: Goodwood House
M Douglas: Manx Mus
M Knutsford: Tatton Hall
M London: Wallace Colln
M Petworth: P House
M Shifnal: Weston Park
M South Queensferry:
      Hopetoun House
M Thetford: Euston Hall
M Wilton: W House
M Winchcombe: Sudeley House
VAN GOGH, VINCENT
M London: Univ of L,

   Courtauld Inst
VATICAN, see CATHOLICISM
VAUGHN WILLIAMS
   MEMORIAL LIBRARY:
   London S
VEGETABLE RESEARCH
   STATION, NATIONAL:
   Wellesbourne S
VELAZQUEZ
M London: Wallace Colln
VENN, JOHN (papers)
S Cambridge: C Univ Colls,
      Gonville & Caius
VENTILATING, see HEATING
VERMEER, JAN
M London: Iveagh Bequest
VERNON PARK MUSEUM:
   Stockport M
VERRIO, ANTONIO
M Bakewell: Chatsworth
VERULAMIUM MUSEUM:
   St Albans M
VESTRY HOUSE MUSEUM:
   London M
VETERAN & VINTAGE CAR
   MUSEUM: Cheddar M
VETERAN CARS, see
   MOTOR VEHICLES
VETERINARY MEDICINE
S Cambridge: C Univ,
      Clinical Vet Med Dept
S Dublin, Eire: Univ Coll
S Edinburgh: E Univ
S Glasgow: G Univ Lib
S Liverpool: Univ of L
S London: Royal Coll of Vets
S   Univ of L Colls,
          Royal Vet Coll
S Weybridge: Central Vet Lab
M Aldershot: Royal Army Vet
      Corps Mus
M Huntly: Adamston Agric Mus
VICTOR BATTE-LAY TRUST
M Colchester: Minories Gallery
VICTORIA & ALBERT
   MUSEUM: London S,M
VICTORIA ART GALLERY &
   MUSEUM: Bath M
VICTORIA JUBILEE
   MUSEUM: Cawthorne M
VICTORY, HMS
M Portsmouth: P Royal Naval Mus
VIKING SOCIETY FOR
   NORTHERN RESEARCH LIB
S London: Univ of L Colls, Univ
VIKINGS
M Douglas: Manx Mus
M Newcastle upon Tyne:
      Mus of Antiquities
M Sumbergh Head: Jarlshof
VINCI, LEONARDO DA
M Grantham: Belton House
M Thornhill: Drumlanrig Castle
VINYL PRODUCTS LTD:
   London S
VISCOUNT WOLSELEY
P East Sussex
VOCATIONAL GUIDANCE
S Cambridge: CRAC/NICEC
S London: Loughton Coll
S   Southgate Tech
S   Waltham Forest, Nat Inst
          of Indust Psychology
VON HUGEL COLLN
S St Andrew's: Univ of St A
VULCANOLOGY
S London: Univ of L Colls, Univ
VULLIAMY COLLN
S London: Institution of
          Civil Engineers
VYNE, THE: Sherborne St John M

W

WADDESDON MANOR:
   Aylesbury M
WADE COLLN (Chinese)
S Cambridge: C Univ, Univ Lib
WAGNER COLLN
S London: Huguenot Lib
WALES
S Aberystwyth: Nat Lib of Wales
S Bangor: Univ Coll
S Cardiff: Welsh Folk Mus
S Lampeter: St David's
   see also WELSH
WALES GAS LIBRARY:
   Cardiff S
WALKER ART GALLERY:
   Liverpool S,M
WALLACE COLLECTION:
   London M

WALLINGTON HALL: Cambo M
WALPOLE, SIR HUGH
M Keswick: Fitz Park Mus
WALTHAM FOREST COLLEGE:
   London S
WALTON, IZAAK
S Keele: Univ of K
S Salisbury: S Cath Lib
M Stafford: Izaak Walton Cottage
WANDSWORTH TECHNICAL
   COLLEGE: London S
WARBURG INSTITUTE:
   London, Univ of L S
WARD, BISHOP SETH
S Salisbury: S Cath
WARING COLLN
S London: Royal Army Med
WARLEIGH WOOD NATURE
   RESERVE & TRAIL:
   Plymouth M
WARWICKSHIRE YEOMANRY
   MUSEUM:
   Stratford upon Avon M
WATCHES, see HOROLOGY
WATER
S Ambleside: Freshwater Bio
S Belfast: Min of Comm
S Brecon: Welsh Nat Water
      Dev Authority
S Leeds: Yorks Water Auth
S London: Confed of Brit Indust
S   Dept of the Environment
S   Institution of Municipal
          Engineers
S   Water Inf Centre
S Newcastle upon Tyne:
      Northumbrian Water Auth
S Reading: Central Water
      Planning Unit
S Stevenage: Water Research
S Wallingford: Hydraulics Stat
WATER INFORMATION CENTRE:
   London S
WATERLOO, BATTLE OF
P Sefton
WATER PLANNING UNIT,
   CENTRAL: Reading S
WATER RESEARCH CENTRE:
   Stevenage S
WATERTON, CHARLES, COLLN
M Wakefield: W City Mus
WATER TOWER: Chester M
WATERWAYS MUSEUM:
   Stoke Bruerne M
WATSON COLLN
S Dublin, Eire: Representative
      Church Body
WATSON COLLN (mining)
S Newcastle upon Tyne:
      N of Eng Inst of Mining
WATSON COLLN
S Stirling: S Univ
WATSON, HENRY, COLLN
S Manchester: Royal Northern
      Coll of Music
WATSON, SAMUEL
M Bakewell: Chatsworth
WATT LIB (local history)
P Inverclyde
WATTEAU, ANTOINE
M London: Wallace Colln
M Oxford: O Univ, Ashmolean
WATTS, DR ISAAC
P London, Hackney
WAVELL, F.M.
M Perth: Black Watch Reg Mus
WAX MUSEUM,
   OSBORN-SMITH'S: Brading M
WAYSIDE MUSEUM: Zennor M
WEALD & DOWNLAND OPEN AIR
   MUSEUM: Chichester M
WEAPONS
M Aldershot: Airborne Forces
M Alexandria: Cameron House
M Alloway: Ayrshire Yeomanry
M Alnwick: 'The Fifth' Reg
M Ashburton: A Mus
M Berwick upon Tweed: King's
      Own Scottish Borderers
M Birchington: Powell-Cotton
M Bury: Lancashire Fusiliers Reg
M Bury St Edmunds: Suffolk Reg
M Caernarvon: Royal Welch
      Fusiliers Reg Mus
M Canterbury: Buff's Reg Mus
M   Queen's Reg Mus
M Chichester: Corps of Royal
      Mil Police Mus
M Culross: Erskine of Torrie
M Dorchester: Dorset Mil Mus
M Durham: D Light Infantry
M Edinburgh: Royal Scots Reg
M   Scottish United Services
M Lichfield: Staffs Reg Mus
M London: Artillery Mus

M   Imperial War Mus
M   Nat Army Mus
M   Queen's Royal Surrey Reg
M Maidstone: Queen's Own
      Royal West Kent Reg
M Nairn: N Literary Inst Mus
M Newcastle: Borough Mus
M   Hobbergate Art Gallery
M Perth: Black Watch Reg Mus
M Preston: Queen's Lancs Reg
M Ripley: R Castle
M St Peters: St P Bunker War Mus
M Shrewsbury: King's Shropshire
      Light Infantry Reg Mus
M   Shropshire Yeomanry Mus
M Warwick: W Castle
M Winchester: Royal Hampshire
M Windsor: Household Cavalry
   see also ARMS & ARMOUR
WEATHER, see METEOROLOGY
WEAVER, HARRIET, COLLN
S London: Nat Book League
WEAVER'S COTTAGE:
   Kilbarchan M
WEAVING, see TEXTILES
WEDGWOOD
S Keele: Univ of K
M Barlaston: Wedgwood Mus
M Mansfield: M DC Mus
M Port Sunlight: Lady Lever Gall
WEDGWOOD COLLN
S Birmingham: B Univ
WEIGHTS & MEASURES
M Arbroath: Signal Tower Mus
M Ceres: Fife Folk Mus
M South Molton: S M Mus
M Warley: Avery Hist Mus
   see also METROLOGY
WEISS, W.H
S Cambridge: C Univ, Music Fac
WELBY HOARD (bronze age)
M Leicester: Jewry Wall Mus
WELDING
S Cambridge: C Welding Inst
S Hebburn: H Tech Coll
S London: Paddington Coll
WELLCOME INSTITUTE FOR
   THE HISTORY OF
   MEDICINE: London S,M
WELLCOME MUSEUM OF
   MEDICAL SCIENCE:
   London M
WELLCOME RESEARCH
   LABORATORIES: London S
WELLINGTON, DUKE OF
M Aldershot: Royal Army Med
      Corps Mus
M Bury: Lancs Fusiliers Reg
M London: Royal Hosp, Chelsea
M   Wellington Mus
M Reading: R Mus
M   Stratfield Saye House
WELLS, H.G.
P London, Bromley
WELSH BRIGADE MUSEUM:
   Crickhowell M
WELSH FOLK MUSEUM:
   Cardiff S,M
WELSH HISTORY
M Abergavenny: A & Dist Mus
M Aberystwyth: Ceredigion Mus
M Bangor: Univ Coll
M Brecon: Brecknock Mus
M Cardiff: Welsh Folk Mus
M Carmarthen: Co Mus
M Llanidloes: L Mus
M Merthyr Tydfil: Cyfarthfa
M Newtown: N Textile Mus
M Swansea: Univ Coll Mus
M Trefecca: Howel Harris Mus
WELSH LANGUAGE
P South Glamorgan
S Aberystwyth: Nat Lib of Wales
S Bangor: Univ Coll
S Cardiff: Univ Coll
S Lampeter: St David's Univ Coll
S Swansea: S Mem Coll
S   Univ Coll
WELSH NATIONAL SCHOOL OF
   MEDICINE: Cardiff S
WELSH NATIONAL WATER
   DEVELOPMENT
   AUTHORITY: Brecon S
WELSH PLANT BREEDING
   STATION: Aberystwyth S
WENTWORTH WOODHOUSE MSS
P Sheffield
WEOLEY CASTLE
   ARCHAEOLOGICAL SITE:
   Birmingham M
WERNHER COLLECTION:
   Luton M
WESLEY COLLEGE: Bristol S
WESLEY, CHARLES & JOHN
P Humberside